ISBN 978-1-5277-6435-4
PIBN 10888685

1 MONTH OF
FREE
READING

at

www.ForgottenBooks.com

By purchasing this book you are eligible for one month membership to ForgottenBooks.com, giving you unlimited access to our entire collection of over 700,000 titles via our web site and mobile apps.

To claim your free month visit:

www.forgottenbooks.com/free888685

English
Français
Deutsche
Italiano
Español
Português

www.forgottenbooks.com

Mythology Photography **Fiction**
Fishing Christianity **Art** Cooking
Essays Buddhism Freemasonry
Medicine **Biology** Music **Ancient
Egypt** Evolution Carpentry Physics
Dance Geology **Mathematics** Fitness
Shakespeare **Folklore** Yoga Marketing
Confidence Immortality Biographies
Poetry **Psychology** Witchcraft
Electronics Chemistry History **Law**
Accounting **Philosophy** Anthropology
Alchemy Drama Quantum Mechanics
Atheism Sexual Health **Ancient History**
Entrepreneurship Languages Sport
Paleontology Needlework Islam
Metaphysics Investment Archaeology
Parenting Statistics Criminology
Motivational

BIOGRAPHICAL

ENCYCLOPÆDIA

OF

NEW JERSEY

OF

THE NINETEENTH CENTURY.

PHILADELPHIA:
GALAXY PUBLISHING COMPANY.
1877.

PREFACE.

HON. RICHARD S. FIELD, in the introduction to his valuable work, "The Provincial Courts of New Jersey; with Sketches of the Bench and Bar" (published .
by the New Jersey Historical Society, 1849), writes: "We know more, I suspect,
of the early settlers of Massachusetts and Virginia than we do of those who first
planted the colony of New Jersey. I am sure we know more of the lawyers and judges
of England prior to the American Revolution than we do of those of our own State. We
are much more familiar with the personages who graced the Court of Queen Anne, than
with those who flourished here at the same time under the rule of her kinsman, Lord
Cornbury." And he continues: "I have been astonished, too, to find how few of the
names of distinguished Jerseymen are to be met with in the American biographical
dictionaries. While they abound with ample notices of second and third-rate men of other
sections of the country, those who have been truly eminent among us seldom find a place
in them. The truth is, our biographical dictionaries have, for the most part, been written
by New England men, and, as it would seem, for New England. We ought to have a
biographical dictionary of our own, and it may be worthy of consideration, whether a
work of this description should not be undertaken under the auspices of our Historical
Society." All this, so true in 1849, has gained added import in the quarter of a century
and more that has since then elapsed. Eminent men then living are now dead, and the
records of their honorable and useful lives, then bright, are now dim or forgotten. And
with such forgetfulness a just appreciation of the events in which they were leaders, the
history which they helped to form, is impossible. We see only one side; we have the facts,
but not the motives. The private lives of statesmen constitute a potent factor in the
moulding of States. Much of the history of the past is sealed to us because we
have no contemporaneous biographical history to give us the needed comprehension of
its inner workings. The lacking quantity that Mr. Field so earnestly deprecates, this
work is in a measure designed to present. That it is as complete and satisfactory as
it should be, the publisher does not claim. He simply offers it as an earnest effort to bring
a valuable contribution to the history of a State, full, both in its past and present, of
material for the historian.

MAY, 1877.

THE

BIOGRAPHICAL ENCYCLOPÆDIA

OF

NEW JERSEY.

AYTON, HON. WILLIAM LEWIS, LL.D., Lawyer and Statesman, late of Trenton, was born in Somerset county, New Jersey, February 17th, 1807. He sprang from a long line of distinguished New Jerseymen. His great-grandfather, Jonathan Dayton, settled at Elizabethtown at least as early as 1725, and about the same time his mother's grandfather built, at Baskingridge, Somerset county, the first frame building in that section. On both sides his ancestors were conspicuous for talents and patriotic services, civil and military. In the war of independence, Elias Dayton, granduncle of William, was a brigadier-general, while Edward Lewis, his maternal grandfather, was a commissary, and served as such during the whole war. Jonathan Dayton, son of Elias, occupies a prominent place in history as a member of the convention which framed the Federal Constitution; as Speaker of the House of Representatives in the Fourth Congress, and as a member of the United States Senate. Either during or soon after the war, Robert Dayton, grandfather of William, moved to a farm near Baskingridge, and resided there until his death. He reared a large family, of whom his son Joel, a man of intelligence and probity, succeeded to the farm. By him, in turn, several sons were left, all of whom enjoyed a liberal education. William, the eldest, in his twelfth year, became a pupil in the academy of the celebrated Dr. Brownlee, then of Baskingridge, but afterwards of New York. After due preparation, he entered Nassau Hall, whence he graduated in 1825. Then he entered the office of Hon. Peter D. Vroom, at Somerville, to study law. His preceptor was then the leader of the Jackson party in the State, and in 1829 was by it made Governor. Although the pupil subsequently occupied no less conspicuous a position among the Whigs,

there grew up between them a warm friendship, only interrupted by death. Licensed in 1830, Mr. Dayton began practice at Freehold, where his high abilities as a lawyer, his dignity, courtesy and moral worth, soon established him in a fine legal and social position. From the first he was outspoken in his Whig sentiments, and when in 1836 the Whigs determined to earnestly contest Monmouth county, a stronghold of Jacksonism, he was urged to lead the ticket as candidate for the Legislative Council. He consented, and the whole legislative ticket, with him at its head, was elected, and, after years of defeat, the Whigs, by a brilliant victory, regained control of the State. The Legislature met in October, the month of the election, and Mr. Dayton at once took rank among the leaders in a body containing many able and distinguished men. This was the commencement of a career which identified him with the history of the State, and made his name a household word within its borders. Placed at the head of the Judiciary Committee, he prepared the law by which the county courts, then greatly degenerated and very inefficient, were raised to a status in which they have since commanded the full confidence of the community. The reform was radical. The courts had been conducted by a large number of the most active and influential politicians in every county in the State. Under the new law they were each to be presided over by a single judge of the Supreme Court. In the face of this great personal influence and interest he succeeded in securing the prompt passage of the measure. That the provisions of the new law might be carried out it became necessary to increase the number of Supreme Court judges from three to five, and the election, under the Constitution, then resting with the Legislature, that body elected him to one of the new judicial seats. Thereupon he removed from Freehold to Trenton, which ever after was his home. Although thus early in life he had been made the recipient of high and unusual honors, he began to consider, after a short service on the bench, whether he was justified, in view of family considerations, in continuing labors so inadequately rewarded as those of a judge in those days, and finally he resigned, having sat on the bench three years, and resumed practice at the bar. He at once became a leader and secured a large and very lucrative clientage. In the summer of 1842, on the death of Senator Southard, he was appointed by Governor Pennington to fill the vacancy in the representation of the State in the United States Senate. He took his seat on July 6th, and when the Legislature met in the following October he was, by the unanimous Whig vote, elected for Mr. Southard's unexpired term. In 1845 he was again, by the unanimous vote of his party, elected for the full term of six years. Entering the Senate at thirty-five, probably its youngest member, he manifested marked discretion. He seldom spoke, and only on an important question, when he always said something of worth and weight. At all times, however, he worked hard for the passage of measures he deemed good and for the defeat of those he thought bad. In the passage of the tariff of 1842 he bore an active part, and his support was of immense value, inasmuch as a previous tariff bill had been vetoed, and this one only passed the Senate by a majority of one. He also, in secret session, approved the treaty negotiated by Lord Ashburton and Mr. Webster for the settlement of the northeastern boundary question. These actions indicate two cardinal features of his public policy: "peace abroad, and the promotion of industry at home." On the opening of the next session the estimation in which he was held was testified by his appointment on the Judiciary Committee, whereon he served until the close of his term, excepting one session. He also served on several other important committees. During his career in the Senate many important matters came up for discussion, and Judge Dayton occupied a very conspicuous position in all. His first speech, made February 15th, 1843, was a most eloquent and forcible defence of the character and credit of the national government, then suffering much in Europe from the failure of several of the States to pay the interest on their public debts. He demonstrated convincingly that the faith and credit of the national government had been preserved without a spot, and far more carefully than those of the European governments. The speech was highly commended as unanswerable and opportune by the press and the entire country. An advocate of cheap postage, he voted in 1844 for the bill to reduce the then current rates. During this same session he made a firm stand for the independence of Senators as against "instructions" from the Legislatures of their respective States. He opposed the resolution giving notice to Great Britain of the termination of the joint possession of Oregon, and after Mr. Clay's defeat under the cry of "54° 40′ or fight," Mr.

Polk's administration negotiated a treaty settling the difficulty on the very terms recommended by Judge Dayton and his associates—the retention of the mouth of the Columbia river, and a compromise respecting the sterile and comparatively worthless region in the extreme northern part of the Territory. An attack being made during the same session on the tariff act of 1842 with a view to its repeal, he made a very elaborate argument in favor of the protective system, and his effort exerted great weight in the satisfactory conclusion reached. He opposed in 1845 the annexation of Texas, believing it was pressed with sectional motives, and to enable one portion of the Union to dominate, against the equities of the Constitution, over another. He again fought for protection in 1846, but Secretary Walker's revenue measure, superseding the tariff of 1842, became law by the casting vote of Mr. Dallas. While disapproving the course of the administration in provoking the Mexican war, he voted for all necessary supplies for its prosecution, though he denounced the proposition to issue letters of marque and reprisal as a resort to a system of legalized piracy, the relic of a barbarous age. Subsequently he strongly supported the ratification of the treaty with Mexico, and defended his course with great power in open Congress, declaring its terms preferable to a prolongation of the war. Upon the much-vexed question of slavery in newly-acquired territory he took the ground laid down in the Wilmot proviso, contending that Congress had the right, and that it was its duty, to prevent the extension of the institution, which existed only by municipal law and could not be carried by the Constitution where it did not previously exist; while he declared the government had no right to interfere with it in the States. During the excitement in the Forty-first Congress respecting the admission of California, and the claims then put forward by the South, he distinguished himself by several speeches, all directed against the extension of slavery in any way, maintaining the right of California to admission independently of any concessions to the slave-holding power, and earnestly opposing the Fugitive Slave Law. During this same session he opposed the reception of a petition praying Congress to take steps for a dissolution of the Union, on the ground that while there was a constitutional right to petition "for redress of grievances," the document in question preferred no such prayer, but asked for the abolition of the government itself—prayed Senators to be treasonable. His term expired with the next session, a short and uneventful one, and Judge Dayton returned home to practise his profession. Unknown to himself, he was nominated for the Vice-Presidency by the Republican National Convention at Philadelphia, in June, 1856, by five hundred and twenty-nine out of five hundred and sixty votes. In February, 1857, he was appointed Attorney-General of New Jersey. In the following year he declined re-election to the United States Senate. During the State campaigns of 1858 and 1859 he rendered, by request, material aid to the Opposition party, formed by the fusion of the supporters of Fremont and Fillmore, sinking all personal considerations to promote the success of the great principles upon which both sections were agreed. At this time he earnestly advocated the homestead bill as a phase of protection and encouragement to American labor. In the National Republican Convention of 1860 he was brought forward as a candidate for the nomination for President, and he occupied a very prominent position as such. When Abraham Lincoln began his administration, in March, 1861, he offered him the position of United States Minister to France. In connection with this offer the following account is given in "Elmer's Reminiscences of New Jersey" of an interview with the President: "It was well known in Washington that President Lincoln entertained a high opinion of the character, abilities and public services of Mr. Dayton, and that if he had been permitted to exercise his own judgment, he would have given him a prominent position in his cabinet. A day or two after the abrupt entrance of the President-elect into Washington, in the month of February, 1861, the Republican delegation in Congress from New Jersey had, by appointment, a formal interview with him at his rooms in Willard's Hotel, to urge upon him a suitable recognition of Mr. Dayton in the formation of his cabinet. Senator Ten Eyck was made the spokesman of the delegation, and he opened the subject with a somewhat elaborate statement of the worth, talents and party claims of the distinguished Jerseyman. Mr. Lincoln's reply was prompt and characteristically candid. 'It is not necessary,' he said, 'to speak to me in praise of Mr. Dayton; I have known him since we served in the different houses of Congress, at the same time, and there is no public man for whose character I have a higher admiration. When the telegraphic wires brought to Springfield the news of my election, my first thought was that I would have him associated with me in council, and would make him Secretary of State. But New York is a great State, and Mr. Seward has many friends, and I was compelled by the pressure upon me to give up the thought. I then desired to arrange for him some other cabinet position, commensurate with his abilities; but Pennsylvania, another great State, you know, was bound to have a place for Mr. Cameron, and I again reluctantly yielded. I then said to myself, Mr. Dayton deserves the best place abroad, and I will send him to the Court of St. James. But New England pressed her claims for notice, and united upon Mr. Adams, and I was driven from that purpose. I then thought of the French mission, and wondered if that would not suit him. I have put my foot down now, and will not be moved. I shall offer that place to Mr. Dayton, and hope it will prove satisfactory to him and his friends.' The interview here ended, and although it was generally understood that the President was surrounded by influences hostile to Mr. Dayton, and jealous of his recognition and advancement, yet he adhered to his resolution, and offered to him the mission to France, which, after some hesitation, he accepted." The nomination was at once confirmed by the Senate, and in due course Mr. Dayton sailed for France and entered upon his duties. These proved to be exceptionally trying, but they found him at all times equal to their mastery, his eminent abilities being no less marked in his diplomacy abroad than in his statesmanship at home. Many difficult and dangerous crises in our relations with France were safely passed while the interests of our government in that country were intrusted to his care, owing largely to his wisdom and personal influence. Among them was the threatened war with England on account of the seizure of Mason and Slidell, wherein that country received the countenance and sympathy of France. Also among them were the many difficult questions arising out of the French invasion of Mexico; the presence in the ports of France of the rebel cruisers, the "Georgia," "Florida" and "Alabama," as well as of the "Rappahannock," which was at last left unarmed in the port of Calais; the building of four clipper ships at Bordeaux and Nantes, and two iron-clad rams at Nantes for the Confederate service, which through the exertions and influence of our Minister were by the French government prohibited from delivery to the Confederates. The value of the last-mentioned service cannot be over-estimated, for had these vessels been successfully launched upon a career similar to that of the "Alabama," there can be no doubt but that American commerce would have been entirely swept from the ocean. From the testimony of French statesmen of the day it is evident that the maintenance of amicable relations between the two governments during Mr. Dayton's term as Minister was largely owing not only to his ability and statesmanship but to his high character and candor of his advice, which always inspired the trust and confidence of the court to which he was accredited. While discharging this high trust death overtook him quite suddenly. He died at Paris, December 1st, 1864. Funeral services were held in the American Chapel, and in addition to the religious exercises addresses were delivered by Mr. Bigelow, then the American Consul, and subsequently Minister to France, and by Professor Labou laye, of the French Institute, in which the highest tributes were paid to his worth and public services.

--◆--

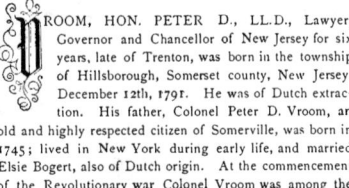ROOM, HON. PETER D., LL.D., Lawyer, Governor and Chancellor of New Jersey for six years, late of Trenton, was born in the township of Hillsborough, Somerset county, New Jersey, December 12th, 1791. He was of Dutch extraction. His father, Colonel Peter D. Vroom, an old and highly respected citizen of Somerville, was born in 1745; lived in New York during early life, and married Elsie Bogert, also of Dutch origin. At the commencement of the Revolutionary war Colonel Vroom was among the

first to raise a military company; he served throughout the struggle, fighting his way up to the rank of Lieutenant-Colonel. He held various county offices, such as clerk of the pleas, sheriff, and justice of the peace, and served for a long term in the Assembly and in the Council. An honored elder in the Dutch Reformed Church, he lived to see his son Governor of the State, and died full of years and honor in 1831. His son, Peter D., received his preparatory education at Somerville Academy, and became a student in Columbia College, New York, in 1806, graduating two years subsequently. Having a taste for law, he read with George McDonald, of Somerville; was licensed as attorney in May, 1813, and as counsellor in 1816; twelve years later he was called to be a sergeant. He began practice at Schooley's Mountain, in Morris county, but after eighteen months removed to Hacketstown, where, however, he remained but two years, transferring his office to Flemington. In these places he enjoyed a fair practice and laid the foundation of his subsequent reputation. During his residence at Flemington he married Miss Dumont, a daughter of Colonel Dumont, of Somerset county, whose sister was the wife of Frederick Frelinghuysen. In 1820 he made another removal, returning to his native county and opening his office in Somerville, where he lived for more than twenty years. Politically a Federalist, he did not participate actively in political movements until 1824, when he became an ardent supporter of General Jackson, being especially attracted to that statesman by his famous letter to President Monroe deprecating partisanship in the selection of a national cabinet. During the years 1826, 1827 and 1829 he served as a member of the Assembly from Somerset county, and in the last-named year he was elected Governor. At that time the Governor was also Chancellor and Ordinary. He was re-elected in the two succeeding years, but in 1832 was defeated by Mr. Southard. In 1833, 1834 and 1835 he was again elected, but in 1836 declined renomination on account of impaired health. His decisions in the Court of Chancery during these years tended to establish securely the character imparted to the court by his predecessor, Chancellor Williamson, and stand, for the most part, unquestioned to the present day. After retiring from the gubernatorial chair he resumed practice at Somerville, but in 1837 he was absent for several months in Mississippi, having been appointed by President Van Buren one of three commissioners to adjust land reserve claims under the Choctaw Indian treaty. In 1838 he became a candidate for Congress, and was elected, but owing to irregularities in some of the returns failed to receive the Governor's commission. The matter was long and bitterly contested, and eventually a decision was rendered in his favor, Congress going behind the broad seal of the State and ascertaining that Mr. Vroom had received a clear majority. This contest is known as the " broad seal war." At the expiration of his Congressional term he made Trenton his home, and his first wife having died, he about this time married a daughter

of General Wall. When, in 1844, a convention assembled to revise the State constitution, he sat as a delegate from his native county; served as Chairman of the Committee on the Legislative Department, and labored conspicuously throughout the work of revision. In 1848 he was associated with Henry W. Green, Stacy G. Potts and William L. Dayton in bringing the statutes into conformity with the new constitution, and in consolidating the numerous supplements. Chief-Justice Green's term expiring, Mr. Vroom was nominated by Governor Fort as his successor, and the Senate promptly confirmed the nomination, but he declined. In 1853 he accepted the mission to the Court of Prussia, and resided in Berlin until 1857, when he was recalled, at his own request, and returned to the practice of his profession. A difficult question with which he was called upon to deal while in Prussia was the claim of Prussian subjects, who after naturalization as American citizens had returned to their native country, to protection against the military law of Prussia. Our government refused protection, on the ground that if such citizens returned voluntarily to the jurisdiction of the country whose laws they had broken prior to naturalization as Americans they must suffer the consequences of their unlawful acts. To convince those who had fallen under punishment and looked to him for relief of the justice of this principle was no easy matter, but Mr. Vroom managed this difficult task with great judgment and success. In 1860 he was placed upon the electoral ticket by the Breckinridge and Lane party, but was defeated. While earnestly opposed to the measures of the northern abolitionists, he was just as strongly opposed to the secession doctrines of the Southern extremists. In the Peace Conference, which met at Washington on February 4th, 1861, he was one of the nine representatives from New Jersey, and was a member of the committee, composed of one representative from each State, to which were referred the various propositions for the restoration of harmony and preservation of the Union. This committee, after many long and protracted sessions, at which Mr. Vroom was a punctual, faithful and active attendant, reported on February 15th, but only failure resulted. The causes of this failure were thus stated by him in an address to the voters of New Jersey, published in 1862: " Radical politicians everywhere opposed the adjustment. The Union men in the border States were earnest in their entreaties. They foresaw and foretold with almost prophetic distinctness what would be the results of a failure. The Crittenden resolutions; the propositions of the Peace Convention, either, if agreed to by Congress, might have saved the country. But secessionists in the South opposed them. The radicals of the North and East opposed them. The great Republican party, everywhere, with some honorable exceptions, were unwilling to abandon their platform. They insisted it should be carried out to the letter, no matter what might be the consequences. Some assured the people that there was no danger; that everything would be quieted in thirty, days, or a few weeks; others did not hesitate to say that blood-letting would be of service to the nation." Herein appear the grounds upon which he opposed the measures of the Lincoln administration. He was a presidential elector in 1862 upon the Pierce ticket. During the excitement over the compulsory draft in July, 1863, he made a speech to a large assembly in Somerset county, which was the means of calming passion and promoting obedience to the law, urging with great eloquence and force that the people were not the judges of the constitutionality of a law. He was a supporter of General McClellan for President in 1864, and his able and earnest efforts contributed greatly to the success of that ticket in New Jersey. In 1868 he was an elector on the Seymour and Blair ticket. Upon the death of his eldest son he took up his office of State reporter of the decisions of the Supreme Court. For several years he was one of the Commissioners of the Sinking Fund. In religious faith he sympathized with the Dutch Reformed Church, of which for many years he was a ruling elder. He was a Vice-President of the American Colonization and Bible Societies. His degree of LL.D. he received from the College of New Jersey in 1850. Possessing a vigorous constitution and iron frame, he continued to prosecute his profession with undiminished powers till within a very short period of his death, which occurred November 18th, 1874.

WILLIAMSON, HON. ISAAC H., LL.D., Governor and Chancellor of the State of New Jersey from 1817 to 1829, was born at Elizabethtown in the year 1767. He studied law with his brother, Matthias Williamson, then, and for many years, one of the leading lawyers of the State. In 1791 he was licensed as an attorney; in 1796 as a counsellor, and in 1804 was called to be a serjeant-at-law. Although in early life he ranked as a Federalist, he did not sympathize with that party in their violent opposition to the war of 1812, and in 1815 he was put upon the ticket for member of the Assembly from Essex county by the Democrats, without his knowledge, and elected a member of the Legislature. On the resignation of Governor Dickerson, after his being chosen Senator in 1817, Mr. Williamson was elected Governor, and was afterwards re-elected every year for twelve years. He was elected a member of the Council (now Senate) from Essex county for the years 1831 and 1832, and in 1832 would undoubtedly have been elected Chief-Justice of the State, made vacant by the death of Chief-Justice Ewing, if he had permitted the use of his name. In 1844 he was chosen a member of the convention which framed the new constitution of the State, and was unanimously elected the President of that body, no other person being nominated. He presided over its deliberations for some time, but his health failed and he was obliged to leave,

and finally to resign the Presidency before the proceedings were closed. Before the close of the year he died at the age of seventy-seven years. Prior to Governor Williamson's entering upon the duties of Chancellor and Judge of the Prerogative Court of the State, those courts were comparatively unimportant. Occasionally an important case was prosecuted in them, but the practice was in many respects very loose, and was understood by very few members of the bar. Chancellor Williamson made himself thoroughly acquainted with the practice of the English courts of equity, after which the Court of Chancery in New Jersey had been originally modelled, and in 1822 prepared and adopted a set of rules greatly improving the business of the court. Moulded by his skill and learning, and dignified by his administration of its peculiar sphere of justice, the court was deservedly held in high repute, and became, and has since continued to be, a most important branch of the judiciary system of the State. Judge Elmer, from whose reminiscences this sketch is culled, says of him: "Mr. Williamson was one of the most thorough-bred lawyers that ever adorned the bar of New Jersey. His learning was almost entirely the learning essential to a great lawyer, which, of course, was by no means confined to the mere technical details of the profession. He was a diligent reader of history; but during his busy professional life he did not allow his mind to be diverted by what is termed light literature; and he altogether abstained from any active participation in mere party politics. He was an able and very successful advocate, and when made Chancellor became a great equity judge.

WILLIAMSON, HON. BENJAMIN, LL.D., Chancellor of the State from 1852 to 1859, son of Governor and Chancellor Isaac H. Williamson, was born at Elizabethtown, New Jersey, and graduated from Nassau Hall in 1827. He studied law and was admitted to the bar in 1830 and made a counsellor in 1833. He commenced and continued the practice of his profession in his native town, and soon rose to eminence. He served with great success as Prosecutor of the Pleas for Essex County for several years, that being at the time the most important office of the kind in the State. In 1852 he was appointed to the highest judicial position in the courts of New Jersey, succeeding Chancellor Oliver S. Halsted, whose term then expired. He filled this position, which his father had done so much to make important and which he had for so many years graced with his learning, with distinguished ability until the expiration of his term, and then resumed the practice of the law. There were few cases of importance or interest, arising in Mr. Williamson's section of the State, in which he was not employed, previous to his appointment as chancellor, and on his return to the bar he at once secured a large and important practice, extending over the whole State. Without disparagement to others, he may be said for years to have occupied the position of leader of the bar. While Mr. Williamson has avoided public office outside the line of professional service, he has, on more than one occasion, been prominently urged by friends as United States Senator, and they only failed of his election by a few votes in 1863 or 1864. In 1860 he was a Delegate at large from the State to the Democratic Convention at Charleston, and in 1861 was appointed one of the delegates to represent New Jersey in the Peace Congress which met in Washington, composed of delegates from every State, and which was called in the hope and for the purpose of averting, if possible, the impending conflict between the two sections of the country. Mr. Williamson has been all his life identified with the interests of the church, of education, and the development of the resources of the State. He has for years served as an officer of the church of St. John's Episcopal Parish and of the Union County Bible Society, as Trustee of the State Normal School, as Director and Counsel for the Central Railroad Company of New Jersey, of the State Bank of Elizabeth, and as Director and Trustee of the New Jersey Southern Railroad Company, as Commissioner of the Sinking Fund of Elizabeth, and in other positions of trust, both public and private. He still lives at Elizabeth, on the place formerly the residence of his father.

OOPER, RICHARD MATLACK, Bank President, Legislator and Judge, late of Camden, born in Gloucester county, New Jersey, February 29th, 1768, was a descendant of William Cooper, one of the first English occupants of a great part of the lands on the Delaware river opposite Philadelphia. This ancestor, born in 1632, and a resident of Coleshill in Hertfordshire, became a convinced member of the Society of Friends, and, with his family, incurring a share of the persecutions to which that sect were cruelly subjected, sought, with others, relief and rest in the "new world," where, in 1678, they landed and located at Burlington, a settlement of West New Jersey, then a few years in existence. In a short time he purchased and removed to a large survey of land at Pyne Point (now Cooper's Point and Camden), opposite the Indian village of Shakamaxon, where, two years later, the famous treaty was made. It was at William Cooper's house at this place, and at Thomas Fairman's at Shakamaxon, that the first Friends' Meetings were alternately held, until the arrival of William Penn in 1682, when "the ancient meeting of Shakamaxon" was removed to the newly-founded city of Philadelphia. The meeting at Pyne Point remained for some time longer, and a quaint old letter of the time, in mentioning this fact, says, "We had then zeal and fervency of spirit, although we had some dread of the Indians as a savage people, nevertheless ye Lord turned them to be ser-

viceable to us, and to be very loving and kinde." He was an active member of the Assembly of West Jersey in the first meeting after its organization in 1681, and in subsequent sessions; and also one of the West Jersey Council of Proprietors at the first meeting of that body in 1687, and thereafter. An accepted minister of the society, he was found amongst those who, on behalf of the Yearly Meeting of Friends, testified against George Keith, in the celebrated controversy which for a time threatened schism in the then infant church. In the history of the family during succeeding generations, several served their State in official capacities, amongst whom may be mentioned Joseph Cooper, chosen to represent Gloucester county in the Assembly for nineteen successive years; and many were prominent in the less public, but no less important stations of ministers and elders in their religious society. The position of the subject of this sketch, as a large landed proprietor and a high personal character, soon brought him into the political field as a successful candidate in several elections for the Legislative Council of New Jersey. In 1813 he became President of the State Bank at Camden, then recently chartered, and held that position by continuous annual elections, until a re-election was declined in 1842, the institution meanwhile proving itself one of the most prosperous in the State. In 1829 he was chosen as Representative to the National Congress, and again in 1831. For several years he served as Presiding Judge of the Gloucester County Courts, and at various times filled other minor local positions of trust and honor, securing in every station the confidence and respect of all classes by his judgment, integrity, and amiable deportment. He died March 10th, 1844.

OOPER, RICHARD MATLACK, M. D., son of Richard M. Cooper, was born at Camden, New Jersey, August 30th, 1816. In 1832, after a superior preliminary training, he entered the literary department of the University of Pennsylvania, graduated with honor in July, 1836, matriculated in the medical department of the same institution in October, 1836, and graduated in 1839, having studied under the supervision of the celebrated physician and medical author, Professor George B. Wood. Inheriting ability of a high order, studious by temperament, and gifted with remarkable powers of observation, he laid during these years of collegiate life and private study a sure foundation for success. Beginning professional practice in his native city under these favorable auspices, by indefatigable labor and study a position was soon won amongst the foremost of his professional brethren. An immense practice in the city and neighborhood and a reputation over and beyond the State resulted, yet at no time did onerous engagements prevent a diligent study to keep pace with medical progress. Declining health gradually circumscribed his

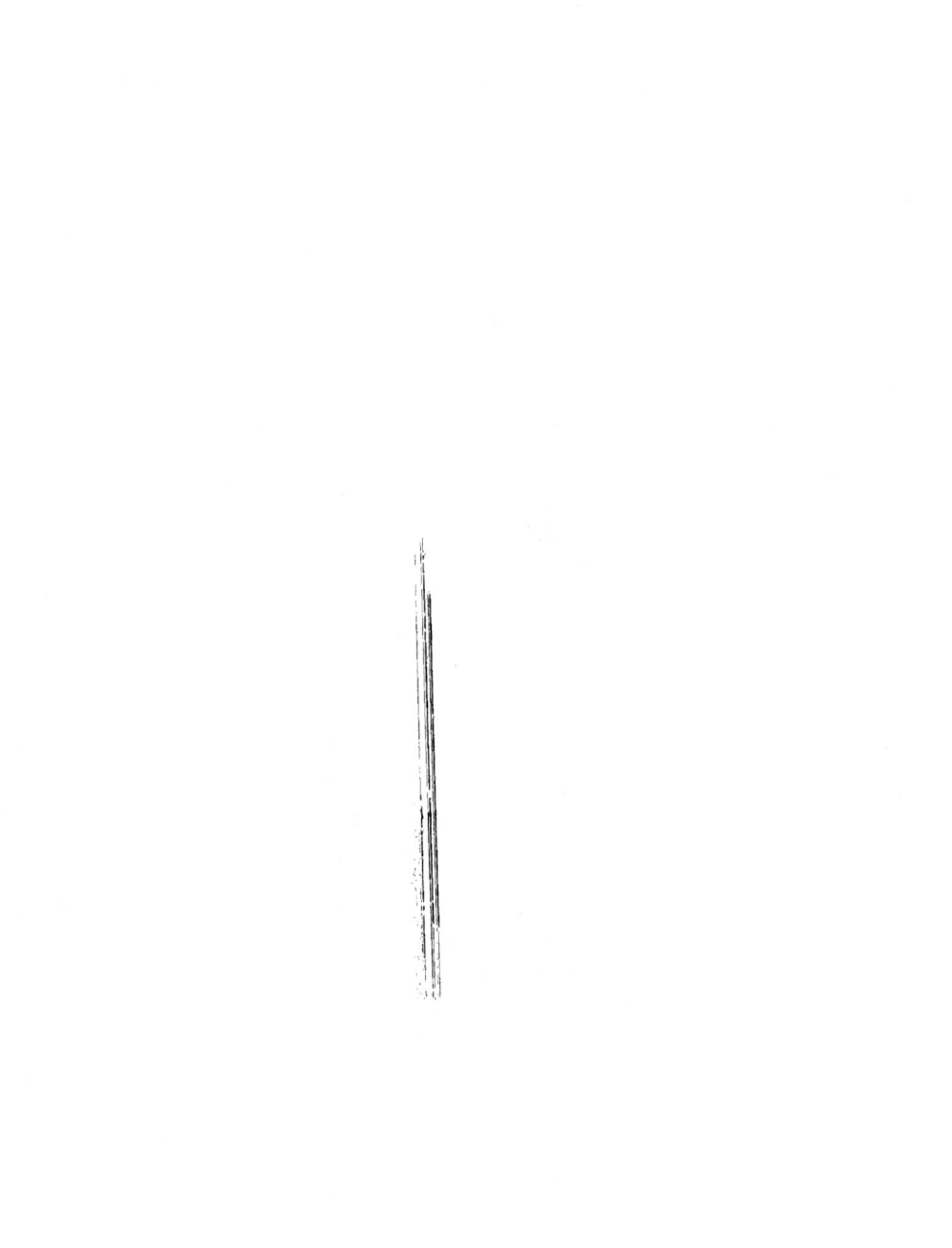

Rich^d M Cooper

William D. Cooper

usefulness, but neither this nor the possession of ample means could induce retirement from the practice of a profession loved for itself and for the good it enabled him to do, especially amongst the poverty-stricken and destitute classes, to whom his charitable services were freely extended. Thus devoted to his calling he naturally took a deep interest in its welfare, and both as president and fellow was an active member of the medical societies of his State, county and city, being a founder of the Camden District Medical Society, in 1845, and of the Camden City Dispensary, in 1865. He also favored the establishment of the Camden Hospital, a project since carried into effect through the instrumentality of his brother, William D. Cooper, Esq. Honorable in every act, generous and kind by nature, of genial manners, a consistent Christian, a skilful physician, an earnest and public-spirited citizen, he died May 25th, 1874, loved, respected, and sincerely regretted.

———❧———

OOPER, WILLIAM DANIEL, Lawyer, son of Richard M. Cooper, was born at Camden, New Jersey, August 30th, 1816, graduated at the University of Pennsylvania in 1836, studied law under the supervision of the Hon. William M. Meredith, of Philadelphia, and was admitted to the bar of that city and Camden in 1841. In practice, though rarely appearing in the courts, he was recognized as one of the most sagacious counsellors in the profession, and a model of straightforward, strict integrity. As a citizen he was public-spirited, and by the judicious management of the large estates of his family lying within the limits of the city, contributed very materially to its growth and improvement, always carefully studying to advance the interests of the community. Benevolent and philanthropic in disposition, the need of a hospital in West New Jersey drew his attention towards establishing such an institution, but death occurring before the realization of this project, his family, in accordance with the wish and plan of their relative, generously donated a large tract of land eligibly situated in the city of Camden, and the sum of $200,000 for the erection of suitable buildings thereon and as an endowment fund for their support. This noble charity, incorporated under the title of the Camden Hospital, will be ready to dedicate to public service during the early part of the present year (1877). Mr. Cooper died February 18th, 1875.

———❧———

EARNY, LAWRENCE, late Commodore of the United States Navy, was born, November 30th, 1789, in the then village of Perth Amboy, New Jersey, his father's family and ancestry having been among the early settlers of that section. From his very boyhood he manifested a fondness for a maritime life, and in his eighteenth year was the re-

cipient of a midshipman's warrant at the hands of President Jefferson and was immediately ordered to join the gunboat flotilla then under the command of Commodore Rodgers, in which he served during the enforcement of the embargo laid upon American shipping in 1807. He was next ordered to the frigate "Constitution," and subsequently to the "President," both of which vessels were attached to the Home Squadron. He remained on the latter vessel until 1810, when he was transferred to the schooner "Enterprise," whose cruising ground extended from Cape Hatteras to the southern point of Florida, and while attached to this vessel received his commission as Lieutenant in the year 1813. In the meantime war had been declared against Great Britain, and to the infant navy of the republic was committed the honor of the flag as well as the protection of the seaboard cities and towns. How well he bore his part in the conflict, the brave and gallant acts he performed, are told not only by contemporaneous writers, but are also recorded by the impartial historian. At the close of the war he continued on the "Enterprise" as her Commander, and for some time thereafter was engaged on a special service. In this new field of operations he was equally successful, not only in benefiting his own countrymen, but also in protecting the merchantmen of friendly nations, who had hitherto been at the mercy of the freebooters and pirates who had, from time immemorial, haunted the islands and keys from Key West down to the Spanish main. Through his active exertions, the band of the noted pirate, Gibbs, was completely broken up, a number of them being captured, although the chief escaped with some of his outlawed companions. Three large vessels were recaptured from the corsairs, of which two, the American ship "Lucius," and the British brig "Larch," were delivered to their respective owners; but the American brig "Aristides" had been previously stranded. Besides these, he captured five schooners, one sloop, and several luggers of the piratical fleet. In fact, he effectually cleared the seas of these marauders, and not only received the thanks of those at home, but his invaluable services were recognized by the civilized world. He remained in the "Enterprise" until that vessel was wrecked, and, after some shore service, was advanced to the rank of Master Commandant in 1825. Towards the close of the following year he was assigned to the command of the corvette "Warren," and sailed February 22d, 1827, to the Mediterranean. It was not long before he was again actively engaged in rooting out the pirates who had been operating for a long time in the Grecian archipelago, to the detriment of all nations whose interests led them there. His exertions not only destroyed their stronghold, but compelled the recipients of a portion of the plunder to disgorge their ill-gotten booty. On the comp'etion of his cruise he returned home, and in 1832 received his commission as Captain, that being in those days the highest rank in the service. For some years he was occupied on shore duty, until 1839, when he was assigned to the frigate "United

States." In the following year he was ordered to the frigate "Potomac," and sailed for the Brazil station. While in harbor at Rio de Janeiro he received the appointment of Commander of the East India Squadron, and in February, 1841, raised his flag on the frigate "Constellation," and soon after sailed for his new sphere of action. He found himself on the Chinese coast in 1842, and was prominently engaged in endeavoring to prevent the contraband traffic in opium. Being instructed by the Navy Department to protect American interests in that distant section of the globe, he adopted the necessary measures to obtain pecuniary satisfaction for those merchants who had been considerable losers when the Dutch factory had been plundered by Chinese. Hitherto all measures had failed in obtaining the desired redress; but he succeeded in making the officials understand that the damages should be promptly arranged, and the amount of indemnity, over a quarter million dollars, was subsequently paid. About this time Great Britain was engaged in concluding a treaty with the Chinese government, which Captain Kearny feared might prove to the disadvantage of the United States, unless steps were taken to obviate it. He accordingly addressed a letter to both the Imperial Commissioners and also to the Governor of the Canton province, who advised him that to the United States would be accorded the same privileges as those which should be granted to Great Britain. Having secured this favorable reply, he communicated these proceedings to the Navy Department; and the Washington government thereupon availed itself of the opening he had thus effected by sending Caleb Cushing as the Commissioner or Special Envoy to the Chinese empire, the latter being clothed with all the necessary power to conclude the treaty with that country, which was ratified in 1845, and went into operation during the following year. The next important service which Captain Kearny effected was to protest against the proposed cession of the Sandwich Islands to the British government. This was in the summer of 1843, while he was on his homeward-bound voyage. He notified both the king and the British commissioner that such action as the former proposed would be inimical to the rights of those Americans who had settled in the islands. The matter was not adjusted when he left Hawaii, but his timely interference had great weight in prolonging the negotiations, which ultimately came to naught. Turning the prow of his ship once more toward the east, and doubling Cape Horn, he speedily made his way toward home, arriving at Norfolk April 30th, 1844, thus closing a sea-service of nearly thirty-seven years. During the remainder of his life he was variously occupied at different stations, including the command of the navy-yard at Brooklyn, New York. He was also President of one of the Naval Courts of Inquiry, and a member of the Light-house Board, as well as of the New Jersey Board of Pilot Commissioners. He was commissioned Commodore, on the retired list, in 1866, and died at Perth Amboy, November 29th, 1868.

EARNY, STEPHEN WATTS, late Major-General United States Army, was born, August 30th, 1794, in the city of Newark, New Jersey, where also he was educated. At the outbreak of the war with Great Britain in 1812, he entered the army as a Lieutenant, and was assigned to a company in the 13th Regiment of Infantry. This command, with several other regiments, was ordered to the frontier during the same year, and crossed over to Canada, where he participated in the action at Queenstown Heights, where he acquitted himself with honor to himself and to the service. He was actively engaged during the entire period of the war, and after peace was declared he was retained in the army, having been promoted meanwhile to the rank of Captain and attached to the 3d Infantry. For the period of eighteen years he was attached to this branch of the service, both as Captain and afterwards Major. In 1833 he attained the grade of Lieutenant-Colonel and was transferred to the United States Dragoons; three years later he became Colonel, and in 1846 was commissioned Brigadier-General, and was appointed to command the "Army of the West," as was then termed the force employed on the Indian frontier. When hostilities commenced with the republic of Mexico, he was ordered by the War Department to march westward with his command. Starting from Bent's Fort, on the Arkansas river, he pressed onward toward New Mexico, which he conquered, and where he established a provisional government in Santa Fé, the then capital. He then took up the line of march across the plains, the Rocky mountains, and the almost unknown regions beyond, until he reached California, and again defeated the Mexican army at the battle of San Pascual, on December 6th, 1846, in which engagement he was wounded twice. Having reached the sea-coast, his command was reinforced by a detachment of sailors and marines; and with these and his dragoons he fought the enemy in the battle of San Gabriel, January 8th, 1847, and also the next day in the engagement on the plains of Mesa, defeating them in both conflicts. He was highly complimented by the War Department for his services in the campaign, and was rewarded with the brevet-rank of Major-General, his commission as such being dated December 6th, 1846, the day when he met the Mexicans in the field at San Pascual. About this time Commodore R. F. Stockton had superseded Commodore Sloat in command of the United States squadron in the Pacific ocean, and the former officer, with his sailors and marines, aided by several hundred Californian settlers, had effectually conquered the Mexicans in and around Monterey. A conflict of authority unfortunately prevailed between Commodore Stockton and General Kearny, which was finally settled by a court-martial. Commodore Stockton returned to the United States overland, leaving General Kearny as Provisional Governor of the then Territory of California, which position he ably filled from March to June, 1847. He shortly afterwards rejoined the army in Mexico,

MAJ. GEN. PHILIP KEARNEY.

J until military operations term
> the United States was ordered
author of a work entitled " Mam
' 183;', and " Laws for the Goven
1846). He died in St. Louis, Oc
e⋅e ᴡʰⁱᶜʰ ʰᵉ had contracted the

PHILIP, late Major-General Unit. ᵢ
dunteers, was born, June 2d, 1815, i ⋅
[New York. On the paternal side hi.
vas Irish, while his mother was partly.
t in descent. He was also a nephew
al Stephen W. Kearny, whose bio-   cᴄ
ay be found immediately preceding.   the,
the best academies of his native city,   Amei
ur years' course in Columbia College.   losing
studied l: v, but being charmed with   superiors
d de⋅ ⋅u⋅ of a more active life than   ploit, and ᴠ
ttᴜᴇᶠ ᴜ' he continued at the bar, he   of that war h
f ⋅ ⋅ ⋅ommission as Lieutenant in a   and was ordered to the Pacinc coast, where he was em-
' ᴡⱼ had been ordered to the West.   ployed in operations against the Indian tribes. He resigned
7. and among the officers was Jefferson   his commission about 1852, and being a man of fortune, he
company: He remained with the com-   travelled throughout Europe and the East. and huaiiy estab-
months, during which time he studied   lished himself in Paris, occasionally visiting the United
d practice of his profession, and availed   States, where he remained each time only for a brief period.
portunity to perfect himself in all those   He served with the French army in 1859, being an aide-de-
ld constitute him a perfect tactician. In   camp on the staff of General Meurice, commanding the
i as one of three officers who were sent   cavalry of the guard, and was present at the battle of Sol-
government to Europe to study cavalry   ferino. For the bravery and gallantry he displayed in that
iission had been obtained from the gov-   campaign, he received from the Emperor Napoleon III. the
or these officers to enter their celebrated   Cross of the Legion of Honor. When the great Southern
tumur, he availed himself of this great   rebellion broke out, he abandoned his Parisian life, and,
e one of the most patient and indefatig-   hastening home, offered his services to the Union govern-
fter thoroughly mastering his profession   ment. After his arrival, early in 1861, he applied to General
nd accompanied the French forces to   Scott, who referred him to the governor of his native State.
ied to the 1st Regiment " Chasseurs   But he failed to receive any commission from the New
ticipated in two battles, where he dis-   York State authorities, and desiring impatiently an oppor-
and gallantry, and won for himself the   tunity to enter the volunteer service, he was finally commis-
his superior officers. He left France   sioned by the Governor of New Jersey, Brigadier-General

afforded them or their leader during the
' until they appeared in sight of the goal
⋅⋅ ⁚ been pressing for so many months.
⋅ever, that their leader was en-
⋅. as the commanding general
⋅v escort. The Mexicans,
⋅ the American cavalry
⋅ed the marsh, the
⋅ nt of one of the
nd pressed
of this
⋅. re-

ce,
the,
Amei
losing
superiors
ploit, and ᴠ
of that war h   ⋅⋅⋅ᴜⁿᵗ ex-
⋅⋅ ⋅ⁿⁿ ᴛʰᵉ army to the United States,

where he remained until military operations terminated; and on his return to the United States was ordered to the West. He was the author of a work entitled " Manœuvering of Dragoons " (1837), and " Laws for the Government of New Mexico " (1846). He died in St. Louis, October 31st, 1848, of a disease which he had contracted the previous year in Mexico.

EARNY, PHILIP, late Major-General United States Volunteers, was born, June 2d, 1815, in the city of New York. On the paternal side his ancestry was Irish, while his mother was partly Huguenot in descent. He was also a nephew of General Stephen W. Kearny, whose biographical sketch may be found immediately preceding. He was educated in the best academies of his native city, closing with the four years' course in Columbia College. After graduation he studied law, but being charmed with military pursuits, and desirous of a more active life than could possibly be attained if he continued at the bar, he sought and obtained a commission as Lieutenant in a cavalry regiment which had been ordered to the West. This was about 1837, and among the officers was Jefferson Davis, captain of a company. He remained with the command about sixteen months, during which time he studied the whole theory and practice of his profession, and availed himself of every opportunity to perfect himself in all those branches which would constitute him a perfect tactician. In 1839 he was selected as one of three officers who were sent by the United States government to Europe to study cavalry tactics; and as permission had been obtained from the government of France for these officers to enter their celebrated military school at Saumur, he availed himself of this great privilege, and became one of the most patient and indefatigable of students. After thoroughly mastering his profession he left the school and accompanied the French forces to Africa, being attached to the 1st Regiment " Chasseurs d'Afrique," and participated in two battles, where he displayed great bravery and gallantry, and won for himself the highest praises from his superior officers. He left France for home in 1841, and on his arrival in the United States was ordered to the staff of General Winfield Scott, in which position he remained until the outbreak of the Mexican war. In the meantime, however, he had received his commission as Captain of United States Dragoons; and being permitted to raise his own company, he journeyed to the western country, where he recruited a superior body of men and horses, himself adding from his ample means an additional bounty to that offered by the government. He was thus enabled to pick his men, and the result was as he desired; his troop being the acknowledged superior of any similar body in that branch of the service. This fact was so apparent that General Scott selected them as his body-guard when he reached the Mexican territory, and no opportunity

for action was afforded them or their leader during the march to the capital until they appeared in sight of the goal toward which they had been pressing for so many months. It was at Cherubusco, however, that their leader was enabled to bring them into action, as the commanding general temporarily relinquished his military escort. The Mexicans, being on the retreat, were pursued by the American cavalry along the narrow causeway which spanned the marsh, the causeway being protected by a battery in front of one of the city gates. Kearny seized the opportunity and pressed forward to prevent the enemy gaining possession of this shelter, and rallying for its and their defence. Though recalled by an officer despatched for that purpose, he hastily made known the situation and was allowed to continue the course he had taken, and reached the Cherubusco gate of the capital, killing all who resisted. On rejoining the American army he was wounded by a shower of grape, losing his left arm. He was highly complimented by his superiors in command for this dangerous and gallant exploit, and was promoted to the rank of Major. After the close of that war he returned with the army to the United States, and was ordered to the Pacific coast, where he was employed in operations against the Indian tribes. He resigned his commission about 1852, and being a man of fortune, he travelled throughout Europe and the East, and finally established himself in Paris, occasionally visiting the United States, where he remained each time only for a brief period. He served with the French army in 1859, being an aide-de-camp on the staff of General Meurice, commanding the cavalry of the guard, and was present at the battle of Solferino. For the bravery and gallantry he displayed in that campaign, he received from the Emperor Napoleon III. the Cross of the Legion of Honor. When the great Southern rebellion broke out, he abandoned his Parisian life, and, hastening home, offered his services to the Union government. After his arrival, early in 1861, he applied to General Scott, who referred him to the governor of his native State. But he failed to receive any commission from the New York State authorities, and desiring impatiently an opportunity to enter the volunteer service, he was finally commissioned by the Governor of New Jersey, Brigadier-General of Volunteers. This was after the disaster at the first Bull Run, and he immediately entered upon his duties with extraordinary ardor. He made the First Brigade of New Jersey the flower of the troops of that State. His organization was thoroughly disciplined, for he was remarkably strict on that point, and from the outset of his campaign until he fell on the field of battle, he was ever the foremost in maintaining his command in a degree of the highest excellence and standing. He was attached to the Army of the Potomac, under General McClellan, and viewed with disgust the halting and hesitating course of that officer. He saw opportunity after opportunity of reaching Richmond slip by, and he could scarcely conceal his opinion of the vacillation and incompetency of his superior general. The change of base which McClellan advised and subsequently adopted was severely criticised by him in confidential letters addressed to his friends, and he emphatically condemned the course pursued as a great mistake. In March, 1862, he was tendered the command of a division ; but as he was unwilling to leave the brigade of Jerseymen, he declined the same. When he arrived at this decision, and returned to camp, his appearance there was the occasion of an ovation spontaneously tendered him by his command. But he was obliged during the Peninsular campaign, in an emergency, to assume command of a division of Heintzleman's corps, and he relinquished his favorite troops, not without a sigh. He participated in the battle of Williamsburg, May 5th, 1862, and arrived in time to support Hooker and his New Jersey troops at a most critical period, thus avoiding what would have proved an irremediable disaster. The bravery he displayed on this occasion won for him the admiration of all beholders. He marched far ahead of his column and hurried them on at the double-quick, driving the enemy before him. So also, at the battle of Fair Oaks, May 31st, he arrived on the scene immediately after the flight of Casey's division, and turned the tide of battle. Again supporting Hooker, he drove back the rebels, who believed themselves victorious until now, and both he and his brother officers desired permission to follow the enemy into Richmond, which might then easily have been captured, but were refused by the hesitating course pursued by the general-in-chief. He foresaw the disasters which afterwards befel the Army of the Potomac; the "change of base," as it was termed, he really called a retreat, and during the whole week which was thus occupied in transferring the immense army to the James river, he was conspicuously engaged in every skirmish which transpired. Particularly was this the case in the battle of White Oak Swamp, June 30th; wherever danger was the greatest he was to be found, rallying his men and inspiring confidence when all seemed disaster and despair. So, likewise, at Malvern Hill, July 1st, he displayed the same undaunted courage and bravery which had made his name renowned as a Bayard, "without fear and reproach." When McClellan again failed to order an advance on Richmond, and commanded the army to retreat to Harrison's Landing, his indignation knew no bounds, and he publicly protested, in the presence of many officers, against so fatal a course being adopted, saying that "such an order can only be prompted by cowardice or treason." He had now received promotion to the rank of Major-General of Volunteers, though he had been for three months in command of a division. His predictions that Pope would be crushed by the rebels were fulfilled by the events that took place at and after the second Bull Run, August 30th. On September 1st was fought the battle of Chantilly, where General Pope, in order to save his army, looked for aid from Generals Kearny, Reno and Stevens, who promptly came to the rescue. The two latter attacked the enemy, but were compelled to retire by an overwhelming force. At this juncture Kearny placed himself at the head of General Birney's brigade, broke the rebel centre, causing them to retreat in great disorder, thus saving Pope's army and the city of Washington. At sunset on that day, while reconnoitring the enemy's position, he suddenly came upon their lines, and his surrender being demanded, he refused. As he turned to fly, he was shot dead, his body falling into the hands of the rebels. The tidings of this fatal event flew far and fast throughout the country on the wings of the lightning, and everywhere a wail went up for the brave man thus sacrificed : he was mourned alike by President and peasant.

———◦◦◦———

OUTHARD, HON. SAMUEL L., LL.D., Lawyer and Statesman, late of Jersey City, was born, June 7th, 1787, at Baskingridge, New Jersey, and was the son of Hon. Henry Southard, formerly of Long Island, but who had removed to New Jersey while a youth, where by his industry he purchased a farm, became a justice of the peace, then a member of the legislature, and for sixteen years represented his district in the lower house of Congress. Samuel was educated in a classical school in his native town, where he had as classmates the late Theodore Frelinghuysen and Joseph R. Ingersoll, of Philadelphia; who were also with him at Princeton College, where he graduated in 1804, being then barely seventeen years of age. After leaving college he began teaching school at Mendham, in Morris county, and subsequently went to Washington, where his father was then occupied with his congressional duties, and who introduced him to Colonel John Taliaferro, a member from Virginia. The latter forthwith tendered him a position in his family as tutor to his sons and nephews, which he accepted; and in the autumn of 1805 he became a resident of Hagley, King George's county, Virginia, that being the name of Colonel Taliaferro's plantation. This country-seat was within a short distance of Fredericksburg; and here he passed five years in instructing his pupils. His leisure hours were devoted to the study of law, under the preceptorship of Judges Green and Brooks, of Fredericksburg; and after due examination was admitted, in 1809, to practise at the bar. He remained in Virginia until 1811, when he returned to New Jersey, and settled at Flemington; and being licensed by the Supreme Court of the State, opened his office, and soon obtained a fair and remunerative practice, eventually attaining a high rank at the bar. His first public position was as Prosecuting Attorney of Hunterdon county; and in 1814 he was appointed State Law Reporter. In 1815 he was elected a member of the General Assembly, having previously attracted great attention in that body, by an argument in opposition to a petition for the repeal of a law granting to Aaron Ogden and Daniel Dod the exclusive right of using steamboats plying between New Jersey and New York, in the waters of New Jersey. After taking his seat in the Legislature he remained but a very brief period, as he was chosen a Judge of the Supreme Court, to fill a vacancy occasioned by the election of Mahlon Dickerson—one of the judges—to the gubernatorial chair of the State. He removed his residence to Trenton, and passed five years on the bench, being also selected as reporter of the decisions of his court. In 1820 he was engaged, in connection with Charles Ewing, to attend to the preparation of the "Revised Statutes of the State," and to superintend their publication. In the autumn of the same year he was elected by the Legislature (as was then the custom) a member of the Electoral College of New Jersey, and cast his vote for that sterling patriot James Monroe, who was also his warm personal friend. In 1821 he was elected United States Senator, and thereupon resigned his position as Judge. He took his seat in that body in February, 1821, having been also selected to fill the vacancy occasioned by the resignation of James J. Wilson, whose term would have expired March 3d, 1821. It was a period of intense political excitement, growing out of the question of the admission of Missouri into the Union, which was opposed by reason of two clauses in her constitution, one being that the Legislature should prohibit the immigration of free negroes, and the other forbidding the abolition of slavery. The House of Representatives had voted against admitting the State, when Henry Clay moved that a joint committee of the House and Senate should be appointed to consider the subject in its various bearings. This course was adopted, and, strange to say, the father, Hon. Henry Southard, of the House—at that time approaching very nearly the close of his Congressional career—met his son, Samuel, of the Senate, then at the very commencement of his high position, to confer together as to the best means to pursue. Samuel L. Southard had prepared resolutions—the identical ones which were afterwards introduced and passed. These he showed to his political friends, among them Mr. Clay; they were approved, and it was understood that they should be presented in the Senate by their author. Mr. Clay subsequently obtained possession of the resolutions by saying that it would be better if something of that nature should first emanate from the lower House. But the verbiage of the resolutions was unaltered; and they were carried in both Houses, thus ending the struggle. From that time Mr. Clay had all the merit of settling the question, while the real originator and author of the measure was quietly ignored. He remained a member of the Senate until 1823, when he succeeded Hon. Smith Thompson as Secretary of the Navy. He remained in this position throughout the remainder of President Monroe's term, and upon the accession of President John Quincy Adams the latter continued him in the same high office, being unwilling to make a change. During these years he also filled for short periods the additional positions of Acting Secretary of the Treasury and Acting Secretary of the War Departments. Early in 1829 a movement was made in the New Jersey Legislature

to re-elect him to his old position of United States Senator; when those opposed to his nomination advanced the singular objection that he was not a resident of the State, such as her constitution implied; and a resolution was actually passed declaring him ineligible, when Senator Dickerson was chosen. A month later Theodore Frelinghuysen, then Attorney-General of the State, was also chosen as United States Senator, and Southard was elected to the vacancy in the attorney-generality thus created. He returned to Trenton with his family, which city again became his residence, and there resumed the practice of his profession. In the autumn of 1832 his partisans controlled the Legislature, and elected him Governor of the State. He held this position but three months, when he was chosen United States Senator. During his occupancy of the gubernatorial office but one term of the Court of Chancery was held. His only message to the Legislature was addressed to them in January, 1833, relative to the Nullification acts of South Carolina, and transmitting to those bodies copies of the same, which he had received from the governor of that State. He also took occasion to concur in the views entertained by President Jackson in his celebrated proclamation issued on the occasion, and which for the time united all parties at the North in one solid column to the support of the man who declared that the "Union must and shall be preserved." From the day he took his seat in the Senate until the close of his life he took a very active part in all the proceedings of that body, although his party were in the minority and in opposition to the government up to 1841. In the autumn of 1838 he was re-elected United States Senator for the full term of six years; and in 1841 was elected President *pro tem.* of that body. After the death of President Harrison, in April, 1841, Vice-President Tyler succeeded to the Chief Magistracy, when Southard filled the position of presiding officer continuously during life; and he was recognized by all parties as most faithful, impartial and able in that high office. When first elected to the General Assembly of his native State, he was elected as a Democrat, in which organization he continued down to the close of his career of a cabinet officer under President Adams. Meanwhile the political creeds or parties had materially changed, and so likewise did their names; and great confusion existed in 1824-25, when both Jackson and Adams were classed as members of the Democratic party, although they were strongly opposed to each other. After the latter had been elected President by the House of Representatives the Jackson party manifested great hostility to him and to his administration; and when General Jackson succeeded him, in 1829, the party in opposition to the Democracy of those days was termed "Anti-Jackson." With the latter Senator Southard affiliated; and when, at the close of the second term of General Jackson's administration, Mr. Van Buren was placed in nomination by the Democracy, and the Whig party was formed, he (Southard) gave in his adhesion to the new organization, which was in effect the same as had opposed the measures of the Jackson dynasty. In 1840 the Whigs succeeded in electing General Harrison to the Presidency by a sweeping majority, and thenceforward for thirteen years were a power in the country, until dissolved by the advent of the Free-soil or Republican organization. In 1838 Mr. Southard was appointed President of the Morris Canal and Banking Company, and thenceforward took up his residence in Jersey City. In religious belief he was a Presbyterian; although not a communicant member, yet he was strongly attached to its principles. He was an earnest advocate for temperance principles, even to the degree of total abstinence. As a counsellor and attorney-at-law he was regarded as skilful and preparing his cases thoroughly; and as a statesman, the high positions he attained is a sufficient proof of his abilities in that direction. While a resident at Hagley, in Virginia, he was married, in June, 1812, to Rebecca Harrow, daughter of an Episcopal clergyman (then deceased); and thirty years after, June 26th, 1842, he died at the house of his wife's brother, in Fredericksburg, Virginia.

TOCKTON, HON. RICHARD, Lawyer and United States Senator, late of Princeton, New Jersey, was born in that place in the year 1764. Coming from one of the ancient and distinguished families of the State, he may be said to have inherited, with a noble name, the qualities which won him fame; his father, named also Richard Stockton, having been an eminent lawyer, one of the justices of the Supreme Court before the Revolution, and a signer of the Declaration of Independence. On the maternal side also his lineage was notable, his mother being a Boudinot, and a woman of superior and highly cultivated mind and literary taste. His classical education he completed at Princeton, from which he graduated before his seventeenth year. Determining to follow his father's profession, he entered the office of his uncle, Elisha Boudinot, at Newark, and after the usual course of study was admitted to the bar as attorney in 1784, when only about twenty years old. In due time he was licensed as counsellor, and was called as sergeant-at-law in 1792. At first his progress at the bar was somewhat slow, but in a few years he had made his quality so manifest that he stood among the first. His practice grew to very large proportions, and no name for many years was so familiar in important causes as his. From the year 1818 until his death he was generally recognized as the leader of the bar, and this distinction was deserved. During his time he was almost the only New Jersey lawyer who argued causes before the Supreme Court at Washington, and these were cases not originating in the State. A well-read lawyer and a diligent student, he was also an eloquent and forcible speaker. He had great power in denunciation, being alike

a master of invective and retort, and crushing in sarcasm. His addresses to juries were magnificent specimens of legal oratory, and have rarely been equalled. Of his efforts scarcely any remain in enduring form beyond an able argument in favor of the New Jersey claims to the waters of the Hudson, appended to the report of a commission, published by order of the Legislature in 1828. In politics he was a decided Federalist of the Hamilton school. As such he sat in the United States Senate, being elected thereto by the Legislature in joint session, to fill a vacancy. He held his seat until 1799. His party losing power, he figured very little in politics for some years thereafter. But when war was declared against Great Britain, and it obtained a temporary majority in the State, providing for the election of Congressmen by districts, he was chosen, in January, 1813, a member of the Thirteenth Congress. Therein he took a leading part, proving himself a worthy contemporary of such men as Webster, Calhoun and Clay. In the affairs of his *Alma Mater*, Princeton College, he always manifested an earnest interest, and from 1791 was one of its Trustees. From Rutgers and Union Colleges he received the honorary degree of LL. D. When a vacancy occurred on the bench of the United States District Court, in 1826, through the death of Judge Pennington, general expectation turned to Mr. Stockton as his most fitting successor. It was known to the President, John Quincy Adams, and Mr. Southard, a member of the Cabinet, that he would accept the nomination, and his fitness was conspicuous. But the administration deemed it inconsistent with their prospects to appoint so pronounced a Federalist, and Mr. Stockton would not permit his friends to bring the least pressure to bear in his favor. The nomination therefore went elsewhere. A man of most imposing personal appearance, and singularly polished address, he came to be known among the junior members of the bar as "the old duke." And, indeed, he was a nobleman in the truest sense. His whole bearing, while free from self-consciousness, was that of a man of the highest distinction. Yet he was very affable and easy of access, but none could approach him without yielding a tribute of respect. He died in 1828.

TOCKTON, ROBERT FIELD, late Commodore United States Navy, and Senator of the United States, was born, 1796, in Princeton, and was a son of the late Hon. Richard Stockton, whose biographical sketch precedes. He was partly educated at the College of New Jersey, in his native town, and while a student the war with Great Britain commenced. He at once left college to enter the navy as a midshipman, and made his first cruise in the frigate "President," commanded by Commodore Rodgers. He participated in several engagements while serving on board that vessel, and bore himself with such bravery and

Yours truly
R. F. Stockton

gallantry as to receive honorable mention in the despatches forwarded by his commander. For these tokens of approbation he was rewarded by receiving, in December, 1814, his commission as a lieutenant. After peace had been declared with England, the United States became involved in war with the Algerine government, and the frigate "Guerriere" was despatched to the Mediterranean, to which ship he had been previously ordered. Shortly after reaching that station he was transferred to the "Spitfire," as First-Lieutenant of that vessel. He soon furnished another example of coolness and bravery by attacking an Algerine man-of-war, aided by a single boat's crew from his own ship, boarding the enemy and capturing their vessel. Early in 1816 he was transferred to the ship-of-the-line "Washington," at that time the flag-ship of Commodore Chauncey, commanding the Mediterranean Squadron, where he remained for some time, being eventually ordered to command the sloop of war "Erie," in which latter vessel he returned home in 1821. After a short stay in the United States he was sent to the coast of Africa, and was permitted to aid the American Colonization Society in their endeavors to secure a site for their proposed colony. His associate was Dr. Ayres, the society's agent, and after considerable delay he succeeded in making a treaty with the natives by which a large tract of land was ceded, and which constituted at one period the original territory of the Republic of Liberia. After this important step had been accomplished he cruised on the coast, overhauling and capturing many slavers, including a Portuguese privateer called the "Marianna Flora," mounting twenty-two guns. This last vessel had commenced the conflict which resulted in her capture; he placed a prize crew on board and sent her to the United States. On her arrival much litigation ensued in the Admiralty courts, it being contended by the counsel for the Portuguese government that Lieutenant Stockton had exceeded his authority in capturing the privateer. A decision, however, was finally reached, by which he was fully exonerated for the course pursued, but the vessel was delivered over to the Portuguese government. On his return home he was next assigned to duty in the West India islands, and assisted in rooting out and breaking the numerous gangs of freebooters and pirates who had long infested those waters. After this important service had been rendered he returned to the United States, and for several years was absent on leave; and during this period identified himself with the movement taking place in his native State relative to the establishment of canals and railroads, chiefly between New York and Philadelphia, and including what is now termed the "United Companies of New Jersey." In 1838 he was ordered to the ship-of-the-line "Ohio," as Flag-Lieutenant to Commodore Hull, with whom he sailed to the Mediterranean, serving in that capacity for about a year, when he was commissioned Captain, and recalled. He had for many years been engaged in solving the problem as to the best mode of apply-

ing steam power to vessels of war, and also to the more effective armament of naval vessels. Up to 1841 the United States navy did not possess a single steam man-of-war, the "Fulton" having exploded some years previously; while the "Mississippi" and "Missouri" steam frigates were still on the stocks. These latter were powerful side-wheelers of 2,500 tons, and were pierced for ten guns of heavy calibre; but, in his opinion, they possessed one fatal mistake, in having the motive power exposed to the chance shot of an enemy. He accordingly submitted to the Navy Department some plans which he had prepared, substituting the screw for the paddle, and locating the boiler and engines below the load or water-line. After much persuasion, notwithstanding that naval constructors had condemned his theories, he received permission from the authorities to build an experimental steam sloop of war. The keel was laid, 1842, in his presence, in the large ship-house at the navy yard, Philadelphia, and he placed a golden eagle at the intersection of the stern post. The vessel, which was of only 700 tons burthen, old measurement, was launched in 1843 and was named the "Princeton." Her engine and boilers were placed below the water-line, in accordance with his plans, the former being of 175 horse-power and consuming sixteen tons of coal in twenty-four hours. The armament consisted of twelve guns, forty-two-pounders, and two large wrought-iron cannon carrying shot of 225 pounds. These latter were named the "Oregon" and the "Peacemaker." The trial trip of the vessel occurred towards the close of 1843, when she made the run from the capes of the Delaware to the eastward, sighting Madeira in eight days and a few hours. Returning home she ascended the Potomac river and reached Washington, where she remained for some time. It was during her stay that the terrible accident occurred, February 28th, 1844, when the great gun called the "Peacemaker" exploded, killing five persons, including the Secretaries of War and of the Navy, besides wounding many others, including the Commodore himself. A court of inquiry subsequently convened, which fully acquitted him of all blame or want of precaution either in the manufacture of the gun or in its management. In the summer of 1844 the vessel returned to Philadelphia, and her officers and crew, at the request of the municipal authorities, landed and assisted in preserving the peace during the formidable church riots occurring in that year. In October, 1845, he sailed for the Pacific with several vessels to reinforce the squadron in those waters, then under the command of Commodore Sloat, whom he relieved while in the harbor of Monterey. At that time the war with the Mexican republic was in progress, and, aware of the importance of acquiring the western coast of that power, he assumed the responsibility of capturing the same. He landed with a force of 600 sailors and marines, and was subsequently joined by several hundred Californian settlers and adventurers, thus forming an earnest and formidable body, who seized upon the territory, over which he established a provisional government. Meanwhile Brigadier-General Kearny had marched overland and had defeated the Mexicans at San Pascual and at San Gabriel, and himself had also established a provisional government. The old feud between the army and navy relative to questions of rank and of supreme command arose, which was finally settled at a court martial convened for the express purpose. Commodore Stockton returned to the United States via the plains in 1847, and in 1849 resigned his commission. In 1851 he was elected by the Legislature of his native State a Senator of the United States, which position he held for two years only, resigning in 1853. During this time he succeeded in introducing a bill for the suppression of flogging in the navy as a punishment; and he also advocated the non-intervention of the United States in the quarrel between Austria and Hungary, in opposition to the solicitations of Cossuth, who at that time was urging not only the people of the United States, but also the two houses of Congress, in support of this measure. In 1856 some of his admirers pressed his claim upon the country as an available candidate for the Presidency, and during the same year his "Life, Speeches and Letters" were published in New York city. Towards the close of his life he lived in retirement at Princeton, having suffered a reverse of fortune; and died in that town, October 7th, 1866.

———

TOCKTON, HON. JOHN P., Lawyer and Legislator, of Trenton, was born in Princeton, New Jersey, August 2d, 1826. He comes of the family so long distinguished in the history of the State for their brilliant qualities and devoted services to the country. After a superior preparatory course he became a student at Princeton College, from which he was graduated in 1843. Adopting the law, he passed through the usual preparation, and was licensed as an attorney in 1846. Three years later he was called to the bar as a counsellor. He very speedily attained a high position in his profession, and in connection therewith received some high trusts, being appointed a member of the Commission for the Revision of the Laws of New Jersey, and subsequently Reporter to the Court of Chancery. In this latter capacity he published three volumes of "Equity Reports" which bear his name. He has been engaged in a number of the leading causes of his time, and was a prominent counsel for the Pennsylvania Railroad Company in the long and intricate litigation rendered necessary by assaults upon the privileges enjoyed by it from the corporations known as the United Railroads of New Jersey. This litigation absorbed an extraordinary attention, and forms the greatest railroad war in the annals of the State. Politically a Democrat, inheriting his principles from a long line of ancestors, he has taken an active and conspicuous part in

politics. In 1858 he was offered by President Buchanan the position of Minister-Resident at Rome, which he accepted and filled until 1861, when he was recalled at his own request. In 1865 he was elected by the Legislature to the United States Senate for the term ending in 1871. A contest, however, arose, and after he had occupied the seat for rather more than a year his election was declared by the Senate to have been informal. He was accordingly unseated, and thereupon returned home to prosecute his profession. In 1868 he was again elected to the United States Senate as the successor of Hon. Frederick T. Frelinghuysen, and took his seat on March 4th, 1869. On the expiration of this term, in March, 1875, he resumed close attention to his profession.

———

HITTINGHAM, EDWARD THOMAS, M. D., of Millburn, New Jersey, was born April 22d, 1821. He is of English parentage. He was educated at the College of St. James, an Episcopal institution in Hagerstown, Maryland, from which he graduated in July, 1849, and pursued his medical studies in the medical department of the University of Maryland, graduating in March, 1852. He first settled in Baltimore, Maryland, whence in 1854 he removed to Millburn, Essex county, New Jersey, where he has since resided, excepting the interval of his military service, extending from the outbreak of the civil war to 1864. He is a member of the Essex County Medical Society, and of the Essex Medical Union, and was formerly a member of the Medico-Chirurgical Society of Maryland. His contributions to medical literature consist principally of his reports as a Surgeon in the army, though these, considering his general culture and professional skill, not to mention the variety and multiplicity of surgical experiences in the field, can scarcely be regarded as unimportant. He was Assistant Surgeon in the United States army during the critical years of the civil war, serving with various commands and in the several campaigns of the Army of the Potomac. He was married in 1859 to Martha G. Condit, daughter of J. D. Condit, of Millburn, New Jersey.

———

OUDINOT, HON. ELISHA, Lawyer and Judge of the Supreme Court of New Jersey, and brother of Elias Boudinot, of whom a sketch appears above, was born in 1742. After a good preparatory education he studied for the bar, and was in due course admitted as attorney, and subsequently as counsellor. He was called to be a sergeant-at-law in 1792. An able lawyer and of exalted character, he attained a high position in his profession. His practice was commenced in Newark, where he chiefly resided during his lifetime. When, in 1798, an act was passed by the Legislature authorizing the appointment of an additional Justice of the Supreme Court, which then consisted of the Chief-Justice and two associates, Mr. Boudinot was elected to the new seat, which he occupied during one term of seven years. In 1804 this law was repealed and the court reduced to its former status, which was maintained until 1838. Mr. Boudinot was widely respected and esteemed, not only as a lawyer and a judge, but as a private citizen. He died in 1819.

———————

HOMSON, JOHN R., late United States Senator from New Jersey, was born, September 25th, 1800, in the city of Philadelphia, Pennsylvania, where he was also educated. After leaving school he entered the counting-house of one of the most prominent merchants in that city, whence he proceeded to China, where he was for several years a resident, largely engaged in the tea trade. While abroad he received from President Monroe the appointment of United States Consul for the port and district of Canton. He returned to the United States in 1825, having amassed an ample competence, and shortly after married a sister of the late Commodore Stockton, and settled in Princeton, New Jersey. He was among the first to manifest an interest in the construction of the Delaware and Raritan Canal, and was the first Secretary of that company, and one of the Board of Directors until his death. He was also an early advocate for the building of the Camden & Amboy Railroad, and subsequently for the various lines of railway which were afterwards known by the name of the "United Companies of New Jersey;" and was also a prominent stockholder and director of the latter. In political belief he was a Democrat of the Andrew Jackson type, and took an active part in the several presidential campaigns occurring after 1828 in that State. In 1842 he was among those who advocated the framing of a new constitution, and he thoroughly canvassed the State in favor of that object. The convention assembled in 1844, during which year he was the Democratic candidate for Governor, but failed of an election. After this period he retired from political life for a while, until 1853, when his brother-in-law, Commodore Stockton, resigned his seat in the United States Senate, and he was chosen for the unexpired term. In 1857 he was again elected to that body for the term of six years, ending March 3d, 1863. But he was not destined to occupy that exalted position for that period. A lingering illness confined him at home for a considerable time, and he died September 13th, 1862. At a meeting of the stockholders of the Delaware & Raritan Canal Company, held at Princeton, May 11th, 1863, Hon. Robert F. Stockton, in his annual report, paid a high tribute to the character and services of Mr. Thomson. He said: "Mr. Thomson was secretary of the Delaware & Raritan Canal Company from its first organization, and a member of the Board of Directors until his decease. Possessed of business talents of the highest order, he devoted himself to the duties of his position with zeal. Industrious, faithful and accurate, for more than thirty years he served the company with a fidelity never questioned, and with an intelligent aptitude for the duties devolved upon him which could not be excelled. In serving the company he served the people of New Jersey, whose State pride is gratified, and whose interests are largely promoted by the success of this great work. He took part, at an important epoch in the history of the State, in urging the adoption of the present Constitution of New Jersey, as a substitute for the imperfect organization of the State government which preceded it, and he closed his career while representing New Jersey in the Senate of the United States, to which distinguished position he was twice elected by the Legislature. Valuable as Mr. Thomson's services were to these companies, distinguished as was his political career, yet by us, who were his companions and friends, he will be regretted for those social qualities of which he was so eminently possessed; his memory will be recalled by the recollection of the delightful hours we have passed in companionship with him. We will mourn on our own account the society of the friend we have since lost, the charm of his conversation, his cheerful smile and pleasant anecdote. His vacant seat leaves a social vacuum that can never be filled. His absence is a loss which we cannot cease to feel with peculiar force on the recurrence of our annual meetings. Identified with the history of the Delaware & Raritan Canal Company from its origin, his name will likewise be remembered in the history of New Jersey, while his memory will be cherished by a large circle of personal friends."

———————

ROWNING, HON. ABRAHAM, Lawyer, of Camden, was born, July 26th, 1808, on his father's farm, in the vicinity of the city, where he has since resided. The family to which he belongs is one of the oldest in the State of New Jersey, and has always occupied a high social position. Its American founder, George Browning, grandfather of Abraham, came immediately from Holland, although of ancient English lineage. He arrived in this country about the year 1735, being then quite young, and settled near Pea Shore, in Camden county. Here he purchased large tracts of land, and devoted himself to agricultural pursuits. He also became extensively interested in the fisheries on the Delaware river. These fishery interests were bequeathed to his heirs and have been handed down from generation to generation, being still retained in the Browning family. George Browning's son, Abraham, following in his father's footsteps, became a farmer also, and continued to reside in the old homestead and to cultivate the lands his sire had acquired. He married Beulah

Genge, who, like himself, was a native of New Jersey, but whose parents were English, arriving in America from London about the year 1760. From this marriage sprang the subject of this sketch and a numerous progeny, in whose veins the mingled Dutch and English blood has flowed to good purpose, the city, the State, and the country alike, deriving benefit from their active, honorable and public-spirited lives. Abraham obtained his earliest education—apart from the training of home influences—at the country schools in the neighborhood of his home. The standard of the common schools of those days was far from high, but the ordinary routine was in his case supplemented by private study. Possessed of a large capacity for acquiring knowledge, and gifted with a studious temperament, he made most effective use of all his opportunities, and laid a solid foundation, broad and deep, for the superstructure of after years. After an elementary course thus satisfactorily pursued, he was placed at the academy at Woodbury, in Gloucester county, then in charge of the Rev. Joseph Jones, and his brother, Samuel Jones. From this he was transferred to the renowned school of John Gummere, in Burlington. This institution was, at that time, one of the most valued educational establishments in the State, and to it nearly all the first families of West Jersey sent their sons. The enlarged advantages here offered Abraham Browning were industriously improved, and he secured a very thorough English and a limited classical education. But mathematics was his forte. It having been determined that he should enter the legal profession, on leaving school he became a student in the law office of Hon. Samuel L. Southard, at Trenton, in 1830. With that gentleman he remained about a year, vigorously prosecuting his preliminary studies, and making it very manifest that, in choosing the course for his career, a very wise decision had been reached. From the first he developed a special and marked aptitude for the calling, and progressed rapidly in the attainment of legal knowledge. At the expiration of a year passed in preliminary study, he entered the law school of Yale College, where he remained between two and three years, gaining for himself a high and eminently deserved reputation for scholarship. Returning home he enjoyed the exceptional advantages of a connection with the office of the well-known Philadelphia lawyer, Charles Chauncey. There he continued, however, but a short time, being admitted to the bar in September, 1834, and immediately thereafter beginning the practice of his profession in Camden. In this city he has ever since resided, laboring in his chosen career. He early became noted for the care and ability with which the business intrusted to his care was managed, and as a natural consequence he made steady and rapid progress through the ranks. With clear perception, a well-trained and well-stored mind, to which constant study was ever bringing valuable contributions, indomitable industry, and never-tiring investigation of detail, he obtained so thorough a mastery over his cases as to be entirely invincible when he advised contest, and to secure

respectful attention for any opinion he might utter. Gradually his successes brought him into the very front of the profession, where to-day he holds a commanding position, enjoying a very large, important and lucrative practice. But while he has reached so proud an eminence, he is not unmindful of the means whereby it was gained. Nowhere in the ranks can a harder student be found ; not one among the aspirants to similar fame devotes more faithful and painstaking labor to his clients' interests. Indeed, the amount of work he does in special cases is simply tremendous. Of course, a lawyer with such qualities and attainments, and of so many and great successes, could not fail of recognition outside of his own State. His aid has been sought in many important issues beyond its borders, and his reputation has become national. While there are very few lawyers in New Jersey who can be classed as his peers, the number is not greatly enlarged even when the range of vision covers the nation. As a constitutional lawyer he is a recognized authority, and his opinion on points of constitutional issue carries great weight everywhere. In railroad cases, also, he is regarded as especially strong, and he has been engaged in many important cases involving difficult and delicate points of railroad law. His famous contest with Hon. Theodore Cuyler, a foeman worthy of his steel, in the Pennsylvania Railroad case in 1871, will long be remembered by members of the profession for the profound legal learning, easy mastery over the mazy difficulties of a peculiarly intricate litigation, readiness of resource, patient endurance and overwhelming strength he manifested. On some of the most celebrated issues of his time his opinion has been called for, and has always been received with respect by the highest, and has exercised great influence in the final decision. To him, in part, New Jersey owes its present constitution, inasmuch as he was an active and prominent member of the convention called in 1844 for the revision of the then existing instrument. He was also the first Attorney-General under the constitution so revised, being appointed to that position by Governor Stratton in the same year. This office he held during the regular term of five years. His successes as a lawyer do not bound his career. He has stepped beyond merely professional boundaries in his studies and researches, and in whatever direction his tastes have led him, the same thoroughness and success have marked his efforts. A notable illustration of this is found in his oration delivered at the Centennial Exposition on the State-day of New Jersey. He had been appointed the historian of the State for the occasion, and his effort will long be treasured and quoted as an exhaustive and complete synopsis of the State's history, elegant in its diction and eloquent in its appreciation of the achievements of his native home. Mr. Browning was married, May 23d, 1842, to Elizabeth, daughter of Hon. James Matlack, of Woodbury, New Jersey, whose American ancestor, William Matlack, was among the Quakers who settled at Burlington, New Jersey, about the year 1670.

Genge, who, like himself, was a native of New Jersey, but whose parents were English, so that in America for a sudden above the .... From this marriage sprang the rubicund .... his eleven .... numerous progeny, in whose veins the noblest French and English blood has flowed to good purpose the city, the State, and the country alike, deriving .... from their active, honorable and public-spirited lives. Abraham obtained his earliest education—apart from the training of home influences—at the country schools in the neighborhood of his home. The standard of the common schools of those days was far from high, but the ordinary routine was in his case supplemented by private study. Possessed of a large capacity for acquiring knowledge, and gifted with a studious temperament, he made most effective use of all his opportunities, and laid a solid foundation, broad and deep, for the superstructure of after years. After an elementary course thus satisfactorily pursued, he was placed at the academy at Woodbury, in Gloucester county, then in charge of the Rev. Joseph Jones, and his brother, Samuel Jones. From this he was transferred to the renowned school of John Gummere, in Burlington. This institution was, at that time, one of the most valued educational establishments in the State, and to it nearly all the first families of West Jersey sent their sons. The enlarged advantages here offered Abraham Browning were industriously improved, and he secured a very thorough English and a limited classical education. But mathematics was his forte. It having been determined that he should enter the legal profession, on leaving school he became a student in the law office of Hon. Samuel L. Southard, at Trenton, in 1830. With that gentleman he remained about a year, vigorously prosecuting his preliminary studies, and making it very manifest that, in choosing the course his career, a very wise decision had been reached. From the first he developed a special and marked aptitude for the calling, and progressed rapidly in the attainment of legal knowledge. At the expiration of a year passed in preliminary study, he entered the law school of Yale College, where he remained between two and three years, gaining for himself a high and eminently deserved reputation for scholarship. Returning home he enjoyed the exceptional advantages of a connection with the office of the well-known Philadelphia lawyer, Charles Chauncey. There he continued, however, but a short time, being admitted to the bar in September, 1834, and immediately thereafter beginning the practice of his profession in Camden. In this city he has ever since resided, laboring in his chosen career. He early became noted for the care and ability with which the business intrusted to his care was managed, and as a natural consequence he made steady and rapid progress through the ranks. With clear .. well-trained and well-stored mind, to which constant study was ever bringing valuable contributions, indomitable industry, and never-tiring investigation of detail, he obtained .. through a mastery over his cases as to be entirely invincible when he advised contest, and to secure

respectful attention for any opinion he might utter. Gradually his successes brought him into the very front of the profession, where to-day he holds a commanding position, enjoying a very large, important and lucrative practice. But while he has reached so proud an eminence, he is not unmindful of the means whereby it was gained. Nowhere in the ranks can a harder student be found; not one among the aspirants to similar fame devotes more faithful and painstaking labor to his clients' interests. Indeed, the amount of work he does in special cases is simply tremendous. Of course, a lawyer with such qualities and attainments, and of so many and great successes, could not fail of recognition outside of his own State. His aid has been sought in many important issues beyond its borders, and his reputation has become national. While there are very few lawyers in New Jersey who can be classed as his peers, the number is not greatly enlarged even when the range of vision covers the nation. As a constitutional lawyer he is a recognized authority, and his opinion on points of constitutional issue carries great weight everywhere. In railroad cases, also, he is regarded as especially strong, and he has been engaged in many important cases involving difficult and delicate points of railroad law. His famous contest with Hon. Theodore Cuyler, a foeman worthy of his steel, in the Pennsylvania Railroad case in 1871, will long be remembered by members of the profession for the profound legal learning, easy mastery over the mazy difficulties of a peculiarly intricate litigation, readiness of resource, patient endurance and overwhelming strength he manifested. On some of the most celebrated issues of his time his opinion has been called for, and has always been received with respect by the highest, and has exercised great influence in the final decision. To him, in part, New Jersey owes its present constitution, inasmuch as he was an active and prominent member of the convention called in 1844 for the revision of the then existing instrument. He was also the first Attorney-General under the constitution so revised, being appointed to that position by Governor ... in the same year. This office he held during the regular term of five years. His successes as a lawyer have not bound his career. He has stepped beyond his professional boundaries in his studies and researches, and in whatever direction his tastes have led him, the same thoroughness and success have marked his efforts. A notable illustration of this is found in his oration delivered at the Centennial Exposition on the State-day of New Jersey. He had been appointed the historian of the State for the occasion, and his effort will long be treasured and quoted as an exhaustive and complete synopsis of the State's history, elegant in its diction and eloquent in its appreciation of the achievements of his native home. Mr. Browning was married, May 23d, 1842, to Elizabeth, daughter of Hon. James Matlack, of Woodbury, New Jersey, whose American ancestor, William Matlack, was among the Quakers who settled at Burlington, New Jersey, about the year 1670.

DEN, AARON, LL.D., Lawyer, Statesman and Governor of New Jersey, was born, 1756, in Elizabethtown, and was the son of Robert Ogden, and the great-grandson of Jonathan Ogden, one of the original associates of the Elizabethtown purchase, and who died in 1732, aged eighty-six years. Aaron received an excellent education, and graduated from Princeton College before he reached the age of seventeen. After leaving college, in 1773, he became a tutor in Barber's grammar school, where among other pupils were to be found William Livingston and Alexander Hamilton. When resistance to British tyranny assumed the character of a revolution, the school was deserted and the pupils with their tutor volunteered in the patriot army. Ogden entered a corps of infantry at Elizabethtown, some time towards the close of 1775. General William Alexander—more familiarly known as Lord Sterling, and, withal, an ardent patriot—had planned an expedition having in view the capture of a large British store-ship near Sandy Hook, and this too while a British ship-of-the-line was anchored in New York harbor. The volunteer company in which Ogden was an officer formed part of this expedition, which embarked in boats and carried the store-ship by boarding. The prize was a valuable one, and the exploit was recognized by Congress, then in session at Philadelphia, who passed a vote of thanks to the commander and the men engaged in the hazardous undertaking. Lieutenant Aaron Ogden participated with his regiment, of which his brother had command, at the battle of the Brandywine, in September, 1777. He was also present at the battle of Monmouth, where he was directed by General Washington to reconnoitre an important position; and upon his report being received, Washington ordered an advance, and the battle was with the Americans. He had already been promoted to a Captaincy; and became subsequently aide to General Maxwell, and also Brigade Major. He greatly distinguished himself at the battle of Springfield, where he held a large force of the enemy in check. During the following winter, while reconnoitring at night what proved to be a large force of British soldiers who were destined to surprise and capture the American troops quartered at Elizabethtown, he received a bayonet wound in his chest; but he managed to reach the garrison, two miles distant, and give the alarm; but he was a long time recovering from the wound, which was a very dangerous one. He subsequently participated in General Sullivan's campaigns against the Indians in 1779, where he again served as an aide to General Maxwell, and when the latter resigned he commanded a company of light infantry under General Lafayette; and was also with the latter in Virginia, and covered the retreat when Lord Cornwallis made his attempt to capture "the boy," as he termed the youthful marquis. He was an active participant in the siege of Yorktown, and received the personal commendation of General Washington. At the expiration of the war, in 1783, he commenced the study of law with his brother Robert, and was licensed as an attorney in September, 1784. He at once commenced the practice of his profession at Elizabethtown, where he made his mark and enjoyed a lucrative patronage; in fact, he was an accomplished lawyer, and took high rank at the bar. He was subsequently created a counsellor, and in 1794 a sergeant-at-law. In 1797 occurred the short war with the French republic, and a provisional army was raised; he received the appointment of Colonel of the 15th Regiment, holding the same a few months, and until the additional troops were disbanded; and from this he derived his appellation of Colonel, by which he was afterwards known. He was a prominent member of the Federal party, and in 1801 was elected by the Legislature United States Senator for two years, that being the unexpired term of Senator Schureman, who had resigned. Prior to his becoming Senator he had been for several years Clerk of Essex county, but the Legislature having passed a law in 1801 that no member of Congress could hold a State office, he was obliged to yield the latter position, although he made considerable effort to retain it. In 1812 he was elected by the Legislature to the office of Governor, which position he retained one year. During his term as the executive of the State, he was nominated by President Madison Major-General of the army, and unanimously confirmed by the Senate. But he declined the appointment, for good reasons, and subsequently was actively engaged in organizing volunteers for the defence of New York when threatened with invasion. He had, some while previous to his becoming a Senator, withdrawn from the practice of the law, and somewhere about 1810 or 1811 he became engaged in steamboat navigation, in conjunction with Daniel Dod, operating a vessel plying between Elizabethtown and New York city. This enterprise proved an unfortunate one, as Fulton and his associates had secured, by an act of the New York State Legislature, exclusive rights to the waters of New York. In 1813 New Jersey retaliated by conferring on Ogden & Dod an exclusive right to navigate the waters of New Jersey by aid of the same power. Livingston, who was an associate of Fulton, sought to have this latter act repealed, and succeeded. Meanwhile, another opponent arose in the person of one Thomas Gibbons, who inaugurated an opposition line to Ogden & Dod. Much litigation ensued, not only as regarded the conflict of the States respecting the waters bounding each, but also as to the rights involved. Colonel Ogden, impressed with the equity and justice of his claims, resisted to the utmost the opposing forces; but all his efforts, which were of the greatest, were unavailing. He lost his fortune, and to add to this, domestic affliction supervened, and he never recuperated. In 1829 he removed to Jersey City, and towards the close of that year was arrested for debt in New York city, where he was in confinement for several weeks, and although his friends offered to settle the amount, he forbade them. As soon as these proceedings were known at

Albany, an act was passed not only forbidding in future imprisonment for debt, where a soldier of the Revolution was concerned, but making this law retroactive, and Colonel Ogden was accordingly discharged. A similar law was also enacted by New Jersey. In his declining years he was provided for by being appointed Collector of Customs at Jersey City, an act of Congress being passed creating that city a port of entry; he held this position until his death, having received his commission from President Jackson, whom he had supported in preference to Adams, whom he regarded as a renegade from the old Federal party, with which he had for so long a period been connected. He was one of the original members of the Society of the Cincinnati, of New Jersey, which was formed at Elizabethtown in June, 1783, and became President of this State society in 1824, being the immediate successor of General Bloomfield. In 1825 he was chosen Vice-President of the general society, and was elected President-General in 1829. He was elected a Trustee of Princeton College in 1803, and was *ex officio* President of the Board during his term as Governor of the State; in 1817 he was again elected a Trustee, holding the position during life. In 1816 his *Alma Mater* conferred on him the honorary degree of Doctor of Laws. He was married, October, 1787, to Elizabeth, daughter of John Chetwood; she died in 1825. He survived her fourteen years, and died in Jersey City, April 19th, 1839, at the advanced age of eighty-three years.

ATERSON, HON. WILLIAM, Lawyer, Jurist and Statesman, was born, *circe* 1745, in the north of Ireland, and when but two years of age came to America. They first located at Trenton, next at Princeton, and finally settled at Raritan, now Somerville, where his father died in 1781. William entered the College of New Jersey, at Princeton, and graduated in 1763. He then studied law with Richard Stockton, one of the signers of the Declaration, and was licensed as an attorney-at-law in 1769. He opened his office at Bromley, in Hunterdon county, but afterwards removed to Princeton, where he became associated with his father and brother in mercantile business. In 1775 he was a delegate in the Provincial Congress, and was Secretary of the same at both its sessions. He was also a member of the Congress which met at Burlington in 1776, of which he was likewise Secretary. When the State government was organized, during the same year, he was made Attorney-General, and his position was a difficult one, as he was obliged to attend courts in different counties, liable at any time to be captured by the British army, which had then invaded the State; he was also at the same time a member of the Legislative Council. In 1780, while still occupied with his duties as Attorney-General, he was named a delegate to the Continental Congress; but he declined the

appointment, inasmuch as he could not faithfully discharge the duties of both stations. When peace was declared, in 1783, he resumed his practice as an attorney, removing his office and residence to New Brunswick. He was named as one of the members of the Convention which met in Philadelphia in 1787 to frame the Federal Constitution. There were two plans presented to that body, one by Edmond Randolph, of Virginia, and the other by William Paterson, the former being favored by the larger and the latter by the smaller States. The result was a compromise by which a general government was formed, partly federal and partly national. After the Constitution of the United States was ratified, William Paterson and Jonathan Elmer were elected by the Legislature of New Jersey Senators of the United States. The former retained his seat but a single year, for in 1790, on the death of Governor Livingston, he was chosen as his successor by the Legislature, and his administration was so successful that at the end of his term he was re-elected without much opposition. In 1792 a law was enacted authorizing him to codify all the statutes of Great Britain which prior to the Revolution were in force in the colony of New Jersey; together with those passed by the Legislature of the Province both before and after the separation from the mother country, so that the work when completed should be presented to the Legislature for re-enactment, should they deem it proper so to do. This work was entered upon by him, and occupied his leisure time and attention for six years; but it was deemed more convenient for the Legislature to act upon the statutes thus prepared as they emanated seriatim from his revision, than to review the whole during a single session. While he was thus engaged, he was nominated in 1793 by President Washington an Associate Justice of the Supreme Court of the United States, an office which he held until his death. He was engaged in the revision of the laws for six years, as stated above, and received for his services the meagre sum of $2,500. The volume thus produced has been long acknowledged to be the most perfect system of statute law produced in any State of the Union. He also greatly improved the practice of the Court of Chancery. During his occupancy of the position of Judge of the Supreme Court many important cases were tried, among them the trials for treason of the persons implicated in the famous "whiskey insurrection" in western Pennsylvania; and also that of Lyon, tried for a violation of the sedition law. His last official act was to preside in the Circuit Court of the United States, at New York, in April, 1806, on the trials of Ogden and Smith for violation of the neutrality laws in aiding Miranda to revolutionize some of the South American States. As he did not agree with the Associate Judge (Talmadge) he left the bench, and the latter proceeded with the trial alone. From this time his health began visibly to decline, and he withdrew from all active official duties. He was an able statesman, an upright judge and a disinterested friend of his country. His religious creed was

... not only forbidding in future
... debt, where a soldier of the Revolution
... reserved, but making this law retroactive, and
Colonel Ogden was accordingly discharged. A similar
law was also enacted by New Jersey. In his declining years
he was provided for by being appointed Collector of Customs at Jersey City, an act of Congress being passed creating that city a port of entry; he held this position until his
death, having received his commission from President
Jackson, whom he had supported in preference to Adams,
whom he regarded as a renegade from the old Federal
party, with which he had for so long a period been connected. He was one of the original members of the Society of the Cincinnati, of New Jersey, which was formed
at Elizabethtown in June, 1783, and became President of
this State society in 1824, being the immediate successor
of General Bloomfield. In 1825 he was chosen Vice-
President of the general society, and was elected President-
General in 1829. He was elected a Trustee of Princeton
College in 1803, and was ex officio President of the Board
during his term as Governor of the State; in 1817 he was
again elected a Trustee, holding the position during life.
In 1816 his Alma Mater conferred on him the honorary
degree of Doctor of Laws. He was married, October,
1787, to Elizabeth, daughter of John Chetwood; she died
in 1825. He survived her fourteen years, and died in
Jersey City, April 19th, 1839, at the advanced age of eighty-
three years.

PATERSON, HON. WILLIAM, Lawyer, Jurist
and Statesman, was born, circa 1745, in the north
of Ireland, and when but two years of age came
to America. They first located at Trenton, next
at Princeton, and finally settled at Raritan, now
Somerville, where his father died in 1781. William entered the College of New Jersey, at Princeton, and
graduated in 1763. He then studied law with Richard
Stockton, one of the signers of the Declaration, and was
licensed as an attorney-at-law in 1769. He opened his
office at Bromley, in Hunterdon county, but afterwards
removed to Princeton, where he became associated with his
father and brother in mercantile business. In 1775 he was
a delegate in the Provincial Congress, and was Secretary
of the same at both its sessions. He was also a member of
the Congress which met at Burlington in 1776, of which he
was likewise Secretary. When the State government was
organised during the same year, he was made Attorney-
General, and his position was a difficult one, as he was
obliged to attend courts in different counties, liable at any
time to be captured by the British army, which had then
invaded the State; he was also at the same time a member
of the Legislative Council. In 1780, while still occupied
with his duties as Attorney-General, he was named a
delegate to the Continental Congress; but he declined the

appointment, inasmuch as he could not faithfully discharge
the duties of both stations. When peace was declared, in
1783, he resumed his practice as an attorney, removing his
office and residence to New Brunswick. He was named as
one of the members of the Convention which met in Philadelphia in 1787 to frame the Federal Constitution. There
were two plans presented to that body, one by Edmond
Randolph, of Virginia, and the other by William Paterson,
the former being favored by the larger and the latter by the
smaller States. The result was a compromise by which a
general government was formed, partly federal and partly
national. After the Constitution of the United States was
ratified, William Paterson and Jonathan Elmer were elected
by the Legislature of New Jersey Senators of the United
States. The former retained his seat but a single year, for
in 1790, on the death of Governor Livingston, he was
chosen as his successor by the Legislature, and his administration was so successful that at the end of his term he was
re-elected without much opposition. In 1792 a law was
enacted authorizing him to codify all the statutes of Great
Britain which prior to the Revolution were in force in the
colony of New Jersey; together with those passed by the
Legislature of the Province both before and after the separation from the mother country, so that the work when
completed should be presented to the Legislature for re-
enactment, should they deem it proper so to do. This
work was entered upon by him, and occupied his leisure
time and attention for six years; but it was deemed more
convenient for the Legislature to act upon the statutes thus
prepared as they emanated seriatim from his revision, than
to review the whole during a single session. While he was
thus engaged, he was nominated in 1793 by President
Washington an Associate Justice of the Supreme Court of
the United States, an office which he held until his death.
He was engaged in the revision of the laws for six years,
as stated above, and received for his services the meagre
sum of $2,500. The volume thus produced has been long
acknowledged to be the most perfect system of statute law
produced in any State of the Union. He also greatly improved the practice of the Court of Chancery. During his
occupancy of the position of Judge of the Supreme Court
many important cases were tried, among them the trials for
treason of the persons implicated in the famous "whiskey
insurrection" in western Pennsylvania; and also that of
Lyon, tried for a violation of the sedition law. His last
official act was to preside in the Circuit Court of the
United States, at New York, in April, 1806, on the trials
of Ogden and Smith for violation of the neutrality laws in
aiding Miranda to revolutionize some of the South American States. As he did not agree with the Associate Judge
(Talmadge) he left the bench, and the latter proceeded with
the trial alone. From this time his health began visibly to
decline; and he withdrew from all active official duties.
He was an able statesman, an upright judge and a disinterested friend of his country. His religious creed was

Painted and Engraved by A.B.Durand.

Baron Ogden

that of the Presbyterian church; and he was a Trustee of their college at Princeton from 1787 to 1802. He was twice married; he left two children, a son and daughter of his first wife, to whom he was united in 1779; his second wife, whom he married in New Brunswick, left no issue. He died at his daughter's residence, September 9th, 1806, in the sixty-second year of his age. His name is perpetuated by the thriving manufacturing city near the falls of the Passaic river.

OOK, GEORGE H., PII.D., LL.D., Vice-President of Rutgers College, Professor of Chemistry, Natural History and Agriculture in that institution, and State Geologist of New Jersey, was born in Hanover, Morris county, New Jersey, January 5th, 1818. His parents were John and Sallie (Mum) Cook. Obtaining his early education at select schools near home, he subsequently became a student at Rensselaer Polytechnic Institute, at Troy, New York, entering in the year 1836 and leaving it in 1838. For a short time thereafter he followed actively the profession of civil engineering, being engaged first along the line of the Morris & Essex Railroad, and then with Ephraim Beach, who was the chief engineer of the Catskill & Canajoharie Railroad an enterprise that never reached completion. In the spring of 1840 he received the appointment of Assistant Professor of Engineering at the Rensselaer Polytechnic Institute. IIis labors in this position met with appreciation in his appointment, in 1842, to the Senior Professorship, and this position he filled with much acceptability. In 1848 he entered the Albany Academy as Professor of Mathematics and Mental Philosophy, occupying the chair until 1851, when his valuable services as an educator led to his selection as Principal of the academy. For two years he retained this post, adding by his able administration to the high reputation enjoyed by the institution, and then accepted a call to Rutgers College as Professor of Chemistry and Natural History, a chair for which he was exceptionally qualified and which he has filled with great advantage to the college. In 1864 he was appointed Vice-President of the college, and this position he occupies at the present time. His attainments as a geologist secured for him the charge of the southern division of New Jersey as Assistant State Geologist, which he held from 1854 until the survey was suspended, in 1856. Some years later, in 1868, he was called upon, by vote of the Legislature, to assume the duties of State Geologist, and he has continued to discharge them until now. In 1864 the Legislature established the State Agricultural College in Rutgers Scientific School, and the science of agriculture was then added to the subjects taught from his chair. He has through life been very active in all educational movements, and enjoys a very high reputation not only in the State but beyond its borders, as an educator and scientist. IIe is an acknowledged authority in geology, and his geo-

logical reports, presented to the Legislature, take rank among the ablest of the State papers. IIe was married, March 26th, 1846, to Mary II. Thomas, a native of New York State.

HERRERD, JOHN MAXWELL, Lawyer, late of Belvidere, was born at Mansfield, now in the county of Warren, but then a portion of old Sussex, New Jersey, September 6th, 1794. IIe was the son of Samuel Sherrerd and Ann Maxwell, his wife, and grandson of John Sherrerd, who emigrated to this country from the city of London in the early part of the last century. He settled at the old homestead, about one and a half miles from Washington, on the line of the Morris & Essex Railroad, where he built a mill and carried on milling, store-keeping and farming, during his life. He was succeeded in his business by his son, who reared a large family, eight daughters and two sons, all but one of whom were, at his death, married and settled within thirty miles of his home. John was the eldest son, and his education was carefully looked after by his mother, who was a woman of strong mind and considerable culture. He prepared for college at Baskingridge, under the care of Dr. Finley, and graduated at the College of New Jersey in 1812, and soon after commenced the study of law in the office of his uncle, Hon. George Maxwell, who, dying during his studentship, appointed him the guardian of his children. On the death of his uncle, he entered the office of Hon. Charles Ewing, afterwards the Chief-Justice of the State, at Trenton, where he was a fellow-student with Hon. Garret D. Wall. He was admitted to the bar as an attorney in November, 1816, and as a counsellor in February, 1831. Immediately on his admission as an attorney, he commenced the practice of law at Flemington, New Jersey, in connection with another uncle, William Maxwell, Esq., and in 1818 he returned to his old home at Mansfield, and practised principally in the old county of Sussex. In 1825 the new county of Warren was erected out of a portion of Sussex, and he, having been appointed the first Surrogate of the new county, removed to Belvidere, the county-seat, in 1826. After this time he constantly resided there, and was ever fully identified with the prosperity of the place. During not less than forty years he was the leader of the bar in the northern part of the State, and continued in active practice until the time of his death. In his earlier days he was an earnest advocate, exceedingly sharp and somewhat testy in his manner of conducting causes, and especially in cross-examination of unwilling witnesses, but during the latter portion of his life he shunned as much as possible adverse litigation and the excitement of the court-room; and as he possessed a remarkable facility of reproducing in writing the exact words of a witness, he was much employed in the business of Master in Chancery, where this faculty came in play. Being descended from decidedly Presbyterian stock, he early in life connected himself with that branch of the church, and while still a law student at Trenton, was sent to Philadelphia as one of a committee from the First Presbyterian Church to examine into the working of the Sunday-school system then just established there. The result of that visit was the organization of a school in connection with the church at Trenton, which is supposed to have been the first one organized in the State of New Jersey. From that time until his death he was an earnest worker in the cause, and at his grave the children of the Sunday-school in Belvidere, of which he was then and had been for a long time the superintendent, paid a touching tribute to his memory by covering his coffin, when lowered to its last resting-place, with bouquets of white flowers. As he had early consecrated himself to a nobler service than that belonging to this world, he cared more for the honor of his Master's kingdom than for earthly honors or distinctions, and consequently never took an active part in party politics nor sought for office. He was, however, at all times decided in his political faith, and was not afraid, at suitable times, to make known his views. An original Jeffersonian Democrat, he became a supporter of John Quincy Adams, was an old-line Whig, and afterwards a Republican. He was ordained an elder in the old Oxford Church, which is one of the first of the organizations of the Presbyterian order in the county, and in 1834 removed his church connection to a new church then first organized under the pastorate of Rev. I. N. Candee, D.D., in which he remained as the ruling spirit until his death. At the organization of this church a plan of systematic benevolence was adopted under the joint management of Dr. Candee and Mr. Sherrerd, which was probably the first scheme of the kind ever worked, although now so popular in the churches. He was an earnest and active Christian, ever ready for any good word or work, though entirely unobtrusive in manner and action. He was married in 1818 to Sarah Brown, of Philadelphia, and though he survived her for more than a quarter of a century, he never formed another matrimonial connection. In his manner and all his social intercourse he was at all times remarkable for his geniality, sprightliness and good-humor. This was especially shown in his treatment of children, of whom he was exceedingly fond, and who loved him in return with enduring affection. He was never happier than when surrounded by them and ministering to their happiness. He died on the 26th of May, 1871, after a short illness brought on by exposure in his garden, in which he insisted upon working more than his failing strength would allow. His funeral was largely attended by old and young, who well knew they had lost one of their best friends. Two of his children survive him, and are both residents of Belvidere. Samuel is now the Law-Judge of the Court of Common Pleas of Warren County. Sarah D. is married to Dr. P. F. Brakeley, long engaged in the practice of medicine at that place. Another son, John Brown, was also a physician, and died in the practice of his profession at Scranton, Pennsylvania, in 1852. He was cut off suddenly and was taken away from a sphere of great usefulness and distinction. He left two daughters, both of them now well married.

HERRERD, HON. SAMUEL, Lawyer and Judge, of Belvidere, was born in Philadelphia, Pennsylvania, April 25th, 1819. His father was John M. Sherrerd, whose biographical sketch appears above, while his mother, Sarah Brown, came from an old Philadelphia family of Friends, after whom Brown street in that city is named. He prepared for a collegiate course at Belvidere and at the Rensselaer Institute, of Troy, New York. He entered the Junior class at Princeton College in 1836, and graduated with the class of 1838. Among his classmates were Dr. Hornblower, the late Oliver S. Halstead, and General Branch, afterward of the Confederate army. Determining to adopt his father's profession, he began his legal studies with him at Belvidere in 1840. After remaining with his father some time, he passed to the law office of Judge H. D. Maxwell, of Easton, and was admitted to the bar in that city in 1842. For a while he practised law at Easton, and then removed South, where he engaged in the iron business. Associated with him in this enterprise were Judge Maxwell and I. I. Albright. Their establishment was known as the Bath & Old Etna Iron Works, near the Natural Bridge, Virginia. The tariff of 1847, resulting so disastrously to the iron industry of the United States, compelled them to stop their works in 1850. Mr. Sherrerd then returned North, and settled at Scranton. The extensive iron and coal interests of that place were just about being developed, and he superintended the construction of its first coal-breaker, and also its first shipment of coal. He occupied first the position of Paymaster and after that of Mining Engineer for the Delaware & Lackawanna Railroad Company, then known as the Leggett's Gap Railroad Company. In 1857 he returned to the practice of law in Scranton, and for a while acted as the Secretary of the Dickson Manufacturing Company. His career in Scranton was eminently that of a man of enterprise and progressive ideas, and his intelligent labors for the development of the great natural resources of the surrounding region won for him the high respect and esteem of the community. During 1867 he returned to his early home, Belvidere, and for a time was connected with the Belvidere Manufacturing Company. After the closing up of that enterprise he was appointed Law-Judge of Warren County, in place of Hon. J. M. Robeson, resigned. This position he still holds. He is regarded as a man of unquestionable integrity, and is highly respected by the bar and his fellow-citizens. He was married in 1847 to Miss Hamilton, a daughter of the late General Samuel R. Hamilton, of Trenton.

ALL, HON. GARRET DORSET, Lawyer, Soldier and Statesman, was born, 1783, in Middletown township, Monmouth county, New Jersey, and was the fourth child of James and —— (Dorset) Wall. On his paternal side, he was of English lineage, his father being the fourth in descent from Walter Wall, who emigrated from Great Britain about the middle of the seventeenth century to Massachusetts, where he resided for a short time, removing thence to Long Island, and eventually settling in Monmouth county, New Jersey, in 1657. His father, James Wall, had been an officer in the war for independence, and was a participant in the celebrated battle of Monmouth, where he personally captured an English officer, who tendered him his sword. Garret was barely nine years old when his father died, leaving a widow and six children, with but slender means of support. At this juncture, his father's brother, Dr. John G. Wall, of Woodbridge, received Garret into his own family, and he resided with his uncle until the latter's death, in 1798. He received a fair education, including instruction in the Greek and Latin languages, until he attained his fifteenth year—the period of his uncle's death—when he removed to Trenton, and at that early age became a student-at-law in the office of General Jonathan Rhea, who, at that period, was clerk of the Supreme Court of the State. His pecuniary means were very limited, but his preceptor gave him employment in the office, which yielded him his principal means of support. He was a careful student, acquainting himself not only with the principles of the common law, but paying particular attention to those bearing upon real estate, the laws of inheritance and titles. In addition to these he familiarized himself with the practice of the court in whose office he was an employé; so that, in after years, his opinions on all matters relating to that practice carried great weight by reason of his thorough knowledge of the subject in question. On arriving at the age of twenty-one years, he was duly examined and licensed as an attorney, and at once commenced the practice of his profession at Trenton, and by his urbane manners, as well as his extensive reading, gradually attained a remunerative line of practice. At first, however, owing either to extreme diffidence, or a seeming want of confidence in himself, he experienced great difficulty in conducting his pleadings; and even after overcoming, in a measure, this hesitating mode of speaking, he never entirely eradicated it. In 1857 he was advanced to the grade of counsellor-at-law, which largely increased his emoluments. He continued diligently engaged in his profession until 1812, when he was elected Clerk of the Supreme Court for the term of five years. This position was doubly important, as it served not only to largely increase his income, but also as a means of introducing him to a widely extended practice. He failed, however, to be re-elected, and returned to the practice of his profession. During his term of service as clerk of the court the war of 1812 with Great Britain transpired; and he, being imbued with a large share of military and patriotic feeling, and also inheriting the same from his father, volunteered his services in a company of uniformed militia, of which he had been for some years a lieutenant. As Captain of the Phœnix Infantry Corps, he was detailed, in connection with other troops, to aid in the protection of the city of New York. He even contemplated resigning his office of Clerk of the Supreme Court to accept a position on Colonel Ogden's staff, had that officer accepted the position of Major-General. In 1820 he was again advanced to the rank of sergeant-at-law, which title enabled him to still further enlarge his growing practice. In 1822 he was elected, on a "Union" ticket, a member of the lower branch of the State Legislature, to represent Hunterdon county in that body, where he distinguished himself by his thorough knowledge of law, both common and statute, which enabled him to take a leading part in that body. He opposed, with great earnestness, the indiscriminate exercise, which the Legislature then possessed, of granting divorces; and succeeded for a time in arresting this species of personal legislation. Up to this time he had been a zealous, earnest member of the Federalist party; but, at length, from conviction he became a pronounced Democrat, or "Republican," as they were sometimes termed in those days, and was among the earliest supporters, in 1824, of General Jackson for the Presidency. In 1827 he succeeded in securing the nomination, on the Democratic ticket, for member of Assembly for Hunterdon county, the office he had held five years previously, notwithstanding the fact that the leaders of that party were strongly opposed to him: but he appealed to the masses, who placed him in nomination, and these elected him at the polls. He at once took the front rank among the Democracy, and two years later he was elected by the Legislature Governor of the State, which high position he, however, declined. In the same year, without any solicitation on his part, he was nominated, by President Jackson, United States District Attorney for New Jersey, which official station he held for several years, discharging its duties with energy and ability. In 1834 he was elected, by the State Legislature, a member of the United States Senate, where he served during the last two years of Jackson's second term, and the entire four years of Van Buren's administration; and to whose policy and tenets he gave an unhesitating support. He was noticeable in his condemnation of the measures put forth in favor of rechartering the United States Bank, and one of the most effective speeches he ever delivered while a Senator was in opposition to the advocates for a continuance of that fiscal institution. After his term expired he returned to Burlington, which town had been his home since 1828, and recommenced his professional duties, which he pursued until stricken by disease. From this attack he partially recovered, and engaged in some important cases. He earnestly advocated the measures which culminated in the assembling of a Constitutional Convention, in 1844, and manifested a great interest in the adoption of the new Constitution which had been framed by them. Although not a member of the body which prepared it, yet he was able to aid the members by his counsel and advice while they were progressing in their work. In 1848 he was made a member of the Court of Errors and Appeals, and in that high tribunal his great learning and research enabled him to reach an impartial conclusion on the various legal questions submitted to that body of learned jurists. He occupied this position until a second attack of his disease ended fatally. He was, as already remarked, a counsellor of the highest ability and learning; while, as a pleader, he entered into the case as if he were the client, not the attorney; and some of his arguments before the jury or court were of the highest eloquence. As a partisan he was remarkably free from party bitterness; and never allowed his friendships to be sundered, though his political belief might condemn the measures advocated by his most intimate and valued associate. He was an earnest advocate for the cause of education, and took a lively interest in the establishment of Burlington College, and was an active member of the Board of Trustees of that institution. He was eminently distinguished for his hospitality and for his willingness to advise all those who sought his counsel, although reaping no pecuniary benefit from it. In fact, he was deemed, by those who knew him best, as entirely too liberal in this respect. He was proud of his native State, and of the leading part she took in the revolutionary war; moreover, as said above, he inherited a taste for military duties, as was evinced by his connection with a volunteer company which dated back to the days of '76. In personal appearance he looked the soldier, and when, in after years, he acquired the title of General, from having held the position of Quartermaster-General of the State, his very step seemed to indicate that he was born to command. He was twice married; his first wife, to whom he was united shortly after being admitted to the bar, was a daughter of his preceptor, General Jonathan Rhea. His second marriage took place in the autumn of 1828. He died in November, 1850.

OWELL, HON. RICHARD; Lawyer, Soldier and Governor of New Jersey, was born, October 25th, 1754 (with his twin brother Lewis), in Newark, Newcastle county, Delaware, and was one of eleven children whose father was Ebenezer Howell, the latter being the son of the founder of the American branch of the family, who left Wales in 1729 and settled in Delaware. Richard and his brother Lewis were educated in Newcastle, and remained there until about 1774, when they removed to New Jersey, whither their father had preceded them some five years previously, settling in Cumberland county, a few miles to the west of Bridgeton. Both brothers at that date were strongly imbued with patriotic ardor, and were of the party who, in November, 1774, disguised as Indians, broke into a storehouse at Greenwich, removed the brig "Greyhound's" cargo of tea, and burned it. For this the party were sued by the owners, but the case never came to trial; for the Whig sheriff had taken care to summon a Whig grand jury, who ignored the bill, although the royalist judge charged them to find a true one. Richard Howell had commenced the study of law, but was obliged to suspend his readings and enlist in the cause of independence. Early in 1775 he was appointed a subaltern officer in a company of light infantry, and in December of that year was commissioned a Captain in the 2d Regiment of the line, commanded by Colonel Maxwell. The regiment was ordered to Canada, and participated in the attack on Quebec, where they were repulsed. However, Captain Howell was promoted to a Majorship, for the valor he displayed on that and several other occasions; and when the New Jersey regiments were reorganized Colonel Maxwell became a Brigadier-General, with Howell as Brigade-Major. They participated in the battle of Brandywine, and where Lewis Howell, Richard's twin brother, served as surgeon; the latter was captured, but fortunately escaped. The day prior to the battle of Monmouth Surgeon Howell died from an attack of fever, without being able to bid farewell to his brother Richard, who was with his command awaiting the expected battle. He shortly after resigned from the army by special request of General Washington, who immediately ordered him to transact certain duties of a private nature, which he could not perform while holding a military commission from Congress. It is generally supposed that the nature of this business was to discover by the best means he could the proceedings of the British commanders. In 1779, having received his license as an attorney, he commenced the practice of law in Cumberland county, where he resided for several years. Early in 1788 he removed to Trenton, and shortly afterwards was elected Clerk of the Supreme Court. He served in this office until 1793, when, William Paterson being appointed a Justice of the United States Supreme Court, Howell was chosen by the Legislature Governor of the State, to fill the vacancy then existing; and as he gave entire satisfaction in that high station he was annually re-elected, almost always unanimously, until 1801, when the Republican or Jefferson party gained the ascendency, and he was succeeded by Joseph Bloomfield. During his incumbency as Governor, in 1794, the famous Whiskey Insurrection broke out in western Pennsylvania, and Governor Howell was named by President Washington as commander of the right wing of the army detailed to operate against the insurrectionists. After marching to the extreme western boundary of Pennsylvania the insurgents were overawed, and did not hazard a battle, and the troops were dismissed by an order of General Washington, dated at Pittsburgh, November 17th, 1794, and shortly afterwards marched back to New Jersey. After his vacation of the gubernatorial chair he returned to the practice of the law, continuing to reside in or near Trenton.

Drawn by C. Fenderich.   Engraved by T. Illman N.Y.

Garret D. Wall

He was married in November, 1779, to a daughter of Joseph Burr, of Burlington county, by whom he had nine children, some of whom died in infancy. Richard, born 1794, was in 1812 a lieutenant of infantry, and was aide to Brigadier-General Pike when he was killed at the blowing up of Fort George in Canada. Another son, William, was a lieutenant in the marine corps; and Franklin was a lieutenant in the navy, and was killed on board the frigate "President." Governor Howell died at his residence, near Trenton, May 5th, 1803.

———◦◦◦———

LOOMFIELD, HON. JOSEPH, Lawyer, Soldier and Governor of New Jersey, was born, 1755, at Woodbridge, Middlesex county, and was the son of Dr. Moses Bloomfield, who was probably descended from Thomas Bloomfield, who lived at Newbury, Massachusetts, in 1638, and afterwards removed to New Jersey. He was educated at a classical school taught by Rev. Enoch Green, at Deerfield, Cumberland county; after leaving which he commenced the study of the law with Cortlandt Skinner, attorney-general of the province, who during the Revolution was a Tory, and left the country with his family after independence had been achieved. In 1775 Bloomfield was licensed as an attorney, and commenced the practice of his profession in Bridgeton. In February, 1776, he received a commission as Captain in the 3d New Jersey Regiment, which was ordered to Canada. On their way thither Captain Bloomfield was ordered to arrest his old preceptor, Skinner, at Perth Amboy, but who, however, had taken refuge on board a British man-of-war. The regiment, on its arrival at Albany, received news of the retreat of the Continental troops from Quebec, and was subsequently marched up the Mohawk valley to restrain the Indians. Thence, in the following November, they repaired to Ticonderoga, where Captain Bloomfield was named Judge Advocate of the Army of the North. There being much sickness and exposure, he fell ill, and on Christmas day left for home. He was subsequently promoted Major of the 3d Regiment. In 1778 he resigned from the army, and in the autumn of the same year was chosen Clerk of the Assembly, and was for several years Register of the Admiralty Court. In 1783 he was elected Attorney-General of the State, was re-elected in 1788, and resigned in 1792. Shortly after his resignation from the army he had removed to Burlington, which became his future residence, except when absent on public service. In 1793 he was chosen as one of the Trustees of Princeton College, which he resigned in 1801. He was General of Militia in 1794, and took the field as commander of a brigade to aid in the suppression of the Whiskey Insurrection in western Pennsylvania, marching with the troops to the district where these troubles arose, and was instrumental in quelling the insurgents without recourse to arms.

In 1792 he had been one of the Electoral College of New Jersey, voting for Washington and Adams for the respective offices of President and Vice-President of the United States; but owing to his opposition of the latter was not appointed an elector in 1796. This opposition to Adams accordingly made him friendly to Jefferson, the avowed leader of the Republicans, since termed Democrats, and he was chosen to succeed Richard Howell as Governor of the State. This was in the autumn of 1801, when he received thirty votes, while his opponent, Richard Stockton, commanded but twenty. In the election, held in 1802, each candidate received twenty-six votes, and the balloting thereafter with different candidates resulted in a tie. Notwithstanding all efforts of compromise nothing resulted, and New Jersey had no governor for a year, the duties of the office being performed agreeably to the constitution by the Democratic vice-president of the Council, John Lambert. In 1803 he received thirty-three votes, while his old opponent could only poll seventeen; and in 1804 he counted thirty-seven votes, and Mr. Stockton sixteen, in all. He was subsequently re-elected, until 1812, without opposition. In June, 1812, war was declared against Great Britain, and he was shortly thereafter appointed a Brigadier-General by President Madison, in the army destined for the invasion of Canada. Early in 1813 his brigade marched to Sackett's Harbor, and a portion of them, under General Pike, crossed into that province, attacked Fort George, were repulsed, and the general killed. General Bloomfield was soon withdrawn and ordered to the command of a military district, with his head-quarters at Philadelphia, where he remained until the close of the war. He then returned to Burlington, where he re-commenced the practice of his profession, and in 1816 was elected, by the Democrats, a member of Congress, and re-elected in 1818, closing his career in that body March 3d, 1821. He was Chairman of the Committee on Revolutionary Pensions, and succeeded in introducing and having enacted the bills granting pensions to the veteran soldiers of the Revolution and their widows. During the period of his serving as Governor he was ex-officio President of the Board of Trustees of Princeton College; and, in 1819 he was again elected a Trustee of that institution, which position he held until the close of his life. He was for many years an active member and President of the "New Jersey Society for the Abolition of Slavery," an organization that must not be confounded with those other societies which afterwards degenerated into societies of a fanatical character. The societies first formed for the abolition of slavery confined themselves to protecting slaves from abuse, and to aiding them to obtain their liberty by legal proceedings. Writs of habeas corpus were procured, and many negroes claimed as slaves were declared by the Supreme Court to be free. Joseph Bloomfield was throughout his whole career a firm Republican, or, as was afterwards styled, a firm Democrat in his political belief; while in Congress he was regarded as a sound legislator; a brave soldier in the field, and in private life an estimable citizen. He was married, about 1779, to Mary, a daughter of Dr. William McIlvaine, of Burlington; she died in 1818. A few years afterwards he married a lady who survived him. He died at Burlington, October 3d, 1825. The inscription on his tomb states the simple facts that he was "A soldier of the Revolution; late Governor of New Jersey."

ENNINGTON, WILLIAM SANDFORD, Soldier, Lawyer, Jurist and Governor of New Jersey, was born in Newark, and was the great-grandson of Ephraim Pennington, one of the original settlers of Newark, who removed in 1667 from the colony of Connecticut. Very little is known concerning the youth of Governor Pennington, excepting that he was apprenticed to his maternal uncle, from whom he was named; and that as the uncle espoused the cause of the royalists, while the nephew was an ardent revolutionist, the indentures were cancelled and he entered the Continental army. He was at first a non-commissioned officer of artillery; and being discovered by General Knox entirely unsupported, during a skirmish, actively loading and firing one of the cannon, and exhibiting so much courage, he was commissioned on the field a Lieutenant of Artillery, to take rank from September 12th, 1778. From his private journal, he appears to have been present at the execution of Major Andre, October 2d, 1780; and was ordered to join a detachment of troops, January 25th, 1781, to assist in quelling a mutiny among the Pennsylvania and New Jersey troops at Morristown, New Jersey. It is believed that he was present during the siege of Yorktown, and that he was wounded in some engagement with the enemy; he had been promoted to a brevet Captaincy when he left the army. After the war he was engaged in business as a hatter, and subsequently embarked in mercantile pursuits in Newark. In 1797 he was elected a member of the General Assembly, which position he held for three years. In 1801 he was chosen a member of the Council, and re-elected in 1802. He was at this period, and subsequently for twenty years, a leading member of the Republican or Democratic party. He had entered, about the year 1800, upon the study of the law with Mr. Boudinot, and in May, 1802, was licensed as an attorney. Before he could be appointed a counsellor-at-law he was elected, in February, 1804, an Associate Justice of the Supreme Court; and in 1806 was appointed Reporter of the same. He retained this position until 1813, when he was elected Governor of the State, being the successor in that office of Colonel Ogden, and was re-elected in 1814. In 1815 he was nominated by President Madison as Judge of the United States District Court for New Jersey, vice Robert Morris (deceased), and was confirmed by the Senate. He held this position until his death, his residence being Newark. He was, as already stated, a true Democrat; yet he regarded John Quincy Adams as the true Republican (democratic) successor of Presidents Jefferson and Madison. He enjoyed the respect of all men, and during his entire career was never known to have an enemy. He was regarded by all as a good citizen, a faithful friend and a just, unswerving judge. He died September 17th, 1826.

ICKERSON, MAHLON, Lawyer, Jurist and Governor of New Jersey, was born in 1771, and was a descendant of Philemon Dickerson, who with his brothers emigrated from England in 1638 and settled originally in Massachusetts. Four of his grandsons and children of his son Thomas removed to Morris county, New Jersey, in 1745, and from these the Dickersons, and Dickinsons, as some term themselves, of New Jersey, are descended. Mahlon was the grandson of one of these four brothers, and the son of Jonatban Dickerson. He graduated from Princeton in 1789; and after leaving college studied law, and was licensed as an attorney in 1793. In the following year he served as a member of Captain Kinney's cavalry company, in the expedition sent to western Pennsylvania to aid in the suppression of the celebrated Whiskey Insurrection. He subsequently, with his brothers, removed to Philadelphia, which for many years thereafter became their residence. In that city he entered the law office of James Milnor, who afterwards was a member of Congress, and who ultimately studied divinity and became a distinguished clergyman of the Episcopal Church. Mahlon Dickerson was admitted to the bar in Philadelphia in 1797. Shortly afterwards he was elected a member of the Common Council; and being an earnest Republican was named by President Jefferson, in 1802, as a Commissioner in Bankruptcy. In 1805 he was appointed Adjutant-General of the Commonwealth of Pennsylvania by Governor McKean, and resigned the same three years after to accept the position of Recorder of the City of Philadelphia, which was, as then constituted, a judicial office, to be held during good behavior, and exercising criminal jurisdiction in the city proper. In 1810 his father died, leaving a valuable estate, and Mahlon Dickerson removed to Morris county, New Jersey, where he continued to reside, except when employed in public business, until the close of his life. He was elected in 1812, and re-elected in 1813, a member of the General Assembly of New Jersey, from Morris county. While thus a representative he was elected by the two houses of the Legislature a Justice of the Supreme Court, and also chosen Reporter of the same, but did not accept the latter appointment. In 1815 he was elected Governor of the State, without opposition, and re-elected in 1816. While occupying the gubernatorial chair, in February, 1817, he was elected United States Senator, and served in that capacity for sixteen years. In

May, 1834, he was named by President Jackson as Minister to Russia, and expected to accept the position, but yielded to the persuasions of Martin Van Buren, who was then an aspirant for the Presidency, and he declined the office and devoted all his energies towards securing the succession in the Presidential office to his friend, Van Buren. In June, 1834, he became Secretary of the Navy, and resigned therefrom in 1838. In September, 1840, he was appointed to succeed Judge Rossell in the District Court, which he held for about six months, when he resigned, and his brother, Hon. Philemon Dickerson, was appointed. He subsequently was President of the American Institute, of New York city. During his term as Senator of the United States he was a leading member of that body, affiliating at first with the Republicans or Democrats, and afterwards became a member of the Jackson and Van Buren Democracy. He was largely interested in the mining and manufacture of iron in Morris county, and so favored a high protective tariff, in opposition to the views of many of his political brethren. He was kind, amiable and highly esteemed as a man of sound judgment and a safe legislator. He was possessed of a large fortune, but had no issue, never having married. He died at his residence in Suckasunny, Morris county, October 5th, 1853, aged eighty-two years.

appointed on the 24th of June to prepare a constitution, of which Jacob Green was the chairman. It consisted, besides the chairman, of John Cooper, Jonathan D. Sargeant, Lewis Ogden, Theophilus Elmer, Elijah Hughes, John Covenhoven, John Cleves Symmes, Silas Condict and Samuel Dick. The constitution was reported on the 26th, and discussed from day to day until the 2d of July, when it was adopted two days before the Declaration of Independence. The convention, on the 22d of June, authorized their delegates " to concur in a declaration of independence and in the formation of a confederacy for union and common defence, making treaties with foreign nations, for commerce and assistance, and taking such action as might appear necessary for these great ends." The Constitution of New Jersey, adopted July 2d, 1776, remained the organic law of the State for nearly seventy years, the second constitution being framed and adopted in 1844. Jacob Green, though pressed to do so, refused to be again a candidate for membership in any legislative body, on the ground that his duty as a minister, except on extraordinary occasions, required his efforts in his parochial charge. He was one of the first Trustees of Princeton College, a position which he resigned in 1764. He remained in charge of his congregation at Hanover for forty-five years, and died there in May, 1790.

REEN, REV. JACOB, D. D., of Hanover, Morris county, was born at Malden, in the State of Massachusetts, in 1712. He graduated at Harvard, and joined the Rev. George Whitfield in his enterprise to Georgia. On reaching Elizabethtown, New Jersey, on their way thither, Mr. Whitfield suggested a change of plan, and Mr. Green, on the advice of Mr. Dickinson and Mr. Burr, remained at that place and studied divinity with the latter. He was soon called to settle in the Presbyterian congregation of Hanover. He married a daughter of Rev. John Pierson, for a long time the pastor of the Presbyterian Church of Woodbridge, New Jersey, and who was a son of Rev. Abraham Pierson, the first president or rector of Yale College, and a grandson of the Rev. Abraham Pierson, one of the first settlers, from Connecticut, of Newark, and the first pastor of the church in that city. Jacob Green, although a clergyman, took a deep interest in the impending conflict between England and the colonies, and was an earnest Whig. On the fourth Tuesday of May, 1776, he was elected from the county of Morris a member of the Provincial Congress of New Jersey, which organized at Burlingtou the 10th of June, 1776, by choosing Samuel Tucker, Esq., President, and William Patterson, Esq., Secretary. On the 21st of June the Provincial Congress resolved that a government be formed for regulating the internal police of the colony, pursuant to the recommendation of the Continental Congress of the 15th of May. A committee was

REEN, REV. ASHBEL, D. D., LL. D., President of Nassau Hall from 1812 to 1822, and one of the originators of the Theological Seminary at Princeton, was born in Hanover, Morris county, New Jersey, July 6th, 1762. He was the son of Rev. Jacob Green, D. D., a biographical sketch of whom appears above. While a youth he served in the local militia at the battle of Springfield. He graduated at the College of New Jersey in 1783, and for the succeeding two years was tutor at Princeton. In 1785 he was ordained a minister of the gospel by the Presbytery of New Brunswick, and during the same year was chosen Professor of Mathematics and Natural Philosophy at Princeton, holding the chair until 1787. In April of the last-mentioned year he became colleague-pastor of the Second Presbyterian Church in Philadelphia, and succeeded to the pastorate on the death of Rev. Dr. Sproat, in 1793. He was a member of the body which adopted the Constitution of the Presbyterian Church of America, in 1788, and was also a delegate to the General Assembly in 1791. From 1792 to 1800 he was, with Bishop White, one of the Chaplains of Congress. In 1809 he had a primary agency in forming the Philadelphia Bible Society. He was chosen a Trustee of Nassau Hall in 1790, and held that office until 1812, when he resigned in order to accept the Presidency of the college. This important trust remained in his charge until 1822, when he resigned and returned to Philadelphia to reside. For twelve years thereafter he edited the monthly *Christian*

Advocate. Recognizing the necessity for the establishment of a theological seminary in connection with the college at Princeton, he became one of its originators, was the first President of its Board of Directors, and a director until his death. He was also a Trustee of the Jefferson Medical College, of Philadelphia. Although he did not give much attention to authorship, many of his discourses, lectures, addresses, etc., were of such a character as to create a great demand for their publication. Among these may be specially mentioned a " Discourse delivered in the College of New Jersey, with a History of the College," published in Boston, in 1822; a " History of Presbyterian Missions," and " Lectures on the Shorter Catechism," two volumes. He was a logical, bold and powerful preacher. As a man, he was possessed of great moral courage, and was characterized by wonderful perseverance and industry. He was an able college president, and, while a strict disciplinarian, commanded the marked regard of the students. For more than half a century he occupied a conspicuous position in the community, and was one of the leading men of the Presbyterian Church. His wife was Elizabeth, daughter of Robert Stockton, of Princeton, to whom he was married on November 3d, 1785. He died in Philadelphia, May 19th, 1848.

---◆◇◆---

REEN, JAMES S., Lawyer, of Princeton, son of Rev. Dr. Ashbel Green, was born in Philadelphia, on July 22d, 1792. He graduated at Dickinson College in 1811, and studied law with Hon. George Wood. He was licensed as an attorney in 1817; was admitted as counsellor in 1821, and received the rank of Sergeant in 1834. He soon acquired a large practice in the courts of the State, and was the Reporter from 1831 to 1836 of the decisions of the Supreme Court, published under his name. He represented Somerset county for several terms in the first branch of the Legislature, then known as the Council, being first elected in 1829, and as such being *ex-officio* a member of the Court of Appeals. On the accession to office of President Jackson he appointed Mr. Green United States District Attorney, which position he filled by successive appointments until the election of President Harrison. He was nominated by President Tyler as Secretary of the Treasury, but, with others, failed of confirmation in the opposition Senate. Under the old constitution the Legislature in joint meeting had the appointment of Governor, who was also Chancellor, and Mr. Green was the candidate of the Democratic party for the position, but was defeated by Governor Pennington. Mr. Green was one of the first directors of the Delaware & Raritan Canal Company, which position he occupied until his death, being also Treasurer of the Joint Railroad and Canal Companies. He was a Trustee of Princeton College from 1828 to the time of his death, and had been Treasurer of the Theological Seminary at that place for many years. He was Pro-

fessor of the Law Department of the college from 1847 to 1855. His death occurred on November 8th, 1862. At the annual meeting of the stockholders of the Delaware & Raritan Canal Company, held in Princeton, May 11th, 1863, the Hon. Robert F. Stockton, in his report, made the following allusion to the loss the corporation had sustained by the death of Mr. Green : "About half a century ago Mr. Green commenced his career at Princeton as an attorney-at-law. To great suavity of manner he united industry, accuracy and precision, a sound judgment and talents eminently practical and efficient. His deportment was always correct, and neither pleasure nor vice impaired his character for steadiness and attention to business. He frequently represented the people in the Legislature. As a legislator he became known throughout the State, and the ' Statute Book of New Jersey' bears witness to his wisdom and sagacity. The cause of common school education had no more meritorious advocate than Mr. Green. In progress of time he took rank with the first men in our State in directing public opinion. He was among the first and most efficient friends of internal improvements in New Jersey, in constructing that noble system of public works which, without imposing on the people the burthen of a State debt, has developed the resources of New Jersey and conferred on her advantages which no other State in the Union possesses. As a politician he was firm, though conciliatory and kind to his opponents. For many years there was no one in the party to which he belonged who enjoyed more completely the public confidence. From the origin of our Joint Companies to the day of his death Mr. Green was an influential member, enjoying the implicit confidence of all connected with them, and holding in them high and responsible positions. His fidelity, industry and sagacity, as a member of our great corporations, will be always gratefully remembered by all of us who survive him. Distinguished as Mr. Green was, as our true, faithful friend, a politician, a legislator and a statesman, it may be perhaps from his labors of love as a philanthropist and a Christian that his memory will be held dear by a large and distinguished circle of friends. I will not attempt, at this time, to enumerate and record all the important services of Mr. Green as a public benefactor. I hope some one more competent to such a task will perform it, because such a history, while it would do but justice to the dead, might be of benefit to the living. But his friends will fondly remember the alacrity with which he went forward to aid every cause by which human suffering could be ameliorated, or religion and public virtue promoted. Whether it was to restore by colonization the emancipated African to his ancestral home, to send the missionary to herald the glad tidings of salvation to pagan nations, to spread abroad the Bible to all destitute people, to build up and foster the Sunday-school, Mr. Green was ever ready to take the advance, to marshal organizations, or to instruct the public mind and direct it to the encouragement and support of any benevolent

Jas. S. Green M.D.

D., of Elizabeth, was born to Elizabeth

enterprise. We care hot how bright may be the fame of other Christians, whether priest or layman, nor how distinguished their piety, no name is more worthy of commendation for a long life of gratuitous and arduous labor in the cause of humanity than that of our deceased friend, James S. Green." By resolution, this portion of the report was published and copies furnished to the family of the deceased.

REEN, JAMES S., M. D., of Elizabeth, was born at Princeton, New Jersey, on July 22d, 1829. He is a son of the late Hon. James S. Green, of Princeton, whose biographical sketch precedes this, and the grandson of the late Rev. Ashbel Green, D. D., LL.D., a distinguished Presbyterian clergyman and one of the Presidents of Princeton College. His mother's maiden name was Isabella McCulloh. He received a collegiate education at Nassau Hall, and graduated in June, 1848. His tastes leading him toward the medical profession, he became a student of medicine under the direction of Dr. John Neill, of Philadelphia, and attended lectures at the University of Pennsylvania, medical department, from which he graduated with the degree of M. D. in April, 1851. Twelve months previous to graduation he had been appointed Resident Physician to the Wills Hospital for Diseases of the Eye, Philadelphia; this position he retained for six months after receiving his degree. In the winter of 1850–51 he was appointed as Assistant Demonstrator of Anatomy in the University of Pennsylvania, and he continued to fill the appointment for a period of three years. During the summer of 1853 he served as Resident Surgeon of the Pennsylvania Hospital. In November of that year he removed to Elizabeth, New Jersey, and commenced a general practice there. In this city he has since resided. Having enjoyed exceptional advantages for study and practice, and having thoroughly improved them, he soon acquired a high professional reputation, and the substantial rewards ordinarily following such an acquisition have not been denied him. At the present time his practice is second to none in the city or neighborhood. But he has never permitted its cares to engross the whole of his attention. He is a man of large public spirit, and from his settlement in Elizabeth he has always manifested an earnest and active interest in its affairs. After the incorporation of the place as a city, he was chosen the first President of the City Council, and in the rapid development of the municipality he has borne a prominent part. This development, while exceptionally rapid, has at the same time been substantial, the improvements under wise administration of public affairs only keeping pace with the requirements of new and expanding industries, and the needs of a growing population. He was married, in April, 1854, to Fanny Winchester, of Baltimore.

REEN, HON. ROBERT S., Lawyer, of Elizabeth, son of James S. Green, was born at Princeton, New Jersey, March 25th, 1831. After a preliminary training, he became a student at Nassau Hall, from which he graduated in 1850. Choosing the profession of the law, he was, after the usual course of study, admitted to the bar in 1853, and became a counsellor in 1856. While residing in his native place he took an active interest in its affairs, and in 1852 served as a member of its council. In 1856 he removed to Elizabeth, and immediately became interested in the movement for the creation of Union county; indeed he was largely instrumental in the passage of the act of 1857 by which it was accomplished, and which designated Elizabeth as the county-seat. During this latter year he was appointed Prosecutor of the borough courts by Governor Newell, and in the following one became the City Attorney of Elizabeth, a position he continued to fill with marked ability for ten years. At the expiration of this period he was elected to the City Council, and served therein by successive elections from 1868 to 1873. He had been elected Surrogate of Union county in 1862, and appointed Presiding Judge of the Court of Common Pleas and county courts in 1868. During the succeeding year he was appointed by Governor Randolph to the Commercial Convention at Louisville as a representative of New Jersey. In his professional capacity he has been connected with some of the most important movements of recent years in the State. Of these the most notable, because of its almost revolutionary and far reaching character, may be mentioned the enterprise designed to deliver the people of the commonwealth from the monopoly long enjoyed by the Camden & Amboy Railroad Company and its successors, the Pennsylvania Railroad Company. An organization was effected, known as the National Railway Company, having for its object the construction of a second railroad between the cities of Philadelphia and New York. At every step the new enterprise was met with opposition and litigation by its established rival. This opposition and litigation culminated in 1872 in the celebrated case before the Chancellor's Court in Trenton. In this suit, which was brought by the Pennsylvania Railroad Company, as lessees of the franchises and road of the Camden & Amboy Railroad, against the National Railway Company to restrain it from operating a through line from New York to Philadelphia, under several charters which were to be used as connecting links of the route, Mr. Green acted as attorney for the defendants. This litigation led, in the succeeding winter, to the fierce contest in the Legislature between the railroad companies and the advocates of free railroads. Bill after bill granting the rights sought by the promoters of the new enterprise passed the House of Assembly, only to be killed or smothered in the Senate. The Assembly had early in the session passed a bill, introduced by Mr. Canfield, of Morris, creating a general railroad law. This measure had gone to the Senate, and been there amended by the striking out of all after the enacting clause, and the insertion of a bill that would have been practically useless. On the return of this amended bill to the House, in the last days of the session, it was referred to a committee, consisting of Messrs. Worthington, Canfield, Letson, Willets and Schenck, who, with Messrs. Cortlandt Parker, Green, Attorney-General Gilchrist, and B. W. Throckmorton, prepared and perfected a measure which was the next day reported to the House by the committee as a substitute for the Senate's amendment. The Assembly passed it, and, after some small alterations, made by a Committee of Conference, it eventually passed both Houses; was signed by Governor Parker and became law. Railroad monopoly privileges, which had been enjoyed under the decision in the case of the Camden & Amboy Railroad Company and the Delaware & Raritan Bay Company, even after the companies had relinquished their rights to exclusive privileges, were by this law destroyed, and under it the Delaware & Bound Brook Railroad was built on the route and partially finished road-bed of the National Railway Company, and in connection with the New Jersey Central and North Pennsylvania Railroads formed a continuous and through line from New York to Philadelphia. With the opening of this road was consummated the release of New Jersey from one of the most oppressive monopolies known to the history of this country, and to Mr. Green the community is indebted in no small degree for its deliverance. His great ability and tireless care in working up the intricate points of the preliminary litigation, and in shaping the subsequent legislation, conduced conspicuously to the final triumph of popular rights. In 1873 he was appointed by Governor Parker, and the nomination received the confirmation of the Senate, one of the commissioners to suggest amendments to the constitution of the State. In this commission he served as Chairman of the Committees on Bills of Rights; Rights of Suffrage; Limitation of Power of Government, and General and Special Legislation. The amendments suggested were substantially adopted by the two succeeding Legislatures and ratified by the people at the general election of 1875. He became a member of the bar of New York in January, 1874, as a partner in the firm of Brown, Hall & Vanderpoel, which afterwards, by changes in its *personnel*, became that of Vanderpoel, Green & Cuming. Politically, he is a Democrat, and was a delegate to the convention at Baltimore which nominated Hon. Stephen A. Douglas for President. He was married October 1st, 1857.

ICKERSON, HON. PHILEMON, Lawyer, Governor and Chancellor of New Jersey, late of Paterson, was born about 1790, and was a son of Jonathan Dickerson and a brother of Mahlon Dickerson, whose biographical sketch appears elsewhere in this volume. He was a resident of Philadelphia for a number of years, during which time he studied law and was admitted to the bar. Having removed to New Jersey, he received his license there as an attorney in 1813; became a counsellor in 1817, and, finally, in 1834 attained the third and highest degree, that of serjeant-at-law. He resided at Paterson, where he entered into the practice of his profession, which eventually became not only extensive but lucrative. In 1833 he was returned to the Assembly as a Representative from Essex county. He was elected by the two houses of the Legislature Governor of the State in 1836, and filled that position a single year. In 1839 he was nominated for Congress, and, as was finally settled by the majority in the Twenty-sixth Congress, was considered elected; but owing to irregularities in some of the returns, the votes were thrown out by two of the county clerks, and when the returns were reported to the Governor the latter issued the commission to his opponent under the broad seal of the State. When Congress met, the disqualified members were admitted, because their opinions happened to coincide with the majority who organized the House; while those who held their certificates, as being duly elected, were denied the seats. Had they been admitted, the very close majority of the administration party would have been destroyed, and the opposition would have gained the political ascendency. This course resulted in the almost entire discomfiture of the power that had so long ruled the Union—the election of 1840 terminating in a regular rout of the Democracy. In 1841, towards the very close of President Van Buren's administration, he was appointed Judge of the District Court of the United States, and held that office during the remainder of his life. He was an ardent supporter of Democratic principles as expounded by Jackson and his successors. His decisions as Chancellor were but few in number, yet none of them were ever reversed in the Court of Appeals. During his service of over twenty years in the United States Court he gave entire satisfaction, and was acknowledged to be an able jurist. He died in 1862.

AGIE, REV. DAVID, D. D., late of Elizabeth, New Jersey, was born in the immediate neighborhood of that place, on March 13th, 1795. His life from his infancy to three-score years and ten was spent near the same locality and among the same people. He was the descendant of a line of Scotch Presbyterians, a class of men distinguished for their strong, good sense; their love of peace and order; their untiring industry and their deep, practical piety. Pride of birth would have been inconsistent with the humility which was a prominent trait of Dr. Magie's character, and yet he felt, and has been known so to express himself, that he was happier having such an ancestry than if he had descended from "loins enthroned and rulers of the earth." His parents, Michael Magie and Mary (Meeker) Magie, were for a long time members of the First

Presbyterian Church in Elizabeth. He inherited from his father his activity and industry, and from his mother her sympathetic and deeply religious nature. As early as eight or ten years of age, a time when most boys think of their sports only, his mind was exercised with the idea of God and thoughts of the world to come. His father was regular in his observance of that time-honored custom of Scotch Presbyterians, the calling around him on the Sabbath day every member of his household and teaching them the "Westminster Catechism." It is impossible to over-estimate the value of such instruction in childhood and early youth, when the heart and mind are wax to receive impressions and marble to retain them. At the age of sixteen he was bereft of his father's care and left to be the staff of a widowed mother and an example to the younger members of his family. From his childhood he had always felt an ardent desire to be a minister of the gospel, and when at the age of eighteen he united with the church the desire became stronger and stronger. His way seemed, however, to be hedged in by many difficulties. His age was an objection; and as the care of the farm devolved on him he did not see how he could be spared. But He who had called him to the high destiny of the ministry made his way clear before him. In 1813 he began to study Latin under Rev. Dr. John McDowell, pastor of the First Presbyterian Church. He entered the junior class of the College of New Jersey in 1815. After graduating with honor, he became a student in the Theological Seminary, in the same place, in the fall of 1817, being then in his twenty-second year. After spending one year in the seminary, he was solicited by the faculty of the college to fill the position of tutor. He accepted the offer, and for two years performed the two-fold duty of teacher and student at the same time. Immediately after graduating he placed himself under the care of the Presbytery of New Jersey as a candidate for gospel ministry. After the usual course of study, he was licensed to preach. He delivered his first sermon in the lecture-room of Dr. McDowell's church, and his second on the following Sabbath in the church proper. The First Church had long been full to overflowing, and just at this time the subject of forming a new society was agitated. The enterprise was successfully carried out, and Dr. Magie was installed pastor of the Second Presbyterian Church of Elizabeth, April 24th, 1821. During the period of his pastorate, which lasted nearly forty-five years, he received many calls from other churches and from many religious boards, but he declined them all, some of them without even mentioning the subject to his people. The relations between him and his congregation were always most happy, and he had no wish to change for a more prominent position. He filled, up to the time of his decease, several positions of honor and trust; as Trustee of the College of New Jersey; Director in the American Board of Commissioners for Foreign Missions; Director in the American Tract Society, and Chairman of the Committee of Publica-

tions; Director in the Theological Seminary at Princeton, etc. The duties of these different positions he performed with the most conscientious carefulness. A man who conquered circumstances, he made himself, under Providence, what he was, a power in the community. Contending in youth with the hardships of a farmer's life, and then grappling with the intellectual difficulties of the student, his powers and capacities developed themselves to a degree far exceeding that of a man nursed in the lap of luxury. Having lived in daily contact with nature, he learned to estimate things according to their true value, and he esteemed men not in proportion to the mere accident of birth or surroundings but according to their integrity and worth. He possessed in a great degree the characteristics of the race from which he sprung, prudence, excellent judgment and a wide knowledge of the affairs of every-day life. Benevolence beamed from every feature of his face, and so wise was he in counsel that many who were not his own people sought his advice upon subjects not spiritual or ecclesiastical. His patriotism during the dark and trying hours of the rebellion was only second to his religion. He was a man of great simplicity and earnestness of manner, which in preaching carried the hearer beyond the speaker to the message he was delivering, a fact which accounts for his successful ministrations through so long a term of years. He finished his earthy career May 10th, 1865. His funeral, which took place a few days after, was largely attended, not only by his brethren in the ministry from other parts of the State, but also by persons of all classes in the community. The bells of the city were tolled; the flags were displayed at half-mast, and everything betokened that his fellow-citizens mourned deeply the great loss they had sustained.

AGIE, WILLIAM J., Lawyer, of Elizabeth, New Jersey, was born in that city, December 9th, 1832. His father, David Magie, D. D., was for nearly forty-five years pastor of the Second Presbyterian Church of Elizabeth, and was also a native of the same town. His mother, née Ann Francis Wilson, was also to the manor born. He entered Princeton College in 1852, and graduated in 1855. Then he studied law in Elizabeth with the late Francis B. Chetwood, and was licensed an attorney in 1856, and as counsellor in 1859. For six years he was associated in practice with his able preceptor, Mr. Chetwood, under the firm-name of Chetwood & Magie. Dissolving this connection he practised alone for a short time, and then formed a partnership with Mr. Cross, the style of the firm being, as now, Magie & Cross. From 1866 to 1871 he was Prosecutor of Pleas for Union county. One of the original incorporators of the First National Bank of Elizabeth, he is at present a Director of that institution; also a Director in the Dime Savings Bank. He is counsel for the Elizabeth Water Company, and was counsel for the New Jersey Railroad until its lease to the Pennsylvania Railroad, and was continued by them until his election to the New Jersey Senate in 1875 from Union county. During the session of 1875-76 he was appointed Chairman of the Judiciary Committee, on which he served with marked ability. In politics he is a Republican, having acted with that party since 1861, but, as a rule, he has eschewed an active part in politics, preferring to devote his time and talents to his profession. He only accepted his senatorial position at the earnest solicitation of his friends. In educational matters he has always manifested an earnest interest, and was a member of the Board of Education of Elizabeth from 1856 to 1861. With others he was instrumental in organizing the Elizabeth & Newark Horse Railroad, and has been a director in that company since its organization, acting also as counsel for it. He is a Director and one of the originators of the Elizabeth Public Library, which, though in embryo, bids fair to be a valuable means of culture to the town. In fact he is and has always been active in all public improvements, and is among the most valuable citizens of Elizabeth. In his profession he takes position in the front rank, being at once an able and well-read lawyer and a high minded gentleman. He was married on October 1st, 1857, to Frances Baldwin, of Elizabeth.

ORNELISON, JOHN MESIER, M. D., Physician, late of Bergen, was born in that town, April 29th, 1802. His parents were Rev. John Cornelison, pastor of the Dutch Reformed Church of Bergen, and Catharine (Mesier) Cornelison, of New York. After acquiring a good preliminary education at the schools of the community in which he lived, he entered Union College, at Schenectady, New York, from which institution he graduated in the year 1822. Shortly after leaving college he entered the office of Dr. Valentine Mott as a medical student. He received his diploma in the year 1825, and at once commenced the practice of medicine in Bergen. After a time he removed to Jersey City, and there continued earnestly engaged until 1862, when he retired from active practice and removed again to his native town of Bergen. Devoted as he was to his profession, and successful as he was in the practice of it, he yet found time and strength for political and official labors. In the year 1832 he was elected by the Democratic party to serve as a member of the Assembly in the State Legislature, and was re-elected in 1833. In the year 1851 he was appointed by the Governor one of the Lay Judges of the Court of Errors and Appeals, to fill the unexpired term of Hon. Garret Wall, and was reappointed for two succeeding terms, holding the position for sixteen years. In 1869 he was elected Mayor of Bergen, and in 1873 was appointed by the Legislature a member of the Board of Works in Jersey City, and was elected President of the

Board. When the war of the rebellion broke out, he became an earnest and active supporter of the national government, and thenceforward remained identified with the Republican party. At the time of his death he was President of the Board of Regents of the Hudson County Hospital. He was married in 1826 to Metta Van Winkle. He died, May 24th, 1875, universally esteemed and universally lamented.

ENNINGTON, WILLIAM, Lawyer, Governor and Chancellor of New Jersey, was born, 1790, in the city of Newark, and was the son of Governor William S. Pennington, whose biographical sketch will be found elsewhere in this volume. William received an excellent classical education in the schools of Newark, and subsequently entered the College of New Jersey, at Princeton, from which institution he graduated in 1813, with honor to himself and to his *Alma Mater*. He at once commenced the study of law in the office of Hon. Theodore Frelinghuysen, and was licensed as an attorney in 1817; three years afterward he was made a counsellor, and in 1834 was appointed serjeant-at-law. He was for several years Clerk of the United States District and Circuit Courts, and in 1828 was elected a member of the General Assembly as a Representative from Essex county. He was, as were also all of his family, friendly to the election of John Quincy Adams for the Presidency, and of course opposed to the principles and policy of Andrew Jackson and his successors. This party were at one time designated as National Republicans, but in 1834 assumed the name and style of the Whig party, and of this latter organization William Pennington was regarded as the leader in New Jersey. In the fall of 1837 he was elected by the Legislature to the office of Governor and Chancellor of the State, and was re-elected continuously until 1843, when the Democratic party had gained the ascendency in the Legislature. During his term as Governor occurred the celebrated "broad seal" difficulty, which created such an intense feeling throughout the country, and particularly in New Jersey; and it is not too much to say, at this distant day, that the action of the majority of Congress, in displacing the Whig members, who bore their commissions as having been fairly returned to that body, and substituting therefor others who had not such commissions, merely because their views were in accordance with the majority when Congress organized, contributed in a great measure to the overwhelming defeat which met the Democratic party in the campaign of 1840. Governor Pennington likewise gave great satisfaction both as Chancellor and Judge of the Prerogative Court, and but one of his decrees was overruled in the Court of Appeal, and that was after he ceased to preside. After his last term as Governor had expired, he returned to the practice of the law, which, prior to his holding that office, had been large and lucrative. During the Fillmore

Alfred Hall

administration he was offered the position of Governor of the Territory of Minnesota, but declined the appointment. When the Whig party had become disintegrated, and a new organization was being formed, he became in a measure identified with it. In 1856 Fremont had been nominated by the Free-soil or Republican party, for the Presidency, with William L. Dayton, of New Jersey, as the candidate for Vice-President; and he supported these nominations because of his firm friendship for Mr. Dayton. In 1858 he was nominated for Congress, but declined the same; but as it was believed he was the only candidate in the then opposition party who could carry the district, he was elected. When the House met in December, 1859, an intense excitement was at once apparent, and everything betokened the coming contest. For two months the organization of the House was suspended, no Speaker being elected; but at last, he received a majority of all the votes cast, and was inducted into that office, which he filled most ably and impartially; indeed, it is not too much to say, that he never had any superior and rarely one equal in such an arduous and difficult position. He was a man gifted with a large share of common sense; and he was thus able to grasp as it were the most difficult questions and render a decision on true and equitable grounds. He was an excellent counsellor, an eloquent pleader, and a most judicious and reliable judge. In religious belief he was a member of the Presbyterian church, and for many years had been the President of the Board of Trustees of the First Church of Newark, prior to 1849, at which time he withdrew to become one of the High Street congregation, then about being formed. He was married, about 1820, to an estimable lady, a descendant of Dr. William Burnet, Surgeon-General of the army, who survived him. He died in February, 1862, his death being ascribed to a large dose of morphine, administered through the mistake of an apothecary.

HALL, ALFRED, Manufacturer, of Perth Amboy, is a New Englander by birth, having been born, May 22d, 1803, in Meriden, Connecticut. On his father's side he is of English and on his mother's side of French extraction. Both his father, Avery Hall, and his mother, Sarah Foster, were natives of Connecticut, his father being a farmer at Meriden. The early education of Alfred Hall was obtained in the public schools of Meriden. Later he removed with his parents to Great Barrington, Massachusetts, and he continued his studies in the schools at that place. During school sessions he worked hard and effectively at his books, and out of school he worked just as hard and effectively on his father's farm. At the age of seventeen he did what one is tempted to believe every New England boy does at one time or another—he began to teach school. For the space of a year he taught the school at the centre of Tyringham,

Massachusetts. At the end of that time he literally started out into the world. His father owned a large tract of land in what was then Medina county, but is now Lorain county, Ohio, about fifty miles southwest of Cleveland, and Alfred and his brother Seldon, who is now a resident of Ohio, started to reach this tract of land and clear a portion of the timber off it, to render the place fit for farming purposes. The brothers performed this journey of seven hundred miles on foot, going by way of Albany and Rochester (the latter place being then a mere collection of log huts), and thence through Buffalo and Cleveland, reaching their destination a month after leaving home. Their first work, after arrival, was to erect a log hut and commence a "clearing;" and in the construction of their cabin not a nail was used, for the conclusive reason that there were no nails in that region. Three months after the brothers had erected their log cabin, the remainder of the family arrived from Massachusetts, making the journey in wagons drawn by oxen, and the clearing in the forest became the family homestead. Alfred Hall, having a natural aptness for mechanical work, was frequently called upon to help his neighbor pioneers in preparing their log homes. He remained at the forest homestead for about a year, assisting with the farm-work, and then he went to Silver Springs, Cumberland county, Pennsylvania, and there resumed his occupation of teacher. He remained there, so employed, for about two years, when he returned to his father's home. He built himself a cabin in the vicinity, and settled down as a hard-working citizen of the community. He remained for several years, during which time he acted as Postmaster, Trustee of the Township, and Justice of the Peace. His occupation as postmaster could not have been very arduous, as in those days two months were required to send a letter to the East and receive a reply, the mails for the most part being carried by men who travelled on foot. At length he removed to Cleveland, and there engaged in the manufacture of building-brick, which business he continued to prosecute, successfully and to a considerable extent, for a period of fifteen years. He took an active part in the public affairs of Cleveland during this residence. He was a prominent worker in the formation of the charter of the town, and subsequently served as an Alderman, and also as a member of Council. When the town was regularly laid out, he was Chairman of the Committee on Streets, etc. Although a Democrat in politics, his public spirit, sterling integrity, and practical ability were so widely and heartily recognized, that he received the support of his fellow-citizens, irrespective of party considerations. In the year 1842, while still in business in Cleveland, he invented and patented a brick-moulding machine, which achieved a fine success and was adopted generally by the trade throughout the country, and is now in use by the firm of which he is the head. Leaving Cleveland, he removed to Coxsackie, New York, where he remained three years. In 1845 he went to England, and during most of that year was occupied in securing patent-rights in that country for his brick machine. He returned to the United States in the latter part of the year, and located at Perth Amboy, where he commenced the erection of buildings for the manufacture of fire-brick. The buildings were constructed of wood, and business could be conducted in them only during the summer months. Ten years later, in 1856, a portion of these buildings was destroyed by fire, and then he at once erected in their place an extensive brick building, comprising all desirable improvements, and in this structure the work is carried on all the year round. The ground-floor is heated by four immense furnaces, by which the bricks are dried; and the upper story is used for the manufacture of Rockingham and yellow ware. The works include, also, extensive kilns for burning the bricks and the ware, the ware being burnt in round kilns, according to the old English style, and the bricks in the square American kilns. These are perfect in their way, embodying many improvements which are the inventions of the proprietor: among them may be mentioned a patent hinge-grate of his invention, which renders the burning much more speedy and less expensive than heretofore. Beside the works at Perth Amboy, the firm of A. Hall & Sons have a similar fire-brick works, of about the same capacity, at Buffalo, New York, and ten miles below Buffalo, at Tonawanda, extensive works for the manufacture of red brick, which produce about 2,250,000 annually, a million of which are of the style of Philadelphia face bricks. When running in full force, the several works employ about 250 men and boys, and produce about 5,000,000 fire-brick and 2,250,000 red-brick annually. The works in Buffalo are in charge of Edward J. Hall, a son of Alfred Hall. Another son, Eber H. Hall, is associated with his father at Perth Amboy. A fine specimen of the colored building-brick, produced by A. Hall & Sons, was presented by the large chimney erected by them adjoining the New Jersey building on the Centennial grounds, and it deservedly attracted much attention and admiration. The manufacture of brick has been very much benefited by various improvements introduced by Mr. Hall, many of them being his own inventions. From 1863 to 1869 he was Mayor of Perth Amboy, and three times he was elected without the opposition of any other candidate. He is, and has been since its organization, a stockholder, Director, and the President of the Middlesex Land Company. He was for many years a member of the Board of Freeholders of Middlesex County, and is President of the Fire-Brick Manufacturers' Association of the United States. During the war of the rebellion he was an active Union man, aiding the government effectively with money and influence. During his residence in Lorain county, Ohio, he married Sarah Buckingham, a native of Connecticut, and in their pioneer home the two sons now associated with him in business were born. Their family consisted of three sons and three daughters, of whom only two sons and one daughter are now living. She died in 1853, highly esteemed by all who knew her. Subsequently he married Pamelia F.

Robinson, a widow with three young children—one son and two daughters—whom he reared as his own. She is a native of New England, and a daughter of Colonel William Pearl, of New Hampshire. Mr. Hall is possessed of literary tastes, and his writings are always graphic and to the point. An article written by him, on the "Manufacture of Fire-Brick," and published in the *Scientific American* in January, 1870, and republished in several English papers, is characteristic. As a public speaker he seldom occupies more than twenty minutes, and is always listened to with earnest attention, as he never speaks unless he has something to say. He is a supporter of the Episcopal church, which he attends with his family, but he is no sectarian, and is not a member of any church. He has liberally aided all religious societies in his vicinity in the erection of their churches, and thinks any religion a good one if it makes those who profess it do what is right.

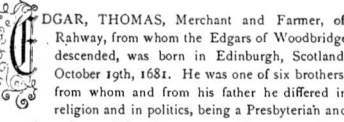DGAR, THOMAS, Merchant and Farmer, of Rahway, from whom the Edgars of Woodbridge descended, was born in Edinburgh, Scotland, October 19th, 1681. He was one of six brothers, from whom and from his father he differed in religion and in politics, being a Presbyterian and opposed to James III. He came to this country about 1720. Many of the Scotch ancestors of New Jersey families came at this period. He was one of the passengers on the "Caledonia" in the last voyage she made. She landed at Perth Amboy, and never went to sea again. Janet Knox, whom he afterward married, was also a passenger on the "Caledonia." He purchased land on Rahway river, and built a house thereon, which is still occupied by some of his descendants. In addition to farming his land he prosecuted business as a merchant, earning in all relations of life a wide reputation for integrity, strict uprightness and devoted piety. He died in May, 1759, leaving three sons and three daughters, from whom have sprung numerous descendants, although the name does not appear in all the families. They have ever been conspicuous for their virtues, industry and domestic habits. Very few of them have been in professional or public life, although the family has from time to time been worthily represented in the army, in law, in medicine, in the pulpit and in politics. As, for example, Clarkson Edgar was a brigadier-general in the war for independence, while another, David Edgar, was a captain of cavalry in the same patriotic contest. Later on, Alexander Edgar selected the medical profession, and served his country by taking part in the quelling of the insurrection in the Mohawk valley. Three other Edgars, William, Samuel and Thompson, were each several times members of the Legislature, wherein they served with great credit to themselves and acceptability to their constituents; and Samuel also held the office of Sheriff of Middlesex

county. Of those now living, David Edgar is a physician in high standing on Staten Island, while Jonathan Edgar enjoys a fine practice and excellent reputation as a lawyer in New York city, and Frank W. Edgar is a rising member of the bar of Northampton county, Pennsylvania. Among the representatives of the family in the pulpit are Rev. Dr. Edgar, of Easton, Pennsylvania, Rev. E. B. Edgar, of Plainfield, formerly of Westfield, and Rev. H. M. Booth, of Englewood. There have been others of this profession, but their names and location cannot be ascertained. Rev. C. H. Edgar, D. D., was seven years head master in the grammar school of New York University; was pastor of the Presbyterian Church in Bridgehampton, Long Island, and has been more than twenty years pastor of the American Reformed Church in Easton, Pennsylvania. He has contributed to the press a tractate on the "Curse of Canaan," some articles in reviews and several sermons. Rev. E. B. Edgar, during his pastorate at Westfield, preached the last sermon delivered in the Old Presbyterian Church of that town. This church was originally located in 1730, a rude log-house being first used; this gave way to a frame building, which in its turn was replaced in 1802-3 by the edifice wherein, on January 26th, 1862, Mr. Edgar preached the last sermon. This discourse, in its historical narrative and related thoughts, proved so interesting that, by general request, its author consented to yield the manuscript for publication, and it now remains among the most cherished archives of the new church. Commerce has attracted the attention of members of the family, and among the names of the successful and honorable merchants of the commercial metropolis of the new world—New York—appear those of several Edgars.

EDGAR, WILLIAM, third son of Thomas Edgar, was born April 20th, 1724, and died April 17th, 1776. He lived and died in the house built by his father, to which he made some additions. His career was that of a merchant and a farmer. Seven children were born to him. Of these were General Clarkson Edgar and Dr. Alexander Edgar, above alluded to. William, the youngest, known as Major Edgar, succeeded to the old homestead; also added some improvements to the structure. After the major's death the house was occupied by his son, William, until his decease, in July, 1866. Then it came into the occupancy of Miss Catharine B. Edgar, daughter of Major Edgar, who, now in her eighty-third year, still continues to reside beneath its shelter. The same house has been owned and occupied by this family more than a hundred and fifty years.

EDGAR, WILLIAM, son of William and grandson of Thomas, known as Major Edgar, was born March 25th, 1768, and died May 22d, 1845, aged seventy-seven years. He married Phebe Baker, great-granddaughter of Admiral Sir John Baker, to whose character and services a memorial column was erected in Westminster Abbey. Phebe Baker was the daughter of Captain Matthias Baker, of whose deeds of daring and narrow escapes in the service of the country the family have traditions; for example, he alone, unsupported by any soldiers, captured a British wagon with stores; which was guarded by a troop of cavalry. A musket is shown and highly prized as an evidence and trophy of the courageous deed. Major Edgar was a merchant, and a farmer in a very extensive way. Considerable attention was given by him to brick manufacture, and a large business in that line resulted. In connection with farming he conducted heavy operations in cattle and sheep. Looking beyond his merely personal requirements, he took an earnest interest in the development of his neighborhood, and, perceiving the necessity for better banking facilities, became one of the originators of the Farmers' & Mechanics' Bank, and its first president. He gained great repute as a manager and as a clear-headed business man of unquestionable integrity. Many estates were intrusted to his care for settlement, and in business disputes among his neighbors he came to be regarded as a general referee. For a number of years he was a member of the Legislature, and he proved himself a devoted and intelligent custodian of the public interests. His title of Major he derived from his rank in the State cavalry. Respected and beloved by the whole community, his death was regarded as a public loss. His family consisted of twelve children, six sons and six daughters, four of whom survive. Matthias B., who died in 1865, aged seventy-five years, held several positions of honor and trust in the Custom House, and was at one time Treasurer of the Illinois Central Railroad. He was a long time one of the leading merchants in New York. Alexander, who died in 1866, aged seventy-four years, was also a merchant, and for many years Public Storekeeper in New York; he held other positions of importance under the city and national government. Clarkson, who died in 1856, aged fifty years, was for a long period a merchant in Louisiana, and a New Jersey farmer. Jennette, who became the wife of Cornelius Baker, late of Elizabeth, and for many years a prominent merchant of New York, died in 1867, aged sixty-seven years. The four survivors are: Miss Catharine B. Edgar, living at the Edgar homestead; John B. Edgar, a farmer who has given much attention to the improvement of stock and to the best methods of agriculture; Rev. Dr. Edgar, of Easton, Pennsylvania, above mentioned; and Margaret, the wife of William W. Cornell, of Poughkeepsie, New York.

EDGAR, WILLIAM, son of Major Edgar, died July, 1866, aged sixty-nine. After some years spent in New York, as a merchant, he and his brother Alexander went, in 1820, to Ohio, into the very forest, to engage in farming. He afterward engaged in business in New Orleans. Securing a comfortable competence he retired, and after the death of his father purchased the homestead, and was largely occupied in agriculture. Always deeply interested in the welfare of his country, and well informed upon all political questions, he nevertheless declined all offers of office, preferring a private life. He was highly esteemed as a good citizen, an affectionate friend, a kind neighbor and a benevolent man. He lived a bachelor. He left the old homestead to be occupied by his sister Catharine.

EDGAR, CAPTAIN GEORGE P., is a son of Alexander and grandson of Major Edgar. He served with gallantry in the war for the Union and received the highest commendation from his superior officers; he was brevetted Major by Governor Fenton, of New York, as he first entered the service with the famous 7th Regiment, of New York city.

EDGAR, SAMUEL, above mentioned, was descended from Thomas through his second son, Alexander. He was highly esteemed as an honorable man, and served as Sheriff of Middlesex county and in the Legislature. Among his children are Jonathan Edgar, Esq., of New York, and Martha, the wife of Dr. Ellis B. Freeman, of Woodbridge.

EDGAR, THOMPSON, was also a descendant from Thomas through Alexander, his second son. He was an honest and benevolent man, and very popular with his party, of which he was the recognized head in his town. He served several times in the Legislature. He died a few years ago, in a ripe old age, beloved by all who knew him.

There are branches of the Edgar family of Woodbridge and Rahway in New York, Missouri, Ohio, Illinois and other parts. There have been hundreds of descendants of Thomas Edgar—scores of them now living. Like their ancestor, most of them have been Presbyterians. Some of the females married Quakers, and thus many of the most estimable of the Society of Friends in Rahway, Plainfield, Philadelphia and elsewhere are descendants of Thomas Edgar, of Scotland.

LEXANDER, WILLIAM COWPER, LL. D., Lawyer, of Princeton, was born in Prince Edward county, Virginia, May 20th, 1806. He was the second son of Rev. Archibald Alexander, D. D., the first Professor in the Princeton Theological Seminary, and of Janetta (Waddel) Alexander, daughter of Rev. James Waddel, Wirts' "Blind Preacher." Having passed through preliminary instruction, he became a student at Princeton College, from which he graduated with the class of 1824. He then took up the study of law, under the guidance of Hon. James S. Green, in Princeton, New Jersey, and was admitted in due course to the bar, in 1827. As a lawyer he took high rank. He mingled actively in politics, his convictions attaching him

to the Democratic party, of which he became a conspicuous leader. In 1853 he was elected to the State Senate, of which he continued, by successive elections, a member until 1868. For four years he presided over that body as its president, and his rule was distinguished for its ability, impartiality, discretion, firmness and dignity. In 1857 he received the Democratic nomination for Governor, but he was defeated with his party. Two years subsequently, in 1859, he was chosen President of the Equitable Life Assurance Society of the United States, and held the position up to the time of his death, August 24th, 1874. He was a member from New Jersey of the famous Peace Congress, held in Washington in 1861, and did his best to secure the objects with which that assemblage was called together. In recognition of his scholarship and public services Lafayette College, Pennsylvania, conferred the degree of Doctor of Laws upon him in 1860. He was never married.

TRATTON, HON. JOHN L. N., President of the Farmers' National Bank, of Mount Holly, New Jersey, was born in that township, November 27th, 1817. His father was John L. Stratton, M. D., a distinguished practitioner of Burlington county, who carried out his profession for more than forty-five years. His mother, whose maiden name was Ann Newbold, descending from an old and influential family, was a native of the same county. His early education was mainly obtained at select schools in Mount Holly. He was prepared for college at Mendham, Morris county, New Jersey, and in the spring of 1834 entered Princeton, from which he graduated in September, 1836. Upon his return to his native town he spiritedly entered upon the study of law, under the guidance of B. R. Browne, Esq., and in 1839 received his license as attorney, and in 1842 as counsellor. He commenced at once the practice of his profession, which he has ever since steadily maintained in the county and State courts. His reputation is that of an able and honorable advocate, and his clientage is very large. In 1858 he was elected to Congress on the Second District, on the Republican ticket. Primarily he was a Whig, and upon the dissolution of that party he identified himself with the Republican organization, of which he has ever since been a prominent member. In 1860 his constituency returned him a second time to the national House of Representatives. His record in these two sessions of Congress shows him to have been an industrious worker, strong in argument, ready in parliamentary law, influential in committee meetings, and at all times faithful to the people whom he so ably represented. Upon the conclusion of his Congressional service he resumed his practice of the law. In 1875 he was chosen President of the Farmers' National Bank, of Mount Holly, to fill the vacancy caused by the death of John Black, Esq., who had served in that responsible position for the remarkable period of fifty-seven years. The institution was organized in 1814, and since Mr. Stratton has been called to its management he has sufficiently shown his ability as a careful financier. For some years past he has served also as President of the Gas Works. He is still actively interested in politics, and gives his good counsel to the organization with which he has been for many years so honorably identified. In 1842 he married Caroline Newbold, of Burlington county, New Jersey.

STRATTON, LIEUTENANT-COLONEL JAMES NEWBOLD, A. M., Judge-Advocate on the Staff of General Gershom Mott, was born, August 26th, 1845, in Mount Holly, Burlington county, New Jersey. His father is the Hon. John L. N. Stratton, a prominent lawyer of that place, and President of the Farmers' National Bank, whose biographical sketch goes before. His mother, Caroline Newbold, was a member of an old and highly respected family of Burlington county. He spent a considerable period of his youth at a select school of Mount Holly, where he acquired an excellent rudimentary education; thence passed into the Lawrenceville High School, where, from 1860 to 1863, he studied the courses essentially preparatory to a collegiate career, and in the fall of the latter year entered Princeton College. Two years after, so rapid and substantial was his progress, he graduated with the class of 1865, and in 1868 received the degree of A. M. He commenced at once, upon leaving Princeton, the study of law in his father's office at Mount Holly, and in 1868 was licensed as an attorney, and in 1871 as counsellor. Since his admission to the bar he has been actively engaged in professional labors at Mount Holly, and has participated in many of the most important cases which have been brought up for adjudication. In politics he is identified with the Republican party, of which, in his locality, he is a leading member. He has served on important committees, and has frequently stumped the State in the interest of Republican candidates. In speaking he is fluent, with a ready memory to reproduce facts in local, State, or national history, and a quick ability to construct from them a powerful argument. He was chosen a delegate to the Cincinnati Convention, in 1876, which nominated for the Presidency the Hon. Rutherford B. Hayes. He fills, and has filled a number of important trusts. At this time he is Solicitor for the First National Bank, of Vincentown, New Jersey. He has for a number of terms served as the legal adviser to the officers of Mount Holly, and has been a director of the Farmers' National Bank, of the same place, and of which his father is president, since 1872. On August 12th, 1873, he was commissioned Major of the 7th New Jersey National Guard, and was, on the 28th of June, 1876, raised to the position of Lieutenant-Colonel and Judge-Advocate. His interest in the advancement of the military interests is decided, and has infused greater activity in the organizations with which he is identified. He is a gentleman not only of ability, but of progressive tendency, and enjoys the esteem of all his fellow-citizens.

PARRISH, JOSEPH, M. D., who is so widely known in connection with the treatment of inebriety as a disease, was born in Philadelphia, Pennsylvania, November 11th, 1818, being the son of the late Dr. Joseph Parrish, of that city. After receiving a liberal education he studied medicine at the University of Pennsylvania, and graduated with distinction in 1844. He married Lydia Gaskill, the daughter of a leading citizen of Burlington, New Jersey, and began practice in that city. Here he achieved rapid success, and in the fourth year of his professional life was appointed Physician to Burlington College and St. Mary's Hall. About this time he started the *New Jersey Medical Reporter*, being its sole editor and proprietor. So ably did he conduct it that the journal attracted the attention of the profession throughout the country, and the New Jersey Medical Society marked their sense of its value by recognizing it as their organ, and making an annual appropriation for its support. Thus firmly established, the *Reporter* still enjoys favor, being published from Philadelphia, and managed by Dr. S. W. Butler, formerly Dr. Parrish's office assistant, and later co-editor. After a residence of some years in Burlington Dr. Parrish was waited upon by a committee of the faculty of the Philadelphia College of Medicine, and invited to accept the chair of Obstetrics and Diseases of Women and Children. At first he declined the offer, but subsequently, at the solicitation of his friends in Philadelphia, he accepted it, and removed thither in 1854. Under the heavy claims of his professorship and a large private practice his health gave way; he resigned his chair, and with his family spent the winter in Alabama, near Montgomery. Failing to realize the anticipated benefit from the change of climate, he sailed for Europe in the following May. A pulmonary complaint had then been developed, and his recovery was deemed doubtful by distinguished physicians. While abroad he conceived a desire to visit Switzerland during the winter, and accordingly, accompanied by his wife and three friends, he made the passage of the St. Bernard Pass in December. The severe weather and concomitant hardships of the trip exercised the most favorable influence upon the invalid traveller, and his health steadily improved therefrom. He passed some time in Rome, and paid frequent visits to the various hospitals and asylums, in the management of one of which he observed a painful carelessness and inhumanity. Expostulating with the authorities of the Insane Department of the San Spirito Hospital for the harshness and severity of their discipline, he was referred to the Prefect of the charities of the city. This led to a further reference—this time to the Pope himself. But official circumlocution rendering a personal interview with the pontiff too difficult, Dr. Parrish drew up an urgent appeal to His Holiness, which he handed in person to Cardinal Antonelli, whose sympathies he enlisted so completely that the appeal reached its destination under most favorable auspices, and elicited from the Pope a reply to the effect that he "was graciously indebted to the young American for his kindly and judicious interest." Soon after a medical commission was appointed to examine the hospitals, and to visit similar institutions in France and Germany. As a consequence, the glaring abuses of power upon the helpless inmates of the asylum, appealed against by Dr. Parrish, were entirely corrected. After nearly a year's foreign travel he returned to Philadelphia, and, his health renewed, proposed to resume practice, for which his advantages, including a Fellowship in the College of Physicians, were unusually good. But the peculiar ability of his writings and lectures, with the success of his practice, marked him out to a large circle of friends as eminently fitted to take charge of an institution for the training of idiots, lately organized under a charter from the State by Bishop Potter and a few philanthropic Philadelphians, and commenced in an experimental way in a rented property at Germantown. Unknown to him, they presented his name to the Board of Directors; the position was tendered to him; he visited the institution, found it in a state of confusion and disorder, became interested, and, accepting the charge, at once gave form and life to the beneficent enterprise. Under his able administration its value was speedily recognized both by the people and the Legislature of the State. From the former came large private contributions, and from the latter liberal appropriations. The Legislatures of New Jersey and Delaware, and the City Councils of Philadelphia, under his influence, voted grants in consideration of the reception and treatment of a given number of children from their respective localities. Having established the institution firmly—it had by this time been removed to Media—Dr. Parrish, in 1863, resigned its charge, notwithstanding the urgent remonstrances of the Board of Directors, conceiving his services to be demanded by his country. Leaving the school, with which his name will ever be identified, he entered the Sanitary Commission, where he was welcomed by being made the recipient of important trusts. Beginning as an inspector of the camps and hospitals about Washington, he was subsequently delegated to travel through the principal towns of Pennsylvania and some other States, holding public meetings and organizing aid societies, with a view to secure much-needed efficient supplies. He also edited the *Sanitary Commission Bulletin*, and so successful was he in the organization of soclelles for the manufacture of garments and the collection of supplies that he was requested by the board to visit the governors and Legislatures of the loyal States and endeavor

to unify and concentrate the work of this valuable auxiliary to the government. This commission he executed with very gratifying results. Subsequently, under a full commission from the President of the United States, he made an extended tour, embracing the numerous camps and hospitals within the Union lines in the West and South, looking after the sick and wounded and distributing with great discretion the supplies of the people through the authorities of the government. For some months he superintended the supply stations at White House and City Point, distributing whole cargoes of clothing, ice and hospital stores. In much of this benevolent labor he found a valuable coadjutor in Mrs. Parrish, who, in addition to her many services in connection with the commission, prepared a little volume entitled the "Soldiers' Friend," containing directions how to find the rests and lodges of the commission; also a choice collection of hymns, of which 50,000 copies were distributed gratuitously in the army and navy. After the surrender of Lee's army Dr. Parrish went to Richmond, and rendered efficient assistance to the Sanitary Commission in providing for the disbanded soldiers of both armies and the multitudes of destitute negroes. Strongly interested in the condition of the newly emancipated slaves, he, accompanied by his wife, made a tour of inspection of schools throughout the Southern States, in connection with the Freedman's Commission. As illustrating the general appreciation of his noble and disinterested labors during and immediately succeeding the war, it may be mentioned that through all these troublous times he travelled without a weapon of any kind. On one occasion, being arrested by a picket in Virginia, the officer before whom he was taken not only instantly released him, but furnished an escort for his safe conduct to his destination. Returning home to Pennsylvania he turned his entire attention to a subject which for many years had occupied his mind—the nature and cure of inebriety. Observation and study had convinced him that intemperance was actually a disease, subject to constitutional causes and amenable to treatment as other diseases are. With this conviction he organized the Pennsylvania Sanitarium for the Cure of Inebriates, locating it at Media, and becoming the President of its Board. In 1870 he called in New York a convention of physicians interested in similar institutions, and the American Association for the Cure of Inebriates was then formed. He was tendered its presidency, but, preferring the secretaryship, Dr. Willard Parker, of New York, was, on his motion, elected president. Two years later the presidency was again tendered him, and he accepted, holding it to this day. In 1872, the association being requested by a parliamentary committee in England to send a delegation to testify before a Select Committee of the English House of Commons, Dr. Parrish and Dr. Dodge, of Binghampton, New York, were appointed, and appeared before the committee, in London, during three weeks, which were occupied in their examination, narrating their experience in the treatment of inebriety and presenting an outline of

American legislation on the subject. A full stenographic report of their testimony was taken and published by the British government, while the committee were so impressed that they made a unanimous report adopting the recommendations of the delegates. Dr. Donald Dalrymple, chairman of this committee, had previously visited the various American inebriate asylums, and speaking, in his report to the House of Commons, of the Media Sanitarium, he says: " I visited the establishment at Media twice, though I only once saw the superintendent, Dr. Parrish, who, from length of experience, accurate knowledge, moderation of views and sobriety of judgment, I place at the head of all those with whom I have had communication." Soon after his return from England he was unexpectedly appointed to negotiate a treaty with the warlike Indians in the territory lying north of Texas, but he visited Washington and declined the commission, though repeatedly urged by the Secretary of the Interior to accept. Six months after his return he accepted the invitation of the trustees of the Maryland Inebriate Asylum, located at Baltimore, to devote a portion of his time to that institution. He found it in a most discouraging condition, but his energy and magnetism soon produced a change for the better, and aroused a lively interest in the benevolent enterprise throughout the State and country. During all these years of active work on behalf of particular institutions he has not been unmindful of the promulgation of his theory in a wider sphere. By able contributions to the public press and to the medical literature of the country, he has attracted large attention to the scientific treatment of idiocy and inebriety, and has secured for himself the position of an authority on these subjects. Among these publications must be specially noticed his " Report to the Legislature on the Criminal and Dependent Population of Pennsylvania," " Philosophy of Intemperance," " Intemperance as a Disease," being a report before the Pennsylvania Medical Society, of which he was first vice-president; " Classification and Treatment of Inebriates," " Opium Intoxication " and " The Pathology of Inebriety," being a lecture delivered before the Medical and Chirurgical Society of Maryland. He has also appeared as a lecturer upon these and other subjects. About the last of October, 1875, he returned to Burlington, intending to devote himself to medical literature, and especially to a further elaboration of the subject of his specialty; but his return, though after twenty years' absence, was greeted by his many friends with much more enthusiasm than was anticipated, and he found himself rapidly falling into an extensive practice, which he could not very well avoid. With the vigor of youth, and the enterprise which he has always manifested in his profession, he is still pursuing a practice that occupies much of his time. He is, however, not so much occupied that he cannot devote a few spare hours to the preparation for the press of a work on the " Pathology and Treatment of Alcoholic and Opium Intoxication." The first to elaborate the theory that inebriety and the opium habit are diseases subject to regular medical treatment in such a way as to secure its acceptance by the medical profession, he has earned the gratitude of all humanitarians and done much to advance the welfare of mankind. Much of his success may be attributed to his great personal magnetism, which attracts support from society and confidence from his patients. Naturally he has been approached by temperance organizations and appealed to by them for co-operation and support. But pursuing his theory simply in its medical aspect he has invariably declined such affiliations, preferring, to use his own expression, " not to dilute his energies" by too much subdivision. The subject, as he views it, is large enough to engage all the powers of any man, and in his devotion to its study on that line he is best serving his generation and posterity. At a recent meeting of the American Association for the Cure of Inebriates, of which he was the founder and which he served as president for three years, he was made Secretary for foreign correspondence, and requested by resolution to communicate with all civilized nations having official correspondence with the United States, and with all heathen nations in which there are Christian missions, through our foreign consuls and ministers, and through the several missions, and propound to them such questions as he may prepare, for the purpose of eliciting and collating reliable facts as to the kind and character of intoxicants used by the several nations and kingdoms of the globe, and of the laws governing their manufacture and sale, as well as the effect on the morals and habits of the people. He is now engaged in this comprehensive service, and when he shall have completed it he will have secured most important facts, which will of course be made the property of the public.

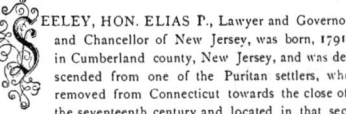

EELEY, HON. ELIAS P., Lawyer and Governor and Chancellor of New Jersey, was born, 1791, in Cumberland county, New Jersey, and was descended from one of the Puritan settlers, who removed from Connecticut towards the close of the seventeenth century and located in that section. While a child, his father removed to Bridgeton and held several county offices beside serving both in the Assembly and Legislative Council of the State. Elias had but a limited education, but entered upon the study of law in the office of Daniel Elmer, and was licensed as an attorney in 1815. He shortly after commenced the practice of his profession, adding to the latter the duties of a conveyancer. He was elected a member of the Legislative Council in 1829, and thereafter re-elected for three successive years; and in 1832 was chosen vice-president of the same. When Governor Southard was elected United States Senator a vacancy was then created in the executive chair, and at a joint meeting of the Legislature, held in March, 1833, Elias P. Seeley was elected to fill the same. During his term of service as Chancellor, the celebrated Quaker case was argued before him, which consumed over a month in the hearing. The result was to affirm the original decree, seven of the judges, including the Governor, being favorable to the decree, while four dissented from the same. After the expiration of his term as Governor, he was again elected a member of the Legislature, in which he served for several years. He was politically opposed to the Democratic doctrines as laid down by Jackson, and toward the close of his life was an active and zealous member of the Whig party. He died in 1846.

SHEDDAN, REV. SAMUEL SHARON, D. D., late of Rahway, was born in Northumberland county, in Pennsylvania, September 13th, 1810. His grandparents came from Scotland, and settled on a farm within a few miles of the Susquehanna river, where the homestead of his family remains until the present time. He pursued his studies preparatory to college at the academy in Milton, Pennsylvania; entered Jefferson College in the year 1830, and graduated two years afterward. Theology he studied at Princeton, and was licensed to preach by the Presbytery of Northumberland in the fall of 1834. Shortly after his license Dr. Sheddan was called to take charge of the church at Muncy for one-half of his time, and to give the other half as a supply to the church in Williamsport, in Pennsylvania. At the end of two and a half years he was called to relinquish his field in Williamsport, and give this half of his time as co-pastor with Dr. Bryson in the church at Warrior Run. Dr. Bryson had been pastor of the church at Warrior Run for about fifty years, and under his pastorate both the grandfather and the father of Dr. Sheddan had become ruling elders. He remained four years and a half as co-pastor with Dr. Bryson, and at the end of that period became sole pastor of the church, then one of the largest churches in the vicinity. He remained at Warrior Run eleven years from the day he became sole pastor of the church. At the end of that time he was unanimously called to the First Presbyterian Church in Rahway, New Jersey. On December 17th, 1835, he was united in marriage with Mary Boyd, daughter of the Rev. Alexander Boyd, of Newtown, Pennsylvania. In the year 1864 he received the degree of Doctor of Divinity from Columbia College, New York. The life of Dr. Sheddan was a most laborious and useful one. During his ministry at Warrior Run, he united the office of teacher with that of pastor, and by unremitting toil carried on successfully both his school and his church. Among other fruits of his labors he prepared for college from twelve to fifteen ministers of the Gospel, many of whom still survive; and through them, though dead, he still speaks. He remained the beloved pastor of the First Presbyterian Church in Rahway, New Jersey, for twenty-two years and a half, and Sunday, at noon, on October 18th, 1874, upon the fortieth anniversary of his ministerial life, he laid down his earthly work to receive his crown.

ELMENDORF, JOHN C., Lawyer, and Treasurer of Rutgers College, was born in Somerset county, New Jersey, in March, 1814. His parents, William C. and Maria (Dumont) Elmendorf, were both natives of the same State. He obtained his elementary education at Somerville; entered Rutgers College in 1833, and was graduated in 1836. Choosing the legal profession, he became a student in the office of Judge S. Nevins, of New Brunswick, and after the prescribed course of study was licensed as an attorney in 1839, and as counsellor in 1842. For fifteen years he served with marked ability and fidelity as Prosecutor of the Pleas for Middlesex County, filling the office under the administrations of Governors Stratton, Newell and Olden. Appointed Treasurer of Rutgers College in 1853, he has discharged the duties of that position for over twenty-three years with distinguished ability, and to the increased prosperity of the institution. He was married on October 6th, 1857, to Maria Louisa Frelinghuysen, of New Jersey.

MURPHY, COLONEL WILLIAM ROBINSON, Supervisor of the New Jersey State Prison, at Trenton, was born at Princeton, New Jersey, November 27th, 1809. His father, William R. Murphy, a farmer by occupation, was a native of Lawrence township, Mercer county, in the same State, and his mother, whose maiden name was Mary Burk, was born in Princeton. John Burk, his maternal grandfather, was a sergeant in the Maryland Line Regiment of Infantry, under General George Washington, and received at Monmouth a wound, which eventually proved fatal. Colonel Murphy's education was obtained in the Princeton common schools. When fifteen years of age he was apprenticed in the cabinet-making trade, to which he devoted himself assiduously, and when attaining his majority, his employer dying, the entire business which the latter had built up in Princeton fell into his hands. He carried this on with good results for eight years, and was compelled then to relinquish it by reason of failing health, retiring for a time from active life. In 1844 he was appointed Postmaster at Princeton, and filled this position acceptably to his fellow-townsmen for many years. In 1852 he was appointed Clerk of Mercer county, and remained in office until the expiration of his term, which comprised a period of five years, winning golden opinions from all classes in the community by the energy, promptitude and fidelity he displayed in the discharge of his duties, and by the urbanity of his deportment.

He had always manifested a deep interest in military matters, was a member of a military organization, and at the time of the breaking out of the late civil war, he was in command of a fine body of men, in discipline and *morale* unsurpassed by any other of like numbers in the State. With this body, acting heartily with him, he was among the first to respond to President Lincoln's call for troops. Governor Olden placed him, successively, in various positions, all comprising important military trusts, and in February, 1862, he received his commission as Colonel of the 10th New Jersey Infantry. In 1863, after resisting for a time pressing importunities to return, he came from the field to supervise the interests of the canal company. In March of the same year he resigned his command, and was appointed Inspector and Collector of the Delaware & Raritan Canal, a joint company with the old Camden & Amboy Railroad. For a few months he served as Superintendent of the Air Line from New York to Washington, the business of which had assumed huge proportions in consequence of its being used as the main road for the transportation of troops and army supplies from the northeast to the seat of war. He retained his connection with the canal company up to 1868. In April of the following year he was chosen to the Supervisorship of the State Prison at Trenton, and it is an excellent commentary on the ability and care with which he has discharged all his onerous duties, that he has continued ever since to fill that position in the midst of great political changes. He is an active Democrat, but allows no partisan zeal to influence him in the fulfilment of the responsibilities laid upon him. He has reformed many abuses in prison discipline, and has originated and rendered practical many beneficial methods of discipline, and has been often rewarded by the commendation of the people. He is a gentleman of engaging manners, versatile in business accomplishments, and firm in action when convinced it is for private and public good. His residence is at Bordentown, and his wife, whose maiden name was Mary Landphier, and her native place, New London, Connecticut, is a lady of many accomplishments, and ably supports him in all his undertakings.

———— ◆◆◆ ————

ARRISON, CHARLES H., Manufacturer of Patent Leather, was born in Parsippany, Morris county, New Jersey, March 12th, 1825. His father, Henry Harrison, originally a manufacturer, was a native of Orange, New Jersey, as was his father before him, Captain Thomas Harrison, a soldier of the Revolution, who died about 1837, at the ripe age of eighty. His mother was Pamela De Hart, of Elizabethtown, New Jersey, a descendant of the De Harts of revolutionary fame; so that revolutionary blood pours into his veins along both lines of descent. He attended the district schools of Morris county until he was twelve years of age, at which period his parents removed to Orange, where he resumed his attendance at school, though only for the winter months, working through the rest of the year on the farm with his father, who had retired from manufacturing, and engaged in agriculture. He continued thus to divide his time between the farm and the school till he was fifteen years old, when he left school, and for a short time gave his whole attention to the farm, after which he went to Newark, and entered the establishment of Colonel D. B. Crockett, for the purpose of learning the art of manufacturing patent leather. In this establishment he remained until 1848, when, having mastered the business, he left for Pittsburgh, Pennsylvania, to take charge of a patent leather manufactory at that place. This position he held till 1850, discharging its duties faithfully and ably. He had now acquired experience as well as skill in his business, and withal a small capital, the fruit of hard labor and self-denying economy. With this stock, of which by far the most valuable part was carried not in his purse, but in his head, he returned to Newark, and laid the foundations—in a small way, indeed, but on the present site—of the extensive and flourishing business which now spreads his name in all quarters of this continent. A little over a year after he set up in business on his own account he associated with him his brother, John D. Harrison, under the firm-name of C. H. & J. D. Harrison. Their united capital was not large, but both were hard workers, with clear perceptions of what should be done, and strong wills and cunning hands to do it. They were determined to succeed, and, as usually follows in such cases, they carried their determination into effect. They have succeeded eminently, standing to-day among the acknowledged leaders of their business in the United States. Their present manufactories, erected on the site occupied at the outset, cover about two acres of ground, and, when running at full force, they employ some one hundred and twenty men, producing twenty thousand hides annually. Their trade, which is steadily increasing, extends now over all parts of the United States, Canada, and the East and West Indies. Not content with their success, they treat it as a stepping-stone to greater achievements in the future. The spurs they won long ago they used only to prick the sides of their ambition, and, in the midst of ripening prosperity, they still maintain the same spirit. With them success is not a sedative, but a stimulant. The senior member of the firm is in politics a Republican, and in 1875 represented the Sixth Assembly District of Essex county in the Legislature, where he displayed the diligence, judgment, and liberality that have characterized him as a business man. He is now one of the School Commissioners of the city of Newark. On the special call of the government during the Gettysburg fight he volunteered his services, and was assigned to duty as Quartermaster of the Provisional Battalion of New Jersey Volunteers, stationed at Harrisburg. He was married in April, 1849, to Marie Brewster, of New Jersey.

ARICK, THEODORE ROMEYN, M. D., of Jersey City, was born, June 24th, 1825, in Dutchess county, New York. His father, John Vreedenbergh Varick, was a native of New York city. His mother, Anna Maria (Romeyn) Varick, belonged to the Romeyn family of Hackensack, New Jersey. Members of this family have, for the last three generations, ministered to the congregation of the Reformed Dutch in that town, and the pulpit is at present filled by one of them. His uncle, Colonel Richard Varick, leaving his profession, that of the law, enrolled himself during the revolutionary war among his country's defenders, and was attached to General Benedict Arnold's staff at the time of that great traitor's defection. Subsequently Colonel Varick became private secretary to Washington, and continued in that office till the close of the war. He was Recorder of New York city from 1783 to 1788; being also, from 1787 to 1788, a member of the Assembly. From 1788 to 1789 he served as Attorney-General for the State of New York. In the latter year he was elected Mayor of the city of New York, holding that office till 1800, a period of eleven consecutive years. He died in 1831, "full of years and of honors," and was buried at Hackensack. In 1832 Dr. Varick's father removed to Jersey City, occupying as a country residence the old homestead. The family lived in Jersey City from 1845 to 1848, in which year they returned to Jersey City. His father died in 1835, previous to their removal to New York. In 1841 Theodore R. Varick entered the collegiate department of the New York University, and in 1843 he commenced the study of medicine in the same institution, graduating in the spring of 1846, before he had attained his twenty-first year. Soon after his graduation he received an appointment as Assistant Physician in the New York City Dispensary, located at the corner of White and Centre streets. In the following year he became one of the corps of attending physicians, and served in this capacity for two years. During this period (in 1847), the ship fever prevailed as an epidemic, and three out of a medical staff of six, succumbing to the disease, fell martyrs to their noble profession. In the fall of 1848 he returned to Jersey City, where he has since resided. In 1851 he became one of the incorporators of the District Medical Society of Hudson County, New Jersey, and is at the present time, except Dr. J. E. Culver, the only surviving one of the charter members. In 1853 he was elected member of the American Medical Association. He is also a Fellow of the New Jersey State Medical Society, having been President of that body in 1864. In that capacity he addressed them upon the occasion of their annual meeting, in a learned and suggestive dissertation upon the "Attributes of Mind, their Development and Effects." He belongs to the New York Academy of Medicine, and has been an honorary member of the New York State Medical Society since 1869. Of the New Jersey Academy of Medicine he was the first President. His address to the society in 1875, upon "The Causes of Death after Operations and Grave Injuries," was reported by the New York Medical Journal in October of that year. He is also connected with the Jersey City Pathological Society, and with the Neurological Society of New York city. In 1869 he was appointed by Governor Randolph to the office of Surgeon-General of the State of New Jersey, and still occupies that position. He is Attending Surgeon to St. Francis' Hospital and also to Jersey City Charity Hospital. In 1867 he reported to the Medical Record a case of "Complete Lateral Luxation of the Radius and Ulna, outward to the Radial Side." The records of medical science contain but thirteen similar cases, those having occurred in France. He also published an article on "Urticarea Produced by Hydrocianic Acid." This was as early as 1847, and in the same year he wrote another paper on the "Use of Nitrate of Silver in Acute Laryngitis." In 1859 he contributed to the medical press an account of the removal of a fibre-cellular tumor from the tongue with the écraseur. In 1869 he recorded a case of "Sub-periostal Resection of the Clavicle." His contributions to the medical literature of his day are numerous and important. Written as they have been at times snatched from the sterner duties of his profession, they show that Dr. Varick is a physician "born, not made;" one who loves science for its own sake as well as for the power it gives him of alleviating human suffering. His scientific researches and experience have made him an authority with the profession, while his election to the many societies of which he is a member is conclusive testimony that his brethren of the medical fraternity think they honor themselves while honoring him. He was married, in 1847, to Adelia J. Woolsey, of Jersey City. His eldest son, William Woolsey Varick, graduated at Bellevue Medical College, New York, in March, 1876, and was appointed assistant surgeon to St. Francis' Hospital, Jersey City.

--◆--

YMMES, HON. JOHN CLEVES, Lawyer, Soldier and Jurist, was born, July 21st, 1742, at Riverhead, Long Island, province of New York. He appears to have received a fair education, though not a classical one, and in early manhood became a school teacher and surveyor. He subsequently studied law, and at the time when the difficulties with Great Britain culminated in the war of the Revolution he abandoned his professional pursuits and entered the Northern army, though exactly in what capacity he served is not recorded. At all events, he was present at and participated in the battle of Saratoga. Shortly after this event he removed to New Jersey, taking up his residence at Newton, in Sussex county, and subsequently was appointed a delegate to the Provincial Congress, and assisted in framing the State constitution of 1776. In February, 1777, he was elected by the joint action of the Council and Assembly an Associate-Justice of the Supreme Court of the State, and

I

Theodore R. Varick M. D.

held that position for several years. In 1784 and 1785 he was a delegate to the Continental Congress at Philadelphia, retaining, however, his seat on the bench. In 1788 he was chosen by the Continental Congress one of the Judges of the Northwest Territory, and shortly afterwards removed to Ohio. As early as 1787 he began to negotiate for the purchase of lands in that Territory; the coveted tracts being about one million acres lying between the two Miami rivers. Finally a contract for that number of acres was signed by himself and others, at sixty-six cents per acre, payable in instalments. But the troubled state of the country, caused by the hostility of the Indians to the proposed settlement, led to their failure in fulfilling the contract. However, in the spring of 1794, in conjunction with Elias Boudinot, Jonathan Dayton and others, he effected the purchase of 248,000 acres, lying between the two Miami rivers, including the sites of the present cities of Dayton and Cincinnati. In the meantime, he established his own residence at the north bend of the Ohio, and laid out a city there to be called after himself; but circumstances led to the adoption of the land around Fort Washington as the site of the "Queen City," and the prospective metropolis at North Bend was destined to fail, although in those pioneer days it was regarded as the rival of Cincinnati. Judge Symmes was one of the most energetic and influential of the early pioneers, and had a method of dealing with the Indians which made them more friendly towards him than to the great majority of his white brethren. Indeed, he was more than once assured by these children of the forest that his life had been thus far spared because of his kindness to them. He married Susanna, daughter of Governor Livingston, of New Jersey, and was the father of two children, a son and a daughter. The son, who bore the same name as himself, was the promulgator of the fanciful theory that the earth was hollow, with openings at the poles, whereby the inhabitants of the interior could enter; and he even petitioned Congress to fit out an expedition to explore those mysterious regions. Judge Symmes' daughter married General, afterwards President, Harrison, who subsequently made North Bend his residence after the death of his father-in-law. Judge Symmes died February 26th, 1814, at Cincinnati, and was buried at North Bend, where twenty-seven years later the remains of President Harrison were also laid. The inscription on Judge Symmes' tomb states, among other facts, that " he made the first settlement between the Miami rivers."

INSEY, HON. JAMES, LL.D., Lawyer and Chief-Justice of the Supreme Court of New Jersey, was born, 1733, in Middlesex county, New Jersey, and was the son of the Hon. John Kinsey, who emigrated from England in 1716 and settled in Middlesex county, which he subsequently represented in the Provincial Assembly, and was

Speaker of the House for many years, his last tenure of that position being in 1733. He shortly afterwards removed to Pennsylvania, where he was likewise chosen a member of the Assembly of that Province; he was an eminent lawyer; a consistent member of the Society of Friends, and for the last seven years of his life Chief-Justice of Pennsylvania. He died in May, 1750, at Burlington, West Jersey. In the same town his son, James, married and settled. In 1772 he was elected a member of Assembly to represent, in connection with a colleague, that city, and soon took a prominent part in the proceedings of that body, being regarded as the leader of the opposition to Governor Franklin. He was appointed one of, the delegates to the Continental Congress, and took his seat in that body, at Philadelphia, September 5th, 1774; he resigned his position, for reasons deemed satisfactory by the Congress, in November, 1775. In 1777 the New Jersey Legislature passed a law requiring attorneys and counsellors-at-law to take the oath or affirmation of allegiance to the new State government; but this he declined taking, and consequently was obliged to relinquish his practice. It is probable that his being a member of the Society of Friends caused his unwillingness to conform to the law as enacted. When Judge Brearly resigned the office of Chief-Justice, the joint meeting of the Council and Assembly, in November, 1789, elected James Kinsey to fill the vacancy, and he was re-elected in 1796, holding the position during life, a period of nearly fourteen years. His first election took place during the administration of Governor Livingston, who was not only satisfied that he was amply qualified for the office, but of his being entirely devoted to the cause of his country. He was thoroughly versed in the doctrines of the law, and of spotless integrity. He died in Burlington, January 4th, 1803, in the seventieth year of his age.

AMPBELL, REV. W. H., D. D., LL.D., Clergyman, Professor and President of Rutgers College, New Brunswick, was born, September 14th, 1808, in the city of Baltimore, Maryland. He received a thorough academical education prior to his entering Dickinson College, at Carlisle, Pennsylvania, from which institution he graduated in 1828. After leaving this seminary he became the Principal of "Erasmus Hall," an institution of learning on Long Island, where he remained for six years. After dissolving his connection therewith he became the pastor of congregations at East New York and Albany, wherein he was settled for a period of nine years. In 1848 he returned to educational pursuits, and accepted charge of the Albany Academy, where he remained three years, and thence was called to and accepted a professorship in the New Brunswick Theological Seminary and Rutgers College; and, September 16th, 1862, was elected President of the latter. Since occupying this prominent position, he has been very active in promoting the interests of the college, and during the years 1863, 1864 and 1865 by his own efforts secured from the churches of the Reformed Dutch Communion, in New Jersey and New York, an endowment fund aggregating $144,000. In 1870, in commemoration of the centennial anniversary of the college, he again secured the additional sum of $121,000 for the purpose of erecting new buildings and establishing professorships, seven of which have been created since he commenced his administration, thus materially enlarging the course of study. As a natural result of this great increase of professorships, the number of students has correspondingly augmented since he accepted the office of President. Several fine buildings have been erected on the college grounds: the Astronomical Observatory; Geological Hall; Kirkpatrick's Chapel and Library; and also outside the grounds a large building used as a grammar school, known as the "Rutgers College Grammar School," and which is under the charge and government of the trustees of the college. As an efficient educator and able administrator, Dr. Campbell is widely known throughout the country; while as a pulpit orator and deeply-read theologian, he likewise occupies a prominent position among the divines of the Reformed Dutch Church.

MITH, ISAAC, Physician, Soldier and Jurist, was born in 1740, and received a liberal education and graduated from Princeton College in 1758. He afterwards studied medicine and became a practising physician. From the very commencement of the troubles with Great Britain he was distinguished for his patriotic services in the cause of his country, and in 1776 he commanded a regiment. During the periods of gloom and dismay he was firm and persevering. He associated valor with discretion, and the disciplined spirit of the soldier with the sagacity of the statesman. In February, 1777, he was elected by the Legislative Council and Assembly, in joint meeting, an Associate-Justice of the Supreme Court of New Jersey, and was thrice subsequently re-elected to the same position, so that he remained on the bench for twenty-eight years, a longer period than it has ever been held by any other person. When his fourth term of office expired, in 1805, party spirit ran high, and, as he was a Federalist, he did not succeed in being re-elected. After he had retired from the bench, he returned to his residence in Trenton, and was appointed the first President of the Trenton Banking Company, which position he held until death. He enjoyed the acquaintance and friendship of both Presidents Washington and Adams, who esteemed him for his many virtues. Endowed with talents of a high order, he united in himself the scholar, soldier, gentleman and Christian. He died August 20th, 1807.

TRATTON, HON. CHARLES P., Lawyer and Law Judge, of Camden county, was born, June 18th, 1828, in Bridgeton, Cumberland county, New Jersey. He is descended from Benjamin Stratton, of East Hampton, Long Island, who removed to Fairfield, Cumberland county, as early as 1715. His parents, Nathan L. and Hannah (Buck) Stratton, were both natives of New Jersey, and the family has always enjoyed a good standing in the State. Having obtained his preliminary education in the schools of Bridgeton, he took an academical course at Perth Amboy, in a boarding-school of high reputation. Thus carefully prepared, he entered Princeton College in 1845, and was graduated with the class of 1848. Then he became a student in the office of Judge L. Q. C. Elmer, of Bridgeton, an able lawyer and judge long and favorably known throughout the State. Under this excellent supervision he prosecuted his legal studies, and, in due course, was licensed to practise as attorney in November, 1852. Three years later he was admitted to the higher rank of counsellor. In the early part of 1853 he removed to Camden, and entered the office of Judge Carpenter, where he remained for about one year assisting the judge in the details of his practice and gaining a valuable experience for himself. On leaving that engagement he began the practice of his profession alone in the same city, where he has since continued to reside. Since the passage of the bankruptcy act he has acted as Register in Bankruptcy. Having established a reputation as a sound lawyer, and manifested a judicial cast of mind, his name was brought before the Legislature in 1872 as a candidate for Law Judge of Camden county, and on joint ballot he was elected for a term of five years. In this capacity he presides over a court created for the trial of a special class of cases, and his conduct thereof has tended to consolidate and increase the estimation in which he was previously held in the profession and in the community generally. In politics he has always been a Republican, and, so far as consistent with the dignity of his official position, he has always accorded an earnest and active support to the Republican party. He was married in 1856 to Clara Cooper, of Trenton.

ESSLER, REV. ABRAHAM, D. D., Clergyman, of Somerville, New Jersey, was born, November 15th, 1800, in Readington township, New Jersey. His father was Cornelius Messler, and his mother Mary (Stryker) Messler. The family are descended from Teunis Thomason Metzellaer, who came to this country from Holland in 1641 with the first ship sent out by the Van Rennselaer manor, at Albany. He seems to have remained only a short time at Albany. In 1642 he was a resident of New Amsterdam, and had a child baptized March 23d. The grandfather of Dr. Messler removed to New Jersey, and settled near New Brunswick, in 1745; his grandfather resided near Sommerville, but finally removed to New Brunswick, and died there in 1806, at the age of eighty years; his father resided on the paternal homestead, near New Germantown, where he died, May 28th, 1843, in the eighty-fifth year of his age. Abraham Messler was prepared for college at New Germantown and at Lamington, under the direction of Rev. Horace Galpin. In the year 1819 he entered the junior class of Union College, from which institution he graduated with honors in the class of 1821. Among his classmates were Rev. Dr. Nevin, of the Reformed Church, of Pennsylvania, Rev. Dr. Austin Yates, of Union College, and President Hickock, also of Union College, Hon. W. A. Campbell, of Cherry Valley, and Governor Seward, of New York. Immediately after his graduation he entered the Theological Seminary at New Brunswick, then under the charge of the Rev. Drs. Livingston and Ludlow. He graduated here in the year 1824, and was licensed to preach, May 27th, 1824. He settled first at Lodi, New York, where he was ordained, April 29th, 1825. He remained there three years, when he resigned and accepted a call from the church of Pompton Plains, New Jersey. There he remained until October, 1832, when he was called to the First Reformed Church, of Somerville, New Jersey. There he has ever since remained, ministering to this congregation through a period of almost half a century. In 1844 the degree of D. D. was conferred on him by Rutgers College. In the year 1854 he travelled extensively in Europe, visiting France, Italy, Germany, Switzerland, England and Scotland. He is a most faithful worker for and with one of the largest congregations in the State, a great portion of which has grown up under his fostering care, and sent off three branches, now flourishing churches; but, in addition to his regular ministerial labors, he has found time and strength to do much arduous literary work. In the year 1836 he wrote a work entitled "Fruits of Early Piety," which was published by the American Sunday-school Union and has had an extensive circulation. In 1872 he published his "Eight Memorial Sermons, with a History of the Reformed Churches of Somerset County." In 1874 his "Memorial Sermon and Tribute of Respect to ex-Governor P. D. Vroom" was published, "a contribution of friendship to departed worth." Beside these publications, with occasional sermons, his contributions to periodical literature have been large. In 1853 and 1854 he published two series of articles for the *Christian Intelligencer* entitled "Christian Ministry, the Reformers before the Reformation, the Confession of Faith," etc., which ran through about 150 numbers of this paper. After his return from Europe he contributed to the same paper a series of articles entitled "Rhine and Rhineland; Holland, Belgium, etc." For over five years he wrote the principal editorials of the *Christian Intelligencer*. During the last year he contributed several articles to that paper, entitled

"Science and the Bible," which have attracted considerable attention. He is now engaged in preparing a "Centennial History of Somerset County." He was married in 1826 to Elma Doremus, an aunt of the well-known Professor Doremus, of New York. He has six children living, his only son being Thomas D. Messler, third Vice-President and Comptroller of Accounts of the Pennsylvania Railroad, Assistant President of the Pittsburgh, Cincinnati & St. Louis Railroad, and President of the Terre Haute & St. Louis Railroad. His eldest daughter is the wife of Hon. Charles W. Swift, of Poughkeepsie, and another is married to John T. Grimsby, of Springfield, Illinois. On the 11th of September himself and wife celebrated their golden wedding, having all their children and grandchildren present at dinner, and in the evening a numerous reception of their friends of the church and congregation, and others.

ORRIS, ROBERT, Chief-Justice of the Supreme Court of New Jersey, was the son of Robert Hunter Morris, also Chief-Justice of the province; the grandson of Lewis Morris, Governor of the same province; and the great-grandson of Richard Morris, an officer of the time of Cromwell, who left England at the period when Charles II. was restored to the throne, and settled in New York, where he died in 1673. Robert Morris was the first regularly elected chief-justice of New Jersey after the State had declared her independence of Great Britain. He was elected at the joint meeting of the Legislative Council and Assembly, held in February, 1777, and continued in that office only two years, when he resigned it. In 1790 he was appointed by President Washington Judge of the District Court of the United States for the District of New Jersey, which he held for the remainder of his life; during the latter part of the time, however, his health was so impaired as to render him unable to preside in court; but the business of the court was so limited that his failure to appear on the bench did not create any special inconvenience to the public interests. He died at his residence in New Brunswick, in 1815.

RIFFITH, HON. WILLIAM, Lawyer and Jurist, was born, 1766, at Bound Brook, Somerset county, New Jersey, and was the son of Dr. John Griffith, of that place. He entered the office of the late Hon. Elisha Boudinot, at Newark, where he pursued his legal studies; and in conjunction with Josiah Ogden Hoffman, afterwards a distinguished lawyer of New York, Gabriel H. Ford, Alexander C. McWhorter and Richard Stockton, who were all law students in the same town, founded the "Institutio Legalis," a species of moot court, which subsequently existed for many years, and served to prepare them and their successors, in a great measure, for the active duties of their profession. William Griffith was licensed as an attorney in 1778; in 1781 as a counsellor; and in 1798 as a serjeant-at-law. He fixed his residence at Burlington, where he married, and in a short time his practice became a very lucrative one, and he enjoyed a deservedly high reputation as an advocate. He was exceedingly well versed in the common law which governs real estate; and he made himself acquainted with most of the land titles of New Jersey. At the close of President Adams' administration, and after the election of President Jefferson, an act of Congress was passed creating six new Circuit courts, each having its own justice and two associate justices. On the very last day, or rather night, of the outgoing administration the Senate acted on the nominations made by the President; and as the entire number were confirmed by the Senate, about midnight of March 3d, 1801, these judges — thus confirmed — enjoyed the soubriquet of "Midnight judges." For the Third Circuit, consisting of the States of Pennsylvania, New Jersey and Delaware, there were selected the late Chief-Justice Tilghman, of Pennsylvania, as chief-justice of the new circuit; Richard Bassett, of Delaware, and William Griffith, of New Jersey. The court thus constituted held two terms, one in May and the other in October, 1801. But these appointments were very unpopular, as they were made in the last hour of an outgoing administration, when the succeeding one was of directly opposite doctrines; and so, when Congress assembled, in December, 1801, one of its first acts was to repeal the courts thus established, and cast adrift the judges so nominated and confirmed. Judge Bassett, however, vigorously protested against these retaliatory measures; but nothing resulted from it, although the course thus adopted by the majority was against the Constitution of the United States, which states that the judges shall hold office during good behavior. Of course there was no alternative but to accept the situation, and Judge Griffith returned to his practice at the bar, but did not long continue therein, as he had become a speculator in the sale of lands; and when the war of 1812 was in progress he embarked in the business of manufacturing both cotton and woollen goods; and, having no experience in that line of business, lost all his fortune, besides being involved far beyond his means; and indeed he was entirely unable to free himself from these incumbrances during the balance of his life. At a later date he became a member of the Legislature, and while in that body was the author of the act "to secure to creditors an equal and just division of the estates of debtors who convey to assignees for the benefit of creditors," which was passed in February, 1820. In the early part of the year 1826 he was appointed Clerk of the Supreme Court of the United States, but he only filled that important station a few months. He was at an early date a member of the Society for Promoting the Abolition of Slavery; and when his father died he, as the executor, refused to allow the slaves to be sold, but took them into his own service, and in 1806 formally liberated them. He was one of the few attorneys and counsellors-at-law in New Jersey who ever became an author. In 1796 he published a "Treatise on the Jurisdiction and Proceedings of Justices of the Peace," with an appendix containing advice to executors, etc. It was regarded as a most valuable work, and several editions were issued. He also published a series of "Essays," in which he showed the defects of the State constitution, and advocated a change, which, however, was not effected until a fourth of a century after his death. In 1820 he became engaged in the publication of the "Annual Register of the United States," which was designed to include not only the officers, but also the laws and regulations of each of the States of the Union; and these to be corrected year by year in supplements issued for the purpose. By way of an introduction, he began to collate the "Historical Notes of the American Colonies and Revolution, from 1754 to 1775," but he never lived to complete it. He died June 7th, 1826.

ALLEN, ROBERT, Jr., Lawyer, of Red Bank, was born in the city of New York, March 2d, 1824. His father, Charles G. Allen, is a native of Middletown, New Jersey; for many years he was engaged as a looking-glass and picture-frame manufacturer in New York city, a business he subsequently abandoned to take up farming in New Jersey. His mother's maiden name was Catherine Trafford, who was born at Rumson village, Shrewsbury township, Monmouth county, New Jersey. Young Robert received excellent educational advantages. After a thorough preparatory training he entered Princeton College in 1842, and took a four years' course, graduating in 1846. His inclination leading him towards the law as a profession, he immediately began study with the late Judge Peter Vredenburgh, at Freehold, New Jersey. After passing through the prescribed preliminaries he was licensed as an attorney in 1851, and in three years was qualified as counsellor. On beginning the active prosecution of his profession he took up his residence at Red Bank, where he has since continued to practise. He is a close and industrious student, and has attained a wide reputation as a learned lawyer. His practice is chiefly in the State and county courts. He is the author of several important acts passed by the Legislature of New Jersey, among them the noted Railroad law of 1874, commonly called the Ten-day law, whereby the New Jersey Southern Railroad, from Sandy Hook through Long Branch and Vineland to the Delaware, was put in reoperation, to the relief of the towns and business centres in the neighborhood of the route of the road and its branches. For a period of five years, from 1867 to 1872, he was State's Attorney for Monmouth county, by commission from the governor, and performed the duties of that office with ready

Wm H. Berry

zeal, ability, and constant fidelity to the public interests. He takes a deep interest in the affairs of the town, and his value as a citizen and popularity as a man are attested by the fact that for three years past he has been chosen its mayor. Among other responsible trusts he holds he is Vice-President of the First National Bank, of Red Bank, and one of the Trustees of the State Normal School, upon whose Board he is now serving his second term. In politics he is a staunch Republican, and has yielded his party good service. Several valuable campaign papers have issued from his pen, as did also the first editorial article in any paper earnestly advocating the nomination of Governor Hayes for President. He was married, February 14th, 1855, to Rebecca S. Crawford, of Middletown, New Jersey.

ERRY, WILLIAM H., Manufacturer, of Woodbridge, is a native of New England, having been born in Litchfield, Maine, September 18th, 1805. He comes of revolutionary stock, his grandfather, Nathaniel Berry, having served throughout the revolutionary war with bravery and distinction. Shortly after December, 1777, Nathaniel Berry became attached to General Washington's Life Guard, a body of men selected for their courage, hardihood and trustworthiness. He died, August 20th, 1850, at Pittston, Maine, in the ninety-fourth year of his age, and his obsequies were celebrated in a manner befitting a man so devoted in his patriotism; he was buried with civic and military honors, and was followed to his grave by large numbers of citizens, who continued to cherish the remembrance of his virtues and services. He was a man of naturally strong character, and retained the use of his faculties to the last. At the time of his death he was the last surviving member of Washington's Life Guard. Nathaniel Berry's son, John Berry, was a farmer, who married Elizabeth Robinson, also a native of Maine. When well advanced in life they removed from Litchfield to Gardiner, Maine, and there their son, William H. Berry, received his education, attending the public schools at Gardiner. He continued his attendance at school until he was nineteen years of age, when he entered upon the active business of life on his own account. On leaving school he entered upon a maritime career, and followed the sea for a period of six years. He commenced his sea-going experiences as a common sailor before the mast, and finished them as first officer. On retiring from the sea he established himself in Jersey City, New Jersey, where he remained for a term of two years, associated with his brother in the business of baling and shipping hay. In the year 1832 he removed from Jersey City to Woodbridge, where he continued in the hay business by himself. This he pursued until the year 1845, also carrying on in the meantime the coal business at Woodbridge. He was the first person to introduce anthra-

cite coal to that community, bringing it from Rondout, on the Hudson river; and it is a curious thing to know that, so slowly did anthracite coal come into general favor, only forty tons of it were sold in the first two years after its introduction into Woodbridge. In 1845 he embarked in his present business, the manufacturing of fire-brick. With his characteristic energy he speedily rendered this one of the leading interests of the community. His conduct of it has been eminently successful, and his operations have been greatly enlarged, the present capacity of the works being three times what it was originally. From time to time, as the pressure of increasing demands rendered it necessary, the manufactory has been enlarged, until now, when running with a full complement of hands, it can produce 1,000,000 fire-bricks per annum, and at a trifling additional cost could be made to turn out 2,000,000 bricks in a year. The works are located on the creek, so that the advantage of water transportation is gained, as well as that of transportation by rail. The reputation of the work done at this manufactory is widespread and of the highest character. William H. Berry, besides devoting himself with energy and eminent success to his private concerns, is a most public-spirited citizen, always taking an active interest in the public affairs of the community in which he resides. For a number of years he has been a member of the Township Committee, and since the year 1873 he has acted as its chairman. In the winter of 1871 he obtained from the Legislature a charter for a Dime Savings Bank, and has held the office of President of the Board of Directors since the organization of the institution. At the present time he is Trustee of the Public Schools, and is engaged in building a school-house which, when completed, will cost between $25,000 and $30,000, and will be an ornament to the village. He was also the first person to erect in Woodbridge scales of heavy draught. During the war of the rebellion he was an ardent supporter of the Union cause, giving time and money freely to aid the administration to subdue the rebellion. He fitted up a portion of one of the factory buildings for drill purposes, and here, for about one year, troops, organized in the vicinity for actual service in the field, were exercised in the army drill. His son, William C. Berry, on the breaking out of the rebellion, organized a company of young men of the village, and in August, 1861, a part of his command joined Company H, 5th New Jersey Volunteers, he himself being commissioned as First-Lieutenant. On the 5th of May, 1862, while leading his men in the battle of Williamsburg, he fell a martyr to his country's cause. His body was recovered and now rests in the Alpine Cemetery, between Woodbridge and Perth Amboy, to await the final coming forth of all that sleep in their graves. William H. Berry was married in May, 1835, to Margaret Coddington, of Woodbridge, New Jersey, whose grandfather, Robert Coddington, was one of a party of three who, during the revolutionary war, captured, off Perth Amboy, a British vessel loaded with stores. It was a bitter

7

cold night in winter when the attack was made. The ice was thick enough along the shores to sustain a heavy burden. The stores were subsequently drawn on the ice to Perth Amboy, together with one of the British cannon, which was used in Woodbridge for many years in celebrating American independence; in 1874 the town committee presented the gun to the New Jersey Museum of Revolutionary Relics, at Morristown, New Jersey. Mr. Berry is a member of the Methodist Episcopal Church. For one-third of a century he has acted as a Trustee of the church at Woodbridge, for the greater part of that time as President of the Board. He has also held the position of class-leader for upward of twenty-five years, and that of Superintendent of the Sunday-school for five years.

———————

OWNE, HON. HUGH H., Farmer, of Rahway, was born at Oak Ridge, Rahway, New Jersey, November 30th, 1814. His parents were Robert H. Bowne, born in Shrewsbury, New Jersey, and Sarah (Hartshorne) Bowne, a native of Milford, Pennsylvania. His educational training was obtained in the High School, New York, at West Town, Pennsylvania, and at John Gummere's celebrated academy at Burlington, New Jersey. For a year subsequent to leaving school he was engaged as a clerk in New York city, but since 1834 he has lived on the Oak Ridge farm. Always a Republican, and an earnest laborer for the success of Republican principles, he has filled many political positions of responsibility and honor. Twice he was elected to represent his district in the State Legislature, and has filled most of the county offices. For the past nine years he has sat on the bench as Lay Judge. He was a Delegate to the Convention which nominated Fremont for the Presidency in 1856, and to that which nominated Lincoln in 1860. Governor Ward appointed him as one of the representatives of New Jersey at the Philadelphia Convention of 1866. He is a man of high character, and is greatly respected in the county.

———————

OPER, JAMES, M. D., Physician, of Millville, New Jersey, was born at Pittsgrove, Salem county, New Jersey, April 24th, 1812. His father, William Loper, was also a native of that section of the State, and was engaged in agricultural pursuits. His worth and integrity being appreciated by the community in which he resided, he was for several years chosen as Justice of the Peace, and for twenty-five years he served as an Associate Judge of the Common Pleas Court of Salem County. He died in 1871 at the ripe age of eighty-eight, respected and esteemed by all who had intercourse with him either in public or private life. The mother of Dr. Loper was Mera Abbott, a native of Glouces-

ter county. She was descended from a family well known in this section of the State. Her grandfather, Rev. Benjamin Abbott, who came from England, was a Methodist divine who for many years travelled an extended circuit in West Jersey, and became widely known and beloved as a Christian teacher. Her father, Jeptha Abbott, following in the footsteps of his father, became a Methodist divine, and labored in that church for many years. The preliminary education of Dr. Loper was obtained in his native county, and after mastering the elementary rudiments he attended the old-established school of Samuel Miller, at Bridgeton; here he acquired proficiency in Latin and Greek, and finished his course of studies. Selecting the time-honored profession of medicine for his future vocation, he immediately commenced studying to that end in the office of Dr. William C. Mulford, of Daretown, Pittsgrove township, and in the fall of 1834 matriculated at Jefferson Medical College, from which he was graduated in the spring of 1836. For a few months he practised at Pittsgrove, but in the fall of 1836 he located at Millville, where he has since resided. Thus, for a period of forty years, has Dr. Loper devoted himself to the arduous labors of an extensive and extended practice. For a long period the only physician of note in the vicinity, he was called upon from far and near to administer to the needs of the sick. Being wrapped up in his professional life, he has avoided and declined participation in political and public office, although having been frequently solicited to accept of positions of honor and trust. He was married, March 15th, 1837, to Rebecca K. Richmond, a native of Pittsgrove. This estimable lady died November 20th, 1869. The issue of this marriage was three sons, all of whom are now deceased.

———————

OPER, WILLIAM F., A. B., and M. D., son of Dr. James Loper, was born, July 18th, 1839, at Millville. After a thorough preparatory course secured at the West Jersey Academy, in Bridgeton, he entered, in 1857, the freshman class of Princeton College, and received therefrom in 1861 the degree of A. B. at the conclusion of a four years' course. Inheriting, as it were, a love for the profession of his father he pursued the regular courses of study at Jefferson Medical College, graduating therefrom in the spring of 1863, and immediately returned to his native town and entered upon his professional career. He died January 15th, 1864, his death being caused by the error of a druggist in furnishing a prescription which he took. Thus, in the flower of life, was cut down one who gave much promise of a bright career; one who would have been an honor to the profession at large, and a joy to the community in which he resided. His professional brethren felt that in his premature death their ranks had lost one who would have rapidly acquired a leading position in the profession, had his life been spared.

PEAR, HENRY, Printer and Stationer, was born, January 26th, 1817, at Boston. His father, a native of the same place, was by occupation a printer, and transacted a large business. His mother, whose maiden name was Elizabeth Fisk, was born in Massachusetts. Mr. Spear's early education was obtained at New Hampton Academy, New Hampshire, which he left when eleven years of age, moving to New York city. Here he entered the printing-house of Spear & Nesbit, and served a full apprenticeship. Upon attaining his majority he commenced business on his own account, and rapidly built up a large printing trade, with which he combined the manufacture and sale of stationery and book-binding. He has been thus engaged ever since, and is now located at the corner of Wall and Water streets, New York. For seventeen years he has resided at Rahway, New Jersey, and has taken great interest in originating and carrying out many local improvements for the embellishment of the town where he resides and the comfort of its citizens. He is a Director of the Rahway Savings Institution, and is prominently identified with a number of other social and business organizations. In 1840 he married Sophia H. Whitman, of Boston.

———◆◆◆———

BERNETHY, SAMUEL, M. D., late of Rahway, was born in Tinicum township, Bucks county, Pennsylvania, February 22d, 1806. His mother died when he was three years of age, and his father before he had reached his thirteenth year.

Being thus early left an orphan, he was sent to pursue his studies with the Rev. Mr. Boyd, at Newtown, Bucks county, Pennsylvania. From there he went to Union College, New York, where he graduated in the year 1827. He commenced the study of medicine with the eminent physician and surgeon, Dr. Delos White, of Cherry Valley, Otsego county. Having laid a foundation of medical knowledge, he entered the Medical University of Pennsylvania, graduating in 1830. Directly after he was appointed Surgeon to the hospital in Philadelphia, and honorary member of the Medical Society of Philadelphia. In March, 1831, he removed to Rahway, where, at the age of twenty-five, he commenced practice. This place remained the scene of his labors until his death, which took place February 13th, 1874. He had an extensive practice, and was widely known as an eminent physician and surgeon. His genius was too great to allow his reputation to be merely local. Neighboring cities and States acknowledged him the peer of their most distinguished practitioners, and brought to him their tribute. Notwithstanding his great merits he was peculiarly unostentatious, and was never known to speak of what he had done, but seemed always to be looking forward to what he could do in the future. Forty-three years as a practitioner would naturally endear one to his patients; but

the rare ability, genial spirit and characteristic unselfishness of Dr. Abernethy endeared him to the people of Rahway in a manner rarely known. He was a bachelor, and could therefore be truly wedded to his profession, not for his own emolument, however, but for the good that through his agency he could do his fellow-creature. He was reticent and reserved in disposition; his silence was proverbial; yet the young as well as the old felt their gatherings incomplete without him. He was truly Rahway's own, and his death caused such a demonstration as was never before seen there. Meetings of the city authorities and of the citizens were called and resolutions passed. His body lay in state in the First Presbyterian Church, from which he was buried, some hours before the funeral, which was largely attended by citizens, officials and the medical profession. Business was suspended, and flags displayed at half-mast showed numistakably that the place of his labors mourned a great man and a good, gone.

———◆◆◆———

ULFORD, HON. DAVID, Judge of the Common Pleas, was born in Linden township, New Jersey, April 12th, 1825, his father, Lewis Mulford, having been born in the same township on August 5th, 1790. The latter was by trade a carpenter, but in 1832 he took up farming, and has since followed it with success and without interruption. His wife was Charlotte Williams, who was born in Union township in 1795. Mr. Mulford's education was conducted in his native township, and the loss incurred by him from the lack of great facilities in those days was made up by his own indefatigable efforts in private study. He followed, with his father, agricultural pursuits until 1858, when he entered business as a coal and lumber merchant. He had been, from the date of his majority, an active and intelligent partisan of the Democracy, and became a leader to the people of his township, who, in 1859 and in 1860, elected him as their representative in the lower house of the State Assembly. In 1862 he was appointed Judge of the Common Pleas for a term of five years, and in 1868 the distinction of a reappointment for a similar period was conferred on him. During his first term Daniel Harris was president judge of the court, and William Gibley and Theodore Kirson, associates. During his second term, David A. Depue was president judge, and William Gibley and Hugh H. Bowne, associates. His service on the bench was marked by a clear knowledge of the letter and a keen appreciation of the spirit of the law, and his rulings and charges were admirable in their summary of facts and their application of laws bearing upon them. For ten years Mr. Mulford has been a Director in the State Bank, for a long period a Director of the National Fire and Marine Insurance Company, and a Manager of the Dimes Saving Institution. For several terms he filled with general approval a seat in the Board of Chosen Freeholders, and for three years acted as one of its

Directors. In his various capacities, as a business man, as a civic official, he has, by his firm integrity and substantial ability, secured the esteem of all brought in contact with him, and is justly regarded as one of the foremost citizens of his township. He was married, in 1847, to Charity O., daughter of Townley Mulford, of Linden.

NDRUS, CHARLES H., M. D., Physician, of Metuchen, was born in Winham, Greene county, New York, October 13th, 1823. He sprang from New England stock, his parents, Sylvester and Elizabeth P. (Clark) Andrus, being both natives of Connecticut. His early educational training he obtained at Roxbury district school, from which he proceeded, in 1840, to Delaware academy, Delphi, Delaware county, New York. At this latter institution he remained a student for three years, becoming during the last a tutor as well as a student, assisting in the instruction of chemistry and Latin. Having selected the medical profession for his life-work, he began the study of its principles under Dr. E. Steel. This he followed up with a two years' course at the College of Physicians and Surgeons, of New York, and then took a single year's course at Berkshire Medical College, Pittsfield, Massachusetts. His degree was conferred by the College of Physicians and Surgeons, of New York, in 1845. Thus carefully prepared for the duties of a medical practitioner, he began practice in his native place, but soon after, in 1846, chose Poughkeepsie, New York, as his field of labor. Here he became associated with Dr. A. B. Harvey, and the connection continued for two years, after which he pursued practice alone until 1857, when he removed to Balston Spa, Saratoga county. In this new sphere he remained until the spring of 1862, when, desirous of contributing his services to the cause of his country, he entered the army as Assistant Surgeon of the 128th Regiment of New York Volunteers. In 1864 his skill and devotion met with recognition in a commission as Surgeon of the 176th New York Infantry, with which he served until its disbandment in April, 1866, the regiment being retained on duty in Georgia after the close of the war. During three months in the year 1864 he was detailed for duty at Sheridan's Field Hospital in the valley of the Shenandoah as Medical Inspector and Operating Surgeon. After leaving the army he resumed practice at Poughkeepsie, where he remained until 1872. In that year he settled in Metuchen, the present scene of his labors. He enjoys a considerable and valuable practice, and is highly esteemed both as a medical man and as a large-hearted and public-spirited citizen. During his residence in Poughkeepsie he served for several years as a member of the Board of Education, and for two terms as Coroner for Dutchess county. In this latter capacity he has also officiated in Middlesex county, New Jersey, for one year. While living at Balston Spa, he was twice elected President of the Saratoga County Medical Association. He was married, October 7th, 1845, to Louisa C. Cowles, daughter of Dr. Jonathan B. Cowles, of Durham, Greene county, New York.

ICKINSON, GENERAL PHILEMON, Soldier and Statesman, was born in 1740, and was descended from Philemon Dickerson, who with his brothers emigrated from England, and landed in Massachusetts in 1638. He was admitted à freeman of the town of Salem in 1641, and removed to Long Island in 1672. He had two sons, Thomas and Peter. Thomas had four sons, all of whom moved to Morris county, New Jersey, about 1745, and from these the Dickersons and Dickinsons, as their names were sometimes written, are descended. During the war of the Revolution, General Dickinson took an early and active part in the struggle for his country, and hazarded his ample fortune as well as his life to establish independence. In the memorable battle of Monmouth, at the head of the New Jersey militia, he exhibited the gallantry and spirit of a soldier of liberty. After the establishment of the national government he became a member of Congress. In the various stations, both civil and military, with which he was honored, he discharged his duties with great zeal and ability. During the last twelve or fifteen years of his life, he retired from active life, passing the remainder of his days at his country-seat, near Trenton, where he died, February 4th, 1809.

OODBRIDGE, REV. SAMUEL M., D. D., Clergyman and Professor of Ecclesiastical History and Government in the Theological Seminary of the Reformed Dutch Church, New Brunswick, was born, April 5th, 1819, in Greenfield, Massachusetts, and is the son of the late Rev. Dr. Sylvester and Elizabeth (Brewster) Woodbridge. His father had been at one period pastor of the orthodox Congregational Church of South Hampton, Massachusetts, whence he removed to New Orleans, where he became pastor of the Second Presbyterian Church for some years previous to his death, which occurred in the autumn of 1862. His mother was a native of Sharon, Connecticut. He received his preliminary education in an academy in his native town, which he attended for five years, and thence proceeded to the city of New York, where he became a pupil in the select academy of William Sherwood. In 1834 he matriculated at the New York University, from which institution he graduated in 1838. He next entered the Theological Seminary of the Reformed Dutch Church, at New Brunswick, for the study of divinity, and received his diploma on the completion of the course in 1841. Shortly after leaving this institution he received a call to become the pastor of the South Reformed

Dutch Church of Brooklyn, which he accepted, and labored there for the period of nine years. Having, at the end of this time, received a call to the pulpit of the Second Reformed Dutch Church of Coxsackie, New York, he removed to that place and became its pastor for two years, 1850 to 1852. In the latter year he assumed charge of the Second Reformed Dutch Church of New Brunswick, where he remained until his appointment, in 1856, as Professor of Mental Philosophy in Rutgers College in that city. He filled this chair with acceptability for the period of three years, when he was chosen as Professor of Ecclesiastical History and Government in the Theological Seminary of the Reformed Dutch Church, New Brunswick, which position he still retains. He was married, February, 1845, to Caroline Bergen, of Brooklyn, New York, who died in 1860. After a widowerhood of seven years, he was united in marriage to Anna W., daughter of Charles P. Dayton, for many years an extensive dry-goods merchant of New Brunswick.

———❖———

PAGE, RICHARD H., M. D., Physician, of Columbus, Burlington county, was born near Medford, in the same county of New Jersey, September 22d, 1828. He is a member of the medical profession by inheritance, as it were, his father, Thomas Page, having been a well-known practitioner in and around Tuckerton, in the same county, while his grandfather, William Page, was also a physician. On the maternal side, also, his descent is from a New Jersey family, his mother being Elizabeth, daughter of Thomas Butcher, of Burlington county. He obtained his early education in the public and select schools of Tuckerton, and from 1843 to 1846 he was a pupil in the Pennington Academy. The study of medicine he began with Dr. Budd, of Mount Holly, and continued under the direction of that gentleman during the summer months. In the winters he attended the regular course of lectures at the University of Pennsylvania, and pursued his readings under the care of Dr. S. G. Morton, of Philadelphia, who was then President of the Academy of Natural Sciences. After a full course at the University of Pennsylvania, he was graduated from that institution with the degree of M. D. in March, 1850. In July of the same year he located in Columbus and began the practice of his profession. From that time he has been actively engaged in the same sphere of usefulness, his practice expanding year by year, and assuming always a more influential and lucrative character. He occupies a high position in the respect and regard of his professional brethren. In the county medical society he has held the offices of Secretary and President, has frequently been a delegate therefrom to the State Medical Society, and was a Delegate to the Convention of the North American Medical Association held in Philadelphia. A public-spirited citizen, he takes an earnest interest in all movements calculated to advance the welfare of the community in which he resides. He lent his energies to the promotion of the Columbus, Kincora & Springfield Railroad, and has been its Treasurer since the organization of the company. In politics, however, he takes no active part, desiring no other distinction than accrues in the strict line of his profession. He was married in 1856 to Elizabeth F. Wills, daughter of Judge Moses Wills, of Columbus.

———❖———

THOMPSON, HON. JOSHUA S., A. M., Lawyer, of Swedesboro', was born in Somerset county, Maine, October 11th, 1815. His parents, James and Susan (Patterson) Thompson, were both natives of that State, where his father followed agricultural pursuits, but his grandfather, John Thompson, belonged to Londonderry, New Hampshire, coming from a long line of ancestors in that section. After a thorough preparatory course in the public schools and academies in his native State, the subject of this sketch entered Waterville College, in the town of Waterville, Maine, an institution of high standing in New England, now known as Colby University. From this college he was graduated in 1839, after a four years' course zealously pursued, with the degree of A. B. In 1844 he received the degree of A. M., in regular course. Electing to join the legal profession, he began the study of law in the office of Hon. Wyman B. S. Moore, at Waterville. Here he enjoyed exceptional advantages in legal training, his preceptor being among the eminent lawyers of the State. Subsequently Mr. Moore became, in 1848, Attorney-General of the State, and, later on, was appointed by the Governor to fill a vacancy in the United States Senate, caused by the death of Hon. John Fairfield. Some years afterwards he was nominated and confirmed as United States Consul-General for the British North American Provinces. Under the guidance of this distinguished lawyer Mr. Thompson completed his legal studies, and was admitted to the bar in his native county, in the State of Maine, in June, 1841. Thereupon he entered into a law partnership with Stephen Stark, Esq., a prominent lawyer of Waterville. This connection lasted, however, for about a year only, the delicate condition of his health, caused by excessive mental labor, constant sedentary habits and the great severity of the winters in that latitude, compelling him to seek a more genial climate for a residence. After due consideration he concluded to settle in Swedesboro', Gloucester county, New Jersey, whither he removed in August, 1842. He could not, however, at once resume the practice of his profession, the rules of the Supreme Court of New Jersey requiring a longer course of study and residence in the State as a condition precedent to admission to its bar. In the meantime, therefore, having had the advantages of a thorough classical education, and appreciating the dignity and value of an educator, he, at the earnest solicitation of the leading men of the town, engaged in teaching in the academy at that place, and continued so occupied for two years, or until his admission to the bar, in September, 1844. This experience naturally aroused a lasting interest in educational matters in the community, and the manifestation of this interest has led to the reposing in him of various educational trusts by the community. Thus, about 1848 he was appointed by the Board of Chosen Freeholders of the county as Examiner of Public School Teachers, and this position, which he was so admirably fitted to fill, he occupied with great acceptability for about eight years. He was also for several years connected with the Board of Education of the county. He headed the first teachers' institute ever held in the county of Gloucester, at the ancient town of Swedesboro'. During this period an agitation was commenced having for its object the passage by the Legislature of a new school law, and the movement was entirely successful. A board of commissioners was appointed to report a new school law, with other revisions. Among other changes introduced by the new measure was the extension of the school-going age. Under the provisions of the old statute the limit was from five to sixteen years. Mr. Thompson entertained the opinion that instruction should be continued to children until they were eighteen years old, and that the school-going age should be extended to that time, believing that during the additional two years the scholars would be so much more alive to the advantages of education, and so much more capable of comprehending their studies, their minds being more expanded and matured, as to make far greater progress than during their earlier life. He would prefer and recommend, in the case of males especially, an extension to the age of twenty-one, rather than to make eighteen the limit. He pressed his convictions on this subject so strongly upon the commissioners appointed by the Legislature to revise the school laws that his recommendation was adopted and the limit extended to eighteen years. He was married, on December 24th, 1844, to Frances Stratton Garrison, daughter of Dr. Charles Garrison, late of Swedesboro'. They have five children. The eldest daughter, Hannah, was married, October 20th, 1869, to George B. Boggs, civil engineer, and Resident Superintendent of the Delaware & Bound Brook Railroad, and live, at Trenton. During this time he had been making an excellent position in his profession, which from the date of his admission, in 1844, he had earnestly prosecuted. So high a rank had he secured by 1847, and so favorably was he regarded by the community generally, that his name was prominently mentioned by the press for a position on the Supreme bench of the State; but, regarding himself as too young in the profession for so exalted a station, he declined judicial honors and refused to take any steps to accomplish the fulfilment of the wishes of his friends. In September, 1848, he was licensed as counsellor-at-law, and on February 22d of the following year he was appointed Prosecutor of the Pleas for Gloucester County by Governor Daniel Haines. Five years later, on the expiration of his term, he was re-

appointed by Governor R. M. Price; again, on March 1st, 1864, by Governor Joel Parker; again, on March 1st, 1869, by Governor Randolph; again, on March 2d, 1874, by Governor Joel Parker. Upon the expiration of his present term he will thus have filled this important position for twenty-five years, the service being continuous, save for one interval, occurring between 1859 and 1864. This is in all probability the longest service ever rendered by any one in the State as Prosecutor of the Pleas, and that the office should have been so continuously held under successive administrations is sufficient testimony to the zeal, ability and fidelity with which Mr. Thompson discharged his functions. The governor makes the nomination to the Senate, and they have the power to confirm or reject, as they may please. So popular and favorably known had he become that, at his last nomination, they confirmed by acclamation, without even referring his name to a committee, as was usual. On July 6th, 1848, at the time of his admission as counsellor, he was made Master in Chancery, and on November 17th, 1874, he was appointed a Commissioner of the Supreme Court. He has ever identified himself with the interests of Swedesboro' and his adopted State, and in all movements tending to their advancement, material and moral, he has taken an active part—in many being the prime mover and leader. In 1854, at the instance of the agents of the Camden & Amboy Railroad Company, he drew up a charter for a railroad from Woodbury to Swedesboro', called the Woodbury & Swedesboro' Railroad Company, and procured its passage through the Legislature, but the road under this charter was never constructed by them, its necessity being removed. In 1866 he succeeded in obtaining from the Legislature a charter for a railroad from Swedesboro' to Woodbury, called the Swedesboro' Railroad, a distance of eleven miles, thus opening railroad communication—the first-mentioned place previously being quite isolated from the rest of the world. This project had been broached by him several years previously, as appears above; but this time he was bound to succeed. He encountered not only opposition and discouragement from all quarters, but in some cases ridicule from those who would neither help build it, nor let others do it. He, however, was well satisfied of its necessity, and of the great advantage to the country through which it would run, and undauntedly pushed the matter step by step, and year by year, until complete success in its accomplishment crowned his public-spirited efforts. Upon the organization of the commissioners and of the Board of Directors he was very fittingly chosen President of both, and has filled that position ever since. The road was opened for travel in September, 1869. The friends of Mr. Thompson, and those who recognize the benefits conferred by the railroad on the country through which it runs, cheerfully acknowledge that, owing its existence to his untiring efforts and unbounded energy, it constitutes the *chef d'œuvre* of his life. At the opening of the great Centennial fair in Philadelphia he was solicited by the school authorities of New Jersey to write a sketch of the history of the old academy in Swedesboro', which was established in 1771, one of the oldest educational institutions in this part of the State. It was a work that required extensive research; and portions of it, together with other school histories of the State, are at this writing (October, 1876) shown in the Main Building of that extraordinary national exhibition. He is engaged in preparing a "History of the Swedes in New Jersey," and of the church established by them in 1703, and of "Swedesboro': its Churches and its Schools." The old Swedes' Church has been changed to an Episcopal Church, and is called Trinity Church. Mr. Thompson has been successively elected a vestryman in the same for some thirty years past, having held that position for a longer period than any member of the Board. To the rising generation especially his life and character present a notable example of energy of purpose and perseverance in doing good to his fellow-man, against any and all obstacles.

HOFF, CAPTAIN JOSEPH D., Master Mariner, of Keyport, was born near that place, in Middletown township, Monmouth county, New Jersey. His father, William Hoff, a farmer by occupation, belonged to one of the oldest families in the county. His mother, Martha Dye, was born in New Jersey, but came of Danish descent. Captain Hoff, when a boy, attended the common schools of his native township, and acquired the elements of a sound practical education. Upon leaving school he was apprenticed to learn the trade of a carpenter, having developed a taste in that direction. After following this occupation for a period of about five years he became interested in ship-building in the town of Keyport, in association with a Mr. Rosevelt, the firm being styled Rosevelt & Hoff. From 1835 to 1838 he was engaged in mercantile pursuits at the same place. In 1839 he received an appointment as an Associate Judge of Common Pleas for Monmouth county, and sat upon the bench in that capacity for a term of five years, discharging his functions with ability, fidelity and general acceptability. During the same period he served as Justice of the Peace. With a great desire to see distant countries, in 1853 he built a large schooner, the "T. A. Ward," and after coasting for two years, to North Carolina, Charleston and the West Indies, he went to Cadiz, Lisbon, Rio de Janeiro, New Orleans, and home. He then commenced the Mediterranean trade, and continued in it for nearly six years, making eleven voyages, or twenty-two passages, without ever an insurance loss; visiting Gibraltar, Malaga, Aden, Denia, and Barcelona, in Spain; Marseilles, in France; Naples, in Italy; Palermo and Messina, in Sicily; Venice, Trieste and Pola, in Austria. At Pola he saw and conversed with Maximilian, who then was Admiral of the Austrian fleet; he was a nobleman by nature as well as birth. At the commencement of the war he sold the schooner to the United States government, and then built a barque in connection with the great firm of A. A. Low Brothers, in 1862, and sailed to China; he visited the ports of Shanghai, Hong Kong, Ningpo, Chefoo, Tientsin, Canton and Whampoa, in China; also Hakodadi, in Japan. In October, 1864, he sold his barque, and in November started for home by the overland route, and touched at Singapore, Penang, Point de Galle, in Ceylon, at Aden, Suez, Cairo and Alexandria, in Africa, and at Malta and Marseilles, where he left the steamer, December 23d, 1864. He then went to Paris, London and Liverpool, and embarked for home in the "City of Baltimore," and arrived, January 23d, 1865, in New York. In 1866 he started on a mining expedition to Colorado, and visited all the principal mines from Cheyenne to Trinidad, and all about the range of the Rocky mountains, but made his home most of the time at Black Hawk and Central City, although he was a great deal at Georgetown, James Creek, Boulder City and Left Hand. He crossed the plains some eight times, four of the journeys being performed in stages. Since then he has made voyages to Venice, Trieste, Bordeaux, New Orleans, Rio and Santos. But after all his travels he says there is no place equal to Monmouth county, New Jersey. He has always been favored by fortune. In all his experience as a sea captain he has never suffered the perils of shipwreck, nor has he ever lost a man from any of his ships. He was married, September 20th, 1837, to Maria Ackerson, a native of New Jersey. A man of very estimable character, he is highly respected and esteemed in a wide circle.

ROBBINS, HON. CHILION, Lawyer and ex-Jurist, was born, December 31st, 1842, in Allentown, Monmouth county, New Jersey, and is a son of Augustus and Lucy (Savidge) Robbins, both of whom are natives of New Jersey. His father was a mason by trade, and the family has for many years been identified with Monmouth county; while his mother is of English lineage, being a descendant of the Leigh family of Great Britain. Chilion was educated in the public schools of his district, and subsequently learned the trade of a mason, which he followed until he was twenty-two years of age. Having determined to follow a professional life, he entered the law office of Judge E. W. Scudder, of Trenton, under whose preceptorship he pursued his studies, and was licensed an attorney in 1866, and a counsellor-at-law in 1869. At first he located in Allentown, where he opened an office and practised his profession with good success until 1872, when he was appointed Presiding Judge of the Court of Common Pleas of Monmouth County, to fill the unexpired term of Judge George

C. Beekman, who had resigned that office. He took his seat upon the bench, March 14th, 1872, and occupied that position until April 1st, 1874. Upon retiring from office he settled in Freehold and resumed his professional duties at the bar, acquiring a large and lucrative practice. He has had charge of several important cases, among which may be mentioned the Ganby murder case, which attracted great attention in that section of the State, and in which he was associate counsel for the prosecution. At present (1876) he is the legal adviser of the "Oyster kings," who are one of the parties concerned in what is known as the "Keyport oyster case."

AMPBELL, HON. CHARLES A., Merchant, of Woodbridge, was born, June 2d, 1836, in Woodbridge township, Middlesex county, New Jersey. He is the son of John H. Campbell, who was himself a native of Woodbridge township, and who was a thrifty and successful farmer in that place. Charles A. Campbell received his education, so far as attendance at school was concerned, in the schools near his home. His studying, like everything else he undertook, was done with energy and with the success that energy brings, so that his limited time and opportunities were made productive of more than usually good results. When he had reached the age of fourteen years he left school and commenced the serious work of life. He went to work on his father's farm, and for several years was engaged in agricultural pursuits. At length he engaged in business in Metuchen, and remained there so occupied for a period of ten years. In the year 1864 he became interested in the clay business at Woodbridge, but in 1865 he sold out his interest in that business and devoted his time and energies to other business pursuits. In the year 1867, however, he again purchased clay banks in the vicinity of Woodbridge, and ever since that time he, in connection with others, has been largely interested as a clay merchant, the style of the firm being C. A. Campbell & Co. The same firm, under the name of the Staten Island Kaolin Company, have large kaolin interests in Staten Island. They have there half a mile of private railroad track for transporting the kaolin from their extensive banks to the river for transportation; and at Woodbridge they built, in 1863, a private railroad track a mile and a half in length, over which to transport their clay from the banks to the Raritan river. Their works are extensive, and up to the end of the year 1873 there were employed at their works about ninety-five men, and the products of their banks are shipped to various points in the Union, North, South, East and West, as well as to numerous places in the Canadas. Notwithstanding the ceaseless activity and great energy which have made him so successful in the prosecution of his private business, Charles A. Campbell has found, and still finds, time and strength to act in promotion of various enterprises, public and corporate. He is a director of the Middlesex County Bank, at Perth Amboy, and has filled that position since the organization of the bank, in 1873. He has held various positions in township and county affairs, such as Commissioner of Appeals, Judge of Election, Town Committee and Freeholder. He is one of the Trustees of the public school now being erected at Woodbridge, a fine graded school, the building for which will cost $25,000; also a director of the Amboy Savings Institution, and is President and one of the largest stockholders of the Masonic Hall Association, of Woodbridge, the building of which was erected in 1873, at a cost of $20,000, and contains a handsome opera house, stores, etc. Moreover, he is the President of the Board of Trustees of a new Congregational Church, whose church structure has recently been completed at Woodbridge. This church is an offspring from the old Presbyterian Church of that place, and he has been a prime mover in its organization, aiding it with both money and influence. Politically he is a Democrat, and in 1875 was chosen by that party in his district to represent them in the Legislature of the State. During his session there he served as a member of the committee to investigate the fees and salaries of all State officers appointed by the Legislature. Woodbridge knows and recognizes him as one of her most enterprising and public-spirited citizens, and among other beneficial acts of his has been the erection of many fine buildings, which add very much to the beauty of the town. He was married in the year 1855 to Susan L. Clarkson, daughter of the late Noe Clarkson, himself an influential and greatly respected citizen of Woodbridge township.

GDEN, HON. ELIAS BOUDINOT D., Lawyer and Jurist, was born, 1800, at Elizabethtown, New Jersey, and was the son of Aaron and Elizabeth (Chetwood) Ogden. His father was Governor of the State, and his biographical sketch will be found elsewhere in this volume. At the age of nineteen Judge Ogden graduated from Nassau Hall, and at once entered upon the study of the law. He was licensed as an attorney in 1824; was admitted a counsellor in 1829, and made a serjeant-at-law in 1837, being the last lawyer raised to that dignity in the State. Immediately after his admission to the bar he opened an office in Paterson for the practice of his profession, and at once took a leading rank among his brother advocates, and was made Prosecutor of the Pleas, which position he held for two terms. He was also elected a member of the Legislature, and again re-elected. He was chosen, in 1844, a member, from Passaic county, in the convention called for the purpose of remodelling the Constitution of the State, and took a leading and active part during its sessions. He was appointed by Governor Haines, in 1848, as one of the Justices

Chas. A. Campbell

of the Supreme Court, and upon the expiration of his term in 1855 was reappointed by Governor Price; and a third time, in 1862, by Governor Olden. He resided in Paterson until 1858, when he removed to Elizabeth and reoccupied the old homestead of his father. His political faith was that of the Democratic party as taught by Jackson, having originally been indoctrinated in the views of the Federalists, and as a Jackson Democrat he deemed it his duty to adhere to the cause of the Union during the period of the great rebellion. One of the decisions of the court, pronounced by him, was to the effect that, as a judge of the State court, he had no authority to interfere for the release of a person charged with an offence against the laws of the United States. His religious faith was that maintained by the Protestant Episcopal Church, of which he was an active and zealous member. He was one of the Trustees of Burlington College. He died in 1865.

———◦◦———

URTS, HON. ALEXANDER, Lawyer, was born, 1799, in the village of Flanders, Morris county, New Jersey, and is the youngest of a family of eight sons, whose father was John Wurts, an extensive iron manufacturer of that county. He died when Alexander was quite young, and the latter then went to Philadelphia, where he resided with his older brothers, and where he prepared for college. He entered Princeton College in 1812 and finished his senior year in 1815, in the seventeenth year of his age. He then returned to Philadelphia and began the study of the law; and likewise devoted some time to travelling. In the winter of 1819-20 he removed to Flemington, New Jersey, where he completed his legal studies and was licensed as an attorney in 1820. He immediately commenced the practice of law in the village of Flemington. In 1824 he was elected a member of the Assembly, in which body he served one year. After three years he again became a candidate, and was elected successively in 1828-29-30 and '31 to the same body; and during the three last years was Speaker of the House. In 1833 he was nominated and elected a member of the Legislative Council, in which he served one year. In 1838 he was the candidate of the Democratic party for Congress on the general ticket, but was defeated, as was the entire ticket. In 1844 the Legislature of New Jersey called a convention to revise the State Constitution. To this convention he was elected from Hunterdon county. When the body assembled he was chosen vice-president, Isaac H. Williamson being elected president; but as the latter was in exceedingly impaired health, the principal burden of the duties of a presiding officer devolved upon the vice-president. And upon the resignation of Mr. Williamson, before the convention adjourned, Mr. Wurts was elected president. The convention framed the present State Constitution, abolished the Legislative Council, and adopted, in its stead, the

State Senate. Their proceedings were ratified by a large majority of the popular vote when submitted to the people. In the autumn of 1844 he was elected the first State Senator from Hunterdon county, and served in that body for a two years' term. In 1848 charges of serious import were preferred against the Camden & Amboy Railroad and the Delaware & Raritan Canal Companies, and the Legislature appointed three commissioners to thoroughly investigate these matters. This commission consisted of Alexander Wurts, of Hunterdon, Aaron Robertson, of Morris, and James S. Hulme, of Burlington counties. The duty was a laborious one, occupying nearly a year in going over the entire work, which consisted of a minute investigation of the books and papers of these companies, covering all their transactions with the State and with the people; and the result was, that the commission, by an elaborate and extended report, fully exonerated the companies from all the charges brought against them, thus entirely allaying all public excitement on these subjects. In 1853 Governor Fort nominated Alexander Wurts as Chief-Justice of the Supreme Court of the State, and his nomination was at once confirmed by the State Senate; but he respectfully declined the appointment. In 1865 his friends again induced him to become the candidate of the Democratic party, to which he was attached, for the State Senate, when he accepted on the assurance that the party could thereby be harmonized. He was accordingly elected and served the usual term of three years. He has been for over twenty years one of the Managers of the State Lunatic Asylum, and President of the Board since 1859. Although he has now, in a great measure, retired from public and professional life, he is often consulted on important legal questions. His unflinching integrity, thorough legal acquirements, and undoubted honesty, give weight to his opinions. There is not probably another man in the State who has been in public life so long as he; and he yet retains the confidence of all parties in a great degree. He was urged, on two or three occasions, by his many Democratic friends to become a candidate for Governor; and perhaps, if he had made the usual efforts put forth by many aspirants for office, would have secured the nomination. But he refused to embark in the canvass.

———◦◦———

AYTON, ALFRED B., M. D., late of Matawan, was born at Basking Ridge, Somerset county, New Jersey, December 25th, 1812. He came of the family so distinguished in the history of the State, which gave to its service and that of the nation the late Hon. William L. Dayton, his brother. Another brother is James B. Dayton, of Camden. He enjoyed educational advantages of a superior character, completing his preparatory training at Princeton College. Having chosen the medical profession, he was accorded the most esteemed aids in his study, and eventually graduated from the College of Physicians and Surgeons, New York, in the spring of 1835. He first settled for practice at Chester, Morris county, New Jersey, but after a few months removed to Matawan, then "Middletown Point," opening his office there in July, 1835. In this location he continued in active practice for thirty-five years, achieving large success and enjoying the high esteem of a very wide circle of patients and friends. He became a member of the District Medical Society in April, 1841, and an idea is afforded of the position he had even then attained in the fact that on admission his examination was waived by a unanimous vote. In the same year he was elected Vice-President of the society, and in the following year its President. A member of the State Medical Society from an early day in his professional career, he was, in 1854, elected to the position of President. In this body, a short while before his death, he appeared as delegate from the district society. Upon the roll of the National Medical Association his name was registered as a permanent member. He possessed oratorical and rhetorical powers of a high order, being a graceful speaker and polished writer. To the medical press he contributed many papers, all of which commanded the respectful attention of the profession. Among them may be specially mentioned the following: "Review of the Principles and Practice of Thompsonianism;" "Mollities Ossium;" "Inversion of the Uterus, with Method of Reduction, and Case Illustrated;" "Cerebro-Spinal Meningitis;" and "Dry Gangrene." A refined and cultivated gentleman, his deportment in all the relations of life was dignified and pleasing. To his medical brethren he was kind, courteous, and honorable, observing the ethical rules regulating professional intercourse with scrupulous care. When, therefore, his death occurred, on July 19th, 1870, from cholera morbus, he was deeply regretted by the profession and sincerely mourned by the community at large, the poor, at whose service he had ever been, especially deploring the loss of an accomplished physician and kind friend.

———◆———

AYTON, RENSSELAER W., A. M., Lawyer, of Matawan, was born at that place, then known as Middletown Point, January 9th, 1843. His father, Dr. Alfred B. Dayton, of wh·m a biographical sketch appears elsewhere in this volume, was an eminent physician, whose long and useful career was closed by death in 1870. His mother, Elizabeth R. Vanderveer, was a native of Somerville, New Jersey. After a thorough preliminary training, the subject of this sketch entered Princeton College in 1860, whence he graduated in 1863. Drawn towards the legal profession, he began reading with Hon. Henry S. Little, of Matawan, who at the present time is Clerk of the Court of Chancery of New Jersey. After fulfilling the prescribed conditions he was admitted to the bar as an attorney on November 8th, 1866, and began practice in association with his preceptor.

This connection was maintained until 1871, when he commenced by himself, and so practised until December, 1874, when he took into partnership Marcus B. Taylor. The firm is known as Dayton & Taylor, and it enjoys a considerable practice in the counties of Monmouth and Middlesex. He is thoroughly in love with his profession, to which he devotes all his time and powers.

———◆———

RROWSMITH, JOSEPH E., M. D., of Keyport, was born in Middletown, Monmouth county, New Jersey, January 23d, 1823. He is descended from a family that has distinguished itself in the service of the State. His father, Hon. Thomas Arrowsmith, was for many years one of the judges of the Court of Errors, and at an earlier period worthily held the office of State Treasurer. His mother, Emma Van Brakle, a native of New Jersey, was the daughter of Matthias Van Brakle, a substantial and much-respected farmer, who was sent by his neighbors to represent them in the Legislature, where he displayed sterling qualities and won the gratitude of his constituents. The subject of this sketch obtained his literary education in the academy at Flatbush, Long Island, then presided over by Professor Campbell, the accomplished scholar and eminent teacher who now serves as president of Rutgers College, New Brunswick. Evincing a taste for medicine, he began his studies for that profession in the fall of 1838 with Dr. Edward Taylor, an old and successful practitioner in his native town. Subsequently he became a student of Dr. Valentine Mott, of New York, at the same time attending lectures at the university of that city, from which he graduated with honor in 1842. After serving for a few months on the staff of Bellevue Hospital, in New York, he, in 1843, located at Keyport, where he has since continued to practise, and has won a foremost position among his professional brethren together with the substantial rewards that attend able and faithful labors. He is an old member of the county medical society, and was at one time its president. In 1864 he was chosen to represent his section in the convention of the American Medical Association.

———◆———

ORNISH, JOSEPH B., Merchant and ex-Senator, of Washington, was born, April 3d, 1836, in Bethlehem, Hunterdon county, New Jersey, his father, Joseph Cornish, Sr., being a merchant and a highly esteemed citizen of Hunterdon. In his boyhood he received such education as could be obtained at the common schools of the neighborhood in which he lived. He studied hard, and at sixteen years of age had obtained a good English education. When he had reached that age he entered his father's store and devoted

Hampton Cutter

himself thenceforward to mercantile pursuits. His great natural aptitude for commercial business and his ardent application to his duties developed him rapidly into a thorough business man, and on the attainment of his majority he became associated with his father as partner in the general country trade. In the years 1863 and 1864 he left mercantile life temporarily to serve as Engrossing Clerk of the New Jersey Assembly, having been elected to that office when in his twenty-seventh year. In the year 1865 he removed to Washington, New Jersey, where he associated himself as partner with his two brothers-in-law, Henry W. and Joseph Johnston, in the dry-goods, grocery, clothing and general country trade, under the firm-name of Johnston, Cornish & Co. They were eminently successful, but in 1869 his partners withdrew to organize an extensive hardware business, and he assumed the entire interest of the old establishment. He still continues the business, which has attained large proportions, and is eminently flourishing. He has always taken a lively and practical interest in political affairs, and is identified with the Democratic party. In the year 1870 he received the Democratic nomination for State Senator, but owing to party dissensions he was not elected. In 1873 he was again nominated for that position by the Democracy, and was elected Senator by the largest vote ever given to any candidate in Warren county. During his three years' term of office he served with eminent satisfaction to his constituents. It was during this term that the great battle over the general railroad law of the State was brought to a conclusion by the passage of the law, and the people of the State are largely indebted to the exertions of Senator Cornish in bringing about the adoption of the measure which practically puts an end to the system of corruption and jobbery formerly so great a source of public danger. He is a shrewd political manager, and at the same time maintains a spotless character, his integrity being without suspicion of taint, and he has never been even seemingly entangled in any disreputable political transactions. He is ambitious, able and honest, and the high esteem in which he is held by his fellow-citizens gives promise that he will in time to come attain still higher political position than he has yet occupied. He was married a number of years ago, to a daughter of Philip Johnston, Esq., a prominent citizen of Warren county, New Jersey.

AN RENSSELAER, LEDYARD, M. D., of Burlington, was born in Burlington, New Jersey, November 20th, 1843. He comes of the well-known Van Rensselaer family of New York, which has for many generations furnished to New York city and State some of their brightest and most useful citizens. His father, Rev. C. Van Rensselaer, D.D., was the son of Stephen Van Rensselaer, a prominent resident of Albany, New York. His mother, Catharine Ledyard Cogswell, was the daughter of Mason F. Cogswell, M. D., of Hartford,

Connecticut, a distinguished physician and surgeon of his time, and the first to perform the delicate and important operation of ligation of the primitive carotid artery in the extirpation of a tumor. Ledyard Van Rensselaer received his classical education at the College of New Jersey, Princeton, from which he graduated in the class of 1866. Making choice of the medical profession, he became a student in the medical department of the University of Pennsylvania, Philadelphia, and graduated in the class of 1869. After taking his degree he went abroad for the purpose of availing himself of the opportunities afforded by the medical institutions of the old world, and spent twelve months with great profit in the hospitals in Vienna and Berlin. Thus prepared for successful prosecution of his profession, he returned to his native city and commenced practice there in 1871. His career has been speedily progressive, and he now enjoys a large and valuable practice. The estimation in which he is held by his fellow-citizens is indicated by the fact that he was chosen Health Officer of the city during the years 1872 and 1873, while his position in the profession is attested by his election to the office of President of the Burlington County Medical Society, which he held from January 1st, 1875, to January 1st, 1876. He is Examining Physician for the Guardian Mutual Life Insurance Company, in Burlington.

UTTER, HAMPTON, Farmer and Clay Merchant, was born, December 25th, 1811, in Woodbridge township, Middlesex county, New Jersey, and is the fifth child of the late William C. and Sarah (Harriott) Cutter, of that section. The Cutter family are of Scotch and English extraction; one, Richard Cutter, with his mother, brother and sisters, arriving in Massachusetts about 1640, and settled in and about Cambridge. A grandson of Richard Cutter, and bearing the same name, and known as Major Richard Cutter, was the first of the name to leave New England and settle in a distant locality. He married Mary, daughter of John Pike, August 20th, 1706. This John Pike was one of the first and most active settlers of Woodbridge. Major Cutter died in 1756, leaving a numerous progeny; and from his fourth child and eldest son, Deacon William Cutter, who died in 1780, Hampton Cutter is the third in descent, being his great-grandson. He received his education in the schools of his native district, and assisted his father in his farming operations until 1836, when he married, and then continued in agricultural pursuits on his own account. In 1845 he commenced to dig kaolin, having discovered a large deposit of this valuable material on his farm. It is used with clay in the manufacture of fire-brick. Several years afterwards he reached a strata of fine blue clay, which also largely enters into the composition of fire-brick; and for many years past he has been engaged very extensively in supplying this valuable article to manufacturers not only of his immediate neighborhood, but also shipping the same to more distant points, large amounts finding their way to Portland, Boston, Albany, Cleveland, etc. Of late years he has associated his sons, Josiah C. and William Henry, with him, under the firm-name of Hampton Cutter & Sons. Aside from his business Hampton Cutter has been for many years called upon to serve the public in various local offices. For the past fifteen years he has been Justice of the Peace, and very recently has refused another term of the said office. Since 1868 he has been a director in the National Bank of Rahway. In religious faith he is a Presbyterian, and has been for twenty-two years one of the Trustees of the old Presbyterian Church of Woodbridge; and in politics he affiliates with the Democratic party. He was married, January 26th, 1836, to Mary R., daughter of Josiah Crane, of Crawford, New Jersey, and has a family of four children, two sons and two daughters.

————◆◆◆————

ONEYMAN, JOHN, M. D., late of New Germantown, Hunterdon county, New Jersey, was born, February 22d, 1798, a few miles from that village. He was a son of James Honeyman, well known as a popular landlord and singing-master fifty years ago, and grandson of John Honeyman, whose exploits in the French and Indian war, under General Wolfe, and during the Revolution, as "the Spy of Washington," are detailed with great interest by Hon. John Van Dyke in the local magazine, *Our Home*, for October, 1873. The subject of this sketch taught the academy in New Germantown when only eighteen years of age, and afterward entered the sophomore class, Middlebury College, Vermont, in 1817. He studied medicine with Dr. William Johnson, of White House, attended lectures at the University of Pennsylvania, and commenced practice in his native village in 1824, fifty years before his death, which occurred January 2d, 1874. He was esteemed far and wide, had a large practice, and by industry and economy accumulated a competence. His character was so extremely dignified and exemplary that it is said of him he never prevaricated, never told an untruth, never uttered a harsh word, never made an enemy. His death created a void in the medical profession which cannot soon be filled.

————◆◆◆————

ONEYMAN, A. VAN DOREN, Lawyer, Litterateur and Journalist, of Somerville, was born in New Germantown, Hunterdon county, November 12th, 1849, and is consequently in his twenty-seventh year. His father, Dr. John Honeyman, mention of whom is made just above, was an esteemed physician of a half century's practice at New Germantown. His great-grandfather, John Honeyman, emigrated from Ireland, fought under General Wolfe, and was a chosen spy of General Washington in the Revolution. On his mother's side he is a descendant of the Van Doren stock, whose ancestry can be traced back in Holland to the fourteenth century. He received but a common school education, then studied law in the office of the late Hon. H. D. Maxwell, of Easton, his brother-in-law, and commenced its practice at Somerville, as a partner of A. A. Clark, Esq., in 1871. In 1873 he projected and carried through the year the publication *Our Home*, a magazine of much local merit, which, however, was not financially sustained by the public. Resuming the practice of the law he formed a partnership with Mr. H. B. Herr, which still exists. In 1874, from hard work and exhaustion, he was obliged to leave business, and spent the summer in Europe, travelling in every country from Ireland to Italy. January 1st, 1876, he purchased the *Somerset Gazette*, and at once enlarged and improved it, with a view to making it the leading literary and family journal in the county. He has written much for the press generally, including the New York *Independent* and *Christian at Work*. He has also written and had printed a "Memorial" of his father's labors as a physician, and likewise issued a small book of poems. In the temperance cause he has been ever active, assailing the rumseller in the courts wherever practicable; and he aided to found and has been thrice elected President of the Young Men's Christian Association of Somerville.

————◆◆◆————

ENSON, DAVID, M. D., of Hoboken, was born in Englewood, Bergen county, New Jersey, July 19th, 1832. He is descended from families long resident in that locality and enjoying always the high regard of their neighbors, both his father and his mother, John J. and Hester (Banta) Benson, being natives of the same place. While he was yet very young his parents removed to Philadelphia, where his education was obtained. As a boy he attended a private collegiate school conducted by Dr. A. L. Kennedy, the present President of the Polytechnic Institute. Having determined to become a physician he entered the medical department of the University of Pennsylvania, matriculating in 1849. Here he prosecuted his studies very assiduously and thoroughly, taking a four years' course, and graduating with distinction in the spring of 1853. After graduation he engaged in practice in New York city for a short time, and then passed several years in travel and observation. On turning his attention once more to his profession, in 1861, he located in Hoboken, and began to earnestly prosecute his practice. Patients soon manifested their appreciation of his skill, care and sympathy, and their circle has widened and widened with every successive year. He is an electrician in practice. In all matters relating to his profession he takes an active interest. He is a member of the District

Charles Ewing

Medical Society of Hudson county, and was its President in 1872. He also belongs to the Pathological Society of Jersey City and to the New Jersey Academy of Medicine. For years he has been the Attending Physician of St. Mary's Hospital, of Hoboken, which is the oldest hospital in the State, and is maintained under the auspices of the "Sisters of the Poor of St. Francis.". During 1871 and part of 1872 he was City Physician of Hoboken, and it was while he was incumbent of the office that the long-to-be-remembered small-pox epidemic prevailed. Throughout the continuance of this dreadful scourge he was unceasing in his efforts to circumscribe its destructiveness, and his indefatigable labors, crowned as they were with a large measure of success, earned for him the gratitude of the whole community. He was married in 1854 to Mary Lyons, of Dublin.

EVINS, HON. JAMES S., Lawyer and Jurist, was born, 1786, in Somerset county, New Jersey. He received a fine classical education, and after passing through the curriculum at Nassau Hall, Princeton, graduated therefrom in 1816. He at once commenced the study of the law in the office of Frederick Frelinghuysen, and received his license as an attorney in 1819, becoming a counsellor in 1823, and named serjeant-at-law in 1837. After his admission to the bar he opened an office in New Brunswick, where he practised his profession and where he continued to reside until 1852. He was elected in 1838, by the joint meeting of the Council and Assembly, a Judge of the Supreme Court of New Jersey, to fill the vacancy occasioned by the death of Judge Ryerson; and on the expiration of his term, in 1845, was reappointed by the Governor for another term of seven years, which expired in 1852. He then removed his residence to Jersey City and resumed the practice of his profession, but not to any appreciable extent. He was a man of generous impulses, of great conversational ability, interspersed with wit and humor; and he was the life of the social circle with whom his lot was cast. He had been trained by pious parents in the evangelical faith, and was ever a believer in the doctrines which had been taught him. He possessed a warm friend in his legal preceptor, Frederick Frelinghuysen, and frequently visited him, and for a long period corresponded with him. Judge Nevins died in Jersey City, in 1859.

WING, HON. CHARLES, LL. D., Lawyer and Jurist, was born, 1780, in Bridgeton, Cumberland county, New Jersey, and was the only son of James and Martha (Boyd) Ewing. He was of Scotch-Irish descent, and was the great-grandson of Finley Ewing, of Londonderry, Ireland, who fought at the battle of the Boyne, and for his gallantry was publicly complimented by King William IH., who also presented him with a sword. One of his sons, Thomas Ewing, emigrated to America in 1718 and settled in Cumberland county, New Jersey, where he died, leaving a numerous progeny, some of whom have been greatly distinguished; among them may be named the late Thomas Ewing, of Ohio, United States Senator, and at one time Secretary of the Treasury. Judge Ewing's maternal grandfather was from the north of Ireland, and emigrated about 1772 to New Jersey, settling in Bridgeton. After a short time he managed to establish himself in a good business, and sent for his family. When these arrived, the following year, they found that he had died but a short time previous. The widow, however, took charge of her late husband's business, and employed as her clerk and assistant James Ewing, who subsequently married her eldest daughter, and the latter died soon after the birth of her son. Charles received a liberal education, and entered Princeton College, from which he graduated in 1798, taking the first honor. He afterwards entered the office of Samuel Leake, with whom he studied law, and in due time received his licenses as an attorney and counsellor-at-law. He was regarded as a most efficient and able advocate, and gained the control of a large and lucrative practice. In 1824 he was elected by the two houses of the Legislature as Chief-Justice of the Supreme Court, to succeed Judge Kirkpatrick, whose term at that time expired. He did not aspire to the position; indeed, he was opposed to any change being made, as the selection of his predecessor had given general satisfaction to the profession, although some complained of his unwillingness to pay much attention to the statutes regulating the proceedings in justices' courts. The change, however, was regarded as an excellent one, as Judge Ewing was a most patient, painstaking and laborious judge, learned both in principles and cases, and prompt in their application. He always took upon himself all the responsibilities of the judge, and ever instructed the jury in matters of law, and guided them, where it was allowable for him to do so, in their estimate of facts and evidence. At the expiration of his seven years' term, so satisfactory had been his course, that he was re-elected by a joint meeting of a Legislature opposed to him in politics; but he only lived a few months of the first year of his second term. In religious faith he was a Presbyterian and a zealous member of that church. When from any cause there was no one to preach, the worship was carried on by the elders, and a sermon read. On these occasions Judge Ewing was always selected as reader, and the discourse he chose was always one of Dr. Witherspoon's. He was excellently well informed on the general literature of the day; and possessed a fine miscellaneous library, in addition to the well-filled shelves of rare and valuable works of legal lore. He was a truly elegant gentleman of the old school; an instructive and agreeable conversationalist, and renowned for his hospitality. He died, August 5th, 1832, being one of the first victims of the Asiatic cholera in New Jersey.

ILL, CHARLES S., Cashier of the National Bank of New Jersey and Clerk of Middlesex county, was born, January 20th, 1840, in the city of New Brunswick, and is the son of the late John B. and Henrietta V. (Chapman) Hill. His father was for many years a banker in New Brunswick; and his mother was the daughter of Thomas Chapman, proprietor and principal of the Holmesburg Academy, near Philadelphia, Pennsylvania. Charles was educated in the best schools of his native place, and when sixteen years old entered the employ of Rolfe & Metler, lumber merchants, of New Brunswick, and continued there some four years. He then removed to Brooklyn, New York, where he became salesman and bookkeeper for the New York Steam Saw-Mill Company, and after a short time effected an engagement with the Park Bank, in the city of New York, which terminated in 1865. In the latter year he was called to New Brunswick and offered the position of Cashier of the National Bank of New Jersey, which he accepted and still retains. Since his return to his native city he has served two years in the City Council as the representative from the Sixth Ward; and in 1872 was elected the County Clerk of Middlesex county for the term of five years. He is also Treasurer of the Union, Raritan, and Manufacturers' & Mechanics' Loan Associations. He was married, October 19th, 1865, to Ellen C. Auten, of New Brunswick, New Jersey.

OTTS, HON. STACY GARDINER, Lawyer and Jurist, was born, November, 1799, in the city of Harrisburg, Pennsylvania, and was of English extraction. He was the great-great-grandson of Thomas Potts, a member of the Society of Friends, who, with his family and in company with Mahlon Stacy and his kindred, left England, 1678, in the ship "Shield," and landed at Burlington, being the first vessel of her class to sail so far up the Delaware. The two families of Stacy and Potts intermarried, and thus the names were interchanged in both. Stacy Potts, the grandfather of Judge Potts, was a tanner by trade, and carried on that business in Trenton. His son removed to Harrisburg, and in 1791 married a Miss Gardiner, a Presbyterian. Shortly after the birth of young Stacy, his father purchased a large tract of land in Northumberland county, Pennsylvania, on which he resided until 1808, when the father and son left for Trenton, pursuing the journey on foot, and consuming only four days in the trip, it being a distance of one hundred and twenty miles. Young Stacy became an inmate of his grandfather's family, who was at that time the mayor of Trenton. He attended school at the Friends' Academy, where he remained four years. During this time he became so captivated with the opportunities of seeing books and papers in a printing office, that he was permitted to enter it as an apprentice. Having also access to a book store, and

becoming a member of a debating club, he cultivated his taste for composition, and soon began to contribute both articles of poetry and prose to the newspapers of the town. He was employed in 1821, when he attained his majority, as editor of a weekly paper, entitled the *Emporium*, and at the same time was a contributor to a Philadelphia monthly magazine, for which he wrote many articles. In 1823 he entered upon the study of the law with Counsellor Stockton, still continuing to devote all his time every day to his editorial duties, which obliged him to do the greater part of his study at night. After reading under his preceptor a short time, he left him to become one of the pupils of the late Garret D. Wall, with whom he remained until he was licensed as an attorney in 1827; he became a counsellor in 1830. In 1828 he was elected a member of Assembly on the Jackson Democratic ticket, and re-elected in 1829. In 1831 he was appointed by the joint meeting of Assembly and Council, Clerk of the Court of Chancery, and was re-elected by them at the expiration of his term in 1836, thus holding that office for ten years. During his incumbency he made the income of the office a very lucrative one; and this was effected by his drafting the necessary decrees, processes, etc., for the solicitors, who gladly paid him their fees for the services so rendered. He was also chosen in 1834 by the Legislature an Alderman, which gave him a seat as Justice of the Court of Quarter Sessions. At the close of his clerkship, his health requiring relaxation, he accompanied his brother, the late Rev. William S. Potts, D. D., of St. Louis, on a visit to Europe. He examined, while in England, the practice in some of the principal courts, and was an interested observer of the legal proceedings of the same; he also visited some of the most remarkable places in Great Britain and also upon the Continent. He returned to the United States in 1841, with his health completely recuperated. In 1845 he was associated, by act of the Legislature, with ex-Governor Vroom, Chancellor Green and Minister Dayton, on a commission to revise the laws of New Jersey, and besides performing his share of the revision, it devolved on him to systematize and arrange the result for publication. Upon the inception of the State Lunatic Asylum, in 1847, he was placed on the first Board of Managers, and was actively engaged in his duties until he was called to the bench. In 1852 he was nominated by Governor Fort and confirmed by the Senate, one of the Justices of the Supreme Court, and took for his circuit the counties of Camden, Gloucester, Ocean and Burlington, the court then consisting of five judges. He served throughout his entire term of seven years, and then retired to private life. He was accounted an excellent jurist, and was deservedly popular with the bar and the public. He was an active member of the Presbyterian Church, and was at different times connected with various boards and institutions of that denomination. While a member of the General Assembly, in 1851, he was made chairman of a special committee to arrange the complicated finances of the church, and his report, published in full, elicited great admiration for its skill and perfectness. He devoted some of his later years to the composition of a work entitled " The Christ of Revelation," designed to trace the scriptural doctrine of the Redeemer from the prophecies to the life and teachings of the New Testament. He had filled the position of Sunday-school teacher and, for a time, Superintendent of the same, for a period of thirty-six years. He became a communicant member of the church in 1822, and was ordained a Ruling Elder in 1836. He received, in 1844, from the College of New Jersey, the honorary degree of Master of Arts. From 1859 his health began to decline gradually, which culminated in his death at Trenton, April 9th, 1865.

YCKOFF, MARTIN, Lawyer and Soldier, of Asbury, Warren county, was born, October 18th, 1834, near White House, New Jersey. The family is of Hollander lineage, and was among the earliest settlers of New Jersey; while some of those living during the period of the American Revolution were engaged in the war for independence. Martin attended the public schools until 1850, when he entered the grammar-school connected with Rutgers College; and in 1852 entered the sophomore class of that college. In 1854 he was chosen one of the junior orators, and graduated with the class of 1855, taking the second honor. Among his classmates were Hon. J. H. Stone, of Rahway, and Milton A. Fowler, now of the New York bar. After leaving college he went to the Southern States, and was engaged in teaching in Virginia between one and two years. In the spring of 1857 he returned to New Jersey and commenced the study of law with Hon. Alexander Wurts, at Flemington, where he remained until admitted to the bar, in 1860. He immediately entered upon the practice of his profession, and had acquired a fair line of patronage when the war of the rebellion broke out. He at once relinquished his law business, and with Captains Bonnel and Allen proceeded to raise a company of volunteers, in which he himself enlisted as a private; and when the company was fully organized and attached to the 3d Regiment, he was elected First Sergeant, and soon afterwards commissioned Lieutenant. At the first battle of Bull Run he had been placed in charge of a supply-train, with which he succeeded in safely reaching Alexandria after the disastrous termination of that battle. When the term of service of his regiment had expired he returned home and removed his residence to Asbury, and there, in the spring of 1862, he commenced again to practise his profession. In the autumn of the same year an additional call for troops was made, and upon the organization of the 31st Regiment of Infantry, he was appointed its Adjutant, and was subsequently attached to the staff of General Paul, with the rank of Captain. He participated in the severe battles fought under Burnside, including Fredericksburg, Chancellorsville, etc., and also

rendered valuable service while with a foraging expedition into Virginia, wherein a large amount of provision and other material was captured. When his second term of service expired Captain Wyckoff again returned to the practice of his profession at Asbury, where he has since remained, and where his clientage has become one of the most lucrative in Warren county. He is a careful, painstaking lawyer, of strict probity, and in the management of cases evinces great shrewdness. He is very seldom or never deceived on the merits of a case, and rarely takes one into court in which he does not succeed. He was of counsel for the Lehigh Valley Railroad Company during the construction of the Easton & Allentown Division. At present he is the legal adviser of the Bloomsburg National Bank and also of the First National Bank at Clinton, besides being the attorney of several manufacturing companies and other corporations. His political views are those of the Democratic party, but he prefers to act independently, never hesitating to oppose the measures or the men of his own party when he believes the public good demands it. He stands high in the estimation of his fellow-townsmen, both as a lawyer and a citizen. In all matters pertaining to real estate he is probably without a superior at the New Jersey bar. He was married in 1862 to a daughter of Hugh Capner, of Flemington; she died in January, 1876.

OUGH, DE WITT CLINTON, M. D., of Rahway, was born at Point Pleasant, Bucks county, Pennsylvania, December 21st, 1826. His father, General Joseph Hough, was a native of Pennsylvania, and followed agricultural pursuits; his mother, Jane Crowell, came from the same State. He obtained his literary education at Newtown Academy, which he attended from 1839 to 1841, having previously received its elements in the schools of his native place. Attracted toward the medical profession, he began preparation therefor as a student under the guidance of Dr. Charles Fronefield, of Montgomery county, Pennsylvania. Having laid a sound foundation of medical knowledge, he entered Jefferson Medical College, Philadelphia, and after a full course graduated therefrom in the spring of 1847. He began practice at Tyler's Port, Montgomery county, Pennsylvania, where he remained one year. Then he removed to Red Hill, Bucks county, where he was engaged for three years. From this place he moved to Frenchtown, New Jersey, where he labored for six years. Seeking a wider field of practice he settled in Rahway in 1857, and met with encouraging success until, on the outbreak of the war of the rebellion, in 1861, desirous of contributing his services to the cause of the Union, he entered the army as Surgeon of the 7th New Jersey Infantry. For three years he accompanied this regiment, and served with it through all its engagements. On leaving the army he resumed the practice of his profession in Rahway, attending during the winter of that year, 1864, a course of lectures at Bellevue Medical College, New York, and availing himself of the advantages of the hospital clinics. Since the conclusion of this additional course of study he has devoted himself to his practice in Rahway, which has grown to large and influential proportions. He has been a member of the Union County Medical Society since its organization, in 1869, and acted as its Vice-President in 1873. Politically he affiliates with the Republican party, and has been honored by it with various important trusts. In 1867 and 1868 he was elected by it to the mayoralty of Rahway, and in 1868 and 1869 to the Legislature. He was a member of the Water Commission of Rahway from 1871 to 1874, and President of the Board during the construction of the works. On January 28th, 1850, he was married to Elmira C. Runkle, of New Jersey.

———

CHENK, WILLIAM HENRY, M. D., Physician, of Flemington, is a native of the place which is now his home, having been born in Flemington, September 21st, 1826. His early education was obtained at the public schools of Flemington and vicinity, and later he attended the grammar school connected with Rutgers College. When he had reached the age when he should select and prepare for a profession, he commenced the study of medicine under the instruction of his father, Dr. John F. Schenk. After completing his course of preparatory reading he entered the University of New York. Here he continued his studies with energy and great success, and when he graduated, in the spring of 1848, he was well qualified for the practice of the arduous profession he had chosen. He returned to Flemington after his graduation, and there entered upon practice in company with his father. He remained there until 1850, when he removed to Ringoes, New Jersey, where he was engaged in professional practice for about a year. At the end of that time he went to New York, and there engaged in the drug business. He remained in this business until the year 1853, when, upon the breaking out of the Australian gold excitement, he went to try his fortunes upon the island continent. In Australia he engaged in mining as well as the practice of his profession, although the latter claimed the principal portion of his attention and efforts. While there he became a member of the Medical Board of Victoria. In the year 1867, after having remained abroad for fourteen years, he returned home by way of England. In 1868 he resumed the practice of his profession in his native town of Flemington, and there he has continued to reside ever since. He has achieved a high position in his calling; his skill as a practitioner is universally recognized, and he is in possession of an extensive and valuable patronage. Politically he is a Democrat, but his highest and most active interest is in his profession, and

politics receives but a minor share of his attention. He was married in Australia, in the year 1862, to Margaret McLean, of Scotland.

———

LLEN, GEORGE A., Lawyer, of Flemington, New Jersey, was born in Westport, Fairfield county, Connecticut, and is a son of the late William Allen, formerly a merchant of that place. The family is of English origin, and were among the early settlers of Connecticut. They were noted for their fidelity and patriotism during the war for independence. Both his paternal and maternal grandfathers served as officers in the revolutionary army, and one participated in the battle of Long Island, where he was taken prisoner by the British and suffered untold privations and hardships at their hands. George A. Allen was being prepared for college at Greens Farms Academy when his father died suddenly, and as his pecuniary affairs were not in a condition to allow his son to pursue a collegiate course, the latter commenced teaching school at Milford, Connecticut, where he continued in this vocation about two years; and thence removed to New Jersey, where he again commenced teaching in a school near Flemington, and was likewise so occupied another two years. At the expiration of this latter period he entered the law office of James N. Reading, then of Flemington (now of Morris, Illinois), and commenced his legal studies. He remained there four years, and in 1844 was licensed as an attorney. He soon became known as an ardent, energetic practitioner, who could be entirely depended upon, both as advisory counsel or in the management of cases, and as such rapidly acquired practice. On the outbreak of the great rebellion he enlisted as a private in the 3d Regiment New Jersey Volunteers on the first call for troops. He was, however, soon promoted to a Captaincy; and the regiment to which he was attached was one of the first in the field, reaching Washington City by the way of Annapolis. On the expiration of the term for which he had enlisted he returned with his regiment to New Jersey. As his extensive legal and private business demanded his attention, he was thus prevented from returning to the field; but throughout the entire period of the war he was active and earnest in his support of the Union cause and in the raising of men and means to carry on the contest. His legal practice still continues a large one, and there is rarely any important case in the county in which he is not engaged. As a chancery lawyer he enjoys a reputation second to none in the State. He prepares his cases with the utmost care, and seldom takes one into court with a single point unguarded, while he will speedily detect any weaknesses, however slight, in his opponent's side. In arguing a case he never displays much oratorical effort, but arranges the facts and circumstances in the most forcible and logical manner, and never allows the judge or jury to lose sight of his main points. He thus invariably puts his

client's case in the best possible light that it is capable of assuming. His undoubted probity and his unswerving devotion to the interests of his clients have placed him at the head of the profession in his section of the State, and have won for him an extensive and lucrative practice, which has yielded him a competency. He assisted materially in the organization of the Hunterdon County Bank, and was at one period President of the same, and also was one of the organizers of the bank at Lambertville, both of which institutions are at present national banks. In 1856 he, with others, founded the *Hunterdon Republican*, and was one of its editors, and still continues one of its proprietors. His political creed was formerly that held by the Whig party, but he became a Republican, and was one of those who brought that organization as a party into existence. In 1872, or thereabouts, when the liberal Republican party was formed, which nominated Horace Greeley for the Presidency, he supported that movement, and at that time retired from the editorial management of the *Republican*, but continued one of the proprietors of that journal. He is a member of the State Editorial Association, and during the Greeley campaign he was one of the State Executive Committee. He was married in 1850 to Mary, daughter of Charles Bonnell, of Flemington. His eldest son, William D. Allen, was admitted to practise at the bar in 1875; and his second son, Charles W., is now (1876) a student in the medical department of Harvard University, Cambridge, Massachusetts.

HETWOOD, FRANCIS B., late Attorney and Counsellor-at-Law, of Elizabeth, was born, February 1st, 1806, at Elizabethtown, New Jersey, and was the son of the late Hon. William and Mary (Barber) Chetwood. His grandfather, John Chetwood, was an Associate-Justice of the Supreme Court of New Jersey, and was of Quaker descent. His resignation from the bench, as stated by one of his contemporaries, was occasioned by "continued and increasing bad health;" but the tradition in his family is that it was "his unwillingness to sentence a man to death." He died in 1806, at Elizabeth, at the age of seventy-two years. Francis B. Chetwood obtained his education in the schools of his native place, and at the proper age commenced the study of the law in his father's office, the latter having been a prominent practitioner in his time. Francis was duly licensed as an attorney in November, 1828, and as a counsellor three years later. He commenced the practice of the law with his father, with whom he continued until the latter retired. He then followed his professional pursuits alone until about 1860, when he formed a partnership with William J. Magie, who had studied with him, the firm's name and style being Chetwood & Magie. After some years this firm dissolved, and he then associated with his son, Robert E. Chetwood, under the style of F. B. Chetwood & Son, and

the firm continued until the death of the senior member. During his lifetime he held a large number of offices of trust and honor in the gift of his fellow-townsmen. He was Prosecutor of the Pleas for the county of Essex; this was prior to the formation of Union county. At an early period of his manhood he was a member of the City Council for several terms; also a member of the State Legislature for two years, and was elected Mayor of the borough, and also Mayor of the city of Elizabeth; in the latter office his administration was characterized by rare executive ability and remarkable industry. He was the projector of the Elizabeth Water and the Elizabeth Gas Companies, and it was owing, in a great measure, to his indomitable perseverance that these works were built, notwithstanding the indifference of some and the opposition of others. He was also one of the originators of the Elizabeth Orphan Asylum and of the Evergreen Cemetery, and was one of the two who purchased the grounds for the cemetery and became personally responsible for their cost. He also assisted in planning the grounds, giving the names to its avenues and paths, beside framing the rules and regulations for the government of the company. He took a warm interest in the growth and prosperity of his native place, which was especially noted for the elegance of the buildings he erected at various times and afterwards disposed of. Some of the finest suburban residences of Elizabeth were planned and erected by him. For many years he held the position of attorney for the old State bank; he lost heavily by the failure of several institutions, and these losses, added to continued domestic affliction, had their effect upon his sensitive nature. He had been long a communicant of St. John's Episcopal Church, in which he served for many years as a vestryman, and at the time of his death was a warden. As a citizen and neighbor he was universally beloved; he was as simple and unostentatious in his manners as he was pure and honorable in his dealings. He always acted in accordance with his convictions, whether they were popular or the reverse; and he left behind him a record that few can equal. He was married, April 3d, 1832, to Elizabeth P. Phelps; he died, January 18th, 1875, leaving a widow, two sons and one daughter, two sons having died some years previous.

HETWOOD, ROBERT E., Lawyer, of Elizabeth, is a native of the place in which he now resides, being born there, December 20th, 1837. On his mother's side he is of New England descent, his mother, Eliza P. Phelps, having been born in Connecticut; but his father, Francis B. Chetwood, was a native of Elizabeth. Robert received the rudiments of his education at the common schools of Elizabeth. He "had a turn for study," and his progress was rapid and thorough. When he had arrived at the proper age he entered Princeton College, and there pursued a three years' course of study. He graduated in the year 1858, and immediately commenced the study of the law. That he should become a lawyer was almost a matter of course. His father was a prominent member of the profession, who had also been mayor of the city, and of the borough before its incorporation as a city. Moreover, the son had a strong natural inclination toward the law, and a thorough fitness for that profession. He entered the office of his father as a student, and prosecuted his studies with vigor and rapid success. He was licensed as an attorney in June, 1861. In June, 1864, he received his license as counsellor-at-law. His progress in his profession was rapid, and he speedily attained a high place at the bar and in the confidence of his professional brethren and of the public. In the year 1874 he was elected to the office of City Attorney of Elizabeth, a position which he still holds. Politically he is of the Republican faith, and has been an active and effective worker in the ranks of that party since his majority. Repeatedly he has been delegate to Republican conventions, and has served the party in numerous other capacities. He was married, March 5th, 1867, to Kate A. McGowan, daughter of Captain John McGowan, of the United States Revenue Service.

RIGHT, GEORGE M., State Treasurer, was born, July 18th, 1817, in Newshoreham, Newport county, Rhode Island, and is a son of William L. and Lucy (Minor) Wright, both of Rhode Island, and both of English descent. His father was for many years a sea captain, but the latter portion of his life was devoted to agricultural pursuits, he having removed to Otsego county, New York, where he died. George received his preliminary education at the district school of Rhode Island, and then became a pupil in a select school at Hartwick, in the same county. When twenty years old he left the academy, and went to New York at twenty-one to better his condition; and being possessed of an active, energetic spirit, he soon advanced himself in the world. He engaged in various enterprises, which all proved successful, as to whatever he undertook he gave all his attention, and allowed nothing to escape his notice which might in the end conduce to his benefit. In 1851 he was the agent for George W. Aspinwall's line of steamers, which position he retained until the death of that gentleman, which occurred in 1853. About that time the Pennsylvania Steam Towing & Transportation Company was formed, in which he became a large stockholder, and has continued as such ever since. From his long connection with the steamboat interests of New Jersey he is more familiarly known as Captain Wright. In 1851 he removed to New Jersey, and resided in New Brunswick for about three years, when he selected Bordentown as his future home, and of which he still continues a citizen. He was elected Mayor of Bordentown in 1858, and held that

position two years. In 1864 he was chosen Senator from Burlington county, and served in that capacity for three years in the Legislature, 1864 to 1867; while a member of that body he was placed on several important committees. For twelve years he filled the post of Inspector and Collector, at Bordentown, for the Delaware & Raritan Canal. During his occupancy of that important position millions of dollars passed through his hands, all of which was satisfactorily accounted for. He is at present a director in the Bordentown Banking Company, as also of the Steam Towing Company. He was appointed State Treasurer in February, 1875. Throughout his whole life he has been noted for his industrious habits, his sterling honesty and unimpeachable character; while he is regarded by his fellow-townsmen as an energetic, public-spirited citizen. He was married in 1848 to Jane M. Bradley, of Richmond county, New York. The old homestead of his father, in New York State, is still in his possession.

OWELL, REV. ISAAC P., late Pastor of St. Mary's Church, Elizabeth, New Jersey, was born, July 16th, 1811, in the city of Philadelphia, Pennsylvania, and was the son of Dr. Abraham and Mary Elizabeth (Rosette) Howell. His father was an eminent physician and a staunch Protestant; while his mother was of French extraction and a zealous member of the Roman Catholic Church. In accordance with the views of his father, he commenced the study of medicine in 1829, but before he had completed his prescribed course of readings his father died—in 1832. At the earnest solicitation of his mother, he entered Mount St. Mary's College, in Maryland, to study divinity and prepare himself to exercise the sacred functions of a priest of the church. He was ordained by the late Archbishop Hughes, March 17th, 1844, and immediately was detailed for duty in Elizabeth. Although that city is the oldest settlement in New Jersey, but few members of the Roman Catholic Church ever resided there until of late years. Less than half a century ago—in 1829—there were but three of that faith sojourning there; when their religions faith was discovered they were obliged to leave, as no employment would be given them. In the course of time, especially when the New Jersey Railroad, and at a later day when the Central Railway were in process of construction, a large influx of laborers professing that faith were added to the population of the town; but there were no services held as yet, and very little probability that any would be needed, as the Roman Catholic population was, so to speak, a floating population. The late Rev. P. Moran, of Newark, then the only priest there, attended to the sick calls of the railroad laborers; and in 1842 Rev. Yldefonso Medrano, then stationed on Staten Island, visited the few scattered members of the fold in and near Elizabeth, and

course of study. He graduated in the year 1858. and immediately commenced the study of the law. That he should become a lawyer was almost a matter of course. His father was a prominent member of the profession, who had also been mayor of the city, and of the borough before its incorporation as a city. Moreover, the son had a strong natural inclination toward the law, and a thorough ...... for that profession. He entered the office of his father .... student, and prosecuted his studies with vigor .... success. He was licensed as an attorney in .... In June, 1864, he received his license .... His progress in his profession was .... attained a high place at the .... professional brethren and ...

he was elected to the office ...

positions ....

....

.... he .... to legislative conventions, and has .... other capacities. He was .... 5th, 1867, to Kate A. McGowan, ... hn McGowan, of the United States Navy.

WRIGHT, GEORGE M., State Treasurer, was born, July 18th, 1817, in Newshoreham, Newport county, Rhode Island, and is a son of William L. and Lucy (Minor) Wright, both of Rhode Island, and both of English descent. His father was for many years a sea captain, but the latter portion of his life was devoted to agricultural pursuits, he having removed to Otsego county, New York, where he died. George received his preliminary education at the district school of Rhode Island, and then became a pupil in a select school at Hartwick, in the same county. When twenty years old he left the academy, and went to New York at twenty-one to better his condition; and being possessed of an active, energetic spirit, he soon advanced himself in the world. He engaged in various enterprises, which all proved successful, as to whatever he undertook he gave all his attention, and allowed nothing to escape his notice which might in the end conduce to his benefit. In 1851 he was the agent for George W. Aspinwall's line of steamers, which position he retained until the death of that .... in 1852. About that time the ....

position two years. Burlington county, years in the Legisla that body he was p for twelve years b ector, at Bordento During his .... dollars passed th family accounted ...town Bankin Company. He .... 1875. Thro ...... industrious

....

.... certain ...... in .... repeatedly ....

Sam ... born J phia, I' Abrahar His fat staunch Protestan traction and a zo Church. In accu commenced the s had completed hi died—in 1832. he entered Mount divinity and prepa of a priest of the Archbishop Hugh was detailed for the oldest settlem the Roman Catho years. Less than but three of that gious faith was th employment woul especially when .... day when the Ce

occasionally celebrated for them the rites of religion; but the prejudice against the church was such that the only place he could procure for the purpose was a low tavern on the outskirts of the town, and his visitations were attended by the most unfavorable circumstances, not only to his own personal interest, but also to the most vital interests of religion. And this was the state of affairs when Father Howell appeared. After considerable difficulty he procured a small room, in a house near the town, in which to celebrate mass. On Palm Sunday, 1844, a congregation of about twenty-five assembled to greet their pastor and assist at the sacred rites of religion. Notwithstanding that he met with opposition, yet there was somewhat of an increase in the congregation during that year, and a collection was commenced in the fall to purchase a lot whereon to erect a church. In April, 1845, the basement wall of St. Mary's of the Assumption was laid, and on the first Sunday in Advent of the same year a substantial brick church, fifty feet square, was sufficiently completed to accommodate the congregation, which had then increased to about 100. In the course of a few years the church became too small for the rapid growth of the parish, and in 1847 the German members of the congregation left and erected an edifice for themselves. In 1851 a substantial brick school-house, two stories high, was erected alongside of St. Mary's Church. In 1858 the enlargement and remodelling of the church and erection of a pastoral residence were commenced; and in the spring of 1862 the work was completed. A beautiful church, 133 feet long and 66 feet wide, with a spacious pastoral residence, are the best evidences of the zeal and charity of the congregation. To this congregation did Father Howell minister until the close of his life. At the outbreak of the great rebellion, in 1861, he promptly espoused the cause of the Union, and induced many of his flock to aid in the defence of their country. He was a man of marked learning and ability, and the founder of the Roman Catholic Church in Elizabeth. He died, August 31st, 1866, and his funeral was attended by all denominations, who had learned to respect and honor him.

QUIER, WILLIAM CRANE, Merchant, of Rahway, New Jersey, was born in that place on January 8th, 1812. He is descended from illustrious ancestors. His grandfather, John Squier, married Hannah Clark, cousin of Abram Clark, one of the signers of the Declaration of Independence; his uncle, Abram Clark Squier, was captured from a privateer by a British cruiser and consigned to the famous New York sugar-house prison, where he died from slow starvation; his father, Jonathan Squier, married Hannah Crane, a niece of General William Crane, of Elizabeth, New Jersey, who distinguished himself as an officer of the revolutionary army. Inheriting from his ancestry an ardent

love of country, he has through life proved himself a public-spirited and useful citizen, always rendering substantial support to all movements calculated to advance the material and social welfare of the nation, in whose creation his progenitors bore so conspicuous and honorable a part. He was educated at the New York University, and the superior advantages he there enjoyed were improved to the full. Shortly after commencing the active business of life he removed to the South, and from 1834 to 1846 was engaged in New Orleans as a merchant. Subsequently he returned North, and since 1852 has conducted business as a merchant in the city of New York, residing at his native place, Rahway. In the progress of this rapidly advancing locality he has always manifested an active interest. He has been President of the Rahway Savings Institution since its organization, in 1853. In the subsequent year he was chosen President and Managing Director of the Passaic Zinc Company, a corporation of the State of New Jersey, engaged in the manufacture of oxide of zinc, spelter and sheet zinc at Jersey City, with mines in Sussex county, New Jersey, formerly owned by Lord Stirling—that is, before the revolutionary war. He has continued to serve the company in that capacity until the present time, and its substantial prosperity is attributable in large degree to the wise and prudent character of his management of its affairs. He was married on November 8th, 1841, to Catherine Craig, daughter of Dr. David S. Craig, a highly respected physician of Rahway (now deceased).

HITE, HON. JOHN MOORE, Lawyer and Jurist, late of Woodbury, was born, 1770, at Bridgeton, Cumberland county, New Jersey, and was the youngest son of an English merchant who had originally settled in Philadelphia and who had married the daughter of Alexander Moore, who had settled in Bridgeton about 1730, and had been engaged there in business for many years and had acquired a competence. She was of Irish descent, and a remarkably handsome woman; and the same may be said of her husband's appearance. She died while her youngest son was but an infant, leaving also two other sons. The widower returned to England; but when the revolutionary war broke out he took the patriot's side, returned to America, obtained a commission in the army, was an aide to General Sullivan, and was killed in the battle of Germantown, Pennsylvania. Alexander Moore, their grandfather, became the guardian of the three boys, and educated them. He died in 1786, and bequeathed to them a large portion of his landed property, including a large tract on the east side of the Cohansey river, upon which the city of Bridgeton is built. Judge White studied law with Joseph Bloomfield, and received his license as an attorney in 1791, as a counsellor in 1799, and as a serjeant-at-law in 1812. He settled in Bridgeton, where he entered upon the practice of his profession, and where he continued to reside until 1808, when he removed to Woodbury, and lived there until the close of his life. He was very successful as an advocate, and was well versed in the common law as applied to matters where real estate was concerned; and, as he had made himself fully acquainted with the surveys located under the proprietors, he was generally charged with cases where boundary lines were involved. He was also, during his professional life at the bar, the Prosecutor of the Pleas of the State for several years in the counties of Cumberland and Salem. During the early part of his residence in Woodbury he was elected a member of Assembly, to represent Gloucester county in that body, and was several times re-elected. He was appointed Attorney-General of the State in 1833, and served in that position during his five years' term, and would have retained the position had it been possible for him to have done so. But when the joint meeting of the Legislature was held, in 1838, another person was elected as his successor, while he was nominated and elected a Judge of the Supreme Court of the State. He served his term of seven years on the bench, and at its close retired to private life. He had married, about the time of his admission to the bar, Miss Zuntzinger, and his family consisted only of one child, a daughter, who died when only about sixteen years old. Judge White's years were protracted beyond fourscore years and ten. He died, 1862, in the ninety-second year of his age.

———◆◇◆———

ARKER, GEORGE W., Division Superintendent of the New York Division of the Pennsylvania Railroad, and a resident of Jersey City, was born in Strafford county, New Hampshire, June 17th, 1828. His father, Benjamin Barker, of New Hampshire, and his brother, Hon. David Barker, member of Congress from New Hampshire, were the originators of the woollen manufacture now so extensively carried on in that section. His mother, Eliza March, was the daughter of Hon. Jonas C. March, a man of public note for many years in New Hampshire. It was in the public schools that the subject of this sketch received all the educational training he ever enjoyed, and, his father having failed in the great panic of 1837, it was necessary that at an early age he should do something for his living. Accordingly at sixteen years of age he began working in a saw-mill. After a short employment there he engaged with the Eastern Express Company as a messenger, and in this occupation he continued for about a year. He then assisted his father in the conduct of a grist-mill and in the manufacture of shoe-lasts. For several years he remained with his father, and in 1851 was appointed Station Agent at Rochester, on a branch of the Boston & Maine Railroad. Here he struck the right track, and made it manifest that his path lay in the direction of railroading. With the Boston

& Maine road he continued for two years, and resigned to become Freight Agent for the Salem & Lowell, and the Lowell & Lawrence Railroads, at Lowell, acting as General Freight Agent as well as Local Agent for both of these roads, which at that time were under the management of William Livingston. In April, 1854, he resigned his position on these roads, and moved to Jersey City to enter the freight department of the Erie Railway, as Assistant Local Freight Agent. After holding this post for one year he was transferred to a passenger conductorship, and travelled in that capacity until September, 1858, when he was dismissed the road by D. C. McCallum for passing some of the family of one of its directors. He was, however, shortly after reinstated by Charles Minot, and ran as Conductor on the Elmira & Canandaigua Branch of the Erie road, where he served for two years, and was then transferred to Chicago as Passenger Agent for the same railroad in that city. At the expiration of two years he resigned that position, and, by request, connected himself with the New Jersey Railroad & Transportation Company, as Conductor. After running in that capacity for twelve months he was made Depot Master at Jersey City, and so continued for about four months, when he was appointed Master of Transportation. In this office he served until 1871, when the Pennsylvania Railroad Company took charge of the United Railroads of New Jersey, when he was appointed Division Superintendent of the New York Division, extending from New York to Philadelphia. In this responsible position he has demonstrated more strikingly than ever before his special fitness to take part in the active operation of a railroad. When he first arrived in Jersey City the entire number of trains centring at that point was only twenty-two daily, a total that included the trains of the Erie, the Morris & Essex, and the New Jersey Railroad & Transportation Companies. Now the Pennsylvania Railroad Company alone run eighty-two passenger trains each way daily from their depots. In this total are included those of the Lehigh Valley, New Jersey Midland, Montclair & Greenwood Lake, and Jersey City & Albany Railroads, all of which are under the immediate supervision of Mr. Barker. On the opening of the Centennial Exposition, at Philadelphia, there were 344 trains handled on the New York Division in twenty-four hours, the movement of seventy-eight of them being directed each way by telegraph. Again, on the occasion observed as New York Day at the Exposition, and for a day or two previous and for a day or two after, there was an immense strain upon the resources of the division and upon the executive ability of its Superintendent, while from about the end of August until after the close of the Exposition the travel on the road was simply enormous, taxing heavily the capacity and endurance of this officer and his assistants. The whole of this extraordinary travel, owing to the system and careful attention of the Superintendent, was conducted on remarkable time and without an accident by which a passenger was injured. Having served in almost every department of a railroad, Mr. Barker is peculiarly qualified to fill his present position, no matter what its emergencies, and having earned it step by step he is a firm believer in and consistent advocate of the system of promotion from the ranks, holding that its adoption secures well-tried and efficient assistants; indeed, to his observance of this principle he attributes in great measure the large success that has attended his management. His position invests him with the control over about 2500 employés, including the shopmen.

E WITT, REV. JOHN, D. D., Professor of Oriental Literature in the Theological Seminary at New Brunswick, was born in Albany, New York, November 29th, 1821. His father, whose name he bears, was a distinguished theologian and instructor, having been for many years connected with the Theological Seminary at New Brunswick, at the same time occupying the Professorship of Rhetoric and Belles-Lettres in Rutgers College, Dr. De Witt, the subject of this sketch, graduated from Rutgers College in 1838, and then entered the Theological Seminary, from which he graduated in 1842. His first charge was the Reformed Church at Ridgeway, Michigan, where he ministered from 1842 to 1844. He then received and accepted a call from the First Reformed Church at Ghent, New York, and labored in that connection with much acceptability and encouraging success until 1848. His next charge was at Canajoharie, Montgomery county, New York, which he held for a very short time, when his health failed, obliging him to desist from professional labor for a year. Upon his recovery he accepted the pastorate of the Reformed Church at Millstone, New Jersey. He continued in this relation from 1850 to 1863. In the latter year he was elected to the Chair of Oriental Literature in the Theological Seminary at New Brunswick. Feeling that in assuming this position he would be laboring in an enlarged field of usefulness, he severed his relations with the church at Millstone, and moved to New Brunswick, and entered upon his duties as Professor. A fine Oriental scholar, he has filled the chair with distinguished ability from that time down to the present writing. He was married, in 1847, to Charlotte L. Gillette, of New York.

ORD, HON. GABRIEL H., Lawyer and Jurist, late of Morristown, was born, 1764, in Morristown, New Jersey, and was a son of Colonel Jacob Ford, whose family residence was the head-quarters of General Washington in the winter of 1779–80, and is still standing, a hallowed memento of "the times that tried men's souls." Judge Ford graduated from Princeton College in 1784, and having made choice of the profession of the law, entered the office of Abraham Ogden, of Newark, whom he selected as his preceptor. During the period of his novitiate he became a member of the "Institutio Legalis," or moot-court, where he had for associates, William Griffith, J. Ogden Hoffman, Richard Stockton, who afterwards became lawyers of renown, both in New York and New Jersey, and who ascribed in a great measure their success at the bar to the practice attained in this mimic court. He was licensed as an attorney in 1789, and subsequently, in 1793, became a counsellor-at-law. In 1818, under an act passed for dividing the State into three judicial districts, he was appointed Judge of one, comprising the counties of Bergen, Morris, Essex and Sussex, and ex officio became President Judge of the several courts of each of these counties. The act was soon after repealed, and subsequently Judge Ford, who had been thus legislated out of office, was chosen an Associate Justice of the Supreme Court, and was twice re-elected, thus holding that position for twenty-one years, and would doubtless have been a fourth time chosen, had not his increasing years and infirm health warned him of the necessity of relinquishing the position. After he had retired from the bench, he was complimented by a series of resolutions, passed by the bar, in which they assured him of the high esteem in which they held him, "of his untiring patience in investigation, his purity, and his independence, which led him at all times to adopt, as a maxim, 'Be just, and fear not.'" He was everywhere regarded as the most efficient and eloquent of the lawyers of New Jersey. After his retirement from the bench he relinquished all professional duties, and passed his remaining years at his seat near Morristown, where he died, August 27th, 1849. His son, Henry A. Ford, is a member of the same bar at which his father was distinguished.

ERRY, GARRETT, Lawyer, was born, January 3d, 1832, at Hamburg, Sussex county, New Jersey, and is a son of Jesse and Elizabeth (Wisner) Berry, both of whom are natives of that county. His rudimentary education was obtained at the common schools of his district, which was supplemented by an academic course of study at the Newton Collegiate Institute; and in 1859 he finally graduated at the New Jersey State Normal School. In the following year he was appointed Superintendent of the State Farming School, at Beverly, in which position he remained one year, and thence removed to Rahway, and assumed charge of the public school in that city for a brief period. Subsequently, in conjunction with W. M. Phelps, he was appointed by the State superintendent, Lecturer and Conductor of Institutes throughout the State, which occupied his attention for the years 1861 and 1862. His leisure hours, meanwhile, had been devoted to the study of the law, having commenced his readings in view of that profession while he was a resident of Rahway in 1860; and in 1863 he was licensed as an attorney, and three years later as a counsellor-at-law. In 1866 he was elected City Attorney for Rahway, and at present (1876) is of counsel for the Union National Bank of Rahway. He has associated with him Mr. Lupton for the practice of the law, under the firm-name of Berry & Lupton, who are favorably and extensively known as able and successful practitioners. In political matters he is a Republican, and has been connected with that party since its organization. He was married, March 24th, 1859, to Lizzie Ludlam, of Dennisville, New Jersey.

OOLITTLE, REV. THEODORE S., D. D., Collegiate Church Professor of Rhetoric, Logic and Mental Philosophy, in Rutgers College, was born at Ovid, Seneca county, New York, November 30th, 1836. His parents were Solomon and Caroline (Satterly) Doolittle, the former being a native of Connecticut, and the latter of New York State. He obtained his early education in the Ovid academy, and having laid a good foundation in that establishment, entered Rutgers College as a student in the fall of 1855, and was graduated in 1859, having pursued a four years' course. Feeling himself called to the ministry, he then became a student in the New Brunswick Theological Seminary, where he prosecuted his theological studies until 1862. In July of that year he accepted a call to the pastorate of a church at Flatland, Kings county, New York, and continued his ministrations for two years. At the expiration of that period he was offered the Chair of Rhetoric, Logic and Mental Philosophy in Rutgers College, which he accepted and still fills. In 1872 he took a tour through Europe, visiting England, Ireland, Scotland, Italy, Belgium and other continental countries, gathering by the way much information in connection with the subjects taught from his chair, and a knowledge of methods in professional instruction which has added greatly to the acceptability of his teaching. On this trip he collected, also, many very fine specimens of ancient architecture. He is a powerful and elegant writer, and his contributions to the *Christian at Work*, of which he is a contributing editor, on the relations of science to religion, lend much interest and attractiveness to the columns of that journal. He was married, September 17th, 1862, to Mary A., daughter of Rev. Benjamin Bassler, of Farmer Village, Seneca county, New York.

HITEHEAD, HON. IRA C., Lawyer and Jurist, late of Morristown, was born, 1798, near Morristown, New Jersey. He received a thorough academical education preparatory to his matriculation at Princeton College, from which institution he graduated in 1816, having as classmates the late Bishop Charles J. McIlvaine, of Ohio, Rev. Dr.

John Maclean, and Judge Nevins, of the Supreme Court of New Jersey. After leaving college he commenced the study of law in the office of the late Joseph C. Hornblower, of Newark, afterwards Chief Justice of New Jersey, and received his license as an attorney in May, 1821; and became a counsellor-at-law three years later. He commenced the practice of his profession at Schooley's Mountain, where he only remained for a short time; and thence removed to Morristown, which became his future residence. He succeeded in building up an extensive and lucrative practice, and was considered to be an able and successful advocate. In November, 1841, he was chosen by the joint convention of the Council and Assembly a Judge of the Supreme Court, and filled the term of seven years for which he was elected. At the expiration of his term in 1848, the politics of the State had changed, and as he was in the ranks of the opposition another succeeded him. He immediately resumed the practice of his profession, and again became very successful. He was subsequently appointed Judge of the Court of Common Pleas in and for Morris County, and occupied the bench for several terms. He was a man of the most unblemished character, and was possessed of such a high degree of integrity that he was continually named by various persons as their executor, especially where the estates happened to be extensive. The business thus intrusted to him occupied his time and attention for many years. As a judge he was greatly respected, and his opinions, as reported, show him to have been a deep thinker, an able logician, and a most impartial jurist. He was a Whig in political doctrine, and being such failed to be re-elected judge in 1848. He was a true Christian, and most charitable in his gifts for objects of a religious and benevolent character. He married about 1822, and was the father of a daughter, who died, as also did his wife, before his own decease. In 1862 he was stricken with paralysis, but recovered. He died at Morristown, August 27th, 1867.

UTTOLPH, HORACE A., M. D., LL. D., Physician and Superintendent of the State Asylum for the Insane, at Morristown, New Jersey, was born, April 6th, 1815, in the township of North East, Dutchess county, New York, and is the son of Warren and Mary (McAllister) Buttolph. His father was also a native of New York, and followed agricultural pursuits; he was of German descent, the founder of the American branch of the family having emigrated from Germany at an early day and settled in Boston, Massachusetts. His mother was of Irish lineage. When Dr. Buttolph was quite young, his father removed to Pennsylvania and located within four miles of the site of the present thriving city of Scranton, which was then known as Slocum's Mill; and the doctor often visited the same, making his way on horseback through an almost uninhabited wilder-

a counsellor-at-law. In
[ne]y for Rahway, and at
e Union National Bank
with him Mr. Lupton for
he firm-name of Berry &
extensively known as his
political matters for is a
...ied with that pers...
...March 24th, 1857, his
ew Jersey.

BOWNE E. S., D. D., ...
...of age of ... and
Rutgers College, was born
..., New York, November
rea... were Solomon and
...die, the former being
latter of New York State.
...in the Ovid academy, and
that establishment, entered
the fall of 1855, and was
sued a four years' course.
...inistry, he then became a
...heological Seminary, where
...indies until 1862. In July
o the pastorate of a church
w York, and continued his
the expiration of that period
...hetoric, Logic, and Mental,
...which he accepted and still
r through Europe, visiting
ly, Belgium and other con-
...the way much information,
taught from his chair, and a
...sional instruction, which has
...ity of his teaching. On this
...ry-line specimens of ancient
...and elegant writer, and his
...at Work, of which he is a
...ations of science to religion,
...veness to the columns of that
ptember 17th, 1862, to Mary
...n Bassler, of Farmer Village,

IRA C., Lawyer and Jurist,
was born, 1798, near Morris-
. He received a thorough
...preparato... to his matricu
College, from which institu-
...n 1816, having as classmates
McIlvaine, of Ohio, Rev. Dr.

John Maclean, and Judge Nevins, of the Supreme Court of
New Jersey. After leaving college he commenced the
study of law in the office of the late Joseph C. Hornblower,
of Newark, afterwards Chief Justice of New Jersey, and received his license as an attorney in May, 1821; and became
a counsellor-at-law three years later. He commenced the
practice of his profession at Schooley's Mountain, where he
...ly remained for a short time; and thence removed to
...Morristown, which became his future residence. He succeeded in building up an extensive and lucrative practice,
...was considered to be an able and successful advocate.
In November, 1841, he was chosen by the joint convention
of the Council and Assembly a Judge of the Supreme Court,
...red the term of seven years for which he was elected.
At the expiration of his term in 1848, the politics of the
State had changed, and as he was in the ranks of the opposition another succeeded him. He immediately resumed
the practice of his profession, and again became very successful. He was subsequently appointed Judge of the Court
of Common Pleas in and for Morris County, and occupied
the bench for several terms. He was a man of the most
unblemished character, and was possessed of such a high
degree of integrity that he was continually named by various
persons as their executor, especially where the estates happened to be extensive. The business thus intrusted to him
occupied his time and attention for many years. As a judge
he was greatly respected, and his opinions, as reported,
show him to have been a deep thinker, an able logician, and
a most impartial jurist. He was a Whig in political doctrine, and being such, failed to be re-elected judge in 1848.
He was a true Christian and most charitable in his gifts for
objects of a religious and benevolent character. He married about 1822, and was the father of a daughter, who
died, as also did his wife, before his own decease. In 1862
he was stricken with paralysis, but recovered. He died at
Morristown, August 27th, 1867.

BUTTOLPH, HOLMES A., M. D., LL. D., Physician and Superintendent of the State Asylum
for the Insane, at Morristown, New Jersey, was
born, April 6th, 1815, in the township of North
East, Dutchess county, New York, and is the son
of Warren and Mary (McAllister) Buttolph. His
father was also a native of New York, and followed agricultural pursuits; he was of German descent, the founder of
the American branch of the family having emigrated from
Germany at an early day and settled in Boston, Massachusetts. His mother was of Irish lineage. When Dr. Buttolph was quite young, his father removed to Pennsylvania
...located within four miles of the site of the present thriving city of Scranton, which was then known as Slocum's
Mills; and the doctor often visited the same, making his
way on horseback through an almost uninhabited wilder-

ness. After a few years his father returned to Dutchess county, New York, where the son attended school until he was fourteen years of age; he afterwards became an inmate of the family of his maternal uncle, Dr. Charles McAllister, of South Lee, Berkshire county, Massachusetts. While residing with his uncle he became a pupil of the Stockbridge Academy, where he completed his education. Having resolved to devote his life to the medical profession, he commenced its study with his uncle, meanwhile teaching school and thus defraying his expenses incident to the same; in fact, the doctor sustained himself from the start, and is, in all respects, emphatically a self-made man. He attended three regular courses of lectures delivered at the Berkshire Medical College, Massachusetts, and graduated from that institution in 1835. Returning to Dutchess county, New York, he at once began the practice of his profession; but only remained there for a brief period, removing thence to Sharon, Litchfield county, Connecticut, where he resided for five years. He then went to New York city, and attended a course of medical lectures in the university of that city, at which time the late Dr. Valentine Mott was the leading surgeon. For some time previous to this period he had been deeply interested in mental science, and in the proper treatment of insane patients, and had already paid much attention to these subjects. As the asylum at Utica was about opening, in the winter of 1842-43, he made an effort to become one of the medical staff. He also visited the leading asylums in the New England States, and after his return was appointed assistant to Dr. Brigham, who had been called to take charge of the Utica Asylum, and he filled this situation about five years. In 1847 he was appointed Superintendent of the New Jersey State Lunatic Asylum, at Trenton; but before he accepted this responsible position, he visited many of the prominent asylums for insane patients in Great Britain, France and Germany, numbering in all some thirty institutions; so that he was enabled to enter upon his duties at Trenton with a full understanding of the best methods to pursue. He held this position uninterruptedly for nearly twenty-nine years, being thoroughly identified with every step of its progress, and relinquished it in April, 1876, to take charge of the State Asylum for the Insane, at Morristown, to which he had been elected in June, 1875. It may be here stated that, while acting as a member of a commission appointed by the Legislature of 1868-69 to select a site and prepare plans for a new institution in the State, Dr. Buttolph, in conjunction with Samuel Sloan, architect, of Philadelphia, arranged the design for a building which, with slight modification of detail, was subsequently adopted by the commissioners for erecting this. In the interim between his acceptance of this new charge and his actual assumption of its duties, he assisted the commissioners charged with the erection of the same, with his "great experience, practical skill, and rare good judgment," and he planned many of the features which render this institution one of the most perfect asylum buildings ever erected. The institution was opened for the admission of patients on the 17th day of August, since which, to this date (November 1st), a period of two and a half months, the large number of 346 have been received. It was commenced in the year 1872, and during that and the following years the sum of over $2,250,000 was expended in its construction. It has an imposing appearance, especially when viewed from the front, which stretches out in a continuous line 1270 feet in extent, each subdivision receding, until the rear of the two wings are about 600 feet distant from the front line of the central projecting edifice. All the buildings are fire-proof as far as stone, brick and iron can make them, and the stairways are of iron and slate. They are generally five stories high, including the basement, the upper story being finished with a mansard roof, ornamented with domes and turrets. The asylum is heated with steam throughout, supplied by eight boilers, which are placed in a building some distance in the rear of the central structure, and which also contains the bake-house, laundry, machine and work shops. To give an idea of the great extent of the edifice, it may be stated that nearly eight acres of floor, over thirteen miles of base-board, 2000 doors, 2500 windows have been placed in the several stories; and the area of the plastered walls is somewhat over thirty-three acres. There are between 4000 and 5000 radiators, and about 3000 registers connected with the heating apparatus; while some eight miles of iron pipe have been laid to convey gas, water and steam. The gas used is made on the premises in a separate building erected for the purpose; while other structures, such as barns, stables, carriage-houses, ice-houses, slaughter-houses, etc., have been put up during the present year (1876). Dr. Buttolph is most enthusiastically devoted to his profession, particularly in his specialty, which, indeed, has been almost a life-long study with him. In 1872 he was honored by Princeton College with the degree of Doctor of Laws. He was married, in 1838, to Catharine, daughter of George King, of Sharon, Connecticut. She died in 1851. In 1854 he was united in marriage to Mrs. Maria R. Gardner, daughter of John Syng Dorsey, M. D., Professor of Anatomy in the University of Pennsylvania.

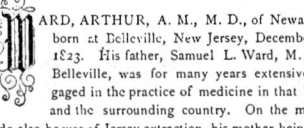ARD, ARTHUR, A. M., M. D., of Newark, was born at Belleville, New Jersey, December 23d, 1823. His father, Samuel L. Ward, M. D., of Belleville, was for many years extensively engaged in the practice of medicine in that locality and the surrounding country. On the maternal side also he was of Jersey extraction, his mother being Caroline Bruen, of Newark. His preliminary education was obtained partly in Newark, whence he proceeded to the Bacon Academy, at Colchester, Connecticut. Having completed his preparation for a university course at this academy he entered Yale College in 1840. At this famous seat of

learning he spent four years in diligent student, graduating in 1844, and having conferred on him in due course the degree of A. M. Selecting the medical profession, he immediately commenced his studies under the tutorship of his father and the eminent physician, Dr. Thomas Cock, of New York, who was one of the founders of the College of Physicians and Surgeons of that city. At this institution he attended lectures, and from it he graduated in the fall of 1847. He at once entered upon the active duties of his profession in Newark, where he practised for óne year, when he took up his residence at Belleville. At this place and in Newark he was successfully engaged until 1865. In that year he returned to Newark to reside, and has continued to practise there with steadily increasing success to the present time. He has now been in active practice for nearly thirty years, and during this period he has devoted himself exclusively to the promotion of the interests of his noble profession, always commanding the respect and esteem of the profession at large, as well as the entire confidence of all who have come under his care. In the medical associations with which he is and has been connected he has always taken an active interest. He is a member of the Essex District Medical Society ; also, the Essex Medical Union. Of the Connecticut Medical Society he is a corresponding member, and for the year 1876 was a delegate to the New Jersey State Medical Society from the district society. He was married in 1854 to Anna C., daughter of Robert Lee, of Rahway.

RAKE, HON. GEORGE K., Lawyer and Jurist, late of Morristown, was born, 1788, in Morris county, New Jersey, and was a son of Colonel Jacob Drake, and his mother was a sister of Jonathan Dickerson, and aunt of Governor Mahlon Dickerson. He received his preparatory education at the hands of Rev. Dr. Armstrong, of Mendham, and subsequently entered Princeton College, from which institution he graduated in 1808, having as classmates the late Bishop Meade, of Virginia, and Judge Wayne, of the United States Supreme Court. After leaving college he made choice of the profession of the law as his future avocation, and chose as his preceptor therein Sylvester Russell, of Morristown. After the usual course of study he was licensed as an attorney in 1812, became a counsellor in 1815, and was appointed serjeant-at-law in 1834. Shortly after his admission to the bar he commenced the practice of his profession at Morristown, where he continued until he was appointed Judge. In 1823 he was elected a member of Assembly, and was re-elected three several times; during his last two terms in that body, he was chosen Speaker of the House. In December, 1826, at a joint meeting of the Council and Assembly, he was chosen Justice of the Supreme Court, to succeed Judge Russell. Shortly after his

appointment he removed to Burlington, where he remained but a short time, however, and ultimately chose Trenton as his residence, and where he remained until the expiration of his term of office. The opinion which he gave in the case of Hendrickson vs. Decow operated against his reappointment, although generally admitted to be correct. This opinion was adverse to the Hicksites' cause, and they helped to elect, in 1833, a large majority of Democrats to the Legislature, mainly to defeat the re-election of Judge Drake. Upon the termination of his office he returned to Morristown, where he resumed the practice of his profession. Religiously he was a Presbyterian, and an active and zealous member of that communion. He died suddenly, while on a visit to his brother-in-law, Dr. Woodruff, at Drakesville, in 1837.

UNT, EZRA M., M. D., of Metuchen, was born in that place on January 4th, 1830. His father, Rev. H. W. Hunt, was for many years the beloved pastor of the First Presbyterian Church, Metuchen, and was a Jerseyman, having been born in Hunterdon county. The family, however, came originally from Westchester county, New York. Having received a superior elementary training, Ezra attended Irving Institute, at Tarrytown, New York, where he continued from 1840 to 1845, and prepared for college. He entered Princeton College in the latter year, and graduated therefrom in 1849. The life of a physician being that to which his tastes led, he then began the study of medicine under the superintendence of Dr. Abram Coles, an eminent practitioner of Newark, New Jersey, at the same time attending lectures at the College of Physicians and Surgeons, of New York, from which, after a three years' course, he received his degree of M. D., in March, 1852. After graduating he located himself in Metuchen, but did not long remain in that place at that time, being, in 1853, appointed Lecturer on Materia Medica and Therapeutics, in the Vermont Medical College, at Woodstock. In the following year he was chosen Professor of Chemistry in the same institution. During 1855 he concluded to resume his profession, and returned to Metuchen. There he was successfully engaged until 1862, when he was impelled by patriotic motives to join the Union army. He entered the service for nine months, as Assistant Surgeon of the 29th New Jersey Infantry. After serving with the regiment for two months he was detached to take charge of the Calvert Street Hospital, Baltimore, where he did duly until the expiration of his term. Returning to Metuchen, he once more resumed the labors of private practice, in which he has since been continuously occupied, and with steadily increasing success. In his profession he enjoys a high reputation, both as a physician and an author. He is a member of the Middlesex County Medical Society, and has been many times a delegate to the State Medical Society, of which he is a Fellow, having acted as its President in 1865. He was one of the delegates who represented the State Medical Society of New Jersey in the Convention of the American Medical Association held in Philadelphia, from June 6th to June 10th, 1876, and was also a delegate from the State to the International Medical Congress, held in Philadelphia in September, 1876. Among the medical works that have emanated from his pen may be mentioned the "Physicians' Counsel," and "Patients' and Physicians' Aid." But he is known in authorship outside of the professional pale. Among the more prominent of his literary works may be named "Grace Culture," published by the Presbyterian Board of Publication, and "A Commentary on the Old and New Testaments," published by Scribner & Co., of New York. Various other works of minor importance have been given to the public by him. During 1863 and 1864 he was a member of the Board of Enrolment from the Third Congressional District. He has been twice married. His first wife, Emma L. Ayres, of Rahway, he espoused in 1853; she died in 1867. The second marriage took place in 1870, and was contracted with Emma Reeve, of Allowaystown, New Jersey.

ROWN, HON. GEORGE H., Lawyer and Jurist, late of Somerville, was born in 1810, and was the son of Rev. Isaac V. Brown, D. D., for a long time principal of a classical academy at Lawrenceville, and where he received a thorough training previous to entering college. He graduated with the class of 1828 from Nassau Hall, and afterwards became an assistant in his father's school, where he remained about two years. Having determined to embrace the legal profession, he entered for a while the law office of Thomas A. Hartwell, of Somerville; but subsequently he became a student in the law department of Yale College. He was licensed as an attorney in 1835, and became a counsellor in 1838. He immediately opened an office in Somerville, which town he likewise made his residence, and continued there throughout his life. His success was a good one from the first, and he soon had the control of an extensive and lucrative business, being a thoroughly able lawyer. He was a member of the convention which assembled in 1844 to frame the new State Constitution, in which body he took an active part. When this new Constitution was adopted, he was nominated by the Whigs as Senator from Somerset county, and was elected, although the county was considered a sound Democratic district. He was elected, in 1850, a member of Congress, but failed to be re-elected in 1852, the district giving a majority to his opponent. In 1861, when Judge Whelpley was appointed Chief-justice, he was nominated by Governor Olden, to fill the vacancy created by such promotion, and duly confirmed by the Senate. The selection was an excellent one, and his course as a Judge was eminently satisfactory; but he was

not destined to continue in the high position which he was so well qualified to fill. He was desirous of resigning, but was urged to remain while there appeared any hope of recovery. But a disease, which baffled the skill of the most skilful physicians, soon after his resignation was accepted, terminated his life in 1865.

LACKWELL, LEWIS S., M. D., of Perth Amboy, was born at Pennington, New Jersey, January 23d, 1833. His parents, Henry and Rebecca (Titus) Blackwell, were both natives of the State, and gave their son a good education. He first attended the academy in Pennington, and afterward the New Jersey Conference Seminary at the same place, the latter being an old-established and popular institution of learning. Being drawn by taste toward the medical profession, he began to read medicine shortly after leaving the seminary, having for his preceptor his brother, Dr. E. T. Blackwell. In 1854 he attended a course of lectures at Vermont Medical College, at Woodstock, Vermont. During the three subsequent years he attended the University of Pennsylvania, and graduated therefrom in the spring of 1857. After graduation he located at Wertsville, Hunterdon county, New Jersey, where, however, he remained only a short time. In 1858 he returned to Pennington, where he practised successfully until 1872, having in the mean time attended a course of lectures in Bellevue Hospital Medical College. During that year he transferred his labors to Bound Brook, New Jersey, and continued in that field for two years, when he located in Perth Amboy, where he is now residing in the enjoyment of a large and growing practice. In 1867 he was elected a member of the Board of Chosen Freeholders of Mercer County, which office he held for two years. His wife, Charlotte Ogden Waters, to whom he was married April 28th, 1859, is a native of Millville, New Jersey.

CHOMP, JOHN, Lawyer, of Somerville, was born, June 2d, 1843, in Readington, Hunterdon county, New Jersey, and is a son of Jacob G. Schomp, a farmer and builder of that county. He was prepared for college at first under private instruction, and at Claverack Institute, New York. He entered the sophomore class of Rutgers College, New Brunswick, in 1859, and had as classmates Judge Reed, A. J. Garretson, and others, since prominent in the legal profession. After leaving college he commenced preparing himself for admission to the bar, with the eminent law-firm of Brown, Hall & Vanderpool, of New York city, where he remained for some time; but as his health began to fail, he abandoned his studies for a year. He subsequently became a student in the office of B. Van Syckel, now one of the

Justices of the Supreme Court of New Jersey, where he remained until his admission to the bar, in 1866. In the early part of the following year he opened an office and commenced practice in Somerville, where he still resides. His ability and integrity have won for him not only the confidence and esteem of his fellow-townsmen, but also a large and lucrative business. He is a Democrat in political faith, and ardently attached to the principles of that party, although he has never sought any official position at the hands of that organization. He has in the past rendered excellent service for the party in eloquently defending its principles and candidates. He is regarded in his profession as a safe counsellor, and judicious in the management of his clients' interests. He was married, in 1869, to Wilhelmina Schomp, of Hunterdon county, New Jersey.

TOCKTON, CHARLES S., DD. S., of Newark, was born in Springfield township, Burlington county, New Jersey, on December 17th, 1836. His parents were Staccy and Eliza (Roselle) Stockton, both natives of the same State. On his paternal side he is descended from the old Stockton family, so long and thoroughly identified with the State of New Jersey. His education was principally obtained at the New Jersey Conference Seminary of the Methodist Episcopal Church, at Pennington, from which institution he graduated with the first honors of his class on July 28th, 1855, being chosen to deliver the valedictory oration on that occasion. Having been attracted to the dental profession, he commenced, in the fall of 1855, the study of dentistry in the office of Dr. George C. Brown, of Mount Holly, New Jersey, with whom he remained for about one year, when he entered the office of Dr. C. A. Kingsbury, a long-established dentist, also of Mount Holly at that time, but more widely known of late years as one of the founders of the celebrated Dental College of Pennsylvania. Having fitted himself for the practice of dentistry, Dr. Stockton, in March, 1857, purchased the property and practice of Dr. Kingsbury, and soon met with flattering success, and was engaged in an extensive and lucrative practice here up to the summer of 1872, when he removed to Newark, purchasing the property there on Cedar street which for many years was occupied by the Messrs. Colburn, the leading dentists of Newark in their day. Here Dr. Stockton again acquired a lucrative and constantly-increasing patronage, which he continues to enjoy, and is in all probability the leading dental practitioner in Newark. Fully appreciating, however, the great importance of being thoroughly learned in the real science and practice of his profession, he availed himself of the benefit of a full course of lectures at the Pennsylvania College of Dental Surgery, where he was graduated with the highest honors, February 29th, 1868. An enthusiast in his profession, Dr. Stockton has taken great pride in elevating the standard of its members, etc. He was actively instrumental in aiding the organization of the New Jersey State Dental Association, in 1870, and has always taken a lively interest in its deliberations. Upon its formation he was chosen Vice-President and elected to deliver the public address at the first annual meeting, which was held at Newark, in July, 1871. His discourse on this occasion embodied a concise history of dentistry from the early ages to the present period, accompanied by a number of excellent practical suggestions touching the elements of professional success. The address received many encomiums from its hearers, and its publication was ordered by the society. At the annual meeting of the society, held at Long Branch in the summer of 1872, he contributed an interesting paper entitled " On What we Live." He has been called upon to act in various official capacities in the State society, viz., Chairman of the Executive Committee of the society and also of the State Board of Examiners. In July, 1875, he was honored with the Presidency of the society, which office he now holds. In February, 1874, he was elected President of the Alumni Association of the Pennsylvania College of Dental Surgery for the ensuing year. Notwithstanding his devotion to his profession, he has also found time to aid and promote in various ways the welfare of the communities in which he has resided. During his sojourn at Mount Holly he represented his church in the Episcopal Diocesan Convention of New Jersey. While not caring for political honors, he has at the same time recognized the duty each citizen owes in this direction, and has, a number of times, been a delegate in the county, State and district conventions of his party. He was married in 1857 to Martha Smith, of Perth Amboy.

RAIG, DAVID STEWART, M. D., Physician, of Rahway, was a native of that place, having been born there, September 22d, 1776. His parents were David Craig and Catherine Terrill, and his grandparents on the father's side were Timothy Craig and Jane Stewart. Through his grandmother he was of Scotch descent, her father, David Stewart, having come to this country from Edinburgh, Scotland, and settled in Woodbridge. David Stewart Craig, in his boyhood, attended a select school in his native place, and his natural aptness and his early habits of hard work rendered his acquisition of knowledge rapid and effectual. It was early decided that he was to enter the medical profession. Indeed that was the hereditary profession of his family. His father, David Craig, was a physician, and his great-grandfather, David Stewart, was the first physician who practised in Woodbridge, where he settled after his arrival from Edinburgh. After his term of attendance at the select school had expired the young David entered at once upon the study of medicine. He was placed in the office of Dr. Samuel Bard, of New York, and continued under the instruction of that practitioner until the completion of his course of study. He received his diploma in the year 1797, when he had just attained his majority. He returned to Rahway and at once commenced the practice of his profession there. He speedily rose in favor, and while still a young man found himself possessed of a large and increasing patronage. His energy in the performance of his chosen work was great; he was an indefatigable student, and kept well up with the progress of medical science, and his skill and success were remarkable. He advanced rapidly to acknowledged eminence, and during fifty years of unremitting practice in Rahway he maintained a leading position in his profession. As a man and a citizen, no less than as a physician, did he win and retain the esteem of those about him. He was public-spirited in a high degree, and all movements for the welfare of the community received his hearty and active co-operation. He was especially active in the removal of the mill-dams, a work which, at the time, awakened the interest and commanded much of the attention of the community in which he lived. He died, November 9th, 1866, widely and sincerely mourned, and his memory is still cherished with high esteem.

ILLY, HON. SAMUEL, M. D., Physician, Statesman and Jurist, of Lambertville, was born, October 28th, 1815, in Geneva, Ontario county, New York, and is a son of William Lilly. He is of English descent, his grandfather, Samuel Lilly, being the emigrant ancestor of the American branch of the family. He was a barrister by profession in England; and, being a fine classical and belles-lettres scholar, on his arrival in America he adopted the profession of a teacher, and established himself at first in New York city, and afterwards went to Albany. At the instance of warm personal friends, he took orders in and became a clergyman of the Protestant Episcopal Church. In the course of time he became Rector of St. John's Church, Elizabethtown, New Jersey; and while there he officiated at the marriage ceremony of Lord Bolingbroke, then a resident of that ancient borough. His son, William Lilly, the father of Dr. Samuel Lilly, was placed at an early age in the extensive house of E. C. Cane & Co., who were engaged in the East India trade, and where he acquired all the information necessary to form the attainments of a successful merchant. He afterwards removed to Geneva, thence to Penn Yan, subsequently to New York city, and finally settled at Lambertville, New Jersey. In 1829 his son Samuel, who at that time was about fourteen years of age, commenced the study of the classics with his uncle, Dr. John Lilly, a prominent physician, who had been a resident practitioner of medicine in Lambertville since 1809; he also received instruction from Rev. P. O. Studiford, D. D., an eminent Presbyterian clergyman. Having decided to embrace the medical profession, he entered the medical department of the University of Pennsylvania, and graduated therefrom with the degree of M. D. in 1837. He immediately entered upon the practice of his profession at Lambertville, and soon acquired the control of an extensive and lucrative business and reputation. He is a leading member of the Hunterdon Medical Society and of the New Jersey State Medical Society, in both of which he has held all the leading offices, and is now Vice-President of the American Medical Association. In 1852 he was elected by the Democratic party to the Thirty-third Congress; and during the term for which he was elected served as Chairman of the Committee on Expenditures of the Post-office Department, and was also a member of the Committee on Agriculture. The Thirty-third Congress has become historical on account of the "Cansas-Nebraska" struggle, and the passage of legislative acts virtually repealing the "Missouri Compromise." His Congressional career was marked by his earnest efforts to check the turbulent passions, promote a better and more fraternal feeling between the sections and allay the stormy passions, which finally culminated in the civil war. He was renominated in 1854, but the Cnow-Nothing movement prevented his re-election. He was, however, chosen to fill several important local offices both in the city and county where he resided. He was elected, in 1849, the first Mayor of Lambertville, and re-elected for three succeeding years. For eight years he was Director of the Board of Freeholders for Hunterdon county. In January, 1861, he was appointed, by President Buchanan, Consul-General to British India, to reside at Calcutta. During his connection with the consulate the civil war, and our relations with England growing out of the Mason and Slidell affair, rendered the administration of the occupant of the position one of great responsibility. Some American merchant vessels, partly loaded with saltpetre, were detained at Calcutta during the Mason and Slidell excitement. Dr. Lilly contended vigorously for the rights of the American traders, who were then allowed to depart. Previous to his leaving Calcutta for the United States, the American merchants resident in that city presented him with a handsome service of plate, in token of the esteem in which he was held by them; and on his arrival at his home, in Lambertville, he was welcomed by an ovation at the hands of his fellow-townsmen. In 1868 he was appointed Judge of the Court of Common Pleas for the County of Hunterdon, and served for the term of five years in that capacity. In 1871 he was appointed one of the Commissioners to locate and build the new State Lunatic Asylum. The site selected was at Morristown, and it is now completed and occupied. It is one of the largest and best designed institutions of the kind on the continent, and reflects credit on the State and the Board of Commissioners. In 1873 he was appointed by Governor Parker one of the Judges of the Court of Errors and Appeals, which position he still retains. He is also a director of the Flemington Railroad Company; President of the Centre Bridge Company, and President of the Lambertville Savings Bank. He is a prominent member of the Masonic order and of the Independent Order of Odd Fellows, in each of which organizations he has held the most important positions. As a man of irreproachable character he is universally respected; and however men may differ with him on political questions, or on public affairs, his most bitter political opponents have never called in question his probity, or his earnest desire for the public good.

IRKPATRICK, HON. ANDREW, Lawyer and Jurist, late of New Brunswick, was born, February 17th, 1756, in Somerset county, New Jersey, and was the third son of David and Mary (McEwan) Kirkpatrick, and a grandson of Alexander Kirkpatrick, the emigrant ancestor of the family. The latter was a native of Scotland, who had removed first to Belfast, Ireland, where he lived a few years, and subsequently, in 1736, sailed with his family to America. He settled in Somerset county, New Jersey, near Basking Ridge, where he died in 1758. His second son, David, was, like his father, a rigid Presbyterian, and of plain and unassuming habits, highly respected for his unswerving integrity and great perseverance; he attained the great age of over fourscore years and ten, and died in 1814. Andrew received the best education attainable in the vicinity of his birthplace, and graduated at Princeton College in 1775. His father had educated him especially to enter the ministry of the Presbyterian Church; and after he left college he commenced the study of divinity with the Rev. Mr. Kennedy, a distinguished theologian, at Basking Ridge; but after a short time he abandoned the idea of entering the ministry and expressed his determination to become a student at law. His father appears to have been much chagrined at the change in his son's views, and declined to assist him in obtaining the instruction needed to attain the desired end; so he was compelled to rely upon his own exertions, and he left home, with his mother's blessing and her parting gift of some golden pieces—the savings of years. He went to Virginia, and became a tutor in the family of Colonel Taliaferro, at Hagley, near Fredericksburg, King George's county, the same household where Hon. Samuel L. Southard subsequently taught; and after remaining there a brief period went to Esopus (now Kingston), in Ulster county, New York; and he afterwards returned to New Jersey, where he obtained a position as teacher of the classics at Rutgers College Grammar School, at New Brunswick. During this whole period he occupied his leisure hours in the study of the law, and subsequently entered the office of William Paterson—afterwards governor—as a regular student, and was licensed as an attorney in 1785. He

located in Morristown, and achieved success from the start; but met with an unfortunate accident two years later—the destruction of his effects, including his library, by fire— and accordingly returned to New Brunswick, which for the future became his residence, and where he acquired an excellent and constantly increasing practice. In 1797 he was elected a member of the Assembly from Middlesex county, and, after serving a short time in that body, was appointed, by the joint meeting of the two houses, an Associate Justice of the Supreme Court, to fill the vacancy occasioned by the resignation of Judge Chetwood. In 1803, after the death of Chief-Justice Kinsey, he was elected Chief-Justice, and was twice afterwards re-elected, thus passing a period of twenty-seven years on the bench of that court, a longer service than any other judge, except Isaac Smith, who only exceeded him by one year. While Chief-Justice he was elected, in 1820, a member of the Legislative Council, the old constitution of the State allowing such a practice; but the session was a brief one, lasting but four weeks, and eventually adjourning without day. His term expired in 1824, and he passed the remainder of his days in comparative retirement, rarely appearing in court, though he occasionally was called upon to give professional advice to some of his old clients. He was noted for his deep knowledge of the old English common law, especially of all that relating to the law of real estate; and his opinions in various cases, where the latter were called in question, are regarded as models of deep learning, sound reasoning and polished language. He became a Trustee of Princeton College in 1809, and seldom failed in his attendance upon the meetings of the Board. He was married, in 1792, to Jane, daughter of Colonel John Bayard, formerly of Pennsylvania, and a distinguished officer in the continental army. Judge Kirkpatrick died in 1831.

ORNBLOWER, HON. JOSEPH C., LL. D., Lawyer and Chief-Justice of New Jersey, was born, May 6th, 1777, at Belleville, Essex county, in that State, and was the youngest son of the Hon. Josiah Hornblower. His father was an Englishman, and a civil engineer by profession, who came to America in 1753. He was a member of the Legislature and a delegate to the Continental Congress; he died in 1809, aged eighty years. Joseph, although unable to obtain a collegiate education, nevertheless received some very valuable instruction in the classical academy at Orange, and he applied himself closely; his father also freely imparted his mathematical learning. His health from childhood was feeble, and when only sixteen years of age he had a paralytic attack, from which he was a considerable time recovering. He subsequently went to New York city, where he entered the employ of one of his brothers-in-law, who was engaged in mercantile business, and remained with him

some time. But having resolved to lead a professional life he returned to New Jersey, and entered the office of David B. Ogden,.of Newark, who at that time was becoming a prominent advocate, and was subsequently one of the ornaments of the profession in New York city. He studied with him for the prescribed term of five years, and was licensed as an attorney in February, 1803, becoming a counsellor in 1806, and ten years later receiving the highest dignity, that of serjeant-at-law. Before his admission to practice he was associated with his preceptor as a partner; his business soon became a large and valuable one, and he early took rank with the first lawyers of the State. In November, 1832, he was appointed, by the joint meeting of Council and Assembly, Chief-Justice of the Supreme Court of New Jersey, to take the place vacated by the death of Chief-Justice Ewing, and was re-elected in 1839, thus serving in that capacity for fourteen years, retiring in 1846. His decisions during this period were marked by learning, legal acumen and high moral principle; they occupy several volumes of the "New Jersey Law Reports." His well-known decision, in 1856, that Congress had no right to pass a fugitive slave law, was one which, though reversed, attracted much attention. In 1844 he was one of the most prominent members of the convention called to frame a new constitution for the State; and he strenuously endeavored to obtain the insertion of a clause putting an end to slavery in the State, in which, however, he was unsuccessful. After his retirement from the bench he resumed the practice of his profession, but not to any very appreciable extent. During his incumbency as Chief-Justice the College of New Jersey conferred on him the honorary degree of Doctor of Laws; and in 1847 he was, by the trustees of that institution, appointed the Professor of Law, with the hope that he would remove to Princeton and assist in building up a permanent school of law; but as no provision had been made for an adequate salary, and as he was unwilling to leave a residence where he had passed so many years, although he accepted the appointment and delivered a course of lectures, there was not sufficient encouragement given him to remain, and he soon after resigned the chair. Politically he was a Federalist, and afterwards became a Whig, and more recently a Republican; he was a strong anti-slavery man, as evinced by his attempt, as already stated, to insert in the State constitution a clause abolishing that institution. In 1856 he was Chairman of the New Jersey delegation and Vice-President of the Philadelphia Convention, which nominated General Fremont for the Presidency on the Republican ticket. In 1820 he was one of the Electors, and cast his vote for James Monroe, and in 1860 was President of the Electoral College of New Jersey, who cast the vote of that State for Lincoln and Hamlin. Religiously, he was for many years a member of the Presbyterian Church, and a ruling elder of the same; he was one of the original members of the American Bible Society; President of the New Jersey Colonization Society;

President of the Society for Promoting Collegiate and Theological Education in the West; and also President of the New Jersey Historical Society from its inception, besides being connected with many of the religious organizations of the day, contributing largely of his means to their furtherance and support. In private life he was a gentleman of urbane manners, a good conversationalist and an interesting companion. He was a thoroughly honest and truthful man, and all with whom he was brought in contact were charmed with his society and his happily expressed sentiments. When a young man, and just admitted to the bar, he married a granddaughter of Dr. William Burnet, who brought him a large family of children, most of whom survived him. She died many years ago. After he had been a widower for some time he married a daughter of Colonel John Kinney, of Morris county, with whom he lived most happily, and who soothed his declining years with the most tender attention. He died at his residence, in the city of Newark, June 11th, 1864, in the eighty-eighth year of his age.

ORRIS, THEODORE FRELINGHUYSEN, M. D., Physician, of Jersey City, was born in New Brunswick, New Jersey, December 30th, 1831. He is descended from revolutionary stock, his great-grandfather, Jonathan T. Morris, having been a commissioned officer in the revolutionary army, who was wounded in the battle of Trenton and died at the head-quarters of General Lafayette, at Morristown, New Jersey. Theodore's father, William Cullen Morris, was a native of New Jersey, and a lawyer. For thirty years he served as Prosecutor of the Pleas for Warren County, in his native State, having his residence at Belvidere. It was at the classical academy at this place that Theodore F. Morris received his education. The habits of hard work and patient study which characterized him later in life were early formed, and enabled him to obtain from his academic course of study such abundant results as do not often follow more ample opportunities. It was almost a foregone conclusion that he should enter the medical profession. His grandfathers, both on the father's side and the mother's side, had been physicians, and had both held the position of President of the New Jersey State Medical Society. It seemed the natural thing for him to do, therefore, to study medicine; and accordingly, when he had reached the age of eighteen, he commenced a course of preparatory reading. In the winter of 1854 and 1855 he matriculated at the University of New York. There he took the fullest advantage of the opportunities afforded him, studied hard and made excellent progress. In the spring of 1855, after passing examination before the Board of Censors, he was licensed by the New Jersey State Medical Society to practise as a physician. He at once settled in Jersey City, and there entered upon a professional career which has been characterized by constant and progressive success. He was admirably adapted by nature to the profession he had chosen, and his culture and acquirements were already large. He speedily became known as a careful and skilful practitioner, who conquered the confidence of the community, and hence he was soon the possessor of a large and valuable patronage. He continued his habits of close study, and thereby kept himself abreast of his profession in its most advanced progress. As a result his patronage grew, and he rose rapidly and steadily to a high rank in his profession, which he has always maintained and in which he has the cordial recognition of his professional brethren and of the community at large. In the winter of 1862 and 1863 he attended a course of lectures at Bellevue College, receiving a diploma from that institution in the spring of 1863. He is a leading member of the District Medical Society of Hudson, and has several times served as the delegate of that society to the State Medical Society. He was a delegate to the convention of the American Medical Association, held in June, 1876. He was one of the organizers of the Jersey City Charity Hospital, and serves on its medical staff. He is also one of the staff of the Hudson County Church Hospital. He acted on the staff of St. Francis' Hospital from the time of its organization up to July, 1873. For several years he was Physician to the Children's Home in Jersey City, and for a number of years acted as City Physician. In the early stage of his practice he served a term of three years as Coroner of Hudson County. In 1863, when the call was made for army surgeons, he at once offered his services, but his efforts to be placed on active duty at "the front" were unsuccessful. He is enthusiastically devoted to his profession, and frequently contributes to its literature. He was married in 1855 to Gertrude Johnson, a granddaughter of Stephen Vreeland.

———◦◦◦———

ROWN, HON. THOMAS S. R., Merchant, Keyport, was born in Middlesex county, New Jersey. His father, Benjamin L. Brown, by occupation a farmer and builder, and his mother, whose maiden name was Susan Brown, were both natives of the same State. His youth was passed on his father's farm, and his education was obtained during this period in the county public schools. When sixteen years of age he was placed to learn the mason's trade, and upon acquiring this he embarked in the coasting trade, in which he was engaged for two years. In the winter of 1846 he settled in Keyport, New Jersey, where he went into business as a mason and builder. This, with marked and constant success, he continued up to 1864, when he entered mercantile life, dealing mainly in hardware, lumber and coal. He has always been an active and influential Democrat, and as such was elected one of the first commissioners of Keyport, a position which he held during 1870 and 1871.

He was a Chosen Freeholder for three years, and in 1866 and 1867 was elected by his party to the Legislature, where he served with good effect for two terms, and headed the Committee on Engrossed Bills the second year. He has been identified with all efforts to secure local improvements, and is esteemed as an active, public-spirited citizen, an excellent official and progressive merchant.

———◦◦◦———

COTT, JOSEPH WARREN, L.L.D., Lawyer, late of New Brunswick, New Jersey, was born, November 28th, 1778, in that town, and was the son of Dr. Moses Scott, and the grandson of John Scott, a native of Scotland, who emigrated to America at an early date, settling in Bucks county, Pennsylvania. Prior to the revolutionary war Dr. Scott removed to New Brunswick, where he resided until his death, engaged in the practice of medicine. During the war for independence he was professionally engaged in the army, and was present at the battles of Princeton and Brandywine. He was created, by a special act of Congress, Senior Physician and Surgeon of the General Army Hospital of the Middle District. He was a warm and intimate friend of Generals Washington and Warren. The latter, it will be remembered, was a physician, and fell at the battle of Bunker Hill. Dr. Scott had given his eldest son the name of the patriot physician, but the child died in its infancy, and he continued the name to his second son. The latter attended the schools of his native town, and also at Elizabethtown, preparatory to entering college. He graduated at Princeton, in 1795, before he had attained the age of seventeen years. He first appears to have selected the medical profession as his future role, and became a student in his father's office. He soon abandoned this, and then entertained the idea of becoming a clergyman. After a short course in theology he again changed his mind, and resolved to embrace the legal profession. With this view he entered the office of General Frederick Frelinghuysen, in New Brunswick, and was licensed as an attorney in 1801, becoming a counsellor three years later, and was finally made a serjeant-at-law in 1816. After his admission to the bar, in 1801, he commenced practice in his native city, in which he continued to reside until the end of his life. He was a most profound lawyer and able barrister and counsellor, and his practice was a large and lucrative one. He was appointed Prosecutor of the Pleas for the County of Middlesex, but beyond this never held any official position. He retired, in a measure, from practice about 1840; but as late as 1857, when nearly eighty years of age, he defended a criminal charged with murder, and made a powerful argument against the validity of the indictment. He was a supporter of General Jackson for the Presidency, and was one of the Electoral College of New Jersey who cast their ballots for that candidate in 1824. He was a prominent member of the Order of the Cincinnati, entering the New Jersey Society in 1825, as the eldest surviving son of his father, Dr. Moses Scott. In 1832 he was elected Assistant Treasurer of the general society, and in 1838 became the Treasurer-general. In 1840 he was elected Vice-President of the State Society, and in 1844 became its President. In 1868, when he had reached the age of fourscore years and ten, he was present at the inauguration of Rev. Dr. James McCosh as President of the College of New Jersey, and with his associate, Judge Herring, were the two oldest living graduates of Princeton College. While he was a student in that institution the Rev. Dr. John Witherspoon was still its president, and as such conferred on him the degree of Bachelor of Arts. On this occasion, one of the first acts of the new incumbent was to make him the recipient of the honorary degree of Doctor of Laws. He was a most accomplished gentleman, well versed in the Latin tongue, and was wont to correspond with his friends in that language up to his latest year; he was likewise an excellent English scholar, and thoroughly acquainted with the old poets. In early life he had been honored by one of the governors of the State as a member of his staff, with the rank of Colonel; and by this appellation he was more familiarly known. He died in New Brunswick in May, 1871, having nearly reached the great age of ninety-three years.

HACKLETON, JUDSON G., M. D., Physician, of Matawan, was born in Belvidere, New Jersey, June 16th, 1836. His father was Hon. Benjamin Shackleton, who, although he was a merchant by occupation, for many years occupied the bench of Warren county, and who now resides in Jersey City. Judge Shackleton's wife was Ellen Stull, a native of Pennsylvania. Their son, Judson, received his education at the select schools of Belvidere. It was early decided that he should enter the medical profession, and accordingly when he left school, at the age of eighteen, he entered the office of Dr. R. Byington, an old and prominent practitioner of Belvidere. He remained here as a student until 1855, when he matriculated at the New York Medical University. His preliminary reading had been diligent and thorough, so he entered the institution fully prepared to avail himself to the utmost of every advantage offered. During his university course he continued his close and studious application, and his progress was rapid and pronounced. He graduated in the spring of 1857, and at once settled at what was then Middletown Point, but what is now known as Matawan. Here he commenced the practice of his profession, and so decided was his natural fitness for his career, and so thorough had been his preparation for it, that he advanced rapidly toward success, and in a comparatively short time found himself in the possession of an extensive and lucrative practice. He entered the army September 20th, 1862, as Assistant Surgeon of the 29th New Jersey Volunteers, and served with that regiment for a period of nine months. With the exception of that interval, his residence and practice at Matawan have been uninterrupted since his settlement there after receiving his diploma. He stands high in his profession, and the entire confidence of the community is accorded to him. He was married, October 26th, 1864, to Cordelia M. Rose, of New York city.

EMKE, REV. HENRY, of Elizabeth, Clergyman and Priest of the Order of St. Benedict, was born, July 27th, 1796, in the Grand Duchy of Mecklenburg, Germany, and is descended from an old Lutheran family. He received his education in the Colleges and University of Mecklenburg-Rostock, and was intended by his family for a medical career. When but a youth and a student he volunteered, as did many of his compatriots, to serve in the army against Napoleon, and was attached to the corps commanded by Blucher, which participated in the battle of Waterloo, and there he witnessed the overthrow of the usurper. After the war was over he resolved to become a Lutheran clergyman, having been reared in that faith; but the lax ideas then prevalent shocked him, as he had been carefully educated in one of the strict old patriarchal families, and he left his home irresolute. He visited Bavaria, and there came under the teaching and advice of some of the leading bishops of the Roman Catholic Church, and having resolved to devote himself to the priesthood, after a severe course of study was ordained in 1826, by the venerable Bishop Sailer, of Ratisbon, in whose diocese he labored for eight years, and then sailed for America in 1834, and was at first stationed in Holy Trinity Church, Philadelphia, where he remained a year; and then became the associate of the Russian Count, Demetrius Augustine Gallitzin (whose father was a Russian prince, and his mother was a daughter of the celebrated general, the Count of Schmettan). Count Gallitzin was one who gave up position and fortune, everything, in fact, to establish a church in the wilderness of Western Pennsylvania. Father Lemke was associated with Count Gallitzin for five years, and until his death, and then became his biographer. He subsequently secured a tract of land in Westmoreland county, Pennsylvania, and then returned to Germany, and brought back with him a colony of monks of the Order of St. Benedict, and founded the Abbey of St. Vincennes, on the above-mentioned land. This body has since grown rapidly, and has three mitred abbots in the United States. In the meantime Father Lemke became a member of the order, and, leaving the colony in Pennsylvania in a prosperous condition, went, in 1856, to Kansas, and inaugurated a mission of that order in the town of Doniphan, which was afterwards transferred to the flourishing priory of Atchison, in the same State. In 1859 he left Kansas, and again visited Germany, where he sojourned a year. Returning once more to the United States, in 1860, he stopped in New Jersey to take charge, for a season, of St. Michael's Church, Elizabeth. This parish was in an enfeebled condition, but he brought it safely through all difficulties, and in the course of five years it had become too small to accommodate its worshippers. In 1865 the congregation was divided, and leaving the German element to retain possession of the Church of St. Michael, he, with the Irish members, commenced the erection of the Convent and Church of St. Walburga, which was regularly chartered in 1868. The convent has a large number of nuns of the Order of St. Benedict, and he is their chaplain, besides acting as pastor to those of his faith in that portion of the city of Elizabeth. On St. Mark's Day, April 25th, 1876, he celebrated his golden jubilee, being the fiftieth anniversary of his induction into the sacred order of the priesthood, on which occasion the little chapel of St. Walburga's Convent was the scene of an unwonted display. Both the pastoral residence and the chapel itself were decorated with arches of green, and the bishops of Newark and Rochester, New York, preceded by nearly one hundred priests, escorted the venerable father and priest to the church. A solemn high mass was sung, a sermon preached by Bishop McQuade, of Rochester, who paid a merited tribute to the veteran priest, and the benediction was given by Bishop Corrigan, of Newark. At the altar a fine golden chalice was presented to him by a pupil of the Benedictine nuns, as the offering of the sisters and their pupils. One of the congregation gave an elegant altar; another, a set of vestments; others, a fine cope; and at the dinner, which followed the services, Vicar-General Doane, in the name of the clergy of the diocese, presented the reverend father with a purse containing nearly a thousand dollars. Father Lemke has now entered his eighty-first year, but is still a hale and hearty man; his appearance is impressive, heightened especially by the long white beard, one of the characteristics of his order.

ONOVER, ROBERT R., M. D., of Red Bank, was born in Freehold township, Monmouth county, New Jersey, October 3d, 1824. His father, Colonel Robert Conover, who died in 1826, was a native of the same township, and followed agricultural pursuits. He served with ability as an officer in the war of 1812. The mother of Robert R. Conover was Gertrude Sutphen, also from Monmouth county, and a granddaughter of David Sutphen, one of the revolutionary patriots who fought so nobly in the memorable battles of which old Monmouth was the scene. Dr. Conover's early education was principally obtained at a boarding-school and academy in Mount Holly. Being destined for the medical profession, he commenced his studies in 1843 under the tuition of his brother, the late Dr.

John R. Conover, at that time of Red Bank. After two years of diligent study he matriculated at the College of Physicians and Surgeons, in New York, where he attended during the winter course of 1845-46. The next course he took at the University of New York, from which he graduated in the spring of 1847, receiving therefrom his degree of M. D. During this session he also was an attendant at the celebrated private school of medicine of Dr. William Detmold. Locating himself in Red Bank, he has since 1847 been engaged in active practice, being associated with his brother until that gentleman's removal to Freehold, in 1858. During the long period in which Dr. Conover has been practising in Monmouth county, extending over a term of thirty years, he has devoted himself exclusively to his noble profession, securing a very extensive patronage, enjoying the entire confidence of his numerous patients as well as the community at large, and commanding the respect and esteem of the most distinguished of his professional brethren. He has for many years been a member of the Monmouth County Medical Society, was its President during one year, and has been several times a delegate to the New Jersey State Medical Society. To-day he stands among the oldest and most highly esteemed practitioners in Monmouth county. He was married, November 25th, 1863, to Anna Maria Throckmorton, of Red Bank.

RAIG, JAMES, M. D., Physician, of Jersey City, was born, January 22d, 1834, in the city of Glasgow, Scotland, and is a son of John and Margaret (McIntyre) Craig. He received a preliminary education in the schools of his native city, and when seventeen years of age emigrated to the United States, and settled for a while in the Northwest. Some time elapsed after his arrival in America before he made choice of a profession, but eventually he selected that of a physician, and for this purpose entered the office of Dr. J. H. Stewart, of St. Paul, Minnesota, where he prosecuted his studies with diligence for about two years. In 1859 he went to New York city, where he matriculated in the medical department of its university, and having passed through the two years' curriculum, graduated therefrom in the spring of 1861. During the same period he attended a course of lectures and study in the celebrated private school of Drs. Thomas and Donaghe, of the same city; and likewise was a participant in two courses of lectures in the New York Ophthalmic Hospital, from which latter institution he received a diploma for that special branch of study. He also attended clinics in the Bellevue and New York Hospitals, receiving therefor certificates. After obtaining his degree he selected Jersey City as his future residence, where he opened his office in the spring of 1861, and where he has remained ever since, actively engaged in professional duties, having acquired a large and remunerative practice,

James Craig, M. D.

and enjoying the confidence of his professional brethren and of the community at large. He has been for years a member of the District Medical Society of Hudson County, and in 1875 was a delegate to the New Jersey State Medical Society from the first-named body. He was the Attending Physician of St. Francis' Hospital, when that institution was in its infancy, and before it was permanently organized. The great pressure of other professional duties forced him to relinquish hospital service. In the present year (1876) he was elected a member of the New York Medico-legal Society. He has at various times contributed papers on medical subjects for publication, and has ever taken a great interest in all that pertains to the advancement of his chosen profession in the city of his residence and the State of his adoption. He was married, December 2d, 1862, to Catharine Nicholson, a native of Portree, Isle of Skye, Scotland.

TRONG, PROFESSOR THEODORE, LL. D., late of New Brunswick, was a son of Rev. Joseph Strong and Sophia Woodbridge, and was born, July 26th, 1790, at South Hadley, Massachusetts. He was graduated at Yale College in 1812, taking the prize in mathematics and a high stand in all his studies, and at once became tutor in Hamilton College, in which institution he was also Professor of Mathematics and Natural Philosophy from 1816 to 1827, when he accepted the same position at Rutgers College, which he held for thirty-five years, from 1827 to 1863. He was one of the original members of the National Academy of Arts and Sciences. From the first the whole strength of his distinguished and cultivated powers of mind was given to mathematical studies. The hardest problems, which had long baffled the efforts of others for their solution, he liked best to attack and conquer. His range, in fact, of mathematical investigation and attainment, spread through the highest sphere of inquiries wherein Newton and La Place had gone before him. He early resolved some difficult questions pertaining to the geometry of a circle, propounded as a challenge to all mankind in "Rees' Encyclopædia," by some distinguished Scotch mathematicians. He completed the solution of cubic equations in a truly scientific way which none of the European mathematicians had ever been able to accomplish. By a most ingenious mode of factoring he devised also a method of extracting any root of any integral number by a direct process. In 1859 he published a "Treatise on Algebra," in which he presented the whole science in original forms of his own, a thorough piece of solid intellectual masonwork. In the summer of 1867 he wrote out largely, if not wholly, at Clinton, New York, a volume on the "Differential and Integral Calculus," full of new processes and results of his own origination. In this splendid treatise he exhibits the highest style of analytic power of mind. For fifty years a teacher of the higher

mathematics, and for nearly sixty an earnest and successful student of them, he bore with him throughout all his long life the characteristics of a man devoted to the highest and best ends of human pursuit. He was industrious, thoughtful, simple-minded, humble, cheerful and happy. He was a man of remarkable gentleness of spirit, and at the same time of great ardor in his moral convictions. He abhorred shams of all kinds and everything like intrigue and mean insinuations and intentions. In conversation, disquisition and debate, of all of which he was quite fond, his eyes and features were always on the move with life. He was a positive patriot, and took a great interest in the political and social questions of the times, and occupied always the advanced positions of the hour in all matters of social reform. He was a man of full height and breadth in his physique, of dark complexion and dark eyes, and of a very intellectual face. He was always very regular in all his bodily habits, and enjoyed generally robust health. He possessed a competency of worldly goods from the beginning of his professional labors, and while his life was checkered with many trials, it abounded in many and great blessings to the very end. He was a man of most decided and unwavering faith in the Word of God; the great facts of revealed religion stood out as clear to his eye as those of mathematical truth, and they were all precious to his heart. He did not indeed join the church of Christ on earth, because of his great distrust of his own heart, until a short time before his death; but he everywhere openly confessed Christ among men all his days, and was a man of childlike faith in God and prayer, and a great lover of the Bible and of good men. He said to the author of this sketch, when almost eighty years of age, when speaking of this beautiful world and of our grandly appointed life in it: "We ought to go through life shouting." He died at New Brunswick, New Jersey, February 1st, 1869. He married, September 23d, 1818, Lucy Dix, of Littleton, Massachusetts, who survived him until November, 1875.

TRONG, HON. BENJAMIN RUGGLES WOODBRIDGE, Counsellor-at-Law and Judge, of New Brunswick, was born at Clinton, Oneida county, New York, February 21st, 1827. He is the son of Professor Theodore Strong, whose biographical sketch immediately precedes this. After a preliminary training, he entered Rutgers College in 1843, and graduated after a full course in 1847. Developing an inclination for the law, he began reading for that profession under the direction of Hon. John Van Dyke, of New Brunswick, but he was not licensed to practise as an attorney until 1852, having in the meantime been attracted to California in 1849 by the gold discoveries. He remained on the Pacific coast for two years, and was one of the first finders of gold in Oregon. On his admission to the bar in New Jersey, he speedily gained himself a good position in

11

the profession, and during his career thereat he was made the depositary of various important trusts. For several terms, extending in all over ten years, he was Corporation Counsel for New Brunswick. He was counsel for the National Bank of New Jersey, and for several large manufacturing companies, and other corporate institutions. At a comparatively early period in his professional life he was appointed a Notary Public and a Master in Chancery. On April 1st, 1874, he was appointed Judge of the Common Pleas, Quarter Sessions, and Orphans' Courts, for Middlesex County, for a term of five years. In politics he is an earnest Republican, but he is not a politician in the ordinary acceptation of the word, though all movements having for their object the promotion of the public welfare receive his hearty and active support. He was married in 1872 to Harriet A., daughter of Hon. Jonathan Hartwell, of Littleton, Massachusetts.

EMPSHALL, REV. EVERARD, D. D., Minister, of Elizabeth, was born in Rochester, New York, August 9th, 1830. His father, Thomas Kempshall, was a merchant of Staines, England, and came to this country in 1812, settling in Rochester when it was only a forest. He was a man universally loved and respected for his integrity of character, and represented his district in Congress from 1839 to 1841. His wife was Emily Peck, of New Haven, Connecticut. Everard, their son, received his education at Williams College, Massachusetts, where he graduated in 1851. He then entered upon a theological course at Princeton Seminary, graduating in 1855. After completing his theological course he entered upon the ministry at Buffalo, where he preached two years. He started the Delaware Street Presbyterian Church there, now known as the Calvary Church. After leaving Buffalo he preached as " a supply " for two years at Batavia, New York. In the year 1861 he was called to Elizabeth, New Jersey, to take charge of the First Presbyterian Church of that place, which pulpit he has since continued to fill to the eminent satisfaction of the congregation. In 1869 he was a member of the Board of Foreign and Domestic Missions. In 1859 he married Charlotte A. Eaton, only daughter of Orsamus Eaton, of Troy, New York. The church in which he now ministers is one of the oldest Presbyterian churches in the country, having been organized more than two hundred years ago. It is supposed to have been founded very shortly after the settlement of the town in 1664-65. The men who founded both the town and the church were, with very few exceptions, from New England. The first minister was Rev. Jeremiah Peck, a native of London, England, and one of the early settlers of New Haven, Connecticut. For the first half century of its existence the church was an independent one, and became Presbyterian not earlier than 1717. It was represented for the first time in the Synod of Philadelphia in 1721. From

1761 to the time of his tragic death in 1781 the Rev. James Caldwell, of revolutionary fame, was pastor of this church. He was shot and killed by the British in Elizabeth. The graveyard attached to the church contains the remains of many illustrious dead.

ANEWAY, GEORGE J., A. M., M. D., Physician, of New Brunswick, is a native of Philadelphia. His parents were Rev. Jacob Janeway, a Presbyterian minister, of Philadelphia, and Martha (Leiper) Janeway, of Pennsylvania. He received his preliminary education at the select schools in Philadelphia, and in the year 1826 entered the University of Pennsylvania as a medical student. He also prosecuted his studies in the office of Dr. Nathaniel Chapman, who was at that time Professor of the Practice of Medicine in the university. Having completed his university course, he went in 1831 to Paris, where he remained a year, completing his medical studies in the best schools of that city. Returning to this country he commenced professional practice in New York city. He remained there until 1847, when he removed to New Brunswick, New Jersey, where he has since resided. He has devoted himself untiringly and with eminent success to the practice of his profession, and has attained in it a high and acknowledged position. He is no less esteemed as a citizen than as a professional man, and during 1871 and 1872 he served as Mayor of the city.

ANEWAY, JACOB J., Manufacturer, of New Brunswick, was born in Middlesex county, New Jersey, March 15th, 1840. He is the son of Dr. George J. Janeway, an old and prominent physician of New Brunswick, and of Martha M. (Smith) Janeway. He received his preliminary education at select schools in New Brunswick, and entered Rutgers College in the year 1855. He remained in that institution during a period of four years, and after leaving it he entered the service of the Sheffield Brothers, druggists, of New York, as Superintendent of their oil warehouse, in Jersey City. About a year later the warehouse was destroyed by fire, and he returned to New Brunswick. In July, 1862, he entered the Union army for the suppression of the rebellion. He organized a company of infantry in New Brunswick, of which he was made Captain. He, with his company, was attached to the 14th Regiment of New Jersey Infantry. The regiment was on detached service in Maryland for some time, and subsequently joined the Army of the Potomac, at Harper's Ferry. When General Grant took command of the Army of the Potomac the 14th was transferred to the 6th Army Corps, under command of General Sedgwick, and served through the war. In the fall of 1864 Captain Janeway was commissioned Major, after

Wm C. Roberts

the death of the gallant Major Vredenbergh, and one week later he received his commission as Lieutenant-Colonel, and he was brevetted Colonel for bravery at the battle of Petersburg, just previous to the surrender of General Lee. At the close of the war he returned to New Brunswick, and there entered the service of his uncle, H. L. Janeway, as Superintendent of the paper-mills there. He continued to act in this capacity until 1872, when he formed the partnership now existing, of Janeway & Carpenter, for the manufacture in all its branches of paper-hangings, which business he has successfully prosecuted ever since. Through an invention of Colonel Janeway's, patented December 15th, 1874, the company are enabled to produce the specialty in paper-hangings known as the "French drawn stripe." By this invention the labor previously done by hand is now accomplished by machinery, and this kind of work, which had previously been almost excluded from market on account of the expense attending hand-work, is produced at a profit. He was married, in November, 1871, to Eliza Harrington, daughter of Henry L. Harrington, of Philadelphia.

OBERTS, REV. WILLIAM CHARLES, D. D., was born, September 23d, 1832, at Galltmai (May's Grove), near Aberystwith, in Cardiganshire, South Wales. His father, Charles Roberts, was a well-to-do farmer, of the class usually known there as "country esquires." He was a man of more than ordinary education and general intelligence, having spent some years in college, at Welshpool, with the view of becoming a clergyman of the Established Church of England. For reasons satisfactory to himself he refused to receive holy orders, married and settled down as a farmer. He held a number of important offices in the shire, and bore the cognomen of Counsellor, on account of his extensive knowledge of law. According to what seems to be a well-founded tradition, the mother of the subject of this sketch belonged to the Welsh branch of the well-known Jonathan Edwards family of this country. She had the name of possessing in an eminent degree the strong qualities of mind and heart common to all the branches of her family. After spending some years in a little school near his father's house, William Charles was sent to Evan's Academy, in town, well known in that section of the principality for the ability of its teachers and the thoroughness of its training. It was an institution modelled after the celebrated Eton and Rugby schools, in England. Owing to the failure in business of relatives, for whom Mr. Roberts had become an indorser, he was so embarrassed that he was compelled to leave his beautiful home. Rather than to accept his altered condition among his old friends, he resolved to come to this country for eight or ten years, landing in New York on the 28th of June, 1849. In less than a week after his arrival on these shores himself, wife

and two children were carried away by the cholera that was then raging in the city, leaving behind in a strange country six orphan children, of whom William was the eldest. Instead of returning home to Wales at the urgent solicitation of relatives and friends, the surviving members of the family decided to spend some time in the United States, two or three of the oldest seeking some temporary employment to supplement the little income left them by their parents. In the providence of God William was led to Elizabethtown, New Jersey, in September, 1849, where he entered the leather establishment of Mulford Brothers. After seeing his way clear to make his home in this country, he entered the school of Rev. David H. Pierson, with the view of carrying out his original intention before leaving Wales of becoming a lawyer or minister of the gospel. In the fall of 1852 he entered the sophomore class in Princeton College, and graduated with honors in 1855. At the close of the final examination he accepted the appointment of tutor in Delaware College, where he discharged the duties of an absent professor. He then commenced the study of law, under Judge Patton, in Pennsylvania, acting at the same time as a private tutor to his children. Convinced that it was his duty to become a minister of the gospel, he entered the Theological Seminary at Princeton, and remained there through the whole course, graduating in 1858. Before leaving the seminary he had accepted a unanimous call to succeed the Rev. Stephen R. Wynkoop, as the pastor of the First Presbyterian Church, Wilmington, Delaware. He was ordained and installed by the Presbytery of New Castle in June, 1858. Whilst at Wilmington Mr. Roberts was married to Mary Louise, the only daughter of E. B. Fuller, Esq., of Trenton, New Jersey, for many years a well-known banker in Natchez, Mississippi. He was appointed by the Synod of Philadelphia one of the Trustees of Lafayette College, at Easton, Pennsylvania. In the autumn of 1861 he accepted a unanimous call to fill the pulpit of the First Presbyterian Church of Columbus, Ohio, rendered vacant by the declining health and old age of the Rev. James Hoge, D. D. There he acted as Chaplain of the State Senate; a member of a committee in the room of Dr. Hoge to found a college, which eventuated in Wooster University, and the Moderator of the Synod of Ohio, in 1864. On account of the ill health of Mrs. Roberts, he was advised by the best physicians of the place to leave Columbus, and seek a settlement on the sea-board, somewhere between New York and Washington. He accepted a call to become a co-pastor with the Rev. Dr. Magie, of the Second Presbyterian Church of Elizabeth, New Jersey. He was installed there by the Presbytery of Passaic, in December, 1864. In consequence of the rapid growth of the city and the great demand for pews in the Second Church, repeated propositions were made to enlarge the old edifice, but they did not meet the views of the majority of the congregation. As the people could not agree on a plan for enlarging the existing church, it was deemed advisable to colonize and occupy the inviting field then opening for a Presbyterian church north of the New Jersey Central Railroad. Ninety-three members of the Second Church, and seven from other churches out of town, were organized, January 31st, 1856, into what is called the Westminster Presbyterian Church of Elizabeth. They gave a unanimous call to the Rev. William C. Roberts, then pastor of the mother congregation. By advice of prominent members of Presbytery, he accepted the call, and was installed March 7th, 1866. The prosperity of the church under his pastorate has been very marked. Its roll of members has swelled from one hundred to four hundred and seventy-five, exclusive of those taken away by death and removals. They have erected, on the corner of Westminster avenue and Prince street, perhaps the finest church edifice in the State of New Jersey, costing, independent of the large tower, about $175,000, all paid for. They have contributed also to outside and benevolent objects over $100,000. Mr. Roberts was elected a Trustee of Princeton College in June, 1866; appointed by the first General Assembly of the united church one of the original members of its Board of Home Missions in May, 1869; he was made Chairman of the deputation sent to the Free Church of Scotland for the year 1874; a member of the Assembly's committee to consider the propriety of holding a general Presbyterian council; he was honored with the title of D. D. by Union College, Schenectady, New York, in June, 1872; he was elected by acclamation the Moderator of the Synod of New Jersey in October, 1875, and appointed a member of the first Pan Presbyterian Council to meet in Edinburgh, July 3d, 1877.

——◆——

ARKER, P. C., M. D., Physician, of Morristown, was born, 1835, in Oneida county, New York, and is a son of G. W. Barker, a merchant, whose wife was a Miss Coe; both parents being also natives of New York State. He received a thorough academical education, and in 1856 commenced the study of medicine in the office of Dr. S. G. Wolcott, of Utica, New York, who holds high rank as an eminent surgeon. He likewise attended the regular course of lectures delivered at the College of Physicians and Surgeons, in New York city, from which institution he graduated in March, 1860, with the degree of Doctor of Medicine. He subsequently became an Assistant Physician at Bellevue Hospital, where he passed a year. In 1861 he commenced the practice of medicine at Cold Spring, Putnam county, New York, being associated with Dr. T. D. Lente. This copartnership continued until 1868, when it was dissolved. He then removed to Morristown, New Jersey, where he settled, and has since been engaged in the control of an extensive medical practice, and is regarded as one of the leading physicians of that place. He has filled both the office of Vice-President and President of the

County Medical Society, and President of the Masonic Hall Association. He was married in 1863 to Anna E., daughter of David L. Barton, of New York.

——◆——

AN ANTWERP, JAMES, Dentist, of New Brunswick, was born, June 19th, 1835, in the city of New York, and is a son of William and Jane (McCollough) Van Antwerp of that city, where the former was engaged in the hardware business. His mother was a daughter of Colonel William McCullough, of Asbury, New Jersey. James at first attended a select school in his native city, and subsequently was a pupil for three years in an academy at Port Colden, New Jersey. He was afterwards placed in a school at Hacketts town, and completed his studies at the celebrated academy of Mr. Vanderveer, in Easton, Pennsylvania. He commenced the study of dentistry under Drs. Miller & Cook, of Brooklyn, New York, where he became fully acquainted with the qualifications necessary to be attained in that vocation. He selected New Brunswick as his future field, and for four years was associated with Dr. A. D. Newell, since which time he has practised his profession alone. He was married, November 1st, 1865, to Phebe R. Stout, daughter of Lewis Stout, of New Brunswick, who died March 6th, 1871. He was again married, April 29th, 1874, to Catharine, daughter of William W. Cannon, and granddaughter of James Spencer Cannon, deceased, formerly a professor in the Theological Seminary at New Brunswick.

——◆——

cKINLAY, WILLIAM, Builder and Real-Estate Operator, of Elizabeth, was born, December 18th, 1814, in Dalmelington, Ayrshire, Scotland, and is a son of Alexander and Mary (McAdam) McKinlay. His education was received at home, and he subsequently learned the trade of a carpenter. He emigrated to America in the autumn of 1838, and settled in Venango county, Pennsylvania, where he devoted himself to agricultural pursuits and building, and was also engaged in a mercantile business. During the years 1863, 1864 and 1865 he was Postmaster at Stewart's Run, Venango county. In 1866 he removed to Elizabeth, New Jersey, where he became interested in real-estate operations, and still continues to reside. He was elected a member of the Assembly in 1872 from Union county. During that session he introduced a bill which after a bitter contest became a law. This bill created a comptroller to advance the interests of the city, curtailing expenses and extravagant outlay. He also served during this session as Chairman of the Committee on Stationery. He was re-elected in 1873 and in 1874. During these sessions he was in both years Chairman of the Committee on Municipal

Corporations, and in the latter year was a member of the joint Committee on the Treasurer's Account and State Prisons. He was a delegate to the State Gubernatorial Convention in 1874; and also a delegate in 1876 to a convention held in Trenton to choose delegates to the Advisory Convention, which met in Philadelphia during that year. He is a Director in the National State Bank of Elizabeth; also of the Elizabeth Fire and Marine Insurance Company, and of the Mechanics' Savings Bank. He takes an active interest in all public improvements, but, at the same time, believes that in cautious action resides a great safeguard to the public welfare, and that no more improvements should be entered into than the times and credit of the city warrant. He was married, March 4th, 1841, to Mary Louisa Abbott, of New York.

ASSAR, REV. THOMAS EDWIN, Clergyman and Pastor of the Flemington Baptist Church, was born, December 3d, 1834, at Poughkeepsie, New York, and is the son of William and Mary (Hogeman) Vassar, of that city. There came to the United States from England in 1796, two brothers, James and Thomas Vassar; the former was the father of Matthew Vassar, the founder of Vassar College; while the latter was the father of William Vassar, and grandfather of Rev. T. E. Vassar. The latter, while preparing to enter college in his native place, was prevented from so doing on account of family misfortunes, which threw heavy cares on him as the eldest son. Having early in life determined to devote himself to the Gospel ministry, he commenced his theological studies with his former pastor, the Rev. Rufus Babcock, D. D., ex-president of Waterville College. When twenty-two years of age, he was ordained a minister of the Baptist church, at Poughkeepsie, and supplied the congregation there for one year, declining a call to become its permanent pastor. He commenced pastoral duties, however, at Amenia, Dutchess county, having received and accepted a call from the society there, and removed thither in 1857, and was settled there for eight years. During this period the congregation granted him one year's leave of absence, and this one year he devoted to service in the field, as Chaplain of the 150th Regiment New York Volunteers. His regiment was mustered into the service in 1862, was attached to the Army of the Potomac till the autumn of 1863, and participated in the severe campaigns of that command, including the battle of Gettysburg. In 1863 he returned to his charge at Amenia, where he continued until 1865, when he received and accepted a call to the pastorate of the First Baptist Church of Lynn, Massachusetts. In 1872 he removed to Flemington, New Jersey, having decided to become the pastor of the congregation in that town, where he still remains. Here, as in his former fields of labor, he has been eminently successful. His

lecture, entitled "Gettysburg," is one of the finest productions of its kind, and has been delivered to many large and appreciative audiences. He is President of the Baptist Sunday School Union of New Jersey, and is an earnest and efficient laborer in that cause. He was married in 1861 to Tamma G. Sackett, of Stanford, Dutchess county, New York.

ILSON, REV. EDWARD, Pastor of the St. James Methodist Episcopal Church, New Brunswick, New Jersey, was born, July 25th, 1820, in the town of Liverpool, England. One of his grandfathers practised law in the city of New York in 1788. He was educated by a private tutor, and also had the advantages of study and school under one of the best Oxford masters. Afterwards he read law and studied military engineering under Generals Pasley and Sandham. In 1840 he came to the United States, where he remained until 1847; during that period he was licensed to preach by the Methodist Episcopal Church in Indiana in 1846. On his return to England he was for some years a District Superintendent of the British and Foreign Bible Society, in the Cornwall and Devon district. For thirteen years subsequently he was the Secretary of the Country Towns Mission Society, London, established by David Nasmith, the founder of City and Town Missions. He also edited the monthly magazine of the society during that period, and increased the society's income from $30,000 to $55,000 per annum. He returned to the United States in 1869, and settled in Metuchen, New Jersey, whence he was called to the pastorate of St. James Methodist Episcopal Church, New Brunswick, and found the congregation laboring under financial disaster, their church edifice having been seized by the sheriff for debt. By his personal influence and exertions he extricated the building from the clutches of the law and placed the property on a sound basis. He was married to an American lady in 1844, during his first visit to this country.

ILLEN, FORREST A., M. D., of Bound Brook, was born in Poughkeepsie, New York, March 23d, 1852, his father being Joseph Gillen, a prominent merchant of that place. He was educated in the common schools, graduating at the Poughkeepsie High School in 1870, after passing with distinction through its various courses of study. Selecting from the professions then presented him that of medicine as his only choice, he entered with avidity upon its study in the office and under the direction of Dr. Cissam, Police Surgeon, of Brooklyn. In the year and a half spent by him under this practitioner's care he made rapid progress both in the theory and practice of medicine, and was well qualified in all requisite preparatory knowledge when enrolled as a matriculant in the New York University in 1872. In this institution he studied three years, graduating from it in February, 1875, with the rank of third in a class of one hundred and twenty-four. Soon after receiving his degree Dr. Gillen removed to Bound Brook, New Jersey, and commenced at once his professional duties, associating for some time with Dr. Fields. Since the close of 1875 he has practised alone, and is gathering around him a large clientele. Though a young man he has already acquired reputation as a careful and skilful practitioner, and no other physician in the same locality enjoys to a greater degree the confidence of those for whom he has been called to prescribe. A number of important operations testify to his ability as a surgeon. Dr. Gillen is an earnest student and a practitioner of progressive impulses, and certainly none other, of his age, has brighter professional prospects.

———◆◆◆———

ILMARTH, FRANK, A. M., M. D., Physician, of East Orange, was born, March 28th, 1841, in Smithfield, Rhode Island, and is a son of Theophilus W. and Delia A. (Mowry) Wilmarth, both natives of that State, where his father was a manufacturer of cotton goods. When Frank was five years old, his parents removed to Oxford, Massachusetts, where he obtained his preliminary education. At about sixteen years of age he was engaged as a teacher of mathematics at Rutgers College Grammar School, in New Brunswick, thus enabling him to prepare himself at the same time to enter college; and he continued a teacher for about three years. Having selected medicine as his future profession, he commenced his studies and had attended one course of lectures at the College of Physicians and Surgeons, New York, when he entered the United States service in 1864, and for three years was engaged in the Surgeon-General's Department, at Washington. During his occupancy of that position he received the honorary degree of Master of Arts, which was conferred upon him by Rutgers College. While a resident of Washington he entered the office of Dr. Thomas Antisell, professor of physiology in the Georgetown Medical College, and a member of the examining board for surgeons and assistant surgeons of the United States volunteer service. In the spring of 1868 he completed his medical studies, and graduated from the College of Physicians and Surgeons, New York. Shortly after receiving the degree of Doctor of Medicine, he became House Physician to the Colored Home Hospital. In the autumn of 1869 he located at East Orange, where he has since practised his profession, meeting with good success, and is now in the control of an extensive medical business, taking much interest in all those matters which tend to promote the honor of the medical fraternity. He is a member of the Essex County Medical Society, and has been its reporter for the past five years. He has also been a delegate to the New Jersey State Medical Society for the same period of time. He is also a member of the Essex Medical Union, and of the New Jersey Academy of Medicine. He is one of the visiting Surgeons to St. Barnabas' Hospital, Newark, and also to the Orange Memorial Hospital. He is a member of the Medical Advisory Board of the Mutual Benefit Life Insurance Company of Newark, succeeding the late Dr. Woodhull in that board. He was married, April 30th, 1874, to Esther P., daughter of Alden Sampson, of New York city.

———◆◆◆———

ULLEN, THOMAS FRANKFORD, M. D., of Camden, was born in Philadelphia, Pennsylvania, September 3d, 1822, being the son of Thomas Cullen, a sea-captain, who for many years was engaged in the India trade. His father was a native of Trappe, Pennsylvania, and his mother, née Margaret Frankford, was born near Philadelphia. When quite young, his parents removed to Mount Holly, Burlington county, New Jersey, and it was in that town he received his elementary education. In 1839 he returned to Philadelphia, where, in the office of Dr. Eber Chase, he commenced the study of medicine preparatory to a collegiate course. In 1840 he matriculated in the medical department of the University of Pennsylvania, and in 1844 graduated with honor. Upon leaving this venerable institution he settled in Newark, Delaware, where he practised with gratifying success until 1847. In 1849 he removed to Camden, New Jersey, where he has ever since resided, and where his professional duties, which have claimed his constant attention, have secured to him the reputation of being one of the ablest practitioners in the State. He is a leading member of the Camden County Medical Society, a Fellow of the New Jersey State Medical Society, having in 1870 served as its President; and has labored with ability and success to promote the interests of his profession in his county and State. His practice embraces both medicine and surgery, and in both branches he has achieved distinction. He holds a membership in the Delaware State Medical Society, and has the merit of having been one of the incorporators of the Camden Hospital. His contributions to the science of which he is an exponent have been important, and in number considerable. He was married in 1858 to Elizabeth Stout, of New Jersey.

———◆◆◆———

EAN, JOHN, Bank President, of Elizabethtown, was born at Ursino, near Elizabethtown, March 27th, 1814. His father was Peter Kean, of the same place, and his mother was one of the Morris family of New York, granddaughter of Louis Morris, one of the signers of the Declaration of Independence. His education was received at Princeton

College, and after his graduation he studied law with Governor Pennington, of New Jersey, but never entered upon professional practice. For a period he was on Governor Pennington's staff, with the rank of Colonel. He has always continued to reside at Ursino, and is identified with all the leading interests of Elizabethtown and vicinity. A man of fine abilities, high culture and eminent social position, he occupies a prominent and leading position as a public-spirited and influential citizen, enjoying the fullest confidence and the highest esteem of the entire community. He was one of the founders, and was the first President of the Central Railroad of New Jersey, and is now acting as New Jersey Director of that company. He is President of the National State Bank, of Elizabethtown, and is connected in various capacities with numerous other institutions. Indeed, he has been and continues to be identified with most of the moneyed institutions of Elizabeth. He was active in the foundation of many of these institutions, and in others his interest was inherited. His duties in connection with these various enterprises occupy his time and attention fully, and he takes no active interest in politics, and has never sought or held public office of any kind. He is one of the wealthiest men in New Jersey, and enjoys the rare distinction of rendering his great wealth beneficial to the fullest extent to the community surrounding him. He is married to a daughter of Caleb O. Halstead, of New York.

IMONSON, JACOB, D. D. S., of Newark, was born on Staten Island, Richmond county, New York, March 8th, 1844. His parents were Jacob and Caroline (Jacques) Simonson. His education, preliminary to his professional studies, was carefully conducted in the public schools and academy at his home, and finally at Kingston Academy, Pennsylvania. His studies in these institutions were comprehensive, and admirably fitted him for his pursuit of professional science. In 1868 he entered the office of Dr. C. E. Francis, a celebrated practitioner in New York city, and under his preceptorship made rapid and thorough progress in his study of dentistry during the two years he remained with him. In 1870 he was entered on the rolls of the Philadelphia Dental College, and at the commencement of 1871 graduated with honors. The theses prepared by him on that occasion were highly commended for their thoroughness in research and their application of methods in professional duties. He supplemented this study by two courses of lectures on descriptive anatomy, at the Philadelphia School of Anatomy, in Philadelphia, and by a course of medical surgery at Blockley Almshouse, under Dr. William H. Pancoast and others. In the summer of this year he commenced the practice of his profession in New York city, and in the fall transferred his office to a more promising field in Newark, where he has since labored with no ordi-

nary degree of success. His researches and studies in a constantly expanding science, his care and attention when called to act or consult, his frequent contributions to the literature of medicine and dental surgery, have all combined to raise him to a leadership in his profession in the city of his residence. He was married in 1871 to Jane Medora Haughwont, of Port Richmond, Staten Island.

WEN, FRED WOOSTER, M. D., of Morristown, was born, October 6th, 1840, on Martha's Vineyard, Massachusetts. His father, Captain William W. Owen, descended from one of the oldest settlers in New England, was born at Wiscassett, Maine, and for many years commanded vessels in the foreign trade. His mother, Adeline Wooster (descended from Major-General David Wooster, who was killed in the revolutionary battle of Danbury, Connecticut, and a daughter of Abel Wooster, M. D., born in Stratford, Connecticut) was born in New York city, and after a life to whose worth and beauty all bore tribute, died at Port Jefferson, Long Island, June 29th, 1867. Dr. Owen attended the French School of the Christian Brothers, the German School of Saint Matthew, and Public School, No. 1, in New York, Mr. Hines' school in Warren, Connecticut, and Saint Mark's Hall, Orange, New Jersey. From 1855 to 1859 he prosecuted classical studies in the Gymnasia of Neuchatel, Switzerland, and Leipsig, Germany. From October, 1859, to May, 1861, he was assistant bookkeeper in foreign houses in New York. In June and July, 1861, he recruited sixty volunteers for the 2d New York Fire Zouaves, and went with that regiment to the war. November 12th, 1861, he was commissioned Second Lieutenant, 38th New York Volunteers. The following extracts from his military history are taken from the records of the United States Signal Corps, and from papers on file in the War Department at Washington: "Was detached for signal duty by Brigadier-General John Sedgwick, December 24th, 1861, and reported for said duty to Major Albert J. Myer, signal officer of the army at Signal Camp of Instruction, Georgetown, District of Columbia, January 1st, 1862;" "February 24th, 1862, was ordered to report for signal duty to General Hooker, on the lower Potomac;" "Lieutenant Owen acted as a Signal Officer during the entire Peninsular campaign, and was frequently mentioned by his commanding officer for efficiency, zeal and gallantry;" "October 23d, 1862, Lieutenant Owen was, by virtue of General Orders No. 42, issued from Head-quarters United States Signal Corps, Camp near Harrison's Landing, Virginia, July 23d, 1862, awarded a set of 'battle flags,' inscribed 'Yorktown' and 'West Point,' for having gallantly carried and used his signal flags in those battles;" "For services at the battle of Antietam and on the pursuit to Shepherdstown, Virginia, Second Lieutenant F. W. Owen occupied the front near Rutlett's House, and bravely maintained it for some hours under an artillery fire." He was promoted to First Lieutenant, 38th New York Volunteers, December 1st, 1862. Captain B. F. Fisher, Acting Signal Officer, in a report dated December 18th, 1862, and covering the battle of Fredericksburg, Virginia, says : " It gives me pleasure to mention the courage displayed and the marked attention given to duty, under the fire of the enemy, by Lieutenant Owen." Upon the expiration of the term of service of the 38th New York Volunteers, early in 1863, the regiment was mustered out, and Lieutenant Owen, having received authority to have the additional names of " Fort Powhattan," "Antietam," and " Fredericksburg " inscribed upon his battle flags, severed, with honor, his connection with the Signal Corps. Immediately after this, upon the recommendation of his colonel, and of Generals Sedgwick and Howard, he was appointed by President Lincoln, Captain and C. S. Volunteers, and continued to serve with the Army of the Potomac in the field from April 30th, 1863, to November 30th, 1864, when disease, contracted in the service, compelled his resignation upon surgeon's certificate of disability, and he was honorably discharged from the service. The following, from his immediate commander, covers his career in his new field of service : " West Point, New York, January 2d, 1867. Brevet Major Fred Wooster Owen served for a long time under my command in the 2d Division, 2d Army Corps, Army of the Potomac. He was most conscientious and assiduous in the performance of his various duties, particularly indefatigable in campaign movements, and most enterprising. I respected him as an officer and as a man. Alex. S. Webb, Lieutenant-Colonel and Brevet Major-General United States Army." At the close of the war Captain Owen received from the United States the brevet of Major, and from the State of New York the brevet of Lieutenant-Colonel, both commissions being " for gallant and meritorious services during the war." In May, 1865, he received from General Howard an appointment in the Freedmen's Bureau. While in Washington, and outside of the government hours, he continued his medical studies commenced the previous year, and attended through the winters of 1865-66 and 1866-67 the courses of lectures of the medical faculty of Georgetown College. July 1st, 1866, he received the appointment as Chief Clerk of the Freedmen's Bureau, and, March 5th, 1867, the degree of M. D. from his *Alma Mater*. August 14th, 1867, he resigned his position in Washington, and was married to Louisa M. Graves, of Brooklyn, a graduate of the Packer Institute. Rufus R. Graves, his wife's father, was born in Sunderland, Massachusetts, November 6th, 1807. In 1830 he removed with his father to Macon, Georgia, and there established a successful business. In 1842 he removed to New York city, and established himself in a business from which he retired, after an eminently successful career, in 1873. He was one of the earliest promoters and managers of the Delaware, Lackawanna & Western Railroad, a Director of the

New Jersey Zinc Company, and of several New York insurance companies. He was interested in all patriotic and benevolent enterprises, and contributed liberally to their support. He died, August 17th, 1876, at his residence in Morristown, New Jersey. November 6th, 1867, Dr. Owen and his wife sailed for Europe, and resided in Paris until November 30th, 1869, during which time the doctor, attached to Dolbeau's service, Hospital Beaujon, prepared for and passed the five examinations of the Doctorate of the Faculty of Paris, receiving his second diploma just before leaving for America. In December, 1869, he settled in Brooklyn, and was appointed, in January, 1870, Adjunct Surgeon Long Island College Hospital. In June, 1870, his wife being an invalid, he removed to Morristown, New Jersey, where he now resides and practises his profession. He is a member and an ex-officer of the Morris County Medical Society, was twice elected Health Physician of Morristown, and is the present County Physician.

VAN AMBURG, REV. ROBERT, Clergyman, of Lebanon, was born, June 9th, 1809, about six miles south of Poughkeepsie, in the southern part of Dutchess county, New York, and is of both Hollander and French descent. His early ocenpatiou was that of husbandry, and in all the varieties of agricultural pursuits he was among the first in labor and success ; even at ten years of age he could handle a scythe with the same ease and agility as any older laborer. The first twenty years of his life were passed in the usual routine of a farmer's life, receiving the education the common schools of the neighborhood afforded. When he had nearly attained his majority, he received a decided religious impression, accompanied by a strong sense of Divine responsibility that he should devote himself exclusively to the service of the Lord. He at once began to prepare himself under the tutelage of the Rev. Eliphalet Price, a very able and worthy Presbyterian minister, at Hughsonville, New York, and from thence he repaired to Whitesboro', in the same State. In 1834 he entered Rutgers College, at New Brunswick, from which institution he graduated in the class of 1837. He subsequently matriculated in the Theological Seminary in the same city, and took his degree in 1840 ; in both institutions the highest honors were conceded to him. When he entered the public ministry, his preaching was so popular and so significantly successful, that he was tendered a call in almost every vacant church where he ministered. He accepted a call to the Reformed Church of Lebanon, New Jersey ; and in a comparatively brief period the congregation grew until the edifice was filled to its utmost capacity. The field of his labors embraced a rich, rural country, thickly settled, about ten to twelve miles square. The calls to duty were frequent, and the duties themselves multiform and various. His labors were numerous, often burdensome, and little time was left him for study or recreation. Years glided by with scarcely any cessation or rest, until August, 1837, when he resigned his charge and went to Fordham, New York, where he became pastor of an old church. The congregation there had been for years agitating the expediency of erecting a new edifice, but internal and external strength was apparently paralyzed, and their efforts resulted in nothing, notwithstanding for seventeen years they had been striving to attain their object. In this state of lethargy he came among them, and instilled new life into the fold; the old, dilapidated structure was filled to overflowing during the first year of his ministry, and in February, 1838, a meeting was called to take measures for the erection of a new edifice. In the following month of August a beautiful brick building was dedicated, free of debt, with the exception of about $1200. This building was soon filled with an interesting worshipping assembly; and his salary was largely increased from the pew-rents. From Fordham he removed to Hughsonville, New York, after the former charge became independent. He was recalled to Lebanon in August, 1853, and almost immediately the old brick church was converted into a new, convenient and elegant frame structure, not surpassed by any church edifice in Hunterdon county; here also his labors were crowned with remarkable success. Great numbers of the middle-aged, as also the young and old, were added to the church; and from the adjoining counties the population flocked to this church, insomuch that all could not obtain sittings, even on ordinary occasions, and it became the largest assemblage of any country congregation in the State. In 1869 he accepted a call to High Bridge, a church of his own organizing, it having grown under his care from a very few worshippers, in an obscure school-house, to a fairly sustaining congregation with a church edifice. When he had become settled as their permanent pastor, the building was found to be too small to accommodate the necessary congregation; whereupon he immediately agitated the question of building a new edifice, and in the face of strenuous opposition he pushed the matter forward, and soon had the corner-stone laid, obtained the means, and speedily there was completed one of the finest specimens of Gothic architecture in the State, which now lifts its spire heavenward, as if indicating its future prosperity and the moral elevation of the surrounding inhabitants. From High Bridge he removed to Lower German Valley, and took charge of the Presbyterian Church at that place. This also was an infant congregation, and under his ministry rapidly advanced in strength and devotion. From Lower German Valley he removed to Annandale, New Jersey, to another congregation which he had organized previously. At this point a large debt had been nearly liquidated in about two years and the number of attendants nearly doubled. He is still their pastor, and much greater good will doubtless be their lot under prayerfully discreet care.

12

He is now in the sixty-eighth year of his age, and is yet as vivacious in spirit, active in labor, and as persevering in his efforts as he was in his youth. He possesses a warm temperament, with great decision of character, accompanied with an energetic spirit that contends earnestly for victory in the battle of life. He makes it a point to preach twice every Lord's day. He is benevolent, and is a generous giver; and his house is where the needy and afflicted are wont to gather.

LIGGETT, REV. JOHN ALBERT, A. M., Clergyman, of Rahway, was born, November 1st, 1834, at Brandywine Manor, Chester county, Pennsylvania, and is a son of Caleb and Jane (Cowan) Liggett; his father was a farmer by occupation. He was educated principally at Lafayette College, Easton, Pennsylvania, from which institution he graduated in the class of 1857. He then entered the theological seminary at Danville, Kentucky, for the three years' course, and in 1860 was settled over a church at Crittenden, Kentucky, where he labored for four years. In 1864 he received and accepted a call from Rahway, to become the pastor of the Second Presbyterian Church of that city, and whose pulpit he has ably filled for the past twelve years. During that period the church membership has been largely increased under his ministry, and is at the present time in a flourishing condition. At one period he was Moderator of the New Jersey Presbytery. He was chosen to deliver the annual address before the Alumni of Lafayette College, June 25th, 1876. He was married, November 13th, 1861, to Mary B., the only daughter of George B. Armstrong, of Kentucky.

CHETWOOD, JOHN JOSEPH, Lawyer, late of Elizabeth (deceased), was born in that city, January 18th, 1800, and was the son of Dr. John Chetwood, a physician of great eminence, who was one of the first victims of the Asiatic cholera, in 1832; his grandfather, Hon. John Chetwood, was an Associate Justice of the Supreme Court of New Jersey. John Joseph received a liberal education preparatory to his entering Nassau Hall, and graduated from that ancient institution in 1818. Immediately after leaving college he entered the office of his uncle, William Chetwood, where he prosecuted his studies for the bar, and was licensed as an attorney in 1821, becoming a counsellor in 1825, and attaining the rank of a serjeant-at-law in 1837. He was for fourteen years Surrogate of Essex County, and also the first Prosecutor of the Pleas for Union County. He was also a member of the Legislative Council before the adoption of the present constitution of the State. He was early identified with the great railroad enterprises of the State, active in the promotion of education and in the support of religious institutions. His practice was large and remunerative. He was a man of generous and genial disposition, a cheerful giver to charitable and benevolent objects. He was a member of the Protestant Episcopal Church, and one of the Trustees of Burlington College. He was married to a granddaughter of General Elias Dayton, and was a resident of Elizabeth, his native place, where he died, November 18th, 1861.

URRAY, REV. NICHOLAS, D. D., Clergyman, late pastor of the First Presbyterian Church, of Elizabeth, was born, December 25th, 1802, at Ballynaskea, in the county of Westmeath, Ireland, and was the son of Nicholas and Judith (Mangum) Murray. His father was a farmer of some property, and exerted considerable influence in the civil affairs of the neighborhood in which he lived; he died in 1806. Nicholas remained at home under the care of his mother until he was about nine years old, when he went to reside with an aunt, his mother's sister, some ten or more miles distant, where he went to school until he reached the age of twelve. He was then apprenticed as a merchant's clerk in a store in Grannarth, near Edgeworthtown, where he remained three years. He was sadly and badly used by his employer, but he bore it bravely for those three years, and then fled to his mother's house. But she disapproved of this step, and urged him to return to the service of his master. He refused to do so, and chose to emigrate to America; telling his brother that he would relinquish all right to any property that he might inherit from his father's estate if he would give him the necessary means to convey him to the United States. His brother, moved by his entreaties, gave him assistance, and he bade farewell to his native land. His parents were of the Roman Catholic faith, and he had been baptized and duly confirmed by the bishop; he had also conformed to the entire discipline of that church, never doubting the religion in which he had been reared. It was in July, 1818, when he arrived in New York, and his entire fortune was about twelve dollars. After finding lodgings he began to look for something to do, and visited store after store, acknowledging that he was perfectly willing to work, and resolved to do anything that was honest to help him to support himself. Among other places he called on the Messrs. Harper, who were then in the printing business in Pearl street. They listened to his story, and accepted him as an apprentice to their business; moreover, he became an inmate of the family of one of the firm, where he was associated with young men of his own age who had been religiously educated, and the influences which surrounded him were very favorable to his own moral improvement. His education and associations in Ireland had not fitted him to fill any position that required culture; but he was ready for any task that he could perform. He labored earnestly and steadily both at the press and at other employment in the printing department, so faithfully that he won the respect of all with whom he came in contact. The firm of J. & J. Harper was then composed of two brothers, James and John. Their two younger brothers, Wesley and Fletcher, who subsequently became members of the firm of Harper & Brothers, were then working at the business with Murray, and were also his companions by night, occupying the same room with him in their mother's house. He continued in this family until the autumn of 1820, when he became a boarder in Mr. Kirk's house, in Liberty street, although he still continued in the employ of the Harpers. He there formed an intimacy with some young men, theological students chiefly, one of whom, who was afterwards known as Rev. J. B. Steele, of the Reformed Dutch Church, proposed to teach him the Latin language. To this young Murray assented, and he made such rapid progress that at the end of six months he was not only able to translate " Virgil," but also possessed some knowledge of the Greek grammar. In the meantime his religious training had not been neglected. He had first abandoned the church of his fathers, and was lapsing into infidelity, when he was brought under the influence of the Methodists. After being a probationary member for a period he became an attendant upon the ministrations of the Presbyterian Church, and finally joined that communion. In the winter of 1820–21 he determined to prepare himself for the work of the gospel ministry, and at that time came under the notice of the Rev. Dr. Alexander Proudfit, of Salem, Washington county, New York, who encouraged him in the views he now entertained; and by means of funds, raised by several benevolent persons connected with the " Brick Church," in New York, he was enabled to prosecute his studies in that direction, having previously connected himself with that congregation, then under the pastoral care of Rev. Dr. Spring. Now that the way was open he entered upon his studies with greater avidity than before; for while he was earnestly seeking the assistance necessary for his support, while prosecuting his studies, he had neglected no opportunities of self-culture, but had been occupied in steadily improving every leisure hour. His associates were those who have since been distinguished in various public and private positions, and with them he mingled constantly. He was yet an apprentice to the Harpers, and his time and services were valuable to them, as he had so thoroughly learned the business; but when he sought their advice and assistance in reference to his future career, they cheerfully cancelled his indentures and bid him God-speed in his new sphere. In the fall of 1821 he went to Amherst Academy, Massachusetts, where he prepared for entering college, under the tutorship of Gerard Halleck, afterwards editor of the New York *Journal of Commerce*. He remained there about nine months, and in

early identified with the great railroad system of the state, active in the promotion of enterprises and of the part of religious institutions. His genius was large and conservative. He was a man of generous and genial disposition, a cheerful giver to charitable and benevolent objects. He was a member of the Protestant Episcopal Church, and one of the Trustees of Burlington College. He was married to a granddaughter of General Elias Dayton, and was a resident of Elizabeth, his native place, where he died, November 18th, 1861.

MURRAY, REV. NICHOLAS, D. D., Clergyman, late pastor of the First Presbyterian Church of Elizabeth, was born, December 25th, 1802, at Ballynaskea, in the county of Westmeath, Ireland, and was the son of Nicholas and Judith (Mangson) Murray. His father was a farmer of some property, and exerted considerable influence in the civil affairs of the neighborhood in which he lived; he died in 1806. Nicholas remained at home under the care of his mother until he was about nine years old, when he went to reside with an aunt, his mother's sister, some ten or more miles distant, where he went to school until he reached the age of twelve. He was then apprenticed as a merchant's clerk in a store in Granaugh, near Edgeworthstown, where he remained three years. He was solicited both to used by his employer, but he bore it bravely for three years, and then fled to his mother's roof, and, as things turned of this step, and urged him to return to the service of his master. He refused to do so, and gave up emigrate to America, telling his mother that he would relinquish all right to any property that he could make from his father's estate if he would give him the means to convey him to the United States. This her love, pierced by his entreaties, gave him assistance, and a sad farewell to his native land. His parents were of the Roman Catholic faith, and he had been baptized and duly confirmed by the bishop; he had also conformed to the entire discipline of that church, never doubting the religion in which he had been reared. It was in July, 1818, when he arrived in New York, and his entire fortune was about twelve dollars. After finding lodgings he began to look for something to do, and visited store after store, acknowledging that he was perfectly willing to work, and resolved to do anything that was honest to help him to support himself. Among other places he called on the Messrs. Harper, who were then in the printing business in Pearl street. They listened to his story, and accepted him as an apprentice to their business; moreover, he became an inmate of the family of one of the firm, where he associated with young men of his own age who had been religiously educated, and the influences which surrounded him were very favorable to his own moral improvement. His education and associations in

Ireland had not fitted him to fill any position that required culture; but he was ready for any task that he could perform. He labored earnestly and steadily both at the press and at other employment in the printing department, so faithfully that he won the respect of all with whom he came in contact. The firm of J. & J. Harper was then composed of two brothers, James and John. Their two younger brothers, Wesley and Fletcher, who subsequently became members of the firm of Harper & Brothers, were then working at the business with Murray, and were also his companions by night, occupying the same room with him in their mother's house. He continued in this family until the autumn of 1820, when he became a boarder in Mr. Kirk's house, in Liberty street, although he still continued in the employ of the Harpers. He there formed an intimacy with some young men, theological students chiefly, one of whom, who was afterwards known as Rev. J. B. Steele, of the Reformed Dutch Church, proposed to teach him the Latin language. To this young Murray assented, and he made such rapid progress that at the end of six months he was not only able to translate "Virgil," but also possessed some knowledge of the Greek grammar. In the meantime his religious training had not been neglected. He had abandoned the church of his fathers, and was lapsing into infidelity, when he was brought under the influence of the Methodists. After being a probationary member for a period he became an attendant upon the ministrations of the Presbyterian Church, and finally joined that communion. In the winter of 1820-21 he determined to prepare himself for the work of the gospel ministry, and at this time came under the notice of the Rev. Dr. Alexander Proudfit, of Salem, Washington county, New York, who encouraged him in the views he then entertained, and by means of funds, raised by several benevolent persons connected with the "Brick Church," in New York, he was enabled to prosecute his studies in that direction, having previously connected himself with that congregation, then under the pastoral care of Rev. Dr. Spring. Now that the way was open he entered upon his studies with greater avidity than before; for while he was earnestly seeking the assistance necessary for his support, while prosecuting his studies, he had neglected no opportunity of self-culture, but had been occupied in steadily improving every leisure hour. His associates were those who had been distinguished in various public and private pursuits, and with them he mingled constantly. He was yet an apprentice to the Harpers, and his time and services were valuable to them, as he had so thoroughly learned the business; but when he sought their advice and assistance in reference to his future career, they cheerfully cancelled his indentures and bid him God-speed in his new sphere. In the fall of 1821 he went to Amherst Academy, Massachusetts, which he prepared for entering college, under the tuition of Gerard Hallock, afterwards editor of the New York Journal of Commerce. He remained there about nine months, and at

N. Murray

the autumn of 1822 entered the freshman class of Williams College, then under the presidency of Rev. E. D. Griffin, D. D. He was a diligent and earnest student, and always acquitted himself well; and he made rapid progress in his studies. During his sophomore year he was elected as the orator of the day on the anniversary of our national independence; and the lofty spirit of patriotism which pervaded his address showed how thoroughly he had become an American in sentiment. He passed through the four years' course of study, and graduated with honor in the summer of 1826. He then accepted for a short time an agency of the American Tract Society, and left New York to fulfil the same in September, 1826. He visited many cities and towns in the interior, where he addressed congregations and organized auxiliary societies. After a service of six or seven weeks he returned, and at once entered the Theological Seminary at Princeton. He remained there for some time, pursuing his studies under the care of the New York Presbytery, with which he had connected himself, occasionally accepting, during his vacations, an agency of the tract society, as a colporteur. On one of these occasions he absented himself from the seminary beyond the specified time, and had neglected to inform the presbytery of his reasons therefor. It appears this body directed the moderator to write him a letter of caution; and his letter in reply, which has been preserved, shows that he was capable of wielding a pen in self-defence, and was also not disposed to compromise himself in the least, nor willing to obey such tyrannical orders. He continued his labors in connection with the tract society in Pennsylvania, and was an efficient laborer in establishing an auxiliary society in Philadelphia. He was thus engaged for about eighteen months, and was enabled to lay up a sufficient store of money wherewith to sustain himself during the remainder of his divinity studies at Princeton. Notwithstanding his absence from the seminary he had kept pace with all the studies of his class during his leisure hours. In fact, so successful was he in this respect that his certificate of dismission from the seminary, given May 7th, 1829, states that he had entered the institution, November 9th, 1826, " and has ever since been a regular student." In April, 1829, he was licensed by the Presbytery of Philadelphia to preach the gospel, and his first sermon was delivered in that city, in the "old Pine Street Church." He then filled a three weeks' engagement in Norristown, Pennsylvania, and proceeded to Wilkesbarre, in the same State, to hold a mission service of two months' duration, at the instance of the Board of Missions of the General Assembly. He was subsequently invited by the churches of Wilkesbarre and Kingston to become their pastor; and, after consulting with friends in Philadelphia, accepted the call. He was frequently during this year perplexed with calls from various sources, urging him to accept pastorates, and the American Tract Society wished him to become their permanent agent; and before he had been even licensed to preach, the Presbyterian Board of

Education elected him their Assistant Corresponding Secretary and General Agent. But having his mind set upon the pastoral office he declined these appointments. He was ordained pastor of the churches of Wilkesbarre and Kingston, November 4th, 1829, and formally installed. He remained in the Wyoming valley about three years and a half, and built up the congregations there, meanwhile receiving and declining a call to act as General Agent of the American Tract Society for the Valley of the Mississippi. In May, 1833, he received a call to become pastor of the First Presbyterian Church, of Elizabethtown, New Jersey, and after some little time accepted the same—urged as he was by his ministerial brethren. He was duly installed, July 23d, 1833. He was the immediate successor of the Rev. Dr. John McDowell, who had been its settled pastor for nearly the twenty-nine previous years. He remained here for nearly twenty-eight years as a faithful minister, and though frequently solicited by other churches to become their pastor invariably declined. Three several times was he tendered the pastorate of the Park Street Church, in Boston, and three times he replied in the negative. From the North and the South, the East and the West, came calls, but to all he unhesitatingly replied, No. His ecclesiastical relations were, first, as a member of the Susquehanna Presbytery, and, secondly, as being connected with the Presbytery of Elizabeth; and he was never absent from any of their meetings, except when abroad, and on one occasion in 1860. He was from 1830 to 1860 a member of the New Jersey Synod, and never missed a single meeting; after a few years' attendance in this body he was elected Moderator. In 1849, in the twentieth year of his ministry, he was chosen Moderator of the General Assembly. He was a faithful, laborious, painstaking presbyter; one who was an earnest, though not an eloquent preacher; and a dignified, learned, and catholic-spirited man. He gave a warm support to the national societies for the circulation of the Bible and tracts, and earnestly labored in their behalf. He was also a noted lecturer, and delivered these in all parts of the Union. He was foremost in everything that tended to advance the welfare of the people. He took great interest in the cause of common school education in the State of New Jersey; and his exertions were felt in the Legislature and in the distant counties. He was among the founders of the New Jersey Historical Society, and at his own request the meeting was called which gave birth to that organization. He also helped to establish the Lyceum and the Orphan Asylum, in his own city. Twice he went abroad and revisited his native island, and also made an extended tour on the continent of Europe. He was celebrated as the author of certain letters addressed to Bishop Hughes, of New York, over the signature of "Kirwan." The first series appeared weekly, commencing February 6th, and terminating May 8th, 1847. When completed they were published in book form, and over 100,000 copies were sold, besides being translated into the German language. His second series of similar letters were begun October 2d, 1847, and were likewise addressed to Bishop Hughes, except the two last, which were addressed to the Roman Catholic people. As Bishop Hughes replied in a series of six letters, addressed to "Dear Reader," Dr. Murray rejoined in a single letter, answering the six of his aulagonist, and ended the controversy. His next essay against the church of his fathers was in a series of letters addressed to the late Chief-Justice Taney, and contained the result of his observations and studies while in the city of Rome, and were published in a volume in 1852, entitled, "Romanism at Home." He also published "Parish and other Pencillings;" "Men and Things as I Saw them in Europe;" "The Happy Home;" "Preachers and Preaching." A posthumous work, containing sermons which he had never delivered, entitled, "A Dying Legacy to the People of My Beloved Charge," and containing discourses "on the unseen and eternal," was issued in the summer of 1861. He was a most pleasant, cheerful companion, his conversation abounding in genial humor, with occasional flashes of wit that enlivened the circle around him. He was liberal to all who called themselves Christians, and especially to those from whom he separated in youth. When one of his brethren remonstrated with him in having subscribed and donated funds for the building of a Roman Catholic church in Elizabeth, he replied that he desired to show his kindly feelings towards those whose faith he opposed. He was alike respected by all his fellow-townsmen, and his death was profoundly felt by all classes in the city of his adoption. He was married, in January, 1830, to Eliza J., daughter of the Rev. Morgan John Rhees, a native of Wales, and a Baptist minister, and was the father of ten children, six of whom preceded him to the grave. He died in Elizabeth, February 4th, 1861.

ARSH, HAMPTON O., President of the National Iron Bank, of Morristown, New Jersey, was born, July 23d, 1831, in Mendham, Morris county, and is the son of John and Caroline (Hudson) Marsh, both of whom are natives of New Jersey; his father is a carriage builder in Mendham. He received a rudimentary education in his native town, and when thirteen years old became a pupil in the Flushing Institute, near Madison, New Jersey, where he remained about one year. Returning home he became a clerk in a mercantile store, and in 1849 went to Morristown, where he filled a similar position for three years. In 1852, having attained his majority, he returned to Mendham, where he became engaged in the manufacture of carriages on his own account, and which he continued until 1859. He then removed to Morristown and embarked in the lumber business in connection with different parties, constituting two firms, up to the year 1867, when he associated himself with George E. Voorhess, under the firm-name of Voorhess & Marsh, hardware merchants, and this partnership continued until 1870, when he disposed of his interests in the establishment. For some time prior to this last-named date he had been a director of the National Iron Bank, formerly a State institution, but which had been established under the national system, May 4th, 1865, with a capital of $100,000. He was elected the President of this institution, January 12th, 1869, and in order to devote his whole time to the interests of the bank, relinquished his business, as above stated, in 1870. The capital stock of the bank, on and after January 1st, 1872, was increased to $200,000, and is at present in a sound and prosperous condition. He is also a director in and Vice-President of the Morris Aqueduct Company; and one of the original incorporators and directors of the Masonic Hall Association, and filled the position of its Treasurer for three years. Upon the organization of the Washington Association, of New Jersey, which has for its object the care and control of the building known as "Washington's Head-quarters," at Morristown, New Jersey, he was chosen one of the Executive Committee of that body. He was a member of the Whig party up to the time of its disintegration; and has since acted with the Republicans. He was married, 1855, to Mary E., daughter of William P. Dayton, a highly respected merchant of New York city, who died in that same year.

ITCHELL, HENRY, M. D., Physician, of Jersey City, was born, August 6th, 1845, in Norwich, Chenango county, New York. His father, Dr. Henry Mitchell, was a native of Connecticut and a nephew of Roger Sherman, one of the signers of the Declaration of Independence, and settled in Chenango county, New York, in 1806. He was a classical scholar of high attainments, a graduate of Yale College, and a man of rare skill and accurate judgment in his profession. In 1827 he was chosen a member of the New York State Legislature, and in 1832 he represented his district in Congress. He was a member of the New York State Medical Society and of the American Medical Association. His wife was Mary Bellamy, of Catskill, New York. Their son, Henry, received his early education in the public schools of Chenango county, and later attended the Catskill Academy and the Phillips Exeter Academy. It was decided that, like his father, he should enter the medical profession. Accordingly, on leaving school, he commenced a preliminary course of medical study in the office of Dr. H. C. Bellows, of Norwich, New York. Having accomplished his preparatory reading he entered Bellevue Hospital Medical College, continuing his private studies under the direction of Professor James R. Wood, of New York city. He graduated in medicine and surgery in October, 1866. Having received his diploma he returned to his home in Norwich, New York, and there entered upon the practice of his profession. In 1869 he held the office of Coroner for Chenango County. He was appointed, September 1st, 1868, Surgeon of the 103d Regiment New York State National Guard, and this position he continued to hold until 1870, when he removed to New Jersey and established himself in Jersey City. There he entered upon the practice of his profession and with an energy and skill that won success. He served for three years as Visiting Physician to St. Francis' Hospital, in Jersey City, and is at present one of the Visiting Physicians to the Hudson County Church Hospital. He is a member of the District Medical Society for Hudson County, and has held official position in that organization during four years. He is also a member of the American Medical Association. He was married, in 1866, to Elizabeth M. Roberts, daughter of Rev. William Roberts, D. D., of New York city.

———◦×◦———

OOKE, HENRY G., A. M., M. D., of Holmdel, was born in that township, Monmouth county, New Jersey, February 3d, 1836. His father, Robert W. Cooke, was a native of Sussex county, and his mother, whose maiden name was Susan Gansevoort, was born at Albany, New York. He was educated in a select school near his home, and in 1850 entered Rutgers College, from which he graduated in 1853, receiving his degree of A. M. from that institution. Immediately after he commenced reading medicine with his father, an eminent practitioner; but within a few months was installed a student in the office of the celebrated Willard Parker, of New York, Professor of Surgery in the College of Physicians and Surgeons of that city. Having completed his preparatory studies, Dr. Cooke became a matriculant in this institution, and in 1857 graduated from it, receiving his degree of M. D. He associated at once in practice with his father, at Holmdel, and soon secured a fine reputation for faithfulness and ability. In 1862 he entered the Union service as Surgeon of the 29th New Jersey Volunteers, and remained with this organization for nine months, when he returned to Holmdel, where he has since been engaged in professional duties, making the old homestead his residence. His father died in 1867, and he succeeded to the large practice which the former had enjoyed for a long period. Dr. Cooke is now prominently identified with the leading medical associations. In 1859 he was President of the Monmouth County Medical Society. In 1868 he was a delegate to the American Medical Association, which convened at New York. He has frequently represented the profession in his county in the State society. He is now a member of the New Jersey Academy of Medicine, and acts as Medical Examiner for a number of leading insurance companies. He has always been devoted to the highest interests of his profession, and the fruit of this devotion is a reputation which secures esteem wherever he is known. His practice is a very large one, and his patrons are among the most influential citizens of the section in which he resides. He was married, on June 8th, 1876, to Maria B. Condrey, of New Rochelle, New York.

———◦×◦———

ORROGH, CLIFFORD T., M. D., Physician, of New Brunswick, is a native of Ireland, having been born in county Cork, August 1st, 1821. His father, John Morrogh, was a gentleman of culture and means, and his mother, Mary (Plowden) Morrogh, was a daughter of Francis Plowden, Esq., the English historian. Clifford Morrogh received his early education at the well-known select school of Porter & Hamlin, in Cork. In the year 1836 he removed to America, and finished his studies in the city of New York. For a period of four years he was engaged in mercantile pursuits in New York; but he had determined on entering the medical profession, and with that purpose he entered, as a student, the office of Dr. John H. Whittaker, who was at that time Demonstrator of Anatomy in the University of New York. Having concluded his course of preparatory reading he attended the regular course of lectures at the university, and graduated from that institution in March, 1847. During his attendance at the university he was chosen by Professor Whittaker to be Demonstrator of Anatomy in his private school, at which there was an attendance of about 200 scholars. In March, 1847, immediately after his graduation, he commenced the practice of his profession in association with his brother, Archibald C. Morrogh, M. D., an eminent practitioner in New York city. He remained with his brother in New York until the fall of 1847, when he removed to New Brunswick, New Jersey, where he commenced to practise independently, and where he has ever since resided. In 1869 and 1870 he went to Europe and spent several months abroad, visiting all the principal hospitals of Italy, England and France, spending most of his time in the latter country. He made another visit to Europe in the year 1873, but this trip was undertaken mainly on account of his health. He has been a delegate to the State Medical Society on various occasions. His army experience, during the war of the rebellion, was brief, but valuable. Immediately after the battle of the Wilderness, and in response to the call of Governor Olden for medical aid, he went to the front, and during a period of three weeks rendered most efficient service there. His standing in his profession is very high, and as a surgeon, particularly, he enjoys a wide and enviable reputation. He has been twice married. In June, 1850, he was married to Mrs. Mary Richmond, who died in the spring of 1871. In the fall of 1872 he married for his second wife Cornelia Perry, of Troy, New York.

ARISON, CORNELIUS W., M. D., Principal of, and Professor of Natural Science in, the Academy of Science and Art at Ringoes, New Jersey, was born, January 10th, 1837, in Delaware township, Hunterdon county, New Jersey. He received a rudimentary education in the public school nearest to his father's farm. At the age of seventeen he began to spend his leisure hours in reading such books treating of science as came within his reach. In the early part of the eighteenth year of his age he purchased Bullion's "Latin Grammar" and "Latin Reader;" and, unaided by an instructor, during the following spring and summer, while at the plow-tail through the day, he made himself acquainted with the declension of Latin nouns and adjectives, and with the conjugation of Latin verbs, and during the evenings tried his skill at translation. In October of 1855 he became an attendant at the Pennsylvania College of Medicine. In the spring of 1856 he commenced a classical course of study at the Flemington High School, then under the principalship of Rev. Jonathan D. Merrill, A. M. He matriculated at the University at Lewisburg, Pennsylvania, in September, 1857, and in September, 1860, was engaged as Teacher of Mathematics and Natural Science in the High School at Flemington, New Jersey. In June, 1861, he became Principal of this institution. In October of the same year he matriculated at the Geneva Medical College, at Geneva, New York, and was graduated M. D. by this institution, January 20th, 1863. He settled at Ringoes, New Jersey, as a physician and teacher, in February, 1863. The seminary at Ringoes was the result of his interest in educational matters in that vicinity. In that institution he was associated with his brother, Rev. A. B. Larison, M. D., who acted as Principal and Instructor in the Languages, while he himself was the Teacher of Natural Science. Upon the death of his brother, A. B. Larison, the principalship of the seminary devolved upon him, and this position he held until September, 1874, continuing still as Teacher of Natural Science. In August, 1874, he was appointed Professor of Natural Science in the University at Lewisburg, Pennsylvania. This position he accepted, and entered upon its duties, September 10th, 1874. Owing to the death of his partner, C. M. Lee, M. D., which occurred in June, 1875, he resigned his position in the university and returned to Ringoes to take charge of his practice again. He has been steadily engaged in the practice of medicine since he first settled at Ringoes, and has the control of a lucrative and extensive business, it being one of the largest in the county. In June, 1876, he was appointed Professor of Zoology in the University at Lewisburg, Pennsylvania. As his duties there would not require his constant attendance, and he could remain at home in his practice much of the time, he accepted the position. He has also organized at Ringoes a seminary, or, more strictly speaking, a school, termed the Academy of Science and Art, and which has every promise of success.

This school was organized to afford an opportunity for a practical education in those departments of science and art that most directly bear upon the rounds of every-day life. The instruction given is of the most practical character, and imparted in the most practical manner; the pupil being constantly required to reduce whatever is taught directly to practice, and to show how it relates to the things of the present. Every facility is given for proper and careful instruction in the different branches taught; and the implements used for imparting a knowledge of the various sciences are of the most perfect and costly character. Especially is this the case in the study of physical geography, where a globe sixty-one inches in diameter, with an uneven surface, shows the ridges, peaks, plains, plateaus, excavations and depressions of the earth's surface, and exhibits in a striking manner the relative altitude of such ridges, peaks, plains, plateaus, etc. Politically he is a Democrat; and religiously a Baptist. He married Mary Jane, daughter of Gershom C. Sergeant, of Flemington, New Jersey, March 25th, 1863. She was one of the first graduates of the New Jersey State Normal School, her diploma bearing date June, 1859.

ORD, REV. EDWARD, Clergyman, and Pastor of the Reformed Church of Metuchen, was born, March 29th, 1821, at Danby, New York, and is a son of Chester W. and B. (Kingsbury) Lord. His father was a native of Salisbury, Connecticut, while his mother was born in Berkshire county, Massachusetts. He received a thorough classical education, and was a student at Williams College, Massachusetts, where he graduated in 1843. Having determined to devote his life to the gospel ministry, he commenced his studies at the theological seminary at Auburn, New York, from which institution he graduated in 1846. He subsequently was ordained and settled over a Presbyterian congregation at Romulus, New York, where he ministered acceptably until 1851, when he received and accepted a call to become the pastor of the Presbyterian Church at Fulton, New York. He labored there for fourteen years. During this period his congregation granted him one year's leave of absence, when he accepted the chaplaincy of the 110th Regiment of New York Volunteers, in August, 1862. The command, after remaining in camp at Baltimore for instruction, which occupied some two months, was sent to New Orleans, reaching that city at the time that General Banks assumed command of the Department of the Gulf. He accompanied the regiment in its march through western Louisiana, and was present during the entire siege of Port Hudson. He was honorably discharged from the service at the expiration of the year, for which period his leave of absence from his congregation extended; and he accordingly returned to Fulton. In 1865 he became pastor of the church at Adams, New York, where he remained until the spring of 1870, when he removed to Metuchen, New Jersey, where he has since resided, as pastor of the Reformed Church. During the thirty years of his clerical life he has been constantly and actively engaged in building up the congregations among whom he has labored, and he has ever felt that he has not labored in vain, as the churches grew and prospered under his ministrations. He was married, in August, 1846, to Mary J. Sanders, of Williamstown, Massachusetts.

CONKLING, EDWARD PAYSON, Lawyer, of Flemington, was born, 1846, in Boonton, Morris county, New Jersey, and is a son of the Rev. C. S. Conkling, a well-known and highly respected clergyman of the Presbyterian Church, who was for several years Superintendent of the Public Schools of Hunterdon County. The family is of English lineage, and is a branch of the Conkling family of New York. Edward obtained his preliminary education at Carversville, Pennsylvania; and in 1864 entered the sophomore class of Lafayette College, Easton, in the same State, and graduated therefrom with the class of 1867, receiving the third honor. After leaving college he taught for a short time at the Susquehanna Institute; and in 1868 entered the office of George A. Allen, of Flemington, to prosecute his legal studies. He remained under the preceptorship of that eminent practitioner until 1871, when he was admitted to practise. For two years he was associated with Hon. John T. Bird, constituting the firm of Bird & Conkling. In 1873 this copartnership was dissolved, and he has since practised alone. He has won for himself a reputation and a practice, during this short period, second to few in the county; and the bar of Hunterdon county is justly regarded as the first in the State. He is a prominent member of the Democratic party, to which he renders efficient service in every political canvass, being an eloquent and logical orator. He is highly esteemed not only by his professional brethren, but by his fellow-townsmen. He is a director of the Flemington National Bank. He was married, 1871, to Jennie Key, of Hunterdon county.

BISPHAM, CHARLES, Retired Merchant, of Mount Holly, New Jersey, and son of John and Margaret Bispham, was born at that place, December 2d, 1798, in the house where he now resides, and where his father also was born. The homestead has been in the possession of the family about one hundred and forty years. Having the misfortune to lose his father when he was but twelve years of age, Charles Bispham was placed in a school in Philadel-

phia under the watchful care of his eldest brother, Stacy B. Bispham, the partner of that noble and Christian gentleman, Samuel Archer, the firm being extensively engaged in the China and India trade. Into the counting-house of this firm he was received on reaching his sixteenth year. Here he remained until he was twenty-one, though his brother lived but two years after his admission. At this time he commenced business on his own account as a super-cargo, making numerous voyages to India, China, Buenos Ayres, Valparaiso, Lima, and various other ports on the Pacific coast. He afterwards entered into association with Mr. Joseph Archer, the son of his brother's partner, in Philadelphia, but the enterprise not proving as profitable as was anticipated, an agreement was made between them that Mr. Archer should join the house of Messrs. Wetmore & Co., Canton, and Mr. Bispham that of Messrs. Alsop & Co., Valparaiso, and that at the expiration of ten years they should make an equal division of the profits. The agreement was carried out, and the division of profits made on their return to the United States, in the latter part of the year 1840. Since that time Mr. Bispham has resided in Mount Holly, employing himself in the improvement of his native town by building, farming, etc. He has always been the President of its railroad, and he is a director in nearly all the institutions of the place. He built a cottage at Long Branch, New Jersey, in 1845, where the family reside during the warm months of summer.

WARD, GEORGE S., M. D., of Newark, was born in Bloomfield, New Jersey, November 11th, 1827. His parents were Bethuel and Rhoda (Freeman) Ward, both natives of the same State. His education was obtained at the Bloomfield Academy, an old-established and well-known institution of learning, where he acquired a thorough preliminary training preparatory to entering college. A prolonged and almost fatal attack of fever, engendered by the nursing of a brother, prevented him from carrying out his design of entering college. Selecting the medical profession, he placed himself under the tuition of the late Dr. John F. Ward, of Newark (a brother), and an eminent and successful practitioner for many years. Matriculating at the College of Physicians and Surgeons, New York, he took there a thorough course, and graduated in the spring of 1849. Locating himself in Newark, he immediately commenced his labors, and by his devotion to his profession has succeeded in building up an extensive and lucrative practice; enjoying the respect of the profession at large as also the esteem and confidence of the community with which he has been identified for more than a quarter of a century. He has for the past twenty years been the Attending Physician to the City Almshouse, performing efficiently the duties of this office to the entire satisfaction of all. He is a member of the Essex County Medical Society. He was married, May 9th, 1850, to Fanny H. Baldwin, of Philadelphia.

———◦✦◦———

ATSON, BERIAH A., M. D., of Jersey City, the third son of Perry and Maria, *née* Place, Watson, was born at Lake George, Warren county, New York, March 26th, 1836. Perry Watson, a native of Rhode Island, was descended from a pioneer family of New England, and was named after his grandfather, who had participated in the battle of Bunker Hill. In early youth he removed to Greenwich, Washington county, New York, where his wife was born. He subsequently led the life of a farmer in this and the adjoining county of Warren, and was highly respected by all who appreciated his stern qualities of industry and honesty. When seven years of age their son was sent to the country district school, which he attended regularly during the summer and winter months, *i. e.*, about eight months during the year, until he was fourteen years of age. His services were now demanded on the farm, as his time was thought too valuable to be spent in the school-room during the summer months. But in this new occupation, to which he reluctantly turned himself, it was soon discovered that he took neither pleasure nor interest. Arrangements were then made with Isaac Streeter whereby he was enabled to continue his studies uninterruptedly. His innate desire for knowledge was such that he never failed to improve every moment by study when not engaged in farm work. Gladly did he take advantage of the stormy weather, which enabled him to leave the irksome duties of farming for his agreeable recitations. These were indeed days of real enjoyment, and the progress made in his studies during this period was even greater than that at any previous time. In the following autumn, just prior to the opening of the winter session of the district school, young Watson took up his residence with the family of Jonathan Streeter, father of Isaac, previously mentioned. Attending the district school, doing whatever was required of him on the farm, passing the evenings in reading and studying his books, thus he occupied the winter months. To understand the advantages of a residence with this family, to which the doctor attributes very largely his success, it may be proper to mention some facts in regard to their peculiarities. Jonathan Streeter and family were strict members of the Society of Friends. Though in early life he had been obliged to labor with his hands for his daily bread, and had been enabled to obtain scarcely four months' instruction at school, he was, however, in the elementary branches far more thorough than many collegiates of the present day. He had, in fact, by his studious application and untiring industry, acquired not only a good education but also enough of this world's goods to be considered wealthy by the community in which he lived. At the time young Watson resided with him he had

attained his sixtieth year, but was still strong and remarkably industrious. There were during this period two other young men living with the family. All were required to be ready for the duties of the day promptly at five A. M. during the whole year. In winter, at this early hour, Mr. Streeter never failed to be seated before the blazing wood-fire, provided with his in-door work, which frequently was the making of a broom from a hickory or birch stick. The moment he was seated he required one of the young men of his household, properly supplied with a book, and with works of reference near him, to read aloud while he himself plied his work. The same system was adopted in the evening, and thus work never ceased till ten o'clock. The reading was conducted with great care; the reader was never allowed to hurry; he was required not only to make his reading intelligible to Mr. Streeter but to understand it himself. If a word were found that he supposed the reader did not understand he was stopped, asked to give its meaning, and if unable to do so, he was requested to refer to the dictionary and read aloud the definition. A similar method was followed with regard to geographical names, the reader being required to locate the place, give all the important facts pertaining to its surroundings and its history, or obtain them by reference before proceeding further. The grammatical construction of sentences was also criticised, and Mr. Streeter was frequently heard citing the rules from Lindley Murray's grammar; a copy of this work at one period in his life he had constantly with him, to be studied at every available opportunity, even when working behind his team in performing his agricultural duties. This work of reading for the old gentleman fell principally to the lot of young Watson. On the closing of the district school he entered a private school, conducted by Warren Fleming, where he remained a few months. During the following summer he left this school and assisted his friend and patron on his farm, still pursuing his studies with the assistance of Isaac and Annie Streeter. In this family the strict rules enforced prohibited all frivolous conversation, but encouraged discussions on scientific subjects. After a residence of two years with this kind-hearted Quaker, who was continually laboring for the advancement of his neighbors' interests, and thus frequently sacrificing his own comfort, he left this hospitable home for the purpose of engaging in a new sphere of activity as a teacher of a public school. The next six months were occupied in teaching, after which he entered the State Normal School, at Albany, New York. From this time until he had attained his twenty-first year he was engaged in study either at school or under a private tutor. A portion of his time, however, was employed in teaching. The object of this was two-fold: firstly, to procure the means necessary for a present livelihood; secondly, that he might secure the funds necessary for the prosecution of his future studies. When he had arrived at his majority he entered the office of the late Dr. James Riley, at Suckasunny, Morris county, New Jersey, where he devoted his

Collins Pub Co. Philad.ᵃ

B. A. Watson M.D.

whole time and attention to the study of the profession he had chosen. In the autumn of 1859 he matriculated in the medical department of the University of New York, from which he was graduated in the spring of 1861. After leaving the medical school he located at White House, New Jersey, where he practised his profession for a short time. In the fall of 1862 he entered the United States service as a Contract Surgeon, after having passed an examination before the Board of Examiners appointed by the Surgeon-General for the Department of New York, of which Dr. Valentine Mott was President, and was ordered to report for duty, September 1st, at Newark, where he was engaged in the army hospital service until March 26th, 1863. He then received a commission from Governor Parker as Assistant-Surgeon of the 4th New Jersey Volunteers, and reported promptly to the commandant of his regiment, but very soon after was detached from that command and ordered to report to Dr. Asch, Medical Director of the Artillery Reserve, and by him directed to take charge of the 4th Artillery Brigade, then located at Falmouth, Virginia. He remained with that command until after the battle of Gettysburg, when he received orders to return to his regiment (the 4th New Jersey), and it was commissioned Surgeon, with the rank of Major, on November 4th. Shortly after this latter date he was detailed as one of the operating surgeons to the 1st Brigade, 1st Division, of the 6th Army Corps, stationed in front of Petersburg, Virginia, at this time. In this capacity he had remained but a few months when he was ordered to take charge of the 1st Division, 6th Army Corps Hospital, and at the same time made Acting Medical Purveyor to the corps. He retained this latter position and continued to discharge the duties of the office until the close of the war, retiring from the service July 10th, 1865. Returning to civil life he made choice of Jersey City as his future residence, and renewed the practice of his profession, which has become large and lucrative. Although actively engaged in practice he still finds time for study, and very few men at any period of life enter into it with more ardor or better success. He has frequently been heard to say to members of his profession: "If you would spend less time in the drug stores; less time in places of amusements; devote every moment, not actually required for the attendance of your patients or the performance of other necessary duties, to study, then, in due time, you would be rewarded and your profession honored." He has little respect for the plea often made by members of the medical profession that the weather is now too cold or too hot for study, and is probably inclined to think that such men are too lazy for their profession. He has not only endeavored to advance himself but has also endeavored to advance the interests of the profession. The passage of the act legalizing dissection of human cadavera in this State was secured principally through the efforts of the doctor and his friend, Dr. J. D. McGill. The same may be also said in regard to the formation of the New Jersey Academy of Medicine.

He is a Fellow of the New Jersey Academy of Medicine; Permanent Member of the American Medical Association; Member of the New York Neurological Society, and also the Jersey City Pathological Society. He is now President of the New Jersey Academy of Medicine, and he likewise held at one time the office of President of the District Medical Society for the County of Hudson, New Jersey. He was appointed Attending Surgeon to the Jersey City Charity Hospital at the time of its organization in 1869, and also appointed Attending Surgeon to the St. Francis Hospital in 1873, and still continues to discharge the duties of both positions at the present time. He has, from time to time, contributed essays and reports of cases to medical literature of the day, among which may be mentioned the following: "A Case of Facial Neuralgia Treated by Extirpation of the Superior Maxillary Nerve;" *The Medical Record*, October 16th, 1871; "A Case of Hæmatoma of the Thigh, Two Operations: Death;" *The Medical Record*, February 20th, 1875; "The Pathology and Treatment of Chronic Ulcers;" New York *Medical Journal*, July, 1875; "A Supposed Case of Rabies Canina Treated with Strychnia and Woorara: Recovery;" *The American Journal of Medical Sciences*, July, 1876; "Femoral Aneurism Treated by Plugging the Sac: Death, Caused by Hemorrhage from Deep Epigastric Artery, on the Eighteenth Day; Autopsy; Remarks;" *The American Journal of Medical Sciences*, October, 1876. He was married, September 24th, 1868, to Phebe A., only daughter of H. M. Traphagen, of Jersey City, and has two children, Myra M. and Henry M. T.

ORTON, REV. LEVI WARREN, Rector of St. Luke's Episcopal Church, Metuchen, was born in Genesee county, New York, October 17th, 1819. His father, Elijah Norton, came of New England parentage, being a native of Connecticut; he was a contractor and builder. His mother, Mary M. Beardley, was a native of New York State. The preliminary education of the subject of this sketch was obtained at Lowville Academy, Lowville, Lewis county, New York. From that institution he proceeded to the Cherry Valley Academy, Otsego county, in the same State, where he prepared for college. In 1840 he entered Union College, Schenectady, where he spent three years. Then, becoming a candidate for holy orders in the Protestant Episcopal Church, he pursued the study of theology for one year under Rev. E. A. Renouf, of Lowville. Thereafter he entered the General Theological Seminary of New York, where his ministerial studies were completed. He graduated in 1846, and on July 26th of the same year, he was ordained by Bishop Delaney, of New York. His first pastorate was at Watertown, Jefferson county, New York, in which place he officiated for seven years as Rector of Trinity Church. Receiving a call from Jamestown, Chatanqua county, in the same State, he removed to that field of labor, in which he remained engaged for seventeen years. During this period his church was twice destroyed by fire, but each time it was rebuilt. In September, 1870, he removed to Metuchen to accept his present charge. He was married, October 15th, 1846, to Elizabeth P. Leonard, of Lowville.

OUGHTON, CHARLES HENRY, Brevet Colonel United States Volunteers, and Collector of Customs for the District of Perth Amboy, New Jersey, was born, April 30th, 1842, in McComb township, St. Lawrence county, New York, and is the second son of William and Eliza A. (Bentley) Houghton, both of whom are natives of that State. His father's family trace their descent from one of three brothers who emigrated from Houghton Tower, Lancashire, England, a few years subsequent to the landing of the Pilgrims, and who settled in Massachusetts, Colonel Charles H. Houghton being the eighth in descent from one of the three brothers. He received a fair education, both in the district and private schools, occasionally assisting in his father's store. In 1853 his father died, leaving a widow and six children without much means. Shortly after this young Houghton found a position in an union store at De Peyster Corners, where he remained several years, winning the confidence and esteem of all. Owing in part to failing health, he left the position, and after active work on a farm obtained a situation in a large dry-goods house in Ogdensburg, where he continued until the outbreak of the rebellion. Although but nineteen years of age he resolved to volunteer, and having obtained his mother's permission, both he and an elder brother commenced raising a company, which was, however, too late to be accepted in the first call for troops. Shortly after the second call was made the company (H of the 33d Regiment, National Guard, State of New York), to which both himself and brother had belonged for four years previously, volunteered in a body, and was the first to reach Camp Wheeler, at Ogdensburg, which camp was named in honor of the Republican candidate for the Vice-Presidency in 1876. Though he enlisted only as a private, yet he was at once promoted to First or Orderly Sergeant of his company, in which capacity he served for over a year. The regiment was designated as the 60th New York Volunteers, and was ordered to proceed to Washington, but was finally posted at the Relay House, where it performed guard duty on the railroad until the spring of 1862, when the regiment was ordered to reinforce General Banks' Corps, after it had been forced back on Harper's Ferry by Stonewall Jackson. While in the section of Virginia around Little Washington, much sickness prevailed in the command ; and he had a taste of the malarial fever which seemed indigenous to the locality. The regiment had a narrow escape from capture after the second battle of Bull Run, but eventually

rejoined the Union forces at Centreville, making a forced march of twenty-eight miles through the rain and mud, and arrived in time to support General Phil Kearny at the battle of Chantilly, September 1st, 1862. He was recommended for promotion to the grade of Second Lieutenant by his colonel shortly before the latter's death at the battle of Antietam, where young Houghton greatly distinguished himself for bravery and coolness while under fire. His regiment became separated from the main body of the Union army, and in joining the latter lost heavily. Young Houghton, seeing the lieutenant-colonel in danger, interposed his own body as a shield, though without that officer's knowledge. The rest of the autumn was passed at London Heights and Harper's Ferry, whence the regiment marched, December 10th, for Fredericksburg, where they passed their time in marching and countermarching, interspersed with an occasional skirmish. They finally removed to Acquia Creek Landing, where they encamped and erected several forts. In the spring of 1863, being desirous to return home on business, Lieutenant Houghton solicited a leave of absence, which not being granted, he for a second time tendered his resignation, which was accepted, the first having been returned him by General Hooker with this indorsement : "Disapproved ; the services of this officer cannot be spared." His regiment accompanied Hooker to Sherman's army, with which they served until the close of the war, his brother and step-brother remaining as privates during the entire two terms of the regiment's service, refusing promotions tendered them. Young Houghton returned home, married, and re-entered the mercantile house at Ogdensburg, in which he had previously held a position ; but he did not continue there any length of time. The 14th New York Artillery was then organizing at Rochester, and its colonel, learning through his recruiting officer of young Houghton's presence in Ogdensburg, immediately tendered him a Captaincy if he would organize a company. About this time he also received a letter of authority from the governor to raise a company, and he accepted the same. The requisite number was soon raised, and among them came his former captain, in whose favor he wished to withdraw, accepting a subordinate position ; but the latter would not permit it and only asked for a lieutenancy. The company thus recruited was probably the largest in number and stature that left the State during the war, numbering 172 officers and men. The regiment performed garrison duty in the forts of New York harbor until the spring of 1864, when they were ordered to the front. At the opening of the great Sanitary Fair in New York city, 1600 officers and men of the regiment participated in the public demonstration, and the whole corps came together for the first time in dress parade at Alexandria, Virginia, numbering nearly 2,300 officers and men. On their arrival at the seat of war they joined the 9th Corps, under General Burnside, and were in time to participate in the first day's fight at the battle of the Wilderness. Captain Houghton commanded the

picket line on the extreme right of the Union army ; at his front were rebel cavalry, and being allowed to reconnoitre, he advanced his line of skirmishers over a mile, and finding no infantry, re-established his line. General Grant's great flank movement to Spottsylvania was next executed, and to Captain Houghton was again assigned the command of the skirmishers, with whom he advanced and drew the fire of the enemy. The latter attempted to dislodge him, but he retained his lines until his ammunition was exhausted, losing heavily, but inflicting greater loss upon the enemy. In an attack, May 31st, near Tolopotamy creek, his battalion was almost surrounded by the enemy, but was happily withdrawn by the major, who followed the suggestion of Captain Houghton. On June 1st the flank movement on Cold Harbor was executed, when his line was the last to be withdrawn, as it was detailed to protect the ammunition trains and artillery. In rejoining the main line they were attacked by the rebels, and a severe engagement, lasting far into the night, ensued. Twice were they driven by a flank attack from the position they sought to hold, until the trains were safe within our main line. Each time they fought their way back, retaking the position again, Captain Houghton being conspicuous in leading the movement of his men, though he had received a contused wound in the left leg, and twice he was in the enemy's l a ids that night, escaping through the darkness. Next followed the great flank movement to City Point, and the 9th Corps was ordered to take the rebel works with the bayonet. This was executed, though great loss ensued, Captain Houghton's company losing heavily, and in the entire regiment but four captains remained. The three battalions were consolidated into two, the first of which Captain Houghton commanded until March 25th, 1865. During the first siege of Petersburg, his regiment occupied the advanced lines and exposed portions during the greater part of the summer of 1864. On July 30th the mine was sprung, when Captain Houghton led the charge upon the works, capturing prisoners and two guns, which he turned upon the rebels, while the other battalion charged beyond the rebel works and captured a stand of colors from a South Carolina regiment. The regiment, not being properly supported, was obliged to withdraw, having suffered a loss of 127 officers and men. Throughout the remaining portion of the year his regiment was continually engaged in the most exposed situations and hazardous operations, especially in the attack and capture of a portion of Mahone's Division, and where he properly won his Majorship. In November, 1864, with his battalion, he assumed command of Fort Haskell, in front of Petersburg, and so continued until March 25th, 1865, the date of the attack on Fort Steadman. The rebels having captured the latter, his position at Fort Haskell became very precarious, as the enemy not only turned the guns of Steadman on him, but also all the batteries lying between those works, which they also captured, and all the guns in their main line. The bombardment of Fort Haskell was terrific ; as many as fifty shells

were seen at one time to fall within it. While repelling the enemy's charge on the works Captain Houghton received his supposed fatal wounds. Before he was removed to the bomb-proof he was again wounded in the head. The attack on Fort Haskell was repulsed, though the rebels outnum. bered the Union men ten-fold, and they were driven back to Fort Steadman, from which it was death to reach their own lines again, aud they ultimately surrendered to the re. mainder of the 14th Regiment, his battalion having made a sortie from Fort Haskell and recaptured the works. Captain Houghton's death was reported among the list of casualties, but his life was spared, though he lost his right leg. After remaining at the field hospital until after the fall of Petersburg, he was removed to City Point, and eventu. ally to Washington, which city was reached on the day President Lincoln died. He remained at Armory Square Hospital for many weary weeks, hovering between life and death, attended by his faithful wife. But his strong will asserted itself and he recovered. Governor Fenton, learn. ing that he had been thrice recommended for promotion, which he did not obtain at the hands of the Democratic Executive, conferred upon him the brevet rank of Lieu-tenant-Colonel, for gallantry at Forts Steadman and Haskell and general good conduct ; and subsequently he was again brevetted as Colonel, for gallant and meritorious services in the field and general good conduct during the war, he hav-ing distinguished himself by some act of bravery in every battle of his regiment, never having been, during his term of service, whether as an enlisted man or commissioned officer, under arrest or court-martial. While at the hospital he was asked if he desired to return home on leave of ab-sence ; but he replied that he would prefer returning to his regiment for duty. The necessary order was given in pen-cil by Secretary Stanton to the adjutant-general, so that the latter could issue it in proper form ; but that official de-clined to make such order, as Major Houghton's condition was such as to be unable to perform any duty ; that there was no precedent for such a course. Again the Secretary of War issued the memorandum, but the adjutant-general de-clined. In the meantime Major Houghton contrived an-other plan, and resolved to put it into execution. On the same day General Marshall (his colonel), commanding the brigade, asked him if he desired to return to camp, saying that he had a position on his staff which he had reserved for him. To this the Major replied by narrating his own efforts to secure a return to duty, and the difficulties in the way. Finally General Marshall, by adopting a certain course, which the Major had studied out, managed to get him returned to duty, and as a member of his military family. It was altogether an exceptional case, and reflects great honor on the then Major for his persistent efforts to return to the field, where others who had lost a limb were discharged from the service. He left the hospital in an am-bulance, and was heartily greeted and welcomed by his comrades in bivouac and battle, who were then stationed in

Forts Mansfield, Sumner, Reno, etc. He was ordered the next day to report to General Marshall for duty on his staff as Inspector-General of the 1st Brigade, Hardin's Division of the 22d Army Corps. Entering immediately on his duties, he remained until he received an order from General Auger, detailing him upon a General Court-Martial, and also upon a Military Commission at the old Capitol Prison in Washington. While engaged in these duties, his regiment received orders for being mustered out of the service; and, upon learning this fact, he decided at once to request the authorities to be relieved from the duty he was performing so that he might accompany his regiment home. He was urged at head-quarters to remain on duty and in service, when he could have been transferred to the regular army, and, in fact, he was so informed. But the war was over, and conscious that his whole duty had been performed acceptably to the government and to his own credit, and also believing that his services were no longer necessary, he insisted on being relieved in time to join the regiment, which was granted, and he reached the depot in time to take the special train that was to convey his regiment homeward. Here again he was heartily cheered by his men. Having reached Rochester the regiment was disbanded, and in taking leave of his men for the last time, many stern and brave hearts softened, and bronzed cheeks were moistened with tears of affection. After a brief sojourn at home, and receiving several offers to engage in business, he was tendered by Hon. Preston King, who had been appointed collector of customs for the district of New York, a position in the civil service, and he entered upon his duties there October 1st, 1865. He remained in the New York Customs Department for about eight and a half years, and where, by strict attention to his duties, he was several times promoted. On April 1st, 1875, he entered upon the duties of his present position as Collector for the District of Perth Amboy, New Jersey, his fitness for the post being conceded by the leading men of the State and indorsed by the press. He was married, August 18th, 1863, in Michigan, to Lavonia, fourth daughter of Colonel John Anderson, the latter being the first white male child born at Paulus Hook (now Jersey City), and the great-grandson of General Schuyler, of revolutionary renown.

ILLS, ALFRED, Lawyer, of Morristown, was born, July 24th, 1827, in that town, and is a son of Lewis and Sarah (Este) Mills, both of whom were also natives of New Jersey. His father was for a long period a merchant of Morristown. His mother was the daughter of Captain Moses Este, a soldier of the revolutionary war, and a participant in the battle of Monmouth, where he was wounded and left on the field. Captain Este was discovered by Colonel Hamilton, who was on the staff of General Washington, and who happened to be riding over the field after the fight was over.

He had him removed at once to a place of safety and cared for; and Captain Este ever after considered that his life had been saved by Hamilton, for he doubtless would have perished had he remained in his suffering condition much longer. Twenty-five years after the occurrence, Alexander Hamilton himself related these facts to the captain's son, Judge Este, who, in turn, nearly seventy years after the battle was fought, made a narration of the rescue to those of the present generation. Young Mills received a thorough academical education at the Morristown Academy, and then matriculated at Yale College in 1844, from which institution he graduated in 1847. He shortly afterwards commenced the study of the law in the office of the late Chief-Justice Edward W. Whelpley, at Morristown, and was licensed as an attorney in 1851, and as a counsellor-at-law in 1854. He immediately entered upon the practice of his profession in his native town, where he has since continued to reside, and where he is engaged in the control of an extensive and lucrative line of business. He has ever been a member of the Republican party; and during the civil war took an active part in sustaining the government both with money and influence. He was appointed Prosecutor of the Pleas for Morris County in 1867, and served in that position for five years. In 1874 he was elected by the Republicans Mayor of Morristown, and served in that capacity until 1876. In the latter year he was the nominee, also of the Republicans, for the Forty-fifth Congress at the election in November, but the Democrats carried the State. He is a Director of the First National Bank of Morristown, and also one of the Managers of the Morristown Savings Bank; and has been since its commencement a Director in the new Library. He was married, September 24th, 1857, to Catharine, daughter of Judge Aaron Coe, of Westfield, New Jersey, who died the same year.

AYLOR, H. GENET, M. D., Physician, of Camden, was born, July 6th, 1837, at Charmantol, the residence of his uncle, General Henry J. Genet, near Troy, New York, and is the son of the late Dr. Othniel H. Taylor, who shortly after his son's birth removed to Camden, New Jersey. The latter received his rudimentary education in the primary schools, and completed the same in the Academy of the Protestant Episcopal Church, in Philadelphia. He then commenced reading medicine under his father's supervision and preceptorship, and also matriculated in the medical department of the University of Pennsylvania, graduating therefrom in the spring of 1860. He immediately thereafter entered upon the practice of his profession in Camden, where he continued until the outbreak of the rebellion. He entered the service in 1861 as Assistant Surgeon of the 8th Regiment, New Jersey Volunteers, and was in active duty in the field with the Army of the Potomac during the first three years of the war; and during his last eighteen months of service he was Surgeon in charge of the Medical Department of the Artillery Brigade of the 3d Corps, Army of the Potomac. On his return to civil life he resumed the practice of medicine in Camden. In 1864 he was appointed a member of the Board of Enrolment, where, as Medical Examiner, he served until the close of the rebellion. He is a member and Secretary of the Camden County Medical Society, a member of the New Jersey Medical Society, and also of the American Medical Association. He is likewise Reporter for the New Jersey Sanitary Association, and a member of the New Jersey Academy of Medicine

---

BERCROMBIE, REV. RICHARD MASON, D. D., Clergyman and Rector of St. Matthew's Church, Jersey City, was born, 1822, in the city of Philadelphia, Pennsylvania, and is a son of the late Rev. James Abercrombie, D. D., one of the assistant ministers of the United Churches of Christ, St. Peter's and St. James', in that city. He was educated in his native city, and graduated in the department of arts in the University of Pennsylvania, July, 1840. Having resolved to devote himself to the ministry of the church, he matriculated in the General Theological Seminary of the Protestant Episcopal Church, in New York city, and after pursuing the regular three years' course in that institution, graduated as Bachelor of Divinity in 1843; and in the same year received the degree of Master of Arts from his *Alma Mater*. His ministerial duties commenced, soon after his ordination, in St. Andrew's Church, Harlem, New York, where he officiated until 1849, when he accepted the rectorship of the Church of the Intercession, at Washington Heights, in the same diocese, and occupied that position until 1852. During his residence at that place he received a call to Trinity Church, Chicago, which he declined. In 1852 he received and accepted a call from St. John's Church, Clifton, Staten Island, of which he was the incumbent four years; and during this time his former parishioners at Washington Heights urged him to return to them once more, but he did not feel inclined to accede to their wishes. He also received, shortly afterwards, a call from Christ Church, Hartford, Connecticut, which he then declined; but upon its renewal he accepted the same, and removed there in 1856. His ministrations there were greatly blessed and he officiated until 1862, when he was stricken down with typhoid fever, and thereupon resigned his charge, having determined to recruit his health by a long vacation, during which he would indulge in travelling. His resignation was accepted, and was accompanied by a substantial token from his parishioners, who in this manner testified their appreciation of his worth and services. Having regained his health, he accepted a call in 1863 to take charge of St. Paul's Church, Rahway, New Jersey, where he so-

journed for nine years. In acknowledgment of his merit the honorary degree of Doctor of Divinity was conferred on him, in 1865, by his *Alma Mater*, the University of Pennsylvania. In 1872 he received a call from St. Matthew's Church, Jersey City, which he accepted and removed thither. He found this parish in a rather precarious condition, which was the result of a combination of unfortunate circumstances; one of these was the fact that the church edifice was located in the lower part of the city, while many of the parishioners had removed further up town, and the other arose from dissatisfaction with a previous rector. Dr. Abercrombie, however, began his ministry of reconciliation, and by means of his energy and perseverance in building up, the congregation returned to the fold, and the fruits of his labor are apparent in the fact that at present there are no sittings vacant in St. Matthew's Church. When the diocese of New Jersey was divided, a few years since, his name was prominently used as a candidate for the new see, but fortunately for his parish he was not elected. He is the President of the Hudson County Church Hospital and Home, in Magnolia avenue, Jersey City, an institution which, although under the control of the Protestant Episcopal Church, is open for the reception of patients of all denominations, and is doing a good work in the community. He is also Dean of the Convocation of Jersey City, in the Diocese of Northern New Jersey. As a talented preacher he is well known in the community wherein his lot is cast, and his sermons show careful thought in their preparation, being delivered with that earnestness of manner which carries conviction to the hearts of his hearers of his sincerity and belief in what he says.

REEMAN, ELLIS B., A. M., M. D., Physician, of Woodbridge, was born in that town, June 18th, 1807, and is a son of Jonathan and Phœbe (Barron) Freeman, his father being engaged in agricultural pursuits. He obtained his preliminary education at the academy in his native town, and in 1825 entered Princeton College, from which institution he graduated in the class of 1827. He then commenced the study of medicine with Dr. Matthias Freeman, an old and eminent practitioner of Woodbridge, and also attended a three years' course at the College of Physicians and Surgeons in New York, graduating from that institution in the spring of 1831. During the following summer, while the Camden & Amboy Railroad was in process of construction, there was considerable sickness among the laborers on the road, and he was requested to go to Amboy, which request he complied with, and practised his profession there until the autumu of that year. He then returned to Woodbridge and opened an office, where he has since continued to reside, and has the control of an extensive medical patronage. He is a member of the Middlesex County Medical Society, and has filled the offices of Treasurer and President of that body. He is one of the Trustees of the "Barron Library," to be constructed in Woodbridge from an endowment fund of fifty thousand dollars, bequeathed for that purpose by the late Thomas Barron, of Woodbridge. For more than twenty years past he has been President of the Board of Trustees of the First Presbyterian Church of Woodbridge, which is one of the oldest religious societies in the country. During the revolutionary war, its pastor, the Rev. Hazel Roe, D. D., was taken prisoner by the British, and carried to Staten Island. Dr. Freeman was married in 1834 to Martha, daughter of Samuel Edgar, of Woodbridge. For three successive years, viz., 1858, 1859 and 1860, he was a member of the Legislature of New Jersey, and for four years just past a member of the Board of Chosen Freeholders of the County of Middlesex.

REEMAN, SAMUEL E., M. D., son of the preceding, is a graduate of the College of Physicians and Surgeons of New York city, where he received his diploma in 1858, and has since constantly resided in Woodbridge, engaged in the practice of medicine. During the two administrations of President Lincoln, and also during a portion of President Grant's, he was Postmaster of Woodbridge. He was married, 1866, to Kate F. Randolph, of New York city, who died in January, 1873.

ARTINE, JOHN D., Lawyer, was born, 1836, near Princeton, New Jersey. He received a good education, and graduated at the Lawrenceville High School in 1858. For several years thereafter he was engaged in teaching school, and in 1861 commenced the study of law in the office of J. F. Hageman, of Princeton. He was licensed to practise law in 1865, and immediately thereafter removed to Somerville, where he opened a law office and speedily acquired reputation and practice; and his business has continued to increase until it now has attained a prominence second to none in this section of the State. He is regarded not only as an excellent counsellor, but an eloquent and able advocate; and, in his addresses before the jury or the court, seldom neglects any point in the cases which are confided to him, besides being ready to detect any weakness or defect in his opponent's argument. He practises in all the courts, and in all the branches of the profession; and during the past ten years has managed some of the most important and intricate cases which have been heard in the courts of his county; noticeably, the Vanarsdale murder case, the Vanderveer will case, and the long-contested water-right case of Ten Eyck vs. Runk, which was finally adjudicated after he became connected with the matter as counsel. He is at present the legal adviser of the Wellsboro' Fire Insurance Company, as also for several building loan associations, and other corporations; and is one of the Board of Directors of the Somerset County Bank. He is highly respected by his fellow-townsmen, as well as by his brethren at the bar. In political faith he is an earnest Democrat, and has done that party good service in several sharply-contested campaigns, but he is no office-seeker, nor has he ever held any public position, except being connected with the School Board and the Town Council. In 1867 he was honored by receiving from Princeton College the degree of Master of Arts. He was married in 1868 to Miss Van Deveer, of Rocky Hill.

ERHUNE, WILLIAM L., Lawyer, of Matawan, New Jersey, Master and Examiner in Chancery, and Supreme Court Commissioner of New Jersey. He is also the Notary Public of the Farmers' and Merchants' Bank, in Matawan, the Counsel and one of the Directors of that institution. His legal practice extends to the counties of Monmouth and Middlesex, in which he has been actively engaged for the past thirty years. Mr. Terhune is a graduate of Rutgers College; studied law with the late Hon. James S. Nevins; was married in 1843 to Margaret, daughter of William Little, former president of the Farmers' and Merchants' Bank, of Middletown Point. His father, the Hon. John Terhune, of New Brunswick, New Jersey, is still living.

MITH, CHARLES McKNIGHT, M. D., Physician, late of Perth Amboy, was born, September 29th, 1803, at Haverstraw, Rockland county, New York, and was a son of Samuel Smith, an attorney and counsellor-at-law. On his mother's side he was the grandson of Dr. Charles McKnight, from whom he was named, and whose biographical sketch appears elsewhere in this volume. He received an excellent education, and having chosen the medical profession for his future career, became a student in the office of Dr. Cornelison, of Haverstraw, whom he selected as his preceptor. He also matriculated in the New York College of Medicine, from which he graduated with honor, April 9th, 1827. He at once entered upon the practice of medicine, selecting as his field of operations the county of St. Mary, in the State of Maryland, but he remained there only a short time, as the prospects were far from encouraging. Returning northward he located in Perth Amboy, where he continued during the remainder of his life. His practice was an extensive one, being confined not merely to the town of Perth Amboy, but extending across the river to South Amboy and its neighborhood, while he had frequent calls from points on Staten Island; and in those days, there being no established ferries,.he underwent considerable exposure in crossing those waters. He took a great interest in political matters, and although he differed from the majority which obtained in his town, yet he was several times elected to different positions in its municipal government, without any solicitation on his part to become a candidate. During the famous Harrison campaign of 1840 he took an active part in favor of the "hero of Tippecanoe," and his services were recognized by the new President, who conferred on him the Collectorship of Customs for the District of Perth Amboy, then regarded as one of the best Federal offices in the State. He retained this position for but one-half the period named in his commission, owing to the disorganization of the party, produced by the return of President Tyler to the Democratic party. At a later period, however, on the accession of General Taylor to the Presidency, Dr. Smith was again appointed to the same office, which he held for the full period of four years. Subsequent to the inauguration of General Grant, in 1869, he was a third time the recipient of the same office, and held it until the expiration of his commission, in 1873, when it was renewed for another term of four years. But his health, which until this period had been unimpaired, now began to fail; and the disorder that threatened him became more and more developed, and notwithstanding he had the best medical skill all was unavailing. For many years he held the position of Health Officer of the city. In religious belief he was a member of the Protestant Episcopal Church, and for thirty years a vestryman of St. Peter's Church. He died, February 3d, 1874, universally lamented by his fellow-townsmen and friends.

ARD, WILLIAM S., A. B., A. M., M. D., of Newark, was born in Bloomfield, New Jersey, July 13th, 1821. His parents, Eleazer D. and Elizabeth (Dodd) Ward, were also natives of New Jersey. His father, the late Dr. Ward, of Bloomfield, was for many years successfully engaged in his profession in that place. After a thorough preparatory course at an excellent academy in Bloomfield, William S. Ward entered Princeton College in 1838, from which he graduated in the class of 1841, receiving in due course the degrees of A. B. and A. M. Selecting the medical profession, he commenced his studies, in 1846, under the guidance of his father, and matriculated at the College of Physicians and Surgeons, of New York, from which he graduated, after a thorough course of three years, in the spring of 1849. Locating himself in Newark, he immediately entered upon the active duties of his profession, where he has been constantly and successfully engaged since that period. He has at different times served as District Physician, in which

position he has given entire satisfaction to the community. During the operation of the Ward Hospital, in Newark, he was connected with its staff as Assistant Surgeon, and shortly after the battle of the Wilderness was detailed for duty at Washington, District of Columbia, where he performed efficient service. Since entering upon the practice of medicine he has devoted his entire time to the interests of his profession, and enjoys the esteem of his professional brethren as well as the respect of the community at large in which he has successfully labored for nearly thirty years. He is a member of the Essex Medical Union. He was married, May 10th, 1850, to Elizabeth H. Stitt, of Philadelphia.

ABRISKIE, HON. ABRAHAM O., LL. D., Lawyer, Jurist and late Chancellor of New Jersey, was born, June 10th, 1807, in the then village of Greenbush, opposite Albany, in the State of New York, and when four years old removed with his parents to Millstone, New Jersey. He received a thorough academical education, and subsequently matriculated at Nassau Hall, Princeton, in 1823, becoming a member of the junior class when only sixteen years of age. He remained in college for two years only, and graduated with the class of 1825. In the same year he commenced the study of law in the office of James S. Green, of Princeton, and was licensed as an attorney in November, 1828; being admitted as counsellor-at-law in 1831. At first he selected Newark as the point where he would practise his profession; but after a residence of less than two years he removed to Hackensack, where he sojourned for nineteen years. Here he was thrown amid a quiet, slow agricultural population, where he gradually matured his intellectual powers, and gathered strength which lasted during life. He gained the confidence of the people, and they in turn trusted him as they had never trusted any one before. In 1838 he was appointed Surrogate of Bergen County, and five years later was reappointed, holding that position for a period of ten years. During his incumbency he not only accurately learned how to frame the statements of executors and administrators, but he acquired a full knowledge of the history of ecclesiastical law, as pertaining to the estates of decedents, which made his counsels valuable in his after life. During the full administration of this office he evinced a method and accuracy which distinguished his life, and the discipline and care about minute details that he acquired in this position lasted him ever afterward; and there was no man in the profession, in litigated causes in the Orphans' Court or Prerogative Court, whose services were more valuable than his. In 1842 he was appointed Prosecutor of the Pleas for Bergen County, and in this position he became master of the principles of the criminal law, so that no one who was really guilty of its infraction ever went unpunished for lack of effort on his part. He was so especially noted for his success in practice of this kind that he was frequently called upon, at later dates, both to prosecute and defend in criminal causes. During his residence in Bergen county he was retained as counsel in many cases before the civil courts, and especially in those involving questions of titles to lands. By this means he became thoroughly familiar with the duties of a practical surveyor, and also with the proprietary history of New Jersey, and understood every patent in the old " Field Book of Bergen County," and the common lands assigned to each patent. He was regarded by the legal fraternity as a most formidable adversary in all those cases where the title to land was involved. Having been a practitioner in the Supreme Court for some years, during which period he had been noted for his thorough research and capacity for patient labor, he was named Reporter for that tribunal, and held that position until 1855. He removed from Hackensack in 1849, and selected Jersey City, in the county of Hudson, as his future, and, as it proved, his final residence. To the people of this county he was no stranger, for Hudson county had been until 1840 a portion of the county of Bergen, of which latter Hackensack was the shire town. In 1850, the year after he had removed, he was nominated for the State Senate and elected, his term of service including the years 1851, 1852 and 1853. While a member of that body he took an important part in legislation, and came in personal contact with many leading men in the State, which proved of great benefit to him afterwards. He was also one of the committee of citizens who framed the voluminous charter of Jersey City, passed March 18th, 1851, some of its provisions being drafted by him. During his senatorial career he was the means of having a good and sufficient lien law and also the " wharf act " passed. He was the author of the " Long Dock charter," which became a law in February, 1856, by which means the company bearing that cognomen were enabled to provide the necessary means to bring the New York & Erie Railroad to their new terminus in Jersey City. During the same year he was elected a director of the New Jersey Railroad & Transportation Company, and held that position until he was made Chancellor, ten years afterwards. He soon became master of the situation, thoroughly conversant with all the affairs of the company, not only as regarded the road, but the rolling stock, the workshops and the multifarious data of so large a concern. He was nominated, in 1859, by Governor Newell for the office of Chancellor of the State, but as the Senate was politically opposed to the governor, they declined to confirm him, and the memorable struggle commenced which left the State for a year without a chancellor. At the next election Charles S. Olden was chosen Governor, but again the Senate was opposed to him; and as he deemed that the interests of the State required that his name should not be submitted to the Senate—although he was his first choice—another was named for the

position. He was finally nominated by Governor Ward, in 1866, and confirmed by the Senate, and formally became Chancellor, May 1st, 1866. The Senate stood eleven Republicans to ten Democrats; of the Republicans one was opposed to him because he was opposed to the great monopoly, the Camden & Amboy Railroad, and this single Republican member was also a member of that corporation. But a young member of the Democratic side of the house, who had in times gone by been the recipient of great kindnesses from his elder brother in the law, voted for his confirmation, and so turned the scales. He performed the arduous duties of Chancellor with a promptness which has never been surpassed by any other officer who has held that position. During his administration business had greatly increased, yet no cause was allowed to linger by reason of a want of time for his examination and decision. And these decisions betoken a positive and independent mind, manifesting great labor and research, and have established for him an enduring fame as a jurist. About the period when the great monopoly, as it was justly termed, was about to cease its arrogant demands, it was rumored that it sought an extension of twenty years, commencing January 1st, 1869, and much discussion prevailed throughout the State. At this juncture a public meeting was held in Jersey City to oppose the renewal of these monopoly privileges, when Chancellor Zabriskie made a speech taking strong ground against the renewal, and declared that, rather than have so odious a contract perpetuated, the people should, with pickaxe in hand, tear up the rails. For this expression of public indignation he earned the soubriquet of " Captain of the Pickaxe Guard." But the independent portion of the community sustained his earnest declaration, and the State has been relieved of the obnoxious restriction. He repeated his speech before a committee of the Legislature at Trenton, and the monopoly extension scheme was dead. It was the crowning act of his life to defeat this giant corporation, and the result is seen already in the free railroad law of the State. He was in all respects a most successful man. His practice was large and lucrative, whereby he was enabled to gain an ample competence. As a lawyer his learning was great and varied, as already detailed; and of his ability as a judge all his compeers bear full witness. He was regarded by business men as eminently sagacious in the management of affairs; and in these particulars not only was his advice sought for, but he was chosen to fill many positions of trust in various institutions. He was, as already stated, one of the directors of the New Jersey Railroad, and held the same position in a bank, a life insurance and trust company, and in the Jersey City Gas Company; also as a Trustee of the old Jersey City Savings Bank, besides in sundry other institutions. When engaged in business he gave his whole attention to the matter before him; and when his labors were over he sought recreation. During his life he was somewhat of a traveller, and more than once visited the old world. Here again his methodical spirit

Galaxy Pub Co. Phila.

Geo. C. Beckman

asserted itself; for, not only was the day of his departure fixed upon, but all the minutiæ of his travels abroad were predetermined before he left his home, and the day of his return thither indicated. He also journeyed through a greater portion of the Union at various times, and he always adhered to the plan which he marked out to pursue. After his term as Chancellor expired he desired to visit the Pacific States, and in company with a friend set out upon what proved to be his last journey on earth. Together they passed from the East to the West, over the great iron highway that binds the Atlantic and Pacific shores of the imperial republic in an unbroken link, passing over the fertile fields, the boundless prairies, the extended plains, the Rocky mountains and the dreary wastes of the great basin intervening between this rocky barrier and the Sierra Nevada, into the golden State and to the shores of the Pacific. After being impressed with the glories of the most sublime natural scenery on the continent they retraced their steps, and on their homeward way he was suddenly stricken by a sickness which proved mortal. He had been reared in the doctrines of the Reformed Dutch Church, and although he had never become a communicant member of that denomination, he was essentially a Christian man. He was a most charitable man, and never wearied in acts of kindnesses; and he was also a most conscientious man, for he took pains to know his duty, and when known he faithfully discharged it. He was a most diligent student, not only well read in law, but in history, the natural sciences, anatomy, medicine and theology; and what he studied at all was thoroughly studied. He died at Trenton, California, June 27th, 1873, and the news of his decease, transmitted by telegraph, produced a most profound impression throughout the State; calling forth eulogia upon his fame not only as a lawyer, Senator, jurist and Chancellor, but also as a private citizen, a neighbor and a friend.

BEEKMAN, HON. GEORGE CRAWFORD, Lawyer and Jurist, at Freehold, was born, July 2d, 1839, on Beekman farm, at the old village of Middletown, in the county of Monmouth. The house where he was born and reared commands a magnificent view of Staten Island, the Narrows, Long Island and the whole expanse of Raritan Bay, with Sandy Hook and the ocean beyond. Here Commodore Bainbridge passed his early youth, with his grandfather, "Squire" Taylor, who then owned this farm. In view of the great ships sailing up and down the blue waters, he doubtless formed an inclination for a life on that element where he afterwards won his fame. Here, too, General Clinton was entertained on his retreat from the battle of Monmouth to Sandy Hook by the Tory owner, whose son, Colonel Taylor, was an active and prominent loyalist. George C. Beekman is the second son of Rev.

Jacob Ten Broeck Beekman and his wife, Anna Crawford. He is seventh in descent from William Beekman, or, as originally spelled, Boeckman, a native of Hasselt Overissel, Holland, who was sent to America by the Dutch West India Company, in 1647, as one of their agents, and was among the earliest magistrates of New Amsterdam. One of his sons, Gerardus Beekman, was a physician at Flatbush, Long Island, a member of Leisler's Council, and afterwards of the Council of New York, from Cornbury's time until his death, in 1723. Between 1709 and 1722 he purchased several large tracts of land on the Millstone and Raritan rivers, in Somerset county, New Jersey; one of his sons and two of his grandsons settled on portions of those lands. From one of these ultimately sprang Rev. Jacob T. B. Beekman, who was born on Ten Broeck homestead, near Harlingen, in the county of Somerset. He was licensed as a minister of the Reformed Dutch Church, but afterward connected with the Presbyterian Church. He helped to found several new churches in Monmouth county, and preached the gospel for half a century. He was faithful to his trust until his death, which occurred, without suffering, April 23d, 1875. His son, George C., attended the common school of his native village until he was thirteen years of age, when he entered the celebrated collegiate preparatory school of Mr. Vandeveer, at Easton, Pennsylvania. He left this school for a private and select school at Jersey City. Mr. Vanderbeek giving up this school, he became a pupil in Kinsley's school, at Astoria, Long Island. In 1856 he matriculated at Princeton College, and graduated in the class of 1859, receiving the degrees of A. B. and A. M. in course. After leaving college he entered the law office of Joel Parker, since Governor of the State for two terms, at Freehold, where he acquired a full knowledge of the law, and was licensed by the Supreme Court at Trenton, in June, 1863, as an attorney-at-law, and as counsellor three years later. He began the practice of his profession at Freehold, where he has since continued, and had up to 1869 an extensive line of business. In this last-named year he was appointed by the Legislature of New Jersey, in joint meeting, Law Judge of the Inferior Court of Common Pleas, the Court of General Quarter Sessions of the place, and Orphans' Court of the County of Monmouth. His appointment was for five years, but the office not being very remunerative he resigned his position at the expiration of three years. While judge none of his decisions were reversed by the higher courts. As a magistrate he was thorough and impartial in the administration of the law, and endeavored at all times to mitigate the severity of the law when it was consistent with the public good. At the expiration of his office there were fewer criminals in the State prison from Monmouth county than from any other county of the State, in proportion to its population. Since resuming the practice of law he has been engaged in nearly every important case which has been tried at the Monmouth bar,

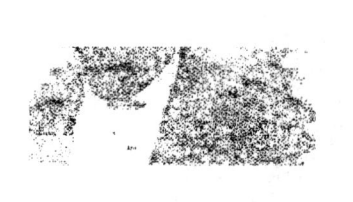

asserted itself; for, not only was the day of his departure fixed upon, but all the minutiæ of his travels abroad were predetermined before he left his home, and the day of his return thither indicated. He also journeyed through a greater portion of the Union at various times, and he always adhered to the plan which he marked out to pursue. After his term as Chancellor expired he desired to visit the Pacific States, and in company with a friend set out upon what proved to be his last journey on earth. Together they passed from the East to the West, over the great iron highway that binds the Atlantic and Pacific shores of the imperial republic in an unbroken link, passing over the fertile fields, the boundless prairies, the extended plains, the Rocky mountains, and the dreary wastes of the great basin intervening between this rocky barrier and the Sierra Nevada, into the golden State and to the shores of the Pacific. After being impressed with the glories of the most sublime natural scenery on the continent they retraced their steps, and on their homeward way he was suddenly stricken by a sickness which proved mortal. He had been reared in the doctrines of the Reformed Dutch Church, and although he had never become a communicant member of that denomination, he was essentially a Christian man. He was a most charitable man, and never wearied in doing kindnesses; and he was also a most conscientious man, for he took pains to know his duty, and when known he faithfully discharged it. He was a most diligent student, not only well read in law, but in history, the natural sciences, anatomy, medicine and theology; and what he studied at all was thoroughly studied. He died at Truckee, California, June 27th, 1873, and the news of his decease, transmitted by telegraph, produced a most profound impression throughout the State, calling forth eulogia upon his fame not only as a lawyer, Senator, jurist and Chancellor, but also as a private citizen, a neighbor and a friend.

EEKMAN, HON. GEORGE CRAWFORD, Lawyer and Jurist, at Freehold, was born, July 2d, 1839, on Beekman farm, at the old village of Middletown, in the county of Monmouth. The house where he was born and reared commands a magnificent view of Staten Island, the Narrows, Long Island and the whole expanse of Raritan Bay, with Sandy Hook and the ocean beyond. Here Commodore Bainbridge passed his early youth, with his grandfather, "Squire" Taylor, who then owned this farm. In view of the great ships, sailing up and down the blue waters, he doubtless formed an inclination for a life on that element where he afterwards won his fame. Here, too, General Clinton was entertained on his retreat from the battle of Monmouth to Sandy Hook by the Tory owner, whose son, Colonel Taylor, was an active and prominent loyalist. George C. Beekman is the second son of Rev.

14

Jacob Ten Broeck Beekman and his wife, Anna Crawford. He is seventh in descent from Willian Beekman, or, as originally spelled, Beeckman, a native of Hasselt, Overyssel, Holland, who was sent to America by the Dutch West India Company, in 1647, as one of their agents, and was among the earliest magistrates of New Amsterdam. One of his sons, Gerardus Beekman, was a physician at Flatbush, Long Island, a member of Leisler's Council, and afterwards of the Council of New York, from Cornbury's time until his death, in 1723. Between 1700 and 1722 he purchased several large tracts of land on the Millstone and Raritan rivers, in Somerset county, New Jersey; one of his sons and two of his grandsons settled on portions of those lands. From one of these ultimately sprang Rev. Jacob T. B. Beekman, who was born on Ten Broeck homestead, near Harlingen, in the county of Somerset. He was licensed as a minister of the Reformed Dutch Church, but afterward connected with the Presbyterian Church. He helped to found several new churches in Monmouth county, and preached the gospel for half a century. He was faithful to his trust until his death, which occurred, without suffering, April 23d, 1859. His son, George C., attended the common school of his native village until he was thirteen years of age, when he entered the celebrated collegiate preparatory school of Mr. Vanderveer, at Easton, Pennsylvania. He left this school for a private and select school at Bergen Hills, then taught by Mr. Voorhees, now a lawyer at Jersey City. Mr. Voorhees giving up this school, he became a pupil in Parker's school, at Astoria, Long Island. In 1856 he matriculated at Princeton College, and graduated in the class of 1859, receiving the degrees of A. B. and A. M. in course. After leaving college he entered the law office of Joel Parker, since Governor of the State for two terms, at Freehold, where he acquired a full knowledge of the law, and was licensed by the Supreme Court at Trenton, in June, 1863, as an attorney-at-law, and as counsellor three years later. He began the practice of his profession at Freehold, where he has since continued, and had up to 1869 an extensive line of business. In this last-named year he was appointed by the Legislature of New Jersey, in joint meeting, Law Judge of the Inferior Court of Common Pleas, the Court of General Quarter Sessions of the peace, and Orphans' Court of the County of Monmouth. His appointment was for five years, but the office not being very remunerative he resigned his position at the expiration of three years. While judge none of his decisions were reversed by the higher courts. As a magistrate he was thorough and impartial in the administration of the law, and endeavored at all times to mitigate the severity of the law when it was consistent with the public good. At the expiration of his office there were fewer criminals in the State prison from Monmouth county than from any other county of the State, in proportion to its population. Since resuming the practice of law he has been engaged in nearly every important case which has been tried at the Monmouth bar,

In his jury trials he has met with remarkable success, and is considered a strong advocate. As a lawyer he is very earnest and faithful to the interests of his clients, often making their cause his own, at a considerable sacrifice of time and means. His political opinions coincide with those of the Democratic party. In 1860 his first vote was cast for the three Douglas electors on the fusion ticket, after erasing the names of the Bell and Breckenridge electors. Since then he has voted the solid Democratic ticket. Since 1860 he has taken an active and earnest part in the several political campaigns which have occurred during that period. He has been a delegate to many State, county and Congressional conventions, and was a delegate to the National Convention at St. Louis, in 1876. Although taking a prominent part in his party as an orator and leader, he is no politician or office-seeker, but contributes his services and means for the success of the principles which he believes to be conducive to the county, State and national welfare. He has also been for a considerable time a prominent member of the Masonic order in his county. In his manners he is plain and unassuming; open in expression of his sentiments; strong in his friendships and enmities, and of a free, generous nature; unyielding and persistent in his opinions, and of an original turn of mind; slow in his judgment, and rather obstinate when he has reached a conclusion. He is of strong, robust form, with an excellent constitution, of which he has never taken much care. He comes of a long-lived race, and has a fair promise of many years of an active and useful life. He is a firm believer in the Scriptures, which he has studied diligently for years, and also believes in special providences. He has, however, but little sympathy for any of the ecclesiastical corporations, and is not a member of any church, although he attends the Presbyterian.

RVERSON, HON. THOMAS C., late Associate-Justice of the Supreme Court of New Jersey, was the third son of Martin Ryerson and Rhoda Hull, and born, May 4th, 1788, at Myrtle Grove, Sussex county, New Jersey, five miles west of Newton, the county-seat. He was a great-great-grandson of Martin Ryerson, of French Huguenot descent, who emigrated from Holland about 1660, and settled at Flatbush, on Long Island; was a member from an early age of the Dutch Reformed Church, as its records still show, and, for those days, possessed of considerable property. On the 14th of May, 1663, he married Annettie Rappelye, a daughter of Joris Jansen Rappelye, who settled on Long Island in 1625, in which year his first daughter, Sara, was born, the first white child born on Long Island. From this marriage have sprung large numbers of the name of Ryerson (besides numerous descendants of the female branches of the family), who are scattered over New York, New Jersey and several other States, and many in Canada,

and in all of them the original Christian name of "Martin" has been kept up, that being the name of both the father and grandfather of Judge Ryerson. His grandfather resided in Hunterdon county, New Jersey, whence his father removed to Sussex about 1770, dying there in 1820, in his seventy-third year; his father and grandfather were both distinguished as surveyors, being deputies of the Surveyor-General of both East and West Jersey, and his father was thus enabled to make very judicious land-locations for himself, and at his death left a landed estate of between forty and fifty thousand dollars. Until the age of sixteen Judge Ryerson remained at home, working on his father's farm and receiving only the common education of the country. In 1800 his father removed to Hamburg, in the same county, where he died, and in 1804 his son began preparing for college at a private school in the family of Robert Ogden. He was an older brother of Colonel Aaron Ogden, a graduate of Princeton College, in 1765, and one of the founders of the Cliosophic Society. He was born at Elizabethtown, practised law there for several years, was in the American army during the war of the Revolution, and, on account of the effect of the sea air upon his health, removed about 1785 to Sparta, Sussex county, five miles from Hamburg, where he owned considerable real estate, and died in that county in 1826, aged eighty years. His fifth daughter, Amelia, married Judge Ryerson, in November, 1814; an older daughter, Mary, was married some fifteen years earlier to Elias Haines, of Elizabethtown, the father of the Hon. Daniel Haines, late Governor, Chancellor, and Judge of the Supreme Court of New Jersey. After some time spent in this private school he finished his preparatory studies at the Mendham (New Jersey) Academy, then taught by the late Hon. Samuel L. Southard, and in 1807 entered the junior class at Princeton, graduating there, in 1809, with the third honor in a class of forty-four. This school acquaintance with Mr. Southard ripened into an intimate and life-long friendship, and a very warm and enduring friendship grew up between him and the late Judge George K. Drake, who was graduated at Princeton in 1808. After graduating he studied law with the late Joh S. Halsted, of Newton, and was admitted to the bar in February, 1814; four years of study with a practising lawyer were then required, even of graduates, and during a part of this time he was out with the New Jersey militia, at Sandy Hook, to resist a threatened attack of the British. Immediately after being licensed he began practising law at Hamburg, marrying in the following November, as above stated, and continued practising there till April, 1820, when he removed to Newton, where he resided till his death, August 11th, 1838, aged fifty years, three months and seven days. For two years (1825-27) he was a member of the Legislative Council of New Jersey, and in January, 1834, was elected by the joint meeting a Justice of the Supreme Court, in place of Judge Drake, whose term then expired. It is well known that Judge Drake had given great offence, but without good reason for it, to the Hicksite Quakers, by his opinion in the celebrated suit between them and the Orthodox Quakers, for which they determined, if possible, to defeat his re-election; to accomplish this they aided, in 1833, in electing a large majority of Democrats to the Legislature, which the year before had a majority of the other party. Although a leading and influential Democrat and politically opposed to Judge Drake, Judge Ryerson, in common with many other Democrats, was strongly opposed to this unjustifiable proscription, a warm advocate of Judge Drake's re-election, and used all his influence with the four Democratic members from Sussex in its favor. He was not in Trenton during that session till after the joint meeting, and his name was brought forward in the Democratic caucus as an opposing candidate, without his consent, and he knew nothing of it till after his election. The leading opponents of Judge Drake, finding that the votes of the Sussex members would re-elect him, resorted to the use of Judge Ryerson's name as the only means of preventing it, and thus, without his knowledge, he was made the instrument of defeating an excellent and irreproachable judge, his own warm personal friend. So strong an impression had. he made upon the Sussex members in favor of Judge Drake that one of them voted for him in joint meeting, notwithstanding his own Democratic caucus nomination, and other Democrats also bolted the nomination, so that, notwithstanding the large Democratic majority in joint meeting, he was elected by only a very small majority. So strong, however, was the Hicksite feeling against Judge Drake that he received but one vote from the members south of the Assanpink. Theodore Frelinghuysen was then in the Senate, his term to expire March 4th, 1835. He also had given great offence to the Hicksites by his able and eloquent speech in the same suit, and to reach him the same combination was continued till the election of October, 1834, and resulted in sending General Wall to the Senate in his place. The news of his election was a complete surprise to Judge Ryerson, and with it came letters from prominent Democrats urging him to accept, and assuring him that his declination would not benefit Judge Drake; that party lines had become drawn, and he could not now under any circumstances be re-elected. He held the matter under advisement till the receipt of a letter from Judge Drake himself, dated February 3d, 1834, urging him to accept, "*and that promptly.*" He said also, " I feel under obligations to you, and my other friends, for your zeal in my behalf; but it has proved ineffectual, and I have no confidence in the success of another effort." And again, " If the place is thrown open, nobody knows into whose hands it may go. I rejoice that it has been so disposed of that we may still confide in the independence and integrity of the bench." This letter decided him to accept, and he was sworn into office, February 25th, 1834, holding it till his death, in August, 1838. Judge Ryerson's course at the bar and on the bench fully justified the opinion of Judge Drake, quoted above, as in all po-

sitions he was a man of the firmest independence and strictest integrity. He was an able lawyer, well read, and was remarkable for a discriminating and sound judgment, an earnest and successful advocate, with great influence over courts and juries in Sussex and Warren, to which counties he confined his practice; and as a Judge it is believed that he enjoyed in a high degree the esteem and confidence of the bench and bar, as well as of the people at large. For the last eight years of his life he was a very devoted member of the Presbyterian Church, his wife having joined it some eight years earlier, and dying three years before him. Her father was for many years an exemplary and very influential elder of the same denomination, and a large number of his descendants have been and are professing Christians. Judge Ryerson was very easy and affable in his manners, delighting in social intercourse and conversation, with a great fund of anecdote; very simple and economical in his personal tastes and habits, spending, however, freely in educating his children, and noted for his liberality to the poor around him and to the benevolent operations of his day. So much did he give away that he left no more estate than he inherited, although in full practice for twenty years before his appointment as Judge. He often said to his children that he desired only to leave them a good education and correct principles, and that they must expect to make their way in life with only these to depend upon. Both as lawyer and Judge he was very painstaking and laborious, conscientiously faithful in the discharge of duty to his clients and the public; having a strongly nervous temperament, the mental strain was too great and resulted at length in a softening of the brain, from which he died after an illness of three months, leaving three sons and a daughter, and a widow, his first wife's younger sister, and since deceased, to mourn an irreparable loss. Two of his children remain, the youngest son, Colonel Henry Ogden Ryerson, having been killed in May, 1864, at the head of his regiment, on the second day's bloody fighting in the battles of the Wilderness, in Virginia. The eldest, Judge Martin Ryerson, died, June 11th, 1875, and is the subject of the following memoir.

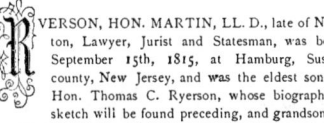

RYERSON, HON. MARTIN, LL. D., late of Newton, Lawyer, Jurist and Statesman, was born, September 15th, 1815, at Hamburg, Sussex county, New Jersey, and was the eldest son of Hon. Thomas C. Ryerson, whose biographical sketch will be found preceding, and grandson of the elder Martin Ryerson, who, in the early history of Sussex, was for many years deputy surveyor, and prominent in the affairs of the county. He received a first-class academical education, which enabled him to matriculate at Princeton College, from which institution he graduated in the class of 1833. He subsequently commenced reading law in his father's office, afterwards continuing his studies with Hon. Garret D. Wall, in Trenton, and concluding his course in the office of ex-Governor Pennington, at Newark. He was licensed as an attorney in November, 1836, and at once commenced the practice of his profession in the last-named city, where he continued a short period, and thence removed to Newton, where he resided during life, with the exception of a few years, when he sojourned in Trenton. He was made a counsellor-at-law in 1839, and acquired distinction in his profession. He was a prominent member of the convention, in 1844, which framed the present constitution of the State. In 1849 he was elected a member of Assembly, when the late Chief-Justice Whelpley was speaker, and served upon the Judiciary Committee; it was mainly through his influence and instrumentality that the charter was obtained for the Farmers' Bank, at Decker-town. Upon an increase of judges in the Supreme Court, he was appointed an Associate-Justice of the same by Governor Brice, and filled the position only three years, ill health compelling him to resign the bench, in 1858. In 1873 he was appointed as one of the Judges of the Alabama Claims commission, a position which he was compelled to resign in January, 1875, by reason of the complete failure of his health. He had likewise been selected by Governor Parker one of the Commissioners to revise the constitution, which he had assisted to frame in 1844; but was also constrained to relinquish the position from the same cause. His political opinions were those of the Democratic party, down to the period when the attempt was made to force slavery in Kansas and Nebraska, and the Democrats surrendered unconditionally to the slave power. At that time he sundered his connection with it, and entered, with all the enthusiasm of his nature, into the work of organizing and building up the anti-slavery sentiment which finally crystallized in the Republican party organization. At the commencement of the recent civil war he was among the foremost supporters of every measure looking to the maintenance of the Union and the vindication of its authority. He was in constant correspondence for many years with many of the most influential men in the country, and, by his counsel and advice, contributed much towards shaping the policy of the government during the critical periods of the war. His mind was well stored with useful information, and his wonderful memory enabled him to draw upon it at will. He engaged actively in the political campaigns which occurred during and immediately after the war, and was instrumental in the revolution in the old Fourth Congressional District, when the Republicans triumphed for the first time. He threw himself with wonderful zeal and energy into that tremendous conflict; and he also did yeoman's service for his party in all the succeeding elections, especially in those of 1868, 1870 and 1872. He would, without hesitation, at a moment's notice, summon a conference of leading politicians from all parts of the State, at Newark, or Paterson, or New-York, and opposition to his

policy was generally in vain. His elan was irresistible and his enthusiasm contagious. In religious belief he was a Presbyterian, and had been for many years a leading member of the congregation in Newton, and of which he had been a ruling elder for ten years; and was likewise frequently selected as a delegate to various church synods and other ecclesiastical bodies. He was also a strong advocate of the temperance cause, and was often called upon to attend conventions of that organization. He was a man of great energy of character, looking with earnest care at all the details of every enterprise in which he was about to engage; and was the energetic and active leader in every local improvement in his native town. As a lawyer he occupied a front rank in his profession; and as a Judge he was regarded by those qualified to give an intelligent opinion as one of the ablest and very best on the bench. He was a kind, considerate, cultivated Christian gentleman, a scholar, a patriot, a genial and invaluable citizen; and in all the elements of intellectual manhood an honor to his native county and State. In 1869 Princeton College, his *Alma Mater*, conferred on him the honorary degree of Doctor of Laws. He was twice married, his wives being sisters; he died, June 11th, 1875, leaving a widow and three children, two daughters and a son.

----◆----

JANVIER, REV. LEVI, Clergyman, late a Missionary of the Presbyterian Board of Missions, was born, April 25th, 1816, at Pittsgrove, New Jersey, and was the son of Rev. Dr. Janvier, a Presbyterian clergyman of eminence. His early education was obtained from his father, and he subsequently entered Lafayette College, at Easton, Pennsylvania, and also studied for a short period at Lawrenceville. In 1835 he entered the junior class of Princeton College, and graduated with the second honor in the class of 1837, being the salutatorian at the commencement. Having become a communicant member of the Presbyterian Church he decided to devote himself to the work of the gospel ministry, and for that purpose entered the Theological Seminary at Princeton. While a student there he offered himself to the Board of Missions, as a missionary to Lodiana, in northern India. Having been duly ordained, he sailed for India, accompanied by his wife, in September, 1841, and reached his destination in the spring of 1842. During the voyage he had commenced the study of the Urdu language, which is largely spoken in Lodiana; and, as he possessed a remarkable facility for acquiring languages, he was able to preach in that tongue soon after his arrival in that country. Some months later he commenced to translate tracts and books, which were published by the mission. He next acquired a thorough familiarity with the Panjabi language, and with the aid of Dr. Newton, of the same mission, undertook the preparation of a Panjabi dictionary, which was completed in 1854. It is a quarto volume of four hundred and thirty-eight pages, in three columns. He continued his labors as a preacher and translator up to the time of his death. He had gone to Mala, in the province of Lodiana, to preach and distribute tracts, and in the evening was met by the fanatic Akali Sikh, who, without the slightest provocation, felled him to the ground with a club. He lingered until the following morning, but was insensible. He died March 25th, 1864. The murderer was arrested, tried, convicted and hanged.

REESE, JACOB R., M. D., Banker and Real-Estate Operator, of Trenton, was born near Hope, Warren county, New Jersey, March 4th, 1826. His father, Isaac Freese, was also a native of the same county, where for some years he was successfully engaged in farming, and afterwards in mercantile pursuits at Hope; his mother was Hannah Read, a daughter of Isaac Read, a wealthy farmer of his day in Warren county. Our subject is of Holland and English extraction, being descended on the paternal side from a family who came originally from a northern province of Holland which bore their name (Freisland). Leaving Holland during the early settlement of the United States they took up a large tract of land in Warren county, New Jersey, and were among the pioneers in that section of the country. The primary education of Jacob R. was obtained in the schools of the neighborhood, followed by an academical course at the Clinton Academy, in Hunterdon county, under the charge of Rev. Albert Williams. From the age of eight years he had been kept a part of each year behind his father's counter, it being his father's wish and design that his son should receive a business, while receiving a school, education. When, therefore, he returned from the academy, at the age of about nineteen, he at once took his accustomed place in his father's country store, but the learning he had obtained made him to want more, and he soon commenced to beg of his father the privilege of studying some profession. His choice was that of law, but the father belonged to the "old fogies" of that early day who believed, honestly believed, that "no lawyer could ever enter heaven," and, earnestly desiring that his son should be a good as well as a useful man, would not consent that Jacob should enter a law office, but would consent that he should study medicine. Arrangements were accordingly made with Dr. Joseph Hedges, then in active practice at Hope, and for more than two years thereafter he diligently pursued his medical studies; afterwards attended two full courses of medical lectures at Philadelphia, and then received his diploma as M. D. Turning his steps westward, he located at Bloomington, Illinois, and immediately entered upon his professional practice. Devoted to his profession, and with an energy which is characteristic of the man, he labored in his chosen path with much success. He soon took rank among the leaders in the medical fraternity of Bloomington, and during his sojourn there, which extended to 1857, enjoyed their utmost respect and confidence, as well as that of the community at large. Within two years from the date of his settling at Bloomington a project was started of establishing a medical college in that city. An organization was effected under the general laws of the State; a large brick building (afterward known as "College Hall") was erected in which to locate a medical museum and deliver the lectures; and a faculty was formed, of which Dr. Freese was made the Professor of Surgery, and also President of the college; but before the institution could get into operation it was concluded that its proximity to the older colleges of Chicago and St. Louis made its support doubtful, if not impossible, and the whole project was finally abandoned as impracticable. Aside from his numerous professional duties in Bloomington, Dr. Freese took a leading and active part in all things tending to the improvement and development of the town. He assisted in erecting in the heart of the city a fine block of buildings for business purposes, which that time were among the finest in the place. In 1857, at the solicitation of his wife, he returned to his native State and located in Trenton. This estimable lady was *née* Lily S. Swayze, a native of New Jersey, to whom he was married December 25th, 1847. She was a lady of more than ordinary ability; possessed with a literary mind, she frequently contributed to the various magazines both in poetry and prose. During the absence of her husband in the army she conducted with marked ability the newspaper which he then owned and edited, the *State Gazette*. She died November 7th, 1871, mourned by a large circle, which had held her in high esteem for her many noble traits of character. On returning to New Jersey Dr. Freese fully expected to follow up in his new home the successes he had already achieved in his profession during his sojourn in the West. Shortly after locating in Trenton, however, he was prevailed upon to purchase the *State Gazette*, one of the oldest newspapers in the State, having been established as far back as 1792, and at the same time another paper known as the *New Jersey Republican*. These papers he merged into one which he issued for a short time under the title of the *State Gazette and Republican*. The latter name, however, was soon dropped, and the paper has since been known as the *State Gazette*. He now relinquished the practice of medicine and devoted himself entirely to the publication of this paper, which he continued to publish and own up to 1866, when he went abroad. In 1858 he was commissioned Lieutenant-Colonel of State Militia. In 1859 he was appointed Bank Commissioner of New Jersey. Soon after the breaking out of the rebellion in the summer of 1861, at the request of the Governor of New Jersey, he accompanied to Washington one of the regiments from this State, expecting in a few days to return home and resume his editorial duties. However, while in Washington, he was prevailed upon to enter the service, and upon tendering himself to President Lincoln he was immediately appointed Assistant Adjutant-General of United States Volunteers, on August 24th, 1861, and at once entered upon active duty. He was assigned to the staff of Brigadier-General Montgomery, who had only a few days previous been appointed Military Governor of the city of Alexandria. Having entered the service of his country without making any provision for the performance of his duties at home pertaining to the management of his newspaper, the emergency was promptly and ably met by his wife, Lily S., of whom we have already spoken. She at once assumed the management of the *State Gazette*, and her administration of affairs was attended by an increase in the circulation of the paper; and while the husband was upholding the government in the field, she through the columns of the press nobly contributed her support to the cause of the Union. In addition to his duties as Assistant Adjutant-General to General Montgomery at Alexandria, Colonel Freese was appointed Provost Judge of the city. Upon the Union troops taking possession the local government of all kind had vacated; merchants had left their stores, and disorder generally reigned. Being possessed of great executive ability he soon created order out of chaos, and his administration as Provost Judge, which continued until January, 1862, was a marked success in every feature. One point therein is particularly noteworthy. As before stated, the merchants generally of Alexandria had closed their stores and fled the town; they were largely indebted to the men of the North for their goods. The creditors had no legal recourse, as all courts of law had ceased to exist in that locality, thus prohibiting the usual procedure in cases of debt. Judge Freese issued a rule or order of the court, in which he stated that where claims were thoroughly and truly established by these Northern merchants they should be allowed to take of the goods of absconded debtors, at an appraisement to be made by disinterested parties, a sufficient amount of the abandoned goods to liquidate their claims; all proceedings to be only by order of the court and under the direct surveillance of its officers. Upon his establishing this precedent many merchants of the North repaired to Alexandria, and were thus enabled to recover thousands of dollars which otherwise would have been lost. His action on this point was a bold one, and though not in strict accordance with the letter of the law, his views on the subject were thoroughly indorsed by President Lincoln and the press of the North in general. Had this precedent established by him been sustained by the government, and carried out in all places when our armies took possession, millions of dollars could have been justly returned to the Northern merchants and the enemy also deprived of immense quantities of supplies. The Attorney-General, however, demurred, and the court was finally discontinued. In January, 1862, Colonel Freese joined the Army of the Potomac, and was attached to the staff of General Heintzelman as Provost Marshal of his division. In this capacity he served up to the battle of Williamsburg, in which engagement he was disabled while serving as an aide to General Frank Patterson, and was compelled to return home. Upon his recovery he returned to the staff of General Montgomery and was stationed in Philadelphia, where he did duty until the spring of 1863. He was then ordered to Cairo, Illinois, where he remained during the summer of 1863, acting as Assistant Adjutant-General and Judge Advocate, being principally engaged in courts-martial. In the fall of 1863 he was sent to Grand Rapids, Michigan, to assist in organizing troops that had been drafted in that State. Here he remained until January, 1864, when he resigned his commission, and returning to Trenton resumed the management of the *State Gazette*. In 1866, having been appointed by President Johnson one of the United States Commissioners to the Paris Exposition, he disposed of his paper and accompanied by his wife, Lily S., and his son, Louie K., started for a tour abroad. They journeyed through all parts of Europe; visited Egypt, Palestine, Syria, Asia Minor and Turkey, and after attending to his duties at the Exposition returned to Trenton in the winter of 1867. Two volumes of his travels were published after his return; the one on Palestine, of which three editions were sold; the other on Egypt. He now determined to engage in the banking business, together with that of real estate, and accordingly established the banking and real estate office of Freese & Co., in which vocation he is at present engaged, having associated with him his two sons, L. K. and H. C. Freese. This establishment was the first of its kind established in Trenton, and under the able management of its founder has proved an entire success. Colonel Freese since his locating in Trenton has always been foremost in all matters of public improvement. Possessing great energy and push, he has striven in various and numerous ways to advance the interests of the city. He is connected with several monetary institutions, among which may be named the State Savings Bank of Trenton, of which he was elected Vice-President and Treasurer in 1869, which position he still holds. In 1866 he was chosen a Director in the First National Bank, and still acts in that capacity. In 1869 he was chosen President of the Standard Fire Insurance Company, of Trenton, and held the office for three years. He was elected President of the Board of Trade in 1870, and lately became Treasurer of the City Railway Company. In politics he was originally a Whig, and such was his admiration of Henry Clay that he named his firstborn after that world-renowned statesman. When, in 1856, that party virtually dissolved, he joined the Republican party, and was one of only six men to hold the first Republican convention ever held in the United States. In 1872 he joined the standard of his old personal and political friend, Horace Greeley, and made many speeches in different parts of New Jersey to secure his election to the Presidency. From 1872 to 1876 he took no part in politics, and only voted for such men and measures as his judgment approved.

When, in 1876, Governor Hayes was nominated for the Presidency, he at once wrote an open letter heartily approving the nomination and fully indorsing the platform adopted at Cincinnati. Though often solicited, never, except in one instance, and then against his most earnest protest, has he permitted his name to be used as a candidate for any political office, nor is he ever likely to permit such use, unless the demand should be for the public good rather than from personal ambition. He was again married, June 9th, 1874, to Mrs. E. P. Nostrand, of New Jersey.

———❦———

URNETT, HON. DAVID, Printer and Journalist, late of Paterson, was born, in the year 1800, at Springfield, New Jersey, where also he was educated. When eighteen years of age he went to New York city, where he learned the trade of a printer, and after becoming thoroughly versed in that art went to Paterson, New Jersey, where he was engaged as a journeyman, and worked at his trade for some three years. In September, 1823, in connection with Mr. Day, he started the *Paterson Intelligencer*. In April, 1845, he was appointed Surrogate of Passaic county. For ten years he was Clerk of the Board of Chosen Freeholders of that county, and was also connected with several banking institutions. He died at Paterson, August 28th, 1873.

———❦———

ITTENHOUSE JOHN P., School-Teacher and ex-Sheriff of Hunterdon County, was born, 1820, near Sergeantsville, New Jersey, and is a son of Samuel Rittenhouse, and a great-grand-nephew of the celebrated astronomer David Rittenhouse; the family is of German descent, and among the early settlers of New Jersey. John attended school until he was twelve years of age, and was then apprenticed to learn the trade of a saddler and harness-maker, and worked at that business until he was sixteen years old, when he relinquished the same and engaged in teaching school. He pursued this latter vocation for ten years quite successfully in New Jersey, Pennsylvania and Ohio. In 1849 he went to California, and was one of the pioneer traders in what is now the city of Sacramento. In company with his partners, he purchased and had recorded in the proper office a title for the first city lot in Sacramento, after the site had been laid off in town-lots, and was situated at the corner of K and Fifth streets. He remained in California somewhat less than a year, but, although successful in his business, he was obliged through failing health to dispose of his interests in Sacramento and return to the States. On his arrival in New Jersey he settled on a farm near Flemington, where he has since continued, except when absent on official duties

elsewhere. In 1855 he was nominated by the Democracy of the First District of Hunterdon county as their candidate for member of Assembly, and was elected by a large majority, and was also re-elected the following year. During his legislative career he filled a position on several important committees, and served as Chairman on that of Public Printing. In 1857 he was appointed one of the Inspectors of Customs for the Port of New York, and filled that position throughout President Buchanan's administration, and during a portion of President Lincoln's first term, relinquishing the office in September, 1862. In 1868 he was appointed Deputy Sheriff, as the sheriff, elected, Richard Bellis, was at that time engaged in business in New York. The entire duties of this responsible position therefore devolved on him. At the expiration of Sheriff Bellis' term in 1871 he was nominated for the office, and elected by a large majority, and served for the three years' term; all parties conceded that his administration was most successful, and that he proved to have been one of the most faithful and efficient officers who ever held that position in Hunterdon county. He was kind and courteous in all his official relations, and never failed in retaining the regard, esteem and confidence of all, even including those persons towards whom his duties were of an unfortunate or perplexing character. His oldest son, H. O. Rittenhouse, is a graduate of the Annapolis Naval School, and is at present a Lieutenant in the United States navy.

———❦———

IKE, BRIGADIER-GENERAL ZEBULON MONTGOMERY, of the United States Army, was born, January 5th, 1779, at Lamberton, New Jersey, and was the son of Zebulon Pike, a brevet-colonel in the service of the United States during the war of the Revolution. He was a lineal descendant of John Pike, who lived at Newbury, Massachusetts, in 1635, and whose son, John, removed to Woodbridge, New Jersey, in 1669, and settled there. Young Pike received an elegant education, including a knowledge of the higher mathematics, and was a thorough master of the Latin, French and Spanish languages. After the purchase of the Territory of Louisiana, which not only embraced the present State of that name but all the lands on the west side of the Mississippi river, now included in the States of Arkansas, Missouri, Iowa and the western shore of Minnesota, President Jefferson in 1805 gave him authority to explore the sources of the Mississippi river. Soon after his return from this survey he was sent on a similar expedition into the interior of Louisiana. He appears to have travelled far beyond the western limit of that Territory, for he was seized by a Spanish force on the banks of the Rio del Norte, who captured all his papers. He returned to the States in 1807. Subsequently he published an account of his expedition to the sources of the Mississippi, etc., which is comprised in an octavo volume, dated 1810. During the war with Great Britain he was appointed a Brigadier-General in the United States army, and commanded the land forces in the attack upon York, Upper Canada. In the explosion of the British magazine he was struck by a large stone, and died in a few hours on board of the commodore's ship. When the British standard was brought to him he caused it to be placed under his head. His wife was a Miss Brown, of Cincinnati; his only daughter married in 1819 J. C. S. Harrison, of Ohio. General Pike died April 27th, 1813.

BURR, COLONEL AARON, Lawyer and Vice-President of the United States, was born, February 6th, 1756, in the city of Newark, and was a son of President Burr and a grandson of President Edwards, of Princeton College. His father died when he was but a year old, and his mother's decease followed in less than a twelvemonth after her husband's. He was thus left an orphan in his very infancy, and the moulding of his character thus left to stranger hands doubtless influenced his whole after life. He received, however, an excellent education, and graduated from Princeton College in 1773. He subsequently commenced the study of law, but before being admitted to the bar the conflict with Great Britain commenced, and when nineteen years of age he joined the Continental army at Cambridge, and accompanied Arnold in his expedition against Quebec. In the year 1776 he was invited to join the military family of General Washington, and accepted the offer; but the commander-in-chief soon lost confidence in him. He retired from military duties in 1779, having reached the rank of Lieutenant-Colonel. He commenced the practice of law in 1782 at Albany, but after a short sojourn in that city removed to New York. He took a prominent part in political matters, and in 1791 he was elected by the Legislature of his adopted State a Senator of the United States, and served in that body until the expiration of his term in 1797, and was a prominent member of the then Democratic party. In 1800 he and Jefferson each had seventy-three votes in the Electoral College for the Presidency. There being no choice, the election for President devolved on the House of Representatives, according to the Constitution. After thirty-five ineffectual trials, Thomas Jefferson was elected on the thirty-sixth ballot, when Colonel Burr was chosen Vice-President. During his term occurred the lamentable controversy with Alexander Hamilton, the challenge and the duel, when the latter fell mortally wounded by the hand of the Vice-President. After the expiration of his term he seems to have meditated the founding of a new empire in the Southwest, this scheme being solely for his own aggrandizement. He journeyed to the West, and having formed an intimacy with the wife of Herman Blen-

nerhasset, endeavored to seek his co-operation in his project through the influence of Mrs. Blennerhasset. The great scheme failed, and Blennerhasset, who was a man of great wealth, was totally ruined, he having made liberal advances of money to promote the matter. Colonel Burr was arrested for treason; tried at Richmond, Virginia, but managed to be acquitted, as no overt act could be proved. For the rest of his life he resided chiefly in New York, living in obscurity and neglect. He had the reputation of being a thoroughly unprincipled, licentious and profligate man, and even his biographer, Davis, has stamped him with infamy. He died at Staten Island, New York, September 14th, 1836.

SOUTHARD, HON. HENRY, Soldier and Statesman, late of Baskingridge, was born, in the year 1747, on Long Island, and was a son of Abraham Southard. When he was about eight years old his father removed to the then colony of New Jersey, and settled at Baskingridge, where the family have since continued to reside. The son received but an ordinary English education, and when a young man was thrown upon his own resources, laboring as a common hired man at thirty cents a day. By his untiring industry he collected enough money wherewith to purchase a farm. His energy and talents distinguished him from the mass, and at an early date he was appointed a Justice of the Peace. Over nine hundred cases were heard by him, and decisions rendered in each of them, and so just were these decisions that there were but four cases appealed. During the war of the Revolution he entered the service and contributed a share towards the attainment of our independence. He was among the earliest members of the State Legislature, subsequent to the adoption of the Federal Constitution in 1789, and usefully served in that body for nine years, and then was elected a member of Congress. This post of honor he held by successive re-elections for twenty-one years, when in 1821, admonished by the growing weight of years, he voluntarily retired, having already passed the ordinary limit of three-score years and ten. A short time previous his distinguished son, Samuel L. Southard, had been elected a member of the United States Senate; and they had the pleasure of meeting in the Joint Committee of the two Houses, upon whom, as a final resort, devolved the settlement of the famous Missouri Compromise, a circumstance probably without a parallel in our political history. Until within three years of his death he had never worn glasses or used a staff, and was accustomed to a daily walk of three miles. His memory was remarkably strong, for he could not only recollect every question which had come before Congress while a member, but could mention the different speakers, and their very arguments. He died within a few days of his distinguished son, June 2d, 1842, at the advanced age of ninety five years.

Wm. H. Hendrickson

CHENCK, JOHN V., A. M., M. D., Physician, of Camden, New Jersey, was born, November 17th, 1824, at a place long known as Six Mile Run, but now called Franklin Park, in Somerset county, New Jersey. His parents were Ferdinand S. and Leah (Voorhees) Schenck, both natives of New Jersey. John Schenck obtained his preliminary education at the common schools in his neighborhood, and subsequently entered upon the usual preparatory course of study before entering college. His preparation being complete, he entered Rutgers College, at New Brunswick, in 1841, and graduated with the class of 1844. After leaving college he at once set about preparing himself to enter the medical profession. With this view he entered the office of his father, who had been for many years a leading practitioner at Six Mile Run. He studied under his father's direction until the year 1845, when he entered the University of Pennsylvania. His studies were prosecuted with the utmost diligence and industry, and his rapid progress in them was remarkable. In the spring of 1847 he graduated from the university, and at once entered upon the practice of his profession in company with his father in his native place. He continued this practice until December, 1848, when he removed to the city of Camden, where he has continued ever since to reside. His success as a practitioner was very rapidly attained, and being based on thorough skill and enthusiastic and unwearied devotion to his profession, it has proved a lasting and increasing success. He rapidly built up an extensive and very valuable practice in Camden, and is among the first—perhaps the foremost—of the profession in that city. His is not a self-seeking professional devotion. He labors constantly to elevate his calling, and always takes a part of unwearied activity in the various medical societies of which he is and has been a member. He is a member of the Camden County Medical Association, and has served two terms as President of that organization. He was elected President of the New Jersey State Medical Society at its annual meeting in May, 1876. He was married, July 6th, 1857, to Martha McKeen, of Philadelphia.

ENDRICKSON, HON. WILLIAM H., Farmer and State Senator, of Middletown, was born, June 3d, 1813, in that town, and is a son of the late William H. and Eleanor (Dubois) Hendrickson. His paternal ancestors were among the pioneer settlers of Monmouth county, having located there as early as 1698, and he still owns and resides upon the old homestead, which has always been in the possession of the family. His education was obtained at the grammar-school of Rutgers College, New Brunswick, which he left on the death of his father, he then being a member of the sophomore class. He has always followed agricultural pursuits, and with marked success. He commands the respect of the community for his sterling worth and integrity of character. In appreciation of these traits he has been honored several times by the people of Monmouth county, who have elected him a member of the State Senate. He was first chosen in 1858, and served until 1861. He was again elected in 1872, and served until 1875, when he was re-elected, so that his term will expire in 1878. During his legislative career he has been a member of the Finance, Printing, and Education Committees, and during his first senatorial term was Chairman of the last-named committee. He has always given his constituents great satisfaction. His election in 1872 was without opposition; and in 1875 his opponent was a gentleman of great popularity in the county. He made no effort whatever to secure the nomination; the office sought him, the people and his party demanding his services. He has been a member of the Board of Freeholders of Monmouth county for eight years, and has been President of the Middletown & Keyport Steamboat Company for the past fifteen years; also a Director of the Farmers' & Merchants' Bank, of Matawan. He was married, February 28th, 1839, to Elizabeth E. Woodward, of Cream Ridge, Monmouth county; she died December 13th, 1865. His second wife is Rebecca C. F. Patterson, to whom he was united June 24th, 1868.

ENDRICKSON, HON. CHARLES DUBOIS, Member of the New Jersey Assembly, was born at Middletown, Monmouth county, New Jersey, July 2d, 1844, and is the oldest living son of William H. and Elizabeth E. (Woodward) Hendrickson, of the same place. He is of the sixth generation to reside upon the property now in the possession of the family; his ancestors being among the first settlers of Monmouth county, and conspicuous during the war of the Revolution for their loyalty and patriotism, taking high rank in the military service, and being distinguished for bravery and devotion to the cause of independence. He received a rudimentary education at the district school-house erected by his father upon his farm near the old homestead, and which he presented to the district. He subsequently passed two years in the Collegiate Institute, at Matawan, New Jersey, and completed his education by a three years' course at the Lawrenceville High School, in Mercer county, in the same State. After leaving school he returned home and remained upon the farm with his parents until his marriage. In the autumn of 1865, with his wife, he made an extended tour, of over three months, through the Atlantic and Gulf States and a portion of the West, visiting many of the prominent cities and places of interest, including nearly all the important battle-fields of the civil war, which had then just concluded, by this means obtaining a personal knowledge of the people, and valuable information concerning the country, together with the results of the civil conflict;

15

Upon returning to New Jersey, he superintended the erection of his family residence, which is built upon the highlands—on a portion of the estate—overlooking Raritan bay,
the Atlantic ocean, Long and Staten islands, New York
harbor, etc., etc., and possessing an extended inland view,
being one of the most beautiful locations on the coast. This
house, with about two hundred acres of land, has been the
means of attaching him to a country life, and to the occupation of an agriculturalist. For three years he conducted
the farm in person, but subsequently leased it, although
maintaining a general supervision over the operations as
managed by his tenant. At an early age he became much
interested in the political movements of the day, and labored
actively and enthusiastically for the candidates of the Democratic party. Although frequently solicited by his friends,
he steadily declined office until the fall of 1874, when he
was induced to allow his name to be presented in the Democratic convention as a candidate for the Assembly, receiving
the unanimous nomination. The Republican party declined
to present a candidate in opposition, and his name was
placed upon both tickets, and in the election he received
nearly the entire vote of the district. In the Legislature of
1874 the Democratic party was in the ascendency. He was
made Chairman of the Committee on Militia, a member of
the joint Committee on the Sinking Fund, and of the House
Committee on Stationery, besides serving on several important special committees. He was renominated in October,
1875, for the Assembly, by the Democratic party, without
opposition. The Republicans making a nomination this
year, after an active canvass he was re-elected by a majority
of 844, carrying every township in the district. Upon the
organization of the Legislature he was chosen the Democratic caucus nominee for Speaker of the House of Assembly, and received the entire Democratic vote for that position; but, as the Republicans had the majority, he failed to
be elected. He was, however, a prominent member of the
Centennial Legislature, and the recognized leader of the
Democratic party, being frequently called to the speaker's
chair, which position he filled with great credit and satisfaction, exhibiting much executive ability. He served as a
member of the Joint Committee on Treasurer's Accounts,
and of the House Committees on Education and the Centennial, and besides was a member of several special committees. When but sixteen years of age he became connected with the State Militia, and served for a number of
years in the ranks. In 1873 he was commissioned a Lieutenant in Company G, 3d Regiment, National Guards of the
State of New Jersey, and retained that position until April
26th, 1876, when he was promoted to the rank of Colonel,
and appointed aide-de-camp upon the staff of his excellency,
Governor Joseph D. Bedle, which appointment he continues
to hold. In 1873 he was appointed, by Governor Parker,
one of the commissioners to examine into the condition of
the deaf, dumb, blind and feeble-minded inhabitants of the
State, and was reappointed in 1874, by the same executive,

one of the commissioners to select sites upon which to erect
institutions for the care of these different classes of defec-
tives, and upon the organization of the commission was
chosen its Secretary. In 1868 he was elected a Director of
the New York & Long Branch Railroad Company, and
after serving for three years in that capacity, resigned. He
gave to that enterprise almost his entire attention for many
months, contributing greatly to its success. At present he
is a Director and Secretary of the Middletown & Keyport
Turnpike Company, and is connected with other minor associations, and is regarded as an energetic, enterprising
citizen, aiding and encouraging the advancement and promotion of all public improvements tending to the development of the section in which he resides. He was married,
October 12th, 1865, to Elizabeth McChesney Rue, at Penn's
Manor, Bucks county, Pennsylvania, by the Rev. David
R. Frazer. He has but one child living, Mary Cor-
lies Hendrickson, who is now (1876) six years of age. A
son of Senator William H. Hendrickson, whose biography
appears immediately before this, there is presented the rather
remarkable coincidence of father and son occupying seats
in the same Legislature during the same session.

VORHEES, JOHN N., Lawyer, of Flemington, was
born, March 4th, 1835, near White House, Hunterdon county, New Jersey, and is a son of the
late Judge Peter E. Vorhees. He received his
preparatory education at the grammar-school of
Rutgers College, New Brunswick, and matriculated at the latter institution in 1850. Having finished the
full curriculum of four years, he graduated with the class
of 1854, which included, among others, Revs. James Le
Fevre and Andrew P. Thompson, of the Reformed Dutch
Church, and James S. Atkin, a prominent member of the
New Jersey bar, now practising at Trenton. Immediately
after leaving college he entered the law office of Hon.
Alexander Wurts, at Flemington, where he prepared for
the bar, to which he was admitted in 1857. He at once
entered upon the practice of his profession in his native
town, White House, where he remained until 1871, when
he removed to Flemington, and became associated with
Hon. John T. Bird, under the firm-name of Bird & Vorhees.
In the following year Chester Van Syckel was added to the
firm, which became Bird, Vorhees & Van Syckel, and continued until the senior partner retired in 1873. The firm of
Vorhees & Van Syckel practised for about a year, when
they dissolved, and the former associated with him his
former student, George H. Large, and this connection still
continues. They control a large and remunerative practice, and among their clients may be named the Easton &
Amboy Railroad Company, and the Delaware & Bound
Brook & High Bridge Railroad Company. The senior
partner has been connected with a number of criminal

cases, noticeable among which are the Rottenburg rioters and Brenner murder cases, in both of which he secured acquittal in the face of the most damaging testimony. He was appointed, by Governor Randolph, Prosecutor of the Pleas, but resigned after holding the appointment a year. His political creed is that of the Democracy, and he has done his party good service, as a speaker at mass meetings and other gatherings. He is, however, no politician; nor has he ever sought or held any office of a political character.

HEBAUD, REV. LEO, Clergyman and Pastor of St. Mary's Roman Catholic Church, Elizabeth, was born, 1839, in the city of New York, and is a son of Edward and Emma (Boisaubin) Thebaud. His father was a merchant in New York city, of which he was a native. His mother was of Jersey birth. He was thoroughly educated at the Roman Catholic College, known by the name of Septon Hall, at South Orange, New Jersey, and being intended for the priesthood, repaired to Italy, where he pursued his theological studies at Genoa, and was ordained by Archbishop Charvaz, of Genoa, in 1867. After his return to the United States, he officiated for five years as assistant in St. John's Roman Catholic Church, at Paterson, and was then transferred to Elizabeth, where he took charge of St. Mary's Church, which is the oldest congregation in Elizabeth, having been founded in 1844 by Rev. Isaac P. Howell, whose biographical sketch will be found elsewhere in this volume. Since his connection with this parish, he has by his earnest labor succeeded in liquidating a debt of $12,000, in which the church building was involved. He is a man of marked ability, an earnest and ready speaker, beloved by his congregation and much respected by his fellow-townsmen.

WARD, HON. FRANK M., of Newton, Senator from Sussex county, was born, November 26th, 1830, in Dutchess county, New York, and is a son of Edward and Annie (Pray) Ward, both also natives of New York State. His father was both a farmer and a manufacturer in Dutchess county. Young Ward received his rudimentary education at the Armenia Seminary in his native county, and subsequently attended an academical institution in Poughkeepsie. Leaving school at an early age, he learned the trade of a millwright, and in 1849 removed to Fond du Lac, Wisconsin, where he commenced operations in that line of business on his own account. He remained there for some time, and then returned to New York, and sojourned at Deposit, New York, until 1855, when he finally located in Sussex county, New Jersey, which he has since made his permanent home, except during 1859 and 1860, when he was en-

gaged in the milling business at Watkins, Schuyler county, New York, and while there was one of the supervisors of the township of Jefferson, in that county. Since his residence in Sussex county, he has been the recipient of several offices in the gift of the people, and has served his constituents to their entire satisfaction. In the autumn of 1865 he was elected by the Democratic party to represent the first district of Sussex in the lower house of the State Legislature, and served as such during the years 1866-67. He was re-elected to the same, and filled that position in 1872-73. In 1876 he was nominated by the same party as candidate for the State Senate, from Sussex county, and also elected. He is a Director of the South Mountain & Boston Railroad Company, which is now in course of construction.

LAWRENCE, CAPTAIN JAMES, of the United States Navy, was born, October 1st, 1781, at Burlingtou, New Jersey, and was the son of James Lawrence, a prominent attorney-at-law of that city. From his earliest years he had a predilection for a seafaring life, which his friends could not conquer. When sixteen years old he received a midshipman's warrant. In the war with Tripoli he accompanied Decatur in the hazardous exploit of destroying the frigate "Philadelphia," which had been captured by that power. He remained several years on the Mediterranean station, and commanded successively the "Vixen," "Wasp," "Argus" and "Hornet." While cruising in the latter vessel off the capes of the Delaware, he fell in with the British sloop-of-war "Peacock," and captured her after an action of only fifteen minutes. This battle occurred February 24th, 1813. On his return to port he was received with great distinction, and was promoted to the rank of Port Captain. In the spring of the same year he was ordered to the command of the frigate "Chesapeake," then fitting out at Boston. While lying in the roads, nearly ready for sea, the British frigate "Shannon," then commanded by Captain Brooke, appeared off the harbor and made signals expressing a wish to meet him in combat. Although laboring under many disadvantages, with a new and undisciplined crew, he yet determined to accept the challenge. He put to sea on the morning of the first day of June, when the "Shannon" bore away. At four o'clock the "Chesapeake" hauled up and fired a gun, and the "Shannon" hove to. A short time after the action commenced Captain Lawrence was wounded in the leg, but he continued on deck giving the necessary orders as if nothing had happened. Then the anchor of the "Chesapeake" caught in one of the ports of the enemy's vessel, and in consequence of this mishap the "Chesapeake" could not bring her guns to bear upon the foe. As Captain Lawrence was being carried below in consequence of receiving a second and a mortal wound in the intestines, he uttered the memorable words, "Don't give up the ship." But after the action had continued eleven minutes the enemy boarded and captured the "Chesapeake." The loss in killed and wounded on the latter was one hundred and forty-six, while the "Shannon" suffered a loss of eighty-six. The "Shannon," with her prize, made sail for Halifax, which port was reached in a short time. Captain Lawrence lingered four days in ex-treme pain, and then died. The British, recognizing him as a true hero, though a fallen one, buried him with all the honors of war. His body, together with that of Lieutenant Ludlow, were subsequently removed by Captain G. Crown-inshield, at his own expense, first to Salem, Massachusetts, and thence removed to New York. Captain Lawrence married the daughter of M. Montaudevert, a merchant of New York. He died June 6th, 1813. His widow survived him, with two children.

OHNSON, THOMAS P., Lawyer, late of Prince-ton, was born, about 1761, in New Jersey, and was the second son of William and Ruth (Potts) Johnson. His father was a native of Ireland, who emigrated to this country in the year 1750, and married Ruth, sister of Stacy Potts, of Trenton; both parents were members of the Society of Friends. When he was quite young, the family removed to Charles-ton, South Carolina, where his father established a flourish-ing boarding-school, and gained much repute by his lectures on various branches of natural philosophy. His fondness for such studies seemed to have been inherited by his son, who, even in his later years, continued to turn his attention to them. His father died at the South, after a residence of some years, when his mother, with her family of five chil-dren, returned to her native State, and with the aid of her brother opened a store in Trenton. In that place Thomas was placed as an apprentice to a carpenter and joiner. After following this business for some time, he was com-pelled to abandon it, owing to his having ruptured a blood-vessel. He then engaged in teaching youth in Bucks county, Pennsylvania, and afterwards in Philadelphia. For this he had rare qualifications. While in Philadelphia a business house took him into partnership, and sent him to Richmond, Virginia, where the firm opened a large store. He became acquainted there with the late Chief-Justice Marshall, and often had the privilege of listening to the first lawyers of the Old Dominion. This probably led him to turn his thoughts to the bar. After a few years the loss of his store and goods by fire caused him to return to New Jersey. He took up his residence in Princeton, where he married, and entered his name as a student of law in the office of the Hon. Richard Stockton. In due time he was admitted to the bar and received his license as an attorney, three years after as a counsellor, and finally attained the rank as a serjeant-at-law. His career at the bar was a most brilliant one; whether arguing points of law, or spreading a

case before a jury, he was always heard with fixed attention or lively interest. He was lucid in arranging and express-ing his thoughts, and well knew how to seize hold of strong points in a case, and when he pleased to touch the chords of feeling, he seldom failed to produce an impression. His style of thought and expression was simple and natural. He was no indifferent spectator of the great political questions, the contests of which have ever divided the wise and good men of the nation. With the majority of the New Jersey bar he belonged to the Washingtonian school, and exerted all his energies in what he honestly believed to be the true interests of his country. He possessed an enlarged acquaint-ance with the principal departments of literature and science, but experimental philosophy and natural history had been his favorite studies. Moreover, he was a good anatomist and no mean chemist, and had a natural fondness for mechanical pursuits; indeed, the products of his skill would not have disgraced the most experienced artists. He was distin-guished by a high sense of moral principle and great kind-ness of heart, and he cherished a warm attachment for his brethren of the New Jersey bar. He entertained a profound regard for the Christian religion, and being fully convinced of its truth, he was not backward in expressing his sense of its importance, and seldom could the scoff of infidelity pass unrebuked in his presence. He married a daughter of Robert Stockton, of Princeton, New Jersey. He died March 12th, 1838.

cKNIGHT, CHARLES, M. D., Physician and Surgeon-General of the American army during the revolutionary war, was born, October 10th, 1750, at Cranberry, New Jersey, and was the eldest son of the Rev. Charles McKnight. His family was originally from Scotland and settled in Ireland at the time of the "Ulster Plantation," at the beginning of the seventeenth century. Dr. McKnight's father was for nearly forty years a much-esteemed and highly respected clergyman of the Presbyterian church, and one of the early trustees of Princeton College. In 1777, he, then being in advanced life, having rendered himself obnoxious to the Tory party, was imprisoned by the British, who treated him with great cruelty. He died shortly after his release, New Year's day, 1778. In this connection it may be stated that a younger brother of the doctor, who was an ardent patriot and an officer of the New Jersey line, was also seized by the British and confined in one of the prison-ships in Wallabout bay, Long Island, now the site of the Brooklyn navy-yard, where he finally perished with the great army of martyrs to the cause of independence. Dr. McKnight received a first-class education, and graduated "candidatum primum" at Princeton College, in the class of 1771. He studied medicine under the celebrated Dr. Shippen, of Philadelphia. At the commencement of the revolutionary war his abilities were so marked as to procure

him the appointment, April 11th, 1777, of "Senior Surgeon of the Flying Hospital, Middle Department." In 1780, although only thirty years of age, he was made Surgeon-General; and from October 1st, 1780, until January 1st, 1782, he served as Chief Physician. The late Dr. John W. Francis, of New York, in an article printed in the *American Medical and Philosophical Register*, thus speaks of him in that connection: "In the discharge of the important and arduous duties of his station, his talents and indefatigable zeal were equally conspicuous. He was pre-eminently faithful in the performance of all these duties, which the perilous situation of his country required and his humane disposition led him to undertake." After the termination of the war he removed to New York city, and was very soon afterwards appointed Professor of Surgery and Anatomy in Columbia College, New York. Dr. Francis speaks of him in this respect: "He delivered lectures on these two branches of medical science to a numerous and attentive class of students, while the profundity of his research and the acuteness of his genius gained for him the approbation of the most fastidious. In a life of constant activity, both as a practitioner and teacher, he continued until he arrived at his forty-first year, when a pulmonary affection (the result of an injury received during the war) put an end to his labors and usefulness." He was distinguished, not only in this country, but also in Europe, for the successful performance of certain most difficult and dangerous surgical operations. President Duer, in his "Reminiscences," thus speaks of him: "Although he was eminent as a physician, he was particularly distinguished as a practical surgeon, and at the time of his death was without a rival in this branch of his profession. Gifted by nature with talents peculiarly calculated for the exercise of the important duties of a surgeon, his education in an especial manner enabled him to attain the highest reputation." He published a paper in the "Memoirs of the London Medical Society," vol. iv, which attracted considerable attention abroad. He was a member of the New York State Society of the Cincinnati. He married Mrs. Litchfield, only daughter of General John Morin Scott, of New York, one of the most zealous patriots of the Revolution, a prominent lawyer and politician of those times, Secretary of the State and a delegate to the Continental Congress of 1782–83. The late John M. Scott McKnight, M. D., of New York city, was his only son. Dr. Charles McKnight died in 1790.

NGLISH, JAMES R., Lawyer, of Elizabeth, was born, September 27th, 1840, in Bernard township, Somerset county, New Jersey, and is a son of Rev. James T. and Mary C. (Jobs) English. He is of Scotch-Irish and English ancestry, and some of his progenitors were the first settlers of Englishtown, Monmouth county, where the family resided for over one hundred and fifty years. His father removed from that place to Liberty Corner, in Bernard township, when a youth, and subsequently became pastor of a Presbyterian congregation, to whom he ministered for thirty-five years. James, the younger, received a thorough education and graduated at Princeton College. He subsequently entered the office of Theodore Little, at Morristown, as a student at law, where he continued until licensed as an attorney in June, 1865. He then removed to Elizabeth, where he commenced the practice of his profession, which has been a large, successful and lucrative one. At the present time he is counsel for many corporations, including large foreign corporations doing business in New Jersey. In political creed he is a Republican, and has taken an ardent and laborious part in various campaigns, and has also been frequently a delegate to county and State conventions. Although frequently solicited to become a candidate for some office in the gift of the people, he has invariably declined the honor of a nomination. He was married, November 9th, 1865, to a Miss Redford.

OODHULL, HON. GEORGE SPOFFORD, Associate Justice of the Supreme Court of New Jersey, was born in Monmouth county, near Freehold, New Jersey. The family has been identified with that county for many years, holding a high social position and enjoying the esteem and respect of a very wide circle. Judge Woodhull's grandfather, Rev. John Woodhull, D. D., was an eminent divine, and for more than forty years pastor of the old Tennent Church, located about three miles from Freehold, while his father, John T. Woodhull, M. D., was for many years a skilful and leading practitioner of the county, and died in the year 1869 at the advanced age of eighty-three. His mother, *née* Ann Wikoff, also belonged to the same county, having been born near Manalapan. He received his early education at home, and after an exceptionally sound and thorough preliminary training, attended Princeton Academy, where he was prepared for Princeton College, which he entered in 1830. At the conclusion of a three years' course he graduated with distinction with the class of 1833. Having made choice of the legal profession he became a student under Richard S. Field, of Princeton, and in due course was admitted as an attorney in 1839. Three years later he was received as counsellor. He began practice at Freehold, where he prosecuted his profession until 1850, when he removed to May's Landing, Atlantic county, and there remained for twelve years. In the year of his removal to May's Landing he was appointed by Governor Haines, Prosecuting Attorney for Atlantic county. This office he held for fifteen years, distinguishing himself by able and faithful service, which led in a few years to his appointment as Prosecuting Attorney for Cape May county also—a position which, in connection with the first, he occupied for ten years. During his residence in Atlantic county, in the year 1856, he was a candidate for the State Senate on the Republican ticket. The county had always been Democratic, and there was little hope of changing the result in that election; but his services in the public behalf, his high abilities as a lawyer and man of affairs, and his popularity as a citizen, enabled him to wield an influence sufficient to turn the current of public opinion. In this year he largely reduced the Democratic majority, and continuing his active efforts year after year he succeeded before he left the county in winning it for the Republican party, and it has since remained true to that allegiance. In 1866 he was appointed, by Governor Ward, Associate-Justice of the Supreme Court of New Jersey, and had assigned to him the Second Judicial District, comprising the counties of Camden, Burlington and Gloucester. A well-read lawyer and a man of evenly-balanced mind, devoted to his profession and to his judicial duties, he attained such a reputation that on the expiration of his term, in 1873, Governor Parker, though differing with him politically, concluded to offer him reappointment. The nomination was accepted, and at once confirmed by the Senate, and the community secured for another term the services of a capable and upright judge. He is highly respected by the profession both as lawyer and judge, while in private life he is esteemed as a polished gentleman and a public-spirited citizen. He was married, in April, 1847, to Caroline Mandeville Vroom, a niece of ex-Governor Vroom.

WOOD, REV. JAMES, D. D., an eminent Presbyterian Clergyman, Teacher and Author, late of Hightstown, was born in New York State, in the year 1800. He was a graduate of the Princeton Theological Seminary, and was ordained pastor of a church in Amsterdam, New York, where he preached for some time. He was subsequently appointed an agent for the Board of Education for the West, and was afterwards elected Professor of Church History in the Indiana Theological Seminary, where he remained for quite a number of years. After resigning from that institution he became Principal of an academy for boys in New Albany, Indiana. His next appointment was that of Assistant Secretary of the Board of Education, at Philadelphia. He was afterwards elected President of Hanover College, Indiana, which position he resigned in 1866, that he might become Principal of the Van Rensselaer Institute, at Hightstown. The primary object of this institution was the education of the children of missionaries. He had entered upon his duties with great zeal, and was making vigorous efforts towards a complete endowment of the institute when interrupted by death. He was the author of an able work entitled "Old and New Theology," setting forth the reasons which led to the division of the Presbyterian Church. A work entitled "Call to the Ministry" was from his pen; besides this, he wrote several other works of a minor character. He was profoundly learned in the specialty of church history, as well as in the history of the Reformation; not only as regarded his own branch of the Reformed church, but in contemporaneous sects and religious bodies. He died at Hightstown, April 7th, 1867.

ELMER, GENERAL EBENEZER, M. D., Physician and Surgeon, Soldier and Statesman, late of Bridgeton, was born, in 1752, at Cedarville, Cumberland county, New Jersey, and was the grandson of the Rev. Daniel Elmer, who removed from Connecticut to Fairfield in 1727. He studied medicine with his elder brother, and was about to establish himself in practice when hostilities commenced between America and Great Britain. In January, 1776, he was commissioned an Ensign in the company of Continental troops commanded by the late Governor Bloomfield, serving in that capacity and also as a Lieutenant in the northern army until the spring of 1777, when, the artillery being reorganized, he was appointed a Surgeon's Mate. In June, 1778, he was appointed Surgeon of the 2d Jersey Regiment, and filled that position until the close of the war, and during the whole period of his career in the army was never absent from duty. After the war he married and settled in Bridgeton, and pursued the practice of his profession. In 1789 he was elected a member of Assembly, and was re-elected for several successive years; and in both 1791 and 1795 was chosen Speaker of the House. In 1800 he was elected a member of Congress, and sat in that body for six years, being twice re-elected. His term of service there was coincident with the period of President Jefferson's administration, of which he was a supporter. He was Adjutant-General of the New Jersey Militia, and for many years Brigadier-General of the Cumberland Brigade. During the war with England, in 1813, he commanded the troops stationed at Billingsport, in New Jersey. In the year 1807, and afterwards, in 1815, he was a member of the Legislative Council of the State, and was chosen Vice-President of that body. In 1808 he was appointed Collector of the Customs for the Port and District of Bridgeton, which office he resigned in 1817. He was reappointed thereto in 1822, and continued in the same until 1832, when he again resigned; and, having then reached the age of fourscore years, wholly declined public business. For a long period of years he had been connected with the Presbyterian Church as an active and leading member. His great characteristic during a long and useful life was his stern integrity; while his benevolence, generosity and kindly acts endeared him to all. He was at the time of his death the President of the New Jersey State Branch of the Order of the Cincinnati, and the last surviving officer of the New Jersey line of the revolutionary army. He died at Bridgeton, October 18th, 1843.

———◆◇◆———

LMER, HON. DANIEL, Lawyer and Jurist, was born, 1784, in Cumberland county, New Jersey. He was the fifth of that name in descent from Rev. Daniel Elmer, pastor of the Cohansey Presbyterian Church, and who died in 1755, leaving several children, whose descendants are still residents of south Jersey. The family is of English origin, and the name was originally Aylmer, one of the family being Baron of the Exchequer, in 1535; and one, John Aylmer, was tutor of Lady Jane Grey, and was consecrated, 1568, Bishop of London under the name of John Elmer. Daniel Elmer lost his father when but eight years of age, and he was placed in the family of his great-uncle, Dr. Ebenezer Elmer, where he resided several years. His education was only such as could be attained in the common schools of the day; but he lost no opportunity of acquiring information, and devoted his leisure hours to study. When about sixteen years old he commenced the study of the law with General Giles, of Bridgeton, who was at that time the county clerk, and young Elmer obtained employment in the office, by which he was enabled to liquidate his ordinary expenses. He remained with his preceptor for five years, and was licensed as an attorney in 1805, as a counsellor in 1808, and twenty years later attained the rank of serjeant-at-law. Immediately after his admission to the bar he opened an office in Bridgeton, where he resided during the balance of his life, except when abroad on professional business. He acquired a large and lucrative practice, especially in the collection of accounts; and, as he was very economical in his habits and made judicious investments with his earnings, gradually acquired an independence. After Judge Dayton resigned, in 1841, he was appointed by the joint meeting of the Legislature a Judge of the Supreme Court, and sat upon the bench for four years. During his incumbency the celebrated Mercer case was tried, and he was the president Judge before whom the criminal was arraigned. The trial created great excitement, especially in Philadelphia, where both the victim, Hutchinson Heberton, and the avenger of his sister's honor, Singleton Mercer, resided. The offence took place on the ferry-boat plying between Philadelphia and Camden, while the vessel was in the waters of New Jersey. Camden at that time was in Gloucester county, and Woodbury the shire town and where the trial took place; Mercer was defended by the celebrated Philadelphia lawyer, Peter A. Browne; and, aside from the feeling in favor of the accused, presented the case so strongly to the jury that, although the State's attorney proved conclusively a clear case of murder,

technically, the jury acquitted the defendant. The latter, however, was ruined morally and physically; and some years after, as if to atone for the crime he had committed, volunteered, with others, as a nurse when Norfolk, Virginia, was smitten with the yellow fever, contracted the fever and died, it is said, a true penitent. Judge Elmer was chosen a member of the convention which assembled to form the new State constitution, and entered upon his duties in that body with his accustomed ardor. He had ever been a laborious advocate and counsellor, and before he had taken his seat on the bench of the Supreme Court he manifested symptoms of overwork. In the winter succeeding the meeting of the convention he had a slight stroke of apoplexy, and which so affected his system as to render it advisable that he should resign his office as Judge. For many years he was President of the Cumberland Bank, of Bridgeton. Politically he was a member of the old Federalist party, and in later years a Whig of the Henry Clay school. In his religious faith he adhered to the doctrines of the Presbyterian Church, and was an earnest and devout member of that denomination. He was married, in 1808, to a daughter of Colonel Potter, and had a family of several children, all of whom, except a son and daughter, died in infancy. Judge Elmer died in 1848.

———◆◇◆———

LMER, HON. LUCIUS QUINTIUS CINCINNATUS, Lawyer and ex-Associate-Justice of the Supreme Court of New Jersey, was born in Bridgeton, New Jersey, where he now resides, February 3d, 1793. His father was General Ebenezer Elmer, M. D., who was also a native of Cumberland county, and who served as a surgeon in the revolutionary army, and during the war of 1812 commanded the militia at Billingsport. His mother was Hannah Seely, daughter of Rev. Ephraim Seely, of Bridgeton. He received his preparatory educational training at various schools in the neighborhood of his home, and then became a student at the University of Pennsylvania. Determining to adopt the legal profession, he studied law with his relative, Hon. Daniel Elmer, of Bridgeton, and in due course was licensed as attorney in 1815. Three years later he was called as counsellor. He began practice in Bridgeton and the surrounding circuits. A good business soon accrued to him, and he began to fill a considerable space in the public eye. Although not a politician, in the general acceptation of the term, he took a lively interest in public affairs, affiliating with the Democratic party, which represented the principles he believed to lie at the root of good government. Naturally, therefore, he was regarded as an eligible candidate for representative positions, and became a member of the lower branch of the Legislature during the sessions of 1820, 1821, 1822 and 1823, serving during the latter year as Speaker of the House. During 1824 he was Prosecutor of the Pleas for

Cumberland County, and at various times for Cape May County also. From 1824 to 1829 he held the appointment of United States District Attorney for New Jersey, and discharged the duties of that office with marked ability and fidelity. In 1843 he was elected to Congress from the First Congressional District, and served for one term. He was appointed Attorney-General of the State in 1850, and held the position until 1852, when he was elevated to a seat on the Supreme bench by Governor Haines. Thereon he sat for fifteen years, his course throughout commanding the confidence and respect of the bar and the whole community. Since 1869 he has ceased all active business. He is known as an author, having put forward several works of much merit and interest. In 1869 he published a "History of Cumberland County," which contains a very interesting account of the earliest settlement of the county, together with a history of the currency of that and the adjoining counties.. Three years later he gave to the public a work entitled "The Constitution and Government of the Province and State of New Jersey, with Biographical Sketches of its Governors from 1776 to 1845." A large amount of valuable information is gathered together in the pages of this work, which was published among the collections of the New Jersey Historical Society. In 1838 he compiled a "Digest of the Laws of New Jersey," which has now reached its fourth edition, although since its second, about which time its author was raised to the bench, it has been known as "Nixon's Digest." Judge Elmer received the degree of A. M. from the College of New Jersey, Princeton, in 1824, and that of LL. D. from the same institution of learning in 1865. He was married, in 1819, to Catherine Hay, of Philadelphia, who still lives.

———

ILDER, SAMSON VRYLING STODDARD, an eminent Philanthropist, late of Elizabeth, was born, in the year 1780, at Bolton, Massachusetts, and was of Huguenot descent. He commenced his mercantile life in Boston, from which city he went, in the course of his business life, to Paris, and in 1813 to London, where he soon formed the acquaintance of the Rev. Rowland Hill and other celebrities of that era. At a very early day he became connected with the Bible and tract societies, and in 1823, when the American Tract Society was organized, he was prevailed upon, after much solicitation, to accept the Presidency. He retired from that office in 1842, having presided over it for nearly nineteen years. Removing to New York, in 1830, he became a prominent banker in connection with the celebrated house of Hottingner, of Paris, and later with the (national) Bank of the United States. At the time when he resigned the presidency of the tract society he was connected with a number of other organizations, from all of which he also retired. He was the author of a number

of religious tracts that obtained a large and world-wide notoriety. He passed the evening of his days in retirement at Elizabeth, and was ever occupied in doing good. He died in that city, April 2d, 1865.

———

ORTER, LUCIUS P., late President of the Norfolk & New Brunswick Hosiery Company, was born, May 14th, 1818, in Coldbrook, Litchfield county, Connecticut, and was the second child and eldest son of Henry Porter, a prosperous farmer of that town. When he was ten years old his father removed to Norfolk, in the same State, and he remained with his father for several years thereafter, and attended the district school. When nineteen years of age he entered a country store as clerk, where he continued some three years, and thence went to Plymouth, where he was similarly employed, first in the store of Paulus Warner, and subsequently in the establishment of Henry Terry, eventually becoming the latter's partner. While connected with this gentleman he first took an interest in the manufacturing business, the firm becoming the owners of the Plymouth Woollen Mills. At this time he was only twenty-eight years old. About two years after he removed to New York city, although he still retained his connection with the mills. In 1851 he, with two other gentlemen, having become possessed of valuable patents—his own being a rubber toy-rattle—organized the New York Rubber Company, which has since become one of the most prominent in the country, and with which he was actively connected as Trustee at the time of his death; and in that business he acquired the principal portion of his wealth. In 1857, with several other capitalists, he organized the Norfolk Hosiery Company, at Norfolk, Connecticut, with a capital of $75,000, of which he was chosen the Treasurer. Two years after the capital was increased to $125,000. This company was organized to carry on the manufacture of fully-fashioned hosiery by steam power, with machinery invented by E. E. and J. K. Kilbourn, the company having purchased their entire right and being the first to introduce this manufacture in this country. E. E. Kilbourn was appointed a superintendent in the company, and elected a director. During the year 1859 he accompanied Mr. Porter on a visit to Europe to introduce the machines, which threatened to revolutionize the methods then in use for knitting by machinery. In 1863 the demand for the company's goods having so increased as to make it necessary to enlarge, a committee was appointed to select an eligible location in some other city, and finally the site now used by the Norfolk & New Brunswick Hosiery Company—which was the name under which the old company was reorganized—was purchased by the corporation, whose capital was fixed at $300,000, and Lucius P. Porter elected President. The latter was so well pleased with New Brunswick that, soon after the mills went into operation, he removed to that city with his family, and resided there until his death. Under his skilful management the company prospered greatly, and in two years the capital stock was increased to $500,000, and in 1869 to $550,000. He continued as the principal executive officer of the corporation, as his management gave entire satisfaction to all interested in its welfare. Upon the organization of the New Brunswick Board of Water Commissioners, in 1873, he was elected President, in which position he continued until his death. He was also a director in the New Brunswick Savings Institution, and was connected with several other corporations in that city. He was for several years an active and leading member of the First Presbyterian Church, and also one of the Trustees of the same. During his residence in his adopted city he effected much for its general prosperity, especially in locating there the largest, if not the most important, of its manufactories, which will remain as a fitting monument to his memory. His death was a sudden one, his illness only lasting a few days; it occurred, April 2d, 1876.

ARON, REV. SAMUEL, Clergyman, Teacher and Author, late of Mount Holly, New Jersey, was born, in the year 1800, at New Britain, Pennsylvania, and was of Welsh-Irish lineage. He was left an orphan at the early age of six years, and was placed under the care of an uncle, on whose farm he labored for several years, and during a portion of the winter months attended the district school. Inheriting a small patrimony from his father, he entered Doylestown Academy at the age of sixteen years, where he remained some four years. He thence removed to Burlington, New Jersey, and connected himself with the classical and mathematical school, both as a student and assistant teacher. After leaving this town he married, and opened a day school at Bridge Point, and subsequently became Principal of a school at Doylestown. In 1829 he was ordained a minister, and became pastor of the Baptist Church at New Britain. In 1833 he returned to Burlington, where he took charge of the High School, and at the same time held the pastorate of the Baptist Society in that place, where he remained eight years. In 1841 he accepted a call to the church at Norristown, Pennsylvania, and removed there. After preaching for about three years he resigned his charge, and shortly afterwards founded the "Treemount Seminary," about three miles from that town, which, under his management, became justly celebrated throughout eastern Pennsylvania and New Jersey, not only in the number of students, but also in the thoroughness of the instruction imparted to them. In the great financial crisis of 1857 he unfortunately became involved, owing to his having indorsed for a friend, and he relinquished the property of the seminary to the creditors. He subsequently removed to

16

Mount Holly, and accepted a call to the Baptist Church there, a position which he retained during the balance of his life. In September of the last-named year, in connection with his son, Charles, he became the Principal of the Mount Holly Institute, continuing in the discharge of his duties up to the time of the brief illness which terminated his useful life. He was twice tendered the presidency of the New York Central College, but declined the honor. He was the author of many improvements in text-books. He died at Mount Holly, April 11th, 1865.

OMERS, CAPTAIN RICHARD, Master Commandant in the United States Navy, was born, 1778, in the township of Egg Harbor, Atlantic county, New Jersey, and was the youngest son of Colonel Richard Somers, a prominent officer in the revolutionary army. He received his preliminary education in the city of Philadelphia, and completed it in a celebrated academy at Burlington, New Jersey. When about sixteen years of age he went in a coasting vessel from Egg Harbor, and during the two following years made sundry voyages. In 1796 he received from President Washington a midshipman's warrant, and made his first cruise in the frigate "United States," then recently built in Philadelphia, which was at that time under command of Captain Stephen Decatur. He formed a lasting friendship with that brave officer, who, although his professional rival, respected and esteemed him highly. In 1801 Somers was promoted to the rank of Lieutenant, and two years later, during the period of the difficulties with the Barbary powers, he was appointed to the command of the "Nautilus," a beautiful schooner of twelve guns, attached to the Mediterranean Squadron, which sailed from the United States in the summer of 1803, and afterwards became so celebrated under Commodore Preble's order. When the United States squadron, under the last-named officer, was blockading Tripoli, in 1804, Lieutenant Somers distinguished himself in its early stages, as well as on the enterprise which cost him his life. On one occasion he was engaged in a gun-boat, within pistol-shot of the enemy, whose strength was five-fold greater than his own; but the foe was obliged to withdraw, and he brought his own boat back in triumph. At another period, as his boat was advancing to her position, he was leaning against the flagstaff, when he saw a shot coming directly towards him, and bowed his head to avoid it. The shot cut the flagstaff in two, and on measuring the remainder it was ascertained that he escaped death only by this timely removal. After several unsuccessful attempts to force the enemy to terms, it was resolved to fit up the ketch "Intrepid," in the double capacity of fire-ship and infernal, and to send her into the inner harbor of Tripoli, there to explode in the very centre of the Turkish vessels. As her deck was to be covered with a large quantity of powder, shells and other missiles, it was hoped that the town would suffer from the explosion, as well as the shipping, and that the panic created by such an assault, in the dead hours of the night, might procure an instant peace, and more especially promote the liberation of the frigate "Philadelphia," whose officers and crew were believed, at that time, to have been reduced to extreme suffering by the barbarity of their captors. The imminent danger of the service forbade the commodore from ordering any of his officers upon it; and Somers, with whom the conception of the daring scheme is supposed to have originated, volunteered to take the command. On the afternoon of September 4th, 1804, he prepared to leave the "Nautilus," with a full determination to carry the ketch into Tripoli that night. Previously to quitting his own vessel he felt that it would be proper to point out the desperate nature of the enterprise to the four men whom he had selected, that their services might be perfectly free and voluntary. He told them that he wished no man to accompany him who would not prefer being blown up rather than to be taken prisoners; that such was his own determination, and that he wished all who went with him to be of the same way of thinking. The boats then gave three cheers in answer, and each man is said to have applied to him for the honor of applying the match. It may be proper to state, in this connection, that at this identical period the enemy were supposed to have almost exhausted their supply of ammunition, and if the ketch had fallen into their hands they would have obtained just exactly what they required, and so prolonged the war; rather than allow them so valuable a prize was another reason why Somers resolved to sacrifice himself and his crew. Being assured of the temper of his companions he took leave of his officers, the boat's crew doing the same; shaking hands and expressing their feelings, as if they felt assured of their fate in advance. Each of the four men made his will, verbally, disposing of his effects among his shipmates, like those about to die. Several of Somers' friends from the other ships visited him on board of the "Intrepid" before he got away. Among these were Stewart and Decatur, with whom he had commenced his naval careér in the frigate "United States." He was grave, but maintained his usual tranquil and quiet manner. At nine o'clock in the evening Lieutenant Reed was the last to leave the ketch for his own vessel. When he went over the side of the "Intrepid" all communication between the gallant spirits she contained and the rest of the world ceased. At that time everything seemed prosperous. Her commander was cheerful, though calm; and perfect order and method prevailed in the little craft. The leave-taking was affectionate and serious with the officers, though the sailors appeared to be in high spirits. Two boats accompanied the ketch to bring away the party just after setting fire to the train: the whole party numbering thirteen, all of whom had volunteered. The ketch was seen to proceed cautiously into the bay, but was soon obscured by the haze on the water. It was not long before the enemy began to fire at the ketch, which by this time was quite near the batteries, though its reports were neither rapid nor numerous. At this moment, near ten o'clock, Captain Stewart and Lieutenant Carrol were standing in the "Siren's" gangway, looking intently towards the place where the ketch was known to be, when the latter exclaimed, "Look, see the light." At that moment a light was seen passing and waving, as if a lantern were carried by some person in quick motion along the vessel's deck, and then it sank from view. Half a minute may have elapsed when the whole firmament was lighted by a fiery glow; a burning mast, with its sails, was seen in the air; the whole harbor was momentarily illuminated; the awful explosion came, and a darkness like that of doom succeeded; the whole was over in less than a minute. The flames, the quaking of towers, the reeling of ships, and even the bursting of shells, of which the majority fell into the water, though some lodged on the rocks, all became silent. The firing ceased, and from that moment Tripoli passed the night in as profound a stillness as that in which the victims of the explosion have lain from that fatal hour to the present time. In the American squadron the opinion was prevalent that Somers and his determined crew had blown themselves up to prevent capture; but subsequent light has rendered it more probable that it was the result of an accident, or perhaps occasioned by a hot shot from the enemy. Thus perished one of the bravest of the brave. Notwithstanding all hypotheses, and all the great efforts of human ingenuity in reasoning, there will remain a melancholy interest around the manner of his end, which, by the Almighty will, is forever veiled from human eyes in a sad and solemn mystery. He was mild, amiable and affectionate, both in disposition and deportment, although of singularly chivalrous ideas of honor and duty. As a proof of the estimation in which he was held, many vessels have been named after him, and among these the clipper brig-of-war "Somers," on which the celebrated mutiny took place when under the command of Alexander Slidell Mackenzie—an event without a parallel in the history of the United States navy.

VAN DEURSEN, WILLIAM, M. D., Physician, late of New Brunswick, was born in that city, May 16th, 1791, where also he was educated, and graduated at Rutgers College, in the class of 1809, with the first honor, and on which occasion he pronounced the valedictory address. He studied medicine in New York city, and after receiving his diploma served as physician and surgeon in one of the hospitals of that city. Subsequently he removed to Monmouth county, New Jersey, where he commenced the practice of medicine, and resided there for several years; but eventually returned to his native city, and there established a reputation for professional skill which he maintained until his retirement from the active duties of his calling. He was the eldest living Trustee of Rutgers College, having been elected to that office in 1823. He died at New Brunswick, February 20th, 1873.

ONTGOMERY, REAR-ADMIRAL JOHN B., of the United States Navy, was born at Allentown, New Jersey, and was appointed from that State, June 4th, 1812, receiving at that date a midshipman's warrant. Early in September of the same year he reported at Sackett's Harbor for duty in the squadron on Lake Ontario, and served successively on board the "Hamilton" and flag-ships "Madison" and "General Pike." He participated in the naval attack on Kingston, Upper Canada, November 10th, 1812, and also in the capture of Little York (now Toronto), April 27th, 1813, and of Fort George and Newark on the 27th of the following month. In conjunction with seven other officers and one hundred sailors he volunteered for service on Lake Erie, August 4th, 1813, and joined the United States brig "Niagara," Captain Elliott, and took part in the general naval action of September 10th, which resulted in the capture of the British fleet. For this service he received a sword and the thanks of Congress awarded to the officers of his grade. He was present during the blockade and subsequent attack on Mackinaw (Lake Huron), in August, 1814, and also, during the same month, at the destruction of a block-house and gun-brig on the British side of the lake. During the last siege of Fort Erie the "Niagara" was employed in protecting communication between the fort and the United States hospitals at Buffalo, and the transportation of troops between the two shores of the lake during the months of September and October. He continued on board that vessel until the close of the war, and returned to New York late in February, 1815, in time to witness the general illumination in celebration of peace. Early in the following month of March, the United States being at war with Algiers, he was ordered to the sloop-of-war "Ontario," at Baltimore, then under the command of Captain Jesse Duncan Elliott, and sailed with the first squadron under Commodore Decatur, May 15th, 1815, for the Mediterranean. He participated in the capture of an Algerine frigate and a man-of-war brig in June, and in the blockade of Algiers to the close of the war, in July, 1815. He continued to serve on board the "Ontario" and frigate "United States" in the Mediterranean until 1817, when he returned to the United States in the store-ship "Alert," and in August of the same year was ordered to the sloop-of-war "Hornet," then preparing for sea at New York. In February, 1818, he was transferred to the sloop-of-war "Cyane," and shortly afterwards promoted to the rank of Lieutenant.

He cruised in the "Cyane," under Captain Trenchard, on the coast of Africa, returning to the United States in 1820, and almost immediately afterwards was ordered to the sloop-of-war "Erie," at New York. He served on that vessel, under Captain Deacon, until her return from a three-years' cruise in the Mediterranean, in November, 1826. After a furlough of some eighteen months, he was placed in 1828 on recruiting service, in which he was engaged during that and the following year. In 1830 he was ordered to the West Indies as Executive Officer of the sloop-of-war "Peacock," Captain McCall. He was subsequently transferred to the flag-ship "Erie," and at a later period commanded that ship on a cruise along the coast of Mexico. In July, 1831, he was relieved from the command of the "Erie" by Captain Clark, and ordered to the flag-ship "Natchez," and returned in her to Norfolk, Virginia, towards the close of August, 1831, when he was detached on leave. From January, 1833, until February, 1835, he was engaged on recruiting service in Philadelphia and New York, when he received orders to join the frigate "Constitution," at Boston, as Executive Officer, Captain Elliott being in command. This vessel sailed March 2d, 1835, for New York, and thence on the 15th of the same month proceeded to Havre, France, to convey Mr. Livingston, the United States Minister, and family to the United States. He returned on the frigate in July and was detached on leave. In March, 1837, he was ordered to the command of the receiving-ship "Columbus," seventy-four, at Boston; and was detached therefrom in May, 1839, and on the 9th of December following promoted to the rank of Commander. In May, 1841, he was ordered to the recruiting rendezvous at Boston, where he continued until February, 1844, when he was detached on leave. In October of the same year he was ordered to the command of the sloop-of-war "Portsmouth," at Portsmouth, New Hampshire, and sailed in her for Norfolk, Virginia, on the 9th of December. From the latter port he put to sea in January, 1845, bound to the Pacific Ocean, where he continued until near the close of the war with Mexico, returning with the ship to Boston, in May, 1848, when he was detached on leave. During this cruise of the "Portsmouth," of three years and seven months duration, the officers and crew under command of Commander Montgomery took possession of and permanently established the authority of the United States at San Francisco, Sonoma, New Helvetia, and Santa Clara, Upper California. They also maintained a blockade of Mazatlan, Mexico, for some months; and in March and April, 1847, took possession of and hoisted the first United States flags at San Jose, Cape St. Lucas and La Paz, in Lower California, which ports were held until relinquished at the close of the war. In October, 1847, in company with the frigate "Congress," Captain Lavallette, he bombarded and captured the fortified town and port of Guaymas, on the Gulf of California. In April, 1849, he was ordered as Executive Officer to the Navy Yard, Washington, from which he was relieved, November 1st, 1851, and placed on leave. He was commissioned as Captain January 6th, 1853. In April, 1857, he was ordered to the command of the new steam frigate "Roanoke," at Norfolk, Virginia, and sailed thence to Aspinwall, returning in August of that year to New York with two hundred and fifty of the deluded followers of General Walker, who had proposed to liberate Cuba. In the following month he was ordered to Washington as a member of one of the Court of Inquiry on Retired Officers. In January, 1858, the court was dissolved, when he was placed on leave. In April, 1859, he was ordered to the command of the Pacific Squadron, and to hoist his flag on the steam-corvette "Lancaster," at Philadelphia. He was relieved from this command by Commodore Charles H. Bell, in January, 1862, and arrived in New York on the 11th of the same month and placed on waiting orders (retired list). In the following month of May he was ordered to command the Navy Yard, Boston, and was transferred to the Navy Yard, Washington, December 31st, 1863. He remained at the Capital until October 13th, 1865, when he was placed on waiting orders. On July 10th, 1866, he was ordered to the command of the naval station at Sackett's Harbor, from which he was relieved September 1st, 1869, and again placed on waiting orders. His last service was, it will be seen, in command of the station where he first made his entree upon his profession fifty-seven years previously. He was promoted to the ranks of Commodore and Rear-Admiral (retired list), and passed the remainder of his days at Carlisle, Pennsylvania, where he died March 25th, 1873.

OUNG, ERENCE D., M. D., Physician, of Bordentown, was born in Newcastle county, Delaware, May 12th, 1827. His father, William W. Young, was a native of Philadelphia, Pennsylvania, who moved into Delaware; he was a manufacturer in quite an extensive way. On the maternal side he is a Jerseyman, his mother having been Julia E. Anderson, of Trenton. The early education of the subject of this sketch was received at the select school of John H. Willets, in Philadelphia, whence he proceeded to the Newark Academy, Newark, Delaware. From that institution he was graduated in 1845, and immediately began the study of medicine with Dr. William R. Grant, Professor of Anatomy in the University of Pennsylvania. He attended the regular course of lectures in that university, and in due course was graduated, on March 8th, 1848. After receiving his diploma he was appointed Resident Physician of Wills Hospital for Diseases of the Eye, in Philadelphia, and the duties of this position he filled for about a year. Then he was stationed at the Pennsylvania Hospital, in the same city, for about a year. On June 25th, 1849, he removed to Bordentown, and opened an office for the practice of his profession. In

that place he has remained ever since, and has developed a large and valuable practice. In the estimation of his brother practitioners and of the general community he holds a high place both as a doctor and as a man. He is a member of the County Medical Society, and has been sent as a delegate to the State Society a number of times.

INKHAM, WILLIAM E., D. D. S., Dentist, of Newark, was born, May 21st, 1844, in the town of Winslow, Kennebec county, Maine, and is a son of Elias and Fannie (Sampson) Pinkham, who are also both natives of that State. He received his rudimentary education in the schools of his native county, and subsequently became a pupil at a Friends' academy in Providence. When sixteen years of age he commenced the study of dentistry at the Boston Dental College, where he attended one course of lectures; and subsequently matriculated at the Philadelphia Dental College, where he completed his studies and graduated in the spring of 1873 with the degree of Doctor of Dental Surgery. He then removed to New Jersey, locating at Newark, where he has since been actively engaged in the practice of his profession. He is a member of the New Jersey State Dental Society.

OWNLEY, ROBERT W., Mayor of Elizabeth, New Jersey, was born, July 13th, 1813, at Springfield, in that State, and is the eldest son of Richard and Hannah Wade Townley, both of whom were also Jersey-born. His father was devoted to agricultural pursuits near Elizabeth, and his family for four generations have been identified with that neighborhood. The old family homestead was destroyed by fire in 1875, having stood for about one hundred and twenty-five years. It was of the old English style of architecture. The family itself is of English origin, being lineal descendants of Lord Charles Townley, of Great Britain. His preliminary education was obtained in a country school-house on the homestead, after which he attended a classical school for two years in Elizabeth, having in view a liberal education. But his tastes and preferences were found to be in the direction of business, and in 1828 he entered a general country store in Elizabeth as clerk, and a few years afterwards engaged in business on his own account. He so continued until 1840, when he removed to Fort Wayne, Indiana, then in its infancy, and became one of the pioneer settlers of that section of the State, which was then largely populated by Indians. He remained there actively engaged in mercantile pursuits until 1859, when he returned to Elizabeth to reside, although he still retained his business interests in Fort Wayne until 1870. Shortly after his return to New

Jersey the great rebellion broke out, when he took an active part in sustaining the Union cause, with both his influence and purse. During the years 1872 and 1873 he was a member of the City Council of Elizabeth; and in 1874 was elected Mayor of the city, being re-elected in 1875 and 1876, filling that position with marked satisfaction to his constituents. He is identified with various charitable and financial institutions in the city, and is highly respected by the community, as being a man of sound principles, broad views, and more than ordinary executive ability.

ARON, JOHN, late Chief-Engineer in the United States Navy, was born in New Jersey, and entered the service from that State in 1840. When the steam-frigate "Powhatan" was nearly completed he was ordered to that vessel as one of her officers, and served in her during the cruise of three years and six months which she made, first in the Gulf of Mexico and thence to China and Japan. On his return to the United States he was variously employed for a period of some years, when he was assigned as Senior Assistant-Engineer on board the "Niagara," which vessel, in conjunction with several British men-of-war, were engaged in laying the first Atlantic cable. Shortly after the war of the rebellion broke out he was ordered to the "San Jacinto," steam-sloop, and was in charge of the engineer department on board that vessel when she captured the rebel commissioners, Mason and Slidell. After his return from that memorable cruise he was Superintendent of the monitors which were in course of building at the iron ship-building yards at Jersey City, and, among others, supervised the building of the "Tecumseh." Before the completion of that vessel he was ordered to the "Onondaga," but preferring to go to sea in a vessel of his own construction, he succeeded in getting detached and ordered to the "Tecumseh," and had left a sick-bed to be present at the engagement during which he lost his life. The monitor "Tecumseh" was sunk in Mobile Bay on the 5th day of August, 1864.

ROWN, HON. JOHN J., President of the First National Bank, of Paterson, New Jersey, was born, in the year 1817, in the city of New York. When he was five years old his parents were compelled to leave New York owing to an epidemic of yellow fever, and they removed to New Jersey, settling in Paterson, which then was but a mere village. They at first intended to return to New York, but finally decided to remain, and his father engaged in the grocery business. John attended school until he was thirteen years old, when he withdrew and became a clerk in a dry-goods store, where he remained about four years. In

1834 he went to New York, where he effected an engagement as clerk to James La Tourette, at that time a noted fur, cap and stock manufacturer, in whose employ he continued for some three years, including the winter of 1836-37, which he passed in New Orleans. Returning to New York, in May, 1837, he found his employer had failed, as had also happened to many other small and large establishments, all of which had gone down before the great financial storm of that year. This failure prevented him from entering into business himself, as he otherwise would have done, and he accordingly went to Paterson. He there found employment as a clerk in a dry-goods store, and a few years later succeeded to his father's grocery business. He carried the latter on until 1844, when he changed his business and embarked in dry-goods on his own account; this venture proved a very successful one, and he continued it for twenty-three years, when he retired in 1867. At the close of his mercantile career he had a large establishment on Main street, and had built up the most extensive business houses of the kind in the city. The First National Bank, of Paterson, was established in April, 1864, but it did not prosper, and during the summer of that year application had been made to the proper authorities to close the institution, and surrender the bonds which had been deposited in accordance with the law. About this time, however, Mr. Brown's attention was called to the matter, when he stepped forward and saved the charter. With some effort, the sum of one hundred thousand dollars was subscribed, a first-class board of directors selected, who chose John J. Brown as President of the bank, which was reorganized in September, 1864, since which time he has continued in that position, and to which he has devoted all his time and talents since he withdrew from active mercantile pursuits. In three months from the time the bank commenced business its capital was increased to two hundred and fifty thousand dollars, and on January 1st, 1868, another sum of one hundred thousand dollars was added. It has a large surplus fund in addition to the present capital of $400,000, and continues to pay its stockholders a handsome dividend semi-annually. He has also been connected with the Passaic Water-Works Company since its organization; and this corporation is greatly indebted to him for the earnest thought, labor and sacrifices which this great work demanded. Through his management the financial difficulties, which ever attend improvements of this nature, have been overcome, and the works have proved a complete success, not only financially but in all other respects. He has also been interested in other measures for the improvement of the city, and among these may be named the Cedar Lawn Cemetery. In conjunction with a number of other gentlemen, he purchased about one hundred acres of land, which was laid out in 1866-67, and dedicated in September, 1867. It is situated on the bank of the Passaic river, about two miles distance from the city. From almost the very organization of Paterson as a city he was chosen one of the Board of Aldermen, and while absent in Europe, was again elected to that office. In 1854 he was selected as the first Mayor of the municipality, but after he had served his term, declined any further nomination. During his mayoralty he projected and carried out the measure for paving the sidewalks, which before this time had been almost entirely neglected. In 1856 he was induced to become the nominee of the Republican party for the Legislature, and was elected. He served in the lower house for one year, but since that period has invariably declined all offices which have been tendered him. He is a man of very active, energetic temperament, system and practical judgment in regard to everything that he does, and of great courtesy and blandness in demeanor to all persons. As a business man and bank director he has no superior, and his earnest spirit and good sense in executive management make him invaluable as a co-worker in all enterprises. He avoids ostentation in every particular, and is as discreet and practical in all his tastes as he is reliable in his character. Socially he is noted for his genial traits, kindness of heart, and steadfastness in the discharge of all moral and religious duties.

AKLEY, LEWIS W., M. D., of Elizabeth, Physician and Surgeon, ex-Surgeon-General of New Jersey, was born, November 22d, 1828, in the city of New York, and is a son of Samuel and Abby (Williams) Oakley, both of whom were also natives of New York, and of English descent. His father was for many years a leading merchant of that city. He received a first-class education, and entered Princeton College, where, after passing the usual course of study in that ancient and celebrated institution, he graduated with the class of 1849. In the same year he commenced the study of medicine and matriculated at the College of Physicians and Surgeons, in New York city, from which he graduated in 1852. He then went abroad for travel and study, remaining a year or more. Returning to the United States, he selected Elizabeth as his residence in 1854, where he has since continued, and controls an extensive practice. At the outbreak of the rebellion he entered the service as Assistant Surgeon of the 2d Regiment New Jersey Volunteers, May 21st, 1861, and was promoted on the 12th of October of the same year to the rank of Surgeon of the 4th New Jersey Regiment. He was transferred to the 2d Regiment, January 2d, 1862, and from that date was Surgeon-in-Chief of the 1st New Jersey Brigade, 1st Division, 6th Corps, until the expiration of the term for which he had enlisted in 1864. He participated with the Army of the Potomac in all the battles of the war in Virginia in which that army was engaged, from the first battle of Bull Run down to the contest at Cold Harbor, frequently performing arduous hospital duty; was in charge of the 6th Corps Hospital during May and June, 1863, and was present at the battle of Gettysburg, July, 1863, and was among the most efficient and esteemed of the surgeons of New Jersey. In 1865 he was commissioned Surgeon-General of the National Guard of New Jersey, with the rank of Brigadier-General, and held that position until 1869. He was married, September 14th, 1853, to Henrietta Badwin, of Elizabeth, and after her death was united in marriage, March 18th, 1863, to Anna, second daughter of Rev. David Magie, D. D., also of Elizabeth, New Jersey.

ALRIMPLE, HON. VAN CLEVE, of Morristown, Lawyer, and an Associate Justice of the Supreme Court of New Jersey, was born, 1821, in Morris county, in that State, and is a son of Joseph and Abigail (Bryant) Dalrimple, both of whom were of Jersey birth. His father was a merchant and a native of Morris county, while his mother was from Essex county. He received an excellent education at the academy in Morristown, and when nineteen years of age left school and commenced the study of the law in the office of Henry A. Ford, an eminent attorney of Morristown, whom he had selected as his preceptor. Having pursued his legal studies for the required time, he was licensed as an attorney in 1843, and advanced to the rank of counsellor-at-law in 1847. He immediately after his admission to the bar commenced the practice of his profession at Morristown, where he at once made his mark, and took a front rank among the legal practitioners in that section of the State. He was appointed in 1852 Prosecutor of the Pleas for Morris county, and filled that position with great ability during his term of office, which expired in 1857. He was nominated as an Associate Justice of the Supreme Court in 1866, and having been duly confirmed by the Senate, took his seat on the bench, which office he has since held. He was a Democrat in opinion and practice until the troubles arose in connection with the repeal of the Missouri Compromise, when he left that organization and united with the Free-soil, afterwards termed the Republican party. He was married, 1853, to Mary Anna, daughter of Dr. Isaac W. Canfield, of Morristown, New Jersey.

IGH, HON. JOHN J., Mayor of Rahway, was born, March 6th, 1829, in Westfield, New Jersey, and is a son of John and Sarah (Meeker) High, which family and their progenitors have been for a long series of years prominently identified with that town. His father, John High, was a captain in the New Jersey Artillery in the war of 1812, and both his grandfathers participated in the war for independence. James Meeker, his maternal grandfather, was of French descent, and during the revolutionary struggle was attached to the staff of General Lafayette. Young High was educated at an academy in Rahway, and in 1846, after leaving

school, went to New York city, where he effected an engagement as a clerk in a wholesale dry-goods house, remaining there six years. Returning to New Jersey he engaged in business on his own account, starting a store for the sale of manufacturers' hardware, and in which he has continued to the present time. He has always taken an active part in politics, and was a Democrat until 1855, since which time he has affiliated with the Republican party. He was elected in 1861 to the Legislature on that ticket, in which body he served one term. Subsequently he was chosen as a member of City Councils, which position he held for four years, and for three years was President of that body. From 1858 until it ceased to exist in 1865, he was a Director of the Farmers' and Mechanics' Bank of Rahway; he is at present a Director in the Rahway Savings Bank, and also of the Rahway Fire Insurance Company. He has been foremost among his fellow-townsmen in promoting the welfare and prosperity of his adopted city, and is regarded by all as a valuable and public-spirited citizen. He was married in 1866 to Anna Sheddan, daughter of Rev. S. S. Sheddan, D. D.; she died in 1872.

———

HUNT, JOHN W., M. D., Physician and Surgeon, was born, October 10th, 1834, in Groveland, Livingston county, New York, and is the son of Elijah and Eunice (Huffman) Hunt; the father, a farmer by occupation, was born in Pennsylvania, but when about two years of age, in 1736, his father, John Hunt, removed with his family from Pennsylvania to Livingston county, New York, and was among the pioneers of that county, all that part of the State being a wilderness. Dr. Hunt is of English descent, his grandfather's father having emigrated from England, one of the New England colonies. His great-grandfather, William Hunt, was born in Rhode Island, married and removed to New Jersey. His grandfather, John Hunt, was born in New Jersey. Dr. Hunt while a youth attended the district school in his native town, where he received a good common-school education. He subsequently became a pupil in the Genesee Wesleyan Seminary, at Lima, New York, where he remained three years. Early in life he expressed a desire to study medicine, which was not encouraged by his parents. His early choice of a profession, however, was not changed, and in the spring of 1856 he entered the office of Dr. Alexander C. Campbell, at Lima, New York, as a medical student. In the spring of 1857 he proceeded to New York city, matriculated at the University Medical College, and attended the summer course of lectures, at the same time receiving instruction in the private classes of Drs. T. Gaillard Thomas and William R. Donaghe. He continued at the university, attending the winter course of lectures of 1857-58, and in the spring of 1858 returned to Livingston county, and assisted Dr. Campbell in his practice

during the summer. His second full course of lectures he attended at the university the following winter, and graduated in the spring of 1859. Soon after receiving his diploma he presented himself with other candidates for examination by the examining board for Internes to Bellevue Hospital. He was one of the successful candidates and was appointed one of the junior assistants on the house staff. As his services were not required at the hospital during his six months' term of junior service (unless a vacancy should occur) he obtained leave of absence and sailed for England, where considerable time was occupied in visiting the English hospitals, chiefly in London. He returned to New York in October, and entered upon his duties on the House Staff of Bellevue Hospital, where he remained until his term of service expired in the fall of 1860. Having determined to make Jersey City, New Jersey, his future home, he at once opened an office there and commenced practice. At the breaking out of the rebellion he was called by his native State to take professional charge of the 10th Regiment, New York State Volunteers, which was one of the first to organize. He responded to the call, and, in May, 1861, was commissioned Surgeon of that regiment, and followed its fortunes until the spring of 1862, when he resigned his State commission for the purpose of accepting a United States commission as "Brigade Surgeon," afterwards designated "Surgeon of United States Volunteers." Immediately thereafter he was ordered to take charge of the "Mill Creek General Hospital," near Fortress Monroe, Virginia, then just established. Here he was actively engaged until the late August, when he was attacked with fever, which confined him to his bed three months; he was sent north on leave of absence, and in January, 1863, being still feeble and unfit for duty in the field, he retired from the service. Early in March following he visited New Orleans as surgeon of a government transport, and returned much improved in strength. In May he resumed practice in Jersey City, and at once took a prominent position among the profession. In 1864 he was appointed Examining Surgeon of recruits drafted into the service. He is an active member of the District Medical Society for the County of Hudson; and as a delegate to the New Jersey State Medical Society for a number of years, he takes a deep interest in the proceedings of that body, and has generally been a contributor to its transactions. He has also at sundry times contributed to the literature of the profession. Dr. Hunt had not practiced long in Jersey City before he recognized the necessity of a city hospital, and in 1866 he began to agitate the subject among the profession and others interested in such matters, but it was without avail until two years later, in 1868, when, with the aid of a few of his professional friends, he prepared and submitted to the Common Council, through a special committee of that body, an ordinance, which was passed, creating the Jersey City Charity Hospital, the first hospital in the State of New Jersey established as a public charity. He was appointed one of the attending surgeons,

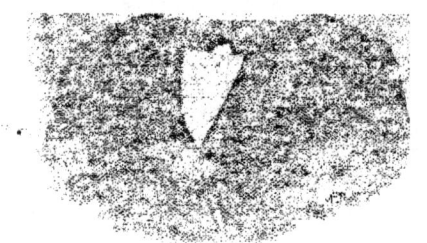

school, went to New York city, where he effected an engagement as a clerk in a wholesale dry-goods house, remaining there six years. Returning to New Jersey he engaged in business on his own account, starting a store for the sale of manufacturers' hardware, and in which he has continued to the present time. He has always taken an active part in politics, and was a Democrat until 1855, since which time he has affiliated with the Republican party. He was elected in 1861 to the Legislature on that ticket, in which body he served one term. Subsequently he was chosen as a member of City Councils, which position he held for four years, and for three years was President of that body. From 1858 until it ceased to exist in 1865, he was a Director of the Farmers' and Mechanics' Bank of Rahway; he is at present a Director in the Rahway Savings Bank, and also of the Rahway Fire Insurance Company. He has been foremost among his fellow-townsmen in promoting the welfare and prosperity of his adopted city, and is regarded by all as a valuable and public-spirited citizen. He was married in 1866 to Anna Sheddan, daughter of Rev. S. S. Sheddan, D. D.; she died in 1872.

HUNT, JOHN W., M. D., Physician and Surgeon, was born, October 10th, 1834, in Groveland, Livingston county, New York, and is the son of Elijah and Eunice (Huffman) Hunt; the former, a farmer by occupation, was born in Pennsylvania, but when about two years of age, in 1796, his father, John Hunt, removed with his family from Pennsylvania to Livingston county, New York, and was one of the pioneers of that county, all that part of the State being then a wilderness. Dr. Hunt is of English descent, his great-grandfather's father having emigrated from England to one of the New England colonies. His great-grandfather, William Hunt, was born in Rhode Island, married and removed to New Jersey. His grandfather, John Hunt, was born in New Jersey. Dr. Hunt while a youth attended the district school in his native town, where he received a good common-school education. He subsequently became a pupil in the Genesee Wesleyan Seminary, at Lima, New York, where he remained three years. Early in life he expressed a desire to study medicine, which was not encouraged by his parents. His early choice of a profession, however, was never changed, and in the spring of 1856 he entered the office of Dr. Alexander C. Campbell, at Lima, New York, as a medical student. In the spring of 1857 he proceeded to New York city, matriculated at the University Medical College, and attended the summer course of lectures, at the same time receiving instruction in the private classes of Drs. T. Gaillard Thomas and William R. Donaghe. He continued at the university, attending the winter course of lectures of 1857-58, and in the spring of 1858 returned to Livingston county, and assisted Dr. Campbell in his practice

during the summer. His second full course of lectures he attended at the university the following winter, and graduated in the spring of 1859. Soon after receiving his diploma he presented himself with other candidates for examination by the examining board for *Internes* to Bellevue Hospital. He was one of the successful candidates and was appointed one of the junior assistants on the house staff. As his services were not required at the hospital during his six months' term of Junior service (unless a vacancy should occur) he obtained leave of absence and sailed for England, where considerable time was occupied in visiting the English hospitals, chiefly in London. He returned to New York in October, and entered upon his duties on the House Staff of Bellevue Hospital, where he remained until his term of service expired in the fall of 1860. Having determined to make Jersey City, New Jersey, his future home, he at once opened an office there and commenced practice. At the breaking out of the rebellion he was called by his native State to take professional charge of the 10th Regiment, New York State Volunteers, which was one of the first to organize. He at once responded to the call, and, in May, 1861, was commissioned Surgeon of that regiment, and followed its fortunes until the spring of 1862, when he resigned his State commission for the purpose of accepting a United States commission as "Brigade Surgeon," afterwards designated "Surgeon of United States Volunteers." Immediately thereafter he was ordered to take charge of the "Mill Creek General Hospital," near Fortress Monroe, Virginia, then just opened. Here he was actively engaged until the last of August, when he was attacked with fever, which confined him to his bed three months; he was sent north on leave of absence, and in January, 1863, being still feeble and unfit for duty in the field, he retired from the service. Early in March following he visited New Orleans as surgeon of a government transport, and returned much improved in strength. In May he resumed practice in Jersey City, and at once took a prominent position among the profession. In 1864 he was appointed Examining Surgeon of recruits drafted into the service. He is an active member of the District Medical Society for the County of Hudson; and as a delegate to the New Jersey State Medical Society for a number of years, he takes a deep interest in the proceedings of that body, and has generally been a contributor to its transactions. He has also at sundry times contributed to the literature of the profession. Dr. Hunt had not practised long in Jersey City before he recognized the necessity of a city hospital, and in 1866 he began to agitate the subject among the profession and others interested in such matters, but it was without avail until two years later, in 1868, when, with the aid of a few of his professional friends, he prepared and submitted to the Common Council, through a special committee of that body, an ordinance, which was passed, creating the Jersey City Charity Hospital, the first hospital in the State of New Jersey established as a *public charity*. He was appointed one of the attending surgeons, and holds that position at the present time. He is also one of the visiting surgeons to the Hudson County Church Hospital. He has always manifested great interest in the institutions with which he is professionally connected, and has devoted to them much time and attention. In fact, in all that pertains to the advancement of his profession or the relief of suffering, he is a zealous worker. He was married in 1866 to N. Adeline Reynolds, daughter of H. S. Reynolds, Esq., of Springfield, Massachusetts.

OGT, LOUIS C., Journalist, late of Morristown, was born in Hamburg, Germany, May 3d, 1808, and was brought to the United States by his parents in his third year. The family originally settled in Philadelphia, but soon removed to New York, where the father found employment on the *Commercial Advertiser*, then owned and edited by Francis Hall and Colonel Stone. Several years later, Louis, then a mere lad, was taken into the same office, and, excepting a short time spent on the New York *Evening Post* as a journeyman, he remained therein until 1838, when he settled in Morristown. By this time his three younger brothers, Henry, George and Charles, had all been received into the *Advertiser* office for the purpose of learning the printing business. Just before Louis Vogt arrived in Morristown the *Jerseyman* had been the organ of the Democratic party in the county. But differences had arisen between the leaders and its editor, which resulted in the paper taking an independent position. This led to the establishment of another paper, which should fill its place, and to the new journal was given the name of *The Democratic Banner*. Mr. Vogt was engaged upon the *Banner*, and continued to edit it until the owners required of him the performance of duties obnoxious to his sense of right and self-respect, when he retired. Encouraged by many friends, who did not approve the course pursued by the *Banner* proprietors in manipulating party affairs, he soon began the publication of the *True Democratic Banner*, the insertion of the word "True" in the heading being designed to distinguish it as the true or only legitimate *Banner* of the two publications. The original *Banner* did not survive the withdrawal of Mr. Vogt, who continued with manly earnestness and vigor to fight the battle of reform within the party, until his efforts were crowned in the rescue of the county from the domination of the opposition. This result was not easily accomplished. He had to contend against powerful and unscrupulous foes within the ranks of the organization, who, when they found temptation after temptation unavailing, resorted to threats and sought to establish a Democratic journal in opposition. But through all he preserved his fidelity to principle and turned a deaf ear to all personal considerations, the while he labored as publisher and printer with indomitable energy and an ability receiving daily wider recog-

nition. As a consequence he achieved his ambition, and established in Morris county a Democratic newspaper upon a firm foundation. As a business man he proved himself the possessor of thoroughly progressive ideas. He was the first to introduce into the county modern improvements in the art of printing, to replace the old-fashioned, slow-going hand presses by better and yet improved appliances, until at last the paper, published in a handsome building erected by himself and furnished with all the latest improvements, was printed by steam-power. Devoted to the printing art, he took great pleasure and pride in gathering recruits into its service from among his relatives and friends, and his advice and assistance were ever ready to render their essays successful. He lived to see his three sons grow up and become established in the business, as well as eighteen near relatives, and nearly all prosperous. He was married, December 28th, 1834, and his wife proved a help-meet in the truest and highest sense. When with years came great affliction, she nursed, sustained, cheered and helped him with a devotion and a skill at once rare and beautiful. Originally a man of great physical power, he experienced the first symptoms of paralysis in his lower limbs about 1850, in a stiffening of the knees, which prevented him from running. These became gradually more aggravated, necessitating the use of a cane, then crutches, and then (in 1862) a wheeled chair, in which he was conveyed to and from the office. But the heat of the summer of 1870 prostrated him, and his visits to the office became fewer, until they ceased altogether in the spring of 1875. He died, December 4th, in the same year. Piety distinguished him through life. At fifteen he became a member of the German Reformed Church, Forsyth street, New York, and he remained in that communion until his departure for Morristown. On arrival there he connected himself with the Methodist Episcopal Church. During long years of suffering he drew from religion a comfort and support which rendered him always resigned and cheerful. His death was a public loss.

LMER, WILLIAM, A. M., M. D., Physician, of Bridgeton, New Jersey, was born in that town, October 5th, 1814. He comes of a long line of physicians, his father and grandfather having both been successful and prominent followers of the profession of medicine. His father, William Elmer, M. D., who died in 1836, was also a native of Bridgeton, where he practised for a period of ten years. The mother of the subject of this sketch was also to the manor born, being Nancy Boyd Potter, daughter of Colonel Potter, of Bridgeton. He was prepared for college at the excellent school of Rev. Isaac Brown, at Lawrenceville, New Jersey, and entered the sophomore class at Princeton College in 1830. From this institution he was graduated in 1832, and honored with the English salutatory oration.

Having early imbibed a taste for the medical profession, and determined to adopt it, he then became a student under Dr. Joseph Parrish, of Philadelphia, and matriculating at the University of Pennsylvania, in 1833, he received his degree therefrom in the spring of 1836. The following eighteen months he spent at Blockley Almshouse, than which few better schools for study present themselves to young practitioners. Of this term he served for one year as Resident Physician, and at the end of that time he was elected as Resident Physician of the Children's Hospital. In July, 1837, he returned to his native place and began a practice there which has been continued down to the present time, and which has been uniformly successful. To-day Dr. Elmer is the leader of the profession in West Jersey, and is thoroughly known throughout that section of the State, honored by his brethren and the community at large. He has always been devoted to medicine, and his devotion and skill have won for him the confidence and esteem of many of the leading physicians outside of the State. He is a Fellow of the New Jersey State Medical Society, and served as its President in 1860; several times he has been chosen President of the Cumberland Country District Medical Society. He was married, December 19th, 1839, to Eliza R. Whiteley, of Wilmington, Delaware, and has four children living, three sons and a daughter; two of his sons are doctors—William Elmer, Jr., of whom a sketch follows, is practising at Trenton; H. W. Elmer, who was graduated from Princeton in 1866, and from the University of Pennsylvania in 1869, is associated with his father in practice.

———

ELMER, WILLIAM, M. D., of Trenton, New Jersey, was born at Bridgeton, New Jersey, December 14th, 1840. His parents were William and Eliza R. (Whiteley) Elmer. His father is now, and has been for many years, a distinguished and leading medical practitioner in the city of Bridgeton. After the usual preparatory course he entered Princeton College, in 1858, and was graduated therefrom in 1861, receiving in due course the degrees of A. B. and A. M. Coming from a long line of physicians, the family for three generations previous having followed that time-honored profession, William Elmer, Jr., matriculated in medicine at the University of Pennsylvania, in the fall of 1861, at the same time becoming a student in the office of Drs. Levick, Hunt and Penrose, practitioners in Philadelphia, who also conducted a private medical class. Pursuing the regular courses at the University of Pennsylvania, he received his degree of M. D. from that institution in the spring of 1863. The eighteen months following was devoted to extending his medical knowledge by a practical course at the Episcopal and Pennsylvania Hospitals. At the expiration of this time he returned to Bridgeton, and was associated in active professional duty with his father

until July, 1869, when he removed to Trenton, in which city he has since resided. Devoted to his profession, he soon took rank among the leaders of the medical fraternity, and enjoys the esteem and confidence of them all, together with that of the community wherein he resides. He is a member of the Mercer County District Medical Society, and at present Vice-President of that body. He is the present Corresponding Secretary of the New Jersey State Medical Society. He was married, in 1869, to Alice Grey, of Columbia, Pennsylvania.

———

CANNON, GARRIT S., Lawyer, of Bordentown, was born in Somerset county, New Jersey, being the son of Rev. James Spencer and Catharine (Brevoort) Cannon, both natives of the same State. His father, whose eminent qualifications and long and distinguished services as a minister received recognition in the degree of Doctor of Divinity, bestowed on him by Union College, was for years Professor of Theology in the Dutch Reformed Theological Seminary at New Brunswick. He held for the same period the chair of Metaphysics in Rutgers College. In both of these departments of science and religion he was an acknowledged authority, and certainly in his time had no superior as a teacher. He died in 1852, having filled the professorship of theology in the seminary for thirty years. His wife was born in Bergen county, New Jersey, descending from a family that had long been settled in the State. The early education of Garrit S. Cannon was conducted at the Rutgers College Grammar School, in New Brunswick. It was here that he made his preparations for an academic career. In 1829 he entered Rutgers College, from which, after passing through all the studies of its comprehensive four years' course, he graduated in 1833. Immediately after leaving college he commenced the study of law in the office of B. R. Brown, of Mount Holly, and in November, 1836, was licensed as an attorney, and three years after as counsellor. Being thus qualified for a professional career, he removed to Bordentown and engaged in practice, which has uninterruptedly engaged his attention ever since. He was appointed to the Prosecuting Attorneyship of the county by Governor Daniel Haines, in 1850, and so acceptably discharged all the varied and weighty responsibilities of this office as to merit a reappointment, in 1855, at the hands of Governor R. M. Price, and a second reappointment at the hands of Governor Joel Parker, in 1865. During this period he more than satisfied all claims of the people against a public functionary, and secured a reputation second to that of no other member of his profession in the State, as an earnest and forcible lawyer and a fearless Prosecuting Attorney. President Pierce honored him, in 1853, with the appointment of United States District Attorney for the State, and President Buchanan reaffirmed the

17

wisdom of his predecessor's choice by reappointing Mr. Cannon to the same office in 1857. As a pleader he is not surpassed by any other in his section of the State. His presentation of the fact and the law of a case; his keen analysis of evidence; his citations of authorities in support of his arguments, are rapid, clear, decisive. Few men are more fluent ·in speech, more thorough in preparation, more brilliant in legal strategy.· Early in life he manifested a deep interest in politics, and identified himself with the old Jeffersonian Democracy. In 1845 he was elected to the lower house of the State Legislature, and served his constituency with ability and zeal. .Though still true to the party of his first and only choice, he no longer is an active leader, devoting all his time to his professional duties. He has given his support to all measures for local governmental improvement, and to enterprises calculated to increase the comfort of his fellow-citizens and to beautify the town in which he resides. He is President of the Gas Company, of Bordentown, and President of the Water Works Company, and has been a director, as well as the attorney, of the Bordentown Banking Company ever since its organization. He is an energetic, public-spirited citizen, and enjoys the esteem of all his fellow-townsmen. In November, 1839, he was married to Hannah Kinsey, daughter of Charles Kinsey, Esq., of Burlington, New Jersey.

INFIELD, HON. CHARLES HARDEN-BERGH, Lawyer and ex-Senator, of Jersey City, was born, November 8th, 1829, in the town of Deerpark, near Port Jervis, New York. He is the fifth son of Henry and Deborah (Westbrook) Winfield. His father was a Pennsylvanian by birth, and by· occupation a farmer. His mother was from Sussex county, New Jersey. He obtained his preliminary education at the district school of Westfall township, Pike county, Pennsylvania, across the Delaware from Port Jervis, and pursued his academical studies at Deckertown, New Jersey, under the care of the late William Rankin. He entered the sophomore class in Rutgers College, New Brunswick, in the fall of 1849, and graduated in 1852, standing fourth in his class. In 1855 he received from his *Alma Mater* the degree of Master of Arts. Having selected the law as his future profession, he entered the law office of the late Chancellor Zabriskie, of Jersey City, in October, 1852. After three years of study under his able preceptor he was admitted to the bar, November 8th 1855. He immediately began the practice of the law in Jersey City, where he has since been constantly engaged in the duties of his profession. At the present time (October, 1876) there remain in active practice but three lawyers who were in their profession in Hudson county when he came to the bar. He ranks high in the criminal branch of his profession, and is expert in the man-

agement of a cause and the examination of witnesses. In 1865 he was counsel in the case of Bonker & Wood *vs.* Randel, Helm & Co. The plaintiffs sued to recover the contract price of an engine, placed in a tug-boat. The defendants insisted that the engine was not constructed according to the contract, and desired to recover their damages. As the law then stood this could not be done; the only remedy was to bring a cross-action. Hence the defence was ruled out; but Mr. Winfield, being convinced of the justice of his claim, carried the case to the Supreme Court, and there succeeded in establishing the principle of recoupment. In 1865 he was elected by the Democratic party of Hudson county to the State Senate for a term of three years, taking his seat in January, 1866. While a member of that body he was its acknowledged leader in debate, and took an active part in all questions pertaining to the welfare of his constituents and the State at large. His opposition to the bill to establish a Board of Police Commissioners for Jersey City was persistent, manly and eloquent, and marked the course which his party has since pursued in its opposition to local commissions for the rule of municipal bodies. Notwithstanding a trained party vote against him, he succeeded in engrafting upon the bill several amendments of importance to Jersey City. Through blunder or fraud these amendments were not incorporated in the bill signed by the Governor and filed with the Secretary of State. This state of facts presented a serious question, and it afterwards came before the Supreme Court on application for mandamus to compel the old police authorities to surrender the police property in their possession to the new Board of Commissioners. Senator Winfield and the present Associate-Justice, Bradley, of the United States Supreme Court, were retained to resist the application. The court granted the writ, and established or confirmed the doctrine, that, without special legislation for that purpose, there was no authority to inquire into the question whether the bill signed by the proper officers, and filed in the office of the Secretary of State, ever passed the Legislature. It was a record behind which they could not go, though admitted to be a fraud and a cheat. Among other important bills which have added greatly to the population and taxable wealth of Hudson county, he sustained ·what was known as the "Harsimus Cove bill." This was to authorize the United Railroad Companies to construct·a spur from their main line, at Bergen Hill, to the Hudson river, at Harsimus, and improve the lands under water. The bill passed, the road elevated above the streets was constructed, the State received $500,000 for the lands under water, and the abattoir and cattle-yards—the largest on the Atlantic seaboard—were built. Previous to his election to the Senate, the Legislature had rejected the Thirteenth Amendment to the Constitution of the United States. During his first year, the Republicans being then in the majority, a resolution to approve the said amendment was brought forward. This was opposed by the Democrats on the ground

that the previous action of the Legislature could not be re-considered. Senator Winfield here proved himself above the mere partisan, and took a decided stand against the views of his own party. He voted for its adoption. During this same session (1866) he took a bold stand against the attempt of the House of Assembly to impeach Chancellor Green and Judge Van Dyke, on the petition of Mr. Charles F. Durant. In 1867 the Legislature approved the Fourteenth Amendment to the Constitution of the United States. This was opposed by Senator Winfield and his party. In the session of 1868, this amendment not yet having received the approval of the requisite number of States, the Democrats being then in the majority, a resolution was introduced to withdraw the approval of New Jersey. This resolution was supported by Senator Winfield in a speech which was pronounced a masterpiece of logic, law and eloquence. As a public speaker he ranks high in the popular favor. His latest effort of decided merit was his Centennial Oration, delivered in Jersey City, July 4th, 1876. In 1872 he published a "History of the Land Titles in Hudson County, from 1609 to 1871," a royal octavo volume of 443 pages, with maps. This work is a thorough and exhaustive compilation, and an acknowledged authority upon the subject. In 1874 he published a "History of Hudson County, New Jersey, from its Earliest Settlement to the Present Time," an octavo volume of 568 pages. Both of these works not only prove a versatility of talent in the author, but exhibit a depth of research and comprehensive grouping of facts which, while they impart valuable information, furnish attractive reading, the true forte of the popular historian. He was married, February 14th, 1856, to Harriet Mc-Dougall Allen, of Schenectady, New York.

AINBRIDGE, COMMODORE WILLIAM, of the United States Navy, was born, May 7th, 1774, at Princeton, New Jersey, and was the son of Dr. Absalom Bainbridge, a highly respected physician, who removed to New York while William was but a child, leaving him under the care of his maternal grandfather, John Taylor, of Monmouth county, where he received his education. He entered the sea-service as an apprentice on board of a merchant vessel from Philadelphia. When eighteen years old, while mate of the ship "Hope," on her voyage to Holland, the crew, taking advantage of a violent gale of wind, rose against the officers, seized the captain, and had nearly succeeded in bearing him overboard. Young Bainbridge, hearing the noise, ran on deck with an old pistol without a lock, and being assisted by an apprentice boy, who was of Irish birth, seized the captain, seized the ringleaders and quelled the mutiny. In July, 1798, he unexpectedly received the command of the United States schooner "Re-

commencement of hostilities with the French (Directory) government. In September of that year, while cruising off Guadaloupe, the "Retaliation" was captured by a French squadron and carried into the port of Basseterre, where she was detained, and Bainbridge with his officers and men were held as prisoners of war until the month of December following, when she was given up. Upon his liberation he returned to the United States with his command, and on his arrival was promoted, first to the rank of Master, and then as Commander; and was thereupon appointed to the command of the brig-of-war "Norfolk," in which vessel he cruised very actively for the protection of our commerce in the West Indies during a large portion of our war with France. In the year 1800 he was commissioned a Post-Captain in the United States navy, and was appointed to the command of the frigate "George Washington," in which he was sent to Algiers with presents, which the government of the United States had agreed to make to that power, which Algiers. The Dey demanded that he should continue his voyage and venture to Constantinople with his presents to the Grand Seignior. To this demand Captain Bainbridge demurred, and protested against this objection, but all remonstrances were in vain; he was assenting to the batteries of Algiers, and a declaration of war on the part of the United States was threatened by the Dey; if he did not comply with this outrageous demand, a valuable and prosperous trade in the Mediterranean was at the mercy of the Algerine cruisers if this threat was executed. After assenting to the demand of the Dey, the "George Washington" sailed with the motley embassy, and arrived in the harbor of Constantinople, November 12th, 1800. When the Turkish officers were informed that it was a United States ship, they replied that they knew of no such nation. Captain Bainbridge, by explaining that America was the new world, was enabled to give them some idea of the United States. He remained in Constantinople for two months, during which time he was treated with great distinction by the Ottoman government, upon whom he made a most favorable impression. Early in January, 1801, he sailed for Algiers, and after fulfilling his mission there returned to the United States. The course he had adopted was fully sustained by the administration, and he was complimented by the President for his forbearing demeanor towards a semi-civilized power. He was next appointed to the frigate "Essex," which was destined to the Mediterranean station; and after the declaration of war by Algiers was transferred to the frigate "Philadelphia." He sailed for the Mediterranean in July, 1803, somewhat in advance of the rest of the squadron. On his arrival at Gibraltar he was informed that two Tripolitan cruisers were off Cape de Gatte, and he sailed at once in quest of them. On the night of August 26th, while under that cape, he fell in with the Moorish frigate "Meshboa," of twenty-two guns and 120 men, having an American brig in company. On examining

COMMODORE

that the previous action of the Legislature could not be re-considered. Senator Winfield here proved himself above the mere partisan, and took a decided stand against the views of his own party. He voted for its adoption. During this same session (1866) he took a bold stand against the attempt of the House of Assembly to impeach Chancellor Green and Judge Van Dyke, on the petition of Mr. Charles F. Durant. In 1867 the Legislature approved the Four-teenth Amendment to the Constitution of the United States. This was opposed by Senator Winfield and his party. In the session of 1868, this amendment not yet having received the approval of the requisite number of States, the Demo-crats being then in the majority, a resolution was introduced to withdraw the approval of New Jersey. This resolution was supported by Senator Winfield in a speech which was pronounced a masterpiece of logic, law and eloquence. As a public speaker he ranks high in the popular favor. His latest effort of decided merit was his Centennial Oration, delivered in Jersey City, July 4th, 1876. In 1872 he pub-lished a "History of the Land Titles in Hudson County, from 1609 to 1871," a royal octavo volume of 443 pages, with maps. This work is a thorough and exhaustive com-pilation, and an acknowledged authority upon the subject. In 1874 he published a "History of Hudson County, New Jersey, from its Earliest Settlement to the Present Time," an octavo volume of 568 pages. Both of these works not only prove a versatility of talent in the author, but exhibit a depth of research and comprehensive grouping of facts which, while they impart valuable information, furnish attractive reading, the true forte of the popular historian. He was married, February 14th, 1856, to Harriet Mc-Dougall Allen, of Schenectady, New York.

AINBRIDGE, COMMODORE WILLIAM, of the United States Navy, was born, May 7th, 1774, at Princeton, New Jersey, and was the son of Dr. Absalom Bainbridge, a highly respected physician, who removed to New York while William was but a child, leaving him under the care of his maternal grandfather, John Taylor, of Mon-mouth county, where he received his education. He entered the sea-service as an apprentice on board of a mer-chant vessel from Philadelphia. When eighteen years old, while mate of the ship "Hope," on her voyage to Holland, the crew, taking advantage of a violent gale of wind, rose against the officers, seized the captain, and had nearly suc-ceeded in throwing him overboard. Young Bainbridge, hearing the alarm, ran on deck with an old pistol, without a lock, and being assisted by an apprentice boy, who was of Irish birth, rescued the captain, seized the ringleaders and quelled the mutiny. In July, 1798, he unexpectedly received the command of the United States schooner "Re-taliation," of fourteen guns, that being the period of the

commencement of hostilities with the French (Directory) government. In September of that year, while cruising off Guadaloupe, the "Retaliation" was captured by a French squadron and carried into the port of Bassetene, where she was detained, and Bainbridge with his officers and men were held as prisoners of war until the month of December following, when she was given up. Upon his liberation he returned to the United States with his command, and on his arrival was promoted, first to the rank of Master, and then as Commander; and was thereupon appointed to the command of the brig-of-war "Norfolk," in which vessel he cruised very actively for the protection of our commerce in the West Indies during a large portion of our war with France. In the year 1800 he was commissioned a Post-Captain in the United States navy, and was appointed to the command of the frigate "George Washington," in which he was sent to Algiers with presents, which the gov-ernment of the United States had agreed to make to that power. While at Algiers the Dey demanded that he should convey his ambassador and retinue to Constantinople with his presents to the Grand Seignior. To this demand Cap-tain Bainbridge demurred, and protested against this ob-noxious request. But all remonstrances were in vain; he was under the batteries of Algiers, and a declaration of war against the United States was threatened by the Dey; if he did not comply with this outrageous demand, a valuable and unprotected trade in the Mediterranean was at the mercy of the Algerine cruisers if this threat was executed. After assenting to the demand of the Dey, the "George Washington" sailed with the motley embassy, and arrived in the harbor of Constantinople, November 12th, 1800. When the Turkish officers were informed that it was a United States ship, they replied that they knew of no such nation. Captain Bainbridge, by explaining that America was the new world, was enabled to give them some idea of the United States. He remained in Constantinople two months, during which time he was treated with great dis-tinction by the Ottoman government, upon whom he made a most favorable impression. Early in January, 1801, he sailed for Algiers, and after fulfilling his mission there re-turned to the United States. The course he had adopted was fully sustained by the administration, and he was com-plimented by the President for his forbearing demeanor towards a semi-civilized power. He was next appointed to the frigate "Essex," which was destined to the Mediter-ranean station; and after the declaration of war by Algiers was transferred to the frigate "Philadelphia." He sailed for the Mediterranean in July, 1803, somewhat in advance of the rest of the squadron. On his arrival at Gibraltar he was informed that two Tripolitan cruisers were off Cape de Gatte, and he sailed at once in quest of them. On the night of August 26th, while under that cape, he fell in with the Moorish frigate "Meshboa," of twenty-two guns and 120 men, having an American brig in company. On examining the Moorish vessel he found that she had captured the brig

"Celia," of Boston, and had her master and crew on board as prisoners. He immediately captured the frigate, and re-captured the brig and returned her to her proper master. The Moorish captain at first declined to show authority for his acts; but when Bainbridge threatened to treat him as a pirate, he produced an order from the Governor of Tangier for the capture of American vessels. Bainbridge carried his prize to Gibraltar, and went in search of another Moorish vessel, but failed to find her. In the meantime Commodore Preble arrived, and the latter, after approving all that his subordinate had accomplished, found no diffi-culty in placing American relations with Morocco on a pacific footing. While cruising in the "Philadelphia" frigate before the harbor of Tripoli, having sighted an enemy's frigate, Bainbridge immediately ran for her, but, unfortunately, going into shoal water, the "Philadelphia" grounded, about three miles from the town. He was im-mediately surrounded by gunboats, and seeing no hope of escape, and after consultation with his officers, surrendered the vessel. This was on the 13th of October, 1803, and the entire ship's company, numbering in all some 315 men, were captured and taken before the Bashaw, who conversed with Bainbridge through an interpreter. After intimating to him that the fortunes of war had brought him into this unpleasant situation, the whole party were ordered to be imprisoned, and were placed in charge of Sidi Mohammed D'Ghies. During their incarceration, which lasted for nineteen months, the Danish Consul, N. C. Nissen, paid them every attention, for which he subsequently received the thanks of Congress and a handsome testimonial from Captain Bainbridge and his officers. Shortly before their release Colonel Lear negotiated a treaty with Tripoli, when they were delivered up and returned to the United States. After reaching home a court of inquiry was called to in-quire into the loss of his ship, and he was honorably ac-quitted. Shortly after the declaration, by Congress, of war with Great Britain, Captain Bainbridge took command of the frigate "Constitution." On December 29th, 1812, while running down the coast of Brazil, he fell in with the British frigate "Java." After an action of two hours the "Java's" fire was completely silenced, and her colors being down, Bainbridge supposed that she had struck. He there-fore shot ahead to repair his rigging, but while hove-to for that purpose discovered that her colors were still flying, al-though her mainmast had gone by the board. He accord-ingly bore down again upon her, and having come close athwart her bows was on the point of raking her with a broadside, when she hauled down her colors, being com-pletely an unmanageable wreck, entirely dismantled, with-out a spar of any sort standing. On boarding her it was found that her commander, Captain Lambert, was mortally wounded (he died the next day), and that the "Java" was so much injured that it would be impossible to take her to the United States. Captain Bainbridge, himself seriously wounded, was assisted by two of his officers to the cot on

which Captain Lambert lay on his own quarter-deck, and a touching scene was witnessed when Bainbridge returned to him the sword he had surrendered. After the prisoners and baggage were removed the "Java" was blown up. She carried forty-nine guns of heavier calibre than the "Constitution," which carried fifty-four, and had a crew of 400 men, having, in addition to her own ship's company, upwards of 100 supernumerary officers and seamen for different ships on the East India station, among whom were a master and a commander in the navy, and also Lieutenant-General Hislop and his two aids, of the British army. General Hislop was a passenger, and had been appointed by the British government as the governor of the Bombay district, and was on his way thither when cap-tured. Between him and Captain Bainbridge a warm friendship was contracted, which continued through life without any interruption. The "Constitution" returned to the United States for repairs, her timbers being much de-cayed. Congress voted to Captain Bainbridge a gold medal, and medals of silver to each of the officers, and dis-tributed the sum of $50,000 to the crew as prize money. It should be stated that the "Java" lost sixty killed and over 100 men wounded; while the "Constitution" had but nine killed and twenty-five wounded. Captain Bainbridge, having been detached from the "Constitution," was ordered to the command of the navy-yard at Boston, where he re-mained until peace was declared. Meanwhile he superin-tended the construction of the "Independence," of seventy-four guns, and after she was launched and equipped he was appointed to the command of a squadron of twenty sail, and had the honor of raising his broad pennant to the mast-head of the first line-of-battle-ship—the "Independence"—that ever adorned the United States navy. This force was intended to act against the Algerines, but peace was con-cluded before it reached the Mediterranean. Captain Bain-bridge, however, settled disputes with the Barbary powers satisfactorily, and then returned home. On his arrival he was named to the command of the vessels afloat at Boston, where he remained until 1819, when he was assigned to the "Columbus," ship-of-the-line, of eighty guns, once more to the Mediterranean station, from which he returned in 1821, this being his last cruise. From that time until his death he was variously employed on important shore duty, com-manding at different times the navy-yards at Boston and Philadelphia, and holding the position of President of the Board of Naval Commissioners. As an officer he had few superiors. Although ardent in temperament, he was cool in danger, and always possessed the confidence of those under his command. His system of discipline, though rigid, was always consistent and just; and he was remark-able for paying the greatest attention to the training of his young officers. The whole of his long and arduous career was most useful to his country and honorable to himself. He died in Philadelphia, July 28th, 1833, and was buried with all the honors of war.

ANEWAY, COLONEL HUGH H., Soldier, late of the 1st Regiment New Jersey Cavalry, was born, 1842, at Jersey City. When but nineteen years old he joined the 1st Regiment of Cavalry, the 16th of the New Jersey line in the war of the rebellion, as Lieutenant of Company L. This regiment was raised by Colonel Halsted, who was superseded six months after it was formed by Colonel Sir Percy Wyndham, a gallant soldier of the British and Italian armies. It formed one of the 1st Brigade of Cavalry, and fought all through the war in the Army of the Potomac. During the winter of 1861–62 the regiment was employed in picket duty and scouting along the left of the line. In this duty Lieutenant Janeway, having at one time ridden in advance of his company, accompanied by a single orderly, was wounded by the enemy and left for dead. With great fortitude he rose and walked back to his command, and, though wounded in seven or eight places, was fit for duty again within a month. He was promoted to the rank of Captain, February 9th, 1862. In April of the same year the regiment joined General McDowell's corps, and was actively engaged thereafter, being attached to the brigade of General George D. Bayard, and doing picket duty until May 25th, when, as it was advancing to the battle of Hanover Courthouse, it was ordered to the valley of Virginia to oppose Stonewall Jackson, and three days later encountered the enemy under General Ashby, near Strasburg, and drove them off. The regiment, reaching Harrisonburg, sustained a defeat, and their colonel was captured by the enemy. Captain Janeway afterwards participated in the battle of Cedar Mountain, in August, 1862, and in the famous raid on Warrenton in October of that year, when sixteen hundred of the enemy were captured besides a large amount of stores. The winter of 1862–63 was passed near Brooks' Station, on the Acquia Railroad, and on the 27th of January, 1863, Captain Janeway was promoted to the rank of Major. On the 13th of the following April the spring campaign opened, when Major Janeway was engaged for some time in command of scouting parties, and afterwards participated in the struggle at Brandy Station, wherein Colonel Wyndham —who had rejoined his command—was wounded, the lieutenant-colonel and senior major killed; so that upon Major Janeway devolved the command of the regiment. In June, 1863, General Lee advanced into Pennsylvania, and the cavalry corps started for Gettysburg on the 27th of that month. The 1st New Jersey Cavalry reached that celebrated battle-field, July 2d, on the second day of the contest, and repulsed an attack made upon it. On the 3d, as the battle opened, the 1st New Jersey was advanced from the extreme rear to the very front, getting just in time to see the rebel cavalry pouring upon our flank. Leaping from their horses, forming line as they touched the ground, and starting at once into a run in the very face of the enemy, they dashed at the nearest cover, where they prepared to check the progress of the entire force arrayed against them. They

did not only that, but drove back the assailing columns. Sent forward as a forlorn hope, to give time for the rest of the division to come up with unblown horses, this little band of one hundred and fifty men, by their undaunted bearing and steady fire, staggered the troops that by a single charge could have ridden over them. Refusing to dismount in spite of the storm of bullets constantly whistling over our men, Major Janeway rode from end to end of his skirmishers, encouraging, warning and directing its every portion, showing here, as on many another field, a coolness and bravery that made him a marked man among men. Advancing from point to point, heralding each charge by a cheer which shook the enemy worse than the bullets of their carbines, for more than a hundred yards the 1st Jersey pushed their little line, and at last, with ammunition exhausted, they still held their ground, facing the rebels with their revolvers. Then Janeway rode back to the reserve, and reported to Major Beaumont the condition of his men, requesting ammunition and reinforcement. A regiment was ordered to their support, but failed to reach them. Finally the 3d Pennsylvania appeared, when the 1st Jersey were at liberty to retire, but the latter would not, and actually borrowed ammunition from the Pennsylvanians, and kept their boldly won position, and cheering till they were hoarse, defied the efforts of the enemy. On the 4th day of July, after a brief repose on the battle-field, they were in the saddle again, chasing the retreating columns of the foe, continuing to have daily skirmishes until the 14th of July, when their horses' feet again trod the "sacred soil of Virginia." From that time forward, and for the three following months, Major Janeway was alternately engaged in scouting and on picket duty. On October 12th the battle of White Sulphur Springs occurred, in which the 1st Jersey participated. Major Janeway had detached some of his command as skirmishers, and was left with only the second squadron as a reserve, when he received a message from Colonel Taylor, commanding the brigade, ordering him to fall back slowly, but the Major replied that "to fall back would expose our weakness and ensure our destruction by the overwhelming force of the enemy," and asked permission to hold his ground until dark, which being granted, he once more addressed himself to the arduous task before him. It was indeed a difficult work, and the hour one of great anxiety. He received word that the enemy were strengthening every minute, that many of his men had exhausted their ammunition, and that the next attack would surely force him back. Fortunately a reinforcement came up, when Janeway led Robbins' squadron into and through the woods, met the rebel charge, while those of his men who had expended their ammunition were safely withdrawn. As the day waned the fighting grew fiercer, but the enemy could not dislodge the Jersey men. When night came they withdrew, when the rebels made an effort to occupy the wood; but the reserve which Janeway had persisted in retaining unbroken, in spite of every apparent crisis, now justified the wisdom of his action.

Galled for hours by a fire which it had been unable to return, it now opened upon the advancing enemy with such vindictive energy, as to force him back behind the cover, incapable of another movement to the front. For half an hour after the retreat the ground was left unoccupied by the enemy, and even then he advanced against the deserted position with skirmishers deployed and a long line of battle formed. ·In an hour from that time the whole of Ewell's corps was camped upon the field of battle, having been detained by the 1st New Jersey until it was too late to close upon the flanks of the Union army. Major Janeway having made his report of the operations of his command, it was thus indorsed : " This report having been referred to me, I take great pleasure in bringing to your notice the gallantry of both officers and men of this command. The conduct of Major Hugh H. Janeway upon three several occasions was commendable in the highest degree, and reflected great credit upon himself and the regiment. John W. Kester, Lieutenant-Colonel commanding." Rejoining the brigade, the regiment proceeded to Fayetteville, where it encamped for the night, and subsequently, while on the march to Auburn, it had another brush with the enemy. While forming a part of the rear-guard of the army still in retreat before the enemy, Major Janeway was directed to remain with his regiment, in order to hold a hill. Taking command in person of the line of skirmishers, he strengthened it by seven companies of his own regiment, turning over the rest to Captain Gray, and then proceeded to make the best disposition of the sixteen companies placed at his disposal. The rebels, however, made no assault, and the force was finally withdrawn. From that time forward until the close of November the regiment was employed only on picket duty. On the 27th of that month occurred a struggle in the Wilderness, in which Major Janeway participated, and he was favorably noticed in the official report. During the winter of 1863-64 the regiment was engaged in picket duty, scouting, and occasionally picking up a few guerillas. On the 4th of May, 1864, the regiment crossed the Rapidan, and was for several days engaged in a series of battles with the enemy in the Wilderness, in which the rebels were worsted ; and from the 9th of the same month until the 25th was with Sheridan in his raid towards Richmond. Major Janeway also did noble service in the manœuvres which resulted in turning Lee's right, and had a narrow escape from being wounded, the ball merely reddening the skin of his forehead. He was promoted, July 6th, 1864, to the rank of Lieutenant-Colonel, and afterwards took up the line of march for the north bank of the James river to aid in the operations around Petersburg. On August 12th, during a skirmish, he was wounded, having lost a finger while using a pocket-handkerchief. On September 1st, 1864, the period of original enlistment of the 1st New Jersey expired, but the regiment was still left as an organization in the field, its honors being duly inherited by hundreds of re-enlisted men and supported by its numerous recruits. At the close of that month, while on picket duty, the regiment charged Butler's South Carolina Brigade, and captured Captain Butler, brother of General Butler, of the rebel army. During the operations of the first three days of October, in which the enemy were repulsed, Janeway was present in an engagement where the heaviest firing of the war occurred, and subsequently assaulted the enemy, inflicting upon him a terrible loss. At this time he was only twenty-two years of age, and the Colonelcy being vacant, he was appointed to it October 11th, 1864, at the written request of every officer of the regiment. Early in December, 1864, it was found that the enemy were receiving large supplies by the way of the Weldon Railroad, and the 3d Division of the 2d Corps, together with Gregg's Cavalry, were detailed to operate upon and destroy the railroad as far as Hicksford. Colonel Janeway, in his report to Governor Parker, stated that his command, though not actually engaged in the struggle at Stony Creek Station, yet did the enemy much damage by destroying large quantities of railroad iron and burning the rebel workshops. On the 9th of December Colonel Janeway near Hicksford dismounted his command and formed a heavy skirmish line on the edge of the woods, near which a large body of the enemy were known to be, and then, with a cheer, dashed upon the rifle-pits in front, and speedily drove the enemy in disorder, occupying their position. In his report he remarks : " During the whole period of my service with the regiment I have never seen officers or men display greater gallantry or more soldierly endurance of hardships." The brave troopers held the pits for three hours, suffering terribly from cold and exposed to a heavy rain, which froze as it fell. Meanwhile the railroad in that neighborhood was being destroyed, and the object of the expedition being accomplished, the forces were withdrawn. For three months thereafter the regiment was in winter quarters near Petersburg, and on the 29th of March, 1865, broke camp and started on the final campaign. Colonel Janeway held the Flatfoot road on that night with his regiment. The next day nothing was done, but on the 31st; from information received from a captured infantry picket, it was found that the rebel Generals Pickett and Bushrod Johnson were in front. Colonel Janeway immediately strengthened and extended his picket lines, and ordered Major Robbins to make a reconnoissance on the left, to ascertain if the rebels were moving around in that direction. Shortly after an engagement commenced, in which the enemy were repulsed and their general (Ransom) fell ; but as they were largely reinforced, Colonel Janeway deemed it prudent to retire. On April 1st and 2d the regiment remained in camp at Dinwiddie Courthouse, and on the 3d pushed on to Wilson's plantation, having crossed the Southside Railroad, where they encamped, and on the 4th marched to Jetersville, which they reached on that afternoon and where they expected to find the enemy. Having bivouacked for the night, on the following day they pushed on after Lee, who was then on the retreat from Richmond, and

advance guard of the rebel army, which General Davies captured. The latter officer then detailed Colonel Janeway to hold a certain road until the captured enemy, property, etc., were properly disposed of, which he did, and this having been effected, the regiment marched to Painesville, where it halted for one half-hour. In the meantime the enemy appeared in immense numbers, and made several charges, which were repulsed; but finally they were obliged to give way before a superior force of the foe, when they fell back, and were finally relieved by the 2d Brigade. Retiring to a point near Amelia Springs, they rested until 2 P. M., when General Davies ordered Colonel Janeway to support two other regiments in a charge. These regiments were repulsed and driven back. Colonel Janeway immediately ordered a charge, and seized the colors of his regiment, and was in the act of carrying them forward, when a bullet entered his brain and he died instantly. This fatal event cast a gloom over the whole regiment. Major Robbins, in his report, says : " His superior we never knew; a brave, skilful officer, a courteous gentleman, a true, earnest patriot—qualities which endeared him to every officer and man of the regiment." Thus fell Colonel Janeway, at the early age of twenty-three years, April 5th, 1865.

ARKER, HON. JOEL, of Freehold, Lawyer, Soldier and ex Governor of New Jersey, was born, November 24th, 1816, in Monmouth county, in the immediate neighborhood of the old battle ground, and is a son of Charles Parker, one of the leading men of the State, who filled many responsible public positions of trust and emolument. Both his father and mother were also natives of Monmouth county. His maternal grandfather, at the very commencement of the revolutionary contest, entered the army as a private, and continued therein until the close of the war, either in the ranks, or as a company officer, distinguishing himself in many battles. His father served a term as sheriff of Monmouth county, and was subsequently elected to the Assembly for five successive years. During his fifth term he was chosen State treasurer by the Democrats on joint ballot of the two branches of the Legislature, and held this position for six

treasurer, and to this Joel not only a considerable period had it in ch retired from the treasury, he purcha county, with the intention of remov balance of his days; but being elect the Mechanics' and Manufacturers' urged to accept that important trust cordingly sent his son Joel to Mc farm, which he did for two or three advantage of his physical developme Princeton College, and after the graduated with honor in the class profession of the law he entered th W. Green, afterwards chief-justice State, where he pursued his studies was admitted to the bar in 1842, an tice of his profession at Freehold, in ing the same year, where he has reside. In 1849 he first took an musters, and attracted much attentio the interest of the then Democratic elected to the Assembly from Mon continued. In the House, being Democratic side, he became the dec especially on all questions having a the first bills which he offered was c by taxing persons as well as real were in the majority that they did n selves on record against the bill, nor it. It was the brand in their mid ened disputation. The former memb lowed the lead of Representative Pa ter was laid over, and the publicat author's speech was ordered in all t —a distinguished compliment to th natural result was to give him a S together with the merits of the mea credit, and perhaps contributed to tl Fort in 1850, besides the final pa which remains on the statute-book at of the session he opposed the usual s dentials," and being defeated, he dec consequently that element still remai declined being a candidate in 1851

reached Paines Cross Roads, where they came up with the advance guard of the rebel army, which General Davies captured. The latter officer then detailed Colonel Janeway to hold a certain road until the captured enemy, property, etc., were properly disposed of, which he did, and this having been effected, the regiment marched to Painesville, where it halted for one half-hour. In the meantime the enemy appeared in immense numbers, and made several charges, which were repulsed; but finally they were obliged to give way before a superior force of the foe, when they fell back, and were finally relieved by the 2d Brigade. Retiring to a point near Amelia Springs, they rested until 2 P. M., when General Davies ordered Colonel Janeway to support two other regiments in a charge. These regiments were repulsed and driven back. Colonel Janeway immediately ordered a charge, and seized the colors of his regiment, and was in the act of carrying them forward, when a bullet entered his brain and he died instantly. This fatal event cast a gloom over the whole regiment. Major Robbins, in his report, says : " His superior we never knew ; a brave, skilful officer, a courteous gentleman, a true, earnest patriot—qualities which endeared him to every officer and man of the regiment." Thus fell Colonel Janeway, at the early age of twenty-three years, April 5th, 1865.

---◦◦◦---

ARKER, HON. JOEL, of Freehold, Lawyer, Soldier and ex Governor of New Jersey, was born, November 24th, 1816, in Monmouth county, in the immediate neighborhood of the old battle ground, and is a son of Charles Parker, one of the leading men of the State, who filled many responsible public positions of trust and emolument. Both his father and mother were also natives of Monmouth county. His maternal grandfather, at the very commencement of the revolutionary contest, entered the army as a private, and continued therein until the close of the war, either in the ranks, or as a company officer, distinguishing himself in many battles. His father served a term as sheriff of Monmouth county, and was subsequently elected to the Assembly for five successive years. During his fifth term he was chosen State treasurer by the Democrats on joint ballot of the two branches of the Legislature, and held this position for sixteen successive years, under different administrations of various parties, being thus retained solely on account of his great financial ability and the faithful discharge of his duties. When he was first elected treasurer, in 1821, he removed to Trenton, where his son Joel was educated, not only in the formal routine of the best schools of that city, but in the more essential branch, practical experience in his father's office. He there received his first lessons of political economy and State wisdom, and from a master than whom the State has never known a better. At that time

the State library was under the care and jurisdiction of the treasurer, and to this Joel not only had access, but also for a considerable period had it in charge. After his father retired from the treasury, he purchased a farm in his native county, with the intention of removing thither to spend the balance of his days; but being elected to the presidency of the Mechanics' and Manufacturers' Bank, of Trenton, and urged to accept that important trust, he consented; and accordingly sent his son Joel to Monmouth, to manage the farm, which he did for two or three years, and much to the advantage of his physical development. He next entered Princeton College, and after the usual course of study graduated with honor in the class of 1839. Selecting the profession of the law he entered the office of Hon. Henry W. Green, afterwards chief-justice and chancellor of the State, where he pursued his studies in that direction. He was admitted to the bar in 1842, and commenced the practice of his profession at Freehold, in his native county, during the same year, where he has ever since continued to reside. In 1844 he first took an active part in political matters, and attracted much attention as a public speaker in the interests of the then Democratic party. In 1847 he was elected to the Assembly from Monmouth county, as then constituted. In the House, being the only lawyer on the Democratic side, he became the decided leader in his party, especially on all questions having a legal bearing. Among the first bills which he offered was one to equalize taxation, by taxing personal as well as real property. The Whigs were in the majority, but they did not want to place themselves on record against the bill, nor did they wish to favor it. It was a firebrand in their midst, that seriously threatened disruption. The former members of both parties followed the lead of Representative Parker. Finally the matter was laid over, and the publication of the bill with its author's speech was ordered in all the papers in the State —a distinguished compliment to the young member. The natural result was to give him a State reputation, which, together with the merits of the measure, redounded to his credit, and perhaps contributed to the election of Governor Fort in 1850, besides the final passage of the measure, which remains on the statute-book at this day. At the close of the session he opposed the usual appropriation for " Incidentals," and being defeated, he declined to take his ratio; consequently that amount still remains in the treasury. He declined being a candidate in 1851, as his practice was so rapidly increasing as to demand all his care and attention. Soon after this he was appointed Prosecutor of the Pleas for Monmouth county, and served the usual term of five years; and this position brought him in contact with some of the highest and brightest practitioners of the State. In 1860 he was chosen a United States Elector by 5,000 majority, and was one of the three northern electors who cast their votes for the Hon. Stephen A. Douglas for the Presidency. For several years prior to the late civil war he had been Brigadier-General of the Monmouth and Ocean Brigade, and taken an interest in military matters. In 1861 Governor Olden, although a Republican, nominated him to the Senate as Major-General of the five counties of Monmouth, Ocean, Mercer, Union and Middlesex, with a view to promote volunteering and to organize the forces. He was unanimously confirmed by the Senate, and the result shows that the confidence thus reposed in him, although a member of the Democratic party, was not over-estimated; his district promptly forwarded several regiments to the field, many of them being his old militia followers. In 1862 his county presented him as their candidate for Governor. But other counties and districts placed their favorites in the field, and not enough votes could be counted for either one. Finally all agreed on Joel Parker, who was unanimously nominated and elected over Hon. Marcus L. Ward by 14,600 majority, being three times as great as any majority ever received by any candidate since the office became elective. He was inaugurated for his term of three years in January, 1863, and will be remembered in all time to come as New Jersey's "War Governor." His administration of the office was distinguished for its financial policy and efficiency in promoting and aiding the general government in the suppression of the rebellion and in keeping up, by personal exertion, the system of volunteering for one year, after all other States were drafting. When he took charge of the State government, the civil account had been for years largely in arrears, but by his checks on extravagance this was not only entirely obliterated, but at the end of his term there was a large surplus in the treasury. In the despatching of troops he was second to none in the country, and for his solicitude for the welfare of all who went into the field he received and merited much public commendation as well as private appreciation. When Pennsylvania was invaded by the rebels he threw into that State regiment after regiment, and that, too, before the Pennsylvanians themselves realized their danger. After the close of his term as Governor he remained at home engaged in his legal business, wholly refusing to become a candidate for any office. In 1868 his State delegation in the National Democratic Convention in New York cast the full vote of New Jersey on every ballot for him as President. He was again solicited in 1871 to become a candidate for Governor, and yielded to the wishes of his friends. In the fall of that year he was a second time elected, and served with approbation for the full term of his office. He manifested a deep interest in the success of the International Exhibition, at Philadelphia, in commemoration of the Centennial of American independence, and favored the subscription of $100,000, which New Jersey made to that object. Personally he is of a commanding appearance, over six feet in height, has an open, ingenuous countenance, and a well-balanced head. He mingles freely with his fellow-citizens of all classes without distinction, and never refuses to befriend the most humble. The middle classes love him for his benevolence, and those more favored for his fine intellect, great executive ability, and, above all,

his unimpeachable honesty. He was married in 1843 to Maria M., eldest daughter of Samuel R. Gummere, of Burlington, New Jersey.

HALL, WILLIAM, President of the Middlesex County Bank, of Perth Amboy, was born, March 10th, 1816, in Somerset county, New Jersey, and is the son of Isaac and Elizabeth (Strimple) Hall. His father followed agricultural pursuits upon a farm which had been purchased by his ancestors direct from William Penn, whose name is signed to the original deed of conveyance. His mother was a native of Wyoming, Pennsylvania, and a daughter of Christopher Strimple, a soldier of the Revolution, also of that place. Young Hall was educated in the district schools of Somerset county, which he attended until he was sixteen years of age, when he began to learn the trade of carriage-trimming in Newark, remaining there until he was twenty-three years old. He then commenced the manufacturing of carriages at Milford, where he continued for several years, and then removed to Greenville, in Sussex county, where he engaged in general merchandising. After a sojourn there for some years he transferred his business to Perth Amboy, which occupied his attention for about twenty-one years, and until the incorporation, in January, 1873, of the Middlesex County Bank, of which institution he was elected President, and has since continued to hold that position. He has also been the President and Treasurer of the Perth Amboy Gaslight Company since its organization in 1871. Of the Middlesex County Land Company he is the Vice-President, and of the Perth Amboy Savings Institution, incorporated in April, 1869, the Treasurer. He has also been a member of the City Council at various times. He was married in 1842 to Charlotte Clark, of Connecticut.

WARD, JOHN W., A. M., M. D., Physician, and Superintendent of the State Lunatic Asylum, at Trenton, New Jersey, was born, February 12th, 1840, in the city of Salem in that State, and is a son of Samuel and Esther (Griffiths) Ward. He received a first-class education at Fairfield, Herkimer county, State of New York, where he pursued a thorough and entire collegiate course, lasting from 1854 to 1862. Returning to New Jersey, he engaged in teaching at Harrisonville, near Salem, which avocation he followed for several months, and during this period decided to adopt a professional life. Adopting that of medicine, he entered the office of Dr. John Kirby, an old and successful practitioner of Salem, and commenced his studies there in autumn of 1863, at the same time matriculating at the University of Pennsylvania, from which institution he graduated

In the spring of 1866, having attended an extra course beyond the number usually required. After practising his profession for about a year he was appointed, May 14th, 1867, as Second Assistant Physician at the New Jersey State Lunatic Asylum, Trenton, which was then under the charge of Dr. H. A. Buttolph. He filled that position with great acceptation for a period of five years, when he was promoted to be First Assistant Physician of the same institution. After acting in that capacity for a term of four years he was appointed, on April 1st, 1876, as Physician in Charge and Superintendent of the asylum, succeeding Dr. Buttolph, who had been transferred to the new State asylum, at Morristown. Though he has been but a few months in charge, his management has given every proof of his ability in all respects, and great success has so far attended his efforts. He has, during his nine years' connection with the institution, devoted his whole time to the thorough study of insanity in all its phases, and has at the same time kept pace with all the literature which has appeared bearing on that disease. His views on the treatment of insanity are those of all of the humane and most advanced authorities on the subject. The institution over which he presides is a model of order and cleanliness in all its departments, and every effort is constantly being made to alleviate and improve the sufferings and mental condition of the inmates. The asylum contains nearly 500 patients. Dr. Ward was married, March 5th, 1873, to Horacana B., daughter of the late Caleb Sager, who for many years was the able and thoroughly efficient steward of the asylum.

---❖---

ITHERSPOON, REV. JOHN, D. D., L L. D., Clergyman, Patriot and President of the College of New Jersey, was born, February 5th, 1722, in the parish of Yester, near Edinburgh, Haddingtonshire, Scotland, and was the son of the minister of that parish. On the maternal side he was a lineal descendant of the celebrated reformer John Knox. When fourteen years of age he entered the University of Edinburgh, as a student, where he remained until nearly twenty-one, when he was licensed to preach the gospel. In the year 1745 he was ordained and settled as minister of the parish of Beith, in the western part of Scotland. He was present at the battle of Falkirk, as a spectator, January 17th, 1746, and was taken a prisoner, although he was subsequently released after being in confinement for two weeks, during which time his health received permanent injury. In 1753 he published, anonymously, "Ecclesiastical Characteristics," or the "Arcana of Church Policy," followed a few years later by "A Serious Apology for the Characteristics," in which he avowed himself the author of the work he defended. In 1756 he published the "Essay on Justification," and in the following year his "Serious Inquiry into the Nature and Effects of the Stage," called forth by the appearance of Home's tragedy of "Douglas." In 1757 he was installed as pastor of the Low Church in Paisley, where he lived in high reputation and in great usefulness, although some opposition was raised by the presbytery of that town on account of their dislike to the "Characteristics." So extensively was he, at this time, known that he was invited to take the charge of different congregations in Dublin, Dundee and Rotterdam. In 1764 he went to London, where he published three volumes of "Essays on Important Subjects." In 1766 President Finley, of Princeton College, died, and the Rev. Dr. Witherspoon was chosen his successor. At first he declined the appointment, but afterwards accepted the same. He arrived, with his family, in Princeton in the month of August, 1768, and shortly after was duly inaugurated. This college had been already presided over by Dickinson, Burr, Edwards, Davies and Finley, all of them men distinguished for their genius, learning and piety. Dr. Witherspoon, by his name, brought a great accession of students to the college, thus considerably raising the reputation of the college. He was also instrumental in obtaining a large increase in its funds, which he raised by subscription. He also accepted the position of Professor of Divinity, in addition to his other duties, and was likewise pastor of the church in Princeton during the whole period of his presidency. But the war of the American Revolution prostrated everything. While the academical shades were deserted, and his functions as President were suspended, he was introduced into a new field of labor. When he landed on the shores of the new world he became at once an American, as if to the manor born. The citizens of New Jersey, who were cognizant of his distinguished abilities, appointed him a member of the Provincial Congress, of New Jersey, which framed the constitution of that State; and in that body he appeared as profound a civilian as he had before been known as a philosopher and divine. From the revolutionary committees and conventions of the State he was sent, early in 1776, as a representative to the Continental Congress. On May 17th of that year, the day appointed by the Congress to be observed as a fast, with reference to the peculiar circumstances of the country, he preached a sermon entitled "The Dominion of Providence over the Passions of Men," which entered fully into the great political questions of the day. He was for the space of seven years a member of that great patriotic, illustrious body—the governing power of the colonies, the Continental Congress—during which period he drew up many of the important State papers of the period. In far-reaching insight into the future, it can safely be said that he had not his superior in that body. He was always collected, firm and wise, amidst the embarrassing circumstances in which Congress was placed. He was one of the glorious fifty-six whose signatures were appended to the declaration that all men are created free and equal, and the only clergyman who signed that immortal document. His signature is also affixed to the Articles of Confederation, adopted by the

States at the close of the contest. But while he was thus engaged in political affairs, he did not lay aside his ministry. He gladly embraced every opportunity for preaching, and his character as a minister of the gospel he ever considered as the highest honor. As soon as the state of the country would permit the college was re-established, and its instruction was recommenced under the immediate care of the Vice-President, Dr. Smith; but during the war the institution had suffered greatly, and the trustees earnestly solicited Dr. Witherspoon to cross the ocean and endeavor to enlist sympathy in its behalf. He accepted the trust confided in him, and returned to Great Britain. His mission thither was not only an utter failure, but he found himself placed in circumstances of the most painful embarrassment. On his return to America he entered into that retirement which was dear to him, and his attention was principally confined to the duties of his office, as President, and as a minister of the gospel. During the latter part of his life he suffered not a little in consequence of having ventured upon some imprudent speculations in Vermont lands. He resided for several year, prior to his death, on his farm, near Princeton, and for the last two years of his life was entirely blind. But during this darkened period he was frequently led to the pulpit, whence he delivered his sermons with his accustomed ease, and always acquitted himself with his usual accuracy and animation. He, however, became more and more feeble, and sank to rest under the pressure of his infirmities. He possessed a mass of information, well selected and thoroughly digested. Scarcely any man of the age had a more vigorous mind or a more sound understanding. As President of the college he rendered literary inquiries more liberal, extensive and profound; and was the means of introducing an important revolution in the system of education. He extended the study of mathematical science, and it is believed he was the first man who taught in America the substance of those doctrines of the philosophy of the mind which Dr. Reid afterwards developed with so much success. He was very distinguished as a preacher. Although he wrote his sermons, and afterwards committed them to memory, yet, as he was governed by the desire of doing good, and wished to bring his discourses to the level of every understanding, he was not confined, when addressing his hearers, within the boundaries of what he had written. Although a very serious writer, he possessed a fund of refined humor and delicate satire. In his ecclesiastical characteristics his wit was directed at certain corruptions in principle and practice prevalent in the Church of Scotland, and it was keen and cutting. He formed a union of those who accorded with him, and became their leader. His reputation, learning and solid judgment were deservedly high. His influence upon the interests of literature was substance of Connecticut, and his talents as a professor were of the most popular kind. He died at his farm, near Princeton, September 15th, 1794, in the seventy-third year of his age. This brief record

of his life seems called for, as in the Centennial year of the nation which he aided in establishing, a fitting memorial of the patriotic clergyman, cast in enduring bronze, was erected and inaugurated October 20th, 1876, in Fairmount park, Philadelphia, by the Presbyterians of the United States, with grand civic and religious ceremonies befitting the occasion. The statue is of heroic size, and is a faithful embodiment of the features of the beloved President of Nassau Hall and signer of the Declaration of Independence.

ROGERS, RICHARD R., M. D., Physician, of Trenton, was born, September 15th, 1823, in West Windsor township, Mercer county, New Jersey, and is a son of Ezekiel and Mary (Runyan) Rogers. He was reared on his father's farm, until he attained his majority, meanwhile acquiring as much education as he could obtain by attending the district school during the winter months. For several years after attaining his majority he was engaged in a general country store; and during this period was also School Superintendent of the township and a Justice of the Peace. In 1852 he was elected Surrogate of Mercer County for a term of five years, and in 1857 re-elected to the same office. During his latter term as Surrogate he pursued the study of medicine, and after attending the usual number of courses of lectures graduated from the University of Pennsylvania in the spring of 1862. He then was appointed, by President Lincoln, the Examining Surgeon for the Second Congressional District of New Jersey, and filled the duties of that office until the close of the war. He also entered upon the practice of his profession in Trenton, immediately after receiving his diploma as doctor of medicine, and has since resided there, meeting with considerable success. In 1872 he was elected by the Republican party to the Legislature, where he served one term. At present (1876) he is a member of the City Council of Trenton. He is a member of the Mercer County District Medical Society, and has also on various occasions been a delegate to the State Medical Society. He was married, in 1844, to Mary A. Hutchinson, of Mercer county.

WHITNEY, REV. GEORGE HENRY, D. D., Clergyman, Teacher, Author and President of the Centenary Collegiate Institute of the Newark Conference of the Methodist Episcopal Church, at Hackettstown, was born, July 30th, 1830, in the city of Georgetown, District of Columbia, and is a son of William Whitney, a native of Connecticut. The family are of both French and English descent, and were among the early settlers of Connecticut; many of them having left their names and impress as among the benefactors of mankind; and notably so was Eli Whitney, the inventor of the celebrated cotton gin. While yet in his infancy his father removed to the city of Washington, where young Whitney obtained his rudimentary education. After leaving school he became a book-keeper in a large establishment; and subsequently, when only seventeen years of age, was the city editor of the *Daily National Whig*. Two years later he removed to Irvington, New Jersey, where he taught a select school for two years. On attaining his majority he became one of the teachers of the Wesleyan Institute, at Newark, where he was thus occupied for three years. On terminating his connection with that institution he entered the Wesleyan University, at Middletown, Connecticut, where he graduated with the class of 1858. Among his classmates were H. P. Shepard, Professor in the Albert University, of Canada; Nathaniel Fellows, Principal of Wilbraham Academy, Massachusetts, and Daniel C. Knowles, Principal of Pennington Seminary, New Jersey. Soon after graduating he was chosen Principal of Macedon Seminary, at Macedon Centre, State of New York; and from 1859 to 1861 occupied the same position at Oneida Seminary, Madison county, New York. In 1861 he joined the Newark Conference of the Methodist Episcopal Church, and was stationed the first year at Somerville, removing thence to Elizabeth, where he sojourned two years, and was transferred to Newton, where he passed three years. Two years were devoted to Plainfield, and two years to the pastorate of Trinity Church, Jersey City. He next was appointed to Passaic, where he ministered for three years, and during his incumbency he was the means of having a fine stone church building erected, at a cost of $80,000. A short time previous to laying the corner-stone of the Centenary Collegiate Institute, which took place September 9th, 1869, he was elected its President. He superintended the construction of the buildings, and during its erection performed pastoral duty, preaching educational sermons and soliciting aid for the completion of the buildings, etc. The institute was finished and dedicated, September 9th, 1874, and he at once entered upon his duties as President of the educational department. The institution opened with large classes, and the attendance has been to the fullest capacity of the edifice ever since. It is designed to afford the amplest facilities for both sexes to receive a superior education; and to prepare young men for the higher classes in college or in the theological seminary. The department for ladies is a regularly chartered college, empowered to confer degrees upon those who complete the prescribed course of study. The edifice, which cost about $200,000, is an elegant and substantial one; and, in taste and adaptation to its purpose, is one of the most admirable structures of the kind in the Union, and, in every respect, impresses the most scrutinizing visitor with the forethought displayed in its construction and the ability of its present management. No detail that adds to the care, comfort or safety of the students seems to have been omitted. The location, overlooking the village of Hackettstown and its beautiful surroundings, is exceedingly attractive. In addition to his other labors Dr. Whitney has written several works, among which may be mentioned "A Bible Geography," the result of years of patient investigation, and which has reached a very large sale. Another work is entitled "Commentary on International Sunday school Lessons;" and he has also contributed largely to various magazines and periodicals. He is at the present time (1876) engaged on a work to be known as "Old Testament Archæology." It is intended to be one of fifteen volumes, and to be published by the Methodist Book Concern, the whole set being entitled "The Theological Library." Since he has been located at this institution, Dr. Whitney has been called to some of the oldest leading institutions of learning in the country; but he has chosen to remain at Hackettstown, to continue the work so auspiciously commenced and successfully carried on. He was married, November 17th, 1858, to Carrie A. Shepard, of Northern New York, who died, December 19th, 1865. After a widowerhood of two years he was again married, December 24th, 1867, to Nettie, daughter of P. M. French, of Plainfield, New Jersey.

———————

PHARO, TIMOTHY, late of Tuckerton, Manufacturer and Merchant, was born, October 30th, 1792, at West Creek, Monmouth (now, Ocean) county, and was the son of Timothy and Hannah Pharo. He was a grandson of James Pharo, who emigrated from England during the latter part of the seventeenth century, and located first in Springfield, Burlington county, but subsequently settled at West Creek. Young Timothy was engaged in agricultural pursuits, having inherited the property which he cultivated, but was required to pay certain legacies, entailed on the property, and this to so considerable an amount as to reduce his original patrimony to a very moderate sum. While he carried on the farm he also engaged in mercantile and other business, among which, and the most lucrative, was the manufacture of castor oil, his own farm supplying much of the raw material. In 1824 his multifarious engagements induced him to abandon his farm and devote his time more exclusively to the former. For a period of over forty years he gave an unceasing, indefatigable energy and attention to the prosecution of various private enterprises and business operations, which resulted in the accumulation of a moderate fortune. He seemed to be possessed with such a discriminating judgment, united to a remarkable energy of will, as to have rendered him peculiarly successful in all his undertakings. His business was always extensive and varied. Assisted by his sons, he operated a grist-mill, saw-mill, general store, ship-building—sometimes having several in progress at the same time—and was also engaged in the wood, coal and lumber trade, thus furnishing employment to a large number of hands. He was a member of the Society of Friends, and belonged to Little Egg Harbor Monthly Meeting. He was a man of honor and strict integrity, truthful and prompt in his dealings, conscientious in the performance of his duties, firm in his attachments, kind to his neighbors, generous to the needy, affable and social in his intercourse; an affectionate husband, a loving and indulgent parent, a public benefactor, a plain unassuming man. He was married, February 18th, 1812, to Hannah, daughter of James Willits, he being then but a little over nineteen years of age. He died at Tuckerton, August 14th, 1854, leaving a widow and five children, three sons and two daughters.

ILSON, BLAKELY, late of Jersey City, Bank President, was born, December 12th, 1815, in the city of New York, where also he received his education. When thirteen years of age he was placed in a banker's and broker's office in Wall street, New York, and rose from one station to another until he became thoroughly conversant with all the details of financial business. He remained in connection with the various operations carried on in that celebrated locality for a period of thirty-five years, when he was elected to the Presidency of the Second National Bank, of Jersey City, which position he ably filled for eleven years. During this period he was also a director in several important insurance companies. In political feeling he was a Republican. During his residence in New York he was Second Lieutenant of a military organization. He was married, in 1844, to Sophia Newkirk. He died, February 13th, 1876, on the river Nile, in Egypt.

UCKER, HON. EBENEZER, Soldier, late of Tuckerton, was born, November 15th, 1757, in the State of New York, and was a son of Reuben Tucker. When he was about eight years old his father removed to the Province of East Jersey, where he purchased the whole of the island called Tucker's Beach, extending from Little Egg Harbor to Brigantine Inlet, ten miles in length, also a plantation near Tuckerton. In 1778 Ebenezer located himself in the settlement called "the middle of the shore," near Andrews' mill, then owned by the Shourds family. During the war of the Revolution he was in the Continental army, and served under General Washington, participating in the battle of Long Island and in other engagements; and also held several important trusts during that eventful period. At the close of the war he purchased the farm of John and

Joseph Gaunt, on which the main portion of Tuckerton is now built. He soon laid out the tract into building-lots, and erected houses. He also entered largely into the mercantile and shipping business, importing his groceries direct from the West Indies, in exchange for lumber. In 1786 the people of the village and vicinity met, and resolved that the village should be called Tuckerton. He was the first Postmaster of this new town; and when the District of Little Egg Harbor was created, which includes Tuckerton, he was chosen the first Collector of the Customs for the same. He subsequently was made Judge of the Court of Burlington County, and occupied that position for several years. In 1824 he was elected a member of the Nineteenth Congress of the United States, and was re-elected in 1826, thus serving in the House of Representatives during the entire period of President John Quincy Adams' administration. He died at Tuckerton, September 5th, 1845, having nearly completed his eighty-eighth year.

HITELY, ROBERT J., M. D., Physician, of Paterson, New Jersey, was born, January 16th, 1825, in that city, and is a son of Henry and Elizabeth (Van Riper) Whitely. His father was a native of the north of Ireland, who emigrated to the United States and settled in Paterson, among the oldest inhabitants of that town, where he was for many years engaged in mercantile pursuits. His mother was a native of Paterson, descended from the early Dutch settlers, who came to eastern Jersey about the year 1680. Young Whitely received a fair education in the schools of his native town, which was completed at Rutgers College, New Brunswick. Having determined upon a professional life, he selected the science of medicine, and in 1843 entered the office of Dr. William Magee, of Paterson, whom he had chosen as his preceptor, and with whom he pursued his studies for four years. During this interval he matriculated at the College of Physicians and Surgeons, of New York city, where he attended upon three separate courses of lectures, and graduated from that institution in the spring of 1846. He at once commenced the practice of his profession in his native place, and was favorably received by his townsmen. In February, 1849, he was prevailed upon to accompany a party to California, as their medical adviser. They sailed from New York in that month, and took the long and circuitous route, rounding Cape Horn, and finally reached their destination. During the winter of 1849–50 Dr. Whitely was successfully engaged in professional pursuits in San Francisco, and the remainder of the time he passed in the practice of his profession in the mining districts of Eldorado and Placer counties. In the spring of 1853 he bade farewell to the Golden State, and turned his face eastward, returning to the Atlantic States by the Panama route, and reached Paterson in May, 1853. He at once resumed his practice after over four years absence, and soon found himself actively and successfully engaged in his professional labors, which he continued until the summer of 1868, when he sailed for Europe. He was absent from home about four months, and during that time visited, among other objects, the various hospitals of Great Britain and Ireland. He also made the tour of Europe in 1870, and was absent from this country some seven months, resuming his practice after his return. He is among the oldest medical practitioners of Paterson, enjoying the confidence, esteem and respect of his professional brethren, as well as of the community at large. He has been connected with the Passaic County Medical Society since 1847, during which time he has served twice as President of that body. He has been since its organization and is at present connected with the medical staff of the Ladies' Hospital, at Paterson; and is also a Director in the Second National Bank of Paterson, having been identified with that institution since 1869.

MARCY, ALEXANDER, M. D., Physician, of Camden, was born in Cape May county, New Jersey, April 16th, 1838. His parents were Samuel S. Marcy, M. D., an old physician of Cape May county, and Thankful (Edmunds) Marcy; the former was a native of Connecticut, who settled in Cape May county in 1817, and practised medicine from that time up to the last year or two. Alexander Marcy entered Amherst College in 1855, and left a junior. He began to study medicine with his father in 1859, and at the same time matriculated at the University of Pennsylvania, from which he was graduated in 1861. He at once located for practice in Camden, New Jersey, and has continued to prosecute his profession in that city to the present time, with steady and increasing success. Devoted to his profession, he seeks to promote its interests, and has always been an active member of the Camden Medical Society, of which he was chosen President for the year 1876. He was married in 1861 to Hannah Mccray, of Cape May, New Jersey.

PEDDIE, HON. THOMAS B., of Newark, Manufacturer, Merchant, and Member of Congress from the Sixth District of New Jersey, is a native of Scotland, as were also his parents, who possessed a moderate independence. He was educated in his native country, and was an earnest reader, especially of the literature of the day. The glowing accounts of the great western republic which from time to time met his eye, inspired him with a wish to view the land so happily described, and he determined to cross the Atlantic and ascertain if such unbounded prosperity existed in the new world. It was in 1833 that he landed in America, and among other towns that he visited was the present city of Newark, then little more than a large village. The situation pleased him so much that he soon determined it should be his future home. At that period it was a town of some manufacturing importance, and he at once selected an avocation which he believed was best calculated for advancement. Entering the factory of Smith & Wright, saddlers, he remained with them for about two years, and having by strict habits of economy laid up a sum of money, the fruits of his earnings, commenced on his own account the manufacture of leather trunks and travelling bags. From the small beginning of two-score years ago, he has steadily augmented his manufacturing facilities, until his establishment is the largest of its kind in the Union, if not in the world. During his long residence in the beautiful city of Newark, he has become prominently identified with her interests, and has contributed in no small degree to her importance as a great manufacturing centre—the third city in the Union in that particular. At the same time he has given some attention to the interests of education. To the institution at Hightstown, New Jersey, which now bears his name, he has contributed largely of his means for its success. Of late years he went abroad, and passed a year in travelling through the greater portion of Europe, paying particular attention not only to many points of interest in Great Britain and Ireland, but also in France, Germany, Austria and Italy; besides which he was an attentive observer of the laws of trade and commerce, and of the particular care taken by the government of Great Britain in fostering the interests of her merchants and manufacturers. On his return home he made an address to the Board of Trade—of which body he had long been a member and at one time President—which is replete with valuable information, being a general review of trade and the industrial pursuits, both mechanical and agricultural, of the different countries he visited. Towards the conclusion of his remarks he became the earnest advocate of a new department at Washington, that of trade and commerce, as an adjunct to the one already added within a few years past, that of agriculture. In political creed he is an ardent member of the Republican party, and has been the recipient of the favors of that organization at sundry times. He was twice elected Mayor of Newark, and twice chosen as a Representative in the lower or popular branch of the State Legislature, where, during the great southern rebellion, he took an active part in support of the general government both with his influence and his purse. He was nominated by the Republicans in 1876 as their candidate for the Forty-fifth Congress from the Sixth Congressional District of New Jersey, and was elected. Being a thoroughly practical man of the people, he will doubtless faithfully represent his constituents in the Federal legislature, and contribute by every means at his command to advance not only their own interests, but that of the country at large; and it is to be hoped that he will be not only the originator of the new department of the government alluded to above, but that he may be early called upon to organize the same.

———

TERHUNE, GARRIT, M. D., Physician, of Passaic, was born in Bergen county, New Jersey, in October, 1801. His parents both came from the same county, in which his father, Richard N. Terhune, followed agricultural pursuits. His mother was Hannah Voorhees. From the common schools of his native place Garrit Terhune received his primary educational training. He fitted for college at the classical school of Dr. Sythoff, and then entered Princeton College, from which he was graduated in 1823. Having determined to adopt the medical profession, he began study therefor immediately upon leaving college, having for his preceptor first the same Dr. Sythoff from whom he obtained his university preparation, and subsequently Professor John W. Francis, of Rutgers Medical College, then in operation in Jersey City, although an adjunct of Rutgers College, of New Brunswick. He graduated in medicine in 1829, and at once began practice in Hackensack. After a short while he removed to Passaic, where he has since followed his profession with much success. He was the first President of the Passaic County Medical Society. In the year 1828 he was married to Elizabeth A. Zabriskie, of St. Johnsville, New York.

———

VOORHEES, PETER L., Lawyer, of Camden, was born in Blawenburgh, Somerset county, New Jersey, July 12th, 1825. He is descended of New Jersey ancestors, his parents being Peter Voorhees and Jane Schenck, daughter of Captain John Schenck. His educational advantages were only such as could be obtained at the common schools of the neighborhood, but of them he made the most diligent use, and acquired the elements of a sound education. Up to his twenty-first year he was occupied on the home farm, but farming not being to his taste, and the law possessing great attraction for him, he determined to follow the latter as his career. Accordingly he entered the office of Richard S. Field, of Princeton, as a student, and in connection with his studies there he, in the following year, 1847, attended the law school then attached to Princeton College, but long since discontinued, having been conducted for about three years only. From this institution he received in due course the degree of LL. B., and subsequently that of A. M. He was admitted to the bar in November, 1851, and located in Camden in October, 1852. In this city he has since resided and practised. One of the oldest practitioners in this section of the State, he is also among the leaders of its bar. This position he has attained by the force of sheer hard work. There may be more brilliant men among his com-

peers, but there is none who is a sounder or better read lawyer, nor is there one who more completely masters every case intrusted to him, who is more successful before the courts, and who enjoys so thoroughly the confidence of his clients and the respect of the profession. For one year he served as City Solicitor of Camden, and he is counsellor, for this section of the State, for the Pennsylvania Railroad Company, although one of its opponents in the great railroad war in New Jersey. He was married in 1855 to Annie F., sister of the late Hon. W. L. Dayton, the distinguished statesman.

———

PRICE, THEOPHILUS T., M. D., Physician, of Tuckerton, was born, May 21st, 1828, at Town Bank, Cape May county, New Jersey, on the estate which had descended from his great-grandfather, William Price, and is a son of John and Kezia (Swain) Price, both of whom were also natives of the same State. The Price family during the revolutionary era were well known as loyal to the patriot cause, and during the war some of them were distinguished for their services, among them William Price, mentioned above, who was a captain in the Continental army and served in the cause of the colonies during that conflict. When young Price was about three years old his father sold his share of the paternal estate to his brother, Captain William Price, and purchased a farm at Swaintown—a short distance from Cold Spring, in the same county—from his father-in-law, Daniel Swain, and the family homestead still remains at that locality. Daniel Swain was descended from one of the oldest and most respected families of Cape May county. Young Price received his rudimentary education in the common schools of the neighborhood, which he attended until he was thirteen years old, when his father placed him in the academy at Cold Spring, which had then been recently founded, and which was carried on successfully for several years by Rev. Moses Williamson, at that place. He there obtained a fair English education, and remained there about three years. The learning which he acquired at that academy was considerably augmented by diligent private study, after leaving school. He next assisted his father on the farm until he was twenty years old, when he commenced teaching school, and one year afterwards began the study of medicine. He subsequently matriculated at the Pennsylvania Medical College, and attended the regular courses of lectures delivered in that institution, from which he graduated in March, 1853. The following month he settled at Tuckerton, having been invited to do so by Dr. Mason, a physician then in practice there, and he has continued to reside there ever since, giving close attention to his profession, and has won for himself a well-merited reputation as a most successful physician and surgeon. He has been for a long period an active and influential member of the Medical Society of Burlington county. During the war he was an earnest supporter of the government, and after the battle of Gettysburg offered his services as volunteer surgeon; they were accepted and he was assigned to duty at Chestnut Hill Military Hospital for one month, when, the wards being relieved of part of their wounded crowds, he returned to his practice. His political creed is that of the Republican party, and he became their nominee, in 1868, as Representative of the Fourth Legislative District of Burlington county, and was elected. During his term of service he introduced and secured the passage of a bill to charter a railroad from Tuckerton to Egg Harbor City; also of an act to charter a company to construct a ship-canal from the river Delaware to Little Egg Harbor river. He was the author of the bill to protect harmless and insectivorous birds, passed at that session; and he introduced a bill to charter an institution for the reformation of inebriates, which, however, failed to pass. In 1870–71 he was actively associated with John Rutherford, A. K. Pharo, and other gentlemen, in the construction of the Tuckerton Railroad, having been a Director and the Secretary of the company from its first organization; and has also been the local Treasurer since its first year. He has also been a Director in the Beach Haven Land Company, and an associate of the gentlemen who have displayed so much energy in establishing that new and growing watering-place. He has also been a Director of Medford, New Jersey, Bank for the past sixteen years. He has ever been a warm friend of education for the masses, and filled for eight years the position of Superintendent of the Public Schools in the township of Little Egg Harbor, where he resides. During that period there were eleven schools under his care, and into them he first introduced several important reforms. In religious belief he is a Baptist, and assisted in founding the Baptist Church at West Creek, of which he was chosen the first deacon. He was one of the founders of the Tuckerton Bible Society, and has been its Treasurer for many years. He has also been a liberal friend to the missionary cause, and he supports and conducts almost entirely a home mission school. He is a member of the New Jersey Historical Society, and is at the present time (1876) President of the Tuckerton Public Library Society, besides which he has also filled several important trusts. A man of literary tastes, he is the author of a number of contributions, both in prose and verse, that have appeared from time to time in the papers. As a citizen he stands high in the estimation of the public, and having been so long identified with the welfare and prosperity of his section, he is regarded by all as a gentleman of the highest intelligence, who aims to do good in all things, and who endeavors, as much as lies in his power, to advance the general interests of the county and of the State. He was married in November, 1854, to Eliza, youngest daughter of Timothy Pharo, one of the most successful business men of Tuckerton, New Jersey, whose biographical sketch will be found elsewhere in this volume.

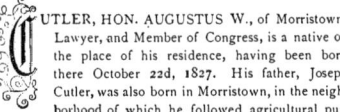

UTLER, HON. AUGUSTUS W., of Morristown, Lawyer, and Member of Congress, is a native of the place of his residence, having been born there October 22d, 1827. His father, Joseph Cutler, was also born in Morristown, in the neighborhood of which he followed agricultural pursuits. On the maternal side he is a descendant of Silas Condit, a member of the Continental Congress, his mother, Elizabeth Cook, being a granddaughter of that distinguished man. Augustus was brought up on the home farm, and obtained his education in the schools of his native place. When the time arrived for the choice of a profession he selected that of the law, and began to study in the office of Governor Haines. In due course he was admitted as an attorney in 1850, and three years later was received as counsellor. He soon won a good standing at the bar, and in 1856 was appointed Prosecutor of the Pleas for Morris county. This position he held until 1861. Ten years later, in 1871, he was elected Senator from Morris county, and served for three years with great credit to himself and advantage to his constituents. During this term he served on the committees on Judiciary and Education. He was a member of the State Constitutional Convention in 1873, and labored faithfully and successfully for the introduction into the organic law of many much needed reforms. In 1875 he was elected to Congress from the Fifth Congressional District, comprising the counties of Bergen, Morris, and Passaic, and did such good service as to secure re-election in 1876. His affiliations have always been with the Democratic party, and he has always exerted a wide influence as an earnest exponent of its best principles. In the advancement of the cause of education he has from early life manifested a deep interest, identifying himself with every movement of educational value. Of the Board of Education of Morristown he has been President since its organization in 1870. He was mainly instrumental in causing the moneys received from riparian rights by the State to be entirely appropriated to the school fund, thus securing a free school system to the State. This question reached a settlement during his term in the State Senate, his earnest efforts conducing in very great degree to the satisfactory result. While there may be more brilliant men at the bar than he, there are few who have won a more solid position by well-directed, hard study, and persistent attention to the interests of his clients and constituents. He was married in 1854 to Julia R. Walker, of Albany, New York.

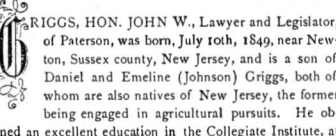

RIGGS, HON. JOHN W., Lawyer and Legislator, of Paterson, was born, July 10th, 1849, near Newton, Sussex county, New Jersey, and is a son of Daniel and Emeline (Johnson) Griggs, both of whom are also natives of New Jersey, the former being engaged in agricultural pursuits. He obtained an excellent education in the Collegiate Institute, at

Newton, and in the autumn of 1865 matriculated at La-fayette College, Easton, Pennsylvania, where he completed his studies, and graduated from that institution with the class of 1868, as Bachelor of Arts. After leaving college he entered the office of Hon. Robert Hamilton, to engage in the study of the law, remaining there until May, 1871, when he removed to Paterson, where he selected as his preceptor Hon. Socrates Tuttle, with whom he continued until the prescribed term of three years' reading was con-cluded, when he was duly licensed as an attorney, in No-vember, 1871, being raised to the rank of counsellor-at-law in 1874. Immediately after his admission to the bar, in 1871, he commenced the practice of his profession in Pater-son, continuing the same on his own account until the winter of 1873, when he became the law partner of his preceptor, Hon. Socrates Tuttle, and is still his associate. In the autumn of 1875 he was elected by the Republican party as the Representative to the lower house of the State Legislature from the First Assembly District of Passaic County, and was re-elected in 1876. During his first term he served on several prominent committees in that body, and took an active part in the preparation of the new Elec-tion law, which went into operation during the winter of 1875-76. Although young in years, he has already achieved a first-class reputation as a barrister and an efficient legis-lator. He was married October 7th, 1874.

RIDGWAY, BENJAMIN, President of the Union Bank, of Mount Holly, was born, July 8th, 1797, in the township of Willingborough, Burlington county, New Jersey, and is the son of the late Benjamin E. and Prudence (Borton) Ridgway, both of whom were also natives of that State. His rudimentary education was obtained in the common schools of the day in the neighborhood of his home; and he completed his studies in the then well-known academy of the late John Gummere, at Burlington, where so many prominent citizens of both New Jersey and Pennsylvania were educated. When twenty years old he left school, and for some years was engaged in assisting his father on his farm. As soon as he attained his majority he commenced taking an active interest in politics, and was elected Asses-sor, which position he held for eleven years, being con-stantly re-elected every year. He was then elected Free-holder, wherein he served his constituency between fifteen and twenty years. In 1842 he was elected a member of Assembly, on the Whig ticket, and so ably did he acquit himself that, in the year following, he was nominated by both parties, and received almost the entire vote of the district, lacking only about ninety ballots of the whole voting population of 5.700. He was ever outspoken on all questions, and voted for that which was for the public weal, irrespective of party. In fact, so great confidence has been placed in his honor and integrity that, during a greater part of his manhood, he has been intrusted with the settlement of many estates throughout the county. Aside from these, and other duties of an official character, his entire life, from the time of his leaving school, in 1817, until the year 1867 —a period of just half a century—has been devoted to agricultural pursuits. In the year last named he disposed of his interests in the farm and removed to Mount Holly. In 1874 he was chosen President of the Union Bank, of Mount Holly, which position he has filled with credit to himself and with great benefit to the institution. He has always taken an active part in all matters pertaining to the improvement of the town, and manifests much interest in everything that tends towards the development of the county and State. Since 1844 he has taken no active part in politics; but his principles accord with those held by the Republican party, and he is held in high estimation by the members of both political organizations. He was married, in 1837, to Margaret B. Fenimore, of Camden county, New Jersey.

RIDGWAY, CAPTAIN JOSEPH R., Soldier, was born, December, 1840, in Willingborough town-ship, Burlington county, New Jersey, and was the son of Benjamin and Margaret B. (Feni-more) Ridgway, both his parents being natives of the same State; and his father's biographical sketch appears above. Joseph's early education was ob-tained at Beverly, and he completed his studies at the Gummere's Academy, in Burlington, the same institution where his father had attended, and presided over by Samuel Gummere, who was a son of John Gummere, who founded the institution. He left school when nineteen years of age, and became of much assistance to his father in the management of his farm. He remained there until the outbreak of the war and the call for the ninety-day men, when he responded, and raised a company in his own neighborhood, which was subsequently known as Company G, of the 3d Regiment New Jersey Infantry, and of which he was elected Captain. He fell at the battle of Fredericks-burg, while gallantly leading his command. His remains were recovered, taken home and buried at Rancocas.

CLARK, AMOS, JR., ex-Member of Congress and Real-Estate Operator, of Elizabeth, was born in Brooklyn, New York, November 8th, 1828. His father, Amos Clark, was a native of Union county, New Jersey, and his mother, whose maiden name was Sarah Meeker, was a native of Springfield, New Jersey. He was educated at an academy in Elizabeth, New Jersey, where he was thoroughly schooled in all the

Amos Clark Jr.

usual branches of study. Upon completing his academic career he engaged in a large wholesale clothing house, and by careful attention and active observation gained in a short time a thorough insight into the methods of conducting business transactions. Soon afterwards he embarked on his individual account, in New York, in the same line, and met with gratifying success. In 1862 he made extensive real estate purchases in Elizabeth, and rapidly augmented these investments, until they had reached proportions which demanded his entire attention. In 1865, therefore, he relinquished his business in New York, and gave his whole time to his interests in Elizabeth, where he settled. Having become one of the largest proprietors of real estate in that city, he was naturally led into an active support of all efforts to carry out long-needed local improvements; and to this end gave liberally of his own means and attention. He became one of the incorporators of the First National Bank, of Elizabeth, and was chosen as its President by the body of stockholders. This office he has continuously held up to the present time, and his sagacious management of its affairs, resulting in its becoming one of the strongest moneyed institutions in the State, is an ample affirmation of his ability as a financier. He was one of the originators of the Elizabeth Horse Railroad, and is very heavily interested in it. He was one of the projectors, and is now President, of the National Fire & Marine Insurance Company, of Elizabeth, having occupied his present position ever since its incorporation. He found time, amid these cares, to carry out a large number of individual schemes, which have given to the city many conspicuous ornaments. A large number of the finest business blocks he erected, prominent among them being the Arcade, which was built in 1869. This substantial and imposing structure contains a fine opera house, a conservatory of music, a Masonic hall and a series of handsome offices. The post-office of the city is also located in this building. Mr. Clark has always evinced a decided interest in agricultural science, and has been for years a prominent member of the New Jersey State Agricultural Society, of which he is at present the presiding officer. Politically, he is identified with the Republican party, and is one of its most influential leaders in this State. He was elected a member of the City Council in 1865, and served until the close of 1866. Union county sent him to the State Senate for the term of 1866-69, where he served his constituency with distinguished ability. In 1872 he was returned as Congressman from the Third District of New Jersey, a district which comprises the counties of Middlesex, Monmouth and Union. During his term he was a member of the committee appointed to thoroughly investigate the District of Columbia frauds, and which unearthed the peculations of Shepherd and his associates. Mr. Clark, in this position, rendered most valuable and conspicuous services. He was an Elector on the Republican ticket in the Presidential campaign of 1872, and a delegate to the convention in Philadelphia which placed General Grant in

19

nomination for a second term. Upon two occasions he has represented his party in Union county at gubernatorial conventions. His irreproachable character, various business capacities, energy in projecting and carrying to complete realization important local improvements, his liberal aid to charities, his important services to his party and to his fellow-townsmen, irrespective of party, have secured for him their lasting regard as a public-spirited citizen and a faithful official. He was married, on October 15th, 1851, to Elizabeth R. Hunter, of Massachusetts.

BLANE, JOHN, M. D., of Perryville, Physician, ex-Senator and Major-General New Jersey Militia, was born, July 7th, 1802, in the township of North Brunswick, Middlesex county, New Jersey, and is the only son of the late Thomas and Elizabeth (Toombs) Blane. His father was a native of the county of Louth, Ireland, and had emigrated to the United States only a short time prior to the birth of his only son. His family were originally from a Spanish or French province, and had migrated to the district of Galloway, the extreme southwest part of Scotland, where they resided for very many years. They were, while residents of this latter country, staunch Presbyterians, members of the Kirk of Scotland, and noted for their adherence to the convictions of right and justice. Although strong Protestants, they believed the cause of the Stuarts a just one, and followed the fortunes of that house to their own sorrow. Early in the eighteenth century the grandfather of Dr. Blane left Scotland for Ireland. His mother, Elizabeth Toombs, was a daughter of George Toombs, of Carlingford, Ireland, and a cousin of John Philpot Curran, the celebrated barrister, her mother having been Elizabeth Curran. When he was but three years old his mother died. He was educated in the schools of Middlesex county; and, in addition to the knowledge he gained there, studied surveying under Hon. Beach Jennings, and was instructed in conveyancing by Richard Harwood, Esq. In the spring of 1820 he opened a school in Hillsborough, Somerset county, where he was engaged in teaching for about one year. During this period he passed his "blank Saturdays" and his leisure days in surveying and drawing deeds, etc. After relinquishing his position as teacher he again became a student in the select school of Abraham G. Voorhees—who was a graduate of Princeton College—at the residence of Rev. Mr. Zabriskie, at Millstone, boarding in the family of the principal. He remained at this locality about one year, and among other matters studied the science of navigation. In the spring of 1822 he had made all the necessary arrangements to go to the West Indies as second mate of the "Howard," a vessel trading from New York; but one of the owners of that craft, desirous of finding a berth for a relative, induced him to withdraw. Moreover, such a course was in opposition to his father's wishes, who desired him to embrace one of the learned professions. He thereupon commenced the study of medicine, under the preceptorship of Dr. William D. McKissack, of Millstone; meanwhile passing one or two days each week in surveying, drafting, etc. In the autumn of 1825 he went to New York city, and became an attendant upon the medical lectures delivered by the professors of the College of Physicians and Surgeons, in Barclay street. These professors were Drs. Wright Post, Samuel Mitchell, William J. McNevin, Valentine Mott, John W. Francis and David Hosack; and this course of lectures was the last delivered by those professors in that institution. During this season he was a student in the office of Drs. Smith and Pendleton, New York city. Returning home he taught the school of his native school district, at Six Mile Run, during the summer of 1826; at the same time reading, or occasionally giving a helping hand to his father on the farm. Towards the close of that year he again went to New York city, where he became an attendant upon the lectures delivered in the Rutgers Medical College, in Duane street. These lectures were delivered by Drs. Hosack, Mott, McNevin, Francis, Godman and Griscom, the first four having been connected with the College of Physicians and Surgeons during the previous year. During this period he was the office student of Dr. Stephen Brown, of Franklin Square, having as his companion the late Surgeon Charles Tripler, of the United States army, then also a student. During both winters, while a resident of New York city, he attended the practice of the New York Hospital, and also that of Bellevue, then a comparatively new institution. In the spring of 1827 he entered into an arrangement with Dr. G. W. Boyd & Co., to superintend their apothecary store, No. 526 Pearl street, New York, and to prescribe and attend upon such calls as might offer. He passed his examination satisfactorily, and received a certificate for the same; but the chancellor having decided that the diploma of the Rutgers Medical School was not a license to practise in the State of New York, he went to Somerville, New Jersey, and was examined there by the Board of Censors, April 26th, 1827, and received their certificate and the diploma of the Medical Society of New Jersey, which entitled him to practise the profession of medicine in New Jersey; and this certificate and diploma, being subsequently filed in New York, removed the disability. He continued in the situation at the store in Pearl street until the close of the year; but, city life having become distasteful, he relinquished the position and returned to his father's farm. Early in 1828 he became the associate of Dr. W. A. A. Hunt, of Clarksville, Hunterdon county, which partnership continued for three years. He then removed to Perryville, in the same county, where for many years he attended to a large practice, never refusing a call, unless forced to do so by circumstances over which he had no control. During his long residence in Hunterdon county he has been re-

garded as one of the leading medical men of the State, and is much esteemed by those who know him best, both as a physician and as a surgeon; and has done much to advance the dignity and character of the profession in the State. In the latter part of 1870 he relinquished to his son-in-law, Dr. N. B. Boileau, his extensive practice, and has since been in comparative retirement, occasionally attending consultations, or prescribing for old friends. It is a singular fact, that there is not a township adjoining the one in which he resides, nor a county adjoining Hunterdon— not even excepting two in Pennsylvania—in which he has not practised. He was a regular attendant upon the meetings of the district medical society of his county, and was one of the commissioners for its reorganization, in 1836, and again in 1846; it has since continued in a flourishing condition. In 1848, and also in 1855, he was its President; in 1859 he was elected Treasurer; and in 1869 was chosen as the historian of the society. Under its auspices he wrote a "History of the Physicians of the County of Hunterdon," and also of several other neighboring and State practitioners. From 1847 to 1861 he was frequently a delegate to the New Jersey State Medical Society, and up to 1865, inclusive, served as one of the Board of Censors of the same, being sixteen times in nineteen terms of that body. In 1855 he was the Chairman of their Standing Committee; and upon reporting the proceedings of that committee, in the session of January 22d, 1856, the society conferred upon him the degree of M. D. In 1859 he was elected their Second Vice-President; in 1860 he became the First Vice-President; and the following year was made President of that body. He has also been on many occasions a delegate to the meetings of the American Medical Association; and from 1855, when he first became a member thereof, until prevented by age and infirmities from attending its meetings, was more punctual in his appearance at its sessions than the majority of its members. At the meeting held in Chicago, in 1863, he served on the Committee on Nominations; and at the session held in Baltimore, in 1867, he was appointed on the Committee on Necrology, and since that period has been annually reappointed. He has ever been a friend to the cause of education, and has been a member of the School Committee and Superintendent of the Township Schools for over thirty years. He has held several township offices, and as chosen Freeholder, which he held for several years, was the Director of the Board, in 1850. For over a half century he has held commissions in the militia of New Jersey. From eighteen years of age, when first subject to military duty, he passed through all the ranks up to that of Major-General; the latter appointment he received in February, 1840. In 1834 he was nominated by the Democrats as their candidate for the State Assembly, and was elected by a large majority; being re-elected during the following year, and served with credit to himself and also to that of his constituents. In 1861 he was nominated by the Democracy as their candidate for State Senator, and elected over Charles Bartles, Esq., by a large majority. He served three years in the Senate, and during his first year in that body was Chairman of the Committee on the Lunatic Asylum; in 1863 he was Chairman of the Militia Committee; while in his last year he was Chairman of the Committee on Education and on the Committee on the State Prison. Here, as in every other position, public or professional, that he has filled, his thorough integrity asserted itself. His record, as a State Senator or other official, as a practitioner, or as a private citizen, in purity of thought or action, has been guided by rare discrimination and judgment. He has been somewhat of a writer in connection with medical matters. His thesis was on the "History of Scarlet Fever;" and as historian of the medical society already alluded to, he has penned the biographies of various physicians; also a "History of the Medical Society of Hunterdon, with its Medical Men;" together with reports of various committees. One of these should be more especially noticed. While a member of the Legislature, in 1837, he opposed the encroachments on the rights of the citizens of New Jersey by the companies then acquiring monopoly powers in the State, and was Chairman of the Committee of Inquiry on that subject. His report, although a minority one, did much towards restraining these companies in their grasping and overreaching acts towards the State; it was their first check in that quarter. His political predilections were in favor of the Democratic principles enunciated by Jefferson, Jackson and Johnson; and although he has had all deference for the opinions of others, he has never failed to give his views, unreservedly, when called upon to do so. He was energetic, industrious and persevering beyond the endurance of his physical ability, for his health was never robust. From 1837 until 1867, a period of thirty years, he conducted the management of his farm, taking it from the hand of nature, in a rough and forbidding condition, and brought it to a fair state of cultivation. He is of temperate habits and dresses plainly. His religious faith is that of the Presbyterian Church. He is now (November, 1876) in the seventy-fifth year of his age, and, among his other acquirements, has learned to grow old gracefully in a pleasant home, surrounded by the most productive farming country of New Jersey. During his long career as a physician he has been the preceptor of many medical men, all of whom were successful and an honor to the profession. Among these may be named Drs. I. S. Cramer, William Labaw, William S. Creveling, Matthias Abel, Levi Farrow, Nathan Case and the late Lewis R. Needham, all of New Jersey; A. S. Combs, of Ohio; the late H. L. R. Wiggin, of Maine; and C. A. Voorhees, of Pennsylvania. Dr. Blane was married, May 28th, 1840, to Cornelia Hunt, youngest daughter of Isaac Smith, of Warren county, and is the father of three children, one son, who died in infancy, and two daughters; one of the latter is the wife of his successor in practice, Dr. N. B. Boileau, and the other married Dr. Nathan Case, now a resident of Riegelsville, Warren county, New Jersey.

ANNON, HENRY R., M. D., Physician and County Clerk of Union County, was born, May 20th, 1821, in Somerset county, New Jersey, and is a son of Rev. James S. and Catharine (Brevoort) Cannon. His father was a native of one of the West India islands, and for many years filled the chair of Professor of Mental Philosophy, etc., in Rutgers College, New Brunswick; his mother was a native of Bergen county, New Jersey. Dr. Cannon received his preliminary education in the grammar school of Rutgers College, and in 1836 matriculated in the college itself, graduating in the class of 1840. Having decided to enter upon the profession of medicine, he became a student in the office of Dr. William Van Deursen, of New Brunswick, with whom he remained for nearly three years, meanwhile attending the courses of lectures delivered in the medical department of the University of New York, and in March, 1843, graduated as Doctor of Medicine. In the autumn of that year he commenced the practice of his profession in Somerset county, and for nine years thereafter was actively engaged therein. In 1852 he opened a drug store in Plainfield, which he successfully conducted until April, 1857, when he was appointed County Clerk of Union County, and has been continually re-elected at the expiration of his term, and is now in the twentieth year of the tenure of that office. This one fact speaks volumes as to his capability, integrity and popularity, the position being the most important office of a leading county. He is also connected with some of the most important corporations of that section, and is a director of the National Fire and Marine Insurance Company, of Elizabeth; also a director of the Elizabeth Horse Railroad; and a director of the Union Manufacturing Company, of Elizabethport. He was married, in 1844, to Emma M. Carkart, of New York city, who died in 1862. He was subsequently united in marriage to Mrs. Mary C. Van Vranken, of Hackensack, New Jersey.

———◦✦◦———

OODRUFF, JONATHAN, President of the Union National Bank, Rahway, was born, September 6th, 1815, in Westfield, New Jersey, of which place his parents, William and Phoebe (Ludlow) Woodruff, were old residents. The Woodruffs and Ludlows settled in the neighborhood of Westfield and were identified with the town before the revolutionary war, in which his maternal grandfather, Jacob Ludlow, was a participant, and shared the dangers and privations of the "Jersey Brigade." Mr. Woodruff was one of a family of ten children, eight of whom (six sons and two daughters) are now living, the oldest being over seventy-three years of age and the youngest over fifty. In 1816 his father purchased a farm about one mile from Rahway, on the old "King George's road," from Rahway to Elizabeth, and there Jonathan passed his boyhood. Rahway at that time was extensively engaged in the manufacture of carriages for the Southern market, and when seventeen years of age he began to learn the trade of carriage-making, and was occupied for four years in mastering all the branches of the business. He then went to New York city, where he engaged in mercantile pursuits for several years, until 1842, when, in connection with his brother Amos, he opened a general mercantile store in Rahway, under the firm-name of J. & A. Woodruff. In the winter of 1845 the firm established a house in Memphis, Tennessee, for the sale of carriages, which they manufactured in their own establishment at Rahway, shipping all their products to the Memphis house for disposal. His brother, Amos Woodruff, took charge of the Memphis branch of the business, while he remained in Rahway. His thorough knowledge respecting the manufacture of carriages, gained in his four years' experience in the business, now proved of great value to him; and the vehicles bearing their stamp soon acquired a wide reputation in the West and Southwest. They carried on this trade with great success until the breaking out of the war, when the firm of J. & A. Woodruff & Co. was dissolved by Jonathan retiring. The business in Memphis is still carried on by Amos Woodruff and William Woodruff (a nephew), under the firm-name of A. Woodruff & Co. In 1865 Mr. Woodruff became one of the first to organize the Union National Bank, of Rahway, and when it went into operation was chosen President of the institution, and has since continued to conduct its affairs. Under his management the bank has successfully withstood all the monetary disasters and financial storms that have visited the country during the past eleven years, since its organization. He has been thoroughly identified with all improvements in the city of Rahway, and has always been ready to aid, both with his time and his means, any enterprise that would promote the public good. He was married, August 9th, 1842, to Alvira, daughter of William and Sarah (Crowell) Martin, whose ancestors came from England and Scotland, and settled in Middlesex county, New Jersey.

EWELL, WILLIAM L., M. D., Physician, of Millville, was born in Bridgeton, New Jersey, March 27th, 1834. His father, James M. Newell, was for many years a prominent citizen of that place, where he edited and conducted the *Bridgeton Chronicle*. The influence he exerted proved of immense advantage to the town and State. He was mainly instrumental in having various public measures adopted, among which may be cited, as of especial importance to the community, the Equalization of Taxes, the Abolishment of Imprisonment for Debt, and the Two Hun-

dred Dollar Exemption Act. He died in 1851. Dr. Newell's mother, Amanda Loper, was a daughter of Judge W. Loper, who for over twenty-five years was an Associate Judge of the Court of Common Pleas of Salem County. His grandfather, James Newell, was for over thirty years engaged in successful ministerial labors in connection with the Methodist Church. He himself received his preliminary training at the Mount Holly Academy, and subsequently attended Princeton College for two years. Having made choice of the medical profession, he began study therefor, in 1856, under the direction of Dr. E. B. Richmond, of Millville, New Jersey, and in 1857 matriculated at Jefferson College, Philadelphia. From this institution he was graduated in 1859, and thereupon settled for practice in Millville. In this sphere of labor he remained until 1862, when he entered the United States service, as Surgeon of the 24th New Jersey Infantry. With this regiment he continued for nine months, when he became Brigade Surgeon (and Surgeon-in-Chief of Kimball's brigade). Subsequently he served as Surgeon-in-Chief of General French's division, Second Corps, Army of the Potomac. On returning to private practice he located at Salem, New Jersey, where he remained for one year. Then, by request, he settled once more in Millville. This was in the year 1864, and he has since been successfully engaged in the same field. He has won an excellent reputation as a skilful and judicious surgeon, and in all departments of the profession occupies a good position. He is a member of the Cumberland County District Medical Society, and was its President in 1875. His brethren sent him as a delegate to the American Medical Association in 1876. He was married, in 1869, to Sallie W. Maylin, daughter of E. W. Maylin, of Millville; she died, January 1st 1876.

HITAKER, JONATHAN S., M. D., Physician, of Millville, was born in Cedarville, Cumberland county, New Jersey, January 20th, 1823. On both paternal and maternal sides he comes from Cumberland county families, his parents, Thomas and Deborah (Sheppard) Whitaker, being natives of that section. He was educated at Claflin's High School, at Bridgeton, New Jersey, and received a thorough fundamental training. Attracted towards the profession of medicine, he began his studies in that science, in 1841, under the superintendence of Dr. Jacob W. Ludlam, at Deerfield, Cumberland county, New Jersey. Having prepared himself for a college course, he matriculated at Jefferson College in 1842, and, taking the full course, graduated in 1845. Upon receiving his diploma he located at Centreton, Salem county, where he engaged in an extensive and laborious practice for some nineteen years. In 1864 he removed to Millville, where he has since resided, and has secured a good practice. He is a skilful physician, and enjoys to the highest degree the respect and esteem of his professional brethren as well as of the community at large. In the medical associations he manifests an earnest interest; he is a member of the Cumberland County Medical Society, and in the present year (1876) was a delegate to the New Jersey State Medical Association. He was married in 1856 to Mary S. Johnson, of Salem county.

RANE, JOB SYMMES, M. D., Physician in the city of Elizabeth, was born, April 23d, 1825, in the town where he now resides. His parents were Job and Mary B. (Woodruff) Crane, both natives of Elizabeth. The family of which he is a representative is an ancient and honorable one. His ancestor, Ralph Crane, accompanied Sir Francis Drake from England to America in 1577. Another ancestor, Sir Robert Crane, belonged to the first company which came to Massachusetts Bay in 1630. His home was in Essex, England. The first resident representative of the family in this country was Stephen Crane, who was born in 1619, and probably came to America from England in 1640. He died there in 1710, and during his life held a number of high offices in church and state. Among other public duties he was chosen, in 1743, to go to England and lay a petition before the king. Job Symmes Crane is the great-great-great-grandson of this distinguished citizen. His early education was obtained at the justly celebrated classical school of Mr. James G. Nuttman, and when he had reached the age of fifteen he entered Princeton College, from which institution he graduated in 1843. After leaving college he taught school for a period of two years and a half at the seminary of S. E. and S. G. Woodbridge, at Perth Amboy. In the meantime he had decided to adopt the medical profession, and at the conclusion of his term of teaching he began with spirit and assiduity the necessary preliminary studies. In due time he entered as a student at the College of Physicians and Surgeons in New York, and in the year 1849 he graduated from the college and received his diploma. He at once returned to Elizabeth, and there commenced the practice of his profession, having been invited to enter into a copartnership with his former preceptor, Dr. George R. Chetwood. He possessed eminent natural qualifications for attaining success in his profession, and his acquired knowledge and practical skill were already great. Hence his progress toward success was rapid, and he speedily attained a large and lucrative practice. He rose rapidly to a high and universally acknowledged rank, and now enjoys the honorable distinction of being one of the leaders of the profession in the community where he resides. For five years after entering upon practice he was associated in partnership with Dr. Chetwood. Later he was associated, for a period of seven years, with Dr. James S. Green. He is a member of the New

Jersey State Medical Society, and was a member also of the Essex County Medical Society, until the formation of the Union County Medical Association. He was President of the last-named society during the second year of its organization. He was married, March 8th, 1854, to Helen B. Watkins, a native of Albany, New York.

UHL, RICHARD S., Lawyer, of Flemington, was born near that place, August 24th, 1839, and is the son of Leonard P. Kuhl, a farmer of Hunterdon county, New Jersey, who was a prominent man in the management of both township and county affairs, and held a number of offices of trust and responsibility. He graduated at Lawrenceville in the year 1860, and in 1861 he entered the law office of B. Van Syckel, Esq., now one of the judges of the New Jersey Supreme Court. He remained here as a student for four years, and was admitted to the bar as an attorney in 1865. He at once commenced the practice of law in Flemington, and was admitted counsellor in 1868. His progress in his profession was rapid, and he soon took rank as one of the leading lawyers of the county. He is a fine and effective speaker, and his management of a case is marked by much ability and skill. He was one of the counsel for the defence in the case of the Pattenburg rioters, a case which attracted much attention a few years since. For a long time he was Secretary of the Hunterdon County Agricultural Society. He has always been prominent in every movement of his town, social, moral, or financial. Politically he acted with the Republican party up to the time when the Liberal Republican movement was inaugurated. Being a warm admirer of Mr. Greeley, he took an active part in his support during his campaign for the Presidency. After that time he gave but little attention to politics, until the Presidential campaign of 1876, when he took an active part with the Democratic party in support of Mr. Tilden.

RELINGHUYSEN, GENERAL FREDERICK, Lawyer, Soldier and Statesman, late of New Brunswick, was born, April 13th, 1753, in Somerset county, New Jersey. He was a son of the Rev. Theodorus Frelinghuysen, a devoted minister of the Reformed Dutch Church, who came from Holland to America in 1720, and preached the gospel in the counties of Somerset, Middlesex and Huntingdon. He received an excellent education and subsequently studied law, being admitted about the time of his attaining the age of twenty-one years. When only twenty-two he was sent by the representatives of the colony of New Jersey as a Delegate to the Continental Congress, which position he resigned in 1777, as appears by a curious letter which he addressed to Colonel Camp, in which he pleads his youth and inexperience in affairs of State as one reason for his withdrawal, in order that an older and more expert individual might be substituted in his place. Returning home he seems to have been instrumental in raising a corps of artillery,.of which he was named Captain, and which volunteered their services to the Continental Congress for a year. During the recesses of Congress, while then a member, and also subsequently, he was in active service, and participated in the battles of Trenton and Monmouth ; and throughout the war was continually engaged, being Colonel of the militia of his native county of Somerset. In 1793, after repeatedly receiving the testimonials of public confidence in various State and county offices, he was elected by the Legislature a Senator of the United States. He continued in that station until domestic bereavements and the claims of his family constrained him to resign in 1796. In the Western Expedition, as was then termed the military force sent into western Pennsylvania to quell the uprising of the people in the notorious " Whisky Insurrection," he was selected by the commander-in-chief to the command, as Major-General, of the New Jersey and Pennsylvania troops. As a civilian he stood in the front rank at the bar of New Jersey, and he died beloved and lamented by his children and friends, leaving to the former the rich legacy of a life unsullied and which had ever abounded in benevolence and usefulness. On the monument erected by his children over his remains, his virtues are recorded in touching language, of which the following is an extract : " At the bar he was eloquent, in the Senate he was wise, in the field he was brave. Candid, generous and just, he was ardent in his friendships, constant to his friends, the patron and protector of honorable merit ; he gave his hand to the young, his counsel to the middle-aged, his support to him who was feeble in years." He died on his fifty-first birthday, April 13th, 1804, and left three sons, John, Frederick and Theodore ; a biographical sketch of the latter will be found hereafter.

FRELINGHUYSEN, HON. THEODORE, Lawyer, United States Senator, and candidate for the Vice-Presidency on the ticket with Hon. Henry Clay, was born in New Brunswick in 1787. He sprang from Dutch ancestry. His grandfather, Rev. John Frelinghuysen, came to the United States from Holland in 1720; and ministered for more than a quarter of a century to the Dutch settlers in Somerset and Middlesex counties. His grandmother, the daughter of a rich merchant of Amsterdam, was a woman of superior intellect, strong will, and devoted piety. His father, Frederick Frelinghuysen, educated at Princeton, was a distinguished lawyer and a member of the Provincial and Continental Congress. He fought during the Revolution ; was a Captain of artillery in the battle with the Hessians at Tren-

ton, and a Colonel of militia in several subsequent engagements with the enemy. In 1793 he was elected Senator of the United States, but resigned in 1796. During Washington's administration he commanded, as Major-General, a portion of the army sent into western Pennsylvania to quell the " Whisky Insurrection." He died in 1804. Theodore graduated at Princeton in that year, and choosing to be a lawyer, studied law with Richard Stockton, and was admitted to the bar in 1808. He followed the profession until 1839, and achieved large success. His attention was always fully occupied, and he was engaged in most of the leading causes of his day. In 1817 he was elected by the Legislature in joint convention, a majority of which differed from him in politics, Attorney-General of the State, and was re-elected, holding the office until elected to the Senate of the United States in 1829. Prior to this, in the year 1826, he had been elected one of the Judges of the Supreme Court of the State, but he had declined the position. As a counsellor, his rapid, correct and comprehensive mind, and exceptionally good judgment, made him very safe, while the same qualities, combined with a most magnetic, persuasive manner as a speaker, won him success as an advocate. In the prosecution of his professional duties, he was always governed by the highest sense of honor and right, never permitting himself to become the advocate of wrong, nor to press for a conviction in a criminal cause, even when public prosecutor, unless the case was reasonably clear of doubt. As a Senator he exercised a powerful influence. His voice was always heard in the Senate chamber on the right side of all questions partaking of a religious or moral character, and he always exerted his best powers for the promotion of all measures which in his judgment were calculated to advance the best interests of the nation. The high integrity of his character and the unquestionable purity of his motives, in connection with his ability, invested him with much power in Washington ; indeed, it is generally conceded that no one man of his day exercised a larger personal influence in the national capital. Early in 1839 he was chosen Chancellor of the University of New York, and after considerable hesitation he accepted the position and removed to New York city. He was moved towards acceptance and the relinquishment of his profession, which that step involved, by the great and growing repugnance he felt to the conflicts of a lawyer, especially in the ability of causes involving disputed facts. In 1844 he was chosen by the Whig party as their candidate for Vice-President, with Mr. Clay, then the great leader of the party, as the candidate for the Presidency. When eventually slavery became the great issue of the day, and the Republican party came into existence, Mr. Frelinghuysen gave it his earnest support. He had never been a pronounced abolitionist, but he heartily disapproved of the system of slavery, and up to the time of his death always did his utmost to prevent it dissolving the Union, and extended his most powerful efforts for the preservation of the nation. It was not permitted him to witness the final triumph of right, but his descendants can regard with pride the part he took in making that triumph possible. In the year 1850 he was chosen President of Rutgers College, and removed to New Brunswick, where he passed his remaining days. His management of this institution was able and judicious, and he was very much beloved by the students. He was a man of deep and earnest piety, and felt at various times in his career strongly drawn towards the ministry of the gospel. By the advice of his friends, however, he continued in his profession, where his spotless integrity and unostentatious piety exercised a powerful influence for good. In religious movements he always manifested an earnest interest, and he labored in a conspicuous post in connection with two great instruments for the promotion of religion, being chosen in 1841 President of the American Board of Commissioners for Foreign Missions, and in 1846 President of the American Bible Society. He died in 1862, at the age of seventy-five years, after a life of singular distinction and usefulness.

AYS, THOMAS, Lawyer, of Newton, Sussex county, New Jersey, was born, October 15th, 1829, in Lafayette township, Sussex county, New Jersey, and is a son of Thomas and Mary (Bale) Kays, both of whom were also natives of New Jersey. His father was a manufacturer by avocation, and died in 1830, leaving a small estate. The subject of this sketch received only a common school education, and when sixteen years of age commenced to learn the trade of pattern-maker, and millwright. He duly served his time until he attained his majority, and became thoroughly versed in all the various details of the business. While learning his trade he spent all his leisure time in study, and became thoroughly conversant with most of the higher branches of education, especially mathematics, and during the same time read law to some extent. In Pebruary, 1852, being then in his twenty-third year, he engaged in copartnership with Dr. Franklin Smith, at LaFayette, in the general foundry, machine and millwright business, in all its branches, and carried on a very heavy business until 1860, when he sold out his interest to his partner. He commenced regularly the study of law with Hon. Andrew J. Rogers, in 1858, and continued it under the preceptorship of Hon. Martin Ryerson and Mr. Rogers until the February term of the Supreme Court of New Jersey, 1863, when he was licensed as an attorney-at-law, and immediately formed a copartnership with Mr. Rogers, the firm being Rogers & Kays. The copartnership continued until April 1st, 1867, when it was dissolved, and he has since conducted the law business alone, having built up a very large and valuable practice. He was licensed as a counsellor-at-law at the February term of the Supreme Court in 1872, and is a master and examiner in chancery, and is also a special master of that court. He has always been a strong sup-

porter of the Democratic party and its principles, and at times active in politics. But he has devoted himself almost exclusively to his profession, and has never sought nor held any political office in the gift of the people. He is a member of the Board of Directors of the Sussex National Bank, of Newton, New Jersey, and was for several years the legal adviser of the Merchants' National Bank, of Newton. He was married, September 24th, 1857, to Amanda E. Slater, of LaFayette, New Jersey. His health became much impaired in 1869 from too close application to his profession, and he has continued to practise law since only by taking a great deal of outdoor exercise. He is naturally of a sturdy constitution and indomitable will, which have enabled him to rise by his own unaided exertions from comparative obscurity to a commanding position in his section of the State, and though in the later years his health has been enfeebled, his strong determination has to a great extent supplied the lack of physical strength.

AMESON, CHARLES MILLER, Journalist, was born in York, York county, Pennsylvania, in 1823. His grandfather, Dr. Horatio Jameson, emigrated to that locality from Scotland, before the revolutionary war, and became a surgeon in the American army. The father of the subject of this sketch, Dr. Thomas Jameson, was also a physician of prominence and extensive practice in York county. Charles, after attending the York County Academy, then under the direction of Rev. Stephen Boyer, entered Marshall College, then located at Mercersburg, in the year 1845, and graduated with the class of 1849. He remained two years in the Theological Seminary, connected with the German Reformed Church, and affiliated with the college, when he was licensed to preach by the Synod of the above-mentioned church, then holding its sessions at Martinsburg, Virginia. Soon after he received a call from a Reformed congregation in Taneytown, Maryland, to become its pastor, which he accepted, and settled in that State. Here he remained but a short time, having received and accepted a call to the Fiftieth Street Reformed Dutch Church, New York. In that charge he remained about twelve years. During the year 1862 he resigned his pastoral charge and purchased a finely-situated farm in Hillsborough township, near Somerville, Somerset county, New Jersey. Upon this farm he took up his residence, and devoted himself to agriculture, at the same time contributing considerably to the press. Latterly he has been writing most of the leading editorials of the *Somerset Messenger,* organ of the Democratic party in Somerset county. In March, 1876, he purchased the *Messenger,* and assumed entire editorial and financial control of the journal, which promises to become even more prosperous than of yore under his able direction. He is a Democrat of the most pronounced type, and with his paper has wielded signal service to the party cause. Well informed upon all current topics, a scholar of large attainments, and a man of well-defined individuality, he not only handles a subject easily and forcibly, but also boldly, impressing his views with weight upon his readers. Socially he is a genial, kind-hearted man, and a very fluent and pleasant conversationalist. He was married in 1857 to Ann Eliza Meserole, of Greenpoint, Long Island.

———◦◦◦———

OWELL, THEODORE P., Leather Manufacturer, of Newark, was born, January 6th, 1819, at Suckasunny Plains, Morris county, New Jersey, and is a son of the late Jacob Drake Howell, an officer in the United States army, who died in 1826, and whose widow still survives at the advanced age of eighty-six years. When young Howell was about nine years of age, he went to Newark, where his uncle, Samuel M. Howell, resided, who received him into his family, and by whom he was reared. He attended school in the academy of Stephen R. Grover, and there acquired a fair English education. Having concluded his studies, he became desirous of learning his uncle's trade, that of tanner and currier, and accordingly entered it as apprentice. He began at the very foot of the ladder, so that he might learn the business thoroughly. In that establishment he acquired a practical knowledge of the trade in all its details, and this thorough acquaintance with its every branch has been the secret of his great success through his long career as a manufacturer. When he attained his majority his uncle admitted him as a partner in the business, under the firm-name and style of S. M. & T. P. Howell, the concern being then located at the corner of Market and Washington streets; and they commenced the manufacture of patent leather on a very small scale. This article is a German invention, and was first made about a century ago. It was soon after introduced into France and England, and first made its appearance in America in 1828, the pioneer being Seth Boyden, of Newark. In 1848 the buildings of the firm having been destroyed by fire, the new establishment was located on the site of the present works, then outside the city limits and surrounded by fields. At the present time there is a larger population beyond it than the whole city then contained. The capacity of the works was considerably larger than the one first inaugurated, and from the amount of forty hides per week, the product has gained to the immense proportion of five thousand in the same space of time. In the new location the firm conducted the business with remarkable success, in connection with other partners admitted from time to time until August, 1855, when the present company was organized, and which consists, in addition to Theodore P. Howell, and his two sons, Henry C. and Samuel C. Howell, of Abraham R. Van Nest, of New York city, an old and successful merchant, who is

president of the organization; Peter Hayden, whose reputation is known throughout the country; Austin Jenkins, one of the leading merchants of Baltimore, now retired from business; and Pollock Wilson, of Cincinnati, all of whom have long been recognized as the leading saddlery hardware men of the United States. Since the company organized, the business has been ever on the increase; new buildings have been erected, and all the novel and improved machinery which from time to time has been invented has been added as required, until, in this Centennial year of the nation, the establishment ranks as one of the largest and finest on the continent, and in the production of its leading specialty, patent leather, is the largest in the world. Many of the prominent leather manufacturers of Newark have learned the business with this company. The works in Newark cover six acres of ground, and manufacture principally the patent and enamelled leather of twenty different varieties and classifications. There are also produced roans, linings, many varieties of harness leather, military buff leather of extraordinary endurance, being tanned with pure cod-liver oil, as are also the buck-skins; and the manufacture of wool mats is a specialty, being sheep-skins with the wool left upon them. A branch manufactory has been established at Middletown, Orange county, New York, which covers two acres, and is designed for the production of boot and shoe leathers, as also for Russia and pocket-book leathers. In addition to these hives of industry, a slaughtering-house has been in operation in New York city for some time, and requires seven city lots for its area. This branch is conducted solely for the purpose of having the skinning done promptly and the hides free from those cuts which arise from the carelessness of workmen. The cattle are not purchased, but simply killed for the wholesale butchers, the hides being retained at their value. The total number of skins used by the company in the course of a year amounts in round numbers to a quarter of a million, one-fifth of these being cattle hides, and the remainder of calf, sheep and deer skins. During all these years the present senior member of the company, Theodore P. Howell, has led a life of untiring industry, devoting the early morning hours to the vast business details, and suffering nothing to interfere with his constant supervision of the manufactory. Nothing bearing directly or indirectly upon this, his life-long study, has been neglected or omitted. He has twice visited Europe to investigate the markets and methods of England and Germany, and thus has familiarized himself with the hide and cattle markets of the world, as well as the modes of manufacture and the qualities of their products; so that he might not only imitate, but improve upon their manner of fabrication. This persistency of observation has resulted in the superior excellence of the goods furnished at his establishment; and his brand of skins is recognized throughout the country as strictly of the first class. Although this great devotion to his private business has been so systematically carried out, yet he has spared time to interest himself in

American Publishing & Engraving Co. New York

Thos. P. Howell

Isaiah Rolfe

promoters for the establishment of the plank road, over which his wagons now daily travel with the goods from his warehouse direct to their destination, thus saving the many expenses attendant upon railway transfer. He has also assisted in the establishment of banks, insurance companies, and other commercial institutions, and was also among those who originated the New York & Newark Railroad, and labored ardently until it was a fixed fact in being a direct route to the great city on the Hudson. He is at the present time a Director of the Mutual Benefit Life Insurance Company, the American Mutual Fire Insurance Company, the Mechanics' Bank, and the Howard Savings Bank.

able to recuperate, and so surmount these difficulties and build up a successful business of twenty years' standing. His political proclivities have been in favor of Republican principles, and in 1870 he was chosen by that party as a candidate for Alderman, and served in that capacity for two terms, or four years, being elected in 1872. In April, 1874, he was elected Mayor of the city of New Brunswick, and in the spring of 1876. In the fall of the same year he was chosen to the Legislature. He was married December, 1832, to Charlotte Mead, of New Jersey.

----—◦•◦—----

OLFE, HON. ISAIAH, Lumber Merchant, Builder, Contractor, and Mayor of New Brunswick, was born, 1809, in the township of South Amboy, Middlesex county, New Jersey, and is the son of Phineas and Sarah (Martin) Wolfe, both of whom were natives of New Jersey. His father, many years since, was captain of one of the packets which were used to convey passengers from Amboy to New York, before the era of railroads, and who were wont to make the journey by stages from Bordentown, which at that time was the terminal point of the steamboats from Philadelphia. Isaiah received his education in the common schools of the day, and when seventeen years of age, went to New Brunswick, where he learned the trade of a carpenter. He labored at this craft until he attained his majority, and becoming dissatisfied with the few opportunities afforded in a country town, repaired to New York in 1831, in order to secure a good position in what he believed to be a larger field of labor; and he remained there until the following summer, when, upon the breaking out of the cholera in 1832, he returned to New Brunswick, and remained three

ILSON, DANIEL M., late of Newark, an eminent citizen and philanthropist, was born, 1803, and in his early life was engaged in mercantile pursuits in New York city, by which he acquired an ample fortune. On his retirement from business, he became a resident of Newark, New Jersey, and from that time identified himself with all of its important interests. He was one of the most active citizens in urging the plank road constructed between Newark and Jersey City, and was the President of the company from its formation. He was also a Director of several financial institutions, and President of the Republican Trust Company, of Newark, from its organization. He was for several years President of the American and Foreign Bible Society, and held other important offices connected with the Baptist denomination. He was also President of the Peddie Classical and Scientific Institute, at Hightstown, to which he was a large contributor. He died at Newark, January 18th, 1873.

----—◦•◦—----

ARMAN, DAVID, M. D., Physician, of Trenton, was born in Franklin township, Warren county,

other matters which have tended to the welfare and progress of the city where he resides. He early recognized the necessity of an improved method of communication with New York city, and was among the earliest supporters and promoters for the establishment of the plank road, over which his wagons now daily travel with the goods from his warehouse direct to their destination, thus saving the many expenses attendant upon railway transfer. He has also assisted in the establishment of banks, insurance companies, and other commercial institutions, and was also among those who originated the New York & Newark Railroad, and labored ardently until it was a fixed fact in being a direct route to the great city on the Hudson. He is at the present time a Director of the Mutual Benefit Life Insurance Company, the American Mutual Fire Insurance Company, the Mechanics' Bank, and the Howard Savings Bank.

OLFE, HON. ISAIAH, Lumber Merchant, Builder, Contractor, and Mayor of New Brunswick, was born, 1809, in the township of South Amboy, Middlesex county, New Jersey, and is the son of Phineas and Sarah (Martin) Rolfe, both of whom were natives of New Jersey. His father, many years since, was captain of one of the packets which were used to convey passengers from Amboy to New York, before the era of railroads, and who were obliged to make the journey by stages from Bordentown, which at that time was the terminal point of the steamboats from Philadelphia. Isaiah received his education in the common schools of the day, and when seventeen years of age went to New Brunswick, where he learned the trade of a carpenter. He labored at this craft until he attained his majority, and becoming dissatisfied with the few opportunities afforded in a country town, repaired to New York in 1831, in order to secure a good position in what he believed to be a larger field of labor; and he remained there until the following summer, when, upon the breaking out of the cholera in 1832, he returned to New Brunswick, and remained three years. Shortly after this, in 1836, he went to Newark, at that period rapidly growing in importance; and for two years thereafter he successfully plied his vocation. With the year 1837 came the celebrated period of financial distress, which overspread the entire country. Returning once more to New Brunswick, he bided his time, and when more prosperous times dawned upon the country, he effected favorable engagements, and resumed his avocation as carpenter, contractor and builder. He continued in this calling until 1853 with encouraging success; and during the latter part of that year became interested in the lumber business, in which he has since continued. Although he has met with many reverses, yet he has, by his energy and indomitable perseverance, surmounted all the disasters that have befallen him. Between 1837 and 1865 he suffered loss by fire on

20

three separate occasions, and once had his business almost ruined by an inundation; in addition to all this, in 1835 a tornado almost demolished a building which he had nearly completed. Although a sufferer by these losses, he was able to recuperate, and so surmount these difficulties and build up a successful business of twenty years' standing. His political proclivities have been in favor of Republican principles, and in 1870 he was chosen by that party as a candidate for Alderman, and served in that capacity for two terms, or four years, being elected in 1872. In April, 1874, he was elected Mayor of the city of New Brunswick, and in the spring of 1876. In the fall of the same year he was chosen to the Legislature. He was married December, 1832, to Charlotte Mead, of New Jersey.

ILSON, DANIEL M., late of Newark, an eminent citizen and philanthropist, was born, 1803, and in his early life was engaged in mercantile pursuits in New York city, by which he acquired an ample fortune. On his retirement from business, he became a resident of Newark, New Jersey, and from that time identified himself with all of its important interests. He was one of the most active citizens in having the plank road constructed between Newark and Jersey City, and was the President of the company from its formation. He was also a Director of several financial institutions, and President of the Republican Trust Company, of Newark, from its organization. He was for several years President of the American and Foreign Bible Society, and held other important offices connected with the Baptist denomination. He was also President of the Peddie Classical and Scientific Institute, at Hightstown, to which he was a large contributor. He died at Newark, January 18th, 1873.

ARMAN, DAVID, M. D., Physician, of Trenton, was born in Franklin township, Warren county, New Jersey, January 29th, 1836. He is of English and German extraction. His parents were Thomas and Elizabeth (Frome) Warman, and his father was a farmer in Warren county. David obtained his early education in the schools of the district, and his classical education was completed at the academy at Belvidere, New Jersey. When about nineteen years of age he commenced teaching school, and continued so occupied for a term of four years. During this period he taught at Harker's Grove a while; also at Little York, and latterly at Harmony, all these localities being within the limits of his native county. Concluding to adopt the profession of medicine, he began his studies in 1859, under the direction of Dr. P. G. Creneling, of Broadway, Warren county. He matriculated at the College of Physicians and

Surgeons, New York, in 1860. At this institution he took one course; the succeeding one was taken at Bellevue Hospital Medical College, from which he was graduated in the spring of 1862. He was among the first graduates of that college. Upon receiving his diploma he settled for practice at Milford, New Jersey, but remained there only about six months. Then he removed to Morrisville, Bucks county, Pennsylvania, where he was engaged until the spring of 1864. At that time he entered the army as Contract Surgeon, and was stationed at Chesapeake Hospital, near Fortress Monroe. Here he was occupied busily from May, 1864, until November of that year, when he retired from the service, and settled down to private practice at Trenton. In this city he has since continued to reside, and has built up a good practice. To all movements designed to advance the best interests of the profession he has always contributed earnest support. He is a member of Mercer County District Medical Society, and in 1871 and 1872 served as its President. At various times he has been chosen as delegate to the New Jersey State Medical Society. He has acted as Secretary of the Trenton Medical Association since its organization, and much of its vitality is owing to his earnest labors on its behalf. In 1862 he was married to Rebecca F. Love, daughter of Rev. Robert Love, of Warren county, New Jersey, and sister of Dr. J. J. H. Love, of Montclair, Essex county, New Jersey.

ULLIVAN, GEORGE R., M. D., was born in Maryland in 1836, being the son of James T. Sullivan, and a grandson of William Sullivan, a native of Pennsylvania, who served with distinction in the revolutionary army. He studied at Newton University, pursuing a comprehensive course, and upon graduating from that institution commenced the study of medicine under the preceptorship of Professor Smith, of Baltimore, and in 1859 received his degree of M. D., from the Maryland Medical College. The year succeeding his graduation he passed in study and medical service in the Baltimore Hospital, securing there a fund of information which became invaluable when he had fully entered upon his professional duties as a practitioner. In 1860 he removed to Flemington, New Jersey, where he successfully labored as a physician until July, 1862, when he was called to the field as Assistant Surgeon of the 15th New Jersey Volunteers. He served with this command two years, passing through all the vicissitudes of one of the most trying campaigns of the great civil war, and embracing nearly all of the perils that visited the army in the Potomac and Shenandoah valleys. In 1864 he was appointed Surgeon of the 39th New Jersey Volunteers, and served with this command until peace was declared, and he was mustered out in June, 1865. Few surgeons rendered more continuous service in the army than Dr. Sullivan, and certainly

none more valuable. The rank and file became deeply attached to him for his intelligent and laborious efforts to save life and mitigate pain, and for his kindness, which was invariable. From the battle-fields of Virginia he returned to his home in Flemington, and resumed his professional duties which the war had interrupted. His practice is extensive, and his services as a consulting physician are frequently solicited from places remote from his home. He has rare ability as a surgeon, and has performed many of the most important operations which have claimed the attention of the profession in the State. He is a gentleman of fine social characteristics and progressive ideas, and manifests an active interest in the material as well as moral welfare of the community in which he makes his home.

 NGLISH, DAVID C., M. D., Physician, of New Brunswick, was born in that city, March 2d, 1842, and is a son of the late Dr. David C. and Henrietta (Green) English, both of whom were natives of New Jersey. The grandfather was also a physician, who devoted himself to the practice of medicine for many years at Englishtown. Young English received his education, first at the public school for two years, after that at one of the private schools until 1859, when he entered Rutgers College Grammar School with the intention of preparing for the college, during the same time spending his spare hours in his father's store (his father being a druggist and practising physician), acquiring a knowledge of medicines. In the summer of 1862 Dr. C. T. Murrogh, of the same place, made a proposition to young English to enter his office as pharmacist and take up the study of medicine. The proposition was favorably received by him, the college course of study for which he was then prepared was with regret abandoned, and he entered Dr. Morrogh's office the same week, where he was engaged for some time. Subsequently he attended a three years' course of study in the College of Physicians and Surgeons, in New York city, and graduated from that institution in March, 1868, with the degree of Doctor of Medicine. For a few months thereafter he was associated with his preceptor, and then commenced to practise his profession on his own account, and has ever since been actively engaged in his native city. On two separate occasions, during Dr. Morrogh's absence in Europe, he assumed charge of his practice. He has been an active member of the Middlesex County Medical Society, having been its President one year, its Reporter to the State Society three years, and is now its Treasurer, having also several times been one of its delegates to the State Society. He was elected by the State Society a delegate to the American Medical Association in 1870 and again in 1873. He was also a delegate to the same at its session in Philadelphia, 1876, from the county society. He was for three years Vice-President of the

New Jersey Microscopical Society. He was elected an Alderman from the Third Ward of the city, and served two years in that body, 1866 and 1867. This is the only political office he has held, all his time that could be spared from his professional engagements having been mostly given to the various benevolent and religious organizations in the city, with many of which he has been identified. He is a member of the First Presbyterian Church, and one of its elders. He was for three years President of the Young Men's Christian Association of New Brunswick, and has several times represented it in the International Young Men's Christian Association Convention, at the meeting of which body in 1875, at Richmond, Virginia, he was elected one of its Vice-Presidents. He is a Director in the Union and also New Brunswick Building Loan Associations. He was married, September 14th, 1870, to Susie C., daughter of Harrison Blake, for many years a prominent lawyer of Cumberland county, Maine, now resident at New Brunswick.

ACKSON JOHN P., late Vice-President and Superintendent of the New Jersey Railroad and Transportation Company, was born, 1805, in New Jersey. He was educated for the bar, and held a high position in the legal profession. He was on two several occasions elected to the State Legislature, and was twice elected Clerk of the County of Essex, a very lucrative office. After his election by the Directors of the New Jersey Railroad as the Superintendent of the Company, he abandoned all participation in the pursuits of political life, and devoted all his energies and thoughts to its service. He was connected with the company from its very organization until the close of his life. He was distinguished for his benevolence and charity, as well as for integrity of character and honesty of purpose. He died at Newark, December 10th, 1861.

OB, ARCHIBALD F., President of the Central National Bank of Hightstown, New Jersey, was born in that town, March 15th, 1831, and is the son of the late Richard M. and Mary F. (Wilson) Job, both of whom were also natives of New Jersey. He is a great-grandson of Peter Job, an officer in the war of the Revolution, who was a participant in the battle of Princeton, and was taken prisoner by the British there, but managed to effect his escape on his horse, and reached his home near Cranberry; and thence returned to the American forces. He was afterwards present at the battle of Monmouth, where he was an aide-de-camp on the staff of General Washington. He returned home after the close of the war and lived many years. Richard M. Job,

father of Archibald, was for many years a prominent miller at Hightstown; the latter part of his life was devoted to agricultural pursuits; he died October 26th, 1874. Archibald's mother was the daughter of Dr. Enoch Wilson, of Hightstown. His rudimentary education was obtained in the common schools of the district, but he afterwards became a pupil in the select school of O. R. Willis, in his native town. When nineteen years old he left school and commenced learning the milling business with his father, and three years after, when twenty-two years of age, his father associated with him under the firm-name of R. M. Job & Son, which they carried on successfully until 1865, when he disposed of his interest in the business and engaged in agricultural pursuits on the farm where he now resides. In June, 1872, he was elected President of the Central National Bank of Hightstown, which position he has continued to hold until the present time. He was married, February 15th, 1854, to Ann Eliza Perrin, who died, January 5th, 1856. He again married, August 17th, 1865, Martha M. Oakley, of Saratoga county, New York, daughter of William J. Oakley, of Middletown, in that State.

ROST, BARTLETT C., Lawyer, of Philipsburg, was born, March 17th, 1833, in the town of Leeds, Androscoggin county, Maine, and is a son of Oliver P. Frost. His family is of English descent, and was among the early settlers of New England. His preliminary education was obtained in the schools of his native town, and when he reached the age of eighteen years, himself became a teacher, which avocation he pursued for some time, and then completed his studies at the Maine Wesleyan University. In 1854 he removed to New Jersey, and recommenced teaching, first at Clarksville, and afterwards at Springtown. Having resolved to devote himself to the profession of the law, he entered the law department of the University at Albany, New York, and also became a student in the office of Peckham & Tremain, and in 1859 was admitted to practise at the New York bar. His name having already been registered in New Jersey as a student-at-law, he returned thither, continued his readings, and in 1860 was licensed as an attorney in that State. He immediately entered upon the practice of his profession at Philipsburg, Warren county, and has met with marked success in building up a large and lucrative business, which extends to all the courts in the State; and for two years was corporation counsel. He is a hard student, and manages his cases with marked ability. In politics he is a Republican, but in 1872 was a liberal Republican and an earnest supporter of Horace Greeley. He was married in 1874 to Mary L. Stockton, of Easton, Pennsylvania, a lady of accomplishment and highly esteemed.

ATHERTON, GEORGE P., Professor of History, Political Economy and Constitutional Law in Rutgers College, New Brunswick, was born, June 20th, 1837, in the town of Boxford, Essex county, Massachusetts, of New England parentage. His father died when he was but twelve years of age, leaving his family in straitened circumstances, and young Atherton obtained work in a cotton-mill, whereby he earned a living for himself, beside affording some support for his mother and young sisters. A few years afterwards he was employed on a farm, where he continued for several years. Meanwhile, when about seventeen years of age, he formed a purpose to obtain a college education, and through the practice of much economy and self-denial obtained enough means to enable him to attend the village academy during the winter, while he labored upon the farm the balance of the year. By incessant application he gained sufficient knowledge to enable himself to become an educator of youth, and secured a position in a district school in New Hampshire for the usual term of eight weeks. His teaching was so successful that when the session was concluded he was invited to remain for nine weeks longer, a private subscription being raised for the purpose. When this extra term ended he had saved sufficient means to enable him to enter Phillips Academy, at Exeter, where he pursued the studies requisite in entering a college, devoting a portion of his time during the winter season in teaching district schools. After thus obtaining his preparatory education, he was appointed a teacher in the celebrated Albany Academy, where he taught with great acceptance for eighteen months, and thus secured means enough to enter college. He matriculated in Yale College, New Haven, in 1860, becoming a member of the sophomore class, and continued through that year and a part of the junior year. During that period the great rebellion had broken out which threatened to destroy the Union, and he felt it to be his duty to be one of the defenders of the flag and of the country. Having explained his purpose to President Woolsey, of Yale, the latter approved of his patriotic course, and consented to his withdrawal from college for a season. He also wrote him an introductory letter to Governor Buckingham, of Connecticut, and the latter, after making proper inquiry, gave him a Lieutenant's commission in the 10th Regiment Connecticut Volunteers. His regiment was assigned to the celebrated Burnside expedition against the rebel positions in North Carolina, and did valiant service in the battles of Roanoke Island, Newbern, etc., in which engagements he participated and commanded the company in the absence of the captain. Immediately after the battle of Newbern he was promoted to the rank of Captain, and served in that capacity for several months, his regiment being engaged only in camp and picket duty during that time. Finding that there was no prospect of active service, he resigned and returned to college. In December, 1862, his regiment was ordered to join the expedition against Charleston, and he again joined his old regiment; the Governor of Connecticut, at the written request of the field and line officers, recommissioned him as First Lieutenant and then as Captain, in which capacity he again entered into the arduous duty of army life and the swamps surrounding the cradle of the rebellion. The malarial fever in time prostrated him, which was followed in turn by the typhoid, and so prostrated his otherwise vigorous constitution that, in accordance with the advice of his physicians, he was again compelled to resign from the army, much against his wishes. Returning to the North, he recuperated sufficiently to enable him to resume his studies once more, and graduated at Yale College. He was afterwards appointed a professor in the Albany Academy, where he remained for three years, and then accepted a professorship in St. John's College, Annapolis, Maryland. He passed about eighteen months in that institution, when he accepted a call to the State University, at Champaign, Illinois, where he also filled the chair as professor. In 1868, through the influence of Professor David Murray, who had made his acquaintance at the Albany Academy, and knew his capacity as an instructor, he was invited to become a professor in Rutgers College, New Brunswick. After much persuasion on the part of his Eastern friends and opposition from his Western associates, he finally accepted the position in Rutgers as Professor of History, Political Economy and Constitutional Law. This was a new chair in the institution, and it is almost needless to say that he has filled it to the entire satisfaction of the trustees, faculty and students of the college. He has not only performed the duties incident to that particular chair, but has been active in all that pertains to the welfare of the institution. He has been repeatedly invited to return to institutions with which he has formerly been connected, besides being offered the Presidency of the Howard and one or more other universities, all of which he has declined, as the duties of his present position are congenial to his mind, besides being otherwise satisfactory to him. In the year 1875 charges of fraud were made in regard to the administration of affairs at the Red Cloud Indian Agency, in Dakota, and three commissioners were appointed by President Grant and three others by the Board of Indian Commissioners to investigate matters. Several distinguished men of both political parties were members of this commission, and among them was Professor Atherton. The commission paid a personal visit to the Red Cloud Agency, and several posts in the Northwest which had transactions with it, and made a thorough investigation of all matters connected therewith. A full and exhaustive report, accompanied by the sworn testimony taken in the case, was made and published, filling a large volume. The commission found various abuses existing, which they detailed, and pointed out by name the persons who were incompetent and guilty, and recommended their discharge from the government service. Some of the more serious were not found to be substantiated by the facts, and corresponding recommendations were made. The report was laid before the Forty-fourth Congress, at its first session, for examination, and Hon. C. J. Faulkner, of Virginia, a member of the opposition, and one of the commissioners, went before the Committee on Indian Affairs and challenged them to go over the work again. The labors of the commission and the report cannot be assailed, as no other commission can go over the work again without arriving at the same conclusions. A large portion of the labor of this commission was performed by Professor Atherton, and the result arrived at as well as the report itself are a sufficient proof of his capabilities and his entire fairness. In all educational matters outside of his college he has been an earnest and active laborer. He is a member of several educational societies, national and State; has participated in several prominent discussions, and has delivered several addresses of great interest and value. He has likewise bestowed much attention on common school matters, and is a warm supporter of the common school system of New Jersey, thereby sympathizing with the masses in all that concerns their welfare. Since his residence in New Brunswick he has been active in every good work that has enlisted the sympathies of the citizens, and is universally respected by all classes of his fellow-townsmen. In the autumn of 1876 he was nominated by the Republican party of the Third Congressional District as their candidate for Representative in the popular branch of the Federal Legislature, and was unanimously indorsed not only by the partisan press of the district but by other journals in distant parts of the country where he had resided. It is a matter of regret that so able a man should have been defeated in the election of November, 1876, and, aside from partisan views, that one so thoroughly competent for the position should have lost the battle.

ARKER, CHARLES G., Brigadier-General, was born at Swedesboro, Gloucester county, New Jersey, in 1835. At an early age he was left an orphan, his father and mother following each other to the grave at a short interval. Some of the friends of the family and a few influential gentlemen took the lad's case in hand and obtained for him an appointment to a vacancy in West Point Military Academy. In this institution he remained for four years, being graduated with distinction in 1858. The class of that year was examined by a Board of Visitors, of which General Robert Anderson was a member. That distinguished officer was much attracted by the bearing and attainments of young Harker, and declared him to be a model of a soldier, and one who would distinguish himself should opportunity offer. He entered the United States army as a Brevet Second Lieutenant of the 2d Infantry, July 1st, 1858, and on August 15th of the same year was promoted to a full Second Lieutenancy. At that time the regiment was engaged on frontier duty; he at once joined it, and served in the command until the summer of 1861. Then he was detailed for special duty at a school of instruction for volunteers in Ohio. So well did he acquit himself in this sphere that he was offered the Colonelcy of the 65th Ohio Regiment, and the permission necessary for its acceptance was given by the Secretary of War. About the same time he was promoted to be Captain in the regular army. On assuming command of the 65th he joined General Buell's Army of the Ohio, and assisted in constructing the military road in eastern Kentucky; participated in the battle of Shiloh and siege of Corinth, and commanded a brigade of the force that drove Bragg beyond the boundaries of Kehtucky. Subsequently, with his brigade, he was attached to General Rosecrans' Army of the Cumberland, and distinguished himself so remarkably at the battle of Stone River that his superior officer recommended his promotion to a Brigadier-Generalship; this recommendation was, however, not then complied with. At the close of the campaign he was granted leave of absence for twenty days, and devoted this period of rest to a visit to his home in New Jersey. To his friends he expressed an earnest desire to take service with the troops of his native State, of whose achievements on behalf of the national cause in the field and in the council chamber he displayed great pride. He would not consent, however, that any efforts should be put forth by his friends to have him promoted and transferred, preferring to sink his personal wishes and to do his duty cheerfully in whatever position he might be employed. His short leave, and it was the only one he obtained during the war, expired, he rejoined his brigade, assuming command as ranking Colonel, and participated in all the operations of the Tennessee campaign. At Chickamauga he made himself a brilliant record under General Thomas, and received credit as largely instrumental with that officer in saving the army. At the critical moment of the conflict his command, sustained in magnificent *morale* by his coolness and soldierly bearing, stood immovable, and repelled, though with heavy loss, every assault of the enemy. The qualities displayed by the young commander in this battle are described by an eye-witness as of the very highest order, as positively heroic. While he did not spare himself in the slightest degree, and had two horses shot under him, he escaped all personal injury, seeming to bear a charmed life. Upon this engagement followed a second and far stronger recommendation for his promotion, and this time the voice of his superior officers could not be disregarded, he received his commission as Brigadier, to date from the battle of Chickamauga. He was engaged in the battles of Mission Ridge and Resaca, on May 7th and 14th respectively, and in each he had a horse shot under him and sustained slight wounds. Writing to a friend after the latter fight, while on the march, near Kingston, Georgia, May 22d, 1864, he says: "You are aware that the great Southwestern campaign under General Sherman is in progress. Thus far we have had several quite severe engagements, in which we have been entirely victorious. In the battle of Resaca, on the 14th instant, I was wounded, though not dangerously. I was struck on the leg by a shell, which exploded immediately after passing me, wounding General Manson and killing my own horse and that of one of my orderlies. It was quite a narrow escape for me. My leg, though slightly cut and painfully bruised, is doing well. I did not leave the field, though unable to exercise full command, for about thirty-six hours. You and my family will be glad to learn that I can walk and ride very well now. I am able to discharge all my duties, and hope to be able to conduct my brave little command, which has so nobly stood by me in so many severe engagements, through the great struggle, or perhaps series of struggles, which will doubtless ensue before the fall of Atlanta. The result of the great battle before us cannot be doubted, though all of us cannot hope to witness the great triumph which must crown the efforts of our magnificent army." These last words would seem almost to have come to his mind in premonition of his own fate, so soon after did he fall while in the full tide of effort to promote the great triumph of which he then wrote. On June 27th, 1864, General Sherman's army assaulted the position of the enemy on Kenesaw mountain; General Harker commanded a leading column in the assault, and, while other generals were mostly dismounted, bestrode his charger, the better to manage his force. Advancing under the full range of the rebel fire, he became an especial target for the sharpshooters. All heedless of this danger, he rode gallantly hither and thither stimulating his men, until mortally wounded. He was carried to the rear, and soon expired, his last words being: "Have we taken the mountain?" Later on, his body was removed to New Jersey and buried in the neighborhood where he passed his early life. Of truly noble personal character, and possessed of a courage and gallantry springing from a rare sense of duty and love of country, he was also a soldier of the highest skill and ability. He was much beloved by his associates and the men of his command, over whom he exerted a powerful influence for good.

WILLIAMSON, NICHOLAS, A. M., M. D., Physician, of New Brunswick, was born, March 9th, 1845, in the city of New York, and is a son of Nicholas and Mary R. (Burlock) Williamson. His father was a native of the State of New York, and for many years was president of the Novelty Rubber Company, of New Brunswick; his mother was born in the island of St. Croix, West Indies. He was prepared at the select school of Professor Gustavus Fischer, in New Brunswick, for Rutgers College, which he entered in June, 1862. But in the autumn of that year he removed to New York, and became a clerk in the Novelty Rubber Company. At the end of three years he was elected the Secretary of the company, which position he still holds.

In 1869 he commenced his medical studies in New Brunswick under the preceptorship of Dr. H. R. Baldwin, and attended one course of lectures at the New York University, and subsequently two complete courses at the College of Physicians and Surgeons in that city, receiving a degree from the university in 1871, and his diploma from the College of Physicians and Surgeons in 1872. He commenced the practice of medicine with his preceptor, Dr. Baldwin, in May, 1871, with whom he was associated for five years. He is a member of the Middlesex County Medical Society, and was its President in 1876. During the same year he was the delegate from that body to the New Jersey State Medical Society. In May, 1875, he was appointed City Physician, and reappointed in 1876. He was married, April 9th, 1874, to Sarah, daughter of Professor George H. Cook, State Geologist.

BALBACH, EDWARD, Sr., Refiner of Precious Metals, of Newark, was born in Baden, Germany, March 19th, 1804. His early studies embraced chemistry, for which he evinced a special fondness, and on growing to manhood he became a refiner of precious metals. This business he prosecuted with moderate success in his native city for a number of years, but the control exercised by European governments over the refinement of ores trammelled the business and prevented its being largely extended. Moreover, Edward Balbach was strongly republican in his views and principles, and for a long time entertained the thought of removing to America. In 1848, when he was forty-four years of age, this idea became a fixed purpose, and he came to this country on a prospecting tour. He was not influenced by the wild stories of great gold discoveries in California, which were beginning to be heard; he thought only of transplanting his business just as he had conducted it at home. With this purpose in view, he was more favorably impressed with Newark, New Jersey, than any other place he visited. Newark was then a city of 35,000 inhabitants, and the manufacture of jewelry was a leading interest. The "sweepings" of the jewelry establishments he ascertained were purchased by speculators, who sent them to Europe to be smelted. The smelting of these sweepings would be a largely remunerative business; he could purchase property cheaply in Newark; the city itself was practically, for his business, a suburb of New York, and it was also convenient to the trade of Philadelphia and Baltimore; and, moreover, the Newark manufacturers would gladly welcome a skilled and reliable man among them, who would rescue them from the spoiling of the speculators. He determined to locate himself in Newark, but hardly had he so decided when he received news that his brother and his brother's wife had both fallen victims to an epidemic, leaving eight orphan children. With characteristic generosity, he at once returned to Europe and adopted

E. Balbach Sr

these eight children as his own. Having done this he came back to Newark, and there, in 1850, erected the first building of what are now the extensive smelting works that have become so famous. He commenced the smelting of jewelers' sweepings. His was the only establishment of the kind in the country; he speedily won the confidence of the trade, and his business grew with great rapidity. His reputation extended, and he received consignments from New York, Philadelphia and other cities. His machinery and buildings had to be increased. Then other demands were made upon his skill and resources; lead from a new mine in New York, and from an old mine reopened in Pennsylvania was sent to him to be smelted. His reputation extended to foreign lands, and in 1861 he received a consignment of silver-bearing lead from Mexico. This established a connection which still continues. The treating of these silver-bearing leads involved the necessity for a more rapid process of desilverizing or separating the silver from the base metals. This new process was devised by Edward Balbach, Jr., a young man of twenty-one, who had long been employed in his father's establishment, and who was at once admitted to partnership. The new process was patented in 1864, and soon became universally known as "Balbach's desilverizing process." It speedily came into general use, and yielded large revenues. The discovery of the great Nevada mine brought so great an increase of business to the Newark establishment that new wharves for the storage of coal and the shipment of products, and new buildings and furnaces for the treatment of ores, were required, these wants were promptly met, and since that time the fires of the great establishment have never been permitted to die out by day or night. Much of the silver ore which comes to Newark is what is known as "refractory," or "base metal," that is, carrying too large a quantity of lead to be amalgamated with quicksilver. This is melted into pig-metal, and from these pigs of base metal Messrs. Balbach & Son extract gold, silver, copper, antimony, nickel and other substances, until there is nothing left but slag and ashes. Vast shipments have come to the firm through the agency of the Bank of California, and great consignments have come from the mines of Nevada, Utah, Colorado, Montana, Idaho, Arizona and Lower California. Frequently also shipments are received from Mexico and South America. Some of these latter ores are very rich, and one lot of five tons from Mexico yielded 29,000 ounces of silver, or more than $6000 to the ton. The Canadian "Silver Islet" mine, of Lake Superior, has sent a great deal of ore to the establishment. The firm also receive large amounts of crude silver bars for separation, as this is the only private concern in the country where this work is done. In short, Messrs. Balbach & Son do the same close work as the government mints and assay offices, and much that the latter have not the facilities for doing. Within the last two or three years a new business has been opened up here, being the preparation of that perfectly pure lead used in the manu-

facture of white-lead. Heretofore this has all been imported from Europe. During the year ending October 1st, 1875, the total value of the products turned out by Messrs. Balbach & Son was $2,890,931.26. For the fiscal year ending June 30th, 1875, the total amount of domestic gold and silver deposited at the Philadelphia Mint was $2,123,711.39. The private smelting establishment has surpassed the parent mint of the government; and notwithstanding all these grand operations, the firm continue to work as faithfully as ever at the sweepings of the jewelry establishments. It is needless to speak of the absolute and unblemished integrity with which the business of the house is conducted. Without the perfect and unquestioning confidence which such integrity inspires their business would be an impossibility. As it is, the bars of silver and gold bearing their stamp pass as current upon Wall street as those of the mint. Edward Balbach, Sr., although he has passed the limit of three-score years and ten, is still an active and energetic man, with the prospect before him of being permitted to give still more years of attention to the great business which his enterprise founded and his prudent care and skill developed.

BALBACH, EDWARD, JR., Chemist, Inventor and Refiner of Precious Metals, of Newark, was born in 1842. He is of German birth and parentage, his father, Edward Balbach, Sr., being a native of Baden. He was an earnest scientific student in his youth, and by the time he had reached the age of twenty-one he was an accomplished chemist. He was employed in his father's smelting works in Newark, and about the time mentioned large quantities of silver-bearing lead were being sent to the works to have the precious metal separated from the base. This process by the old methods was slow and wasteful one, and he commenced a series of elaborate experiments to devise some process in which these objections should disappear. The result was a most valuable invention, known as "Balbach's desilverizing process," which has come into universal use and has brought rich revenues and a world-wide reputation to the house of Balbach & Son. Under the old process the whole volume of lead containing gold or silver had to be "cupelled," or oxidized into "litharge," a slow and laborious work, involving great loss of lead. By the new process the lead containing the precious metals is first melted with a sufficient quantity of zinc to take up the gold or silver present, those metals having a greater affinity for zinc than for lead. The melted mass is then poured into moulds of proper size and allowed to cool. These prepared masses are then placed in a furnace with an inclined hearth, and heated to a degree just sufficient to melt the lead without melting the other metals, the melted lead being drawn off into kettles. This lead contains no particle of gold or silver, although it still bears traces of zinc, and must be still further treated before it becomes pure lead. The mass remaining in the furnace consists of zinc, gold and silver, with a small portion of lead remaining. The mass is placed in black-lead retorts, and freed from zinc by distillation. This leaves again a mass of lead, gold and silver, but the precious metals which were before distributed throughout a ton of lead are now distributed through only sixty pounds. To this mass of sixty pounds of base metal the old process of cupelling is now applied, and the pure gold and silver obtained. Through this process the establishment of Messrs. Balbach & Son is enabled to smelt twenty-five tons of ore in one day, and to desilverize seventy-five tons of bullion. Edward Balbach, Jr., is still a young man. He has fine natural endowments, and by culture and experience is thoroughly qualified to achieve even greater scientific results than he has yet done.

AYLOR, OTHNIEL HART, M. D., Physician, late of Camden, was a native of Philadelphia, in which city he was born, May 4th, 1803. He was of English ancestry, both his parents, William Taylor, Jr., and Mary E. Gazzam, being natives of Cambridge, England. They removed to America in 1793 and settled in Philadelphia, where for more than forty years William Taylor was engaged in extensive mercantile business. In his early years Taylor attended elementary schools in Philadelphia and Holmesburgh, Pennsylvania, and in Baskingridge, New Jersey. He studied earnestly and effectively, and made rapid progress. In the year 1818 he entered the literary department of the University of Pennsylvania, and there pursued the more advanced studies of a general education. He had decided upon entering the medical profession, and in the year 1820 he became a student in the office of Thomas T. Hewson, M. D., the distinguished physician and surgeon. At the same time that he was pursuing his studies in Dr. Hewson's office, he received a course of instruction in the medical department of the University of Pennsylvania. He completed his university studies in the year 1825, and graduated with the class of that year. After graduating he at once entered upon the practice of his profession in the city of Philadelphia. He brought to the work he had chosen a combination of qualifications as valuable as rare. He was energetic and patient; he was progressive and prudent; he worked ceaselessly, and always had leisure to meet the necessities of others; he studied continuously and practised cautiously; he had much knowledge and so much modesty that his knowledge was never obtruded. Such a combination in the long run makes success, and success came to him. Soon after he entered upon the practice of his profession, he was appointed one of the physicians of the City Dispensary, in which capacity he served many years. About the same time he was elected out-door phy-

sician to the Pennsylvania Hospital, a position which he held for a term of eight years. In the year 1832 the Asiatic cholera made its first appearance on this continent, and it afforded him a signal opportunity to show his qualities, not only as a medical practitioner, but as a man. He distinguished himself by volunteering to serve in the city hospitals which the municipal authorities established to meet the emergency, and at the same time he acted as one of the committee of physicians appointed by the City Councils as consulting physicians to their sanitary board. The hospital specially in his charge was the St. Augustine Hospital, on Crown street, and the number of cholera patients reported by him as under treatment in that hospital was five hundred and twelve. He had also been elected as one of a commission of medical men who were sent to Montreal to study the character and treatment of cholera on its outbreak in that city, and before its appearance in our own cities; but being unable to accompany the commission, he declined in favor of Dr. Charles D. Meigs. When the hospitals were closed, after the disappearance of the cholera, he with seven other physicians, who had also been in charge of cholera hospitals, received, by vote of the City Councils, a testimonial for the services rendered the city, each being presented with a service of silver, the inscription testifying that the gift was bestowed "as a token of regard for intrepid and disinterested services." In the meantime Dr. Taylor had attained a very extended private practice and achieved recognition as a man already eminent in his profession. His arduous and unceasing labors told inevitably upon his health, and at length, in the year 1838, in consequence of impaired strength, he temporarily relinquished the practice of his profession, and removed from Philadelphia to Fontaintown, Pennsylvania. He remained there until 1841, when he removed to Caldwell, Essex county, New Jersey, and in 1844 he took up his residence in Camden. In the meantime he had resumed practice with the recovery of his strength, and in Camden his medical career was, from the first, one of great success and distinction, and he very soon possessed a very large share of the practice of the city and vicinity. He continued actively engaged in the work of his profession until about a year before his death, when, owing to his rapidly failing strength, he was obliged to relinquish his practice entirely. His fatal illness commenced with a severe attack of pneumonia early in the winter of 1864. The effects of this attack were manifested in a rapidly developed disease of the lungs, which resisted all efforts to check it, and resulted in his death, September 5th, 1869. Added to his eminent qualities as a professional man, Dr. Taylor possessed rare personal characteristics which won for him not only the respect and esteem, but the warm affection of all who came within his acquaintance. He was for many years a member of the Protestant Episcopal Church in Camden, and was known as a consistent Christian gentleman. Beside the regular routine work of his practice, his general labors in the line of his profession were various

and exacting. He was an active member of the Camden County Medical Society from the time of its organization; acted as Vice-President of the body through many successive terms, and prepared and delivered numerous addresses before the society. In 1852 he was the President of the State Medical Society, and consequently a Fellow of the same till his death. Moreover he was the author of many exhaustive treatises on medical subjects, published in various leading medical periodicals. In 1832, the year in which he so distinguished himself during the cholera visitation, Dr. Taylor married Evelina C. Burrough, of Gloucester county, New Jersey.

INSEY, CHARLES, Lawyer, of Burlington, New Jersey, was a son of Chief-Justice Kinsey. He studied law with William Griffith, Esq., at said place, and after being admitted to the bar by the Supreme Court, opened his office there and continued to practise his profession until he was appointed Surrogate of the County of Burlington, when he removed to the county-town, Mount Holly. After his term of office expired he returned to Burlington, resuming practice there until he died. He was a conscientious, well-read lawyer, and was noted for the purity of his life and character.

ESICK, REV. JOHN F., D. D., of Somerville, was born in the State of New York, June 28th, 1813, and when he was about two years of age his father removed to Catskill. The Mesick family are of old German origin, the first of the name having settled in the town of Claverac in 1719. The father of John Mesick was Peter Mesick, a merchant. At a proper age John attended the classical academy at Catskill, his teacher being the Rev. Carlos Smith, an eminent Greek and Latin scholar. In 1831 he became a communicant of the Reformed Dutch Church at Catskill, then under charge of the Rev. Dr. Wykoff; during the same year he entered Rutgers College, graduating with the class of 1834, and numbering among his classmates Dr. Chambers, of New York. Immediately after leaving college he entered the theological seminary, where he was graduated July 5th, 1837. The same year he was ordained and installed pastor of the Reformed Dutch Church of Rochester, New York, remaining there until December 17th, 1840, when he became pastor of the German Reformed Salem Church, of Harrisburg, Pennsylvania. In 1855 he accepted a call to the Second Reformed Church of Somerville, New Jersey, of which he took ministerial charge February 15th of the same year, and where he still officiates. Under his efficient leadership this church has greatly prospered, having almost doubled its membership, built a chapel, and enlarged the church edifice at a cost of several thousand dollars. He was married, September 5th, 1839, to Jane Perrine, daughter of Dr. William Perrine, of Philadelphia. His eldest son, William, is a graduate of Rutgers and is practising law in Philadelphia; he was first admitted to the New Jersey bar, and afterward prepared himself with Hon. F. C. Brewster for the Pennsylvania bar.

OOPER, REDMAN, Merchant and Importer, was born, January 1st, 1818, at Mantua Creek, about four miles below Woodbury, New Jersey. He is of the seventh generation, in line, from English ancestors, William and Margaret Cooper, of Coleshill, parish of Amersham, Hertford county, England, who came to America in 1679. They were members of the Society of Friends. A certificate to visit and settle in the new world was granted them by their Meeting on December 5th, 1678. After arrival, for a short time, they resided in Burlington. In 1682 they removed to Pyne Point, now Cooper's Point, so called from William Cooper, at one time the largest land-holder in New Jersey, owning two miles down the Delaware river, and two miles up Cooper's creek, on the south side. Redman is the son of David Cooper. He received a fair education in the schools at Haddonfield and Woodbury, and improved to the utmost what advantages were offered. On September 24th, 1834, he moved to Philadelphia, and obtained a position in the store of Isaac Barton & Co., on Second street, at that time one of the largest retail stores, of dress goods, in the city. Desirous of further knowledge, he gave all his spare time to reading. After coming of age he remained with Barton & Co., in the capacity of clerk, until 1847, when, with a limited capital of about $700, he started in business on his own account, purchasing a part of the interest held by his brother in the firm. In the year 1851 the nature of the business was changed, the house confining itself to shoe-stuffs, upholsterers' and carriage-manufacturers' goods, and a few years later dropping other branches in order to make a specialty of shoe-stuffs. On January 1st, 1867, the senior retired from active business, the firm then changing to Armstrong, Wilkins & Co. They are now the largest importers and jobbers of leather and general shoe goods in the United States, their sales amounting to from one to one and a quarter million of dollars per annum. The subject of this sketch is the senior partner of the firm, as well as its general financial manager. The extended operations in which it is constantly engaged, in supplying the markets of this country by importations from abroad, are under his care, and the excellent reputation which it sustains in European markets, as well as in this country, is largely owing to the weight of his personal character. Prior to the consolidation of the city of Philadelphia, he

21

resided in what was known as "Chestnut Ward," and in its affairs was always active and influential, identifying himself with the "Henry Clay Whig" party. His best efforts were ever exerted for the advancement of Philadelphia in growth and influence, every movement tending in that direction finding in him an earnest upholder and advocate. When the question of the city subscribing to the stock of the Pennsylvania Railroad arose, he was deeply interested, and well understood the importance of supporting the road. His political influence was employed in behalf only of those pledged to its support, and by the aid of such men as he, the road was brought into successful operation. Some twenty-five years ago he removed from "Chestnut Ward," and since that date has taken no part in politics except to vote for those whom he thought would best serve the interests of the community at large. November 1st, 1849, he was married to the daughter of Joseph Cowperthwait, formerly cashier in the United States Bank.

ROWN, ABRAHAM, Lawyer, of Mount Holly, New Jersey, was born in Recklesstown, Burlington county. His education was acquired at a classical school kept many years ago at Bordentown by Burgess Allison. After completing his education he commenced the study of law, and on receiving his license to practise he removed to Mount Holly, where he resided until his death. Soon after his removal there he was appointed Surrogate of the county, which office he held by reappointment for a continuous period of seventeen years. He was a profound lawyer, and a wise counsellor, a man of great integrity of character, and exercised a widespread influence in his native county. He was one of the original Directors of the Camden & Amboy Railroad Company, and held the same when he died.

OWENHOVEN, HON. CHARLES T., Lawyer, and ex-Judge, of New Brunswick, was born in that city, December 1st, 1844. The family originally came from Holland in the latter part of the sixteenth century, and were people of large possessions. His father, Nicholas R. Cowenhoven, was born on Long Island, while his mother, Annie Rappleyea, was a native of New Jersey. The advantages of a good education were afforded him. At first he attended the select schools of New Brunswick; subsequently he entered Rutgers College, matriculating in 1858, and being graduated in 1862. He then began the study of law, having determined upon adopting the legal profession. His studies were conducted in the office and under the supervision of A. V. Schenck, Esq., in New Brunswick. In due course he was licensed as an attorney in 1865, and as counsellor in

June, 1869. During the last-named year the office of Law Judge for the County of Middlesex was created by act of the Legislature, and he was appointed to fill the position. For a period of five years thereafter he sat upon the bench, and discharged the various functions of his office with marked ability. Indeed, during that time not a single decision of the many given was ever appealed. Further testimony to his quality as a judge is superfluous. This record is the more remarkable inasmuch as he was in all probability the youngest judge who ever sat on the bench in the State. In this position he was the Presiding Judge of the Court of Common Pleas, Orphans' Court, and Court of Quarter Sessions. At the expiration of his term he returned to private practice, in which he has been very successful. In December, 1870, he was married to Ella A., daughter of Henry Towle, of New Brunswick.

OTT, REV. GEORGE SCUDDER, D. D., of Flemington, was born, November 25th, 1829, in the city of New York, where the family had resided for several generations. His father was Lawrence S. Mott, and his mother's maiden name was Vail. One of his ancestors had to flee from the city of New York on its occupation by the British; another was killed at the Indian battle of Minisink. George prepared for college at a private school in his native city, entered the sophomore class of the University of New York in 1847, and graduated in 1850, taking fourth honor. Among his classmates were Vaughn Abbott, Esq., of New York city, Prof. H. H. Baird, and the Rev. D. Zabriskie, of the Congregational Church. Entering Princeton Theological Seminary in the autumn of 1850, he graduated in 1853. During the same year he accepted a call to the Second Presbyterian Church of Rahway, New Jersey, and remained five years. He was then called to the Presbyterian Church, at Newton, New Jersey, where he continued for nine years. In 1869 Dr. Mott removed to Flemington, New Jersey, having consented to take charge of the Presbyterian Church of that place, and there he still resides. In 1873 he was elected Professor of Sacred Rhetoric in Lincoln University, Pennsylvania, but declined the proffered position. In 1874 Princeton College conferred on him the degree of D. D. He has written several valuable books, among which—published by the American Tract Society—may be named the "Perfect Law," which has been translated into Spanish and Portuguese; also a tract, "Holding on to Christ"—of this over two hundred thousand copies have been printed. The Presbyterian Board of Publication has published of his works, "The Prodigal Son," and several tracts, viz.: "Gaming and Gambling," "There is no Passing," "Eating and Drinking Unworthily," "Nurse Them at Home." A book entitled "Resurrection of the Dead" has been published for him by Randolph. These efforts evince much thought and depth of reasoning, and are of a high order of literary merit. In 1854 he was married to Isabella, daughter of John Acken, Esq., of New Brunswick, New Jersey. He is a fervent and zealous pastor, as well as one of the ablest workers in the field of didactic Christian literature, as may readily be inferred from the practical character of the titles of his productions above mentioned.

PHARO, HON. JOSEPH W., Merchant and State Senator, late of Tuckerton, was born, March 14th, 1813, in that town, and was a son of the late Timothy Pharo, whose biographical sketch will be found elsewhere in this volume. He received an excellent education, partly at the celebrated Friends' school at Westtown, Chester county, Pennsylvania, and partly at the equally excellent academy of John Gummere, in Burlington, New Jersey. When he was nineteen years of age, his father placed him in his store, devolving the principal care and management of the business upon him. He remained there until 1840, when he went to New York city, and entered into the wholesale dry-goods jobbing business with George Barnes, the firm being known for several years as Barnes & Pharo. This business soon became a very large one, the sales extensive; and during the first ten years of this partnership, the junior member of the house travelled extensively through the Western States, chiefly on business connected with the firm. After the death of his father, he dissolved his connection with the firm in New York, and returning, in the spring of 1857, to his native town, he erected there a commodious and tasteful residence, and adorned its surroundings with useful and ornamental gardens and shrubbery. He now entered into business with his brother, A. R. Pharo, constituting the firm of J. & A. R. Pharo, carrying on an extensive general trade in stores, mills, lumber, wood, coal, ship-building, agriculture, etc., etc. They were also largely interested in the coasting trade, and probably represented a larger interest in coasting vessels than any other family in the State. His talents for business were of the highest order. Few men possessed the comprehensive grasp of mind to survey so readily all the advantages and difficulties bearing upon any subject to which his powers were directed, and none perhaps arrived more quickly at a judicious and correct conclusion. For this reason his judgment and advice were universally sought by the community for several miles around his residence, and to all who came to him for this purpose, he was the safe, judicious and valuable counsellor, the impartial, just and reliable arbiter. His success in business was but the natural consequence of his industry, his application to, and his superior capacity for, it. He seemed to find his greatest pleasure in the executive management and

direction of a large business; and the accumulation of wealth was with him but the result of commendable employment, and not a sordid pursuit. In the fall of 1861 he was elected State Senator from Burlington county by a very popular vote. His legislative career, though of short duration, was promising and satisfactory. He occupied a prominent position on several important committees, and was one of the special committee of the Senate to meet the governors of Pennsylvania, New Jersey and Delaware, with a joint committee from the Legislature of each of these States, to consult relative to the coast defences. His illness prevented him from being present at the meeting of this committee, much to his regret. He was, in religious opinion and belief, a member of the Society of Friends; having a birthright in that society, and thoroughly educated in their principles, he always properly conformed to their discipline and worship. He was strictly moral in deed and word, regular, exact and systematic in his habits, scrupulously neat and particular in his personal appearance, and guarded in his language and expression. He embodied in a high degree the character of a pure, high-minded gentleman. His education was liberal, his principles sound, his judgment vigorous, prompt and discriminating, his mind was well stored with valuable and diversified information, and combined with a calculating, comprehensive business tact were high integrity of purpose and honesty of principle. His popularity in his neighborhood was universal. To the poor, the needy and the destitute, his hand was ever open, and his heart ready to respond to the voice of distress. He was their charitable donor and their sympathizing benefactor. To his relatives and intimate acquaintances he was the warm-hearted, genial and cheerful companion and faithful friend; and to all around he was the dignified gentleman, the generous neighbor, and the honest man. He was married in December, 1839, to Beulah H., a daughter of Benjamin Oliphant, of Mannahawkin. He died at his residence in Tuckerton, April 16th 1862.

CANNON, REV. JAMES SPENCER, D. D., S. T. P., was born in the city of New York, and was placed, when a small boy, by his father, in the family of Colonel Elias Brevoort, at Hackensack, New Jersey, to be educated. Shortly after this his father was lost at sea in his own vessel, and by his death his son was left an orphan. Colonel Brevoort, who was an officer of the Revolution, adopted the child as his own, and had him thoroughly educated at the classical academy of Dr. Peter Wilson, at Hackensack. At the age of sixteen he united himself to the Reformed Dutch Church, at the latter place, and shortly after commenced his theological studies under Dr. Jacob Freligh. At the age of twenty-one he was ordained as a minister of said church, and shortly after, having married one of the daughters of Colonel Brevoort, was called to the Dutch Reformed Church at Six Mile Run, in Somerset county, near New Brunswick, and continued there as the pastor of that large congregation, ministering to them with great fidelity and acceptance for twenty-five years, until he was elected by the General Synod of that church to the Professorship of Pastoral Theology in their seminary at New Brunswick; here he discharged for thirty years, and until his death, which occurred in 1852, not only his duties in this station, but also the duties of Professor of Metaphysics and Philosophy in Rutgers College, in the same city, to which he had been elected by the Trustees of that institution. He died, lamented and beloved by all who ever knew him. As a teacher he was eminent and successful; as a preacher he was attractive and eloquent; as a Christian and a man he was a model in all respects. After his death his "Lectures on Pastoral Theology" were published by Scribner & Co., of New York, in a large volume, which is regarded everywhere as a standard work in this department of theology.

ARD, HON. MARCUS L., ex-Governor of New Jersey, was born, November 9th, 1812, in the city of Newark, where his paternal ancestors have resided since 1666. The Wards are of English stock, and Joyce Ward, widow of Stephen Ward, with four children, originally settled in Connecticut. Her son, John Ward, was among the thirty families who originally settled the shore of the Passaic, and laid, in the present city of Newark, the foundations of a prosperous community. His son, of the same name, who accompanied his father to the new settlement, was shortly after married to Abigail Kitchell, the granddaughter of the Rev. Abraham Pierson, the pious and eloquent pastor and teacher of the emigrants, in honor of whose birthplace the name of Newark was given to the settlement. From this stock Governor Ward is descended, and it is not too much to say that during seven generations this family have been distinguished by the highest qualities of integrity and personal honor. In early life Governor Ward entered into trade, and soon became connected with the financial institutions and public enterprises of the city. Their success and wise management have been measurably due to the prudence and judgment which such men have uniformly exhibited, and Newark is especially noted for the strength of its financial institutions. Slow in growth, until a recent period, it has ever maintained some of the characteristics of its Puritan settlers, and this has been manifested in its banks, its insurance companies, its schools, and even in its conservative government. During his business life Governor Ward gained, and has ever since maintained, that reputation for honesty, integrity and prudence which lies at the base of his character. This confidence he has retained through the passage of years, the virulence of party warfare, and through the strongest test, that of public position and administrative responsibility. Governor Ward's political associations were with the Whig party, but he was among the earliest to recognize the necessity of a stronger organization to curb the growing domination of the South. He supported Fremont and Dayton in the Presidential campaign of 1856, but his attention was not seriously drawn to political subjects until the summer of 1858. In that year the exciting contest between slavery and freedom called him to Kansas, and while there he fully saw and appreciated the importance of the struggle going on in that territory. He gave while there his prudent counsel and his liberal contributions to the Free State party, and on his return to New Jersey he engaged warmly in the work of rousing public attention to the pending issue. At a time when party spirit was at its height, his representations were received with the confidence which his character always inspired. He was deeply interested in the political contest of the ensuing autumn, and none rejoiced more sincerely over the result in New Jersey which secured a United States Senator and an unbroken delegation in the House of Representatives against the Lecompton fraud. In 1860 the growing political influence of Governor Ward began to be felt and acknowledged, and he was unanimously chosen a delegate to the National Republican Convention, the proceedings of which culminated in the nomination of Abraham Lincoln. In the contest which ensued he bore his full part, and when the result was reached he felt amply repaid for all his exertions. He neither challenged nor sought to avoid the consequences of that success. When the signal was given for that revolt which had long been preparing in the Southern States, it found him ready for any services or sacrifices which were necessary to defend the right. He was neither discouraged by defeats nor unduly elated with transient successes, but his efforts were directed to one end, the preservation of the Union. At the outbreak of hostilities he led in the call for a public meeting to sustain the government. As the struggle increased in importance, and drew into the ranks of the patriot army regiment after regiment of New Jersey troops, Governor Ward saw the absolute necessity of sustaining the families of the volunteers during their absence. Alone and unaided he devised and carried out that system of relief the advantages of which were felt in every county of the State. The pay of the volunteer was collected at the camp and passed over to the wife and children at home; if killed or wounded, the pension was secured; and this continued until after the close of the war, without a charge of any nature upon these sacred funds. Hundreds and thousands of families were preserved from want and suffering by this wise and considerate scheme, and of all the means devised to sustain the State none was more potent than this. But his active exertions did not terminate here. It was through his efforts and influence with the general government that a hospital

Marcus L. Ward

for sick and wounded soldiers was established in Newark, and in view of his loyal action his name was bestowed upon it. "Ward's Hospital" became known as one of the best controlled institutions of the kind in the country. His sanitary arrangements were fully appreciated. These constant and unwearied services brought Governor Ward into immediate contact with Mr. Lincoln and his cabinet, by whom he was ever regarded as entitled to the highest consideration. In 1862, so strongly did his services impress the Republicans of the State, he was unanimously nominated for Governor; but in the absence of so large a portion of the loyal voters, and in the deep depression of that memorable year, he was defeated. This did not change his unswerving loyalty or affect in any manner his constant and unwearied labors for the right. In 1864 he was a delegate at large to the National Republican Convention, at Baltimore, which renominated Mr. Lincoln, and in the ensuing election he was placed on the Republican ticket as a Senatorial elector. The close of the war and the defeat of the rebellion was to him a source of unmixed gratification, and it brought to him a strong personal popularity, evinced upon every occasion. As regiment after regiment of the soldiers returned to their native State they manifested their appreciation of his loyal conduct and services, and even political opponents admitted his sincerity and patriotism. This was to him the happiest period of his life. In 1865 he again received the Republican nomination for Governor, and after an unusually exciting contest he was elected by a large majority. His administration was one of the best New Jersey has ever known. His executive ability was fully demonstrated, and his honesty and fidelity were unquestioned. Every department of the public service, so far as his influence could reach it, was economically and faithfully administered. The laws passed by the Legislature were carefully scanned, and pardons for criminal offences were granted only when mercy could be safely united with justice. To his administration New Jersey was deeply indebted for many important measures affecting the interests of the State. The present Public School act was passed upon his strong and urgent representations, and its advantages have been felt in the increased educational facilities of the State, and the more thorough character and development of its schools. The riparian rights of the State were called by him to the attention of the Legislature, and a commission secured through which its large and valuable interests have been protected. His constant and persistent representations to the Legislature, in his various messages, of the mismanagement of the State prison under all political parties, contributed largely to the passage of an act removing it, as far as possible, from partisan government, and the result has been large savings to the State. Various other public acts and measures, having an important bearing upon the growth and well-being of the State, were urged and sustained by him, and whenever adopted they were found to have increased its prosperity and development. The close of his administration found him stronger than ever in the confidence of the people of the State he had so worthily served. In 1864 Governor Ward was placed upon the National Republican Committee, and in 1866 he was chosen Chairman. In this capacity he made the preliminary arrangements for the convention, in 1868, which nominated General Grant. He took a decided part in the campaign which followed, and his services and efforts were fully acknowledged. During the few succeeding years Governor Ward lived in comparative retirement, but was frequently called to duties of a public character. He was the first President of the Newark Industrial Exposition, and by his efforts contributed largely to its success. The "Soldiers' Home," at Newark, was originally established through his exertions, and as one of its managers he has given it to the present hour his constant and unwearied service. It was the first, as it is now the only State institution of the kind. It seemed natural and proper that the man who during the war had protected the interests and families of the loyal soldier, who had provided him with the care and attendance of a hospital when sick and wounded, should, when the war was over, still secure him, crippled and maimed, the comforts of a "soldiers' home." During the Presidential campaign of 1872 Governor Ward was nominated for Congress from the Sixth District of New Jersey, and was elected by over 5,000 majority. Upon taking his seat in the House of Representatives he was recognized as one of its most valuable members. He was placed on the Committee on Foreign Relations, and on the few occasions on which he addressed the house he commanded attention by the clearness of his reasoning and the thorough honesty of his convictions. In 1874 Governor Ward was unanimously renominated for Congress by the Republicans of his district, but the condition of the country was unfavorable for success. Financial disaster disturbed all the marts of trade, and the large manufacturing district he represented was most severely affected. Thousands of laborers were unemployed, and the hope that a political change would return prosperity governed their action. The tidal wave which swept over the strongest Republican States submerged his district also, although, as usual, he stood the highest on the Republican ticket. The confidence and attachment of the people were never shown more clearly than in the regret and disappointment which this defeat occasioned. After the expiration of his Congressional term he was tendered by the President the important post of Commissioner of Indian Affairs, but it was declined, while fully appreciating the compliment thereby conveyed. Here this brief record of his life might be closed, but the sketch would be imperfect if reference were not made to some of the peculiar traits which distinguish him. He is not a politician, in the common view, but he is an earnest Republican and a man of the most positive convictions. He is justly popular among all classes, because respect and attachment to him are based on his sterling qualities and generous nature. His deeds of considerate charity have been as numerous as they have been blessed. Many a struggling artist has received from him the generous order which did not degrade, and many a home has been brightened by blessings secured through him. Few men have brought to their public duties the conscientiousness which characterizes Governor Ward. Every act is governed by that law of justice and of right which will bear the closest scrutiny. Popular in the highest and purest sense of that term, he will not sacrifice his judgment or his convictions to the caprices of the multitude. He knows how to recognize the difference between generosity and a betrayal of financial trusts. His manners are engaging, but they are the result of the native kindness of heart which characterizes him. His charities have frequently been pursued for years, unknown to the world, but he chooses his own ways of doing good. When our statesmen shall reach preferment because of the qualities which should command it, when high principle, personal integrity and unquestioned ability are made the basis of public life; when the true shall be preferred to the false, and the substantial to the pretentious, such men will constitute the real strength of the State.

ALDWIN, MATTHIAS W., Locomotive Engine-builder and founder of the Baldwin Locomotive Works, of Philadelphia, was born in Elizabeth-town, New Jersey, December 10th, 1795. His father, William Baldwin, was a carriage-maker by trade, and at his death left his family a comfortable property, which by the mismanagement of the executors was nearly all lost. His widow was thus left to her own exertions for the maintenance of herself and family. To the necessity for economy and self-reliance thus imposed, young Baldwin probably owed the first development of his inventive genius. From early childhood he exhibited a remarkable fondness for mechanical contrivances. His toys were taken apart and examined, while he would produce others far superior in mechanism and finish. When sixteen years old he was apprenticed to Woolworth Brothers, jewelry manufacturers, of Frankford, Pennsylvania, and while serving his time he commanded the respect and esteem of both his associates and employers. Having mastered all the details of the business, thus becoming a finished workman, and having attained his majority, he found employment in the establishment of Fletcher & Gardiner, Philadelphia, who were extensive manufacturers of jewelry. He soon became the most useful man in the shop, his work being delicate in finish and his designs characterized by great originality and beauty. In 1819 he commenced business on his own account; but in consequence of financial difficulties, and the trade becoming depressed, he soon abandoned it. His attention was then drawn to the invention of machinery; and one of his first efforts in this direction was a machine whereby the process of gold-plating was greatly simplified. He next turned his attention to the manufacture of book-binders' tools, to supersede those which had been, up to that time, of foreign production. He associated himself for this purpose with David Mason, a competent machinist, and the enterprise was a success. Indeed, so admirable were the quality and finish of the tools, especially as they were of an improved make, that the book trade was soon rendered independent of foreign manufacturers. He next invented the cylinder for printing of calicoes, which had always been previously done by hand-presses; and he revolutionized the entire business. The manufacture of these printing rollers increased so greatly that additional accommodations were necessary. Here again he effected an improvement, first using horse-power as a substitute for the hand-machinery and foot-lathes, which in its turn gave way to steam-power. The engine purchased for this purpose not meeting his wishes, he built one himself, from original drawings of his own. This little engine of six-horse power, and occupying a space of six square feet, is still in use, driving the whole machinery of the boiler shop in the locomotive works on Broad street, Philadelphia. It is over forty years old. His genius in this respect being soon recognized, he received many orders for the manufacture of stationary engines, which they became his most important article of manufacture. When the first locomotive engine in America, imported by the Camden & Amboy Railroad Company, in 1830, arrived, he examined it carefully and resolved to construct one after his own ideas; and after urgent requests from Franklin Peale, the proprietor of the Philadelphia Museum, built a miniature engine for exhibition. His only guide in this work consisted of a few imperfect sketches of the one he had examined, aided by descriptions of those in use on the Liverpool & Manchester Railway. He successfully accomplished the task, and on the 25th of April, 1831, the miniature locomotive was running over a track in the museum rooms, a portion of this track being laid on the floors of the transepts, and the balance passing over trestle work in the naves of the building. Two small cars, holding four persons, were attached to it, and the novelty attracted immense crowds. The experiment resulting well, he received an order to construct a road locomotive for the Germantown Railroad. He had great difficulty in procuring the necessary tools and help. The inventor and his mechanic worked himself on the greater part of the entire engine. It was accomplished, finally, and on its trial trip, November 23d, 1832, proved a success. Some imperfections existed, but these being remedied, it was accepted by the company, and was in use for twenty years thereafter. The smoke-stack was originally constructed of the same diameter from its junction with the fire-box to the top, where it was bent at a right angle and carried back, with its opening to the rear of the train. This engine weighed five tons, and was sold for $3,500. Two years elapsed before he ventured upon building another, as he had seemingly insurmountable difficulties to encounter; there were so many improvements to be made, and the lack of skilled labor, and above all of the necessary tools and machinery, was so great, that he almost abandoned the work. In 1834 he constructed an engine for the South Carolina Railroad, and also one for the Pennsylvania State Line, running from Philadelphia to Columbia. The latter weighed 17,000 pounds, and drew at one time nineteen loaded cars. This was such an unprecedented performance that the State Legislature at once ordered several additional ones, and two more completed and delivered during the same year; and he also constructed one for the Philadelphia & Trenton Railroad. In 1835 he built fourteen; in 1836, forty. Then came the terrible financial panic of 1837, which ruined so many houses throughout the land; he also became embarrassed, but calling his creditors together, he asked and obtained an extension, and subsequently paid every dollar, principal and interest. His success was now assured, and his works became the largest in the United States, perhaps in the world. Engines were shipped to every-quarter of the globe, even to England, where they had been invented—and the name of Baldwin grew as familiar as 'a household word.' He was one of the founders of the Franklin Institute. He was an exemplary Christian, and of a charitable and benevolent disposition. He died, September 7th, 1866.

RICK, SAMUEL REEVE, Architect and Civil Engineer, was born, November 1st, 1809, in Woodstown, Salem county, New Jersey. He is of Quaker parentage; the son of Joseph (Jr.) and Elizabeth (Smith) Brick, and the fifth in the line of descent from John Brick, who as early as 1690 settled at Cohansey, where he purchased extensive tracts of land. For it appears when Joseph Miller resurveyed Samuel Demming's large tract of land on Gravelly run or the southern branch of Stoe creek (it being the boundary line between Salem and Cumberland counties at this time), Miller said he was assisted by John Brick and his two sons; and that the difficulty they had to contend with proved more chargeable than he expected it would be to the proprietor. John Brick soon afterwards purchased the whole tract. His son, John Brick, Jr., who was the first President Judge of Common Pleas of Cumberland county, New Jersey, married, in 1729, Ann Nicholson, of Elsinboro' (who was born November 15th, 1707). They commenced life together at Cohansey, and had eight children. Previous to his death he purchased a large quantity of land lying on the south side of Alloway's creek; part of a neck of land, called "Beesley neck," he devised to his second son, Joseph. John Brick, Jr., died, January 23d, 1758, and his widow some twenty years thereafter. Joseph Brick married, first, Rebecca Abbott, of Elsinboro', about 1758, and they re-

sided together for a short time on his property on Alloway's creek, when they removed to a farm in Elsinboro', which had been left to his wife by her father, Samuel Abbott. Their family consisted of two daughters, Anne and Hannah, and one son, Samuel. His first wife died, November 16th, 1780, and he afterwards married Martha Reeve, and removed to Cohansey creek, where he resided until his death. By Martha Reeve he had two sons, named Joseph and John Brick; the eldest son of Joseph married Ann Smart, of Elsinboro'. Joseph married Elizabeth, daughter of David Smith, a resident of Mannington. He was a native of Egg Harbor, and removed from there to Salem county when he was at middle age. He was greatly respected for his uprightness and quiet deportment among the people of the neighborhood in which he dwelt. Joseph and his wife had five sons, among whom was Samuel Reeve. He received his primary education in Salem, and subsequently at the school in Mannington. In accordance with the custom of those days, he was at the age of fourteen years regularly indentured as an apprentice, which was done at Philadelphia, to one Robert Evans, a member of the Society of Friends, to learn the business of bricklaying, and, as customary then, he became an inmate of Friend Evans' household. He remained with his preceptor and master until he attained his majority, and became a thorough master of the trade and calling which he had acquired. He then carried on the business as master for ten years, after which he commenced to study in the city of Philadelphia the principles of architecture, and also of civil engineering. Having given his whole attention to these new and important subjects, and become thoroughly proficient in their various details, he commenced the practice of his new profession, which he still continues. He has paid particular attention to the construction of gas-works, and has superintended the erection of many of these important improvements in various and distant parts of the country, in British America as well as in the United States. His labors in this direction may be understood and appreciated when it is stated that their fruits dot the streets of larger and smaller localities of the several States of the Union, from Maine to Florida. He holds at present the position of President of the Richmond County Gas Light Company, at Stapleton, New York. He also served for three years as a Trustee of the Philadelphia Gas Works. His political life commenced as a faithful adherent to the doctrines of the Whig party as expounded by the statesman, Henry Clay, and he was nominated by that party and elected as one of the Commissioners of the (old) District of the Northern Liberties, Philadelphia county. Since the dissolution of that party he has given his adherence to Republican principles. He is a life-member of the Historical Society of Pennsylvania. He was married, March 23d, 1831, to Esther, daughter of James Gardiner, who was a prominent soldier of the war of the Revolution, and has had eight children, six of whom are now living. He is also Consulting Engineer of several works in the United States. His son, Joseph, is in the fifth generation of that name.

OLLES, ENOCH, Real Estate Operator, late of Newark, was born in Connecticut, in the year 1779. In his early life he followed the sea for his livelihood. The vessel in which he sailed was detained in Charleston harbor during the embargo, early in this century. Thereupon he returned North, and engaged in the shoe business in Newark. Subsequently he was for over forty years principally engaged in real estate operations on a gradually increasing scale. Through the rapid growth of the city, which he had been shrewd enough to foresee, he amassed by these operations a large fortune. A very public-spirited man, he took a deep interest in municipal affairs, and was active in all movements calculated to advance the city's interests. He was for a long period on the Town Committee, and was a member of the first Common Council of the city, elected in 1836. He also served in a similar capacity in the years 1837 and 1840. By his enterprise and active efforts on behalf of the community, and his many estimable qualities, he won the esteem and regard of a large circle. He lived to a good old age, dying in his adopted city on June 29th, 1865.

ARISON, REV. GEORGE HOLCOMBE, M. D., Clergyman and Physician, of Lambertville, was born, January 4th, 1831, in Delaware township, Hunterdon county, New Jersey, and is a son of Benjamin Larison, a farmer of that vicinity. He passed his boyhood on his father's farm, attending the district school, where he received his rudimentary education, and subsequently became a teacher of the same. In 1853 he entered the University of Lewisburg, Pennsylvania, from which he subsequently received the honorary degree of Master of Arts. Having resolved to embrace the profession of medicine, he commenced his studies with Hon. Samuel Lilly, M. D., as preceptor, and attended the lectures delivered at the medical department of the University of Pennsylvania, from which latter institution he graduated in 1858 with the degree of Doctor of Medicine. He immediately entered upon the practice of his profession at Dolington, Bucks county, Pennsylvania, and the following year he removed to Lambertville, New Jersey, where he has since resided, and has now the control of an extensive and lucrative practice. He is a member of the Hunterdon County Medical Society, and was for seven years its Secretary. He is also a member of the State Medical Society, and was elected its Third Vice-President in 1872; and presided over the one hundred and ninth an-

nual meeting, held at Atlantic City, May 25th, 1875, when he delivered the annual address. This was a remarkably able effort, wherein he reviewed the healing art and the advancement of the profession in a manner that proves not only his acquaintance with the classics, but also with the sciences. Previous to his being elected President of this body he had held the positions of First, Second and Third Vice-President before he was chosen President of that body. While he was its Third Vice-President he wrote an essay entitled "Diseases Prevalent in the Valley of the Delaware," which was well received by the medical fraternity, and was published by the State Medical Society among its transactions. During the prevalence of the small-pox in Lambertville, in 1863–64, he attended ninety-nine cases, and only lost four. One of these he buried at midnight, and with his own hands. He subsequently prepared a paper on "Small-pox and its Treatment," for the medical society, in 1864, which was well received by the profession, and filed with the important papers of the society. His practice is a general one, but he makes a specialty with obstetrics, and has so far attended over 1000 cases successfully; he has also achieved great success in surgical cases. He has, on two occasions, been a delegate to the Pennsylvania State Medical Society, and at one of its sessions delivered an address before that organization in the city of Carlisle. In 1862 he was elected Town Superintendent of Schools, and has filled that position both under the town and the city organization to the present time, being continuously re-elected, on the Democratic ticket, although parties have had a variety of changes during those years; the schools are in a prosperous condition, and now number over 1400 pupils. He was for seven years a member of the City Council, and has held all the grades of office in the New Jersey State Militia, from Second Lieutenant to Brigadier-General, excepting that of Lieutenant-Colonel. He is now Surgeon on the staff of Colonel Angel's well-known regiment—the 7th Regiment New Jersey National Guard. During his attendance at the University of Lewisburg he became a member of the Baptist Church, and he is now a regularly ordained clergyman of that denomination. He has a congregation at Solebury, Pennsylvania, over the Delaware river, to whom he has ministered every Sunday morning and evening for the past seven years. The church is mainly of his own ingathering; it had a membership of about twenty when he commenced his labors, and has now increased to over 120. He has been connected with the Reading Association of the Baptist Churches. At the organization of this body, at Reading, Pennsylvania, he preached the opening sermon, and was chosen Moderator of the meeting. His leisure hours at times have been taken up in teaching both preparatory to college and in the medical profession. Rev. J. H. Chambers, A. M., now pastor of the Olivet Baptist Church, in Philadelphia, was prepared for college under his instruction, and entered the freshman class in the University at Lewisburg, Pennsylvania, where he graduated as the valedictorian of the class of 1872. As a medical preceptor he has given instruction to the following persons : William D. Wolverton, M. D., who graduated in 1861, and after a satisfactory examination before the Army Board was admitted as an assistant surgeon into the regular army, where he still holds an honored position ; Professor C. W. Larison, M. D., of natural sciences in the University at Lewisburg; A. B. Larison, M. D., assistant surgeon of volunteers; F. Fisher, M. D., of Somerset county, and E. E. James, M. D., of Montandon, Pennsylvania, a son of Professor C. S. James, of the University at Lewisburg, Pennsylvania. Taking all things into consideration, he probably accomplishes as much real good to the community as any other man in Hunterdon county. As previously stated his medical practice is large and lucrative, and has placed him in a comparatively independent position; and he is the owner of some of the most valuable real-estate in and around Lambertville, the results of his professional labor. He still has time to cultivate literature, and at the same time to be a very agreeable and well-informed conversationalist; and he never parts with any one without fully understanding the motive for which he has sought an interview. He was married in 1859 to Sarah Q., daughter of Caleb F. Fisher, of Ringoes, New Jersey.

expiration of his second Congressional term he resumed the practice of his profession in Flemington. Mr. Bird is an earnest, working Democrat, and renders his party great service on the stump. During the late rebellion he was known as a war Democrat, doing his utmost to assist the government in raising troops, besides taking an active part in every measure tending to destroy the rebellion. The bill for increasing the pay of members of Congress, which was passed while he was a member, met with his determined opposition, and after it became a law he turned his portion of the back-pay into the United States treasury. He is eminently in favor of judicial reform, having written several works on the subject which have attracted much public attention. He is a member of the Presbyterian Church and an earnest worker in behalf of Sabbath schools; he was also for some time President of the Hunterdon County Bible Society. There is no member of the Democratic party in that part of the State held in higher regard by his party, or more generally respected by his political opponents ; he is also greatly esteemed by his brother practitioners. Mr. Bird is attorney for the Hunterdon County National Bank, and is engaged in most of the leading cases coming before the Hunterdon county courts. He was married in 1854 to Annie, daughter of Thomas Hilton, of Hunterdon county.

IRD, HON. JOHN T., of Flemington, Lawyer and ex-Member of Congress, was born in Bethlehem township, Hunterdon county, New Jersey, August 16th, 1829. His father was James Bird, a farmer of the same county. He attended the public schools of his neighborhood, and spent three years at a classical academy at Hackettstown, New Jersey, then under the direction of John S. Labar. After leaving school he began preparing for the bar with the Hon. A. G. Richey, then residing at Asbury, New Jersey. Mr. Bird was admitted to the bar during the November term of 1855, and for three years practised at Bloomsburg, in his own State. In 1863 he was appointed, by Governor Parker, Prosecutor of the Pleas for Hunterdon county; he then removed to Clinton, New Jersey, remaining there until 1865, when he changed his residence to Flemington. In the meantime his practice had grown to be one of the largest in the county. As Prosecutor of the Pleas he served for five years. In 1868 he was elected by the Democratic party to the Forty-first Congress, and re-elected in 1872. While in Congress he took an active part in all the leading questions of that body, was an earnest and eloquent speaker, and a ready, effective debater. His speeches were printed, and give evidence of a thorough understanding of the various subjects under consideration ; in particular may be mentioned his speech on civil service, delivered in 1872, this effort being considered by the opposition the ablest that had been delivered upon the question in Congress. On the

22

IDCOCK, HON. JAMES NELSON, State Senator, of White House, Hunterdon county, was born at Mechanicsville, New Jersey, February 8th, 1836. He is of English extraction, and the founders of the family in this country settled in New Jersey in an early period of its history. His father was John G. Pidcock, and his mother, before her marriage, was a Ramsey. When about five years of age he removed with his parents to Lebanon, New Jersey, and during the early years of his boyhood he attended the public schools in that place and vicinity. When he had reached the age of thirteen he left school and went to work with an engineering corps on the Belvidere Delaware Railroad. He was engaged in the location and construction of this road until 1851. In that year he went South, and he had turned his experience with the engineer corps to so good account that he took charge of the construction of a division, twenty-five miles long, of the Mobile & Ohio Railroad. The portion of the work under his control was in the State of Mississippi, and the resident chief-engineer was Mr. Foote. He remained in the South until the year 1857, when ill health, together with the financial troubles of the Mobile & Ohio Railroad, caused him to resign his position and return home. Shortly afterwards he became a member of the firm of William E. Henry & Co., and contracted for the building of several miles of the Allentown & Auburn Railroad. After working about eight months in fulfilment of this contract, the financial disaster of that memorable year involved the corporation in such trouble that the work was stopped. He and his partners lost heavily, but paid off all their indebtedness. During the remainder of that disastrous year, instead of remaining idle and complaining of hard times, he planned new enterprises, and in company with J. E. Voorhees and J. F. Wykoff, engaged largely in the purchase of clothing at forced sales in New York, and disposing of the purchases by wholesale and at auction through the country. These operations resulted in handsome profits. He next engaged in business as drover and stock dealer, and his business and profits steadily increased until 1861. Then came the war, and the financial depression that accompanied its early stages caused the failure of so many of his customers that he lost all that he had saved in more prosperous years, and he had literally to commence business anew, with no other capital than the energy and perseverance that are so strongly characteristic of him. He chose to continue in the stock business and did so with fair success until 1865. Then, in company with J. N. Ramsey and Richard Bellis, he commenced business in New York and Jersey City, as live-stock commission merchant. He continued in this way until 1868, losing in the meantime $18,000 through the defalcation of a bookkeeper in the employ of the firm, and then became sole proprietor of the business, which, under his judicious management and through his great enterprise, became one of the largest of its kind in New York and its vicinity, averaging 300,000 head of live-stock, sheep and lambs, a year, and comprising, beside the large ·cal trade, heavy consignments from the South and West. In 1875 he entered into association with Mr. Philip S. Kase, under the firm-name of Kase & Pidcock, the present head-quarters of the business are at the Central Stock Yards of Jersey City. Politically James N. Pidcock is a Democrat, but previous to the year 1873 he had taken no more active part in politics than that of a citizen desirous of serving the public by helping to put good men in office. In that year he was urged by his friends to allow the use of his name as Democratic candidate for State Senator. He consented and received the caucus nomination ; but owing to the unusually light vote cast at the election, and the fact that one of his caucus rivals used his influence for the Republican candidate, Mr. T. A. Potts, together with the Central Railroad directing its employés to support Potts, he was defeated. In 1876 he was again a candidate, and this time was elected Senator by a majority of 1,675 over one of the most popular Republicans in the county. He is largely interested in real estate, owning over 1,800 acres of valuable land in his native township, within a radius of five miles of White House, besides holding a half interest in about 800 acres more. He has been largely instrumental in the improvement of the village of White House, selling property for building purposes on ten years' time, and then advancing to the purchaser a large part of the money necessary to erect buildings thereon. Property now valued at over $100,000 has been disposed of on this plan, and not a pur-

chaser has been distressed or any of the property taken back. He was married in 1862 to Fanny A. Faulks, of Elizabeth, New Jersey.

———◆◆———

HOTWELL. This family is one of the oldest in New Jersey. Abraham Shotwell, the first of the name of whom there is an account, is believed to have been of English origin. His name is the fourth in the list of the inhabitants of Elizabethtown and the jurisdiction thereof, who took the oath of allegiance to King Charles the Second, and his successors, etc., beginning the 19th of February, 1665. In the contentions between the people and Governor Carteret, he was bold and outspoken against the governor's usurpations. He became the victim of Carteret's wrath, his house and grounds were confiscated, and he himself driven into exile. A portion of this property includes the whole east side of Broad street, from the Stone Bridge to a point seven hundred and ninety-two feet north of Elizabeth avenue, the Courthouse and First Presbyterian Church being on the opposite side of the street. He retired to New York and appealed to the Lords Proprietors. In the meantime he returned to his home, sustained by his townsmen. His appeal was not sustained, and he was informed by orders from the Proprietary Government that he must depart the town, and should he return that he would be subjected to severe indignities. His property was sold at public auction, August 25th, 1675, for £12, to Thomas Blumfield Carpenter, of Woodbridge, who resold it a fortnight later, for £14, to Governor Carteret. Shotwell obtained a grant of land from the New York government, and died in exile. Daniel, who settled on Staten Island, was probably his son. John, another son, married, in New York, October, 1679, Elizabeth · Burton. The property so arbitrarily wrested from Abraham Shotwell was restored to his son, John, on May 12th, 1683; he petitioned the Council for its restoration, as the following will show : "At a meeting of Council held the 10th day of May, Anno Domini 1683, The petition of John Shotwell being here read, and upon reading thereof it being alleged that the lands for w'ch he desires a survey and patent is now or late in the possession of Elizabeth Carteret, w'w, the relict and executrix of the late Governor, Captain Philip Carteret, deceased. Its agreed that the further consideration thereof be deferred till the next Seventh Day morning, being the 12th instant, at 8 of the clock in the fforenoon, and that notice then be given to the Widdow Carteret that she may then appear, and if she has aught to allege against the substance of the petition she may then be heard." "Elizabeth Towne, May 12th, 1683. The matter of John Shottwell's petition came here into debate, and the Widdow Carteret being also here present, and in writing gave in two papers as her answer to the substance of the said petition. And it being asked the said Widdow Carterett if she desired any tyme to offer or object anything against the substance of the petition, she said she had no ffurther answer than what she gave in writing. And it appearing that Abraham Shotwell was the possessor, occupant, clearer and improver of the land mentioned in the petition, and that John Shottwell is the said Abraham Shottwell's sonne and heire; It is therefore agreed and ordered that the Deputy Governor issue out a warrant to the Surveyor General and his deputy, to survey the same lands and make return thereof, in order that the said Shottwell may have a pattent thereof, according to the concessions." The next official account of John Shotwell is found in the "Records of Friends," as follows: "At a monthly meeting, the 19th of ye 11th month, 1709, held att Nathaniel Fitz Randolph's, (Woodbridge) New Jersey. Our friend John Shotwell hath requested this meeting to have a meeting settled at his house (Statten Island) once every quarter, to which this meeting consented, and it is to begin ye first First Day, in ye next First Month, and so to continue quarterly." Respecting a meeting held at the same place the 21st, Third month, 1713, the following entry appears: "The meeting that was appointed att John Shotwell's, att Statten Island, is found inconvenient to be on ye day it was appointed, and the time of holding it is changed to ye second First Day, in ye Fourth, Seventh, Tenth and First months." John Shotwell died in 1718 at Woodbridge, where he resided at the time. In his will he is called "John Shotwelt, of the Towne of Woodbridge, in ye County of Middlesex, and Province of New Jersey, yoeman." His will was proved at Amboy, October 5th, 1719, before John Barclay. John Kinsey, his trusty and well beloved, and his son-in-law John Laing, are the executors named. In it he directs all his lands to be sold, and all goods indoors and outdoors, husbandry utensils and joiners' tools, cattle and horses, and his negro, Tom, are to be disposed of. After making bequests to his sons, John and Abraham, and daughter, Elizabeth Laing, and Sarah Smith, wife of Benjamin Smith, he orders the balance to be put out on interest for the use and benefit of his well-beloved wife. Joseph Shotwell, who married Mary Manning, in Woodbridge, in 1716, was no doubt a son of Daniel Shotwell, of Staten Island. The following certificate appears on record, referring to John Shotwell, Sr., son of John formerly of Staten Island: "From our Monthly Meeting, held att Philadelphia the 29th day of ye Eighth month, 1708, to the Monthly Meeting of Friends at Woodbridge, greeting: Whereas, John Shotwell, who came from your parts to serve an apprenticeship in this city, which being fulfilled and he intending to return to ye place of his former abode, hath regularly applied to this meeting for a certificate concerning his conversation (whilst among us) and clearness with respect to marriage. These are, therefore, according to ye wholesome and necessary discipline of truth, to certify on his behalf that, after due inquiry made, we find his conversation has been orderly and his diligence in keeping to meetings commendable as becomes our holy profession, and as to his clearness relating to marriage, we have no cause to think him under any engagements of that kinde. So, recommending him to your care, with desires for his prosperity in ye blessed truth, we dearly salute you and take leave. Your affectionate friends and brethren. Wm. Southby, Saml. Carpenter, Griffith Owens, Richard Hill, Wm. Hudson, Thom. Story, Nicholas Waln, Thom. Griffith, Ralph Jackson, Hugh Dewbury, David Loyd, Christopher Blakeburne, Nathan Stanberry, Anthony Morris." In the Eighth month, 1709, John Shotwell applied for a certificate on account of marriage, to carry to Flushing, Long Island, which was immediately granted, and in the following month the Flushing "Records" show that John Chatwell, or Shotwell, of Staten Island, and Mary Thorne, of Flushing, were married. The same record shows that in Ninth month, 1712, his brother Abraham married Elizabeth Cowperthwaite, daughter of John Cowperthwaite, of West Jersey. Abraham after his marriage resided in the neighborhood of Metuchen. Immediately after his marriage John Shotwell settled on the northerly bank of Rahway river, long known as Shotwell's Landing, now better known as Rahway Port, and lying within the limits of the city of Rahway; he also acquired a tract of land adjacent to his residence, where he died in 1762. His eldest son, Joseph, was born in 1710, married at Flushing, Long Island, in 1741, located where the National Banking House of Rahway now stands, and was a prominent merchant a century and a quarter ago. The land lying between the North and Robinson's Branch of Rahway river, now known as Upper Rahway, was his farm. Soon after the close of the revolutionary war two of his sons opened and maintained a direct trade with Bristol, England, shipping flaxseed and other produce and receiving in return dry goods, by means of a small vessel that navigated a portion of Rahway river. Before the close of the century they succeeded (what was at the time regarded a great and doubtful undertaking) by means of the race way leading to Milton Lake, in obtaining sufficient power to run successfully what have since been known as the Milton Mills, and to a descendant of one of the above Rahway is largely indebted for many of the improvements more recently made. John the second, son of John Shotwell, of Shotwell's Landing, was born in 1712. Soon after attaining his majority he started for the West, and eventually reached and settled the premises now owned and occupied by John Taylor Johnson, President of Central Railroad of New Jersey, now in the bounds of Plainfield city, but at that time known as the vicinity of Scotch Plains. And here it may not be improper to remark that the mountain beyond and the Short Hills, that bound the beautiful plain on the east, were occupied and settled before the plain, which, being covered with a stunted growth of scrub oaks, was regarded as of little value for agricultural purposes. At the time of which this is written the present growing and beautiful city of Plainfield had not an existence. There was a Plainfield, a neighborhood or locality, but it was some two or three miles to the eastward, in the township of Piscataway, county of Middlesex; the Plainfield of to day is in Union, formerly Essex county. In the year 1788 Friends decided to build a new meeting house, and the structure yet stands near the depot in Plainfield. The name by which the old town had been called was transferred to the new one, and thereafter the present Plainfield had a name and a record. John Shotwell acquired a large tract of land between Scotch Plains and Plainfield, extending from the mountain to the Short Hills. By his first wife, a daughter of Shobel Smith, of Woodbridge, he had one son, John Smith Shotwell, two of whose sons at one time resided at Turkey, now New Providence; another, fifty years ago, was a prominent auctioneer and merchant in New York. By his second wife, a daughter of William Webster, Jr., he had a numerous family of children. Two sons occupied portions of the original homestead; one went to Sussex county, and another to Canada; the youngest son, Hugh, settled in Harrison county, Ohio. Abraham, the third son of John of Shotwell's Landing, was born in 1719, married at Flushing, Long Island, and settled on the bank of the river, between Staten Island and the Landing, on lands believed to have been originally taken up by his father, which are yet owned and occupied by a grandson. Jacob, the fourth son, married at Flushing, Long Island, and was a merchant in Rahway. The house he occupied is yet standing in a good state of preservation, having been substantially built on oak frame covered with cedar shingles. Alexander Shotwell, a grandson, has long been a resident of the State of Alabama. Samuel, the fifth son, resided in what is now Grand street, near the Landing; his descendants are to be found in the northern part of the State. Benjamin, the sixth son, married at Flushing, Long Island, and inherited the homestead at the Landing, which descended through three generations and finally passed into the hands of strangers. Benjamin Lundy, one of the most persistent of abolitionists, the publisher of the *Genius of Universal Emancipation*, was a grandson of Benjamin Shotwell. The descendants of Abraham Shotwell may be found in every part of the Union and also in Canada, but few of them are aware of the suffering and privation he endured more than two centuries ago for his love of liberty and outspoken opposition to oppression and tyranny.

HOTWELL, ABEL VAIL, Retired Merchant and Secretary and Treasurer of the Rahway Insurance Company, was born, October 18th, 1814, in that place, and is a son of Abel and Elizabeth (Vail) Shotwell. His father carried on a tannery in Rahway for many years, and which was quite an extensive one for those days. His mother was a native of Somerset county, New Jersey, and fifth in descent from Edward Fitz Randolph, a native of

Nottinghamshire, England, born about the year 1617, and who came to Plymouth, Massachusetts, in 1630, it is supposed, with his parents. Edward Fitz Randolph was married, by Rev. John Lathrop, pastor of the Scituate and Barnstable Church, May 10th, 1637, to Elizabeth Blossom, born in Leyden, 1620, to which city her parents had escaped to avoid the persecutions of the English, and who also came to America the same year, landing at Plymouth from the celebrated "Mayflower." About the year 1668, Edward came to Piscataway, New Jersey, where he soon after died, after which his widow married Captain John Pike, of Woodbridge. Their son, Nathaniel, married Mary Holby, at Barnstable, Massachusetts, in November, 1660, and about the year 1667 he removed with his family to Woodbridge, New Jersey. In 1693 he represented that place in the Assembly held at Perth Amboy. From 1705 until 1713—the year of his death—Friends' Meetings were held in his house (which is said to have stood near the black walnut tree on the place recently owned by John Barron, deceased, near the railroad depot, Woodbridge). His son Edward married Katherine, daughter of Richard and Margaret Hartshorne, of Middletown, New Jersey. This Richard Hartshorne represented Monmouth county in the Provincial Assembly, and was Speaker of the same. He was also high sheriff of the county, and a member of the governor's council. Their son Edward was born May 7th, 1706. On July 26th, 1734, the monthly meeting of Friends at Woodbridge furnished Edward Fitz Randolph, Jr., with a certificate to Flushing, Long Island, Meeting, on account of his marriage with Phebe, daughter of James Jackson, of that place. Phebe was one of a family of twenty-two children, nineteen of whom grew up and married. Edward Fitz Randolph and Phebe his wife resided on the farm now owned and occupied by their great-grandson, Robert C. Vail, now in Raritan township (formerly Woodbridge), situated about midway between Rahway and Plainfield. One or more sharp skirmishes occurred on this farm during the war for independence. On one occasion a party of American militia, being closely pressed, retreated into the low grounds called "Ash Swamp," followed by the British cavalry, whose horses soon became mired to the saddle girths, when the Americans, who had taken shelter behind the trees, killed and wounded many of the enemy. The children of this last couple were six in number, two sons and four daughters. The fourth child, Catharine, married one John Vail, and the fifth child, Margaret, married his brother, Abraham Vail. The offspring of this last-named pair were Ephraim Vail, now living (November, 1876) in the ninety-third year of his age. He resides in the house his father built—as he was accustomed to say—in the year the war broke out in Boston, 1775. Ephraim's sister, Elizabeth, married Abel Shotwell. In connection with this generation of the family, an interesting historical fact deserves mention in this place. At a period during the revolutionary war, when the opposing forces were manœuvring between the mountains and the Short Hills, General Wash-ington attended by his staff rode up to the house of John Vail (who had married Catharine Fitz Randolph), and asked for a guide to lead them to some prominent place on the mountain where a good view could be obtained of the country below. Edward Fitz Randolph, a younger brother of Catharine Vail, happening to be at the house, volun-teered his services to guide the party, when one of the general's staff, or attendants, dismounted, and Edward took his place in the saddle. He led the general and his staff to what has since been known as "Washington's Rock," a prominent and conspicuous place on the face of the moun-tain, some two or three miles south of Plainfield. Imme-diately after the general and staff had left Vail's seat for the mountains, a boy was despatched to a neighboring pasture-field, where a horse was soon caught, and the general's dis-mounted attendant at once followed in rapid pursuit. This Edward Fitz Randolph subsequently purchased and resided on the farm adjoining his brother-in-law, John Vail, where he died about the year 1830. The farm of John Vail, where Washington called for a guide, is now owned and occupied by his grandson, Jonah Vail. Captain Nathaniel Fitz Randolph, of revolutionary fame, who resided in Woodbridge, was a cousin. Hartshorne Fitz Randolph, an uncle, settled prior to the Revolution in Morris county, and from him the township of Randolph is named. The wife of the late Hon. Thomas Corwin, of Ohio, is a granddaugh-ter of Hartshorne Fitz Randolph. Abel Vail Shotwell, the sixth in descent from the pilgrim of the "Mayflower," re-ceived a common school education in his native town of Rahway, and in 1830 effected an engagement as a clerk in a mercantile establishment there. Four years later he com-menced business on his own account, and was actively en-gaged therein until 1863. In 1868 he became connected with the Rahway Fire Insurance Company, which has been in existence since 1836. For the past ten years he has been Second Vice-President of the Rahway Savings Bank, and also Secretary to the Board of Directors of the National Bank of Rahway, which position he has held since the or-ganization of the bank in 1865. He was for many years a Director in the old Farmers' and Mechanics' Bank of Rahway, which was chartered in 1828, and wound up its affairs in 1865, since which period it has ceased to exist. When the city government of Rahway was formed in 1858, he was chosen to represent the First Ward in the City Coun-cil. He was married, November 2d, 1859, to his second cousin, Rosetta Shotwell Ebert, of Hamilton, Ohio, grand-daughter of Hugh Shotwell, formerly of Scotch Plains, New Jersey, and also, on her father's side, great grand-daughter of Colonel Michael Smyser, of York county, Pennsylvania, an officer in the war of the Revolution. Colonel Smyser was captain in Colonel Swope's regiment, and was one of the captured at Fort Washington, on the Hudson, November 16th, 1776. York county sent him seven times to the House, and he served two terms in the State Senate.

HOTWELL, JACOB R., Retired Merchant, was born, October 8th, 1813, in the city of Rahway, New Jersey, and is a son of the late Joseph D. and Elizabeth (Fitz Randolph) Shotwell. He is the great-grandson of Joseph Shotwell, one of the early settlers of East Jersey, and a grandson of Henry Shotwell, who was born in that province about 1751 and died in 1824. His house was the resort of the minis-ters of the Society of Friends, and was always open to re-ceive and welcome them. The family were leading mem-bers of that society, and have been identified with Rahway for very many years. Joseph D. Shotwell, son of Henry, was born in the city of New York, April 6th, 1782, and died December 7th, 1856; he married Elizabeth, daughter of Jacob Fitz Randolph, of Blazing Star, a member of the old family bearing that name, so familiarly known in New Jer-sey; the latter died November 26th, 1839, aged eighty-five years. Jacob R. Shotwell was educated partly at the Friends' Select School, in Rahway, and thence passed to the celebrated Westtown Boarding School, near Philadel-phia, also under the control of the same denomination, com-pleting his studies in Gummere's Collegiate School, at Bur-lingtou, where he graduated in 1831. Returning to Rahway he engaged there in mercantile pursuits, in which he was actively occupied until 1860, when he retired. He was one of the founders of the Rahway Gaslight Company, and has been its President since its organization in 1857. He is Vice-President of the Rahway Savings Institution; one of the incorporators and a Director of the Hazelwood Ceme-tery, of Rahway; a Director of the Jersey City Fire In-surance Company; a member of the Board of Commission-ers of Fisheries of the State of New Jersey. He was one of the incorporators of the Rahway Public Library, which was organized in 1858 and incorporated in 1864, and is now under the direct and able management of an association of the ladies of Rahway. He was also Chairman of the Com-mission appointed by act of Legislature to lay out "streets, avenues and squares" in the city of Rahway. He was a member of the first Board of Water Commissioners under an act of the Legislature, for supplying the city of Rahway and places adjacent with pure and wholesome water, and labored assiduously and successfully to accomplish that ob-ject. He is a life-member of the American Pomological Society, and has all his life taken an active interest in horti-culture, landscape gardening, and their kindred pursuits. He has been for many years a member of the New Jer-sey Historical Society. He has been thoroughly identi-fied with every public improvement, and has done much to advance the interests of the city. In politics he was an old-line Whig; and has acted with the Republican party since its organization. He was married, September 30th, 1841, to Elizabeth B., daughter of Hugh Hartshorne, of Locust Grove, near Rahway; she died May 1st, 1846. December 7th, 1848, he married his second wife, Martha, daughter of Daniel Stroud, of Stroudsburgh, Monroe co., Pa.

SHOTWELL, ABRAHAM F., President of the National Bank of Rahway, New Jersey, was born, August 6th, 1817, in that city, and is a son of John and Sarah (Freeman) Shotwell, both of whom were natives of New Jersey. His father was a farmer by occupation, and the old Shotwell homestead, near Rahway, is still occupied by the family, the land having been originally purchased by them from the Indians. There is quite a curiosity on the lands in the shape of a pear tree which has borne fruit yearly for the last two centuries, and never once failed during all that time. His mother was of the Freemans of Woodbridge, likewise an old Jersey family. He received his education at a select school in his birthplace known as the "Rahway Athenæum," from which he graduated in 1834. After leaving school he went to New York city, where he was engaged in mercantile pursuits for several years. He subsequently returned to Rahway, and from 1858 to 1865 was Cashier of the Farmers' and Mechanics' Bank, of that city. Upon the organization of the National Bank of Rahway, in 1865, he was elected its President, and has ever since occupied that position. He is also a Director of the Rahway Savings Bank. He was married in 1845 to Mary J. Wood, of New York.

these two were the only medical practitioners in the entire neighborhood. He brought to his new profession high natural qualifications, thorough professional training, a zealous enthusiasm and an unflagging energy. As a result, he speedily built up a very large practice, extending over a considerable portion of the country surrounding Flemington. The success attending his practice was great, and his reputation as a skilled physician and surgeon rested on a secure and permanent foundation. · Since 1820 he has been connected with the Somerset and Hunterdon County Medical Societies. He has been President of the latter association, and is now an honorary member of it. Through all his long career he has been highly esteemed by his professional brethren, and by all in the community in which he has lived. Politically he has taken no more active part than is required of every good citizen. His political sympathies are with the Democratic party. He was married in 1820 to Miss Van Deursen, of New Brunswick, New Jersey, sister of Dr. Van Deursen of that city. She died in 1848, and in 1850 he married Miss Churchill, of Portland, Connecticut. She died in 1865. His son, Dr. W. H. Schenk, is one of the leading physicians of Hunterdon county. Another son has long been connected with journalism in New Jersey.

SCHENK, DOCTOR JOHN FRELINGHUYSEN, Physician, of Flemington, was born in Neshanic, Somerset county, New Jersey, June 6th, 1799. He is of Dutch descent, his ancestors having come to this county from Holland and settled in the Millstone valley. His father, Dr. Henry H. Schenk, was an assistant surgeon in the revolutionary army, during the latter part of the war for independence. On the mother's side his grandfather was Jacob R. Hardenberg, first President of Queen's (now Rutgers) College. The early education of Dr. Schenk was obtained in the schools of Neshanic and vicinity, and subsequently, when he had passed through the proper course of preparatory training, he commenced the study of medicine, reading under the direction of his brother, Dr. Jacob R. Schenk, and Dr. Vanderveer. Subsequently he attended a regular course at the College of Physicians and Surgeons, in New York, graduating in due form. He was licensed to practise in the year 1820, and established himself as a practitioner at North Branch. He remained there but a short time, and then removed to Readington, New Jersey. His stay at the latter place was also brief, and in 1822 he removed to Flemington, where he has ever since continued to reside, and where for more than half a century he was engaged in active professional practice. In 1870 he retired from regular practice, and since then his professional labors have been confined to an occasional consultation with his son, Dr. W. H. Schenk. When he first established himself in Flemington there was but one other physician in the place, and for a long time

---

SCHENK, J. RUTSEN, Journalist, of Somerville, was born, May 23d, 1831, at Flemington, New Jersey, and is a son of Dr. John F. Schenk. His education was received at the public schools of his native town, and when he reached the age of seventeen years he was apprenticed to the printing business in the office of the *Hunterdon Democrat*, then under the editorial charge of George C. Seymour. He passed through all the grades of the business, and when he attained his majority he founded a Democratic newspaper at Woodstown, Salem county, New Jersey, which is still known as the *Woodstown Register*. He was successfully connected with this journal, as both editor and publisher, for about a year. In 1857 he established a Democratic organ at Middletown Point—now Matawan—which he conducted with marked ability until the breaking out of the rebellion. He was appointed by President Buchanan Postmaster of that town in 1859, which position he retained until 1861. Under the call for nine months troops he assisted to organize the 29th Regiment New Jersey Volunteers, from Monmouth county, and entered the regiment as a private. He was promoted from the ranks to the grade of First Lieutenant for good conduct, and at the close of the term for which he enlisted was mustered out of the service in June, 1863. During the same year he purchased the *Hunterdon Gazette*, which he published successfully until 1865, when he disposed of the concern, and it was finally merged with the *Hunterdon Democrat*. In the winter of 1867 he founded the *Constitutional Democrat* at Clinton,

... until 1869; it is now ...
... purchased the *Somer-*
... of Somerset county,
and ... the spring of 1876,
when he ... proprietors. He is
an unwave... party, and at the
present time ... man of the Somerset County ...

RICHARD... ...RGE, Mayor of Dover,
New Jer... ... 1833, in Pottsville, Pennsylvania. ... a common school education, and at ... early age was thrown on his
own resources. When about eighteen years of
age he went to New Jersey, where he found employment in an iron mine, and, being a remarkably industrious and observant young man, speedily won the respect
and esteem of his employers. He seemed to be innately
cognizant of the ... of iron ore in hitherto unsuspected
localities, and ... er he has selected any particular spot,
which ... indicated a bed of this valuable ore,
subsequent operations have proved that he never was
mistaken in his survey. In 1852 the northern region of
New Jersey was under the control of the Glendon Iron
Company, and the energy and good judgment which young
Richards displayed soon won recognition, and in 1853 he
was made Superintendent of their numerous mines. But
even this responsible position did not deter him from aiming to become still more prominent in the community, and
he steadily rose, until in 1860 he became identified with
the largest iron interests of the State. At the present time
he holds perhaps the most prominent position of any citizen
of New Jersey who has embarked in the iron business. He
is President and Director of the Ogden Iron Company;
the Ogden Mine Railroad Company; the Hibernia Mine
Railroad Company; the Morris County Machine and Iron
Company; a Director of the Chester Iron Company; Director, organizer and chief owner of the National Union Bank of
Dover; Director of the Delaware & Bound Brook Railroad
Company, and other institutions of a similar character. His
interests in the Lehigh valley compass its vast trade for iron
ore. He is the senior partner in the firms of George
Richards & Co.; Richards, Beach & Cox, and Richards,
Simpson & Co., who control the largest retail trade in that
State. He was State Director of the United Railroads of
New Jersey in 1871 and 1872, and his duty was to super-
vise the large trust funds of the State invested in those
securities. During his term of office the great question of
the lease of those roads to the Pennsylvania Company arose.
His answer ...

taken was that under a somewhat blind a...
ture, passed, however, for the purpose, it ...
the old companies to make the lease,
subsequently to obtain further legislation
He labored earnestly and successfully
of the monopoly and its adherents, and
energies towards the establishment of ...
travel, which culminated in the passage of
law. In political feeling he is an arden...
Republican party, but has persistently d...
nations for any prominent position. ...
yielded to the persuasions of his fellow...
coming their Mayor, and was the first one
after its creation, and has been ever since
has also taken a deep interest in the pro...
ture, and is a member of the State soci...
holds a membership in Washington's Hon...
which the ancient building at Morristow...
served. In private life he is social, genero...
is unobtrusive in his charities, and know...
money, as those who have formed it only c...
heart, are ever open to the deserving. He
family in a beautiful mansion in Dover, ...
respect a happy house. He was married i...
beth Anna McCarty, of Morris county, Ne...

ADRAIN, ROBERT, LL.D., Prof...
... matics in Rutgers College, was
... fergus, Ireland, September 30th,
... of French ancestry, his father havi...
... of France who left that country
... tion of the edict of Nantes.
... brothers, Donald and Hugh, he settled in t...
of Ireland, and there set about solving the ...
ing a livelihood in a strange land, and ...
methods. In their native country the th...
been manufacturers of mathematical inst...
their new home this branch of industry pro...
resuls, so they turned their attention in v...
in the effort to earn sufficient bread. A...
prises, they travelled through the coun...
here and there as they went. The ma...
one; there was no lack of will, but ...
Success was won at last, but before ...
came into greatly reduced circumstan...
Robert for a time sailed a small v...
Ireland to the neighboring ... d t...
subsistence for himself and ... pendent...
was a man of fine cultiv... and was rem...

New Jersey, and managed that paper until 1869; it is now the *Clinton Democrat*. In 1871 he purchased the *Somerset Messenger*, the Democratic organ of Somerset county, and conducted it with great success until the spring of 1876, when he disposed of it to the present proprietors. He is an unwavering member of the Democratic party, and at the present time (November, 1876) is Chairman of the Somerset County Executive Committee.

RICHARDS, HON. GEORGE, Mayor of Dover, New Jersey, was born, 1833, in Pottsville, Pennsylvania. He received a common school education, and at an early age was thrown on his own resources. When about eighteen years of age he went to New Jersey, where he found employment in an iron mine, and, being a remarkably industrious and observant young man, speedily won the respect and esteem of his employers. He seemed to be innately cognizant of the presence of iron ore in hitherto unsuspected localities, and wherever he has selected any particular spot, which in his judgment indicated a bed of this valuable ore, subsequent investigations have proved that he never was mistaken in his surmises. In 1852 the northern region of New Jersey was under the control of the Glenden Iron Company, and the energy and good judgment which young Richards displayed soon won recognition, and in 1853 he was made Superintendent of their numerous mines. But even this responsible position did not deter him from aiming to become still more prominent in the community, and he steadily rose, until in 1860 he became identified with the largest iron interests of the State. At the present time he holds perhaps the most prominent position of any citizen of New Jersey who has embarked in the iron business. He is President and Director of the Ogden Iron Company; the Ogden Mine Railroad Company; the Hibernia Mine Railroad Company; the Morris County Machine and Iron Company; a Director of the Chester Iron Company; Director, organizer and chief owner of the National Union Bank of Dover; Director of the Delaware & Bound Brook Railroad Company, and other institutions of a similar character. His interests in the Lehigh valley compass its vast trade for iron ore. He is the senior partner in the firms of George Richards & Co.; Richards, Beach & Co., and Richards, Simpson & Co., who control the largest retail trade in that State. He was State Director of the United Railroads of New Jersey in 1871 and 1872, and his duty was to supervise the large trust funds of the State invested in those securities. During his term of office the great question of the lease of those roads to the Pennsylvania Company arose. His answer as State Director, on behalf of his State, in the memorable litigation which ensued, though decided adversely by Chancellor Zabriskie, was subsequently sanctioned by the Court of Errors and Appeals. The point taken was that under a somewhat blind act of the Legislature, passed, however, for the purpose, it was not lawful for the old companies to make the lease. It was necessary subsequently to obtain further legislation upon the subject. He labored earnestly and successfully against the efforts of the monopoly and its adherents, and devoted his best energies towards the establishment of competing lines of travel, which culminated in the passage of the free railroad law. In political feeling he is an ardent member of the Republican party, but has persistently declined all nominations for any prominent position. He has, however, yielded to the persuasions of his fellow-townsmen in becoming their Mayor, and was the first one to fill that office after its creation, and has been ever since re-elected. He has also taken a deep interest in the promotion of agriculture, and is a member of the State society; and he also holds a membership in Washington's Home Association, by which the ancient building at Morristown has been preserved. In private life he is social, generous and kind. He is unobtrusive in his charities, and knowing the value of money, as those who have earned it only can, his hand and heart are ever open to the deserving. He resides with his family in a beautiful mansion in Dover, which is in every respect a happy home. He was married in 1860 to Elizabeth Anna McCarty, of Morris county, New Jersey.

ADRAIN, ROBERT, LL.D., Professor of Mathematics in Rutgers College, was born at Carrickfergus, Ireland, September 30th, 1775. He was of French ancestry, his father having been a native of France, who left that country after the revocation of the edict of Nantes. With his two brothers, Donald and Hugh, he settled in the northern part of Ireland, and there set about solving the problem of gaining a livelihood in a strange land, and by unaccustomed methods. In their native country the three brothers had been manufacturers of mathematical instruments, but in their new home this branch of industry promised but meagre results, so they turned their attention in various directions in the effort to earn sufficient bread. Among their enterprises, they travelled through the country teaching school here and there as they went. The struggle was a brave one; there was no lack of will and no lack of courage. Success was won at last, but before that time the family came into greatly reduced circumstances, and the father of Robert for a time sailed a small vessel from the north of Ireland to the neighboring islands, and thereby gained a subsistence for himself and those dependent upon him. He was a man of fine cultivation, and was remarkable for his brilliant wit and his great and versatile powers of conversation. After coming to Ireland he married, and a family of five children gathered about him. The eldest of these was Robert. He early developed an intellectual quickness and aptitude that amounted to genius. This his father was quick to perceive, and determined him to make every possible exertion to give the boy a thorough education and fit him for the ministry. He carried this purpose into effect so far as lay in his power. Robert Adrain was placed at school, where his precocity and thirst for knowledge endeared him to all his instructors, and insured his wonderfully rapid progress in his studies. But when he was only fifteen years old both his father and mother died, and he was thrown wholly upon his own resources. His experience as a pupil ended and his experience as a teacher began almost simultaneously. Young as he was, he opened a school at Ballycarry and commenced teaching for a livelihood. It was through this necessity that his wonderful talent for mathematics was developed. One day he was looking through an old arithmetic and noticed a series of algebraic signs at the end of the book; he did not know the meaning of these, and at once determined to find it out; by his own efforts he mastered the task, and in a short time he was able to solve any problem in arithmetic by algebraic processes. This was the first step in the mathematical career which ultimately resulted so brilliantly. His success in teaching was so great that a Mr. Mortimer, a man of great wealth and influence in the town of Cumber, engaged him as an instructor of his children. His position here was a pleasant one, but not of long duration. The Irish rebellion of 1798 broke out; Mr. Mortimer, an officer of the government, learned that the young tutor in his employ was at the head of an Irish company; he was greatly enraged and offered fifty pounds for the young man's capture, at the same time sending out emissaries after him in every direction. The next day Mr. Mortimer was mortally wounded in the battle of Saintfield, and the pursuit, so far as he was concerned, came to an end. The result would probably have been the same in any case, however, for young Adrain was a genuine Independent, and spoke his mind in regard to his own party as well as others. He opposed some measure proposed in his division of the army, and in resentment of this opposition one of his own men treacherously wounded him in the back, producing such injuries that there seemed no possibility of recovery. This gave rise to the statement that he was dead, and all efforts for his capture came to an end. He recovered, after much suffering, and by assuming the disguise of a weaver he was enabled to escape to America. Arriving in New York he found the yellow fever prevailing there. He heard, moreover, that employment as a teacher could be obtained in New Jersey; so he hastened across the Hudson river and walked all the way to Princeton, seeking employment. He found it, and on the day of his arrival obtained a position in the Princeton Academy. He remained there two or three years, and then removed to York, Pennsylvania, and became the Principal of the York County Academy. While here his mathematical talents and accomplishments were brought before the public by frequent contributions to the *Mathematical-Correspondent,*

published in New York, and, although still a young man, received several of the prize medals awarded for the best solutions of problems published in the columns of that periodical. In 1805 he removed from York to Reading, Pennsylvania, and took charge of the academy at that place. While here he was offered the editorship of the *Mathematical Correspondent,* and also the mathematical school, in New York, of Mr. Baron, proprietor of the *Correspondent,* but both offers were declined. Shortly afterwards he himself commenced the publication of a mathematical periodical, called the *Analyst,* which he continued to publish for two or three years, and which was characterized by brilliant ability and great culture. The publication of this periodical made him extensively and favorably known throughout the country as an able and leading mathematician, and in the year 1810 he was called to the Professorship of Mathematics and Natural Philosophy in Queens (now Rutgers) College, at New Brunswick, New Jersey. Shortly after going to New Brunswick the degree of Doctor of Laws was conferred upon him, and in 1812 he was elected a member of the American Philosophical Society; in the following year of the American Academy of Arts and Sciences, and subsequently of several of the philosophical societies of Europe. Besides fulfilling his college duties he edited the third American edition of Hutton's "Course of Mathematics." In the fall of 1813, upon the death of Dr. Kemp, he was elected to supply his place as Professor of Mathematics and Natural Philosophy in Columbia College, New York, the choice being made without any application on his part. He accepted the position, and in New York became the centre of a brilliant collection of mathematical talent and culture. All gathered about him, and all did him honor as their rightful leader. His contributions to the literature of mathematical science while in New York, and subsequently, were voluminous, and all were marked by a force and clearness, a profound and exhaustive knowledge, and an elegance of style that won for them universal admiration and commanded the respectful attention of the scientists of the world. In 1825 he commenced editing the *Mathematical Diary,* a work superior to anything that had ever been previously published in this country. He continued this editorial work until 1826, when he relinquished his position in Columbia College and returned to Rutgers, the change being made necessary by the delicate state of his wife's health. His departure from Columbia College was the occasion of great regret among his brother professors and the students of the institution, and many were the fitting and substantial tokens of their regard that they bestowed upon him at parting. He remained at Rutgers only two or three years, when, in response to pressing solicitations, he accepted a professorship in the University of Pennsylvania. He was also Vice-Provost of that institution. He retained this professorship until 1834, discharging its duties with the ability that characterized all his work. His wife's health, however, compelled her to remain at their country home, near New Brunswick, New Jersey, and in the year named, that he might be more with her and their family, he resigned his position and went to his New Brunswick home. At his departure the trustees and faculty of the university passed resolutions of regret at his leaving them. The habit of teaching was strong upon him and he could not remain at home in idleness, so after two or three years he moved to the city of New York and taught in the grammar school connected with Columbia College. This he continued to do until within three years of his death; then, yielding to the entreaties of his family and friends, he relinquished the work of teaching forever, and returned to New Brunswick. Although several very flattering offers of positions were made to him, he refused them all. It was not long before his clear mind began to grow clouded and his strong faculties to fail, and the painfulness of this fact was increased by his keen appreciation of it. On the 10th of August, 1843, he breathed his last, surrounded by his family, and mourned sincerely by all to whom his name had become so familiarly known. The mourning was not simply that one of the brightest intellectual lights had disappeared, but that a man who won the love of all who came in contact with him was no more.

DRAIN, HON. GARNETT B., A. M. and A. B., Lawyer, of New Brunswick, was born in the city of New York, December 20th, 1815. His father was the celebrated Professor Robert Adrain, of Rutgers College, a native of Belfast, Ireland, and his mother was Annie (Pollock) Adrain, a native also of Belfast. Professor Adrain came to this country about the year 1800, establishing himself first at Princeton, New Jersey, and later at New Brunswick. There his son, Garnett, received his education. He attended first the Rutgers College Grammar School, and in the year 1829 entered Rutgers College. He graduated from that institution with the class of 1833. After his graduation he entered the law office of his brother, Robert Adrain, who was then a leading lawyer in New Brunswick. Here he pursued the necessary course of study to fit him for the profession he had chosen, and was licensed as an attorney in 1836. Three years later, in 1839, he was licensed as a counsellor. He at once entered upon the practice of his profession in New Brunswick, and has continued in active and eminently successful practice there to the present time. He speedily took high rank in his profession, and holds a commanding position at the bar. In politics he is a Democrat of the old school. He was an ardent adherent of Stephen A. Douglas, and concurred with him in the position he took on the Lecompton Compromise issue. In 1856 he was nominated for Congress by the Democrats of the Third District, and was elected and served his term. In 1858 there was a "bolt" from the regular Congressional convention of Democrats at Somerville, and he was put in nomination by the bolting convention. He went through the canvass as a Douglas Democrat, and was elected a second time to Congress, gaining a handsome majority over William Patterson, of Perth Amboy, the regular Democratic nominee. His career in Congress was an active one, and was characterized by great ability and high toned earnestness. His speeches were pointed, eloquent and effective, and his influence, on some of the issues presented during his terms of service, was strongly felt. Among the more noteworthy of the speeches delivered by him during his terms in the House of Representatives were: one on the "Treasury Note Bill," on the 22d of December, 1857; one on the "Neutrality Laws," January 7th, 1858; another against the "Admission of Kansas," March 20th, 1858; one on the "Impeachment of Judge Watrous," December 13th, 1858; one on the "Election of Speaker," December 14th, 1859; one on the "Organization of the House," January 6th, 1860, and one on the "State of the Union," January 15th, 1861. Since his retirement from Congress at the end of his second term he has not taken any active part in politics. He was married, January 3d, 1838, to Mary Griggs, daughter of Joseph C. Griggs, Esq., who was for many years one of the leading merchants of New Brunswick.

AN LIEW, REV. JOHN, D. D., Clergyman and late Pastor of the Reformed Dutch Church, at Readington, was born, September 30th, 1798, in Neshanic, Somerset county, New Jersey, and was a son of Dennis and Maria (Suydam) Van Liew. His ancestors emigrated to America from Holland at an early day, and were among the first settlers on Long Island. He received a first-class academical education preparatory to entering Queens (now Rutgers) College, New Brunswick, from which institution he graduated with the class of 1816. Having resolved to devote himself to the gospel ministry, he matriculated at the Theological Seminary of the Reformed Dutch Church connected with the college, and was licensed to preach by the Classis of New Brunswick in June, 1820. In the summer of the same year he commenced his ministerial labors at the Presbyterian Church of Meadville, Pennsylvania, and was ordained its pastor by the Presbytery of Erie, August 22d, 1821. This relation continued until June 21st, 1824, when, on account of impaired health, it was dissolved, and the next day he was dismissed to the Presbytery of New Jersey. In the spring of the following year, his health having improved, he accepted a call to the Presbyterian Church of Mendham, New Jersey, where he remained until 1825, when his relations with this congregation were dissolved by reason of his health again failing him. He then made the tour of the Southern States, spending several months in travel, extending as far south as Georgia, and returned

23

home with renewed health. He shortly afterwards received and accepted a call to the pastorate of the Reformed Church of Readington, New Jersey. At that place he remained and labored faithfully and successfully for forty-three years. His relations with this congregation terminated in 1869, owing to a severe cold he had contracted the previous winter, which, with advanced age, so far enfeebled him as to render his further efficiency in the manifold labors of his large parish entirely beyond his powers of endurance; and, to the great regret of his congregation, he resigned his pastorate, and was succeeded by Rev. J. G. Van Slyke. The church resolved to continue his salary during life, and it was the earnest wish of the congregation that he would continue to meet and worship with them, and also preach as often as his health would permit; but their hopes in this respect were not realized. While on a visit to his son-in-law, J. F. Randolph, at Bloomfield, who insisted on his remaining with him until his health was in a measure restored, he gradually failed, and on October 18th, 1869, he calmly passed away. His life and ministerial services at Readington had very much endeared him to that congregation, and his death was deeply felt by them. The funeral discourses were delivered by Rev. Dr. A. Messh and Rev. Joseph P. Thompson, who eloquently and touchingly noticed the long period of his pastorate. He was married, June 20th, 1827, to Anna M., daughter of Dr. H. S. Woodruff, of Mendham, New Jersey.

AN LIEW, CORNELIUS S., of Washington, Superintendent of the Morris Canal, was born, August 18th, 1828, in Readington, New Jersey, and is the eldest son of the late Rev. Dr. John Van Liew, whose biographical sketch will be found above. The family are of Hollander descent; the original emigrant ancestor settled near Fort Hamilton, on Long Island. Tredvick Van Liew, great-grandfather of Cornelius, settled at Three Mile Run, in Middlesex county, New Jersey, where his son, Dennis, resided when the war of the Revolution commenced. He was then a young man of nineteen, and after serving a short time as a substitute for a neighbor, who desired the opportunity to harvest his crops, he assisted to organize and became a member of a volunteer cavalry organization, who equipped and furnished themselves; and in this capacity served till the close of the war. His military equipments are still in the possession of his grandson. Cornelius was educated at the grammar school of Rutgers College, New Brunswick, under the direction of Rev. W. J. Thompson, having previously been for two years under his tutelage before entering the school. He was fully prepared to enter the junior class; but, instead of taking a collegiate course, he determined to devote himself to business pursuits; and

effected an engagement as clerk in a general retail store at Morristown, where he remained four years. Subsequently, in connection with his brother-in-law, J. F. Randolph, he embarked in a general country trade at Somerville, where they continued four years, and then purchased a mill for the manufacture of paper at Bloomfield, New Jersey. The firm occupied the mill and transacted a very good business for nine years. In the fall of 1861 the mill was burned, and in the following spring he removed to the old homestead—his grandfather's farm, at Neshanic—where he resided until 1869, when he located at Washington, and was elected, by the Board of Directors, Assistant Superintendent of the Morris Canal. He has the charge of the canal interests on its western division, from Lake Hopatcong to Philipsburg. He is highly esteemed by his fellow-townsmen as an amiable and valuable citizen, and as a business man of rare foresight and ability. His residence at Washington bears good evidence of a fine architectural taste. His political predilections are favorable to the principles held by the Republican party. He was married, January 3d, 1856, to Sarah, daughter of Hon. David Oakes, of Bloomfield; she died, June 1st, 1858. He was a second time married to Susan, daughter of James Moore, also of Bloomfield, April 3d, 1862.

WAYZE, JACOB L., Cashier of the Merchants' National Bank, of Newton, New Jersey, was born, March 3d, 1824, in the village of Hope, Warren county, and is a son of Israel and Mary Ann (Lowrance) Swayze, both of whom were also natives of New Jersey. On his father's side he is of Welsh descent, and his mother's family were of Hollander ancestry. The Swayze family emigrated to America about 1660, and a portion settled on Long Island, while others located, at a later date, in both Warren and Morris counties, New Jersey. Young Swayze received his education in the common schools of his native county, continuing to attend them until he was thirteen years old. He then assisted his father in farm work for about a year, and subsequently entered the country store of his uncles, at Hope, as a clerk. In June, 1842, he purchased the interests of the partner of one of these uncles, continuing the business under the firm-name of C. & J. L. Swayze until January, 1845, when the other uncle disposed of his share of the concern to his nephew, and the latter became sole proprietor. He carried on the establishment until the spring of 1847, when he relinquished the business, and afterwards went to New York city, where he effected an engagement in a wholesale dry-goods house as clerk. He remained there for about four months, and, returning to New Jersey, at first located in Stanhope, Sussex county, and once more started in business, carrying on a general country store until the spring of 1854, when he sold out the concern. He then resolved to lead a professional life, and removed to Trenton in May, 1854, where he at once commenced the study of law under Hon. Martin Ryerson as his preceptor, with whom he remained about one year, when Mr. Ryerson removed to Newton. He then entered the office of Mercer Beasley, now Chief-Justice, and finished his studies preparatory to admission to the bar under the instruction of the latter for about three years, and was admitted as an attorney at the June term of 1858, and at once entered upon the practice of his profession at Trenton, where, however, he remained but a short time. In the autumn of the same year he went to Newton, where he again followed mercantile pursuits, and so continued until the spring of 1865. He was active in organizing the Merchants' National Bank, of Newton, is its largest shareholder, and was elected Cashier, March 6th, 1865, at the first meeting of its directors. Although of Whig parentage on his father's side, his political creed up to 1854 was that of the old Jackson school, and never differed with the principles of the Democratic party, except on the question of slavery. He has always been a radical anti-slavery man, and a zealous advocate of free trade and direct taxation. He joined the Republican movement in 1856, being one of its earliest members, and adhered to the organization until 1872, when he espoused the cause of the Liberal Republicans and Democrats, and supported the claims of Horace Greeley for the Presidency, and has continued to act with the Democratic party since. He was a member of the Constitutional Commission that proposed amendments to the constitution, in 1873, and introduced a number of measures of reform, several of which were adopted in whole or in a modified form, and are now incorporated into the constitution of the State. He labored earnestly, industriously and zealously in favor of every reform measure that was introduced. He favored an elective judiciary, the abolition of the Court of Chancery, the abolition of capital punishment, woman suffrage, the equal taxation of all kinds of property, and no exemptions even for churches and institutions of learning, the election of State officers by the people, measures to prevent bribery at elections and several other reforms; and he opposed a change of representation in the Senate and the creation of any new offices. He was married, September 10th, 1860, to Joanna Hill, daughter of the late Jonathan Hill, of Sussex county.

ANDERSON, HON. AUGUSTUS E., Lawyer, was born, February 15th, 1832, in Littleton, Middlesex county, Massachusetts, and is a son of Ira and Asenath (Hatch) Sanderson; his maternal grandmother was Mary Webster, a relative of the late Hon. Daniel Webster. The Sanderson family, of Massachusetts, are descendants of Edward and Robert Sanderson, who settled in Watertown, Massachu-

setts, about 1630. They have been noted for their adherence to the customs of the Puritans. The family genealogy is liberally interspersed with those who have been prominent in the church and local affairs of State. George W. Sanderson, a brother of Augustus E., and a member elect to the Legislature of Massachusetts, now holds the position of Clerk of the District Court of Northern Middlesex, Massachusetts, and owns and resides on a farm near Littleton, which has been in the occupancy of the Sanderson family over 120 years. The present generation is the sixth in descent from Edward Sanderson, one of the emigrant ancestors. Augustus E. Sanderson was educated at Appleton's Seminary, Mount Vernon, New Hampshire, now called the McCullock Institute. In 1854 he removed to New Jersey, and taught school near Lebanon; at the same time he commenced the study of the law with M. D. Trefren. He was licensed as an attorney in 1858, and made a counsellor-at-law in 1863. Immediately after his admission to the bar he opened an office in Lebanon, in 1858, and at once commenced to practise his profession. He was for a number of years Superintendent of Schools for the township where he resides, and otherwise identified with the local politics of the town and county. In 1870 he received the Democratic nomination for member of Assembly, and was elected by a large majority. He was renominated and elected in 1871. During both sessions he served on the Judiciary Committee; and as the Democrats were in a minority, his being assigned to that important committee was highly complimentary. Although a Democrat, he is not an aggressive politician, and during the civil war was an earnest advocate for the cause of the Union. During his career in the Legislature his course was very generally approved by all parties. He advocated the general railroad bill, which subsequently became a law. He introduced the first free school bill, which was afterwards supplemented by the Runyon bill, and subsequently passed; it is at present the existing school law of New Jersey. During his entire residence in the State he has commanded the respect of his fellow-townsmen, as well as the members of the profession at large. He was married, in 1856, to Mary A. Groendyke, of Lebanon, New Jersey.

LIET, JOSEPH, of Washington, Lawyer and Law Judge of the Courts of Warren County, New Jersey, was born in Franklin township, of that county, and is the son of Daniel Vliet, and a grandson of Garrett Vliet, Major-General of New Jersey Militia, and whose division performed escort duty on the occasion of the visit of General Lafayette to Trenton, in 1825. The family was among the earliest settlers of the Musconetcong valley, and several of his ancestors participated in the war of the Revolution. He was educated principally in his native county, and in 1845 entered the law office of Hon. A. G. Richey, where he commenced his preparation for the bar, to which he was admitted as an attorney, January 3d, 1850, and in 1852 was appointed a Master in Chancery. He was licensed a counsellor in 1855, which entitled him to practise in the Supreme courts. He was appointed, by Governor Price, Prosecutor of the Pleas for Warren County, which position he held for the usual term of five years. After an interval of five years —during which time the position was filled by Colonel James M. Robeson—he was again appointed by Governor Randolph, in 1865; again, in 1870, by Governor Parker; and a fourth time, in 1875, by Governor Bedle. After receiving his license as an attorney, in 1850, he practised his profession for one year at Asbury, and then removed to Washington, where he has since resided. He was elected the first Mayor of Washington, after its incorporation as a borough, and served in that position for three years. He is attorney for the First National Bank, at Washington; and was of counsel for the Morris & Essex Railroad Company in Warren county, during its construction and until it was merged into the Delaware, Lackawanna & Western Railroad. During the long period that he has filled the position of Prosecutor of the Pleas he has tried over twenty homicide cases; noticeable among which was that of the Rev. Jacob Hardin, convicted and executed for the murder of his wife. In this case he was assisted by James M. Robeson and the late Hon. William L. Dayton, Attorney-General of the State. During his long service the great variety of criminal business of which he has had charge has been ably managed, and there is probably not a single instance where an indictment of his preparing has been quashed through a defect in the bill. As a lawyer he ranks equal to any in the country, and is highly respected by the bar and also by his fellow-townsmen. Politically he is a Democrat, although too deeply engrossed in and devoted to his profession to be an office-holder or office-seeker, outside of his professional appointments. He has been twice married. His first wife was Miss Crevley, of Bloomsburg, New Jersey, who died in 1872. In 1874 he was married to Martha Voorhees Losey, of Pittsburgh, Pennsylvania. In February, 1877, he was appointed Law-Judge of Warren county.

BYINGTON, WILLIAM WILBERFORCE, of Newark, General Agent for New Jersey of the Mutual Life Insurance Company, of New York, was born, December 26th, 1840, at Potsdam, St. Lawrence county, New York. His father was the Rev. John Byington, born at Great Barrington, Massachusetts, and his mother, Catherine (Newton) Byington, was a native of Vermont. His father was a clergyman of the Methodist Episcopal Church, but withdrew from it because he believed its position on the slavery ques-

tion not sufficiently pronounced, and he was one of the leading men in the organization of the Wesleyan Methodist Church. Mr. Byington's boyhood was spent on his father's farm, in northern New York, on which he acquired a fine physical constitution, as well as the earnest political convictions of his father. But while yet a lad he was ambitious for a better education than the district school of a small town could afford, and at the age of sixteen he went to Battle Creek, Michigan, where an elder brother resided, and spent a year at the public school. At the age of seventeen he taught his first school, and from that time for four years he supported himself entirely by teaching in the winter, while attending school in the summer. At the age of twenty-one he graduated with a high rank at the State Normal School of Michigan, winch was then, as now, celebrated for the thorough drill which it gave its pupils. Immediately on his graduation he was called back to Battle Creek to take charge of one of the schools there, and a year after was called to the mastership of the Houghton Union School, of Detroit, one of the finest in that city, which position he held for three years. At the end of this time he resigned, on the ground that teachers were not properly paid for their services, and received the highest testimonials for his remarkable ability and success. At the age of twenty-six he now went into the life insurance business, and spent about three years in travelling in that interest in the West. In 1870 he removed to New York city, where he was an insurance broker for four years. Being a man who could not but give the whole of his fine abilities and intense energy to thoroughly understanding and prosecuting his business, he made a careful study of the science and history of life insurance, and gained considerable reputation as a very vigorous writer on this subject. It was in 1872 that he issued what was a great desideratum, his first "Synopsis of Ten Years of Life Insurance Business," which he has since issued annually. It gave all the statistics of all our American companies for ten years, and had an immediate sale of about 40,000 copies. In the beginning of 1874 Mr. Byington was invited by the Mutual Life Insurance Company, of New York, to the responsible post of General Agent for the State of New Jersey. He thereupon moved to Newark, in this State, and has devoted himself ever since to its duties. Being a man of very positive convictions, he has not hesitated to take a pronounced position in fighting against everything, especially in the insurance business, which he saw to be an injury to its truest interests, and his familiarity with the general subject and his command of a sharp and telling style have made his work in this line very successful. Physically, Mr. Byington is a man of large frame and well-proportioned figure. He is an active and public-spirited citizen, taking great interest in every good cause; in politics he is an earnest Republican; and is a communicant of Trinity Protestant Episcopal Church. He was married, December 25th, 1865, to Kate M. Preston, of Battle Creek, Michigan.

ULVER, JOSEPH EDWIN, M. D., Practising Physician of Jersey City, was born, February 9th, 1823, in Groton, New London county, Connecticut. His parents were Joseph and Permelia Lamb Culver. For several generations his ancestors on both sides were natives of Connecticut. His early education was obtained at the public schools of his native place. The schools there, however, were of a very high character, and afforded him large opportunities for advancement in his studies. He was of a specially studious disposition, and from the first made the utmost of the opportunities afforded him. Not only did he industriously perform the regular mark of school study, but he availed himself of every leisure hour at home to prosecute additional studies. It was well that he possessed this persevering energy, for when he was only two years old his father had died, and it was inevitable that the fatherless boy should as early as possible depend upon himself for support. He was only ten years of age when the responsibility of self-support came upon him, and from that time forward he has earned his own livelihood. The ambition that characterized him continued to manifest itself in his devotion to books, and he read and studied what time could be spared from work and sleep. Such progress did he make in this way that when he was only sixteen year of age he passed the necessary examination and taught a public school in his native town. Succeeding satisfactorily he continued in this employment for several years during the winter months, and thus he obtained the means to advance his own education. In the summers of 1839 and 1840 he was a student at the Connecticut Literary Institution located at Suffield. Here in the latter year, by request of the principal, he wrote and delivered an oration on "Political Fame," on the occasion of the annual commencement. He obtained a fair knowledge of the Latin language and a smattering of the Greek, and attempted the study of the French without a teacher, and of course without a pronunciation. But scientific pursuits claimed his chief attention. For the pure and mixed mathematics he always cherished an especial fondness, and in these branches he never needed the assistance of a tutor; albeit he never failed to solve the most difficult test problems submitted to him by his teachers and schoolfellows. His reading extended to every department of human knowledge, but a strong preference for the natural sciences now led him for a few years to devote all his leisure time to conjoined study and experiment. And when at length he decided to enter the medical profession he was already quite familiar with what was then known of electricity and galvanism, optics, acoustics, chemistry inorganic and organic, human and comparative physiology, human anatomy, materia medica, toxicology, hygiene, and the history of medicine. In the year 1847 he matriculated at the Berkshire Medical College, at Pittsfield, Massachusetts, where he attended one course of lectures. The following spring he went to New York city, where he attended for one year the excellent private school of Dr. John H. Whittaker, and also for several months the private surgical school of Dr. William Detmold. In the fall and winter of 1848 he attended the course of lectures at the College of Physicians and Surgeons in New York city, and received his diploma therefrom in the spring of 1849. After his graduation he went to live in the southern part of North Bergen, subsequently Hudson City, and now included in the municipality of Jersey City. Here he at once entered upon the practice of his profession, in which he has ever since been actively engaged. He rapidly achieved success in the career he had chosen, and his practice soon extended into every city and township in Hudson county. In the summer of 1849 he was chosen physician for the townships of Bergen and North Bergen, and also for Hudson county, which positions he continued to fill for several consecutive years. Having been examined and licensed by the Medical Society of New Jersey, he became a member of the Passaic District Medical Society, and in 1850 was a delegate from that body to the State Medical Society. By the State Medical Society he was empowered to organize the District Medical Society of Hudson County, which accordingly was chartered in 1851. He wrote the constitution and by-laws of the Hudson District Medical Society. He compiled and published in 1873 "A Documentary History of Recent Discussions in the District Medical Society for the County of Hudson." He has held every office in the gift of said society, and he is at the present time the appointed historian and custodian of its archives. In 1871, 1872 and 1873, he was one of the Standing Committee of the Medical Society of New Jersey. He is a charter member of the New Jersey Academy of Medicine, Vice-President, and Chairman of Committee on Admissions. One of the founders of the Jersey City Pathological Society, he was also its first President. For many years he has been a member of the New York Pathological Society, and he has belonged to the Neurological Society of New York city since its reorganization. He is one of the attending physicians of St. Francis Hospital, having been on the staff since its organization. In years past he has written more or less of the reports of the Hudson District Medical Society, which have been published annually in the "Transactions of the Medical Society of New Jersey." Aside from this he has contributed from time to time to the literature of his profession. In 1868 he published, in the transactions of the State Medical Society, "A Case of Choleraic Dysentery—Death by Septicæmia;" in 1869 a paper on the hygrometer, being a plea for its general use in epidemiological observations. In 1876 he published, in The American Journal of the Medical Sciences, "A Case of Hydrophobia," in which the symptoms and post mortem appearances were carefully noted and an attempt made to lay the foundation of a rational treatment of this disease on its pathological conditions. He is a thorough scholar and a close professional student, taking an ardent and active interest in all matters pertaining to his chosen calling. His profession, however, has not absorbed all his attention and energies. He has taken a strong and practical interest in general educational matters. During four years of his residence in Hudson City, he filled the position of City Superintendent of Public Schools, and for one year he was one of the County Board of Examiners of Public School Teachers. When he entered upon the duties of the former office, in 1860, Hudson City had not a school building nor a school worthy of the name. He assisted the city to borrow twenty thousand dollars, with which three commodious schoolhouses were built and furnished. He classified the pupils according to their studies and proficiency, and graded the departments accordingly. He wrote the rules and regulations for the government of the schools, and the by-laws adopted by the Board of Education. The system of school management organized by him has never been changed essentially. Three years after it was put on trial the State superintendent pronounced the schools of Hudson City the best in Hudson county, and the schools of Hudson county the best in the State. Moreover, he is active in the general duties of citizenship, and in the year 1860 he was elected Treasurer of Hudson City, the duties of which position he performed for a period of eight years. Before the issue of war-bonds was authorized by State legislation, Hudson City had borrowed more than one hundred thousand dollars, for the payment of which the lenders held no other security than the signature of the Treasurer and the integrity of the city officers. For these eight years the bonds of Hudson City were very acceptable at the banks and among capitalists. He is one of the Trustees of the Hudson City Savings Bank, appointed by the act of incorporation. The by-laws adopted by the trustees, under which the bank management is controlled, the trustees permanently organized, and the duties of their chosen officers defined, were written by him. The Hudson County Hospital was chartered in 1860 through the joint efforts of Drs. T. R. Varick and J. E. Culver. There were ten regents, who appointed a staff of four regular physicians. Subscriptions to the amount of twenty-five thousand dollars, more or less, were found to be obtainable, when the war of the rebellion put a stop to further progress. Soon after the war ceased, however, the project was revived. About this time, without the knowledge of the staff and the surviving regents, an amendment to the hospital charter, doubling the number of regents, was hurried through the Legislature. Upon the heels of this sharp practice the new quota of regents was filled, and they were then brought to sanction a second amendment legalizing the appointment on the hospital staff of irregular practitioners. At this juncture the District Medical Society demurred and appointed a committee to wait upon the regents and protest against this infringement of vested rights. Dr. Culver wrote and presented theirs on this occasion. It was published by order of the District Medical Society. Ignoring the staff elect, the regents now appointed a new one, far greater in numbers and not inconveniently squeam-

ish about their associates. The hospital, prematurely put to work, ran a feeble race for two years, and fell dead. Recently it has been resuscitated, but with fewer patients than attendants it languishes, and is itself a fearfully expensive example and victim of chronic disease. The following original essays by Dr. Culver may be mentioned: Thesis for graduation, on certain physiological relations and uses of the oxides and oxysalts of iron; papers read before the District Medical Society—1. "On Digestion;" 2. "On the Origin and Relations of Urea, Uric Acid and Uric Oxide in Vertebrates and Invertebrates;" 3. "On Pepsin;" 4. "Concerning the Effects of Zinc Oxide on those who Manufacture and Use it;" 5. "On Putrefaction" (read on retiring from the presidency of the District Medical Society): papers read before the Academy of Medicine—1. "Experimental and Rational Researches Concerning the Pigment of Jaundice;" 2. "A New Method of Testing for Bile-Pigment in Urine and Other Liquids,"

———————

CLARK, HON. ALVAH A., of Somerville, Lawyer and Congressman, was born, September 13th, 1840, at Lebanon, Hunterdon county, New Jersey. He is the son of Samuel Clark, who removed to New Germantown, in the same State, when Alvah was quite young. Mr. Clark kept the hotel at this place, and his son assisted him in the business in all the capacities necessitated by the exigencies of a country hotel. At the same time the lad attended school as much as his duties would permit, and having determined upon following a learned profession he made the best use of all his opportunities. The profession he had fixed his mind upon was that of the law, and so steadily did the fire of ambition burn within him that at the age of nineteen he had succeeded in preparing for college, studying part of the time with Rev. D. Blauvelt, of Lamington. Circumstances, however, not permitting him to take a collegiate course, he entered the law office of Hon. J. C. Rafferty in 1859, and there remained two years. At the expiration of that term he passed to the office of I. N. Dilts, Esq., in which he continued to study and acquire a knowledge of the practical details of the profession, until he was admitted as an attorney in 1863. Thereupon he at once opened an office at his old home, New Germantown, and began practice. After laboring in this sphere for three years, he removed to Somerville, where he has since continued. His practice has grown to be a large and profitable one in all branches of the profession. He is a well-read lawyer, and devotes great care to the preparation and management of his cases. To these circumstances, in connection with his great natural ability, his marked success, whether in chamber practice or before the courts, is to be attributed. Several corporations have secured his services as attorney, among which may be mentioned the Bound

Brook & Delaware Railroad Company, the Hamilton Land Improvement Company, and the Dime Savings Bank of Somerville. Politically he belongs to the Democratic party, and as a political organizer is one of the strongest men in the organization. In 1876 he was a candidate for the Democratic nomination in the Fourth Congressional District, and succeeded in making it in one of the sharpest contests ever known in the district. The campaign which followed was unusually bitter and was fought with great determination on both sides. In the result Mr. Clark was elected by a majority of over five thousand, a statement which sufficiently attests the estimation in which he is held. A polished, courteous gentleman, a good speaker, and more important still, a good debater, he will prove a valuable acquisition to the Democratic side of the House of Representatives. His law practice has consisted largely of contested cases; one of the most important of these was the Vandeveer will case. He was married in 1864 to Anna Van Debeek, of Somerset county, New Jersey. A truly self-made man, he presents some of the finest characteristics of the best class of self-made men, being at once self-reliant and energetic, modest and moderate.

NIGHT, EDWARD C., President of the Central Railroad of New Jersey, Merchant and Importer of Philadelphia, was born in Gloucester, now Camden, county, New Jersey, December 8th, 1813. He comes of a family intimately associated with the early history of Pennsylvania and New Jersey. His ancestor, Giles Knight, of Gloucestershire, England, came over in the ship "Welcome," with William Penn, sailing from England on September 30th, 1682. He settled in Byberry, and died in 1726; Mary, his wife, died in 1732. Their son, Thomas Knight, then lived in New Jersey, on a place belonging to Titian Leeds, the almanac maker. The parents of E. C. Knight, Jonathan and Rebecca Knight, were members of the Society of Friends, to whose tenets he himself still adheres. His father was a farmer and died in 1823. He worked on a farm until 1830, when he obtained a situation in a country store at Kaighn's Point, New Jersey. In that occupation he continued until September, 1832, when he engaged as clerk in the grocery store of Atkinson & Cuthbert, South street wharf, Philadelphia, on the Delaware. At this period, while quite young, an incident occurred which indicated the character of the future man. He was receiving but four dollars a week, when, engaged in his duties, he observed a man being carried down the Delaware upon the ice. He labored to persuade several men, who were standing near, to attempt his rescue. Their reply was, "He will be no loss to the community. Let him go." Offering, out of his own little purse, a dollar apiece to two men, if they would rescue him, they succeeded in saving him from his perilous posi-

tion and placing him upon dry ground. The moral was not lost on the preserver. He reasoned that if a man's life were worth two dollars, it would be well to have that amount always in his pocket for emergencies. In May, 1836, he established himself in the grocery business on Second street, in the same city, giving his mother an interest in the concern. The firm was sufficiently prosperous to enable them, in 1844, to appropriate a sum large enough to pay the balance due by the estate of his father, which proved after his death to be deficient about twenty per cent. About this time he became interested in the importing business, acquiring a share in the ownership of the schooner "Baltimore," which was at once placed in the San Domingo trade, making regular trips between Cape Haytien and Philadelphia, freighted principally with coffee. In September, 1846, he removed to the southeast corner of Water and Chestnut streets, and for over thirty years has been engaged, at first alone and then as the principal partner of the firm of E. C. Knight & Co., in the wholesale grocery, commission, importing and sugar refining business. In 1849, this house became, and thereafter continued to be, interested to a considerable extent in the California trade; it sent out the first steamer that ever plied on the waters above Sacramento City. The business at present is principally that of sugar-refining, for which purpose the firm occupies two large houses at Bainbridge street wharf on the Delaware, and that of importing molasses and sugar from Cuba, together with teas from China. As affording some idea of the close attention Mr. Knight has always paid to business, it may be mentioned that during thirty-seven years no one but himself has ever signed a note for the firm, and for years he worked sixteen hours per day. During the last thirty years he has embarked in many enterprises, and discharged the duties of many positions outside of his ordinary business. He was President of the Luzerne Coal and Iron Company; was a Director in the Lackawanna & Bloomsburg Railroad Company; Director of the Southwark Bank in 1840, and for several years thereafter—also the Bank of Commerce and the Corn Exchange Bank, and a member of the Board of Trade; was appointed by the city as one of the Trustees of City Ice Boats, and served for twenty years; also a Director in the Girard Life Insurance and Annuity Trust Company; and in 1859 he made several inventions in sleeping cars, put them into operation, and subsequently sold his interests in the patents to incorporated companies. He also served as President of the Coastwise Steamship Company, that built in Philadelphia the vessels "John Gibson" and "E. C. Knight." For years he served as a Director in the Pennsylvania, the North Pennsylvania, the Trenton & West Jersey Railroads. In the project for establishing a second line of railway between Philadelphia and New York he took a warm interest, and when eventually brought to a successful issue in the construction of the Delaware & Bound Brook Railroad, which, in connection with the New Jersey Central and North Pennsylvania Railroads, gave a second continuous and through line between the two great cities, he was chosen President of the new road. About the middle of the year 1876, a change in the management of the New Jersey Central being deemed advisable, Mr. Knight was asked to lend the strength of his name and his great financial and executive abilities to the corporation as its President. He consented to do so, and has since that time been laboring faithfully to restore the road to its former prosperity, and with good prospects of success. Up to the close of the year 1876 he had served for some time the Guarantee Fidelity and Trust Company as its President, but the affairs of the New Jersey Central occupied so much of his time and attention that he then resigned the presidency, continuing, however, associated with the direction of this Philadelphia institution in the capacity of Vice-President. He is also a Director of the Union League, the Insurance Company of the State of Pennsylvania, and the Merchant's Fund. He was also Chairman for seven years of a committee of the Pennsylvania Railroad Company, to assist in establishing a line of American steamships between Philadelphia and Europe. Of the company which has grown out of that movement he was first President. This company contracted with Cramp & Sons for four ships of over three thousand tons each. All of them are now in service—the "Pennsylvania," the "Ohio," the "Indiana," and the "Illinois," and have proved first-class vessels, while two more are being built. This enterprise has conferred marked advantages upon Philadelphia, and his efforts in bringing matters to their present satisfactory condition have met with high appreciation at the hands of the mercantile community and of all who are concerned for the material prosperity of the city of Philadelphia. In politics also he has been prominent, acting latterly with the Republican party. In 1856 he was nominated by the American, Whig and Reform parties for Congress, in the First District of Pennsylvania. He was an elector from the same district on the Presidential ticket when Abraham Lincoln was first elected President. He was a member of the convention assembled in 1873 for the purpose of revising the Constitution of the State of Pennsylvania, in which his long and varied business experience rendered his advice much sought and his influence potent for good. His name is a synonym for integrity and honor.

AN FLEET, HON. DAVID, Judge, of Flemington, was born in Readington, Hunterdon county, New Jersey, August 13th, 1819, and is a son of William T. Van Fleet, of that place. He is of Dutch descent, his ancestors having come from Holland in the year 1600. He received in his youth such education as the common schools of the neighborhood afforded, and for a time he followed the occupation of school teacher, and then

that of a clerk in a store at Centreville, New Jersey. His integrity of character and high personal qualities won and retained for him the esteem and respect of the community in which he resided, and in 1848 he was elected to the New Jersey Legislature. His services in that body were so well appreciated by his constituents that, in 1849, he was re-elected. In 1853 he engaged in mercantile pursuits on his own account in Centreville, and did a prosperous business. At the Presidential election of 1856 he was chosen one of the electors for President Buchanan, and in 1859 he was elected Surrogate of Hunterdon county. Up to this time, and until the breaking out of the war of the rebellion, he acted with the Democratic party, and he was elected to the various positions to which he was chosen by a Democratic constituency. When the war broke out, however, he became a Republican, and with that party he has ever since been identified. In the year 1869 he was appointed by President Grant one of the Inspectors of Customs for New York, but resigned the position after holding it for one year. In 1872 he was appointed one of the Common Pleas Judges of Hunterdon county, which position he still holds, and which he fills in a thoroughly able and satisfactory manner. He is a master in chancery, and is trustee for a number of estates, as well as a Director of the Hunterdon County National Bank. He is a man of strong religious convictions, and is a consistent member of the Methodist Episcopal Church. He was married in 1845 to Susan A. Cole, daughter of David O. Cole, Esq., of Readington, New Jersey.

OORHEES, J. VRED, Lawyer and Prosecutor of the Pleas, was born at Somerville, New Jersey, August 5th, 1819. His family was an old one of Dutch extraction, several of whose members won distinction by their services in the patriotic cause during the revolutionary war. Nicholas Voorhees, his father, was a gentleman of high standing and sturdy integrity, and a staunch supporter of the Dutch Reformed Church. He married Sarah Dumont, a descendant of a well-known French Huguenot family. The subject of this sketch prepared for college at the Somerville Academy. Advancing rapidly, he was able to enter the junior class of Rutgers College, where he graduated in 1840, with high standing. Having determined upon the study of the law, he entered the office of the late Judge Brown, at Somerville, in 1841, where he remained, a diligent worker, until after his admission to the bar in 1844. He at once entered upon a lucrative practice, and was licensed as counsellor in 1848. He was married in 1858 to Annie R. Borden, of Mount Holly, New Jersey. He lived a life of quiet industry and usefulness until the outbreak of the rebellion, when he at once took a prominent part in the stirring events of 1861, and in the fall of 1862 went to the front with a commission as

First Lieutenant and Quartermaster of the 30th Regiment of New Jersey Volunteers. Here he participated in all the hard service of camp life, until failing health compelled him to resign. After some time spent in recruiting his energies, he reopened his office in Somerville, where he has since remained. In 1872 he was appointed by Governor Parker Prosecutor of the Pleas for Somerset County, which office he still holds. He is also attorney for the Somerset County Bank and for the Bound Brook & Delaware Railroad. Mr. Voorhees is a man highly respected, both as a citizen and an official, and for his integrity of character.

EWITT, HON. SILAS WRIGHT, Lawyer and Member of the State Legislature, was born in Warren county, New Jersey, in the year 1846. He prepared for a collegiate course in Blairstown, New Jersey, and then entered Lafayette College, Pennsylvania, in the year 1865. After a full four years' course he was graduated in the class of 1869. Among his classmates were Rev. Walter Q. Scott, of Philadelphia, and Messrs. William Patton and R..E. James, of the Pennsylvania bar. Selecting the profession of law for his life career, he commenced his legal studies in the office of J. F. Dumont, Esq., at Phillipsburg, New Jersey, and was admitted to practise in that State in 1873. Two years previously, however, he had been admitted to the bar of Pennsylvania, after a course of study in the office of Messrs. Armstrong and Lynn, at Williamsport, in the same State. His political opinions led him into association with the Democratic party, on whose behalf he has always labored actively and with much effect. In the fall of 1876 he became a candidate for election from his district to the State House of Representatives, and after a spirited contest was elected by a considerable majority, although in the previous year the Democratic nominee had been defeated. This attests his popularity in the district, and indeed he is widely respected for his abilities and esteemed for his personal qualities.

OOD, RICHARD D., Merchant and Manufacturer (cotton and iron), was born in Greenwich, Cumberland county, New Jersey, March 29th, 1799. His ancestors, who came from Gloucestershire, England, were among the original settlers of Philadelphia; one of them, Richard Wood, arriving in this country, with some of the earliest Quaker emigrants, in the latter part of the seventeenth century, here located, while his grandson, also named Richard, moved to Cumberland county, New Jersey, of which he became one of the Judges and a Justice of the Peace in the reign of George II. He also represented his county in the Legislature of the State, as did also some of his descendants, who were men of marked intelligence and influence. Passing through the limited course of instruction of the country schools of that period, he acquired a fair degree of elementary education. For some years after leaving school he was employed as an assistant in his father's store, where the town library was kept, and this being placed under his care, gave him the opportunity of indulging in reading of a varied character. Of the advantage here afforded him he diligently availed himself, thus gratifying his taste and fostering the habit of continually adding to his store of information by constant and judicious reading, which, even in the press and manifold occupations of his after life, he always preserved. A little before attaining his legal majority he left his native place to begin the battle of life at Salem, New Jersey. A successful career of two years in that place enabled him to establish himself in Philadelphia. To this city he removed in 1823, and uniting with Mr. William L. Abbott and S. C. Wood, under the firm of Wood, Abbott & Wood, he started in life as a city merchant at what is now No. 309 Market street. With this house, under all its various changes of title, he remained connected to the day of his death. Commencing with but limited means, in competition with established houses of large capital and unlimited credit, who had been accustomed to extend long credits to their customers, with correspondingly large profits, the firm of Wood & Abbott inaugurated a system of selling for cash and at only five per cent. advance on cost, under which, by rapidity of sales and a frequent turning of the capital they possessed, the new house succeeded in equalizing profits with their more powerful competitors. From that time forward the labors and influence of Mr. Wood were felt in almost every undertaking having for its object the advancement of the material prosperity of Philadelphia. He was the first to introduce the bleaching and dyeing of cotton goods on a large scale for this market, in competition with the established and powerful corporations of New England. Even while carrying on this extensive business he found time to embark in other enterprises. The advance of the town of Millville, in New Jersey, is due to his farsighted sagacity; about the year 1851 he became actively interested in that place, and establishing there a large cotton factory, bleaching and dye works, as also extensive iron works, he gradually built up the town to a manufacturing depot of importance. The first to appreciate the fact that southern New Jersey would hear the extension of railroad improvement, he built the Millville & Glassboro' Railroad, and afterwards exerted a powerful influence in the building of the Cape May road, with the various branches that contribute to the usefulness of that line and the convenience of its passengers and freight patrons. About 1851 he also started the manufacture of cast-iron gas and water pipe, under the firm of R. D. Wood & Co., whose products have entered a large proportion of the cities of the Union.

He was the owner of the original tract upon which is built the town of Vineland, New Jersey, and it is owing to the generous and liberal terms with which he treated the founder of that thriving place, that the project was carried out. About 1867 he erected large factories at May's Landing, New Jersey, and also constructed a mammoth dam on the Maurice river at Millville. He was, also, at critical periods in their history, a powerful supporter, at one time, of the Schuylkill Navigation Company, promoting confidence in it by liberal subscriptions to its stock and loans when they were looked upon with suspicion and doubt; and, at another time, of the Pennsylvania Central Railroad, when it was of the most critical importance that its then President (Samuel V. Merrick) should be seconded, as he was, in his efforts to carry forward to completion that great undertaking, by men in its directorship of just such personal influence, fertility of resource and force of character as Mr. Wood. In fact, he was one of the projectors of this great railroad, as well as one of the reorganizers and largest owners of the Cambria Iron Works, at Johnstown, Pennsylvania. He was long a Director of the Philadelphia Bank; was one of the founders of the Union Benevolent Association of Philadelphia, and held directorships in numerous other railroads, corporations, and public institutions. Mr. Wood's talent and goodness of heart alike were proved by his conspicuous ability in the power of moulding persons who at different times joined his enterprises as assistants. He rarely separated from those men, but developed and applied their powers until they became useful members of his different firms, or sometimes left him, upon the completion of their business education, for the creation of individual fortunes. From the laboring man to the possessor of business talent, he perceived the qualification of every applicant, and constituted himself the life-long friend of all who were suited to aid him; so powerful was his influence and disposition to promote the advancement of enterprising and deserving young men, that possibly a hundred of Philadelphia's wealthy and honored citizens owe their first success in business to a partnership in one of the various enterprises inaugurated and prosecuted by Mr. Wood. His agreeable relations in society depended largely upon his even and pleasant temper, conversational powers, ready and well-stored memory, and natural urbanity. Educated with the Society of Friends, of which he was a life-long though not active member, he ever displayed the sobriety and justice of apprehension common to that sect. Of his religious character, it may be said that he felt far more than he showed, having a dislike to formality and bigotry quite equal to his love for true heartfelt Christianity. He died April 1st, 1869. Out of his fortune of several millions, he devised numerous bequests to charitable objects and public institutions, among which were $5000 to Haverford College, $500 to the Union Benevolent Association of Philadelphia, and $500 to the Shelter for Colored Orphans. He was a benefactor not only to the community in which he lived, but to the entire country; and benefits of his enterprise and examples will be strong in their influence for good in generations yet to come.

 IXON, JAMES HARRIS, A. B. and A. M., Lawyer, of Millville, was born in Cedarville, Cumberland county, New Jersey, January 30th, 1836. His father was George W. Nixon, who followed the occupation of a farmer in the same county, of which also his mother, Martha Harris, was a native. He obtained his preparatory educational training at Harmony Academy, Bridgeton, which is now known as West Jersey Academy. Having fitted himself for a university course, he entered Princeton College in January, 1855, and was graduated in June, 1858, with the degree of A. B. In due course he received the degree of A. M. in 1861. After graduation he engaged in teaching school for three years, making an engagement at the Lawrenceville High School. Having a taste for the legal profession, he began to study law with the Hon. J. T. Nixon, then of Bridgeton, but now United States District Judge, and residing at Trenton. Having complied with all requirements he was admitted as an attorney in November, 1863, and as counsellor three years subsequently. In the month after admission as attorney he located at Millville, and commenced the practice of his profession, which he has continued to prosecute at the same place ever since, with a steadily increasing success. His affiliations have always been with the Republican party, and in the fall of 1864 he was elected to the popular branch of the Legislature on the ticket of that organization. He served in the House for four years, during the last two of which he acted as Chairman of the Judiciary Committee. In 1868 he was elected to the Senate, where he served one term of three years. Since that time he has devoted himself to the prosecution of his profession, only permitting the use of his name in politics during the present year, when he was one of the Presidential electors upon the Republican ticket. He has given especial attention to the criminal law, and occupied considerable space in the public eye during the celebrated Landis trial, on which occasion he was of counsel for the defendant.

 AGONER, HENRY G., M. D., Physician and Surgeon, of Somerville, was born in Hunterdon county, New Jersey, August 16th, 1829, his father being William Wagoner, a farmer and manufacturer in that county. In his youth he received a classical education, studying for the most part under private tutors. Having decided to enter the medical profession, he entered upon a preparatory

... John Manners, of Clinton, ... University of Pennsyl... he went ... New Jersey, where he ... the practice of ... successful ... to Somerville, New Jersey, ... His skill as a practitioner ... qualities rendered him ... extended largely ... portion of the ... produced by his large practice ... strength, and in 1864 ... obtain the assistance of a partner. ... with himself Dr. J. S. Knox, ... possible withdrew from active practice ... to recruit his wasted strength. The partnership endured until 1873, when, by the retirement of Dr. Knox, he again assumed the entire labor of his large practice. He is a member of the State and County Medical Societies, and ranks among the foremost of his profession in this part of the State. Withal he is a courteous and accomplished gentleman, and is esteemed for his personal and ... qualities no less than for his great professional learning and skill. He is a prominent member of the Masonic fraternity, has been Master of Solomon's Lodge and High Priest of Keystone Chapter, which he was instrumental in organizing. He was married in 1854 to the daughter of Philip R. Dakin, M. D., of Wilmington, Ohio. She died July, 1876.

ALSEY, HON. GEORGE A., ex-Member of Congress, of Newark, was born in Springfield, Union county, New Jersey, December 7th, 1827. During a period extending back to 1694, his ancestors had resided in that neighborhood. They were farmers, and in his youth he himself was accustomed to the labors of the farm. His parents, however, removed to Newark, and a new career opened before him. He went as an apprentice into the establishment of Messrs. Fisher & Tucker, manufacturers of patent leather, and mastered all the details of that business. Subsequently an opportunity presented itself to enter into the wholesale clothing business in connection with Southern firms, and the opportunity was promptly accepted. He speedily developed into a prudent, enterprising and successful business man, and the qualities which have since gained him reputation and honors were brought into strong relief. His energy found new avenues of employment, and he became connected with various banking and insurance institutions of Newark. When the war of the rebellion broke out in 1861 the firm of which he was the head suffered crushing reverses, its property being all swept away by the secession of the Southern States. Notwithstanding this, the obligations of the firm were finally met. His prompt fulfilment of every personal duty and obligation made it natural that his fellow-citizens should turn to him for active co-operation in public affairs, where his high integrity would be so strongly felt. In 1860 he was sent to the State Legislature from the district in which he resided. Notwithstanding the fact that he was largely interested in Southern trade, and had intimate business associations with Southern men, he was an active and earnest Republican from the time of the organization of the party in New Jersey. He was one of the minority in the Assembly of the State, but his integrity, judgment and high business qualities gave him a large influence in that body, and during the session they marked the opening of the rebellion, he was one of Governor Olden's strongest aids. In 1861 he was re-elected to the Assembly. In 1862, upon the organization of the Internal Revenue Bureau, he was appointed Assessor for the Fifth District of New Jersey, his sphere of duties comprising one of the largest manufacturing districts in the State. Through his influence many of the harsher provisions of the revenue law were ameliorated. At the close of the war he was selected by the Revenue Commissioners of their Southern States for the purpose of instructing in their duties the newly-appointed revenue officers, but the requirements of his own district compelled him to decline the appointment. Through all the years of the war he cordially sustained the administration of President Lincoln. In 1866 President Johnson sought to remove him from office, but the Senate refused to confirm his successor, and he retained the assessorship. This attempt to remove him, added to the high reputation he had ... directed the attention of the Republicans of his district to him as their best choice for Congress. He was ... unanimously, and elected by a large majority, although the district had been previously largely Democratic. In Congress he maintained the high character he had previously acquired, and was freely consulted upon questions affecting the manufacturing and financial interests of the country. His services to his district were constant and invaluable, and were rendered alike to Democrats and Republicans. He served on the Committee on the District of Columbia, and was chairman of one of the Joint Select Committees on Research, and served with Senators Edmunds and Buckalew on the sub-committee of that body, "to examine the method of printing and issuing bonds, notes and other securities," the results of which secured important reforms in the Treasury Department. In 1868 he was again unanimously renominated for Congress, but was defeated, although his popularity was so great that his vote in his district largely exceeded that of General Grant. When Mr. Boutwell assumed the position of Secretary of the Treasury under President Grant's administration, he tendered the important office of Register to Mr. Halsey, but the position was declined by him, as, on retiring from Congress, he had actively resumed his business as manufacturer of

course of reading with Dr. John Manners, of Clinton, New Jersey, and graduated from the University of Pennsylvania in the spring of 1853. After his graduation he went to Stanton, New Jersey, where he entered upon the practice of his profession. He remained there in active and successful practice until 1859, when he removed to Somerville, New Jersey, where he has since resided. His skill as a practitioner and his estimable personal qualities rendered him exceedingly popular, and his patronage extended largely and rapidly, embracing Somerville and a large portion of the surrounding territory. The strain produced by his large practice was too severe for his physical strength, and in 1869 he found it necessary to obtain the assistance of a partner. He therefore associated with himself Dr. J. S. Knox, now of Chicago, and so far as possible withdrew from active practice, in the endeavor to recruit his wasted strength. The partnership endured until 1873, when, by the retirement of Dr. Knox, he again assumed the entire labor of his large practice. He is a member of the State and County Medical Societies, and ranks among the foremost of his profession in his part of the State. Withal he is a courteous and accomplished gentleman, and is esteemed for his personal and social qualities no less than for his great professional learning and skill. He is a prominent member of the Masonic fraternity, has been Master of Solomon's Lodge and High Priest of Keystone Chapter, which he was instrumental in organizing. He was married in 1854 to the daughter of Philip R. Dakin, M. D., of Wilmington, Ohio. She died July, 1876.

ALSEY, HON. GEORGE A., ex-Member of Congress, of Newark, was born in Springfield, Union county, New Jersey, December 7th, 1827. During a period extending back to 1694, his ancestors had resided in that neighborhood. They were farmers, and in his youth he himself was accustomed to the labors of the farm. His parents, however, removed with him to Newark, and a new career opened before him. He went as an apprentice into the establishment of Messrs. Halsey & Tucker, manufacturers of patent leather, and mastered all the details of that business. Subsequently, an opportunity presented itself to enter into the wholesale clothing business in connection with Southern firms, and the opportunity was promptly accepted. He speedily developed into a prudent, enterprising and successful business man, and the qualities which have since gained him reputation and honors were brought into strong relief. His energy found new avenues of endeavor, and he became connected with various banking and insurance institutions of Newark. When the war of the rebellion broke out in 1861 the firm of which he was the head suffered crushing reverses, its property being all swept away by the secession of the Southern States. Notwithstanding this, the obligations of the firm were finally met. His prompt fulfilment of every personal duty and obligation made it natural that his fellow-citizens should turn to him for active co-operation in public affairs, where his high integrity would be so strongly felt. In 1860 he was sent to the State Legislature from the district in which he resided. Notwithstanding the fact that he was largely interested in Southern trade, and had intimate business associations with Southern men, he was an active and earnest Republican from the time of the organization of the party in New Jersey. He was one of the minority in the Assembly of the State, but his integrity, judgment and high business qualities gave him a large influence in that body, and during the scenes that marked the opening of the rebellion, he was one of Governor Olden's strongest aids. In 1861 he was re-elected to the Assembly. In 1862, upon the organization of the Internal Revenue Bureau, he was appointed Assessor for the Fifth District of New Jersey, his sphere of duties comprising one of the largest manufacturing districts in the Union. Through his influence many of the harsher provisions of the revenue law were ameliorated. At the close of the war he was selected by the Revenue Commissioner to visit the Southern States for the purpose of instructing in their duties the newly-appointed revenue officers, but the requirements of his own district compelled him to decline the appointment. Through all the years of the war he cordially sustained the administration of President Lincoln. In 1866 President Johnson sought to remove him from office, but the Senate refused to confirm his successor, and he retained the assessorship. This attempt to remove him, added to the high reputation he had gained, directed the attention of the Republicans of his district to him as their best choice for Congress. He was nominated unanimously, and elected by a large majority, although the district had been previously largely Democratic. In Congress he maintained the high character he had previously acquired, and was freely consulted upon questions affecting the manufacturing and financial interests of the country. His services to his district were constant and invaluable, and were rendered alike to Democrats and Republicans. He served on the Committee on the District of Columbia; was appointed one of the Joint Select Committee on Retrenchment, and served with Senators Edmunds and Buckalew on the sub-committee of that body, "to examine the method of printing and issuing bonds, notes and other securities," the results of which secured important reforms in the Treasury Department. In 1868 he was unanimously renominated for Congress, but was defeated, although his popularity was so great that his vote in his district largely exceeded that of General Grant. When Mr. Boutwell assumed the position of Secretary of the Treasury under President Grant's administration, he tendered the important office of Register to Mr. Halsey, but the position was declined by him, as, on retiring from Congress, he had actively resumed his business as manufacturer of

patent leather. He was not permitted to remain permanently in retirement, however, and in 1870 he was again
nominated for Congress, and was elected by a majority of
over three thousand. This brilliant triumph brought him
more prominently than ever before the country, and on
taking his seat in the House he was assigned to the Chairmanship of one of the most important committees, the duties of which he performed with the fidelity and ability characteristic of him. It was due mainly to his watchfulness of
the interests of his district and State, that the new court
house and post-office at Trenton, and the post-office at
Jersey City, were secured, and that the improvements in
the Passaic and other rivers of the State were authorized.
At the close of this Congress he received from the people of
Hudson county, wholly irrespective of party, a valuable testimonial of their appreciation of the high official services he
had rendered. In 1872 he was urged to again accept a
nomination for Congress, but declined. He was not permitted to retire to private life, however. Upon the retirement of Governor Ward he was chosen President of the
Newark Industrial Exposition, and was the real as well as
the nominal head of that enterprise. In connection with
Governor Randolph and others he has been prominent in
preserving the future Washington's head-quarters at
Morristown, and is at present one of the Commissioners of
the new Lunatic Asylum at Morris Plains. Previous to the
last gubernatorial convention, he was prominently named as
a fitting nominee for the position of Governor. His friends
believed that he possessed in a pre-eminent degree the
qualities necessary to success, and in that belief the delegates
who assembled at Trenton on the 27th of August, 1874,
concurred most cordially, and nominated him by acclamation
for the high position named. The nomination was made
without the faintest solicitation on his part, and was in every
way most honorable to him, showing unmistakably the high
esteem in which he is held as a citizen, and the admiration
accorded to his public career. In this year, however,
occurred the tidal wave which proved so disastrous to the
Republican party, and the Democrats succeeded in electing
his opponent. Since that time he has been chiefly engaged
in the management of his extensive business, but he has not
lost his interest in public affairs. At the New Jersey State
Republican Convention in May, 1876, he was appointed a
Senatorial Delegate to the National Republican Convention
held at Cincinnati.

VREDENBURGH, HON. PETER, LL.D., Lawyer,
was born, 1805, at Readington, Hunterdon county,
New Jersey, and was the son of Dr. Peter Vredenburgh, of Somerville. He graduated at Rutgers
College, in 1826; studied law; was licensed as
an attorney in 1829; and began practice at Eaton-
town, Monmouth county, and in a year removed to Freehold,
where he continued until his death. In 1837 he was made
Prosecutor of the Pleas for Monmouth county, and held
that position for fifteen years. This office brought him in
conflict with the best legal talent, and it was soon discovered that he possessed a high order of intellect, stored with
a thorough knowledge of the great principles of jurisprudence. From that time his professional success was assured. He at once took rank with the foremost practitioners
of the county, and the Supreme Court reports of that period
prove that from the year 1840 to his appointment as Judge,
he was concerned in all cases of magnitude in Monmouth
and Ocean counties. In the discharge of his duties as
Prosecutor of the Pleas, he displayed signal ability. He
was peculiarly fitted for the position. If he had doubts of
the guilt of a prisoner, he frankly said so, and consented to
an acquittal. But he was a terror to evil-doers. His clearness of perception enabled him to detect falsehood in evidence and sophistry in reasoning; and he would weave
around the guilty such a web of circumstances that the most
eloquent defender of the accused could not destroy, nor
deliver the culprits from the penalty of their crimes. Prior
to the adoption of the new Constitution of New Jersey, he
served as a member of the Legislative Council, being the
representative from Monmouth county. In 1855 he was
appointed one of the Associate Justices of the Supreme
Court by Governor Price, although of opposite politics; and
in 1862 he was reappointed to the office by Governor
Olden, thus holding the position for fourteen years, discharging the duties of the office ably and acceptably, and
sustaining a reputation as second to no one on the bench.
Many of his decisions are regarded as among the ablest
reported, and all bear evidence of having been most carefully prepared. To the discharge of the duties of this office
he brought a mind in the maturity of its powers, improved
by long study and experience. When a young man he
took an active part in politics, and was an ardent member
of the Whig party; in later years, although a Judge, he
sympathized with the Republicans. At the commencement
of the civil war, the passions of the people of Monmouth
county were aroused to a state of frenzy, and insults and
outrages were inflicted on many citizens under the impression that the party sympathies of Judge Vredenburgh would
sustain them; while the aggrieved were on the point of
taking the law into their own hands, and meet violence
with violence. At this critical time the Judge, rising above
the passions and prejudices of the hour, divesting himself of
all personal and partisan feelings, proved himself a wise
and fearless magistrate. His famous charge to the grand
jury, and their action, taught the violent that there still was
law; and the aggrieved that the law could protect. For
this he was denounced by some, harsh names were given,
and still harsher threats were made; but time has fully vindicated his action. At the close of his second term of office
he resumed the practice of the law, but his health soon
began to fail. This was increased by the death of a favor-

ite son, Major Peter Vredenburgh, Jr., who was killed in the battle of Winchester, Virginia, the sacrifice he laid upon the altar of his country, to maintain the right, and to preserve the Union: consequently, he was compelled to abandon his practice. For a time he found partial solace and comfort in reading; but soon his sight failed, and that source of pleasure to a cultivated mind was denied him. At length, in the hope of prolonging life, he was induced to seek a more genial clime, but all was unavailing. He held during his active life various minor public positions of trust and honor, and at the time of his death he was one of the Commissioners on Riparian Rights. He died in the city of St. Augustine, Florida, March 24th, 1873.

REDENBURGH, MAJOR PETER, Lawyer and Soldier, son of Judge Vredenburgh, whose biographical sketch appears above, was born at Freehold, New Jersey. He received a liberal education, studied law, and was admitted to the bar, where he soon achieved a good position. In August, 1862, being then in his twenty-seventh year, he determined to offer his life in the cause of country, being impelled to this course by the early disasters of the war and the obvious necessity for patriotic action on the part of the best blood in the land. Descended, on both sides, from men found among the gallant defenders of Harlem and Leyden, he could not resist the call on behalf of liberty and the nation. At this time the 14th Regiment New Jersey Volunteers was being largely recruited in his own county, and on August 25th, 1862, he received a commission as Major in that regiment. It was with some hesitation, however, that he accepted so high a rank, being wholly ignorant of military science. But his natural ability manifested itself in a singularly easy mastery of his duties, and he at once established for himself a character unrivalled in the regiment as a capable and efficient officer. His command passed the greater portion of the first year at Frederick City, Maryland, and for six months of this period Major Vredenburgh acted as Provost-Marshal of the city, exhibiting in that capacity marked executive ability. September 5th, 1863, he was appointed Inspector-General of the Third Division of the Third Corps by General French, and was so attached to the staff of General Elliot until October 4th, 1863, and then on that of his successor, General Carr, until December 4th following. A week later General French appointed him Inspector-General of the Third Corps, then consisting of about twenty-seven thousand men. He proved himself exceptionally valuable as a staff officer. Considering his lack of previous training, military or engineering, his topographical eye was exceptionally accurate, while his disregard of danger, his self-confidence and enterprising performance of duty, gave his services conspicuous importance. When towards the spring of 1864 the Third Division

of the Third Corps, to which Major Vredenburgh belonged, was transferred to the Sixth Corps, he remained at the head-quarters of his division on the staff of General Ricketts. In General Grant's advance across the Rapidan on May 4th, 1864, he bore himself gallantly. A member of his regiment thus describes his conduct: "Our Major had done gloriously; all day he had been in the saddle; all day he rode backward and forward through the storm of leaden hail. Was there an order to carry to that part of the division that wavered under a galling fire of the enemy, who to carry it but young Vredenburgh? Who could take it as well? His eagle eye took in the field at a glance. How our boys would shout as they saw him dashing with the speed of an arrow from one end of the line to the other—for he rode swiftly; he was a splendid horseman." On the following day, and during the whole of that terrible campaign of the Wilderness, at Crump's Creek and Spottsylvania, he displayed most daring courage, high address and active energy. Again, at the battle of Cold Harbor, his conduct commanded the highest praise from his superior officers, and won from his soldiers the significant title of "Commander of the Sixth Corps." Early in July the 14th regiment, withdrawn from Petersburg, returned to Frederick City, and crossing the Monocacy river on the 8th of that month, fought nearly alone the hard-fought engagement known by that stream's name. The Major was at that time attached to the staff of General Ricketts, and many spectators of the fight assert that he displayed more bravery than any man in the field. On this day Lieutenant-Colonel Hall, commanding, and every captain in the regiment who successively took command, were either killed or wounded. Thereupon the Major asked to be returned to his regiment, and under his command, on September 18th, 1864, after much marching and counter-marching, it proceeded from its works at Berry-ville, in the direction of Winchester, and near Opequan again engaged the enemy. The charge was made at eight in the morning, through a galling fire of ball and shell. Major Vredenburgh led his men, having previously declared his intention to lead them to the enemy's intrenchments. While gallantly pushing forward he was struck by a fragment of shell and killed instantly. His last words were: "Forward, men! Forward, and guide on me!" Thus nobly died one who had nobly lived.

LDEN, HON. CHARLES S., ex-Governor of New Jersey, was born, February, 1797, at the old homestead at Stony Brook, near Princeton, which has been in the possession of the family since 1696. After receiving a fair English education, he entered his father's store as a clerk, but subsequently removed to Philadelphia before attaining his majority, and entered the mercantile house of Matthew Newkirk, on Second street near Arch. After some years' service as a clerk, he was taken into the house as a partner, and was finally intrusted with the management of the branch house of Newkirk & Co., in New Orleans, where he remained from 1825 to 1834. Having acquired a large fortune, he returned to New Jersey, and purchased a farm near Princeton, where he settled down, and gave his attention to agricultural pursuits. He was subsequently elected to the State Senate in 1844, and re-elected in 1847, serving altogether six years in that body. In 1856 he took an active part in the Presidential campaign in support of the election of Millard Fillmore, but subsequently allied himself to the Republican party, and in 1859 became the nominee of that organization for Governor; he was elected by a majority of 1,651 votes over his Democratic opponent, General E. R. V. Wright. Although possessed of liberal conservative principles, and being in favor of a conciliatory course towards the South, he gave an enthusiastic and unfaltering support to the national government on the outbreak of hostilities. His record during this trying period was of the purest, noblest and most patriotic character. His honesty was never doubted, and his administration of the affairs of his native State during a three years' term gave full satisfaction to all classes. Beside those of Governor and State Senator, he held many other positions of honor and trust during his career. At one time he was a member of the Court of Errors and Appeals, and the Court of Pardons, and he was also a Commissioner of the State Sinking Fund. An old-fashioned legislator, he was always careful, thoughtful and discreet while serving the State in any capacity. He died April 7th, 1876.

ARNED, SAMUEL P., M. D., of Woodbridge, was born in New York city, June 9th, 1836, his parents being William and Mary (Phillips) Harned. He received his education at the New York public schools, and at the age of sixteen entered the dry goods trade. In 1856 he removed to Woodbridge, New Jersey, and there became associated with his father in the management of a general store. This connection continued for eighteen months, when the father withdrew, and Mr. S. E. Ensign entered the firm as junior partner. The firm of Harned & Ensign existed for six years, but during this time Dr. Harned was preparing himself for the duties of his intended profession. Procuring the requisite text-books, he studied medicine in such leisure time as he could take from his business, and having attended the necessary courses of lectures at the University of New York, he received his degree in 1868. During the two years previous to his graduation, he was an office student with Professor Benjamin Howard, who held the chair of Surgery in the University, and in the year subsequent to his graduation he attended a special course of lectures by Prof. Alfred L. Loomis upon "Physical Diagnosis." Upon the receipt of his degree he established himself at Wood-

bridge, where he has built up an extensive and lucrative practice. He has for several years held the position of Township Physician; has been one of the Coroners of Middlesex county, and is a prominent member of the Middlesex County Medical Society. On the 12th of October, 1859, he was married to Rebecca S., daughter of James Bloodgood; she dying in 1869, he was again married, December 10th, 1874, to Fannie S. Bloodgood, a sister of his first wife.

OUGHERTY, ALEXANDER N., A. M., M. D., Physician, of Newark, was born, January 1st, 1822, in the city of his present residence. His parents are Alexander N. Dougherty, a leather merchant and a native of New York, and Sarah (Congar) Dougherty, of Newark. Dr. Dougherty's education was commenced in the private schools of Newark, and the instruction here received was supplemented by a regular four years' course at Oberlin College, Ohio, from which institution he graduated in the fall of 1841, with the degree of A. B., followed in three years by that of A. M., which degree was also conferred upon him by Princeton College, in 1865-66. In the choice of a profession he was decided by a strong natural bias, and the inclination which the possession of such bias brings, to determine upon that of physician and surgeon, and with characteristic zeal and energy he entered upon the task of fitting himself for the career he had chosen. After thorough and effective preliminary study he entered the Albany Medical College, where he attended a course of lectures. After this he went through the regular course at the College of Physicians and Surgeons, in New York, of the alumni of which he is now Vice-President. Graduating here in the spring of 1845, he entered at once upon the practice of his profession in Newark, the city of his birth. He remained in Newark, actively engaged in professional duties, until the breaking out of the war of the rebellion in 1861, when he entered the army of the United States, and commenced a new career of more than ordinary brilliancy. He went into the government service as Surgeon of the 4th New Jersey Volunteers, receiving his commission from Governor Olden. Soon afterwards he passed examination at Washington, was made Brigade Surgeon of Volunteers, and was assigned for duty under General Kearny, with whom he served until the spring of 1862. At that time he became Surgeon of General N. J. T. Davis' brigade, and with that organization served through the Peninsular campaign, and also at the battle of Antietam. In this engagement he acted as Medical Director of the Second Army Corps of the Army of the Potomac, under command of General Sumner. After the battle of Antietam he was duly commissioned as Medical Director of the Second Corps, and did duty in that capacity until shortly before the battle of Fredericksburg, when he was promoted to the position of Medical Director of the Right

Grand Division of the Army of the Potomac, comprising the Second and Ninth Corps. This was the highest and most responsible position attained by any officer of the volunteer medical staff. Upon the dissolution of the Grand Division, he was retransferred to the Second Corps, as its Medical Director, and served in this capacity until October, 1864, when his services were solicited and obtained by General Hancock, and he became Medical Director of the Veteran Corps, and when that officer was placed in command of the Army of the Shenandoah, Dr. Dougherty accompanied him as his chief medical officer. He served here until he was transferred to the Department of West Virginia, of which department he was Medical Director until he was mustered out of service in October, 1865. In the campaign before Petersburg he was made Brevet Lieutenant-Colonel, and at the close of the war he received the brevet rank of Colonel. He did not go unscathed through the duties of his varied and responsible duties in the war; he was wounded at the battle of Spottsylvania. After the close of the war he served for a period of six months as surgeon on the Pacific mail steamers, and at the end of that time returned to Newark, where he resumed his private practice. His preference is for surgery, and his services in that department of the profession are much in demand. He has been one of the attending Surgeons of St. Barnabas Hospital, in Newark, since the opening of the institution. He is connected with various medical societies, county and State, and has several times been a delegate to the American Medical Association. He was married in 1850 to Henrietta Arrowsmith, of Morris county, New Jersey.

UNT, HENRY FRANCIS, M. D., of Camden, was born in Cranston, Providence county, Rhode Island, March 28th, 1838. He is the eldest son of Joshua Hunt, who for many years was a well-known cotton manufacturer. His ancestors were among the earliest settlers of that State; having come over from England and settled in Newport in 1654. His ancestors on his mother's side were among the leading men of the State during the revolutionary war, and have always been prominent in public affairs. He received his preliminary education in the public schools of Providence and at Smithville Seminary. In 1854 he entered Providence Conference Seminary, where he commenced a collegiate course of study. Here he remained three years, when his father's business suffering from the financial crisis of that period, he abandoned the idea of college. Entering his father's business house, he assisted in conducting affairs with the intention of preparing for a commercial life. During the two years he remained here he pursued his studies privately, endeavoring to supply whatever was lacking in his education. Finding commercial life not suited to his tastes, he decided to enter upon the study of medicine. This he commenced in the office of a distinguished allopathic physi-

cian, where he continued for two years, attending a partial course of lectures in Bellevue Hospital College, New York. At this time his attention was called to the system of homœopathy, which he had seen practised with the most successful results, during an epidemic of diphtheria. Giving the principles a thorough examination, he became convinced of the superiority of the new school over the old, and entered at once upon the study, in the office of Dr. Okie, of Providence. He attended two full courses of lectures at the Homœopathic Medical College of Pennsylvania, where he graduated with the class of 1864. The decease of J. R. Andrews, M. D., of Camden, leaving a vacancy in the field there, Dr. Hunt immediately assumed charge of the extensive practice already established. Dr. Andrews was the pioneer of homœopathy in Camden, where he had labored faithfully and successfully for over twenty years. Here Dr. Hunt found his duties very arduous. From the first day he assumed them, they demanded his closest attention, and most faithfully and earnestly has he discharged his duty. He has always appreciated the responsibility of his position, and has allowed himself but little time for recreation since the commencement of his professional life, and has kept himself well posted in the literature of both systems of medical practice. He has been punctual in his attendance at the meetings of the several medical societies of which he is a member, and has aided in making these meetings interesting by the contribution of valuable papers. He was one of the founders of New Jersey State Homœopathic Medical Society, of which he was afterward President, and aided in securing a liberal charter for the same, conferring all the privileges upon the homœopathic physician that are enjoyed by the allopathic. He also assisted in organizing the West Jersey Homœopathic Medical Society, of which he was afterward President. These societies have aided materially in the spread of homœopathy in the State. He has been a delegate from these societies to the American Institute of Homœopathy every year since he joined that body. In 1866 he was married to Theresa Hugg, of Camden, daughter of the late William Hugg, Esq. He has filled satisfactorily to his numerous patients the position left vacant by the death of one whose ministry had secured him the most enviable reputation. His practice has increased until it has become one of the most lucrative in the city. He has succeeded in winning the confidence and esteem of the entire community, by his Christian character and professional ability.

IDGWAY, HON. CALEB G., of Burlington, Merchant, and State Senator, was born in Springfield township, Burlington county, New Jersey, April 4th, 1836. His ancestors were amongst the early settlers of the State, and of that class of English Friends, the cultivated and industrious yeomanry, to whom the citizens are indebted for its promi-

nence in advanced agriculture, horticulture and social accomplishments. He was educated in the schools of Burlington
city, whose fame for thorough, practical mental training
has been so long established. At the age of fourteen, when
his father died, he was apprenticed in a dry goods and grocery store, where he faithfully discharged every duty for
three years. Then he was taken into the employ of a German importing house in Philadelphia, where, after a few
years of diligent application to business, he was promoted
to the full agency of one of the largest dry goods firms in
Europe. His business qualifications, and agreeable, social
manners, are fully appreciated by his employers, and are
rewarded by special marks of consideration. At the age of
thirty he commenced his political career by his election to
the Common Council of the city of Burlington, and although
from local causes and interests the political complexion is
variable, his positive conservative character has secured his
re-election, until he has served in that office for ten consecutive years; during the last two he has been successively
chosen to preside over the deliberations of that body. In 1872
he was elected to represent Burlington township in the board
of chosen freeholders of Burlington county; his ability was
recognized by his constituents, and he was rewarded by a
re-election in 1873; his services and business qualifications
increased his popularity throughout the county, and made
for him the prominence that merit deserves. On the 18th
of September, 1876, he received the unanimous vote of the
Democratic Convention of Burlington county for State
Senator, and after one of the most exciting and closely contested elections ever held in the county, against one of the
most popular candidates of the opposite party, he secured
his election to fill the seat that only twice before has been
occupied by a Democrat, the Republican majority in this
county ranging from eight hundred to twelve hundred.

AINES, HON. DANIEL, Lawyer, Jurist, Governor
and Chancellor of New Jersey, was born, 1801, in
the city of New York, and was the son of the late
Elias Haines, for many years a highly respected
and successful merchant of that city, who married a
daughter of Robert Ogden, of Sussex county, New
Jersey, and a sister of Governor Ogden. His grandfather,
Stephen Haines, was distinguished during the revolutionary
era for his earnest patriotism and sufferings for the cause;
and accordingly incurred the hatred of the Tories. The
latter, aided by an armed band, surrounded his dwelling,
and captured him with his sons, all of whom they took to
New York, and imprisoned them in the celebrated "Sugar
House," where they remained for a long time, enduring
untold sufferings. Daniel was educated partly in New
York, and at the academy in Elizabethtown: he matriculated
at Princeton College, and graduated from that institution in
1820. After leaving college he entered the law office of

Thomas C. Ryerson, at Newton; and was licensed as an attorney in 1823, as a counsellor in 1826, and finally reached the
highest rank—that of serjeant-at-law—in 1837. He made
choice of Hamburg, Sussex county, as his residence, and
there he commenced the practice of his profession in 1824.
The same year witnessed the nomination of Andrew Jackson
for the Presidency, in which he took an active part in forwarding the interests of the organization which placed him as the
leader of the same. Both Federalists and Democrats pronounced in favor of the hero of New Orleans, so that Sussex
county became the stronghold of the Democracy, and ever
gave the heaviest majorities, for that party, over any county in
the State. In 1839, a matter of local interest to Sussex county
having arisen, he was tendered a nomination to the Legislative Council of the State, which he accepted, and was accordingly elected. At this time the "broad seal" contest was
waging, in which he also became engaged. The refusal of
the Speaker of the House of Representatives—R. M. T.
Hunter, of Virginia—to receive the resolutions passed by
the New Jersey Legislature the previous year, incited the
Whigs to renew the contest the following year; and a series
of resolutions were prepared and introduced into that body
denouncing the action of the National House of Representatives as virtually reading New Jersey out of the Union.
To Daniel Haines was assigned the part to oppose these
resolutions, and he ardently contested the right as well as
the propriety of the Legislature to pass them. But the
Whigs having a large majority, the resolutions were carried.
The debate, in which he bore so prominent a part, served to
bring him forward as a leader of the Democracy; he was
re-elected a member of the Council, but declined another
nomination. In 1843 he was elected, by the two houses of
the Legislature, Governor and Chancellor of the State; and
he was the last Governor elected by the joint action of the
two houses. He was earnest in advocating a change in the
Constitution of the State, and labored earnestly for the passage of a law which should authorize the calling of a Convention for that purpose. He was also the warm friend of
the free school system, and recommended the same to the
Legislature and the people of the State. After the new
Constitution was framed and passed by a vote of the people,
he was continued in the office of Governor, etc., until his
successor, Governor Stratton, was inaugurated in January,
1845, having declined the nomination as candidate in the first
election under the new Constitution, whereby the people
voted directly for the Governor. In 1847, however, he accepted the nomination of his party and was elected. At the
expiration of his term of office he resumed the practice of
the law until November, 1852, when he took his seat on
the bench of the Supreme Court of the State, having been
previously nominated to that office and confirmed by the
Senate: at the close of his term, he was reappointed, so
that he retained that position for fourteen years. For several
years he was President Judge of the Newark circuit, the most
important in the State; and when his term of office was

about to expire, he received an elegant testimonial of respect from the members of its bar. As already stated, Governor Haines was an ardent supporter of the measures of General Jackson and his successors in the Democratic school of politics. He had been, previous to 1824, a believer in the doctrines of the Federal party as promulgated years previous, and he regarded General Jackson as being the true successor of the Federalistic school. He retained his Democratic sentiments down to the period of the great rebellion, voting, in 1860, against the Republican party, and in favor of the "Union Democratic Ticket." After the election of Abraham Lincoln, he earnestly advocated every measure which might be adopted to prevent the war; but when the Southern States seceded, and the flag was fired upon at Fort Sumter, he wheeled into the line in support of the Union, and used all his influence to raise men and means to carry on the war for the restoration of the Union. His two sons, and a son-in-law, with his entire approbation, volunteered for the cause, and one of the former gave his life to his country. Notwithstanding this, he was a warm supporter of General McClellan and Horatio Seymour when nominated in opposition to Lincoln and Grant; and he has steadily opposed the reconstruction acts of the Republican party, as being, in his estimation, a clear violation of the Constitution. He has ever been a warm friend of education for the masses, and for every measure which will advance the establishment of public schools. He was named, in 1845, one of the Commissioners to select a site for the State Lunatic Asylum, and was a member of the first Board of Managers of the same. In 1865 he was appointed a Trustee of the "Reform School for Juvenile Delinquents," at Jamestown, when he was elected and still continues President of the Board: he was also appointed, during the same year, a Commissioner to select a site for the "Home for Disabled Soldiers," and afterwards was named as one of its managers. In 1868 he was selected as one of the Commissioners on the State Prison system of New Jersey and of other States, "and to report an improved plan for the government and discipline of the prison." Governor Randolph appointed him, in 1870, as one of the Commissioners to the National Prison Reform Congress, which convened at Cincinnati; and by that body he was named one of a committee having for its object the organization of a National Prison Reform Association, and an International Congress on Prison Discipline and Reform. In the former, he was made one of the corporators, and also one of the Vice-Presidents. In religious belief he is a Presbyterian, and for many years a communicant member and a ruling elder. He has been on various occasions a Commissioner to the General Assembly, and has ever been an earnest advocate for the union of the two great divisions into which that church became divided. He is also prominently identified with those societies auxiliary to the church of his choice, especially in Sunday-school work, and the Bible Society. For many years past he has been one of the Board of Trustees of Princeton College. [Died, Jan. 26th, 1877.]

25

STRATTON, BENJAMIN HARRIS, M. D., late of Mount Holly, New Jersey, was born in that place, February 6th, 1804. He was the son of Dr. John L. and Anna H. Stratton, the latter being a daughter of Dr. James Stratton, of Swedesboro, Gloucester county, in the same State. Dr. John L. Stratton was a Jerseyman, having been born in Fairfield, Cumberland county, February 23d, 1778. He enjoyed good educational advantages and improved them; his medical studies he pursued under the direction of Dr. James Stratton; he graduated from the University of Pennsylvania in the year 1800, shortly after located in Mt. Holly, and there successfully pursued his profession, with an interruption of only six months, until a few years before his death, which occurred on August 17th, 1845. The son, Benjamin Harris, was prepared for college at Baskenridge, which then enjoyed a high reputation as a preparatory school, and graduated at Princeton College in September, 1823. Very soon thereafter he commenced the study of medicine with the father, and graduated at the University of Pennsylvania in the spring of 1827. Soon after graduating he entered into partnership with his father as a medical practitioner. They continued together until a few years before the father's death, when the infirmities of age, made premature by his onerous life-work, caused the father to retire from active practice; and the son, in addition to the labor, hardships and responsibilities of an already large and increasing practice, assumed the duties laid aside by the father; and how well, conscientiously and successfully they were performed, the love, veneration and respect of the community he served so long most eloquently declare. He continued his professional labors through all the changes and vicissitudes of a half century up to the commencement of his last illness, and then unwillingly laid them aside only at the commands of his attending physicians. After several months of confinement and suffering with a complication of diseases, borne with the resignation of a Christian gentleman, he died December 29th, 1875, aged seventy-two years. He was a high-toned, honorable gentleman, just and upright in all his dealings, possessing a high sense of integrity, from which he never swerved. He was a cheerful, genial companion, warm and true in his friendships, and compassionate and considerate of the feelings of others. In his professional life the same characteristics that distinguished him as a man—honor, honesty and integrity—were prominent, with an enthusiastic love for his calling that was shown in his practice, in his daily intercourse with physicians, in the meetings of the medical societies, and in his observance of the laws of medical etiquette. As a physician, through all the years of his practice, he held a prominent position among those of the State. He was one of the founders of the Burlington County Medical Society in 1829, was elected President several times, and served as Treasurer for many years. He was almost always present at its stated meetings, and actively participated in the proceedings, and when young physicians were elected as members, he would extend to them a cordial greeting, and in all their after professional intercourse with him, be to them friend, guide and counsellor. He was a member and regular attendant of the meetings of the New Jersey State Medical Society, and was elected President in the year 1838. As a practitioner, he was successful in the treatment of diseases, and not only won the confidence of his patients by his skill, but their hearts by his kindness and sympathy. He was noted for his ready resource in the use and adaptation of "domestic remedies" as adjuncts in the cure of disease, and as a prescriber of officinal standard remedies in their combinations and adaptability to the ailment under treatment he had few or no superiors. He acquired a high reputation as an accoucheur, and was very skilful in the use of the forceps. And amid all his labors he was a close student of the current medical literature of the day, and thus kept pace with the material advancement of medical science. He was married May 11th, 1829, and left a widow and two daughters. At a special meeting of the County Medical Society a preamble and series of resolutions were adopted setting forth the honor and esteem with which his labors and character inspired his professional brethren.

TEARNS, JOHN O., for many years Superintendent and Engineer of the Central Railroad of New Jersey, was born in Billerica, near Boston, Massachusetts, August 3d, 1805. He was the son of John Stearns, and one of a family of four sons and two daughters. For educational advantages he was indebted only to the district schools, which were only permitted to claim part of his time, the remainder being passed on his father's farm. This property had been in the family for several generations, descending to his father from his earlier ancestors through John O.'s grandfather, Hon. Isaac Stearns. From his sixteenth to his twentieth year the subject of this sketch was engaged in mechanical pursuits; thereafter he was employed in a subordinate capacity in the construction of the Blackstone Canal, in Rhode Island, and of Fort Trumbull, Connecticut. A few years subsequently he made a contract for the building of locks on the Chesapeake & Ohio Canal, and followed with another for constructing the macadamized turnpike road from Harper's Ferry up the valley of the Shenandoah to Smithfield. In 1832 he began his career as railroad contractor by taking several sections on the Philadelphia & Columbia Railroad. From that time he was continuously engaged in building roads in different parts of the country until the formation of his permanent connection with the Central Railroad of New Jersey. He built as many as twenty different roads; among the more important may be mentioned the Camden & Amboy Railroad, in New Jersey; the Philadelphia & Trenton, in Pennsylvania; the Philadelphia, Wilmington & Baltimore; the Baltimore & Ohio; the Philadelphia & Columbia; the Delaware & Atlantic; the Tioga, in Pennsylvania; the Blossburg & Corning, in New York; the Elizabethtown & Somerville, now the Central Railroad of New Jersey. His most extensive operations were conducted in connection with the last mentioned railway, his services being almost exclusively devoted to it after the year 1842 until his death. The original line extending from Elizabethport to Somerville was built by him and his partner, Coffin Colkett. They afterwards leased the road and operated it; when it was sold under foreclosure of the mortgage, they bought it in and organized for its operation a new company of which John O. Stearns was elected Superintendent, and also a member of the Board of Directors. After a while a scheme was projected for the extension of the line to the Delaware, and a company was formed for the purpose under the title of the Somerville & Easton Railroad Company. Mr. Stearns took a very active share in floating this enterprise, and upon the organization became a member of the Board of Directors. In this capacity he rendered very efficient assistance in urging forward the construction of the line. When in 1849 the two companies were consolidated under the style of the Central Railroad of New Jersey, his valuable services were secured to superintend the whole road, and he retained his seat at the newly-organized Board. Subsequently to the title of Superintendent that of Engineer was added, and the duties of this arduous and responsible position he continued to discharge with marked ability and fidelity during life. At the time of his death the company was about to raise him to the Vice-Presidency. For twenty years previous to this event he had been engaged somewhat extensively in the iron, lumber and mining business in New York and Pennsylvania. These operations he opened by the purchase, in 1842, of the property of the Lycoming Coal and Iron Company of Pennsylvania, consisting of coal and iron mines, a large rolling mill, iron foundry, lumber mills, timber lands, with improvements, etc., which had cost a company of capitalists from Boston nearly half a million of dollars. Mr. Stearns, however, acquired it at a greatly reduced price. After operating the whole for several years, he disposed of all but the timber lands and lumber mills, which he continued to work upon a much larger scale than formerly up to the period of his death. He also devoted much time and thought to, and was at considerable expense in projecting, plans for the development of the iron resources of New Jersey. Indeed, he was pre-eminently a man of affairs; his activity and sagacity in business were remarkable, and no less so was his administrative ability, as is illustrated by the circumstance that at one time he was engaged in, and brought to successful completion, the construction of as many as seven different roads. In character he was singularly upright and unselfish. It is very rare to find a man declining an increase of compensation for services, yet when the Central Railroad Company, in just appreciation of his untiring devotion to their interests, proposed to raise his

salary, he objected on the ground that he was already paid as much as he thought was merited. The company, however, insisted, disregarding his protest, and carried their point. He was very generous in disposition, and out of the abundance of his means was always ready to help not only public enterprises but private charities. By his fellow-citizens he was naturally held in very high esteem, those admiring him the most who knew him best. He died at his residence in Elizabeth, in November, 1862, leaving behind a record of unimpeachable integrity in all his dealings.

TEARNS, JOSIAH O., late Superintendent of the Central Railroad Company of New Jersey, was born in New Hampshire in the year 1831. He commenced railroad life as a conductor on the Pennsylvania Railroad, from which he subsequently transferred his services to the New Jersey Central, in which company he was the Assistant Superintendent until 1862, when he succeeded his relative, John O. Stearns, as Superintendent. He was indefatigable in the discharge of his duties to the company, and was universally esteemed for his liberality to the poor, and also for his many social virtues. He died at Elizabeth, August 29th, 1867.

ARRAND, ANDREW JACKSON, of Raritan, was born in Warren county, New Jersey, March 25th, 1826. His father, John Farrand, a native of Connecticut, died while Andrew was still an infant, and at a very early age the lad was thrown entirely upon his own resources. He worked upon a farm until his sixteenth year, studying in the winters at the neighboring public schools, and thus acquiring—aided too by persevering home study—a fair English education. At the age of sixteen he applied himself to shoemaking, but when nineteen years old relinquished this to take up the business of tailoring. Establishing himself at Philipsburg, his business constantly increased, growing eventually into a large manufactory employing from twenty-five to thirty hands. In 1858, after thirteen years of close application to trade, failing health compelled him to enter upon some business calculated to less severely tax his bodily and mental powers, and he accordingly sold out his clothing manufactory and purchased an interest in the Philipsburg Agricultural Works, becoming a member of the firm of Reece, Lake, Melick & Co. Of this concern the present Screw Mower and Reaper Company is the outgrowth—a manufacturing company having establishments at Philipsburg and Raritan, New Jersey, from which over one thousand machines have been turned out in the course of a single season, beside extensive works at Lewistown, Pennsylvania. Of this company Mr. Farrand is the Sec-

retary and Treasurer. He was one of the organizers, and the first President of the Raritan Savings Bank; is President of the Raritan Building Loan Association No. 1, and a Director in Association No. 2. He is largely interested in real estate, both at Raritan and Philipsburg. Farrandtown, north of Raritan, takes its name from him, he having there purchased a tract of land and caused it to be laid out in building lots of convenient size, assisting with his own means intending settlers to erect dwellings. By his wise liberality many deserving workmen have here been provided with comfortable homes. Upon removing to Raritan he was elected a member of the town council, and in this position—as also when holding similar office at Philipsburg—he evidenced a remarkable knowledge of the needs and methods of civic government. In 1875 he was named in the Democratic State Convention as candidate for State Senator, but his nomination was lost by a single adverse vote—a result that would certainly not have been reached had he made the slightest effort to gain the honor. He was warmly urged by his friends for the nomination for member of Congress from the Fourth New Jersey District, his sterling integrity and extensive business knowledge, and knowledge of the requirements of the country, peculiarly fitting him for such a position. As an inventor, he has considerably added to the effectiveness of the screw mower and reaper, many of the most important attachments to that machine being his own patents; indeed, as now manufactured, it is claimed by the company that for simplicity of construction, convenience in handling and lightness of draft, the reaper is probably unsurpassed. In substantiation of this assertion, it is affirmed that the reaper took the first prize in a competitive trial with eight machines of other celebrated makers held at the Chester county agricultural fair. In addition to his other enterprises, Mr. Farrand has two boot and shoe stores; one at Raritan, in which his eldest son is the active partner, and one at Philipsburg, in which Mr. Godfrey is partner. He also owns a considerable amount of real estate in both towns. He was married in 1850 to Miss Duckworth, of Hunterdon county.

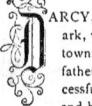

ARCY, JOHN S., M. D., Physician, late of Newark, was born, February 24th, 1788, in Hanover township, Morris county, New Jersey. His father was for many years an eminent and successful practitioner of medicine in that county, and he entered upon the study of the same science with him and succeeded to his extensive practice, in which he likewise met with great success. In 1832, when the Asiatic cholera first made its appearance in this country, he removed to Newark, and by his skill and promptness in the treatment of that terrible disease, and by his unselfish devotion to his patients, and sympathy for their sufferings, he soon attained a more extensive practice than any other in

the State, and which finally impaired his own vigorous constitution. In 1849 he made an overland journey to California, merely for the improvement of his health; but although the expedition was in other respects successful, his
health was rather impaired than benefited by the trip. On
the incorporation of the New Jersey Railroad and Transportation Company, he was elected its President, and held
the office until death, a period of over thirty years. His
political creed was that of the Jackson school of the Democracy, and very early in life he was elected a member of the
State Legislature, in which he served several years; and at
a subsequent date, while yet a resident of Morris county,
was United States Marshal for the District of New Jersey,
having been appointed to that office by President Jackson,
and continued to hold that position during the subsequent
administration of Martin Van Buren. He exerted great influence in his party throughout the State, although he was
averse to holding office. He was for many years a prominent member of the Masonic order, and for some years held
the office of Grand Master of the Grand Lodge of the State.
He died in Newark, of paralysis, October 22d, 1863.

———————

 OOPER, SHERMAN, M.D., of Westfield, was
born in Croydon, Sullivan county, New Hampshire, August 20th, 1833, his parents being Lemuel P. and Laura (Whipple) Cooper, both natives
of New Hampshire. He was educated at the
public schools at Rome, and at the Kimball Union
Academy at Meriden, graduating from the latter institution
in 1852. Electing the profession of medicine, he attended
a course of lectures at Dartmouth College in 1855, and read
in the office of Professor David S. Conant in New York.
In 1856-7 he attended lectures at the New York Medical
College, and in the latter year was appointed assistant surgeon to the hospital on Blackwell's Island. In 1858 he
was made chief of staff at that hospital. In the subsequent
year he entered upon the practice of his profession at Clare-
mont, New Hampshire, and continued in successful practice until the breaking out of the war. In 1861 he entered
the United States service as surgeon of the 6th Regiment
New Hampshire Volunteers, and served with credit for
three years. In the spring of 1865 he returned to Clare-
mont, and during the succeeding five years was actively
engaged in the duties of his profession. In 1866-7 he held
the chair of Assistant Professor of Surgery in the University
of Vermont. In the latter year he received his degree of
M. D. from the University of New York. In October, 1871,
he removed to Westfield, where he has since continued in
successful practice. He was elected Coroner for Union
county in the fall of 1875. He has been for several years
a prominent member of the Union County Medical Society.
On the 23d of June, 1858, he was married to Celia Pierson,
of Westfield.

CRIVENS, ZEBULON W., M.D., late of Long
Branch, was born in Petersburg, New York, September 1st, 1826. After a good preliminary
training, he entered the Literary University, New
York, from which he was graduated with honor
in 1849. From his early childhood he was a
hard student and a literary aspirant, possessing a retentive
mind that never grew weary in its pursuit after knowledge.
It was very natural therefore that he should incline toward
a learned profession. He chose that of medicine, and began
reading under the direction of Dr. A. H. Hull, of Berlin,
New York, and took a full course at the Albany Medical
College, from which he was graduated in 1852. The practice of his profession he opened in his native town, Petersburg, where he pursued it for twelve months. For a similar
period he labored at Eagle Mills, in the same State, whither
he removed from Petersburg. In 1854 he succeeded Dr.
Jacob Vanderveer, at Long Branch, in a laborious and increasing practice, extending over a section of country four
miles wide and sixteen miles long. But his reputation was
not thus limited, called, as he often was, miles away to hold
consultations with neighboring physicians in critical cases.
He was a man of large perceptions and excellent judgment;
devoted to his profession, sacrificing everything else to its
pursuit, even his life; for although a large, stalwart man,
possessing great bodily vigor and vitality, he had to succumb before the heavy labors he imposed on himself. A
careful and successful general practitioner, he especially excelled in surgery, and was remarkably successful in his operations. He died February 11th, 1876, from pneumonia,
complicated with other diseases. By all who knew him he
was not only respected but beloved.

———————

OBS, EUGENE, M.D., late of Springfield, was
born at Liberty Corner, Somerset county, New
Jersey, February 23d, 1821, being the son of
Nicholas C. and Margaret C. Jobs. After an ordinary country school education, he commenced
life as a teacher, and also as an assistant to his
father in his store. Attracted toward the medical profession, he began to study medicine with Dr. Smith English,
at Manalapan, Monmouth county, and in due course matriculated at the University of Pennsylvania, medical department, from which he was graduated April 4th, 1844.
He was licensed to practise in New Jersey, at Elizabeth,
by the Board of Censors of the Medical Society of New
Jersey, for the Eastern District, September 11th, 1844.
Practice he commenced at Springfield, Union county, in the
spring of 1845, and there he continued uninterruptedly until
his death. On October 28th, 1846, he was married to
Mary L., oldest daughter of Thomas C. Allen, of Connecticut Farms, Union county, who died September 12th, 1863,

leaving two sons and two daughters. He was a member of the Presbyterian Church, joining the communion in Springfield in 1848, and remaining a consistent member through after life. He died suddenly, of apoplexy, May 22d, 1875. Patient, industrious and ambitious, his incessant toil, his great exposure and many hardships overtaxing the brain and body, brought on the fatal attack. He fully appreciated the duties, responsibilities and privileges of his profession, honoring it in all his actions. Although his practice became very large, it was not especially remunerative, but his poor patients ever received from him the same careful attention extended to the rich. He recognized his calling as one enabling him to do good, and never neglected an opportunity of helping the afflicted and poor. He enjoyed a high reputation as a skilful physician, and was very highly respected and esteemed in a large neighborhood for his sterling character and social qualities.

ATZMER, WILLIAM H., Railroad Promoter and Manager, was born, July 22d, 1807, near Somerville, Somerset county, New Jersey. On the paternal side he is of German descent, his father having emigrated from Coburg in 1794, and settled first in Bustleton, near Philadelphia, and later in Somerset county, New Jersey, where he had charge of the Campbell Mills. His limited means did not permit him to furnish his son other educational advantages than those of a country village, but these were so well used that at the age of twelve years the latter was qualified to fill the situation of clerk in a country store. A year later he entered a more extensive establishment at Somerville. Here he remained for five years, displaying such business qualifications that the entire management of the house was confided to him, and the proprietor was desirous that he should acquire a partnership interest. To this, however, his want of capital was a bar, and believing that the knowledge of some trade would render him more secure of winning success in life, he left the store and entered a printing office in the same town. The opportunities for self-culture which such a position offers were not neglected by him, and he soon acquired not merely a practical acquaintance with the trade but a general knowledge of science and literature. Thus provided, a rational ambition prompted him to seek a wider field than that of a country village, and, supplied with high testimonials of character and ability, he applied successfully to the wealthy steamboat firm of Stevens Brothers, of New York city, for a situation. At that date, 1830, they controlled the principal trade of the North river, and they placed him as chief clerk on the "North America," then the finest boat afloat on the New York waters, where he distinguished himself by his executive skill and agreeable manners. The brothers Stevens were at this period engaged in constructing the

Camden & Amboy Railroad, a charter of which had been granted by the Legislature of New Jersey in 1830. In 1833, having completed the eastern sections of the line, they transferred him to the steamboat route between New York city and South Amboy, which position he occupied about three years. After the completion of the road from Amboy to Camden a responsible position was assigned to him in the office in Philadelphia by the same firm. Its duties he fulfilled so satisfactorily that soon not merely the management of the Philadelphia office but of the whole interests of the company were intrusted to him. It is not easy at this day, when the railroad system is thoroughly organized and acknowledged successful, to appreciate how onerous and responsible those duties were. The Camden & Amboy Railroad was the first great through line completed in this country. By many sound and cautious men it was deemed a hazardous and even chimerical experiment, likely enough to bankrupt its stockholders. The respective rights of the public and the road were yet undefined; costly litigation was unavoidable, and the immense labor of organization had all to be performed without the light of precedent or example. The company justly recognized that one mind must control the whole, untrammelled by interference or conflicting opinion, and the brothers Stevens rightly judged that such a mind could be found in their late employé. Hence for years he may be said to have been the autocrat of the road, appointing and deposing any subordinate officer, carrying his plans and wishes through the Board of Directors with little opposition, and, withal, using this extensive authority with such discretion that neither employés nor stockholders ever preferred just grounds of complaint against his management. The company obtained control, early in its history, of the Philadelphia & Trenton Railroad, to secure the direct all-rail route between Philadelphia and New York, and ran a steamboat, first to Bristol and then to Tacony, in connection with this line. They also became proprietors of the ferry between Philadelphia and Camden, and of several freight and ferry lines on the Delaware. From these beginnings the road extended the area of its branches in all directions, so that it finally received the transportation of nearly one-half the territory of New Jersey. The smaller connecting roads, which were from time to time constructed, were supplied with funds and credit by the Camden & Amboy, and generally managed in accordance to the advice of its efficient superintendent. Nor was his influence bounded by the limits here defined. The Belvidere & Delaware Railroad, one of the important connecting branches of the Camden & Amboy, approaches the vast coal regions of Pennsylvania. The extension required to unite this with the coal fields was the Lehigh Valley Railroad and its branches, projected by Judge Packer, of Pennsylvania; and certain privileges and assistance essential to that important undertaking were, by Mr. Gatzmer's advice, granted the Lehigh Valley Company by the Camden & Amboy, services warmly acknowledged by Judge Packer. In 1867 Edwin

A. Stevens having resigned the Presidency of the Camden & Amboy Railroad Company, that honor was conferred, by unanimous consent, on him, who for thirty-seven years had been the faithful and successful steward of the company's interests. In this year the New Jersey Railroad and Transportation Company was amalgamated with the Joint Companies of New Jersey, and the public works of the State, embraced in the Delaware & Raritan Canal Company, the Camden & Amboy Railroad Company, and the New Jersey Railroad Company were managed by a Joint Board, through the respective presidents. He was appointed Chairman of the Passenger and Freight Committee, and Secretary of the Joint Board and Executive Committees, which positions he held until the lease of the works to the Pennsylvania Railroad Company. To this lease he was opposed, and stated the reasons for his opposition in a forcible argument, entitled, " Views upon the Proposition to Lease the Public Works of New Jersey to the Pennsylvania Railroad Company ; read before the Joint Board of Directors, at their meeting at Trenton, New Jersey, April 20th, 1871." The lease, however, was finally ratified and executed by the presidents of the companies, by directions of the Joint Board, his views of its inexpediency remaining, nevertheless, unchanged. In May, 1872, his official connection with the United Canal and Railroad Companies of New Jersey, and as President of the Camden & Amboy Railroad Company, ceased. His connection with the Lehigh Valley Railroad Company, of which he was a Director as early as 1853, continues, and he was elected unanimously its Consulting Manager. When twenty-two years of age he married Eliza A. Campbell, of New York city, and has had the pleasure of witnessing an exemplary family grow up around him. His personal character has not merely been conspicuous for fair dealing and sincerity, qualities essential to the posts he has filled, but also for uniform courteousness, and a freedom from the irritability which so frequently mars the manners of the best men when overworked and weighted with the cares of a complex business. The capacity of very rapid labor, and the power of occupying the mind with more than one topic of attention at a time, are traits he has manifested in a universal degree, and explain the facility with which he could transact, without errors, such varied affairs.

ARISON, REV. ANDREW B., late of Ringoes, was born, December 31st, 1841, at Sandy Ridge, Hunterdon county, New Jersey. He was the third son of Benjamin Larison, and his boyhood was passed upon his father's farm. He prepared for college at Flemington High School, of which his brother, C. W. Larison, was at that time principal, and in October, 1861, entered the medical college at Geneva, New York. He graduated thence in 1864, and immediately

entered the United States army as an Assistant Surgeon, serving until the end of the war. When mustered out of the service he entered the freshman class in the university at Lewisburg, Pennsylvania, and continued his studies until, having reached the last term of his senior year, failing health compelled a total cessation from labor. A series of hemorrhages from the lungs, superinduced by an attack of pleuro-pneumonia while in the army, threatened his life, but after a few months of rest his strength seemed restored and he was ordained a minister of the Baptist Church, in February, 1870. He was immediately called to the pastorate of the church at Ringoes, New Jersey, an office that he held until his death. In January, 1870, in connection with his brother, Cornelius W. Larison, he founded the seminary at Ringoes, taking the position of Principal, and holding the chairs of Moral Science and Languages. His death occurred September 25th, 1872, and although the term of his ministry comprehended less than three years, upwards of eighty new members were added to the church through his exertions. Few men, laboring for so brief a period, have left so distinct an impress upon the moral tone of the community in which they have lived. Mr. Larison was married, October 6th, 1869, to Catherine B. Brown, a graduate of the University Female Institute, Lewisburg, Pennsylvania, who was to him an excellent helpmate, both in pastoral duties and in the duties of the seminary.

EAVITT, JOHN, M. D., of Baptistown, was born in New Hampshire in the year 1819. After a good New England education he moved to New Jersey, where he became a school teacher in New Hampton. At the same time, having determined to adopt the medical profession, he began to read medicine with Dr. R. M. McLonahan, of that place. Having prepared himself for a college course, he proceeded to New York, pursued a full course and graduated. Upon receiving his diploma, he opened an office in Asbury, Warren county, New Jersey, where he practised from 1846 to 1847. In the latter year he removed to Ohio, where he prosecuted his profession for a short time. But he tired of the West, and returned to New Jersey and located in Finesville, Warren county. There he remained until 1854, when he took up his residence in Baptistown, Hunterdon county, where he continued actively engaged until his death. An extensive practice rewarded his labors, his skill and care. He married Miss Smith, daughter of James Smith, who with two children, a daughter and a son, survive him. After moving to Hunterdon county he became a member of the District Medical Society for that county ; in 1860 he was chosen its President, and also one of its Board of Censors. He was very conservative in practice. Unobtrusive in his manners, beloved by his patients, and warmly esteemed by the community in which he lived, he was also highly respected by his professional brethren. Religiously he was a Presbyterian. He died October 20th, 1875.

PHELPS, HON. WILLIAM WALTER, Lawyer and Member of the Forty-Second Congress, was born in August, 1839. The Phelps family were early merchants of New York, and were noted for their culture as well as for their business conquests. They reaped wealth through wise and fair dealing with their fellow-men. Phelps' father, John Jay Phelps, rose to affluence in days when Moses Taylor, Commodore Garrison, William E. Dodge, and other men whose names are now historical in commerce, were his friends and competitors. The elder Phelps is remembered as a financier of great shrewdness in his immediate dealings with events, but who, in common with all truly large-minded men, had a faculty for planning and executing projects that were not only intended to produce riches, but to surprise and charm by their originality and vastness. It was he who with consummate judgment decided that the coal regions of Pennsylvania, in which he had invested much money, should be connected with tide water at New York by the railway which is known as the Delaware, Lackawanna & Western. Our greatest men are not merely planners; they are also executors; and if we count the really successful men of our century we may say of them that in no project which they contemplated were they less willing to become responsible with their own money or reputations, than they were to invite the trust of others. So that it may be said that John Jay Phelps was an investor and not what we in our day are likely to call, with the falling inflection, a "speculator." Of the railway which he projected, he was President for many years. Carlyle says that self-esteem is one of the greatest qualities of men; and when this capitalist became in August, 1830, the father of a son, he was proud enough to borrow time from his wide enterprises to devote to the development of the boy's character. Nor was he mistaken either in his plan or in the character of the child; for while William Walter Phelps inherited the quick intelligence of his father, he early in life developed a passion for "mere culture" for its own sake—that brooding over what Emerson calls the "beautiful in doing," and what Matthew Arnold would call the literary instinct. At Yale College, William Walter Phelps became one of the most popular of the undergraduates, mainly because he united the habits of the scholarly recluse, when duty called for them, with a sturdy interest in the social demands of the institution. It is perhaps his leading characteristic that his nervous-sanguine temperament leads him to take a practical interest in whatever surrounds him. So lasting is the memory of his active workings for his *Alma Mater* that when he was only passing his thirtieth year he was chosen a Fellow of Yale by a vote which led that of even William M. Evarts. He early showed readiness for debate; and he was both in and out of college one of the few really great speakers whom that stern and jealous institution has produced. Men who are powerful in speaking are seldom good writers, as Charles James Fox has suggested; and those who fashion their thoughts into a graceful style of writing usually fail, as Addison did, when they ascend the rostrum. There are few exceptions to this rule, Wendell Phillips being one, and William Walter Phelps being another, in our country and our generation. Yet, wisely, Mr. Phelps does not plunge into the arena of popular literature. His style of speaking, when reproduced in print, possesses the true literary quality, resembling very much that of Sargent S. Prentiss, who was popular as an orator in the generation just preceding ours. Without this literary quality Phelps might have unduly developed his ready practical talent, so that, while he would not have been lacking in force as a debater, his quality of learning might not have acquired for him the liking of that by-no-means-weak element in politics which is sometimes called doctrinaire. It is the spirit of the poet chastening the action of the executor: the blue depth that gives picturesque color to the hurtling cataract. Wirt, Story, Phillips, and Phelps have had more lasting power in politics than turbulent speakers like Randolph and Tom Marshall and Butler and Cox. The quality that our speakers with the literary instinct possess is powerful because it charms. The campaign speaker who rouses cheers at every stamp of his brogans and every sweep of his hand is forgotten in a day; but in true intelligence there is somewhat the same sort of conservation of force which exists in physics; and as in poetry "a thing of beauty is a joy forever," so in politics a word spoken with that intelligence which transcends commonplace, is like bread cast upon waters and returning after many days. The Englishman whom Phelps most resembles is Canning, whose life was very much like that of our Jerseyman, so far as the latter has lived long enough for us to make the comparison. There are the same microcosmic word, the same graceful phrase, the same melodic period, the same merciless sarcasm, and the same reverence for the subject. It was said of Canning by his enemies in sarcasm that contained genuine praise that his rhetoric could not hide the sinews of his oratorical power. The same may be said of Phelps. But it can never be said of Phelps, as Canning's enemies said of him, that he is ever tawdry. Phelps' European journey was a visit to the shrines of great men, mainly in literature; and newspaper men have no need to cease their liking for him when we tell them that he went with reverential footsteps to Thackeray's habitual scenes. Columbia Law School furnished him with the means of attaining a thorough legal education, and there, as at Yale, he won the honors of his class. He immediately upon graduating became known for his skill in financial and railroad law, a branch of his profession in which S. L. M. Barlow and Governor Tilden have proved so successful. Among his clients were capitalists like Moses Taylor,

George Bliss and William E. Dodge. Soon after he began to achieve distinction in his profession his father died, leaving him so large a fortune that he was compelled to give exclusive attention to the interests which it involved. He had already chosen New Jersey as his place of residence, and had purchased a farm in Bergen county, including a thousand acres of land, reaching from the Hudson river to the town of Hackensack. His manner of life among his neighbors, though never lacking the gracefulness which makes the outer sign of a gentleman, was and continues to be unassuming, cordial and democratic. He is emphatically a hearty man. The present writer has said otherwhere that a man of great powers cannot find substantial success in public life unless he has had a background of country life. Burke used to raise turnips for recreation; Bismarck hides himself on his farm; and Webster found his best ideas while leaning over the fences watching his fat oxen. Phelps' most valuable help in the study of politics has been his New Jersey country life. It was in 1870, just after he had assumed the responsibility of being thirty years old, that Judge Ryerson discovered that if John Hill was to be elected to Congress in the Fifth District, the vote of Bergen county, which has been Democratic from the time when the memory of man runneth not to the contrary, should be weakened; and in his despair, which bred ingenuity, he determined to appeal to the farmer-lawyer of the Hackensack valley. William Walter Phelps was so practical in his response, working with all his nervous energy and frank independence of character, that he reduced the Democratic vote two-thirds, and elected Hill. Thereafter, Phelps became known as the man in his district who could make large majorities. He is the only Republican within our knowledge who ever had a Democratic majority in Bergen county. In Passaic county his popularity was comparatively as great. When, in 1872, he was elected to Congress, he began at once to win honors for his State; so that men who marvelled whence this young man had so suddenly sprung began to say in the Paterson shops and on the hillsides of Morris that the Fifth District of New Jersey was able to send to Washington a man who could honor it with his learning and his brilliancy. Certainly no man in the State ever made so substantial a fame in so short a time. In Congress he rose so high above the conception of him existing in some minds that he was a mere man of money, that constituents who gloomily doubted at the intrusion of one who was almost a stranger, began to applaud when the whole country learned to admire him. He at once made himself popular among the members by several amusing speeches which, tearing the nap from a good deal of shoddy politics, left it threadbare for the study of men. The use of wit in debate is by no means to be reprehended when it serves its purpose of good; and by its use alone is humbug sometimes best exposed. When Phelps' satire was keenest and when his humor was bubbling over, his friends never ceased to respect him, and his enemies, vying with his friends in respect, never wished to hate him. The honesty of the man's faith and the sincerity of his manner gave him a power which is never attained through any of the arts of the demagogue. From the days of Horace Greeley in Congress, the discussion of the franking abuse had been carried on in a ponderous way. When the question arose during the term of Phelps' service, he immediately attacked it with the argument *reductio ad absurdum*. By a stroke of policy which no one had theretofore conceived, he laughed the measure down. In Congress a measure is usually doomed if it is one that can be laughed at. Ridicule, notwithstanding Mr. Carlyle, is a power in oratory, and nothing suffers more severely than when it suffers from contempt. Phelps understood this, and with skill he used his talent for mockery with success. A man is known and respected in Congress for the committees to which he is consigned. There are a few committees that command the power of the House; and there are some tag-end committees that are of utter insignificance. Even in these latter a man like Blue-Jean-Wilhams may be useful. But Phelps—though he was a new and almost untried man, whose youthful face was in great contrast with those of men much older than he—was assigned to the Committee on Banking and Commerce, one of the foremost in the House. This was an honor which his district appreciated; and he used his advantages well. His skill as a financial lawyer was displayed in the work of the committee room by the clearness of his reports. This was at a time when the impending panic was threatening to demand all sorts of wild and dangerous exploits in financial legislation; and among those who stood forward as champions of a sensible and valuable currency none carried greater power or commanded higher respect than Phelps. He argued his questions with surprising skill; sometimes cleaving his obstacle with the sword of Richard —sometimes cutting the floating veil with the dexterous scimetar of Saladin. Above all, he was clear. His speech in which he defined "value" was one of the clearest and ablest expositions in political economy that have ever been produced. The present writer, at the time of its utterance, suggested in a public journal that it be used as a text-book in colleges. It had great influence everywhere; and Phelps received not only praise from hurried, practical politicians who saw his effect, but commendation from scholarly recluses who were studying the problem within college walls. So far as the speech was intended to go, that is, concerning the subject of "value" and its distinction from "price," it stands, for clearness of exposition and for originality of illustration, in advance of the chapters devoted to the subject by either Cairns or Mill. It may be said without exaggeration that, during the two years of Phelps' service in Congress, he did as much as any statesman, not excepting even Schurz or Sherman, to prepare the way for honest money. He belonged to that small, powerful, well-organized band who by their energy and genius legislated so that hard times should not be prolonged beyond their natural period. In 1874 the Democratic tidal wave swept everything before it; and the Fifth District was not excepted from its effects. No Canute could have kept it back. William Walter Phelps was defeated by only five votes. Hundreds of Republicans, standing pulseless and pale in the agony of a panic which was credited to the administration, did not go near the polls. There were jealous men who saw that Phelps' genius made their talents appear ignoble, and they said that "this boy" had shot up like a rocket and must come down like a stick. There were still others who thought that he did not bow low enough to the demands of demagoguery. He could not truckle to low arts. There were enough of those who wished him to do so, to defeat him. There were five. It is a matter of surprise that in the tidal sweep over a district filled with a working population which is sensitive to hard times and which always lays them at the door of the party in power, he was almost elected. His popularity almost made him an exception. During his last term in Congress he worked with unabated vigor. His voice was frequently welcomed by men who were glad to hear his clear exposi-tions. His fame grew. It was during that session that he was one of the committee, of which Mr. Wheeler, the Re-publican candidate for Vice-President, was another, that investigated the political affairs of Louisiana. He found that there was great fraud in that State, and he had the manhood to denounce it, and the ability to make his words have effect. Republicans began to call him "independent," because he was essentially not partisan; and because he naturally had a reverence for what rights the States had re-tained for themselves, and because he disliked Federal interference in local elections, he was sometimes called a Democrat. There were negroes who believed he was not their champion, because in the consideration of measures relating to civil rights he thought that white men, too, had some rights of choice. He has always been in favor of the utmost freedom that can be given to individual men in con-sistency with civil order. But for his "too independence," as some one called it, he would have been re-elected. After Congress adjourned Mr. Phelps was so ill from the effects of overwork that he was compelled to seek health in Europe. While he was there, his name was again men-tioned for the Republican nomination for Congress in his district; but he made no efforts to obtain it. Even some of the Democrats wished to second the nomination, because they admired his independence, and wished that his bril-liancy should honor the district. But he made no efforts to se-cure either, and as many men wished the office, there was no one to fight for him in his absence. He is far from being a politician in the sense of being a schemer. He carried his county by his open, personal appeal to men's judgment and honesty. He refused to come home to win the nomination, as he could have done. "I will not stand in any one's way," said he. When he returned, restored in health, and strong in his wish to see the country restored to harmony and prosperity by the wisdom and magnanimity and higher

judgment of its statesmen, his name was mentioned as one of that number. His financial position, which at one time made him a proposed candidate for Secretary of the Treas-ury, and his conservative views in regard to Southern poli-tics, were thought to be valuable. His name was mentioned as that of one who should succeed Mr. Frelinghuysen in the Senate; and men in both parties were anxious to have him as a candidate. But he said, at least to the present writer: "I should be glad to serve New Jersey, if my service were at any time valuable; but I am not going to sacrifice my self-respect or the respect of others, by resort-ing to any tricks for promotion. Honor earned in that way is a flimsy thing, and no popular applause can satisfy a man who is not true to himself." These were the words of a Jerseyman who is truly great.

BULLOCK, EDWARD R., Lawyer, of Flemington, was born October 17th, 1818, in Falls township, Bucks county, Pennsylvania. His parents, Isaac Bullock and Sarah (Burton) Bullock, were de-scended from English Quakers. When he was ten years old, his father died, occasioning him to withdraw from the schools, which he had previously attended, and engage as a farm hand, in which capacity he remained until he was sixteen, when he became an appren-tice to a marble-cutter in Trenton, New Jersey, with whom he stayed as such apprentice five years, though he continued in the marble-cutting business, while working at all, until the summer of 1842, attending meanwhile, during the winter as occasion permitted, a school kept by his uncle at Wilmington, Delaware. At this latter date he went to Easton, Pennsylvania, the seat of Lafayette College, pre-pared himself for matriculation, and was duly matriculated in that institution, remaining, however, only one year. In the spring of 1844 he removed to New York, where he worked at his trade till 1846, when he returned to Easton, working there one year, and then going to Flemington, New Jersey, at which place he set up the marble-cutting business on his own account. In 1853, at the age of thirty-five, he began to read law with A. O. Van Fleet, now Vice-Chan-cellor, and was admitted to the bar in 1857. He settled at Flemington, and soon commanded a fair practice. In 1868 he was appointed, by Governor Ward, Prosecutor of the Pleas for Hunterdon county, holding the office about four years, and then resigning it. He was admitted to practise in the United States District Court in 1867, and in 1870 was appointed United States Commissioner. His advance-ment in the profession, like his preparation for it, has been gradual, but thorough and sure. The qualities indeed that shaped his earlier career, so checkered and eventful as to have been almost romantic, could hardly fail to inspire the admiration and trust of his fellow-citizens, and in the long run to assure his solid triumph. It is pleasant to contem-

26

plate the hero of such trials and struggles safe at last in the haven of success. Mr. Bullock was married in 1844, when his battle of life waxed hottest, to Janet, daughter of James Pollock, of Easton, Pennsylvania, who thus became his helpmeet in his days of care not less than in his palmy days. His eldest son, Captain James I. Bullock, of the 15th New Jersey Volunteers, was lost with the steamer General Lyon, while serving on detached duty, escorting troops from Hart Island to Wilmington, North Carolina. His second and only surviving son, John A. Bullock, is a member of the New Jersey bar. Mr. Bullock is in politics a Republican, and, although no politician, his convictions are not on that account the shallower, but possibly all the deeper. At any rate he is a very earnest supporter of the principles of his party.

RIMES, JOHN, M. D., late of Boonton, was born at Parsippany, Morris county, New Jersey, in 1802. After a course of medical study he received a certificate to practise from the State Medical Society in 1827. He first settled in Newfoundland, New Jersey; but in 1833 removed to Boonton, where he continued to practise until his death, on September 12th, 1875. He was remarkable for his strong convictions, and the boldness and pertinacity with which he followed them. At an early period he became a fearless and outspoken advocate of the anti-slavery doctrine, and played an important part in the agitation of that question. He frequently aided slaves to escape, and his house was what was termed a station on the " Underground Railroad." This conspicuous advocacy of a then unpopular cause subjected him to much annoyance; he was frequently ill treated and mobbed, and once arrested by the sheriff of Essex county, for aiding in the escape of fugitive slaves. He gave bonds, but for some reason was never tried. So devoted a laborer was he in the cause of human freedom that he was chosen President of the first Anti-Slavery Society in the State. In 1844 he published the New York *Freeman*, which was maintained until 1850, when other journals took up and advocated abolition. He was also an early and strong advocate of the temperance cause, and strongly condemned the use of stimulants as practised in the profession twenty years ago. It was a satisfaction to him that he lived to see his views on this subject adopted in great measure by his medical brethren, and his abolitionist doctrines indorsed by the country at large. Through nearly the whole of his adult life he abstained from animal food, and in himself he presented a very strong argument in favor of his theory, being exceptionally vigorous in both mind and body, performing with comparative ease the duties of a large and laborious practice, and when an old man doing more professional work than most young men are able to endure. Owing to his pronounced opinions on the slavery and temperance questions, his grave, quiet manner, and plainness of dress, he was somewhat unpopular for the greater part of his life. But all, whether in or out of the profession, recognized his ability as a practitioner. He performed many important surgical operations, and in both surgery and obstetrics was for a long time considered authority in his section of the State. Always a man of honor, truth, and the strictest morality, he was ever respected, and as life advanced he conquered the high esteem and love of a very large circle.

AMILTON, GENERAL SAMUEL RANDOLPH, Lawyer, late of Trenton, was born at Princeton, then in the county of Middlesex, New Jersey, June 7th, 1790. He was the son of John Ross and Phebe Hamilton, who were old residents of that place and neighborhood. He graduated at the College of New Jersey in 1808. Studied law with Governor Williamson at Elizabeth. Was admitted to the bar as an attorney-at-law of the Supreme Court of New Jersey in 1812. In 1823 he was admitted as Counsellor, and was called as a serjeant-at-law in 1837. May 20th, 1818, he was married to Eliza, daughter of Morris Robeson, of Oxford Furnace, now in Warren county. He commenced the practice of law at Princeton, but soon removed to Trenton, where he continued to reside until his death. In his profession he enjoyed a large practice which extended to almost every county in the State, and engaged his attention during the whole of his business career. He stood high in his profession, and was remarkable among his brethren and friends for great geniality and an extended hospitality. During his whole life, his house was the gathering point of the members of the profession from different parts of the State, when on business at the capital. He was a life-long Democrat in politics, and in 1836 was nominated by his party as a candidate for Congress, but in that year the Whigs triumphed for the first time in several years, and he was, with the remainder of the ticket, defeated by about six hundred votes. For many years he was Quartermaster-General of the Militia of the State, an office which he filled with great acceptance to those with whom he came in contact, and care for the interests of the State, until a few years before his death, when he resigned, and was succeeded by General Lewis Perrine. He was appointed Prosecutor of the Pleas of Mercer county by Governor Fort, and held the office at the time of his death. He was also elected by his fellow-citizens as Mayor of the city of Trenton. For many years he was a Trustee of the First Presbyterian Church of Trenton, and always took an active part in the promotion of its interests and of the cause of religion in general, and during the latter years of his life was a member in full communion of that church. He at all times took a deep interest in education, and on his death-bed the interests of the schools of the city seemed to bear more heavily upon him than any other care. He died on the 13th of August, 1856 at the age of sixty-six, leaving a widow and four children. His eldest son, Colonel Morris R. Hamilton, though admitted to the bar, has never practised law, but for the most of his life has been connected with the press. Two other sons devoted their attention to agricultural pursuits, and his daughter married Samuel Sherrerd, of Belvidere, New Jersey. He was buried with military honors in consideration of his connection with public affairs, the military and city government.

EAN, JOHN W., Merchant, of Philipsburg, was born at Stewartsville, Warren county, New Jersey, March 7th, 1839. He was educated at the public schools of his native county, and at the age of seventeen years entered the store of his father in Stewartsville, where he remained for six years. In 1862 he removed to Philipsburg and purchased an interest in the manufacturing business, conducted under the firm-name of Reece, Lake, Melick & Co. In the same year the concern was made a stock company, and Mr. Dean was elected Secretary and Treasurer. In 1862 he was also elected Mayor of Philipsburg, a position to which he was re-elected for three subsequent terms. In 1870 he resigned his offices of Secretary and Treasurer in the company, although still retaining his interest in the enterprise, and engaged in mercantile pursuits in Philipsburg. He continued in business upon his own account until the death of the gentleman elected as his successor in the secretaryship and treasuryship of the company, when, at the urgent solicitation of his fellow-stockholders, he again accepted, and has since continued to hold, the double office. He has held various local offices in Philipsburg besides the mayoralty, and is now freeholder from the first ward of the borough. His affiliations have constantly been with the Democratic party. He has been for many years a consistent member of the Presbyterian Church, and is the leader of a fine choir in the church at Philipsburg. His musical ability is, indeed, somewhat exceptional, and beside being choir leader he is leader of a musical association of some local celebrity known as the "Old Folks." He was largely instrumental in the building of the Philipsburg street railway, and is one of the most public-spirited citizens of the town. In 1861 he was married to Kate Melick, of Philipsburg.

OODHULL, ADDISON W., late of Newark, was born in Monmouth county, New Jersey, in the year 1831. He was a son of Dr. John Woodhull; Judge Woodhull of the Supreme Court is his brother. After a sound preliminary training he entered Princeton College, from which he was graduated in 1854. His taste lying in the direction of

medicine, he studied for that profession, and in due course received his degree. He acted as Penitentiary Physician on Blackwell's Island in 1856, and during the following year moved to Newark, where he settled down to practice. A physician of high ability, and a gentleman whose character commanded confidence, he had by 1861 built up a fine practice, but he abandoned it and left a young wife in response to the call of his country, becoming Assistant Surgeon of the 9th New Jersey Regiment. Subsequently he was detailed as Surgeon and Chief of Hospital at Beaufort, North Carolina, during Burnside's campaign, and afterwards served with Rosecrans and Sherman during the latter part of his grand march to the sea. After his return home he held various positions of honor and trust, being physician of the county jail for several years; President of the Newark Medical Association, of the Essex County Medical Society, one of the first physicians of St. Michael's Hospital, a member of the Board of Examiners for Pensions, and, at the time of his death, a medical examiner for the Mutual Benefit Life Insurance Company. He was a religious man and belonged to the Presbyterian communion. Of the South Park Presbyterian Church he was a prominent member and ruling elder, and a teacher in the Sunday-school, which appointed a committee to prepare a suitable memorial on his decease. The teachers of the two schools attended the funeral in a body. In social as well as professional life he had the confidence and esteem of every one. Of high literary attainments, he was a lover of the arts, and was very skilful in his profession. Faithful to every trust, and a man of most attractive character, his loss was sincerely mourned in a large circle. He died May 14th, 1876, leaving a wife and four children.

ORBERT, A. T. A., Major-General United States army, and now United States Consul-General at Paris, entered the military academy at West Point in 1851, and after passing through the regular course of instruction, graduated in 1855 as Second Lieutenant of infantry. He was attached to the 5th Regiment, then stationed in Texas, and served during the succeeding six years on the frontier of that State, in Florida, in Utah and in New Mexico. In April, 1861—his appointment to a first lieutenancy having reached him two months earlier—he was ordered by the Secretary of War to report for mustering duty to Governor Olden, of New Jersey. In the following August he was made Captain and Assistant Quartermaster, and until September he discharged the functions of mustering officer. The quota of troops from New Jersey demanded by the general government being then filled, Captain Torbert received permission from the War Department to accept the colonelcy of one of the regiments which he had assisted to muster in, and was accordingly appointed by Governor Olden to the command of the

1st regiment. On the 17th of September he assumed command at Camp Seminary, Virginia, and during the winter following he devoted himself to drilling and disciplining his men. When McClellan opened the campaign, in March, 1862, with the advance upon Manassas, the 1st New Jersey was one of the most efficient commands in the entire army. The regiment participated in that advance, and also in the subsequent operations upon the Peninsula, being engaged at West Point, Mechanicsville and Gaines' Mill, and also in the series of fights and skirmishes attendant upon McClellan's change of base. So well did Colonel Torbert handle his command during this trying and disastrous period that in the following August he was promoted to be Brigadier-General and assigned to the command of the 1st Brigade of the 1st Division, 6th Corps, then stationed at Alexandria, Virginia. Under McClellan, and subsequently under Pope, the brigade took part in the Maryland campaign, being engaged in the fight at Crampton's Pass (where General Torbert was slightly wounded), in the battle of Antietam, and in the battle of Fredericksburg, December 13th, 1862, bearing in the latter a prominent part. In January, 1863, General Torbert was ordered home on sick-leave, and so, to his infinite regret, missed the second Fredericksburg fight. He rejoined his brigade in June, and served (under the sequent commands of Hooker and Meade) through the Maryland and Pennsylvania campaigns, bearing a distinguished part in the battles of Fairfield and Gettysburg. In April, 1864, he was promoted to the command of the 1st Cavalry Division of the Army of the Potomac, and in the following month the command of all the cavalry in that army was transferred to him. This force numbered about 3,000, the main body being with Sheridan on the Richmond road. As a cavalry officer he took part in the following battles: Milford Station, May 21st; North Anna, 24th; Hanovertown, 27th; Hawes's Shop, 28th; Old Church, 30th; Cold Harbor, 31st and June 1st; Trevillian Station, 11th; Malloway's Ford Cross Road, 12th; White House and Tanstall's Station, 21st, and Darbytown, 28th. After this rapid series of engagements, his force was comparatively inactive for a month, and on the 30th of July was ordered to proceed, via City Point and Washington, to Harper's Ferry and there effect a juncture with Sheridan. On reporting to Sheridan, that officer made him Chief of Cavalry of the Middle Military Division, a staff appointment, his immediate command consisting of the 1st and 31 Cavalry Divisions of the Army of the Potomac—commanded, respectively, by Generals Merrit and Wilson—and the 2d Cavalry Division of the Army of the Shenandoah, commanded by General Averill At Winchester, Torbert was in command until Sheridan's arrival, and he was also in command at the battles of Kearneysville, August 25th; Opequan, September 19th; Mount Crawford, October 2d; Toms River, October 9th; took part with his division in the general engagement of Cedar Creek, October 19th, and was present at the fight near Middletown, November 12th.

He commanded at the battles of Liberty Hills, December 22d, and Gordonsville, December 23d. In April, 1865, his many gallant services were recognized by his appointment to the command of the Army of the Shenandoah, a position for which he had been rendered eligible the previous September by promotion to the rank of Brevet Major-General. He was in command of this army until July, when it was disbanded, and he was then ordered to the command of the military district of Southeastern Virginia, with head-quarters at Norfolk. In December, 1865, he was mustered out of the volunteer service, falling back to his rank in the regular army, with the added brevet rank of Major-General. After his brilliant career in active service, General Torbert had small liking for military life in times of peace, and he therefore, November 1st, 1866, resigned his commission. His record is one of the brightest upon the New Jersey page of the history of the war, and it is all the brighter because by birth and association he had every temptation to array himself upon the side of treason. His loyalty was, indeed, more than once assailed, but he permitted his actions to confute the words of his opponents, and regardless of evil tongues and envious hearts did his duty as became a true soldier and a gallant gentleman. When the New Jersey contingent was called out, as mustering officer he rapidly worked the raw material into manageable shape, and having placed the troops in the field, he commanded his regiment, brigade, division and army with constant courage, almost constant success and always constant honor. On the conclusion of the war he retired to private life for a while. He is now (January, 1877) and for some time has been United States Consul-General to France.

————◆◆◆————

ARTRANFT, REV. CHESTER D., A. B., A. M., Clergyman, was born in Frederick township, Montgomery county, Pennsylvania, October 15th, 1839, his father, Samuel Hartranft, being an extensive flour merchant of Philadelphia, and a member of the family to which General J. F. Hartranft, Governor of Pennsylvania, belongs. His mother was Sarah, daughter of Adam Stetler. The Stetlers were among the earliest settlers of Frederick township, and the family is one of considerable antiquity, its founder in America, Christian Stetler, having immigrated to this country in 1720. Educated in early youth at the Philadelphia public schools, he graduated with credit from the High School in 1856, and in 1857 entered the University of Pennsylvania, and there for a year applied himself to the higher branches of study. His education was completed at a select school in Pottstown, Pennsylvania, whence he graduated in 1861. Naturally of a serious temperament, he had determined upon the ministry as his profession, and in pursuance of this determination he entered, immediately upon the completion of his secular studies, the Theological Seminary of the Reformed Dutch Church, at New Brunswick, New Jersey. Here he remained for three years, passing through the regular course and receiving his degree and license to preach in 1864. He was in the same year called to the pastoral charge of the South Bushwick Reformed Church, in the eastern district of Brooklyn, where, until October, 1866, he labored to excellent purpose. On the date last named he removed to New Brunswick, New Jersey, to assume the pastorate of the Second Reformed Dutch Church, a position which he still holds and very acceptably fills. On the 10th of July, 1864, he was married to Annie F., daughter of the Rev. Dr. Bergh, of Philadelphia.

CALLISTER, ROBERT, Major-General, was, in many respects, a representative officer in the late war. Residing at Oxford, New Jersey, he was, in 1861, engaged in a business of magnitude, and was, moreover, considerably beyond middle age.

His interest, as well as the inclinations natural to his time of life, prompted him to refrain from entering actively into the conflict following upon the shot thrown across Charleston bay by the rebel batteries into Fort Sumter; but his patriotism was stronger than his love of wealth or of ease, and immediately upon the call for troops to serve for three years or the war, when it became evident that the government was dealing not with a mere local revolt but with a general rebellion, he raised a company and reported for duty at the State capital. Upon being mustered into the service, he was appointed Lieutenant-Colonel of the 1st Regiment New Jersey Volunteers, but during the ensuing year was for the greater portion of the time the commanding officer, and as such led the regiment in the numerous battles in which it was engaged. In July, 1862, he was promoted to Colonel, and appointed to the command of the 11th Regiment New Jersey Volunteers, a position he held for more than two years, until appointed Brevet Brigadier-General "for gallant and distinguished services at Boydton Plank Road." He had, however, been acting Brigadier-General for a considerable period previous to his promotion. In October, 1862, as senior officer, he took command of the 1st Brigade of the 2d Division, 3d Corps, to which the 11th New Jersey was attached; he was temporarily in charge of the 2d Brigade of the 3d Division of the 2d Corps, commanding it in numerous engagements; and on the 24th of June, 1864, he was placed in command of the 3d Brigade, 3d Division, 2d Corps. He remained in this command until the end of the war, being raised to the brevet rank of Major-General in March, 1865, and mustered out of the service on the 6th of June of the same year. General McAllister's battle record would be a record of almost all the important engagements of the war. From the first Bull Run—through the fights of Gaines' Mill, Charles City Cross Roads, White Oak Swamp, Malvern Hill, Fredericksburg, Chancellors-

ville, Gettysburg, Jacob's Ford, Kelley's Ford, Locust Grove, Mine Run, the Wilderness, Spottsylvania, the North Anna, Coal Harbor, Petersburg, Deep Bottom, Strawberry Plains, Weldon Railroad, Reams' Station, Boydton Plank Road, Hatcher's Run—General McAllister led his men with that coolness and steadiness of purpose that marked him as one of the most reliable officers in the whole army, and in the final battles before Richmond he manifested the same admirable qualities. His quiet nerve was the prime secret of his success; his remarkable self-possession under the most trying circumstances invariably enabling him to bring out his command if not victorious at least with credit. Another cause of his efficiency as an officer was the personal attention that he gave to details. He not only issued orders, but he assured himself that his orders were carried into execution, and this habit of exactness was constantly productive of the most beneficial results; his subordinate officers were prompt in obedience and his men placed in him a firm reliance. Nor did he confine himself to raising only the standard of discipline in his commands; a thorough Christian himself, he constantly sought to inculcate morality and a love of religion among the men whom he led so intrepidly into battle, and the influence that he thus exerted was productive in the most marked manner of good results. As said at the outset, he was a representative American soldier; a private citizen who went out to battle from a high sense of duty; who fought with the utmost gallantry wherever fighting was to be done, and who carried the Christian faith of the household into the stormy atmosphere of the camp.

TRYKER, NELSON D. W. T., M. D., late of Monmouth Junction, was born September 11th, 1802. He was the son of John Stryker, Jr., and grandson of John Stryker, Sr., of revolutionary memory, who brought him up, as both his parents died when he was quite young; and before he was fully grown up both his grandparents died. Left thus to himself, he entered a printing office, where he spent some time. This business, however, was not to his taste, and he forsook it for merchandising, being for some years associated in partnership with his only brother, John, in the conduct of a store at Six Mile Run. But as he advanced in manhood he was attracted toward the medical profession; commenced the study of medicine with Dr. Ferdinand S. Schenck, of Six Mile Run; attended lectures in Rutgers Medical College, in New York, and was graduated therefrom. Forthwith beginning practice, he settled at what was then known as Long Bridge, now Monmouth Junction, and there continued actively engaged until a short period before his death, which occurred October 20th, 1875. He built up an extensive practice, and won the respect and esteem of all with whom he came in contact as a conscientious and careful practitioner, while his qualities as a man gained him a very large circle of devoted friends. A member of the Reformed Church, he was a devoted Christian. He was married three times: first, to Miss Williamson, daughter of George Williamson, of Three Mile Run; after her death, to Miss Pumyea, her cousin, and daughter of John Pumyea, of the same place; and after her death, to Miss Stout, daughter of John Stout, also of the same neighborhood. Of these marriages only one child, a son, named after his father, born of the third wife, survives.

ECKMAN, CHARLES A., Brevet Major-General, was born at Easton, Pennsylvania, December 3d, 1822. When war was declared against Mexico he entered the army as First Lieutenant of Company H, 1st Voltigeurs, and was engaged in several of the most important battles fought during that conflict—National Bridge, Contreras, Cherubusco, Molino del Rey and Chapultepec—and was present at the capture of the City of Mexico. When mustered out of the service at the end of the war, he entered the employment of the Central Railroad Company of New Jersey as conductor, and remained in this position until the breaking out of the rebellion. Under the call for troops for three months' service, he raised a company in Easton; was commissioned Captain, and was assigned with his command to the 1st Pennsylvania Regiment. Under the call for troops to serve for three years or the war, he again volunteered, but this time at Philipsburg, New Jersey. Governor Olden, appreciating his military qualities, appointed him Major of the 9th Regiment New Jersey Volunteers, and his subsequent conduct in the field amply justified such selection. His conspicuous gallantry in action gained him rapid promotion, and in but little more than a year he was raised to the rank of Brigadier-General. His bravery amounted almost to rashness; but he held that an officer's duty is not to follow but to lead, and that he was not justified in ordering his men into danger that he himself was not willing to be exposed to. Notwithstanding his constant defiance of death, he was never wounded, his only mischance being his capture and imprisonment in 1864. His detention at Richmond was not of long duration, and upon his return in May he was placed in command of the 2d Division, 18th Corps, and was engaged at the capture of Fort Harrison, one of the fiercest fights of the war. Having with his own division captured two regiments and four pieces of artillery, he was suddenly, General Ord, his senior officer, having been wounded, placed in command of the entire attacking column, and his able management of the forces at his disposal won for him the warm commendation of General Grant. On the consolidation of the 10th and 18th Corps, he was placed in command of the 1st Division of the 25th (colored) Corps, and very soon after, General Weitzel being temporarily relieved, became commander of the entire corps.

Perhaps General Heckman's greatest military achievement was the moulding of this corps, greatly disorganized when it reverted to him, into effective form. When General Weitzel returned he appointed General Heckman Chief of Staff, a position held by the latter until the 25th of May, when, the war being virtually at an end, he resigned his commission. In acknowledgment of his gallant conduct and efficient services, he received, after his retirement to private life, the brevet of Major-General, dating from the capture of Fort Harrison.

AGE, THOMAS, M. D., late of Tuckerton, was born at Cross Roads, Burlington county, New Jersey, June 8th, 1798. He received a liberal education, and inclining toward the medical profession entered upon his studies under the direction of Dr. Joseph Parrish, of Philadelphia. In due course, he matriculated at the University of Pennsylvania, medical department, from which he was graduated in the spring of 1821. Soon after graduating he became associated in partnership with his father, and together they labored in the performance of the duties appertaining to a large practice extending over a wide and populous district of country, and taxing their powers of endurance to the utmost. This connection existed for about twelve years, when the failing health of the son necessitated its dissolution. He then removed to Tuckerton, in the same county, and engaged in mercantile pursuits in connection with the limited practice of his profession. The latter he continued for several years, but finally confined himself to a consulting practice. A few years before the outbreak of the rebellion he had successfully engaged in the milling and lumber business in Virginia. When the war began he encountered many vicissitudes and dangers, but finally succeeded in disposing of his movable property at an immense sacrifice, and entirely abandoning his real estate, he started for his home in New Jersey, thus losing the results of years of toil. On his way he was unexpectedly detained several weeks at Norfolk, as parole prisoner, during which time his family heard nothing from him; at last, through the influence of some Southern gentlemen, who had formed for him a warm friendship by reason of his upright business habits and gentlemanly, genial manners, he was granted a permit to pass the lines, and reached home safely. He afterward engaged in the drug business at Tuckerton, and continued it until his death, which occurred February 18th, 1876. He was a successful physician, and very progressive in his tendencies, adopting in his treatment many years ago methods that only very recently have become general. As a business man he always bore a character for the highest integrity, and proved a safe counsellor and adviser to his neighbors. His ability and personal qualities won the entire confidence of the community, by which he was chosen to represent its interests in the State Legislature for one term.

Giles. Pat & Boston

Wm Dolton

... ...eting the affairs of the estab- ... ...oss until he attained his majority. ... he first wholesale grocery house in ... ...ng in which he began operations was ... ...for him, and adjoined his present location, ... treet. It had a frontage of thirty-three feet, ...ed to a depth of one hundred and five feet, being ...e the finest edifice of its kind in the city. Here, ...standing his situation betwixt the two largest cities ... country, and the consequent rivalry into which he ...ought with the great wholesale grocery houses of both ...dly built up a profitable and far-extending trade; his ...pplication to business, supplemented by untiring ...a thorough business tact, enabling him to succeed ...ere that, undertaken by a man of less resources ... by one having a less comprehensive grasp of ... theories, would assuredly have failed. With each ... year his business rapidly increased, and during the ...cade his annual sales have averaged more than a ... of dollars. In 1865 he admitted into his partner, ...brother-in-law, Jonathan H. Blackwell, and since ...e the style of the firm has been William Dolton & ...uding it necessary in 1872 to increase his facilities ...ness, he erected a new building that is, without ex- ...the finest ever put up in Trenton for business pur- ...and it stands to-day as a monument to its founder, ... in all probability done more to advance the com- ...and other interests of the city than has any one ...dividual. The building is thirty-nine feet front by ...drawn and thirty deep, and has four floors, besides an ...basement. The portion used by the firm is valued ...housand dollars, and is in every respect admirably ...to the numerous requirements of the several branches ...business carried on within its walls, a business that ... from the coal regions to the Atlantic ocean. The ...joining the wholesale department, and containing ...office, Adams' express office and several mercantile ...ments, is valued at one hundred and fifty thousand Always alive to the advancement of the interest of ...nunity for which he has already done so much, he ...e a wise provision in the erection of his block by ... the upper floors in suites for dwellings, thus en- ...amilies of refined tastes to enjoy comfortable ...ith all modern conveniences, at a small rental.

... ...gaining for himself greater independence and increased despatch ...and shipment of freights; and although his ... .strongly opposed, he, with others, persisted in the public until at last a substantial victory ... completion of the Bound Brook line. To h... honor of being one of the original incorpor... that of being one of the first to advise the built... In 1864 he advocated the increase of bankir... the city, and to that end was one of the found... No... ... ...etton, an institution in w... ... ... years. This bank has ... a million, and has the entire confidence of the munity. In various ways beside this banking ...dgment and business insight have been ... ...eteen ... commercial and monetary pr... ... ... and still is President of the ... ...mpany, of Trenton, an organiza ... ...hundred and twenty thousand... Directors ... ...Merchants' Transportation Com ...ciation ... ...a line of steam-propellers ... York, Trenton and Philadelphia; and to ... ...mainly due the organization of the Trenton ... ...of which body he is President. His remarka... ...merchant and financier must be attribute... ...derstanding of commercial affairs; to his ... ...out details as well as determining general pr ...above all, to his life-long habits of industry, ...qualities, he has been enabled to carry his ... through the several financial panics that hav the country since his business ...er began; to them that he is now, in the ...of his life, ...tive successful American ... ... He was n... 19th, 1860, to Elizabeth ... ...well, of Ho... Jersey.

HON. ... SAMUEL CARY, M. ...

...was born at Bucking ... Pennsylvania, in the year 17... ...son of Joseph and Mary Thornton ... ...dents of that place. After a ... ... he became a pupil in the ... ...where he studied assiduously and ... Medicine presenting itself ... ...

He was twice married, and left two sons by his first and two daughters by his second marriage.

OLTON, WILLIAM, Wholesale Grocer, was born in Trenton, New Jersey, April 6th, 1831, his parents being Edward and Mary (McVey) Dolton. Educated at one of the leading select schools of his native town, he began his business career, at the age of sixteen years, in a general store owned by his father, conducting the affairs of the establishment with marked success until he attained his majority. In 1858 he established the first wholesale grocery house in Trenton. The building in which he began operations was specially erected for him, and adjoined his present location, upon Warren street. It had a frontage of thirty-three feet, and extended to a depth of one hundred and five feet, being at that time the finest edifice of its kind in the city. Here, notwithstanding his situation betwixt the two largest cities of the country, and the consequent rivalry into which he was brought with the great wholesale grocery houses of both, he rapidly built up a profitable and far-extending trade; his close application to business, supplemented by untiring energy and thorough business tact, enabling him to succeed in a venture that, undertaken by a man of less resolute purpose, or by one having a less comprehensive grasp of commercial theories, would assuredly have failed. With each passing year his business rapidly increased, and during the past decade his annual sales have averaged more than a million of dollars. In 1865 he admitted into his partnership his brother-in-law, Jonathan H. Blackwell, and since that date the style of the firm has been William Dolton & Co. Finding it necessary in 1872 to increase his facilities for business, he erected a new building that is, without exception, the finest ever put up in Trenton for business purposes, and it stands to-day as a monument to its founder, who has in all probability done more to advance the commercial and other interests of the city than has any one other individual. The building is thirty-nine feet front by one hundred and thirty deep, and has four floors, besides an attic and basement. The portion used by the firm is valued at fifty thousand dollars, and is in every respect admirably adapted to the numerous requirements of the several branches of the business carried on within its walls, a business that extends from the coal regions to the Atlantic ocean. The block adjoining the wholesale department, and containing the post-office, Adams' express office and several mercantile establishments, is valued at one hundred and fifty thousand dollars. Always alive to the advancement of the interest of the community for which he has already done so much, he has made a wise provision in the erection of his block by arranging the upper floors in suites for dwellings, thus enabling families of refined tastes to enjoy comfortable homes, with all modern conveniences, at a small rental.

Precisely this need has long been felt in Trenton, and in satisfying it he has not only advanced his own interests but has greatly ministered to the welfare of his fellow-townsmen. He is the undoubted and acknowledged leader of commercial affairs in Trenton, and during his business career, extending over a period of more than twenty-five years, he has embraced every opportunity to promote the prosperity of the city. Appreciating the advantages to be gained by increased railroad facilities, he was among the first to counsel the building of a new line between Philadelphia and New York by way of Trenton, thus gaining for residents of Trenton greater independence and increased despatch in the receipt and shipment of freights; and although his proposition was strongly opposed, he, with others, persisted in forcing it upon the public until at last a substantial victory was won in the completion of the Bound Brook line. To him belongs the honor of being one of the original incorporators, as well as that of being one of the first to advise the building of the road. In 1864 he advocated the increase of banking facilities for the city, and to this end was one of the founders of the First National Bank of Trenton, an institution in which he served as Director for several years. This bank has a capital of half a million, and has the entire confidence of the business community. In various ways beside this banking enterprise his judgment and business insight have been utilized in the furtherance of commercial and monetary projects. In 1872 he was elected and still is President of the Standard Fire Insurance Company, of Trenton, an organization having a capital of three hundred and twenty thousand dollars; he is a Director of the Merchants' Transportation Company, an association running a line of steam-propellers between New York, Trenton and Philadelphia; and to his energy was mainly due the organization of the Trenton Board of Trade, of which body he is President. His remarkable success as a merchant and financier must be attributed to his clear understanding of commercial affairs; to his power of working out details as well as determining general principles, and, above all, to his life-long habits of industry; having these qualities, he has been enabled to carry his business safely through the several financial panics that have swept over the country since his business career began; and it is due to them that he is now, in the prime of his life, a representative successful American merchant. He was married, June 19th, 1860, to Elizabeth W. Blackwell, of Hopewell, New Jersey.

HORNTON, SAMUEL CARY, M. D., late of Moorestown, was born at Buckingham, Bucks county, Pennsylvania, in the year 1791, being the son of Joseph and Mary Thornton, respected residents of that place. After a preliminary training he became a pupil in the Doylestown Academy, where he studied assiduously and took a good position. Medicine presenting itself to his mind as the profession most consonant with his tastes and sympathies, he began to read the text-books under the direction of Dr. Wilson, of Buckingham. He entered the medical department of the University of Pennsylvania, and at the conclusion of a full course was graduated from that time-honored institution in the spring of 1816. Directly after graduation he settled in Moorestown, Burlington county, New Jersey, and opened an office for the practice of his profession. In this place he remained until his death, a period of forty-two years, engaged uninterruptedly in professional duties. By his skill and attention as a physician, and his estimable qualities as a man and a citizen, he endeared himself to a very wide circle. His death occurred March 19th, 1858.

ILTS, ISAIAH N., Lawyer, of Somerville, was born at Schooley's Mountain, Morris county, New Jersey, August 3d, 1824, and is the son of Daniel Dilts, a highly respected farmer of that neighborhood. After attending the public schools of his native place, where he manifested an aptness for acquiring knowledge, he fitted for college at Morristown, and then entered the sophomore class in Lafayette College, Easton, Pennsylvania, in 1841. From this institution he was graduated in 1844, taking the highest honors of his class. Shortly after graduation, having chosen the profession of the law for his life career, he began reading therefor with the late Senator Jacob W. Miller and ex-Chief Justice Whelpley, then law partners at Morristown. With these eminent lawyers he continued a student until his admission to the bar in 1847. During the same year he commenced the practice of law in Morristown. Three years later, in 1850, he received his counsellor's license, and having pursued his profession in the town for six years, he, in 1853, removed to Somerville, where he has since resided. He holds several professional appointments, being Supreme Court Commissioner, United States Commissioner, and Special Master in Chancery. His practice is a general one, and takes him into all the State and Federal courts. A lawyer of sound and extensive learning, he is held in high estimation by his professional brethren and much consulted by them. He is also a gentleman of fine literary taste and culture, not only retaining but cultivating the knowledge of the classical and foreign languages acquired in college days, and keeping thoroughly abreast of the literature and thought of the age. Of a quiet, scholarly disposition and bearing, the first impression conveyed to a stranger by his appearance would be that he was a college professor. His literary writings have been numerous, consisting largely of contributions to various periodicals and magazines. He is also an eloquent and impressive speaker. Previous to the organization of the Liberal party he affiliated with the Republicans, but when that event occurred, and Horace Greeley was nominated as its standard bearer in the Presi-

dential campaign of 1872, he entered warmly into the movement, as did so many of the truest and most consistent Republicans, who regarded that candidate as the ideal of political integrity and worth. To the canvass he lent his best energies, and while success did not crown the movement, he, with his associates, feels proud of the course he then pursued. He was a delegate to the Republican National Convention at Cincinnati in 1876, and supported Hayes and Wheeler for President and Vice-President. Although he is deeply interested in political affairs, enters into a campaign with great earnestness, and by his eloquent and effective speaking wields a powerful influence, he has invariably declined office or nomination for office. He was married, April 23d, 1856, to Ellen, youngest daughter of the late Judge Vandeveer, and sister of Mrs. W. L. Dayton. She died in 1875.

ERRENCE, HERREN A., M. D., of New Hampton Junction, was born in Cork, Ireland, August 28th, 1848. He is descended from a brother of Brian Boru, the most celebrated of the native Irish kings. Several of his ancestors were officers in the revolutionary wars of Ireland, always on the side of Irish liberty. Both his great-grandfathers were executed for having taken up arms against the British in 1798. A great-uncle of his, a clergyman, studied at the famous University of Louvain, where, on the occasion of a visit by the Lord-Lieutenant of Ireland, he so won the regard of that functionary by the fluency with which he conversed in the different languages that his excellency, on taking leave, not only complimented the youth in warm terms, but promised him his services, if needed, in the future. A sad occasion for them arose not many years after, when the father of the gifted young man, then in orders, was condemned to death for disloyalty to the British crown. Repairing to the Lord-Lieutenant, who, to do him justice, proved as good as his word, the son flew with a reprieve to the castle in which his father was confined, but, alas, too late! the authorities, hearing of his success with the Lord-Lieutenant, and thirsting for blood, having had the unhappy victim led forth to execution before the coming reprieve could reach them. The father of the subject of this sketch was an Irish gentleman and landholder. His mother was a sister of the vicar-general of the diocese of Cloyne. He received a classical education, and prepared for the church, under the tutorship of D. Reardon, LL.D., in Cork. He, however, relinquished the church in favor of the medical profession, but before he finished his studies became involved in the Irish revolutionary movement of 1864 and 1865; was arrested, with a number of others, imprisoned, tried and condemned to exile for a period of five years. Choosing this country as his land of exile, he came to the city of New York, travelled extensively through the country, and finished his medical studies, so that by the expiration of his term of exile in 1873, he was able to return to Ireland, as he did, with hardly a chasm in his professional course, which he at once renewed in its higher branches at Paris, London and Dublin, graduating finally at the Royal College of Surgeons in the latter city. Receiving a license to practise in the three kingdoms, he became in 1874 clinical assistant to Sir William Wilds, in St. Mark's Hospital, Dublin, from whom he bears testimonials, as well as from Drs. Kid, Ruyland, Churchill, and the other leading medical professors in the various institutions wherein he was student or assistant. During his stay in his native land at this time, his political friends, mindful of his devotion to the Green Isle, nominated him for the office of coroner for the district including the city of Cork, one of the most important and lucrative elective offices in the county, but such was his antipathy to British rule that he declined to recognize it by holding office or standing for office under it. He was offered a surgeon's commission in the army of Don Carlos, but was prevented, by the opposition of friends, from accepting it. In 1875 he returned to the United States and established himself in his profession at New Hampton Junction, New Jersey, where he has already built up a large and remunerative practice, extending from Somerville to Easton. He has performed a number of operations that have attracted much public attention, notably one recorded in the *Catholic Citizen* of September 4th, 1875, performed on the arm of a lady of New York city, which resulted in bringing about a cure after medical skill had long been baffled. For so young a man his career has been noteworthy, and promises, if he lives, to lead up to one of great usefulness and distinction. He indeed is still but a youngster, having measured scarcely half of the sunny side of his prime.

—————◦⊶◦—————

TOKES, CHARLES, Farmer, of Rancocas, son of David and Ann Stokes, born in Willingborough, now Beverly, in the county of Burlington, New Jersey, traces his genealogy from Thomas Stokes, of London, England, who was born in 1640, married Mary Barnard, daughter of John Barnard, October 30th, 1668, and settled in Burlington county, New Jersey, soon after the making of "the concessions and agreements of the proprietors, freeholders and inhabitants of the Province of West New Jersey, in America." To this instrument he was a party. This constitution or form of government for the province was thus characterized in a letter to Richard Hartshorne, by William Penn, Gawen Lawrie, Nicholas Lucas and others, dated 25th of Sixth month, 1676: "There we lay a foundation for after ages to understand their liberty as men and Christians, that they may not be brought in bondage but by their own consent, for we put the power in the people, etc., etc." In it was established a representative form of government, trial by jury, and liberty of conscience,

all concisely but fully set forth, especially the last, which commences with the memorable declaration, that no "men nor number of men upon earth hath power or authority to rule other men's consciences in religious matters," etc. Altogether it formed "the common law or fundamental rights and privileges of West New Jersey," and it has been but little improved in this or any other country since its promutgation, though two centuries have elapsed. Thomas Stokes became the proprietor of a farm on the north side of the north branch of the Rancocas river, about three miles west of Mount Holly, and had three sons, John, Thomas and Joseph, all of whom were farmers. The two latter were heads of large families of children, by whom the name has been widely extended. John, who married Elizabeth Green, daughter of Thomas Green, and granddaughter of Arthur Green, of Bugbroke, county of Northton, England, became proprietor of a farm on the north side of the Rancocas river, less than two miles westerly of his father's location. He had but the one son, John, who married Hannah, daughter of Jervas Stockdale, and succeeded his father on his farm on the Rancocas. He left three sons, John, David and Jervas. David married Ann, the daughter of John and Elizabeth Lancaster, of Bucks county, Pennsylvania, and succeeded his father on the homestead farm on the Rancocas; he had four sons, named Israel, John L., Charles and David Stokes, but no daughters. Charles Stokes married Tacy, daughter of William and Ann Jarrett, Montgomery county, Pennsylvania, October 18th, 1816, erected buildings and commenced business on a part of the homestead farm on the Rancocas river. They had two sons, Jarrett and William, and three daughters, Hannah, Alice and Annie, married as follows: Jarrett married Martha, daughter of William and Hannah Hilyard; William married Annie, daughter of James and Rebecca McIlvaine; Hannah married Charles, son of Joseph and Martha Williams; Alice married William, son of John R. and Letitia P. Parry; and Annie married Chalkley, son of John and Ann Albertson; all forming an unbroken succession of farmers, including a space of nearly two centuries and continuing to the present time. Charles Stokes, the subject of this sketch, received his school education mostly at Friends' School at Rancocas. At a time when but few aspired to anything further than such branches as were thought necessary to qualify for the ordinary business of life, he, having a taste for study and the acquisition of knowledge, with a few others of about the same time of life, availed themselves of an opportunity which presented, and took a deep interest in advanced studies, particularly of a mathematical character. These tended to enlarge the views and stimulate in his mind a desire to obtain useful knowledge from every available source. Books of a character to gratify this desire were but few and hard to be obtained in the vicinity of his residence. No library existed nearer than Burlington, five miles, where was an ancient and good collection of books for that day. In addition to this he was proffered by Joshua Wallan, a venerable

27

citizen of Burlington, the free use of his extensive and excellent private library. He now commenced a study of history, seeking to make himself acquainted with the rise and fall of nations, and the acts of distinguished characters who had signalized themselves in the different departments of life. Love of liberty and aversion to tyranny of every description appeared to be inwrought in his nature, and he felt his mission to be to cherish and support the one and discountenance the other on every proper occasion and · by all suitable means. He endeavored to make himself acquainted with the history, constitution and laws of his State and country, to judge of the acts of such as were in power to administer them, calmly and without excitement, and in his own judgment mete justice to all. In his early life he became impressed with the conviction that Infinite Wisdom was not unmindful of man after his introduction into this life, but that by His omniscience and omnipresence was always with him as a sure and unfailing rule to rightly instruct him in all things in matters of duty, furnishing ability to perform it, providing the terms were accepted. This conviction, deeply engraven, had much influence in moulding his character and pursuits. He endeavored in all things so to conduct himself that his mind would be at ease and avoid remorse, being satisfied that this rule of life gave all the liberty necessary for its enjoyments, and would qualify for its duties. Agriculture was the pursuit chosen by him. He labored on his father's farm during the summer months, teaching a school the balance of the year. This was continued for several years, keeping him in sympathy with the manual laborer, and also brightening what he had acquired of school learning, and furnishing opportunities for extended improvement. About the twenty-fifth year of his life he married Tacy Jarrett, daughter of William and Ann Jarrett, as before stated; an acquisition of great importance to him as a faithful partner in the vicissitudes of life, wise in admonition and steady in support in times of trial. To her he thinks he owes much for whatever he may have accomplished, and what ever enjoyments he may have possessed. They commenced life on a part of the old Stokes farm, near the present village of Rancocas, she performing the duties of housewifery, he managing and laboring on the farm, and occasionally surveying land, writing and taking acknowledgments of deeds, etc., being a Master in the Court of Chancery, settling estates, and performing the duties of township offices, as Township Committee Clerk, Chosen Freeholder, etc. In the fall of 1830, without his wish or desire, he was elected a member of the House of Assembly for the county of Burlington. After taking his seat the first duty that presented to his mind was to have repealed an enactment to pay a chaplain for services at the State prison; and this was effected on the ground that the constitution as it then stood prohibited the payment of money for the support of a ministry, etc. In those days New Jersey did not have any clergyman to open the session of the Legislature with prayer. The old sentiments embodied in the "concessions and agreements" had not become entirely obliterated in the minds of the people, and legislative bodies left the important matter of approaching Infinite Mercy in supplication to the individual members. It is believed by Mr. Stokes to have been quite as well done and with more safety to our religious liberties than by the present method. In 1831 the constitution required the Legislature to be elected and meet in the fall of the year; the custom being to meet, organize, perform a few official acts, and adjourn to an early day in the ensuing year. At this adjourned session in 1831, Dr. William B. Ewing, an old and influential member from Cumberland, moved that J. Hancock (a worthy member from Morris) should open the session with prayer. Charles Stokes objected to the right of the House, by resolutions or otherwise, to direct a member to perform an act of this kind, stating that if any member should find it to be a duty to engage in the solemn act of public invocation, he would be among the last to object. Hancock arose and stated that such was his case, but he did not wish to impose upon the House without consent. Charles Stokes then withdrew his objection, whereupon Hancock knelt, and the House arose, as by common consent, without vote. The prayer was impressive and accompanied by due solemnity. When the House was about to close *sine die* and the members to separate to their several homes, Hancock made a short address suited to the occasion, and said that if there was no objection he would address the Throne of Grace in supplication. The House (without vote) manifested their approval by rising, and a fervent prayer was uttered by Hancock; immediately the Speaker pronounced an adjournment without day, and the members separated to their respective homes with much friendly feeling. At the preceding session of the Legislature two companies were incorporated : one to unite by canal the waters of the Delaware and Raritan rivers; the other to construct a railroad from Camden to Amboy, under the names of Camden & Amboy Railroad Company and Delaware & Raritan Canal Company. Stock was taken; both companies organized and commenced operations. In the session of 1830–31 the canal company asked for additional powers to enable them to build a railroad on the bank of their canal. This was vigorously opposed by the railroad company, and upon this point the House of Assembly was nearly equally divided. The result was the introduction of a bill to unite the two companies under the name of the "Delaware & Raritan Canal and Camden & Amboy Railroad and Transportation Companies." This was opposed by Charles Stokes on the ground that the location of the works and the union of two such companies would concentrate a power not to be managed or controlled by the State. The union was sanctioned by the Legislature, and at the ensuing session an act was passed prohibiting any other railroad being built to compete in business with the works of the joint companies, thus giving the exclusive right of transportation and travel between New York and Philadelphia, which for many years greatly retarded the improvement of the State. During all this time Charles Stokes, always a friend of the companies, but steadily and unyieldingly opposed to their monopoly privileges, with a few others, by availing themselves of every suitable opportunity, at length had the great gratification of seeing the State enfranchised and freed from the incubus which had paralyzed every effort in the way of railroad improvement. The State school law underwent a revision during this session calculated to remove all sectarianism in schools, and to preserve to parents control over the education of their children. In this subject Charles Stokes took a deep interest at the time, and has so continued, now for more than half a century, on all proper occasions protesting against the tendencies of the age as apprehended by him—the assumption of powers by the State in controlling the education of the children—as calculated to subvert our dear-bought liberties, both civil and religious. At the close of the session he retired to an active private life, positively refusing to be again a candidate, until the public became much divided in regard to the policy of Andrew Jackson, President, concerning the Bank of the United States. His refusal to allow the bank further to receive the revenues of the government on deposit created much excitement and dissatisfaction with a large portion of the community; so much so that but comparatively few would speak in advocacy of his measures. That there might be no doubt as to his opinion, Charles Stokes permitted his name to be used as a candidate for Council in the State Legislature in connection with others who approved of the policy of the President. They were defeated then, as was expected, but the public sentiment subsequently became so much changed upon the subject, that in the fall of 1836 he was returned a member of the Legislative Council. Having discharged this trust in such a way as to meet his own approval, he declined a further candidacy and again resumed his former avocations. On February 23d, 1844, the Legislature of New Jersey passed an act providing for an election of delegates to meet in convention to frame a constitution for the government of the State. Charles Stokes was elected a member of this body, and on May 14th of the same year took his seat at the organization of the convention, which was composed of men distinguished for talent and high moral worth, selected with the intention that party preferences should be balanced. Early in the session Richard S. Field offered a resolution "that the sittings of the convention be opened every morning with prayer, and that the clergymen of the city of Trenton and its vicinity be invited to officiate on such occasions." Charles Stokes said that he appreciated the importance of the service for which they were assembled, and the necessity for Divine assistance to enable them to wisely perform their duties. They were in their seats representing different sections of the State, the whole people, and the interests of all. Different views, no doubt, were entertained with regard to the proper mode of offering prayer; and each one

was entitled to his opinion; and no man, nor number of men, had a right to impose religious services upon another, contrary to what he believed to be right. The provisions of the 18th and 19th sections of the constitution of 1776, which they had bound themselves by solemn asseveration to maintain, guaranteed this protection, and up to this day had been sacredly observed. If now, on this momentous occasion, they should sanction the principle embraced in the resolution offered by the member from Mercer, they would open a door for practices, for legislation, leading to a subversion of liberty of conscience, to a union of church and state; Legislatures would have imposed upon them prayers, perhaps gratuitously in the beginning, but soon compensated by enforced taxation. He believed the mind should always be in the attitude of prayer, that men should "pray without ceasing," that they should do their own praying, and not by proxy. R. S. Field replied that a constitutional convention was a rare occasion, might not again occur for a century, and its gravity would not only justify, but demanded an extra solemnity to mark its proceedings; that it could not be quoted as precedent by the Legislature, not only because the character of the bodies were unlike, but the constitution would prohibit it. The resolution passed; the clergy were introduced and officiated. The first ensuing Legislature followed the example of the convention, and this practice has been continued without exception; first with a present of stationery, but of late with pecuniary compensation added. Thus a usage has been established which Mr. Stokes believes forebodes no good to the religious liberties of the people. There were various other subjects which engaged the attention of the convention, in which Charles Stokes took a deep interest, among which several may be mentioned. In the bill of rights and privileges is a provision that the rights of conscience to worship shall be inviolably maintained. The paragraph upon this important subject was prepared by him, and unanimously adopted by the convention. The funds of the State set apart for the maintenance of public or free schools, at his suggestion, were so guarded that they should be "for the equal benefit of all the people of the State." This provision was intended and understood at the time by the convention that the Legislature should not have power to prescribe any terms, sectarian or otherwise, that would deprive any portion of the people of the State of their part of the school funds, nor take from parents and guardians of children the great right to educate their children in their own way, at the expense of their share of the funds. This protection was held sacred for a time, but at length was disregarded by the Legislature and a system introduced which, in the opinion of Mr. Stokes, establishes principles subversive of justice and equity and religious liberty. The use of oaths was objected to by him as unnecessary and without effect in insuring performing services or in speaking truth, demoralizing in tendency, by frequent appeals to the great Creator as necessary to be honest, to speak the truth, or be believed. He held that such as had not principle to do right without the formality of an oath, would not hesitate at perjury, provided there was no penalty. Let the penalty for false testimony remain, and oaths be abolished, said he, and the cause of morality would be promoted and the public better served. With this sentiment many of the most eminent of the convention united, and were it not that the constitution of the United States required the States to conform to the practice, the probability was strong that the provision would not have been retained in the constitution of the State. Under the military laws of the State fines were imposed upon such as did not train in the militia, however scrupulous or religiously conscientious they might be, and if the pecuniary fine could not be recovered, the penalty was imprisonment in the county jail. Charles Stokes requested Judge I. Hornblower to offer an amendment in the proper place to abolish the imprisonment; which he willingly agreed to do, with the addition of "in time of peace." With this addition the amendment was adopted, and forms a part of the constitution, affording great relief to a worthy portion of the community. He advocated equality in taxation; that the burthens borne by the agricultural community should be shared by trades and professions. This proposition, just and proper in his eyes, was of a nature not to be readily adopted by the convention, and, of course, failed. The convention, having been in session about forty days, were ready to close their labors and submit the constitution which they had framed to the people of the State for their approval or rejection. Alexander Wurts, their president, congratulated them upon the happy result of their labors, and the uniform spirit of harmony which marked their deliberations, stating that the members had faithfully discharged their duty by conforming to the honorable and patriotic example set them by their constituents. In the spirit of harmony and kind feeling thus indicated and manifested, it was but natural and to be desired that entire unity should characterize the final vote of approval. Charles Stokes sympathized with this feeling, and so expressed himself to the convention, and desired to do nothing to interrupt it. He had considered the matter well. He thought they had prepared a good constitution; perhaps as well suited to the condition of the people of the State as they could offer; but there were principles involved to which he could not give his assent. The military powers conferred, he was fully aware, could not be dispensed with by the body of the people with the views actuating them, and he was not about to censure them; they had an equal right to their opinions that he claimed for himself. He believed, however, in the existence of a principle which, if permitted to govern our actions, would end contention, strife and wars. Believing in the potency of such a principle, and in the duty to maintain it in action, he could not consistently impose upon others a duty he could not discharge himself. He was impelled, therefore, to kindly ask the convention to release him from participating in the final vote of approval. He asked this not only on the ground

stated, but because he did not wish to mar the remarkable harmony which had prevailed in their deliberations by a negative vote. The request was kindly received, a full sentiment expressed that consistency demanded it should be made, and by unanimous vote it was granted, and he was requested to put his reasons in shape, that such might be placed on the record. This he gave in the following terms: "On account of the military features contained in the constitution." Thus ended his labors here, and he returned to his home in peace, and so far as he knows with the kind feelings and friendship of his fellow-members. Here again he engaged in the duties of an active business life, in all things endeavoring to be governed by that influence which hitherto he had found to be a safe conductor. His leisure time was much occupied in reading, with the view to gain instruction in all matters appertaining to the welfare of man. In his opinion the existence of an Infinite Creator is manifest by His works, and His attributes by the gracious impressions and teachings made upon the mind. He does not seek to imagine form, nor to determine locality, but to be satisfied with the Scripture doctrine, that such things as are revealed belong to us; but such as are secret and not revealed belong to the great Fountain of Knowledge. And so to conform his life and actions as to be in harmony with this power, this intelligence that permeates all things, constitutes the leading purpose of his life. With him it removes the bane of sectarianism, and enables him to recognize fellowship with all whose hearts are in harmony with the Divine Nature, and qualified for the discharge of duties, not only of religious but of civil life. He endeavors to keep himself informed of the proceedings of his State and of the general government, and has occasionally written articles upon public subjects, some of which have been printed over his own proper signature. Prompt to form opinions upon measures touching the public welfare, he has been careful in his manner of expressing them. Solicitous to discharge his duties rightly in social and business life, and without anything especial to mark the last thirty or more years, he may be said to have acted the part of a good citizen. He is remarkably preserved in health and vigor, both of body and mind, although now of the advanced age of eighty-six years. On Saturday, October 21st, 1876, there were assembled at his residence a large number of relatives and friends to celebrate the sixtieth anniversary of his marriage with his wife, Tacy. The reading of the certificate of marriage drawn up according to the usage of the Society of Friends, dated 18th day of Tenth month, 1816, signed by the parties themselves and by sixty-three witnesses, was followed by that of a memorial prepared by the children, and by their desire to be appended to the certificate, bearing the names of their parents, their children, children-in-law, grand and great-grandchildren, to the number of fifty-two, and of their friends who were present to the number of twenty-four. Charles Stokes then addressed the meeting, expressing his sincere feeling of gratitude to those who had so largely con-

William Parry

RREY, HON. WILLIAM, of Cinnaminson, New
Jersey, Civil Engineer, Surveyor,
Master in the Court of Chancery, and
the Court of Common Pleas, for
county, was born, October 9th,
Mootestown, in that county, and is a son of
R, Parry and Laetitia P., his wife, both of whom were
ives of Pennsylvania, but removed to New Jersey in 1816,
and settled on the farm where their son now resides. John
R. Parry was born, October 30th, 1783, married Laetitia P.
Smith, daughter of Thomas Smith, had five children and
died February 8th, 1845. John R. Parry was son of John
Parry, 2d, who was born December 13th, 1754, married
Elizabeth Roberts, and had two sons; John Parry, 2d, was
son of John Parry, 1st, who was born July 28th, 1721, married Margaret Tyson, and had seven children ; John Parry,
1st, was son of Thomas Parry, gentleman, who was born
about the year A. D. 1680, in Caernarvonshire, North Wales
— where the family had been seated for many generations—
came to America near the close of the seventeenth century,
married in 1715 Jane Morris, by whom he had ten children,
and was the founder of the Parry family in Pennsylvania.
He settled in what is now Montgomery county, Pennsylvania, and had ten children, all born between 1716 and 1739.
To this family Lieutenant-Colonel Caleb Parry, of Colonel
Atlee's Continental Regiment, belonged ; he lost his life at
the battle of Long Island in 1776. Major Edward Randolph Parry, of the United States army, who was commissioned in 1861, resigned in 1871, and died in 1874 of injuries incurred during the late civil war, was also of this
family, a more full history of which is to be found in "The
History of Bucks County, Pennsylvania," published by
W. W. H. Davis. William Parry's preliminary
... obtained at the Friends' school in the neigh-

tributed to the joyousness of the occasion. Judge Naar, of Trenton, being present, made some brief remarks, adverting to the beneficial moral effects upon the young people present of such an occasion. Following the example of their honored progenitor they might look for useful and honored lives, without stain or reproach, as his had been, and might hope at the age of eighty-six years, to which he had arrived, to be surrounded by descendants as worthy and respectable as those who then surrounded him. Judge Naar was followed by Mary S. Lippincott, of Moorestown, New Jersey, who, in a happy and graceful manner, alluded to her life-long connection with Charles and his wife, and her affectionate regards for them and their descendants. It is hardly possible to imagine a more interesting occasion; the love and affection between the relatives, the simplicity of manners of all, from the youngest to the oldest, the absence of ostentation and display—all gave a charm to it which will long be remembered.

ARRY, HON. WILLIAM, of Cinnaminson, New Jersey, Civil Engineer, Surveyor, Conveyancer, Master in the Court of Chancery, and Judge of the Court of Common Pleas for Burlington county, was born, October 9th, 1817, near Moorestown, in that county, and is a son of John R. Parry and Laetitia P., his wife, both of whom were natives of Pennsylvania, but removed to New Jersey in 1816, and settled on the farm where their son now resides. John R. Parry was born, October 30th, 1783, married Laetitia P. Smith, daughter of Thomas Smith, and had five children and died February 8th, 1845. John R. Parry was son of John Parry, 2d, who was born December 13th, 1754, married Elizabeth Roberts, and had two sons; John Parry, 2d, was son of John Parry, 1st, who was born July 28th, 1721, married Margaret Tyson, and had seven children; John Parry, 1st, was son of Thomas Parry, gentleman, who was born about the year A. D. 1680, in Caernarvonshire, North Wales —where the family had been seated for many generations— came to America near the close of the seventeenth century, married in 1715 Jane Morris, by whom he had ten children, and was the founder of the Parry family in Pennsylvania. He settled in what is now Montgomery county, Pennsylvania, and had ten children, all born between 1716 and 1739. To this family Lieutenant-Colonel Caleb Parry, of Colonel Atlee's Continental Regiment, belonged; he lost his life at the battle of Long Island in 1776. Major Edward Randolph Parry, of the United States army, who was commissioned in 1861, resigned in 1871, and died in 1874 of hardships incurred during the late civil war, was also of this family, a more full history of which is to be found in "The History of Bucks County, Pennsylvania," published by General W. W. H. Davis. William Parry's preliminary education was obtained at the Friends' school in the neighborhood; and he subsequently attended the academy of

Benjamin Hallowell, also a Friend, at Alexandria, Virginia, where he remained until 1837. In the following year he commenced the nursery business on the homestead farm, which he has ever since continued to cultivate and which is generally known throughout the country by the name of Pomona Nursery, and is the most extensive establishment of its kind in the State, comprising over three hundred acres in cultivation, about one hundred of which are usually devoted to growing small fruits. His residence stands among the stately old trees which he planted in his younger days; and many of more recent introduction have since been added. An avenue of near half a mile in length, bordered at a distance of several rods on each side with broad belts planted with a general collection of hardy ornamental trees and evergreens. The various nursery fields are separated merely by driveways or trees, and the proprietor is dispensing with fences, where not needed to enclose his own stock, finding this plan more convenient, as well as more economical and pleasing to the eye. Every new fruit which comes before the public is thoroughly tested on these grounds, and in sufficient quantities to give a thorough trial of its merits, previous to being disseminated. Many fruit farms in the United States have been supplied with trees and plants sent from here, and the annual yield of their rich products is a continual reminder to their owners of Pomona Nursery, from whence the stock was obtained. From 1850 to 1870 he was a practical civil engineer, surveyor and conveyancer; and during that period he located and superintended the construction or improvement of over thirty different turnpike roads, and whilst engaged in surveying several large tracts of land in the interior of the State, one of which contained 40,000 and another 50,000 acres, which without convenient means of reaching market was of but little value, he became fully impressed with the importance of railroads in this State, which contained two million acres of unimproved land; and by writing and speaking in their favor and against the policy of maintaining the exclusive privileges of the joint companies, which prohibited the construction and use of any railroad in this State without their consent, or to compete with them in business, he contributed largely to effect a change in public sentiment. He was elected a member of the Legislature in 1854, and re-elected the two following years; and during the time he was in that body, served on many important committees and was Speaker of the House of Assembly during the session of 1855. He took an active part in the railroad war against the monopoly and in favor of granting railroads wherever needed to develop the resources of the State and bring thousands of acres of land, naturally fertile though uncultivated, within reach of markets. The whole subject of exclusive or monopoly privileges in railroading was so thoroughly agitated and discussed, that a law was passed fixing the time when the exclusive or monopoly privileges of the joint companies should cease, determine and end. " That after the first day of January, 1869, it should be lawful without the consent of the Delaware & Raritan Canal and Camden & Amboy Railroad and Transportation Companies (called the joint companies) to construct any railroad or railroads in this State, or to compete in business with the railroads of said joint companies." From that time all legal restraints against building railroads in New Jersey have been removed, and in 1873 a general railroad law was passed, and the people left at liberty and encouraged to build railroads wherever the public good required. Being a member of the Whig party whilst in existence, he was chosen President of the first Republican Convention which assembled in the State. It was held in Newark, April, 1856, to organize the Republican party, at which convention resolutions were passed taking strong grounds against the repeal of the Missouri Compromise, and to resist the aggressive spirit of slavery, and to accept the issue thus forced upon the free States, regarding the momentous issues at the then approaching election to be whether slavery or freedom should be national, and in favor of admitting Kansas as a free State. He is identified with the interests of the county and State, and is foremost in all matters that pertain to the welfare of the public. He contributed more largely than any other person towards erecting and maintaining the public free school in the district, where more than one hundred scholars are regularly taught free of charge. He now holds many honorable positions in the State. He was the International Judge from New Jersey in the department of pomology, at the late Centennial Exposition, held in Philadelphia. He is a member of the New Jersey State Board of Agriculture; is one of the Managers of the New Jersey State Geological Survey; is President of the West Jersey Surveyors' Association; is President of the State Board of Visitors to Rutgers Scientific College for the benefit of Agriculture and Mechanic Arts; is President of the Westfield and Camden Turnpike Company; is President of Rake Pond Cranberry Company; is Vice-President of the American Pomological Society; is a member of the Horticultural Societies of both New Jersey and Pennsylvania, and an honorary member of the Pennsylvania Historical Society; and at the present time is Judge of the Court of Common Pleas and Master in the Court of Chancery. He is highly respected and esteemed by the community where he resides, and in fact by all those who have the pleasure of his acquaintance. March 23d, 1843, he married Alice, daughter of Charles Stokes. She has been a constant and faithful helpmate through all the vicissitudes of life; wise in counsel, mild and exemplary in deportment, performing household duties in a Christian spirit; ever mindful of their dependence on Infinite Wisdom, whom she believed would at all times rightly direct those who obey Divine admonitions. To her he thinks he is mainly indebted for whatever good he has accomplished or happiness attained. They had seven children, as follows, viz.: Charles, married Anna Sill; Hannah, died at the age of fourteen years; John R., William, Oliver, Howard, and Tacie Parry.

ERVIS, HOWARD, M. D., of Junction, was born, October 6th, 1829, near Ringoes, New Jersey. His father was Garret Servis, a prominent citizen of Hunterdon county, who was for three years sheriff, was twice elected to the New Jersey Legislature, and was for several years postmaster at Clinton. His mother was Susan Stout, a granddaughter of John Hart, one of the signers of the Declaration of Independence. Dr. Servis was educated solely by his father. In 1856 he entered the medical department of the University of Pennsylvania. Being over twenty-one years of age at the time of entering he was required to take but two terms, and in 1858 received his degree. He at once established himself at Fairmount, Hunterdon county, New Jersey, and soon built up an extensive practice. With unusual professional ardor he determined, after having been in active practice for two years, to resume his academic studies; and he accordingly in the winter of 1860 attended a special course of lectures at the University of Pennsylvania. He returned to Fairmount, but at the end of a year he removed to New Hampton, and succeeded to the practice of Dr. McLenahen, a prominent physician whom failing health compelled to give up professional labor, and at whose request Dr. Servis made the change. With such indorsement, he succeeded to the full practice of Dr. Lenahen, and has since considerably increased it, and has won the respect and esteem of the community in which he resides, both as a useful citizen and as an eminently successful physician and surgeon. He was married, June 12th, 1867, to Belinda, daughter of Philip Johnston, Esq., of Washington, New Jersey.

OBINS, HON. AMOS, late of New Brunswick, Legislator, was born in the fourth ward of the city of New York, August 30th, 1815. He was educated at a boarding-school in Connecticut, and in his later youth served as a clerk in the dry-goods house of J. & N. Robins, Pearl street, New York, the junior member of the firm being his father, the senior his uncle. In his early manhood he superintended the construction of the railroad from Vicksburg to Jackson, in Mississippi. He afterwards purchased a farm near Metuchen, Middlesex county, New Jersey, on which he lived until 1866, when he removed to New Brunswick, where he died June 27th, 1871. He married, in Metuchen, Margaret, daughter of Mr. William Ross. For sixteen years Mr. Robins occupied as a public man a large share of the admiring attention of his county and State. Under President Buchanan he filled the office of Collector of the Port of Perth Amboy. In 1856 and 1857 he represented the second district of Middlesex county in the Assembly. He represented Middlesex county in the Senate from 1862 to 1871, having been elected for three consecutive terms. He was twice elected President of the Senate—in 1864 and in

1870; and in 1868 was President *pro tem.* during the illness of the permanent President. In this latter year he was a prominent candidate in the Democratic State Convention for the nomination for the office of Governor, but, after a very close contest, was defeated by Theodore F. Randolph. Mr. Robins was equally estimable in public and in private, never in either relation betraying a friend or shunning an enemy, and, above all, never breaking his faith or his word. His character was at once strong and balanced. The elements in him were so mixed that, although each was strenuous, the whole was harmonious. A staunch and thoroughgoing Democrat, he was a tolerant partisan and a whole-souled citizen. Of intense prejudices, and, for that matter, of intense feelings in general, he was forgiving, magnanimous, and just. Stern of will, he was genial in spirit, making him alike trusted and beloved. A shrewd man of the world, he carried his heart on his sleeve, leaving the political daws, at their pleasure, to peck at it or to wonder at it, which last they generally were drawn to do. His perfect frankness and integrity, conjoined with his astuteness, was often indeed a marvel to those of his friends who had not yet penetrated, as he himself had, to the fruitful truth that a firm stand on these qualities lends inspiration to policy, and that, while the trickster needs surpassing resources of mind, and after all must fail in the long run, the address of the upright man is in the end invincible. Though it would not be well, if it were possible, to be honest because honesty is the best policy, it is well to realize that honesty is the best policy, for it does no harm to honesty and infinite good to policy; and in this point of view the public career of Amos Robins shines forth, in the apt words of one of his oldest and closest friends, as "a beacon light to all young men entering on a political course." Their attention cannot be too frequently or too carefully directed towards it.

ROBINS, WRIGHT, of Metuchen, a Retired Merchant of great public spirit, brother to the subject of the preceding sketch, was born in the city of New York, November, 1823. His father, Nathan Robins, a native of New Jersey, was a sea-captain previously to the war of 1812, when he abandoned the sea, and engaged, with his brother John, in the wholesale dry-goods trade in New York city, the firm, J. & N. Robins, at 426 Pearl street, becoming one of the most extensive in its day. His mother was Elizabeth Hassan, of Connecticut. In 1840 his father retired from active business, and took up his abode in Metuchen, New Jersey, where he built a fine homestead, and died in November, 1859. The son laid the foundations of his education in the public schools of the city of New York, completing the edifice in the collegiate school at Poughkeepsie, New York, which he entered at the age of sixteen, and from which he graduated five years later. He then returned to New York

city, and, having just passed his majority, entered as an active partner the establishment of his father and uncle, in which relation he continued for about sixteen years, the entire charge of the immense business devolving on him for the last few years of this period, which was closed by the death of his uncle, the senior member of the firm; whereupon, his father being also dead, he closed up the affairs of the house, and removed to the old homestead in Metuchen, New Jersey, where he has since resided, devoting his time and means to the development of the town, and now and then relieving the tension of his generous enterprise by the delights of foreign travel. He takes his ease with dignity, sweetening it with a life of beneficence and charity. He was married, in 1855, to Delia Dally, County Longford, Ireland.

STOKES, N. NEWLIN, M. D., was born near Moorestown, Burlington county, New Jersey. His parents, like himself, were natives of New Jersey, his mother, Nancy E. Stokes, having been born in the same county as himself. His father, Nathaniel N. Stokes, was a farmer. The ancestors of both were English Quakers, one of whom, Joseph Stokes, came to this country in William Penn's time, and settled as a farmer in the county above mentioned. The subject of this sketch was educated at the Quaker school in West-Town, Chester county, Pennsylvania. He began the study of medicine in 1851, with his uncle, Dr. John H. Stokes, of Moorestown, now deceased, a physician of excellent repute, who practised his profession at Moorestown for more than forty years. The nephew attended the regular course at the Jefferson Medical College, Philadelphia, studying during the winter months in the office of Dr. Da Costa, of that city. Receiving his diploma in March, 1854, he immediately entered upon the practice at Moorestown in partnership with his uncle, continuing in this relation until 1869, when his uncle, on account of his failing health, retired from practice, throwing the double burden on the shoulders of the nephew, which, however, proved broad enough and strong enough to carry it with ease and distinguished success. Dr. Newlin Stokes is in fact one of the most esteemed and successful physicians in the wide region of his practice. He is devoted to his profession, which, in return, has bestowed abundant favors upon him. He has been President of the Burlington County Medical Association, and has many times represented the county in the State Association. He was also a delegate to the National Medical Convention that met in Philadelphia in June, 1876. He is examining surgeon for a number of prominent life insurance companies, among which may be mentioned the Providence, John Hancock, and National. He was married in 1861 to Martha E. Stokes, of Stroudsburg, Pennsylvania.

OBBINS, HON. GEORGE R., M. D., Physician and Member of Congress, late of Hamilton Square, was born in Monmouth county, New Jersey, September 24th, 1808. After a good literary education, having decided to follow the medical profession, he studied medicine under the direction of Dr. John McKelway, then a prominent practitioner of Trenton. His preliminary studies completed, he matriculated at the Jefferson Medical College, Philadelphia, from which he was graduated at the conclusion of a full course. After graduation he opened an office in the village of Fallsington, Bucks county, Pennsylvania, where he practised for twelve months. In the spring of 1837 he removed to Hamilton Square, Mercer county, New Jersey, and there he lived engaged in active professional duties for nearly thirty-eight years. Upon the organization of the Mercer County District Medical Society in 1848, he became one of its members, and was chosen its Treasurer, a position he continued to fill with much acceptability. He always manifested a deep interest in public affairs, and in 1854 received the nomination in the Second Congressional District of New Jersey; was elected, and gave such lively satisfaction to his constituents by his labors in the House of Representatives as to secure a re-election in 1858. Professionally, he was a successful man, his skill, care, and many estimable qualities securing him a large and widely extended practice, with the confidence and affection of his patients. His death occurred February 22d, 1875, and was regretted by a large circle which had benefited by his professional and public-spirited labors.

———————

AMSEY, JOHN, Brevet Major-General, was one of the many soldiers sent out from New Jersey to the late war, who, by gallantry in the field and marked ability in handling troops, rose to the rank of a general officer. Entering the service as First Lieutenant of Company G, 2d Regiment —under the call for volunteers to serve for three months— the election of his Captain to the colonelcy of the regiment raised him to the rank of Captain, and in this capacity he served during the term of his enlistment. When the regiment was withdrawn, Captain Ramsey recruited a company for the three years term, was commissioned Captain, and was attached to the 5th Regiment. The 5th—as was the case with almost all of the New Jersey regiments—was engaged in active service during the entire war, and Captain Ramsey had ample opportunity for displaying his soldierly qualities. In May, 1862, for "distinguished gallantry at Williamsburg," he received his commission as Major, and on the 21st of the following October he was made Lieutenant-Colonel. The colonelcy of the 8th Regiment falling vacant in April, 1863, he was raised to that position; and in December, 1864, was brevetted Brigadier-

General. In April, 1865, he received the further promotion of Brevet Major-General, and two months later, the war ended, he was mustered out of the service. General Ramsey saw his first active service under McClellan on the Peninsula, taking part in the various battles of that campaign, and participating in the siege of Yorktown and in the memorable change of base. In the second Bull Run, and in the battles of Bristow, Chantilly, McLean's Ford, Fredericksburg, Chancellorsville, Gettysburg, the Wilderness and Petersburg—not to mention a dozen or more of less important engagements—he bore a distinguished part, being thrice wounded and on several occasions honorably mentioned in official reports. As a commander he united, in a remarkable degree, prudence and dashing bravery; and this combination of soldierly qualities secured him the confidence of his men and made him a rarely successful officer.

———————

ETSON, JOHNSON, Merchant and Manufacturer, of New Brunswick, New Jersey, was born in that place, December 8th, 1806. He is the son of Thomas and Ann Letson, both of whom were natives of New Jersey, the former having been born at the Raritan Landing, October 12th, 1763, the latter at Piscataway, in 1774. The father, while yet a young man, removed to New Brunswick, in which he established the leather manufacturing business, pursuing it until about 1832, when he retired to his farm at Three Mile Run, where he resided till his death, May 13th, 1851. The mother died in New Brunswick, October, 1856, at the house of her son, the subject of this sketch. Young Johnson was educated in New Brunswick, closing his education at the grammar school auxiliary to Rutgers College, in the main building of which it was then held, under the Rev. John Mabon, D. D. His education, though not polite, was solid, like the understanding it trained, and afforded, on the whole, a fair preparation for the long and active and useful life before him. When about the age of fourteen, he went to New York as clerk in a hardware store, and remained there in that capacity for some three years, after which he returned to New Brunswick, where he served in the same capacity until 1827, when he again went to New York, engaging this time in the book business, which he pursued for about two years, and then sold out, returning once more to his native city. The needle in his life's compass now began to rest; and, seeing his way clearly, he followed it henceforward steadily. In March, 1830, he started the hardware business in Burnet street, New Brunswick, and prosecuted it there till 1855, a quarter of a century, when, content with his large success, and preferring perhaps a more retired and quiet life, he disposed of all his interests in it, and has since devoted himself mainly to the discharge of his duties as an officer of various corporations, conspicuously the duties devolving on him as President of the New

Brunswick Rubber Company, an office which he has held since the organization of the company in 1850. In conjunction with several other gentlemen he organized, in 1863, the Norfolk and New Brunswick Hosiery Company, of which he was then made one of the Directors, a position he has ever since held. On the organization of the National Bank of New Jersey, he was chosen a Director, and has remained one to the present time. He was also chosen a Director of the Willow Grove Cemetery Association on its organization, and, after serving a number of years in that capacity, was elected its President, which he continues to be. There would seem to be no relief for him when he has accepted an office at the hands of a corporation. Such is the sense of his business capacity and of his general trustworthiness, that, if he serves once, he has no choice but to serve ever. Corporations never die, and they will not let him resign. Glorious servitude, in which the fetters are forged of honor, and fastened by esteem! Mr. Letson has never taken an active part in politics, although long ago he served as a member of the City Council for several years, and was always identified with the Whig party before it dissolved, as he has been with the Republican party since. He is indeed as little of a politician as is consistent with good citizenship, his catholic tastes and his broad feelings chafing against the limitations set up by political organizations. In September, 1830, he was married to Eliza L., daughter of Cornelius and Eliza W. Shaddu, of the city of New York.

AIL, BENJAMIN A., Lawyer, of Rahway, was born near Rahway, Middlesex county, New Jersey, August 15th, 1844. His father, too, Benjamin F. Vail, was a native of New Jersey, as also his mother, who was a Miss Martha C. Parker. His education was begun in West-Town, Chester county, Pennsylvania, and finished at Haverford College, in the adjoining county, from which institution he graduated in the class of 1865. Entering the law office of Parker & Keasby, Newark, he studied the requisite term, during the winter of 1867-68 the Columbia Law School in New York city, and was licensed as attorney in November, 1868, and as counsellor in 1871. He began the practice at Rahway, where he has since pursued it, achieving a proud success, and establishing himself, both as a man and a lawyer, in the confidence of the community. He served as a member of the Rahway Common Council during 1870 and 1871. In the fall of 1875 he was elected to the Assembly on the Republican ticket. He is a Director of Rahway Savings Bank, and Counsel for the Rahway Railroad, in which he is also a Director, and of which he was one of the projectors. He is an honorary member of the New Jersey Historical Society. He is a rising man, and bids fair to rise high enough to make his mark among the loftiest names of the State.

28

SZARD, JACOB, M. D., of Glassborough, was born in Glassborough, Gloucester county, New Jersey, May 23d, 1829. His father, Rev. Joseph Iszard, an Episcopal minister, was also a native of Gloucester county, in which he preached for many years. His mother was Mary Swope, daughter of Mr. John Swope, of Squankum, now called Williamstown. He was educated at home and at the Pennington Seminary, both excellent seats of learning, and turning out in his case, as in that of so many others, jointly or separately, a thoroughly educated man. When about the age of twenty-one, he engaged in teaching school at Malaga, in Gloucester county, where he continued in this pursuit for some nine months, when he transferred the sphere of his calling to Bowenstown, a few miles below Bridgeton, remaining there for three winters. He next taught one season at Swedesborough, and then removed to Clarksborough, teaching in that place, as Principal of the village academy, for about four years and a half. Leaving Clarksborough, he returned to Glassborough, in which he served as Principal of the public schools, until the summer of 1868, when he decided to become a homœopathic physician, and accordingly entered the office of Dr. D. R. Gardner, of Woodbury, New Jersey, with whom he prosecuted his studies for two years, attending meanwhile the regular course at the Hahnemann Medical College, from which he graduated in the spring of 1870. He at once opened an office in Glassborough, where he has since resided, practising with notable success. His independence of character, combined with his conservative instincts, his intellectual training, and his varied experience, renders him a bold and at the same time a safe practitioner. His high merits are widely recognized. Immediately after graduating, he connected himself with the Homœopathic Medical Society of West Jersey, and has always taken an active part in its transactions, serving in 1875 as its President, and being at present the Chairman of its Bureau of Practice. He was married in 1854 to Eliza, daughter of Mr. Solomon H. Stanger, a well-known citizen of Glassborough, the family having been among the original settlers of the town.

ARNES, ORSON, M. D., late of Paterson, was born in Baldwinsville, Onondaga county, New York, in the year 1830. His early education was obtained in his native place at a private school conducted by Professor Stilwell. On leaving this establishment he completed a course of study at the Syracuse Academy. With his mind thus carefully trained, he took up medical reading in 1848, under the superintendence of Dr. J. V. Kendall; subsequently becoming a pupil of Dr. D. T. Jones, a physician of celebrity in western New York. He matriculated at the Albany Medical College, took three full courses of lectures, and graduated therefrom in 1854. Thereupon he made an extensive tour through the Western States, at the conclusion of which he returned to his native State, and began the practice of his profession at Succa Falls. About two years later he was persuaded to remove to Athens, Pennsylvania, where he built up a large practice. In September, 1861, he married the daughter of Charles Danforth, of Paterson, New Jersey, and two years subsequently, after the death of that lady's brother, Captain Charles Danforth, removed to Paterson, where he gradually worked together a large and lucrative practice. Thoroughly devoted to his profession and the interests of his patients, he won for himself a high reputation among his brethren and the fullest confidence of those who experienced his ministrations. His characteristics as a practitioner were rapid analysis, ready judgment, and prompt and decided action. Courageous and hopeful himself, his firm tread and self-reliant air inspired hope when despair was rapidly settling down upon the mind of his patient, while his ready sympathy incited the warmest attachments between himself and his patients. A man of fine natural abilities, of commanding presence, pleasing address, and a good conversationalist, he was welcomed and at home in any society. By nature he was a politician. While never seeking political preferment, he was deeply interested in every contest, national, State and municipal, and exercised considerable influence over the result in his neighborhood. In December, 1874, he was prostrated by an attack of pneumonia. From this he made a good recovery, but exposing himself too early by a return to professional labors, he brought on acute rheumatism, which resulted in disease of the heart and general dropsy. Death released him from great suffering, July 23d, 1875. The esteem in which he was held was manifested in the tributes of respect paid his memory by his numerous friends and professional brethren.

MITH, WILLIAM A., M. D., of Newark, was born, March 30th, 1820, in Guilford, Chenango county, New York. His parents were natives of Connecticut, and removed to Chenango county in 1804, when it was a wilderness. His father, Samuel A. Smith, was a farmer, although at various times he filled positions of honor and trust, having been for several terms Sheriff of Chenango county, and having also represented the county in the Legislature. He died at Guilford, in the eighty fourth year of his age. The mother was Wealthy Phelps, of Colebrook, Connecticut. After a thorough preparatory course in the academy of his native town, the son entered Geneva College, where he finished his literary education, and in the spring of 1847 graduated from the medical department of the same institution, at that period one of the best medical schools in the State, having among its faculty Professor F. H. Hamilton, late of Bellevue, New York, who filled the chair of surgery, and Professor Webster, the well-known anatomist. Settling himself at Sidney Plains, Delaware county, New York, he was actively and successfully engaged in his profession there for five years, when he removed to Norwich, the county-seat of Chenango, where he acquired an extensive practice, which he was pursuing at the outbreak of the rebellion, in 1861. In this emergency he promptly tendered his services to the government, and was assigned to duty as Assistant Surgeon of the 89th Regiment New York Volunteers, raised under the auspices of the Hon. Daniel S. Dickerson, though he was soon promoted to a full Surgeoncy and put in charge of the 103d New York Regiment, with which he did active and efficient service. On May 3d, 1863, while on duty with the regiment, then stationed at Suffolk, Virginia, he was very severely and almost fatally wounded, the ball entering just below the heart and coming out at the spinal column, between the hips. In the following autumn, believing himself totally unfitted for further service, he resigned his commission and returned home; but in January, 1864, having sufficiently recovered, he again took the field, and was appointed Surgeon of the 47th New York Regiment, then stationed at Hilton Head. Here he remained only a short time, when he was ordered to Jacksonville, Florida, to assume charge of the hospital there, which he soon reorganized and put in effective order. This was just previous to the battle of Olustee, in which the Union troops were fearfully slaughtered, and 1,500 of the wounded came under his immediate care at Jacksonville. He continued on duty at this place until July, 1864, when he came up to the Savannah river, and was ordered to superintend, on behalf of the government, the exchange of prisoners held in that vicinity. In this line of duty he was engaged at various places, having meanwhile charge of the General Prison Hospital at Newport News until his appointment as Health Officer for Norfolk, Virginia, in which capacity he rendered valuable service till September, 1865, when, the war being over, he was ordered to his regiment, to be mustered out of service with his comrades. Returning with a shattered constitution from the field in which he had served his country so faithfully and heroically, he took up his residence in Newark, New Jersey, intending, on account of his health, to engage in an office practice only; but, in spite of himself, he was soon called into active professional duty, on the full tide of which he is now fairly launched, ranking, by common consent, among the leading practitioners of that city. He is a member of the New Jersey Academy of Medicine, as also of the Essex County Medical Union, and during his term of practice in his native county in New York he was honored with the Presidency of the medical society of the county. He is a staunch Republican in politics, with the practical side of which he has not been wholly unconnected, having been chosen in 1868 to represent the Eighth Ward in the City Council, revolutionizing

ıtlv after, the 4th

at the same time the politics of the ward, which previously had always chosen a Democratic councilman. In 1875 he was again chosen to fill the same position, which he now holds. He was married, August 30th, 1847, to Elizabeth Wade, of Guilford, New York, who is still living. Two children are the fruits of the union.

——◦✦◦——

RUBB, GENERAL E. BURD, Soldier and Iron-Master, of Beverly, was born, November 13th, 1841, in the city of Burlington, and is the son of the late Edward Burd and Euphemia B. (Parker) Grubb. His father was a native of Lancaster county, Pennsylvania, an extensive miner of iron ores and manufacturer of pig-iron, who died. August 27th, 1867, at Burlington, where he had passed many years of his life; and his mother was also a Pennsylvanian by birth, the daughter of Isaac B. Parker, of Carlisle. General Grubb received his preliminary education in the grammar school of his native city, which he entered in 1851, where he remained several years, and then matriculated in the college, from which he graduated with the first honor in 1860. In April, 1861, the great rebellion broke out, and after the three months' men had been mustered into service, President Lincoln, on May 3d, 1861, called for three years' men, or during the war, of which New Jersey was to furnish three regiments. During the same month General Grubb entered the service as Second Lieutenant of Company C, 3d Regiment, and went into camp at Camp Olden, near Trenton. On June 28th, 1861, the three regiments left Trenton, and reported to General Scott, at Washington, the next day. In the following month of July the 3d Regiment formed one of the reserve regiments which moved forward with the army to participate in the battle of (first) Bull Run; and on July 17th its colonel, George W. Taylor, was ordered to march to a point on the Orange & Alexandria Railroad, which was being repaired. On the 21st of the same month, in conjunction with other regiments, the 3d was forwarded to Centreville, in obedience to orders from General McDowell. By this time, however, the battle of Bull Run had been fought and lost, and no further advance of the 3d was necessary than to Fairfax, which they had reached. Shortly after, the 4th New Jersey Regiment was added to the other three regiments, and the whole force, constituting the First Brigade, was placed under the command of Brigadier-General Philip Kearny, who lost no time in thoroughly drilling and moulding his command, bringing it forward as few others in the army at that time had done, and made it renowned for its most perfect discipline and suited to all the requirements of the service. On August 29th the 3d Regiment, while reconnoitring near Cloud's Mills, fell into an ambuscade of the enemy's pickets, and lost two men. During the fall and winter months the brigade was mainly occupied in drill and ordinary camp duties, General McClellan, the Commander-in-Chief, being ever preparing to move, but ever halting. He had succeeded in inducing President Lincoln to suspend the order for an advance on or before February 22d, 1862, and to change all his plans for taking Richmond. Meanwhile General Kearny, who had been ordered, March 7th, to advance to Burke's Station, on the Orange & Alexandria Railroad, for the purpose of guarding the laborers, discovered that the enemy were about to evacuate Manasses; and without orders he took the initiative, and on the 9th, after a skirmish with the enemy, entered the abandoned works of the enemy at Manasses, the 3d Regiment being the first to take possession and hoist the regimental flag, and an immense amount of stores was captured, besides a number of rebel cavalry. About this time Lieutenant Grubb had been promoted to a First Lieutenancy and assigned to Company D, of the same regiment. Early in April the brigade was attached to the First Division of the First Army Corps, and moved to a point on the Orange & Alexandria Railroad, to engage the attention of the enemy while McClellan transferred the main body of his army, by transports, to the peninsula. It subsequently returned to Alexandria, and embarked, April 17th, for the mouth of York river, the new place of rendezvous. At this time, General Kearny having been assigned to the command of a division, Colonel Taylor, of the 3d Regiment, was placed in command of the brigade. Lieutenant Grubb was assigned to duty on Colonel Taylor's staff, where he remained until the death of that officer. On May 4th the rebels evacuated Yorktown, and the next day the New Jersey brigade were advanced to meet the rebels, and successfully held them in check, and on the 15th joined McClellan's army, near the White House, and thence advanced to the Chickahominy. During the battles of Hanover Court House, Fair Oaks and Gaines' Mills they were engaged in picket duty, but on June 27th, the day the battle of Gaines' Mills was fought, they arrived in time to take part and greatly relieve the Union forces, which had been sorely pressed by the enemy; succeeding in successfully repulsing three repeated charges of the rebels. Nevertheless, the day was lost, and the New Jersey brigade, which numbered 2,800 men when they went into the fight, had left but 965 to answer the roll-call. The remnant of the brigade was withdrawn to the woods, where, after a brief rest, it was marched towards Savage Station and Harrison's Landing, pausing to share in the battle of Malvern Hill. After passing through White Oak swamp and across White Oak creek the command had halted for dinner, when the rebels advanced from out the woods, and with six pieces of artillery commenced a galling fire. The position of the Jersey troops was at this time a perilous one, being directly between the fire of the rebels and the main body of our forces. The Jerseymen were quickly formed into line of battle, and General Taylor immediately sent Lieutenant Grubb up the road to General Slocum's head-quarters for orders. The road which he was compelled to take was directly in the range of the rebel batteries, and the ride was consequently a most perilous one; but he dashed on, reaching his destination safely. Not finding General Slocum, he was compelled to return; but orders being imperatively necessary, he was again obliged to repeat his ride through that rain of shot and shell. With death staring him in the face at every bound of his horse, the gallant aide again went back, and this time succeeded in getting orders. The battle was an artillery one, the fire passing over the Jersey troops, who lay flat on their faces. After reaching Harrison's Landing, July 1st, General McClellan was ordered, on July 3d, to withdraw his forces to Acquia creek, but he did not obey the order for a week; and General Lee, of the rebels, taking advantage of the delay, pressed the Union forces heavily. The Jersey brigade did not embark from the peninsula until July 20th, and landed at Alexandria on the 24th, marching to Cloud's Mills, where it remained until the 26th. The next day it went by rail to Bull Run bridge and encountered the enemy; and General Taylor, without either cavalry or artillery to support him, had to bear the brunt of the battle, and that, too, under a scorching, torrid sun. He was, however, only obeying orders transmitted to him, and he was as far as possible nobly sustained by his men; but the day was again lost to the Union forces, and here General Taylor was wounded and eventually died. Speaking of the valor displayed by the Jersey troops, Stonewall Jackson said he had rarely seen a body of men who stood up so gallantly in the face of overwhelming odds as General Taylor's command. After the battle in which General Kearny was killed and Jackson repulsed, General Pope withdrew the army to their entrenchments on the south bank of the Potomac, the First Brigade resuming its old position at Camp Seminary. Here Colonel Torbert succeeded General Taylor, and Lieutenant Grubb, who had escaped all dangers, though continually exposed, was assigned to a position on his staff, having previously refused a promotion as Captain of Company B. Subsequently, in the operations against the enemy, Torbert's Jersey brigade covered themselves with glory in the great charge at Crampton's Pass of the South Mountain, Maryland, where they annihilated Cobb's Legion and drove the rebels from their defences, capturing the position, September 14th, 1862. The enemy lost 15,000 men, and Lee recrossed the Potomac, leaving his dead on the field. The First Brigade remained in Maryland until October 2d, and then returned into Virginia, where it was inactive until ordered to take part in the movement against Fredericksburg. The 15th and 23d Regiments were now added to the other regiments composing the First Brigade, and on November 24th, 1862, Lieutenant Grubb was promoted to Major of the latter regiment, to fill a vacancy, and on the 26th of the following month was again promoted to the Lieutenant-Colonelcy of the same. Meanwhile, on the 12th of December, the brigade crossed the river to take part in the battle of Fredericksburg, and after various manœuvres gained an important position, but being unsupported was compelled to withdraw. After the termination of the conflict the brigade covered the falling back of the Union forces, being the last to leave the field on the left of the lines. Colonel Torbert, in his official report, states that "Major Grubb of the 23d deserves great credit for the manner in which he fought a part of his regiment." Another authority says that "it was due to him that the right of the regiment, when thrown into confusion by the terrible fire to which it was subjected, was rallied and led into the thickest of the combat at Fredericksburg." After remaining in winter quarters for four months, partially recruiting their strength, the command was engaged in the battle of Chancellorsville. And here the same writer, speaking of Colonel Grubb, states that "always at the head of his regiment, mounted until his horse was shot from under him, then on foot, still animating the men and leading them on—himself the farthest in the front and the last to leave the field—seeming to bear a charmed life, he moved from point to point, calm and cool, the men nerved to daring by his example, until further exertion no longer availed." The 23d Regiment was one of the last to leave the field after the main forces had withdrawn. Afterwards the regiment went into camp at White Oak Church, and as the time for which they had enlisted was about drawing to a close, and they were in hourly expectation of receiving orders to march to Washington, they received orders to again cross the Rappahannock. A mutiny had almost broken out in the regiment, when Colonel Grubb addressed them, at evening parade, so forcibly that they reconsidered their action, and said they would go. The following day, June 4th, 1863, they marched and reached the river, which, having crossed, in the course of a single night they threw up a breastwork in front of the city and heights of Fredericksburg, upon which the enemy opened fire, but without inflicting any loss. Each day the works were strengthened, and finally orders were received to march for home. Having reached Beverly, New Jersey, a short delay ensued before the men could finally be mustered out. Late in June, however, Lee advanced into Pennsylvania, and Harrisburg was threatened. When Governor Parker's proclamation was issued, less than half of the 23d Regiment was in camp. Colonel Grubb, after assembling the men, asked all who would follow him to the assistance of a sister State to step forward, when the entire force volunteered. The regiment was received with hearty cheers in Philadelphia, but after reaching Harrisburg, whither they had been carried by rail, they found no excitement there; moreover, were very coolly received—and they the first regimental organization to reach the city. They were at once set to throw up rifle pits on the banks of the Susquehanna, and from the Colonel down they worked with a will; but before the labor was completed they were recalled to Beverly, and on June 27th were disbanded. Colonel Grubb was the most popular officer of the regiment; while being a strict disciplinarian, he still managed to so ingratiate himself in the affections of his command that duty soon became with all a work of love, and he never asked his men to face any dangers which he was unwilling to share. In July, 1863, he was commissioned by the Governor to take command of the camp at Beverly, where he recruited and sent to the front the 34th Regiment. By Governor Parker's request he raised, and once more returned to active service with, the 37th Regiment; this was to be for one hundred days, but they were in the field for a longer period. They left Trenton, June 28th, 1864, and after reaching City Point, where they reported to General Grant, were ordered by him to report to General Butler, at Bermuda Hundred. Landing at the Point of Rocks, July 1st, they were assigned to various duties, including picket and garrison duties. On August 28th they marched to the extreme front of Petersburg, where they did duty in the trenches until their term of service had nearly expired, and on September 25th they were highly complimented in general orders, by Major-General Birney, as being unexceptionably a superior regiment of "hundred days men." On March 5th, 1865, Colonel Grubb was made Brevet Brigadier-General of Volunteers, for meritorious service before Petersburg. On his return to civil life he settled down in his native city of Burlington, where he resided until about 1873. He became a member of the Common Council, and was President of that body for two years. He also was chosen a Trustee of St. Mary's Hall, and also of Burlington College. By his prudent management, aided by R. S. Conover, of Princeton, the last-named institution is in a flourishing condition. On the death of his father, in 1867, General Grubb was called upon to assume the charge of immense iron interests in Pennsylvania, which his father had formerly controlled. Among these are some of the most important pig-iron furnaces in Dauphin, Lancaster and Lebanon counties. Among his numerous interests are the famous Cornwall ore banks of Lancaster county, which at one time were owned by the family exclusively; a portion of these, however, they disposed of: their title to these lands was received direct from William Penn. He has travelled extensively through the old world, and his wife was the first white woman who passed through the entire length of the Suez canal, the trip being made in company with her husband on Baron Lesseps' steam yacht, he having letters of introduction to that celebrated engineer. On his return to the United States, General Grubb wrote an account of his voyage, which was published in *Lippincott's Magazine*, and extensively copied. Socially, he holds a high position, and is a member of the Philadelphia Club, the Reform Club, the New York Yacht Club, and has taken two of the Bennett prize cups. He has ever been an active member of the Republican party, and takes great interest in all matters pertaining to the welfare of the community among whom his lot is cast. Some three years since he removed to Beverly, where he resides in a most delightfully situated country-seat, with a park of twelve acres, handsomely laid

out and fronting the river. He was married, in 1868, to Elizabeth Wadsworth, daughter of Rev. Courtlandt Van Rensselaer, an eminent Presbyterian clergyman, of Albany, New York.

EMLEY, HON. OLIVER HAZARD PERRY, President of the Mount Holly National Bank, was born, May 23d, 1814, in New Hanover township, Burlington county, New Jersey, and is a son of the late Hon. John and Beulah (Warren) Emley, both of whom were also natives of the same State. His father was a member of the lower house of the Legislature from 1831 to 1840, and during his last two years of service in that body was elected Speaker of the same. He died in 1855, on the old homestead, which has now been in the possession of the family for two hundred years; and during that entire time has never been conveyed in any other way than by the last will and testament of the then owner. Oliver received his education at the district school of his native township, attending the same until fifteen years old, and subsequently assisted his father on the farm; indeed, he has been constantly devoted all his life to agricultural pursuits. His political creed was first that of the Whig school; and after the disintegration of that organization he affiliated with the national Republicans. He has always taken an active part in political matters, but never sought office. In 1848, however, he was appointed, by the Legislature, Judge of the Court of Common Pleas for Burlington County, which position he held for five years. He was also selected by Chancellor William Pennington a Master in Chancery, and has also had the settlement of many estates. He had filled the post of Director of the Mount Holly Bank for some ten years prior to his election as President, in March, 1875, to fill the vacancy occasioned by the death of Thomas D. Armstrong. He is also a Director of the Mercer County Insurance Company. He was married, in 1851, to Achsah Swaim, of New Jersey.

HOFFMAN, JAMES P., Merchant, of Clinton, was born, December 11th, 1811, in Lebanon, Hunterdon county, New Jersey. After attending the common schools for the usual time he began the business of life at the age of fifteen, as a clerk for Oscar Pillette, in Allamuchy, Warren county, from which he removed with his employer to Basking Ridge, Somerset county, where he served him in the same capacity. In 1830 he went to Clinton, entering the establishment of Bray & Taylor, extensively engaged in the grain and general mercantile trade at that place. Having graduated, so to speak, in his chosen line of business, he organized, in 1839, the firm of J. P. Hoffman & Co., at the head of which he embarked at Clinton in the general country-store business, which he has conducted ever since, remaining chief through all the numerous changes of the junior partners, and making the firm one of the most prosperous and substantial of the kind, as it is the oldest, in Hunterdon county. He is a sagacious, energetic, thorough-going business man, noted for his honesty not less than his enterprise, and is held, it scarcely need be added, in high esteem by the community. He has been twice married; the first time to Miss Syler, daughter of the late Peter Syler, who died several years ago; and subsequently to Miss King, daughter of the late William King, of Pittstown, New Jersey. His eldest son is at present associated with him in business.

OORIIEES, NATHANIEL W., was born at Mine Brook, Somerset county, New Jersey, June 29th, 1829. He entered Rutgers College in 1844, graduating with credit in 1847. Having read law in the office of the Hon. Richard S. Field, of Princeton, he was admitted to the bar in 1852. Instead, however, of entering upon the practice of his profession, he accepted a position in the Princeton Bank, of which Mr. Field was at that time president. In 1856 a banking company was organized at Clinton, New Jersey, and in this he was offered the position of cashier. Accepting the office he identified his own with the fortunes of the institution, and under his efficient management its financial success was of the most satisfactory character. In 1875, when the First National Bank of Clinton was founded, he was elected to the cashiership, a position that he still retains. Mr. Voorhees, belonging to a family that for many years has been prominent in the public affairs of New Jersey, early gave a considerable portion of his attention to politics, and had he been so minded he could on several occasions have received high offices in the State government. In 1860 he was a delegate to the National Republican Convention at Chicago, and in the convention—as well as during the subsequent civil war—was an earnest supporter of Mr. Lincoln. In 1862 he was elected a member of the State Republican Executive Committee, a position that he held for several successive years. In 1873, a vacaney occurring on the bench of the Court of Common Pleas of Hunterdon county, he was appointed Judge for the unexpired portion of the term, filling the position so satisfactorily that he was offered the appointment for the succeeding full term; this, however, he declined. In 1874 he was urged by his personal and political friends to permit his name to be presented as a candidate for the State Treasurership, a position for which he was especially fitted by the natural bent of his mind and by his extended training as a financier; but the nomination was lost to him by a single vote, and was gained by the then incumbent, the Hon. Josephus Sooy. In 1875 Mr. Voorhees was, without his knowledge, named as a candidate for the office of Secretary of the New Jersey Senate, and upon the assembling of that body was elected to the office. He was again elected in the succeeding year. Occupying so prominent a position in the political affairs of the commonwealth, so heartily respected by the community in which he is best known, and so generally regarded as a financier of exceptional ability, Mr. Voorhees, as has been already said, could without difficulty command so large a share of the popular vote as to assure his election to almost any State office, or to a position in the national government. That he has persistently refused to put himself in the way of such preferment can only be accounted for on the ground that he possesses much more than the average amount of modesty. He was married, November 1st, 1854, to Naomi, daughter of Samuel Leigh, Esq., of Clinton.

AXWELL, HON. JOHN PATERSON BRYANT, Lawyer, Journalist and Congressman, late of Belvidere, was born at Flemington, New Jersey, September 3d, 1804. He was the son of Hon. George C. Maxwell, who was for some time a representative in Congress from New Jersey. His ancestor, Anthony Maxwell, came to this country from the north of Ireland in the early part of the last century, and settled in Hunterdon county. He had two sons: William, who at the commencement of the revolutionary war was a major in the British army and stationed at Detroit; in order to join the Continental forces he traversed the wilderness on foot, and was afterwards promoted to a generalship and died a bachelor some time after the war; the other son, John, was married and left a large family; during the war he raised a company in old Sussex county and continued to serve with his company until the close of hostilities. Sussex county was not remarkable for the loyalty of its inhabitants, and when he presented himself at the camp with his company, it is said General Washington exclaimed in surprise: "What! are there any Whigs in Sussex?" He died at Flemington at a good old age, about 1825. George C. was his eldest son, and is believed to have lived and died at Flemington. He graduated at Nassau Hall in 1792, was licensed as attorney-at-law in 1797, as counsellor in 1800, and called as serjeant in 1816. He was married to Miss Bryant and died quite young, while a member of Congress. He left but two children, John P. B. and Anna Maria, the widow of William P. Robeson, deceased, and mother of the Secretary of the Navy. John P. B. graduated at Nassau Hall in 1823, studied law with Chief-Justice Hornblower, and was admitted to the bar of New Jersey in May, 1827, as an attorney-at-law, and as a counsellor in 1830, when he settled in the practice of his profession at Belvidere, the county-seat of Warren county. He soon turned his attention to politics, was for a time the editor and proprietor of the *Belvidere Apollo*, the Whig paper of the county. He was strong in his political beliefs, but courteous in all his dealings with his opponents. In 1838 he was a candidate of the Whig party for Congress, and was one of the members kept from what they claimed to be their seats by the famous "Broad Seal Controversy." In 1840 he was elected and took his place in the Congress that assembled in 1841, after the log cabin campaign which resulted in the overwhelming election of General Harrison and the Whig ticket generally. As a member of Congress he was more useful than showy. His great modesty and retiring habits kept him from making any attempts at display, but no one was more useful in the committee room than he was, and his career, though not particularly brilliant, was exceedingly honorable. In September, 1834, he was married to Sarah Browne, a young lady of an old family in Philadelphia, to whom he was tenderly attached. Their union, however, was not destined to be of long duration. At the time of their marriage his bride was far gone in consumption, and survived but five weeks after the ceremony. The death of one in whom his life was so much wrapped up cast a shadow over all his future life and caused him to look for his chief happiness beyond this world. He was a member of the Presbyterian Church at Belvidere, and one of its earnest supporters and most liberal contributors. In 1842 he was elected a Trustee of the College of New Jersey, and died at Belvidere, November 14th, 1845.

AN SYCKEL, BENNETT, Associate Justice of the Supreme Court of New Jersey, was born, April 17th, 1830, in Bethlehem, Hunterdon county, New Jersey. He is the third son of the late Aaron Van Syckel. Prepared for college at Easton, Pennsylvania, he was matriculated at Princeton in 1843, entering the sophomore class and graduating in 1846, in the same class with his brother, Dr. S. Van Syckel, of Clinton, and D. A. Depue, now one of the judges of the Supreme Court of New Jersey. Immediately after graduating he entered the law office of Alexander Wurts, of Flemington, in which he remained until he was admitted to the bar in 1851, when he at once began the practice of his profession at Flemington. His professional zeal and ability soon won for him a high reputation at the bar. A hard student, a close thinker, and a forcible speaker, his cases were prepared with thoroughness and presented with the best effect, a cause intrusted to him never failing to strike the court or jury with all the power of which the law and the facts admitted. His forensic abilities are unquestionably of the first order. He pursued his profession at Flemington until 1869, when he was appointed to a seat on the bench of the Supreme Court of the State, a station to which he was reappointed in 1876, and which he now occupies, exemplifying in the discharge of his judicial duties, as formerly in his practice, that profound

learning and spotless integrity which have made the judiciary of New Jersey known and honored throughout the land. He was married in 1857 to Miss Sloane, daughter of W. H. Sloane, of Flemington.

EFFREY, OSCAR, Lawyer, of Washington, was born, August 31st, 1838, at Lockport, New York. His father, Joseph Jeffrey, a merchant of Lockport, died when Oscar was an infant. His mother, whose maiden name was Adeline Baush, removed with him to Jersey City, New Jersey, where, some time after, she also died, leaving him an orphan in his eleventh year. Soon afterwards he removed to Warren county, acquired there a good common-school education, and at the age of eighteen entered as clerk the store of Mr. Robert Blair, at Johnsonburg, in that county, in which he remained eight years, beginning meanwhile, however, the reading of law under the direction of David Thompson, of Newton. In 1864 he became a student in Mr. Thompson's office, and in the same year was admitted to the bar, receiving his license as counsellor two years later. In 1865 he established himself at Washington, Warren county, where he now lives, and in which he has built up, with rapidity, a large and increasing practice, extending to all the courts of the State. His professional abilities and attainments and his unspotted and fearless integrity are recognized wherever he is known. Although still young he occupies a commanding position in his profession, into which he has the satisfaction of reflecting that, under Providence, he has raised himself by his own efforts. In politics he is a Republican, and though not a thick-and-thin partisan, much less an office-seeker, throws himself with zeal into a political canvass. He is a member of the Methodist Episcopal Church and Recording Steward of the Quarterly Conference. The cause of religion has few workers more earnest or unsleeping than he. Mr. Jeffrey was married in 1872 to Emma L. Wild, of Paterson, New Jersey.

AN SYCKEL, SYLVESTER, M. D., of Clinton, was born, February 21st, 1826, in Union township, Hunterdon county, New Jersey. He is the son of the late Aaron Van Syckel and Mary (Bird) Van Syckel, the family being originally of Hollandish extraction. He was prepared for college at the academy of the Rev. John Vanderveer, at Easton, and entered Princeton in 1842. Graduating in 1846, he entered the office of the celebrated Dr. Valentine Mott as a private pupil, at the same time attending lectures at the University of New York—the faculty of this institution then including Drs. Mott, Draper, Mathson, Bedford, Payne and others scarcely less celebrated. In 1849 he received his degree, and was appointed Assistant Physician at Bellevue Hospital. At the end of six months he was made House Physician, and a little later was made House Surgeon. From Bellevue he was appointed by Governor Clark to be one of the Quarantine Hospital physicians, and in this capacity served through the ship-fever epidemic of 1850, an epidemic during the continuance of which Dr. Doane and several other of the medical attendants died at their work. Dr. Van Syckel himself, worn out by sickness and over exertion, was finally compelled to resign, and for the reestablishment of his health moved to Clinton, New Jersey, where he soon acquired a large practice. Since 1851, when this change was made, he has become thoroughly identified with the town and its interests, and has for many years held a leading place among its physicians. During the civil war he was offered the position of Surgeon to the 31st New Jersey Regiment, but sickness in his family compelled him to decline the proffered position. Appreciating his professional qualities, he has been appointed by several of the most prominent of the life insurance companies to guard their interests in the capacity of Examining Physician. He was married, March 24th, 1853, to Mary E., daughter of John Carhart, of Clinton.

———◆◇◆———

LLISON, MICHAEL E., Methodist Clergyman, of Washington, was born in 1818 in Burlington county, New Jersey. His ancestors were of English descent, but at the period of his birth had resided in New Jersey for several generations. He was educated at Lawrenceville, Mercer county, and at the Methodist Seminary in Pennington, at which latter institution he taught for two years. In 1842 he was entered by the New Jersey Conference to preach, and began his ministration on the Parsippany and Fairfield circuit, after which he was stationed successively at Dover, Orange, Haverstraw, New York; New Brunswick, Hoboken, the First Church at Paterson; St. Paul's, Jersey City; Clinton street, Newark; Trinity, Staten Island; St. Paul's, Newark—the largest church in that city—Simpson, Jersey City, and again at Hoboken. For four years he was Presiding Elder in Morristown District. In 1873 he was stationed at Washington, New Jersey, where he has since remained. He has been the Secretary of the Newark Conference for the last thirteen years. In 1857 he visited Europe, travelling extensively in England, Ireland, Scotland, Germany and Italy, meanwhile enriching his correspondence the columns of the *Christian Advocate*. He has been an unwearied and efficient worker in his church, which justly regards him as one of its ablest ministers. Of fine native abilities, well-trained intellectually, and rich in that diversified experience assured by the rules and methods of the church, and of which, as may be seen from this outline of his services, he has drunk to the full, he is among the best equipped and most effective preachers in the State. He was married in 1844 to Ann Whittaker, only daughter of John Whittaker, of Trenton.

———◆◇◆———

ANN, PHILIP H., Banker, of Washington, was born in 1819 in Mansfield township, Warren county, New Jersey. He was educated at Schooley's Mountain, and spent the early years of his manhood in agricultural pursuits. In 1854 he was elected Surrogate of Warren county, holding the position until 1859, when he engaged in the general mercantile business in Washington, pursuing it for three years. In 1864 he was appointed one of the judges of the Court of Common Pleas for Warren County, an appointment renewed in 1869, holding the office for ten years. In 1865, in conjunction with S. T. Scranton, J. C. Swayze, William Shields, George W. Taylor, J. V. Matteson, W. Winter and others, he organized the First National Bank of Washington, of which he was elected the first Cashier, a place he has filled ever since. The bank, as happens often in the case of capable and trusted cashiers, has been largely under his management, the ability and fidelity of which are sufficiently shown by the high character and prosperity of the institution. For a number of years he was a Director of the Phillipsburg Bank before its conversion into a national bank, and he has served several terms in the Belvidere and Washington Town Councils, and held many other positions of public trust. In politics he is a Democrat and a great favorite with his party, as indeed he is with his fellow-citizens in general. Intelligent, steadfast, just, sensible and genial, he is a man to win golden opinions from all classes of people. He was married in 1845 to Miss Dunham, daughter of the Rev. Johnson Dunham, of New York.

———◆◇◆———

ODGSON, WILMER, M. D., of Keyport, was born in Columbia, Virginia. His father, Joseph Hodgson, a merchant of Columbia, was a native of Washington, District of Columbia. His mother was Anna Pannill, of Virginia. Receiving his primary education in his native town, he entered Hampden Sidney College in 1858, in which he was pursuing his studies at the outbreak of the civil war in 1861, when, like thousands of other young men in the South, he exchanged the academic text-book for the manual of arms and joined the Confederate army, serving with distinguished gallantry throughout the war. In 1864 he began the study of medicine under Dr. F. B. Watkins, an eminent physician of Richmond, Virginia, and after attending a regular course of lectures at the Medical College in Richmond, went abroad, where he spent several months, industriously prosecuting his studies. On his return he attended a course of lectures at the College of Physicians and Surgeons of New York, and in 1867 began the practice of his profession in Keyport, Monmouth county, New Jersey, where he has since continued it, making it steadily larger and more lucrative. Few physicians of his age are so fully equipped by training and experience. In the natural course of things a professional career of usefulness and distinction undoubtedly awaits him.

RICK, RILEY ALLEN, Manufacturer, was born in New York city, October 7th, 1837, his parents, of Welsh descent, being natives of Burlington county, New Jersey. Receiving his preliminary education in the schools of New York, he entered Harvard College, graduating in the class of 1858. Immediately upon graduating he succeeded to the business founded by his father in 1832, the manufacture of cast-iron pipes for water and gas, which he has since then successfully carried on. The business also included the making and erection of gas works, and among the heaviest contracts that he has filled may be mentioned the building of the works of the Central and Suburban Gaslight Companies of New York. In the latter, as well as in the People's Gaslight Company, of Albany, New York, he has been for a number of years a Director, and has been associated in the same capacity with the Merchants' Exchange National Bank, of New York. For more than two years he was upon the direction of the New Jersey Southern Railroad Company, being at the same time Secretary of that corporation. For many years he has been prominently connected with various religious and benevolent associations, and is now a Trustee of St. Luke's Hospital Association, of the New York Bible Society, and a Director of the Young Men's Christian Association of New York. In 1866, associated with Mr. Robert Campbell, of New York city, he founded the town of Bricksburg, in Ocean county, New Jersey, and has devoted a great portion of his energy and no small part of his wealth to its establishment and development. The town now numbers upwards of one thousand inhabitants, and its flourishing condition is the best testimonial to the liberality, foresight and business ability of its founder. He was married, January 10th, 1861, to Anna Stone, daughter of Charles H. Brown, Esq., of Boston, Massachusetts.

HILLIPS, WILLIAM W. L., A. M., M. D., Physician, of Trenton, was born in Laurence township, Mercer county, New Jersey, February 19th, 1829. His father, George Phillips, was a native of the same place and carried on farming there, while it had been the family residence for many years. His mother, Abigail Ketcham, came from Mercer county, having been born at Pennington. After obtaining a good

preparatory training at a private school, William entered Princeton College in 1845. He pursued the three years' course, and graduated in 1848, and received the degrees of A. B. and A. M. in due course. His tastes leading him to the medical profession he began his studies with a view to its adoption under the direction of Dr. John McKelway, of Trenton, who still lives at the advanced age of eighty-nine years. He matriculated at Jefferson College in 1848, and graduated in the spring of 1851. On receiving his diploma he settled at Trenton and commenced practice, which he continued with encouraging success until the fall of 1862, when he felt his services were needed in support of the national cause, and he entered the army as Surgeon of the 1st New Jersey Cavalry. From this time until 1864 he continued in active service, and rose to be Surgeon-in-Chief 2d Division Cavalry Corps of the Army of the Potomac. He returned to Trenton in the fall of 1864, having been disabled for active field service, and resumed private practice. His friends and former patients welcomed him back, and soon he found himself surrounded by a more extensive practice than before. He had charge of the troops which were quartered in the vicinity of Trenton until their removal in the summer of 1865. The city was at that time and always had been a rendezvous for drafted men, and his hands were kept pretty full. Dr. Phillips ranks among the leading practitioners of Trenton, and is very highly respected by his medical brethren, while the general community honors him for his many estimable qualities, both as a physician and a citizen. He is a member of the Mercer County District Medical Association, and has served as its President several times. Frequently he has been sent as a Delegate to the meetings of the New Jersey State Medical Association, and for the past three years has acted as Treasurer for the body. For eight years he has been Physician to the New Jersey State Prison, and was re-elected in April, 1876, for a term of three years additional. He is a member of the State Health Association of New Jersey, the United States Pension Examining Surgeon for his district, Medical Examiner for the New York Mutual Life Insurance Company. His religious views are those of the Presbyterian Church, and he is a member of the Fourth Church of Trenton, and President of its Board of Trustees. He was married in December, 1851, to Margaret S. McKelway, daughter of his professional preceptor; she died in 1857, and he married a second time, in 1865, his wife being Meta R. McAlpin, of Philadelphia.

ERCHANT, SILAS, President of the Merchants' Fire Insurance Company of Newark. The world in these latter days is largely ruled by self-made men. As the power of caste has been broken, and the privileged classes have lost their control in society, the individual has come to be measured for what he is worth, and thus merit in a homespun coat com-

29

pels, much more largely than formerly, the same degree of respect as when clothed in royal purple. With this enlargement of the sphere of human action stimulus has been given to the development of native ability among all conditions of men, and as a result we find in all the walks of life those who have made their way from the lower to the higher stations by the assertion of sheer innate force and the utilization alike of inherent qualities and passing opportunities. Silas Merchant, the subject of this sketch, belongs to this class of self-made men. His early opportunities were meagre and limited. The foot of the ladder was for him planted among harsh conditions. Born in Reading, Connecticut, on the 13th of December, 1808, his childhood was spent in Morris county, New Jersey, whither his parents removed in March, 1809. Here he was employed on a farm until the age of twenty. His only means of acquiring an education were such as were afforded by the country schools of that period, and these, which taught merely the primary studies in a most superficial way, he was able to attend only in the winter months. But such opportunities as he possessed he improved to the utmost, his naturally vigorous mind steadily developing under the influence of study, so that when manhood was reached he was thoroughly prepared to grapple with its duties and responsibilities. When twenty years of age, in the year 1828, Mr. Merchant, quitting the farm on which he had been reared, went to Georgia, where he was employed as a clerk in a mercantile establishment until 1832, when he returned to New Jersey. He was married in that year to Electa Heaton, daughter of John H. Heaton, and granddaughter of Hon. David Ayres, of Flanders. Three children were subsequently born to him, all of whom are now deceased. Locating in Newark, he engaged in the wholesale clothing manufacture, his house being the second in that business established in that city. He continued in this business almost continuously until 1863, a period of over thirty years. His business relations being largely with the South, and more particularly with Virginia, the breaking out of the rebellion and the consequent interruption of intercourse and destruction of commercial values in the seceding States, stripped him of the accumulations of years of industry and enterprise; but, accepting the adverse fortune with cheerful courage, he paid every dollar of his indebtedness, balanced his books, and went forward over the wreck to new labors and new experiences. In November, 1860, Mr. Merchant had been elected President of the Merchants' Fire Insurance Company of Newark, and having closed out his manufacturing business, he addressed himself with characteristic vigor to the duties of his new position, withdrawing entirely from political life in order the more completely to meet its requirements. Realizing that insurance is, in fact, a practical science, he familiarized himself with its principles, its methods, and its conditions of prosperity, gathering up meanwhile the lessons of experience, and his administration has, as a natural sequence, been throughout exceptionally successful. From being one of the smallest, his company has come to be one of the largest and most substantial in a city which numbers in its list of fire insurance corporations several of national prominence. As an underwriter, Mr. Merchant has held steadily to the view that the primary object in insurance should be to afford the largest security alike to policy-holder and stockholder at the least possible cost; that the duties of the insurer and the insured are reciprocal; that the full benefaction of the system can only be realized where all transactions are controlled by the spirit of the golden rule; and if he could have the selection of his own epitaph, it would probably be that in the responsible position he now occupies in connection with this great interest, he had faithfully adhered to the requirements of that sublime command. While Mr. Merchant's career has been largely that of a man of business, he has for over a quarter of a century been actively and prominently identified with public affairs. He was an active member of the old-time School Committee of Newark, and upon the creation of the present Board of Education, charged with the management and control of the entire educational interest of the city, he was chosen to that body, serving until 1860, when he voluntarily withdrew. A warm friend of education, he was among the first to urge that larger recognition of its claims which, for a time stubbornly resisted by a false and niggardly conservatism, has in these larger days incarnated itself in comprehensive laws, in liberal appropriations, and in generous policies, all contemplating the largest possible diffusion of the benefits and blessings of sound education among the masses. In 1852 Mr. Merchant served as a member of the lower House of the State Legislature, where he occupied a leading position, acting on the Committees on the Judiciary, Lunatic Asylum, and Education—three of the most important in the entire list. In all the political struggles of the middle period of his life, Mr. Merchant bore a conspicuous part. During this period of active participation in public affairs, his influence in the State was positive and well defined. A sagacious adviser, with rare powers of discrimination as to the character and motives of his contemporaries, his counsel was often sought by the leading men of his party, while in many important crises he was largely influential in determining the policy, not only of his party, but of the State as well. Thus, in 1859, at a critical moment in the political history of the State, he defeated a movement to hand over the so-called American party to one of the rival organizations, and by his sagacity and courage enabled it to maintain both its influence and independence, and so to dictate nominations and a policy which secured to the State a conspicuously wise and loyal administration during the troublous period which soon followed. In all these matters Mr. Merchant's influence was greatly heightened by his facility as a writer, in which he is excelled by few men not of the purely professional and literary classes, and also by his ability as a speaker. At one period in his life he was a liberal contributor to the public

Galaxy Pub. Co. Philad.ᵃ

Henry R Baldwin M.D.

... of public interest, but ... ... topics. His style ... ... being neither obscured by ... ... nor weakened by displays of tinsel rheto-... As it ... ... earnest, direct, and argumentative, ... to the ... rather than to prejudice and passion, ... conviction rather than at the mere ... of his hearers. It has been said by Emerson that every man's life is full of judgment days; and it is true. We are all of us tried and measured, oftener than we think, in the bar where our peers sit in judgment. But to the just and upright man, the man who has lived a clean life, using his gifts for the benefit of his fellows, standing bravely at all times for the right, keeping always in view the day of final review, these days of human judgment have no terror. To such they can be days of victory only. They bring the laurel and the crown, and so even here afford a compensation for all the disappointments and pains and sorrows of life. So Mr. Merchant finds it in the mellow autumn of his days. He has lived a useful, pure and upright life, and he has his reward in the confidence and esteem of his fellows. They rank him as one who can be depended upon to stand inflexibly in defence of law and justice and order whenever and by whomsoever assailed. They know him as one who bestows liberally of his substance to the suffering and the poor, and who is ever ready to help the weak against the cruelty of the strong. They recognize him as a self-made man, who never forgets that he came himself from the ranks of the humble and the obscure, and that it is his duty to help, in so far as he may, the ascent of the deserving who aspire as he did to loftier heights. With such an estimate of his life and career, the subject of this sketch may well be content, for it will make luminous his last days here, as it will no less surely shed a lustre over his memory when he is gone.

———————

BALDWIN, HENRY R., A. M., M. D.., of New Brunswick, was born in the city of New York, September 18th, 1839. His father, Eli Baldwin, M. D. and D. D., was for many years a distinguished minister of the Reformed Church, and was a descendant of the Baldwins who settled in Newark, New Jersey, prior to 1764. His mother, whose maiden name was Phebe Van Nest, was a native of New York city. His youth was passed in the select schools of the latter place, and in his sixteenth year, 1845, he was enrolled on the lists of Rutgers College, from which, having passed through its entire course, he graduated in the class of July, 1849. Directly after receiving his degree of Master of Arts, he entered upon the study of medicine with Dr. George J. Janeway, at New Brunswick, and completed his preparations and a college course of medicine in the office of Drs. Parker and Watts, of New York. He then attended the regular course of lectures at the College of Physicians and Surgeons in that city, and from it received, on March 4th, 1853, his diploma as Doctor of Medicine. Immediately upon the culmination of these studies, he was honored by his preceptor, Dr. Robert Watts, who at that time was professor of anatomy in the College of Physicians and Surgeons, with the appointment of Clinical Assistant, and filled this position with great capacity for a period of six months. During this period he also acted as junior at the Bellevue Hospital, and continued in this position, and as House Physician, eighteen months. This service was of great benefit to him, as it enabled him to render his studies immediately practical. In fine, he became an able and careful practitioner before he had entered upon his professional career. In October, 1854, he commenced practice at Stapleton, Staten Island, being associated with Dr. William C. Anderson. His health failed him, and shortly after he was reluctantly compelled to relinquish this field, in which his success had been marked. As the needed change he accepted the surgeoncy of the steamship "Baltic," of the Collins Line, in August, 1855, and discharged its duties most acceptably, and with benefit to his health, for some months. In December of that year he settled in New Brunswick, New Jersey, and was married, on December 27th, 1855, to Elizabeth Van Cortland Rutgers. Here he has ever since been in active practice, and is recognized among the leaders of the profession in the State. He is prominently identified with the New Jersey Medical Society, having acted as its Treasurer from 1867 to 1875, and now serving as its First Vice-President. At the revival of the Middlesex County Medical Society he filled the positions as President and Vice-President in regular succession. He is as energetic and useful a citizen as he is efficient and attentive as a physician. All measures for public improvements, all methods for advancing the educational interests of his section, have invariably received his support. He has served as Alderman of the city of New Brunswick and as one of the Board of Chosen Freeholders. He was one of the incorporators of the New Brunswick Water Works, and for twelve years was a distinguished member of the Board of Education for that city, and in addition served for two years as its Treasurer. He is a gentleman of progressive ideas and fine social qualities, and is esteemed wherever known.

———————

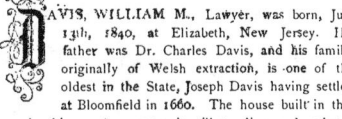

DAVIS, WILLIAM M., Lawyer, was born, July 13th, 1840, at Elizabeth, New Jersey. His father was Dr. Charles Davis, and his family, originally of Welsh extraction, is one of the oldest in the State, Joseph Davis having settled at Bloomfield in 1660. The house built in that year by this remote ancestor is still standing, and—what is much more singular in this country of quickly varying fortunes—still remains in the family. He received an English and classical education at Elizabeth, and subsequently

journals, writing upon all subjects of public interest, but with especial effect upon certain favorite topics. His style is clear, compact and logical, being neither obscured by profuse verbiage, nor weakened by displays of tinsel rhetoric. As a speaker he is earnest, direct, and argumentative, appealing to the reason rather than to prejudice and passion, and aiming to produce conviction rather than at the mere entertainment of his hearers. It has been said by Emerson that every man's life is full of judgment days; and it is true. We are all of us tried and measured, oftener than we think, at the bar where our peers sit in judgment. But to the just and upright man, the man who has lived a clean life, using his gifts for the benefit of his fellows, standing bravely at all times for the right, keeping always in view the day of final assize, these days of human judgment have no terror. To such they can be days of victory only. They bring the laurel and the crown, and so even here afford a compensation for all the disappointments and pains and sorrows of life. So Mr. Merchant finds it in the mellow autumn of his days. He has lived a useful, pure and upright life, and he has his reward in the confidence and esteem of his fellows. They rank him as one who can be depended upon to stand inflexibly in defence of law and justice and order, whenever and by whomsoever assailed. They know him as one who bestows liberally of his substance to the suffering and the poor, and who is ever ready to help the weak against the cruelty of the strong. They recognize him as a self-made man, who never forgets that he came himself from the ranks of the humble and the obscure, and that it is his duty to help, in so far as he may, the ascent of the deserving who aspire as he did to loftier heights. With such an estimate of his life and career, the subject of this sketch may well be content, for it will make luminous his last days here, as it will no less surely shed a lustre over his memory when he is gone.

ALDWIN, HENRY R., A. M., M. D.., of New Brunswick, was born in the city of New York, September 18th, 1829. His father, Eli Baldwin, M. D. and D. D., was for many years a distinguished minister of the Reformed Church, and was a descendant of the Baldwins who settled in Newark, New Jersey, prior to 1764. His mother, whose maiden name was Phebe Van Nest, was a native of New York city. His youth was passed in the select schools of the latter place, and in his sixteenth year, 1845, he was enrolled on the lists of Rutgers College, from which, having passed through its entire course, he graduated in the class of July, 1849. Directly after receiving his degree of Master of Arts, he entered upon the study of medicine with Dr. George J. Janeway, at New Brunswick, and completed his preparations and a college course of medicine in the office of Drs. Parker and Watts, of New York. He then attended the regular course of lectures at the College of Physicians

and Surgeons in that city, and from it received, on March 4th, 1853, his diploma as Doctor of Medicine. Immediately upon the culmination of these studies, he was honored by his preceptor, Dr. Robert Watts, who at that time was professor of anatomy in the College of Physicians and Surgeons, with the appointment of Clinical Assistant, and filled this position with great capacity for a period of six months. During this period he also acted as junior at the Bellevue Hospital, and continued in this position, and as House Physician, eighteen months. This service was of great benefit to him, as it enabled him to render his studies immediately practical. In fine, he became an able and careful practitioner before he had entered upon his professional career. In October, 1854, he commenced practice at Stapleton, Staten Island, being associated with Dr. William C. Anderson. His health failed him, and shortly after he was reluctantly compelled to relinquish this field, in which his success had been marked. As the needed change he accepted the surgeoncy of the steamship "Baltic," of the Collins Line, in August, 1855, and discharged its duties most acceptably, and with benefit to his health, for some months. In December of that year he settled in New Brunswick, New Jersey, and was married, on December 27th, 1855, to Elizabeth Van Cortland Rutgers. Here he has ever since been in active practice, and is recognized among the leaders of the profession in the State. He is prominently identified with the New Jersey Medical Society, having acted as its Treasurer from 1867 to 1875, and now serving as its First Vice-President. At the revival of the Middlesex County Medical Society he filled the positions as President and Vice-president in regular succession. He is as energetic and useful a citizen as he is efficient and attentive as a physician. All measures for public improvements, all methods for advancing the educational interests of his section, have invariably received his support. He has served as Alderman of the city of New Brunswick and as one of the Board of Chosen Freeholders. He was one of the incorporators of the New Brunswick Water Works, and for twelve years was a distinguished member of the Board of Education for that city, and in addition served for two years as its Treasurer. He is a gentleman of progressive ideas and fine social qualities, and is esteemed wherever known.

AVIS, WILLIAM M., Lawyer, was born, July 13th, 1840, at Elizabeth, New Jersey. His father was Dr. Charles Davis, and his family, originally of Welsh extraction, is one of the oldest in the State, Joseph Davis having settled at Bloomfield in 1660. The house built in that year by this remote ancestor is still standing, and—what is much more singular in this country of quickly varying fortunes—still remains in the family. He received an English and classical education at Elizabeth, and subsequently read law in the office of the Hon. H. D. Maxwell, at Easton. In 1864 he was admitted to practise at the Penn sylvania bar, and after reading for a year in the office of Hon. J. G. Shipman, of Belvidere, he was admitted in 1865 to practise at the bar of New Jersey. In the same year he established himself at Philipsburg, and since that time he has built up for himself an extensive practice ranging through all the courts of the State. He is a staunch member of the Republican party, but has never sought nor accepted office, preferring to devote his entire time to the duties of his profession. He was married, April 25th, 1866, to Elizabeth W., daughter of the late Dr. Frederick S. Weller, of Paterson, New Jersey.

1863, when he relinquished it in order to accept the post of Surgeon to the Board of Enrolment of the Fifth Congressional District of New Jersey. This latter office he retained until the final suppression of the rebellion, returning to private practice in 1865. In 1870 he was appointed one of the staff of St. Michael's Hospital, and in the same year Physician to the Essex County Home for the Insane, both of which appointments he continues to hold. He is a member of the New Jersey and Essex County Medical Societies, and is a Director of the Germania Fire Insurance Company of Newark. He was married, April, 1859, to Eveline, daughter of Reynier Van Giesson, of Mount Clare, New Jersey.

CROSS, JEREMIAH A., M. D., of Newark, New Jersey, was born, February 21st, 1827, in Schobarie county, New York. His father, Lemuel Cross, a carpenter and subsequently a country storekeeper, never succeeded in rising above very moderate financial circumstances. From the very outset of his career the lad had his own way to make in the world. Educated at the district school, he worked with such perseverance that he fitted himself to pass an examination for teacher, and having passed was duly licensed. During the next four or five years he was alternately a teacher and a pupil, attending the best available schools when he had laid by sufficient money, earned at teaching, to pay his way, and spending all of his leisure time in study. A considerable portion of this extra study was directed into legal channels, he having about this time determined upon law as a profession, a determination that was nullified by subsequent circumstances. His school education was finally finished by attendance during two or three terms at Canajoharie Academy. When twenty-five years old, he left New York and took up his abode at Franklin, Essex county, New Jersey, and here, abandoning his intention to enter at the bar, he began the study of medicine in the office of Dr S. Daley. Setting himself at the acquisition of his profession with the same earnestness of purpose that had marked his previous student life, in the fall of 1854 he entered the medical department of the University of Michigan, and in 1856 the Albany Medical College, receiving his degree in the spring of that year. In August of the same year he established himself in Newark, New Jersey, and in a very brief period built up for himself an extensive and highly profitable practice. Immediately after the battle of Williamsburg, in 1862, he joined the little company of surgeons who volunteered from New Jersey to go to the front and care for the wounded; and during his absence the United States Army Hospital at Newark was established. To this institution he was appointed, upon his return, Assistant Contract Surgeon, a position which he held until December,

CONGAR, HON. HORACE N., of Newark, Lawyer and ex-Secretary of State, was born in Newark, July 31st, 1817. His ancestors on the paternal side originally settled at Woodbridge, and from this place they migrated to different parts of New Jersey and New York. His mother was a granddaughter of Rev. David Bostwick, who was for many years pastor of the Wall Street Presbyterian Church in New York, and one of the leading divines in the State. The subject of this sketch, after being engaged in teaching school for a number of years, and reading law in the office of Cornelius Boice, Esq., at Plainfield, and Lewis C. Grover, Esq., at Newark, took his license as an attorney, and commenced the practice of his profession in his native place. He had always taken an interest in politics, and his strong anti-slavery convictions led him, as early as 1848, to join in the premature movement of that year for the overthrow of existing parties by the foundation of a Free-Soil party. He was a delegate, with Hon. George Opdyke and others, from New Jersey to the Buffalo convention, and sustained the nominations of Van Buren and Adams by speech and pen in the campaign which followed. For a period afterwards he acted with the Free-Soil wing of the Whig party, and in 1850 became the acknowledged editor of the Newark Daily Mercury. Under his guidance this journal became the leading political paper of the State. It was a troublous time for leadership, and it required a strong will and a determined hand to guide and shape public opinion and to control the warring elements of political strife, but success was measurably obtained and secured. During the period from 1850 to 1860 the Mercury was in the front of the anti-slavery fight, and its editor enjoyed the confidence and friendship of all the well-known leaders in the cause. In 1860 he was a delegate to the National Convention at Chicago, and advocated to the last, with unflagging energy, the selection of Mr. Seward for President. The choice of Mr. Lincoln, however, was entirely satisfactory, and received his earnest support, and the nominations were ratified by the American people. Upon the formation of the administration of Mr. Lincoln, Mr. Seward was appointed Secretary of State, and, without solicitation, he tendered to Mr. Congar the position of United States Consul at Hong Kong, then one of the leading appointments in the East. This position was accepted by him, and from 1861 to 1865 he was absent in China, where his services were duly appreciated and acknowledged by the government. In 1865, in consequence of impaired health caused by the climate of southern China, Mr. Congar was compelled to tender his resignation, which was accepted by the State Department. With this acceptance was transmitted his appointment, by the President, as Commissioner of Emigration of the United States under the then existing law. Returning to the United States through Europe he assumed, in the summer of 1865, the duties of his new office in Washington. Connected with the State Department he was twice commissioned as Acting Assistant Secretary of State, during the illness of the Hon. F. W. Seward, consequent upon the injuries received by him from the assassin, Payne. In the spring of 1866 Mr. Congar was appointed, by Governor Marcus L. Ward, Secretary of State of New Jersey, and he resigned his position in Washington and removed to Trenton. Here he discharged the duties of his office with care and fidelity until 1870, when he was tendered the position of Vice-President in that sterling old company, The Mutual Benefit Life Insurance Company, at Newark, New Jersey. He accepted the offer, resigning the office of Secretary of State, and removing to his old home. He continued in this position for three years, when he found his health badly affected by the confinement of office life, and was obliged to resign. He was subsequently tendered, by President Grant, the position of Consul to Prague, Bohemia, and he spent two years in Europe, returning in the fall of 1875, after resigning his consulship.

TRYKER, JAMES D., Banker, of Lambertville, was born, January 7th, 1800, in Bethlehem, Hunterdon county, New Jersey. Having received a good common-school education, he became at the age of sixteen a clerk in the general country store of Samuel Brittain, at Frenchtown, where he remained for three years, after which he went to Bucks county, Pennsylvania, and took charge of his brother's store there, remaining one year. In 1821 he returned to New Jersey, and went into his brother's store at Flemington, remaining there until 1823, when he engaged in business with Mr. Wilson Bray, at Everittstown. He removed to Frenchtown in 1825, and in the year following to Lambertville. There he united with his brother in establishing a general retail business, under the name of S. D. & J. D. Stryker, the two meanwhile becoming interested in the lumber trade, in favor of which they, in 1848, closed their mercantile business, launching exclusively and extensively into that traffic, purchasing large tracts of timber in the Lehigh

regions of Luzerne and Monroe counties in Pennsylvania, erecting mills near White Haven in that State, and selling lumber by wholesale at their mills and at Philadelphia. The business, managed with great judgment and energy, as it was, proved exceedingly profitable. When the Lambertville Bank was organized, in 1858, he was made a Director, his brother, S. D. Stryker, having been chosen president, to which office, on the death of his brother in 1863, he succeeded, and still holds it. He is also President of the Lambertville Gas Company, and a Director of the Waterpower Company of Lambertville. Experienced, discreet, faithful, and crowned with success, he has in a high degree, as he deserves, the confidence and esteem of his fellowcitizens. He has been for many years an elder of the Presbyterian Church at Lambertville.

ILL, JOHN, President of the National State Bank of Camden, was born July 9th, 1795. His greatgrandfather came to this country from or near London when quite a young man, and settled near the present limits of the village of Haddonfield, New Jersey; he was a relative of John Haddon, who became possessed of large landed estates in West Jersey. Elizabeth Haddon, a daughter of John Haddon, came to this country when about nineteen years of age, and settled on a part of her father's property. Some years later she married John Estaugh, a member of the religious Society of Friends, who was travelling in America in the service of the ministry. By the records it appears that John Gill, in connection with John Estaugh, assumed control of these large estates, which was so satisfactory to John Haddon that he made a gift of a tract of land to John Gill, in recognition of his valuable services. This tract embraced a portion of that now included in the village of Haddonfield. John Gill died in 1749, leaving a son, John, who took charge of his affairs, and who, after the decease of Elizabeth Estaugh, in 1762, acted as one of the executors of her estate, her husband, John Estaugh, having died in Tortola, one of the West India islands, while there on a religious visit about twenty years previous. John Gill resided most of his life on the property owned by his father, and appears to have been a very active business man, and participated to a considerable extent in the political affairs of the country. He married Amy, daughter of David Davis, of Salem county. He died in the year 1794, leaving six children—one son, John Gill, and five daughters. The son, John, married Annie Smith, and occupied the old homestead the greater part of his life. He did not take so active a part in public affairs as his father, except that his name appears quite frequently on the meeting records of the Society of Friends, of which he was a member. He died in 1837, leaving two children, one son and one daughter.

A noticeable feature in the genealogy of this family is, that for several generations there has been but one son, to whom was always given the name of John Gill, after the first comer. John Gill, the subject of the present sketch, was born on the property that had been in the family name for so many years, and at the age of twenty two married Sarah Hopkins, of Haddonfield. About ten years later he purchased a large farm in the neighborhood and removed to it. After the death of his father, in 1837, he went to the old Gill property in the village of Haddonfield, where he now resides. As the owner of considerable landed estate he has always shown a lively interest in agricultural affairs, and for many years took an active part in the matters of the neighborhood. He was elected a member of the House of Assembly of New Jersey in 1832, and to the Senate in 1849. On the 8th of November, 1842, he was elected President of the State Bank, at Camden, New Jersey, and occupied the position by continuous annual elections till the final conversion of the bank into a national institution on the 2d day of June, 1865. He has continued to be President of the National Bank as he had been of the State bank, and has accordingly held that position for the space of thirty-five years, and may well be considered a veteran bank president. It is in a large degree owing to the care, fidelity, oversight and close attention on the part of John Gill, that the institution he represents has become one of the foremost in the State. Shortly after he became its president, by reason of heavy losses in former years, its solvency was greatly questioned, and the value of its capital stock became much reduced, but the high social position held by Mr. Gill, and the devotion of much of his time and services, at once restored confidence in the bank, and since that time it has steadily improved. For the past few years, on account of the infirmities of age, he has not taken an active share in the labors of the institution he represents, but his interest increases with each succeeding year, and he now points with pride to the bank, as having braved the financial storms for sixty-five years.

MERY, WILLIAM P., Merchant, of Flemington, was born near Flemington, July 17th, 1811. After receiving an ordinary English education, at the age of fourteen years he was given a position in the store of Samuel D. Stryker, a prominent general dealer in Flemington. Here he remained during the ensuing seven years, developing marked mercantile ability and thoroughly mastering the intricacies of the business, besides acquiring the confidence and esteem of the community. Upon attaining his majority he at once established himself in business upon his own account, engaging in a general retail trade that rapidly expanded until it became the most flourishing in the county. His personal popularity had much to do with his success, but its essential

cause was the honorable character of his dealings. Although shrewd at a bargain, and always properly alive to his own interests, he was always eminently just, and his customers never suffered from relying upon his word. A member of the Presbyterian Church, of the Hunterdon County Bible Society, an earnest worker in Sunday-schools, and prominent in all undertakings for the advancement of Christianity, his business and private life were entirely in accord, and both were equally to his honor. In 1864, having amassed a considerable capital, he sold his business and engaged in an extensive lumber trade, his dealings covering northeastern New Jersey and the adjacent counties of Pennsylvania, the latter section being in charge of one of his sons. Another son is engaged in the wholesale dry-goods trade in New York, and a third established as a barrister at Trenton. Into this more extended sphere of operations he has carried the same qualities which assured his success in his Flemington store, and he is generally regarded as one of the leading men in his section of the State. It was largely owing to his energy and public spirit that the Flemington railroad was built, and he was equally prominent in the organization of the Hunterdon County National Bank. In both of these corporations he is at present a Director.

RAFFERTY, JOHN C., Senator from Hunterdon county from 1856 to 1859, was born at Woodbury, Gloucester county, New Jersey, December 29th, 1816. His father was William Rafferty, D. D., President of St. John's College, Annapolis, Maryland, a native of Ireland and a graduate of Glasgow University; his mother a Miss Chandler, of Orange county, New York. His father died in 1830, and his mother when he was an infant. After his father's death he attended school at Pittsfield, Massachusetts, for a year; in 1832 entered the sophomore class at Yale, and graduated in 1835. He commenced the study of the law in the office of A. D. Logan, Esq., in New York city, attended the law school at Cambridge from 1837 to 1838, Judge Story and Professor Greenleaf being the instructors, and was admitted to the bar in New York in 1838. In 1841 he married Laura E. Ogden, a daughter of O. W. Ogden, who was United States Marshal of New Jersey under Jefferson, Madison, Monroe and John Q. Adams. Upon his marriage he settled in New Germantown, New Jersey, and engaged in agriculture and milling. In 1855 he was chosen State Senator for Hunterdon county, and upon the expiration of his term as Senator, in 1859, was unanimously elected Secretary of the Senate, and in 1860 re-elected to the same position. In March of the same year he was appointed by the State Democratic Convention one of the senatorial delegates to the Democratic Convention at Charleston, Hon. William Wright, ex-Chancellor Williamson, and Hon.

James Wall being the other senatorial delegates. In 1862 he moved to Flemington, the county-seat, and resumed the practice of the law. In 1863 he was appointed by Governor Parker State Military Agent for New Jersey at Washington, and continued to fill said position until March, 1866, when he returned to Flemington. In 1867 he was appointed County Superintendent of Public Schools by the State Board of Education for a term of three years. Three years later he was again elected Secretary of the State Senate. He is now engaged in the practice of the law at Flemington.

ATES, HENRY J., Manufacturer, of Newark, was born in New York city, December 7th, 1819. He is the son of Thomas Yates, also a manufacturer, who in 1817 came to this country from Sheffield, England, his native place, and settled in the city of New York, where he married Hepseber Thacker, likewise of English birth. The son received his education at the public schools of New York, and at private schools in that city, attending one or the other until he was fifteen years of age, when he went to Newark and entered the service of William Rankin, a hatter, with whom he learned hatting. In 1843, having mastered his trade, he formed a partnership with Mr. Vail, under the name of Vail & Yates, the firm doing a large and flourishing business, which it continued till 1857, when the partnership was dissolved, and the present firm of Yates, Wharton & Co. was formed. Of this firm and its operations, Bishop, in his work on "American Manufactures," thus speaks: " In 1857 the firm of Vail & Yates was dissolved, and Mr. Yates made his present prosperous connection with Mr. John Wharton, well known as one of the most skilful of practical manufacturers at that time in the business. The energy and discrimination displayed by the old firm were not wanting in the new one. The careful regard to material and finish, with the special study of chemical effects, was rather increased than neglected, and tended not only to the profit of the establishment, but likewise to the advancement of the national industry which was thus represented. In 1861 the operations of the firm, by the growing demand for its specialties, justified a move of which the wisdom has been amply evidenced in the greatly enlarged sale of their productions. This was the establishment of a central depot in New York city, through which the market could be more directly and conveniently reached. The number of hands employed by this firm, which varies with the fluctuations of business, is never less than two hundred, and at times reaches five hundred. The machinery operated by them comprehends every improvement known, though no patents for specialties have recently issued to them, notwithstanding the fact that some of the most important innovations in this manufacture have originated in their factories." . Mr. Yates

was an old-line Whig, but has been an active member of the Republican party ever smee its formation. He is not, however, a hide-bound partisan, and consequently enjoys the respect of both parties alike. As a citizen, he is public-spirited, liberal and just. He has never sought office, but at the earnest solicitation of his political friends he has consented to serve the city of Newark, having been elected Alderman of the Fourth Ward, and subsequently, in January, 1876, Mayor of the city, an office which he has administered with fidelity as well as ability, and which he still fills. He is a Director in the Newark City Bank, the Fireman's Insurance Company of Newark, the Prudential Friendly Society, and the Newark Industrial Institute. Although not yet an old man, he has won, by his own energy and intelligence, all the more substantial prizes of life, crowned by the good opinion and confidence of his fellowmen. He was married in 1842 to Sarah A. Condit, of Bloomfield, New Jersey, daughter of Moses Condit, Esq.

HELPLEY, HON. EDWARD W., Lawyer and Chief Justice of the Supreme Court of New Jersey, was born in 1818, at Morristown, and was the only son of Dr. William A. Whelpley, a native of Massachusetts, who married a daughter of General John Dodd, of Bloomfield, father of the late distinguished Amzi Dodd, formerly prosecutor of the pleas of Morris county. Dr. Whelpley, in removing from Massachusetts, settled first in Bloomfield, but eventually made Morristown his residence. He was a gentleman of great refinement of character and manners, and of elegant learning; he died in 1828. Judge Whelpley was but ten years old at his father's death, and his mother attended carefully to the education of her son. He had a most precocious intellect, which he evidently inherited chiefly from his mother, whose family were noted for their superior mathematical attainments. He received his rudimentary education in his native place, and attended a school in which his grandfather had at one time been a teacher; and he completed his studies at Princeton College, from which institution he graduated with the class of 1834, being at that time but little over sixteen years of age. Being too young to enter upon the study of the law, he passed two years in teaching school at the Mendham Academy. He then entered the office of his uncle, Amzi Dodd, and commenced his legal studies, and remained with him until his death, in 1838, when he continued his reading under Amzi Armstrong, who proved an efficient preceptor. Having attained his majority, he was licensed as an attorney in May, 1839, and at once entered upon the practice of his profession in Newark, where he remained for two years. On the election of the late Hon. Jacob W. Miller to the United States Senate in 1841, he removed to Morristown and became his law partner, under the firm name of Miller & Whelpley; and while the senior member was almost constantly absent on official duties, the business was conducted solely by the junior partner. He soon achieved a wonderful success, and rose to eminence in his profession. He was elected in 1847 a member of the Legislature, and re-elected the following year; and during 1848 was chosen Speaker of the House, which position he filled with marked efficiency and ability. In 1858 he was appointed, by Governor Newell, a Judge of the Supreme Court, in place of Judge Ryerson, who had resigned in consequence of ill-health. In 1860 Governor Olden selected the then chief-justice, Hon. Henry W. Green, for the post of chancellor, and elevated Judge Whelpley to the vacant Chief-Justiceship; this office he retained until his death. Before he became a judge, he was an earnest politician and an adherent of the Whig party until its disintegration, and then became a decided Republican. He was a member of the National Convention which nominated General Fremont for the Presidency, and was actively instrumental in the nomination of William L. Dayton for the Vice-Presidency. He was a most able, thorough and pains-taking lawyer, thoroughly versed in the common law. His mind seemed to be so constituted as to enable him to grasp, as if by intuition, the most intricate legal questions, and with unerring precision and certainty discern the principles by which they were solved. His intellect was strong, vigorous, highly cultivated, and well trained. But while these characteristics were most marked, he had admirable moral traits. He was a man of gravity; he felt the responsibilities of life, and met them. He was no trifler. He had integrity, which, at the bar and on the bench, was beyond all suspicion. He expounded the law as he understood it, clearly, logically and firmly. This gave him his influence, and made him a safe counsellor and a good judge. In addition to his great professional learning he was also an ardent lover of general literature, a close student and a classical scholar; a genial companion and a true gentleman, whom every one respected. He was a member of the South Street Presbyterian Church of Morristown, having formally joined that congregation about a year preceding his death. He married, in 1841, a daughter of Dr. Absalom Woodruff, of Mendham, and left a family of three daughters and one son. He died at Morristown, February 21st, 1864.

————◆————

AYARD, SAMUEL JOHN, Lawyer and Littérateur, of Camden, was born at New Rochelle, Westchester county, New York, September 26th, 1801. His ancestors were of Huguenot descent (both paternal and maternal), having left France for America about the middle of the seventeenth century. His grandfather, John Bayard, and his father, Samuel Bayard, were born at Bohemia Manor, in the State of Delaware. John Bayard, his grandfather, was a member from Pennsylvania of the Continental Congress, Colonel of the 1st Regiment of Cavalry of Philadelphia, and served in the army through the revolutionary war, and was afterwards Speaker of the Legislature of Pennsylvania under her first constitution. The father of Samuel J. was a lawyer, several years in practice in Philadelphia. After the negotiation of Jay's treaty with Great Britain in 1794, he was appointed by General Washington, Agent of the United States for the prosecution of American claims provided for by that treaty. On his return to the United States he resided for a few years with his father-in-law, Lewis Pintard, at New Rochelle, where Samuel J. was born. In 1806 Mr. Bayard (the father) removed to Princeton, New Jersey. Samuel J. graduated at Princeton College in 1820. He studied law with Richard Stockton and was admitted to the bar in 1823. In 1826, at the solicitation of his cousin, Commodore R. F. Stockton, he became editor of the *Princeton Patriot*, a newspaper which Commodore Stockton got up for political purposes. The *Patriot* soon became a popular and leading paper in New Jersey. Mr. Bayard in his paper urged the construction of the Delaware & Raritan Canal and a railroad across the State, four years before charters for those works were granted. He also advocated a change of the constitution of New Jersey, and got up a large State convention, which urged the Legislature to authorize the election of delegates to a State convention to form a new constitution. But in the fall of 1827 he left the State for the West, and no change of the constitution took place until 1844. His discussion of the subject in 1826, however, created a popular demand for a new constitution, and furnished the arguments which led to the adoption of the present excellent constitution of New Jersey. Going to Ohio in 1827, he was admitted to practise at the bar of that State. But his taste for politics excited by his experience in New Jersey soon interrupted his professional pursuits. Having attended a Democratic State Convention at Columbus, he drew the resolutions and address adopted by the convention, and thus made known his capacity for producing political effect. He was soon after invited to become the editor of a daily paper in Cincinnati, the only daily Democratic organ in the State. He conducted this paper for a year, and acquired in that time reputation and influence throughout the State. He relinquished in 1833 all the advantages of that position to engage in a real estate purchase at Seneca Falls, Seneca county, New York. At this time he was appointed, by President Jackson, and confirmed by the Senate, Secretary of the commission for running the boundary line between Mexico and the United States, but did not accept the appointment. In the same year that he removed to New York, Mr. Bayard married Jane A. Dashiell, the daughter of the Rev. George Dashiell, then living near Louisville, Kentucky, though originally a distinguished clergyman of the Episcopal Church of Maryland. In 1836 Mr. Bayard was appointed, by Governor Marcy, and confirmed by the Senate of New York, a Judge of the Court of Common

Pleas for Se.... ....ing a ....ncellor in New York he was the P.....g .... c ....urt. He resigned this ....ice after a .... In 1840 he took an active part in ..... of .... for President. He wrote a popular ....,.... several campaign songs for Mr Greeley's .... In 1849, at the instance of his New Jersey .... he returned to that State and conducted several .... in the interest of the Canal and Railroad Companies, against which the anti-monopolists were waging a fierce war. He became editor of the *New York State* in 1850, and distinguished himself in advocating the conspicuous measures of that year. George Wilkes, the editor of the *Police Gazette*, which had the largest ex-ent ... of any paper in New York, is known to have .... that Mr. Bayard's articles on the compromise were ..... copied in other papers than those of all the rest of the New York city papers. In 1851 he again resumed his residence in New York, and wrote for almost every Democratic paper in the State, sending his articles by mail. The Democratic party succeeded in carrying the State that year for the first time in ten years. In 1854 Mr. Bayard was appointed Secretary of the Camden & Amboy Railroad Company, which position he held until the Pennsylvania Railroad Company leased the works of the United Railroad and Canal Companies. He received in 1864 the Democratic nomination for Congress in the First Congressional District of New Jersey, and met with the unanimous support of his party. In 1872 he was President of the straight-out Democratic Convention at Baltimore, which inaugurated the Democratic movement against Mr. Greeley's nomination. He was a prominent member of the Louisville Straight-out Convention, which nominated Charles O'Conor for President, and drew the resolutions adopted by the convention. Mr. Bayard in 1856 published a " Life of Commodore Stockton," which Mayor Conrad (a very competent critic) pronounced the best biography in the English language, excepting only Southey's " Life of Nelson." His only son was General George D. Bayard, who was killed, December 15th, 1862, in the battle of Fredericksburg. In 1873 Mr. Bayard published a life of his son, of which the late William B. Read, literary editor of the *New York World*, in an extended review in that paper, writes as follows : " Without meaning in any way to be extravagant, we express the candid judgment that this little duodecimo of but 300 pages ought to be in the hand of every American military student and of every American soldier. It is a perfect chrysolite— this short life of twenty-seven years. There is no flaw. The literary execution of the book is eminently graceful— the aged father writing about his dead boy—and nothing of the cant which makes such a life as Captain Vickars' so offensive. There is praise implied in a clear statement of personal experiences, but none of that doting eulogy which a parent might be pardoned for indulging in. There is a liberal use of familiar correspondence, but a strict suppression of those details with which surviving relatives are so

30

apt to drug their readers. We know no better specimen of judicious and effective writing." At the present time (1877) Mr. Bayard is a resident of the city of Camden.

VOORHEES, FREDERICK, Counsellor-at-Law, of Mount Holly, was born on a farm about one mile west of Blawenburgh, Somerset county, New Jersey. His parents were Peter Voorhees and Jane (Schenck) Voorhees, the latter being a daughter of Captain John Schenck. He studied the earlier branches of education at a common school near Stoutsburgh, about one mile west of his home. Preferring to adopt a learned profession, he at a comparatively early age began the study of Latin, Rev. T. De Witt Talmadge, the popular pastor of Brooklyn, New York, being a fellow-pupil. Their instructor was Mr. Talmadge's brother, Rev. James K. Talmadge, then pastor of the Dutch Reformed Church at Blawenburgh, and they continued their studies under his direction from November, 1847, until he resigned his pastoral charge about one year thereafter. Frederick Voorhees then returned home and for a while took partial charge in the management of his father's farm. Returning to his classical studies, he placed himself under the tuition of Rev. Theodore B. Romeyn, who succeeded Mr. Talmadge in the pastorate of the Dutch Reformed Church at Blawenburgh. At this time he added the study of Greek to that of Latin. He completed his preparation for college under the instruction of Rev. J. B. Davis, then of Titusville, New Jersey, in the summer and fall of 1852, and entered the Freshman class of Princeton College at the commencement of its second term, in February, 1853. Soon after entering college he joined the Cliosophic Society, one of the two literary institutions connected with the college. He graduated from the college in June, 1856, with an average grade on all studies of ninety-seven and nine-tenths, standing fifth with one other in a graduating class of seventy-nine students. In mathematics he ranked first, and was accorded the honor of the Mathematical Oration at the College Commencement. Determining to follow the legal profession, he began the study of law with his brother, Peter L. Voorhees, at Camden, in June 1856. Three years subsequently, at the June term of the Supreme Court of the State of New Jersey, 1859, he was licensed as an attorney-at-law and solicitor in chancery. In November of that year he removed to Mount Holly, and took charge of the law practice of Hon. John C. Ten Eyck, who was then about leaving for Washington to take his seat as United States Senator. This trust he continued to discharge until the expiration of Mr. Ten Eyck's term, in 1865, when he surrendered it to him, and then opened an office for himself in the same town. His great abilities as a lawyer and counsellor had by this time become generally recognized, and he found himself at once in

Pleas for Seneca county. Being a counsellor in New York he was the Presiding Judge of the Court. He resigned this office after a few years' service. In 1840 he took an active part in favor of General Harrison for President. He wrote a popular biography of him, and several campaign songs for Mr. Greeley's *Log-Cabin* paper. In 1849, at the instance of his New Jersey friends, he returned to that State and conducted several newspapers in the interest of the Canal and Railroad Companies, against which the anti-monopolists were waging a fierce war. He became editor of the *New York Globe* in 1850, and distinguished himself in advocating the compromise measures of that year. George Wilkes, then editor of the *Police Gazette*, which had the largest exchange list of any paper in New York, is known to have said that Mr. Bayard's articles on the compromise were more copied in other papers than those of all the rest of the New York city papers. In 1851 he again resumed his residence in New Jersey, and wrote for almost every Democratic paper in the State, sending his articles by mail. The Democratic party succeeded in carrying the State that year for the first time in ten years. In 1854 Mr. Bayard was appointed Secretary of the Camden & Amboy Railroad Company, which position he held until the Pennsylvania Railroad Company leased the works of the United Railroad and Canal Companies. He received in 1864 the Democratic nomination for Congress in the First Congressional District of New Jersey, and met with the unanimous support of his party. In 1872 he was President of the straight-out Democratic Convention at Baltimore, which inaugurated the Democratic movement against Mr. Greeley's nomination. He was a prominent member of the Louisville Straight-out Convention, which nominated Charles O'Conor for President, and drew the resolutions adopted by the convention. Mr. Bayard in 1856 published a "Life of Commodore Stockton," which Mayor Conrad (a very competent critic) pronounced the best biography in the English language, excepting only Southey's "Life of Nelson." His only son was General George D. Bayard, who was killed, December 15th, 1862, in the battle of Fredericksburg. In 1873 Mr. Bayard published a life of his son, of which the late William B. Read, literary editor of the *New York World*, in an extended review in that paper, writes as follows: "Without meaning in any way to be extravagant, we express the candid judgment that this little duodecimo of but 300 pages ought to be in the hand of every American military student and of every American soldier. It is a perfect chrysolite—this short life of twenty-seven years. There is no flaw. The literary execution of the book is eminently graceful—the aged father writing about his dead boy—and nothing of the cant which makes such a life as 'Captain Vickars' so offensive. There is praise implied in a clear statement of personal experiences, but none of that doting eulogy which a parent might be pardoned for indulging in. There is a liberal use of familiar correspondence, but a strict suppression of those details with which surviving relatives are so

30

apt to drug their readers. We know no better specimen of judicious and effective writing." At the present time (1877) Mr. Bayard is a resident of the city of Camden.

VOORHEES, FREDERICK, Counsellor-at-Law, of Mount Holly, was born on a farm about one mile west of Blawenburgh, Somerset county, New Jersey. His parents were Peter Voorhees and Jane (Schenck) Voorhees, the latter being a daughter of Captain John Schenck. He studied the earlier branches of education at a common school near Stoutsburgh, about one mile west of his home. Preferring to adopt a learned profession, he at a comparatively early age began the study of Latin, Rev. T. De Witt Talmadge, the popular pastor of Brooklyn, New York, being a fellow-pupil. Their instructor was Mr. Talmadge's brother, Rev. James R. Talmadge, then pastor of the Dutch Reformed Church at Blawenburgh, and they continued their studies under his direction from November, 1847, until he resigned his pastoral charge about one year thereafter. Frederick Voorhees then returned home and for a while took partial charge in the management of his father's farm. Returning to his classical studies, he placed himself under the tuition of Rev. Theodore B. Romeyn, who succeeded Mr. Talmadge in the pastorate of the Dutch Reformed Church at Blawenburgh. At this time he added the study of Greek to that of Latin. He completed his preparation for college under the instruction of Rev. J. B. Davis, then of Titusville, New Jersey, in the summer and fall of 1852, and entered the Freshman class of Princeton College at the commencement of its second term, in February, 1853. Soon after entering college he joined the Cliosophic Society, one of the two literary institutions connected with the college. He graduated from the college in June, 1856, with an average grade on all studies of ninety-seven and nine-tenths, standing fifth with one other in a graduating class of seventy-nine students. In mathematics he ranked first, and was accorded the honor of the Mathematical Oration at the College Commencement. Determining to follow the legal profession, he began the study of law with his brother, Peter L. Voorhees, at Camden, in June, 1856. Three years subsequently, at the June term of the Supreme Court of the State of New Jersey, 1859, he was licensed as an attorney-at-law and solicitor in chancery. In November of that year he removed to Mount Holly, and took charge of the law practice of Hon. John C. Ten Eyck, who was then about leaving for Washington to take his seat as United States Senator. This trust he continued to discharge until the expiration of Mr. Ten Eyck's term, in 1865, when he surrendered it to him, and then opened an office for himself in the same town. His great abilities as a lawyer and counsellor had by this time become generally recognized, and he found himself at once in the enjoyment of an extensive and valuable practice, which during subsequent years he has enlarged and consolidated until its proportions and character give him rank as the leader of the bar in his section of the State. He is a man of great tenacity of purpose, and when once a client has placed a cause in his hands, he may rest assured that so long as any legal resource remains it will never be given up. Many of his successes are due to this persevering pursuit of the means provided by the law for the protection of rights and property. To this marked characteristic he unites a profound knowledge of the principles and traditions of law, and being a forcible and prudent speaker, he commands the respectful attention of all the courts in which he practises and of his professional brethren. He has never taken any active part in politics, and is still unmarried.

———◆———

EWELL, HON. WILLIAM J., Railroad Manager and Legislator, of Camden, was born in Ireland in 1835. Coming to this country at a comparatively early age, he has become thoroughly identified with its interests. On the outbreak of the war of the rebellion he felt impelled to give his services to the national cause, and was mustered into the army as Captain of the 5th New Jersey Regiment, August 28th, 1861. It became at once manifest that he was actuated by true military spirit. He showed a comprehension of the necessities of the service and promptly adapted himself to its requirements, proving himself a disciplinarian of a high order and an invaluable support to his superior officers. He participated in all the engagements in which his regiment took part down to the battle of Spottsylvania, in May, 1864, always exhibiting conspicuous courage, and the fine soldierly qualities of ready apprehension and fertile resource in emergencies. In the battle of Chancellorsville, General Gershom Mott being wounded, Sewell, by this time Colonel of the 5th, succeeded to the command of the brigade, and, leading it forward at a critical moment, achieved one of the most brilliant successes of the war, capturing eight colors from the enemy and retaking the regimental standard of a New York regiment. His bearing throughout this most severe engagement was exemplary, and at once placed him among the ablest and bravest soldiers of the republic. At Gettysburg he won fresh laurels. Both at Chancellorsville and Gettysburg he was wounded; in the latter battle severely, while commanding the skirmish line in front of the 3d Corps, during the attack of Longstreet in the second day's engagement. His commission as Lieutenant-Colonel of the 5th Regiment was dated July 7th, 1862, and that as Colonel on October 21st following, both promotions being made on the recommendation of Colonel Starr, himself a gallant and efficient soldier. On September 30th, 1864, Colonel Sewell, who had been compelled by sickness, arising from long exposure, to temporarily leave

the service in July, was made Colonel of the 38th Regiment, then about organizing, and with it returned to the field, where he remained until the summer of 1865. He was made Brevet Brigadier-General of volunteers April 9th, 1866, " for gallant and meritorious conduct in the battle of Chancellorsville," and no honor was ever more worthily or justly bestowed. At the close of the war he was brevetted Major-General for meritorious services. On the election of Hon. Joel Parker as governor of the State, in 1872, General Sewell was appointed a member of his personal staff, a position which he held with his army rank in accordance with a special act of the Legislature. In the same year he was elected to the State Senate from Camden, polling 5,022 votes out of a total of 7,399, and considerably increasing the previous Republican majority. He took a conspicuous position in the Senate ; in the session of 1874 he was Chairman of the Committees on Soldiers' Children's Home, Militia, Riparian Rights, and Centennial. As chairman of the last-named committee he was one of the first to suggest that the State and national governments be asked for direct appropriations to the Centennial Exposition, and the first to give practical force to the suggestion by procuring from the New Jersey Legislature a subscription of $100,000 to the stock of the enterprise. In this measure he was ably-supported by Governor Parker and Thomas H. Dudley, Esq. During the same session he was also a member of the Committees on Municipal Corporations, and Revision of the Laws. Re-elected in 1875, he served during the session of 1876 in the distinguished position of President of the Senate. A staunch Republican and a man of high principle, he has made for himself an enviable political record.

———◆———

ARPENTER, THOMAS PRESTON, Lawyer and Judge of the Supreme Court of New Jersey, late of Camden, was born on April 19th, 1804, at Glassboro', Gloucester county, New Jersey, where his father, Edward Carpenter, was then living and operating the glass-works now owned by the Whitneys. He was a descendant of Samuel Carpenter and Thomas Lloyd, both well-known men in the early days of Pennsylvania. His father dying when he was quite young, Mr. Carpenter spent his early life with his grandfather, at Carpenter's Landing (now Mantua). After receiving a liberal education he studied law with Judge White, of Woodbury, and was admitted as an attorney in September, 1830. On October 26th, 1838, he was appointed Prosecutor of the Pleas of Gloucester county, and took a prominent part in several very important trials, especially the one known as the "Mercer trial" (March, 1843). On February 5th, 1845, he was appointed, by Governor Stratton, one of the Associate Judges of the Supreme Court of the State ; his circuit comprising Burlington, Camden and Gloucester counties. On his retirement (after seven years) from the judgeship he devoted himself to the practice of his profession, principally as a counsellor, and was eminently successful. At the breaking out of the rebellion he joined the Union League of Philadelphia, and gave his entire sympathies to the Union cause. In 1865 he was active in promoting the success of the Sanitary Fair, occupying as he did the position of President of the New Jersey Auxiliary. He was an earnest Christian, and in the church (Protestant Episcopal) he always held an honored position, being for many years Vestryman, Warden and Deputy to the Diocesan and General Conventions. He was not only an able lawyer, but amidst the cares of an active practice he was thoroughly versed in classical and general literature. He died at his home in Camden, New Jersey, on March 20th, 1876. He was greatly respected throughout the State of New Jersey, of which he was at the time of his death one of the best-known citizens. As a Judge of the Supreme Court he was held in high esteem by his associates, and by the bar of the State, for his ability, learning, and for the uniform good judgment which he brought to the consideration of cases. In the counties where he presided at circuits, and which he visited during his term of office at regular periods, his genial manners and kindly intercourse with the people made him very popular. Judge Carpenter was interested and active at home in all schemes which affected the prosperity and welfare of his town. In the church, at the bar, and in society, he was, during his life, one of the most prominent men of his native State.

 KILLMAN, CHARLES A., Lawyer, of Lambertville, was born, December 16th, 1827, in Hopewell township, Mercer county, New Jersey. One of his paternal ancestors, Captain Skillman, came to this country from England in 1664, and assisted in capturing New York from the Dutch, settling afterwards on Long Island, whence a descendant of the fourth degree, the great-grandfather of the subject of this sketch, removed to the Millstone valley in New Jersey, where he engaged in agricultural pursuits and in the vicinity of which the family has since resided. Charles entered the sophomore class of Princeton in 1845, graduating in 1848, when he immediately began the study of the law under William Halstead, of Trenton. He was admitted to the bar in 1851. In 1852 he removed to Lambertville, in which place he has since lived. His practice is extensive and profitable. In 1858 he was appointed by Governor Newell, Prosecutor of the Pleas for Hunterdon county, a position which he held for four years, performing its duties with such vigor and fidelity as to win general acceptance. He is solicitor for the Belvidere Delaware Division of the Pennsylvania Railroad, Vice-President of the Lambertville National Bank, as also its attorney, and a Director of the Lambertville Gas Company. He enjoys a high reputation, not only as a lawyer and an officer, but as a man and a citizen.

 EWLIN, JOHN W., Journalist, of Millville, New Jersey, son of John and Mary A. (Williams) Newlin, was born in Philadelphia, August 19th, 1833. Educated in the Philadelphia public schools, and in Anthony Bolmar's academy, Westchester, he entered the office of the Westchester *Register and Examiner*, subsequently known as *The Village Record*, as an apprentice to the trade of printing. He soon rose to be foreman of the paper, and after holding this position for some time, accepted an advantageous offer to enter the office of the *Chester County Times*, since styled the *Chester County Republican*. Here he remained for upwards of seven years. Upon the breaking out of war, he entered the United States volunteer army as Sergeant-Major of Battery B, Pennsylvania Artillery, being engaged in active service for some seventeen months, mainly in the Shenandoah valley. Resigning from the army, he established (in 1864) the Millville *Republican*, an enterprising, liberal journal, that he has since its foundation conducted with marked ability. An earnest Republican himself, his paper has been constant in maintaining the doctrines of that party, and has played an important part in securing the success of its candidates in West Jersey. He has for a number of years been prominent in educational matters; is now President of the Millville Board of Education, a position that he has acceptably filled for the past eight years, and for three years has served as Superintendent of the Board of Instruction. From 1865 to 1870, when the district was consolidated, he was Assistant Assessor of Internal Revenue, and during the sessions of 1871-72-73-74 was Assistant Secretary of the State Senate.

HITEHEAD, WILLIAM A., of Newark, is a gentleman widely known in New Jersey as an historian and antiquarian. He was the originator of the New Jersey Historical Society, of which he has been from the first and is still the Corresponding Secretary, and his pen has been most prolific in contributions to its annals. Principal among these are his "History of New Jersey Under the Proprietors," and "Contributions to the Early History of Perth Amboy," etc., each being a volume of several hundred pages, replete with evidence of the industry, research and ability of their author. Besides these interesting and useful labors, he has for many years kept a daily record of the weather, including thermometrical and barometrical observations, monthly statements of which have been published in the Newark *Daily Advertiser*. On this subject, as well as upon the history of the

State, Mr. Whitehead is an established authority. These employments, which have given him large fame, are the recreations of a life devoted to close and daily labor. At sixteen he left school and entered a bank, of which his father was cashier. In early manhood he joined an elder brother then engaged in mercantile pursuits at Key West. He was appointed collector and lived there several years, employing his spare time in close study and self-development. At his father's death he returned to the North, and entered into business in Wall street, which he relinquished and became successively Treasurer of the Haarlem Railroad; Secretary of the New Jersey Railroad, and Treasurer of the American Trust Company, at Newark, a position he still fills. Mr. Whitehead is the father of the Newark Library, as well as of the New Jersey Historical Society. He has accepted no public office except that of a member of the Board of Public Education, in which he was for years very efficient. It is believed he was the first to suggest a city hospital, and he has ever been foremost in local benevolence. He is now about sixty-six years old, and full of health and energy. He was born in Newark, within a few steps of where he resides. His wife is a daughter of James Parker, late of Perth Amboy. He has had several children, of whom three grew up. One son is a distinguished Episcopal clergyman, Rev. Cortlandt Whitehead, of Bethlehem, Pennsylvania.

OYNTON, CASSIMER W., Manufacturer, of Woodbridge, son of Gorham L. and Louisa (Bassford) Boynton—his father being the proprietor of large tracts of timber land, an extensive builder and owner of saw-mills, and for a number of years surveyor-general of the lumber interests of the State—was born in Bangor, Maine, February 14th, 1836. Educated at the Bangor public schools, at the Lawrence Scientific school, Cambridge, and at the Rensselaer Polytechnic Institute, Troy, New York, remaining at the latter for three years, he received a thorough training as a civil engineer; indeed, during the last two years of his course at Troy, he was Assistant Teacher of Mechanical Engineering. Shortly after his graduation, in 1857, he was appointed Assistant Engineer and placed in charge of the western end of Bergen Tunnel, remaining upon that important work until its completion. He was then engaged to finish the construction of the San Francisco Water Works, and under this appointment he built two large reservoirs and put up the necessary pumps, one of which is one of the highest single lifts—three hundred and ten feet through a half mile of pipe—in the country. In connection with the water works, he also built an aqueduct three thousand feet long, through solid rock, beneath the fort on Black Point. This was completed in 1862, and for two years thereafter he was engaged as a mining engineer in Sonora and Mexico. From 1864 to 1866 he was

again professionally engaged in San Francisco. In the early part of the latter year he returned to the Atlantic coast, and, after some months passed in examining mill sites, finally selected property at Woodbridge, and, in partnership with Mr. J. P. Davis, there erected extensive works for the manufacture of brick drain-pipe and tile. The works as at present existing, having been several times added to during the eleven years that they have been in operation, comprehend two down-draft kilns (sixteen and a half feet in diameter by eleven feet high, and fourteen and a half feet in diameter by ten feet high) with all adequate appliances; employ a large force of men, and have an out-put during the height of the busy season of about one thousand dollars' worth of finished pipe, etc., per day. The location is peculiarly eligible, the property having a frontage of eleven hundred feet upon Woodbridge creek, and another of six hundred and fifty feet upon Staten Island Sound; the latter permitting the erection of wharves at which vessels of the largest draught can safely lie even at the neap tides. The market for the product of the works is mainly found in the Eastern States, but a considerable business is also done in supplying other portions of the country; in New York there is a very general demand for the Woodbridge hollow bricks (used for roofing fire-proof buildings), and the larger portion of the drain-pipe used in Prospect Park, Brooklyn, and in the capitol grounds at Washington, came from the Woodbridge factory. Beside the hollow bricks above referred to, the firm makes a specialty of a small pipe for under-draining, so constructed, with a loose-fitting collar, as to permit the entry of water at the joints, but effectually barring the entry of sand, a very obvious improvement upon the common variety. Mr. Boynton has filled various positions of trust and honor in Woodbridge, and, having done so much to stimulate its business activity, is naturally regarded as one of the most useful inhabitants of the town. He was married, December 20th, 1866, to Eunice A. Harriman, of Georgetown, Massachusetts.

UMONT, JOHN F., Lawyer, was born, November 11th, 1824, near New Germantown, New Jersey. His family is of Huguenot extraction, his ancestors having left France shortly after the massacre of St. Bartholomew, though it was not until as late as 1710 that his ancestors came to this country, settling on their arrival here in Somerset county, New Jersey. His grandfather, William Dumont, served in the revolutionary army, taking part in the battle of Monmouth, and becoming after the war one of the judges of Hunterdon county. His maternal grandfather, John Finley, of Amwell township, Hunterdon county, New Jersey, was also a revolutionary officer, a commissary. His father, John W. Dumont, was a farmer in the vicinity of New Germantown, Hunterdon county, from which he removed to Warren

county, and thence to the State of Illinois. The son spent the first eighteen years of his life on a farm, attending meanwhile, as occasion offered, the common school of the neighborhood, in which he acquired his early education, and afterward taught school himself, spending the time not thus occupied in study and the education of himself as a self-made man. In 1845 he entered the law office of S. B. Ransom, of Somerville, New Jersey, remaining there till he was admitted to the bar in 1849. He practised at New Germantown until 1852, when, having been licensed as counsellor and appointed Prosecutor of the Pleas for Hunterdon county, he removed to Flemington, where he remained four years, after which he resigned his office as Prosecutor, and in the spring of 1856 removed to Phillipsburg, Warren county, New Jersey, at which he still resides. His practice is large and valuable. He stands, by common consent, at the head of the Phillipsburg bar. He is a lawyer such as clients love; tenacious of their rights, zealous for their interests, and sure to contest with unflinching energy and skill every point in a case. In politics, he is a Democrat; was a supporter of the war for the Union. He has never suffered political ambition to step between him and his profession, having never sought a political office. He was married in 1853 to Anna E. Cline, daughter of the Rev. David Cline, a Lutheran minister, formerly of West Camp, Ulster county, New York, now of Clarksville, New Jersey.

———◦◦———

REGANOWAN, AMBROSE, A.M., M.D., of South Amboy, Middlesex county, New Jersey, was born in Camborne, county of Cornwall, England, February 14th, 1836. His parents are John and Ann Treganowan, of the same county; his mother's maiden name was Ann Clymo; she is still living. He is the youngest of four children, all sons, and, besides this immediate family and their relatives, there is not another family of Treganowans, and their pedigree is lost, except what is related in some curious and romantic traditions. His father died before his recollection. The family are largely identified with the mining interests of that county, some of its copper ore mines being the most famous in the world. The doctor's early education was received at a select academy for boys in the town where he resided, conducted by one Mr. William Bellows, a Quaker, and a former resident of New York city. At the early age of fourteen years he commenced his preparation for the medical profession, by being indentured for seven years to the celebrated surgeon, Alfred Prideaux, Esq., of Siskeard, about forty miles from his native town, in the same county. After fulfilling about three years of his articles of engagement, however, he grew restive, and evinced a determination to go to America. His family, seeing his determination, succeed in cancelling his articles of indenture, and equipped him with an abundant outfit and the necessary means. He

left the shores of old England in the year 1853, from the port of Penzance, in the ship "Marquis of Chandos," Captain Colenzo commanding (an old friend of the family), with a faithful mother's prayer to heaven for the protection of her "wayward child." It was not dreamed but that he would return again to England in the same ship, after his curiosity had been satisfied and the reconciling influences of a year's absence from home and its comforts had mollified his roving nature. But he left the good old captain and the ship on her arrival at New York, and after a few days entered the drug store of Eugene Dupy, corner of Houston street and Broadway, where he performed the duties of translator in the English prescription department. In 1854 he went to Philadelphia, and resumed his regular medical studies, under the preceptorship of Professor James Bryan, Professor of Surgery in the Philadelphia College of Medicine, in Fifth street, below Walnut. After being in Philadelphia but a short time he received letters of introduction from England to Professor Dunglison, Professor of Therapeutics in the Practice of Medicine in Jefferson Medical College, who had known the young student's family in England, and who took a deep and earnest interest in his behalf, giving him much private instruction and wise counsel, although he was a candidate for the degree of Doctor of Medicine in another college. During the years of his study in Philadelphia he supported himself, purchased his college tickets and bore other expenses attending his studies, by connecting himself with the press as reporter, but especially as a stenographic reporter, in which he then excelled. Dr. Treganowan graduated from the Philadelphia College of Medicine in the year 1857 with honor and high distinction, and commenced his professional career at Beverly, New Jersey, meeting with proud success, but was soon compelled to abandon that field on account of failing health, his medical friends and advisers recommending him to some location on the seaboard. He removed to South Amboy in the year 1860, where he has been actively engaged ever since, commanding a large and responsible practice. His love for his chosen profession is very strong, founded on qualifications and tastes which characterize him as the "natural physician." The doctor's biography may be said to have but just commenced. As a general practitioner, he is sound in diagnosis and quick in application; as an obstetrician, he has few superiors; as a surgeon, he is bold and fearless, but few men in general practice having a larger experience. The doctor has some peculiarities which make him decided enemies, but his hosts of friends are more than is necessary to neutralize this bitter ingredient in the mixture of his daily life and duties. A more considerate man of his brother physicians' feelings and honor cannot be found; his honor, generosity and forgiving nature cannot be excelled. In 1862 he entered the army as Surgeon of the 14th Regiment New Jersey Volunteers, and remained in the service about two years. Much of the time he was on detached duty in charge of field hospitals in the Army of the Potomac, doing all that a brave man and surgeon could do. In 1864 his health failed him, and his resignation from the service became imperative. After a few weeks rest at home, he again began the usual duties of his profession at Amboy. For a number of years previous to the lease of the old Camden & Amboy Railroad Dr. Treganowan was a salaried surgeon in their employ, which position he still holds in the service of the Pennsylvania Central Railroad Company. He is Examining Surgeon for most of the important life insurance companies for his neighborhood. He is fondly attached to the medical society of the county, and has, at various times, held all the offices appertaining to that society; has been repeatedly a delegate from the State Medical Society of New Jersey to other State medical societies; was appointed delegate to the American Medical Convention, held in San Francisco in 1869, and also to the International Congress, held in Philadelphia, June, 1876; is member of the New Jersey Microscopical Society, etc., etc. Notwithstanding the numerous and arduous duties of his profession as a country practitioner, he devotes much time to journalistic and other literary pursuits, both for home and foreign publication. The true extent of the doctor's labors in this department of mental culture is something far beyond the idea of his most intimate friends, and little do they and the community at large think, whilst enjoying some literary treat, that it is from the doctor's pen, as he has always refused to identify himself with his writings. Some of his poetic writings are of the highest order of thought and expression. He is a P. M. member of the ancient order of Freemasons, and has written some most beautiful Masonic odes. He is also associate editor of the *South Amboy Argus*. Dr. Treganowan was married in 1855 to Constance Gordon, daughter of the late Judge Thomas F. Gordon, historian and legal writer, so well known to the people and the legal profession of the United States, and a granddaughter of Count Reseau, once an eminent physician of Philadelphia, who fled to America, somewhere about the year 1782, during the revolution in France. The doctor is a member of the Episcopal Church; passionately fond of music, himself being a good musician.

URNET, HON. JACOB, LL. D., was the son of Dr. William Burnet the elder, of Newark, New Jersey, and the grandson of Dr. Ichabod Burnet, a native of Scotland, who was educated at Edinburgh, removed to America soon after his education was finished, and settled at Elizabethtown, New Jersey, where he practised his profession with great success as a physician and surgeon until his death, in 1773, at the advanced age of eighty. Dr. William Burnet was born in 1730, educated at Nassau Hall during the Presidency of the Rev. Aaron Burr, and graduated in 1749, before that institution was removed to Princeton. He studied medicine under Dr. Staats, of New York, and practised it with success until the difficulties with the mother country became alarmingly serious, when he took an active and leading part in resisting the encroachments of the British government. He was a member of the Newark Committee of Safety, composed of himself, Judge J. Hedden, and Major S. Hays, until, in 1776, he was elected a member of the Continental Congress. He resigned that position to accept an appointment as Surgeon-General of the Eastern Division of the American army, which position he filled with distinction until the close of the war. Dr. Burnet died in 1791, in the sixty-first year of his age. Jacob Burnet, his sixth son, was born in Newark, New Jersey, February 22d, 1770; was educated at Nassau Hall, Princeton, under the Presidency of Dr. Witherspoon, and graduated with honor in September, 1791. He remained there a year as a resident graduate, and then entered the office of Judge Boudinot, of Newark, as a student of law, and under that distinguished lawyer laid the foundation for his future attainments in his profession. He was admitted to the bar by the Supreme Court of the State in the spring of 1796, and proceeded at once to Cincinnati, in the neighborhood of which his father had made considerable investments. At that time Cincinnati was a small village of log cabins, including about fifteen rough, unfinished frame houses with stone chimneys. There was not a brick house in it, and only about 150 inhabitants, and the entire white population of the Northwestern Territory was estimated at about 15,000 souls. In 1798 it was ascertained that the Territory contained 5,000 white male inhabitants, and was entitled to enter upon the second grade of Territorial Government provided for under the ordinance of 1787. This provided for a General Assembly, consisting of representatives elected by the citizens of the Territory, and a Legislative Council of five persons, nominated by the lower House and appointed by the President by and with the advice and consent of the United States Senate. Judge Burnet was appointed by President John Adams a member of the first Legislative Council, together with James Findlay, Henry Vanderburgh, Robert Oliver and David Vance. He remained a member of this body until the organization of the State government in 1802–3. The practice of his profession, which obliged him to travel over the whole settled portion of the Territory as far as Detroit, in Michigan, on the north, and Vincennes, in Indiana, enabled him to become acquainted with the Territory and the people by personal observation, and in the Legislative Council he was able to use the information thus acquired to good purpose in shaping legislation to meet the wants of the rapidly-growing population of the Territory, and was himself the author of most of the important measures adopted by the Legislature. When it was proposed to go into a State government, Judge Burnet believed the step premature and opposed the action, and when the State was formed he retired from active participation in politics and devoted himself to the practice of his profession. His talents, ripe scholarship, and brilliancy as an advocate secured for him from the first an extensive and lucrative practice, and enabled him to assume and maintain the foremost position at the bar, until, in 1817, he retired from the practice of the law. In the year 1821 he was persuaded to accept an appointment by the Governor to the bench of the Supreme Court of the State, and was subsequently elected by the Legislature to the same place. In 1828 he resigned his position on the bench and was elected to the United States Senate to fill a vacancy occasioned by the retirement of General William H. Harrison, and accepted the position on the condition that he should not be considered a candidate for re-election, but on the expiration of his term be permitted to carry out his long-cherished purpose of retiring to private life. His term expired in 1833, and from that time until his death, in 1853, at the advanced age of eighty-three years, he took no further active part in public affairs. As a lawyer and legislator Judge Burnet was without doubt the most influential and prominent person in the section of country he represented and with which his interests were identified. Educated amid the stirring scenes of the Revolution, and the scarcely less stirring scenes connected with the discussion and adoption of the Federal Constitution; brought into association with Washington and Hamilton and other leaders of the struggle for independence, through his father's intimacy with and friendship for them; with great natural ability united to thorough scholarship, and having with it all strong and decided convictions and great energy and persistence in enforcing them, he was eminently qualified to take the leading part he did in developing the resources of the great Northwestern Territory and in shaping its institutions. As a lawyer he was the acknowledged leader of the bar in the West. Within the period of twenty years—which was about the extent of his practice at the bar—few men have engaged in more important causes or with more uniform success. His fame as an advocate was coextensive with the West, and the story of his forensic efforts is perpetuated in the traditions of his profession. About the time also of his appointment to the Supreme bench of Ohio he was elected to fill the Professorship of Law in the University of Lexington, Virginia, and received from that institution the honorary degree of Doctor of Laws, an honor subsequently conferred upon him also by his own *Alma Mater*, Nassau Hall. It has already been stated that while in the Territorial Legislature Judge Burnet was the author of most of the necessary legislation. During the session of 1799 alone he prepared and reported the following bills: "To regulate the admission and practice of attorneys-at-law;" "to confirm and give force to certain laws enacted by the Governor and Judges;" a bill making promissory notes negotiable; a bill to authorize and regulate arbitrations; a bill to regulate the service and return of process in certain cases; a bill establishing courts for the trial of small causes; a bill to prevent trespassing by cutting of timber; a bill providing for the appointment of constables; a bill defining privileges in certain cases; a bill

to prevent the introduction of spirituous liquors into certain Indian towns; a bill for the appointment of general officers in the militia of the Territory; a bill to revise the laws adopted or made by the Governors and Judges; a bill for the relief of the poor; a bill repealing certain laws or parts of laws, and a bill for the punishment of arson. He was also appointed to prepare and report rules for conducting the business of the Legislative Council, and an answer to the Governor's address to the two Houses at the opening of the session. Also to draft a memorial to Congress in behalf of purchasers of land in the Miami country, and a complimentary address to the President of the United States. After the formation of the State government he succeeded, by his researches into the laws of Virginia and his lucid demonstration of the same, in settling in favor of the State of Ohio the right which Kentucky controverted of arresting criminals on the river between the two States. Under the system established for the sale of the public domain by the law of 1800 and acts supplementary thereto, an immense debt was contracted and became due to the government of the United States from the people of the West, exceeding the entire amount of money in circulation in the West. The debt had been accumulating for twenty years, and was swelling daily with increasing rapidity. The first emigrants to the West, and the greater part of those who followed them from time to time, were compelled by necessity to purchase on credit, exhausting their means to the last dollar in raising the first payment on their entries. The debt due the government in 1820 at the different Western land offices amounted to $22,000,000, an amount far exceeding the ability of the debtors to pay. Thousands of industrious men, some of whom had paid one, some two, and some three instalments on their lands, and had toiled day and night in clearing, enclosing and improving them, became convinced that they would be forfeited and their money and labor lost. This appalling prospect spread a deep gloom over the community, and it was evident that if the government attempted to enforce its claims universal bankruptcy would ensue. Serious fears were felt that any attempt on the part of the government to enforce its claim would meet with resistance, and probably result in civil war. Judge Burnet, at this crisis of affairs, gave the matter his most earnest attention, with a view of devising a plan of relief, and was able to mature and propose a plan which met the approval of all the sufferers, and so commended itself to Congress and the government that it was speedily adopted. The evils threatened were thus averted, and the prosperity and rapid settlement of the country greatly promoted. At a very early period he recognized the importance to the trade and commerce of the West of the unobstructed navigation of the Ohio river, and especially the importance to the trade of the upper Ohio of removing the obstruction caused by the falls in the river at Louisville. He was one of the first to advocate the construction of a canal around the falls, and was appointed by the State of Indiana one of several commissioners for carrying out this project, in which he took a warm and active part. Considerable progress was made in the work when the rival project of a canal on the Kentucky shore was started, which met with more general favor. This caused the abandonment of the Indiana canal, and the canal on the Kentucky shore was constructed, thus removing one of the most serious obstructions to the navigation of the upper Ohio. The construction of a canal from the Ohio river, at Cincinnati, to Lake Erie, at Toledo, Ohio, thus affording water communication between the commerce of the lakes and the Ohio and Mississippi valleys, was another matter that enlisted his warmest support. Under an act of Congress, making a large grant of public land in aid of this project, considerable progress was made in the work, when it was found that certain conditions and restrictions in the original grant were such as to greatly embarrass, if not to defeat, the completion of the work, which greatly languished and was about to be abandoned. Judge Burnet, on taking his place in the Senate, secured the appointment of a committee of the Senate to take into consideration the modification of the original grant so as to remove its objectionable features, and appearing before the committee in behalf of the measure. His representations were so effective that he was requested by the committee to draw up a report embodying the principal facts in support of the claim, and also a bill to carry it into effect. The committee presented the report and bill, with a recommendation that it should pass. It did pass both Houses and became a law during the session, and without doubt secured the completion of the canal. In the Senate he was the friend and associate of Adams, Clay and Webster, and was especially the friend and admirer of the latter, with whom he occupied a desk in the Senate chamber. When General Haynes, of South Carolina, made his celebrated speech on nullification, which elicited Mr. Webster's more celebrated reply, Mr. Webster was absent from the Senate, and it was remarked that in his reply he answered General Haynes' points seriatim, as if he had been present and heard them. Judge Burnet, who heard Haynes' speech, took full notes of it and gave them to Mr. Webster, who was thus prepared to make his reply as if personally present. No one was more delighted with Mr. Webster's unanswerable rejoinder than the amateur reporter who had assisted to call it forth. With the close of his term in the Senate his public career ended. In full vigor of mind and body, with brilliant prospects of political preferment before him if he would but seek it, he chose rather to spend the remainder of his days as a private citizen. He was not ambitious of place; he was driven to accept office from a sense of duty, and not by ambition. As soon as the duty was discharged he returned to private life. In the year 1837, at the request of a friend, he wrote a series of letters detailing at some length such facts and incidents relating to the early settlement of the Northwestern Territory as were within his recollection and were considered worth preserving. These letters were laid before the Historical Society of Ohio, and ordered to be printed among the transactions of that institution. A few years later, at the solicitation of many personal friends, he revised and enlarged these letters and put them in a form more convenient for publication, and in 1847 published his "Notes on the Northwestern Territory," which is a very valuable contribution to the history of this region. He was married on the second day of January, 1800, at Marietta, Ohio; to Rebecca Wallace, daughter of the Rev. Matthew Wallace, a Presbyterian clergyman, with whom he lived in wedlock fifty-three years, and who outlived him fourteen years. By her he had eleven children, five of whom arrived at maturity and survived him at his death. In appearance he was rather above medium height, erect in form, with animated countenance and piercing eyes. His manners were dignified and courteous to all. Reared in the school of Washington and Hamilton, he had the manners of that age. His colloquial powers were uncommonly fine. He expressed himself in ordinary conversation with the precision, energy, and polish of an accomplished orator. His opinions were clear, sharply defined, and held with great tenacity. His friendships were ardent and lasting. Time or outward changes made with him no difference. He who once won his friendship, unless proved to be unworthy, enjoyed it for life. It is related of him that when Aaron Burr was in Cincinnati seeking to enlist in his treasonable designs as many prominent persons as possible, he sought an interview with Judge Burnet, who, although unaware of Burr's designs, yet peremptorily refused to receive him, giving as his reason that he would never shake the hand of the murderer of Hamilton, his father's friend and his own. In morality and integrity he was above suspicion both in his public career and in private life. He was a firm believer in the truth of Christianity and the inspiration of the Bible; and. although a Presbyterian both from conviction and preference, he was far removed from anything like sectarian bigotry. Ministers of all denominations were at all times welcome and honored guests in his house. On the 10th of May, 1853, in his eighty-fourth year, with his mind still vigorous, his memory still unimpaired, and his bodily vigor such as to give promise of still more advanced old age, he died at his home in Cincinnati, of acute disease, after a comparatively short illness.

KENT, JOSEPH CHARLES, of Phillipsburg, Iron Manufacturer, was born in Chenango county, New York. He is the son of William St. George Kent, a merchant of Chenango, who came to this country from England. When he was still a boy, his father removed to New York city, where the son was educated at St. Luke's Classical School, then under charge of Professor Patterson. After leaving school he was for some time employed in the office of Mr. Seabury

Brewster, a retired merchant of wealth, with extensive interests in real estate and stocks demanding his attention. Subsequently he studied chemistry with Mr. George Jeffries, during his stay with whom he was called upon by his friend, Mr. A. S. Hewitt, to go to Phillipsburg, New Jersey, to assist in superintending the manufacture of iron at the Cooper Iron Works, named in honor of Peter Cooper, one of the principal members of the Trenton Iron Company, which set up the establishment. Accepting this call, he went to Phillipsburg in 1848, the year in which the furnace was completed, and became the Assistant Superintendent, successfully applying his knowledge of chemistry to the mixing of ores and the general manufacture of iron. On the resignation of the General Superintendent, Dr. G. G. Palmer, in 1853, he was chosen to succeed him, and has since filled the place, although in 1867 the works changed hands and name, being purchased by a Philadelphia company, and named Andover Iron Company, after one of the principal mines. Since his connection with the works they have been greatly enlarged, their present capacity being 35,000 tons yearly; at the same time they have kept fully up with all the modern improvements. The ores used are mainly magnetites from Morris county, New Jersey, and the iron is of very superior quality. Ascribing to these advantages their proper influence, great credit is, nevertheless, due to him for the fact that the works have been running steadily through all the recent dull period, when so many establishments in other places have been forced to close; and this credit the fact itself, indeed, speaking plainly of skill, intelligence and fidelity in the management, renders in no equivocal way. In politics he is a Republican, and an earnest supporter of the principles of the party. As a man and a citizen he is universally esteemed. He married Frances B. Banks, of Pennsylvania.

DENHEIMER, WILLIAM HENRY, D. D., Bishop of Northern New Jersey, was born in Philadelphia, August 11th, 1817. He graduated at the University of Pennsylvania in 1835, and at the General Theological Seminary of the Protestant Episcopal Church, in New York, in 1838. In the same year he entered Holy Orders, being ordained deacon in the Protestant Episcopal Church. In 1841 he received Priest's Orders, and was instituted Rector of St. Peter's Church, Philadelphia. He subsequently became, in 1859, Bishop of New Jersey. On the division of the diocese, in 1874, he elected to take charge of Northern New Jersey, and established his residence at Newark. Soon after he took a voyage to Europe for the benefit of his health, which had become very much impaired. Indeed, he is now (1877) quite an invalid, owing to fracture of the patella of both knees. He is the author of numerous works, of which the following are chief: "The Origin and

Compilation of the Prayer-Book," 1841; "The Devout Churchman's Companion," 1841; "The True Catholic no Romanist," 1842; "Thoughts on Immersion," 1843; "The Young Churchman's Catechism," 1844; "Ringelburgius on Study;" "Bishop White's Opinions," 1846; "Essay on Canon Law," 1847; "The Clergyman's Assistant in Reading the Liturgy," 1847; "The Private Prayer-Book," 1851; "Jerusalem and its Vicinity;" a series of familiar lectures (eight) on the sacred localities connected with the week before the resurrection, 1855. In this last work he gives the results of his meditations among the holy places during a visit to Jerusalem in 1851-52. It is a most valuable book, and deeply interesting to the devout Christian. Bishop Odenheimer has confirmed, during the seventeen years since his consecration, 17,277 persons.

BARRON FAMILY, Woodbridge. Among the earliest settlers in New Jersey was Ellis Barron, one of a party of English emigrants reaching this country about 1690. Making his home at Woodbridge (now in Middlesex county) he married a daughter of Ephraim Andrews, and from this union the present large family is descended. Mr. Barron, according to the early records, agreed to build a church for the settlers for one hundred pounds. The contract was broken after he had expended eighty pounds on stones and timber (see " Dally's History "). Ephraim Andrews was included in 1673 among the original freeholders to whom the patent for the town was granted in 1670; he served in 1679-81, and again in 1693, as an officer of the township court, and was a Deputy to the General Assembly in 1687. Both founders of the Barron line in this country were therefore intimately associated with the early history of the New Jersey colony. Samuel, the only male child issue of this marriage, of whose birth record exists, was born in Woodbridge in 1711. He seems to have received a good education for that early day, the public school facilities of the town being quite remarkable, the second school of the kind established in the State being provided for here; the first was at Newark. Inheriting a considerable property from his father, he showed great energy and enterprise in adding to it. He raised a large family, handsomely providing for all his children. In 1774, as shown by the town records, he was appointed Chairman of the Committee of Freeholders. He died at Woodbridge in 1801, and in his will—a long and curious document—after disposing of two farms, three houses, a tan-yard and buildings thereof, certain freehold rights, etc., he bequeaths his four slaves— Benjamin, Robert, Sharper and Cornelius. Woodbridge seems, indeed, to have been rather a slave-holding place, for, nine years later, 230 slaves are included in a census of the town, and even so recently as 1840 there were seven slaves owned within the township limits, while one was in

31

the possession of the Barron family so late as 1859, supported by them in his old age as the law of the State required. Samuel Barron was twice married; by his first wife, Elizabeth, he had three sons and two daughters— Ellis (commissioned a Captain in the 1st Middlesex Regiment of the Continental army, January 10th, 1776), Mary, John and Samuel. By his second wife, Johannah, he had one son, Joseph. Ellis married Sarah Stone; Mary married Jonathan Clawson (the grandparents of the late well-known Judge Clawson, of Staten island); John married Nancy Coddington (having issue, Samuel and John E., late prominent citizens of Woodbridge, and Johanna, now living); Samuel studied medicine, and to complete his studies sailed for Europe in the "very fine East Indiaman, Grand Duke of Russia," as stated by him in a letter to his father, dated, "Off Sandy Hook, September 3d, 1780." He never returned. It is thought that he lost his life in the English service on the Mediterranean. Joseph remained in Woodbridge and became one of its most prominent citizens, a deacon in the church and a man stirring in business affairs. In his generation Woodbridge was one of the most important towns in east New Jersey. Standing upon the old king's road between Philadelphia and New York, the Elm Tree Inn was a famous stopping-place, and Woodbridge was honored by the reflected glory of its excellent hostelrie. Washington—that most persistent sleeper, the rival of the seven of Ephesus—is reported to have slept there on his way to New York to be inaugurated President. Concerning several of the early Presidents, and various distinguished statesmen and soldiers, a similar legend obtains; and it is matter of undoubted historic fact, that President Adams, on his way to Washington to take the oath of office, did, indeed, pass a night beneath the rustling branches of the great elm tree. As a means of increasing and facilitating travel, the king's road was turnpiked, and among the prime movers in this enterprise, as well as one of the original incorporators, and subsequently President and Treasurer of the Woodbridge Turnpike Company, was Joseph Barron. Turnpike building was then as active an interest as canal building was some few years later, or as railroad building is now, and in various works of this character he invested very considerable sums of money. Toward the close of his career he was prominent in urging before and getting passed by the New York Legislature a bill providing for the erection of a bridge across Staten Island Sound at Blazing Star, and although the bill was defeated in the New Jersey Legislature, there is no doubt but that the bridge would have been built, had not railways come into existence, and a specific scheme for laying a line of metals from Jersey City to New Brunswick rendered the bridge project of none effect. But the invention of railways did something more than kill the bridge at Blazing Star; it distracted the line of travel that for so long had flowed past the Elm Tree Inn, and left Woodbridge village stranded far beyond the high water mark of travel. Joseph

Barron did not live to see the decline of his native town; the "Sessions Book" of the old Woodbridge church says, "Deacon Barron died July 4th, 1831, greatly lamented as a citizen and a useful member of the church." He married Fanny, daughter of Thomas Brown, of Woodbridge, an excellent woman, who survived him by more than a quarter of a century, her death occurring in October, 1857, in her ninety-second year. Ten children were the issue of this marriage : Samuel, Thomas, John, Rebecca, Joseph, Fanny, Johannah, Christian, Mary and Jane. (1) Samuel married Rebecca White, having issue, Harvey and Maria; Harvey married and left one son, Harvey; Maria died single; Samuel died in his twenty-seventh year. (2) Thomas, the founder of the Barron Library at Woodbridge, was born June 10th, 1790, dying unmarried, August 31st, 1875. (3) John was born October 18th, 1792; he married, June 16th, 1824, Mary, daughter of Colonel Richard Conner, of Staten Island, having issue, Frances M., John C., and Maria L. Frances married John H. Campbell, and is now living, a widow, at Woodbridge; John C. married Harriet M., daughter of Rev. Albert Williams, of San Francisco, California, and is now living in New York; Maria married Charles D. Fredericks, Esq., of New York. (4) Rebecca died in early life. (5) Joseph married Charity, daughter of Abel Clarkson, Esq., having issue three children, only one of whom, Joseph, is now living. (6) Frances married twice : first to H. Woodruff, second to I. S. Jaques, having by her second husband several children. She is now a widow. (7) Johannah married Dr. Charles Young, dying without issue. (8) Christian died in early life. (9) Mary, now dead, married Jared Woodhull, having issue one child, now married to James P. Edgar, and resident at Woodbridge. (10) Jane married Josiah Doremus, of Newark, New Jersey, dying without issue. In the town of Woodbridge, the real estate granted with freehold rights to Ellis Barron nearly two hundred years ago, still remains in the possession of his descendants. The Episcopal rectory, purchased from the executors of the late Samuel Barron, has the original walls of Holland brick as when built and occupied by the first Samuel Barron in the early part of the eighteenth century, the first house built of brick in New Jersey. The fine old seat now known as the Barron homestead, and owned by Dr. John C. Barron, was the property of Joseph Barron, the grandfather of the present owner. The mansion was erected and the grounds laid out by him about 1800. The Barron Library, a handsome memorial building of Belleville brown stone, appropriately stands upon a corner of this property, having been built from an endowment fund of $50,000 bequeathed by the late Thomas Barron. In this and many other directions the influence of the Barron family upon the town and neighborhood of Woodbridge has always been beneficial, being steadily cast in favor of the development of its resources and the advancement of the social condition of its population.

Thomas Baum

ARRON, THOMAS, second son of Joseph and Fanny (Brown) Barron, was born in Woodbridge, June 10th, 1790. Receiving a common-school education, he became at the age of fourteen years a clerk in his father's store, and rapidly developed a prodigious aptitude for business. In a very short time he was intrusted by his father with commissions to buy and sell in New York, and in the execution of his trusts his sagacity and youth frequently excited the favorable comment of the merchants with whom he dealt. When nineteen years old he was admitted as a partner into his father's business, continuing as such during the ensuing five years. At the beginning of this period he was fired by a desire to fit out a trading boat on the head-waters of the Mississippi and trade down to New Orleans; and although, at the urgent solicitation of his parents, he abandoned this scheme, it is worthy of note, inasmuch as it points to the fact that even then his regard was fixed upon the commercial possibilities of the Southwest. For a man of his mercantile ability, the narrow range of a country store was, of course, far too limited; and although he gave over his trading project, his eventual departure from Woodbridge to one or other of the great commercial centres was a patent necessity. In 1814, being then twenty-four years old, he took up his abode in New York. After being for a short time a partner in the house of J. C. Marsh & Co., he entered the firm of Laing & Randolph, then one of the leading houses in the West India trade. He made two voyages to the West Indies, and it is probable that these tended to strengthen his belief in the business opportunities then afforded by the Southwest. Be this as it may, in the spring of 1817 (or 1818) he dissolved his connection with Laing & Randolph, formed a partnership with J. I. Coddington, and embarked, in the fall of the same year, in business in New Orleans. The success of the firm fully justified his highest expectations, and was mainly due to his own individual sagacity and foresight; realizing this fact, at the end of five years he purchased, for $50,000, his partner's interest, and thereafter conducted the business singly and to his single profit. The house of Thomas Barron & Co. became, during the twenty years of its existence, one of the best known and most highly respected in the entire southern country. Its agencies extended from Georgia and Florida to the head-waters of the Mississippi, and thence south again to Texas, and its representatives were in London, Liverpool and New York. It was the boast of the head of the house that he had never refused to pay a just debt, and that never, during his entire business career, had one of his notes gone to protest. In the business community he was regarded as a man of exceptional quickness of perception and of rarely sound judgment, and he was constantly solicited to accept positions of public trust and honor. These, almost uniformly, he declined. In New Orleans he was a Director of the Louisiana branch of the United States Bank, and later, in New York, he accepted a few corporation offices; but his desire ever was to avoid offices of every sort. In 1827, having amassed a handsome competence, he withdrew from active business life, delegating the greater portion of the conduct of the firm to his junior partners, and spending his summers in the North. A few years later he entirely severed his business connections, and thereafter led a quiet, honorable life, devoted to unostentatious philanthropy, to study, and to his favorite sport of fishing. For a man of his originally limited education and subsequent mercantile habit of life, the extent and character of the studious tendencies which he developed in later years were quite remarkable. History, geography and natural history were for many years his favorite fields of research, but during the last decade of his life these were to a great extent supplanted by astronomy; during this period the books which he most constantly read were the works of Herschel and Humboldt. Outside of professedly scientific circles, there were few men better read than was he, and few were better able to arrange and utilize their mental acquisitions. Naturally his disposition towards subjects of this nature brought him into contact with the reading and thinking men of the day, and led to his election to membership in various of the learned societies. For many years he was a member of the New York Historical Society, being during the latter portion of his life one of the oldest seven members who, under the society's constitution, nominate the candidates for office. He was also a Fellow of the American Geographical Society and of the American Museum of Natural History, a corresponding member of the New Jersey Historical Society, etc. Although rarely writing for publication, he was a voluminous writer for his own entertainment and edification. For upwards of thirty years he kept a daily journal, and beside this, numerous commonplace books, in which he noted, with comments, matters or events which seemed to him particularly interesting. His thorough business training was manifested in his keeping, almost to the day of his death, his private accounts in a full set of double entry books. Perhaps in no better way can a comprehensive presentment of his character be given than by reproducing bodily the following letter (written under date of New York, September 2d, 1875) to Dr. John C. Barron, by William Pitt Palmer, Esq.: "It is with the sincerest regret that my state of health and the imperative commands of my physician prevent a detail of such reminiscences of your late uncle as the excellence of his character calls for from one of his oldest friends. A wise moralist has said that the life of the humblest person, truthfully written, would be interesting to every thoughtful reader; how much more so, then, must be the memoir of one so truly noble as was your venerable uncle! I have known many able and honored men, but few whom I have loved with ever growing affection. Your uncle was one of these rare few, and while I live his memory will live in my heart with the dearest of its lost idols. Our acquaintance began in 1835, not long after his return from New Orleans, whither he had gone, a mere youth, early in the present century; where he had remained, without once returning to his northern home, until he had won the modest fortune which satisfied his largest wishes. Ily his quiet persistence in the path of duty and honor, the young stranger gained the respect and confidence alike of merchants and planters in that strange community of alien h bits and alien languages, often visited by pestilence and always liable to scenes of violence and bloodshed. Under all the circumstances of time and place his courage and perseverance were simply wonderful, and justly merited the success which a citizen to the manor born could hardly have expected, however favored by nature or local advantages. Returning to New York he took a large house on St. John's Park, mainly to gratify, as was said, an art-loving friend, whose pictured treasures required a breadth of mural accommodation quite beyond their owner's means to supply. Here the two friends lived for some time, and when the friendly partnership came to an end, your uncle bought the modest houses in Walker street, near Broadway, in one of which he resided for many years, until his final removal to Washington Place, where you subsequently became his chosen companion. From our earliest acquaintance in 1835, your uncle was accustomed to visit our office almost daily, where he met congenial friends whose intercourse was like that of brothers. He almost always came to my desk for a little friendly chat about business or other matters in which he felt a personal interest. If I knew of any one needing assistance, he took it as a favor to be informed of the case and be allowed to share in its alleviation. He took a very great interest in the late civil war from its inception. The firing on Sumpter shocked him exceedingly, for no man loved his country more dearly or more clearly saw the inevitable horrors to follow the dreadful collision. Knowing the Southern people well, and the vast means and the stern patriotism of the North, he never doubted the final issue of the contest. He was very earnest in his support of the Sanitary Commission, and when General Grant told the country he could end the war with less expense of blood and treasure if he could have another prompt reinforcement of the armies, your uncle made instant inquiry where recruits could possibly be had, and despatched two to headquarters at a heavy cost. Long after, when an agent of the State offered to reimburse a part of the expense, he refused to listen to the proposal, feeling amply repaid with the consciousness that he had but done his duty. He had already contributed largely towards the equipment and comfort of several New York regiments. Since the close of the dreadful struggle he has largely aided the Military Post Library Association in the effort to furnish the frontier garrisons of our scattered soldiers with reading matter most appropriate to their mental and moral needs. I had only to suggest some object worthy of his charitable regard, to enlist his prompt and generous action. There was a daily beauty in his life through all the years of our long acquaintance. To see him anywhere, at home or abroad, to listen to his kindly greeting, and feel the warm pressure of his friendly hand, was like a benediction. The charm of his character was its evident sincerity. You always knew that his interest in any person or cause was of the heart. The gentle honest eyes made that clear at a glance. I think his temper was naturally quick and strong, but I never saw him for a moment mastered by it. A cheerful serenity was his habitual manifestation, no matter how disturbing were the circumstances which tested its equability. When the box containing the chief securities of his large fortune had been stolen from the custody of his aged friend, the only impatience I saw him manifest was not so much on account of the lost treasure as of his friend's shamefaced hesitation in disclosing the alarming news to him. And when, after long months of costly detective searches and the friendly offices of his old correspondents, Messrs. Baring Brothers, of London, the lost box was finally restored to him with its hundreds of thousands uninjured, save by the elements to which the robbers had been obliged to expose them in their hurried evasions at home and abroad, his chief gratification seemed to be not the recovery of the treasure, but the kind remembrance and unsolicited interest of the friends beyond the sea, whom he had never seen. Not that he did not justly value the recovery of the stolen property, but that he recognized in those efforts the higher and nobler value of human friendship and integrity. As the traits of your uncle's character rise before my failing sight, I feel truly grateful that memory has made them a part of my very being. His bodily presence for so many years was a blessing that even death cannot take from me. It made the world lighter to my eyes for forty years, and though it be now withdrawn forever, the charms of its twilight beauty will go with me to the end of my days. The manes of such a man as he are not alone to abide where his mortal relics are laid to rest; but as living memories their real dwelling place is in the human hearts made grateful for the teachings, the examples, and the loving-kindnesses of the dear ones they are never more to see on earth. But we will not, my dear friend, despair of again seeing that beloved face in some happier sphere, clothed with immortality and beaming with tenderest welcome. In that fond hope I remain ever, faithfully yours." Thomas Barron died August 31st, 1875, but the good that he did lives after him. His will was munificent in its bequests : to the New York Historical Society, $10,000; to the New Jersey Historical Society, $5,000, and his portrait by Durand; to the New York Eye and Ear Infirmary, Juvenile Asylum, Association for Improving the Condition of the Poor, American Female Guardian Society, and Home for the Friendless, $5,000 each, and for the foundation of a public library in his native town of Woodbridge, $50,000. This last and most generous bequest has assured a worthy monument to the donor, his most enduring as well as most fitting memorial being the Barron Library. As has been already stated, the library building stands upon a portion of the old Barron property, and is not less an ornament than

John Barron

greeting, and feel the warm pressure of his friendly hand, was like a benediction. The charm of his character was its evident sincerity. You always knew that his interest in y person or cause was at the heart. The gentle honest ... made that clear at a glance. I think his temper was ... quick and strong, but I never saw him for a moment mastered by it. A cheerful serenity was his habitual manifestation, no matter how disturbing were the circumstances which tested ... ability. When the box containing the chief securities of his large fortune had been stolen from the custody of his agent friend, the only impatience I saw him manifest was just so much on account of the lost treasure as of his friend's ... hesitation in disclosing the alarming news ... and when, after long months of costly detective ... and the friendly offices of his old correspondents. M... Baring Brothers, of London, its lost box was finally restored to him with its hundreds of thousands uninjured, ... by the elements to which the robbers had been forced to expose them in their hurried evasions at home and abroad, his chief gratification seemed to be not the recovery of the treasure, but the kind remembrance and ... of the friends beyond the sea, whom he had never seen. Not that he did not justly value the recovery of the ..., but that he recognized in those efforts the higher ... value of human friendship and integrity. As the ... of your uncle's character rise before my failing sight, I feel ... grateful that memory has made them a part of my ... being. His bodily presence for so many years was a ... that even death cannot take from me. It made the world lighter to my eyes for forty years, and though ... withdrawn forever, the charms of its twilight beauty ... with me to the end of my days. The manes of such ... he are not alone to abide ... his mortal relics are laid to rest; but as living memory their real dwelling is ... is in the human hearts made grateful for the teaching, the examples, and the loving-kindnesses of the dead ones they are never more to see on earth. But we will not, my dear friend, despair of again seeing that beloved face in some happier sphere, clothed with immortality and beaming with tenderest welcome. In ... that fond hope I remain ever, faithfully yours." Thomas ... Barron died August 31st, 1875, but the good that he did lives after him. His will was munificent in its bequests ... In the New York Historical Society, $10,000; to the New ... Jersey Historical Society, $5,000, and his portrait by ... Deceased, to the New York Eye and Ear Infirmary, Juvenile ... Asylum, Association for Improving the Condition of the ... the Military Post; American Female Guardian Society, and Home for ... the ..., $5,000 each, and for the foundation of a ... public library in his native town of Woodbridge, $50,000. ... last and most generous bequest has assured a worthy ... to the donor, his most enduring as well as most ... the Barron Library." As has been ... the library building stands upon a portion of ... and is not less an ornament than

John Barron

John C. Barrow M.D.

a substantial benefit to the town. It is built of Belleville brown stone, from designs submitte i, .. competition, by the well-known architect of New York, J. C. Cady. It is 44 feet square, with a height of 38 feet from the ground-floor to the roof-peak; a tower, abutting from the main front, is surmounted by a steeple, the whole having a height of 81 feet. The interior is divided into a book room 40 by 20 feet; a reading room, 20 by 23.6; a trustees' room, 13 by 6.8; a hall, 8 by 9, and a vestibule, 8.6 by 8.6; all of the ceilings have a height of 28 feet. The arrangement and fittings of the several rooms are in accordance with the latest improvements in library architecture and furniture, and the collection of books is already large and fairly representative of the classes of light and solid literature commonly in demand. Such a creation as this library cannot be too highly valued, for, apart from all consideration of present pleasure and profit, its existence cannot but have a sure and an exalting influence upon the moral tone of the town in all future time. Had the sole result of Thomas Barron's life been the foundation of the Barron Library, his life would have been well ended, and his fortune would not have been gathered in vain.

BARRON, JOHN, third son of Joseph and Fanny (Brown) Barron, was born at Woodbri in the family homestead, October 18th, 1792. His education was mainly obtained in his native place, being finished by attendance upon lectures in New York whilst passing two years in that city (in 1809–11) learning the trade of cabinet-making. Upon his return to Woodbridge he built a large manufactory, and made preparations for carrying on his trade upon an extensive scale. His venture was in advance of the times, and unable to dispose of his wares near at home, he sought a market for them in New Orleans, having some knowledge of this city from his brother Thomas, who had been resident there for several years. Going south by sea, he was fairly successful in his sales, and these being completed he returned to the North by the circuitous stage and post route then existing. The journey was partly one of pleasure, partly one of business, and in both respects was satisfactory in its results. The limited demand in his immediate neighborhood for cabinet ware, and his own failing health, induced him to abandon his manufactory and enter upon a freer, more outdoor life. To this end he purchased a farm on the then outskirts of Woodbridge, and in agricultural pursuits he passed the remainder of his days. Until 1858 the farm remained as when he cultivated it, but since then, in common with other outlying portions of Woodbridge, it has undergone an entire change. Barron avenue divides it, the Congregational church stands upon land that formed a portion of it, and a large section, purchased by the Hon.

Charles A. Campbell, has been covered with handsome buildings. In politics, as in everything else, John Barron was a man of decided opinions. An old-line Whig, he spoke out his views with no uncertain voice, and in warmly contested elections his influence was always an important factor in the success of the Whig ticket in Middlesex. In the Polk-Tyler campaign he was especially active, his energy having a very considerable influence upon the vote in his section of the State. Being much depressed by the loss of his wife in 1851, his feeble health grew feebler day by day till his death, which occurred October 16th, 1853.

BARRON, JOHN C., M. D., New York, son of John and Mary (Conner) Barron, was born in Woodbridge, November 21, 1837. After receiving preliminary education at a select school in his native town, he entered Burlington College, at Burlington, New Jersey, the institution being at that time under the rectorship of the Rt. Rev. George W. Doane, D. D., bishop of the diocese of New Jersey. In 1858 he passed hence to Yale College, studying in the scientific department, and at the same time attending lectures in the eminent private school of Drs. Jewett, Hooker and Knight. In 1860 he entered the College of Physicians and Surgeons, New York, graduating thence in 1861. In April of that year, immediately upon receiving his degree, he entered the United States Volunteer Army as an Assistant Surgeon, being passed by the Board of Army Medical Examiners, sitting at Albany, and assigned to the Mechanics Rifles. This position was declined on account of being tendered the Assistant Surgeoncy of the 69th New York Regiment, then in the field. This regiment was among the foremost to offer their services to the general government early in 1861. Dr. Barron, immediately upon his appointment, with a detachment of the regiment, proceeded to Washington, and was sworn into the service of the United States, going at once to active work with the regiment, then the advance-guard in Virginia, and as stated in the publications of the day, "showing his devotion to the cause by donating one thousand dollars for medical supplies, etc., to the hospital department." The 69th saw much service, being at Blackburn's Ford, and at the first Bull Run battles, at the latter losing in killed and wounded nearly two hundred men. He held his commission until the following August. In June, 1863, he re-entered the army, being assigned Assistant Surgeon of the 7th New York Regiment, N. G. S. N. Y., and serving with the reserves called out in 1863 to repel the advance of Lee. In July, 1869, he was promoted to the Surgeoncy. In June, 1871, he resigned from the regiment and was appointed Surgeon-General of the 1st Division, N. G. S. N. Y., with the rank of Colonel, on the staff of Major-General Alexander Shaler. He was married, June 23d, 1869, to Harriet M., daughter

a substantial benefit to the town. It is built of Belleville brown stone, from designs submitted, in competition, by the well-known architect of New York, J. C. Cady. It is 44 feet square, with a height of 38 feet from the ground-floor to the roof-peak; a tower, abutting from the main front, is surmounted by a steeple, the whole having a height of 81 feet. The interior is divided into a book room 40 by 20 feet; a reading room, 20 by 23.6; a trustees' room, 13 by 6.8; a hall, 8 by 9, and a vestibule, 8.6 by 8.6; all of the ceilings have a height of 28 feet. The arrangement and fittings of the several rooms are in accordance with the latest improvements in library architecture and furniture, and the collection of books is already large and fairly representative of the classes of light and solid literature commouly in demand. Such a creation as this library cannot be too highly valued, for, apart from all consideration of present pleasure and profit, its existence cannot but have a sure and an exalting influence upon the moral tone of the town in all future time. Had the sole result of Thomas Barron's life been the foundation of the Barron Library, his life would have been well ended, and his fortune would not have been gathered in vain.

ARRON, JOHN, third son of Joseph and Fanny (Brown) Barron, was born at Woodbridge, in the family homestead, October 18th, 1792. His education was mainly obtained in his native place, being finished by attendance upon lectures in New York whilst passing two years in that city (in 1809–11) learning the trade of cabinet-making. Upon his return to Woodbridge he built a large manufactory, and made preparations for carrying on his trade upon an extensive scale. His venture was in advance of the times, and unable to dispose of his wares near at home, he sought a market for them in New Orleans, having some knowledge of this city from his brother Thomas, who had been resident there for several years. Going south by sea, he was fairly successful in his sales, and these being completed he returned to the North by the circuitous stage and post route then existing. The journey was partly one of pleasure, partly one of business, and in both respects was satisfactory in its results. The limited demand in his immediate neighborhood for cabinet ware, and his own failing health, induced him to abandon his manufactory and enter upon a freer, more outdoor life. To this end he purchased a farm on the then outskirts of Woodbridge, and in agricultural pursuits he passed the remainder of his days. Until 1858 the farm remained as when he cultivated it, but since then, in common with other outlying portions of Woodbridge, it has undergone an entire change. Barron avenue divides it, the Congregational church stands upon land that formed a portion of it, and a large section, purchased by the Hon.

Charles A. Campbell, has been covered with handsome buildings. In politics, as in everything else, John Barron was a man of decided opinions. An old-line Whig, he spoke out his views with no uncertain voice, and in warmly contested elections his influence was always an important factor in the success of the Whig ticket in Middlesex. In the Polk-Tyler campaign he was especially active, his energy having a very considerable influence upon the vote in his section of the State. Being much depressed by the loss of his wife in 1851, his feeble health grew feebler day by day till his death, which occurred October 16th, 1853.

ARRON, JOHN C., M. D., New York, son of John and Mary (Conner) Barron, was born in Woodbridge, November 2d, 1837. After receiving preliminary education at a select school in his native town, he entered Burlington College, at Burlington, New Jersey, the institution being at that time under the rectorship of the Rt. Rev. George W. Doane, D. D., bishop of the diocese of New Jersey. In 1858 he passed hence to Yale College, studying in the scientific department, and at the same time attending lectures in the eminent private school of Drs. Jewett, Hooker and Knight. In 1860 he entered the College of Physicians and Surgeons, New York, graduating thence in 1861. In April of that year, immediately upon receiving his degree, he entered the United States Volunteer Army as an Assistant Surgeon, being passed by the Board of Army Medical Examiners, sitting at Albany, and assigned to the Mechanics Rifles. This position was declined on account of being tendered the Assistant Surgeency of the 69th New York Regiment, then in the field. This regiment was among the foremost to offer their services to the general government early in 1861. Dr. Barron, immediately upon his appointment, with a detachment of the regiment, proceeded to Washington, and was sworn into the service of the United States, going at once to active work with the regiment, then the advance-guard in Virginia, and as stated in the publications of the day, "showing his devotion to the cause by donating one thousand dollars for medical supplies, etc., to the hospital department." The 69th saw much service, being at Blackburn's Ford, and at the first Bull Run battles, at the latter losing in killed and wounded nearly two hundred men. He held his commission until the following August. In June, 1863, he re-entered the army, being assigned Assistant Surgeon of the 7th New York Regiment, N. G. S. N. Y., and serving with the reserves called out in 1863 to repel the advance of Lee. In July, 1869, he was promoted to the Surgeoncy. In June, 1871, he resigned from the regiment and was appointed Surgeon-General of the 1st Division, N. G. S. N. Y., with the rank of Colonel, on the staff of Major-General Alexander Shaler. He was married, June 23d, 1869, to Harriet M., daughter of Rev. Albert Williams, of San Francisco, California. After spending a year in Europe, including an extended tour of the eastern countries and a trip of seven hundred miles up the river Nile, he returned and settled in New York city, where he now resides.

ILLIAMS, REV. ALBERT, Minister in the Presbyterian Church. Among the earliest settlers of New England, in 1629, was Robert Williams, "the ancestor of the Williams family in America," and one of the founders of the town of Roxbury, Massachusetts. Thence a branch of the family removed to Connecticut, and from that colony came to New Jersey, as one of the first settlers of the town of Newark, the ancestor of the subject of the present sketch. Of the succeeding generation, his great-grandfather, Samuel Williams, was born in 1714, in that part of Newark now the city of Orange. After his marriage to Mary Harrison, of the same place, he entered upon lands in what is now West Orange, securing the titles of the aborigines and New Jersey proprietors. In the course of time he became possessed of a large landed estate, embracing some hundreds of acres. His death occurred, April 2d, 1812, in the ninety-ninth year of his age. In a memorial published at the time, in the *Newark Sentinel of Freedom*, among other personal notices, honorable testimony to his worth was borne in the following tribute: "He retained in a remarkable degree the use of his mental faculties to the last. In the relations of husband, parent and neighbor, he discharged his duty with great fidelity. Throughout his life he uniformly expressed a high respect for the institutions of our holy religion, and was always a cheerful and generous supporter of the gospel. As long as any live who knew him he will be affectionately remembered." In the line of descent now traced was his son Jonathan, who inherited a goodly portion of the estate adjoining the homestead, whose only son, Nathan, as the chief heir, succeeded to him in his landed possessions. Upon these paternal acres members of this venerable family are now living, represented in the sixth generation. The worth of good citizenship and the virtues of quiet rural life, with an almost exceptional feature of longevity, are special traits and distinctions belonging to the successive generations of this family. Albert, the subject of the present memoir, the son of Nathan and Catharine Wade Williams, was born, April 29th, 1809. Early intended for a liberal education, his preparatory instruction was shaped to that end, his final elementary studies being pursued in the grammar school of Mr. Calvin S. Crane, Caldwell, and in the Bloomfield Academy, presided over by the Rev. Amzi Armstrong, D D., and the Rev. Albert Pierson. Entering Princeton College, he was graduated in that institution in the class of 1829. His professional training was obtained in the Theological Seminary of Princeton.

He was licensed to preach the gospel in October, 1832, by the Presbytery of Newark; and in October, 1834, was ordained to the gospel ministry by the same presbytery, being sent under the appointment of the American Seamen's Friend Society, as a Chaplain to seamen in the port of Mobile. Four years were spent in this service, during the first year of which period he caused the formation of the Mobile Port Society, thus relieving the parent society of the expense of the chaplaincy. On the 6th of September, 1837, Mr. Williams was married to Mary Parker Havens, daughter of Henry B. Havens, Esq., of Sag Harbor, New York. Three children, Henry Wade, Harriet Mulford and Albert, were born to them. In November, 1838, Mr. Williams was called to the pastorate of the Presbyterian Church of Clinton, Hunterdon county, New Jersey. At that time the congregation was small, but under his ministry many families were attracted to it, and from being a recipient of missionary aid it became self-supporting and prosperous. Having completed a period of ten years in this relation, he tendered his resignation and obtained his release. About this time the movement to California, consequent upon the gold discovery, commenced. More from the solicitation of others than his own original promptings, under the impression that where the world goes the church should go, Mr. Williams decided to throw himself into the new field of Christian enterprise then opening up in California. Accordingly, on the 5th of February, 1849, as one of the second company of pioneers, *via* the new steamship mail route across the Isthmus of Panama, he sailed from New York in the steamer "Crescent City," for Chagres, New Grenada. Spending four weeks in Panama, waiting for the arrival of the steamer "Oregon," from New York *via* Cape Horn, on the 13th of March he sailed on board that ship for San Francisco, where he arrived on the 1st day of April. He found in San Francisco a population, transient and more or less permanent, of between 3,000 and 4,000. In that city, as throughout California, the theme, excitement and business were centred in the acquisition of gold. The government of the country was still of the old Mexican régime, as stipulated in the treaty of Guadaloupe-Hidalgo. No church or other social organization had been formed to embody the ideas of American civilization. Religious services had been held, but no formal church organization of the Protestant order had been effected. Among the fellow-passengers of Mr. Williams in the "Oregon" were a number of gentlemen, between whom and himself a warm and attached friendship was formed. Before their arrival at San Francisco the organization of a church in that city was projected. With the encouragement and co-operation of these gentlemen, and others who had been longer in the city, Mr. Williams, hindered by unavoidable delays from an earlier beginning, on the second Sunday of May commenced holding a religious service in the public school house, and on the following Sunday, May 20th, he organized the First Presbyterian Church of San Francisco, the first Protestant church of that city; and at the present time the oldest in California. Singularly fortunate in the excellent character of the membership of his church and congregation, he was also greatly aided by their prominent social position in its subsequent growth and prosperity. Having the advantage of being the first in the order of time, it is only due to fact to say, that owing to this circumstance and other favorable influences the First Presbyterian Church of San Francisco, mother of Presbyterian churches in that city and its vicinity, continued to be for years the leading Protestant religious society; and although not the first to erect a church edifice, yet it was the first to build one possessing a characteristic and imposing ecclesiastical architecture. While bestowing a careful attention upon the interests of his immediate pastoral charge, he was not content to confine his influence within that sphere. Accordingly he assisted, and in not a few instances led, in the various measures for either relief or amelioration in the body politic. Not as a politician, but as a friend of good order and social improvement, he gave freely his advice to those who in '49 were shaping the formation of the municipal and State governments, and especially in behalf of the interests of public education. In the more direct line of benevolence, he was prominent in the formation, in '49, of the Bible, Tract, Temperance, Benevolent, and Seamen's Friend Societies, which thus early were brought into efficient operation. It is to the First Presbyterian Church, through its pastor and the ladies in his congregation, that the establishment, in February, 1851, of the noble institution of the Ladies' Protestant Orphan Asylum, of San Francisco, is chiefly due. In 1852 the pastor, together with W. W. Caldwell, Esq., senior ruling elder of the First Presbyterian Church, by correspondence, induced the Presbyterian Board of Foreign Missions to establish the Presbyterian Chinese Mission of San Francisco, the First Church contributing largely to the erection of its mission house. In a similar exercise of public spirit Mr. Williams was ever gratified, when his friends and parishioners bestowed their charities upon worthy objects for the general good, and particularly in church building and church extension. Not to say in general, in those early days there was a series of public movements which enlisted more or less his interest; there were also at intervals special events involving a more intense agitation, in reference to which he could not remain indifferent. Such were the exciting scenes of the "Hounds'" outrages in 1849, the afflictive visitation of cholera in 1850 and 1851, and the irruption of crime, calling for the interposition of the Vigilance Committee of 1851. What with the ordinary routine of pastoral duties, these extra occasions imposed a burden of severe and exhausting labor, too great to be borne. Without cessation, without relaxation, without any vacation to break the force of oppressive cares, which may be safely regarded as fourfold, it is not strange that the pastor's health gave way in a serious indisposition. This failure of health began to show itself in 1853. And

still he continued at his post and in the discharge of his constantly recurring duties until the autumn of 1854, when, by his own convictions and medical advice as well, he sought and obtained relief by the resignation of his pastorate, which had continued through a period of five and a half years, on October 8th, 1854. The sympathy and respect for the retiring pioneer pastor, not only of his congregation, but also of the community in general, were shown in numerous notices and letters, called forth by this change of relation. A committee of the congregation, addressing him by letter, said : . . . . "In acceding to your request for a dissolution of the pastoral relation, the parish had no fear that their action, under the circumstances, would be misconstrued to indicate any want of respect and affectionate regard for you, or any forgetfulness of your long, arduous, faithful and successful efforts in behalf of their church, and of Christian education in the city. . They knew that, as the first and only pastor of the early established and first Protestant church in San Francisco, your consistent Christian character, your devotion to your high and responsible office, your zeal, energy, and successful labor were too widely known and well appreciated to allow, either in the parish or out of it, a thought that your attachment to the church with which you had so long been identified had grown cold, or that the church had lost its affectionate regard for you. But with this the parish was not satisfied: they were unwilling that the pastoral relation should be dissolved without a direct communication of the kind and friendly feelings entertained towards you by them; of their sense of obligation to you, under Providence, for the establishment of their church, and its continuance during all the vicissitudes and embarrassments of our city, and without a hearty assurance of their respect and earnest good wishes for the future. . . . . Though you cease to be the pastor of the First Presbyterian Church of San Francisco, it will never be forgotten that you were its founder, and for more than five years its faithful guide; that you have labored in season and out of season for its prosperity; and that under your zealous but prudent supervision the church, and the great doctrines of which it is the exponent, have been commended to the people of San Francisco and the State. Wherever life may lead you in the future, bear with you the conviction that your labors with us have not been in vain; that your name will ever be associated with our church; and that those who have known you here will remember you with grateful recollections." From the testimonial of the ruling elders of the church a brief extract is taken : " We have great comfort and satisfaction in looking back over the five years and upwards in which you have, with the most unremitting diligence, watched over the interests of the church and society, in all that concerned their welfare and progress, both spiritual and temporal; and have great pleasure in bearing testimony to your fidelity and constant devotion to the best interests of the church and congregation. The sick have been visited—and those who were in prison are witnesses of your counsel, warning and admonition—the poor and friendless have been objects of your care and solicitude—the afflicted have been comforted in their distress and anguish of mind, and the dying have been directed to the ' Lamb of God which taketh away the sins of the world.' In all the relations you have sustained in the church and congregation, your bearing has been honorable, manly and independent, and characterized by meekness, charity and a Christian spirit. When we have, as a community, been passing through scenes of unusual violence and bloodshed, you have remained at your post, unmoved by popular tumult and disorder, faithfully declaring ' all the counsel of God.' . . . . We beg also to assure you of our high respect for your uniform courtesy, kindness and counsel in the relation you have sustained to us as members of your session, in which unity and the most entire harmony has prevailed. Feeling sure that should you leave us, you will carry with you the best and kindest sympathies not only of the church and congregation, but of the community among whom you have moved and mingled in this city, we affectionately commend you and your family to the Great Head of the church, praying that he will richly reward your labors of love among us, and do for you and them ' exceeding abundantly above all that we ask or think.' " One of the many friendly published expressions of regard for Mr. Williams paid him the following tribute: "Among others leaving us is the Rev. Albert Williams—a man who for five years past has been with us; been interested for us; and has fulfilled in our midst a high and holy calling. During that time many are the young and loving pairs he has united in the sacred bonds of wedlock; he has sprinkled the brow of infancy with the token of love and mercy, and pressed the seal of pardon and acceptance on the heads of repentant sinners; he has prayed by the bedside of the dying, and wept with the bereaved at the graves of the dead; he has week after week raised his voice against crime, violence and oppression in the land, and in clear, emphatic language shown the way of duty and of safety. Nor is it by precept alone that he has taught; for he has lived the lessons he has inculcated, and set a beautiful example of Christian consistency; unostentatious, meek and benevolent, like the Master he professes to serve, he has gone about doing good; and now, with enfeebled health, but a good conscience, he returns to his early home for that quiet and repose which he so really needs." And from another source this also: "The Rev. A. Williams has been for five and a half years one of the most prudent, though zealous, ' soldiers of the cross' that ever visited California, and his departure, as well as the cause therefor, has occasioned his congregation and friends profound regret. As he was beloved and reverenced by all with whom he came in contact, even so will he be long remembered as the founder of the Presbyterian church in this city." Mr. Williams, with his family, spent the winter of 1854-55 in the Sandwich Islands. He visited all the group, and con-

tributed a series of descriptive letters to the *Presbyterian,* of Philadelphia. In the spring of 1855 he returned, *via* San Francisco and Panama, to the east, and for the four years following made his residence in Princeton, New Jersey, during which time his eldest son passed through the academic course at Nassau Hall. Such was the degree of his nervous prostration that the whole of that period of rest was necessary to bring back his impaired health. Though resting he was not inactive, but by writing for the press and occasional preaching he sought to be useful. While the social revolution was in progress in San Francisco, in 1856, although away from the State, Mr. Williams took a deep interest in the movement, and wrote for one of the eastern papers an article on the subject, which was acknowledged to have had a marked effect in creating a correct public sentiment concerning the action of the Vigilance Committee of that year, and was particularly referred to by a leading periodical in San Francisco in the following appreciative terms: "Our citizens are indebted to the Rev. Albert Williams, late pastor of the First Presbyterian Church of this city, for a timely letter published at the East, in relation to our local difficulties. His intimacy with our affairs gave weight to his opinion among those with whom he is familiar, or to whom he is known in eastern circles." In the summer of 1859 he made a second removal to California. At this time it was his desire to engage in efforts for the promotion of higher education in the State. But influences which he could not control prevented the gratification of that wish, and again he entered into the special work of the ministry, and for another five years and more served gratuitously a mission church in San Francisco. And again, while retaining his connection with San Francisco, he had a home for his family in Princeton, during which time his younger son passed through college. Thus he has, by frequent repassing, either alone or with members of his family, had a double home in California and New Jersey. For the past six years it has been his special work, among other things, as one of the Trustees of the California Prison Commission and as Chairman of its Visiting Committee, to preach gratuitously each alternate Sunday, during the greater part of that time, to the prisoners in the State Penitentiary at San Quentin. The experience gained in his observations and intercourse among the prisoners enabled him to render valuable aid in carrying through the Legislature of 1875-76 very important reforms in the government of the State Prison. One of these enactments removes the immediate management of the prison beyond the sphere of politics. Another provides that prisoners shall receive one-tenth of their earnings, one-half of the amount payable, and, if they so desire, to be received by them weekly, and the other half to be retained for them until the time of their discharge. Mr. Williams early became a member of the Society of California Pioneers, was for many years its Chaplain, and, as a special compliment, has been constituted one of its few Honorary Life Mem-

... prostration that the whole of that period of
bring back his impaired health.
... ... he was not inactive, but by writing for the
... .sional preaching he sought to be useful.
... ... revolution was in progress in San Fran-
... ..., although away from the State, Mr. Williams
... interest in the movement, and wrote for one
... ... papers an article on the subject, which was

bers. In this outline sketch it remains to add, and may be noted as one of the features of this active life, that it has ever been a habit of Mr. Williams to pursue a general course of reading, with a special taste and preference for subjects of a practical and at the same time philosophical character. In later, no less than earlier, years it has been his constant aim to gather that he may impart. Thus, neither is his leisure idleness, nor his rest inactivity. His retirement, if such it may be styled, is filled with busy labors. And, as a fitting close of this brief sketch, it is proper to subjoin a sentence forming part of a personal item in a late San Francisco journal: "Although he (the Rev. A. Williams) may not be technically a pastor, yet as long as his life is continued he will be found employed in essays of utility and benevolence."

———

STE, DAVID K.,. Jurist, was the son of Moses and Ann Este, of Morristown, New Jersey, and was born October 21st, 1785. Captain Este, his father, was severely wounded at the battle of Monmouth, and would have died from exposure but for the personal attentions of Colonel Hamilton, aide to General Washington, who found him among the dead and dying, and provided him with food and medical assistance. He was subsequently Collector of Revenue under President Adams, and died at the age of eighty-four. David K., his son, received his elementary education in his native town, and entered Princeton College, where he pursued the full course of studies, and graduated with distinction in 1803. In April, 1804, he commenced to read law in the office of Gabriel Ford, Esq., at Morristown, and after thorough preparation was admitted to the bar of the Supreme Court at Trenton, in May, 1808. He commenced practice in Morristown at once, and after continuing there one year as a lawyer he removed to Cincinnati, Ohio; but with the intention of making his practice a very general one, covering all the courts in that judicial district, including the United States District and Circuit Courts at Chillicothe, and subsequently at Columbus, he opened an office in Hamilton in order to be centrally located. In the spring of 1814 he located in Cincinnati, and established himself at the corner of Mam and Fifth streets, and by careful attention to his business and the exercise of rare legal talent, he soon secured a very large and influential clientage. In 1817 he formed a partnership with Bellamy Storer, and this business relationship continued until 1821. In 1830 he admitted Ezekiel Haines as an interest in his large and increasing business, and this partnership existed until Mr. Este was made President Judge of Hamilton county, and after the organization of the Superior Court, in 1837, he was appointed its judge. Upon the expiration of his term, in the spring of 1845, he retired from public and professional

32

life. His career at the bar and on the bench was a distinguished one. He was profoundly read in civil and criminal law, his knowledge of the science being constantly improved by continuous research. He was as indefatigable a worker as a student, and gave to all the business intrusted to his care his close attention. He was especially forcible as a pleader, and had rare power for the analyzation of evidence in order to present it clearly to the jury and the court, forming from it a plain and easily understood exposition of the continuity of circumstances involved in the case. He was skilful in the interpretation of the law, and logical in his arguments, which were models of rhetorical expression. His decisions from the bench were accepted as authority, and were characterized by an entire absence of personal bias. He was at all times firm in his support of the integrity of the law. These qualities won for him the sincere respect of the entire community, and his retirement from professional duties was regarded as a public loss. His career was closely identified with the growth and prosperity of Cincinnati. He was zealous in his efforts to secure public improvements, and to make the city attractive, not alone as a place of residence, but as a good field for capitalists, in the way of increasing mercantile and commercial traffic. The first building erected by him was his own residence on Main street. Subsequently he erected fourteen structures on the same thoroughfare and Ninth street, three on Sycamore street and one on Fourth street. In 1858 he reared a handsome stone residence on West Fourth street, which he occupied at the time of his death. In the fall of 1819 he was married to Lucy Ann, daughter of General William Henry Harrison. She died in April, 1826, having been the mother of four children, three of whom died when quite young. The surviving daughter became the wife of Joseph Reynolds, of Baltimore, and died in 1869, at the age of forty-seven years, leaving seven children. In May, 1829, Mr. Este married Louisa Miller, daughter of Judge William Miller, by whom he had seven children, four living at the present time. Even when ninety years of age he took a great interest in the course of public affairs. For many years he was Senior Warden of Christ Church. He died in the early part of the year 1876.

———

OLLINS, REV. JOHN, Minister of the Pioneer Methodist Episcopal Church in Ohio, was born, November 1st, 1769, in New Jersey. Early in life he became an earnest and devout member of the Methodist Church, and determined to become a preacher, a resolution which he carried into effect with characteristic energy. His earlier efforts in his chosen vocation as a preacher gave little promise of his future eminence. So small was the evidence they gave of special qualification that his wife, solicitous for his reputation and usefulness, advised him to desist, believing that he could never succeed. He replied to her, in all candor, that he thought her predictions quite likely to be correct, but nevertheless, although he might never be a successful preacher himself, he purposed to continue trying until he should be instrumental in converting some one who would be a preacher. His subsequent career showed how un-founded were his wife's misgivings, and how wise was his own determination. In the year 1801 he visited the North-western Territory, now the State of Ohio, and in the follow-ing year he removed his family to the West, and settled on a farm in Clermont county, Ohio, on the east fork of the Little Miami river, about twenty-five miles east of Cincin-nati. In 1804 he preached the first Methodist sermon ever preached in Cincinnati. The meeting was held in an upper room, and the congregation comprised twelve persons. He also preached the first Methodist sermons heard in Ripley, Dayton and Urbana. In 1807 he travelled the Miami Circuit, in connection with B. Larkin, an excellent preacher. In 1808 he travelled the Scioto Circuit, and in 1809 and 1810 the Deer Creek Circuit. He was next assigned to the Union Circuit, which embraced the towns of Lebanon and Dayton. In the years 1819 and 1820 he was Pre-siding Elder of the Scioto District. In 1821 and 1822 he was stationed in Cincinnati. The following year he was stationed in Chillicothe, and in 1824 he was appointed to the Cincinnati District, and afterwards to the Miami Dis-trict. He continued to travel in this district during the years 1825, 1826 and 1827. Next he was transferred to the Scioto District, where he labored from 1828 to 1831. In 1832 and 1833 he was on the New Richmond Circuit. He returned to the Cincinnati station in 1834, and in 1835 he travelled the White Oak Circuit. This was the last cir-cuit he ever travelled. On the minutes of the Ohio Annual Conference of 1836 he was returned as superannuated, which relation remained unchanged until his death. He died at Maysville, Kentucky, at the residence of his son, General Richard Collins, August 21st, 1845. His last words were, "Happy, happy, happy!" On his death the official members of the church at Maysville passed resolu-tions expressive of their grief at his loss, and of the highest appreciation of his labors and eminent qualities as a gospel minister. It may truly be said of him that he was one of the most eminent and eloquent preachers in the early days of Methodism in southern Ohio. He married Sarah Black-man, a woman of great energy and force of character, and whose life was an embodiment of the Christian virtues. She was a sister of Leander Blackman. In the spring of 1797, shortly after her husband assured her of his deter-mination to "keep trying to preach until he had converted some one who would preach successfully," her brother Leander was converted through the agency of her hus-band. This was in 1800, and the new convert at once entered the ministry and worked in it with extraordinary power, earnestness and success until his death, some four-

teen years later. No more devoted, zealous, eloquent, or successful preacher labored in the church than he. His eloquence is described as something wonderful. His pres-ence was commanding and attractive, his voice rich, melodi-ous and greatly expressive, and the fervor of his utterances almost irresistible. None could listen to him unmoved, and during the time of his ministrations thousands were converted through his agency. As early as 1809 he was Presiding Elder in the Cumberland District of the Metho-dist Episcopal Church, embracing all of West Tennessee, part of Middle Tennessee, on the Elk and Duck rivers, Madison county, in the Mississippi Territory, and all of Kentucky below the mouth of Green river, with the counties of Ohio and Breckinridge, above Green river. To this day many an old pioneer remembers the sympathy excited and the profound sorrow felt in Cincinnati and throughout the Methodist Church when his death occurred, in 1815. It was a few days after the adjournment of conference in Cincinnati. He and his wife were crossing the Ohio river in an open ferry-boat. The horses on the boat became frightened, and, running together, forced several of the pas-sengers overboard into the river. Leander Blackman was among the number. He swam for some time, but before help reached him he sank and was drowned in full view of his agonized wife. His body was recovered and followed to the grave by a vast concourse of friends.

CLARK, SAMUEL S., M. D., of Belvidere, was born in Flemington, New Jersey, November 8th, 1825. He is a son of the Rev. John F. Clark, and a grandson of the Rev. Joseph Clark, D. D. The last named was a student at Princeton Col-lege at the breaking out of the revolutionary war, and, entering the colonial army, served with distinc-tion on General Washington's staff. The war ended, he returned to Princeton, completed his education, took holy orders, and was for many years pastor of the First Presby-terian Church at New Brunswick. Dr. Clark's great uncle, General John Maxwell, commanded the New Jersey battal-ion in the war of the Revolution, thus giving him a doubly patriotic ancestry. He received his preparatory education at the school of the Rev. John Vanderveer, at Easton, and in 1841 was admitted to Lafayette College. After re-maining here two years he entered the junior class at Princeton, and graduated in 1845. Among his classmates at Princeton were Judges Depue and Van Syckel, of the New Jersey Supreme Court, and his cousin, Hon. George M. Robeson, late Secretary of the Navy. After passing through the regular three years' course in the medical de-partment of the University of New York, he received his degree in 1848, and in the same year established himself at Belvidere, where he has since resided. He has an exten-sive practice, and his professional reputation is unchallenged.

He is a member of the United States, New Jersey, and Warren County Medical Societies. In politics he was a Whig until the formation of the Republican party, when he became and has since continued a member of that organization. He is a partisan, however, from a sense of duty only, having never sought nor held any public office save that of Superintendent of the Draft in Warren county, an appointment that came to him, unsolicited, from Governor Olden, and which he held only until a provost-marshal was appointed in his stead. His practice has of late so greatly increased that he has been compelled to seek the assistance of a medical partner, and has accordingly associated with him Dr. McGee, a young gentleman of ability and ranking well in the profession Dr. Clark was married in 1854 to Jane C., daughter of James C. Kinney, M. D., of Warren county.

REECE, LEWIS C., Banker, was born, June 19th, 1817, in Phillipsburg, New Jersey. He was educated at the Phillipsburg public schools, and upon completing his education was given a position in the carriage manufacturing business carried on by his father. In this business he remained during the succeeding thirteen years, displaying a considerable amount of mechanical ability and a good understanding of commercial affairs. In 1849 he was elected Surrogate of Warren county, holding the office for the full term of five years, and some years later was elected Judge of the Court of Common Pleas. In 1856 the Phillipsburg Bank was founded under a special charter, and of this institution he was chosen Cashier, an office that he still continues to hold. Under his management the bank has been exceptionally successful in its operations, especially since 1865, when it was reorganized under the national banking law. Mr. Reece was married, August 23d, 1848, to Sarah A., daughter of Andrew Lomison, late of Mount Bethel, Pennsylvania.

LEIGH, JOHN T., Banker, of Clinton, was born in 1821, in Hunterdon county, New Jersey. He is the son of Samuel Leigh, whose father, of the same name, served in the war of the Revolution, the Leigh family being one of the oldest in New Jersey. He received a fair common-school education, and at the age of twelve became a clerk in the large mercantile establishment of Peter Dayton & Son, in New Brunswick, assisting in that and similar establishments in New Brunswick until 1844, when he removed to Clinton, New Jersey, where he established himself in the general mercantile business, which he pursued successfully for five years, selling out at the expiration of that period on account of failing health. Since 1849 he has been engaged in va-

rious enterprises, which he has so conducted as to increase at once his fortune and his reputation, placing him easily in the front rank of the business men of the community. He was one of the founders of the Clinton Bank, now the Clinton National Bank, of which he was chosen one of the first Directors, and is at present the Vice-President. He is a member of the Baptist church, of which he is a zealous and liberal supporter, having been chiefly instrumental in securing for the society its handsome edifice in Clinton. In politics he is a Democrat, though not an extremist, being often found in opposition to the pet schemes of his party. He is, however, a steadfast adherent to the cardinal principles of the Democracy. He was elected Mayor of Clinton on the Union ticket. He has been twice married; first, in 1843, to Miss Van Syckel, daughter of Aaron Van Syckel, who died in 1860, and again, in 1862, to a daughter of William Van Syckel. His eldest son, B. O. Leigh, is at present the efficient Cashier of the Clinton National Bank.

LONGWORTH, NICHOLAS, Lawyer, Vine-grower and Horticulturist, was born, January 16th, 1782, in Newark, New Jersey. His father had been a Tory during the war of the Revolution, and his large property had been entirely confiscated in consequence. Young Longworth's childhood was passed in comparative indigence, and while yet a boy he went to South Carolina as a clerk for an elder brother; but the climate proved unfavorable to his health, and, returning to Newark, he resolved to study law. Believing that the region then known as the Northwest Territory offered the best opportunity of success to young men of enterprise, he removed thither in 1803, and, fixing upon the little village of Cincinnati as his residence, he continued his legal studies in the office of Judge Jacob Burnet. His first case after admission to the bar was the defence of a horse-thief, receiving for his fee two copper whiskey-stills. These he bartered for thirty-three acres of land, Central avenue being its eastern boundary. Owing to the great influx of emigration this land in process of time arose to the value of over two millions of dollars. From the time of his arrival in Cincinnati he held to the idea that the log village of that day would become the metropolis of the future. He was outspoken and decided on this point. His convictions determined all his actions in this direction; but they were the merest visions to the old men around him. While a student in Judge Burnet's office he offered to purchase the judge's cow-pasture, and, thinking to obtain it on a long credit, proposed to pay five thousand dollars for it. The judge reproved him sharply for what he was pleased to term the folly that would assume such a debt for such worthless investment; but he lived to see the cow-pasture valued at one and a half million dollars. When

Mr. Longworth began the practice of law he was known as the attorney who would always take land for fees; and during his connection with that profession all his earnings were invested in lands in and around Cincinnati, so that he became, in the course of a few years, a large lot and land-owner and dealer. At that time property was held at a very low figure; many of his lots cost him but ten dollars each, while vast tracts represented but a lawyer's fee. He had for some years given much attention to the cultivation of the grape, with the view of making wine; and at first attempted, though with but little success, the acclimation of foreign vines. He tried about forty different varieties before the idea occurred to him of testing the capabilities of our indigenous grapes. In 1828 he withdrew from the practice of his profession and commenced experimenting upon the adaptation of native grapes to the production of wine. Two of the varieties—the Catawba and the Isabella—seemed to him to possess the best qualities for wine in that climate and soil, and he gradually adopted these throughout his vineyards, though not entirely to the exclusion of others. He had two hundred acres of vineyards, and extensive wine-vaults in the city, where the vintage of each year was stored by itself to ripen. He also purchased wine and grape-juice in large quantities, to be converted by his processes into the wine of commerce. These vineyards eventually became profitable to him, and to the thousands of wine-growers and vine-dressers who emigrated from the wine countries of Europe and established themselves on the hill-slopes of the Ohio, in the vicinity of Cincinnati; but for some years his expenditure was greater than his income from his vineyards. He did not, however, confine his attention to the culture of the grape. He was also much interested in the improvement of the strawberry, and published the results of his numerous experiments on the influence of the sexual character of the strawberry in rendering it productive. Cincinnati he made famous for strawberry culture; and from him the celebrated "Longworth Prolific" derives its name. In private life he was a genial, kindly, but very eccentric man, dressing always in the extremest simplicity and plainness, often to the extent of shabbiness. He was singularly unostentatious in his display of wealth and in his personal habits. He was never accused of meanness nor of illiberality. He was public-spirited and useful; his brain ever teeming with valuable suggestions to the people. He contributed largely to public charities; but his name was rarely found on published lists of contributors to charitable enterprises. His gifts were made in secret, and oftenest to those whom he termed "the devil's poor"—the vagabonds and estrays of social life. Many citizens of Cincinnati cannot fail to remember the winter when he gave hundreds of men work in his stone quarries on the Ohio river, above the city; or, indeed, of his donating, each week, a sack of meal to a large number of equally poor women. It was no delight or virtue to him to help those who could possibly receive sympathy or aid from others. He had also a sys-

tem, which he studiously carried out, of selling his land to poor tenants on long time, thus enabling them to pay for it gradually, often deeding to widows of tenants half of the property leased by their husbands: in this way favoring poor men in securing homes for themselves. He was a benefactor to poor authors and poets, the liberal patron of art and the friend of Hiram Powers. He was a life-long Whig, but held no identity with any political party, and was certainly no politician. He had as little care and respect for politicians as for preachers, being a determined, but a silent, opponent of the latter. Nevertheless, he was a man of high moral rectitude and a firm believer in the Christian religion; and he attended the ministrations of Rev. Dr. Wilson until the death of that eccentric Presbyterian clergyman. For some time Mr. Longworth was President of the "Pioneer Association of Cincinnati." A very honorable action was taken by that body on the occasion of his death; as was also the case in the meeting of the Cincinnati bar. He died in that city, February 10th, 1863.

UDLOW, ISRAEL, First Surveyor of the Northwest Territory, now Ohio, was born, in the year 1765, at Long Hill Farm, near Morristown, New Jersey, where his father, Cornelius Ludlow, resided. He was of English ancestry, his grandfather having left Shropshire, England, at the time of the restoration of the Stuarts, to escape the persecutions of the crown, as the Ludlow family had espoused the cause of the Parliament, and had taken a prominent part in the affairs of the commonwealth. Sir Edmund Ludlow, the head of the family at that time, was banished from England, and died in exile at Vevay, Switzerland. In 1787 Israel Ludlow received the following letter from the Surveyor-General and Geographer of the United States: "To Israel Ludlow, Esq.: Dear sir: I enclose an ordinance of Congress, of the 20th instant, by which you will observe they have agreed to the sale of a large tract of land, which the New Jersey Society have contracted to purchase. As it will be necessary to survey the boundary of this tract with all convenient speed, that the United States may receive the payment for the same, I propose to appoint you for that purpose, being assured of your abilities, diligence and integrity. I hope you will accept it, and desire you will furnish me with an estimate of the expense, and inform me what moneys will be necessary to advance to you to execute the same. I am, dear sir, yours, Thomas Hutchins, Surveyor-General of the United States." He accepted the appointment, received his instructions and an order on the frontier posts for a sufficient escort to enable him to prosecute the surveys; but the extreme weakness of the military force in the Northwest Territory—as Ohio was then called—left him in a very hazardous and exposed condition. His great energy, bodily strength and personal beauty, however, soon attracted the attention and admiration of the Indians, and won friends and safety for his little band, where the tomahawk and scalping-knife would, but for these, have been used against them. There are letters still preserved from General Joseph Harmer, addressed to Israel Ludlow, of date of 1787, and August 28th, 1788, which speak of the impossibility of affording him an adequate escort, and of the danger of his pursuing the survey at that time; but such danger and privations incurred by him did not deter the prosecution of the work. In 1789 he became associated with Mathias Denman and Robert Patterson in the proprietorship—to the extent of one-third—of the settlement about Fort Washington, which was to be called by the whimsical name of Losantiville, a compound word, intended to express "the city opposite the mouth of the Licking." To it, however, was given the more euphonious appellation of Cincinnati by Israel Ludlow, in honor of the Cincinnati Society of revolutionary officers, of which his father was a member, and which society was much criticised at that time. Late in the autumn of 1789 Colonel Ludlow commenced a survey of the town, which has since become the "Queen City of the West." In 1790 White's, Covolt's, and Ludlow Stations were created. The latter was near the north line of the town plot of Cincinnati, and a block-house was the first tenement erected there. As the Indians had become very savage and ferocious, strong forts were built, and military placed therein for the protection of the few whites who had ventured to settle in their neighborhood. So dangerous was the situation that persons who ventured beyond a certain limit of these forts fell victims to the brutality and ferocity of the savages. In 1791 General St. Clair's army was encamped at Ludlow Station, along what is now called Mad Anthony street, and the present site of the Presbyterian and Christian Churches. From thence, on September 17th, 1791, St. Clair proceeded to the Big Miami, and erected Forts Hamilton and Jefferson, and on November 4th following was fought the bloody and unfortunate battle called "St. Clair's Defeat." Israel Ludlow, now Colonel Ludlow, pursued his surveys under great difficulties, but completed them, and May 5th, 1792, made a full report of the same, and of all the expenses incident thereto, which were accepted by Alexander Hamilton, Secretary of the Treasury of the United States. In December, 1794, he surveyed the plot of a town adjacent to Fort Hamilton—hence the name —and was sole owner. In November, 1795, in conjunction with Generals St. Clair, Dayton and Wilkinson, he founded the town of Dayton. Previous to this, however, General Wayne had succeeded General St. Clair—after the latter's defeat—and prosecuted the Indian war until its termination in 1795, when emigration commenced again, and new towns and farms spread through the yielding forest. On November 10th, 1796, Colonel Ludlow married Charlotte, second daughter of General James Chambers, of Chambersburg, Pennsylvania, and on the 20th of the same month they started on their journey to Cincinnati. After a tedious ride over the mountains they reached the Monongahela river, and descended in a small boat to the vicinity of Pittsburgh, where they embarked on the waters of the Ohio. Colonel Ludlow was soon afterwards appointed to establish and survey the boundary line between the United States and the Indian Territory, agreeably to the treaty of Greenville, made by General Wayne, in 1795. It was a most dangerous undertaking, and while absent from Ludlow Station, which he had made his residence, his wife was in constant dread of hearing that some fatality had befallen his little party. In fact she could not anticipate any happiness while separated from her "beloved Ludlow," as she calls him, especially during his constant absence from the fort upon his arduous duties. She writes to him in 1797 of her increased fear for his safety, upon hearing that the Shawnees had appointed a chief, unknown to him, to attend him; and she urges him not to relax his vigilance for one moment. Her distress of mind can be better imagined than described when she learned than he was unable to obtain an escort, and at the same time knowing the great importance of the boundary being established, both to the government and to the settlers. It is a fact that he made a great part of the surveys with only three active woodsmen as spies, and to give him notice of danger. He died in January, 1804, at his home at Ludlow Station, after four days' illness. The house still remains in a good state of preservation, notwithstanding it is now eighty-six years old; and his great-grandchildren may stand in the room where he died and resolve to imitate his virtues. He was not permitted to witness the wonderful results of the enterprise to which his untiring industry was directed in forwarding. That he had a prescience of its importance is shown by his large entries of land in the region tributary to Cincinnati. Looking forward to a long life, he felt its immediate object was to lay the broad foundation of pecuniary fortune. Modesty was a well-known trait of his character. With an eye quick to discern, and energy to have applied, every measure conducing to the prosperity of the territory and the city, he was himself indifferent to his own political advancement, and willing to wait until the fulfilment of his plans. Thus it is, without legislative record of the facts, his name is not known in a manner commensurate with his services to the infant colony and youthful State. He was no politician in the clamorous sense of the term. He was a man for the times in which he lived, and possessed a peculiar fitness for the capacious sphere of his influence. His life was illustrated by a series of practical benevolences, free from ostentation, and the laudation of scarcely other than the recipients of his disinterested kindnesses. The shock created by the announcement of his death was great. The inhabitants joined the Masonic fraternity in paying the closing tribute of respect to his memory, and an oration was pronounced by Hon. John Cleves Symmes. Among his numerous descendants several have occupied prominent positions in Ohio and other Western States.

TILLMAN, CHARLES H., M. D., Physician and ex-Mayor of Plainfield, was born in Schenectady, New York, January 25th, 1817. The family is of English descent, the founders of the American branch having settled in Massachusetts in 1680. Afterwards a portion of the descendants of these settlers removed to Rhode Island, at what is now the village of Stillmanville, and others settled in the State of New York. From these Dr. Stillman is descended. His father, Joseph Stillman, was a widely known ship builder, and his older brother, Thomas B. Stillman, was one of the origina- tors—and up to the time of his death, which occurred some ten years since, was one of the proprietors—of the celebrated Novelty Works, of New York. All the members of the family were more or less celebrated for their skill in the mechanic arts. Charles H. Stillman was fitted for college at the academy of Schenectady, New York, and in the year 1832 entered the sophomore class of Union College. He graduated with the class of 1835. Among his classmates were Professors Foster and Pierson, of Union College. Immediately after graduating he commenced a course of preparatory study, with a view to entering the medical pro- fession. He studied first at Schenectady, and then read for three years with Dr. Delafield, of New York. He graduated from the College of Physicians and Surgeons, in New York, in the year 1840, and for two years after his graduation he was Physician and Oculist of the Eastern Dispensary. In 1842 he removed to Plainfield, New Jersey, where he has since resided, actively engaged in the practice of his profession. His advance to the front rank of medical practitioners was rapid and brilliant. His high natural abilities, joined to his sterling personal qualities and his thorough professional culture, and the enthusiasm with which he devoted all his energies to the calling he had entered upon, soon placed him among the foremost of his profession, and now his practice is among the largest and most valuable in the State. He has been for many years Surgeon of the Central Railroad of New Jersey, and his great skill as a surgeon has won the cordial recognition not only of the community at large, but of all in the profession. Next to his devotion to his profession is his practical ear- nestness in forwarding the educational interests of the com- munity in which he resides. It was largely through his instrumentality that the public schools of Plainfield, which rank now among the best in the State, have been brought to their present high standard. In 1847 he was elected a member of the School Board, and he held that position until 1867, when the revised school laws of the State took effect. He was elected a member of the first School Board under the new law, was chosen President of the Board at its first meeting, and has continued to fill the position from that time to this. He is a member of the State Medical Society and President of the Medical Society of Union County. He is also a Director of the City National Bank, of the Washington Fire Insurance Company, the City

Savings Institute and various other corporations. Politi- cally he is an ardent Republican, but enjoys the high esteem and perfect confidence of his fellow-citizens of all parties. In 1872 he was nominated by both political parties for the office of Mayor of Plainfield. He was, of course, elected to the position, and administered the duties of the office for two years. He was married, in 1842, to Mary E. Starr, of Hamilton, New York. His eldest son was for a time Assistant Professor of Chemistry in Stevens' Institute, Hoboken, New Jersey, and is now pursuing his studies in Germany. His second son is now House Physi- cian in St. Francis' Hospital, New York, and a third son is in his senior year at Rutgers College.

————

AYLOR, LEWIS HAZELIUS, of High Bridge, Iron Manufacturer and Railroad Promoter, was born in 1811, at the old historic mansion of the Taylor family, near the town of High Bridge, New Jersey, and is a son of Archibald and Ann (Bray) Taylor, and grandson of Robert Taylor, who came to America from Ireland in 1757. His grand- father, soon after his arrival, became connected with the Union Iron Company, then owned by the wealthy English laud proprietors and iron masters, Allen & Turner, and superintended by Colonel Hackett. After the death of the latter, Robert Taylor became his successor in the super- vision of the Union Iron Company, and continued to occupy that position until the suspension of the works, about the year 1782. The furnace of that company was the first erected on the continent of America, although the precise date cannot now be determined, but it was prior to the year 1700. The house where Robert Taylor resided is still standing, uniquely connected with and forming a part of the modernized mansion where his grandson now re- sides. In one room of the older portion, one hundred years ago, Governor John Penn and Attorney-General Benjamin Chew, the last colonial officials of Pennsylvania, were placed as prisoners of war, under charge of Robert Taylor, by the Continental Congress. Two volumes of " Memoirs," by Sir John Dalrymple, Baronet, which were presented to Robert Taylor by Governor Penn, are now in the possession of his grandson. In another room Robert Taylor died, in 1821, and in the same room his son Archi- bald was born, in 1780, and died in 1860. Lewis H. Taylor, son of Archibald, was partly educated at the Hart- wick Seminary, then under the superintendence of his uncle, the Rev. Lewis Hazelius, D. D., from whom he was named, where he passed three years; he completed his education under private tutors at home. On reaching manhood he engaged in mercantile and various other pur- suits until 1849, when the announcement was made that the newly acquired territory of California was the long-looked.

for Eldorado. In company with his brother, General George W. Taylor, he started for the Pacific coast, taking passage on the steamer "Crescent City," on her first trip via the isthmus, and was among the first colony of miners or pioneers of California. On their arrival in the land of gold, they were engaged in various enterprises, and while there contracted for and furnished the timbers for building the first wharves of San Francisco. They remained in California until 1852. On his return to the Atlantic States he built a forge on the site of one of the old pre-revolutionary works of the Union Iron Company, which has been enlarged at different times, a car-wheel foundry added, and in 1869 the whole concern was incorporated by the name of the Taylor Iron Company. These works have increased materially, until they are now one of the largest industrial establishments of the kind in the United States, manufacturing car-wheels, car-axles and all varieties of car and locomotive forgings; and it is the only concern in the country which manufactures both car-wheels and axles and "fits" them. The first President of the company was Lewis H. Taylor, who still holds the position. The works are located near the beautiful village of High Bridge, on the south branch of the Raritan river, and at the junction of the High Bridge Railroad and the Central Railroad of New Jersey. There are about two miles of railway which connect the different shops of the company with the Central Railroad, for which a separate charter was obtained in 1871. This gives admirable facilities for operating the works, receiving material, shipping the products, etc. In June, 1874, Mr. Taylor, in conjunction with Edward C. Knight, of Philadelphia, and others, became interested in the Delaware & Bound Brook Railroad. This road was built under the general railroad law of New Jersey, and the route selected was that originally surveyed for the National Air Line Railroad, which last named company had commenced the construction, but through the need of a proper organization and bad management had failed. Lewis H. Taylor was Managing Director of the Delaware & Bound Brook Railroad, and to his energy and capability is due, from the people of New Jersey and the travelling public in general, the credit of the early completion of this road and the first successful attempt to establish a through line between the cities of New York and Philadelphia, in opposition to the New Jersey monopoly, controlled by the Pennsylvania Railroad. The Pennsylvania company had thrown every obstacle in the way of an early completion of the Delaware & Bound Brook Railroad, contesting it in the courts in every possible manner. This opposition culminated into what has passed into the history of New Jersey as the "frog war." The Delaware & Bound Brook Railroad crosses the Mercer & Somerset Railroad—a branch of the Pennsylvania Railroad—on the same grade at a point near the village of Hopewell. As Mr. Taylor was unable to arrange for the right of way across that road—the Pennsylvania company refusing to make any concessions—he had the right of way condemned

in the usual manner and the award of the commissioners paid into court. On the 9th of November, 1875, the Delaware & Bound Brook Railroad brought up the first locomotive engine and stationed it on a siding at the crossing. On the evening of the same day the Pennsylvania company also brought up an engine and placed it immediately on the crossing of the point intersected by the two roads, only moving it away long enough to allow the Mercer & Somerset trains to pass, and, then returning immediately to its post.' Work on the Delaware & Bound Brook Railroad necessitated a crossing at once, and on Wednesday evening, the 6th of January, 1876, a large force of their men appeared on the ground. When the Pennsylvania company's patrolling engine passed off on a siding to allow a regular train to traverse the main road, and as soon as the latter had passed the point of intersection, each man with a crosstie upon his shoulder rushed upon the track, and in a second of time had formed an impassable bulwark. The switch-tender was frightened from his post by this unexpected demonstration of the Delaware & Bound Brook force, and the gang immediately commenced operations with a will, and soon had the Mercer & Somerset track torn from its bed, and were putting in the frog. This state of affairs was at once telegraphed to the officials of the Pennsylvania Railroad Company, and engine 336 was ordered to be run from Millstone at its greatest speed, and if possible to be tumbled into the gap. The engineer of No. 336 obeyed orders, and with his engine proceeded on its dangerous mission, at a speed never before attempted. It fairly flew past Hopewell into the throng of astonished workmen, and, shivered and wrecked, it fell into the pit dug by the Delaware & Bound Brook men, but failed by six inches in reaching the point where the Bound Brook men were putting the frog into position, and which by midnight they had securely laid. Amid the cheering of the victors the engine of the Delaware & Bound Brook Railroad Company moved upon the crossing thus legally secured. The failure of No. 336 to effect its object was flashed over the wires, and another engine, in its place, was at once ordered to the front to assist if possible in pushing the Delaware & Bound Brook engine from the crossing; but on the arrival of the second engine it was apparent that the crippled condition of No. 336 would not admit of such a proceeding. Affairs remained in this position until the following day, when each company brought to the field a force of over 1,000 men—Irishmen armed with the proverbial pick-handles, and Italians with the stiletto or a revolver under their belts. Mr. Taylor, assisted by Messrs. Francis H. Saylor, Chief Engineer, and George B. Boggs, Division Engineer, had the Delaware & Bound Brook men under their control, and Counsellor Browning, of Camden, advised them to defend their position by force, if circumstances rendered such a course necessary, and this course they were fully resolved to adopt. Both parties encamped upon the line, and on the following day Counsellor Browning petitioned the Chancellor for a mandamus to compel the Mercer & Somerset branch of the Pennsylvania Railroad to remove their obstruction. Meanwhile, passengers over this latter road were obliged to be transferred above and below the obstruction. These transactions were witnessed by hundreds of spectators. The Governor of New Jersey ordered the 7th Regiment of the National Guard, under Colonel Angel, to proceed to the disputed territory to preserve the peace. The Delaware & Bound Brook company continued to hold possession until the Chancellor's decision came, and this decision virtually gave them all they had contended for. The road was opened for public travel May 1st, 1876. It is a double track road, and has a passenger traffic fully equal to its capacity. Its completion was a signal victory over the Pennsylvania company and the railroad monopoly that had for years held the State, and virtually controlled its Legislature. The opening of the new line, making a direct route of travel between New York and Philadelphia, was hailed with delight all over the State, and to Lewis H. Taylor was justly awarded the honor of having been the instrument in procuring the long sought for disenthralment of the State from a gigantic monopoly. In 1873 he was instrumental in procuring a charter to construct a railroad from High Bridge, on the New Jersey Central, to Chester, in Morris county. This was afterwards consolidated with the Longwood Valley Railroad. Work was commenced on the High Bridge road in 1874, and completed in 1876 to Port Oram, in Morris county. This road, it is intended, shall reach the Hudson river, and there connect with eastern lines, so forming a direct route from the coal fields of Pennsylvania, via the Central Railroad of New Jersey, to the manufacturing towns of New England. The first President of this corporation was Lewis H. Taylor. He is also a Director of the Union Iron Company, of which his son, W. J. Taylor, is President. In politics, he is an ardent Republican, and has labored earnestly for the welfare of that party. He rendered efficient service to the Union government during the rebellion in raising troops. A serious affection of the eyes, as well as pressure of business devolving on him—owing to the absence of his brother, General George W. Taylor, who was one of the first to proceed to the front after the commencement of hostilities, and also of both his sons—prevented him from taking the field himself. Although so firm a Republican, he has steadily refused any office in the gift of the people, or any nomination thereto. In the autumn of 1876, however, his Republican friends induced him to accept the nomination for State Senator for the intensely Democratic county of Hunterdon, and although defeated, he polled a vote by several hundred greater than the balance of the Republican ticket. He was married, in 1835, to Jane C., daughter of William Johnston, of Philadelphia, and has four children now living: W. J. Taylor, of whom a sketch appears in another portion of this volume; one daughter is married to O. W. Chrystie, one of the officers of the Taylor Iron Works; and the other is the wife of W. H. Stevenson, senior partner of the house of W. H. Stevenson & Co., of Philadelphia, in which Lewis Taylor, Jr., his youngest son, is a junior partner. His second son, Archie, at the commencement of the war, enlisted as a private in Duryea's Zouaves, and served with that organization until just previous to the battle of Big Bethel, when he was promoted to a Lieutenancy and transferred to the 3d Regiment of the First Brigade New Jersey Volunteers. Before his twentieth year he was commissioned Captain, and distinguished himself, through all the hard fighting of the First Brigade, for bravery and fine soldierly qualities. He was killed at the second battle of Fredericksburg, near Salem Church, at the age of twenty years and eleven months.

———◆◆◆———

PENNINGTON, LOT S., M. D., and Pioneer Farmer of Illinois, was born in Somerset county, New Jersey, November 12th, 1812. His parents were Elijah Pennington and Martha (Todd) Pennington. His earlier education was acquired primarily at an academy located in Somerville, Somerset county, New Jersey, and afterward in an educational establishment of Basking Ridge, in the same county and State. At the completion of his probationary course of studies he decided to embrace the medical profession, and prepared himself for it while residing in New Jersey and in New York city. In 1836, believing that in the West was to be found a wider field for the profitable exercise of skill and industry, he removed to Jerseyville, Jersey county, Illinois, and there entered temporarily upon the active practice of his profession. He went subsequently to Macoupin county, and occupied himself professionally, and with success, at Brighton, Woodburn and Bunker Hill, until 1839, at which date he removed to Sterling, where he practised medicine for one year. In 1840 he purchased a tract of land, and applied his attention to farming and agricultural pursuits. In 1841 he commenced the cultivation of fruit and ornamental trees, in the first instance with a view to supply his own requirements only; but that limited beginning was destined to undergo a speedy development, and he ultimately found himself in a position to command an extensive nursery business, and which, in fact, he did subsequently carry on for a period of fifteen years, meeting with great and merited success. His was the second nursery established in northern Illinois, and at the present time he has over 800 acres of the finest land in the State of Illinois, all under high cultivation. He has devoted the latter portion of his life to scientific farming and kindred pursuits, and in apposite knowledge is unsurpassed. The nursery business, from which he retired in 1855, was encompassed with innumerable difficulties in this section, in the earlier days, when the country was sparsely settled and in almost a primitive and virgin condition; the depredations of swarms of wild rabbits made it all but impossible to preserve the trees, while the intensely severe winter of 1842–43 was extremely injurious to all vegetable growth. His lands were located on the boundary of the prairie, and the lucessantly recurring prairie fires necessitated the constant exercise of great caution and vigilance; and it was necessary, in order to arrest the progress of such fires, to hedge the farm about with a cordon, or belt of land, thoroughly plowed, of 200 yards in breadth. In 1861 he was appointed a member of the Board of Supervisors of Whitesides county, in which capacity he has since continued to act with energy and ability. He was married, in 1837, to Ann P. Barnett, daughter of John Barnett, of Brighton; she died in 1866. He was again married, in 1868, to Ruth A. Morrison, daughter of William and Mary Anne Galt, and widow of Dr. William Morrison, of Lancaster county, Pennsylvania.

———◄●►———

cOILL, STEWART, Agriculturist, was born near Trenton, New Jersey, February 18th, 1788, and was the oldest of eight children, whose parents were Neill McGill and Elizabeth (Larrison) McGill. The former, a native of county Antrim, near Belfast, Ireland, was engaged through life in school-teaching and surveying, and while still a young man emigrated to America. He sympathized with the colonies in their resistance to the rule of Great Britain, and took an active part in common with the insurgent patriots. While the Hessians were in winter-quarters at Trenton, prior to their capture by General Washington, they made a descent on his property, and appropriated to their own uses his cattle and other valuable possessions. He died in Hunterdon county, New Jersey, in 1814, at the age of seventy-two years. His mother was a native of New Jersey, and daughter of Rodger Larrison, an active participant in the revolutionary war. She died in 1823. His earlier education was limited, and received at the common schools located in the neighborhood of his home. While in his twelfth year he went to live with Judge John Corryell, of Hunterdon county, New Jersey, with whom he remained for about three years, during this time attending school for a term of three months or more. He subsequently worked for three years as an apprentice under Luke Hebdon, of Trenton, New Jersey, at the shoemaking trade, afterward opening a shoe-shop at Lambertville, New Jersey, where he engaged also in harness-making; he remained there through the ensuing year. Up to 1811 he worked in New Jersey and in New York city, removing later to Ohio, where, July 3d, 1811, he settled finally in Colerain township, Hamilton county. He travelled west on foot through Pennsylvania to Pittsburgh, and thence on a flat-boat to Cincinnati, where he landed July 2d. The battle of Tippecanoe, in the second war with England, had been fought,

and becoming imbued with the prevalent popular excitement he entered the volunteer service in 1812, under the command of General Hull, and was taken prisoner at the time of that officer's surrender at Detroit. At the expiration of a few weeks he was released on parole, and returned to his home in Hamilton county, where he has since resided, occupied mostly in agricultural pursuits. In 1821–22 he served as constable and assessor of chattel property, and in 1823 was elected Justice of the Peace, which office he held for nine years. He also held at various times the offices of Trustee, Township Clerk and Assessor of Real Estate for Colerain and Springfield Townships. In 1824 he was elected Treasurer of the School and Ministerial Funds of his township, which office he held for twenty-five years. In 1838 he was elected a Director in the Colerain, Oxford & Brookville Turnpike Company, whose road was then in the course of construction. In 1840 he was elected Treasurer of said company, which position he held, with the exception of a year or two, until November, 1865. Upon retiring from said position the committee (consisting of the president, secretary and one other director) appointed to settle his accounts passed a resolution expressing their satisfaction that in " accounts extending over a period of nearly a quarter of a century, and amounting to several hundred thousand dollars, no discrepancy had ever appeared, nor had a single dime ever been unaccounted for." He has also settled the estates of more deceased persons than any other man in his part of the county. In politics he is attached to the Republican party; he cast his first vote for President for James Monroe. In 1824 he voted for John Quincy Adams. In 1826 or 1827 he became a strong Jackson man, and took a leading part in organizing the Jackson or Democratic party in Colerain township, and was a delegate to the first convention held by that party in Hamilton county. He voted for General Jackson in 1828, and again in 1832. But in 1833, not approving the course General Jackson had taken, he left the Democratic and joined the Whig party, to which he adhered until it died, after which he became a Republican. In his younger days he took an active part in politics, although he never sought office. In 1833 he was nominated as a candidate for County Commissioner, but was defeated by a few votes. In 1836 the Whigs nominated him for the Legislature, but he was not elected. He was nominated several times afterwards for the same office, sometimes accepting and at others declining to be a candidate; but as his party was in the minority he never was elected. He was married, October 5th, 1823, to Sarah Johnson, widow of Alexander Johnson and daughter of Elias Hedges, an early settler from Morris county, New Jersey, who settled at Dunlap's Station, on the Big Miami river, Hamilton county, in 1805, by whom he has had three children, two of whom are still living, a son and daughter. He lost his wife in April, 1854, and has never married again; his son, Amzi McGill, has been twice elected a member of the House of Representa-

33

tives of Ohio, and has served one term as County Commissioner of Hamilton county, Ohio, and has held various other trusts of greater or less importance.

USLING, JAMES F., Counsellor-at-Law, Master in Chancery and Notary Public, of Trenton, was born at Washington, Warren county, New Jersey, April 14th, 1834. His parents were Gershom and Eliza B. Rusling. In March, 1845, while he was still quite a lad, his family removed to Trenton, New Jersey. He entered the New Jersey Conference Seminary at Pennington, in October, 1850, and graduated there with the honors of his class, in October, 1852. Immediately afterwards he entered the junior class, at Dickinson College, Carlisle, Pennsylvania, and graduated there with second honors in July, 1854. In September following he was elected Professor of Natural Science and Belles Lettres in Dickinson Seminary, Williamsport, Pennsylvania, and read law under Hon. Robert Fleming while teaching there. He was admitted to the Pennsylvania bar in 1857, but subsequently returned to Trenton, and was admitted to the New Jersey bar in June, 1859. He soon acquired a satisfactory practice, but was diverted from it by the civil war, and in August, 1861, entered the Union army as First Lieutenant, 5th Regiment New Jersey Volunteers. In June, 1862, he was made Captain United States Volunteers, by President Lincoln, and in May, 1863, promoted to Lieutenant-Colonel. Early in 1865 he was brevetted Major, Lieutenant-Colonel and Colonel, for "gallantry and good conduct," and promoted to be full Colonel United States Volunteers, and Inspector Quartermaster's Department. In 1866 he was further brevetted Brigadier-General " for faithful and meritorious services " during the war. He served with the Army of the Potomac from August, 1861, to November, 1863: at Yorktown, Williamsburg, Fair Oaks, Glendale, Malvern Hill, second Bull Run, Chantilly, Fredericksburg, Chancellorsville, Gettysburg, Bristow Station, Rappahannock, etc.; and the remainder of the war in the Department of the Cumberland, where, as Chief Assistant-Quartermaster of that department, under Generals Thomas and Sherman, he contributed much to our success at Chattanooga, Kenesaw, Atlanta, Franklin, Nashville, etc. In 1865-66, while Inspector of the Army, he was sent through nearly all of the late rebel States, to observe affairs, reduce government expenditures, etc.; in 1866-67 he was ordered overland to the Pacific, to inspect all military depots and posts en route, and return by the isthmus, with a view to reductions, cheapening supplies, etc. On his return he retired from the army, in September, 1867, and soon after resumed the practice of law at Trenton, New Jersey. While in the army he was so fortunate as to secure the confidence of Generals Sickles, Mott, Hooker, Meigs, Thomas, Sherman and Grant, and his promotions were made chiefly on their recommendations. In 1868 he was nominated for Congress by the Republican party, but failed of election—his district as then constituted being heavily Democratic. In 1869 he was appointed United States Pension Agent for New Jersey, by President Grant, and in 1873 was reappointed. Meanwhile he has continued the practice of his profession, more or less, since 1867, and has been admitted to practise in all the State and Federal courts in New Jersey. General Rusling has also shown considerable literary talent. He has been a frequent contributor to the newspapers and magazines, and in 1874 published a book entitled "Across America; or, The Great West and the Pacific Coast," being the results of his observations and adventures through 15,000 miles of travel, while making his overland tour of inspection, in 1866-67. This has already passed through three editions, and its sale continues. The Boston Post declared it "A really charming volume." The New York Christian Advocate said: "The narrative' is lively, the style forcible, and the facts reliable." The Philadelphia North American, in alluding to it, said: "General Rusling has written a capital book, in a capital way. The best-read persons will gain something from it, and to those unacquainted with recent travel it will be a liberal education." The New York Tribune pronounced it "A series of faithful, if not brilliant, sketches of personal incident and adventure, and it strikingly illustrates the development of utility, intelligence and material success in the great West and on the Pacific coast." The New York World said it was "Not the usual routine of brigadier book-making, but it treats one to some new views of life among army people and miners." The San Francisco Bulletin said: "It abounds in incidents of travel, and occasionally of perilous adventure, marked by shrewd observations and sharp but good-natured hits at our social peculiarities." These are only a few of the many notices of it. Altogether, the press seems to have taken very kindly to it, doubtless much to the gratification of its author.

OFFMAN, THEODORE J., Lawyer, of Clinton, was born in Clinton township, Hunterdon county, New Jersey, his father being the late R. H. Hoffman, a prominent farmer, merchant and real estate operator. Under the tutorship of the Rev. Robert Van Amburg he was prepared for college, the point to which he had carried his studies enabling him to enter Rutgers, in 1848, in the sophomore class. Graduating in 1851, he immediately began the study of law in the office of S. B. Ransom, then of Somerville, a leading practitioner at the Jersey City bar. Admitted to practise in 1854, he established himself at Asbury, New Jersey, where he remained until 1860, acquiring in that time a prominent position in his profession. He was a staunch adherent to the Republican party, and a warm supporter

Nathaniel Niles

ton College, under the presidency of Rev.
the only clergyman appearing among th
Declaration of Independence. A

of President Lincoln, and in 1863, when the war was at its height, he sacrificed his professional prospects and enlisted as a private in the 8th New Jersey Regiment. He served with credit through the severe campaigns of the Army of the Potomac nearly two years, and was, with his regiment, honorably mustered out of the service after the surrender of Lee at Appomattox. He resumed the practice of law at Clinton, New Jersey, where he has since remained. Mr. Hoffman has been engaged in a number of notable suits in the New Jersey courts; that, perhaps, which gained him greatest credit, being the celebrated case of John F. Styne *vs*. The Central Railroad of New Jersey, a case in which he was one of several counsel, and in which he gained a substantial verdict for his client. Mr. Hoffman was married, February 22d, 1855, to Amanda, daughter of the late Aaron Van Syckel.

ILES, HON. NATHANIEL, of Madison, Lawyer, was born, September 15th, 1835, at South Kingston, Rhode Island. He is the son of Rev. William W. Niles, of the Protestant Episcopal Church, and grandson of Judge Nathaniel Niles, of Vermont. The latter was graduated at Princeton College, under the presidency of Rev. Dr. Witherspoon, the only clergyman appearing among the signatures to the Declaration of Independence. A second Nathaniel Niles, uncle of the subject of this sketch, successively represented the United States at the courts of France, Sardinia, and Austria. Nathaniel Niles, of Madison, was educated at home by his father and also at Phillips Academy, in Massachusetts. He settled in New Jersey in 1854, and then afterwards studied law in the office of the late Francis B. Cutting, of New York, in which State he was admitted to practise in 1857. He removed in 1859 to Madison, where he was married to Anna, daughter of Lewis Thompson, of Morris county. He is a large property holder in this and Union county. His political belief is Republican, on which ticket he was elected in 1870 for the lower House of the State Legislature. He served on the important Committees on Railroads and on Education, and originated a number of useful laws. Amongst these, two call for special notice as of lasting importance. The first, which was finally passed over the veto of the governor, swells the State school fund, by transferring to it all moneys derived from the sale of riparian lands, and reads as follows: "An act to increase the school fund of this State. 1. Be it enacted by the Senate and General Assembly of the State of New Jersey, That all moneys hereafter received from the sales and rentals of the land under water belonging to this State, shall be paid over to the trustees of the school fund and appropriated for the support of free public schools, and shall be held by them in trust for that purpose, and shall be invested by the treasurer of the State under their direction, in the same manner as the funds now held by them are invested, the same to constitute a part of the permanent school fund of the State, and the interest thereof to be applied to the support of public schools in the mode which now is or hereafter may be directed by law, and to no other purpose whatever. 2. And be it enacted, That all acts and parts of acts, inconsistent with this act, be, and the same are hereby repealed. 3. And be it enacted, That this act shall take effect immediately. Passed, April 6th, 1871.' Prior to the passage of this act, the total school fund of the State was only half a million dollars. Since its passage the fund has been increased from this source to nearly two and one quarter million dollars, and in the next decade is expected to amount to five millions. The income of it will doubtless at no very distant day entirely relieve the people from the annual school tax. It now affords relief from taxation to more than $100,000 annually. The second law encourages the formation of free school libraries by donating out of the State treasury the sum of twenty dollars, with which to purchase books the first year in each and every school district in which the additional sum of twenty dollars shall be raised for that purpose by voluntary contribution, and ten dollars annually thereafter upon the like conditions. Under this act some four hundred libraries are now in operation. Mr. Niles was re-elected in 1871 by an immensely increased majority, and on the organization of the House was chosen Speaker. He is Vice-President of the American Trust Company of Newark, and also Trustee for several large estates.

ISHER, SAMUEL WARE, D. D., LL. D., Clergyman and College President, was born at Morristown, New Jersey, on April 5th, 1814. His father was an eminent Presbyterian minister, for many years in charge of the church at Morristown, then one of the largest in the State; and afterward for twenty years the pastor of the Presbyterian Church in Paterson. He was the first Moderator of the General Assembly of the New School body after its separation from the old, and was long recognized as one of the most earnest workers in the church, to whose welfare his life was consecrated. To the example and counsels of such a father was naturally owing something of the tastes and tendencies of the son. Dr. Fisher was early initiated into the modes of thought and action common to the great body with which he was connected. Its traditions were all familiar to him from boyhood. The choice of a profession to a young man is sometimes difficult; the result of anxious deliberation, the conclusion reached through much doubt and conflict. To him it was easy; a profession to which his life had been naturally and divinely shaped; the most satisfying and best, he thought, which can be chosen by man. His desires and wishes, his purposes and ambitions, if the word may be used in its better sense, opened out in the direction of work for and through the Presbyterian Church. Here was ground ample and noble, whose every hillside and vale were familiar to him, and it is perfectly natural that he should always have felt himself most at home with the congregations and presbyteries, the synods and assemblies of this powerful body. He was graduated at Yale College in 1835, spent a year in Middletown, Connecticut, pursued his theological studies at Princeton for two years, and completed them afterwards at Union Theological Seminary in New York. Immediately after leaving the seminary he became the minister of the Presbyterian church in West Bloomfield, New Jersey. During his ministry of a little more than four years in this place his fidelity was crowned with two revivals of religion. From there he removed in 1843 to a larger and more trying field of labor, being installed on the 13th of October in that year as pastor of the Fourth Presbyterian Church of Albany. This position was one of unusual delicacy and difficulty. The church was probably, at that time, the largest in the whole denomination, having more than nine hundred names upon the roll of its communicants. The important work of his predecessors he supplemented by other work quite as important in forming a complete and sound Christian character, and a vigorous and active Christian church. The work that he did there has not lost its value by the lapse of years, nor is the estimation of its importance in the judgment of the most judicious observers less than at first. The extent of his reputation as a vigorous and effective preacher may be indicated by the fact that, in October, 1846, he was called to succeed the most popular, the most widely known, and the most powerful preacher of the New School body, in the Second Presbyterian Church of Cincinnati, Dr. Lyman Beecher, and entered on the duties of the service in April, 1847. It was not a small thing then for a minister still young, comparatively unknown, to follow in pulpit ministrations the most renowned pulpit orator, the most powerful controversialist of the West; not an easy task, with prudence, skill, commanding vigor, and above all, with Christian fidelity and with a view to the broadest Christian success, to maintain his position, to secure the confidence, the good-will, the sympathy of a large and unusually intelligent congregation, of various political affinities, trained to vigorous and discriminating thought. Here was not only opportunity but imperative demand for large and exhaustive labor. Here were conflicting opinions to harmonize, critical minds to satisfy, plans for Christian labor to be formed, machinery to be organized and put in motion, new evils to be met by new methods, the life and vigor of the church itself to be maintained in the midst of peculiar temptations, and so a larger and completer Christian household gathered and inspired. This was the work which he performed. The difficulties of his position stimulated his energy. He was in the full vigor of every faculty. The field of labor was broad and full of encouragement. His words were not spoken to the empty air, but came back laden with the murmurs of approving voices. He became

an intellectual and moral power in the city. The young gathered about him, and he prepared more than one series of discourses particularly adapted to their tastes and wants. One of these series, "Three Great Temptations," published in 1852, went through six editions. In no other place did he labor continuously so long as in Cincinnati, and to this period he afterward looked back as on the whole the most successful and fortunate of his life. He was in his chosen employment, his manly energies at their highest vigor; a working church, trained and stimulated by large foresight, in full sympathy with him, accepting his leadership, and cheerfully co-operating in Christian word and work. His ministry in this church was eminently successful—one hundred and seventy-eight persons having been added to the church by profession and two hundred and forty-eight by letter during the eleven years of his pastorate. His character was a rare combination of mildness and energy. He possessed the faculty of discovering the capabilities and most valuable characteristics of those with whom he associated, and of infusing into them the ardor and zeal which animated his own heart. He developed the latent energies and abilities of the Second Presbyterian Church and congregation in a remarkable degree, and by his skill in organizing and combining individual talent into congenial association for Christian work, accomplished great results for the cause of his Master. Thus quietly operating, he put in motion various plans and organizations in the church which resulted in great and lasting usefulness. Among them was the Young Men's Home Missionary Society, so successful in establishing Sabbath schools, providing for vacant churches, and other works of a similar character. He awakened an unusual interest in Foreign Missions by appointing different members of the church to make reports at the monthly concerts on the condition of the important foreign stations. He held regular meetings at his own house of the younger members of the church for devotion, consultation and advice. In numerous ways he was constantly leading on the church in matters of Christian enterprise. During the eleven years of his service in the great commercial city of Ohio, his mind had not been growing narrower, nor, engaged as he constantly was in duties most important and exacting, had he forgotten the claims of science and letters, or failed to meet the demands upon his time and talents necessary to their encouragement. The schools, colleges and professional seminaries of the State, and of neighboring States, heard his voice and felt his influence whenever he could say a word or lift a finger for their help. It was natural also that, occupying so prominent a place, he should have been called upon for various public services, and become of influence in the larger assemblies of the church. In 1857 the New School General Assembly of the Presbyterian Church met at Cleveland. Of this learned and able body Dr. Fisher was chosen Moderator. The subject of slavery had been discussed in more than one General Assembly, and the system strongly condemned. The southern members had as frequently protested against these deliverances, and in 1856 did not hesitate to acknowledge that their views in respect to the evil of slavery had materially changed, and they openly avowed that they now accepted the system, believing it to be right according to the Bible. This position the assembly at Cleveland pointedly condemned, while yet expressing a tender sympathy for those who deplore the evil, and are honestly doing all in their power for the present well-being of their slaves, and for their complete emancipation. These ideas of the two parties were too radically antagonistic, too deeply held, too frequently and publicly affirmed to allow fraternal co-operation. The southern synods thereupon withdrew, and formed themselves into a separate body, called the United Synod of the Presbyterian Church. It was in reference to this secession that, in the sermon before the General Assembly of 1858, in Chicago, with which, as retiring Moderator, he opened the sessions of that body, Dr. Fisher used these strong and generous words: " Fathers and brethren, ministers and elders, we assemble here amidst the brightness of scenes of revival, scenes such as the church of Christ, perhaps, has never enjoyed so richly before. But as my eye passes over this audience, a shade of sadness steals in upon my heart. There are those who have been wont to sit with us in this high council, whose hearty greeting we miss to-day. Taking exception to the ancient, the uniform, the oft-repeated testimony of our church, as well as to the mode of its utterance, respecting one of the greatest moral and organic evils of the age; deeming it better to occupy a platform foreign, indeed, to the genius of our free republican institutions, yet adapted, in their view, to the fuller promulgation of the Gospel in the section where they dwell, they have preferred to take an independent position ; and while we cannot coincide with them in their views on this subject, while we know that this separation has been precipitated upon us, not sought by us, yet, remembering the days when, with us, they stood shoulder to shoulder against ecclesiastical usurpation and revolution, when in deepest sympathy we have gone to the house of God in company, and mingled our prayers before a common mercy-seat, we cannot but pray for their peace and prosperity. We claim no monopoly of wisdom and right. If in our course hitherto we have been moved to acts or deeds unfraternal or unbefitting our mutual relations—if in the attempt to maintain our ancient principles and apply the Gospel to the heart of this gigantic evil, we have given utterance to language that has tended to exasperate rather than quicken to duty, we claim no exemption from censure, we ask the forgiveness we are equally ready to accord." From the delivery of this able and weighty discourse on the " Conflict and Rest of the Church," of the style and spirit of which the above brief extract may give an imperfect notion, he went directly to Clinton, New York, having been already consulted respecting the presidency of Hamilton College. He entered upon his duties at the opening of the fall term of

1858, the ceremonies of the inauguration not taking place until the 4th of November. The college had risen far above its earlier difficulties, and under a wise administration had for many years enjoyed an honorable reputation for thoroughness of instruction and discipline, but its resources were still insufficient, and its appeals for aid had not been quite loud enough to reach the ear of the wealthy and the liberal. To the period of his presidency dates the growth of a greater confidence in the college, the endowments of its professorships and charitable foundations, and prizes for the encouragement of good learning, bearing honored names in this and in neighboring communities, never to be forgotten. From this period dates also the effective enlargement, almost the new creation of the general funds of the college, and an impetus and direction imparted to the liberality of the generous and noble-minded which has not ceased, but has yielded but the first-fruits of an increasing harvest. During his presidency the efficiency of the college instruction was increased. Under his influence and in accordance with his wishes the Bible assumed a more prominent place as a part of the regular curriculum, a place which it has ever since retained, for the advantage of all. His views of the ends and methods of education are contained in several addresses which he delivered at different times, and which were afterwards collected and published. The very subjects of these are suggestive of broad and careful thought. They are such as " Collegiate Education," " Theological Training," " The Three Stages of Education " (by which he discriminates child-life, the school and society), " Female Education," " The Supremacy of Mind," " Secular and Christian Civilization,' " Natural Science in its Relations to Art and Theology." These addresses are eloquent and sound. The most complete of them, perhaps, is his inaugural, in which he endeavors to develop his idea of what he calls the American collegiate system. The whole address is an argument for breadth and loftiness of culture. The scheme which it defends and enforces is noble and generous to the last degree. In 1862, in the midst of the civil war, occurred the semi-centennial celebration of the founding of Hamilton College, a memorable occasion, marking the age and progress of the institution as with a tall memorial shaft visible from afar. The address of Dr. Fisher is an admirable sketch of the college history, portraying in picturesque language the events of its early and later life, with enthusiasm and faith commending it to the good will of its alumni and friends, and predicting its future prosperity. " It was," he said, " amid the smoke and thunder of war that, fifty years ago, the foundations of this college were laid ; and when they passed away, lo ! on the hill-top had sprung into being a power mightier than the sword, more glorious than its triumphs. It is amid the heavier thunder and darker clouds of this dread conflict, when all that to us is most precious is in peril, that we celebrate our semi-centennial jubilee. This thunder shall roll away and the cloud disperse before the uprising patriotism of twenty millions of freemen and the red right arm of the Lord of hosts." That was indeed to the nation an hour of darkness, when the light was as darkness, but he never "bated one jot of heart or hope," or failed to act up to his patriotic faith. After a service of eight years in Hamilton College, he was solicited to accept again the position of pastor by the Westminster Church of Utica, New York, and was installed as pastor November 15th, 1867. For nearly four years of active and progressive work the church enjoyed the ministrations and stimulating energy of this able, active, and untiring pastor. There was yet one other occasion not to be forgotten in which he bore a prominent part in a great and memorable public service, whose influence is incalculable; viz., the measures which led to the reunion of the separated branches of the Presbyterian Church. There was no object, perhaps, nearer his heart, none which more moved his enthusiasm. The disruption had taken place in 1837, just before he entered upon his ministry. His father was the first Moderator of the New School Assembly. The doctrines and the men, the causes and the consequences, he had heard discussed from his boyhood, and in the reunion of the two branches of the church he was relied upon as among the most judicious counsellors in the very delicate and difficult questions that impeded its progress and threatened to prevent its consummation. He was one of the able committee of conference appointed by the two assemblies, which reported the plan of reunion in 1869. Nor does he seem to have doubted the beneficent result. In behalf of the joint committee, he proposed the resolution for raising $1,000,000, immediately afterward raised to $5,000,000, as a memorial fund. His last work, to which he gave himself with all the confidence and enthusiasm of his nature, was to prepare a paper for the General Assembly of 1870, an assembly which he was never to see. He received the Doctorate of Divinity from Miami University in 1852, and the Doctorate of Laws from the University of the city of New York in 1859. As a preacher he must be held to rank among the ablest of the Presbyterian body. With all that may be said by way of detracting criticism, it must still be allowed that our religious communities move along a pretty high level of intellectual experience and of religious feeling. To satisfy the reasonable demands of our congregations requires a continuous intellectual exertion, which, when we come to measure its force, is something startling. It is not a wonder that so many poor sermons are preached, but rather that there are so many good ones. But Dr. Fisher moved above, far above the common level. Within the ample dome of that forehead it was felt, at sight, there dwelt a powerful brain. He brought to his discourses a mind well stored and well disciplined. There was a fulness and richness of thought which left little or nothing in that direction to desire. An intellectual hearer could not fail to be attracted by his vigor. His style was often bold, sometimes picturesque, almost always clear and direct. His words were well chosen and exuberant. Thus full and weighty in matter, affluent in language, with no ambiguity of expression, fertile in imagery and illustration, with a voice clear and penetrating, and a manner somewhat authoritative, it is not surprising that he was constantly sought for to address public bodies on important occasions, a duty which he always performed with dignity and to the satisfaction of his hearers. The subjects of his discourses were various, and as his mind was mainly occupied with grand and lofty themes, so there was a certain nobleness, freedom, and power of development, the natural and necessary fruit of his general studies and habits of thought. No man could ever listen to him when engaged upon those great themes with which his soul was filled, without a persuasion that he spoke from absolute conviction of the truth and an overwhelming sense of the importance of the message he bore as an embassador of Christ and a "legate of the skies." His ordinary discourses were full of thought as well as of feeling. Those who heard the course of sermons on the "Epistle to the Hebrews," and on the "Life of Christ," need not be told that a more remarkable series of discourses has seldom been heard from an American pulpit. There were public occasions also when he discussed great topics with a fulness and a power that left nothing more to be said, and with results of conviction in the minds of his auditors that nothing could shake, nothing even disturb. There are several of his discourses that would alone make a distinguished reputation for any man, and that are to be ranked among the highest efforts of the pulpit of his day. But not in the pulpit only did he shine. So unusually is marked excellence as a preacher combined with an equal excellence as a pastor, that it would not have been strange if he had proved comparatively inefficient in pastoral work. Nevertheless he did prove to be an exceptionably good pastor. He gave living demonstration that one man may be both great preacher and good pastor. In all the families that made up his congregation, his name was a household word. Carrying everywhere an atmosphere of cheerfulness and sunshine, no one ever met him in social life without feeling the charm of his manners and conversation. Slow to condemn and quick to sympathize, shrinking instinctively from wounding the feelings of any, and prompt in all offices of kindness and love, he won the hearts of his people to a most singular degree. Never was any pastor more universally beloved. The minister most covetous of the love of his people might well be satisfied with the measure of affection accorded to Dr. Fisher. A prince he was, not by virtue of any patent of nobility bestowed by an earthly monarch, but by the direct gift of Heaven, with the royal signet of the giver legibly impressed thereon; a prince in intellect, a prince in large and liberal culture, but over and above all, a prince in active sympathies, warm affections, and a great human heart going out impulsively toward all that pertained to man, however lowly, or sin-stained, or despised, and devoting his best powers and faculties to the good of the world and the glory of God. It was in the practical and persistent consecration of the gifts and graces with which he was endowed to these large and beneficent ends, that he earned the title, secured the honors, and obtained the rewards of a prince and a great man in Israel. Such, most imperfectly, and in the merest outline sketched, was Dr. Samuel Ware Fisher up to the day and hour when, at the flood-tide of his influence, and apparently in the meridian fulness of his intellectual and moral powers, he was, by the mysterious stroke of an unseen hand, suddenly struck down, leaving him with the bounding pulse of life faintly fluttering, the bright eye dimmed, the eloquent tongue mute or incoherent. His half-executed plans, his high expectations, his large purposes arrested, nothing remained for him but with childlike trust and sweet patience to await the final summons, which, January 18th, 1874, at Cincinnati, Ohio, came in kindness to call him home. The temporary torpor of his faculties was at once dispelled, the clouds and the shadows that gathered about his setting sun have all been dissipated, the darkness has passed, and light perennial and eternal beams on him, for, in his own beautiful words, "Another Teacher, infinitely wise and good, is now leading him up the heights of knowledge, and in a moment he has learned more than men on earth can ever know."

EGHTE, HON. RYNIER H., ex-State Senator, near Somerville, was born on the farm where he now resides, April 22d, 1811. He is of Dutch descent, his ancestors having come to this country from Holland in the seventeenth century, and settled in Somerset county, New Jersey, where they purchased large tracts of land. The farm on which he was born and now lives has been in the family for two hundred years, and was the property of his grandfather, who passed his life as a farmer. In his boyhood Rynier H. Veghte received a substantial business education, studying diligently and improving to the utmost the opportunities afforded him. When he had reached the age of fourteen he went to New York city, and there took a situation in a jobbing and importing crockery house. In the year 1834 he organized the firm of Veghte & Lippincott, and engaged in the jobbing and importing of crockery, earthenware, etc. In the disastrous fire of 1835 their store was destroyed and he lost nearly all his property. He then accepted a position in the establishment of John Wright, Jr., who was engaged in the crockery business, and remained there for two years. At the end of that time he became a partner in the firm of Wright, Skiller & Co. In 1842 the style of the firm was changed to Veghte, Bergh & Burtis. He was eminently successful in business, and continued actively engaged in it until 1857, when he retired from business and took up his residence on the old homestead near Somerville, which has since been his home. In the fall of 1860 he was nominated by the Democrats for the position of State Senator. He was elected by a handsome majority, and served a three years term. During his term of office he was one of the Committee on Corporations, of which his unquestioned integrity and his large business experience made him a most valuable member. Although acting with the Democratic party, he is not and never has been a partisan or a politician in the ordinary acceptation of the term. When the war of the rebellion broke out, all his sympathy and influence were given to the administration in its defence of the government, and he was an earnest and practical friend of the Union soldiers in the field. When the war closed his sympathies were still warm and active in behalf of the wounded and disabled defenders of the country. In 1876, at the urgent solicitation of many leading citizens, he accepted an independent nomination for Congress, in opposition to the regular Democratic nominee. He was defeated at the polls, but the vote he received was a large and very flattering one, and he carried his own county by a majority of several hundreds, the remainder of his ticket being greatly in the minority there. He is a man of sterling integrity, and possesses the confidence of his fellow-citizens in a high degree. He is a Trustee of the State Normal School; a member of the State Board of Education; President of the Home for Disabled Soldiers; a leading Director of the Somerset County Bank, and President of the Somerset County Agricultural Society. He was married, in 1835, to Maria Theresa Fredericks, of New York.

EGHTE, JOHN O., Banker, of Somerville, son of Rynier Veghte, originally educated for the bar, but by choice a farmer, and the descendant of a Hollandish family resident in New Jersey from colonial times, was born near Somerville, October 13th, 1824. Having received an academical education at Plainfield, New Jersey, under the supervision of the well-known Ezra Fairchild, he entered the sophomore class of Rutgers College, whence he graduated in 1844. In the year of his graduation he was entered at the New Jersey bar, but after reading law for upwards of a twelvemonth, he became convinced that the legal profession was not to his taste. Abandoning his studies, he was engaged in mercantile pursuits for some four years, and was then appointed Teller in the Somerset County Bank. In banking he found a congenial pursuit, for which his exceptional financial ability well fitted him, and having served as Teller and as Cashier, was finally, in 1873, upon the resignation of Mr. Joshua Doughty, elected to the Presidency of the corporation, a position that he still holds. Prominent in the East Jersey division of the Democratic party, he was urged in the State convention of 1872 as a Congressional candidate, but was defeated by filibustering on the part of his rivals.

In the convention of 1876 he was again presented by his friends as a candidate and was again defeated. On both occasions a large majority of the delegates from Somerset were his supporters; and he was entitled, moreover, by party usage to the nomination. His success in 1876 would have been of essential service to the State, as his financial knowledge would have been well employed in the adjustment of the various monetary matters discussed in the ensuing session of the Legislature. In local politics he has been more successful, having been elected County Treasurer of Somerset in 1850, and since continuously re-elected to that office, which he ably fills. Among his fellow-townsmen he is highly esteemed for his integrity and business ability, a feeling testified to by his selection as trustee for a number of valuable estates. He married Sophia Veghte.

FITCH, CHARLES F., Lawyer, of Phillipsburg, was born in 1844 at Edmeston, Otsego county, New York, whither his father, Ransom Fitch, a merchant, had removed from Pittsfield, Massachusetts. The Fitch family, it may be mentioned, were among the early settlers of this old New England town. He was educated at the Mansfield, Pennsylvania, Normal School, and upon his graduation studied law and was admitted to practise at Easton, Pennsylvania. He subsequently read in the office of Judge Depue—now of the New Jersey Supreme Court—at Belvidere, and in 1867 was admitted to the New Jersey bar. Establishing himself at Phillipsburg, he soon acquired an extensive practice, and has been, since 1873, Solicitor for the town. Since 1872 he has owned a controlling interest in the Warren *Democrat*, published at Phillipsburg.

BEDLE, HON. JOSEPH DORSETT, Lawyer, ex-Associate-Justice of the Supreme Court of New Jersey and Governor of the State, was born at Matawan, Monmouth county, New Jersey, January 5th, 1831. He comes of an old American family on both sides, his maternal ancestors having emigrated to this country from Bermuda upwards of 150 years ago. His father, Thomas J. Bedle, whose immediate ancestors were Jerseymen, was a merchant, a Justice of the Peace for upwards of twenty-five years, and a Judge of the Court of Common Pleas for the county of Monmouth. His mother, Hannah Dorsett, descended from a family that was among the early settlers of Monmouth county. Governor Bedle obtained his early educational training in the academy at Matawan, then known as Middletown Point. He was attracted toward the legal profession, and at an early age commenced his law studies under the very able direction of Hon. W. L. Dayton, in Trenton,

in 1848. With this gentleman he remained for three or four years, during this period attending the regular course of lectures at the Law School, Ballston, New York. One winter he passed at Poughkeepsie, New York, in the office of Thompson & Weeks, and was admitted to the bar of New York State, as attorney and counsellor, in the spring of 1852. Returning to New Jersey, he passed a short time in the office of Hon. Henry S. Little, at Matawan, and was admitted to the bar of that State in January, 1853. He began the practice of his profession in New Jersey, at Matawan, where he remained for two years. In the spring of 1855 he removed to Freehold. Here he soon made his value felt, and won a place among the leaders of the bar. A large and valuable practice fell to him, and he was on the high road to wealth, when, in 1865, he was offered by Governor Parker a seat on the Supreme bench of the State. A high sense of the dignity of this position and of his duty to the community caused him to accept the appointment. His commission bore date March 23d, 1865. His term expiring in 1872, he was reappointed by Governor Parker, the reappointment doing honor to the governor as well as to the recipient, so worthily had he performed all the functions of his high office. On accepting the first appointment he moved his residence to Jersey City, that he might be at a convenient distance from all parts of his district, which comprised the counties of Hudson, Passaic and Bergen. Just before the close of his first term—in 1871—he was prominently named as a candidate for Governor, but he himself took no steps whatever to secure the nomination, rather discountenancing the movement in his favor. Notwithstanding, his name was again brought forward in the canvass of 1874, and he received a unanimous nomination at the hands of the Democratic State Convention. He accepted the nomination only at the earnest and persistent appeal of the party, and then declared that as he had been nominated without any effort on his part, so he must be elected, if at all. The party had assumed the responsibility of the nomination, and it must also undertake the labor of the campaign. This course he was constrained to adopt, not from any lack of disposition to serve the political organization with which he had always been affiliated, or unwillingness to assume the dignity and responsibility of administering the government of his State, but simply from a high sense of the impropriety of any action having a political bearing by one holding judicial office. To this declaration he adhered most strictly throughout the campaign, and it would certainly seem as though his high-minded determination were fully appreciated by the people at large, for he was elected by one of the largest votes ever cast for governor in the State, although his opponent, Hon. George A. Halsey, was one of the most popular men in the State. Most unmistakably was he called to his honorable post by the popular voice, and he has not disappointed the great expectations formed of him. His administration from the first has been marked by ability, prudence, and a patriotism

... ... attorney and counsellor, in the spring
... ... Returning to New Jersey, he passed a short time
... ... of Henry S. Little, at Matawan, and was
... ... the bar of that State in January, 1853. He
... ... practice of his profession in New Jersey, at Matawan ... remained for two years. In the spring of
... ... removed to Freehold. Here he soon made his
... ... won a place among the leaders of the bar.
... ... considerable practice fell to him, and he was on
the high road to wealth, when, in 1865, he was offered by
Governor Parker a seat on the Supreme bench of the State.
A sense of the dignity of this position and of his duty
to the ... readily caused him to accept the appointment.
His commission bore date March 23d, 1865. His term expiring in 1872, he was reappointed by Governor Parker, the
... honor to the governor as well as to
the great, so worthily had he performed all the functions
of his high office. On accepting the first appointment he
removed to Jersey City, that he might be at a
convenient distance from all parts of his district, which comprised the counties of Hudson, Passaic and Bergen. Just
before the close of his first term—in 1871—he was prominently named as a candidate for Governor, but he himself
took no steps whatever to secure the nomination, rather discountenancing the movement in his favor. Notwithstanding, his name was again brought forward in the canvass
of 1871, and he received a unanimous nomination at the
hands of the Democratic State Convention. He accepted
the nomination only at the earnest and persistent appeal of
his party, and then declared that as he had been nominated
without any effort on his part, so he must be elected, if at
all. The party had assumed the responsibility of the nomination, and it must also undertake the labor of the campaign. This course he was constrained to adopt, not from
any lack of disposition to serve the political organization
with which he had always been affiliated, or unwillingness
to assume the dignity and responsibility of administering
the government of the State, but simply from a high sense
of impropriety of any action having a political bearing
while holding judicial office. To this declaration he adhered firmly throughout the campaign, and it would
seem as though his high minded determination
to be sustained by the people at large, for he was
by a larger vote than ever cast for governor in
the State. His opponent, Hon. George A. Halsey,
... a popular man in the State. Most un-
... he was elected to his honorable post by the
... and he has not disappointed the great ex-
... him. His administration from the
... has been marked by ability, prudence, and a patriotism

that knows nothing but the public welfare. He has proved himself a statesman of large views and noble aims, and stands to-day more firmly entrenched than ever in the respect and esteem of the community. In 1861 he was married to Althea, daughter of Hon. Bennington F. Randolph, of Freehold. In the fall of 1875 the College of New Jersey conferred on him the degree of LL. D.

UCE, WILLIAM, Lawyer, of Belvidere, was born in Sussex county, New Jersey, October 19th, 1837, being the son of William Luce. Both his parents were natives of Warren county, in which their families were among the pioneer settlers. When William was about a year old, his father died. He attended the public schools and assisted on a farm until attaining his twentieth year, when he married Hulda Reed, daughter of Isaac Reed. After his marriage he was for three or four years engaged in teaching and farming. But these avocations not being wholly to his taste, and his ambition drawing him toward the legal profession, he became, in 1866, a student in the office of Judge J. M. Robeson, at Belvidere. Four years later he was licensed to practise as an attorney, and in 1874 he was called as a counsellor. By dint of good ability and careful attention he built up a very considerable practice, and acquired an honorable position at the bar of his county. He was notably successful in criminal cases, and during 1876 defended several capital cases so ably as to secure the acquittal of the defendants. He was counsel for the Board of Chosen Freeholders of Warren county, and filled the position with much acceptability. Politically, he was a Democrat, and took an active part in the advancement of the interests of that party. He was wholly a self-made man, working into the profession, and to a good position therein, by his own unaided ability and persevering energy. He died in the early part of 1877.

INABERRY, JOHN S., M. D., Physician and Surgeon, of Mountainville, was born near Schooley's Mountain Springs, Morris county, New Jersey. He is son of John Linaberry, a farmer of that county; his mother was Elizabeth (Rodenbaugh) Linaberry. He comes of good revolutionary stock, his grandfather on the maternal side having fought in the war for national independence. John S. Linaberry attended the public schools in Hunterdon county, to which his father had removed while John was yet a small boy. Having acquired the elements of a sound education, he engaged for a short time in teaching. With a desire for seeing something of the country, and especially of the West, he started out in the fall of 1854,

and employed about three years travelling through several States. For a considerable part of this time he was a student at Ann Arbor University, Michigan. In the spring of 1858 he returned to New Jersey, and began the study of medicine with Dr. William S. Crevling, entering, in the fall of the same year, the University of the City of New York, where he graduated with the class of 1861, in company with Drs. Cline, Taylor and Henry, prominent physicians of the South, and Dr. B. A. Watson, of New Jersey. The faculty of the institution at that time consisted of Professors Valentine Mott, D. D., LL. D.; Martin Paine, D. D., LL. D.; J. W. Draper, D. D., LL. D.; G. S. Bedford, M. D.; A. C. Post, M. D.; W. H. Van Buren, M. D.; J. G. Metcalf, M. D. Soon after graduating Dr. Linaberry settled at Mountainville, New Jersey. His medical studies had been pursued with an especial view to service in the navy, and he had therefore given particular attention to surgery and epidemic diseases. This line of study peculiarly fitted him for the professional labors that devolved upon him on his settlement at Mountainville, for he was almost immediately called upon to grapple with that most insidious disease, diphtheria, which had assumed an epidemic form not only in that neighborhood, but over a considerable extent of country. His treatment proved so successful that he was called in consultation with physicians much beyond the limits of his usual practice. At the present time his practice by steady growth has become one of the largest in the county. Repeatedly he has been asked to settle in some of the larger towns of the State, but he has so far preferred to remain amid the scenes of his early professional successes. While manifesting a strong partiality for surgery, his practice is a general one in all branches of the profession. He is a gentleman of high culture and social worth. While his political opinions are those of the Democratic party, he takes no active part in politics, simply discharging his duties as a citizen in accordance with his sense of what is due from each member of the community. He was married, in 1862, to Ellen Robinson, of Hunterdon county, New Jersey.

ARTLES, CHARLES, Lawyer and Bank President, of Flemington, was born at New Germantown, Hunterdon county, New Jersey, March 18th, 1801. The family were among the early settlers of the county, and have largely contributed toward its development. His grandfather, while serving in the cavalry of Frederick the Great, was captured by the French, but succeeded in effecting his escape; proceeding by way of Amsterdam, he reached London, whence he managed to get to this country, stopping first in Philadelphia, but finally settling at New Germantown. Charles' father was Andrew Bartles, who married a Miss Plumb, of New Brunswick, New Jersey. His grandfather, on the maternal side, was a lieutenant in General

34

Washington's army, and was with it in Morristown while his home in New Brunswick was occupied by British officers. A table on which these British officers messed is still in the possession of Charles Bartles. Both his grandfathers were manufacturers of forged iron. At a later day Mr. Andrew Bartles removed to the head-quarters of the Susquehanna, and built the first flour mill in that vicinity, shipping his products by rafts and boats to Baltimore. He projected a route by canal from that point, but the plan fell through owing to the discovery of the shorter one to the seaboard, now represented by the Erie Canal. Charles Bartles was educated at the common schools, and fitted for college at Lamington, New Jersey. He became a student in Union College, and graduated with the class of 1821, among his classmates being Governor Seward, of New York, and Rev. Dr. Messler, of the Reformed Church, of New Jersey. In the spring of 1822 he entered the law office of Nathaniel Saxton, at Flemington, New Jersey, as a law student, and was admitted to practise three years subsequently. He was now fairly launched upon a career, having reached his vantage point by his own unaided efforts, for his friends were unable to assist him either to secure a college course or legal training. In this preparation, however, he had incurred a certain pecuniary indebtedness, and to its liquidation he immediately devoted himself, cancelling the whole by the time his twenty-fifth year was attained. His practice was begun, and was continued until 1854, at Flemington, Hon. Alexander Wurts, P. J. Clark, William Maxwell, Nathaniel Saxton and himself then constituting the Hunterdon county bar. In 1832, in connection with A. Van Syckel, he engaged largely in real estate operations, which were continued until 1860. During this period they handled farming property amounting in value to over a quarter of a million of dollars, and all these sales were settled without the foreclosure of a mortgage, the return of a property, or the distress of a purchaser in any way. In 1853 he turned his attention to railroad matters, and finally succeeded in securing the construction of the Flemington Railroad, giving Flemington direct railroad communication with Philadelphia, and conferring most substantial advantages not only on the town itself, but on a large tract of intervening country. A year later, in company with J. Reading and Mr. Fisher, he engaged in the lumber business, and purchased large tracts of pine timber in Pennsylvania, on Bennett's branch of the Annamahanoy, erecting mills both there and at Williamsport. They disposed of their lumber largely to wholesale dealers. The investment proved exceedingly profitable, for, in addition to the timber on the land, a large portion of the property was found to be underlaid with coal, and it is now accessible to railroads. Mr. Bartles is officially connected with several incorporated enterprises. In 1858 he was elected President of Hunterdon County National Bank, one of the soundest financial institutions in the State. He is a Director of the Belvidere & Delaware Railroad, and of the Flemington

Railroad; of the latter he was President until it became a part of the Pennsylvania Railroad. In politics he was a Democrat up to the outbreak of the late war; since that time he has acted with the Republicans. He has been twice married. His first wife, to whom he was united in 1833, was Eliza Hart, daughter of Neil Hart; she died in 1844. His second wife, who still survives, was Miss Randle, daughter of Daniel W. Randle, of New Hartford, New York.

COOK, GENERAL WILLIAM, Chief Engineer of the Camden & Amboy Railroad, a leading citizen of New Jersey, late of Hoboken, New Jersey, was a native of this State, and a graduate of the United States Military Academy at West Point. Immediately after graduating he entered the Engineer Corps of the army, and served for several years, being employed principally upon government explorations and surveys. In 1830 he left the army to accept the position of Engineer of the Camden & Amboy Railroad Company, in which position he remained until his death, which occurred April 21st, 1865.

CONDIT, SILAS, an eminent citizen of New Jersey, late of Newark, New Jersey, held, during the course of his long and useful life, numerous offices of importance. He was an active and valued member of the State Legislature; from 1831 to 1833 was a representative in Congress; was a member of the convention which formed the present Constitution of New Jersey; and in 1856 was an Elector on the Fillmore ticket. He was a man of spotless private character; was at all times intimately identified with the development of his section and State; and at a critical moment was ever willing and prompt to place a helping shoulder to the wheel of state. He died in Newark, New Jersey, December 28th, 1861, aged eighty-four years.

ROWE, COLONEL JOHN, late of New Brunswick, New Jersey, was born in that place, November 15th, 1809. Upon the outbreak of the war with Mexico, having some military knowledge, and feeling that his country needed the services of every gallant and useful citizen, he accepted the command of the 4th Ohio Regiment and proceeded to the seat of war, where he served efficiently with his comrades in arms until the disbandment, in 1848. Upon the opening of the rebellion he once more tendered his sword in behalf of the Union, and, upon the organization of the 12th Regiment, was unanimously chosen as its Colonel. His force, united with the Cox brigade, was then put in motion, and advanced up the Canawha river. The only battle necessary to clear the Canawha valley of the rebels was fought by the 12th Regiment, and under his command. He was killed at Carnifex Ferry, September 10th, 1861, at a time when, recognizing the vital importance of the coming contest, he was zealously occupying himself in planning certain measures designed for the consideration of his superiors, and tending to illustrate his views concerning the southern outburst.

United Foreign Mission Society. In May, 1825, he was appointed as successor to Mr. Lewis, Secretary for Domestic Correspondence. In the same year he visited the Indians in the western part of New York and in Ohio, returning thence ultimately with his health seriously impaired. The society being now about to be merged in another, he was chosen Assistant Secretary of the American Bible Society. While stricken down by mortal sickness, his mind was still occupied incessantly in musing over the great work to which he had devoted his life and energies, and his thoughts were all for those yet unconverted. He died, January 12th, 1826, aged thirty two years.

RNOLD, GEORGE ("McArone"), Editor and Poet, late of Strawberry Farms, New Jersey, was widely known as the author of the "McArone" papers and several biographical works, and by various contributions to *Vanity Fair, The Leader*, and other journals. He was also the author of several poems of remarkable sweetness, and in his literary essays exhibited much poetic feeling, keen insight into human nature, and a delight in genial, unobtrusive sarcasm. During the progress of the late war of the rebellion he did honorable service in the cause of the country, and for a long time performed military duty at one of the forts on Staten Island. The "McArone" papers attracted much attention and excited great comment at the time of their publication, and at once brought their author favorable recognition. He died at Strawberry Farms, November 3d, 1865.

RANE, REV. JAMES C., Missionary, late of Morristown, New Jersey, was born in that place, January 11th, 1794. In 1805 he removed with his father to New York, and while there served an apprenticeship at a trade. Thrown amidst many temptations, he soon found himself beset by vicious companions and blamable tendencies; but, in consequence of the remembered lessons of a deceased mother, experienced severe and constantly recurring rebukes of conscience. In 1813, finally, he turned, in anguish of mind, to piety, and sought consolation in religious fervor and devotion. Thenceforward he experienced the strongest desires for the conversion of the heathen; and, determined to become a missionary, he, while still an apprentice, attended the lectures of Dr. Mason, and was directed in his studies by Rev. J. M. Matthews. In April, 1817, he was ordained, and a few days after repaired as a missionary to the Indians in Tuscarora village, where he continued to labor until September, 1823, when he was appointed General Agent of the

ARON, REV. SAMUEL, a Baptist Clergyman, Teacher and Author, late of Mount Holly, New Jersey, was a native of New Britain, Pennsylvania, and of Welsh-Irish extraction. Left an orphan at the early age of six years, he was placed under the care of an uncle, upon whose farm he worked for several years, spending a portion of the winter months in a district school. Inheriting a small patrimony from his father, he entered the academy at Doylestown when about sixteen years of age, and there pursued a course of studies in the higher branches. While in his twentieth year he connected himself with the classical and mathematical school at Burlington, New Jersey, as a student and assistant teacher, and subsequently, after his marriage, opened a day-school at Bridge Point, later becoming Principal of an academy at Doylestown. In 1829 he was ordained as a minister, and became pastor of the Baptist Church at New Britain. In 1833 he took charge of the Burlington High School, holding at the same time the pastorate of the church in that place. In 1841, accepting a call to the church at Norristown, Pennsylvania, he removed thither, and after preaching about three years resigned the pastorate, and, removing to the suburbs, founded the Treemount Seminary, which, under his judicious management, became widely and favorably known throughout eastern Pennsylvania and New Jersey, not only for the number of its students, but for the thoroughness of the instruction afforded them. Finding himself involved in the financial crisis of 1857, through indorsements for a friend, he gave up Treemount to his creditors, and removing to Mount Holly accepted a call to the pastorate of the Baptist Church, a position he retained till the time of his decease. In September of the same year he, in co-operation with his son, Charles Aaron, became the Principal of the Mount Holly Institute, and continued engaged in the charge of his responsible duties as educator up to the time of the brief illness which terminated an honorable and useful life. He was twice tendered the Presidency of the New York Central College, but on each occasion deemed it for the best to decline the proffered honor. He was the author of many valuable improvements in text-books, and was admirably qualified to preside as spiritual guide, and also as tutor in the higher departments of learning. He died at Mount Holly, New Jersey, April 11th, 1865, aged sixty-five years.

ITGREAVES, HON. CHARLES, Lawyer, Banker, Legislator, of Phillipsburg, was born, April 22d, 1803, at Easton, Pennsylvania, but has resided at Phillipsburg, New Jersey, since 1805. His father was the Hon. William Sitgreaves, a prominent citizen of that place, his mother belonging to a family of Scotch descent. His own family, proper, is English, his great-grandfather having emigrated to this country. He was educated at Easton, and in 1821 entered the law office of his uncle, the Hon. Samuel Sitgreaves, one of the most distinguished men of Pennsylvania of his time—long a leading member of Congress; manager of the celebrated Blount impeachment case; commissioner to settle the claims of and against England under the Jay treaty, and counsel for the United States in the John Fries case, impeached for high treason. Under the care of this eminent barrister and statesman Mr. Charles Sitgreaves had every advantage for study and for acquiring a practical knowledge of the working rules of his profession. He was admitted to the Pennsylvania bar in 1824, and began practice at Easton; subsequently he was admitted to the bar of New Jersey, and practised in the courts of both States. Entering into politics in New Jersey, he was elected to the Assembly in 1831 and 1833. He was elected a member of the State Council in 1834; he was at one time Vice-President of that body, a position corresponding with that of the present Speaker of the Senate. During the years 1852-54 he was a member of the State Senate, and at this period wrote and published his "Manual of Legislative Practice and Order of Business," which was adopted by the Legislature. While in office he secured the passage of bills abolishing public executions, and making certain household goods exempt from execution. In 1864 he was elected to Congress from the Third District, and two years later was re-elected. During his Congressional service he was attached to the Committee on Military Affairs; strongly opposed the Republican basis of reconstruction, and against that basis made one of the strongest speeches of the session. He has been repeatedly urged as a candidate for Governor of the State. When Phillipsburg was incorporated, in 1861, he had the honor of being elected the first Mayor of the city. For many years he was an active member of the New Jersey State Militia, commanding, with the rank of Major, an independent uniformed battalion. Up to the time of his first election to Congress, he was Trustee of the State Normal School, from 1855 to 1864. When the Belvidere, Delaware & Lackawanna Railroad Company was organized, he was elected to the Presidency of that body, holding the position until 1873, when the company was consolidated with the Pennsylvania Railroad Company. He still remains upon the Board of Direction of the old organization. In 1856, upon its foundation, he was elected President of the Phillipsburg Bank—now the Phillipsburg National Bank—a position that he still holds. He was married, October 25th, 1825, to Jane Louisa, daughter of Samuel De Puy, Esq., of Milford, Pennsylvania. His son, Mr. Charles Sitgreaves, Jr., served with distinction during the late war as Captain in the 1st Regiment New Jersey Volunteers.

TODDARD, JOHN F., Professor, late of Kearny, near Newark, New Jersey, was born in Greenfield, Ulster county, New York, July 20th, 1825. His early years were passed upon a farm, with only such limited means of education as the common school afforded. As years advanced the desire for an increased and more liberal store of knowledge grew stronger within him, and he spent several months in the academy, and at eighteen commenced teaching. Later he entered the New York State Normal School, and upon his graduation therefrom, in 1847, entered upon his life work as an educator. His fondness for mathematical science gave him a remarkable facility for clearness in teaching, and his enthusiasm won the interest of his pupils, arousing them to thought and study, and in turn fitting them for the work of teaching. He delivered a series of lectures before his normal classes and teachers' institutes, in which with great earnestness he set forth the noble and high purpose of the teacher. His remarkable success as an author is evinced by the great popularity of his series of mathematical text-books—a popularity scarcely inferior to that of any other series in this country. As an enduring testimony of his love for mathematical science, he left a fund to Rochester University, furnishing a gold medal worth one hundred dollars to the student who should pass the best examination in mathematics, provided he reached a certain absolute standard, which standard was so high that at one examination the medal was not awarded. He died at Kearny, near Newark, New Jersey, August 6th, 1873, aged forty-eight years.

ENRY, ALEXANDER, Pioneer and Traveller, late of Montreal, Canada, was born in New Jersey, in August, 1739. In 1760 he accompanied the expedition of Amherst, and was present at the reduction of Fort de Levi, near Ontario, and the surrender of Montreal. In descending the river he lost three boats, and saved his life only after great exertions by clinging to the bottom of one of them. Immediately after the reduction of Canada his enterprising and energetic spirit induced him to engage in the fur trade, which he pursued for several years. In 1760 he visited the upper lakes, and during sixteen years travelled in the north-western parts of America, often an actor in these years in scenes of extreme peril and romantic adventure. In 1809 he published in New York an interesting volume of description and reminiscences under the title of "Travels in Canada and the Indian Territories between the Years 1760 and 1776." He was a man of warm affections; a dauntless pioneer and hunter, and possessed an observant and inquiring mind.

FORMAN, SAMUEL R., A. M., M. D., of Jersey City, was born in Freehold, Monmouth county, New Jersey, May 22d, 1835, his parents being John F. T. and Francinchy (Smock) Forman, both natives of the same State. He entered Princeton College in 1851, and was graduated therefrom in 1854. The medical profession being his choice for a life career, he prosecuted his studies at the College of Physicians and Surgeons, in New York, and after a full course received his diploma from that institution in 1857. Immediately after graduation he became attached to the Bellevue Hospital as Interne Physician, and continued so occupied for eighteen months. He then began private practice, opening his office in Hoboken, where he labored until the outbreak of the war. Desiring to contribute his part toward the maintenance of the Union, he entered the army as Assistant Surgeon, and was appointed to duty on the supply steamers to the Gulf Squadron, serving in this direction until nearly the close of the war. Returning to private practice, he settled in Bergen, now annexed to Jersey City, where he still continues to pursue his profession, and has met with good success. He is yet a hard student, and has the reputation of a scientific man in his profession. An upholder of the dignity of the medical practitioner, he is a working member of the Hudson County District Medical Society. He is connected with the Hudson County Church Hospital. In 1860 he was married to Mary W. Alling, of Newark, New Jersey.

STANSBURY, EDWARD A., an eminent citizen of New Jersey, late of Haledon, New Jersey, was born in Vermont, in 1811, and after being graduated at an Eastern college was for several years engaged in the editing of a newspaper. He subsequently entered upon the active practice of law in New York, and in 1856 removed to Haledon, or, as it was then called, to Oldham. Here he became an active and zealous worker in the Republican party, and a staunch

advocate of abolitionory measures. In 1866 he was elected to the Assembly by the Republicans of the Third Assembly District, Passaic county, serving one term. In 1872 he became a prominent mover in supporting the measures of the Liberal Republican party. He died in Haledon, New Jersey, November 4th, 1873, aged fifty-seven years.

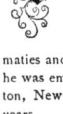

DEAN, JAMES, LL. D., late of Burlington, New Jersey, was a graduate of Dartmouth, in 1800, where he early attracted attention by his masterly attainments in various branches of positive knowledge. He subsequently filled the position, in Vermont University, of Professor of Mathematics and Natural Philosophy, branches of learning which he was eminently qualified to teach. He died at Burlington, New Jersey, January 20th, 1849, aged seventy-three years.

FRANKLIN, WILLIAM, the last Royal Governor of New Jersey, son of Benjamin Franklin, the celebrated patriot, statesman and philosopher, was born in Philadelphia about 1731. In childhood he was, like his father, remarkably fond of reading, and in disposition was enterprising and adventurous. During the progress of the French war (1744-1748) he endeavored to go to sea in a privateer, and, failing in this intention, obtained a commission in the Pennsylvania forces, with which he served in one or two campaigns on the Canadian frontier, and before he had attained his twenty-first year was promoted to a Captaincy. After his return to Philadelphia he obtained official employment through the influence of his father. From 1754 to 1756 he acted as Comptroller of the General Post-office, and during part of the same period was also Clerk of the Provincial Assembly. In 1757 he accompanied his father to London, where he studied law, and was admitted to the bar in 1758. In 1762, while yet in Europe, he was appointed Governor of New Jersey, to which province he returned accordingly in 1763. In the revolutionary contest he remained loyal to Great Britain, and several of his letters, containing strong expressions of Tory sentiments, having been intercepted, he had a guard put over him, in January, 1776, to prevent his escape from Perth Amboy. He finally gave his parole that he would not leave the province, but in June of the same year issued a proclamation as Governor of New Jersey summoning a meeting of the abrogated Legislative Assembly. For this he was placed under arrest by the Provincial Congress of New Jersey, and removed to Burlington as a prisoner. He was shortly after sent to Connecticut, where he was detained and strictly guarded for a period extending over more than two years. In November, 1778, however, he was exchanged for Mr. McKinley, President of Delaware, who had fallen into the power of the enemy. After his liberation he remained in New York till August, 1782, when he sailed for England, in which country he continued to reside until his decease. In remuneration of his losses, the English government granted him eighteen hundred pounds, and in addition a pension of eight hundred pounds per annum. His steadfast adhesion to the royal cause led to an estrangement between him and his father, which continued after the revolutionary conflict had terminated. In 1784, however, he made advances toward a reconciliation, which drew from his father the declaration that he was willing to forget as much of the past as was possible, and to look over bygone actions; yet in 1788, in a letter to Dr. Byles, his father still speaks of existing differences and misunderstandings. In the will of Benjamin Franklin is found the following: "The part he acted against me in the late war, which is of public notoriety, will account for my leaving him no more of an estate he endeavored to deprive me of." His appointment to the Governorship of New Jersey was due mainly to the friendship and kindly influence of the Earl of Bute, who had strongly recommended him to Lord Halifax as a deserving subject, and one worthy of confidence in the troublous hour of riot and rebellion. He died in England, November 17th, 1813, aged eighty-two years.

————◆◆◆————

ARCALOW, CULVER, Merchant, of Somerville, New Jersey, son of William and Ann (Vorhees) Barcalow, grandson of Colonel Farrington Barcalow, an officer in the New Jersey militia during the war of 1812, and a descendant of a Hollandish family settled in New Jersey during the early portion of the colonial period, was born at Flemington, Hunterdon county, October 23d, 1823. His father, a chairmaker, removed his place of business to Somerville in 1825, there following his trade and at the same time keeping a hotel, the son the while attending the schools of the town. In 1833 the elder Barcalow was compelled by failing health to pass a winter in Florida. Impressed by the business opportunities offered in the South, he returned to Somerville, had a large quantity of goods manufactured, and with these, and accompanied by his family, returned to Florida in 1835 and established himself as a grocer and general dealer in St. Augustine. His trade prospered exceedingly, amounting to more than $50,000 per year, but his health continued to decline, and during the last year of his life almost the entire charge of the business fell upon his son, then a mere lad, scarcely fourteen years old. In 1837 the establishment at St. Augustine was broken up and the family started northward; but at Charleston the elder Barcalow died. Having brought the party safely home to Somerville, the son became a clerk in a hotel in that place,

a position that he held during the three following years. In 1840, the last year of his service, he took an active part in politics, being a warm supporter of Harrison. In 1841 he accepted the position of clerk in the Merchants' Hotel, New York; and here he fell in with certain members of the Shaker community, in converse with whom he became convinced that the raising of poultry on a large scale for the New York market might be made highly remunerative. Acting promptly upon this conviction, he returned to Somerville, purchased a suitable piece of ground, and erected a hennery two hundred feet long, with a glass roof and suitably furnished. Unfortunately the venture was not successful, and in the ensuing year he abandoned it altogether. After making a trip to Ohio and assisting in purchasing and bringing East a drove of horses, he accepted, in March, 1843, a position in the dry-goods establishment of the Hon. William G. Steele, of Somerville. This he relinquished a year later and purchased the drug store on the site of his present place of business. Of the drug trade he had no knowledge whatever, and his capital amounted to but $250. But he was quick to learn, and the Hon. George H. Brown, who had a well-founded confidence in his ability, gave him all necessary financial assistance, frequently indorsing paper for him in blank. His business flourished apace, and in 1854 he invested his surplus capital in the erection of a large dry-goods store. This he leased to Messrs. Steele & Shipman, and upon their relinquishing it a year later, he utilized it as a book store, associating with himself for this purpose a practical book dealer, J. R. Vanslike, and placing him in charge of the establishment. Two years later, in 1857, he enlarged his operations still further. The book store was divided and the book trade confined to one side, the other side being set apart for the sale of dry goods. In this scheme he associated with himself a Mr. Lumson, an experienced dry-goods dealer, and, as in the book-store, placed his capital as an offset to his partner's experience. In 1859 he bought Mr. Vanslike's interest in the book firm, and in 1860 Mr. Lumson's interest in the dry-goods firm, himself managing both houses. At this time also he conducted an extensive painting business, in which he employed some twenty hands, and had the management of a large farm that he had purchased. Finding the charge of these various concerns somewhat onerous after conducting them for a year alone, he took into partnership in the dry-goods and book business Mr. J. L. Sutphen, and in 1866 Mr. W. J. L. Potter was admitted into the firm. In 1869 he retired altogether from these branches of trade. Over and above the commercial operations already detailed, he has taken an active interest in promoting local enterprises, and is a leading stockholder in the Somerset County Bank and First National Bank of Somerville. In real estate his operations have been extensive. In 1875 he erected the fine block now occupied by the Somerville post-office, *Unionist* printing office, and a music store, and another block in which is his own drug store, together with various other mercantile establishments and a fine public reading-room. All of these buildings are lighted with gas, the only gas used in the town. During the late war he rendered efficient service to the government. At the first call for troops, in 1861, he raised, almost wholly at his own expense, a full company of one hundred men, and throughout the war his zealous loyalty was altogether exemplary. In politics he was a firm Whig until the dissolution of the Whig party, and since then he has been a not less firm Republican. In 1855 he was elected Treasurer for Hunterdon county, holding the office for two years, and in 1856 he was elected a Delegate to the convention that nominated Fremont and Dayton. In 1861 he was appointed Postmaster at Somerville, holding the office for a term of ten years and discharging its duties in a manner wholly satisfactory to the public. For several years he has had charge of the interests of the Pennsylvania Railroad Company, a corporation in which he is an extensive stockholder, in the New Jersey Legislature. He was married, April 30th, 1845, to Catherine, daughter of the Rev. J. C. Van Dervort, of Cinderhook, New York. He still continues at the head of the drug business, having associated with him his son-in-law, G. S. Cook, and his son, J. V. Barcalow. His career, begun under such adverse circumstances, yet terminating so successfully, is proof of his sound judgment and rare business ability, and looking back over the record of his life, he can say what can be said by but few men, that with scarcely an exception his great schemes for fortune have gone well.

EASLEY, FREDERICK, D. D., late of Elizabethtown, New Jersey, was formerly Provost of the University of Pennsylvania. He was a masterly writer on episcopacy, and on moral and metaphysical subjects, in which he exhibited much learning, studious research, and a notable manner of dealing with many of the conflicting and perplexed questions of the day. He ever found enjoyment in the discussion of spiritual and kindred topics, and in the line of argument bearing upon the varied relations of life and matter as related to the great problem of the future, was an able and logical disputant. He died in Elizabethtown, New Jersey, November 2d, 1845, aged sixty-eight years.

EATTIE, JOHN, M. D., General and Physician, late of Trenton, New Jersey, son of Charles Beattie, the celebrated missionary of Neshaminy, Pennsylvania, was a native of Bucks county, Pennsylvania, and was graduated at Princeton in 1769. After studying medicine, under the supervision of Dr. Rush, he entered the army as a soldier. Upon attaining the rank of Lieutenant-Colonel,

he fell into the hands of the enemy at the capture of Fort Washington in 1776, and suffered a long and rigorous imprisonment. In 1779 he succeeded Elias Boudinot as Commissary-General of prisoners. After the war he settled at Princeton, New Jersey, as a physician, and was also prominent for a time as a member of the State Legislature. In 1793 he took a part in the deliberations and actions of Congress, where he displayed talents of a highly commendable nature. For ten years he officiated as Secretary of the State of New Jersey, succeeding Samuel W. Stockton in 1795, and during a period of ten years acted as President of the Bank of Trenton; and in Trenton he died, April 30th, 1826, aged seventy-seven years. Also for many years he was a Ruling Elder in the church, and distinguished for his earnest and charitable piety.

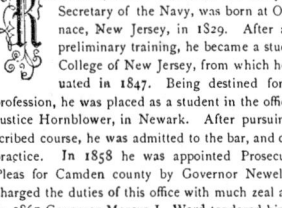

OBESON, HON. GEORGE M., Lawyer, and ex-Secretary of the Navy, was born at Oxford Furnace, New Jersey, in 1829. After a thorough preliminary training, he became a student at the College of New Jersey, from which he was graduated in 1847. Being destined for the legal profession, he was placed as a student in the office of Chief Justice Hornblower, in Newark. After pursuing the prescribed course, he was admitted to the bar, and commenced practice. In 1858 he was appointed Prosecutor of the Pleas for Camden county by Governor Newell, and discharged the duties of this office with much zeal and fidelity. In 1867 Governor Marcus L. Ward tendered him the nomination as Attorney-General of the State, which he accepted, and the same being confirmed, he entered the office and served therein until President Grant, in 1869, offered him the Secretaryship of the Navy, which he accepted, and held until 1877.

LEMENT, DR. KNUT JUNGBOHN, a Danish linguist and historian, late of Bergen, New Jersey, was born in the island of Amrom, Southern Frisia, Denmark, December 4th, 1803. He was educated primarily at the universities of Ciel and Heidelberg, and in 1835 became Doctor of Philosophy. Subsequently, at the expense of the Danish government, he took a tour of three years through the British islands and the continent, and on his return to Denmark became a professor in the University of Ciel. Here he delivered courses of lectures on history, politics, economy and criticism, which attracted wide-spread attention and won him great renown. He published twelve or thirteen elaborate works, historical, linguistic, critical, political, and descriptive, and, though somewhat too much inclined to peculiar and improbable speculations in his linguistic theories, always maintained a very high reputation as an author and scholar. He had taken an active part in the question of the Schleswig-Holstein duchies, and, when they were given up, emigrated to the United States, where he had resided since 1866. He died at Bergen, New Jersey, October 7th, 1873.

ONDIT, REV. AARON, late Pastor at Hanover, died in Morristown, New Jersey, in April, 1852, aged eighty-seven years. For a period extending over nearly forty years he officiated as pastor at Hanover, where his presence and pious labors were productive of great good. During this time he preached over ten thousand sermons, brought about nine or ten memorable revivals, received into his church six hundred and forty-four persons, eleven of whom became preachers, and baptized one thousand and fifty-five. Four of his sons also were ministers, one of whom, Rev. Joseph Condit, of South Hadley, died September 19th, 1847, aged forty-three years. He was a man of excellent parts, an indefatigable spreader of gospel truths, and one that, having once decided conscientiously, pursued his way through all difficulties and over all obstacles, upheld by an abiding faith in his mission and its end. Living to a good old age, exemplifying in his daily life the doctrines he preached, he was venerated and beloved by young and old, not only in the immediate neighborhood where he resided, but in a very wide circle. His influence was exceptionally potent for good.

UBBARD, WILLIAM H., M. D., of Red Bank, was born in Middletown, Monmouth county, New Jersey, September 30th, 1812. His parents were Elias and Nellie (Hendrickson) Hubbard, both natives of the same county. The lad obtained his education at the paid schools and academies of his native county, and a fitting age, having manifested a taste for the medical profession, he began to read medicine under the direction of his uncle, Jacobus Hubbard, a practitioner at Tinton Falls, in the same county. With this preceptor he prosecuted his studies until 1834, in which year he was graduated from the College of Physicians and Surgeons of New York. Commencing practice in connection with his preceptor, he, after twelve months, succeeded him, and continued to pursue the duties of his profession in the locality for a period of twenty-two years. In 1856, being solicited by citizens of the towns of New Utrecht, Gravesend, Flatbush and Flatlands, Long Island, to take the place of two eminently successful practitioners, Drs. Dubnice and Crane, who had lost their lives in the discharge of their duty during the epidemic then raging so fatally, he quickly responded to the call of duty, and remained in that field of labor six years. During that period he had access to the various public institutions of Kings county, viz.: the hospital, almshouse, lunatic asylum, and prison; and became intimately associated with the physicians and surgeons connected therewith. In 1862 he transferred his labors to his native county, settling in the village of Red Bank on July 8th, of that year. In this place he has since remained, and has built up an excellent practice. A well-read and careful practitioner, he enjoys the respect and esteem of his professional brethren. He is a member of the Monmouth County Medical Society, and served as its President in 1856. On October 20th, 1836, he was married to Ellen Cook, of Shrewsbury township, Monmouth county, New Jersey.

UBBARD, DR. CHARLES, Dentist, of Red Bank, son of Dr. William H. Hubbard, whose sketch appears above, was born at Tinton Falls. His education was received at Holmdel Academy, under the instruction of N. H. Whyckoff and Thompson, A. M., and at Monmouth School, under the tuition of Professor W. W. Woodhull. In 1858 he began to study the principles of dentistry, and devoted three years and a half to practical studies under the care of Dr. J. B. Brown, of Brooklyn. After passing the necessary examination, he opened his office at Red Bank, where he has since practised his profession, and has met with much success, being considered by members of his profession and his patrons entitled to a position in the front rank of practitioners of dentistry.

ACKEY, WILLIAM M., Lawyer, was born, March 6th, 1837, in Oxford township, Warren county, New Jersey, his father being John Mackey, Esq., a descendant of one of the oldest of the county families. He was prepared for college under private tutors and entered the sophomore class at Princeton in 1858. In 1861 he graduated, his class including J. R. Emery, Esq., now of the New Jersey bar, the now Rev. J. M. Ludlow, Rev. John DeWitt, and others not less well known, and for a short time was engaged in teaching. Deciding upon the study of law, he was entered in the office of the late J. M. Sherrerd, Esq., at Belvidere, from whence he passed to that of Judge Scudder, at Trenton. He was admitted to the bar in November, 1864, and at once established himself at Belvidere, rapidly acquiring an extensive practice. This of late years has been greatly extended, and ranges through all the courts of the State. He is a member of the Democratic party, but has never made a business of politics. Previous to the passage of the present school law, he was Superintendent of Schools for Belvidere, and in 1873-74 he was Mayor of that city. He has been for many years a consistent member of the Presbyterian church. He was first married, in 1864, to Catherine Keyser, daughter of George Keyser, of Oxford, New Jersey.

CCLELLAND, REV. ALEXANDER, D. D., Professor of Biblical and Oriental Literature in the Theological Seminary, New Brunswick, New Jersey, late of that place, was born in Schenectady, New York, and was a graduate of the Schenectady Union College. He was for several years pastor of the Rutgers Street Presbyterian Church, New York city, and while there was conspicuous among the local preachers for his learning, uprightness, and eloquence. He subsequently held a professorship in Dickinson College, Carlisle, Pennsylvania. During the last nineteen years of his life, however, he was connected with the Theological Seminary at New Brunswick, as Professor of Biblical and Oriental Literature. He was a pious and scholarly gentleman, well versed in Eastern lore, and an ardent Christian guide and spiritual exhorter. He died at New Brunswick, New Jersey, December 19th, 1864, aged sixty-nine years.

ERSELES, HON. JACOB M., ex-State Senator of New Jersey, late of South Bergen, New Jersey, was for three years an active and prominent member of the Legislature, for three terms officiated as Sheriff of Hudson county, and was the pioneer in establishing various stage and city railroad lines in that section. He was a man of extended practical views and prompt in the furtherance and culmination of selected projects. He assisted substantially in the development of the various interests centring and growing in Hudson county, and was identified with the growth and increase of that section of New Jersey. He died of paralysis, at South Bergen, New Jersey, January 2d, 1865.

CUDDER, JOHN, M. D., Missionary, late of Wynberg, Cape of Good Hope, was born in New Brunswick, New Jersey, but at an early day removed with his parents to Freehold, where he acquired his preliminary education. He was graduated in 1811, and in December, 1819, went to Tillipally as a missionary physician. He was subsequently ordained, however, and during the ensuing sixteen years labored zealously at the station of Pandeteripo, in Ceylon. In 1836 he, with Mr. Winslow, was sent to the city of Madras, where it was purposed to use a religious press in the Tamul language. From 1843 to 1847 he was in the United States, promoting the cause of missions by visiting the various charges, everywhere addressing congregations and Sabbath schools with the most impressive ardor and earnestness. He was educated in the Dutch Reformed Church, of which he was the pioneer missionary, and throughout his long and useful life remained one of its most devoted sons. His appeal to the youth of America in behalf of the heathen was published in 1846; also, a tract, entitled "Provision for Passing over Jordan," excited much favorable comment throughout the country, and in religious circles abroad. By his wife, Harriet Scudder, he had fourteen children, of whom seven sons and two daughters survived him. Six of the sons devoted themselves to foreign missions, three of whom were, at the time of his death, in India, at Arcot, seventy miles from Madras. He was an exhorter of persuasive powers, firm in the right, and of indomitable perseverance in the path selected as the true one, and the great good accomplished by him in his lifetime is still thriving, and daily bearing fresh fruit. He died at Wynberg, January 13th, 1855, aged sixty-one years.

LENKER, LOUIS, Brigadier-General of United States Volunteers, late of New Jersey, was born in the city of Worms, in the Grand Duchy of Hesse-Darmstadt, where, in his youth, he was apprenticed to learn the trade of jeweller. Upon attaining his majority, however, he enlisted in the Bavarian Legion, which was organized to accompany the newly elected king, Otho, to Greece. From a private he rose to the rank of Sergeant, and when the legion was disbanded in 1837, he received with his discharge the higher rank of Lieutenant. He then returned to Worms, whence, after a brief stay, he went to Munich in order to attend medical lectures, with the view of becoming professor of medicine. He afterwards abandoned this intention, however, and entered into commercial pursuits. In 1849 he became a leading member of the revolutionary government in his native city, and having been appointed Commander of the National Guards, took an active and zealous part in the popular movements of that period. After the repression of this revolutionary outburst, he retired to Switzerland, and being ordered to leave the country, embarked at Havre for the United States, and settled on a farm in Rockland county, New York. Subsequently he removed to New York city, where he continued engaged in mercantile affairs until 1861. Upon the outbreak of the rebellion, he raised and organized the 8th Regiment of New York Volunteers, with which he marched to Washington, having been commissioned its Colonel, May 13th, 1861. After being encamped for some time on Meridian Hill, the regiment was incorporated with others into a brigade, of which he was appointed commander. The brigade was then attached to

35

General McDowell's army, as a portion of Colonel Myles's Fifth Division. During the battle of Bull Run this division acted as a reserve, and for his services at that time he was commissioned a Brigadier General, August 9th, 1861. He then remained with the Army of the Potomac, command-ing a division until the commencement of the Yorktown campaign, when he was ordered to western Virginia. June 8th, 1862, he was an active participant in the battle of Cross Keys, but was shortly after relieved of the command, and succeeded by General Sigel. He was subsequently ordered to Washington, where he remained for some time, and, March 31st, 1863, was mustered out of service. He died in New Jersey, where he was widely known and re-spected, October 31st, 1863, aged fifty-one years.

MITH, HON. ISAAC, Professor, Judge and Member of Congress, late of New Jersey, was a graduate of Princeton College, in 1755, and acted in that institution in the capacity of tutor. From 1795 to 1797 he was a representative in Congress from New Jersey, and in the latter year was appointed by President Washington a Commis-sioner to treat with the tribe of Seneca Indians. He was also a Judge of the Superior Court of New Jersey. He was a man of polished attainments, of profound judicial learning, and of unassailable rectitude.

XTON, ADAM, Cracker Manufacturer, of Trenton, the son of William and Mary (Turner) Exton, was born in Euxton, Barth, Lancashire, Eng-land, July 5th, 1823. His education was ob-tained under circumstances of the utmost diffi-culty: at eight years of age he was placed at work in a cotton mill, and his only opportunities of learn-ing were at a Sunday-school and at night-schools. The small fee demanded at the latter he paid with earnings gained by working over-time at the mill, his regular wages being given, intact, to his parents. His progress was as rapid as his exertions were earnest, and the limited range of study at his command was utilized to the best advantage. His reading was directed mainly to books of travel, and especially to those treating of travel in the United States. Everything relating to America had to him the deepest interest, and before he was sixteen years old his determina-tion was fixed to emigrate from England to this country so soon as his savings should be sufficient to pay his passage. In 1841 his object seemed in a fair way of being attained, as his father promised him and his brother William, who was also desirous of coming to America, that if they would wait until the following spring he would emigrate with his entire family to the United States. But winter wore away

and no preparations were made for departure; and when, in the early spring, his father said that they had better wait another year, he determined to take the matter into his own hands. His brother William, two years his senior and his confidant in all his plans, readily fell into his views, and without acquainting their father with their intentions they made their arrangements for the voyage. They had saved enough from their wages to pay their passage, and every-thing seemed to work in favor of their undertaking. They left Liverpool, in a sailing vessel, April 4th, 1842, and on the 10th of the following May they landed in New York. Philadelphia was fixed upon as their first location, but as they chanced to remember that one Robert Sumner, a friend of their father's, was living in Paterson, New Jersey, they determined to see him before adopting any definite plans. The morning after their arrival in America they went out to Paterson, found Sumner, and were cordially re-ceived by him. But he was unable to put them in the way of gaining employment, and they concluded to follow out their original intention, and proceed to Philadelphia. As their stock of cash was not large, they left such things as they could not conveniently carry with their friend, and started to make the journey on foot. The parting advice that they received was to take any sort of work that they could get: for at this period, so soon after the financial panic of 1837, business of every sort was utterly stagnated. On arriving at Trenton they encountered Joshua Wright, a member of the Society of Friends, who was favorably im-pressed by the younger brother's appearance, and offered him employment upon the farm of his (Wright's) brother-in-law, William Lee. Upon this farm, some three miles out of Trenton, he remained for eighteen months, a warm attachment, which has increased with each since-passing year, springing up between him and the Lee family. Manu-facturing prospects having meanwhile—under the protective tariff of 1842—materially improved, and his tastes leaning strongly towards mechanical employment, he determined in the fall of 1843 to leave the farm. It was much against the wishes of his employer, as well as against his own feelings, that he carried this resolution into execution; but he felt that in living a farm life he was doing an injustice to him-self, and that it was his duty to engage in some employment wherein he would have an opportunity to rise. He soon obtained a position in a manufactory of prints, where he re-mained for upwards of a year, and where, by working over-time, he averaged eight and a half working days per week. At the end of the year he was offered a much better place in an adjacent cotton mill, the superintendent of which was acquainted with his ability and skill, and this position he held until he entered upon the especial line of manufacture in which he has been so eminently successful. In the early part of 1845 (February 17th) he had married Elizabeth Aspden, an excellent woman, who proved a trusty coun-sellor in all his future undertakings. A year later he pur-chased a tract of land 50 feet front by 150 feet deep, upon

Adam Exton

and no preparations were made for departure; and when, in the early spring, his father said that they had better ... another year, he determined to take the matter into his ... hands. His brother William, two years his senior and ... confidant in all his plans, readily fell into his views, and ... about acquainting their father with their intentions they ... made their arrangements for the voyage. They had saved ... from their wages to pay their passage, and every... declined to work in favor of their undertaking. They ... ..., in a sailing vessel, April 4th, 1842, and on ... ... of the following May they landed in New York. ... ... was fixed upon as their first location, but as ... ... to remember that one Robert Sumner, a ... ... their father's, was living in Paterson, New Jersey, ... determined to see him before adopting any definite ... The morning after their arrival in America they ... ... Paterson, found Sumner, and were cordially re... ... him. But he was unable to put them in the way ... ... employment, and they concluded to follow out ... ... original intention, and proceed to Philadelphia. As ... stock of cash was not large, they left such things as ... they could not conveniently carry with their friend, and ... ... to make the journey on foot. The parting advice ... that they received was to take any sort of work that they ... ... get: for at this period, so soon after the financial panic of 1837, business of every sort was utterly stagnated. On arriving at Trenton they encountered Joshua Wright, a member of the Society of Friends, who was favorably impressed by the younger brother's appearance, and offered him employment upon the farm of his (Wright's) brotherin-law, William Lee ... ... this farm, some three miles out of Trenton, he remained for eighteen months, a warm attachment, which has increased with each since-passing year, springing up between him and the Lee family. Manufacturing prospects having meanwhile—under the protective ... of 1842—materially improved, and his tastes leaning ... ... towards mechanical employment, he determined in ... ... of 1843 to leave the farm. It was much against the ... ... of his employer, as well as against his own feelings, ... carried this resolution into execution; but he felt ... ... a farm life he was doing an injustice to him... ... was his duty to engage in some employment ... ... would have an opportunity to rise. He soon ... ... in a manufactory of prints, where he re... ... ... of a year, and where, by working over... ... ... eight and a half working days per week. ... ... year he was offered a much better place ... ... cotton mill, the superintendent of which was

Adam Exton

which he erected a pair of frame houses, and in the winter of 1846, in one of these houses, he started a bread, cake and cracker bakery. He had associated with him at the outset of this enterprise his wife's brother, Richard Aspden; but Mr. Aspden died within a twelvemonth, and he was left to carry on the business alone. This he did with infinite energy, particularly directing his attention to the development of his cracker trade, and such was his success that in 1850 he found it advisable to drop all other branches of his business and confine himself to cracker-making alone. At this time he conceived the idea of constructing a machine that would mould crackers better than the work could be done by hand, and pursuing his investigations in this direction he not only succeeded in inventing a moulding machine entirely satisfactory in all its workings, but also one not less satisfactory for rolling and docking. Upon both he took out letters patent in 1861, and by the vastly increased productive power thus given to his establishment he was able to meet the rapidly increasing demands of the trade. In 1866 he took out letters patent upon two other machines, the one for making fancy crackers, the other for making scroll biscuit, the two more than trebling his capacity of out-put in these departments. Various inventions of a labor-saving character have since been patented and put into use, and as it now stands the manufactory—a large building, covering a lot 150 feet square—is one of the most completely furnished of its class in the country. The Exton crackers are almost universally known, and the high degree of excellence to which their manufacture has been carried has been certified to by awards of the juries of numerous competitive exhibitions—the award of the judges of the Centennial Exhibition being among the number. The annual out-put ranges from $150,000 to $200,000, and the market supplied extends over a very large portion of the globe. In 1872, in evidence of his appreciation of the faithful service that had long been rendered to him by his brother John, and by his son-in-law William H. Brockaw, Mr. Exton admitted them as partners into his business, allowing to each a one-quarter share. From each he took notes of hand representing the full amount of capital thus bestowed, charging on these seven per cent. per annum interest, and allowing the profit above this rate to dissipate the principal. Under this arrangement the firm-name was changed to its present style, Adam Exton & Co. Having thoroughly identified himself with his adopted country, Mr. Exton has for years taken a warm interest in its welfare, and especially has his public spirit been shown in forwarding all schemes for the improvement of the city of Trenton. The erection of the fine Washington market-house may be cited as a notable instance in which his means and influence were used for the public good; and this is only one of many similar schemes in which he has been prominently engaged. Naturally, he is held in high esteem by the people of Trenton; and this feeling, combined with the high respect entertained for his business ability, has led to his election to numerous offices of trust and honor. For many years he was a member and was prominent in the transactions of the City Councils, serving as Chairman of the Highway Committee; since its organization he has been connected with the Trenton Board of Trade, and in 1876 he was elected by the stockholders of the Trenton Horse Railway Company to be President of that corporation. In short, his brilliant business career—a career due entirely to his indomitable industry and perseverance—is fitly crowned by the respect and esteem of his fellow-citizens.

OWELL, DAVID, LL. D., Judge, late of Providence, Rhode Island, was born in New Jersey, and graduated at Princeton College, 1766. Removing to Rhode Island, he was appointed Professor of Mathematics, and afterward of Law, in the University of that place. Devoting himself to the practice of the law at Providence, he was subsequently chosen to fill the position of Judge of the Supreme Court. He was also a member of the old Congress, and in 1812 was appointed District Judge for Rhode Island, which office he sustained till his death, in 1824, aged seventy-seven years. He was a jurist of excellent attainments; upright in his relations with the general community; scholarly in the wider and better acceptation of the term; and one well provided with knowledge, not only of a general, but also of a positive and scientific nature.

KOWN, HARVEY, Brevet Major-General United States Army, of New Jersey, was born in Roxbury, New Jersey, in 1795, and in 1818 graduated from West Point. Entering the artillery branch of the service, he became First Lieutenant of the 4th Artillery, August 23d, 1821. April 10th, 1835, he was promoted to the rank of Captain; January 9th, 1851, he was made Major in the 2d Artillery, and subsequently rose successively to a Lieutenant-Colonelcy in the 4th Artillery, April 28th, 1861; to a Colonelcy in the 5th Artillery, May 14th, 1861; and on the following September 28th was tendered the position of Brigadier-General of United States Volunteers. August 1st, 1863, he finally retired from the service. He won the brevets of Major, November 21st, 1836, for "gallantry and general efficiency" during the progress of the Florida war; of Lieutenant-Colonel for valuable service rendered at Contreras, August 20th; and Colonel, for gallantry at the gate of Belen, city of Mexico, September 13th, 1847—being also engaged at Monterey, Vera Cruz and Cerro Gordo. He was engaged in the repulse of the rebel attack on Santa Rosa Island, Florida, October 9th, 1861, and was brevetted

Brigadier-General United States army, November 23d, 1861, for gallantry in the engagement between Fort Pickens and the rebel batteries, November 22d, 23d. August 2d, 1866, he was brevetted Major-General United States army for his efficient services in suppressing the memorable and outrageous riots in New York city of July 12–16, 1863, on which occasion he won enviable distinction as a loyal citizen and a fearless yet careful soldier.

UDLOW, REV. JOHN, D. D., LL. D., Professor of Biblical Literature and Ecclesiastical History, late of Philadelphia, Pennsylvania, was born in Aquackanonk, New Jersey, December 13th, 1793, and graduated from the Union College in 1814. His grandfather, Richard Ludlow, was an officer in the revolutionary army. After pursuing for some time a course of legal studies, he entered the New Brunswick Theological School. During one year he acted in the capacity of tutor at Union College, and upon the completion of his preparatory studies in 1817, became pastor of the Reformed Dutch Church in New Brunswick. In 1818 he was appointed Professor of Biblical Literature, and from 1823 to 1834 officiated as pastor of the church in Albany, New York. From 1834 to 1852 he filled the position of Provost of the University of Pennsylvania, and in the latter year took the Chair of Ecclesiastical History in the Theological Seminary of the Reformed Dutch Church, New Brunswick, New Jersey. He died at Philadelphia, Pennsylvania, September 8th, 1857, distinguished for his profound learning as a theological student, and his rare qualities as an educator and spiritual counsellor.

OTY, LOCKWOOD L., Colonel, Lawyer, late of Jersey City, New Jersey, was born at Groveland, New York, May 15th, 1827. His early years were spent in his native village, and, upon attaining his twenty-first year, he entered a law office in Geneseo, New York, where he entered upon a course of legal studies. Upon the outbreak of the rebellion he became actively engaged in procuring enlistments, and acted in the capacity of Military Secretary for Governor Fenton. He also founded the State Military Bureau at Albany, New York, which collected the history of the volunteer regiments, and provided for the care of the sick and wounded. In 1871 he received from President Grant the appointment of Pension Agent of New York city, which position he held until prolonged ill health compelled his resignation but a few weeks previous to his death. He was an earnest and intrepid worker in the defence of the Union, and possessed unusual and excellent administrative abilities. He died in Jersey City, aged forty-six years.

OD, ALBERT B., D. D., Professor of Mathematics, late of Princeton, New Jersey, was born in Mendham, in the same State. After pursuing with diligence the usual course of studies at 1822, and in 1829 was chosen Professor. His method of teaching was both original and notably effective, and as exponent and demonstrator he was equalled by but few. He was also an eloquent preacher, and a writer of considerable merit. He died at Princeton, New Jersey, November 20th, 1845, aged forty years.

EILSON, COLONEL JOHN, Revolutionary Officer, and Member of the Continental Congress, late of New Brunswick, New Jersey, was born in that place, or near it, March 11th, 1745. He was educated in Philadelphia, Pennsylvania, and afterward, from 1769 to 1775, was engaged in mercantile pursuits in his native town. In 1775 he raised and organized a company of patriot volunteers; August 31st, of the same year, he was appointed Colonel of a regiment of minute-men; and until September 18th, 1780, continued actively engaged in repelling British inroads, and in furthering the cause to which he was ardently attached. He was then appointed Deputy Quartermaster-General for New Jersey. Early in 1777 he planned and successfully executed the surprise of a British post at Bennett's Island. In 1778 and 1779 he was a zealous and influential member of the Continental Congress; and in the New Jersey Convention to ratify the Federal Constitution, he distinguished himself as an energetic and efficient supporter of the important measures then held under discussion. He died in New Brunswick, New Jersey, March 3d, 1833.

BEEL, REV. DAVID, D. D., Missionary to China, Author, late of Albany, New York, was born in New Brunswick, New Jersey, June 12th, 1804, and received his preliminary education chiefly at his native place. In 1826 he was ordained to the ministry, and during the ensuing two years his field of labors was Athens, New York. His health failing, in consequence of severe parochial labor and incessant study, he went in October, 1829, as a missionary to China, and thence to Java, Batavia, Singapore and Siam. In 1833 he visited Europe, and on his return home published " The Claims of the World to the Gospel," " Residence in China," from 1829 to 1833; and in 1838 " Missionary Convention at Jerusalem." In 1839 he again went to Canton, China, but the " Opium War " precluding his usefulness in that quarter, he visited Malacca, Borneo, and various other places, settling finally for a period at Kolong-soo. In 1845, his health again becoming seriously enfeebled, he returned, after having begun a mission at Amoy in 1842, to New York, vainly hoping by means of rest and tranquillity to renew his shattered energies. In the "Memoirs" by Rev. G. R. Williamson, he is spoken of as one "well qualified for his work by great practical judgment, good sense, and persevering energy." He died in Albany, New York, September 4th, 1846. His presence and pious labors in China and Java were markedly beneficent in their influence on the natives of those places with whom he was brought into contact, and his tireless efforts to supplant heathenism and fetich worship by the holier creed of Christianity were not barren of good results.

ENNINGTON, HON. ALEXANDER C. M., late of New York city, was a native of Newark, New Jersey, where his youth was spent, and his early education and training obtained. Upon the completion of a preliminary course of studies, he turned his attention to law and legal text-books, and acquired a considerable store of judicial learning, which was afterward of essential service to him both in public and in private life. He served two terms in the State Legislature, and from 1853 to 1857 served as a representative in Congress from New Jersey. His was a far-seeing and enterprising mind; and he was endowed with an energy and quick directness of character which often seconded ably the aims and desires of his co-workers and constituents. He died in New York city, January 25th, 1876, aged fifty-six years.

---

cWILLIAM, REV. JAMES M., a Presbyterian Clergyman and Teacher, of Scottish birth and education, late of Deckertown, New Jersey, was born in Aberdeen, Scotland, July 22d, 1818, and educated at King's College, in that city. In 1835 he emigrated to the United States, and began teaching at Lafayette, New Jersey. After a short time spent in this occupation he was persuaded by the Rev. Dr. Schaffer to enter the Theological Seminary at Princeton. After graduating thence he was called to preach at Oxford, New Jersey, and there ordained in December, 1842. He remained in this pastorate for eleven years, then visited Scotland, and on his return settled at Monroetown, Pennsylvania. Here, in conjunction with Samuel F. Colt, he founded at Towanda the Susquehanna Collegiate Institute, of which he soon afterward became Principal. With the exception of a brief absence, in the pastorate, he remained in charge of this institution until 1866, con-

stantly maintaining a deservedly high reputation as a teacher, especially in the classics. Upon retiring from the Institute in consequence of the impaired health of his wife, he organized a church at the little mining town of Barclay, Pennsylvania, on the summit of the Alleghenies, where he remained for about three years. At the expiration of that period he received a call to Deckertown, New Jersey, which he accepted. In this field of labors he closed his career, September 20th, 1873, aged fifty-five years.

HITEHEAD, REV. CHARLES, D. D., Reformed (Dutch) Clergyman, late of Perth Amboy, New Jersey, was born in 1801, and spent his youthful days in Philadelphia, Pennsylvania. In 1823 he graduated from Dickinson College, and later from the New Brunswick Theological Seminary. In 1826 he was licensed to preach by the Classis of Philadelphia. After a short settlement in the Presbyterian Church at Batavia, New York, he removed in 1828 to the Reformed Church at Hopewell. He subsequently officiated as pastor at Somerville, New Jersey, Fishkill and Walden, New York, and of churches in Houston street, New York, Poughkeepsie and Washington Heights. From 1861 until the time of his decease he presided as Chaplain of the New York City Hospital. At the time of his death, July 13th, 1873, he was spending a summer vacation at Perth Amboy, New Jersey, where he died in the pulpit, aged seventy-two years.

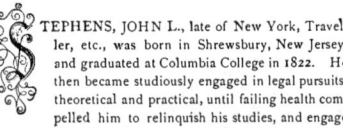TEPHENS, JOHN L., late of New York, Traveller, etc., was born in Shrewsbury, New Jersey, and graduated at Columbia College in 1822. He then became studiously engaged in legal pursuits, theoretical and practical, until failing health compelled him to relinquish his studies, and engage in travel to restore an enfeebled constitution. From 1834 to 1836 he visited Europe, Greece and Turkey. In 1839 President Van Buren sent him as ambassador to Central America, for the purpose of negotiating a treaty, and the final arrangement of various State affairs. He was intimately connected with the movement which led to the establishment of the initial lines of steamers to Europe; was a Director in the Ocean Steam Navigation Company, and President of the Panama Railroad Company. The winter of 1851 he passed on the Isthmus of Darien. The iron track between the Atlantic and Pacific coasts will, in its history, be constantly associated with his name, for his was one of the energetic and far-seeing natures which, seeing infinite good in the speedy development of the railway system, pushed on the tardy and the fearing. He published incidents of travel in Egypt, etc., in 1837; in Greece and

Turkey, etc., in 1838; in Central America in 1841; and later a work descriptive of Yucatan. He died in New York, October 13th, 1852, aged forty-six years.

ENDERSON, HON. THOMAS, Statesman, Judge, Lieutenant-Governor of New Jersey, late of New Jersey, was born in that State, and graduated from Princeton College in 1761. In the course of his honorable and varied career he filled many offices of prominence and trust; was for some time Judge of the Court of Common Pleas; from 1779 to 1780 acted as a delegate to the Continental Congress; and under the constitution, from 1795 to 1797, was a representative in Congress from New Jersey. Also, at one time, he filled the position of Lieutenant-Governor of his State. He was intimately identified with the growth and the development of the interests of New Jersey; and, through his eminent usefulness as a vigilant statesman, won an enviable place in the annals of that State.

ICHEY, HON. AUGUSTUS G., Lawyer, of Trenton, was born, March 17th, 1819, in Warren county, New Jersey. His parents were William Richey, a successful farmer, himself a native of Warren county, and Mary (Godly) Richey, daughter of William Godly, of Spring Mills, Hunterdon county, New Jersey. His education, after he ceased attendance at the common schools, was obtained at Lafayette College, at Easton, Pennsylvania, which he entered in 1834. The institution at that time was under the direction of Dr. George Junkin, and was conducted on the " manual labor system." Under this system the students were required to devote three hours each day to manual labor of some kind, and the work so performed, besides its presumed effect as a discipline and a preparation for practical life, was counted as a partial compensation for the tuition received by the student. He remained here until 1840, when he graduated. Among his classmates were a number of gentlemen who have since become eminent in life, among whom may be mentioned W. Henry Green, D. D., Professor in Princeton Theological Seminary, and who was elected President of Princeton College, but declined the honor; also Dr. T. C. Porter, Professor of Natural History at Lafayette College, and Dr. Charles Elliott, Professor of Hebrew in Chicago Theological Seminary. In the autumn of the same year he commenced the study of the law. He prepared for the profession with Colonel James N. Reading, of Flemington, a very able and prominent lawyer of his time. He studied with Colonel Reading until February, 1844, when he was licensed as an attorney. Three years later he was licensed as counsellor. He settled at Asbury, Warren county, New Jersey, where he entered upon the full practice of his profession.

From the first he achieved a decided success. His natural abilities were of a high order; his training had been thorough and complete; his integrity was above question, his industry was tireless, and his devotion to his profession very great. These facts constituted a claim to general confidence and esteem that could not but be acknowledged and acted upon, and as a consequence patronage came to him very rapidly. He remained at Asbury until the spring of 1856, when he removed to Trenton. There he has since continued to reside, actively engaged in the practice of his profession. His legal brethren, as well as the people at large, speedily acknowledged his claims to a high professional position, and he long ago became one of the leaders of the bar in the city of his residence, a position which he still continues to hold, and which all are glad to acknowledge. He has always been noted as a close and steady laborer in his profession, and for the sound and safe advice he gave his clients. Politically, he is a Republican, but up to the year 1863 he had taken no active part in politics, and had never sought public office. In that year the Republicans of Mercer county urged him to become their candidate for the State Senate. He consented, and was elected by a majority of over three hundred, although, in the previous election, the Democrats had triumphed. He served in the Senate a term of three years, taking an active part in the proceedings, and making for himself an enviable record. During two years of his term he was Chairman of the Judiciary Committee. It was during his term as Senator that the constitutional amendments were adopted. He is an enterprising and public-spirited citizen, and takes an active interest in the welfare and progress of the community in which he lives. For many years he has been closely and actively identified with many of the institutions and enterprises of Trenton and vicinity. For nearly twenty years he has been a Director of the Mechanics' National Bank of Trenton, and acted as Counsellor for the institution; he is a Manager of the Trenton Savings Fund Society; a Director of the Trenton Gas Company; a Director of the Delaware & Bound Brook Railroad Company, between New York and Philadelphia, and is one of the counsel for the road, as well as counsel for the Easton & Amboy Railroad Company. He has also been prominently and actively allied with the temperance movement, and at one time was President of the New Jersey State Temperance Society. He is a devoted and influential member of the Presbyterian Church. For many years he was a ruling elder of the First Presbyterian Church of Trenton. This position he continued to hold until 1875, when the Prospect Avenue Presbyterian Church was organized, and he became a ruling elder in that body. He is also an earnest Sabbath-school worker, and is a regular teacher of an adult Bible class. He was married in 1844 to Anna G. Farley, eldest daughter of Hon. Isaac G. Farley, who was a prominent citizen of Hunterdon county, New Jersey, and who, for many years, represented his district in Congress.

LMER, JONATHAN, Physician, Magistrate and Senator, late of Burlington, New Jersey, was born in Cumberland county, New Jersey, in 1745, and was a graduate of the University of Pennsylvania. He entered upon the practice of medicine shortly after the termination of his preparatory studies, and rapidly won a leading position in the profession in his native county. During the progress of the revolutionary struggle he acted in various offices of trust and distinction; was Sheriff, Surrogate and Judge. In the years 1776-77-78-81-82-83-84 and '87, he was a member of the Continental Congress; and from 1789 to 1791 was a United States Senator from New Jersey. He was a member of the celebrated Philosophical Society, and was a scholarly and accomplished gentleman. He died in Burlington, New Jersey, in 1817.

ALL, CHARLES, D. D., late of Newark, New Jersey, was born in the State of New York, and graduated at Hamilton College in 1825. For many years he presided earnestly and efficiently as Secretary of the American Home Missionary Society, in co-operation with Dr. Badger. He was principal Editor of the *Home Missionary*, and in that capacity brought to his field of labors admirable discretion and an untiring interest. He died at Newark, New Jersey, October 31st, 1853, aged fifty-five years.

OWELL, HON. DAVID, LL. D., Judge, Professor of Natural Philosophy and Mathematics, Attorney-General of Rhode Island, late of Rhode Island, was born in New Jersey, January 1st, 1747, and graduated from the New Jersey College in 1766. Upon removing to Rhode Island, he was, in 1769, appointed Professor of Natural Philosophy and Mathematics; and, from 1790 to 1824, presided as Professor of Law in Brown University, of that State. He then established himself in the practice of the law at Providence, Rhode Island, and rapidly rose to an eminent and leading position in the profession. He filled, for some time, the office of Attorney-General of the State, and was a Judge of the Supreme Court. From 1782 to 1785 he acted as a member of the Continental Congress, and, after the reorganization of the general government, was appointed a Commissioner for settling the eastern boundary of the United States. He afterward officiated as District Attorney, and from 1812 to the time of his decease was District Judge for Rhode Island. He was a man of notable wit, learning and eloquence, a distinguished classical scholar, and a pungent and effective political writer. The superiority of his attainments as a jurist was conceded by all, and his opinions on points of law involving intricate or perplexing questions, and on the varying positions assumed by his country in its internal and external policy, were always received with deserved attention and respect. He died July 29th, 1824. His son, Jeremiah Brown Howell, United States Senator from Rhode Island, 1811 to 1817, was born in 1789, and died in 1822.

LACKFORD, HON. ISAAC NEWTON, Jurist, Judge, late of Washington, District of Columbia, was born at Bound Brook, New Jersey, November 6th, 1786, and graduated from the New Jersey College in 1806. Upon completing his legal studies under the supervision of Gabriel Ford, of Morristown, New Jersey, he removed to Indiana in 1812, and settled in Vincennes. In 1813 he became Clerk of the territorial Legislature, and in the years 1814-15 presided as Judge of the First Judicial Circuit. In 1816 he occupied the position of Speaker of the first State Legislature, and from 1819 to 1835 officiated as Judge of the Supreme Court of Indiana; and, from March, 1855, till his decease, as Judge of the United States Court of Claims. His "Reports," of which there are in all eight volumes, gave enviable credit to the State abroad, and are masterly productions. He died in Washington, District of Columbia, December 31st, 1859.

RMSTRONG, REV. JAMES FRANCIS, Clergyman, late of Trenton, New Jersey, was born in West Nottingham, Maryland, April 3d, 1750, and graduated from the New Jersey College in 1773. His studies in theology were prosecuted under the guidance of Rev. John Blair; and he was licensed to preach in 1777. He served as Chaplain through the war of independence, and was a zealous supporter of the patriot cause. He died at Trenton, New Jersey, January 19th, 1816, widely known and highly respected as an upright citizen and a painstaking and learned minister of the Gospel.

RMSTRONG, JAMES F., Captain in the United States Navy, was born in New Jersey, November 20th, 1816. He became Midshipman March 7th, 1832; December 8th, 1842, was promoted to a Lieutenancy, and, April 27th, 1861, received his commission. During this year he commanded the steamer "Sumter," and July 16th, 1862, was made Captain. From 1862 to 1864 he was in command of the steamer "State of Georgia," of the North Atlantic Blockading Squadron. April 25th, 1862, he was actively engaged at the bombardment and surrender of Fort Macon, and in 1864 commanded the steam sloop "San Jacinto," of the East Gulf Blockading Squadron. From 1865 to 1868 he had charge of the Pensacola Navy Yard. In the attack on Fort Macon the following officers were in co-operation with him: Commander Samuel Lockwood, of the steamer "Daylight," Lieutenant-commanding A. Bryson, of the gunboat "Chippewa," and Lieutenant Edward Covendy, of the bark "Gemsbok;" and on this occasion he performed efficient service in aiding to secure the casemated work at the entrance of Beaufort harbor.

OLLESON, ELIAS, Merchant, late of New Brunswick, was born in Piscataway, New Jersey, October 28th, 1782. He was a descendant, through the Mollesons of Piscataway, of Gilbert Molleson, merchant, of London, one of the proprietors of East Jersey, who signed the surrender of the government of the province to Queen Anne, April 15th, 1702; he was a Scotchman, resident in the English capital, a man of considerable property, and a Christian. At an early age he entered into business in New Brunswick. October 28th, 1825, he was ordained a Ruling Elder in the Presbyterian Church, of which he continued a prominent and valuable member during life. He was much respected in all circles.

ASSINI, CARLO, Composer, Music-Teacher and Writer, late of Irvington, New Jersey, was born in Cuneo, Piedmont, in 1812. Obtaining distinction as a violinist, he went with an operatic company to South America, became Director, and afterward settled as a teacher of music, vocal and instrumental, in New York city. Among his best-known works are: "The Art of Singing," published in 1857; "Melodia Exercises," published in 1865; "Method for the Tenor," published in 1866; "Method for the Baritone," published in 1868; and the "New Method," published in 1869. He composed a large number of pieces, many of them characterized by great sweetness and rich fertility of invention. He died at Irvington, New Jersey, November 26th, 1870.

ADWALLADER, COLONEL LAMBERT, Revolutionary Patriot, late of Trenton, New Jersey, was born in that city in 1741. During the contest with Great Britain he commanded a Pennsylvania regiment, and was an active participant in the defence of Fort Washington, November 16th, 1776. At its capture by the enemy he was taken

prisoner, and subsequently retired to his estate, near Trenton, New Jersey. From 1784 to 1787 he was an honored member of the old Congress; from 1789 to 1791 was a Representative in Congress from New Jersey, and again from 1793 to 1795. He died in Trenton, New Jersey, September 13th, 1823.

ONDIT, LEWIS, M. D., an eminent citizen of New Jersey, late of Morristown, New Jersey, was born in that place in March, 1773, and was a skilful and widely-known physician. From 1805 to 1810 he was a member of the New Jersey Legislature, in the two latter years officiating as Speaker two terms. In 1807 he was a Commissioner for settling the boundary line between New York and New Jersey, and was a Representative in Congress from 1811 to 1817, and from 1821 to 1833. He was also at one time Sheriff of Morris county, New Jersey. He died at Morristown, New Jersey, May 26th, 1862.

ONDIT, JOHN, M. D., Soldier and Surgeon during the revolutionary war, Statesman, late of New Jersey, was born in 1755. For several years he. was a member of the New Jersey Legislature, and from 1799 to 1803 was a Representative in Congress from that State. From 1803 to 1817 he was an active worker as Senator in Congress; and again was a Representative during the years 1819-20. He died May 4th, 1834.

ARD, SAMUEL, M. D., LL. D., late of New Jersey, was born in Philadelphia, Pennsylvania, April 1st, 1742. On his passage to Edinburgh, Scotland, where he studied medicine, he was captured by the French, September, 1761, and owed his release, five months later, to Dr. Franklin, who was then a resident of London. After a tour through Scotland and England, he returned home in 1767, having gained the annual medal given by Professor Hope for the finest collection of plants. He then, in connection with his father, entered upon the active practice of his profession in New York, organized a medical school which was united to King's College, and in that institution took the Chair of Physic in 1769, subsequently becoming Dean of the faculty. In 1770 he married his cousin, Mary Bard; in 1772 purchased his father's establishment and business, and in 1795 took Dr. Hosack into partnership with him. In 1774 he gave a course of clinical lectures; in 1791 was instrumental in causing the establishment of a public hospital, of which he was appointed Visiting Physician; and in 1813

Edward D. P. Kelley, M.D.

was appointed President of the College of Physicians and Surgeons. While the seat of government was in New York city, he was Washington's family physician. In 1798 he retired to his country-seat in New Jersey, but on the approach of the yellow fever pestilence, returned to his former station as medical practitioner in New York. He was then himself laid low with the disease, but, carefully nursed by his wife, soon recovered. He was a skilful horticulturist as well as an eminent physician, and a patient and ingenious student of nature. Besides many addresses and discourses, he published: "The Shepherd's Guide;" "De Viribus Opii," 1765; "On Anguia Suffocativa," in vol. i. "American Philosophical Transactions;" and "Compendium of Midwifery," in 1807. His "Life," published by John McVicar in 1822, contains much matter of a valuable and interesting nature. His degree of M. D. was obtained at the University of Edinburgh in 1765; that of LL. D. was conferred on him by the New Jersey College in 1815. He died in New Jersey, May 24th, 1821.

--- ◆ ---

ELLEY, EDWARD B. P., M. D., Physician, of Perth Amboy, New Jersey, was born, July 4th, 1835, in the town of Lebanon, Pennsylvania, and is the son of Hon. James and Mary (Walton) Kelley, both of whom were natives of Pennsylvania. His father was for many years an eminent lawyer of Lebanon, and at one time Judge of the Court of Common Pleas in that county; the latter portion of his life was spent in agricultural pursuits. During the war of 1812 he served as the colonel of a regiment from Lancaster, Pennsylvania. Dr. Kelley's grandfather, James Kelley, was a colonel in the revolutionary war, and participated in many of the struggles of those eventful times. He was wounded at the battle of the Brandywine, and subsequently mortally wounded at the battle of Germantown. Edward B. P. Kelley was educated at the public schools, and when nineteen years old he graduated from the High School of Harrisburg. He then removed to Philadelphia, where he passed two years in the drug business. Having determined to embrace the medical profession, he prosecuted his studies in that direction under the preceptorship of his brother, Dr. Charles B. P. Kelley, a prominent practitioner of Mount Joy, Lancaster county, Pennsylvania. While a resident of Philadelphia, from 1856 to 1858, he matriculated at the Jefferson Medical College in that city, and also at the Vermont Medical University, at Burlington, Vermont, at which places he alternated his medical courses, and received his degree of M. D. from the Vermont University in 1857, and the following year received a diploma from the Jefferson Medical College. He was subsequently appointed Resident Physician and Surgeon of the Philadelphia Hospital, and served therein during a portion of the years 1858 and 1859. In the autumn of the latter year he sailed for Eu-

rope, where he sojourned for nearly two years, meanwhile visiting the various hospitals in England and on the continent. On his return to the United States he was appointed Medical Inspector for United States Volunteers of the State of Pennsylvania. In August, 1861, he was made Medical Director of the 6th Corps of the Army of the Potomac, with the rank of Colonel, being attached to the staff of General John Sedgwick, and after to that of his successor, General H. G. Wright. He was in active service during the entire period of the war of the rebellion; and at the battle of Gaines' Mills he was wounded by a piece of shell in the face and hands, besides being captured by the enemy. He endured for three months the horrors of the Libby prison. During his connection with the medical corps of the army he was placed in charge of the corps hospital, at Alexandria, Virginia, and in the corps hospital at Fredericksburg, in the same State, subsequent to the battles of the Wilderness. From thence he was transferred to the general hospital at City Point, and was finally in charge of the corps hospital in front of Petersburg, near Fort Hell. After being mustered out of the service, he settled at Perrineville, New Jersey, where he was associated with Dr. T. J. Thomason for seven years, and practised his profession. In 1873 he removed to Perth Amboy, where he has since resided, being actively and successfully engaged in professional pursuits. He was married, October 15th, 1873, to Fannie J., a daughter of Jirah J. Bulkeley, a retired merchant, formerly of Hartford, Connecticut, but now a resident of Cranberry, New Jersey.

--- ◆ ---

AILEY, GAMALIEL, M. D., Proprietor and Editor of the *National Era*, Abolition Advocate, late of Washington, District of Columbia, was born at Mount Holly, New Jersey, December 3d, 1807. Removing to Philadelphia, Pennsylvania, at the age of nine years, he there entered upon a course of medical studies when he had finished his earlier school education, and in 1828 received his degree of M. D. He then sailed to China as physician of a ship, afterward beginning his career as editor on the *Methodist Protestant*, in Baltimore, Maryland. In 1831 he removed to Cincinnati, and in that city acted as physician to the Cholera Hospital during the prevalence of the epidemic. In 1836, in connection with J. G. Birney, he conducted the first anti-slavery newspaper in the West, the Cincinnati *Philanthropist*. Upon two occasions their printing-office was attacked by a riotous mob of malicious persons, the press tossed into the Ohio river, and the books and papers burned. In 1837 he became sole editor of the *Philanthropist*, the organ of the Liberal party, and was a principal leader in the presidential canvass in 1840. In the following year his press was again destroyed by a mob, which, after doing much wilful harm, was dispersed by the

36

military. January 1st, 1847, he began to edit, at the capital, the *National Era*, a newspaper of decided anti-slavery principles. In 1848, a mob, for three consecutive days, besieged his office. "Addressing the multitude in a speech remarkable for its coolness and its independent spirit, the mob, that had proposed to tar and feather him, was disarmed by his eloquence." In the *Era* was originally published "Uncle Tom's Cabin." He died, June 5th, 1859, on board the outgoing steamer "Arago."

———

ATEMAN, DR. EPHRAIM, Member of Congress, and United States Senator, late of Cumberland, New Jersey, was born there, in 1770. While serving as a mechanic's apprentice, he devoted his spare hours to the study of medicine, and rapidly acquired a large and varied store of medical knowledge. Subsequently he won distinction in the profession as a skilful physician, and became widely known through his many successes secured under adverse circumstances. For many years, also, he was an active member of the New Jersey State Legislature; from 1815 to 1823 was in Congress; and from 1826 to 1829 served ably as United States Senator. He was a public-spirited and liberal citizen; upright in all the relations of life, public and private; and ever zealous in the cause of his State and country. He died in Cumberland, New Jersey, January 29th, 1829.

———

OOD, REV. JAMES, D. D., an eminent Presbyterian Clergyman, Teacher, and Author, late of Hightstown, New Jersey, was a native of New York State, and graduated at Princeton Theological Seminary. After preaching for a time in Amsterdam, New York, he was appointed Agent of the Board of Education for the West. He was subsequently for many years Professor of Church History in the Indiana Theological Seminary, and upon his resignation became principal of an academy for boys, in New Albany, Indiana. His next appointment was that of Assistant Secretary of the Board of Education at Philadelphia, Pennsylvania. He was afterward elected to the Presidency of Hanover College, in the same State, which position he resigned, however, in 1866, that he might become principal of the Van Rensselaer Institute, at Hightstown, New Jersey. The primary object of this institution was the education of the children of missionaries. He had entered upon the discharge of his new and important duties with great zeal and energy, and was making vigorous efforts toward a complete endowment, when stricken down by death. He was the author of an able work entitled "Old and New Theology," setting forth the reasons which led to the division of the Presbyterian Church. He published also an interesting

volume known as "A Call to the Ministry," and several other treatises, essays, pamphlets, and sermons, bearing on moral, theological, and kindred subjects; all of which contain sterling food for thought, and much matter of a valuable and suggestive nature. He died at Hightstown, New Jersey, April 7th, 1867, aged sixty-seven years.

———

VANS, AUGUSTUS O., Journalist and Politician, late of Hoboken, New Jersey, was born in Binghampton, New York, in 1831. While in his twentieth year he moved to Brooklyn, there finding employment in a subordinate capacity on the New York *Tribune*, and finally as reporter of the New Jersey *News*. Finding his residence in Brooklyn inconvenient, he removed to Hoboken, New Jersey, and soon after took charge of the *Hudson County Democrat*, of which he retained the proprietorship until March, 1873. For one or two years he occupied the position of City Clerk of Hoboken; in 1855 was elected to the Assembly of New Jersey, and again elected in 1866, when he was chosen as Speaker of the House. He died in Hoboken, New Jersey, September 28th, 1873, aged forty-two years.

———

RISCOM, JOHN, LL. D., Physician and Chemist, late of Burlington, New Jersey, died there February 26th, 1852, aged seventy-seven years. He presided for some time as Professor of Chemistry and Natural Philosophy in New York Institute, where he was admired and respected for his profound acquirements and his rare technical abilities. In addition to his attainments as physician and scientist, he possessed a varied store of literary knowledge, and was himself a writer of no mean calibre. In 1823 he published "A Year in Europe in 1818–1819," 2 vols.; and at a later date, "A Discourse on Character and Education." His criticisms and judgments concerning the current literature of his day were the offspring of a ripe and keenly discriminating perceptive power, and by those who knew his worth, were accepted as guides wholly reliable and trustworthy.

———

INNICKSON, HON. THOMAS, Judge, and Member of the First Congress, late of Salem county, New Jersey, was born in that place, and there received a classical education and mercantile training. He served in the revolutionary war at the battles of Trenton and Princeton, in the capacity of Captain, performing gallant and efficient service. For many years he was an honored member of the Council and Assembly of New Jersey, and the Presiding Judge of the Court of Common Pleas. During the progress of the Revolution he was a vigilant correspondent of the Committee of

Safety; and a Representative in the First Congress, after the adoption of the Constitution, from 1789 to 1791, and again from 1797 to 1799. In the fourth Presidential election, 1801, he was one of the Electors from New Jersey. His name is honorably associated with the history of his State, and he occupies in its annals a proud place as soldier and as statesman.

———◆◇◆———

OYDEN, SETH, Inventor, Leather Manufacturer, etc., late of Middleville, New Jersey, was born in Foxborough, Massachusetts, November 17th, 1788. In 1813 he engaged in the leather manufacturing business in Newark, New Jersey, and invented a machine for splitting leather. In 1819 he began the manufacture of patent leather, and in 1826 made the first malleable iron. He subsequently perfected the first locomotive with the driving-rod outside the wheel; produced the first daguerreotype in America; invented the process of making spelter; discovered the art of making Russian sheet-iron; and patented a hat-body doming machine used in all the hat manufactories in the United States. After passing through a life and career of peculiar usefulness to his fellow-beings, he died at an advanced age, in Middleville, New Jersey, March 31st, 1870. He was a man of singular fertility of invention in mechanical matters, and was richly endowed with resources in all things relating to the practical side of science and mechanics. His mind was constantly occupied in endeavoring to produce the maximum of results with the minimum of means; and he was only completely happy when engaged in essays and experiments tending to illustrate the power and value of a fresh method or new idea.

———◆◇◆———

OGGS, CHARLES STUART, Rear-Admiral United States Navy, of Brunswick, New Jersey, was born in Brunswick, New Jersey, January 28th, 1810, the nephew of Captain James Lawrence. He entered the navy, November 1st, 1826; and September 6th, 1837, was promoted to a lieutenancy. During the progress of the war with Mexico he was on the " Princeton," of Commodore Conner's squadron; was present at the siege of Vera Cruz, and commanded the boat expedition which destroyed the ",Truxton" after her surrender to the Mexicans. September 14th, 1855, he was made Commander, and assigned by the Secretary of the Navy .o the United States mail steamer " Illinois," which he commanded during the ensuing three years. He afterward filled the position of Light-House Inspector for California, Oregon, and Washington Territory. In 1861, at the outbreak of the Southern rebellion, he was ordered to the gunboat " Varuna," of Farragut's Gulf Squadron; and in the assault on the Mississippi forts, destroyed six of the Confederate gunboats, finally losing his own vessel, however, after

setting his antagonist in flames and driving her ashore. He then returned to Washington as bearer of despatches; was ordered to the command of the new sloop-of-war " Juniata;" and July 16th, 1862, was promoted to the rank of Captain. July 25th, 1866, he became Commodore, commanding the steamer " De Soto," of the North Atlantic Squadron, during the years 1867–1868. He became Rear-Admiral in July, 1870, a high rank deservedly attained through his gallantry and ability in action.

———◆◇◆———

ARD, JOHN, Physician, late of Hyde Park, New York, was born in Burlington, New Jersey, February 1st, 1716, and was of a family which had been driven from France in consequence of the revocation of the edict of Nantes. Peter Bard, his father, a merchant, came to Maryland in 1703, but soon moved to New Jersey, where he acted for many years as a Privy-Councillor, and second Judge of the Supreme Court. He received the rudiments of a classical education at Philadelphia, Pennsylvania, was for seven years a surgeon's apprentice in that city, and there also began a lasting friendship with Dr. Franklin. In 1746 he established himself in New York, and rapidly won a leading rank among the practitioners of the city and its environs. In 1750 he assisted Dr. Middleton in the first recorded dissection in America. In 1759 he was appointed to take measures to prevent the spread of ship-fever, and selected Bedloe's Island for a hospital, of which he took charge. In 1778 he withdrew from the city; but, at the close of the war, resumed practice there, and in 1788 became first President of the New York Medical Society. In 1795, during the prevalence at New York of the yellow-fever epidemic, he remained at his post, and made himself eminently useful in a trying and perilous time. In May, 1798, he relinquished his professional labors, and sought the tranquillity of private life. At his decease he left an essay on malignant pleurisy, and also several valuable papers relating to the cause and phases of yellow-fever, which were finally published in the "American Medical Register." He died at Hyde Park, New York, March 30th, 1800.

———◆◇◆———

INLEY, ROBERT, D. D., Presbyterian Divine and Philanthropist, late of Athens, Georgia, was born in Princeton, New Jersey, in 1772; graduated from the New Jersey College in 1787; and in 1817 had conferred on him by that institution the degree of D. D. James Finley, his father, came from Scotland to this country in 1769. From 1793 to 1817 he was connected with the New Jersey College as tutor, or Trustee; and, June 16th, 1795, was ordained pastor at Basking Ridge. He originated the plan of colonizing emancipated blacks in Africa, and was instrumental in forming the constitution and in organizing the Colonization Society. In July, 1817, he was installed President of Franklin College, in Athens, Georgia, where he died, October 3d, 1817. During his lifetime he published various sermons, and several excellent papers relating to the methods and results of colonization, in which he was ever warmly and generously interested.

OLDEN, EDGAR, M.D., Newark, New Jersey, was born in 1838 at Hingham, Massachusetts. He is the son of Asa H. and Annie L. Holden, his father being a manufacturer of malleable and cast-iron cannon. In 1847 he entered the Hingham Academy; in 1852 James Hunting's Boarding School, at Jamaica, Long Island; was Assistant Teacher in the Rev. J. Pingry's Boarding and College School in 1855; graduated at Princeton College in 1859, receiving the degree of A. M. in 1862; and in 1861 graduated at the College of Physicians and Surgeons of New York. In the latter year he was commissioned a Surgeon in the United States navy, by Abraham Lincoln. In 1862 he became a member of the New Jersey State Medical Society; of the Essex District Medical Society, and of the New York Society for the Advancement of Science; and in 1864 a member of the American Medical Association. In the same year he was commissioned as Assistant Surgeon in the United States army. In 1865 he was made a Medical Adviser of the Mutual Benefit Life Insurance Company, and in 1869 President of the Board of Advisers. He visited foreign countries in 1871, and in 1873 was Clinical Physician to St. Michael's Hospital. In 1870 he visited the principal cities and health resorts of the United States. In 1873 he received the Stevens Triennial Prize from the College of Physicians and Surgeons of New York. In 1874 he was Consulting Surgeon to St. Barnabas Hospital. In 1875 he became a member of the New York Laryngological Society, receiving in the same year the degree of Doctor of Philosophy from Princeton College. He was also a member of the Executive Committee of the International Medical Congress held in that year. His contributions to literature, medical and popular, have been frequent and of a high order, his medical papers embracing: "A Singular Case of Sloughing, with Loss of the entire Scapula, with Recovery," read before the Essex Medical Union, 1861; "Certain Diseases of Men of War," published in the *American Journal of Medical Science*, 1864; "Antecedent Diseases in Cases of Heart Disease and Apoplexy," published in the same journal, 1864; "Cancer and Tubercle: their Relations," pamphlet; "Nitrous Oxide and its Relations," published in the *American Journal of Medical Science*; "Ostracism for Consumption," published in the same journal and in pamphlet form; "Successful Treatment of Asthma," in the same journal; "Vaginal and Vulval Varices," published in

the *New York Medical Record*; "Relations of Cardiac Pathology to the Sphygmograph," read before the New York State Medical Society, and published as a pamphlet; "Anomalies of Cardiac Pathology," *American Journal of Medical Science*; "The Sphygmograph," for which the Stevens Triennial Prize was awarded by the College of Physicians and Surgeons of New York, published in book form, and "Influence of Certain Occupations," *American Journal of Medical Science*; while of his popular papers we may mention: "Cruise of the Passaic;" "Chapter on the Coolie Trade," and "Cruise of the Sassacus," published in *Harper's Magazine*; "Journal of Iron-Clad Cruisers;" "The Three Chimneys," published in *The Chimney Corner*, and "Our Pedestrian Tour," all illustrated in pen and ink. He married in 1861 Kate Hedder, daughter of Jotham Hedder, of East Orange, and afterwards Helen Stewart, daughter of Mr. John Binger, of Orange.

UCKER, COLONEL ISAAC M., Lawyer, late of Newark, New Jersey, was a resident of that city, a leading member of the legal profession, and a man of much influence throughout the State. In 1856 he was a member of the State Republican Executive Committee. "He was a true patriot, and his services to his regiment were most valuable." He was killed in the battle of Gaines' Mill, shot by the enemy while being borne wounded from the field, June 27th, 1862.

ARKLEY, ALBERT WATSON, late of Camden, was born in Leacock, Lancaster county, Pennsylvania, October 25th, 1825, and died September 25th, 1875. His early life was passed principally in Columbia, Pennsylvania, and he received his education at Lafayette College, Easton, Pennsylvania. He moved to Camden in 1846, and was first employed in the counting-house of J. W. & J. F. Starr. He remained with this firm about two years, when he accepted a clerkship in the State Bank, and held that position till 1854, when he was appointed assignee of the estate of W. W. Fleming, of Atsion. In the settlement of this large estate, which he managed most successfully, he laid the foundation of his future business career, and became widely known in Camden and Burlington counties for those gentlemanly courtesies which distinguished his conduct in after life, and drew about him a corps of true and admiring friends. He next interested himself in procuring a charter for a new bank in Camden, which he succeeded in doing through the aid of influential friends at Trenton. When the Farmers' and Mechanics' Bank (now First National) commenced business, he was elected President, in which capacity he served for some time. He shortly afterward became deeply interested in the affairs of the Camden & Amboy Railroad Company, of which he was an efficient Director. Here he was recognized as a man of ability, and was intrusted with many delicate transactions, and from that time till the united roads were leased by the Pennsylvania company, he divided his labors between Trenton and Washington to prevent legislation antagonistic to that company. At Washington, by his genial manners and kindly nature, he became one of the most influential and popular men at the national capital, and during the war gave many a New Jersey soldier occasion to remember him with gratitude for leaves of absence, extensions of furloughs, and for grateful delicacies while sick or wounded in the hospitals. This patriotic work was continued, without ostentation and almost unknown, except to the recipients of his favors, until the close of the war. His interest in the New Jersey roads continued till the time of his death. He was also a large stockholder in the Camden & Philadelphia Steamboat Ferry Company. At a very early day he saw the value and capabilities of that corporation and became interested in it, and it is in a measure due to his efforts that this ferry has improved so greatly and increased its facilities for travel to such an extent, and also that the ferries of Camden have within the past few years made such great progress. He was a very benevolent man, and seemed to take delight in conferring favors on other people, and at each Christmas which has elapsed since his death more than one poor family has missed its accustomed turkey, and more than one coal bin and flour barrel have lacked replenishing from the same cause. He attended the First Presbyterian Church, of Camden, and took great interest in its prosperity, and it is largely owing to his exertions that the present edifice was erected. State and party lines seemed to offer no barriers to Mr. Markley's friendships; they were coextensive with the country, and few men in New Jersey were better known than he, or could number so extended a list of friends. The President, the cabinet, senators and members of Congress, governors of States and State officers, all esteemed him for his social and gentlemanly qualities, and these gave him a commanding position, which he used most unselfishly. In proof of this, it may be stated that notwithstanding all the patronage at his command he never held any office, except that of a bank and railroad official.

RANDOLPH, JOSEPH FITZ, Judge, an eminent jurist of New Jersey, late of Jersey City, was born in Freehold, Monmouth county, in 1803. After obtaining an ordinary school education, he entered upon the study of law, and in 1825 was admitted to the bar. For some years he acted as State's Attorney for the county; was a representative in Congress from 1837 to 1843; was a member of the conven-

tion which framed the State Constitution in 1844, and in 1845 was appointed a Judge of the Supreme Court of New Jersey for seven years, after which he resumed the practice of his profession at Trenton. He was a member of the Peace Congress in 1861. He was a jurist of consummate ability, and, through wide and varied experience and close reading, had acquired a remarkable fund of legal lore, and also knowledge in abundance of worldly and literary matters distinct from his profession. He died in Jersey City, March 19th, 1873.

VAN NEST, PETER, REV., Methodist Itinerant Minister, late of Pemberton, New Jersey; died there, September 17th, 1850. For a period extending over fifty-four years he was widely known as a zealous and untiring itinerant preacher and exhorter; and during this extended space of time was instrumental in producing many enthusiastic revivals, and in advancing with fearless ardor the interests of Christianity and his church.

FRAZEE, JOHN, Sculptor and Architect, late of New Bedford, Massachusetts, was born in Rahway, New Jersey, July 18th, 1790, and in early life was actively employed as a stone-cutter, and also as a farmer. Upon removing to New York he rapidly acquired distinction through the beauty and high finish of his monuments, tablets and ornamental mantels, and also the delicacy of his lettering. Turning his attention to sculpture, he produced a mural tablet and bust of John Welles, for St. Paul's Church, a most elaborate and artistically finished piece of work, which attracted much attention. In 1834, at the request of the trustees of the Boston Athenæum, he modeled a series of busts of eminent men in that city, which now adorn its library; they were of Webster, Bowditch, Prescott, Story, J. Lowell, and T. H. Perkins. He also produced heads of John Marshall, Jackson, Lafayette, De Witt Clinton, Jay, Bishop Hobart, Dr. Milnor, and Dr. Stearns. He was also architect of the New York Custom House, in which he was an officer for some time. He died at New Bedford, Massachusetts, March 3d, 1852.

MACCULLOCH, GEORGE P., was born in Bombay, India, in December, 1775. The son of a Scotch officer in the East India service, he lost both parents in his childhood, and at the age of five years was taken from India to Edinburgh, where under the care of his grandmother he completed his education at the University of Edinburgh, having as his instructor in mathematics the illustrious Professor John

Playfair, and as his preceptor in Latin the scarcely less famous Dr. Adams, whose Latin Grammar still survives in our colleges and schools. On the completion of his education, he left Edinburgh for London, where he embarked in mercantile pursuits, becoming the head of an extensive house connected with the East India trade, his partner being Francis Law, grandson of John Law, the celebrated financier, and brother of James Alexander Bernard Law, Count de Lauriston, and favorite aide-de-camp of Napoleon. Shortly after the close of the French Revolution, he spent a year in Paris, where his intimacy with the Count de Lauriston, and his familiarity with the Continental languages, speaking fluently, as he did, French, German, Spanish and Italian, brought him into daily contact with the leading men of those eventful times, and afterwards led to his selection by the London merchants for the conduct of some very important and delicate negotiations in Holland during the Napoleonic wars, in the discharge of which task he passed as a German through Napoleon's army without exciting a suspicion of his nationality or his mission. In 1802 he went as the confidential agent of the directors of the East India Company to the city of Madrid, where he passed the winter in conducting several mercantile negotiations of great delicacy. At this time, young, accomplished, able, a man of the world, versed alike in business and in affairs, he occupied a noble vantage-ground for a career in either commerce or diplomacy, but the unsettled state of Europe clouding for the time his business prospects in London, and his health being impaired, he resolved to emigrate to this country, a resolution he executed in 1806, reaching New York, with his wife, Martha Louisa Edwina Sanderson, having married in 1800, and two children, in July of the former year. Coming to New Jersey in search of a quiet home, he found the object of his search in Morristown, where he built the house in which he lived for all the long remainder of his life, and in which he died, surrounded from first to last by his family, and by

> . . . . "that which should accompany old age,
> As honor, love, obedience, troops of friends."

A few years after he settled in Morristown he lost a large part of the property he had brought with him, and in 1814, with his accustomed spirit, he established in that town an academy for boys, which he conducted with distinguished success for some fifteen years, many of the most eminent men of the country receiving their early training from him. But the great achievement of his life, the one that above every other entitles him to the gratitude of New Jersey and the respect and admiration of posterity, is the Morris Canal, which he projected, and did more than any other man, well nigh as much as all other men, to carry into execution. As this enterprise forms, and must ever form, a prominent chapter in the history of the New Jersey iron manufacture, not to say in the history of New Jersey itself, no apology is needed for giving here, with some particularity, an account of its origin and construction, especially as the account is from the hand of the originator himself, and is thus doubly deserving of incorporation into this sketch. Many years before his death, in compliance with a request of Mr. Cadwallader D. Colden, then President of the Morris Canal Company, he wrote to that gentleman the following communication, which, in justice to the dead as well as the living, should have a permanent place in the records of the State: " Lake Hopatcong," he says in this communication, " in former times commonly called the Long Pond, had always been a resort for sportsmen, but never attracted serious attention, excepting as an advantageous forge and mill seat. Its supposed dimensions were greatly exaggerated, and the only remark produced by its location was concerning the facility with which its water, leaving the bed of its natural outlet towards the Delaware, could be made to inundate Suckasunny plain, and seek an issue towards the Hudson. The Erie Canal was about thirty-five years ago an object commanding deep interest. By pouring the produce of the lake and western counties into the New York market, it seemed to threaten destruction to the agriculture of northern New Jersey, unless some mode of transportation cheaper than teams and turnpikes could be invented. Presiding over the Agricultural Society of Morris County, my mind was naturally turned to this emergency, and, during the repose of a fishing party on the banks of the lake, the project occurred to me of converting this vast reservoir, so aptly situated, into a canal, to penetrate New Jersey in conneeting the Delaware and Hudson rivers. The immense utility of such a communication was obvious, but the topography of the region to be traversed, the obstacles to be encountered, the expedients for surmounting an uncalculated and enormous elevation, were all involved in utter obscurity. The naked project, when started for public discussion, was for these reasons treated rather as the aberration of a dreamer than as the anticipation of a sane mind. Gradually, however, the idea worked its way into the reflective men of the community. Self-interest enlisted the warm advocacy of the population near the course of the projected canal; men of liberal ideas everywhere desired to give fair investigation to so novel a scheme; opposition was finally circumscribed to that most respectable class of personages who understand nothing which they cannot see, believe nothing which they cannot touch, and patronize nothing which they cannot coin into dollars. I had prepared public opinion by a series of essays in the county newspaper. Nothing definite was, however, known of the altitude to be overcome, the soil to be excavated, the undulations to be levelled, the course to be pursued, the difficulties to be surmounted, the expedients to be adopted. All was mere guess, and the calculations were very congenial to the data on which they were predicated. I saw the necessity of walking over all the difficult locations, accompanied by the most intelligent men of the respective vicinities, and with Professor Renwick, of New York, to whom the plan had

... its origin and construction, especially as the account is
... from the hand of the originator himself, and is thus doubly
... of incorporation into this sketch. Many years
... before his death, in compliance with a request of Mr. Cad-
... D. Colden, then President of the Morris Canal
... Company, he wrote to that gentleman the following com-
... which, in justice to the dead as well as the
... should have a permanent place in the records of the
... of "Lake Hopatcong," he says in this communication,
... commonly called the Long Pond, had al-
... been a resort for sportsmen, but never attracted serious
... attention, excepting as an advantageous forge and mill seat.
Its supposed dimensions were greatly exaggerated, and the
... remark produced by its location was concerning the
... with which its waters, leaving the bed of its natural
... towards the ... could be made to inundate
... and ... thirty-five years ago an object
... By pouring the produce of the
... western countries into the New York market; it
... to the agriculture of northern
... mode of transportation cheaper
... could be invented. Presiding
... of Morris County, my mind
... emergency, and, during the
... banks of the lake, the pro-
... projecting this vast reservoir, so
... to penetrate New Jersey in con-
... rivers. The immense
... is obvious, but the topog-
... the obstacles to be en-
... surmounting an uncalculated
... involved in utter obscurity.
... for public discussion, was
... the aberration of a dreamer
... team as the ... mind. Gradually, however, the idea ... the reflective men of the
community. ... the warm advocacy of
the ... of the projected canal; men
of liberal ... to give fair investigation
... to ... was finally circumscribed
... in 1814 ... personages who understand
... nothing which they ... those nothing which they
cannot touch, and ... which they cannot coin
into dollars. I had ... opinion by a series of
... essays in the county newspapers. ... definite was,

Strauss Feh. D. Phila. Pa.

been explained. Thus an approximation to some definite idea was obtained, but still mathematical certitude was wanting, without which no practical result was to be expected. A regular survey was indispensable, but I could not myself afford it; a private subscription to the necessary amount was clearly impossible, and there remained only to obtain legislative aid. Hence arose the necessity of organizing the friends of the enterprise into a sort of party, and of electing assemblymen favorable to a liberal grant. This was effected in the teeth of much opposition, ridicule, and suspicion. I accompanied our legislators to Trenton, and, assisted by Mr. Cobb, of Morris, and Mr. Kinsey, of Bergen, succeeded in obtaining a grant of $2,000 for a survey. It must be confessed, so narrow and uncertain was the information we could convey, that this generous grant seemed to many of the very men who made it a sacrifice to get rid of clamorous and indefatigable enthusiasm rather than seed sown to be in due time matured into a magnificent harvest. Such were affairs in the winter of 1822. Mr. Renwick had already, like myself, gratuitously and at his own expense gone over the whole line, and the operations of the ensuing year were now concerted with him. Be it here broadly stated, that, up to the time when the Morris Canal became a Wall street speculation, he was considered, by every person connected with the enterprise, as its chief engineer, and that without his zeal, talent and science it would not, within our day and generation, have emerged beyond a scheme transmitted to a more liberal and enlightened posterity. In April, 1823, I went to Albany, and, with Governor Clinton's countenance, obtained from the Legislature of New York a grant of its engineers to join in the Morris survey. But even this co-operation did not seem to me sufficient to counteract the apathy of friends or the prejudices and party spirit of opponents. I therefore wrote to Mr. Calhoun, then Secretary of War, for the aid of General Bernard and Colonel Totten, heads of the United States engineer department. This re-inforcement, with the volunteer services of General Swift, constituted a weight of authority sufficient to overpower cavil, ignorance and hostility. From Albany I proceeded with Judge Wright, Chief Engineer of the Erie Canal, to Little Falls, for the purpose of engaging Mr. Beach to take the levels and survey the route, having previously conversed with him, and agreed with Professor Renwick to intrust him with that task. The spring and summer of 1823 were spent by me in collecting topographical and statistical information, as also in reconnoitring the various routes, in company with the inhabitants of their vicinity. Here a singular fact should be stated, that the plain, good sense and local information of our farmers staked out the most difficult passes of the boldest canal in existence, and that in every important point the actual navigation merely pursues the trace thus indicated. In July, 1823, Mr. Beach appeared for the first time on the scene of action, guided by Mr. Renwick, to whom the deliberative department was confided. The Morris Canal was to be constructed on novel principles, and upon scientific deliberation its success was completely dependent. Governor Clinton, with Judge Wright, and General Bernard, with Colonel Totten, successively took a rapid view of the line at all its hazardous points; were informed of the peculiar obstacles of each location; the expedients proposed to surmount these obstacles; the capabilities of the country; the objects of the enterprise, and its probable results. Their remarks on these subjects, submitted by me to their consideration, are embodied in their several reports presented to the Legislature of New Jersey, and, with the documents of Messrs. Renwick and Beach, all forming part of the General Report, dated November, 1823, drawn by me, as President of the Commission. Our uniform object had been, as shown in the Commissioners' Report, to induce the Legislature to adopt the canal as a State concern, but the design proved absolutely impracticable, through local interests, jealousies, and a most laudable dread of public debt. The only remaining expedient for executing the enterprise was to raise a company, endowed with privileges and banking powers sufficiently liberal to allure subscriptions. The summer of 1824 was spent in sustaining through the press and otherwise the spirit which had been roused, and in preparing a suitable charter for the contemplated company. It may be well here to remark, that, anticipating the danger of throwing the whole concern into the control of mere foreign capitalists, this draft of a charter provided that a certain number of directors should be chosen resident in each county penetrated by the canal. An unfortunate collision with the advocates of the Raritan Canal, then in agitation, delayed the passage of our charter; it was December; my academy had been in session several weeks, and I was constrained to return home, with assurances from the Morris members of the Legislature that the affair should be strenuously urged. Several gentlemen from Wall street had volunteered their good offices, and very kindly took part in the Trenton lobby after my departure. Upon their suggestion the draft of the charter was transformed into its present shape, nor did I receive the most distant hint of any alteration until the bill was finally passed. A company was formed, and myself included in its direction. The precarious position of a canal coupled to a bank and directed by men of operations exclusively financial was obvious. The interests of the country, and the development of the iron manufacture, were merged into a reckless stock speculation. I did all in my power to arrest this perversion, but soon found myself a mere cypher, standing alone, and responsible in public opinion for acts of extravagant folly which I alone had strenuously opposed at the Board of Directors. My course would have been to resign my seat at once, but, anxious for an enterprise in which not only all my feelings but all my property were enlisted, and still hoping that prudence and even a far-seeing self-interest might ultimately prevail, I clung to the sinking ship until every hope of safety had vanished, and then vacated my seat by selling out, thus saving myself from ruin, if not from loss. From the moment the charter, altered without my knowledge, was obtained, the whole affair became a stock-jobbing concern; the canal a mere pretext; my effort to recall the institution to its duty was regarded as an intrusion, and every pains was taken to force me to retire. Although nominally the chief of the canal department, everything was done without my concurrence; obstacles were opposed to all my inquiries, and there seemed a universal dread of my seeing or hearing of any transaction. The result was that the canal, after years of delay, amidst gross blunders and most lucrative contracts, was completed at a cost of about $2,000,000, while a responsible contract was rejected to execute the whole for $850,000. Fortunes were lost and gained; loans borrowed and squandered; the property devolved upon foreign capitalists; criminal justice inquired into its management, the bank exploded, after an attempt to involve New Jersey in a ruinous responsibility, and the canal remained an inefficient blot upon the map of the State. After numerous vicissitudes, the management has at length devolved upon gentlemen who understand the public as well as their own private interests, when honor and intelligence bid fair to redeem the charter of the institution, rendering it not only lucrative to the stockholder, but a blessing to the country whose natural resources it now calls into activity. While the foregoing events were in progress, I was the object of unmeasured abuse and misrepresentation by persons who sought to convert my labors into wealth and aggrandizement for themselves; let me therefore be permitted to state what those labors were. Not only was the project itself first conceived by me, but I employed five years in exploring the route, and conciliating friends. The newspaper articles, the correspondence to obtain information, the Commissioners' report, and an endless catalogue of literary tasks, were from my hand. I claim to have, single-handed, achieved the problem of rendering popular and accomplishing a scheme demanding vast resources, and stigmatized as the dream of a crazed imagination. The abuse and misrepresentation are long since forgiven; the loss is forgotten. The enterprise seems now in a fair way to realize that public advantage which was ever the sole object in my mind, and I deem the sacrifice of a few years of comfort and repose as most amply remunerated. What was done was done to repay the hospitality of my adopted country." Never, surely, did public benefactor dispel from his shining name the mists and shadows of detraction with a keener vigor or a nobler dignity. The vindication is not less historical than biographical, and as such, to repeat what was said above, it has a twofold claim to the spare accorded it here. It is plain that his accomplished man in his day did "the State some service." Nay, it would hardly be too much to say that at a critical period in the history of New Jersey he was to the commonwealth what leaven is to dough; he leavened the whole mass. In 1830 he was appointed one of the Board of Visitors of the Military Academy at West Point, and in 1842 was reap-

pointed, discharging his official duties on both occasions with the zeal and fidelity which were a part of his character. Personally, he was one of the most attractive and estimable of men. He, indeed, was in all respects a remarkable man: remarkable in his native gifts, in his culture, in his attainments, in his experience, in his achievements, in his masculine sense, in his vivid sensibilities, in his sparkling humor, in his gentleness, in his exquisite breeding, in the grace and variety and charm of his conversation, in his broad and progressive spirit, in his undrooping energy, in his lofty and spotless integrity, in his length of days, and in the health and happiness and honor that followed him throughout. He died in June, 1858, his wife, with whom he had lived for fifty-eight years, surviving him, as also the two children, his only children, who came with him to this country in the dawn of the century—a son, Mr. Francis L. Macculloch, of Salem, and a daughter, wife of the lamented Jacob W. Miller, of Morristown, formerly United States Senator from New Jersey.

CHUREMAN, HON. JAMES, Revolutionary Patriot, Mayor of the city of New Brunswick, New Jersey, late of that place, was one of its leading and most prominent citizens. In the opening of the revolutionary contest, he graduated at Queens College. On a certain occasion, as the anecdote is told in the "New Jersey Historical Collection," the militia were suddenly called out to go against the enemy; their captain made a speech urging them to volunteer, but not one complied; he then stepped out from the ranks, and, after volunteering himself, addressed them with such persuasive eloquence that a company was instantly formed, which went to Long Island, and there did gallant and efficient service in the conflict between the patriots and the royalist troops. In the course of the war, he was taken prisoner by a party of mounted British, near what is now Bergen's Mills, on Lawrence brook, three miles south of New Brunswick. He was then temporarily confined in the guard-house in New Brunswick, which stood near the Nelson mansion, where he was supplied with nutritious food through the kindness of Mrs. Van Deusen. He was transferred from there to New York, and imprisoned in the sugar-house of that city, with his comrade, George Thomson. Philip Kissack, a tory, touched by their forlorn and suffering condition, furnished them with money, with which they purchased food, and thus kept themselves from starvation and ultimately death. Finally, they bribed the guards to give them the privilege of walking about and exercising in the yard attached to the house; and one night, having supplied them with liquor in which there had been placed a quantity of laudanum, they dug through the wall and escaped to the upper part of the city, near where the old prison stood. There they managed to secure a small fishing-boat, and with a single oar paddled across the Hudson to Powles' Hook, and thence proceeded to Morristown, where they were welcomed by their patriot brothers-in-arms. In 1786-87 he was a delegate to the Continental Congress, and a member of Congress from his State, 1789-91, 1797-99. From the latter year until 1801 he served as a United States Senator; and subsequently became Mayor of the city of New Brunswick, New Jersey. He was again a representative in 1813-15. He died in New Brunswick, New Jersey, January 23d, 1824, aged sixty-seven years.

E BOW, JAMES DUNWOODY BROWNSON, Journalist and Statistician, an eminent citizen of New Jersey, late of Elizabeth, was born in Charleston, South Carolina, July 10th, 1820, and in 1843 graduated from the Charleston College, in his native State. His father was a merchant of good standing and repute. He was for seven years employed in a mercantile house, but after graduating devoted himself to the study of law, and in 1844 was admitted to the Charleston bar. Subsequently he became editor of the *Southern Quarterly Review*, Charleston. One of his articles, entitled "Oregon and the Oregon Question," attracted much attention both at home and abroad, and occasioned a debate in the French Chamber of Deputies. In the latter part of 1845 he removed to New Orleans, Louisiana, and there established his *Commercial Review*. After a short term as Professor of Political Economy and Commercial Statistics in the University of Louisiana, in 1848, he was for three years the Chief of the Census Bureau of the State, and collected and published valuable statistics of the population, commerce and products of Louisiana. Upon his appointment, in March, 1853, as Superintendent of the United States Census, he collected and prepared for the press a large part of the material for the quarto edition of the "Census of 1850." He was a warm supporter of the material and intellectual interests of the South; was a member of nearly every southern commercial convention since 1845, and presided over that held at Knoxville, Tennessee, in 1857. He contributed many articles on American topics to the new edition of the "Encyclopædia Britannica;" delivered various addresses before literary, agricultural and other associations, and was one of the founders of the Louisiana Historical Society, since merged in the Academy of Science. In the years of commotion preceding the outburst of the rebellion he put forth many virulent denunciations of the Northern States and their institutions; and throughout the contest, though his *Review* was necessarily discontinued, his voice and pen were incessantly busied in lauding the aims and actions of the Confederacy. At the conclusion of the war, however, he was brought to admit the superiority of the free to the slave labor system, and

urged upon the Southern States the wise policy of encouraging immigration. He afterward re-established his *Review*, first in New York, later in Nashville. His "Encyclopædia of the Trade and Commerce of the United States," two volumes, 8vo., was published in 1853; his "Southern States: their Agriculture, Commerce, etc.," in 1856; and the "Industrial Resources of the Southwest," compiled from his *Review*, three volumes, in 1853. His "Compendium of the Seventh United States Census" also deserves approving mention. He died in Elizabeth, New Jersey, February 27th, 1867.

UFFIELD, REV. GEORGE, son of George Duffield, D. D., and grandson of George Duffield, D. D., an ardent revolutionary patriot and chaplain of the old Congress, of Ann Arbor, Michigan, was born in Carlisle, Pennsylvania, in 1818. Upon the completion of a course of preparatory studies, he entered Yale College and graduated from that institution in 1837. In 1840 he was ordained to the ministry, and settled for some time in Bloomfield, New Jersey, where he soon became known as a diligent student and earnest preacher. He then removed to Brooklyn, New York, and was engaged in that field of labor until 1852, when he assumed the pastorate of the Central Church, Northern Liberties, Philadelphia, Pennsylvania. For some years past he has officiated at the Presbyterian Church, Ann Arbor, Michigan. He has written many hymns, but will be chiefly remembered for the one, "Stand up for Jesus."

OX, REV. SAMUEL HANSON, D. D., LL. D., Presbyterian Divine, Writer on Religious Subjects, of New York, was born in Leesville, New Jersey, August 25th, 1793. He commenced the study of law in 1811, afterward studied theology, and finally, July 1st, 1817, was ordained by the New Jersey Presbytery. From 1820 to 1833 he officiated as pastor of the Spring Street Church, New York; from 1834 to May, 1837, presided as Professor of Sacred Rhetoric at Auburn, New York; and from that time until 1854, when by the failure of his voice he was obliged to relinquish his charge, was pastor of the First Presbyterian Church of Brooklyn, New York. July 10th, 1834, having openly taken sides with those favoring the abolition of slavery, and aided in founding the Anti-slavery Society, he was one of the sufferers by a mob, which attacked and sacked his church and house. He was successively an ardent advocate of abolition, temperance, colonization, New School Presbyterianism, and the aims and measures of the Evangelical Alliance. He won high rank as a writer and preacher;

and has been frequently a delegate to the religious anniver-saries held in London, England. Among his more notable works are "Quakerism not Christianity," and "Interviews, Memorable and Useful, from the Diary of Memory," New York, 1853. In all measures pertaining to political move-ments, in the South and North, as related to the slavery question, he was an unflinching and eloquent partisan of freedom; and was a prime mover in many important steps taken to remove from his country its chief disgrace and blemish. The well-known Bishop A. C. Coxe is his son.

OMAYNE, NICHOLAS, M. D., Lecturer on An-atomy and Medicine, late of New York city, was born in Hackensack, New Jersey, in September, 1756. He studied under Dr. Peter Wilson, and completed his medical education at Edinburgh, where he published a dissertation "De Genera-tione Puris." He subsequently spent two years in Paris, and also visited Leyden, returning about the year 1782 to New York, where he commenced his professional career. He gave private lectures on anatomy, and taught many professional branches with remarkable success. Upon re-linquishing his labors in this direction he again visited Europe. Later, on account of his connection with the scheme of Blount's conspiracy, he was incarcerated for some time. He was first President of the New York Medi-cal Society, in 1806; and in 1807 was made first President of the College of Physicians and Surgeons, which he had been instrumental in founding. In that institution he gave instruction in anatomy and the institutes of medicine. He died in New York city, July 21st, 1817.

ACCLINTOCK, REV. JOHN, D. D., LL. D., Clergyman, Author, late of Madison, New Jersey, was born in Philadelphia, Pennsylvania, in 1814, and graduated from the University of Pennsyl-vania in 1835. He subsequently became a mem-ber of the New Jersey Conference, and after being a short time in the Methodist ministry was, in 1837, elected Professor of Mathematics in Dickinson College, but in 1839 was transferred to the chair of Ancient Languages. While residing at Carlisle he made a translation, in co-operation with Blumenthal, of Neander's "Life of Christ;" and with Professor Crooks began the preparation for publication of a series of Greek and Latin text-books. From 1848 to 1856 he filled the position of editor of the *Methodist Quarterly Review*, and later was appointed a delegate of his church to the English, Irish, French and German Conferences. He was also present at the World's Convention at Berlin, in 1856. On his return from Europe he was elected President

of the Troy Union, and was during a brief period pastor of St. Paul's Church, New York. In June, 1860, he sailed for Europe again, and took up his residence in Paris, France, in order to take charge of the American chapel es-tablished in that city. From its organization, in 1867, until the time of his decease he was President of the Drew Theo-logical Seminary, in Madison, New Jersey. For several years, in connection with Dr. Strong, he was occupied in preparing the "Cyclopædia of Sacred Literature," three or more volumes of which have been completed and pub-lished. He published also "Analysis of Watson's Theo-logical Institutes;" "Temporal Power of the Pope;" and "Sketches of Eminent Methodist Ministers," 8vo., 1854. In 1855 he edited and published "Bungener's History of the Council of Trent." He died at Madison, New Jersey, March 4th, 1870.

EESE, HON. FREDERICK H., was born Octo-ber 21st, 1823, in the city of Newark. He grad-uated at Princeton College with the class of 1843, and immediately began preparation for the New Jersey bar, to which he was admitted in 1846; he was made Counsellor in 1849. In 1860 he was elected by the Democrats to the New Jersey Legisla-ture, and was re-elected in 1861. During his second term he served as Speaker, and made an excellent presiding offi-cer. In 1864 he was appointed Presiding Judge of the Court of Common Pleas of Essex county, and was reap-pointed in 1869; he resigned in 1872, and resumed his law practice. In the campaign of 1874 he was nominated by the Democrats as their candidate for Congress, and, al-though the district (Essex county) had two years previously given a Republican majority of nearly six thousand, he was elected.

ADAL, REV. BERNARD H., D. D., LL. D., Methodist Clergyman, Scholar and Author, late of Madison, New Jersey, was born in Maryland, in 1815, and was graduated from the Dickinson College. Joining the Baltimore Conference in 1835, he preached in Maryland, Virginia and Delaware; afterward in Washington, Philadelphia, Brook-lyn and New Haven. About 1850 he became a Professor in the Asbury, Indiana, University; was for one session Chaplain of Congress; and on the organization of the Drew Theological Seminary became Professor of Church His-tory, and on the death of Dr. McClintock, acting President. While a resident of Indiana he published essays on "Church History" in the *Methodist Quarterly Review*, which marked him as one of the ablest writers of his denomination. He was a forcible writer, and a chief contributor to *The Meth-odist*. He died at Madison, New Jersey, June 20th, 1870.

PGAR, ELLIS A., Superintendent of Public Instruction for the State of New Jersey, son of David and Hannah (Whitehead) Apgar, his father of German, his mother of English descent, was born at Peapack, Somerset county, New Jersey, March 20th, 1836. Receiving his preparatory education at the district schools of Somerset county, he entered the State Normal School at Trenton in 1854, and graduated thence in 1857. For several years he was engaged as a teacher in various public schools in different parts of the State, and then entered Rutgers College. In 1866 he graduated from this institution, taking the prize for mathematics. Previous to his graduation he was elected Professor of Mathematics in the State Normal School, a position that he held concurrently with and subsequent to his course at Rutgers. In 1866, under an act of the New Jersey Legislature, a State Board of Education had been created, and at the first meeting of this Board, held March 29th, 1866, he was elected State Superintendent of Public Instruction. To this office he has since been continuously re-elected. Shortly after he had entered upon the discharge of his duties, he became impressed by the necessity for a change in the method then existing for the supervision of the public schools, and his first work was to frame a bill, subsequently passed by the Legislature, which provided for the creation of county superintendents and examiners, thus making a radical change in the organization of the department of public instruction. His reforms, from this time onward, were constant. In his annual report for 1863 he urged that a tax should be levied sufficient to make all public schools in the State free; and this demand was practically acceded to in 1871, when an act, which he himself framed, making the public schools free during nine months in each year, was passed by the Legislature. By his energetic efforts, supported as they have been by the State Board of Education and by enlightened citizens in all portions of the State, the school system of New Jersey has been raised to an equality with the best in the country; and during the ten years ending with the year 1876 the value of school property in the State has increased from $1,645,000 to $6,205,000—a gain of $4,560,000. At the Centennial Exhibition a fit opportunity was afforded for making a display of this very remarkable and gratifying progress, and applying himself with characteristic zeal to collecting the necessary material, the New Jersey section was one of the most brilliant in the Department of Instruction. The following table of totals, from his report upon the New Jersey exhibit, best presents his success upon this particular occasion, and is also an effective summing up of the almost unexampled results of his years of earnest, well-directed labor: number of colleges represented, 2; number of private schools represented, 33; number of public ungraded schools represented, 1,184; number of public graded schools represented, 230; number of high schools represented, 8; number of public schools unrepresented, 120; total number of public schools in the State, 1,542; number of public school teachers in the State, 2,810; number of public school teachers who furnished work, 2,690; percentage of school teachers who furnished work, 95 per cent.; number of pupils who furnished work, 14,000; number of specimens from public schools, 16,150; number of specimens from colleges and private schools, 1,512; total number of specimens exhibited, 17,662. In the above particular attention should be directed to the large percentage of teachers furnishing work, and to the great number of specimens from all sources, as these figures are capital proof of how well he is in accord with the teachers and scholars under his control. The total percentage of work exhibited, it should be stated, was greater in the New Jersey section than in the section of any other State represented in the Department of Instruction. His eminent success in massing and arranging the New Jersey exhibit has caused his appointment to the position of Superintendent of the Department of Education in the Permanent International Exhibition to be held in the Main Centennial Building at Philadelphia. Notwithstanding the many and laborious duties connected with his official position, he has produced several valuable scholastic works, among which may be mentioned a system of map drawing now largely in use; a fine set of geographical wall maps; an excellent volume upon "Plant Analysis," and "A Brief History of New Jersey, for School Use"—the last named supplying a long felt want in the New Jersey schools, and being an example that promoters of education in other States would do well to follow, State history being a matter at present entirely too much neglected. He was married, December 25th, 1867, to Camilla, daughter of Mr. Israel Swayze, of Hope, Warren county, New Jersey.

———————

ADDEN, HON. HOSEA F., Merchant, Shipbuilder and State Senator of Tuckahoe, was born in Millville, Cumberland county, New Jersey, November 2d, 1817. He is the son of Hosea Madden. His family are of English descent, but have lived in New Jersey for four generations. He received a good English education at the public schools of his native county, and, his school-days over, learned the art of glass-making. In 1844 he removed to Tuckahoe, Atlantic county, where he engaged in building vessels for the river and coasting trade, and in the general mercantile business—pursuits in which he speedily acquired a reputation for integrity, faithfulness and administrative ability, laying the foundations for the universal confidence and respect with which his fellow-citizens have long regarded him, and which they have repeatedly manifested by the public trusts they have conferred upon him. In 1853 he was elected Sheriff of Atlantic county, holding the position for three years. He was a member of the Board of Chosen Freeholders of the county for nineteen years, during a considerable part of which time he was Director of the Board. At one time and another he has filled all the principal offices of his township. His popularity is solid, beginning at home in his town, and extending through his township and his county out into the commonwealth at large. This was shown at his more especial entrance into political life in 1874, when he was nominated by the Democrats of Atlantic county for the office of State Senator and elected, although the county usually gave a Republican majority of from three hundred to four hundred. As the Senatorial term lasts three years, he still holds the office of Senator, the duties of which he discharges with marked vigor, industry and thoroughness. He is Chairman of the Committee on Engrossed Bills, of the Committee on Passed Bills, and of the Centennial Committee, and is, besides, a member of the Committee on the State Prison, of the Committee on Railroads and Canals, and of other important committees. The estimation in which he is held by his colleagues may be inferred from the positions they have assigned him. Sound in his judgment, practical in his views, thoroughly investigating every measure upon which he is called to act, and fearless in going ahead when he is sure he is right, he is a careful and at the same time an independent legislator, and, consequently, a safe and wise one. Well does he merit the wide esteem he enjoys. He was married in 1842 to Catharine Birch, of Cumberland county, New Jersey.

UNNELL, THOMAS G., Editor and Politician, Newton, Sussex county, New Jersey—son of David Bunnell, farmer, a descendant of William Bunnell, an English emigrant and settler in New Haven, Connecticut, in 1634, and, less remotely, of Solomon Bunnell, who migrated from New England and established the New Jersey branch of the family about the time of the French and Indian war—was born at Walpach, Sussex county, March 14th, 1834. Having received a substantial common school education, he was for a time employed upon his father's farm. Agriculture, however, was not to his taste, and his predilection for journalism was early displayed in a series of ably written articles, mainly political, contributed to the county paper, the *Sussex Herald*. His writings having attracted a considerable amount of attention, he was offered, early in 1867, the position of local editor upon the paper, and this he held until August of the same year, when, in company with several other prominent Democrats, he became a part owner of the publication. The *Herald* is one of the oldest papers published in New Jersey, having been founded in 1829 by Grant Fitch, father of Charles W. Fitch, of Washington, District of Columbia. Selected by his associates in the purchase to be editor, Mr. Bunnell succeeded to the post so ably filled by the Hon. Henry C. Kelsey, who had relin-

quished journalism in order to accept the position of Secretary of State of New Jersey, and his management, notwithstanding his comparative freshness in the editorial harness, was of a character to gain the *Herald* increased respect and authority. He has since continued to conduct the paper with marked ability, and it is now one of the leaders of political thought not only in Sussex county but throughout a large portion of East Jersey. Naturally, he himself has taken a prominent part in local and State politics, and has held a number of the higher local offices. He is at present Chairman of the Newton Town Council, having been elected by a handsome majority at the close of a spirited contest. In February of the present year (1877) he was elected without opposition Engrossing Clerk of the State Senate. He was married, September 19th, 1857, to Mary A., daughter of Mr. Jonas Smith, of Sussex county.

OMEYN, REV. THEODORE DIRCK, D. D., Clergyman, Professor of Theology in the Dutch Reformed Church, son of Nicholas Romeyn, brother of Rev. John Brodhead Romeyn, D. D., late of Schenectady, New York, was born at Hackensack, New Jersey, January 23d, 1744. His early studies were directed by his brother, Rev. Thomas Romeyn, then a minister in Delaware. He graduated at Princeton in 1765; was ordained by the Cœtus over the Dutch Church in Ulster county, May 14th, 1766; and afterwards installed at Hackensack, New Jersey, where he remained until his removal to Schenectady, New York, in November, 1784. In 1797 he was appointed Professor of Theology in the Dutch Church. The establishment of the Union College at Schenectady is to be ascribed principally to his earnest and untiring labors and efforts. He was twice offered the Presidency of Queen's College, New Jersey, but, after careful consideration, deemed it fitting to decline on both occasions. His colleague, Rev. Mr. Meyer, represents him as "a son of thunder" in the pulpit. He was importantly instrumental, also, in promoting the independence of the Dutch churches, or their separation from the jurisdiction of Holland. He died at Schenectady, New York, April 16th, 1804.

---

cPHERSON, HON. JOHN RHODERIC, United States Senator from New Jersey, Stock-raiser and Dealer, of Hudson City, was born, May 9th, 1833, in Livingston county, New York, and is a son of Daniel and Jane (Calder) McPherson, both also natives of New York State, and both of whom are of Scottish descent. He received his education at the Geneseo Academy. After leaving school he became engaged in farming and stock-raising, continuing in those avocations until he was twenty-five years of age. He then removed to New Jersey, and located at Hudson City, where he became interested in stock-dealing, and was also one of the proprietors of the stock-yards in that city, which were constructed by him during 1863 and 1864. He was also the designer and constructer of the buildings used by the Central Stock-Yard and Transit Company at Harsimus Cove, New Jersey, and as such they have proved a grand success, and are believed to be the most perfect system of stock-yards now in existence, while the abattoir is unrivalled. These cover an area of twenty-two acres, and are built entirely on piles, over fifteen thousand of these huge timbers being employed. The tide water ebbs and flows daily over the entire space covered by the structure. It has a daily capacity for seven thousand head of cattle, with all the facilities for yarding, feeding, and watering the same. On the extreme end of the works, and fronting the Hudson river, the abattoir for slaughtering sheep and cattle is constructed, together with the chambers for the storage of live sheep. It has a storage capacity of twenty thousand sheep daily, and a daily slaughtering capacity of ten thousand sheep and two thousand cattle. At this institution all parts of the animal are utilized, so that no portion whatever is allowed to be wasted; and as everything is manufactured while in a perfectly fresh condition, no offensive odor is emitted therefrom. It must be remembered that this establishment is located in the very heart of the city, and in its daily operation it may be considered a fair settlement of the question that stock-yards and abattoirs are not necessarily nuisances. There is another feature of this great institution, and one that commends itself to public favor, which is the fact that no live-stock are permitted to pass through the streets of Jersey City or New York in their distribution from these yards, all being delivered by means of the boats of the company to the butchers in New York and Brooklyn. The company have also an extensive store-room and abattoir for hogs on the west bank of the Hackensack river, where all these animals are removed from the cars, slaughtered, and the product sent to the docks of the company in cars provided for the purpose, as no live hogs are permitted to enter the institution on the Hudson river, which measurably accounts for the entire absence of anything of an offensive nature. Mr. McPherson was also one of the originators and also one of the proprietors of the abattoir and stock-yards at West Philadelphia. He is at the present time the lessee of all the stock-yards on the Erie Railroad, located at Buffalo, Port Deposit, Oak Cliff, etc., and is the inventor of a new stock-car for feeding and watering cattle while in transit. This latter invention has proved a most valuable one, and is being brought into use on a majority of the principal roads over which live-stock are transported. He has taken an active part in political matters, and is a Democrat in principles. From 1863 to 1869 he served as a member of the Board of Aldermen of Hudson City, and was President of that body for the last four years of his connection with the Board. He was elected by the Democratic party as Senator from Hudson county, and served in the sessions of 1872-73 and '74. During his legislative career he took a decided stand against the railroad monopolies of the State, and was a firm and unflinching advocate of the general railroad law, which was passed while he was a Senator. He served on various important committees while a member of that body, among which were Municipal Corporations, Banks, Insurance and Commerce. In 1873 he was instrumental in obtaining the charter for the Central Stock-Yard and Transit Company, above described. He was one of the organizers and the first President of the People's Gas Light Company of Hudson county, incorporated in 1870. In January, 1877, he was elected to represent the State in the United States Senate as the successor of Hon. Frederick T. Frelinghuysen. He was married, in 1868, to Ella J. Gregory, of Buffalo, New York.

———————

TOCKTON, REV. THOMAS HEWLINGS, Clergyman, Editor, Author, late of Philadelphia, Pennsylvania, was born at Mount Holly, New Jersey, June 4th, 1808. He began to write for the press at the age of sixteen, and studied medicine in Philadelphia, but in May, 1829, commenced preaching in connection with the Methodist Protestant Church. In 1830 he was stationed at Baltimore, and in 1833 was elected Chaplain to Congress, and re-elected in 1835 and 1837. Subsequently until 1838 he resided in Baltimore, Maryland, and in addition to discharging his pastoral duties compiled the hymn-book of the Methodist Protestant Church, and was for a short time editor of the church newspaper, the *Methodist Protestant;* but, unwilling to submit to restrictions sought to be imposed upon him in its discussion of slavery by the Baltimore Conference, he resigned his position and removed to Philadelphia, Pennsylvania, where he remained till 1847, as pastor and public lecturer. He then settled in Cincinnati, Ohio, and while residing there was elected President of Miami University, but declined; and in 1850 returned to Baltimore, where he was for five years associate pastor of St. John's Methodist Church, and for three years and six months temporary pastor of an Associate Reformed Presbyterian Church. From 1856 to 1868 he was pastor of the Church of the New Testament, and also performed much literary labor. He had a high reputation for eloquence, and edited with marked ability the *Christian World* and *Bible Times.* He was in the van in all forms of social progress, and an intrepid pioneer in the anti-slavery party; was ardently opposed to all forms of ultra sectarianism, and by voice and pen sought the promotion of Christian brotherhood and union. Memoirs of him have been published by Rev. Alexander Clark and Rev. John G. Wilson. He was again Chaplain to the United States House of Representatives in 1859-1861;

and in the following year filled the Chaplaincy of the United States Senate. He published an edition of the New Testament in paragraph form; many pamphlets, sermons and addresses; "Floating Flowers from a Hidden Brook," 1844; "The Bible Alliance," 1850; "Sermons for the People," 1854; "The Blessing," 1857; "Stand up for Jesus," 1858; "Poems, with Autobiographic and other Notes," 1862; "The Peerless Magnificence of the Word of God," 1862; and "The Meditation of Christ." He died in Philadelphia, October 9th, 1868.

RICE, HON. RODMAN M., ex-Governor of New Jersey, was born in Sussex county, New Jersey, November 5th, 1816, and studied at the New Jersey College—protracted illness preventing his graduation, however, from that institution. He afterward pursued a course of legal studies; in 1840 was appointed Purser in the navy; is said to have been the first person to exercise judicial functions under the American flag, on the Pacific coast, as alcalde; was made Navy Agent there in 1848; from 1851 to 1853, after his return to the East, served as a member of Congress from his native State; and in 1861 was an influential delegate to the Peace Congress. He caused the establishment in New Jersey of a normal school, and was warmly and generously interested in the development of the State militia system.

LARK, J. HENRY, M. D., Physician and Author, late of Montclair, New Jersey, was born in Livingston, New Jersey, June 23d, 1814, and graduated from the University of New York in 1841. He then entered upon a course of medical studies in New York and Europe, and finally established himself in the practice of his profession at Newark, about 1846, there gaining speedily a high reputation as a scholar and physician. For several years he officiated as President of the Essex County Medical Society. His "Sight and Hearing" was published in 1856; and was followed in 1861 by "The Medical Topography of Newark and its Vicinity." He died at Montclair, New Jersey, March 6th, 1869.

ALDWELL, REV. JOSEPH, D. D., Scientist, Author, Professor of Mathematics, late of Chapel Hill, North Carolina, was born in Leamington, New Jersey, April 21st, 1773. In his youth, while at school, he exhibited a noteworthy fondness for mathematical science, and won distinction as a diligent and talented student. He afterward studied for the ministry, was engaged for a time in teach-

ing school, and in 1796 was chosen presiding Professor of the infant University of North Carolina, also performing the duties of Mathematical Professor. September 22d, 1796, he was licensed to preach. In 1804 a presidency was created, to which he was chosen, and which was held by him until the period of his decease. Upon his election to this office he vacated the Mathematical chair for that of Moral Philosophy. In 1824 he visited Europe in order to direct in person the construction of a valuable philosophical apparatus, and also to make a selection of needed books for the library. "To him North Carolina is indebted for various internal improvements of his suggesting, as well as to his services in the cause of education." In 1822 he published a "Treatise on Geometry," and in 1825 the "Letters of Carlton." He died at Chapel Hill, North Carolina, January 24th, 1835.

IXON, JOSEPH, Inventor, late of Jersey City, New Jersey, before he had attained his twenty-first year, made a machine to cut files, and in various ways exhibited unusual skill and talent as a practical artisan. He afterward learned the printer's trade, that of wood engraving, then lithography, and ultimately became a thorough chemist, optician, and photographer. He was probably the first person to take a portrait by the camera, and first used the reflector, so that the object should not appear reversed. He built the first locomotive with wooden wheels, but with the same double-crank which is now in common use. He originated the process of photo-lithography; and to guard against abuses of this process invented the system of printing in colors on bank-notes, and patented it, but never received any benefit from his idea, all the banks having used it without pay. He perfected the system of making collodion for the photographers, and aided Mr. Harrian in the mode of grinding lenses for common tubes. He is the father of the steel-melting business in this country; is widely known as the originator of the plumbago crucible as now made; and his establishment in Jersey City is the largest of the kind in the world. The versatility of his mechanical genius, aided by unflagging energy and an intelligent appreciation of the pressing needs of the general community, has produced notable and welcome results. He died in Jersey City, New Jersey, June 14th, 1869, aged seventy-one years.

IMPSON, JAMES H., Brigadier General, Colonel of Engineers United States Army, and Author, of New Jersey, was born in that State, about 1812, and graduated from the Academy at West Point in 1832. In 1848 he secured at the New Jersey College the degree of A. M. Entering the 3d Artillery, he was appointed Aid to General Eustis,

Rodman M. Price

in the Florida war of 1837-38. He subsequently attained the following positions: July 7th, 1838, First Lieutenant of the Topographical Engineers; March 3d, 1853, Captain; March 3d, 1863, Major in the Engineering Corps; June, of the same year, Lieutenant-Colonel; March 7th, 1867, Colonel, having previously accepted, August 12th, 1861, a Colonelcy in the 4th Regiment of New Jersey Volunteers. He took an active part in the peninsular campaign; was engaged at West Point and Gaines' Mills, where he was captured, June 27th, 1862; from August, 1862, to June, 1865, was Chief-Engineer of the Department of the Ohio; and March 13th, 1865, was made Brevet Brigadier-General of the United States Army. He published "Journal of a Military Reconnoissance from Santa Fé to the Navajo Country, in 1849," 8vo., 1852; "Shortest Route to California," 8vo., 1869; "Report ou the Union Pacific Railroad and Branches," 8vo., 1865. His gallantry in time of action, always characterized by a comprehensive shrewdness which enabled him to take advantage of every passing circumstance, and his skill and attainments in the art of engineering, contributed to make him a reliable leader in the field and a valuable assistant in general military operations.

REENWOOD, MILES, Manufacturer, of Ohio, was born in Jersey City, New Jersey, March 19th, 1807. In 1817 he removed to the West with his father, and settled finally near Cincinnati, Ohio. In 1832 he commenced, on the Miami canal, the Eagle Iron Works, which speedily became the most extensive manufactory in the West. In 1846 it was destroyed by fire, but was soon after entirely rebuilt. He was one of the originators of the Ohio Mechanics' Institute, and an active worker in all that related to its interests and development, contributing largely toward defraying the expenses attending the erection of their present handsome building. He was also mainly instrumental in introducing steam fire-engines, fully appreciating their importance as safeguards of large and crowded cities.

UMMINGS, REV. MOSES, Minister, Editor of the *Christian Messenger* and the *Palladium*, late of New York city, was born at Haverhill, Massachusetts, and entered the ministry at eighteen years of age. His initial fields of labor were throughout New Jersey and New York, and in both States he was famed for his ardor, his energy, and his many good works. In 1854 he assumed editorial charge of the central denominational organs, the *Christian Messenger* and the *Palladium*, resigning his position in the spring of 1862. He was a determined opponent of slavery, and while

deprecating the action of the Southern branch of the church in 1853, was firmly opposed to all compromise or fellowship with slaveholders. As a friend and admirer of Horace Mann, he took the warmest interest in his peculiar educational views, and, during Mr. Mann's presidency of Antioch College, his measures were steadfastly defended and supported by the denominational organs. He died in New York city, January 6th, 1867, aged fifty-one years.

RMSTRONG, REV. WILLIAM JESSUP, D. D., Secretary of the American Board of Foreign Missions, late of New York, was born at Mendham, New Jersey, October 29th, 1796. His degree of A. M. he received from the New Jersey College in 1816, and that of D. D. in 1840. Under the careful guidance of his father, Rev. Dr. A. Armstrong, he acquired his preliminary education, and also, in all probability, the bias which afterward exercised so important an influence on his life and career. After three years of theological study he was sent to Albemarle county, Virginia, as a missionary. Subsequently he officiated for three years as pastor of a church in Trenton, New Jersey. From 1824 to 1834 he filled the pastorate of the First Presbyterian Church in Richmond, Virginia, and in the course of the latter year was appointed Secretary of the Presbyterian Board of Foreign Missions for Virginia and North Carolina; at the same time he was given the appointment of General Agent of the American Board of Missions for these States. In the following September he was appointed successor to Rev. Dr. Wisner, Secretary of the American Board. In April, 1838, after a residence of two years and a half at Boston, he removed to New York. A memoir of his life, with a collection of his sermons, well-digested and ably written productions, edited by Rev. Hollis Read, was published in New York in 1853, and in it is given an interesting account of his useful and varied career. He was drowned in the memorable wreck of the steamer "Atlantic," November 27th, 1846.

NDERSON, JOSEPH, Judge, Statesman and Revolutionary Soldier, late of Washington, District of Columbia, was born in New Jersey, November 5th, 1757. In his youth he received a good education, and at the completion of his preparatory studies turned his attention to the theory and practice of law. In 1775 he was appointed an ensign in the New Jersey Line, and fought at Monmouth as a Captain. In 1779 he took an active part in the expedition of Sullivan against the Six Nations, in 1780 was at Valley Forge, and in the following year was a participant at the siege of York. After the termination of the contest with Great Britain, he received the brevet of Major, for gallant and meritorious conduct on the field. He then entered upon the practice of his profession in Delaware, and in 1791 was appointed, by Washington, Judge of the territory south of the Ohio river. In this position he remained until the formation of the constitution of Tennessee, in which he assisted in a manner that won him warm commendations from the highest quarters. From 1797 to 1815 he was an influential member of the United States Senate from Tennessee, serving upon many important committees, and acting on two occasions as President *pro tem.* of the Senate. From 1815 to 1836 he was First Comptroller of the United States Treasury. As a statesman and political leader he was remarkably shrewd and far-seeing; and the various measures promulgated or supported by him at sundry crises in the development of his section, stand as eloquent witnesses to his abilities. He died at Washington, District of Columbia, April 17th, 1837.

OLLOCK, REV. HENRY D., D. D., Clergyman, late of Savannah, Georgia, was born in New Providence, New Jersey, December 14th, 1778, and graduated from the New Jersey College in 1794, where he subsequently acted as tutor from 1797 to 1800. May 7th of the latter year he was licensed to preach, and in the following December became pastor of a church at Elizabethtown, New Jersey. In December, 1803, he was appointed Professor of Divinity at New Jersey College. From 1806 till the time of his death he officiated as Pastor of the Independent Presbyterian Church, at Savannah, Georgia. As a preacher he had a brilliant reputation, and was widely esteemed for his many excellent qualities of mind and heart. He received the degree of D. D. from Harvard University in 1806. In 1822 his sermons were published in four volumes, 8vo., at Savannah, with a memoir by his brother, S. K. Kollock. He died at Savannah, Georgia, December 29th, 1819.

INDSLEY, REV. PHILIP, D. D., Educator, Professor of Archæology and Church Polity, and of Languages, late of Nashville, Tennessee, was born in Morristown, New Jersey, December 21st, 1786, and graduated from the New Jersey College in 1804. April 24th, 1810, he was licensed to preach, and in 1807-8-9 and '12 was tutor at Princeton College. In 1813 he became Professor of Languages in that institution, in 1817 was made Vice-President, and in 1823 was chosen President, but declined the proffered honor. In December, 1824, he accepted the thrice-tendered Presidency of the University of Nashville, and "through his efforts, the standard of education was raised to a level with that of the oldest and best-endowed colleges of the

Atlantic States." In October, 1850, he resigned this office, and during the last four years of his life resided at New Albany, Indiana, two years of that time being spent as Professor of Archæology and Church Polity in the theological seminary there. Such was his reputation that, between 1820 and 1839, he was at different times offered the presidency of ten different colleges and institutes of learning. In May, 1834, he was elected Moderator of the General Assembly of the Presbyterian Church, then in session at Philadelphia, Pennsylvania. His works, edited by L. I. Halsey, D. D., a well-known and talented clergyman, were published in Philadelphia, three volumes, 8vo., and have deservedly been called a well of desirable knowledge and true learning. The degree of D. D. was conferred on him by Dickinson College in 1828. He died at Nashville, Tennessee, May 25th, 1855.

OLLOCK, SHEPHERD, Revolutionary Officer, Editor, Judge, Late of Philadelphia, Pennsylvania, was born in Lewiston, Delaware, in 1750. At the outbreak of the struggle with Great Britain he was commissioned a Lieutenant, and was an active participant at the battles of Trenton, Fort Lee, Short Hills, and other places of minor importance. In 1779 he resigned his position in the army and established a newspaper, the *New Jersey Journal*, at the village of Chatham. In 1783 he removed his press to the city of New York, and there established the *New York Gazetteer*. He afterwards, in 1787, removed to Elizabethtown, New Jersey, and revived the *New Jersey Journal*, which he edited for more than thirty-one years. The office of Judge of Common Pleas he held for about thirty-five years, and acted as Postmaster at Elizabethtown until 1829. He died at Philadelphia, Pennsylvania, July 28th, 1839.

NOWLTON, MINER, Soldier and Author, late of Burlington, New Jersey, was born in Connecticut in 1804, and graduated at West Point in 1829. Entering the 1st United States Artillery, he became First Lieutenant July 23d, 1835; April 21st, 1846, was promoted to a Captaincy, and October 26th, 1861, retired from the service. In the years 1830-31-32-33 he was Assistant Professor of Mathematics at West Point; from 1833 to 1837 acted in the capacity of Assistant Teacher of French; and from 1837 to 1844 was Instructor of Artillery and Cavalry. He was one of the compilers of "Instruction for Field Artillery," adopted March 6th, 1845, for the United States army; was Aide-de-camp to Marshal Bugeaud in Algeria in 1845, and in the ensuing year served efficiently on the Rio Grande during the Mexican war. He was the author of "Notes on Gunpowder, Cannon and Projectiles," published in 1840; and "Instructions and Regulations for Militia and Volunteers of the United States," in 1861. Also, in 1857, he was President of the Common Council in Burlington, New Jersey. He died at Burlington, New Jersey, December 25th, 1870.

OOKE, EDWIN T., Brevet Brigadier-General of United States Volunteers, Secretary of Legation to Chili, late of Santiago, Chili, was a native of New Jersey, and entered the United States service at the commencement of the war, in 1861, as a Captain in the 2d New York Light Cavalry. By distinguished gallantry he rose to the command of his regiment, and ultimately to the post of Chief of Staff in General Kilpatrick's Cavalry Division. In 1863 he was associated with Colonel Dahlgren in command of the force which was sent to enter Richmond from the south, and had his horse killed under him by the same volley which terminated Dahlgren's life. Being taken prisoner, he was confined for several months in one of the gloomy underground cells of Libby Prison, where deprivation of proper food, light and warmth, completely shattered a once vigorous and powerful constitution. From Libby Prison he was transferred to other places of detention in various parts of South Carolina and Georgia. Finally, after a terrible experience of eighteen months as a prisoner in rebel hands, he obtained his liberty and returned home, utterly lacking the health and strength with which he had set out to assist in upholding the cause of the Union. He then accepted the position of Secretary to the Chilian Legation, hoping that the salubrious climate of that country might restore his impaired energies. The hope proved delusive, however, and he sank gradually into an incurable decline. After a year of constant illness and growing debility, he died at Santiago, August 6th, 1867.

UNROE, JOHN, Brevet Colonel United States Army, late of New Brunswick, New Jersey, was born in Scotland, and graduated from the academy at West Point in 1814. Entering the artillery branch of the service, he became Captain March 2d, 1825, and Brevet Major, for gallantry displayed in the campaigns against the hostile Indians of Florida, February 15th, 1838. August 18th, 1846, he was promoted to the rank of Major of the 2d Artillery, having, in July of the same year, served as Chief of Artillery to General Taylor. February 23d, 1847, for efficient service performed at Buena Vista, Mexico, he was brevetted Lieutenant-Colonel, and Brevet Colonel after the battle of Monterey, Mexico, in the following May. In 1849 and 1850

38

he presided as Military and Civil Governor of New Mexico, filling that responsible office in an able and creditable manner; and November 11th, 1856, was made Lieutenant-Colonel of the 4th United States Artillery.

HAMBERLIN, OCTAVIUS P., Lawyer, of Flemington, was born in Delaware township, Hunterdon county, New Jersey, in 1832. He is the son of Mr. A. Chamberlin, a farmer of that county, who formerly held the sheriffalty, and other important public trusts. He spent the greater part of his youth on his father's farm, attending the neighboring schools as occasion offered, but on the whole with such good result that he was able in 1855 to enter the University at Lewisburg, Pennsylvania, from which he graduated in 1859. Immediately after graduating he began the study of the law under George A. Allen, at Flemington, New Jersey, and was admitted to the bar in 1864, forthwith beginning a practice which has grown steadily larger and more lucrative to the present time. In 1872 he was appointed by Governor Parker, Prosecutor of the Pleas for Hunterdon county, an office which he still fills. He enjoys a reputation, in the profession and out of it, for solid ability and unspotted integrity. Every interest and every trust confided to him is certain to be guarded with unfailing skill and scrupulous fidelity. He is a forcible and persuasive advocate, as well as a patient and sagacious counsellor and a faithful attorney. In politics he is a Democrat, and warmly attached to the principles and traditions of his party. He belongs, in fact, to that class of stout-hearted and strong-headed lawyers, to which civil freedom in all countries and ages has been so largely indebted.

ASTON, HUGH M., Lawyer, of Somerville, was born at Basking Ridge, Somerset county, New Jersey, September 29th, 1819. He is the son of William B. Gaston, a merchant of Basking Ridge, the family, settled in New Jersey for the last century and a half, being of Huguenot descent. He was educated at the Somerville Academy, read law with the Hon. George H. Brown, of Somerville, and was admitted to the bar in 1844, at once opening an office in Somerville, and entering upon the practice of his profession. He was soon recognized as a man of sterling ability as well as of unyielding integrity, and consequently of high promise in the profession, the result being that his practice grew with rapidity until it comprehended more or less directly nearly every important case in the rich and populous region in which he lives, a clientage to which years have certainly brought no shrinkage, but rather new growth and more assured steadiness. The promise discerned in him at the outset of his professional career he has fully redeemed. He stands to day among the acknowledged leaders of the bar, not more sought and trusted by clients than admired and respected by associates, one characteristic of his practice having always been a zealous regard for the honor and dignity of the profession, sharp practice being in his estimation the equivalent of dishonorable practice, befitting perhaps a sharper, but not a lawyer worthy of the name. His professional standard, like his personal standard, has been high, and the verdict of his fellow-citizens, in and out of the profession, is that he has nobly lived up to both. For a number of years, it may be stated here, he was Prosecutor of the Pleas for Somerset county. In politics he was a Whig as long as the Whig party existed; but when it passed away he joined the Republican party, to which he has ever since adhered with zealous and unflinching fidelity. It of course was not to be expected that the temptations of political life would pass by such a man without assailing him, and it was almost as little to be expected that he would turn away from even the fairest and most honorable of them, but, though he consented to be a candidate for the office of Presidential Elector in 1872, he refused to stand for the State Senate, declining not the offer of the nomination merely, but the nomination itself, and, having thus resisted the tempter, has since been free from his importunities, agreeably to the assurance of the Apostle James. He finds in his profession his true sphere of action, and is content, as well he may be, with its honors and emoluments, not to say its labors, which surely are multiplied and various enough. In addition to his ordinary practice, now very extended and important, he is attorney for several of the leading corporations in his section of the State, including the First National Bank of Somerville and the Easton & Amboy Railroad. He is, however, emphatically a worker, sparing no pains in preparing his cases, and no zeal or vigor in presenting them. It would have been strange if such energies, guided by such abilities, had not been crowned with success. In 1862 he formed a partnership with James Beyen, which still subsists, the firm-name being Gaston & Beyen. He was married, in 1849, to Frances M. Prevost.

ILKINSON, JAMES, M. D., of Bergen, Jersey City, was born, April 27th, 1837, at Accrington, England, and is the son of John and Elizabeth (Hayes) Wilkinson. Brought to the United States in infancy, he was reared and educated by his uncle at New Brighton, Staten Island, New York. His education was received chiefly at private schools, more particularly at the boarding school of Rev. Thomas Towel, at Clifton, Staten Island, and at the celebrated Classical Institute of Solomon Jenner (so well known to old New Yorkers), in Henry street, New York city. His classical education was finished at the University of the City of New York. On the completion of his literary course he

went abroad, making the tour of Europe, and on his return he entered the office of Professor James R. Wood, with whom he remained three years, a diligent and painstaking student. He matriculated at the College of Physicians and Surgeons, New York, in 1855, and graduated in the fall of 1858 from the above mentioned college. He at once entered upon the practice of his profession at Bergen, New Jersey, where he has ever since resided, and where he has been constantly engaged in the control and exercise of a very extensive and lucrative practice. Dr. Wilkinson has devoted his life exclusively to his professional business, and has had at all times a large and remunerative practice. His labors have been untiring; he has never allowed himself to be restrained by heat or cold, darkness or storms. To this persistency has he owed mainly the success of his life, and he has prospered in the world, and has deserved to do so. In 1860 he married Lizzie Y. Burton, of Staten Island. In 1875, the doctor's health becoming somewhat impaired by the incessant strain of the ceaseless routine of professional life, he visited Europe, and returned in full, vigorous health to his accustomed duties. Few have brought such indomitable zeal and perseverance to the practice of medicine, and few have reaped the rewards of their labors so generously as the subject of this sketch.

SBORNE, REV. ETHAN, Presbyterian Minister, Revolutionary Soldier, late of Fairfield, New Jersey, was born in Litchfield, Connecticut, August 21st, 1758. At the age of seventeen he volunteered as a soldier in the revolutionary army, served in the campaign of 1776, and was in the retreat through New Jersey. While in his twenty-seventh year he was licensed as a minister, and from December, 1789, to 1844, was settled at the Old Stone Church, Fairfield, New Jersey. He died at Fairfield, New Jersey, May 1st, 1858.

INES, REV. ENOCH COBB, D. D. (Middletown, 1853), LL. D. (Washington College, 1859), Educator, Scholar, Author, of New Jersey, was born in Hanover, New Jersey, February 17th, 1806, and was graduated from the Middletown College in 1827. Upon the completion of a preliminary course of studies, he became Principal of an academy at St. Albans, and afterward assistant teacher in a female seminary at Alexandria, Virginia, subsequently opening and presiding over a school in Washington City. He was then employed in teaching on board the "Constellation," in which vessel he visited the Mediterranean. In 1833 he took charge of the Edgehill school, Princeton, New Jersey, in 1838 became Professor of Languages in the Central High School, of Philadelphia, Pennsylvania, and in 1844 founded

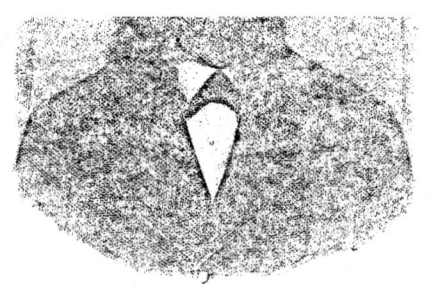

James Wilkinson M.D.

ay among the acknowledged leaders of the bar, not more ought and trusted by clients than admired and respected by associates, one characteristic of his practice having always been a jealous regard for the honor and dignity of the profession, sharp practice being in his estimation the equivalent of dishonorable practice, befitting perhaps a sharper, but not a lawyer worthy of the name. His professional standard, like his personal standard, has been high, and the verdict of his fellow-citizens, in and out of the profession, is that he has nobly lived up to both. For a number of years, it may be stated here, he was Prosecutor of the Pleas for Somerset county. In politics he was a Whig as long as the Whig party existed, but when it passed away he joined the Republican party, to which he has ever since adhered with ardor and unflinching fidelity. It of course was not to be expected that his candidature in any from when the direct and most favorable ... through he committed to ... a Presidential Elector in 1872, ... for the State senate, declining not the offer of the nomination merely but the solicitation itself, and having thus resisted the tempter, has more been than his importunities, agreeably to the advisement of his Apostle issues. He finds in his profession ... and is content, as well he may be, ... emoluments, not to say its labors, which ... and various enough. In addition to ... very extended and important, he ... the leading corporations in his section the First National Bank of ... Railroad. He is; ... sparing no pains in presenting them. ... such energies, guided by such ... with success. In 1862 he ... which still subsists, ... Boyce. He was married, in ...

... D., of Bergen, Jersey ... 1837; at Accrington, ... of John and Elizabeth ... to the United ... and educated by ... Staten Island, New ... chiefly at private ... school of Rev. ... and at the cele- ... well known ... New York city. His ... versity of the City ... literary course he

went abroad, making the tour of Europe; and on his return he entered the office of Professor James R. Wood, with whom he remained three years, a diligent and painstaking student. He matriculated at the College of Physicians and Surgeons, New York, in 1855, and graduated in the fall of 1858 from the above mentioned college. He at once entered upon the practice of his profession at Bergen, New Jersey, where he has ever since resided, and where he has been constantly engaged in the control and exercise of a very extensive and lucrative practice. Dr. Wilkinson has devoted his life exclusively to his professional business, and has had at all times a large and remunerative practice. His labors have been untiring; he has never allowed himself to be restrained by heat or cold, darkness or storms. To this persistency has he owed mainly the success of his life, and he has prospered in the world, and has deserved to do so. In 1860 he married Lizzie Y. Burton, of Staten Island. In 1875, the doctor's health becoming somewhat impaired by the incessant strain of the ceaseless routine of professional life, he visited Europe, and returned in full, vigorous health to his accustomed duties. Few have brought such indomitable zeal and perseverance to the practice of medicine, and few have reaped the rewards of their labors so generously as the subject of this sketch.

SBORNE, REV. ETHAN, Presbyterian Minister, Revolutionary Soldier, late of Fairfield, New Jersey, was born in Litchfield, Connecticut, August 21st, 1758. At the age of seventeen he volunteered as a soldier in the revolutionary army, served in the campaign of 1776, and was in the retreat through New Jersey. While in his twenty-seventh year he was licensed as a minister, and from December, 1789, to 1844, was settled at the Old Stone Church, Fairfield, New Jersey. He died at Fairfield, New Jersey, May 1st, 1858.

INES, REV. ENOCH COBB, D. D. (Middletown, 1853), LL. D. (Washington College, 1859), Educator, Scholar, Author, of New Jersey, was born in Hanover, New Jersey, February 17th, 1806, and was graduated from the Middletown College in 1827. Upon the completion of a preliminary course of studies, he became Principal of an academy at St. Albans, and afterward assistant teacher in a female seminary at Alexandria, Virginia, subsequently opening and presiding over a school in Washington City. In 1829 he was employed in teaching on board the "Constellation," in which vessel he visited the Mediterranean. In 1833 he took charge of the Edgehill school, Princeton, New Jersey, in 1838 became Professor of Languages in the Central High School, of Philadelphia, Pennsylvania, and in 1844 founded

James Wilkinson M.D.

a boarding-school at Burlington, New Jersey, where he continued engaged in professional labors during the ensuing four years. In January, 1849, he was licensed to preach by the Congregational Board of Rhode Island, and has since preached in various places on the eastern coast and elsewhere. In 1853 he was appointed Professor in Washington College, Pennsylvania; and in July, 1859, took charge of a literary institution styled the "City University of St. Louis." He has latterly been engaged in the mission for an organization of an International Prison Congress. He has published, "Two Years and a Half in the American Navy," 2 vols., 1832; "Hints on a System of Popular Education," 1837; "How Shall I Govern My School?" 1838;- "Commentaries on the Laws of the Ancient Hebrews;" "A Trip to Boston," 1838; "A Trip to China," 8vo.; "Monthly Journal of Education;" "Essay on the Advantages of Studying the Classic Languages;" "Lecture on Education as a Source of Wealth;" "Treatise on Regeneration," 1863; "Essay on Temptation," 1865; and "Promises of God," 1868. He has also contributed frequently to the various religious and literary periodicals of the day; and has written several excellent essays and addresses, which have been published in the current journals, or in pamphlet form.

ARDNER, COLONEL CHARLES K., United States Army, Editor, late of Washington, District of Columbia, was born in Morris county, New Jersey, in 1787, and May 3d, 1808, became Ensign in the 6th Infantry. He then occupied successively the following ranks and positions: Captain, 3d Artillery, July, 1812; Brigadier-Major to General Armstrong, August 4th, 1812; Assistant Adjutant-General, March 18th, 1813; Major, 25th Infantry, June 26th, 1813; Adjutant-General, April 12th, 1814; Brevet Lieutenant-Colonel, for distinguished services, February 5th, 1815; Major, 3d Infantry, and Adjutant-General, Division of the North, resigned March 17th, 1818. He was an active participant in the battles of Chrystler's Fields, Chippewa, and Niagara, and was present at the siege and defence of Fort Erie. In 1822-23 he edited the New York *Patriot*. September 11th, 1829, he was appointed Senior Assistant Postmaster-General; from July, 1836, to March, 1841, acted as Auditor of the Treasury; from March, 1845, to July, 1849, was Postmaster at Washington City; and from the latter date till 1853 served as Surveyor-General of Oregon. He was subsequently employed in the Treasury Department at the capitol until 1867. He was a shrewd and intrepid soldier; a wise administrator in civil, political, and financial affairs; and an able writer on special topics. His "Compendium of Infantry Tactics" was published originally at New York, in 1819; his "Dictionary of the Army of the United States," also in New York, in 1853; second edition in 1860. He was the father of the rebel General Gardner, who surrendered Port Hudson, July 9th, 1863. He died at Washington, District of Columbia, November 1st, 1869.

MITH, REV. SAMUEL STANHOPE, D. D., conferred by Yale College in 1783, LL. D., conferred by the Harvard University in 1810, Scholar, Clergyman, Author, late of Princeton, New Jersey, was born in Pequea, Lancaster county, Pennsylvania, March 16th, 1750, and graduated from the New Jersey College in 1769. His earlier education was acquired in his father's academy, and in his sixteenth year he entered Princeton College, where he took his degree of Bachelor of Arts. He then became an assistant in his father's school, and in 1770-73 was engaged as tutor at Princeton, pursuing at the same time the study of theology. He was licensed to preach by the Presbytery of New Castle, being ordained in 1774; and spent some time as a Missionary in the western counties of Virginia. For the purpose of securing his educational services there, a seminary was established of which he was made Principal, and which afterward became the Hampden-Sidney College. After being at the head of that institution for a few years, he was appointed, in 1779, Professor of Moral Philosophy at Princeton, and was succeeded in Virginia by his brother, John Smith. Upon establishing himself at Princeton, where the ravages of the war had been most severely felt, dispersing the students, reducing the building to a state of dilapidation, and greatly embarrassing the institution financially, he made great exertions and pecuniary sacrifices to restore it to prosperity; accepted the additional office of Professor of Theology; and in 1786 that of Vice-President of the college. In the previous year he delivered an anniversary address, which was subsequently expanded into a work on the "Causes of the Variety in the Figure and Complexion of the Human Species," 8vo., published in 1787. In 1786 he was associated with other clergymen of the Presbyterian Church in preparing the form of presbyterial government which is still in force. In the absence of Dr. Witherspoon as a member of Congress, much of the care of the college devolved upon him, and, after his death in 1794, he was elected his successor. In 1812, however, he resigned that office in consequence of repeated strokes of palsy, and for several years occupied himself in preparing his works for the press. Besides two "Orations," and eight miscellaneous sermons in pamphlet form, and the work above mentioned, he published, "Sermons," 8vo., 1799; "Lectures on the Evidences of the Christian Religion," 12mo., 1809; "A Comprehensive View of the Leading and most Important Principles of Natural and Revealed Religion," 8vo., 1816; "On the Love of Praise," 1810; "A Continuation of Ramsay's History of the United States, from 1808 to 1817;" and "Lectures on Moral and Political Philosophy." His "Sermons," with a memoir of his life and writings, were published in 1821, 2 vols., 8vo. His wife was a daughter of Dr. Witherspoon; and his daughter was married to I. M. Pintard, Consul at Madeira. He was distinguished for his acquaintance with ancient and modern literature, and for his eloquence and popularity as a preacher. He was courtly in person and manners, and wrote with notable elegance and perspicuity. He died at Princeton, New Jersey, August 21st, 1819, "vacating a place and station difficult to fill."

———————

UDLEY, THOMAS H., Lawyer, of Camden, was born in Evesham township, Burlington county, New Jersey, October 9th, 1819, his father, a farmer, being the descendant of an English family resident in this country since the latter part of the seventeenth century. His life, until he attained his twenty-first year, was passed upon the Evesham farm; his education being received at the district schools, but being, by reason of his naturally studious habits, much more thorough and comprehensive than usually results from such training. His father died in 1820, and his home education was received at his mother's hands. A woman of much refinement and culture, she stimulated his predisposition to study, and constantly sought to strengthen in him his always strong love of truth for truth's sake. To her training he rightly ascribes his successful career, and to her also may be attributed, in part at least, that sterling integrity which has ever been his most prominent characteristic. Determining upon law as a profession, he entered the office of the late William N. Jeffers, Esq., in Camden, and in 1845 was admitted to the New Jersey bar. From the outset of his legal life he held a conspicuous place in his profession, his naturally acute mind, together with his sound training in the principles and practice of law, uniting to make him unusually successful as a barrister. But a few years after his admission he was one of the leaders of the New Jersey bar. In politics he was from early manhood deeply interested, and from his incisive, analytical habit of mind, has always possessed a very remarkable insight into the determination of political events. Until the dissolution of the Whig party he was one of its staunchest members; since that event he has been a no less earnest Republican. When the war between the States broke out he did not shrink from it, but welcomed it; he had foreseen it for years, and had constantly opposed the various compromises effected between the two parties for the purpose of staying what so very few then saw to be an inevitable evil. To a man of his stern uprightness and intense honesty only decisive action was tolerable. There was a great national wrong to be righted, and a wrong that delay could only increase. The battle

was to be fought, and he wished to fight it at once. Elected in 1860 a delegate at large to the Chicago Convention, he had, and used to good purpose, the opportunity that he had so long hoped for to bring to issue the great question that for years had divided the nation. Of his action, and of the result of his action in that convention, the story is thus told by Charles P. Smith, Esq., of Trenton: "It was conceded early in the session of the convention that there were four doubtful States—New Jersey, Indiana, Illinois and Pennsylvania—and it was necessary to carry at least two of these States in order to nominate a candidate other than Mr. Seward. New Jersey presented Mr. Dayton, Pennsylvania presented Mr. Cameron, and Indiana and Illinois Mr. Lincoln. Mr. Seward was the first choice of a majority of the New England States, but the event disclosed that they preferred the triumph of principle to the success of their favorite. A committee of these States, headed by ex-Governor Andrew, waited upon the New Jersey delegation at their rooms, and declared that Mr. Seward was their choice, but if he could not carry the doubtful States they were willing to go for any one who could, but added: 'Gentlemen, you see our difficulty; you are not agreed among yourselves, but present three different candidates. Now, if you will unite upon some one man who can carry them, then we will give him enough votes in the convention to nominate him. If you continue divided, we shall go into the convention and vote for Mr. Seward, our first choice.' It was narrowed down to this: the four doubtful States must unite upon a candidate, or Mr. Seward would be nominated. The convention assembled Wednesday morning, without change in this state of affairs. Mr. Dudley was assigned a place on the committee to frame a platform, and kept busy until Thursday noon. At that time the four doubtful States assembled at Camden Hall, to endeavor to unite upon some person. Ex-Governor Reeder presided. It was a noisy assemblage, and it very soon became evident that nothing could be accomplished as affairs then stood. Mr. Dudley then proposed to Mr. Judd, of Illinois, that the matter should be referred to a committee of three from each of the four States. He made a motion to this effect, which was carried. Among those appointed were Judge David Davis, Caleb B. Smith, David Wilmot and William B. Mann, of Pennsylvania. On the part of New Jersey, Judge Ephraim Marsh, Hon. F. T. Frelinghuysen and Mr. Dudley. The committee met at six o'clock in Mr. Wilmot's room, and were in session until nearly ten o'clock P. M. before anything was accomplished. At that time it seemed that an adjournment would be carried without arriving at an understanding. The time had been consumed in talking and trying to persuade each other that their favorite candidates were the most available and best qualified. It was then that Mr. Greeley went to the door, and, finding no agreement had been reached, telegraphed to the *Tribune* that Mr. Seward would certainly be nominated the next morning as the Republican candidate.

Finding that the committee was about to separate without achieving any result, Mr. Dudley took the floor, and proposed that it should be ascertained which one of the three candidates had the greatest actual strength before the convention, and could carry the greatest number of delegates from the four States in the event of dropping the other two. Judge Davis stated as to Mr. Lincoln's vote on the first ballot, and the probable vote of the Illinois delegates in the event of Mr. Lincoln being dropped—that is, how they would break. The committee from Indiana and Pennsylvania also reported how the votes of their States would be cast if Lincoln and Cameron were both dropped. The New Jersey committee made a similar statement as to the strength of Judge Dayton. It was understood that a portion of the New Jersey delegates would drop Mr. Dayton, after giving him a complimentary vote, and go for Mr. Seward. This examination revealed the fact that of the three candidates Mr. Lincoln was the strongest. Mr. Dudley then proposed to the Pennsylvania committee that for the general good and success of the party they should give up their candidates and unite upon Mr. Lincoln. After some discussion Mr. Dudley's proposition was agreed to, and a programme arranged to carry into execution. A meeting of the Dayton delegates from New Jersey was immediately called at James T. Sherman's room, at one o'clock that night. Most of the delegates who sustained him were present. Judge Marsh and Mr. Frelinghuysen, evidently not believing it possible to carry out the plan, did not attend the meeting. Thus Mr. Dudley was the only one from the committee present. He explained what had been accomplished, and after talking the matter over they approved his action. It was understood that Judge Dayton was to receive one or more complimentary votes, and then the strength of the delegation to be thrown for Mr. Lincoln. It was also arranged that Mr. Dudley was to lead off in voting for Mr. Lincoln, and then they were to follow. The Pennsylvania delegation likewise adopted the plan, first giving Mr. Cameron a complimentary vote. The agreement of the committee was not generally known the next morning when the convention assembled. On the first ballot the entire New Jersey delegation voted for Mr. Dayton. The next, that portion who favored Mr. Seward voted for him, while the majority voted for Mr. Dayton. When New Jersey was called on the third ballot, Mr. Dudley stated that he should vote for Mr. Lincoln, and was immediately followed by all the New Jersey delegates save one. The result is known. New England did what she promised, and Mr. Lincoln was nominated. It was the action of the committee from the four doubtful States which undoubtedly secured Mr. Lincoln's nomination. But for this Mr. Seward would have been nominated, and there is little doubt just as surely been defeated. This is a plain narrative of the manner in which the nomination of Abraham Lincoln was brought about. It cannot be disguised that had it not been for Mr. Dudley's energy and tact in the committee of doubt-

ful States, the nation, in the emergency which so soon followed, would not have had the service of that great and good man at the helm." After Mr. Lincoln's election, but before his inauguration, Mr. Dudley visited him at his home in Springfield, and for almost an entire day the two were closeted together, discussing measures and men. As was to be expected, their views upon all leading questions of right and policy were identical; in some matters of detail, and in regard to the fitness of certain men for the discharge of certain important trusts, they differed. Mr. Lincoln named the cabinet that he had partially decided upon forming, and the several presumptive members were critically discussed. It is a notable fact that the men to whom Mr. Dudley took exception were not among those eventually selected by the President for his counsellors. When at last the long talk was ended, the President elect, rising, said : "Well, Mr. Dudley, what can I do for you ?" "Nothing, Mr. Lincoln; you have not an office in your gift that I would accept." The grave face of the future President lighted up with a smile as he replied: "Give me your hand; you are the first man I have yet seen who didn't want an office!" Fortunately, for the cause of the Union, this renunciation was nullified by subsequent circumstances. Broken down by hard work, Mr. Dudley was ordered by his physician to seek recuperation in travel, and early in 1861 he left this country for Europe. While in Paris he was suddenly called upon by Minister Dayton—the New Jersey candidate for the Presidency, to whom Mr. Lincoln had given the ministry to France—to fill the position of Consul to Paris, the then incumbent, an appointee of Mr. Buchanan's, being a declared secessionist, and Mr. Bigelow, the Consul appointed by Mr. Lincoln, not having arrived. The ad interim appointment was, at the urgent request of the minister, accepted, and its duties were exactly and ably discharged. In the fall of 1861 Mr. Dudley returned to America, but his journeyings had not been attended with the beneficial result hoped for, and his physician forbade him to resume the practice of his profession; assuring him that only by a residence abroad of several years' duration could his health be entirely restored. He was not the man to willingly enter upon a life of idleness, nor did his circumstances warrant him in so doing. He applied to Mr. Lincoln for a diplomatic appointment, and was at once made Consul to Liverpool. At the time of his application but two positions remained to be filled on the diplomatic list, the Ministry to Japan and the Liverpool Consulate. The latter the President had intended offering to his friend, Governor Kroener, of Illinois, and he therefore urged Mr. Dudley to accept the former. But it was absolutely necessary that Mr. Dudley should be within available distance of the best medical advice, and when the President was informed of this fact, he immediately ordered his commission to be made out to Liverpool. So, by a series of apparent mischances, he was despatched as the representative of the United States at the chief commercial port of England, there to serve his country with a zeal and efficiency unsurpassed by any of her sons during the dark years of the civil war. The position of Consul at Liverpool during the rebellion was second, of all diplomatic appointments abroad, only to that of Minister to the Court of St. James. As a nation England was the professed friend of the United States; as a people the English were the avowed friends of the Southern Confederacy. Liverpool was the centre whence radiated the substantial aid tendered to the American rebels by their British allies. The position of our Consul at this port was therefore one of the greatest consequence and of the greatest delicacy. In his efforts to enforce the maintenance of the neutrality professed by the government to which he was accredited, the utmost diplomacy was necessary to avoid bringing to open war the openly expressed hostility between the two countries. Everywhere his endeavor to check the flow of supplies to the confederacy met with determined resistance—on the part of the people declared; on the part of the government thinly veiled under the cloak of legal technicalities. But his individual determination was almost equal to the task of crushing the united efforts of his opponents. Acting under his orders, a force of upward of 100 men policed the ship-yards of England and Scotland; he himself, *incognito*, constantly visited the shipping centres, and during the four years of the war not a keel was laid down in the United Kingdom that was not within twenty-four hours thereafter registered on the books of the Liverpool Consulate. In every case wherein the facts justified the belief that the ships in course of construction were intended for the use of the confederacy, he submitted full statements, with corroborative proof, to the British government; and each stage in the construction of such ships was noted and made the subject of an additional communication. Nor was his zeal unattended by personal danger. Again and again he received anonymous letters in which he was assured that unless he ceased his opposition to the extension of assistance to the Confederate government his life would be taken; he was warned, specifically, that if he endeavored to crush certain schemes to this end, his death would instantly ensue; and he was informed that if he was found in certain spots designated he would be shot on sight. But threats had small effect upon his stern nature. He had been charged with a high duty, and that duty he fulfilled with a calm determination, and an utter forgetfulness of self such as few other men would have been capable of. The result of his unflinching labors was as satisfactory as the labors themselves were heroic. Outside of those directly engaged in its overthrow, no one man contributed more largely to the downfall of the Southern Confederacy than did he, by stopping the British source of rebel supplies. He remained constantly at his post until November, 1868, when he returned to the United States for a brief visit; during this visit a banquet was given in his honor, at which the eminent men of his State and party were present. Three years

later he again returned to America, and, wearied by his decade of arduous official life, tendered his resignation of his Consulate. But the government was compelled to request his services for a little time longer. The case of the United States, to be laid before the Joint High Commission at Geneva, was in course of preparation, and his assistance was essential in assembling and arranging evidence. He withdrew his tender, and set himself with his usual energy to the work assigned him. In order to facilitate his labors, his son, Mr. Edward Dudley, was appointed Vice-Consul to Liverpool, and was charged with the immediate business of the Consulate. Having assisted in the compilation of the case to go before the Geneva tribunal—supplying the material upon which the judgment in favor of the United States was rendered — he finally, in 1872, returned to America, tendering his resignation, to take effect upon the appointment of his successor. No better presentation of the respect and eventual esteem which he won for himself in England, can be given than the following extract from the Liverpool *Post* of September 4th, 1872: "A Liverpool gentleman last night, out of the fulness of his heart—always open to good sympathies—took upon himself the pleasing office of expressing to Mr. Dudley, who is about to leave Liverpool, the feelings with which his course as American Consul is regarded by those who have observed its tenor. It is impossible to regard such an event as Mr. Dudley's departure without reflecting on the remarkable contrast that is presented between the state of things in which Mr. Dudley resigns his office, and that in which he undertook it. He left his country 'with four millions of human beings held in bondage,' and he returns to it when there is not a slave upon its territory, nor a man, woman or child who does not enjoy a liberty as perfect as that of the air they breathe. The aspect of Liverpool society in reference to the United States presents almost as great a contrast. Within two or three days after Mr. Dudley's arrival in Liverpool the 'Trent' difficulty broke out. There are few among us who do not remember the excitement which this produced—the irritated state of feeling upon which the news of the seizure of Mason and Slidell fell like sparks upon tinder; and the strong disposition shown, especially amongst the higher and mercantile classes, to favor, by every means short of actual belligerency, the cause of the Southern Confederation. We look back now upon this period with eyes greatly clarified by the course of subsequent events. These events were so necessarily sequent upon the conditions of the great conflict which was then commencing that it seemed to some, who spoke out at that time, impossible to anticipate any other results; but this was not the general feeling. And an American Consul, bound by his position to perform difficult duties, to make a strong stand on behalf of his country, and to resist every attempt, whether direct or insidious, to aid that great country's enemies, held no enviable position. None that have known Mr. Dudley will hesitate to confess that throughout the embarrassing period of the civil war, while his firmness and shrewdness were continually exhibited on behalf of his country, he was found constantly courteous and just. No one brought into communication with him ever left him without a satisfactory explanation of his motives, and so far as it was possible for persons approaching difficulties from opposite points of view to understand each other. All who had business with the American Consulate, even in the most difficult period of Mr. Dudley's service, found that to transact it was to deal with a true gentleman, and one who was both a man of business and a statesman. All the untoward circumstances which rendered that period so trying have now passed away, and one scarcely meets in society an avowed partisan of the confederacy which once looked so formidable. As a matter of partisan politics, one would not revive the recollection of a time when the American civil war was a great ground of polemical difference; but much more was involved in the conflict than any mere partisanship; and to appreciate for a moment the intense feeling of satisfaction with which a politician of Mr. Dudley's calibre returns to America, now that the great work of President Lincoln is consolidated, is to understand that the principles at stake in the war were of permanent importance, and may well be regarded even now with interest and enthusiasm. There is much to be thankful for in the present state of the English mind as to American politics. It is a consolatory thing to reflect that the higher classes in this country have been brought, if only by the teachings of success, back again to that faith in the doctrines and practice of freedom which wavered so sadly during the civil war. Mr. Dudley's return to America will make many reflect wisely upon this subject, who may hitherto have given it little consideration; while his personal qualities and the recollection of many pleasing dealings with him, even in the most unpleasing times, will secure for him from the commercial community of Liverpool very good wishes and a permanent interest in his public career." Coming from an English journal, albeit a journal of Liberal proclivities, this testimonial to Mr. Dudley's official life in England is something of which the nation has good reason to be proud. His reception at home was as flattering as was the manifestation of good will attending his departure from Liverpool. As an instance of the many marks of respect accorded him by his fellow-countrymen may be presented the following resolutions, read at a reception tendered to the Hon. George M. Robeson: "*Resolved*, That the Republicans of Camden, whilst reaffirming their confidence in and pledging their support to President U. S. Grant, heartily commend the able administration of home and foreign affairs for which his appointees are more directly responsible. *Resolved*, That among these agents and chief advisers, New Jersey points with pride to Hon. George M. Robeson, Hon. Thomas H. Dudley, Hon. A. G. Cattell, Hon. F. T. Frelinghuysen, Justice Bradley, and other eminent statesmen, diplomats and jurists, who acquired an enviable national reputation. *Resolved*, That while we feel just cause or State pride in the distinction achieved by those honored sons of New Jersey, we tender a cordial welcome to Hon. Thomas H. Dudley, who returns to our midst after an absence of many years, voluntarily closing his honorable and eventful public mission with the successful termination of the Geneva arbitration, to which result he so materially contributed by a firm and patriotic discharge of duty in a hostile land, when so many failed or faltered at home." Since his return to America, Mr. Dudley has been engaged in the practice of his profession in Camden, New Jersey, residing upon his beautiful country-seat, a few miles from that city. His shrewd business ability has caused him to be frequently called upon to act as a corporation officer, and he is at present President of the Pittsburgh, Titusville & Buffalo Railroad Company, and of the New Jersey Mining Company, besides being a member of the Boards of Direction of the Camden & Atlantic Railroad Company, West Jersey Railroad Company, Camden & Philadelphia Ferry Company, and People's Gas-light Company, of Jersey City. He was also a member of the Centennial Board of Finance.

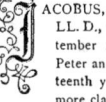ACOBUS, MELANCTHON WILLIAMS, D. D., LL. D., was born at Newark, New Jersey, September 19th, 1816. He was the eldest son of Peter and Phœbe (Williams) Jacobus. In his fifteenth year he entered Princeton College, sophomore class, and three years later graduated with first honors from that institution. One year later he matriculated at the Theological Seminary at Princeton, and on completing his course was appointed Assistant Professor in the Hebrew department. Here he remained a year, when, in answer to a unanimous call, he assumed charge of the First Presbyterian Church, of Brooklyn, New York. He was installed in 1839, and to him this church owes its perpetuity and success. In 1850, his health failing, he visited Europe, and with his wife went into Egypt, Palestine and Syria, returning home by way of Constantinople and Greece. During his absence he was elected Professor of Oriental and Biblical Literature in the Theological Seminary at Allegheny, Pennsylvania. Resigning his ministerial work, he assumed the duties of his chair in 1852, and continued actively engaged therein until ill health obliged him, in 1866, to make a second tour in Europe. He is the author of many and valuable works upon theological subjects; in 1848 he published a volume of Notes on the New Testament, entitled "Matthew with the Harmony;" subsequently, "The Catechetical Question Book," "Mark and Luke," a "Commentary on St. John's Gospels," and "The Acts of the Apostles." In 1864–65 two volumes on Genesis were issued by him, and in 1873 the first volume on Exodus, entitled "Egypt to Sinai." These, with many other

works and pamphlets, are now accepted as among the stan-dard theological literature of the day. In 1852 the degree of D. D. was conferred upon him by Jefferson College, Pennsylvania, and in 1867 he was created an LL. D. by his *Alma Mater*. At the General Assembly of the Old School Presbyterian Church, in New York, May, 1869, he was chosen Moderator, and he also occupied a most important position in the Assembly of 1870. For some years he filled the position of Secretary of the General Assembly of the Presbyterian Church. January, 1840, he married the eldest daughter of Samuel Hayes, M. D., of Newark, New Jersey.

AN SANTVOORD, GEORGE, Lawyer and Author, late of Troy, New York, was born in Belleville, New Jersey, December 8th, 1819. His father was Rev. Staats Van Santvoord. He was graduated at Union College in 1841, during the ensuing three years devoted himself to the study of law at Kinderhook, New York, then removed to the State of Indiana. He subsequently returned to Kinder-hook, and there continued actively engaged in professional labors from 1846 to 1852. He afterward resided at Troy, New York, until the time of his decease. In 1852 and 1856 he was elected to the Assembly of New York, and in 1859 became District-Attorney of Rensselaer county, New York. He has published, in addition to numerous contri-butions to periodical literature, "Life of Algernon Sidney," 1851; "Principles of Pleading in Civil Actions under the New York Code," 8vo., 1852 and 1855; "Indiana Jus-tice," 1845, and a recent edition thereof; "Lives of the Chief-Justices of the United States," 8vo., 1854; "Prece-dents of Pleading," 8vo., 1858; and "Practice in the Su-preme Court of New York, in Equity Actions," 1860-62. He also wrote, for the "Democratic Review," lives of prominent and leading French revolutionists, including those of Robespierre, Danton and Carnot. His father, who was pastor of the Dutch Reformed Church at Belleville, New Jersey, was a man of sterling attainments, an exemplary minister, and a highly-respected citizen. He was accident-ally killed at East Albany, New York, by being run over by a train of cars, March 6th, 1863.

UCKER, HON. JOSEPH, a prominent citizen of New York, late of that city, was born at Eaton town, New Jersey, but removed to New York in 1805, and there engaged in business as a master mason or builder. He was an active participant in many of the actions and engagements attending the war of 1812, and served fourteen years in the State militia. He was twice elected, on the old Whig ticket, to fill the office of Alderman; in 1836 was strongly urged to accept the nomination of a Representative in Congress, but declined; in 1840 was on the Whig electoral ticket, and in 1842 was a member of the New York State Assembly. Throughout the city and the State he was known and re-spected as an useful and upright citizen; and had he been endowed with a greater measure of ambition, might have aspired to offices of trust and distinction with every proba-bility of success. He died at New York city, in the eightieth year of his age.

ILLEDOLER, REV. PHILIP, D. D., Prominent Clergyman of the Dutch Reformed Church, President of Rutgers College, New Jersey, Au-thor, late of Staten Island, was born in Farming-ton, Connecticut, September 22d, 1775, and was of Swiss parentage. While engaged in study at Edinburgh, he became distinguished as a scholar, particu-larly in the application of chemistry to the pursuits of life. The Highland Agricultural Society having offered a pre-mium of fifty sovereigns for the best analysis of oats, he was the successful competitor. In May, 1795, he became minis-ter of the Reformed Church in New York; from 1810 to 1813 was pastor of the Third Presbyterian Church in Phila-delphia, Pennsylvania; from 1813 to 1820 officiated in Rutgers Street Collegiate Church, New York, and from 1825 to 1835 was President of Rutgers College, New Jer-sey, acting at the same time as Professor of Moral Philoso-phy in that institution. He was one of the founders of the Bible Society, and at different times published many lec-tures, addresses, essays and treatises. He died at Staten Island, September 22d, 1852.

ARICK, COLONEL RICHARD, Lawyer, Revo-lutionary Soldier, one of the founders of the American Bible Society, and President of that body, late of Jersey City, New Jersey, was born in Hackensack, New Jersey, March 25th, 1753. On the commencement of active and open hos-tilities between the colonies and the mother country, he was occupied in his profession, as lawyer, in New York city, and entered the patriot service as Captain in McDougall's regi-ment. He was afterward Military Secretary to General Schuyler, who then commanded the northern army, and subsequently was appointed Deputy Muster-Master-General, with the rank of Lieutenant-Colonel. He remained with that army until after the capture of Burgoyne, in October, 1777, when he acted as Inspector-General at West Point until after the discovery of Arnold's meditated treason. He then became a member of Washington's military family,

J. Fenimore Cooper

n t as h Secretary until near the close
n w After the e acuation of the city by the British
N er 25th, 1783, he was appointed Recorder of the
city of New York, which office he held until 1789, when he
took the position of Attorney-General of the State and at a
later date that of M yor, which he held until 1801. He
had been appointed in 1798 with Samuel
I n s, at the result of their
c bt e which b ars ti names
e ntly pleased for so time as
of the e of Assembly. He was one of the
n man l ely, and on the res g
Jay, who succeeded his Boudinot, was se-
r l i In y. for many is he was a
nber of tian church, and was dig ified in his
man er a fixed in his principles, political and religious.
"In pe son he was tall (over six feet in height and of i i-
posing presence." In he graveyard at n xed to the ch c
at Hackensack, New Jersey, is a tall granite monument, r
the rear of the building, bearing the following in i j i.
"In memory of Colonel Richard Varick form erly Mayor of
the city of New York and, at he s de ease,
President of the American Bible Soci p
25 h of March, 53, c 30th f v, 18 a ed

hold, having h w 1 h tle hi ndelity and success
his management, that in ause the sagacity of the great
Pennsylvania Con p v vis of faul as, indeed, i v v
seldom is. He is also a r the w e Nation
Bank. He takes a ecided and a e in est in the n
perity of Lambertville and its people, inch ung
the employés of the Belvidere Delaware Railroad.
all efficient officers, he s human men and believes that
the labor not only is w rthy of h r bu is voit y,
sides, of that combined go el am good he a
which is above all money value. exc pt perhaps to the give,
who i a ro t about way usual y g ts s k a back in
each, proving that if he e nce is qt e tightened self-
interest, it is entirely consistent with Since 1841 he has
been a member of the Presbyter an c h and for several
years an Elder cting also. during c l r of
he inc of h men l p as S er
I L h d nected h the c h.
a friend of he temperance cause, which, unlike
son f its apostles, he s e by pre x ple,
too. ersonally he is a courteous and man.
C gent eman. He was married, Au t. 8 3,
Co lia Cor e, Lambertville.

NDERSON, JOHN A.; Su inte f e l
videre Railroad and its b ic
6th, 1 9 n Fle ng on, H r y
New Jersey. I e is the son of john
su , a merchant of Lambertvi e. His f i
old residents of Hunterdon coun. l n n
r ous to er m i ge, hav n, been Miss A ex er
n ted to the I l m gs, from whom the own of
Flen n ton takes its nam. He was educated at private
scho Hunterdon and at the Doylestown (Pennsylvania)
A adca he 4th f July, 1848. e tered the eng ee
corps of Ashbel W l e engaged in locating the Belvidere D ware Railroad, Martin Coryell being at that
time Mr. Welsh's chief assistant He continued a member
of the corps til the road was located and built, when he
served as a clerk in the w rking departmen subs qu n l
becom g Assistant Supe intendent, an fin l y on Mr
Welsh's resignation of the superin tendenc v, in 1871, he
was appo nted Superinten H contr s uch extending
to the Iercei & S erset and the Flemingt n branches.
On the consummation of the lease of the U i c Rai roads
to the Pe sylvania Railroad in 1872, when the m i e
me of these ro ds passed t he Pennsy vania Con p y
h gh he stock rem ined in the hands of he U te
C ies he was re ai c as Superint ndent of wh t
then d s gnaeled as he Belvidere Delaware Division o
the United h aus of Ne Jersey This po ition he still

v t 'the five sons a e ungest but o e
of ch il en of Juc rm Cooper. In
his in aue he was re n ved, w th the fam ly, to
Coo e town, whe s eral e evi sly, his father
had, by he extinguishme it irc n t es, be n s
cessed of ex eusive tra of and on the shores of Lake Otego le ad w er q hanna, and nearly in the
geog ph a ei r e X c. In this desolate wilderness, civil zed sett m nts, h
lven mous on re t pon care r f remarka le
success and n f e y erect ng the imposing hall w h h
figures so p r e alt in the r n s, and su sec ently
le me t e al eating place, of his sen the sou h rn

re a kable energy and b an s sk I as his a enturou
enc unter of the toil an l t s from er l fe at such a
time ou l indica e b i d a strength an sagac ty
f nd wh h added t h t wealth com g from the
j l e tlem n f the cour r at the close of th ev
n rv war g e a l is family a kind an l le ree f
infl e ce fo ma y e s a jus lied in all t at r on, an
which reacted v y, a n alt get e h p i, upon the
c c ta e f he f i ly. Traces f the indepe d
n c n o soy h ute, engendered by the suns e
s ch c ion and influence are to be detected in any pa
s h of the history and the writings of the you

and acted as Recording Secretary until near the close of the war. After the evacuation of the city by the British, November 25th, 1783, he was appointed Recorder of the city of New York, which office he held until 1789, when he took the position of Attorney-General of the State, and, at a later date, that of Mayor, which he held until 1801. He had been appointed, in 1786, in conjunction with Samuel Jones, Reviser of the State laws, and the result of their combined labors was the volume which bears their names, issued in 1789. He subsequently presided for some time as Speaker of the House of Assembly. He was one of the founders of the American Bible Society, and on the resignation of John Jay, who succeeded Elias Boudinot, was selected to fill its Presidency. For many years he was a member of a Christian church, and was dignified in his manners and fixed in his principles, political and religious. "In person he was tall (over six feet in height) and of imposing presence." In the graveyard annexed to the church at Hackensack, New Jersey, is a tall granite monument, in the rear of the building, bearing the following inscription : "In memory of Colonel Richard Varick, formerly Mayor of the city of New York, and, at the time of his decease, President of the American Bible Society. He was born, 25th of March, 1753; died 30th of July, 1831; aged seventy-eight years, four months, and five days."

NDERSON, JOHN A., Superintendent of the Belvidere Railroad and its branches, was born, June 6th, 1829, in Flemington, Hunterdon county, New Jersey. He is the son of John H. Anderson, a merchant of Lambertville. His family are old residents of Hunterdon county, his mother, previous to her marriage, having been a Miss Alexander, nearly related to the Flemings, from whom the town of Flemington takes its name. He was educated at private schools in Hunterdon, and at the Doylestown (Pennsylvania) Academy. On the 4th of July, 1848, he entered the engineer corps of Ashbel Welsh, then engaged in locating the Belvidere Delaware Railroad, Martin Coryell being at that time Mr. Welsh's chief assistant. He continued a member of the corps until the road was located and built, when he served as a clerk in the working department, subsequently becoming Assistant Superintendent, and finally, on Mr. Welsh's resignation of the superintendency, in 1871, he was appointed Superintendent, his control as such extending to the Mercer & Somerset and the Flemington branches. On the consummation of the lease of the United Railroads to the Pennsylvania Railroad in 1872, when the management of these roads passed to the Pennsylvania Company, although the stock remained in the hands of the United Companies, he was retained as Superintendent of what was then designated as the Belvidere Delaware Division of the United Railroads of New Jersey. This position he still

holds, having shown by the ability, fidelity, and success of his management, that in his case the sagacity of the great Pennsylvania Company was not at fault, as, indeed, it very seldom is. He is also a Director of the Amwell National Bank. He takes a decided and active interest in the prosperity of Lambertville and its people, including especially the employés of the Belvidere Delaware Railroad. Like all efficient officers, he is a humane man, and believes that the laborer not only is worthy of his hire, but is worthy, besides, of that combined good feeling and good treatment which is above all money value, except perhaps to the giver, who in a roundabout way usually gets his kindness back in cash, proving that if benevolence is not enlightened self-interest, it is entirely consistent with it. Since 1846 he has been a member of the Presbyterian church, and for several years an Elder, acting also, during a considerable part of the time of his membership, as Superintendent of the Sabbath school connected with the church. He is, moreover, a devoted friend of the temperance cause, which, unlike some of its apostles, he supports by precept and example, too. Personally he is a courteous and estimable man, a Christian gentleman. He was married, August 31st, 1853, to Cornelia Coryell, of Lambertville.

OOPER, JAMES FENIMORE, Novelist, late of Cooperstown, New York, was born in Burlington, New Jersey, September 15th, 1789, and was the youngest of the five sons, and youngest but one of seven children of Judge William Cooper. In his infancy he was removed, with the family, to Cooperstown, where, several years previously, his father had, by the extinguishment of Indian titles, become possessed of extensive tracts of land on the shores of Lake Otsego, the head waters of the Susquehanna, and nearly in the geographical centre of the State of New York. In this desolate wilderness, far from any civilized settlements, the adventurous pioneer entered upon a career of remarkable success and influence by erecting the imposing hall which figures so prominently in the romances, and subsequently became the final resting-place, of his son, on the southern shore of the lake. "Judge Cooper was not only a man of remarkable energy and business skill, as his adventurous encounter of the toils and perils of frontier life at such a time would indicate, but possessed a strength and sagacity of mind which, added to the great wealth accruing from the rapid settlement of the country at the close of the revolutionary war, gave him and his family a kind and degree of influence for many years unequalled in all that region, and which reacted thus, and not altogether happily, upon the character and tastes of the family. Traces of the independence, not to say hauteur, engendered by the sunshine of such position and influence, are to be detected in many passages both of the history and the writings of the youngest

39

son, and which perhaps contributed to the personal troubles and collisions of his later years." His mother, to whom in personal aspect as well as in mental and moral traits he bore a striking resemblance, was the daughter of Richard Fenimore, of New Jersey, of a family of Swedish descent and personal distinction. She, like her husband, was endowed with rare energy of character, possessed a cultivated and brilliant intellect, and is said to have found great pleasure in general and especially in romantic literature. Her thoroughness as a housekeeper, personal beauty, and family consequence, made her to a notable degree a sharer in the influence of her husband, both in the household and in the surrounding community. Respecting his birth and ancestry, Mr. Cooper wrote the following letter to a friend: " HALL, COOPERSTOWN, December 6th, 1844. Sir: I was born in neither of the places you mention, but in the last house but one of the main street of Burlington, as one goes into the country. There are two houses, of brick, stuccoed, built together, the one having five windows in front, and the other four, the first being the last house in the street. In this house dwelt Mr. Lawrence, my old commander, Captain Lawrence's father, and in the four-window house my father. My father was a native of Pennsylvania, but he lived several years in Burlington. In 1785 he first visited this part of the world, having a large tract of land on the shores of Lake Otsego. In the winter of 1785-6 he commenced the settlement of his tract, or Cooper's Patent, as it was called, and in 1788 this Cooperstown was regularly laid out. That year my father had a house built here, and my mother passed the summer in the place. But it was still too new to tempt her to remain here, and in September, 1789, I was born at the residence I have mentioned. In 1790 the family came here for a permanent residence. My claims on New Jersey, however, go a little further. My father having been elected to Congress in 1794, and that body then sitting in Philadelphia, he brought my mother and such of the children as were not at school as far as Burlington, where he left them. Being the youngest child, I remained with my mother, and by these means commenced Latin with a well-known Irish pedagogue in Burlington, of the name of Higgins. I was twice with this man: once in 1796, and again in 1798. On each occasion I remained about a year in Burlington. My mother was a Jerseywoman, and strongly attached to her native State. In 1798 her reluctance to return to this place was so strong that my father actually purchased a house in Burlington, with the intention of leaving my mother in it; but so great was the grief of my brother and myself at the idea of giving up our lake and haunts at this place, that she abandoned her own wishes to ours, and consented to return. I am inclined to think that my father, whose interests in New York were very large, was afraid to go through the same risks again, for we returned to Burlington no more. I am only remotely connected with Gloucester. William Cooper, who became possessed of the property on Cooper's creek, and around

Camden, in 1687, and in whose descendants most, if not all of it, still remains, was my direct ancestor. But our branch of the family passed into Pennsylvania long before the Revolution, where my father, grandfather, and I believe my great-grandfather, were born. The latter, however, may have been born in Gloucester, though he certainly died in Bucks. I have always understood he had properly distinct from that on which he lived, and have always supposed it was at or near the old family homestead. This is all matter of tradition, though it is tradition pretty accurately obtained. John Cooper, the uncle of the late Richard Matlack Cooper, and my grandfather, were first cousins, as were Marmaduke Cooper, Isaac's father, and my grandfather. You will see by this how near I come to your county. I am a New Yorker by education, interests, property, marriage, and fifty-four years residence; but New Jersey has, and ever will have, a near hold upon my feelings. My ancestors, in various directions, were among her first settlers, and, though William Cooper, the root of us all, first settled at Burlington in 1679, he went so soon to Gloucester that I have always regarded that county as the real nest of the whole brood. If I ever spoke of Gloucester as my place of origin, it must have been in reference to the facts here mentioned. My father maintained some intercourse with his Gloucester county kinsmen, but I have known less. I have known the two Captains Cooper of the navy, father and son, and we recognize the relationship; and I saw the late Richard M. Cooper once or twice, as well as William Cooper, but this is nearly the extent of my acquaintance in that quarter of the country. There are two hamlets that are called Cooperstown at no great distance from you, I believe—one the property of Isaac Cooper, who inherited his father Marmaduke Cooper's large fortune; and the other once belonged to my father, whence its name. I certainly was not born in it, however, nor do I remember ever to have seen it, though I may have passed through it when a boy. I cannot be mistaken as to the place of my birth, as my mother often pointed it out to me when a school-boy in Burlington, and it was often mentioned in our family discussions. I so well recollect the place that I went to it without a guide a few years since, and finding the house, I inquired of an old blind gentleman who was seated on the adjoining stoop, if my father had not once lived in that house. This person, whose name was How, and whose family owned all three of the houses, my father and Mr. Lawrence being their tenants, recollected all about it, and remembered the births of two, if not three children, in the house. It was the last house my father occupied in Burlingtou, and I being the youngest child born there, of course I was right. My sister, who was also born in Burlington, but in a different house, being several years my senior, confirms all these impressions. In addition, I well remember that Dr. Hartshorne, of Burlington, has often been mentioned to me as the professional man who did me the favor to act as accoucheur. Thus, you see, I cannot claim a sentence in your forthcoming work. There will be plenty of the name without me, however; and I shall certainly obtain the book, and no doubt find much information and amusement in it. If you think proper, however, simply to state that I am of Gloucester county stock originally, I shall be one of the last to deny it. The fact is not of much importance to the world, but it has some interest with myself. ·Very respectfully, your servant, J. FENIMORE COOPER." Amid the rude experiences and the perilous incidents of a frontier life he passed his youth until, at the age of thirteen, he was sent from home to be entered in the freshman class of Yale College. The youngest pupil in that institution, and too young to secure the benefits or escape the perils of college life, his career there seems to have given no indications of the lustrous future which lay in store for him. At the close of his third year as student he voluntarily left the college, and entered the United States navy as a common sailor, in which capacity he was employed about two years, chiefly on board the "Sterling." He was then promoted, first to the rank of Midshipman, and before the close of his sea-life to that of Lieutenant, remaining partly with the sloop-of-war "Wasp," and later, for a time, in a vessel on Lake Ontario. That the varied and vivid experiences of this naval life had a powerful influence, if not in determining his career, at least in preparing him for it, is obvious from the perfect familiarity with ocean aspects and seamanship which is displayed in his nautical romances. In 1811 he resigned his post as Lieutenant and removed to Mamaroneck, Westchester county, New York, and was a resident of that place when, a few years afterwards, he began his career as author. It is narrated that, while reading aloud to his wife a newly-published English story of domestic life, and yawning over its tiresome pages, he exclaimed that "he could write a better novel himself." "You had better try," was the response, and it pushed him into a current of thought whose ultimate result was his transformation into the leading novelist of his time and country. After a few weeks of secret labor, he astonished his wife by reading to her the opening chapters of "Precaution." "The style, scenery and spirit of the book readily betray its origin, and when completed it gave but little satisfaction to the author, or pleasure to the reader." It was, however, warmly praised by partial friends, who listened to its chapters as they were successively completed, and through the intervention of Charles Wilkes was published in 1819, and at the expense of the author, who had little faith in its excellence as a literary production. Though at least equal to the average novel of the day, it was so imitative as to have passed for a long time as a work of English origin, and for many years was not acknowledged by its author, and never, with his approval, included among his works. "But it did the great service of awakening to consciousness the real powers of the man. The resolution to write another work of fiction was soon formed, and everything favored the choice of the fortunate theme." The country was emerg-

ing from the war with Great Britain, while popular tastes and associations pointed to the still more exciting experiences of the revolutionary days as a desirable subject of delineation. Then, breaking free from the trammels of precedence and conventionality, he ventured upon the virgin soil of a domestic tale filled with characters familiar to Americans, and depending for its interest upon scenes in which a large part of his contemporaries had actually participated. The composition of the work was kept secret until near its completion, when again the warm counselling of listening friends induced him to undertake its publication. For some time a publisher was sought in vain, and when, finally, Charles Wiley consented to assist him in his aims, it was only at his own expense, but could find no one who would accept the responsibility. Thus, though begun soon after the appearance of "Precaution," three years elapsed before "The Spy" was put into the hands of the public. It had, as it deserved, an immediate and brilliant success. "The novelty of its subject, the originality of every feature, the exciting and familiar scenes, the well-known characters hardly disguised by the thin veil of fiction, the pungent incense to national pride and patriotic feeling, and withal the rough vigor and manly quality of the style, were well fitted to the popular habits and tastes." In the States it met with cordial yet cautious praise by critical littérateurs, but was eagerly read by the general mass of the community, while in England it took the reading public by storm, and rapidly won a popularity rivalling even that of the Waverly novels, then at the very zenith of their success. It ran rapidly through many editions both at home and abroad, and has probably received a greater number of translations and attracted a more widespread admiration than any similar work ever written in English, being at a later period translated even into Persian, Arabic, and other Oriental languages. This stroke of fortune necessarily determined the character of his future life and labors; and, relinquishing his profession, he gave himself to authorship with remarkable diligence and earnestness. After an interval of two years was produced the "Pioneers," and in its preface he has given its real motive and inspiration. He says: "I wrote my first work because it was said I could not write a grave tale; so to prove that the world did not know me, I wrote one so grave that nobody would read it. I wrote the second to see if I could not overcome this neglect of the reading world. The third I have written exclusively to please myself." The "Pioneers" lacks the stirring turmoil and favorite characters of the "Spy," but is still one of the ablest of his productions. With the exception of the "Bravo," it was his favorite, and from beginning to end its composition was a labor of love. It found a publisher at once, but at home was far less immediately popular than its predecessor; but in Europe its striking portraiture of American scenery, and the new phases of life it presented, secured it a warm welcome, and at the time contributed sensibly to the reputation of American literature. Within a year after the "Pioneers" appeared the "Pilot," and its immediate occasion is said to have been the perusal of Scott's "Pirate." This, in its first success, outran all its predecessors, and gained at a bound a position which no subsequent work of the kind has been able even to contest. Said the *Edinburgh Review:* "The empire of the sea is conceded to him by acclamation." Two years later appeared "Lionel Lincoln," which, though carefully and elaborately written, with the "Spy" as its model, was, in comparison with preceding works, received with a degree of coolness that displeased and piqued him. Then came "The Last of the Mohicans," perhaps the most exciting, best sustained, and popular of his achievements upon a field he has held as peculiarly his own. Never before had the romance of Indian character, or the author's dramatic powers been so successfully exhibited. A universal popularity at once greeted its appearance, and it was immediately reproduced in almost every civilized language, and it contributed in a greater measure to the general impressions of the Old World regarding aboriginal life in the New than all other works combined. In 1827 appeared the "Red Rover," generally esteemed the most dramatic and powerful of his sea tales; and in 1828 the "Prairie," "scarcely less interesting as a romance, or less triumphant as a work of art than 'The Last of the Mohicans.'" Between the production of these two tales he visited Europe with his family, where he remained till 1833, and his residence there occasioned some of the most unpleasant passages of his life. Warmly devoted to his country and her institutions, he was prompt in resenting, in every country, the disparaging slanders and imputations which Europe, at that nascent period of American existence, harbored and disseminated; and yet this very love of country rendered him the more painfully sensitive to the faults of principles and conduct by which his countrymen continually brought down ridicule upon themselves and the United States. Indignant at the virulence of those opposed to republicanism, he was scarcely less so at its allies for their errors and inconsistencies. "These faults he felt it was both his right and duty to correct. His literary position, and the consciousness of unquestionable patriotism, gave him, as he thought, the right to expect that well-meant rebuke of obvious evils would be both welcome and effective." In accordance with this idea he wrote "The Letters of a Travelling Bachelor." But however laudable the real and avowed purpose of this step, the effect was anything but beneficial or desirable, and this work was only the beginning of a series "which it would

have been equally to his credit and comfort to have left unwritten." His "Residence in Europe," the "Letter to My Countrymen," "Homeward Bound," "Home as Found," and "The Monikins," gave such deep and general offence at home that it required all the recollections of his genius and the splendid merits of his earlier publications to reconcile an indignant public to his apparent censoriousness and assumption. While this series was in progress, and he to all appearances engrossed in literary and political discussion, the "Bravo" was sent forth, received with applause in America, and in Europe with mingled eulogiums and denunciations. In his own estimation it was his ablest work, and, except the "Pioneers," most completely expressed the convictions of his understanding and his most cherished sentiments. Alternating with various political works, he also published, while still in Europe, "The Wept of Wish-ton-Wish," "The Heidenmauer," and "The Headsman of Berne." On his return home he found himself a centre for attack of the entire press of the country in consequence of the tone of the works before mentioned, and was overwhelmed with cutting criticism, which only too often was characterized by vindictive hatred and an offensive personality wholly unmerited. But, beyond the satires contained in his fictions, no word of defence was published by him to the many charges of his political enemies until full five years had elapsed. Then was published his "Naval History of the United States," the only historical production of his pen except a series of naval biographies published in a magazine. "This was a work of great labor and research, and was regarded by the author with a partiality which . . . . the public judgment has hardly confirmed. . . . . . This work, following the personal tales and essays referred to, and in a few particulars taking novel and unpopular views, elicited from the press attacks of such violence and personality as to provoke the author into the most remarkable series of legal prosecutions ever known in the annals of literature, and which continued for several years to absorb the larger share of his time, and best energies of his mind." Particularly did his recital of the battle of Lake Erie clash with many of the accepted and favorite opinions of the public, in seemingly detracting from Perry's accustomed honors in this exploit, and in assigning to Elliott an unexpected if not the chief merit in the affair. But, whatever may be the truth of the case, it is generally agreed that his position was taken in fair intent, and has the sanction of the award of three competent arbitrators to whom was submitted the whole question as the result of the legal prosecutions. The law of libel when these suits were begun was undefined and almost nugatory: practically, there was but little defence of private character against the most wanton assaults of the press; and if the restraints of the law of libel were at all justifiable, then was presented occasion for giving it a new definition and needed force. " . . . . . And from all that transpired of Cooper, nothing is more clear than that the correction of this great evil was the leading motive for plunging into the sea of troubles which awaited him. . . . . But the immunity of personal character he believed in, and, after a contest of years, established." During this period some twenty distinct suits for libel were brought by him, and in all, or nearly all, he met with success. He was thus chiefly instrumental in bringing about a reform in the habits and manners of the press, and in reviving the practical efficiency of a safeguard that had been much and blamably neglected. While occupied in conducting these libel suits in person he published " The Pathfinder," which, renewing the scenes and characters of his most popular tales, was warmly welcomed by a divided community. After the issue of " Mercedes of Castile " came the last of the Leather-Stocking Tales, " The Deerslayer," which was greeted with enthusiasm scarcely inferior to that which heralded " The Spy " or " The Pilot." About 1844 he became interested in the political questions growing out of the tenure of lands in certain portions of the State of New York, and the organized refusal of the tenants or occupants to pay the accustomed rent toll. Every instinct of personal feeling, as well as political conviction, arrayed him strongly against the novel doctrines, and led to the preparation of the "Littlepage" tales—"Satanstoe," " The Redskins," and " The Chainbearer "—which, " had they advocated the popular side of the question, would have been regarded as models of their kind." From the termination of his suits till the time of his decease he was constantly occupied in literary labors, and there appeared in rapid succession " The Two Admirals," 1842; " Wing-and-Wing " and " Ned Myers," in 1843; " Wyandotte," " Afloat and Ashore," and " Miles Wallingford," in 1844; " The Crater," in 1846; " Jack Tier " and " Oak Openings," in 1848; " The Sea-Lions," in 1849; and " The Ways of the Hour," his last, in 1850. While engaged in the following year upon a work of historical character, after a few months' rapid decline, his extraordinary physical powers gave way, and he died, to the surprise and grief, not less of his family than of the public. Personally, he was of massive and compact proportions, with a countenance "glowing with manly beauty," and eloquent of intellectual strength. In his social traits, so far as his innate reserve and strong predilections would permit, he was magnanimous and hospitable. " Frank, generous, independent, and not over-refined either by native constitution or culture, enemies were as plentifully made as easily reconciled by his singular admixture of opposing qualities." Although his works, for some cause, secured him but a limited remuneration, they have had an unparalleled sale, both at home and abroad. Not only have all the chief stories been reproduced as they appeared in numerous editions in France, Germany, Russia, and many other European countries, and were circulated largely and continuously in Great Britain, but they had and still have an unceasing sale in the United States and the Canadas, also the settled portions of Australia, and the English sections of East India. His " Battle of Lake Erie " was pub-

lished in 1843; and a comedy written by him was performed at Burton's Theatre, New York, in 1850; he published also "Gleanings in Europe," six volumes, and " Sketches of Switzerland." He was married, January 1st, 1811, to Susan de Lancey, sister of the Bishop of the Western Diocese of New York, a woman of great excellence of character, cultivated tastes, and unaffected piety. Susan Fenimore Cooper, his daughter, was author and editor of several popular works, chiefly descriptive of rural life. The first, " Rural Hours," was published in 1850, and is an excellent and interesting volume; in 1854 it was followed by " Rhyme and Reason of Country Life;" and in 1858 by her " Tribute to the Character of Washington." He died at Cooperstown, New York, September 14th, 1851.

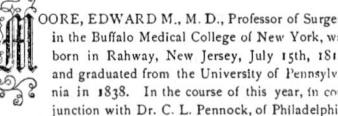

OORE, EDWARD M., M. D., Professor of Surgery in the Buffalo Medical College of New York, was born in Rahway, New Jersey, July 15th, 1814, and graduated from the University of Pennsylvania in 1838. In the course of this year, in conjunction with Dr. C. L. Pennock, of Philadelphia, Pennsylvania, he performed a series of original experiments relative to the heart, and the condition and phases of that organ under certain conditions, which attracted much attention in medical circles. Removing to Rochester, New York, about 1840, he rapidly acquired a high reputation in his profession, and a leading position among the eastern practitioners. He was for many years Professor of Surgery in the Buffalo Medical College, where he won the admiration and respect of all by his sterling attainments as a lecturer and teacher.

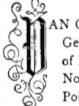

AN CLEVE, HORATIO PHILLIPS, Brigadier-General of Volunteers in the United States army, of Minnesota, was born in Princeton, New Jersey, November 23d, 1809. He graduated at West Point in 1831, after having passed through a course of preparatory studies at Princeton College. He then obtained a commission as Brevet Second Lieutenant in the 5th Infantry, but resigned in 1836. He subsequently resided temporarily in Missouri and Ohio, afterward removing to Michigan, where he was principally occupied in agricultural pursuits, although occasionally employed as a civil engineer. In 1856 he removed to Minnesota, and there, until 1861, pursued the vocation of farmer. July 22d, 1861, he received a commission as Colonel of the 2d Regiment of Minnesota Volunteers, and was ordered to Kentucky to assist in upholding the menaced cause of the Union in that section. This regiment he commanded at the battle of Mill Spring, January 19th, 1862, and for gallantry displayed during that action was appointed Brigadier-General of Volunteers, March 21st, 1862. He also commanded a brigade in Crittenden's division, before Corinth, through northern Alabama; and at Louisville took command of the division, on Crittenden's promotion, October 1st, 1862. Upon joining Rosecrans, in the following December, he was an active participant at the battle of Stone River, where, after having rendered distinguished and efficient service, he was painfully wounded. September 11th and 13th, 1863, he was engaged at Ringgold, Georgia, and Gordon's Mills; took part in the battle of Chickamauga, September 19th and 20th, 1863; and from 1863 to 1865 was in command of Murfreesboro', Tennessee. He has since acted as Adjutant-General of the State of Minnesota, a position to which he was appointed in January, 1866.

ENNINGTON, SAMUEL HAYES, M. D., Newark, son of Samuel and Sarah (Hayes) Pennington—his father being for many years an influential member of the New Jersey Legislature; his maternal grandfather, Major Samuel Hayes, a distinguished militia officer in the revolutionary service—was born at Newark, October 16th, 1806. Having graduated from the Newark Academy, he entered Princeton College in 1823, receiving from that institution the degree of A. B. in 1825, and A. M. in 1828. In the latter year he began the study of medicine under his maternal uncle, Dr. Samuel Hayes; subsequently attended lectures under the Rutgers Medical Faculty of Geneva College, and in 1829 received his degree of M. D. Entering into partnership with his uncle, at Newark, he succeeded to his practice in 1839, and during the ensuing thirty years led an active professional life. During the latter portion of this period he was a recognized leader of the medical profession in East Jersey, and his consulting practice was very extensive. Some twelve years back he began the gradual circumscription of his professional duties, and has now for a considerable period ceased to practice save in a small circle of old and attached friends. In the Medical Society of the State he has been an active member, contributing largely toward the promotion of its interests and taking a leading part in moulding and directing its policy. In 1848 he was elected its President, filling the position in such a manner as to give very general satisfaction. He is also a member of the County Medical Society. His professional standing has been recognized outside of his State by his election to honorary membership in the Connecticut Medical Society, and outside of his country by his election to corresponding membership with the Medical Society of Munich and with the Royal Botanical Society of Ratisbon. He has for many years been prominent in educational matters, and his labors in this connection have been persistent and to good effect. In 1845 he was elected a member of the Newark

Board of Education, being continuously re-elected until 1862, when he refused renomination. In 1855 he was elected President of the Board, both parties uniting in his nomination and giving him their undivided vote. He held the office uninterruptedly until his retirement, in 1862. In 1833 he was elected a member of the Board of Trustees of the Newark Academy, and in 1854 became President of that body, a position that he still holds. In 1856 he was chosen a Trustee of Princeton College, and about the same time a Trustee of the Presbyterian Theological Seminary at the same place, the duties of both of which trusts he has since continued to discharge. In his several different relations with education in the State, he has displayed a broad liberality, and has done excellent service in advancing the welfare of the institutions in the government of which he has been concerned. For nearly thirty years he has been President of the Newark City Bank—of which he was one of the founders—retaining his position through its change from a State to a national institution, and displaying in its management a sound business ability. Under his care the bank has become one of the most successful financial corporations in the State. Dr. Pennington has not aimed at a reputation for authorship, his efforts in that direction having been limited to addresses and essays, on medical, educational and kindred subjects, demanded by his official position in the societies and boards with which he has been connected. These have given evidence of careful consideration, and borne marks of the scientific and classical culture to which he is known to have devoted much of his leisure.

MITH, SAMUEL J., Poet, late of Burlington, New Jersey, was born in that city in 1771. Possessing a large inherited income, he lived tranquilly on his estate during the major portion of his life, dividing his time and attention between literature, agricultural pursuits and public benefactions. A volume of his poetry was published, 8vo., 1836. Two of his lyrics, noted for their beauty, are in the "Lyra Sacra Americana." He died in Burlington, New Jersey, in 1835.

AN SYCKEL, AARON, Merchant and Real-estate Dealer, late of Van Syckelville, was born, May 26th, 1793, at Mount Pleasant, Hunterdon county, New Jersey. His father, after whom he was named, was a farmer. His grandfather came to this country from Holland, and settled in Ringwood township, in Hunterdon county. Young Aaron received a good business education in the common schools of the neighborhood, and when still quite young entered upon a mercantile career. For a long time he kept a country store in Bethlehem township, but eventually his mercantile career, prosperous in its sphere, opened into a cognate career of greater profit to himself as well as of greater benefit to the community. In 1832 he, in company with Charles Bartles, of Flemington, engaged extensively in the real estate business, in which they continued to operate heavily up to 1860, more farms and farming lands having passed through their hands in the intervening period than were handled by any other parties in that section of the State, not a single acre of which, be it recorded to the signal credit of this firm, out of all the thousands, amounting in value to hundreds of thousands of dollars, being ever taken back, sold under foreclosure, or made in any way the occasion of distressing a purchaser for payment. This remarkable feature was due not more to the considerateness and humanity with which they conducted their business than to their plan of operating, which was to sell property on credit to those only in whose integrity and energy they had confidence, and then to see the purchaser through adverse times, helping him to tide over temporary difficulties, a policy indeed equally beneficial to themselves, to the purchaser, and to the community at large; yet not on this account the less worthy of praise, since it requires exceptional qualities of head and heart to perceive self-interest in the interest of all. Between the two members of the firm the utmost confidence existed throughout their connection, each buying property when and where he chose, the one not consulted having the privilege of taking a half-interest in the purchase or not, at his pleasure. Mr. Van Syckel, as might be inferred from what has been said, was distinguished alike for his integrity, his judgment, his knowledge of human nature, and his good feeling. He consciously wronged no man, seldom made a mistake in his estimate of the value of lands or merchandise, measured with unfailing accuracy the motives and abilities of all with whom he had business relations, and the honest and industrious poor invariably found in him a safe counsellor and a sympathizing friend, his generous forbearance towards those struggling to secure a home, not to mention his more generous aid, being gratefully remembered in many a happy family that but for him might now be plunged in misery. He never deceived, was rarely deceived himself, and the dew of his charity, like the rain of heaven, fell upon the just and the unjust. He was married, November 30th, 1816, to Mary Bird, of Hunterdon county, who died September 11th, 1863. Of their ten children, five only are now living, four sons and one daughter. His eldest son, Joseph, is President of the Clinton National Bank, and an esteemed citizen as well as an efficient officer. His second son, Sylvester, is a physician of Clinton, standing in the front rank of his profession. Bennett, his third son, is one of the Judges of the Supreme Court of New Jersey, and is regarded as a lawyer and jurist of the first order. His youngest son, Chester, is a member of the Hunterdon county bar, and bids fair to attain the highest prizes in the

profession. His only daughter living is the wife of T. J. Hoffman, a prominent lawyer of Clinton. Mr. Van Syckel was through life a pronounced Democrat, and, considering his acknowledged abilities and his high standing among his fellow-citizens, it should perhaps be set down as one of his titles to distinction that he never either held or sought an office. He died, January 4th, 1874, leaving, as the fruit of rare business qualifications and wise economy, a large fortune, which, having bequeathed a handsome fund for the endowment of the Bethlehem Baptist Church, he divided equally among his children. It is the memory of such as he that smells sweet and blossoms in the dust.

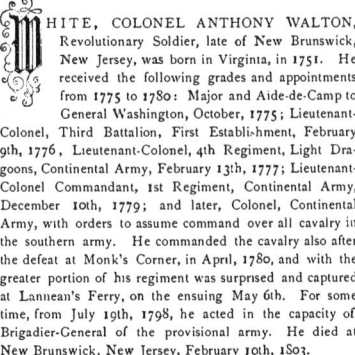

HITE, COLONEL ANTHONY WALTON, Revolutionary Soldier, late of New Brunswick, New Jersey, was born in Virginia, in 1751. He received the following grades and appointments from 1775 to 1780: Major and Aide-de-Camp to General Washington, October, 1775; Lieutenant-Colonel, Third Battalion, First Establishment, February 9th, 1776, Lieutenant-Colonel, 4th Regiment, Light Dragoons, Continental Army, February 13th, 1777; Lieutenant-Colonel Commandant, 1st Regiment, Continental Army, December 10th, 1779; and later, Colonel, Continental Army, with orders to assume command over all cavalry in the southern army. He commanded the cavalry also after the defeat at Monk's Corner, in April, 1780, and with the greater portion of his regiment was surprised and captured at Lannean's Ferry, on the ensuing May 6th. For some time, from July 19th, 1798, he acted in the capacity of Brigadier-General of the provisional army. He died at New Brunswick, New Jersey, February 10th, 1803.

ADDELL, REV. JAMES, D. D. (degree conferred by the Dickinson College, in 1792), eloquent Presbyterian divine, father-in-law of Rev. Archibald Alexander, D. D., late of Louisa county, Virginia, was born in Newry, Ireland, in July, 1739. His parents emigrated with him to the United States during his infancy, and settled on White Clay creek, Pennsylvania. He was educated at the classical school of Rev. Dr. Finley, in Nottingham, Maryland, and in that establishment at a very early age acted as assistant tutor. Subsequently he was engaged in teaching for a time at Pequea, Lancaster county, Pennsylvania. He was also engaged as assistant to President Smith, of the Hampden-Sidney College, and President S. S. Smith, of the New Jersey College, where he was very popular with the students, and admired also by the inhabitants of the town. He began the study of medicine, but having been induced by the celebrated preacher, Rev. Samuel Davies, to enter the ministry, he devoted himself to the study of theology, and in 1761 was licensed as a probationer at Tinkling Spring, Virginia, by the Presbytery of Hanover. He was ordained in June, 1762, and accepted a call from the churches of Lancaster and Northumberland, Pennsylvania, but resigned his charge in 1776, and removed to the valley of the Shenandoah. In 1785 he settled on a large estate, purchased by him in Louisa county, which he called "Hope-well," and preached in various churches in that region during the remaining twenty years of his life. Shortly after his last removal he became blind. His reputation as a preacher and pulpit-orator has become widespread through the well-known description of his preaching given by William Wirt, early in the present century, in the volume entitled "The British Spy." Mr. Wirt heard him after he had become blind and paralytic, but says that "he exceeded all that he had been able to conceive of the sublimity of Massillon, or the force of Bourdaloue." At his death he ordered all his manuscripts to be destroyed. He died in Louisa county, Virginia, September 17th, 1805.

ICHENOR, HON. ISAAC, LL.D., Judge, Governor, late of Bennington, Vermont, was born in Newark, New Jersey, February 8th, 1754, and graduated from the New Jersey College in 1775. While studying law at Schenectady, New York, early in 1777, he was appointed Assistant Commissary-General, and stationed at Burlington, New Jersey, where he entered upon the practice of his profession, and soon became prominent in public affairs as an able exponent of his political views, and as promoter or opposer of the measures and movements of those in power. From 1781 to 1784 he served as a Representative in Congress; in 1782 was the Agent of the State to Congress; acted as a member of the State Council from 1787 to 1792; from 1791 to 1794 held the position of Judge of the Supreme Court; was Chief-Justice in the years 1795 and 1796; a member of the Council of Censors in 1792 and in 1813; Commissioner for adjusting the controversy with New York in 1791; Senator in 1796 and 1797; Governor from 1797 to 1807, and from 1808 to 1809; and again United States Senator from 1815 to 1821. He died at Bennington, Vermont, December 11th, 1838.

AMPBELL, E. L., Lawyer, of Trenton, was born February 2d, 1833, near Belvidere, Warren county, New Jersey. His parents were natives of New Hampshire. Reared partly on a farm and partly in Belvidere, he was educated at Lafayette College, Pennsylvania, from which he graduated in 1855. After his graduation, he engaged in teaching at Belvidere, teaching successively in the Classical Academy

and the Female Seminary of the town. In 1860 he was admitted to the bar, and entered upon the practice of the law at Belvidere. But fate had ordained that his first laurels were not to be won in the forum. On the fall of Sumter in April, 1861, and the consequent call for 75,000 three months' troops, he immediately took an active interest in the raising of men. Finding that the only way to get anything done was to lead, he led accordingly, calling a public meeting on the 18th of April, and enlisting himself in advance not only of all the rest of the meeting, but of all the rest of the county. This was a kind of eloquence nobly adapted to the occasion, and not easily resisted, the result being that a company, with him as its Captain, was formed by the next night. His company was ordered to Trenton by Governor Olden on the 27th of April; but, the brigade assigned to New Jersey being full, and overflowing to the extent of eleven companies, the greater number of the company returned to their homes, while he enlisted in Company D, of the 1st New Jersey (three years') Volunteers, then just ordered, serving successively for some days as private, corporal, and sergeant. Whilst thus engaged, he received from Governor Olden, unsolicited and unanticipated, authority to raise a three years' company, which he at once acted upon by re-organizing his first company, effecting the work so promptly that the company was mustered in on the 28th of May, 1861, being enrolled as Company E, of the 3d New Jersey Volunteers. In less than a month afterwards his company, forming a part of the 1st Brigade, was at the front, receiving the baptism of fire and blood on the banks of the Chickahominy. Through this sanguinary campaign and the succeeding one, he served at the head of his company, and as Acting-Major of the regiment, until he received, on the battle-field of Chantilly, September 2d, 1862, a commission as Lieutenant-Colonel of the 15th New Jersey Volunteers; when, with the view of joining his new regiment at Washington, he tendered the resignation of his Captaincy, which, however, the corps commander refused to accept until the operations of the command became less active. After the battle of Antietam, in which he was wounded in the head, his resignation was accepted, and, September 27th, 1862, he joined his regiment at Washington, already on its way to the front. He served as Lieutenant-Colonel of the 15th—assigned to the 1st Brigade, containing his old regiment, the 3d—until the 16th of February, 1865, when he was commissioned as Colonel of the 4th New Jersey Volunteers, having previously been brevetted Colonel from the 19th of October, 1864, for "conspicuous gallantry" in the battle of Cedar Creek. In this battle he was severely wounded, the incident bringing into strong relief not merely his coolness, but the devotion of his men. "During the action," says Foster, "Colonel Campbell was struck by a bullet which shattered his left arm, but he kept command until the greatest danger was over, when, weak from the loss of blood, he was forced to mount an orderly's horse and leave the field. The word flew along the line, 'Colonel Campbell is wounded,' and even in the excitement of the hour the men turned from the observation of the enemy to follow him with their eyes. As he rode away he lifted his uninjured hand and motioned to them, which they interpreted to mean, ' Hold on.'" In February, 1865, while still suffering from this wound, he was ordered by General Meade to join his staff as Judge-Advocate-General of the Army of the Potomac, a position which he filled until the army was mustered out of service, when he rejoined his regiment, mustered out on the 12th of July, 1865, and conducted it home. His military record, as may be seen, is thoroughly a fighting one. He was a fighting soldier, and commanded a fighting regiment in a fighting brigade, which latter indeed he also commanded in many memorable engagements, including particularly Sheridan's immortal battles in the Valley, being in fact brevetted Brigadier-General, April 9th, 1865, for "gallant and meritorious services." To him at least war was a reality, as will be readily acknowledged by those who learn, that, out of the one hundred and fifty or one hundred and eighty original officers in his brigade, he was the only one left with the body so early as October, in 1864. He served in the Army of the Potomac, at the front, throughout the war, from Bull Run to Appomattox; never missing a battle, and, with a single exception, never missing a skirmish; never being absent from the front but eight or ten days each winter when well, and never so much as three months altogether, even when wounded; and, what perhaps is most remarkable, never asking a promotion or encouraging a friend to ask it for him. Evidently he went into the army to fight. And certainly he took the right way to get fighting to do. He chose his comrades shrewdly. Of the 1st Brigade, to which his regiment belonged, and which he commanded on many a famous field, Foster, in his history of "New Jersey and the Rebellion," thus speaks: "But the memory of this scarred and storied command still remains. On a score of fields it had exhibited the rarest heroism. In discipline, in sturdy, faultless courage, in unwavering and sublime devotion, it justified, down to the latest field, the high expectations of that knightly soldier who made it what it was. Tried in many a fierce and pitiless fire, it had never faltered. Exposed, sometimes, to peculiar hardships, thinned by disease, weakened by heavy loss, it never for an hour lost its faith in the cause. The hospital devoured and the trench swallowed up many of its bravest and best, but the 1st Brigade, even when but a remnant of its strength remained, was still undaunted. No danger appalled, no privation dismayed, no losses disheartened the veterans who with a lofty pride fought and died for Freedom's sake. When at last, with torn standards and lean ranks, it marched from the field, where it had helped to achieve an honorable peace, it was welcomed home with right royal greeting; the people hailing it with glad acclaim, and with it rejoicing that the sound of war had ceased from the land. To-day, scattered in all the walks of life, those of its members who yet survive perform the old duties and bear the old burdens, familiar

before they ever marched a field; but their proudest boast is that they once fought with Kearney and the grand old Army of the Potomac, for the flag which to him and to them was dearer than all things else." Of his regiment the same historian says: " In all the qualities of courage, endurance, and devotion to duty, this was among the foremost of New Jersey regiments; to have fought in its ranks on the ghastly fields where it won celebrity may well be counted an honor at once lustrous and imperishable." And, finally, this historian says of the man himself: " Lieutenant-Colonel Edward Campbell had come out of the battle of McClellan's Maryland campaign with honor, and joined the 15th Regiment on the march to Bakersville. Here, upon the sickness of Colonel Fowler, he took command, which he held during most of the time the regiment was in the service, leading it in nearly every great battle in which it participated. One who served with the regiment says, ' If the 15th ever performed any efficient service for the country, or by its conduct reflected any honor upon New Jersey, it was due more to Edward L. Campbell than any other man. His bravery, integrity, capacity, and diligence, stamped the regiment with a character whose value was known in many critical junctures and hard-fought battles.'" The records show that his command suffered more than any other New Jersey regiment in the field. At the close of the war he returned to Belvidere, and renewed his practice, but was compelled to leave it off in the course of two or three months, in consequence of his impaired health. About this time Governor Ward sent for him to take charge of the State Military Agency at Trenton, a trust which he at first declined, but, on the Governor's insisting, accepted, believing that the business could be soon closed up. It, however, engaged him for two years; at the end of which time, his health meanwhile having gradually recovered, he returned to his profession, and was presently fully engaged in successful practice. He is now the City Solicitor of Trenton.

READING, JAMES NEWELL, Judge, was born in Flemington, Hunterdon county, New Jersey, August 8th, 1808, his father being Joseph Reading, a farmer. His first studies were pursued in a common school and then a grammar school, after which he entered Princeton College, in the junior class, in 1827, and graduated in 1829. He then studied law with Governor S. L. Southard, in Trenton, and was admitted to the bar of New Jersey in 1832. He practised law in his native town from that time until 1850. He was married February 10th, 1835, to Sarah C. A. Southard, niece of the Governor. For fifteen years he was Prosecuting Attorney for Hunterdon county. In 1850 he went to Jefferson county, Missouri, and was there as President of a lead mining company for two years. He then returned to New Jersey, settled up his private business and moved to

Morris, Illinois, where he now resides. He was led to the place by the opportunities it presented for engaging in land business, which he had observed on his way to Missouri. His voice had nearly failed him, and he followed his profession only partially, saving his voice thereby and ultimately recovering it fully, when he again resumed his practice in full. He engaged at once in a land business, and continues in it to this day. In 1865 he was elected County Judge of Grundy county, which position he has held for ten years. He was also a member of the Legislature from the same county for one term, and for a period Clerk of the Circuit Court in the county. During his residence in New Jersey he was at one time Colonel of a regiment of militia. From 1869 to 1871 he resided in Chicago and practised law with Judge Wallace, after which he returned to Morris. The Judge is a gentleman very generally respected in his county, and highly esteemed for his worth of character.

ILLYER, REV. ASA, D. D., Prominent Presbyterian Clergyman, late of Orange, New Jersey, was born in Sheffield, Massachusetts, April 6th, 1763, and graduated at Yale College in 1786. September 29th, 1789, he was ordained at Bottle Hill, New Jersey, and in 1837 sided with the New School, whose views concerning various religious tenets and observances met with his approval. His degree of D. D. was conferred on him by the Allegheny College in 1818. He died in New York, August 28th, 1840.

cLEAN, REV. DANIEL VERCH, D.D., Presbyterian Clergyman and Author, late of Red Bank, New Jersey, was born in 1801. For several years he performed the duties of the pastorate of the Old Tennent Church, Freehold, New Jersey, and from 1854 to 1864 was President of Lafayette College, Easton, Pennsylvania. Up to the time of his decease, after his withdrawal from Easton, he presided as pastor over a church at Red Bank, New Jersey, where he died, November 23d, 1869.

ACLEAN, JOHN, M. D., Chemist, Physician, Scientist, Author, late of Princeton, New Jersey, was born in Glasgow, Scotland, in March, 1771, and was the son of an eminent Scotch scholar and surgeon. After studying in various cities, he commenced the practice of surgery at his native city in 1791. In 1795 he came to the United States, and was appointed Professor of Chemistry and Natural History in the College of New Jersey, and subsequently of Natural Philosophy and Mathematics, which position he resigned, however, in 1812, having been appointed Professor of Natural Philosophy and Chemistry in William and Mary College. His principal publication was " Lectures on Combustion; " while his various papers bearing upon the controversy with Dr. Priestley, and published in the " New York Medical Repository," attracted much attention, and elicited favorable criticism from those interested in the discussion. He died at Princeton, New Jersey, in February, 1814.

IERSON, HON. ISAAC, M. D., Prominent Physician, late of Orange, New Jersey, was born in New Jersey, August 15th, 1770, and was educated at Princeton College, where he graduated in 1789. Subsequently he became a Fellow of the College of Physicians and Surgeons of New York. During a period extending over forty years he was actively engaged in professional labors as a medical practitioner, and won honorable distinction through the many successes attending his conduct of cases of a very critical and perplexing nature. Besides attending to his duties as a physician, he always evinced a warm interest in the current political questions and movements, and was earnest in his advocacy of those measures which seemed to him best fitted to advance the welfare of his State and the leading interests of his fellow-citizens. From 1827 to 1831 he was a Representative in Congress from his native State. He died in New Jersey, September 22d, 1833.

LEXANDER, REV. JOSEPH ADDISON, D. D., Learned Divine and Author, son of Dr. Archibald Alexander, and brother of Dr. James Waddell Alexander, late of Princeton, New Jersey, was born in Philadelphia, April 24th, 1809, and graduated from the New Jersey College in 1826. From 1830 to 1833 he served as Adjunct Professor of Ancient Languages and Literature in his *Alma Mater ;* and from 1838 to 1852 was Professor of Biblical Criticism and Ecclesiastical History at Princeton Theological Seminary. He was subsequently transferred to the Chair of Biblical and Ecclesiastical History, which he held until the time of his decease, performing its responsible duties with vigor and rare ability. The degree of D. D. was conferred on him by the Marshall College, Pennsylvania. He published : " A Translation of and Commentary on the Psalms," three vols. ; "A Critical Commentary on the Prophecies of Isaiah," and an abridgment of the same; a volume on primitive church government, and numerous excellent essays in the " Biblical Repertory " and " Princeton Re

John broes

view." He also aided Dr. Hodge in the preparation of a commentary on the New Testament. He was a linguist of unusual powers, and the possessor of a large and valuable store of philological learning. In the "Memoir" published by H. C. Alexander in 1869, is presented an interesting account of him and his labors in various fields, as educator, writer and professor. He died at Princeton, New Jersey, where he was universally respected and admired for his many gifts and acquirements, January 28th, 1860.

FLEMING, CHARLES E., Lieutenant-Commander United States Navy, was born in New Jersey, and in January, 1835, was appointed from New York. In 1862 he received his commission as Lieutenant-Commander. His total sea-service extended over a period of about nineteen years. He commanded the gun-boat "Sagamore," in the Gulf Squadron, during the late war, and subsequently the "Penobscot," At the time of his death, at Mount Holly, New Jersey, in the fifty-second year of his age, he was ...

ALEXANDER, REV. ARCHIBALD D. D. (transferred to the New Jersey College, 1850), Presbyterian Divine, Itinerant Missionary, Professor of Theology, Author, late of Princeton, New Jersey, was born in Rockbridge county, Virginia, April 17th, 1772. His grandfather, Archibald Alexander, came from Ireland to Pennsylvania in 1736, and about 1738 settled in Virginia. At the age of ten years he was sent to the academy of Rev. William Graham, at Timber Ridge meeting-house. At the expiration of six or seven years from this time he assumed the duties of tutor in the family of General John Posey. Subsequently he entered upon a course of theological studies, was licensed to preach October 1st, 1791, and during the ensuing seven years labored zealously as an itinerant missionary in his native State. Succeeding Dr. Smith in the Presidency of Hampden-Sidney College in 1796, he finally resigned that office and also his pastoral charge in 1801. In the following year he resumed his position at Hampden-Sidney College, but owing to the insubordination and refractory spirit of the students under his charge, accepted a call from the Pine Street Church, Philadelphia, where he was installed pastor, May 20th, 1807. From 1811 until the period of his decease, he presided as Professor of the Theological Seminary at Princeton, New Jersey. He was the author of "Outlines of the Evidences of Christianity," published in 1823; "Treatise on the Canon of the Old and New Testaments," published in 1826; "Counsels of the Aged to the Young," published in 1833; "Lives of the Patriarchs," published in

1835; "Essays on Religious Experience," published in 1840; "History of the Log College," published in 1846; "History of the Israelitish Nation," published in 1852, and "Moral Science," in the course of the same year. He published also a memoir of his old instructor, Rev. William Graham; "History of the Presbyterian Church in Virginia," and many biographical sketches of eminent American clergymen and alumni of the College of New Jersey, and contributed to the "Biblical Repertory," and other periodicals of a literary and religious character. At his demise he left a number of manuscript works, which will probably be published at no distant date. His son, Rev. James Waddell Alexander, D. D., a distinguished Presbyterian clergyman and author, published his "Life" in New York in 1854. He died at Princeton, New Jersey, October 22d, 1851, after a career of eminent usefulness, and pious and scholarly labors.

CROES, JOHN, D. D., Bishop of the Protestant Episcopal Church in New Jersey, late of New Brunswick, was born in Elizabethtown, New Jersey, of parents who had emigrated from Germany, June 1st, 1762. His father intended to instruct him in some mechanical employment, but observing his early and precocious fondness for study and reading, gave him finally the option of learning a trade or proceeding in education by means of his own exertions. He somewhat hesitatingly chose the latter alternative, but his endeavors in this respect were, for a considerable time, retarded by the war of the revolution. Three or four years subsequently he was called upon to take up arms in the cause of his country, and he continued engaged in martial pursuits, with occasional intervals of rest, until the peace in 1782. He then resumed his studies with increased interest, and with that diligence and energy which marked his course through life continued his efforts towards the speedy acquisition of a thorough and liberal education. By tireless perseverance he rapidly acquired a good knowledge of the Latin and Greek languages, at the same time laying the foundation of an unusually accurate knowledge of the English tongue and its higher literature. Having made these acquisitions, he endeavored to be of some use of instruction, thereby riveting more firmly the knowledge he had gained, and procuring the means of supporting himself while studying divinity. In 1790 he was ordained Deacon, and in 1792 Priest, by Bishop White. The first years of his ministry he spent in Swedesboro, in connection with the church of that place, but in 1801 he received an invitation from Christ Church, New Brunswick, and St. Peter's Church, Spotswood, to become their pastor, and at the same time was elected Principal of the academy in New Brunswick. In 1808 he resigned the charge of the academy, having previously resigned that of the church at Spotswood, and devoted himself solely to the church in New Brunswick. In 1815 he was elected,

view." He also aided Dr. Hodge in the preparation of a Commentary on the New Testament. He was a linguist of unusual powers, and the possessor of a large and valuable store of philological learning. In the "Memoir," published by H. C. Alexander in 1869, is presented an interesting account of him and his labors in various fields, as educator, writer and professor. He died at Princeton, New Jersey, where he was universally respected and admired for his many gifts and acquirements, January 28th, 1860.

LEMING, CHARLES E., Lieutenant-Commander United States Navy, was born in New Jersey, and in January, 1835, was appointed from New York. In 1862 he received his commission as Lieutenant-Commander. His total sea-service extended over a period of about nineteen years. He commanded the gun-boat "Sagamore," in the Gulf Squadron, during the late war, and subsequently the "Penobscot." At the time of his death, at Mount Holly, New Jersey, in the fifty-second year of his age, he was unemployed.

LEXANDER, REV. ARCHIBALD, D. D. (conferred by the New Jersey College, 1810), Presbyterian Divine, Itinerant Missionary, Professor of Theology, Author, late of Princeton, New Jersey, was born in Rockbridge county, Virginia, April 17th, 1772. His grandfather, Archibald Alexander, came from Ireland to Pennsylvania in 1736, and about 1738 settled in Virginia. At the age of ten years he was sent to the academy of Rev. William Graham, at Timber Ridge meeting-house. At the expiration of six or seven years from this time he assumed the duties of tutor in the family of General John Posey. Subsequently he entered upon a course of theological studies, was licensed to preach October 1st, 1791, and during the ensuing seven years labored zealously as an itinerant missionary in his native State. Succeeding Dr. Smith in the Presidency of Hampden-Sidney College in 1796, he finally resigned that office and also his pastoral charge in 1801. In the following year he resumed his position at Hampden-Sidney College, but owing to the insubordination and refractory spirit of the students under his charge, accepted a call from the Pine Street Church, Philadelphia, where he was installed pastor, May 20th, 1807. From 1811 until the period of his decease, he presided as Professor of the Theological Seminary at Princeton, New Jersey. He was the author of "Outlines of the Evidences of Christianity," published in 1823; "Treatise on the Canon of the Old and New Testaments," published in 1826; "Counsels of the Aged to the Young," published in 1833; "Lives of the Patriarchs," published in

1835; "Essays on Religious Experience," published in 1840, "History of the Log College," published in 1846; "History of the Israelitish Nation," published in 1852, and "Moral Science," in the course of the same year. He published also a memoir of his old instructor, Rev. William Graham; "History of the Presbyterian Church in Virginia;" and many biographical sketches of eminent American clergymen and alumni of the College of New Jersey, and contributed to the "Biblical Repertory," and other periodicals of a literary and religious character. At his demise he left a number of manuscript works, which will probably be published at no distant date. His son, Rev. James Waddell Alexander, D. D., a distinguished Presbyterian clergyman and author, published his "Life" in New York in 1854. He died at Princeton, New Jersey, October 22d, 1851, after a career of eminent usefulness, and pious and scholarly labors.

ROES, JOHN, D. D., Bishop of the Protestant Episcopal Church in New Jersey, late of New Brunswick, was born in Elizabethtown, New Jersey, of parents who had emigrated from Germany, June 1st, 1762. His father intended to instruct him in some mechanical employment, but noting his early and precocious fondness for study and reading, gave him finally the option of learning a trade or procuring an education by means of his own exertions. He unhesitatingly chose the latter alternative, but his endeavors in this respect were, for a considerable time, retarded by the war of the revolution. Three or four years subsequently he was called upon to take up arms in the cause of his country, and he continued engaged in martial pursuits, with occasional intervals of rest, until the peace in 1782. He then resumed his studies with increased interest, and with that diligence and energy which marked his course through life continued his efforts towards the speedy acquisition of a thorough and liberal education. By tireless perseverance he rapidly acquired a good knowledge of the Latin and Greek languages, at the same time laying the foundation of an unusually accurate knowledge of the English tongue and its higher literature. Having made these acquisitions, he undertook the business of instruction, thereby riveting more firmly the knowledge he had gained, and procuring the means of supporting himself while studying divinity. In 1790 he was ordained Deacon, and in 1792 Priest, by Bishop White. The first years of his ministry he spent in Swedesborough in connection with the church of that place, but in 1801 he received an invitation from Christ Church, New Brunswick, and St. Peter's Church, Spotswood, to become their pastor, and at the same time was elected Principal of the academy in New Brunswick. In 1808 he resigned the charge of the academy, having previously resigned that of the church at Spotswood, and devoted himself solely to the church in New Brunswick. In 1815 he was elected, by the convention of the church in Connecticut, Bishop of that diocese, but this appointment he declined. In the same year he was chosen Bishop in his own State, and was consecrated to that office in November. In this responsible station his industry, ability, and zeal were abundantly manifested. Almost every year he visited all the churches in the diocese, and by his judicious management of the missionary fund, assisted importantly in resuscitating several old and decayed congregations, and in establishing several new ones. He was a self-made man, humanly speaking, and to himself alone was he indebted for his solid and brilliant attainments, and a reputation lustrous and free from stain or blemish. Industry, energy, a mind never darkened by despondency, and an unswerving uprightness, were his distinguishing characteristics. His sermons, charges and addresses always bore the stamp of earnest piety, sincere meditation, and a rare and genial reliance on the beneficent rulings of an inscrutable Providence; while, as a writer, his style was pointed, logical and direct. He died at his residence in New Brunswick, July 30th, 1832.

REVLING, ADAM W., Merchant, was born near Washington, Warren county, New Jersey, December 4th, 1826. His father, Samuel Crevling, was a farmer in Warren county. The family were among the early German settlers of New Jersey. Adam was educated in the public schools, and at the age of fourteen began his mercantile career as clerk in a store at Asbury, New Jersey, after which he engaged in the same capacity at Washington, and then at Oxford, subsequently returning to Washington, where he continued as clerk only one year longer, when, in 1848, he set up business on his own account, and has prosecuted it ever since with steadily increasing success, until it is now probably one of the largest retail businesses of the kind in New Jersey, his yearly sales amounting to from $150,000 to $200,000. In the work of building up and conducting this vast business he has had successively a number of partners. The health and vigor of the main stem may be seen in its flourishing offshoots. Mr. Crevling devotes his entire time to his special business, with such ramifications as it has made into real-estate and building operations, which of late years have in fact diverted a considerable portion of his energy and capital, though in these, as in the principal channel of his business, prosperity has waited on his ventures. He is a Republican in politics, but, whilst keenly alive to his duties as a citizen, takes little interest in the ordinary strife of parties. He is a member of the Presbyterian church, in which he is conspicuous for his activity and zeal. He was married in 1848 to I. A. Bodine, of Warren county. His eldest son is at present associated with him in his business, which, extensive as it is, and unpropitious as the times have long been,

shows no signs of decline, a strong testimony to the ability and character of its experienced head.

BBETT, HON. LEON, of Jersey City, Lawyer and Statesman, was born in Philadelphia, October 8th, 1836, his birthplace being within a hundred yards of the old tree under which William Penn made his treaty with the Indians, known in history and tradition as the "Treaty Tree." His great-grandfather, born in 1730, a Quaker and a farmer, emigrated when a young man to Pennsylvania, and settled in the vicinity of Philadelphia, where he and his descendants lived as farmers until 1830, when the latter began to disperse, the father of the subject of this sketch removing to Philadelphia. Although a man in moderate circumstances, he gave a liberal education to his son, Leon, who, after a term at one of the common schools, graduated in 1853, as Bachelor of Arts, at the High School of Philadelphia, and in 1858 received the degree of Master of Arts. Immediately following his graduation he entered the law office of the Hon. John W. Ashmead, then United States District Attorney for the Eastern District of Pennsylvania, where he remained until of age, when he opened a law office of his own. Having practised a year in Philadelphia, he removed to New York, where, though he had powerful competitors around and before him, and no friends at his back, he advanced so rapidly in his practice that it soon grew too great for his management single-handed, and he formed a partnership with the distinguished patent and admiralty lawyer, Wm. J. A. Fuller, the firm of Abbett & Fuller at once taking rank among the first law establishments of the metropolitan city. Their practice has become immense, and is steadily increasing from year to year. On the 8th of October, 1862, the anniversary of his birth, he was married to a young lady of Philadelphia, signalizing the event by transferring his residence from New York to Hoboken, thereby becoming a citizen of New Jersey, and involuntarily drawing down on himself the necessity of a political career. Being a Democrat, strict and staunch, and a popular speaker of great spirit and effectiveness, the Hoboken Democracy, rejoicing in his steadfastness and his eloquence, pressed him early into their service, and in 1864 elected him to the Assembly, in which he represented Hoboken for two consecutive terms, making, during the first term, a singularly able and judicious speech on the Thirteenth Amendment, which attracted wide attention, extorting the admiration even of his political opponents. During both terms his Democratic colleagues showed their high appreciation of his ability by recognizing him as their leader. Besides representing Hoboken in the Assembly, he served it as Corporation Counsel for three years, resigning in 1868, the Common Council of the city adopting on the occasion resolutions warmly acknowledging his services and regretting their

Leon Abbett

ENGRAVED BY J A O'NEILL HOBOKEN

Leon Abbett

termination. He was also Corporation Attorney for the town of Union over two years, when his increasing business constrained him to resign, though he is still retained by the township in all its more important cases, as he is by Hoboken. He is now the Corporation Counsel for Bayonne, having held the office since Bayonne became a city. In April, 1876, he was appointed Corporation Counsel by the Board of Finance and Taxation of Jersey City, whither he had removed on the expiration of his second term as Representative of Hoboken in the Assembly. He was Chairman of the Democratic State Convention which met at Trenton in 1868 to nominate presidential electors and a governor, and acquitted himself as a presiding officer with signal distinction, insomuch that the dispersing delegates bore his name and praise to all quarters of the State, preparing the Democrats of the Assembly, when he next appeared in that body, which he did in 1869, as the Representative of the First District of Hudson, to nominate him for the office of Speaker by acclamation, as they did, renewing the honor in 1870 with additional emphasis, in attestation of the completeness with which he had met their expectations, a tribute crowned, it should be added, by the consenting eulogies of the press without respect to party. On taking his seat at this election he delivered a speech memorable for its bold and sagacious views on taxation, contending that the prosperity of New Jersey depends principally on the attraction of capital, and not hesitating to suggest that the State, like England and France, should impose no tax on personal property invested in manufactures and shipping, or on money at interest. New Jersey has not yet come up to this advanced position, but there are statesmen of rank who hold with Mr. Abbett that it is the true position, and that the legislation of the State should move in the direction of it. At all events the suggestion of the policy illustrates the strength and independence of his character. The same traits find an illustration equally apt in his views on the subject of naturalization, which pass beyond, not merely the general opinion, but the opinion of his own party, liberal as that is, going to the length of abolishing the present system altogether, and requiring a simple oath of allegiance as the condition of naturalization. It is unnecessary to say that the existing rights and privileges of the adopted citizen have in him a fearless and thorough-going defender. In 1869 he was unanimously elected the successor of Judge Randolph as President of the Board of Education, holding the place until the reorganization of the board. He was in 1872 a Delegate at large to the Democratic National Convention at Baltimore, and one of the Secretaries of the body, in which he voted for Senator Bayard, and against Mr. Greeley, whose nomination he believed would be vivifying to the Republicans, but suicidal for the Democracy. He again, in 1876, was Delegate at large to the Democratic National Convention at St. Louis, and Chairman of the New Jersey delegation, which he led for Parker, whose claims he had previously advocated in the State convention with an ability and fervor that endeared him anew to the Democracy of the State. His services as a legislator have been important as well as conspicuous, and can hardly be said to have ended with his membership, seeing that his abilities and influence, since the expiration of his membership, have been exerted with marked effect in promoting good legislation and opposing bad. The general corporation act of 1875, the most liberal in the United States, was drawn by him, and passed under the pressure of his influence, as was the act of 1876 to increase railroad taxation; while Jersey City, his present home, owes it chiefly to him that she has not suffered still greater evils from the partisan charter, which probably would never have become a law if his energetic and unsleeping opposition could have been made within the Legislature instead of without. He is a popular orator of uncommon force and fire, a debater of large resources and practised skill, and a political leader of consummate sagacity and unquailing spirit. From the opening of the McClellan campaign in 1864 to the present time he has done distinguished and brilliant service on the stump in every national and local field that has been fought. In person he is below the medium height, but of a solid, well-knit frame, surmounted by a head and neck of classical proportions. The physique proclaims the man. He was elected to the Senate from Hudson county in 1874 by a majority of 5,000. The Democracy being in a majority in 1877, he was chosen President of the Senate, which office he now holds, and fills with marked ability and discretion.

TONE, HON. J. HENRY, Lawyer and ex-State Senator, of Rahway, New Jersey, was born in that place, November 19th, 1835. He was educated at Rutgers College. Selecting the legal profession, he began his studies therefor under the direction of Hon. Cortlandt Parker, of Newark, and was admitted to practise in November, 1859. He formed a copartnership with Mr. John P. Jackson, under the style of Stone & Jackson. The office of the firm is in Newark, and he still continues the senior partner therein. A public-spirited man, he has been called upon to occupy many positions of trust and responsibility. He is a Director in the Rahway Gas Company and the Rahway Savings Institution. In the administration of public affairs he has borne a prominent part. He has been a member of the Rahway Common Council, and served the community ably and faithfully for two years as Mayor of the city. For several years he has been attorney for Rahway. He was elected to the State Senate from Union county in the fall of 1872 on the Republican ticket, reversing the result of the previous Senatorial election, in which the county had gone Democratic, and polling a large vote. In the session of 1874 he was Chairman of the Committees on Judiciary, Banks and Insurance, Fisheries, and Soldiers' Home, and a member of that on Education. Although an earnest Republican, he is by no means a mere partisan, his course being always dictated by a desire to promote the best interests of the people.

————

ORMAN, GENERAL DAVID, Revolutionary Patriot, late of New Jersey, was born near Englishtown, in this State. During the progress of the contest with Great Britain he was distinguished as an intrepid and able supporter of American rights and measures, and exercised over his fellow-citizens, and in a manner productive of the most beneficial and desirable results, the powerful influence acquired by him at an early date. At the memorable battle of Germantown he commanded the Jersey troops, and at all times possessed in a high degree the confidence and esteem of Washington. He subsequently filled the position of Judge of the County Court, and for some time acted as a member of the Council of State. In person he was impressive and commanding, and, possessing a fearless disposition and a will firm almost to stubbornness, was as a check and a constant terror to the wood-robbers and tories, toward whom he exercised a severity and harshness that could be justified only by the perils environing the loyal and honest, and the troublous circumstances surrounding the earnest efforts of a sorely-tried State and government. "Wo to the guilty culprits who fell in his power; without waiting for superfluous ceremony the gallows was generally their fate." His complexion was dark and swarthy, and such was the aversion and wholesome fear he inspired in the minds of the spy and footpad that he acquired the name of "Black David," and sometimes "Devil David," "in contradistinction to David Forman, the Sheriff." Throughout his long life and varied career he was a shrewd and loyal observer of all passing events touching upon the interests of his fellow-citizens and the growing institutions of his country, and a prompt and efficient mover wherever and whenever he deemed his counsel or his services needed and desired. In the "New Jersey Historical Collections" is paid him, and justly, a high and enviable compliment: "Were it not for his exertions the county would have suffered far more from its intestine enemies." He died about 1812.

————

LEXANDER, REV. JAMES WADDELL, D.D., an eloquent Presbyterian Clergyman, Author, Editor, Professor of Rhetoric and Belles-lettres, late of Virginia Springs, was born near Gordonsville, Louisa county, Virginia, March 13th, 1804, and graduated from the New Jersey College in 1820. He was the eldest son of Rev. Archibald Alexander, D. D., also an eminent Presbyterian divine, and writer on religious and church subjects. From 1825 to 1827 he was a minister in Charlotte county, Virginia; from 1829 to 1832 officiated as pastor in the church at Trenton, New Jersey; and from 1844 to 1851 presided over the Duane Street Church, New York. Subsequently he was elected pastor of the Fifth Avenue Church. From 1830 to 1833 he filled the position of editor of the *Presbyterian*, a church organ published in Philadelphia, Pennsylvania; in 1833-1834 was Professor of Rhetoric and Belles-lettres in the New Jersey College; and from 1849 to 1851 Professor of Ecclesiastical History and Church Government in the Theological Seminary, Princeton, New Jersey. The degree of D. D. was conferred on him by Lafayette College, Pennsylvania, in 1843, and by Harvard College in 1854. He published a volume of sermons entitled "Consolation;" "Thoughts on Family Worship;" "The American Mechanic and Workingman;" a biography of his father, Dr. Archibald Alexander; "Discourses on Christian Faith and Practice," 1858; a volume of "Sacramental Discourses;" "Gift to the Afflicted;" "Geography of the Bible;" "Plain Words to a Young Communicant;" and "The American Sunday School and its Adjuncts;" also numerous contributions to *The Biblical Repertory* and *Princeton Review*, and several of the publications of the American Tract Society. He wrote for *The Literary World* over the signature of "Cæsariensis." After his decease two volumes of his letters and remains were edited and published by Dr. Hall, of Trenton, New Jersey, a man of excellent repute and fine scholarly attainments. He was a preacher of persuasive powers, of fervent piety, and tireless in his self-accepted task of Christian enlightenment and moral teaching. He died at the Virginia Springs, July 31st, 1859.

————

E HART, COLONEL WILLIAM, Officer in the Revolutionary army, Lawyer, late of Morristown, New Jersey, was born in Elizabethtown, New Jersey, December 7th, 1746, and was the son of Dr. Matthias De Hart. Before the outbreak of the contest between the colonists and Great Britain he was actively engaged in professional labors as a legal practitioner, but relinquished his vocation at the approach of open hostilities. November 7th, 1775, he received the appointment of Major in the 1st New Jersey Battery, and in the course of the ensuing year was promoted to the rank of Lieutenant-Colonel. September 6th, 1780, he again received a Lieutenant-Colonelcy in the 2d Regiment, Continental army. Before the close of the war he resigned his commission, and in Morristown, New Jersey, resumed the profession of the law. He was a leading member of the bar where he practised, and was noted for his brilliant sallies of wit and humor, which seemed ever ready to flash forth at an instant's warning, and at the slightest provocation. In 1779 he acted as President of the St. Tammany Society. Two of his brothers, also, were efficient partisans of the patriot cause, one of them having been aide to General Wayne before he was killed at Fort Lee, in 1780. He died at Morristown, New Jersey, June 16th, 1801.

———◆◇◆———

FRENEAU, PHILIP, distinguished Poet and Journalist of the revolutionary period, late of Monmouth, New Jersey, was born in New York city, January 2d, 1752, and graduated from the New Jersey College in 1771. His grandfather, Andrew Freneau, was a merchant of New York; and Peter Freneau, his father, was a dealer in wines and liquors. The family was of French Huguenot extraction. He was educated at Nassau Hall, New Jersey, where James Madison was his room-mate and intimate personal friend. While still in his boyhood he exhibited considerable satirical power and facility in versification, and when at college wrote "The Poetical History of the Prophet Jonah," in four cantos. He intended originally to apply himself to the study, and ultimately practice, of law, but afterward changed his purpose and engaged in a seafaring life; and in 1776 went, in a mercantile capacity, to the West Indies where he remained for some time. During the contest with Great Britain his pen was constantly launching forth its tirades of sarcasm and invective against the blind policy and tyrannous measures of the mother country, and his political burlesques in prose and verse were extensively circulated and relished. "Some of his verses, descriptive of memorable events on land and sea, are genuine specimens of the national ballad." In 1780, while on his way again to the West Indies, he was captured by a British cruiser, and subjected to a long and cruel confinement on board the prison-ship "Scorpion." This term of intolerable captivity, whose torments and privations were heightened by an uncalled-for harshness and severity on the part of his jailers and the superior officers in command, he has commemorated in his poem, "The British Prison-ship." On his release he became a frequent contributor of patriotic verses to The Freeman's Journal, of Philadelphia, Pennsylvania. But from this pecuniarily profitless occupation finally he turned to mercantile affairs, and made several voyages to the West Indies. For several years after the conclusion of the war he was employed alternately also as newspaper editor and sea-captain. In 1791 he assumed the editorial duties of the New York Daily Advertiser. Upon the establishment of the Federal government at Philadelphia, he was appointed French translator in the Department of State, under Jefferson, and at the same time became editor of the National Gazette, of Philadelphia, which was made the vehicle of bitter and incessant attacks upon the policy and administration of Washington. It is not positively known, however, that he is responsible for all the articles on this subject; and, according to his own statement, the most severe and caustic of the series were written or dictated by Thomas Jefferson, In October, 1793, the National Gazette was discon̄ued, and retiring to New Jersey in the course of this year he started, May 2d, 1795, at Mount Pleasant (near Middletown Point), The Jersey Chronicle, which lived for about twelve months. While residing there he also printed an edition of his poems. Subsequently, after editing for a year, in 1797, and at New York, The Timepiece and Literary Companion, a journal devoted to belles-lettres and general news, he resumed his former employment as master of a merchant vessel. The second war with Great Britain reanimated his slumbering muse, and in pungent and stirring verse he chronicled the successes of his countrymen and satirized the defeats and victories alike of his old adversaries and persecutors. The remainder of his life was spent in retirement at his residence in New Jersey, with frequent visits to Philadelphia and New York, where his acquaintance with eminent statesmen and literary characters was very extensive. He enjoyed the friendship of Adams, Franklin, Jefferson, Madison and Monroe, and for a long time was in constant correspondence with the last three celebrities. He lost his life by exposure and cold, while going on foot in the night, during a heavy snow-storm, to his residence, near Freehold. "His productions animated his countrymen in the darkest days of '76, and cheered the desponding soldier as he fought the battles of freedom." Although comparatively unknown to the present generation of readers, he was a true poet, and an able writer of essays and political articles. His poems embrace all the popular forms of composition, and exhibit notable excellency in fluent versification. His humor is finely illustrated in his numerous satirical poems, and in the political squibs and lampoons which he produced with remarkable facility. Campbell and Scott borrowed from him with no sparing hands, while Jeffrey predicted that the time would come when his poetry, like "Hudibras," would "command a commentator like Grey." Many of his smaller poems possess great elegance of diction, and in the preceding half century were much admired and eulogized by both the critical few and the mass of general readers. His patriotic songs and ballads were everywhere sung with enthusiasm by the revolutionary heroes, and in England were regarded as powerful incentives to disaffection and rebellion. In the "New Jersey Historical Collections," he is briefly described as "a man of naturally fine feelings, but an infidel in sentiment." He published "A Translation of the Travels of Abbé Robin," New York, 1783; "Poems," Philadelphia, 1786; "Miscellaneous Works," 1788; "Poems written between 1768 and 1794," Mount Pleasant, New Jersey, 1795; "Letters on Various Subjects," etc., by Robert Slender, Philadelphia, 1799; a new edition of his "Poems," 1809; and "Poems written between 1797 and 1815," two volumes, New York,

1815. An edition of his "Revolutionary Poems," with a memoir and notes by E. A. Duyckinck, was published in New York in 1865. Peter Freneau, his brother, edited and published at Charleston, South Carolina, 1795 to 1810, the *City Gazette*, a Democratic newspaper. He died, or "perished miserably," at Monmouth, New Jersey, December 18th, 1832, in the eightieth year of his age.

UNT, WILSON PRICE, Pioneer Traveller, the hero of Irving's "Astoria," late of St. Louis, was born in Hopewell, New Jersey, in the house still standing, probably, on the property of Benjamin S. Hull, and served an apprenticeship in the store of his uncle, Abraham Hunt, of Trenton, New Jersey. His adventurous and enterprising spirit brought him to the notice of John Jacob Astor, of New York, who planned an enterprise across the mountains. The conduct of the contemplated expedition was assigned to him, he being one of the partners of the company organized, and ultimately the head of the establishment located at the mouth of the Columbia. June 23d, 1810, articles of agreement were entered into by him, in connection with J. J. Astor, Alexander McKay, Duncan McDougal, and David McKenzie, acting for themselves, and for the several persons who had already agreed to become, or should thereafter become, associated under the firm of "The Pacific Fur Company." He was then appointed an Agent, for the term of five years, and selected to reside at the principal establishment on the northwest coast. In the latter part of the following July he repaired to Montreal, the ancient emporium of the fur trade, and made extensive preparations for the work in hand, engaging Canadian voyageurs, and laying in supplies of ammunition, provisions, and Indian goods. The expedition then set forth from St. Anne's, and made its way up the Ottawa river, and along the smaller lakes and rivers, to Michilimackinac, arriving at Mackinaw, at the confluence of Lakes Huron and Michigan, July 22d. Here he remained for some time, seeking to complete his assortment of goods, and to increase his number of voyageurs. August 12th he finally left Mackinaw, and pursued the usual route to Prairie du Chien, and thence down the Mississippi to St. Louis, where a landing was effected, September 3d. October 21st he took his departure from St. Louis, and soon arrived at the mouth of the Missouri, reaching the mouth of the Nodowa, after a season of suffering and peril, November 16th. January 1st he set off to return on foot to St. Louis, and arrived at his destination on the 20th of the same month. Here he was greatly impeded in his plans by the opposition of the Missouri Fur Company, which saw in him and his expedition rivals and keen competitors. April 17th he was again with his party at the station near the Nodowa river, where the main body of the company had been quartered during the winter.

May 10th he arrived at the Omaha village, and encamped in its neighborhood, but on the 15th set forward toward the country of the Sioux Tetons. June 11th he encamped near an island below the Arickara village, and there commenced a trade with the Indians under the regulation and supervision of the local chieftains. July 18th he took up his line of march by land across the tributaries of the Missouri, and over immense prairies destitute of trees and human life, skirting the Black Hills, and pursuing a westerly course along a ridge of country dividing the tributary waters of the Missouri and the Yellowstone. January 31st he arrived at the falls of the Columbia, and encamped at the village of Wishram, situated at the head of the long narrows. Eventually, after experiences and trials of a most formidable and disheartening character, he arrived safely at Astoria, the distance from St. Louis to that place, by the route taken, being upward of thirty-five hundred miles. August 26th, 1813, after a sojourn of six days at Astoria, he set sail in the "Albatross," and arrived at the Marquesas, where he learned that the British frigate "Phœbe" had sailed, with the "Cherub" and the "Raccoon," for Columbia river. This intelligence alarmed him greatly, since the errand of the hostile vessels could have for end only the demolition of Astoria, and the interests which he had been so zealously promoting there. November 23d he proceeded to the Sandwich Islands; and January 22d set sail for Astoria, intending to remove the property thence as speedily as possible to the Russian settlements on the northwest coast, to prevent it from falling into the hands of the British. February 28th he cast anchor, in the brig "Pedler," in the Columbia river; soon after landed; and upon settling various complicated business arrangements, and laboring loyally in the interest of J. J. Astor, set sail again April 3d, and bade a final adieu to Astoria. In Irving's "Astoria," may be found the following lines: "The absence of Mr. Hunt, the only real representative of Mr. Astor, at the time of the capitulation with the Northwest Company, completed the series of cross-purposes. Had that gentleman been present, the transfer, in all probability, would not have taken place." On his return from the fur region, he settled at St. Louis, where he died in 1842.

---

cNEVEN, WILLIAM JAMES, Author, Professor in the College of Physicians and Surgeons, or in the Medical School connected with Rutgers College, New Jersey, from 1808 to 1830, late of New York city, was born in Galway county, Ireland, March 26th, 1763. He was educated at the Colleges of Prague and Vienna, at the latter of which he graduated in 1784. He became a zealous member of the Society of United Irishmen, and after an imprisonment—in consequence of his connection with it, and ensuing results—of four years, was liberated, and passed the summer of 1802 in travelling through Switzerland on foot, of which journey he published an account entitled "A Ramble in Switzerland." He subsequently acted in the capacity of Captain in the Irish Brigade of the French army, but resigned his commission, and emigrated to the United States, arriving at New York, July 4th, 1804. From 1808 to 1830 he presided as Professor in the College of Physicians and Surgeons, or in an establishment dependent on the Rutgers College, New Jersey. In 1812 he was appointed, by Governor Clinton, Resident Physician; and, in 1840 was again nominated to the same office; and, during the prevalence of the cholera epidemic of 1832, was actively employed as one of the medical council. He published an "Exposition of the Atomic Theory;" "Pieces of Irish History," 8vo., 1807; "Use and Construction of the Mine Auger," London, 1788; and an edition, carefully prepared, of "Brande's Chemistry;" besides occasional essays and addresses on various subjects. He was also a valued contributor to the current medical and scientific journals. He died at New York city, July 12th, 1841.

ARTIN, LUTHER, LL. D., Lawyer, Educator, Revolutionary Patriot, Judge, Statesman, late of New York, was born in New Brunswick, New Jersey, in 1744, and graduated from the New Jersey College in 1766. He was subsequently engaged in teaching school at Queenstown, Maryland; then entered upon a course of legal studies; and was admitted to the bar in 1771. He afterward commenced the practice of his profession in Accomac and Northampton counties, Virginia; and, after his admission as attorney in the courts of Somerset and Worcester, rapidly attained an extensive and lucrative clientage. In 1774 he became a member of the commission to oppose the claims and exactions of Great Britain, and a member also of the Annapolis Convention. He published an answer to the address of the brothers Howe; also "An Address to the Inhabitants of the Peninsula between the Delaware river and the Chesapeake." February 11th, 1778, he was appointed Attorney-General of Maryland; and in 1784–85 acted as a member of the old Congress. Strongly influenced by his political ideas and principles, he wrote many pungent and violent essays against the Democratic party of his time; and in 1804 was one of the defenders of Judge Chase, who was impeached in the House of Representatives for alleged misdemeanor. He was likewise the personal and political friend of Burr, whose acquittal he was instrumental in procuring, when on trial for alleged treason in 1807. In 1814 he was appointed Chief Judge of Oyer and Terminer, for Baltimore, Maryland; and in 1818 was given the appointment of Attorney-General of the State. Although a member of the convention which framed the Federal Constitution, he violently opposed the adoption of that instrument, advocating the equality of the States, and con-

tending that a small State should have as many Congressmen as a large one. He is the Author of "A Defence of Captain Cresap from the Charge of Murder made in Jefferson's Notes;" and "Genuine Information, etc., of the Convention at Philadelphia," etc., 8vo., published in 1788. He was a loyal and upright citizen, although a man of strong prejudices and passionate temperament; an unflinching friend to those he esteemed, and an outspoken enemy when opposed by political adversaries. He died at New York city, July 10th, 1826.

ALL, JOSEPH LLOYD, Bank-Lock and Safe Manufacturer, was born, May 9th, 1823, at Salem, New Jersey, and is the second son of Edward and Anna (Lloyd) Hall. He removed with his parents to Pittsburgh, Pennsylvania, in 1832. His educational advantages were very limited, as he began to earn his own living at eight years of age; and although his early tastes inclined him to mechanical pursuits, yet circumstances combined to prevent their gratification. In 1840 he engaged in a steamboat enterprise, and continued in that business upon the Mississippi river and its tributaries until 1846, when he returned to Pittsburgh and formed a copartnership with his father, under the firm-name of E. & J. Hall, and embarked in the manufacture of fireproof safes. This industry was undeveloped, and they also found such strong competition from the wealthy and long-established Eastern houses in the same line, that they determined to remove to Cincinnati, which they carried out in 1848. In that city they established the nucleus of the present immense manufactory, and both father and son toiled in their little workshop from day to day with indefatigable patience and energy. They labored assiduously to educate the public mind to a fuller appreciation of the great security obtained by the use of fire and burglar-proof safes, and stemming the current of opposition with a rare and admirable pertinacity for years, they finally triumphed over adverse circumstances and stood on a firm foundation. In 1851 his father disposed of his interest in the business to William B. Dodds, and the firm of Hall, Dodds & Co. succeeded; they employed, at that time, a force of fifteen hands, and produced about two safes per week. This firm was dissolved in 1857, and was thereafter followed by others in succession, in all of which Joseph L. Hall was the senior partner and chief executive. The Hall Safe and Lock Company was organized in May, 1867, of which he was chosen President and Treasurer, and, as formerly, still exercises a rigid surveillance over all the practical operations of the works. This is said to be the largest safe manufacturing establishment in the world, and is probably more than four times as large as any similar concern in the United States. It employs some six hundred mechanics of consummate skill and experience, and has a capacity for turning out about fifty safes each working day. He has devoted his mechanical genius to the perfection of the arti-cles manufactured by the company, and his many improve-ments attest his aptness and fitness for the task. He is the patentee of some thirty well-known and valuable inventions in bank locks and safes. He has built some of the largest safes ever constructed, and, without exception, they have preserved their contents intact during the severest tests. The manner in which his five hundred safes passed the terrible ordeal at the great fire in Chicago, October, 1871, is a sufficient proof of their reliability. The company have branch houses in every important city in the Union, and the reputation of the safes and locks is limited only by the confines of civilization. At the outbreak of the late civil war, in 1861, he undertook the execution of a contract to alter, for the United States government, within thirty days, five thousand Austrian muskets, and performed the work so satisfactorily and efficiently, that he was awarded many other contracts during the war. He never aspired to nor accepted a public office, although often solicited to become a candidate. He has been for many years an active, zeal-ous, and consistent member of the Methodist Episcopal Church, and is at present one of the most liberal supporters of St. Paul's Methodist Episcopal Church, of Cincinnati. Such is the record of a man who, by dint of indomitable energy and native genius, won his way to a proud and en-viable position in the business and social world—a position which his generous and hospitable nature well fits him to grace. He was married, in early manhood, to Sarah Jane Jewell, of Pittsburgh, Pennsylvania, and this union has been blessed with twelve children, three sons being now associated with him, all of whom are active and efficient business men—the oldest, Edward C. Hall, having filled the position of Vice-President of the company.

ORGAN, GENERAL DANIEL, a distinguished Officer of the American army in the war of the Revolution, late of Winchester, Virginia, was born in Hunterdon county, New Jersey, 1736. He was of humble parentage, and was unable to secure any but a very elementary and limited education. At the age of seventeen he left his father's farm, and in 1755 joined the expedition of General Braddock against the French and Indians on the Ohio, acting as a teamster or private soldier. While thus engaged, in the spring of 1756, he knocked down a British lieutenant who had insulted him, and for this violation of military rules was sentenced to receive five hundred lashes. He was ac-customed, however, in after life, to maintain jestingly that the drummer had miscounted the number and still owed him one. "One can hardly conceive of his surviving such a severe punishment, and perhaps there was some favor shown by the men who administered it." The officer here spoken of afterward made him a public apology. About

the same time he also received a painful wound, which dis-figured his countenance for life. Returning to Frederick, now Clarke county, Virginia, whence he had removed in early life, he resumed his career as a backwoods farmer and a leading pioneer, until the outbreak of the Revolution. Previously, in 1757, he served in the militia, and distin-guished himself in the defence of Edward's Fort. In 1758 he was made an Ensign, and while carrying despatches was waylaid and severely wounded by Indians, escaping by presence of mind and the fleetness of his horse, from whose back he was taken insensible. After the peace he was much addicted to gambling and dissipation, and gained notoriety as a sturdy pugilist; but before 1771 had reformed, became a man of good morals and substance, and in 1774 commanded a company in Lord Dunmore's expedition against the Indians. Immediately after the battle of Lex-ington, he in less than a week enrolled ninety-six men, the nucleus of his celebrated rifle corps, and led them to Boston, reaching the American camp, after a march of six hundred miles, in three weeks. He was early-appointed to com-mand a troop of horse in Virginia, and with this company marched to the patriot lines at Cambridge in the summer of 1775. General Washington, who knew him well, had great confidence in his bravery and loyalty, and detached him to join the expedition of Arnold against Canada in the following autumn. No officer was more valiantly promi-nent than Morgan on that memorable occasion, and when Arnold was wounded in the first assault he assumed the command. Although successful in that part of the field where he held command, he was compelled by the fall of Montgomery and the defeat of his division to surrender; or, as it is otherwise narrated, he was taken prisoner with others when General Montgomery was slain. While in the hands of the British he was offered the rank and pay of a Colonel in the royal service, which he indignantly rejected. Soon after his release, toward the close of 1776, Washing-ton gave him command of a rifle corps, the 11th Virginia, with which he was detached to the assistance of Gates, then opposing the enemy in its advance from Canada; and took a most important part in the victory attending the surrender of Burgoyne, near Saratoga. During Washington's retreat through New Jersey in 1776, and the campaign in the same State in 1777, he also rendered valuable services. Upon joining the main army, after the action at Saratoga, he was employed by the commander-in-chief in several perilous en-terprises, which he conducted with equal courage and judg-ment; and for his services on the occasion referred to, the Virginia Legislature voted him a horse, pistols, and sword. He was an active participant also in the severe skirmish which took place near Chestnut Hill with a part of Corn-wallis's division. During a part of 1778 he was in com-mand of Woodford's brigade; and March 20th, 1779, was made Colonel of the 7th Virginia regiment, but resigned that position in the following June. In the battle of Bemus's Heights, which had precipitated the surrender of the British commander, his riflemen took a leading and efficient part; yet their chief was unnoticed by Gates, in his official account of the occurrence, and an attempt was even made to induce him to join the Conway cabal against Washington, which he scornfully repelled. After the defeat at Camden he joined the remnant of Gates's army at Hillsborough, and, October 1st, was placed in command of a legionary corps. Continuing in active service in the North until the summer of 1780, he was then made Brigadier-General and transferred to the southern army. At this period he found his health declining, and wished to retire from the army, but was induced to remain with the forces in the South in order to harass and repel the British, who were making depredations on the inhabitants. Shortly after Greene assumed the command, in December, he was detached to the country watered by the Broad and Pacolet rivers. Pursued by Colonel Tarleton, he withdrew to the Cowpens, where, January 17th, 1781, he gained a brilliant victory over that renowned officer, capturing or destroying nearly the whole of his force. A gold medal testified the appreciation of Congress of his skill and bravery on that occasion; he was also honorably noticed by this body, in connection with Colonel Howard, Colonel Washington and General Pickens. He then followed up the action at Cowpens by a series of well-conceived manœuvres which seriously embarrassed Cornwallis. Before the close of the campaign, however, he was compelled, by repeated and severe attacks of rheumatism, to retire to his home in Virginia. In 1794 he commanded the army sent against the insurgents in western Pennsylvania, aiding importantly in quelling the Whiskey Insurrection that had broken out in that locality. From 1795 to 1799 he was a member of Congress. In 1800 he removed to Winchester, where he resided until the time of his decease. In 1799 he published an address to his constituents, vindicating the administration of Mr. Adams. The latter part of his life was passed in much physical suffering, and he died in Winchester, Virginia, July 6th, 1802. His oldest daughter was married to General Presby Neville, of Pittsburgh. His son, Willoughby Morgan, Colonel United States army, died at Fort Crawford, Upper Mississippi, April 4th, 1832. A "Life of Morgan" was published by James Graham, 12mo., in 1859.

OXE, JOHN REDMAN, M. D., Medical Editor and Author, late of Philadelphia, Pennsylvania, was born in Trenton, New Jersey, in 1773. He studied medicine under the guidance of the celebrated Dr. Rush, and also in London, Paris and Edinburgh. Upon his return to the United States he settled in Philadelphia, Pennsylvania, in 1796, and there entered upon the practice of his profession. In 1798 he filled the position of Port Physician, and during the yellow fever visitation performed efficiently, and with noteworthy

energy and ability, the duties of his office. He was for several years a physician of the Pennsylvania Hospital, and of the Philadelphia Dispensary; from 1809 to 1818 he was Professor of Chemistry in the University of Pennsylvania, and from 1818 to 1835 Professor of Materia Medica in that institution. He was the introducer into Philadelphia of the system and practice of vaccination. He published "On Inflammation," 8vo., 1794; "Importance, etc., of Medicine," 8vo., 1800; "Combustion, etc.," 8vo., 1811; "American Dispensatory," 8vo., 1827; "Refutation of Harvey's Claim to the Discovery of the Circulation of the Blood," 8vo., 1834; "Female Biography;" and "Recognition of Friends in Another World," 12mo., 1845. He also edited "The Philadelphia Medical Museum," six volumes, 8vo., 1805, new series, 1811; and "The Emporium of Arts and Sciences," five volumes, 8vo., 1812. "He never had a day's illness throughout the course of his long and busy life, and lived far beyond the average term of man, while keeping intact his rare powers of mind, and his great age excepted, with its attendant feebleness, haleness of body" He died in Philadelphia, March 22d, 1864, without any appreciable disease, aged ninety-one years.

OOD, GEORGE B., M. D., LL. D., Physician and Author, was born in Greenwich, Cumberland county, New Jersey, March 13th, 1797. He was educated at the University of Pennsylvania, where he graduated in 1815 with the degree of A. B., and in 1818 with that of M. D. He was Professor of Chemistry in the Philadelphia College of Pharmacy from 1822 to 1831; Professor of Materia Medica in the same college from 1831 to 1835; Professor of Materia Medica in the University of Pennsylvania from 1835 to 1850; Professor of the Theory and Practice of Medicine in the same from 1850 to 1860; and a physician in the Pennsylvania Hospital from 1835 to 1859. He is the author of numerous and valuable works, chiefly relating to his profession, which rank among the classics of the medical sciences. His first important work, "The Dispensatory of the United States," was written in conjunction with Franklin Bache, M. D., and the original edition was published in Philadelphia, in 1833 (8vo., 1073 pages). This at once stamped him as a man whose research and knowledge of his profession were of the highest order; it was thoroughly exhaustive in its description of the many medicinal agents peculiar to American practice, indicating minutely their various properties and effects. It has gone through thirteen editions, the last being in 1870 (8vo., pages xii. 1810), about 150,000 copies having been sold. Before 1830 there had not been any United States pharmacopœia or standard list of medicines and their preparation whose authority was generally recognized. In the year mentioned two such lists were offered to the public, one prepared in New York, the other chiefly the work of Dr. Wood. In a severe review Dr. Wood completely demolished the first of these, and by writing the "United States Dispensatory" caused the authority of the other to be universally acknowledged. In 1847 he published a "Treatise on the Practice of Medicine" (two volumes, 8vo). It ran through six editions, the last being in 1867. He also published in 1856 a "Treatise on Therapeutics and Pharmacology," or materia medica, which had three editions, the last being issued in 1868 (two volumes, 8vo., 1848 pages), and a volume containing twelve lectures, six addresses and two biographical memoirs, in 1859. It consisted of lectures and addresses on medical subjects, delivered chiefly before the medical classes of the University of Pennsylvania. He has also written "The History of the Pennsylvania Hospital;" "History of the University of Pennsylvania;" "Biographical Memoirs of Franklin Bache," etc. In the first and last of these pamphlets will be found an account of Wood and Bache's "Dispensatory and United States Pharmacopœia," of which he, in connection with Dr. Bache and others, was editor of the editions of 1831, 1840, 1850 and 1860. In 1872 these memoirs, with the addition of the History of Christianity in India, of the British Indian Empire, of the Girard College, and other papers, were collected into a volume entitled "Memoirs, Essays and Addresses." In 1865 he endowed the Auxiliary Faculty of Medicine in the University of Pennsylvania, consisting of five chairs: one of Zoology and Comparative Anatomy, one of Botany, one of Geology and Mineralogy, one of Hygiene, and one of Medical Jurisprudence, all of the subjects to be especially considered in their relation to medicine.

ERGEN, HON. JAMES J., Lawyer, Somerville, son of John J. Bergen, merchant, and descended from a Hollandish family, the founder of which in America was one Hansen Bergen, a shipbuilder, who settled at Breuklyn in 1633, was born at Somerville, New Jersey, October 1st, 1847. At the time of the revolutionary war several of his ancestors served with credit in the continental army, and his family has for many years been prominent in the affairs of East Jersey. Under the tutorship of Mr. Butler, of Somerville, he received a classical education, and in 1864 began the study of law in the office of Hugh Gaston, Esq., a leading practitioner of the same town. Admitted to the New Jersey bar in 1868, he practised for a year in Plainfield, and then, returning to Somerville, entered into partnership with his former legal preceptor, thus establishing the firm of Gaston & Bergen. His ability as displayed at the bar gave him prominence in public affairs, and in 1875 he received the Democratic nomination to the lower house of the State Legislature, and was elected by a handsome

majority. In the Assembly he proved himself to be strong in debate, and also, as a member of the Committees on Revision of the Laws, State Printing, etc., to possess to an exceptional extent the power of formulating and organizing. The duties of his office were so well fulfilled that in 1876 he was again nominated, and was elected by an increased majority. On the rearrangement of committees, at the beginning of the session, he was assigned as a member of the Judiciary, on State Prison, and on Elections. During this session a bill was introduced into the Senate, and passed by that body by a unanimous vote, making a writ of error in capital cases a writ of right; thereby radically changing the criminal law and practice of the State. Against this measure, upon its introduction into the House, he spoke at length and forcibly, but the bill was passed over his protestation, and was referred to the governor for approval. Governor Bedle returned it with his veto, based upon a line of argument practically identical with that used in opposing it by Mr. Bergen, and upon a subsequent reconsideration in the Senate the veto was sustained. Mr. Bergen, it should be observed, was the only member of the Legislature who spoke in opposition to the bill, previous to its being vetoed by the governor. In March, 1877, he was appointed, by Governor Bedle, Prosecutor of the Pleas for Somerset county.

AYTON, HON. GEORGE, of Rutherford, Merchant and Senator from Bergen county, was born in Westerloo, Albany county, New York, October 2d, 1827. He is a member of the same family with the late William L. Dayton, United States Senator and Minister to France, their common ancestor having been Samuel Dayton, of Long Island, High Sheriff there from 1723 to 1728, whose son, Jonathan, the first settler of the name at Elizabethtown, New Jersey, and one of the first of any name. His family indeed has given to the country some of the ablest and most brilliant of its statesmen. He received a thorough English education, and in his twentieth year became a clerk in a mercantile house in New York city, where he is now one of the leading merchants. He has come up from the counter; and that, perhaps, is one reason why he has ascended so high, and is stationed so securely. A poet may be born, not made; but a merchant, even if born, requires a great deal of making, and this he has had. Beginning with the A B C of trade, he took a full course of practice, mastering the business at every stage, until he ranks to-day among the lords of commerce, if not among the princes. But commerce, steadily and successfully as he has pursued it, has not absorbed all his energies of mind or character. For the last twelve years he has taken an active part in the politics of his section, and has been chosen to fill a number of responsible offices. He has been for many terms a member of the Township Committee, of which in late years he has been President; and in 1874 he was elected, by a flattering majority, to represent Bergen county in the State Senate, in which he has attained an enviable prominence as a legislator. Thoroughly informed, able, prudent, vigilant and firm, he is recognized by his colleagues as a leader, and by the public as one who promises to rival the political distinction and influence of his lamented kinsman. He, at any rate, has crossed the threshold of what bids fair to be a useful and distinguished public career. It may be mentioned here, that, while he is a member of the Senate of New Jersey, his brother, J. C. Dayton, by a pleasant coincidence, is a member of the Senate of the neighboring State of New York, representing the district which includes the city of Albany. The mantles of the elder Daytons would seem to have fallen on successors who have the ability as well as the inclination to wear them.

LUMMER, HON. CHARLES S., Merchant and State Senator, of Pedricktown, was born, December 2d, 1839, in Sharptown, Salem county, New Jersey. He is a son of Samuel Plummer, United States Marshal for New Jersey, the family being old residents of Salem county. He was educated in the public schools of the county; and, deciding to lead a mercantile career, embarked in 1864 in merchandising at Pedricktown, where he still pursues the business, which, under his energetic and skilful management, has developed into an extensive one. His mercantile career proved so successful that he was soon led into a political career, the ability and integrity with which he had conducted his private business occasioning his fellow-citizens to call him into the public service. In 1870 the Republicans of Salem county nominated him for the Assembly, but the district being strongly Democratic he was defeated, though running in his own township greatly ahead of the general ticket. But neither he nor his party was content to rest in defeat. In 1875 he was nominated for the State Senate, and this time was elected, carrying his own township, which usually gave a Democratic majority of over 200, by a majority of 110. He is now fairly launched on the political waters, under signs that are favorable to a prosperous course. He has served in the Senate as Chairman of the Committee on the Treasurer's Accounts, and on the State Prison Committee, of which he is at present a member, as he is of other committees of importance. With youth, energy, ability, business skill, the confidence of his party, and the regard of the people, irrespective of party, there would seem to be no good reason why he should not achieve success in politics as well as in commerce. Certain it is, that his future is bright with promise. He has been twice married—to Hannah A. Heritage, in 1861; and, in 1865, to Anna M. Black.

EAMING, HON. JONATHAN F., Physician, Dentist and State Senator, of Cape May Court House, was born in Cape May county, New Jersey, September 7th, 1822. His family, of English extraction, were among the early settlers of New Jersey, Christopher Leaming, from whom he is sixth in the line of descent, having emigrated from England in 1670, and settled in Cape May in the year 1691. He attended Madison (New York) University, from which he passed to Brown University, Rhode Island, where he remained until 1844, subsequently entering Jefferson Medical College, at which he graduated in 1846, and in the following year married Eliza H. Bennett, of Cape May Court House. Immediately after graduating he began the practice of medicine in his native county, and pursued it with signal success for fourteen years, when, its extent and laboriousness and the attendant cares beginning to undermine his health, he was compelled to relinquish it. Unwilling, however, to forego absolutely those struggles with disease in which he had acquired such distinction and displayed such mastery, he compromised with his professional tastes and aptitudes by turning to dentistry, which he has practised ever since, except when interrupted by the public duties to which his fellow-citizens from time to time have called him. His excellent sense, popular sympathies and wide experience of life admirably fit him for political service, and it is not a matter of surprise that he has been called to discharge it; it would have been more surprising if he had not been, among a people who rightly think that no man, whatever his profession or his rank, is too good to serve them, if he has the ability. In 1861, accordingly, he was elected a member of the New Jersey Assembly, in which he served one term, when, in 1862, he was elected to the State Senate for a full term of three years. During this term he was Chairman of the Committee on Education, and a member of several other important committees. His course as a legislator fully justified the expectations of his friends, placing him among the most useful, enlightened and judicious members of the Legislature. In 1868 his popularity received a new stamp by his election to the office of Surrogate of Cape May county for a term of five years, upon the expiration of which, so ably and acceptably had he filled the place, he was re-elected for another full term, which, however, he did not serve out, being re-elected also to the Senate in 1876, and decided to resign the Surrogateship and to accept the Senatorship, which he now holds, having resigned the former office on the 1st of January, 1877. In the Senate he is a member of the Committee on Commerce and Navigation, on Miscellaneous Business, and other important committees, and would no doubt occupy a much more prominent position in the business of the body were it not that he is now one of the minority, to whose members the majority, on grounds quite other than those of qualification, are not accustomed to assign the foremost places. After this it is hardly necessary to say, for the benefit of contemporary readers at any rate, that he is a Republican in politics, though it may not be unnecessary to add that his zeal for his party, always strong, has never been more ardent or more active than it now is. No carpet-knight or summer-bird is he. In 1858 the degree of A. M. was conferred on him by the University at Lewisburg, Pennsylvania, and in 1860 the degree of Doctor of Dental Surgery by the Pennsylvania College of Dental Surgery. He has been for forty years a member of the Baptist Church.

REEN, HON. HENRY WOODHULL, LL.D., of Trenton, Lawyer, and ex-Chancellor of the State, was born near the city of his residence, on September 20th, 1804. After receiving a thoroughly sound preliminary training, he entered Princeton College, and was graduated from that institution in 1820, being then only sixteen years of age. The profession of the law seemed to be naturally indicated for his life career, and he accordingly began his studies therefor soon after his graduation, entering the office of the late Chief-Justice Charles Ewing. Under so distinguished a preceptor he acquired a very sound legal knowledge, and was admitted to the bar in due course in November, 1825. His marked abilities, his deep learning and devotion to his profession, soon placed him in the front rank at the bar, where it was early admitted that he had few equals. As a counsellor, also, he enjoyed the highest consideration. A man of earnest mind and public spirit, he could not fail to take a strong interest in political affairs, and his name was sought to strengthen the ticket of his party—the Whig. He thus became a candidate for the State Legislature in 1842, and was elected by a considerable majority. But legislative service had no attractions for him, and he declined further nominations in that direction. In 1844 he was chosen a member of the Constitutional Convention, and rendered valuable assistance in the revision of the organic law. Two years subsequently his pre-eminent qualifications pointed him out as a fitting member of the bar for elevation to the Supreme Bench as Chief-Justice, and the position being offered to him he accepted it, and served for two full terms, of seven years each, with great distinction. In 1861 Governor Olden singled him out for yet more distinguished honor, tendering him the appointment of Chancellor of the State. The nomination was accepted, and Judge Green occupied the position until he had nearly completed a full term, when ill health necessitated his resignation, much to the regret of the entire legal fraternity and the community at large. As Chancellor he added greatly to his previously very high reputation as a jurist, his opinions being received with marked acceptance, and cited throughout the country as those of very few American jurists have been. Thirty years ago he published three volumes of reports of cases decided in the Court of Chancery. Educational matters always en-

listed his warmest sympathies and active co-operation. He was the second oldest living member of the Board of Trustees of Princeton College, and at the time of his death was, and for some time previously had been, the President of the Board of Trustees of the Theological Seminary at Princeton. His religious views attracted him to the Presbyterian Church, of which he was a devoted and highly valued member. His death occurred in Trenton, on the night of December 19th, 1876.

IXON, HON. JONATHAN, Associate Justice of the Supreme Court of New Jersey, comes of English parentage, and was born in the city of Liverpool, England, July 6th, 1839. There he remained until reaching his eighth year, attending public schools for two or three years. At that time the family removed to Maryport, in the county of Cumberland, where Jonathan's education was continued in the public schools. In the spring of 1848, his father, desirous of improving his fortunes, came to the United States, whither his family followed him in July, 1850, and settled in New Brunswick, New Jersey. During December of the same year, Jonathan became an inmate of the home of Cornelius L. Hardenbergh, a lawyer, who suffered from the misfortune of blindness. To him the lad acted as attendant and amanuensis for nearly five years, or until September, 1855, in the meantime receiving much care and attention from the family, who highly appreciated his intelligence, devotion and ambition. His education was continued under their fostering care, a son, Warren Hardenbergh, giving especial attention to his tuition. So prepared, he was enabled to enter Rutgers College in 1855, and, after a full course assiduously pursued, he was graduated from that institution in 1859. After graduation he entered the office of his friend and quondam tutor, Warren Hardenbergh, as a student at law, and prosecuted his studies under these auspices for about twelve months. Mr. Hardenbergh then removed to New York, and Jonathan Dixon transferred his allegiance as student to George R. Dutton, and subsequently, upon that preceptor in his turn seeking New York as a field of action, to Robert Adrain, all of these gentlemen being members of the bar at New Brunswick. While acquiring a knowledge of his chosen profession, Jonathan Dixon secured the means of living by teaching in public and private schools. In due course his industry and perseverance brought him to the point toward which his attention had been steadily fixed, and he was admitted to practise. His admission as attorney occurred in November, 1862; three years later he was called as counsellor. About a month after being admitted, or in December, 1862, he removed to Jersey City, and entered the office of E. B. Wakeman in a clerical capacity. Here his abilities and love of his profession led, in the spring of 1864, to a partnership with his employer which was maintained for a period of just twelve months. For five years thereafter Mr. Dixon conducted an independent practice, which proved quite successful; so much so, indeed, that in 1870 he concluded that it was advisable to form a new partnership. This he did with Gilbert Collins, the style of the firm being Dixon & Collins. The firm met with uninterrupted success, and from the first occupied a high position at the bar. In April, 1875, he was offered a seat on the Supreme Bench of the State, and, accepting the appointment, his commission was issued, bearing date April 8th, 1875. In the exercise of the judicial functions he has always commanded the respect and confidence of the bar and of the community at large, his decisions evidencing learning, research, independence and impartiality. He is indeed actuated by the true, judicial spirit, and worthily sustains the exalted reputation of the State judiciary. During his career at the bar, he held several positions of a public character. In 1863 he was Corporation Counsel for the town of Bergen, and again in 1869 the same honorable position was enjoyed by him for the city of Bergen. During 1871 he discharged the duties of a similar office in Jersey City. Politically he has always been an earnest Republican, and his abilities and valuable services have always been relied upon to good purpose in all emergencies until his elevation to the bench, since which time he has simply discharged, in an unostentatious and conscientious manner, the political duties devolving upon every member of the community. In the year 1864 he very efficiently promoted the Republican cause as President of the Union League of Jersey City. He was married, September 12th, 1864, to Elizabeth M. Price, of New Brunswick.

LARK, REV. SAMUEL ADAMS, D. D., Clergyman, late of Elizabeth, was born in Newburyport, Massachusetts, on the 27th of January, 1822. His father, Thomas March Clark, was one of the descendants, probably, of Captain Thomas Clark, who was an early settler in the Plymouth colony. His mother, Rebecca Wheelwright, was descended from the Rev. John Wheelwright, a distinguished Puritan clergyman, who was educated at Cambridge University, England, and who, after varied experiences, including banishment from Braintree, now Quincy, Massachusetts, for errors of doctrine, and the founding of the town of Exeter, New Hampshire, died in extreme old age near Newburyport. The parents of Dr. Clark were prominent in the town where they lived, for a period of more than fifty years. They were members of the Presbyterian Church. His father was the President of the Howard Benevolent Society from the year 1816, when that institution was organized, until his death in the year 1851; and his mother for more than thirty years was the President of the Newburyport Orphan Asylum. His early home was consecrated to good works and to Christian hospitality. Before his birth his mother had organized a Youth's Missionary Society. She held the meetings in her own house. She induced the boys connected with the society to make monthly contributions, and so young Clark breathed, in his earliest childhood, the best possible domestic and Christian atmosphere. The brevity of this sketch precludes an extended notice of the virtues of his parents and the character of his home during his boyhood; but, as he owed to these parents and to his early Christian culture nearly all that made his character so precious, even the shortest record of his life should recognize the excellent stock from which he sprang, and the influences which surrounded him in his childhood. The only surviving members of this Newburyport family are the brothers of the deceased : the Rt. Rev. Thomas M. Clark, D. D., Bishop of the Diocese of Rhode Island; the Rev. Rufus W. Clark, D. D., of Albany, New York, and the Rev. George H. Clark, D. D., of Hartford, Connecticut. Dr. Clark studied theology at the seminary in Alexandria, Virginia. After completing his studies he took charge in Philadelphia of a new mission which afterwards was the Church of the Mediator. He was, for a short time, minister of the Episcopal Church, at Plymouth, Massachusetts, and while there he was called to be Assistant in St. Ann's Church, Brooklyn, Long Island, and also to the rectorship of the Church of the Advent, in Philadelphia. In the spring of 1848 he became the Rector of the latter church, and he held this position until April, 1856, when he was called to the rectorship of St. John's Church, Elizabeth, New Jersey. A minute of the vestry of the Church of the Advent, and a tribute from the Sunday-school of that church to his memory, after a separation of eighteen years, indicate that he was held in "grateful remembrance" for his "Christian zeal and loving interest in all the work and people of his charge." While a resident of Philadelphia, Dr. Clark married Sarah Henry, daughter of John S. Henry, Esq. His wife and six children survive him. Soon after taking orders he published the "Life of the Rev. Albert W. Duy," and subsequently published the "History of St. John's Church, Elizabeth." He was elected to represent the Diocese of New Jersey in the last two General Conventions, and at the time of his death was the President of the Standing Committee of the Diocese. He received the title of Doctor of Divinity from Rutgers College, New Jersey. And now, after this mere outline of an active and useful life, the writer would attempt a true portrait of a beloved brother. The materials for this portrait may, in part, be found in the tributes given by others to his memory. There are surely few clergymen whose Christian character and faithful services elicit, when they die, such sympathetic recognition as his death drew forth. That the vestry of his church and the convention of his diocese should pass the common resolutions was to be expected, but it was not to be expected that other, and even distant corporations and societies, should give expression to their grief.

The local editors, too, naturally would deplore his loss as "that of a brother and a personal friend," and mark the day of his going from them as "a day of general mourning," but this "man of warm sympathies," who "always had an ear for the tale of human suffering," to "whose heart the orphan and the poor widow never appealed in vain," whose "catholicity of spirit and freeheartedness led him constantly to overleap all narrow sectarianism and all party boundaries," left his name to be recorded even in distant parts of the land, associated with all which makes life precious and good. Ample was the testimony to his "great ability and earnestness," to "his industry and willingness to assume duties and responsibilities," to "his judicious counsel, his earnest zeal, his cheerful faith," to his "good humor and personal magnetism," to "his universal kindness," to his "winning the love and respect of all who knew him," and the loss was mourned "as children mourn the loss of a dear parent." It was with no common grief that the members of the vestry of St. John's Church, with some of whom he had been pleasantly associated for nearly twenty years, put on their records that they had lost "a beloved personal friend, the church a most conscientious, devoted rector, the community one always in sympathy with them in projecting and doing good; that he had always manifested the most generous and Christian spirit; had been unremitted in his labors, often to an extent far beyond his physical strength; that he had preached the Gospel with faithfulness, warned the unwary, visited the sick; that the young, for whom it was his peculiar delight to labor, had lost a dear friend and counsellor; the poor, a most generous benefactor; the afflicted, a sincere sympathizer; and that no act could be recalled which did not increase the pleasant remembrance of him who was our joy and comfort at all times." While it cannot be claimed that Dr. Clark possessed the qualities of a great preacher, it may truly be said that he was a very effective Christian teacher. He knew what he wished to say, and his sermons were marked by plainness, good sense and strong feeling. Thoughts came to him quickly, and he wrote with rapidity, not stopping to elaborate his style, and seldom, if ever, revising or correcting. He was honest, conscientious, fearless, and was an instructor who was successful in the best meaning of that word. There was a warmth and a glow about him in the pulpit which attracted his hearers. There was that which is superior to profound reasoning and to classic language—the earnest, clear presentation of all Christian duties, and of all Christian hopes and consolation. This, the real calling of a preacher, loyal to his Master, he well fulfilled, guided by the noblest of all principles, and by a true, pure heart. In one of his anniversary sermons, delivered in St. John's Church, Dr. Clark says, "A more efficient ministry might have made a more efficient people;" and in his diary, a few days after he became the Rector of the Church of the Advent, in Philadelphia, he wrote, "I am intrusted with a precious charge. May God grant that I may be a faithful shepherd, a vigilant watchman, a fear-

less preacher, an humble follower of Jesus, and a successful ambassador to my dear people." A more efficient ministry than that which marked his life is seldom secured in any parish, and the prayers which he offered at the beginning of his ministerial life were graciously answered. He was, indeed, a faithful shepherd, a vigilant watchman, a fearless preacher, an humble follower of Jesus, and a successful ambassador. The writer often remonstrated with him for his unceasing labors, but the anxiety of friendship could not keep him from his work. And with what fidelity, with what kindness, and sympathy and gentleness that work was done, those only can know who saw his face, and heard his voice, when they were in trouble and in sorrow. It should be recorded, too, that his philanthropy constantly carried him outside of his parish duties, and that many benevolent institutions found in him an advocate and a supporter. He was the life of every social company into which he entered, and the life of his own home. His buoyancy was never abated; it was perpetual, and was commonly mingled with the kindness of his heart. There was hardly an hour when he did not do good by creating a laugh, and he would sometimes brush away his tears at the very time of saying funny and cheering things. He was tenderhearted as a child, he was truly pious, he was remarkably faithful in Christian duty, at home as well as abroad, and yet he was an incessant blaze of fun; indeed, a most remarkable depositary of "comic animation." Nothing repressed him. "An apt conjunction of satin and lawn" never disconcerted him; he would light up the face of a grave bishop, or start the wrinkles on a judge, with the same careless indifference, as to himself, which he showed when he made a crowd of children happy. Introduced to the venerable mother of the President of the United States, he asked her if she had sons, and then where they lived; and on learning that one lived in Washington, he wished to know what he did there. Hearing a very thin clergyman complain of being followed and annoyed by dogs in the streets, and seeing half-a-dozen other clergymen standing with sober faces and half-open mouths, listening to this recital and not knowing what to say, he said, "The dogs think he's a bone." Approached, while in conversation with a bishop's wife by a very large clergyman, it was impossible for him, with his faculty of looking at and presenting things in their odd relations, not to say, "Permit me, madam, to present to you a portion of my friend, the Rev. Mr. ——." His aged female parishioners were often "lambs," or "brides." His dog, goat, parrot, dead owl, hens, and the pencil-marked eggs on his breakfast table, were prolific sources of merriment to him and to his guests and his family. The habit of getting off funny things was as natural and as irresistible with him as the habit of breathing. And he was never ill-natured, nor vulgar, nor irreverent in his wit, nor did he speak in it many idle words; his fun was more useful than the solemn advice of others; he would give a needed lesson, sometimes a long-remembered lesson, while he sent his hearer away laughing. "It is probable," said a friend, who preached a memorial sermon in St. John's pulpit, "that he is chiefly remembered by many as a cheerful man. Was there ever another who had such a kind and mirthful word for every one? Did any one ever scatter so much sunshine along the very streets through which he passed?" But "this cheerfulness," adds his friend, "was as little the manifestation of a heart that could not profoundly feel, as it was of a mind that could not strongly think." The portrait cannot be complete; a sketch, the lines not fully filled. "There was so much of him to go," said his brother, the Bishop of Rhode Island, and all those who were nearest to him respond, "so much of him to go." He carried a charm about him. He was a delightful companion. His activity, energy, inflexibility in principle, firmness in duty, won respect; his personal character, his generosity, his sweetness, his piety, won love. His soul was white and clear from his early boyhood, and he kept it so to the very end. The long and successful rectorship of Dr. Clark in St. John's Church terminated with his death, on the 28th of January, 1875; and not only the people of his parish, but the people of the city, of all classes and of all creeds, deplored the irreversible event. It may be doubted if any citizen had so many friendships, and it is certain that no possible loss in the community could have been more deeply or universally lamented. A hundred clergymen, it is supposed, attended the funeral services. The large church was filled with mourners. Bishop Stevens and Bishop Scarborough were in the chancel and made addresses. The bells of the city were tolled. A noble life had ended; a great heart had ceased to beat. The congregation of St. John's has placed a memorial tablet within the church edifice, and, by vote of the vestry, a monument has been erected, in Laurel Hill cemetery, Philadelphia, over the grave of this beloved minister.

ARTIN, HON. ALEXANDER, LL.D. (degree conferred by Princeton College), Soldier and Statesman of the revolutionary war, Governor of North Carolina, Author, late of Danbury, North Carolina, was born in New Jersey, about the year 1740, and studied at the New Jersey College, graduating from that institution in 1756. In 1721 his father had emigrated to the colonial settlements from Tyrone county, Ireland, and settled in New Jersey, where, it is supposed, he resided until the time of his decease. In 1772 he removed to North Carolina, and settled eventually in Guilford county, in that State. He served as a member of the Colonial Assembly, was actively engaged for some time as Colonel of a Continental Regiment, took a prominent part in the battles of Brandywine and Germantown, was State Senator in 1779–80–81–82–85–87 and '88, served as

Speaker of the Senate at the close of the war, and, while acting in this capacity, as Acting Governor in 1781-82; from 1782 to 1785 and from 1789 to 1792 was Governor of North Carolina; in 1788 was a member of the Convention to adopt the Federal Constitution; and from 1793 to 1799 was an active and influential member of the United States Senate. According to Wheeler, "he was vain of his literary attainments, and published in the North Carolina *University Magazine*, poetical tributes to General Francis Nash and Governor Caswell." However this may be, he was certainly an upright and honored citizen, a man of unusual scholarly attainments, and an earnest worker in the interests of his country. At the time of his death he was a Trustee of the University of North Carolina. He died at Danbury, North Carolina, in November, 1807.

ILL, THOMAS, D. D., LL.D., Clergyman, Mathematician, Author, of New Jersey, was born in New Brunswick, New Jersey, January 7th, 1818. His father, a tanner by trade, was for many years a Judge of the Superior Court of Common Pleas, and on both the paternal and the maternal side he is of English extraction. He was left an orphan at the age of ten, and two years later was apprenticed to the printer of the *Fredonian* newspaper, passing the ensuing four years in its office. While in his seventeenth year, after spending from ten to twelve months in a common school, he entered an apothecary's shop, where he served for three and a half years. In 1843 he was graduated at Harvard College, in 1845 completed his term of residence at the divinity school, and on Christmas of the same year was settled at Waltham. He is a Unitarian of the evangelical school, "but so little sectarian, or strictly denominational, that he was then invited to deliver the address before the Society of Christian Inquiry in the orthodox College of Burlington." In 1859 he succeeded Horace Mann in the Presidency of Antioch College, Yellow Springs, Ohio; and in 1862–68 was President of Harvard University. He has been a frequent contributor to the periodical and occasional literature of the day, having written poems, reviews, translations, essays, for *The Christian Examiner*, *The Religious Magazine*, *The Phonographic Magazine*, *The North American Review*, and *The Atlantic Monthly*. He has also published sermons, lectures, and addresses, and contributed several valuable papers to "The Proceedings of the American Association for the Advancement of Science." He wrote also the greater part of the articles on mathematics, etc., to be found in Appleton's "Cyclopædia," and published an "Elementary Treatise on Arithmetic," "Geometry and Faith," and "First Lessons in Geometry." It is, however, in his investigations in curves that he has exhibited a remarkable originality and fertility. He has added to the number of known curves, and simplified their expression in an admirable manner; and, by going beyond the common methods of using co-ordinates, and presenting novel combinations, has greatly extended the field of research. "It is understood that he has now in manuscript a work on curves of great value and importance."

———◆◆◆———

PPLEGATE, JOHN S., Lawyer and Bank President, of Red Bank, was born in Middletown, Monmouth county, New Jersey, August 6th, 1837. He comes of good old Jersey stock, his ancestors on both sides as far back as the year 1700 being also natives of Monmouth county, and at the period of the Revolution were active Whigs and soldiers in that heroic struggle. His parents, Joseph S. and Ann (Bray) Applegate, followed agricultural pursuits, and their son grew up amid the quiet and health-giving surroundings of farm life. His preliminary educational training was obtained in the neighboring schools, where he made good use of his opportunities. Being destined for a learned profession, his parents sent him to college, his course being taken at Madison University, at Hamilton, New York, from which he graduated in 1858, after four years study, receiving the degree of A. B. Choosing the law for a career, he pursued his studies for a time at Red Bank, and afterwards entered the office of Hon. W. L. Dayton, at Trenton. Under the superintendence of that learned lawyer and polished advocate he prosecuted his studies until his preceptor was offered and accepted the responsible position of Minister to the Court of France. Then he removed to Jersey City and completed his term of study with E. B. Wakeman. In due course he received his license as an attorney in November, 1861, and subsequently, at the February term of 1865, he was admitted as counsellor. He began and has always continued practice at Red Bank, and is acknowledged to stand among the leaders of the bar in that section. His practice lies principally in the State and county courts. He is a man of large public spirit, and has always manifested an active and intelligent interest in all projects which in his judgment would tend to the advancement of his town. Additional banking facilities being a plain necessity of the locality, he initiated a movement which resulted in the organization, in 1875, of the Second National Bank of Red Bank. His executive ability and financial standing marked him out as eminently fitted for the successful conduct of the new enterprise, and he was accordingly elected the first President of the institution. This post he has since continued to fill, and under his management the bank has secured an assured financial position and the high favor of the community. In politics he is and has always been an earnest Republican, devoting himself at all times to the promotion of his party's success in the simple faith that the country's welfare is inseparably bound up in the supremacy of Repub-

lican principles. In 1862 he was commissioned as President for Monmouth county of the Union League of America and he organized a chapter of that patriotic organization in nearly every township of the county. He was a member of the Republican State Executive Committee in 1865, and in that capacity rendered most efficient service to the cause. In 1865 he was married to Deborah C. Allen, daughter of Charles G. Allen, a prominent citizen of Red Bank.

———◆◆◆———

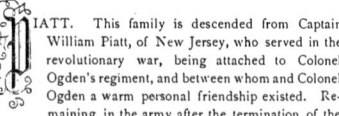

IATT. This family is descended from Captain William Piatt, of New Jersey, who served in the revolutionary war, being attached to Colonel Ogden's regiment, and between whom and Colonel Ogden a warm personal friendship existed. Remaining in the army after the termination of the war, he was detailed a member of General Arthur St. Clair's command in the campaign against the Miami Indians. This war, it will be remembered, was undertaken for the purpose of freeing the Ohio region from hostile Indians, being the first organized attempt at driving the native tribes westward. St. Clair was given command of the northwestern army, and was also appointed Governor of the Northwestern Territory. In the spring of 1791 he took the field, and during the ensuing summer Generals Wilkinson and Scott were gradually advanced with a force of some eight hundred men; the whole army numbered some fifteen hundred. In November the entire force was concentrated, and on the 4th of that month St. Clair ordered a general attack to be made, himself commanding the attacking body. The result was eminently disastrous; more than six hundred of the regulars were killed, and the remainder were utterly routed—the most signally destructive battle fought with the Indians since the defeat of Braddock. In this battle Captain Piatt unquestionably perished, but no reliable information of a definite character as to his fate ever reached his family. When last seen by his retreating comrades he was severely wounded, and was supporting himself against a tree, and his last request was that he might be given a loaded musket so that his life should be sold dearly. By his wife, Sarah, daughter of John Shotwell, of Shotwell's Landing, New Jersey, he had three children: William, Jemima and James. William studied medicine; upon graduation established himself in New York, and was for many years a leading practitioner in that city. Jemima, who was said to bear a striking resemblance to her gallant and unfortunate father, was a distinguished preacher in the Society of Friends, and was well known throughout the American branch of that religious organization. She married her cousin, Elijah Shotwell, of Plainfield, New Jersey. James removed in early life to Ohio, where he married, was a considerable land-owner, and a man of something more than local prominence. From him the noted Colonel Don Piatt, editor of the Washington *Capitol*, is descended. In New

John S. Applegate

Sharp Pub Co. Phila.

John S. Applegate

Jersey, New York and Ohio numerous representatives of the family are now living.

COOPER, JAMES E., Commander in the United States navy, late of Haddonfield, New Jersey, was the son of Benjamin and Elizabeth Cooper, of Gloucester county, New Jersey, both of whom belonged to the Society of Friends. His mother's maiden name was Hopenrie. His father was fourth in descent from William Cooper, who in the early part of the seventeenth century settled at Old Newton, Gloucester county, which has continued to be the seat of his descendants down to the fifth generation. The descendant who forms the subject of this sketch has a double claim to the remembrance and reverence of his countrymen, having won laurels as a soldier in the war of the Revolution, and as a sailor in the war of 1812. He entered "Lee's Legion" in his seventeenth year, and continued in it until the peace of 1783, serving with credit and distinction under both Lee and Marion. And distinction in such a service meant what it would require a volume to express. He took part in the storming of Stony Point; in the surprise and capture of the British garrison at Paulus Hook; in the battle of Guilford Court-House, North Carolina; in the successful operations against Forts Watson, Motte and Granby, South Carolina; in the surprise and capture of Fort Galphin, Georgia; in the triumphant attack on Augusta, Georgia; in the siege of Fort Ninety-Six, South Carolina; and in the battle of Eutaw Springs, South Carolina. His courage and urbanity made him a favorite in the army, and won the full confidence of his illustrious commander, who selected him as the bearer of despatches to Congress, and likewise to the Commander-in-Chief, the immortal Washington, who had selected the " Legion " for his body-guard at the battle of Germantown, and with whom it was always in high favor. He was also chosen by Lee to carry a flag of truce to the British commander. The seal to his military distinction was thus set by the hand of "Legion Harry" himself, him of whom General Greene declared that "few officers in Europe or America" were "held in so high a point of estimation," and that "no man in the progress of the southern campaign had equal merit with him." To have served under such a commander, and received his commendation, was in itself a splendid distinction. After the peace he turned his attention to mercantile pursuits, and, entering the mercantile marine, he made the voyage to China in 1784, soon becoming a ship-master and ship-owner, proving that he could prosecute the arts of peace as vigorously and skilfully as those of war. But though he had beaten his sword into a tiller, he showed in due time that he was as ready to wield the tiller as he had been the sword, against the enemies of his country; for, on the breaking out of the second war with Great Britain, he

again offered his services, and in May, 1812, was appointed Sailing-Master in the United States navy, in which capacity he served during the war, being honored by President Madison, after its close, with a Lieutenant's commission, dated April 22d, 1822, an especial mark of favor, no other promotions having occurred at the time, or for many years thereafter. In 1841, September 8th, he was appointed Master Commander in the navy, and continued actively in service for many years afterwards, until in his seventy-third year he was ordered on duty at the Navy Asylum in Philadelphia, in the performance of which light and not uncongenial service he passed smoothly down the long decline of his life. He died at his residence in Haddonfield, New Jersey, February 5th, 1854, in the ninety-third year of his age, the last survivor of "Lee's Legion," as he had been among its first members in all soldierly achievements and all manly qualities. He was twice married: first to Rebecca Morgan, daughter of Crlfith Morgan, who died in 1812, and by whom he had eleven children; and November 26th, 1818, to Elizabeth Clement, daughter of John Clement, of Haddonfield, a descendant in the fourth degree from Gregory Clement, of London, the regicide. By his last wife he had one child.

COOPER, BENJAMIN, Commodore in the United States navy, was the son of Commander James B. Cooper, the subject of the foregoing sketch. Entering the navy as Sailing-Master in 1809, he served with honor under Captain Lawrence on board the " Hornet " in her action with the " Peacock," February 22d, 1813, and December 9th, 1814, was appointed Lieutenant. In 1828, April 24th, he was made Master Commander, and February 28th, 1838, Captain. He died at his residence in Brooklyn, June 1st, 1851. His remains were interred in Greenwood cemetery, with military honors, Captains Stringham, Sands, Bell, Engle, and other naval officers acting as pall-bearers. He was a distinguished officer, an eminent citizen, and a pure and highminded man, a worthy son, in all respects, of the gallant and honored legionary to whom it was given to fight for his country with equal effectiveness in two wars and on two elements.

CORNELL, REV. WILLIAM, D. D., was born in 1834 in Seneca county, New York. He was the son of a farmer in moderate circumstances, and achieved his education under difficulties, which, however, disappeared one after another, and sometimes in troops, before his strong love of knowledge and resolute will. He was prepared for college by the Rev. Dr. Brown, subsequently a missionary in Japan, and entered Rutgers in 1855, with the ministry in view as his vocation. By selling books, and turning to such other avocations as offered themselves, he worked his way through the college and the seminary, and graduated with honors, winning the esteem alike of his teachers and of his associates. His first charge was at Montague, Sussex county, New Jersey, from which, after remaining one year, he went to Freehold, where he also remained a year, teaching in the institute, his health not permitting him to preach. From Freehold he went to Woodstown, Salem county, remaining five years, and faithfully preaching during the whole period; after which, his health again failing, he removed to Somerville, in 1868, and founded his "Classical Institute for both Sexes," which he conducted until his death. The seat of the institute for the first year was at the northern end of Somerville, but he subsequently purchased a lot on South street, where he erected a handsome building, which included his home as well as his school-room, and where he died. His school speedily gained a widespread reputation, and drew to it pupils from far and near. He was especially successful in training young men for college, his pupils, as was often remarked by Dr. Campbell, President of Rutgers, knowing their classics so well that it was almost idle to examine them. Throughout the eight years of arduous labor which he spent in teaching at Somerville, he occupied the pulpit on the Sabbath whenever possible, feeling that his higher mission was to preach the gospel, and finding in the fulfilment of this mission his chief delight. Nothing but sickness which utterly precluded his attendance ever prevented his preaching when called upon. And his services were not unfruitful. At Lebanon, where he long ministered to a flock without a shepherd; at Raritan, where he filled a vacancy in the pulpit of the Third Reformed Church, and everywhere indeed that he preached, he gained hearts not only for himself, but for his Master. His characteristics as a clergyman were marked and admirable. "As a minister," to quote the apt words of one who knew him well, "he was faithful; as a preacher he was full of power. His sermons were first carefully prepared, and then rewritten, so as not to present an erasure or a blot. His language was simple, like the language of the gospel, but direct, incisive, and full of hope to the believer. Whether he preached the terrors of hell or the allurements of heaven, he faithfully portrayed the whole word. Earnestness, a profound belief in all he uttered, and simplicity of diction were his strong points in preaching, and they are the points which will make any preacher strong and powerful." His zeal and sincerity were of the purest type. The vice of worldliness had no place in his character. He never preached for effect, except the effect of saving human souls, esteeming all else as vanity and foolishness. A proof of this at once striking and touching was afforded by an incident of his closing days. Requesting that his sermons should be brought to him, that he might direct what should be done with them, he deliberately looked at each, saying: "This

one converted a poor woman to God; don't destroy this; here is one which I know saved a young man's soul, for he told me so; keep that," and so on through them all. Those which he knew had converted somebody he wished preserved; but all the rest he ordered to be burned. Rarely has a soul ascended to its Maker so completely purged from the taint of earth. He died, September 11th, 1876, lamented keenly by all who knew him, and most by those who knew him best. Previously to accepting his first charge at Montague he was married to Julia Smith, of Middlebush, who survives him.

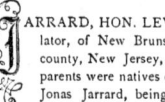ARRARD, HON. LEVI D., Merchant and Legislator, of New Brunswick, was born in Warren county, New Jersey, August 3d, 1824. Both his parents were natives of the same State, his father, Jonas Jarrard, being in his time an extensive manufacturer of wagons, plows, etc.; his mother's maiden name was Ereminah Dalrimple. The district schools of Warren county gave him educational training up to his fourteenth year, when he entered a mercantile establishment in the same county. After clerking in this connection for about four years he removed to Morris county, where he was similarly engaged for the ensuing three years. Then he commenced business on his own account, locating at Mount Freedom. By this time he had attained his twenty-first year. He successfully conducted this undertaking for two years, and then, encouraged by his success, he sought a more extensive field of operations. This he found at Parryville, Pennsylvania, in the neighborhood of Mauch Chunk. Here he pursued a prosperous career until 1850, when he again determined upon a further extension of business. For this purpose he removed to New Brunswick, New Jersey, and opened upon the river front one of the most extensive ship-chandleries in the State. This enterprise he continues to carry on, embracing all branches of ship-supplying, and it to-day occupies a front rank among concerns of its class. Since locating in New Brunswick he has become interested in and owner of vessels doing business along the Delaware & Raritan Canal. But he has not permitted his own personal interests to absorb all his energies. A man of large public spirit and decided convictions, he has taken an earnest interest in politics, local, State and national. In hearty sympathy with the principles of the Republican party, he has ever been found among its most active members, and his high intelligence, delicate tact and superior executive ability, combined with great personal magnetism, won for him, years since, the position of a leader in his section. Numerous illustrations are afforded of his popularity and influence. In 1857 and 1858 he was chosen one of the Aldermen of the city. In 1864 he was chosen to represent Middlesex county in the popular branch of the Legislature, and by successive elec-

tions served through the sessions of 1864, 1865 and 1866. Again, in 1868, he was returned to the same body, and served during the sessions of 1868 and 1869. His course in the Assembly marked him out as eminently fitted for a higher trust, and accordingly, in 1870, he was chosen as Senator for Middlesex county, and this position he held, to the marked satisfaction of his constituents and with honor to himself and the party he represents, for two terms, being re-elected in 1873. During his long term of service in both branches of the Legislature he introduced many measures of great importance; among which may be cited "A Bill for the Education and Maintenance of the Deaf and Dumb, Blind, and Feeble-Minded of the State." This was presented during the session of 1876. It provided for the establishment of three institutions: one at New Brunswick for the deaf and dumb; another at Trenton for the blind, and a third at Bordentown for the feeble-minded. Passed by both chambers, it encountered a veto at the hands of Governor Bedle, but nevertheless came very near enactment, only two votes being lacking to pass it over the veto. The measure was then divided into three separate bills, all of which passed the Legislature, but failed to become law, the governor withholding his signature. During his career in the Senate he served upon the Committees on Municipal Corporations, Railroads and Canals, and Reform School, being Chairman of each; he also acted on many other important committees in both branches of the Legislature after his first entrance into the legislative halls. As a legislator he was always a hard and efficient worker, guarding carefully and untiringly promoting the immediate interests of his constituents, and protecting those of his party generally from aggression by representatives of a different faith from other counties. He has always been a devoted advocate of the maintenance of the Union, and during the rebellion he was among the staunchest supporters of the administration, labored to his utmost for the successful prosecution of the war, and contributed largely of his means in caring for the widows and orphans of the soldiers. He was a district Delegate to the Republican National Convention at Chicago, in 1868, and also a Delegate at large to the Philadelphia Convention, in 1872. As a citizen of New Brunswick he has always been distinguished for his ready and generous aid to all movements for the improvement and development of the city. He is one of the Directors and largest stockholders in the Masonic Hall, one of the finest and most extensive structures in the city, containing an elegant opera house, handsome assembly rooms, and lodge rooms of the order, and a large number of lawyers' offices, etc. The erection of the building was commenced in 1870, and completed in 1874, at a cost of $285,000. He has been a Director and stockholder in most of the loan associations of New Brunswick, and holds the same relations to the New Brunswick & Cranberry Turnpike Company. It will thus be seen that his life has been an exceptionally busy one, and not only so,

but one whose activity has redounded very largely to the advantage of the city in which his lot has been immediately cast, and to the welfare of the community at large, the influence of a well-spent life widening and widening continually, and comprehending a sphere far more extended than is directly recognized. He was married on August 31st, 1844, to Jane Trowbridge, daughter of David Trowbridge, of Mount Freedom, Morris county, who for many years served as a justice of the peace in that county, and was much respected.

ALL, REV. BAYNARD RUST, D. D., Educator, Author, late of Brooklyn, New York, was born in Philadelphia, Pennsylvania, in 1798. In 1820 he was graduated from the Union College, and subsequently studied, and also graduated, at the Princeton Theological Seminary. He was for several years pastor of a church, and President of a college in Bloomington, Indiana; and afterward pastor of a congregation, and principal of a flourishing academy in Bedford, Pennsylvania. At various times he was connected with educational institutions in Bordentown and Trenton, New Jersey, and Poughkeepsie and Newburgh, New York. In 1852, or thereabout, he removed to Brooklyn, New York; officiated for some time as Principal of the Park Institute; and during the last few years of his life found pleasure and occupation in preaching to the destitute and the lower classes, and in administering, to the extent of his ability, to their spiritual comforts and material needs. He published a "Latin Grammar" in 1828; "The New Purchase," in 1843; "Something for Everybody;" "Teaching a Science;" and "Frank Freeman's Barber Shop," 1852. He possessed an extensive circle of friends and admirers in the States of New Jersey and New York, and wherever he was known was loved and respected for his unostentatious good deeds and charities, and his many abilities, natural and acquired. His "Latin Grammar" has been frequently and warmly eulogized as a scholarly production; and his story of "Frank Freeman" had at one time quite an extended popularity. He died at Brooklyn, New York, January 23d, 1863.

URAND, ASHER BROWN, Painter and Engraver, of New Jersey, was born in Jefferson, New Jersey, August 21st, 1796. His paternal ancestors were Huguenots. He learned the art of engraving in the shop of his father, a skilful watchmaker. In 1812 he was apprenticed to Peter Maverick, engraver, with whom, in 1817, he became a partner. His engraving of "Trumbull's Declaration of Independence," his first large work, cost him three years of labor, but at once brought him into favorable notice. The national portrait gallery contains many of his heads; and his "Musidora" and "Ariadne" are excellent specimens of art. After ten years' practice as a painter, he relinquished engraving in 1835, and devoted himself chiefly to landscape-painting. His pictures are pleasing in color and tone, and evince a high degree of poetic feeling and appreciation. The principal of his figure-pieces are, "An Old Man's Reminiscences," "The Wrath of Peter Stuyvesant," "God's Judgment on Gog," "The Dance on the Battery," and "The Capture of André." Among the more notable of his landscapes are, "The Morning and Evening of Life," a pair, "Lake Scene—Sunset," "The Rainbow;" wood-scene, "Primeval Forest," "In The Woods," "The Symbol" from Goldsmith's "Deserted Village," "Franconia Mountains," and "Reminiscences of Catskill Cloves." In 1854 he painted a portrait of the poet, William Cullen Bryant. He has filled with marked ability the office of President of the National Academy of Design. His son, John Durand a scholarly gentleman, and one well-versed in art and artistic matters, has for several years past conducted *The Crayon*, a monthly publication specially devoted to the fine arts.

IVENS, JOHN U., of Belvidere, Lawyer, was born in the village of Vernon, Sussex county, New Jersey, May 25th, 1834. His father was John Givens, the name also of his grandfather, who was a soldier in the war of 1812. After the usual attendance at the common schools, he entered the academy of William Rankin, at Deckertown, New Jersey, becoming afterwards a teacher, teaching in the public schools of Warren county for about nine years, towards the close of which period he began the reading of law, under the instructions of the Hon. A. J. Rogers. In 1862 stimulated by patriotism, and not unmindful of his descent from a soldier, he enlisted in the 31st New Jersey Infantry, and was subsequently promoted to a Lieutenancy. On the expiration of the term of service of the 31st, and the mustering out of the regiment, he assisted in organizing the 2d New Jersey Cavalry, of which he was commissioned First Lieutenant. His regiment was sent to the Southwest, where it was engaged in the several battles with General Price, and also in the capture of Mobile. In all those engagements, as in all subsequent ones, he showed himself a worthy descendant of the soldier of 1812. At Egypt Station, in acknowledgment of his bravery on the field, he was assigned to the Captaincy of Company H, made vacant by the death of Captain Gallagher, killed while assaulting a stockade at that place. His entire record in the war is one of gallantry and soldierly conduct. At the close of the war he resumed his legal studies, under Thomas Rays, of Newton, and was admitted to the bar in 1870, having previously, however, served two terms in the New Jersey Assembly, so impatient were the people to express their sense of his abilities and

of his brilliant military record. On his admission to the bar he settled at Belvidere, where he has already acquired a large practice which is steadily increasing. Since 1873 he has been associated in the practice with Mr. Harris, under the firm-name of Givens & Harris. In politics he is a Democrat, devotedly attached to his party, and, as may be readily believed, cherished by his party in return. By many of his political friends of Warren he was pressed as a candidate for Congress at the late election, and no doubt would have received the nomination, had not another quarter of the district claimed it, on the ground of geographical rotation, not a very intelligible ground perhaps in the light of reason, but potent enough in the somewhat mixed light that "beats upon" the average voter. But he is still young, and can well afford to bide his time. He undoubtedly has a political future.

OTTER, WILLIAM S., was born February 26th, 1833, at Pottersville, New Jersey. He is the son of Samuel Potter, a farmer of that place, whose father, Colonel Jonathan Potter, was long connected with the New Jersey militia, and whose grandfather and great-grandfather both served through the revolutionary war, the latter as Colonel, the former as Captain. The family, one of the oldest in the State, is of English extraction. As early as 1696 it had struck its roots deep and spread them wide in the soil of New Jersey, if we may judge from the ancient records of Newark, the grant for the site of the public buildings of the town in that year describing the property granted as being bounded on the west and south by lands of Samuel Potter. The family is thus not only one of the oldest in the State, but identified with the origin and growth of its chief city. Young William attended the public schools until he was fourteen years of age, when he entered as clerk a mercantile establishment at Morristown, where he remained one year, after which he served six years in the same capacity at Pottersville. He then undertook farming near Freehold, following it until 1855, at which time he embarked in the manufacture of mowing machines and agricultural implements in general, prosecuting the business for two years. Having quit it, he resided for a short time in Freehold, from which he removed to the city of New York, and engaged in business there. At the outbreak of the civil war, he, having meanwhile become a member of the celebrated 7th Regiment, went with his comrades to the defence of the national capital, and remained with the regiment until the term of enlistment expired. On his return he removed to Pluckemin, New Jersey, of revolutionary fame, and, in company with his brother, carried on merchandising. While residing in Pluckemin he was elected a member of the Town Committee, of which he was made Chairman, a position in which he rendered valuable aid in filling the quotas of the town. In 1867 he was elected by the Democrats Surrogate of Somerset county, and filled the office for five years, to the satisfaction of all parties, his trained business capacity and varied experience of life admirably fitting him for the complex and responsible duties of the place. He was re-nominated by his party in 1872, but, with the rest of the local Democratic ticket, shared the general disaster attending upon the Greeley campaign. He has been for four years a member of the Somerville Street Commission, and Secretary of the Somerset County Agricultural Society, since its organization in 1870. He is also a Director of the Somerville Building Loan Association. He is now engaged as a contractor and in the insurance business. He is, besides, at present Secretary of the Speaker of the New Jersey Assembly. He was married in 1863 to Miss Van Derbeck, of Lamington, New Jersey.

URAND, JAMES M., of Newark, Diamond-Broker and Manufacturer of Fine Jewelry, was born in Essex county, New Jersey, March 23d, 1813. He is a son of Henry Durand and Electra Baldwin, natives of New Jersey, with which the family, on both sides, have long been identified. He was educated at South Orange. Leaving school at the age of sixteen he went to New York city to learn the trade of watch-case making, after learning which he settled at Camptown, New Jersey, now known as Irvington, one of the suburbs of Newark, where he associated himself with his uncle, under the firm-name of C. & J. M. Durand, for the manufacture of watch-cases and machinery in all its branches, he superintending the former part of the business, and his uncle the latter. In 1837 he retired from the Camptown establishment, and removed to Newark, becoming the company in the firm of Taylor, Baldwin & Co., jewelry manufacturers. This firm was succeeded by that of Baldwin & Co., in which he was also the company, the latter firm being succeeded in turn by that of Baldwin & Durand, the business of the three firms together continuing for a period of thirteen years. Between the retirement of Baldwin from the last mentioned firm and the forming of the present firm there were two other firms, Durand & Annin, and Durand, Carter & Co., the latter expiring in 1862, when the present one, Durand & Co., was formed, he being, as will be observed, the only constant quantity throughout these combinations, a fact due in part no doubt to circumstances, yet in some measure expressive of the stability and persistence of his strongly marked character. It is seldom mere accident that leads one to keep his place in the figure during so lively a change of partners. A firm foot and a level head are apt to have something to do with it. Certain it is at any rate that he has both of these requisites to a successful business career, as also that his own career has been in fact eminently successful. For forty years he has been a leading manufacturer in Newark, and his prosperity, instead of standing still or waning, is increasing year by year, not even the present hard times materially checking it, although his business is in itself restricted and exclusive, diamonds being a very dispensable sort of luxury to the million, and hardly an absolute necessity even to the upper ten thousand. His establishment, which is large and admirably arranged for its purposes, employs, when running at full force, some 150 men, the products being of the finest jewelry, and the annual sales, in good times, amounting to over $600,000. He trades directly with the retailers, supplying houses in all quarters of the United States, though of course not many houses in any one quarter, the commodities being too costly for general use. It speaks well for his business, and still better, perhaps, for his management of it, that it successfully weathered the late financial storm, and has steadily held on through the succeeding dead calm, ready to catch the first breath of the returning breeze, and go forward at the old rate of speed or at a higher one. Of his marked abilities as a business man there can be no question. That they are not questioned by his fellow-citizens may be inferred from the various trusts to which at different times he has been called, having been an Alderman of the Ninth Ward for two years, and being at present one of the Trustees of the American Trust Company, of Newark, a Director of several of the most prominent Fire Insurance Companies in that city, and President of the Merchants' National Bank. He was married in 1832 to Sarah Ann Carroll, of New York city.

UNTER, REV. ANDREW, D. D., Chaplain in the Revolutionary Army, Professor of Mathematics and Astronomy, late of Burlington, New Jersey, was born in New Jersey *circe* 1750, and studied at Princeton College, graduating from that institution in 1772. During the conflict between the colonies and Great Britain he labored with fearless zeal as an encouraging counsellor and spiritual exhorter among the men of '76, and, at a later date, engaged in teaching in a classical school at Woodbury. He was then occupied for a time in agricultural pursuits, and the cultivation of a farm, on the Delaware near Trenton. From 1804 to 1808 he presided as Professor of Mathematics and Astronomy in his *Alma Mater;* and, in the course of the following year, became the head of an academy in Bordentown, New Jersey. He afterwards accepted a Chaplaincy in the Washington navy-yard. In the Trenton newspaper, of Monday, December 30th, 1799, is the following notice: "The Rev. Mr. Hunter, who officiated yesterday for Mr. Armstrong, after reading the President's proclamation respecting the general mourning for the death of General Washington, gave the intimation in substance, as follows: 'Your pastor desires me to say on the present mournful occasion, that while one sentiment—to mourn the death and honor the memory of General Washington—penetrates every breast, the proclamation which you have just heard read, he doubts not, will be duly attended to; yet believing, as he does, that he but anticipates the wishes of those for whom the intimation is given, Mr. Armstrong requests the female part of his audience in the city of Trenton and Maidenhead, as a testimony of respect for, and condolence with Mrs. Washington, to wear for three months, during their attendance on divine service, such badges of mourning as their discretion may direct.'" His second wife was Mary Stockton, a daughter of Richard Stockton, signer of the Declaration of Independence. He had an uncle, also Rev. Andrew Hunter, who was a pastor in Cumberland county, New Jersey, 1746–1760. He married Ann Stockton, a cousin of Richard Stockton, and died in 1775. His widow was buried in the Trenton church-yard, in October, 1800, and the funeral sermon on that occasion was delivered by President Smith. He was a loyal and learned divine, a man of excellent parts, scrupulous in the performance of every duty, and tireless in his efforts to improve the moral condition of those around him, and to promote the welfare of his State and country. He died in Burlington, New Jersey, February 24th, 1823.

IRK, HON. WILLIAM HENRY, Builder and State Senator, of Newark, son of the late John H. Kirk, and descended from a Hollandish family, resident in New Jersey from early colonial times, was born in New York, 1813. Having received a sound English education in New York, he moved with his parents to New Jersey, whence they had originally come, and which they had always regarded as their home. Here he served an apprenticeship to the trade of carpentry, subsequently studied architecture, and eventually established himself as an architect and builder. His business, founded on the substantial basis of a thorough knowledge of its details, rapidly increased; his reputation for reliability extended, and his operations spread far beyond the limits of the town to which they were at first confined: among his works are to be included many of the finest public and private buildings in the State. Occupying so conspicuous a position in business circles, he naturally became prominent in public affairs. In 1871 he was elected one of the Chosen Free-holders of Essex county, and this was followed in 1873 by his election, on the Republican ticket, to the Legislative Assembly of the State. In the lower house he quickly made his presence felt by his able and determined opposition to the Reformed School Bill, a measure introduced in the interest of the church of Rome; his action being so well to the liking of his constituents that he was re-elected in the following year. During his second term the Roman Catholic Protectory Bill was introduced, and was met by him with determined opposition. Owing to his efforts the bill was greatly reduced in its demands, but he was unable to bar its passage. Carried up into the Senate, the effect of his vigorous denunciation of the bill in the House—aided by his personal appeals to Senators—awakened a spirit of resistance that in the end determined in its defeat; and the constitutional amendment of 1875 removed the matter beyond the chances of future legislation. In the year that he won this substantial victory he was nominated State Senator, and so entirely had his conduct received the popular approval that he was elected by an altogether unprecedented majority of some 4,000. In this election the whole Romanist interest of the district was brought to bear against him, making his success the more striking, and the more strikingly convincing of the esteem in which he is held. As a Senator he has evinced the same strong qualities that made him a leader in the lower house, and he is regarded in Newark as a worthy representative of the first city of the State.

ACWHORTER, REV. ALEXANDER, D. D.— conferred by Yale College in 1776—an eminent Presbyterian divine, late of Newark, New Jersey, was born in Newcastle county, Delaware, July 15th, 1734, and graduated from the New Jersey College in 1757. His father, Hugh MacWhorter, was a native of Ireland. In 1759 he settled near Newark, New Jersey; and from 1764 to 1766 was employed by the Synod of New York and Philadelphia in a mission to North Carolina. In 1775 he was sent by Congress to the western counties of North Carolina, to persuade the numerous royalists of that State to adopt the patriot cause, and aid in resisting the growing tyranny of the mother country. Near the close of 1776 he hastened to the army encamped on the Pennsylvania shore, opposite Trenton, to consult concerning the protection of New Jersey, and was present at the council of war which advised the passage of the Delaware, and the surprise of the Hessian troops. In 1778, at the solicitation of General Knox, he accepted the Chaplaincy of his artillery brigade, and enjoyed friendly relations with Washington during the few months that he held this office. In 1779 he accepted a pastorate and the Presidency of Charlotte Academy, in Mecklenburg county, North Carolina; but the place being captured by Cornwallis, he lost his library and furniture, and, fearing further attacks, was recalled, and finally reinstalled at Newark, New Jersey. In 1788 he was a prominent actor in the settlement of the confession of faith, and the formation of the constitution of the Presbyterian Church of the United States. He was for thirty-five years a Trustee of the College of New Jersey; and, after the burning of the college buildings in 1802, the collection of funds for a new edifice was chiefly due to his influence, and personal solicitations in New England. In 1800 he published a "Century Sermon," describing the settlement and progress of the town of Newark, New Jersey, and its environs; and in 1803 a collection of sermons, in 2 vols., 8vo. His deep religious impressions began to influence him strongly when but sixteen years of age; and after being ordained in 1759 he was minister of the First Presbyterian Church, with slight interruptions, for a period extending over nearly a half century. He possessed

Romeo F. Chabert M.D.

Chabert. M.D.

a vigorous and sound intellect; and was respected for the extent of his learning, and his earnest piety as a minister. His wife, Mary (Cumming) MacWhorter, was a sister of Rev. A. Cumming, of Boston, Massachusetts. In the "History of Newark," by Dr. Stearn, is found a full account of his life and labors, as patriot and pastor, through the troublous days of the struggle for independence down to the time of his decease. After a career of remarkable usefulness, and experiences of a varied and suggestive nature, he died at Newark, New Jersey, July 20th, 1807.

ACON, REV. GEORGE B., late of Orange, New Jersey, was born in New Haven, Connecticut, May 23d, 1836, and was the son of the venerable Dr. Leonard Bacon. A delicate boy and youth, his studies were more or less interrupted. After due preparation he became a student at Yale College, as a member of the class of 1856, but was unable to complete the usual course of study on account of ill health. He received, however, his degree in due time. After leaving college he sailed with Commodore Foote to Japan, and before his return home visited also China and Siam. After this season of foreign travel, which greatly benefited his health, he entered the ministry of the Congregational Church, and in 1861 accepted a call to the pastorate of the church in Orange. "The Valley Church," Oliver Johnson says in *The Orange Journal*, "was the chief scene of his life and work, to which he lovingly gave his service by giving his whole heart. It was precious to him beyond all expression. He would have faithfully loved and served any flock of the Lord Jesus over which he might have been set in charge, for his nature was tenderness, sympathy, and fidelity; but this church was his first charge, and he their first pastor, ordained among them in 1861, when he was twenty-five years of age. He and they had wrought upon each other from the beginning with a subtle interchange, an unconscious reciprocation of mental, moral, spiritual influence, until the union had become in their mind and his sacred almost as wedding-bonds." Dr. Bacon was a valued contributor to the press. He died September 15th, 1876.

HABERT, ROMEO F., M. D., Physician, of Hoboken, is a native of London, England, in which metropolis he was born, August 9th, 1828. His father, Xavier Chabert, was born in Avignon, France, and was an officer under Napoleon Bonaparte; his mother, Mary Ann Falser, was a native of Bristol, England. In the year 1830 the family removed to the United States, and established their residence in the city of New York. The education of Romeo Chabert was

43

obtained at the celebrated French school of Peugnet & Brothers, in New York city. The medical profession had been decided upon, and in the year 1854 he commenced the study of medicine, matriculating at the New York University. He graduated from the university in the spring of 1856, having had the advantage of studying under Dr. Valentine Mott, and soon afterwards commenced professional practice in New York. He remained there one year, and during that time he attended and graduated from the New York Ophthalmic School. In 1858 he removed to Hoboken, and there he has since resided, actively engaged in professional labors, and at present stands in the front rank. He is connected with the New Jersey State Medical Society, the District Medical Society of Hudson county, the New Jersey Academy of Medicine, and the Jersey City Pathological Society. He has been a delegate from the State Medical Society of New Jersey to those of New York and Massachusetts, and was a delegate to the American Medical Association, in 1864, from the Hudson County Medical Society. For one year he acted as the Physician for the city of Hoboken, and one year Superintendent of Public Schools. For fifteen years he has been connected with St. Mary's Hospital, of Hoboken, in the capacity of Attending Surgeon, and during the last two years he acted as Consulting Surgeon. This hospital, it may be remarked, is the first charity hospital founded in the State. In 1860 Dr. Chabert was commissioned Division Surgeon of the Second Division New Jersey State National Guard, under General E. R. V. Wright. He is enthusiastically attached to his profession, is still a close student, and is a hard and earnest as well as an eminently successful worker. He was married, October 21st, 1847, to Harriet A. Hope, of New York.

IELD, HON. RICHARD STOCKTON, LL. D., Jurist, Judge, Attorney-General of New Jersey, late of Princeton, New Jersey, was born at Whitehill, Burlington county, New Jersey, December 31st, 1803, and graduated from the New Jersey College in 1821. The history of his family descent is veiled in some obscurity, but it is given as certain that he was descended from the same family as John Field, the celebrated English astronomer of the middle of the sixteenth century, who was the first to avail himself of the Copernican system as a basis for calculations for practical purposes, in his "Ephemeris Anni 1557 currentis, Juxta Copernici et Reinhaldi Canones fideliter per Joannem Field." This work, which was of considerable magnitude, was undertaken at the suggestion of the famous Dr. Dee, and was probably the first publication which gave to the discoveries and researches of Copernicus the attention and prominence they merited. He was born about the year 1520, and was a son of Richard Fielde, of Ardsley, who, it is asserted, was a grandson of William Fielde, or Feld, of Bradford, who died in 1480. In 1555, the year preceding the publication of his first "Ephemeris," he was admitted Fellow of Lincoln's College, Oxford. About 1560 he married Jane Amyas, a daughter of John Amyas, of Kent, and removed from London, where he had been living, to Ardsley, where he died in 1587. He published an "Ephemeris" for 1558, and another for 1559, in each of which he sustained with increasing force and earnestness the value of the system that he had been instrumental in introducing into his native country. "It was in recognition of the great service which he had thus rendered to the cause of science that he received a patent in 1558, authorizing him to wear as a crest over his family arms *a red right arm* issuing from the clouds and supporting a golden sphere, thereby intimating the splendor of the Copernican discovery. There is a seal in the possession of the family at Princeton which was no doubt handed down from one generation to another: on one side is the family coat-of-arms; on another is the crest before referred to—an arm supporting a globe; and on the third side ' R. F.,' the initials of the name of Robert Field, the emigrant ancestor of the family in this country. John Field had nine children, from the second of whom, Mathew, born at Ardsley, in 1563, it has been attempted to trace the American family of that name. This, however, is considered to be erroneous, while it is admitted that the American family are descended from William of Bradford, the supposed great-grandfather of the astronomer, which, if correct, would make Richard Fielde, the father of John, and John Fielde, the known ancestor of the emigrant, first cousins." William Fielde, deceased in 1559, had a son, also William, who died in 1619, leaving Robert, born about 1605, who married, May 18th, 1630, Elizabeth Taylor, with whom he came to New England in 1635, or nine years later. In 1645 he removed with his family to Newtown, Long Island, and with others received from Governor Keift a patent for a tract of land known as the Flushing Patent, which was dated October 10th, 1645. He had five children; the second, Anthony, died in 1691, and had two children, the eldest of whom, John, settled in Bound Brook, New Jersey, in 1685, and was the founder of the family in that State. His direct descendants, as far as they can be traced, are Robert Field, born January 6th, 1694; married Mary, daughter of Samuel and Susanna Taylor, by whom he had Robert, born May 9th, 1723, and married Mary, daughter of Oswald and Lydia Peale. He died January 29th, 1775, and had posthumous issue, Robert C. Field, born April 5th, 1775. He graduated at Princeton College in 1793, and in 1797 married Abby, daughter of Richard Stockton and Annis Boudinot. He died in 1810, leaving five children. He was also a nephew of Richard Field, one of the signers of the Declaration of Independence. In the year following his father's death he removed with his family to Princeton, where Mrs. Field's family resided, and there received his

education, being eventually graduated with high honors by Princeton College. He then entered upon a course of legal studies with his maternal uncle, the eminent jurist, Richard Stockton, and in February, 1825, was admitted to the bar. He afterward removed to Salem, in his native State, where he was engaged in professional labors until 1832, the date of his return to Princeton. For several years he was a member of the State Legislature, and in February, 1838, received from Governor Pennington the appointment of Attorney-General, which office he resigned, however, in 1841. He was an influential and leading member of the convention which met at Trenton, May 14th, 1844, and formed the present constitution of the State; and when, in 1851, it was resolved to form an association of the surviving members of that convention, he was chosen to deliver the address at its first annual meeting. That address, delivered February 1st, 1853, has been printed, and contains an eloquent memorial of the great convention which, sixty-six years before, met in Philadelphia, and, with Washington as its President, formed the Constitution of the United States. In the New Jersey Historical Society, whose third President he was at the time of his death, he always took a warm and generous interest; and to its publications contributed his most elaborate work, "The Provincial Courts of New Jersey, with Sketches of the Bench and Bar." It forms the third volume of the "Collections," and was the subject of two discourses delivered by him in January and May, 1848. At the meeting of the society, in September, 1851, he read a valuable paper on the "Trial of the Rev. William Tennent for Perjury, in 1742," which was printed in the proceedings of the meeting; and to the *Princeton Review*, July, 1852, contributed the leading article on "The Publications of the New Jersey Historical Society," noticing especially "The Papers of Governor Lewis Morris." In 1851 he was elected one of the Executive Committee, and held this position until 1865, when, on the elevation of Hon. James Parker to the presidency, at the decease of Hon. Joseph C. Hornblower, he became Vice-President. In 1868, on the death of the former, he succeeded him in the Presidency. At the annual meeting, in January, 1865, he delivered an "Address on the Life and Character of Chief-Justice Hornblower;" and at the January meeting, in 1869, a similar one on his predecessor, President Parker. He was also deeply interested in the public education system of his State and country, and upon the organization of the State Normal School, in 1855, was chosen President of the Board of Trustees. This position he filled with admirable energy and ability until the day of his decease, and every annual report made to the Legislature by the board was made by him. For several years he presided as Professor in the law school connected with Princeton College, "which owed its very existence to his energy and talent," and in 1859 his *Alma Mater* conferred upon him the degree of Doctor of Laws. During the conflict between the North and South "he was a staunch supporter of the government," and took a decided stand relative to certain constitutional views and theories, which he upheld with energy and warmth. July 4th, 1861, by request of his fellow-townsmen, he delivered an oration, with "The Constitution not a Compact between Sovereign States" as his subject and point of departure. On the death of Hon. John R. Thomson, a Senator in Congress from New Jersey, he was appointed, in the following November, by Governor Olden, to fill the unexpired term. January 21st, 1863, he was appointed, by Lincoln, Judge of the United States District Court for the District of New Jersey. While serving as a member of the Senate he delivered a speech, "or rather argument," on the discharge of State prisoners, January 7th, 1863, which excited the attention of a large portion of the Republican party, and its supporters of the press. He therein defended the position that the right to suspend the writ of habeas corpus was vested in the President, and not in Congress. On taking his seat upon the bench of the United States District Court he delivered "a most learned and excellent charge" to the grand jury, which has since been printed in a pamphlet of twenty-four pages. In his judicial life he has been described by District-Attorney Keasbey as "a wise, upright and fearless and merciful judge." The same gentleman then continues: "Only one decision of his was ever reversed; that was one in which the Supreme Court were at first almost evenly divided, and ordered a new argument. . . . . He had a keen perception of the real point and merits of a case. . . . . He was fully acquainted with the fountains of English eloquence, and his mind was so stored with the fruits of his learning that he had a rare facility of expression. He always preferred to charge juries or decide cases on the spot. He could always do it better than if he stopped to think or write. I think that if we could reproduce simply his addresses to prisoners about to be sentenced, they would be striking models of manly and tender exhortation." He cherished a warm admiration for Lincoln, and, February 12th, 1866, the anniversary of the President's birthday, at the request of the Legislature of New Jersey, delivered an excellent oration on the life and character of that great citizen and statesman. At the Centennial Celebration of the American Whig Society of the College of New Jersey, in June, 1869, he delivered his last public address, "and it is one marked by great purity of style and graceful erudition," on his favorite theme of education. His various contributions to the New Jersey "Collections," and his numerous discourses and addresses, are valued additions to American special literature, and contain much material of permanent interest to the general student, as well as to the historian and antiquary. In April, 1870, while in the discharge of his duties on the bench, he was stricken with a paralysis, and after uttering some incoherent remarks fell senseless from his seat. He was then carried from the court-room to his home, where, after lingering a few weeks in a totally unconscious state, he died, May 25th, 1870. In 1831, while

residing at Salem, he married Mary Ritchie, by whom he had five children. She died, September 8th, 1852. He is thus described by Charles Henry Hart, LL. B., historiographer of the Numismatic and Antiquarian Society of Philadelphia: "One of the most striking points of his character, and one to be fondly cherished, for it reveals better, perhaps, than any other could, the inmost recesses of his heart, was his warm love of nature and of nature's works. The spacious grounds about his residence at Princeton were remarkable for the rich collection of trees and flowers there cultivated, comprising specimens from the remotest parts of the earth. These he tended with an almost parental affection, and the name of each, with its peculiarity and locality, was firmly fastened on his memory. He attended the services of the Protestant Episcopal Church, and in its councils was an active worker, being repeatedly a Delegate both to the Diocesan and General Conventions, etc."

ROBESON, JAMES M., Lawyer, born November 1st, 1819, near Belvidere, the county-seat of Warren county, New Jersey, was admitted to the bar in the year 1848, and held the office of Prosecutor of the Pleas for the county of Warren for a term of five years. He was appointed by the Legislature of the State of New Jersey, in 1872, Law Judge for the county of Warren for the term of five years, which office he held for two years, and resigned and returned to the practice of the law in his native county of Warren.

PARKE, BENJAMIN, Jurist, Judge, President of the Indiana Historical Society, late of Salem, Indiana, was born in New Jersey in 1777. He was one of the earliest of those hardy and enterprising Western pioneers who carried civilization with them into the lonely wilds of the Indian country, and settled in Indiana in 1799 or 1800. He was a delegate to Congress from that Territory in 1805–1808; and subsequently was appointed by Mr. Jefferson a Judge of the District Court, which office he held until his decease. He was for several years President of the Indiana Historical Society, and during his administration of its affairs ably assisted in promoting its development and prosperity. He died at Salem, Indiana, July 12th, 1835. His name is associated with the early annals of his adopted State; and he was always a prime mover in the various measures devised and carried into execution to assist in the furtherance of its general interests.

FORCE, PETER, Historian, Journalist, late of Washington, District of Columbia, was born at Passaic Falls, New Jersey, November 26th, 1790. William Force, his father, a revolutionary soldier, moved to New York city in 1793. In that place he learned the printer's trade, and in 1812 was chosen to fill the Presidential Chair of the Typographers' Society. In November, 1815, he removed to Washington, where he began the publication of *The National Calendar*, in 1820, and continued it with varying success till 1836. From November 12th, 1823, to February 2d, 1830, he published also *The National Journal*, a political newspaper, which was the official organ during the administration of John Quincy Adams. He served for several years as City Councilman and Alderman; from 1836 to 1840 presided as Mayor of the city of Washington; rose by successive steps to the rank of Major-General of Militia in 1860, and was Vice-President, then President, of the National Institute for the Promotion of Science, at the capital. In 1833 he made a contract with the United States government for the preparation and publication of a documentary history of the American colonies, of which nine folio volumes have since appeared, covering the period from March, 1774, to the end of 1776, and embodying original documents illustrating the history of the Revolution. He prepared a tenth volume, which is, however, yet unpublished. This important work occupied him for over thirty-five years, and in its prosecution he gathered a collection of books, manuscripts, maps, and papers relating to American history, which in completeness and value is not equalled by any other collection in the world on the same subject. He has published also four volumes of historical tracts, relating chiefly to the origin and settlement of the American colonies; " Grinnell Land," 1852; and " Record of Auroral Phenomena," 1856. His collection, MSS., books, etc., now forms a part of the Congressional Library. His son, Manning Ferguson Force, who graduated at Harvard University in 1845, was a Brigadier-General in the war for the Union, appointed August 11th, 1863; and March 13th, 1865, for distinguished services, received the appointment of Brevet Major-General. He died at Washington, January 23d, 1868.

POLLOCK, REV. SHEPPARD (OSCIUSCO, D. D., Presbyterian Clergyman, Professor of Rhetoric and Logic, Author, brother of Rev. Henry Kollock, D. D., late of Elizabethtown, New Jersey, was born in that place, June 29th, 1795, and graduated from Princeton College in 1812. He subsequently filled the position of Professor of Rhetoric and Logic in the University of North Carolina. In June, 1814, he was licensed to preach, and in May, 1818, was ordained pastor of the Presbyterian Church in Oxford, North Carolina. From 1825 to 1835 he filled the pastorate of the Presbyterian Church in Norfolk, Virginia, and afterwards was zealously occupied in pastoral labors in Burlington and Greenwich, New Jersey. In 1822 he published an edition of " Henry Kollock's Sermons, with Memoir," four vols., 8vo.; and at different periods: " Ministerial Character," " Best Method of Delivering Sermons," " Eulogy on Edmund M. Mason," " On Duelling," " On the Perseverance of the Saints," and " Pastoral Reminiscences," New York, 12mo., 1849. He died at Elizabethtown, New Jersey, April 7th, 1865.

DE CAMP, REAR-ADMIRAL JOHN, United States Navy, late of Burlington, was born at Morristown, New Jersey, in 1812. On October 1st, 1827, he received the appointment of Midshipman in the navy, from the State of Florida, and was first put on active service in the sloop " Vandalia," on the Brazilian Squadron, in 1829-30. He was promoted to Passed Midshipman on June 10th, 1833. In 1837 he was on duty on the frigate " Constellation," of the West India Squadron, and on February 28th, 1838, was appointed Lieutenant. He was again on the Brazilian station in 1840, being attached to the sloop " Peacock," and to the sloop " Boston," of the same squadron, during 1845–46. In the war with Mexico in 1846–47 he distinguished himself at the battle of Vera Cruz. In 1850 he was ordered to the Pacific Squadron on the sloop " Falmouth," and in 1854 to the coast of Africa, attached to the frigate " Constitution," receiving his commission as Commander on September 14th, 1855. Subsequently he was appointed Lighthouse Inspector, and was attached to the Brooklyn navyyard in that capacity. He was next appointed to the store-ship " Relief," and in 1861, on the outbreak of the rebellion, he was ordered to the command of the steam sloop " Iroquois," on the West Gulf Blockading Squadron. The " Iroquois," which was one of the fleet of Flag-Officer Farragut, which made the passage of Forts Jackson and Philip on April 24th, 1862, had been placed on picket duty about a mile in advance of the main squadron, on the night of the 23d. In the passage of the forts she was in the second division, under Captain Bell. Early on the morning of April 24th the " Iroquois " hotly engaged the forts, and shortly after four o'clock a rebel ram and a gunboat, which had run astern of her, poured into her a destructive fire of grapeshot and langrage, the latter being composed mostly of copper-slugs. Driving off the gunboat with an 11-inch shell and a stand of canister, the " Iroquois " proceeded, and in a little while, still under a terribly severe fire from Fort St. Philip, as she was passing that fort, she was attacked by five or six rebel steamers, but giving each a broadside of shell as she passed, succeeded in completely destroying them. Four miles farther down the river she captured forty rebel soldiers and a well-equipped gunboat. The

"Iroquois" during the fight was badly injured in her hull, besides having eight of her men killed and twenty-four wounded. From this time forward Commander De Camp took active part in all the engagements on the Mississippi up to and including the capture of Vicksburg. He was commissioned Captain July 16th, 1862, for gallantry at New Orleans. In 1863-64 he commanded the frigate "Wabash," of the South Atlantic Squadron, and was commissioned Commodore September 28th, 1866. He was placed in charge of the "Potomac," store-ship, during 1866-67 at Pensacola, and performed his last active duty as commander of the same vessel while she was stationed at Philadelphia as receiving-ship in 1868-69. He was made Rear-Admiral of the Retired List on July 13th, 1870. Eighteen of the forty-three years he was in the service he passed in active duties at sea, being known during that time as one of the bravest and ablest of the old school of naval officers. An illustration of his bravery is given in the fact that, on one occasion, while ill, he caused himself to be fastened in the chains of his vessel during an engagement, and lost part of one of his ears by a piece of shell from a rebel mortar. In 1871 Admiral De Camp took up his residence in Burlington, and, as regularly as his impaired health would permit, attended the service there of St. Mary's Episcopal Church, having, during the closing years of his life, given serious attention to religious matters. A day was fixed for his public baptism in that church, but the event had to be postponed by reason of an attack of illness. He was, however, baptized by the Rev. Dr. Hills, rector of St. Mary's, while lying on his sick-bed, on June 14th, 1875. He died ten days after, aged sixty-three years, and was buried at Morristown, New Jersey.

---

cWHORTER. This family is of Scotch extraction, the name, as originally written, and as still written in Scotland, being McWhirter. The ancestors of the American branch of the family belonged to a small clan that bore the name of McWhirter, and, with other lowlanders, emigrated in the early part of the seventeenth century to the north of Ireland. Of their history little or nothing is known prior to about 1700. Records exist showing Hugh McWhirter to have been settled, at the beginning of the eighteenth century, as a linen merchant, at Armagh. In 1730, at the solicitation of his son Alexander, he emigrated to America. He settled in the county of New Castle, where he became a prominent farmer and an elder in the Presbyterian Church. By his only wife, Jane, he had eleven children. He died in 1748. Of his numerous children, the eldest, Alexander, who had been educated for the Presbyterian ministry and had spent two years at the University of Edinburgh, died in 1734 without issue; John migrated to North Carolina, where he married; and Nancy married Alexander Osborn; and Jane, John Brevard, of the same province. The youngest of the eleven children, Alexander, was born July 15th (O. S.), 1734, the year of the death of his elder brother, after whom he was named. He also was educated for the ministry, and became a very prominent divine of the Presbyterian Church. In 1758 he married Mary, daughter of Robert Cumming, of Freehold, High Sheriff of the county of Monmouth, and sister of General Cumming, of the Continental army. He died July 20th, 1807. His children were: 1. Mary, who married Samuel Beebe, a merchant of New York; 2. Ann, who married the Rev. George Ogilvie, rector of the Episcopal Church at New Brunswick; 3. Alexander Cumming McWhorter—the first to change the name from McWhirter—born in 1771, died October 8th, 1808, a distinguished member of the New Jersey bar, and one of the most prominent citizens of Newark; 4. John, who married Martha Dwight, of Newark, by whom he had three children; all of these died without issue. Alexander C. McWhorter married Phœbe, daughter of Caleb Bruen, of Newark; by her he had six children: I. Alexander Cumming, born January 7th, 1794, died August 26th, 1826; he married, in 1818, Frances C. G., daughter of United States Senator John Lawrence, having by her several children, all of whom died save Alexander. Alexander married and abode in New Haven. His marriage was without issue. II. George H., born 1795, died 1862. He married, in 1819, Margaret T., daughter of United States Senator John Lawrence, and abode in Oswego, New York, becoming a prominent citizen of that place. He had issue two sons: 1. Alexander C., who married Cecilia Bronson, of Oswego, and had issue one son, Alexander C.; and 2. George Cumming, unmarried. III. Julia Anna, born 1798, died 1846; married 1826 died without issue. IV. Mary Cumming, born 1800, died 1861; married to Josiah B. Howell, by whom she had five children. V. Frances Cornelia, died in childhood. VI. Adriana V. B., born 1808, died 1863; married, 1835, to Herman Bruen, having issue Adriana and Herman.

ILLER, HON. JACOB W., Lawyer and Statesman, late of Morristown, was born in November, 1800, in German Valley, Morris county, New Jersey. He received an excellent education, and, having resolved to devote himself to the profession of the law, entered the office of William W. Miller, an elder brother, who died in early manhood, but whose eloquence still lingers in the traditions of the bar of the State. With this brother he studied the prescribed course of five years, when he was admitted to the bar, at which he soon acquired a large and lucrative practice, particularly in the higher courts, acquiring also distinction as a counsellor. As a lawyer he was remarkable for industry, faithfulness, tact, fervent and impressive oratory, and, above all, common sense, a kind of sense more rare than genius, if not more valuable, and which marked his career in the Senate not less than at the bar, stamping indeed its sage imprint on his whole life. He at one time was associated in the practice of law with Mr. Edward W. Whelpley, a young and gifted attorney, who afterwards became Chief-Justice of the Supreme Court of New Jersey. In 1838 he entered public life, the Whigs having nominated him for the State Senate and elected him by a large majority. He represented his district in the Senate of the State for two years with such usefulness and distinction, that at the close of the term, in 1840, he was elected to represent his State in the Senate of the United States, discharging his duties on that high theatre, then crowded with the most illustrious figures of our parliamentary history, so ably and acceptably that, on the expiration of his term, in 1846, he was re-elected, serving two full terms in the upper house of the first legislative body in the world, when that body, in both branches, was at the zenith of its glory. It may be justly said to the credit of his character and his powers, that in a Senate which included Clay, Webster and Calhoun, with Benton, Wright, Grundy, Berrien, Mangum, Crittenden, Buchanan, McDuffie, Corwin, Reverdy Johnson, Cass, Rives, Pearce and Bayard, he was not thrown into the back-ground, but stood throughout among the principal figures of the scene, commanding their respect, enjoying their friend-ship, and participating with honor in their most renowned debates. He, however, spoke but seldom, reserving him-self in general for the more important questions of debate, content as for the rest with a vigilant attention to the busi-ness of legislation, including a diligent study of proposed or pending measures, practising as a statesman the industry, thoroughness and fidelity that had characterized him as a lawyer. It was partly on this account, perhaps, that when he did speak, he spoke with great effect, but certainly much more on account of the knowledge, fairness, ability, wisdom, and eloquence with which he spoke. Towards the close of his first term in the Federal Senate, the annexation of Texas came up in that body, and upon this question he de-livered one of the ablest and most impassioned of his speeches, opposing the measure as contrary to the Constitu-tion, dangerous to the public peace, and dishonorable to the national character, declaring that, for these reasons, he would "reject Texas, were she to bring with her the wealth of the Indies," and concluding with a telling citation of the report made by Aristides to the Athenians on the stratagem that Themistocles had secretly devised for their benefit: "Nothing could be more *advantageous*, but at the same time nothing could be more *unjust*." A question still more momentous came up as his second term approached its close, the Compromise of 1850, that is to say; and in the discussion of this complex question, in all its aspects and at all its stages, he bore a prominent and effective part. Op-posing the combination of the several measures of compro-mise into a single measure, he supported, after the rejection

of the combination, known as the "Omnibus Bill," some of the measures when put upon their passage separately, and, on the passage in this manner of all of the measures, sustained the compromise as a whole, though not entirely approving every part of it, deeming it, all things con-sidered, a scheme of pacification, in which the best interests of the Union were involved. On this point his position was distinctly and happily stated in one of his latest speeches in the Senate: "But, whatever opposition I may have felt it my duty to make," he said, "to any or either of the meas-ures embraced in the compromise while under discussion, yet, as soon as they were enacted into laws, it became my duty, as it is the duty of every good citizen, to sustain them with as much fidelity as if I had voted for each and all of them. In saying this, I but express the common sentiment of the people of New Jersey, who have always shown their devotion to our republican institutions by a cheerful sub-mission to the voice of the majority, when that voice is ex-pressed in constitutional law. I am now opposed to all further agitation upon this subject. The quiet of the country, and even the sanctity of Congress, demand that we should cease our disputations. Sir, my abhorrence of agi-tation upon this subject is such that it may even carry me beyond my instructions; for I go against agitation on either side of this question, agitation as well by those who were in favor of the compromise as by those who were against it, agitation from the North as well as from the South, agita-tion in State Legislatures and in the halls of Congress. Of all miserable agitation the most miserable is agitation after the fact. It is the cry of alarm after the danger is passed, for the mere love of the excitement. To revive a spent whirlwind that it may blow down a few more trees, to rouse the sleeping lion merely to hear him roar again, may suit the tastes of some, but they who indulge in this kind of ex-citement may find that there is more danger than amuse-ment in the play." Fully to appreciate the point of this lively sally, it should be borne in mind that the occasion of the speech was the presentation of certain resolutions of the Legislature of New Jersey, under the recently-acquired con-trol of the Democratic party, instructing the New Jersey senators " to resist any change, alteration or repeal" of the compromise, instructions which the Whig Senator not un-naturally construed as implying a very unnecessary reflection upon his fidelity to the measure, and treated with derision, as gratuitously feeding the very agitation they condemned. What he thought of this sort of agitation, in whatever quar-ter raised, he had told unequivocally enough in an oration delivered in his home at Morristown the previous July. " I will not say," he observed, on that occasion, "that those men who are continually compassing the government with wordy threats of violence, or horrifying their imaginations with the dissolution of the Union, may be legally chargeable with the desire to bring about the death of our king, the constitution. Yet they are justly chargeable with that moral treason which disturbs the confidence of a loyal peo-

ple in the safety and stability of their government, and undermines their allegiance. Let us not be moved by the cry of fanatics, nor alarmed at the threats of secessionists; they are as the angry waves which vainly howl about the battlements and spend their fury upon the unshaken towers of our political fortress. Politicians may fret and fume; State conventions may resolve and re-resolve; and Congress itself become the arena of fearful agitations; but above and around, as in a mighty amphitheatre, in undisturbed and undismayed majesty, stands the American people, with steady eye and giant hand, overlooking all and governing all; and wo! wo! to the man, and destruction to the State, that attempts to resist their supreme authority." Something of prophecy had those ringing words. It was about this period of his senatorial career that the landing of Cossuth on our shores called forth from him two or three of the most admirable speeches of his life. Drawing a broad distinction between Cossuth as a private individual and as a political agitator, he contended that the brilliant but unfortunate Hungarian should be generously welcomed in the former relation, but in the latter let severely alone, grounding his argument on the Washingtonian policy of non-intervention in the domestic affairs of foreign countries. "Sir," he exclaimed, in one of these speeches, "it is said that we have a great mission to perform; that it is our duty to interfere, not only by the expression of sympathy, but in some other way, which gentlemen do not exactly define, in the cause of distressed humanity in Europe. We have a great trust to execute and a great duty to perform; but, like every other duty, domestic, social and political, it is limited; it has its errand. If we go beyond that, if we turn crusaders, for the purpose of executing that trust and performing that duty in other lands, like all crusaders we may get great honor, we may be renowned in chivalry and song, but we shall neglect the great duties which we have to perform at home, where we can perform them to the advantage of mankind. The altar of our liberty has its own temple. It is here. Here let the oppressed of every land come to worship. Here let them come if they desire to get rid of oppression at home, or to warm their patriotism to return to renewed efforts abroad. Let them come; but let us not take away that altar from our own temple and carry it off into the wilderness of European revolution, there to be taken by the Philistines, or its fires to be quenched forever beneath an ocean of blood. No, sir; it is here that our duty is to be performed." And to his inspired common sense the whole country did instant justice, plaudits reaching him on account of these speeches, from all quarters of the Union. He had touched with a master's hand the common sense and common sensibilities of the people. With the expiration of his second term, in 1852, ended the line of able and accomplished senators that the Whigs of New Jersey furnished to the Union—Frelinghuysen, Southard, Dayton, Miller—a line never renewed; for, when power again passed from the hands of the Democracy of New Jersey, the

Whig party was no more. Against this result no man struggled more zealously or more gallantly than the last Whig senator of the State. In the presidential campaign of 1852 he upheld the Whig banner in a succession of masterly speeches; and when that radiant standard had gone down in what proved to be irretrievable defeat, he still, bating no jot of heart or hope, endeavored to rally the flying squadrons, reform the broken lines, refill the skeleton regiments, and reinforce the army in general, publishing as late as December, 1854, with this view, a series of strong and eloquent papers, insisting on the maintenance of the Whig organization and the Whig principles, but recommending, as a concession to the spirit of the times, the substitution of the name "American," and the enlargement of the platform so as "to condense into one efficient power the feeble fractions" into which the people were subdivided. But events were too powerful for his logic, and in 1855 he abandoned the struggle, of which he at last realized the hopelessness, and cast in his lot with the Republican party, to which with characteristic steadfastness he adhered for the remainder of his life. But the end was near, and the passage to it thickset with infirmities, so that he was not able to do all that he fain would have done for his country in the crisis of her fate. Yet he did much, with both voice and pen, cheering the despondent, convincing the doubtful, shaming the lukewarm, applauding the ardent, and quickening all. One of the most statesmanly and unanswerable disquisitions that ever appeared on the question of secession came from his pen in the closing days of 1860. He felt no misgivings, even when face to face with the deadly peril. His conviction that the Union would be victoriously maintained was clear and abiding. He foresaw the triumph of his country, but, alas! he did not see it. Sinking beneath increasing infirmities, he died at Morristown, September 30th, 1862, leaving a wife, daughter of the lamented George P. Macculloch, and a large family of sons and daughters, one of the former being in the navy, distinguished for gallant conduct in the civil war, and two lawyers of New York, of high abilities and attainments. His eldest daughter is the wife of Mr. A. Q. Keasby.

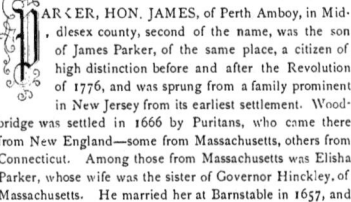

ARKER, HON. JAMES, of Perth Amboy, in Middlesex county, second of the name, was the son of James Parker, of the same place, a citizen of high distinction before and after the Revolution of 1776, and was sprung from a family prominent in New Jersey from its earliest settlement. Woodbridge was settled in 1666 by Puritans, who came there from New England—some from Massachusetts, others from Connecticut. Among those from Massachusetts was Elisha Parker, whose wife was the sister of Governor Hinckley, of Massachusetts. He married her at Barnstable in 1657, and had several children there before his removal to New Jersey. One of his sons was also named Elisha. He was possessed of much property and was a prominent citizen. Governor Hunter, in 1717, made him a member of his Privy Council. His action in so doing was attacked by a clergyman of the English Church resident in Pennsylvania, upon the ground that Mr. Parker was a Puritan ; and defended by the assertion of his high standing and because the governor designed, by new appointments, including this, to establish the Court of Chancery, after some delay the government at home indorsed his plan, and thus that court was established. Perhaps this position led Mr. Parker to the adoption of religious connections more common in the case of public officers. Whatever the cause, this gentleman's children became Episcopalians, and their descendants since have always been earnest and influential in that denomination. John Parker, son of the last named, was born November 11th, 1693. He married a daughter of Dr. John Johnstone, a person of note, and was a member of the Governor's Privy Council from 1719 till his death in 1732. He was a man of education and influence. James Parker, his son, born January 29th, 1723, was also a leading citizen. He entered the provincial military service and embarked for the northern frontier in the French and Indian war, as Captain of a company raised in Middlesex county. Afterwards he became a merchant in New York, but resided in New Jersey. He was an active member of Governor Franklin's Privy Council, and was elected to the Provincial Congress, but did not take his seat. For a long period, likewise, he filled the position of Mayor of Amboy. After the Revolution, in 1789, he was a candidate for Congress, nominated by what was known as the Conservative party of that day. He was a man of large landed property and of vigorous intellect. He was one of the founders of the American Episcopal Church in New Jersey, a leading member of the Board of Proprietors, then a most important body, from whom all land titles came, and in every walk of life an active and conspicuous citizen. He died in 1797, leaving several children ; among them James Parker, who was born March 1st, 1776, and who died April 1st, 1868. This gentleman was a man of great ability and public note. He was graduated in Columbia College, New York, in 1793, second in his class. Destined for mercantile life, he entered the counting-room of John Murray. The death of his father called him, at twenty-one years old, to take his place as the virtual head of his family. The large landed interests he had to manage compelled him to acquire an intimate practical knowledge of law, for which his sagacious mind largely fitted him, and this caused him to be regarded generally as a lawyer of eminence, though in fact he never practised the profession. He entered public life in 1806, when thirty years old, by becoming a member of Assembly. He was re-elected eight successive years ; then, after one year's interval, four years more, and again in 1827–28. He was a leader in the Legislature and

in the State. A Federalist, he was nevertheless not a partisan. And his independence, integrity, and remarkable capacity, made him exceedingly influential. He was a statesman as well as a speaker. Many of the best-known statutes of the State were prepared by him. He was among the originators, if not himself the author, of the Fund for Free Schools. It is written of him, " When the history of the great movement on behalf of popular education in our State comes to be written, the first and the highest place in it will be assigned to James Parker."—(Historical address by Hon. R. S. Field.) He was a leader in measures for the prohibition of the domestic slave trade, which the gradual abolition of slavery actually encouraged, by leading owners to anticipate the period and export their slaves to other States. Both as a member of the Legislature, through which he caused the passage of efficient laws, and as Foreman of the Middlesex Grand Jury, in punishing offenders, he did much to protect the negro and to protect the State from disgrace. He was one of the originators of the Delaware & Raritan Canal. He entered the Legislature in 1827 in order to carry through that enterprise, and succeeded. He was a Director of that company until his death. Mr. Parker was thrice appointed a Commissioner to settle the boundary between New Jersey and New York; once as early as 1806, when but thirty years old; again in 1827, his colleagues being John Rutherford, Richard Stockton, Theodore Frelinghuysen and L. Q. C. Elmer; and finally in 1829, with Messrs. Frelinghuysen and Elmer. And in all these commissions Mr. Parker was a leading actor. The return of Federalists to influence, which distinguished the nomination of General Jackson, brought Mr. Parker again into national politics. He was an Elector in 1824 and gave his vote for Jackson, but J. Q. Adams was elected by the House of Representatives. In 1829 General Jackson appointed him Collector of Perth Amboy. In 1832, and again in 1834, he was elected, by general ticket, a member of the House of Representatives. He served with distinction, winning the cognomen of Honest James Parker, distinguishing himself as a champion of the right of petition and as a guardian of the finances of the Union. Mr. Parker was a Trustee of Princeton College from 1825 to 1829, and of Rutgers during a much longer period. He was Mayor of Perth Amboy for many years, and till the very end of his long life was useful and public-spirited. His views were ahead of his day. He was younger in sentiment and opinion than most of his junior contemporaries. After leaving Congress and until his death, he was first a Whig, and then a Republican, a staunch supporter of the Union and of emancipation. He died April 1st, 1868. This gentleman had three sons, all worthy of mention among Jerseymen. James Parker, his eldest, died in Cincinnati in 1861, where he was distinguished as a lawyer and a Judge. He had early settled in Ohio, and occupied various useful stations there during his life. William Parker, his second son, died in 1868, not long after his father, at Aspinwall, Central

America, where he had lived for several years as Superintendent of the Panama Railroad. He was a civil engineer of distinction. He had a leading part in the construction of the Boston & Worcester Railroad, of which he was long the Superintendent. He likewise aided in the building of the Morris Canal, the Juniata Canal, the Georgia Railroad, and others; and was President of the Boston & Lowell, and at one time Superintendent of the Baltimore & Ohio Railroad. He was beloved and valued, in and out of his profession.

ARKER, HON. CORTLANDT, Lawyer, of Newark, third son of Hon. James Parker, whose sketch precedes, was born at Perth Amboy, in June, 1818. At the age of five he lost his mother, but her place was filled by a sister of the celebrated lawyer, David B. Ogden, of New York, whom his father married, and whose gentle influences were very influential in the formation of his character. After passing through such schools as existed at that day in Perth Amboy, and acquiring the elements of Latin and Greek under the tuition of Mr. Patterson, he entered, in 1832, the freshman class of Rutgers College, at New Brunswick, whence he was graduated, after a four years' course, with the first honor, and was selected to deliver the valedictory. The graduating class of this year—1836—was among the most distinguished that ever left Rutgers College, numbering such men as Justice Bradley, of the United States Supreme Court, Senator Frelinghuysen, Governor Newell, and others of their stamp of intellect. On leaving college Mr. Parker entered upon the study of law in the office of Theodore Frelinghuysen, in Newark, and prosecuted his studies under that direction until his preceptor's appointment as Chancellor of the University of New York, when he became a student with and completed his course under the auspices of Amzi Armstrong, whose early death deprived New Jersey of one of her brightest lights. In September, 1839, Mr. Parker was admitted to the bar, and established himself in Newark, where he still resides, engaged in the practice of his profession in connection with his son. About the same time, two of his classmates, Justice Bradley and Senator Frelinghuysen, opened law offices in that city, and all three rapidly rose in reputation as able lawyers and advocates. Mr. Parker has held only one public office, that of Prosecutor of Pleas of Essex county from 1857 to 1867, but for many years he has occupied a position among the foremost at the bar of his native State. His distinction is almost exclusively professional, except that he has always been a leader in the Whig and Republican parties. To the latter he attached himself at its formation in 1856. During the civil war he was active and intense in his support of the government and the nation, laboring industriously with voice and pen for the maintenance of the Union and the settlement upon a sure and lasting foundation of all the

44

questions involved in the strife. Since the termination of the war he has been an earnest and consistent Republican, and the favorite of a very large section of his party for the highest political honors. A most decided repugnance to the use in any form of the means by which office is often secured, and an unwavering belief in the essential soundness of the principle that office should seek the man, rather than man the office, have so far kept him in private life and deprived the country of his valuable services. He was nominated by Governor Newell as Chancellor of the State, and it is understood that at another time he was tendered a seat on the Supreme Court bench, but he declined. On several occasions his eminent professional services have been secured by the State. The duty of revision of the laws was devolved upon him by sundry acts of the Legislature, and was performed to the satisfaction of that body and also of the community at large. He also acted as Commissioner to settle the disputed boundary between New Jersey and Delaware. He was tendered the post of Commissioner under the Alabama treaty, but declined it. There have been very few important litigations in New Jersey of late years in which he has not borne a part, and always conspicuously. Both as a man and as an advocate his popularity is very wide. Among other distinguished services rendered by him to the State in the line of his profession, and nearly related thereto, must be mentioned the part he took in the movement which culminated in the passage of the general railroad law, which has done much to purify the source of legislation by removing from the law-making power the opportunities of corruption. In this movement he was, from the first to the last, the leader, and to his able guidance its success is in very great degree attributable. Progressive in his views upon all subjects, he is frequently in advance of public sentiment, but when occasion has demanded the effort the community has seldom failed to respond to his leadership. A member of the Episcopal Church, he has occupied a prominent position therein, representing it in two General Conventions, and being a delegate and active debater in every Diocesan Convention since attaining his majority. His own college and also that of New Jersey have conferred on him the degree of LL. D. In educational matters he has ever manifested an unflagging interest, and is now a Trustee of Rutgers College. As a public speaker he is peculiarly successful, always commanding the closest attention and wielding a potent influence. Many of his addresses have been published in pamphlet form, and their publication has contributed to his reputation as a sound, logical and cogent speaker. Among them may be mentioned: an address at Rutgers College, on "True Professional Success;" the centennial address of the Phi Beta Kappa Society, on "The Open Bible, the Source and Stay of American Freedom;" several Fourth of July addresses, delivered during the civil war, each ably discussing the question of the day; an historical address on Philip Kearny, and another on Abraham Lincoln. Though absorbed in the labor of a very extensive practice, Mr. Parker has always found time for literary employment, and for discussions, more or less careful, of public affairs.

LARK, GEORGE A., Manufacturer, of Newark, New Jersey, and Paisley, Scotland, was born in Paisley about 1823. He was the second son of John Clark, of the great firm of James & John Clark, cotton thread manufacturers, and the grandson of the John Clark who, in 1812, founded the business. About 1840 he entered, as a lad, into the employment of the firm of Kerr & Co., at Hamilton, Ontario, and after remaining with this house for some four years, returned to Paisley and began the manufacture of shawls. In 1850 he relinquished this business and was then admitted as a partner with his brother-in-law, Mr Peter Kerr (who was drowned at Long Branch in 1869) in the manufacture of cotton thread. Subsequently his firm was merged into that of the Clarks, and in the latter he retained a partnership until his death, and it was mainly owing to his energy and business ability that the resources and operations of the establishment were so vastly developed. At the commencement of the business, about 1812, the Paisley works were so inconsiderable, that one man, turning a crank, furnished all necessary motive power, and the sale of manufactured goods was limited to but a small portion of the United Kingdom; at his death the Paisley works gave employment to upwards of 2,000 operatives, 1,000 more were employed in the works at Newark, and the business of the firm extended over almost the entire globe. The American branch of the business is wholly due to him. In 1856 he came to this country to take charge of the general agency of the firm for the United States and Canada, his head-quarters being fixed in New York. The consumption of cotton thread being greatly stimulated by the increased use of sewing machines, and the firm being placed at a disadvantage, by reason of the high protective tariff, in competing with American manufacturers, he determined upon the establishment of a branch of the Paisley works in the United States. To this end he founded a factory at Newark, New Jersey, in 1864, and in the fall of that year began operations, on a small scale, in a hired building at the corner of Front and Fulton streets. At the same time he put under contract the extensive works on Clark street, personally superintending their erection, and in many ways improving upon the Paisley model. At the end of eighteen months the buildings were completed, and in the spring of 1866 Clark's O. N. T. spool-cotton became an established manufacture in America. At the head of this great industry, giving employment to so large a number of people and affecting so beneficially the prosperity of the city, he naturally became one of the most prominent men in Newark, and his advice and assistance were sought in furthering various commercial enterprises and undertakings for the public good. In religious matters he was equally conspicuous. An earnest Christian—one who made practical Christianity a part of his daily life, and who constantly sought, by precept and example, to uphold and diffuse its doctrines—he was one of the most active adherents of the North Reformed Church of Newark, and of his large fortune he at all times gave freely for the promotion of religious and benevolent projects. His genial, kindly nature made him not less esteemed socially than in commercial and religious circles. Never ostentatious in his hospitality, he was always liberal and gracious, and his friendships were warm and unwavering. In a word, in the various relations of life, he was a man, acquaintance with whom conferred an honor. His death, from heart disease, occurred suddenly, on the 13th of February, 1873, and was the cause of widespread and very sincere sorrow. Appropriate action was taken by the Newark Board of Trade, of which he was a prominent member; by the Directors of the People's Insurance Company, of which he was a Director, and by the Burns Society, of Newark, of which he was President at the time of his death. Funeral services were held in the North Reformed Church, attended by representatives of the above-named organizations, and by the leading citizens of Newark; and in all ways possible respect was shown to his memory. His remains, sent back to Scotland, rest in the cemetery of his native town of Paisley.

WING, HON. JAMES, late of Trenton, Merchant, at one time Mayor of the city, one of the founders of the Trenton Library and Academy, was the father of Chief-Justice Ewing, and the tenth child of Thomas and Mary Ewing. He first moved to Trenton, as a Representative of Cumberland county in the Legislature in 1774, and removed his residence there in 1779. He was subsequently, under Congress, Auditor of Public Accounts, Commissioner of the Continental Loan Office for New Jersey, and Agent for Pensions. From 1797 to 1803 he officiated as Mayor of Trenton, and was importantly instrumental in securing the establishment of the city's library and academy. During several years he sustained a partnership relation with Isaac Collins, and engaged extensively in general mercantile pursuits. He was also a corporator, commissioner and secretary of the society, incorporated March 15th, 1796, to make the Assanpink navigable from the Trenton Mills to the place where it intersects the stage-road from Burlington to Amboy; and probably was in the company which, February 3d, 1797, descended the stream in the boat "Hope," from Davidstown, where the upper lock was situated, to Trenton, in three hours, and so opened one-half of the proposed line of navigation. "It may have been a revival of this scheme

.... Parker has always found time for
.. .., ... f .. discussions. more or less care-
.....r.

LARK, GEORGE A., Manufacturer, of Newark,
New Jersey, and Paisley, Scotland, was born ..
I .. l.y about 1823. He was the second son of
John Clark, .. the great firm of James & John
t l..k, cotton thread manufacturers, and the
grandson of the John Clark who, in 1812,
first .. .d the business. About 1840 he entered, as a lad,
into the employment of the firm of Kerr & Co., at Hamil
.. .., Ontario, and after remaining with this house for some
four years, returned to Paisley and began the manufacture
.. ..l.. In 1850 he relinquished this business and was
then admitted as a partner with his brother-in-law, Mr
Peter Kerr (who was drowned at Long Branch in 18..)
the manufacture of cotton thread. Subsequently his ....
was merged into that of the Clarks, and in the latter he
tained a partnership until his death, and it was mainly owe..
to his energy and business ability that the resources and op...
ations of the establishment were so vastly developed. A. ..
commencement of the business, ... the .... and the
works were so inconsiderable, that ....
furnished all necessary motive power, and the ....
factured goods was limited to but a ....
United Kingdom ; at his death the ....
ployment to upwards of 2,000 operatives ....
employed in the works at Newark .... and the ..
business of the firm extended over .... the ..
....erican branch of the business .... here ..
... . came to this country to take charge of the gen-
.... of the firm for the United States and Canada,
....ters being fixed in New York. The township-
.... already being greatly stimulated by ....
.... machines, and the .... the
.... reason of the high price ....
....erican manufacturers, he ....
.... of a branch of .. .. . l.y w ....
.... this end he ....
.... 1864, and in the .... that res..
.... in a hire. .... at the
....
....
.... relative ....
....'s model. At the .... ..
....s were completed, and ....
.... spool-cotton because ....
.... At the f.... .... ..
.... imprisonment to so large ....
.... an beneficially the prospe.. ..
.... of the most ....
.... advice and assistance .... ..

thering various commercial enterprises and undertakings
for the public good. In religious matters he was equally
conspicuous. An earnest christian—one who made practi-
... Christianity a part of his daily life, and who constantly
... by precept and example, to uphold and diffuse its
....—he .. .... of the most active adherents of the
North Reformed Church of Newark, and of his large fortune he always .... give freely for the promotion of religious
and benevolent projects. His genial, kindly nature made
him .... socially than in commercial and re-
.... Never ostentatious in his hospitality, he
w.. .... al and gracious, and his friendships were
.... wavering. In a word, in the various relations
.... was a man, acquaintance with whom conferred
.... His death, from heart disease, occurred sud-
.... the 13th of February, 1873, and was the cause of
.... and very sincere sorrow. Appropriate action
.... on by the Newark Board of Trade, of which he was
.... ent member; by the Directors of the People's In-
....rance Company, of which he was a Director, and by the
.... Society, of Newark, of which he was President at the
.... of his death. Funeral services were held in the North
R.f.rmed Church, attended by representatives of the above-
named organizations, and by the leading citizens of Newark ;
and in all ways possible respect was shown to his memory.
His remains, sent back to Scotland, rest in the cemetery of
his native town of Paisley.

....

WING, MON JAMES, late of Trenton, Merchant,
at one time Mayor of the city, one of the
founders of the Trenton Library and Academy,
was the father of Chief Justice Ewing, and the
tenth child of Thomas and Mary Ewing. He
first moved to Trenton, as a Representative
of Cumberland county in the Legislature in 1774, and removed his residence there in 1779. He was subsequently,
under Congress, Auditor of Public Accounts, Commissioner of the Continental Loan Office for New Jersey, and
Agent for Pensions. From 1797 to 1803 he officiated as Mayor
.... .. and was importantly instrumental in securing the
.... of the city's library and academy. During sev-
.... sustained a partnership relation with Isaac Col-
.... extensively in general mercantile pursuits.
He w.. a.... .... r, commissioner and secretary of the
.... March 15th, 1796, to make the Assan-
.... Trenton Mills to the place where it
.... from Burlington to Amboy; and
.... in the .... which, February 3d, 1797,
.... steam in the boat " Hope," from Davids-
.... ver l. .. was situated, to Trenton, in
.... d one .... line of
.... have been a .... scheme

that was contemplated in November, 1814, when a public meeting was called to form an association to supply the town with firewood by water." September 5th, 1808, he was elected a Trustee of the Trenton Presbyterian Church, and ordained an Elder, September 21st, 1817. He continued in both offices until his decease, which took place October 23d, 1823. In accordance with his known objections to the practice, no stone was placed to indicate the spot of his interment, which is in the churchyard of the city with whose history and interests his name is so intimately and honorably identified.

OSWELL, REV. WILLIAM, Clergyman, late of Trenton, was born in New Jersey, and had been for sixteen years pastor of the Baptist Congregation of Trenton and Lamberton, when, in 1823, he issued an address to its members, on account of his adoption of some new tenets, which in several points favored the doctrine of Swedenborgianism. His address was answered by an elaborate letter from Rev. John Burtt, first editor of *The Presbyterian*, in Philadelphia, who was then engaged in spiritual labors in Trenton and the vicinity. The First Baptist Church of Lamberton was opened November 26th, 1803, on which occasion the initial sermon was delivered by Dr. Staughton. His church, or chapel, was known as the "Reformed General Baptist Meeting House," was built, of bricks, in eleven weeks, and opened October 19th, 1823; the dimensions were fifty-four feet by forty. He died June 10th, 1833, at the age of fifty-seven. His grave is in the rear of the building where he last preached, afterward the Second Presbyterian Church. Near to it is that of another prominent Baptist minister, Rev. Burgess Allison, D. D., who died while on a visit to Trenton, February 20th, 1827.

RITTAIN, JOSEPH, late of Trenton, New Jersey, was a prosperous Shoe Manufacturer, and one of the leading men of property of this city. He was the principal owner of the lot on which the State House is built. In January, 1792, he conveyed two and a quarter acres to the commissioners of the State for the nominal price of five shillings; and in February of the same year three-quarters of an acre for sixty-seven pounds and ten shillings. On the same day William Reeder, whose name is also among the signatures of the instrument then drawn up, conveyed one-quarter of an acre for the same purpose, at the price of sixty-two pounds and ten shillings; and George Ely half an acre for one hundred and twenty pounds. He was a prominent and valued member of the Presbyterian Church in Trenton, from 1809 to 1813, "when his connection ceased in consequence of his having embraced doctrines too much at variance with those of our communion for his comfortable continuance." He was a man of strong convictions, slow in conception, but earnest in execution; while, even by those with whose opinions his own were far from harmonizing, he was respected and esteemed. He died in the early part of the present century.

ALLAS, HON. ALEXANDER JAMES, Statesman, Financier, late of Trenton, New Jersey, was born in the island of Jamaica, June 21st, 1759. He was the son of a Scotch physician, and obtained his earlier training and education at Edinburgh and Westminster. His mother becoming a widow, and again marrying, he was prevented from obtaining any share of his father's property, and in April, 1783, quitted his native place, and settled in Philadelphia. In the following June he took the oath of allegiance to the State of Pennsylvania, and in July, 1785, was admitted to practise as an advocate in the Supreme Court, and subsequently became a practitioner in the United States courts. He engaged also in literary undertakings, wrote for the public journals, and at one time edited *The Columbian Magazine*. In January, 1791, he was appointed, by Governor Mifflin, Secretary of Pennsylvania, and in December, 1793, his commission was renewed. He was afterwards constituted Paymaster-General of a force which he accompanied in an expedition to Pittsburgh. In December, 1796, he again became Secretary of State of Pennsylvania, and on the election of Jefferson to the Presidency, in 1801, was appointed United States Attorney for the Eastern District of Pennsylvania, and occupied that post until his removal to Washington. October 6th, 1814, he was made Secretary of the United States Treasury, then in an involved and embarrassed condition, and in that highly responsible and important position exhibited remarkable ability and well-directed energy. In March, 1815, he undertook the additional duties of the War Office, and successfully performed the delicate and difficult task of reducing the army. In 1816 peace and tranquillity being restored, and the financial condition of the country being improved under the influence of the National Bank, which he had so long and zealously endeavored to establish, he resigned his post and resumed the practice of the law. He published: "Features of Jay's Treaty," 1795; "Speeches on the Trial of Blount;" "Laws of Pennsylvania," with notes; "Reports," four vols., 1806–7; "Treasury Reports;" "Exposition of the Causes and Character of the war of 1812–15," etc. His son, Captain James Alexander Dallas, United States navy, was born in 1791, and died in Callao bay, June 3d, 1844, commanding the Pacific Squadron; he entered the navy in 1805, in 1812 served under Rodgers in "The President," later, under Chauncey, on Lake Ontario, and accompanied Porter in his cruise for the extermination of the West India pirates.

George Mifflin Dallas, LL. D., another son, was born in Philadelphia, Pennsylvania, July 10th, 1792, and died there December 31st, 1864; he attained high distinction as a criminal lawyer, and as an able statesman and diplomatist; was Mayor of Philadelphia, United States Senator, Attorney-General of Pennsylvania, Ambassador to Russia, Minister to England, and, 1845-49, Vice-President of the United States. Throughout the eastern and middle sections of the United States Secretary Dallas was admired and esteemed for his abilities, which were of a most varied and thorough nature, as jurist, statesman, and financier; but particularly in New Jersey and Pennsylvania, with whose interests and history he is more especially identified, was his reputation widespread and enviable. He died in Trenton, New Jersey, January 16th, 1817. A grandson, George M. Dallas, son of the Vice-President, is a resident of Philadelphia, and a lawyer of high standing at the bar of that city. He was a member of the convention assembled toward the close of 1872 for the revision of the constitution of the State of Pennsylvania.

———◆◇◆———

BELLEVILLE, NICHOLAS JACQUES EMANUEL DE, M. D., late of Trenton, New Jersey, was born at Metz, France, in 1753, pursued a course of studies in medicine under the supervision of his father, passed seven years as a student, and practitioner in some cases, in the schools and hospitals of Paris, and, in 1777 came to this country, landing first at Salem, Massachusetts. Previously, while in the south of France, where he usually resided during the rigorous season, on account of the feeble state of his health, he was introduced to Count Pulaski, who had just come from Italy, where he had found the place of safety needed on account of the persecution following the active part he sustained in endeavoring to restore to Poland her ancient liberties. "The count was then on the eve of his departure for this country, and having taken a liking for the doctor, invited him to accompany him. For some time he hesitated, by reason of his want of money, but the gentleman at whose house he was, when informed of this fact, told him if a hundred guineas would be sufficient for his purpose, he would supply him, and that his father could reimburse him. He further supplied him with everything necessary for the voyage, and on the last day of May, 1777, he left Paris and embarked at Nantes, on the 9th of June, for the United States."—(Notes of Philemon Dickinson.) He sailed in a sloop-of-war, mounting fourteen guns, with a crew of one hundred and five men, and carrying about sixteen hundred stand of arms destined for the American troops. After disembarking at Salem, he remained there for a few days, then removed to Boston, at that time the centre of attraction for both Americans and those strangers who chanced to be in the colonies, or who had come from France and Germany in the roles of spectator and chronicler, or sympathizer and participant. He afterward attended Pulaski, in the capacity of surgeon, in the different parts of the country to which he went for the purpose of recruiting a legion, which the count was authorized to raise by the Provincial Congress. While thus engaged, he was a resident of Trenton, New Jersey, for some time, and there became acquainted with Dr. Bryant, an eminent and skilful practitioner, who bestowed on him many warm marks of friendly interest, and endeavored to persuade him to relinquish army life and settle in the city, offering to do all in his power to introduce him into lucrative practice. He declined the proposition for the time, however, preferring to accompany Pulaski to the South. While stationed there he received from Dr. Bryant a pressing letter, repeating his counsel, and urging his abandoning military and roving for civil and settled life, representing the improbability of his succeeding there so well as by establishing himself permanently in the practice of his profession. This letter he showed to the count, who told him it was not his wish to stand in the way of his advancement, and advised him, if he thought the doctor's advice sound and timely, to accept and act upon it without delay. He did so, after careful deliberation, and in the fall of 1778 returned to Trenton, where he remained until his decease. He was on several occasions called to attend the exiled king of Spain, at Bordentown, and once, at least, was his almoner—February 5th, 1831—when the Female Benevolent Society, of Trenton, acknowledged fifty dollars " from the Count de Survilliers by Dr. Belleville." He was a pew-holder and an occasional attendant at the Presbyterian church, " but was too fond of his elegant edition of Voltaire to relish the gospel;" his wife, however, was a communicant, and a pious and exemplary woman. He was a resident of Paris in 1774, when Louis XVI. came to the throne, and often told of his hearing the populace cry—in allusion to the wish of Henry IV., that every peasant might have a fowl for his pot-pie— " Poule-au-pot! Poule-au-pot!" He was buried in the Trenton churchyard, and one of his pupils, Dr. F. A. Ewing, in addition to a discriminating obituary in the *State Gazette*, of December 24th, 1831, furnished the inscription for his tomb: "This stone covers the remains of Dr. Nicholas Belleville. Born and educated in France; for fifty-four years an inhabitant of this city. A patriot warmly attached to the principles of liberty; a physician eminently learned and successful; a man of scrupulous and unblemished integrity. On the 17th day of December, A. D. 1831, at the age of seventy-nine years, he closed a life of honor and usefulness; by all respected, esteemed, lamented." General Philemon Dickinson, with whom he was on terms of familiar friendship, held him in high and affectionate consideration, and to him more than to any other he confided the details of his private life and social relations.

WING, HON. MASKELL, Lawyer, late of Greenwich, was born in Trenton, New Jersey, January 30th, 1758. He belonged to what is now the widespread family of Ewing in New Jersey, Pennsylvania, Ohio and Maryland; Thomas Maskell, of England, married Bythia Parsons, of Connecticut, in 1658; Thomas Stathem, of England, married Ruth Udell, in New England, in 1671, and Maskell's son married Stathem's daughter; while in 1720 their daughter became the wife of Thomas Ewing, who had recently come to Greenwich, West Jersey, from Ireland; their eldest son was Maskell Ewing, born in 1721, who was at different times Justice of the Peace, Clerk and Surrogate of Cumberland county, Sheriff and Judge of the Pleas, and died m 1796; one of his ten children was Maskell Ewing, of Trenton. In his youth he assisted his father in the clerkship at Greenwich, and before he had attained his twenty-first year was elected Clerk of the State Assembly. This appointment necessitating removal to Trenton, New Jersey, he resided in that city, engaged in the performance of his official duties, during the ensuing twenty years. He was for a time Recorder of the city, and also pursued a course of legal studies under the supervision of William C. Houston. In 1803 he removed to Philadelphia, and in 1805 to a farm in Delaware county, Pennsylvania. He represented that county in the State Senate for six years. He died while on a visit to Greenwich, August 26th, 1825. His son, Maskell Ewing, who was born in 1806, was a lieutenant in the army, and has died within a few years. Among the branches of the Ewing stock was the family of Rev. John Ewing, D. D., Provost of the University of Pennsylvania from 1779 to 1803, and pastor of the First Church, of Philadelphia.

UNT, GENERAL PETER, Merchant, late of Charleston, South Carolina, was born in New Jersey in 1768, or thereabout. He was engaged extensively in mercantile affairs at Lamberton, where he established a large storehouse, when it was the depot for the trade of Trenton, and at the time of his decease was in partnership with Philip F. Howell. He was identified with the interests and development of the Presbyterian Church in Trenton, New Jersey, and was one of the Trustees elected to supply the vacancies made by the death of Moore Furman, and Isaac Smith, whose daughter he had married. In 1797, Jonathan Doane having contracted to erect a State prison at Trenton, he, in conjunction with Moore Furman, conveyed the ground on which the jail (now arsenal) was built. The measurement was more than eight and one-quarter acres; the consideration, £369 1s. He resided on the estate since occupied by his son, Lieutenant W. E. Hunt, of the United

States navy. He died at Charleston, South Carolina, March 11th, 1810, having spent the winter there in the hope of recovering his health and renewing his enfeebled energies. The Rev. Dr. Hollingshead had a highly satisfactory conversation with him on the day of his death, when he said; "I have no reluctance or hesitation to submit to all the will of God in the article of death; I freely commit my soul into the hands of my Redeemer, and leave my surviving family to the care of a holy and gracious Providence." He was buried with military honors at Charleston, South Carolina, after services in the Circular Church; and in the Presbyterian church porch at Trenton, New Jersey, there is a cenotaph commemorating him.

OW, REV. SAMUEL B., D. D., Educator, Presbyterian Clergyman, afterward pastor of the First Reformed Dutch Church, of New Brunswick, was born in Burlington, New Jersey, and educated at the University of Pennsylvania, where he was graduated in 1811. He acted as tutor for a short time in Dickinson College; then presided as master of the grammar school of his university; in 1813 was licensed by the Presbytery of Philadelphia, subsequently passing a session at the Princeton Seminary, and, November 1st, 1814, was ordained and installed pastor at Solebury, Bucks county. He was identified with the three schools organized under the title of "The Trenton and Lamberton Sunday Free School Association," whose establishment dates from about the opening of the year 1816. "From April to October the school consisted of ninety scholars. On the 27th of October it was divided into three; and it is with peculiar pleasure the association notice those two nurseries of mercy, the Female and African Sunday-schools, which have arisen since the establishment of their own." A column of a newspaper of October 4th, 1819, is occupied with a report of the Trenton Sabbath Day-school, which opens by saying: "Nine months have now elapsed since, by the exertions of a few gentlemen, this school was founded." In February, 1821, the same society reports that it had four schools, the boys', the girls', the African and that at Morrisville. The last school had, in November, 1819, eleven teachers and 116 scholars. The "Female Tract Society" furnished tracts monthly to the schools, while the "Juvenile Dorcas Society" supplied clothing to the children. He was installed over the Trenton congregation, December 17th, 1816, on which occasion Dr. Miller presided and Dr. Alexander preached: 2 Cor. iii. 16; the former giving the charge to the pastor, and Rev. P. V. Brown the charge to the congregation. This pastorship was happily and usefully continued until April, 1821, when a call from the First Church, of New Brunswick, was laid before the presbytery, and he was installed in that city in the following June. The additions to the communion of the church in these five years were fifty-six on their first profession, and thirty on certificates from other churches. In October, 1823, he became pastor of the Independent Presbyterian Church, of Savannah; and in 1830 was made President of Dickinson College. He afterward returned to New Brunswick, however, upon a call to take the pastoral charge of the First Reformed Dutch Church in that city. He was followed, as pastor over the Trenton church, by the late William Jessup Armstrong, D. D., son of Rev. Dr. Amzi Armstrong, of Mendham and Bloomfield, New Jersey.

———◦◦◦———

SMITH, BENJAMIN, late of Elizabethtown, Merchant, Trustee, President of the Board of the Presbyterian Church of Trenton, also its Treasurer, was elected "a Deacon for Trenton," May 6th, 1777, and was an Elder in 1806, and probably for some years before. From the "Minutes of the Trustees," March 19th, 1814, and from other sources, are gathered the following items: For many years he was a valued Trustee and President of the Board, as also Treasurer for the church, all of which offices he filled with faithfulness. At his funeral a sermon was preached by his pastor, Rev. Dr. John McDowell, from the words, "Lord, I have loved the habitation of thy house, and the place where thine honor dwelleth." This text had been selected by himself for the purpose, and his will directed the same to be inscribed on his tomb. Among the legacies of his will was one of $2,500 for the endowment of a scholarship in the Theological Seminary at Princeton, New Jersey, which was realized in 1839, upon the decease of his widow. It stands the twenty-sixth on the list of scholarships, and bears the name of its founder. "Our departed friend," said Dr. McDowell, "loved the house of the Lord, and he has told the speaker that this evidence has often encouraged and comforted his soul, when he could get hold of scarcely any other. His conduct in this respect corresponded with his profession. Through a long life he manifested that he loved the Lord's house. It was taught him, I have understood, from his childhood. At an early age he became the subject of serious impressions, and hopefully of divine grace." He was first received into the Elizabethtown Presbyterian Church, under the ministry of Rev. James Caldwell, in 1765, when he was eighteen or nineteen years of age. Subsequently he removed to Trenton and connected himself with the church in that city, where for a long time he acted in the office of Ruling Elder. During the latter part of the time of his residence in Trenton the congregation erected a new house of worship, and in the attendant movement and measures he took a deep and active interest. About the year 1814 he returned to Elizabethtown, and in the decline of life again renewed his connection with the

local church. He was then elected a Ruling Elder, which office he executed with fidelity until his decease, in the seventy-ninth year of his age. " He manifested his love to the house of God by his constant attendance on its worship until his last short illness; and he manifested it in his will by leaving a bequest for the support of its worship, and remembering other congregations in the town. His last words were, 'Welcome sweet day of rest.'" While the church building was in course of erection at Trenton he also bestowed much of his time, contributed liberally of his means, and went abroad soliciting aid for its completion; while the example set by him of energy and determination spurred on the indolent to fresh exertions, and operated beneficently in awakening general attention to a worthy and laudable undertaking. He died in Elizabethtown, New Jersey, October 23d, 1824.

———◦◦◦———

PEAKE, SAMUEL, Lawyer, late of Trenton, was born in Cumberland county, New Jersey, November 2d, 1747, and received his preparatory training in the two celebrated schools of Fagg's Manor and Pequea. Rev. John Blair, Dr. R. Smith and Enoch Green gave him certificates, 1767–1769, "of proficiency in different branches, and of his high religious character." After teaching three years, or more, in Newcastle, Delaware, he received, in May, 1772, testimonials from Thomas McKean and George Read—two of the three Delaware signers of the Declaration of Independence—George Munro, John Thompson and Rev. Joseph Montgomery. He then entered Princeton College, and in September, 1774, took his Bachelor's degree. In March of the same year President Witherspoon gave to him a written certificate of his qualifications to teach Greek, Latin and mathematics, to which he appended: "I must also add that he gave particular attention to the English language while here, and is probably better acquainted with its structure, propriety and force, than most of his years and standing in this country." He decided, however, not to resume the employment of teaching, but entered upon a course of legal studies, first with Richard Howell, afterward governor of the State, then with Charles Pettit, of Burlington, and with their certificates and that of Thomas McKean, afterward Governor of Pennsylvania, secured his license as an attorney in November, 1776, beginning the practice of his profession in Salem. In October, 1785, he removed to Trenton, where he rapidly acquired an extensive business, and took a leading position among the prominent practitioners of the town. " He paid unusual attention to the students in his office; regularly devoting one hour every day to their examination." He was proverbially systematic in his business affairs; and even into the more private relations of his social and religious life carried a notable method and preciseness, of which the following may be cited as an example: " 1. Be it remembered that Samuel Leake, on Sunday, the thirteenth day of October, in the year of our Lord one thousand eight hundred and eleven, in the Presbyterian church in Trenton, received the Lord's supper; James F. Armstrong then being minister of the gospel, and administering the supper in that church." Entries in the same form, with the proper dates, follow as to each of the semi-annual communions until October 1st, 1815, when the record is that " Dr. Miller preached the action sermon; Dr. Alexander administered the ordinance; Mr. Armstrong was sick and absent." The paper continues to make a formal register of each attendance at the Lord's supper until it closes with that on January 2d, 1820, two months before his decease; he also prepared similar documents for each of his daughters as they in turn became communicants. He died, March 8th, 1820, in the seventy-third year of his age. The Supreme Court being in session at the time, the bar not only resolved to attend the funeral, but recommended to their brethren throughout the State to wear the customary badge of mourning and respect. His epitaph is as follows: "Sacred to the memory of Samuel Leake, Esquire, Serjeant-at-Law. Died March 8th, A. D. 1820, Æ. 72. Educated to the bar, he attained the highest degree of eminence; distinguished for candor, integrity, zeal for his clients, and profound knowledge of jurisprudence, he fulfilled the duties of his station with singular usefulness, 'without fear and without reproach.' Deeply versed in human literature, and devoutly studious of the words of sacred truth; he lived the life of a Christian, and died the death of the righteous."

POLLOCK, JAMES, Dyer, noted Presbyterian Exhorter, Elder of the Trenton church, late of Trenton, was born in Beith, Ayrshire, Scotland. He was one of the most valued parishioners of Rev. James Waddel Alexander, and was "of those who are the glory of the Presbyterian churches." He resided in a small house on Mill Hill, and was employed as a dyer in one of the woollen factories on the Assanpink; and thus is described by the eminent divine already mentioned.: " His figure was somewhat bent, and his hands were always blue, from the colors used in his trade. But his eye was piercing and eloquent; his countenance would shine like a lantern from the light within; and the flame of his strong and impassioned thought made his discourse as interesting as I ever heard from any man. He had the texts of Scripture, as many Scotchmen have, at his finger-ends, and could adduce and apply passages in a most unexpected manner." The great Scottish writers were his familiar friends, and one of his favorite volumes was Rutherford's " Christ Dying and Drawing Sinners to Himself,"

while for Calvin's " Institutes " also he had high respect and admiration. His acquaintance with the reformation history of Scotland was remarkable, being such as would have reflected credit upon any learned clergyman. " Unlike many who resembled him in attainment, he was inwardly and deeply affected by the truths which he knew. His speech was always seasoned with salt, and I deemed it a means of grace to listen to his ardent and continuous discourse. He was certainly a great talker, but without assumption or any wearying of competent hearers. His dialect was broad west-country Scotch, and while I was resident his sense of the peculiarity kept him from praying in the meetings, though none could otherwise have been more acceptable. Having from my childhood been used to Scotch Presbyterians, and knowing how some of the narrower among them will stickle for every pin of the covenanted tabernacle, and every shred and token, as if ordained in the decalogue, I was both surprised and delighted to observe how large-minded he was, in respect to every improvement, however different from the ways of his youth. I have witnessed his faith during grievous illnesses, and I rejoice to know that he was enabled to give a clear dying testimony for the Redeemer whom he loved."—(Letter.) He died in Trenton, New Jersey, in 1858 or 1859. He was widely known and esteemed in the Presbyterian circles of this city, Burlington and other towns of the State, and by his excellent labors in the cause of religion accomplished a large measure of good among those who came within the scope of his influence.

ANDERSON, ALEXANDER, M. D., the first Engraver on Wood in America, late of Jersey City, was born near Beekman's Slip, New York, April 21st, 1775, two days after the first bloodshed in the war for independence had occurred at Lexington and Concord. His father was a native of Scotland, and differed in politics from the major portion of his countrymen in America at that time, who were generally noted for their loyalty to the king and an uncompromising adherence to the royal cause. While the revolutionary crisis was approaching, and collisions between colonial and British authorities and wishes were increasing in frequency, he steadfastly advocated the rights of the Americans, and was fearless and outspoken in his denunciation of English usurpation and tyranny. At the time of his son's birth he was the publisher of a republican newspaper in the city of New York, called *The Constitutional Gazette.* This he continued to publish in opposition to the ministerial papers of Rivington and Gaine until the close of 1776, when the British took possession of New York city. The " rebel printer " was then compelled to fly, with his books and printing materials, nearly all of which were lost or destroyed before he reached a place of absolute safety in Connecticut. He was originally a physician, having graduated, M. D., at Columbia College, New York, and was the pioneer engraver on wood in America, the "virtual inventor" of the art on this side of the Atlantic. His name has been familiar to booksellers and readers in the United States since the opening of the present century; and the "mysterious little monogram, 'A. A.,' in the corners of wood-cuts in educational and text-books has attracted the attention of millions of children in our schools, and at our firesides when experiencing the delight of his pictures." In 1804 he published "A General History of Quadrupeds," with numerous wood-engravings. Among his best known works are forty illustrations of Shakspeare, and those in "Webster's Spelling Book." After his decease B. J. Lossing prepared a memorial lecture of him as pioneer engraver and publisher; and in *Harper's Weekly*, February, 1870, are shown an early and a late specimen of his skill in engraving, the first entitled "The Beggar at the Door;" the second "Alexander Anderson," a portrait of himself, executed in his eighty-first year. It depicts him as a hale, though wrinkled and furrowed, large-featured and bright-eyed man, with a snow-white beard and kindly compressed lips. He died at the residence of his son-in-law, in Jersey City, January 17th, 1870; and in his death "the bookmakers' craft and the world of book-readers have lost a long-familiar friend: a man whose genius, not meteoric in splendor, but planet-like in its effulgence, has burned in our firmament with steady lustre for almost three generations." His "William and Amelia in the Orchard" is a quaint representation of two damsels, a lad playing on a pipe, and a small dog, executed at an early day, and one which presents a fair sample of his initial efforts in the line of art.

ROVER, LEWIS C., of Newark, was born in Caldwell, in the county of Essex, New Jersey, in 1815. His grandfather, Rev. Stephen Grover, served in the continental army, and upon the conclusion of peace resumed his clerical studies. He settled in Caldwell early in life, and remained the pastor of the Presbyterian church in that place until his death, in 1836. He was a man of strong personal characteristics, and was the trusted coadjutor of the many eminent and gifted preachers of the time. The subject of our sketch was a favorite of this venerable and worthy gentleman, whose reputation is still held in high esteem through the large and extensive parish which he ruled and guided. In 1827 Stephen R. Grover, the father of Mr. Grover, took up his residence in Newark, where he became a lawyer of excellent standing. He represented the county of Essex in the State Senate from 1845 to 1848, and discharged the duties of the position with credit and faithfulness. Upon

the removal of the family to Newark, Lewis C. Grover, although quite young, took immediate hold of the real responsibilities of life. He obtained a situation in the State Bank, and afterwards in the large establishment of Messrs. Shipman, Robinson & Co., where he acquired that clear and accurate knowledge of business which has been invaluable to him in his progress through life. While engaged in these pursuits he found time to pursue branches of study in which he became well grounded, the advantages of which he has always felt. His reading, too, was extensive and sound, and his quick, retentive mind carried with it the fruit of culture and study. During this period and afterwards he became connected with the literary institutions of his place of residence, and derived great advantage from his contact with other minds. During this time his inclinations became more decided in favor of a profession, and after some hesitation he became a law student in the office of his father, giving to the study all the resolution of his character. In 1840 he obtained his attorney's license, in the same class as F. T. Frelinghuysen and Joseph P. Bradley, and he almost immediately stepped into a successful and lucrative practice. His activity and energy were proverbial, and his management of causes, and his zeal in behalf of his clients, are remembered and noted. It is not to be supposed that, with his earnest characteristics, he should long remain a stranger to political action. The political contest of 1838 culminated in what was designated the Broad-Seal contest, and in this Governor Pennington enlisted the aid of Mr. Grover in the scrutiny of the polls in this section of the State. This drew him into early association with all the trusted Whig leaders of the State, and laid the foundation of those vigorous efforts which characterized his course in later years. From 1838 to 1848, the close of his connection with political pursuits, he was a bold, earnest and uncompromising Whig, conversant with the political action of his party, and always influential with the younger elements composing it. It was a period when Newark and the county of Essex were changing their character without altering their convictions, and the conflict of what was new with what was old was a necessary feature of that change. The political contests of those times, too, were the wars of the giants. They were tremendous struggles for supremacy between two equal parties, and they called out the energies of young and old to an extent never since equalled. Mr. Grover was prominent and active in the great Presidential struggles of 1840, 1844 and 1848, giving of his labors, means and speech to the success of the Whig organization. In the year 1848 he was placed upon the Whig ticket for Assembly in the county of Essex, and was elected by a large majority. In that body he immediately took an active and leading position. Mr. Whelpley was elected Speaker, and Mr. Grover took the Chairmanship of the Judiciary Committee. In the House were Martin Ryerson, John T. Nixon, William F. Day, and others prominent in the State, and it may be easily under-

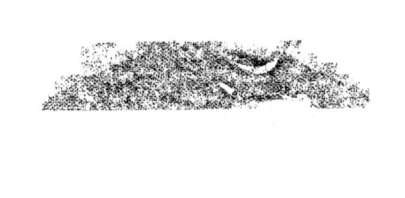

McLeay Pub. Co. Phila.

stood that it required great capacity and energy to stand at the head with such association. In 1845 Mr. Grover had obtained from the Legislature of New Jersey the charter of the Mutual Benefit Life Insurance Company, and in its organization he was made counsel of the institution. From small beginnings it gradually accomplished a success which was real and permanent, and it began to need a vigorous and capable mind. Mr. Grover was invaluable in his position, but the constant demands upon his time and attention by his professional and political pursuits detracted from his usefulness, and at the close of his first session in the Legislature it was proposed by the officers and directors that he should abandon politics and give his attention almost exclusively to the affairs of the company. To a young man of great promise and much ambition this was not a pleasant alternative; but, having decided that the work of his life must be in life insurance, he complied with all its conditions with scrupulous fidelity. Withdrawing from active life, he directed his attention entirely to the success of the company, extending and enlarging its business, and securing it from that irresponsible control which would have destroyed its usefulness. During many years his history would be simply a history of the progress of the company. But while Mr. Grover, in accordance with his engagements, withdrew from the field of political aspirations, he did not lose his interest in public questions. He has not been the less a patriot because he did not take part in political quarrels, for none were more active in sustaining the country in its hour of peril, or more anxious that faithful and honorable men should control its destinies. The friend of law and order, of temperance and religion, of humanity and right, his influence has been frequently potent for good. We are thus brought up to a period in his career when the real success and object of his life became apparent even to himself. His life, indeed, became merged in that of the great company with which he was connected as counsel, Vice-President and President. Its success and prosperity became assured with every passing year, and finally its management and control became a great responsibility, requiring the best energies of his mind and strong character. When the Mutual Benefit Life Insurance Company was formed, life insurance was but little understood or appreciated. Its varied and complex problems had scarcely been reduced to an exact science, and its adaptation to the fresher and newer life of the United States was a question only to be solved by experience. This company proceeded upon careful general principles, its growth was real rather than rapid, and the experience of over thirty years proves the wisdom of its management and the soundness of its mathematical and business control. It is not too much to say that Mr. Grover has always been found equal to the demands made upon him, and that in the complicated management of the company he has proved himself worthy of the confidence reposed in him. To-day the institution over which he presides is regarded as among the strongest in the country.

45

This field of duty, however important, withdraws a person from public observation, and necessarily circumscribes a life within a comparatively narrow boundary; but when we look at the success, the results and the advantages springing from such an institution, it assumes new importance and stronger claims. Within its protecting care are shielded the widow and the fatherless, and its blessings are distributed far and wide. Thus a life devoted to such labors becomes ennobled by results, and we learn to appreciate the patient toil and untiring energy which leaves its mark in blessings scattered through a whole community. This sketch would be wanting in portraiture if we did not refer to the moral and religious culture which distinguishes Mr. Grover. From his youth this private and public conscientiousness has become a part of his life and character, and has been felt in all his connection with business-affairs. His charities have been large, constant and beneficent, and they have been governed by no narrow boundary of creeds. Human want and suffering have always been sufficient to make a claim on that large and comprehensive charity which recognizes the unvarying law of the Christian faith.

URMAN, HON. MOORE, Merchant, first Mayor of Trenton, late of Trenton, New Jersey, was born in 1730, or thereabout, and was an active participant in the war of the Revolution, a loyal and eminently useful citizen both in private life and as a State officer, and a leading spirit in all that concerned the interests of his State and welfare of his fellow-citizens. During the days of conflict between the colonies and the mother country his enterprising character would not permit him to look on with indifference at passing events of such importance, and he at once declared for the patriot against the royal cause. He served as Deputy Quartermaster-General and in other capacities; and by appointment of the Legislature, upon its incorporation, in 1792, became the first Mayor of Trenton, an honor which he bore with energy and uprightness. June 12th, 1760, he was elected a Trustee of the Trenton Presbyterian Church, and Treasurer in 1762. He subsequently removed to Pittstown, and thence to Philadelphia, Pennsylvania. Upon his return to Trenton from the latter city, he was re-elected to the Board, in 1783, and continued in it until the time of his decease. Though so long connected with the temporal affairs of this Presbyterian congregation, he was not a communicant until November 1st, 1806. He died at Trenton, New Jersey, March 16th, 1808, in the eightieth year of his age. He had made a written request of Mr. Armstrong that, in case he should be called to officiate at his funeral, he would speak from the words, "Into thine hand I commit my spirit: thou hast redeemed me, O Lord God of truth," Psalm xxxi.; and his request was faithfully followed in the body of the discourse, to which the pastor added as follows: "This congregation well know his long and faithful services as a zealous supporter and Trustee of the concerns and interests of this church. In the Revolution he was known as a faithful friend of his country, and was intrusted by government and the commander in-chief of our revolutionary army—whose friendship was honor indeed—in offices and in departments the most profitable and most important. When bending beneath the load of years and infirmities, how did it gladden his soul and appear to renew his life to see this edifice rising from the ruins of the old one and consecrated to the service of his God! And did you not see him, shortly after its consecration, as a disciple of his Redeemer, recognizing his baptismal vows, and in that most solemn transaction of our holy religion stretching his trembling hands to receive the symbols of the body and blood of our Lord and Saviour, and in that act express the sentiment of the words selected by himself for the use of this mournful occasion, 'Into thine hand I commit my spirit: thou hast redeemed me, O Lord God of truth'"? Peter Hunt, his son-in-law, a prosperous and influential merchant of Trenton, was afterward elected a Trustee to supply the vacancy occasioned by his death. He was buried within the shadow of the church he held in such warm affection, and his gravestone may still be seen in its porch.

----◆----

RELLET, STEPHEN, eminent Quaker Preacher and Missionary, of Burlington, New Jersey, was born in France, in 1773. His parents being of the household of Louis XVI., he was nurtured in the bosom of the Roman Catholic Church, and educated at the Military College of Lyons. While in his seventeenth year he became one of the body-guard of the king. After the execution of that monarch he evaded the searches of those evilly disposed to every one and everything savoring of royalty, and escaped to Demerara. In 1795 he proceeded to New York, where, chancing to attend a Quaker meeting, he was so attracted by the primitive, simple demeanor and doctrines of the Friends that he determined to join their society. In the following winter he removed to Philadelphia, and during the prevalence of the yellow fever in that city, in 1798, ministered with efficient zeal and rare magnanimity to the sick, the dying and the afflicted. "He was as an angel of mercy to the plague-stricken; unfearingly braved the most virulent types of diseases, contagious and infectious; and spent freely of his substance, time and exertions to rescue those whom, in several cases, their very friends, relations and physician had abandoned." During this terrible and trying season he became impressed with the idea that it was his duty to go abroad, and preach

and publish the gospel, as he held it, to all his fellow-creatures, but did not at once act upon the conviction that had taken firm hold upon him. In 1799 he settled in New York and engaged in mercantile pursuits for a brief period, not yet resolved to accept the role of itinerant preacher, but still uneasy in his mind and unsettled in his deliberations. Eventually he set himself to the pious and self-appointed task, and in 1800 made an extensive tour through the Southern States as far as Georgia, and in 1801 through the various States of New England, and the towns and villages of East and West Canada. In 1807, continuing his ministrations with unflagging ardor, he went to the south of France, and in that historic country, where religion and its adjuncts have for centuries exercised a prime and ruling influence, stirred and thrilled the people by his pleadings, his denunciations, and his eloquent exhortations. In 1812 he travelled in England on his philanthropic mission, and also in Germany. In 1816 he found a fresh field of labors in Hayti; and in 1818, 1819 and 1820 made an extended tour through Norway, Sweden, Russia, Greece and Italy, ever holding the same great end steadfastly in view—the awakening of all to the sacredness and importance of a Christian life, and the peril of worldly pleasure and immorality. At Rome he entered the papal mansion, and standing before the head of Roman Catholicism, with his companion, William Allen, addressed him with the warmth and enthusiasm of an early apostle. On this notable occasion his Holiness, Pope Pius VII., received him with kindness, and even listened to his exhortations "with the greatest respect and courtesy." While in Russia he was granted an audience also with the Czar, and in the palace of that powerful monarch "spoke out valiantly and beseechingly for the cause of pure religion." In August, 1820, he returned to his home in this country, to which he was deeply attached. In 1831-1834 he made another extended missionary excursion through Europe; and in the course of the latter year retired to Burlington, New Jersey, where he resided permanently until the time of his decease. He married the eldest daughter of Isaac Collins, also a member of the Society of Friends, and an eminent citizen of Trenton, New Jersey, where he established and edited the famous pioneer newspaper of the State, The New Jersey Gazette, published in opposition to the royalist organs of New York city. His singular career as a convert from the faith of Rome, and his change from the position of body-guard of Louis XVI. to a devoted Quaker minister and an itinerant missionary, have been commemorated in a printed discourse by Dr. Van Rensselaer; while his "Memoirs," by Benjamin Seebohn, were published (two volumes, 8vo.) in 1860, and are a storehouse of marvellous experiences, facts and fancies of a highly suggestive nature, and revelations of the inner life and meditations of one whose nature, standing out in bold relief from among the listless and incredulous of his kind, was full of the fire of piety, and desirous of the salvation of all mankind. He died at Burlington, New Jersey, November 16th, 1855.

———◆◇◆———

MITH, REV. JOHN, former Pastor of the Trenton Presbyterian Church, was born in Wethersfield, Connecticut, in 1795–1800. He was a graduate of Yale College, 1821, and of the Andover Theological Seminary, and a licentiate of the Congregational Association of East Fairfield. In December, 1825, he was chosen by the congregation of the Trenton Presbyterian Church to fill the vacancy occasioned by the death of Rev. Dr. William Jessup Armstrong; in the ensuing February was received by the Presbytery, and March 8th was ordained and regularly installed. In that service Dr. Carnahan presided; Dr. Hodge preached, 1 Cor. i. 21, and both the charges were given by Rev. E. F. Cooley. In this pastorate he continued less than three years, yet in that time fifty-nine persons made their first profession. Twenty-six of these were received at the communion of April, 1827, two of whom afterward entered the ministry, viz., Rev. George Ely, pastor of Nottingham and Dutch Neck, who died August 14th, 1856, and Rev. George Burrowes, D. D., pastor of Kirkwood, in Maryland, professor in Lafayette College, and pastor in Newtown, Pennsylvania. During his ministry some confusion was created by the indiscreet, however sincere, zeal, in what they called the cause of Christ, of two or three superserviceable ministers and candidates, who desired to introduce those measures for the promotion of the work of a pastor that had, then at least, the apology of being too new to have taught their warning lessons. An attempt was made to form a distinct congregation, and separate meetings were held for a time, and even a small building erected, which was put into connection with the German Reformed Church; but the Presbyterians gradually returned, and no effort was made, or probably designed, to produce a schism. In August, 1828, he requested a dissolution of the pastoral relation, which was granted by the Presbytery, and in the following February was detached from that body and took charge of a Congregational church in Exeter, New Hampshire. He afterward exercised his ministry in Stamford, and other towns of Connecticut, and large numbers of persons of both sexes have, through his labors and persuasions, become united with the churches he has served. While residing in Trenton, New Jersey, he was married to a daughter of the late Aaron Dickinson Woodruff, Attorney-General of the State of New Jersey. In the churchyard at Trenton is a tablet bearing the following inscription, commemorating a noteworthy bringing to God of one of eleven new communicants, in April, 1828: "Here lie the remains of Jeremiah D. Lalor, who departed this life March 8th, A. D. 1845, aged thirty-two years. To those who knew him the remembrance of his virtues is the

highest eulogy of his character. He had devoted himself to the service of God in the ministry of reconciliation, and when just upon the threshold of the sacred office was removed by death from the brightest prospects of usefulness to serve his Maker in another sphere." And, as a learned divine of the same church has remarked, "This is but one of many examples illustrating his surpassing usefulness in a sphere of beneficent labors and good actions."

———◆◇◆———

OLLINS, ISAAC, Printer and Publisher, late of Burlington, New Jersey, was born in Delaware, February 16th, 1746. His father emigrated to the United States from Bristol, England. In his boyhood he served an apprenticeship to the printing business, and at its completion removed to Philadelphia, where he worked as a journeyman during the ensuing eighteen months. At the expiration of this time he entered into partnership relations with Joseph Cruikshanks, and in 1770 settled in Burlington, New Jersey, having been chosen colonial printer to George III. In 1771 he commenced the printing and publishing of almanacs, and continued that series of works for nearly a quarter of a century. He was also at this time the publisher of several other useful and needed books. On his removal to Trenton, New Jersey, in 1778, he projected what was in the publishing business of that time a great enterprise, namely, the publication of an octavo family Bible; and the putting forth of the entire work was then considered so adventurous an undertaking that it was deemed necessary to secure extraordinary encouragement and inducements in advance, and, accordingly, the first edition of the Scriptures, that of John Aitken, was recommended to the country by a resolution of Congress. This was on September 12th, 1782, just five years after the report of a committee on a memorial had stated that to import types and print and bind 30,000 copies would cost £10,272 10s., and therefore recommended the adoption of a resolution authorizing the importation of 20,000 Bibles. In 1788 he issued proposals to print a quarto edition of the Bible, in 984 pages, at the price of four Spanish dollars, "one dollar to be paid at the time of subscribing." Thereupon the Synod of New York and New Jersey, November 3d, 1788, warmly indorsed the matter, and appointed Dr. Witherspoon, President S. S. Smith, and Mr. Armstrong to concur with committees of any other denominations, or of any other Synods, to revise the sheets, and, if necessary, to assist in selecting a standard edition. This committee was authorized to agree with him to append Ostervald's "Notes," if not inconsistent with the wishes of other than Calvinistic subscribers. In 1789 the General Assembly appointed a committee of sixteen to lay his proposals before their respective Presbyteries, and to recommend that subscriptions be solicited in each congregation, and report the number to the next Assembly. This recommendation was reiterated in 1790 and 1791. Thus sustained, the quarto edition of 5,000 copies was published in the course of the latter year. Ostervald's "Practical Observations," which added 170 pages of matter, were furnished to special subscribers. "Collins' Bible" was so carefully revised that it is still a standard. He and his children assumed the roles of careful proof-readers, and it is stated in the preface of a subsequent edition, after mentioning the names of several clergymen who assisted the publisher in 1791, "Some of these persons, James F. Armstrong in particular, being near the press, assisted also in reading and correcting the proof-sheets." The following, taken from Dr. Hall's excellent work treating of Trenton and the Presbyterian church of that city, is an item of interest and value : "As an instance of the weight which the most incidental acts of the Assembly carried at that early period of its existence, I would allude to a letter to the Moderator of 1790 from the Rev. David Rice, often called the Presbyterian Pioneer, or Apostle of Kentucky, in which he states that having received from Mr. Armstrong, as clerk of the Assembly, a notification of the action in reference to the Collins Bible, he had procured the calling of a special meeting of the Transylvania Presbytery, 'that we might be in a capacity to obey the order of the General Assembly.' 'Such is our dispersed condition' that it was some weeks before the meeting could convene. 'After two days' deliberation on the subject,' they found that a compliance was impracticable, and on Mr. Rice was devolved the office of explaining the cause of the delinquency. One of the difficulties was that of sending a messenger to Philadelphia in time for the Assembly to give their advance subscription money ; 'the want of horses sufficient for so long a journey, or of other necessaries, laid an effectual bar in our way.'" In order to secure the utmost accuracy in the typography of his Bible, the whole was subjected to eleven searching and careful proof-readings, the last of which was by his daughter, Rebecca ; and so free from errors was this edition of the Scriptures, that it became at once the standard for all critical appeal, when the English translation alone was concerned. The American historiographer of printing, according to Hall, makes no mention of the quarto edition of 5,000 copies published in 1791, but speaks only of his octavo New Testament of 1788, and Bible of 1793–94. He also printed in Trenton 2,000 copies of Sewel's "History of the Quakers," of nearly 1,000 pages folio; Ramsay's "South Carolina," 2 vols., and other large and important works. Moreover, the first newspaper issued in New Jersey was printed by him at Burlington, December 5th, 1777 ; subsequently it was transferred to Trenton, and published there from February 25th, 1778, to November 27th, 1786, excepting a suspension of nearly five months in 1783, when it was finally discontinued. He was the conductor as well as proprietor of the paper, the title of "editor," indeed, not having superseded that of "printer," and it was established to counteract the anti-republican tendency of Rivington's

Royal Gazette, of New York. Governor Livingston was a correspondent of the *Trenton Gazette* as long as it remained in his hands. December 9th, 1777, the Legislature exempted him, "and any number of men not exceeding four to be employed by him at his printing office," from militia service during the time they were occupied in printing the laws, or the weekly newspaper. In 1779 he vindicated the liberty of the press in a signal and notable manner, considering the time and circumstances bearing on him, by refusing to give the name of a political correspondent on the demand of the Legislative Council. His reply was : "In any other case, not incompatible with good conscience or the welfare of my country, I shall think myself happy in having it in my power to oblige you." There was a paper-mill in Trenton before the time of the publication of his Bible. In December, 1788, it was advertised by its proprietors, Stacy Potts and John Reynolds, as "now nearly completed." The manufacturers issued "earnest appeals for rags ; in one of their publications presenting to the consideration of those mothers who have children going to school the present great scarcity of that useful article, without which their going to school would avail them but little." In January, 1789, the *Federal Post,* otherwise known as the *Trenton Weekly Mercury,* printed by Quequelle & Wilson, was obliged to have its size reduced "on account of the scarcity of demy printing paper." The "Trenton School Company" originated in a meeting of citizens, held February 10th, 1781, the capital being $720, divided into thirty-six shares. A lot was then purchased and a stone building erected, one story of which was occupied in 1782 ; in the following year it was enlarged and the endowment increased ; in 1785 it was incorporated, and in 1794 its funds were replenished by means of a lottery ; and in 1800 the girls' school of the academy was removed to the school-house belonging to the Presbyterian church. "The public quarterly examinations were usually closed with exercises in speaking in the church, and the newspapers tell of 'the crowded and polite audiences' which attended, usually including the Governor, Legislature, and distinguished strangers." Among the latter, in 1784, were the President of Congress, Baron Steuben, and members of the Congress and Legislature. Of this academy he was one of the leading and active founders, and although nine of his children were educated within its walls, he refused to take advantage of his right as a stockholder to have them instructed without further charge. In 1796 he removed to New York, but in 1808 returned to his former home in Burlington. His wife, Rachel Budd, was great-granddaughter of Mahlon Stacy, an eminent citizen of New Jersey, and the original proprietor of the land on which the academy now stands. "It is a remarkable fact in the history of his family of fourteen children that, after the death of one in infancy, there was no mortality for the space of fifty years." His eldest daughter was married to Stephen Grellet, whose singular career as a convert from the faith of Rome, and the position of bodyguard of Louis XVI., to

Gilson Bros Co Philad.

C. Doughty

an ardent Quaker minister and missionary, has been commemorated in a printed discourse by Dr. Van Rensselaer.
In 1848 his surviving family "printed for private use a ......
memoir of their venerated parents," and therein may be ...... found a more extended and minute account of the life and .... the Old State
works of this useful and distinguished citizen. His children .....
have cherished the religious sentiments of their parents and ....
united with the Friends, while the sons turned their atten-..... tion and energies to the vocations of their father, and through .....
out the United States ..... thousands of books bearing
the imprints of the various houses of which this generation .....
of publishers has been possessed, Henry at Burlington,
New Jersey, March 21st, 18..

EOMANS, REV. JOHN ....
terian Clergyman, of ...... State in 1800-1804, and ....
College, 1824, and also .....
March 16th, 1834, the .....
ton Church chose as ....
Henry, but the call was declined. On ......
6th a second choice was made, and he ......
of a Congregational church in Pittsfield ....
elected to fill the vacant pulpit. He was ....
by the Presbytery, and installed October .....
that service Rev. David Comfort preached ....
Alexander preached, 1 Cor. xi. 1, and ....
and A. Alexander gave the charges. His ....
is to be dated from September 11th, 1834, ...
when he entered on the Presidency of L ....
Pennsylvania. "To his energy and influence ....
to the enterprise of the congregation, is .....
of the commodious church which is now ....
congregation." The corner-stone of the .....
laid May 2d, 18.., and services were ..... for the dedi ....
January 19th 18... The preceding .... services ..... placed in its central part. The dimensions are, one .....
length; 62 feet breadth, ... feet ..... 120 feet. On the after-
noon of the same day ..... preached, and Dr. A. Alexander administered the Lord's supper; three deacons and
three elders were .... ordained, James Pollock, Aaron
A. Hutchinson, Thomas A. Ewing, M. D., John A. Hutchinson, Benjamin S. Unthow, and Joseph G. Brearley. ....
In the evening an eloquent sermon was delivered by ....
J. W. Alexander. In April, 1857, a church was organized
by a committee of Presbytery in Bloomsburg, then a suburb
of Trenton, and the place of worship was the building
erected by those who followed Rev. William Boswell in
his secession from the regular Baptist denomination, and
which was vacated upon his death in 1853. This mission
was zealously conducted for a year by Rev. Charles Web-

prior to the eighteen
substantial business col-
age of eighteen years in
portion of the next three
sale dry goods house of
York. He then went ....
for about a year in a .....

an ardent Quaker minister and missionary, has been commemorated in a printed discourse by Dr. Van Rensselaer. In 1848 his surviving family "printed for private use a memoir of their venerated parents," and therein may be found a more extended and minute account of the life and works of this useful and distinguished citizen. His children have cherished the religious sentiments of their parents and united with the Friends, while the sons turned their attention and energies to the vocation of their father, and throughout the United States to-day are thousands of books bearing the imprints of the various firms with which this generation of publishers has been connected. He died at Burlington, New Jersey, March 21st, 1817.

EOMANS, REV. JOHN WILLIAM, Presbyterian Clergyman, of Trenton, was born in this State in 1800–1804, and graduated from Williams College, 1824, and also at the Andover Seminary. March 16th, 1834, the congregation of the Trenton Church chose as pastor Rev. Symmes C. Henry, but the call was declined. On the following June 6th a second choice was made, and he, being then pastor of a Congregational church in Pittsfield, Massachusetts, was elected to fill the vacant pulpit. He was then duly received by the Presbytery, and installed October 7th, 1834. In that service Rev. David Comfort presided; Rev. J. W. Alexander preached, 1 Cor. xi. 1, and Drs. B. H. Rice and A. Alexander gave the charges. His actual ministry is to be dated from September 11th, 1834, to June 1st, 1841, when he entered on the Presidency of Lafayette College, Pennsylvania. "To his energy and influence, not less than to the enterprise of the congregation, is owing the erection of the commodious church which is now occupied by the congregation." The corner-stone of the new building was laid May 2d, 1839, and services were held for the first time January 19th, 1840. The preceding structures stood upon the western part of the church lot: the present one was placed in the central part. The dimensions are, 104 feet length; 62 feet breadth; steeple 120 feet. On the afternoon of the same day Dr. How preached, and Dr. A. Alexander administered the Lord's supper; three deacons and three elders were also then ordained, James Pollock, Aaron A. Hutchinson, Francis A. Ewing, M. D., John A. Hutchinson, Benjamin S. Disbrow, and Joseph G. Brearley; and in the evening an eloquent sermon was delivered by Rev. J. W. Alexander. In April, 1837, a church was organized by a committee of Presbytery in Bloomsburg, then a suburb of Trenton, and the place of worship was the building erected by those who followed Rev. William Boswell in his secession from the regular Baptist denomination, and which was vacated upon his death in 1833. This mission was zealously conducted for a year by Rev. Charles Web-

ster, 1837, and was then suspended until the formation there of the Second Church of Trenton. He had a seat in the General Assembly of 1837, when the decisive acts were adopted which resulted in the division familiarly known as the Old School and the New School, the latter portion forming a distinct congregation. "No disturbance was produced in the Trenton congregation by this revolution; with entire unity it remained in the ancient fraternity of the churches of the New Brunswick Presbytery." The following is a portion of a letter written by him to the Rev. John Hall, D. D., an eminent divine, and the historian of the church in Trenton: "The building of the church fairly led the way to the construction of tasteful architecture in the place. The court house was built at the same time, but the draft of the church helped to determine the form of that; and the row of cottages beyond the canal, and some other handsome dwellings which followed in the course of improvement, were built by the men who came there to build the church. I shall never forget the cordial and earnest way the trustees and others of the congregation, and indeed the whole body, engaged in the work. I have scarcely known a people who resolved to appropriate so much to the erection of a house of worship in proportion to their means at the time. They went through the work without one case of personal disaffection arising out of their proceedings, and their zeal and labor have since proved a great blessing to them and to others. . . . . We had during my ministry there no occasion which was signalized as a revival. The accessions to full connection were, if I rightly remember, more or less at every sacramental celebration of the supper. Sometimes, perhaps, the records will show, twenty or thirty in a year; perhaps even on a single occasion twenty. . . . . But many are far more decisive than I am inclined to be in aiming at the kind of awakenings which are frequent in some parts of the Church, and published with so much avidity in the papers." The total additions to the communion in his pastorate were seventy-two on examination, and eighty-five on certificate. June 1st, 1841, he entered on the Presidency of Lafayette College, Pennsylvania.

OUGHTY, JOSHUA, retired Merchant and Bank President, of Somerville, was born, 1799, in Morris county, New Jersey, and is a son of the late Major-General Solomon Doughty, of the New Jersey State Militia. The family is of English descent, and were settled in New Jersey prior to the revolutionary war. Joshua Doughty received a substantial business education, and when he reached the age of eighteen years he left home, and during the greater portion of the next three years was engaged in the wholesale dry-goods house of Doty & Halsey, in the city of New York. He then went to the Southern States, and sojourned for about a year in Mobile, Alabama. Leaving that city, he engaged in business on his own account in Appalachicola, Florida, where he opened the first store and sold the first goods ever offered in that town. He continued this venture for about two years, when he removed to Franklin, Alabama, where he again embarked in business, carrying on a general country trade, and remained there until 1836, when he closed up his business in the South, and returned to New Jersey, where he selected Somerville as his future residence, and purchased property in that town. In 1838 he built a store, and again entered into a general trade in which he continued to be interested until 1866. He procured, in 1848, the charter for the Somerville County Bank, and immediately upon its organization he was elected its first President, and held that position uninterruptedly for twenty-five years, resigning in 1873. This bank is one of the most substantially prosperous institutions of the kind in the State; and its present high standing is due, in a great measure, to his judicious management in former years. It still retains its organization as a State bank. He is a prominent member of the Democratic party, and in 1860 was one of the delegates to the National Convention at Charleston, where he supported Mr. Guthrie for the Presidency; but when that body adjourned to Baltimore, he supported Breckenridge. In 1863 he was nominated, by the Democracy of Somerville, as their candidate for State Senator, and elected to the same by the largest majority ever given to a Democrat in that county. While in the Senate he served on the Committee on Treasurer's Accounts, and during his first year, when the majority in that body was Democratic, he was Chairman of the said committee. He has been, for a number of years, President of the Raritan Water-Power Company. He is a man of stern integrity, rare business discernment, and has done much to advance the material prosperity of Somerville; indeed, he is perhaps one of its largest real estate owners. He was married, in 1835, to Susan M., daughter of Colonel Isaac Southard, and a niece of the late Senator Samuel L. Southard.

cDANOLDS, JAMES S., State Librarian, Trenton, was born in Branchville, Sussex county, New Jersey, July 11th, 1841. Having received a thorough common school education, he entered, as a clerk, a store in Branchville, and subsequently obtained a clerical position in New York. In the latter he remained until the breaking out of the war, when he enlisted in the 7th New Jersey Regiment, Colonel Joseph Revere. With this organization he remained until the 15th of August, 1862, when he was commissioned a Second Lieutenant and assigned to Company D, in the 15th New Jersey Regiment. In March, 1863, he was promoted to be First Lieutenant, and in March, 1864, to be Captain—his successive advances being the reward of faithful and efficient service. Two months later (May 12th) his career

in the army was cut short at the battle of Spottsylvania, where he was wounded in both legs and in the head. His right leg was so severely injured as to render amputation necessary, and after spending four months in hospital, he was (December 15th, 1864) honorably discharged from the service. Up to the time of his discharge he had taken part in all the hard fighting in which both regiments—during his respective connections with them—had been engaged, and his army record was thoroughly creditable to his patriotism and soldierly ability. Soon after his discharge from the army he opened a general store in Branchville, and was employed in mercantile affairs until the fall of 1871, when he was appointed an officer in the register department of the New York Post-Office. Still retaining his residence in New Jersey, he discharged the duties of this responsible position until March, 1872, when he was appointed State Librarian of New Jersey. Admirably fitted by his clerical training for an office of this sort, his management of the library has been of the most satisfactory character, and his ability was acknowledged by his reappointment in January, 1876, for a further term of three years. In politics, as may be inferred from his war record, he is an earnest Republican, heartily devoted to furthering the interests of his party. He was married, January 1st, 1866, to Frances, daughter of Mr. John Hendershot, of Sussex county.

ILLS, GEORGE MORGAN, D. D., Clergyman, Scholar, Historian, etc., the youngest of six children—four daughters and two sons—of Horace and Almira (Wilcox) Hills, was born in Auburn, New York, October 10th, 1825. His parents were natives of Connecticut, his father's birthplace being near Hartford, and that of his mother near New Haven. They carried the influences of religion and learning with them to their western home, where for thirty years they were prominent in whatever gave Christian refinement to the place. The subject of this notice was prepared for college exclusively in select schools and under private tutors, and very early evinced great promise in oratory and belles-lettres. When fourteen years of age he revised with his parents to the city of New York. At seventeen he set to music Coxe's ballad, "Carol, Carol, Christians," which is believed to have been the first Christmas carol sung in this country. He was graduated with honors at Trinity College, Hartford, Connecticut, in 1847, his oration at the Commencement, on "Berkeley, Bishop of Cloyne," being so marked, that, at the solicitation of several distinguished literary gentlemen present, was published. He immediately became a candidate for holy orders in the Diocese of Western New York. After three years' study in divinity, he was made Master of Arts in course, was ordained Deacon in Trinity Church, Buffalo, New York, by Bishop De Lancey, and took charge of Grace Church, Lyons, New York.

The next year he was advanced to the priesthood, by the same prelate, in Trinity Church, Geneva, New York, and instituted into the rectorship at Lyons. On the 7th of October, 1852, in St. Bartholomew's Church, New York, he was united in marriage, by his brother, the Rev. Horace Hills, Jr., with Sarah, the eldest daughter of the late John Dows, of the firm of Dows & Cary, New York. In 1853 he was called to Trinity Church, Watertown, New York, where he remained with great acceptability and success until he was chosen Rector of St. Paul's Church, Syracuse, New York. He entered upon his duties there in May, 1857, and the congregation increased so rapidly, that the next year the church building was enlarged and otherwise improved. In 1861, accompanied by his wife and two other relatives, he made an extensive tour through Europe, which occupied nearly a year, during which he contributed every week "Letters from Europe" to the columns of the *Gospel Messenger*. He had personal acquaintance with Bishop Wilberforce, Dean Hook, Canon Harold Browne, and other dignitaries of the Church of England, and the memorable pleasure of an interview with the only survivor of those present at the consecration of Bishop Seabury, and of receiving from the Bishop of Aberdeen, Scotland, the gift of a portrait of one of Seabury's consecrators. Returning to his parish in 1862, he was elected by the Convention of Western New York a Trustee of the General Theological Seminary, and subsequently placed by that body on their "committee for the examination" of the students. In 1863 he was elected by the diocesan convention as one of four clergymen appointed to represent that body in the General Convention of the Protestant Episcopal Church, which he subsequently did in Philadelphia in 1865, where he was a member of the "committee on the prayer-book." In 1863, at the request of the rector of that parish, he laid the corner-stone of Christ Church, Jordan, New York. In 1864, at the request of Bishop De Lancey, he preached the sermon at the consecration of St. George's Church, Utica, New York. In 1865 he preached a sermon commemorative of Bishop De Lancey, entitled, "The Wise Master-Builder," which, after being repeated by request, was printed. In the following autumn, at the suggestion of Bishop Coxe, he organized "The Onondaga Convocation," a voluntary association comprising the clergy in the counties of Onondaga, Cayuga and Cortland. In 1867, in addition to the care of his large parish, he inaugurated a very promising mission among the Onondaga Indians, at their "reservation," eight miles from Syracuse, preparing for them a mission service, their own language being on one page and its translation into English on the opposite, fitting them up a chapel, preaching to them through an interpreter every Sunday afternoon, baptizing adults and children, presenting a class for confirmation, and marrying, with Christian rites, some who had been living for years in pagan concubinage. The attachment of these Indians to him became very great, and their chiefs and principal men gave him the

name of Sa-go-ya-ta-gaia-ha-ha, "The great worker to save souls." In December, 1867, by commission from Bishop Coxe, he laid the corner-stone of St. James' Church, Cleveland, New York. In August, 1868, on nomination of Bishop Clarkson, he was elected one of the Trustees of Dacota Hall, at Yancton, Dacota Territory. The same month, by appointment of Bishop Coxe, he preached in St. Paul's Cathedral, Buffalo, New York, before the last convention of the undivided Diocese of Western New York. The sermon, entitled, "The Record of the Past an Incentive for the Future," was printed by request, and very widely copied and circulated in the church papers. As a member of the preliminary committee for the erection of a new diocese in central New York, he offered, in behalf of the church-people of Syracuse, an episcopal residence to cost not less than $20,000, and his own parish church for the cathedral of the new diocese, if its primary convention would give it the name of the "See of Syracuse," and its bishop make that city his seat. A month later, when the new diocese came into existence, and was named "Central New York," he was chosen President of its first Standing Committee, and at its special convention, in January, 1869, he was among those prominently balloted for as bishop of the diocese. In May following, by request of the Trustees of the Syracuse Home Association, he laid the corner-store of the new building for that institution. In August he was appointed by Bishop Huntington as President of the Fourth District Convocation, and organized the clergy and lay representatives from the counties of Oswego, Madison and Onondaga, in accordance with a new canon, dividing the diocese into convocation districts. In October he was elected Financial Secretary of the Diocesan Board of Missions. In January, 1870, he was made First Vice-President (the bishop being president) at the organization of The Church Brotherhood of Syracuse, and prepared an "Office of Devotions" for the opening of its meetings. In the midst of these labors, and holding so many positions of responsibility, he was unexpectedly called to the rectorship of the venerable parish of St. Mary's Church, Burlington, New Jersey. The pressure was very strong, and the attractions very great. He resigned all his offices and trusts in the Diocese of Central New York, and accepted the parish in New Jersey in September, 1870. "An Historical Sketch of St. Paul's Church, Syracuse, New York," which he printed soon after, shows that during his thirteen years' rectorship in that parish, there was a total of baptisms, 616; confirmed, 397; communicants added, 603; marriages, 205; burials, 212; a gain in the Sunday-school of 200 children, and offerings amounting to $123,565.58. Complimentary resolutions were presented to him by his vestry, and $1,000 in money as a parting gift. The Standing Committee of the Diocese of Central New York likewise, through their secretary, addressed him a public letter, expressive of their deep sense of loss by his removal, and bearing testimony to his valuable labors for the church in that diocese. Meanwhile he was received by his New Jersey friends with every demonstration of cordiality and confidence. Bishop Odenheimer completed his college of Examining Chaplains by appointing him to its only vacancy, and shortly afterwards made him Lecturer on Homiletics and Pastoral Theology in Burlington College; and on Sunday, December 4th, 1870, he was solemnly instituted by Bishop Odenheimer into the rectorship of St. Mary's parish, in the presence of a large congregation, including the rectors, teachers and pupils of St. Mary's Hall and Burlington College, most of whom remained after the communion office to add their bidding of "God-speed" to that of the wardens and vestrymen. On the 13th of July, 1871, he received the honorary degree of Doctor of Divinity from his *Alma Mater*, Trinity College. In October following he was made a member of the Board of Missions of the United States. In the same year he was placed on the Indian Commission of that board. In June, 1873, he was chosen by the trustees of that institution a Fellow of Trinity College; and in July, 1874, he was elected Sub-Dean of the House of Convocation of that body. On September 29th following, he was appointed by Bishop Odenheimer, Dean of the Convocation of Burlington, of which he had previously been both Treasurer and Secretary. At the special convention of the Diocese of New Jersey for the election of a bishop, and such other officers as might be needed to put the diocese in full working order, he received several ballots for Bishop of New Jersey, and was elected Secretary of the Standing Committee of the Diocese, with power to make all the arrangements necessary for the confirmation and consecration of the bishop-elect. He was also appointed Chairman of a special committee of five to respond, on behalf of the diocese, to the farewell letter of Bishop Odenheimer. At the convention in May, 1875, he was elected Registrar of the Diocese. On the 6th of October, 1875, by appointment of Bishop Scarborough, he laid the corner-stone of St. Faith's Church, Red Bank, Gloucester county, New Jersey. In January, 1876, he prepared an "Office for the Benediction of the Old Church of St. Mary, in Burlington," which was used by Bishops Scarborough, Odenheimer, and others, on February 2d following, at the reopening of the venerable fabric, restored and beautified for parish purposes. May 30th, 1876, in St. Michael's Church, Trenton, New Jersey, by appointment of Bishop Scarborough, he preached the sermon at the opening of the ninety-third annual convention of the Diocese of New Jersey. The subject was, "The Transfer of the Church in America from Colonial Dependence to the Freedom of the Republic," from St. Matthew xxi. 43. By unanimous vote of the convention it was published. On the 1st of June he issued his great historical work called, "History of the Church in Burlington, New Jersey; comprising the Facts and Incidents of Nearly Two Hundred Years." It is a handsome octavo of 739 pages, showing extraordinary research, universally praised by scholars and people of culture, and for it he was in ne-

diately made a member of the Historical Society of Pennsylvania. In June, 1876, Dr. Hills was elected Dean of the House of Convocation of Trinity College, Hartford; and in July following he was elected a Trustee of Burlington College and St. Mary's Hall. During his rectorship in Burlington seventy additional sittings have been made in the church, the organ doubled in size, a handsome rectory purchased, and a Guild founded for all departments of church work, in which there is now a large, active membership. Dr. Hills has three sons and a daughter.

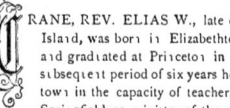

RANE, REV. ELIAS W., late of Jamaica, Long Island, was born in Elizabethtown, New Jersey, and graduated at Princeton in 1814. During a subsequent period of six years he acted at Morristown in the capacity of teacher, and officiated at Springfield as minister of the gospel. In 1825, in the course of a noteworthy revival, eighty or more persons were enrolled among the members of his church, and much abiding good was accomplished. From 1826 until the time of his death his field of labors was in Jamaica, Long Island, where, in the memorable revivals of 1831 and 1839, which produced in many noted instances the most surprising and desirable results, seventy-four and seventy-six persons were secured to the church as permanent and exemplary members. His death, which came upon him suddenly, found him environed by good works and excellent projects. He died November 10th, 1840, aged forty-four years.

ARD, LESLIE DODD, M.D., of Newark, son of Moses D. and Louisa Ward, was born at Madison, New Jersey, July 1st, 1845. Both lines of his ancestors, the Dodds and Wards, have been for many years prominent in East Jersey, the families centring in Newark and vicinity. His uncle, Ira Dodd, took a leading part in furthering the building of the railroad uniting Bloomfield and Newark, and was for a time President, as also one of the original corporators of the company by which the line was built. Various other of his relations have been engaged in important public and private enterprises in New Jersey and elsewhere. In New York his family name is well known, his cousin being senior member of the publishing house of Moses Dodd & Co. He was educated at the Newark Academy. In the early part of 1864 he enlisted in the 37th New Jersey Regiment, obtaining the rating of Orderly Sergeant. In the latter part of the same year he retired from the service and began the study of medicine in the office of Dr. Fisher, of Morristown. Later, he attended lectures at the College of Physicians and Surgeons of New York, receiving his degree of M. D. from that institution in 1868. Establishing himself at Newark, he was fortunate at the outset of his career in being associated with Dr. Lott Southard, a physician of high standing and well established reputation. This connection, which continued for two years, gave him the basis of an extensive and lucrative practice: a practice which has since continuously increased. In the profession he is regarded with general favor, and is an active member of the State and county medical societies. For the past five years he has been Visiting Surgeon to St. Barnabas Hospital, Newark; is County Physician to Essex county, and is Medical Director of the Prudential Insurance Company. He was married, March 5th, 1874, to Minnie, daughter of James Perry, one of the leading manufacturers of leather, of Newark.

ICKS, ELIAS, eminent Quaker Preacher, Founder of the Hicksite Departure, Itinerant Preacher and Exhorter of New Jersey, Pennsylvania, Maryland, Ohio, New York, etc., late of Jericho, Long Island, was born in the township of Hempstead, Queens county, Long Island, March 19th, 1748, and was the son of John Hicks and Martha Hicks, who were descended from reputable families; his father was a grandson of Thomas Hicks, who has honorable mention in the journal of Samuel Bownas; neither was a member in strict fellowship with any religious society until shortly before his birth; his father then joined in membership with Friends; " . . . . but as his residence was mostly at some distance from meeting, and in a neighborhood where very few Friends lived, my associates, when young, were chiefly among those of other religious persuasions, or, what was still worse for me, among those who made no profession of religion at all. This exposed me to much temptation; and though I early felt the operation of divine grace, checking and reproving me for my lightness and vanity, yet being of a lively, active spirit, and ambitious of excelling in my play and diversions, I sometimes exceeded the bounds of true moderation, for which I often felt close conviction and fears on my pillow in the night season." When eight years of age he removed with his father to the south side of Long Island, near the seashore, and there settled on a farm. Five years later he was placed with one of his elder brothers, his mother having died two years previously; and subsequently was apprenticed to learn the trade of a house-carpenter and joiner. His master at that period, though an orderly man and a frequent attendant at Friends' meetings, "was yet in an eager pursuit after temporal riches, and was of but little use to me in my religious improvement. We had to go from place to place, ... to attend to our work, and I was thereby introduced into hurtful company, and learned to dance and to pursue other frivolous and vain amusements." At the expiration of his

apprenticeship, however, he gradually withdrew from the company of his former associates, became more widely acquainted with Friends, and was more frequent in his attendance of meetings; and although this was in some degree profitable to him, he, according to his own statement, yet made but slow progress in his religious improvement. "The occupation of part of my time in fishing and fowling had frequently tended to preserve me from falling into hurtful associations; but through the rising intimations and reproofs of divine grace in my heart, I now began to feel that the manner in which I sometimes amused myself with my gun was not without sin; for although I mostly preferred going alone, and while waiting in stillness for the coming of the fowl, my mind was at times so taken up with divine meditations that the opportunities were seasons of instruction and comfort to me; yet, on other occasions, when accompanied by some of my acquaintances, and when no fowls appeared, which would be useful to us after being obtained, we sometimes, from wantonness or mere diversion, would destroy the small birds which could be of no service to us. . . . . But I was led to consider conduct like this to be a great breach of trust, and an infringement of the divine prerogative. It, therefore, became a settled principle with me not to take the life of any creature, except it was really useful and necessary when dead, or very noxious and hurtful when living." In the spring of 1771 he settled on the farm of his wife's relations, and assisted in the cares and labors incident to agricultural life; with those worthy people he remained during their lives, and the place eventually became his settled residence. He had then the benefit of the company of several Friends, by whose example he was frequently incited to seriousness and piety; "yet, having entered pretty closely into business, I was thereby much diverted from my religious improvement for several years." But about the twenty-sixth year of his age he was again, through divine grace, brought under deep concern of mind, and again permitted to see truly into the perilous state he had been approaching. "My spirit was brought under a close and weighty labor in meetings for discipline, and my understanding much enlarged therein. . . . . About this time I began to have openings leading to the ministry, which brought me under close exercise and deep travail of spirit; for although I had for some time spoken on subjects of business in monthly and preparative meetings, yet the prospect of opening my mouth in public meetings was a close trial; but I endeavored to keep my mind quiet and resigned to the heavenly call, if it should be made clear to me to be my duty." The yearly meeting was held steadily during the revolutionary war on Long Island, where the royalists were in power; yet Friends from the Main, where the American army ruled, had free passage through both armies to attend it, and any other meeting they were desirous of attending, except in a few instances. "This was a favor which the parties would not grant to their best friends, who were of a warlike disposition; which shows what great advantages would redound to mankind were they all of this pacific spirit. I passed myself through the lines of both armies six times during the war, without molestation, ... and although I had to pass' over a tract of country, between the two armies, sometimes more than thirty miles in extent, and which was much frequented by robbers, a set in general of cruel, unprincipled banditti, issuing out from both parties, yet, excepting once, I met with no interruption even from them." In consequence of sundry discussions, concerning the acceptance or refusal of a sum of money taken from the British by some Friends, as rent for the use as an arsenal of the cellar in the New York meeting house, he was, in 1779, appointed to act with others in settling the affair at the next yearly meeting of Pennsylvania. On the following September 9th he set out on his errand; passingly attended meetings at Harrison's Purchase and Oblong; and after a short sojourn at Nine Partners attended also the meetings of New Marlborough, Hardwick and Kingwood, and arrived in Philadelphia on the 25th, on which day he presented himself at the yearly meeting of ministers and elders. A subsequent attack of fever prevented him from being present, however, when the subject that chiefly interested him was discussed, but the result was the advising of the return of the money whence it had come. He afterward attended successively the meetings of the following places: Byberry, Middletown, Wright's Town, Plumbstead, Buckingham, Drowned Lands, Nine Partners, Oswego, Appoquague, Peachpond, Amawalk and Purchase, thence proceeding to his home. March 4th, 1781, he went to Flushing, crossed the sound to Frog's Neck, on the ensuing day attended an appointed meeting at Westchester, and at the expiration of a fortnight arrived at Little Nine Partners; thence set forward for Saratoga—since called Easton—and upon arriving at his destination attended in succession the four meetings of that place, New Britain was next visited, also Shapaqua, Mamaroneck, and Westchester again. In the fall of 1781 he was prostrated with sickness for three months, and when he was reduced nearly to the lowest state of bodily weakness a prospect opened on his mind to pay a religious visit to some parts of the island where no Friends lived, and among a people who were regarded by many as wanting in grace and godliness. Accordingly, upon recovering his health, he went to Jamaica in August, 1782, and there had a very favored meeting with a considerable number of the inhabitants. He also found a later field of labors at Flatlands, Gravesend, New Utrecht and Springfield; and in the fall of 1782 attended the quarterly and other meetings on the Main. Late in 1783 he was present with his brethren at Nine Partners, Oswego and Perquage; June 13th, 1784, he repaired to Herricks, thence to Success, Little Plains, Jamaica, Fresh Meadows and other places, and spurred himself to great exertions to win the native Indians from their perilous condition to a true and righteous life. New York and Staten Island were visited by him in 1790; also Vermont; in 1791 he returned to his native place; in the course of the same year he made a general visit to Friends of the New York yearly meeting; in 1792 he was an active spirit at various meetings of ministers and elders; and in 1793 he travelled in a proselytizing spirit and intent through New England and Vermont. July 26th, 1795, he left home in order to join a committee of Friends, appointed by the yearly meeting of ministers and elders, to visit the quarterly and preparative meetings, and Friends individually, in those stations throughout the yearly meeting. "A concern having arisen in that meeting, occasioned by the many obvious deficiencies and departures amongst us as a people, from the purity and simplicity of our holy profession, a minute was issued and recommended to the inferior meetings, setting forth the ground of this concern, and for the purpose of stirring up and encouraging Friends to a diligent search and labor, that the many hurtful disorders might be removed, and a right reformation, from these prevailing weaknesses, effectually take place." December 12th, 1797, he departed for New York, having in view the visiting of New Jersey, Delaware, Virginia, etc.; and while on his way attended meetings at Shrewsbury, Squan, Squancum, Barnegat, Little Egg Harbor and Stephen's Creek. On Saturday he took part in a meeting at Cape May, New Jersey, thence rode to Morris river, and attended another appointed at the house of Isaac Buzby, a man inclining to Friends and their teachings. In the afternoon he visited Henry Rulon, where, on the next day, he was present at an appointed meeting. He then passed on to Greenwich, Cohansey Creek, Salem, Woodstown, Penn's Neck, Mullica Hill, Upper Greenwich and Woodbury; also Newtown, Haddonfield, and many other places in New Jersey, in all times and circumstances eminently exalting the truth, and holding forth the doctrines of the gospel in the demonstration of the spirit. Sundry towns and villages in Delaware, Maryland and Virginia were then visited, and their inhabitants exhorted to lead pure and upright lives, fitting children of grace. In the meetings at Northwest Fork, Marshy Creek, Centre, Greensborough, Tuckahoe Neck and Tuckahoe, especially, was good seed sown and good fruit gathered. Three of the above meetings in New Jersey were held in meeting-houses belonging to a people under the denomination of Nicholites, who were noted for great self-denial, particularly in regard to dress and household furniture. "They appeared one in principle with us, their faith and doctrine being founded on the manifestation and influence of the divine light, inwardly revealed. Most of them, of late, have requested to be joined in membership with Friends, and have been received. . . . . They appeared to be a plain, innocent, upright-hearted people; and I felt a concern lest they should be hurt by the great and prevailing deficiencies manifest amongst us, by many turning away from the purity and simplicity of our holy self-denying profession." He was afterward for some time zealously employed in pious labors in New Jersey, notably at Upper Evesham, Haddonfield, Moorestown, Rancocas, Mansfield Neck, Burlington, Mansfield, Bordentown, Stony Brook, Plainfield, Rahway and Newark. He was absent from home in this journey about five months and two weeks, rode over 1,600 miles of varied country, and attended about 143 meetings. In 1799 he travelled through Connecticut; in 1800 revisited Oblong and Nine Partners, also Long Island in certain neglected parts; and again, in 1801, stirred up by his eloquence and ardor the people of New Jersey and Pennsylvania. In the fall of 1803 he performed a visit to Friends of Upper Canada, and some other of the northwestern parts of the yearly meeting, and attended meetings at Adolphustown, Sophiasburg, Hallowell, West Lake, Kingstown, Earnest and Palmyra; also in Pleasant Valley, the Branch, Chestnut Ridge, Poquague and New York. Three months were consumed in this journey, and in that time he rode about 1,575 miles. In the spring of 1806 he again set out on a proselytizing tour through Long Island, Staten Island and New York; and on the following December 8th started for Brooklyn, where he was present at an appointed meeting, "which was a solemn comfortable season;" thence he passed on to Mamaroneck, etc., and attended an appointed meeting at Peekskill. Meetings were subsequently had at Troy, Albany, Otego, Cazenovia and Woodstock; also in various parts of New Jersey, where the good work met with desirable encouragement, notably at Burlington, Deruyter, Bridgewater and Brookfield. February 9th, 1807, he rode to New York, and from there returned to his home and fireside, having been absent about two months, attended forty-five particular meetings, nine monthly meetings, one quarterly meeting and two meetings for sufferings, and travelled upwards of 700 miles. October 10th of the same year he again set out on his errand of righteousness, and from that time forward, until 1810, went about, on foot or in the saddle, or wagon, as itinerant missionary, through the cities and rural places of New Jersey, New York and Pennsylvania, everywhere accomplishing great good and leading his kind into the path of virtue and uprightness. The year 1810 he spent mostly at home, except performing a visit to some of the neighboring inhabitants, "not in membership with us." He was absent in this service a few weeks in the spring, and in the summer performed a visit to the half year's meeting at Canada, by appointment from the yearly meeting. The year 1811 also was passed at or near his home, in attending local and adjacent meetings; and the winter and spring of 1812 were consumed in visiting the neighboring inhabitants, not of his society, holding in all twenty-eight meetings in private houses. Early in 1813 he once more left his family, and, after holding several meetings in different parts of Long Island, travelled through the bordering parts of Connecticut, where none of his society resided. The concluding months of this year were occupied in fulfilling engagements at or about

his home, and in visits to Friends in the Middle and Southern States; also especially in laboring in New Jersey, at Newark, Elizabethtown, New Brunswick, Plainfield, Rahway, East Branch and the Mount; and at Rancocas, Burlington and Newtown. During the years 1814 and 1815 he was variously occupied in Long Island, New Jersey and New York. January 3d, 1816, he set out for New England, and upon arriving at Bridgeport, Connecticut, "had a small though comfortable meeting;" afterward meetings were held successively in Seabrook, Epping, Lee, Dover, Berwick, Portland, Falmouth, Windham, Gorham, Durham, Cape Elizabeth, Scarborough, Rochester, etc.; also at Newport, Rhode Island, Tiverton, Swansey, Providence, etc. In this journey he was from home nearly three months, travelled upwards of 1,000 miles, and attended fifty-nine particular, three monthly and two quarterly meetings. Engagements at and about home, and within Westbury quarterly meeting, fill the year 1816 and part of 1817; also a visit to some parts of the yearly meetings of Philadelphia and Baltimore. "First day, the 31st, we attended Pearl street meeting in the morning, and that at Liberty street in the afternoon. On second day afternoon we proceeded on our journey to Newark, New Jersey, ... where we attended a meeting at the fourth hour. . . . I had had several meetings there before; but this was larger than usual for the place. There is no member of our society residing in the town, the inhabitants being principally of the Presbyterian order. The next day we attended a meeting appointed for us in Elizabethtown, New Jersey," and later one at Plainfield, one at Rahway and one at Mendham. He afterward journeyed through Pennsylvania, Rhode Island, Maryland and Delaware, where his presence and example proved of beneficent and enduring value to all that were brought within the radius of his influence. The major portion of the year 1818 was devoted to spiritual and temporal affairs in the vicinity of his farm in Long Island, within the limits of Westbury quarterly meeting, and in a visit to some parts of the yearly meeting of New York. He then continued at or about home until the opening of 1819, attending the meetings as they came in course. About this time, at the meeting at Westbury, he was led to open to Friends "the three principal requisites to the being and well-being of a Christian: The first being a real belief in *God* and *Christ as one undivided essence,* known and believed in, *inwardly* and *spiritually*. The second a complete passive obedience and submission to the divine will and power inwardly and spiritually manifested. . . . . The third, it is necessary to meet and assemble often together for the promotion of love and good works, and as good stewards of the manifold grace of God." In January, 1819, he proceeded to New York, and thence to West Farms, Mamaroneck, White Plains, Purchase, etc.: also to Poughkeepsie, Hudson, Claverack, Kline Kiln, Troy, Plustown, etc., and to Tappan on the way home: on this journey he was absent fourteen weeks, attended seventy-three meetings, and three quarterly and four monthly meetings, and travelled 1,084 miles. From this time to 1823 his life and career is summed up succinctly thus: "Journey to Ohio, in 1819. Visit to the neighboring inhabitants in the same year. Visit to Farmington and Duanesburg quarterly meetings, in 1820. Visit to some parts of Pennsylvania, and to Baltimore, in 1822. Visit to some of the lower quarterly meetings, in 1823." Then comes this significant entry in his "Journal:" " . . . . It was a time of deep exercise to me, being led in the line of searching labor, pointing to a reform in manners and conduct; and showing the fallacy of all ceremonial religion in the observation of days, and complying with outward ordinances; which do not in the least tend to make the comers thereunto a whit the better, as it respects the conscience, but lead the observers thereof into a form, without the power." Then ensued: "Visit to Baltimore to attend the yearly meeting, in 1824. Visit to the inhabitants of the eastern part of Long Island, in 1825. Visit to Scipio quarterly meeting, in 1825. Visit to Southern and Concord quarterly meetings, in Pennsylvania, in 1826. Visit to the families of Friends in Jericho and Westbury monthly meetings, in 1827. Visit to Friends in some parts of New Jersey, Pennsylvania and Ohio, in 1828. On this journey, in New Jersey, at New Garden, Friends had a trying time, as those called Orthodox, although they were but a small part of the meeting, had undertaken to disown a number of Friends; but Friends did not acknowledge their authority, nor consider their disownments of any effect, and they all came together as usual in the quarterly meeting. The Orthodox strove hard to get Friends to withdraw, but they refused, and proceeded with the business of the meeting, which those called Orthodox interrupted for a time; but finding that Friends would not give way, they finally left the meeting and retired to a school-house, and Friends had a comfortable season together, and conducted their business in much harmony and condescension, and were evidently owned by the Head of the Church." Subsequently: "Continuation of his visit to Friends in some parts of New Jersey, Ohio, Indiana, Maryland and Pennsylvania, in 1828. Decease of his wife in 1829. Visit to Friends in the yearly meeting of New York, in 1829. Letter to Hugh Judge, in 1830."—"In the twenty-second year of my age, apprehending it right to change my situation from a single to a married state, and having gained an intimate acquaintance with Jemima Seaman, daughter of Jonathan and Elizabeth Seaman, of Jericho, and my affection being drawn toward her in that relation, I communicated my views to her, and received from her a corresponding expression of affection; and we, after some time, accomplished our marriage at a solemn meeting of Friends, at Westbury, on the 2d of First Month, 1771." His mental powers continued strong and vigorous to the end of his labors, and during the last two years of his life he travelled extensively in the work of the ministry. "On First day morning, 14th of Second Month, 1830, he

was engaged in his room, writing to a Friend, until a little after ten o'clock, when he returned to that occupied by the family, apparently just attacked by a paralytic affection, which nearly deprived him of the use of his right side and of the power of speech. Being assisted to a chair near the fire, he manifested by signs that the letter which he had just finished should be taken care of." He then signed to all to sit down and be still, seemingly sensible that his labors were brought to a close, and only desirous of quietly waiting the final change. His theological writings were principally in an epistolary form; "Elias Hicks: Journal of his Life and Labors," was published in Philadelphia, Pennsylvania, in 1828; and in the same year also a volume entitled "Sermons."

AYLOR, GEORGE W., Brigadier-General, was the third son of Archibald S. Taylor, and was born, November 22d, 1808, at Fairview—the family seat—Hunterdon county, New Jersey. When fifteen years old he entered the celebrated military school of Colonel Allen Partridge, an institution that had very much the reputation then that West Point has now, and three years later graduated with credit. He entered the navy as a midshipman, November 1st, 1827, and made a cruise of three years up the Mediterranean in the sloop-of-war "Fairfield," Captain Foxal A. Parker. Returning to the United States, he tendered his resignation, which was accepted, December 19th, 1831, and engaged in mercantile pursuits. Love of adventure was with him, however, an engrained instinct, and when war was declared against Mexico he offered his services to the government, notwithstanding the fact that his political opinions caused him to condemn the war on the double ground of right and policy. He was commissioned First Lieutenant of the 10th Regiment United States Infantry, and while in Mexico, serving with the army of General Z. Taylor, he was promoted to and commissioned Captain. After the surrender of the city of Mexico he returned to his home, but only for a short period. In February, 1849, he sailed for California as President of the New Jersey Trading & Mining Company, and for three years remained upon the Pacific coast. Returning in 1852 he took a prominent part in politics, being a Whig of the straitest sect, and in 1858 was strongly urged for the Congressional nomination. Immediately upon the call for troops, in May, 1861, he vigorously bestirred himself in raising companies in Hunterdon county; and having been in this matter highly successful, he himself started—with a patriotic heroism singularly picturesque as relieved against the prosaic formalism of this nineteenth century—alone to offer himself, mounted and equipped, as a volunteer upon the staff of some general already at point with the enemy. Governor Olden, however, spoiled this gallant romance by calling the errant soldier to a halt, and commissioning him Colonel of the 3d New Jersey Regiment, then in course of organization at Trenton. He accepted the commission, rapidly reduced the raw mass placed under his orders to a seemly military body, and on the 8th of June marched with his command to Washington. Consolidated with the three other New Jersey regiments raised at the same time, his force became a part of that hard-fighting organization, the First New Jersey Brigade—the brigade that, at the very outset of its career, helped to check the fleeing troops and reform the shattered divisions after the first battle of Bull Run. He was the first to discover the retreat of the Confederates from Manasses, and with the 3d New Jersey was the first to occupy this stronghold. In the early summer of 1862, the brave Kearny having been promoted to be an officer of division, Colonel Taylor, as senior officer, assumed the command of the brigade; and on the 10th of June in that year he was commissioned Brigadier-General. Seventeen days later the brigade was engaged in the desperate fight of Gaines's Mill, occupying the centre of the line of battle, and holding its ground for at least an hour after both flanks had been driven back by the enemy. The action, although ending in defeat, was one of the most honorable of the war, the cool heroism of the New Jersey troops—shown in contending single-handed against an entire army—being in every way worthy of veteran soldiers, and quite unprecedented when it is remembered that but a little time before they had been utterly untrained to the ways of war. Without support, and unable even to procure orders, the brigade fought on alone, and three times charged and broke the enemy's lines. The battle lasted until nightfall, and only when further resistance became hopeless did General Taylor draw off his men, leaving more than 1,000 dead or wounded upon the field. Nearly as many more were taken prisoners, 500 men of the 4th Regiment, refusing to retreat, being surrounded and captured in a body. The next day the brigade fell back to Harrison's Landing, remaining in that vicinity until McClellan effected his change of base in the following August. On the 24th of that month it took up position at Cloud's Mills, and three days later it was sent forward by rail to Bull Run bridge, and thence advanced for the purpose of dispersing a rebel force, reported to be small, concentrated near Manasses Junction. Instead of a few regiments, General Taylor found himself confronted with the whole of "Stonewall" Jackson's command. The action that followed lasted for more than an hour, during the whole of which time the brigade was exposed to a steady fire from front, and to a raking cross fire from batteries masked until the engagement began. Compelled to retreat, the troops fell back in good order until they reached the bridge, where the reserves—the 11th and 12th Ohio Regiments—were stationed, and here another stand was made. But Jackson's forces still pressed forward; the brigade was without artillery, without cavalry, the men were exhausted by forced marches and by the excessive heat; finally, General Taylor was himself severely wounded in the leg. A retreat was ordered. The command retired to Cloud's Mills, and the general, leaving his brigade for the first and last time, continued on to Alexandria. At the hospital there his leg was amputated; but he was broken down by all that he had passed through, his constitution was shattered by malaria contracted during the peninsular campaign; and although the operation was successfully performed, it sapped the last remnant of his vital force. On September 1st he died, and in his grave lies buried as brave a soldier as ever drew a sword.

———◆○◆———

NEWTON, HON. ISAAC, First Commissioner of Agriculture, late of Washington, District of Columbia, was born in Burlington county, New Jersey, in 1800, and passed his early years on a farm, attending school during a few months of the winter seasons. After his marriage he settled on a farm in Delaware county, Pennsylvania, which, under his ceaseless care, became celebrated for its neatness, order and productiveness; and he eventually took place in the front rank of the model farmers of the State. At an early period he became an influential and valued member of the State Agricultural Society, and was among those who urged upon Congress the importance of establishing an agricultural bureau. On the election of Abraham Lincoln the measure he had so ardently and wisely advocated was finally adopted, and he received an appointment to preside over the new department as its Commissioner. The act of Congress was approved May 15th, 1862. He possessed an extensive and practical acquaintance with agricultural matters and methods, and the various systems of farming; and was eminently qualified for the position which he was called upon to fill. He died at Washington City, June 19th, 1867.

———◆○◆———

FOSTER, REV. DANIEL REQUA, eighth Pastor of the Hopewell Presbyterian Church, of Pennington, New Jersey, was born, September 22d, 1838, at Patterson, Putnam county, New York, and is the son of Edmund Foster and Ann Eliza Foster. In January, 1849, he was received into the full communion of the church. He was prepared for college at the Peekskill Academy; in 1863 he took the degree of A. B. at the College of New Jersey; and in 1866 that of A. M. In the latter year also he graduated at the Princeton Theological Seminary; April 24th, 1866, was licensed as a probationer for the gospel ministry, by the Presbytery of Connecticut, at Bridgeport, and entered upon the performance of his duties as pastor-elect in the Presbyterian church of Phelps, New York, June 1st, 1866. He was ordained to the work of the gospel ministry, and installed pastor of the church at Phelps, on the following July 29th, by the Presbytery of Rochester city. In October, 1869, his pastoral connection with the church at Phelps was dissolved. He then entered on his ministerial duties at the Pennington Church on the first Sabbath of October, 1870. Having received a cordial and unanimous call from the people, he was installed pastor, April 17th, 1871, by a committee of the Presbytery of New Brunswick. January 25th, 1874, the church was destroyed by fire, shortly after the dismissal of the congregation, and a new church opened, January 14th, 1875. In the opening of the ensuing year a gracious revival cleansed and purified the spiritual atmosphere of his pastorate, and by February 20th, 1876, between forty and fifty persons joined the church. As a result of his labors, one hundred and eighty-one persons of both sexes have been added to the roll of communicants on profession, besides twenty-six by certificate.

———◆———

cILVAINE, RT. REV. CHARLES PETTIT, D. D., LL. D., D. C. L., Bishop of Ohio, was born in Burlington, New Jersey, January 18th, 1799, his father being Hon. Joseph McIlvaine, at one time a Representative of the State in the United States Senate. His mother's parents, Bowes Reed and Mrs. Reed, were residents of the same place. Bowes Reed was brother of Joseph Reed, of Philadelphia, confidential secretary of General Washington. Joseph McIlvaine, grandfather of the bishop, served through the war of the Revolution, and attained the rank of Colonel in the patriot army; he resided at Bristol, where his remains now repose. The bishop lived in Burlington until his ordination as deacon, and the graves of four generations of his family—from the parents of his mother down to the daughter of his sister, Mrs. Commodore Eugle—are in the churchyard of St. Mary's in that town, with that of his wife's parents and many of her relatives. He was baptized in the old church in his fifteenth year, by Dr. Wharton. The baptism was delayed thus long through his mother entertaining conscientious scruples about presenting her children for baptism while not a communicant herself. He received his education, preparatory to college, in the Burlington Academy, an incorporated institution; the building stood on the ground now occupied by the new edifice of St. Mary's Church, which it was taken down to make room for. Rev. Christian Hanckel, D. D., afterwards of Charleston, South Carolina, was one of his tutors, succeeding his brother John as master of the school. From this institution he passed to Princeton College, from which he was graduated in 1816. Thereupon he became a candidate for orders, but being too young to be ordained, he remained—except for a period of about eighteen months passed in the Theological Seminary of Princeton—in Burlington, reading under Dr. Wharton. During this period he organized the

Sunday-school of St. Mary's Church, one of the first Sunday-schools organized in the United States. He himself, in a letter to Rev. Dr. Hills, now rector of St. Mary's Church, gives the history of this organization as follows: "While I was in college in Princeton, one of my classmates, John Newbold, of Philadelphia (who in graduating became a candidate for orders, but died before he could be ordained), on returning to college from a vacation, brought to us students an account of a Sunday-school he had attended in Philadelphia. It was in the very beginning of Sunday-schools in this country. He brought specimens of the blue and red tickets used. A number of students in the college formed a Sunday-school Society, and raised a fund of about four hundred dollars, of which I (then in my seventeenth year) was made treasurer. We set up four schools in and about Princeton. I and John Newbold, and (I think) the present Dr. Hodge, of Princeton, and the present Bishop Johns (a classmate of Dr. Hodge, and both a year before me), were teachers in different schools. My first extempore address was then made to the school I was detailed to, in a barn of what was called Jug Town, a suburb of Princeton. Going home in 1816, the project of the Burlington school originated. Such a thing had never been heard of in Burlington. I first obtained Dr. Wharton's approbation, and then began to talk it up. Mr. Aikman, the clerk of the church, co-operated. . . . . The organization took place, and the school was always held in the academy as long, I believe, as Dr. Wharton was rector, and how much longer I do not know. The organization took place in the spring of 1816. Consider that I was then only seventeen years of age, and therefore almost all concerned, except as pupils, must have been older. And as I am now in my seventy-fourth year, it is not likely that anybody lives who was actively concerned in those things then. I was not aware that my name has been taken by one of the classes, but am much pleased to know it now." He was the first Superintendent of the school, and held that position for one year, between his graduating and returning to Princeton to enter the Theological Seminary. Mr. Aikman was his successor. While a candidate for orders the bishop officiated as lay-reader at Bristol, during a vacancy in that parish. He was ordained a Deacon by Bishop White, July 4th, 1820, and then went to his first parish, Christ Church, Georgetown, District of Columbia. After officiating there for about two years he received Priest's orders from the hands of Bishop Kemp, of Maryland. He remained in this charge until 1825, officiating during part of the time as Chaplain of the Senate. In the last-mentioned year he was appointed, through the friendly offices of John C. Calhoun, Professor of Ethics and Chaplain in the United States Military Academy, West Point. This position he relinquished to become Rector of St. Anne's Church, Brooklyn, New York. In 1831 he was appointed Professor of the Evidences of Revealed Religion and Sacred Antiquities in the University of the City of New York. On

Chas. P. McIlvaine

October 31st, 1832, he was consecrated Bishop of the Protestant Episcopal Diocese of Ohio. He continued in the active discharge of his episcopal duties until the consecration, in 1859, of the Rev. S. T. Bedell, D. D., as assistant bishop; but subsequent to that date he was frequently incapacitated for active work by failing health. His career as Bishop of Ohio, without being especially eventful, was characterized by untiring energy and the most gratifying results. For many years he resided at Gambier, in the midst of the educational institutions under his episcopal supervision, acting directly as President of Kenyon College from the commencement of his episcopate to 1840. He was perhaps best known to the world as an author. During his incumbency of the professorship in the University of the City of New York, he delivered, in 1831, a course of lectures on the "Evidences of Christianity." At the request of the University Council these lectures were published in a collected form in 1832, and have had an immense circulation, being reprinted in London and Edinburgh, while several different editions have been published in this country. In 1841 he published a work entitled, "Oxford Divinity Compared with that of the Roman and Anglican Churches, with a Special View of the Doctrine of Justification by Faith." Although this work has now dropped out of sight, it attracted universal attention at the time of its publication, when the celebrated tractarian controversy was at its height. The *Edinburgh Review* characterized the work as one of the best "confutations of the tenets of the Oxford school," of which Dr. Pusey was the head. This work, and the other labors of his life, rendered the bishop the recognized champion of evangelical principles in the Protestant Episcopal Church. Among his other more important works were: "The Sinner's Justification before God," 1851; "The Holy Catholic Church," 1844; "The Truth and the Life," 1854. Numerous volumes of sermons were given by him to the world, and he also contributed many valuable articles to the leading religious periodicals of the day. The bishop was a man of large and liberal views. During his incumbency of the rectorship of St. Anne's Church, Brooklyn, he became involved in a controversy with the bishop of the diocese, who endeavored to repress a clerical prayer-meeting, and to prevent his clergy from identifying themselves with "mixed institutions," like the American Bible and Tract Societies, in which he took a decided stand on the liberal side, and for many years he acted as President of the American Tract Society. His influence was not restricted to the circle of his church, but was widespread. At the opening of the rebellion he was, because of his high standing, selected by President Lincoln and Secretary Seward to visit Europe on a confidential mission, and contributed largely towards counteracting the intrigues of the Confederate emissaries in Great Britain. The late Archbishop Hughes and Thurlow Weed, it will be remembered, also visited Europe about the same time, and on a similar mission, at the request of the administration.

A high recognition of Bishop McIlvaine's influential stand. ing was his reception of the degree of Doctor of Civil Law from the University of Oxford in 1853, and that of Doctor of Laws from the University of Cambridge five years later. As a pulpit orator he had few equals. With a commanding presence, a clear, penetrating, trumpet-like voice, an extraordinary power of accurate extemporaneous expression, and a profound insight, he possessed rare qualifications for effectiveness on the platform and in the pulpit. He died in Florence, Italy, on March 13th, 1873.

DAYTON, JONATHAN, a Distinguished Civilian of New Jersey, late of Elizabeth, was born, October 16th, 1760, at Elizabethtown. He graduated at the College of New Jersey in 1776, and in February of the same year entered the Continental army as Paymaster of the 3d New Jersey Battalion, commanded by his father. He subsequently served a time on the staff of General Maxwell, commanding the New Jersey Brigade, and on the 1st of May, 1779, was commissioned as Major and Aide-de-Camp on the staff of Major-General Sullivan, accompanying the latter officer in his expedition of that year against the western Indians. In 1780 he rejoined the Jersey Brigade, being commissioned, March 30th, as Captain in the 3d Regiment. While on duty at Elizabeth, November 4th, 1780, he was taken prisoner by the British, together with his uncle, General Matthias Ogden. After his exchange he served with the 1st New Jersey Regiment, which, with the remainder of the brigade, landed near Williamsburgh, Virginia, on September 21st, 1781, and engaged in the siege of Yorktown. He was soon detached for duty in a command under General Lafayette, whom he aided in storming one of the British redoubts, and was present at the surrender of Lord Cornwallis, October 19th, 1781. In the winter of 1781-82 he was stationed in East Jersey, and especially distinguished himself in a skirmish December 5th, which resulted in the retirement of a force from Staten Island which attacked Elizabeth. He served to the end of the war with undimmed credit, and became an original member of the Society of the Cincinnati. In 1787 he was appointed one of the delegates from New Jersey to the convention at Philadelphia for the purpose of framing the Federal constitution. He took part in the deliberations, and on the 17th of September, 1787, affixed his name to that noble charter, being one of the youngest, if not the youngest, of the signers. After the Revolution he had been repeatedly elected to the Legislature of New Jersey, and in 1790 was elected Speaker of the House. In 1791 he was chosen as a Representative in Congress, and was repeatedly re-elected until he had served for eight successive years. He was active in legislation, and became one of the most prominent leaders of the Federalist party. In 1795 he was elected Speaker of the

House of Representatives, and in 1797 re-elected by a vote of seventy-eight to two. When a war with France was looked upon as probable, in 1798, he was commissioned by President Adams as a Brigadier-General of the regular army. The happy settlement of that difficulty brought his military services to a close. He was soon after elected to the Senate of the United States, and served with distinguished reputation from 1799 to 1805. An intimacy in boyhood, and his later association with him in the Senate of the United States, led him to be a devoted friend and admirer of Aaron Burr. So strong was their regard that, in 1803, he undertook a duel in his behalf, sending a challenge to De Witt Clinton, afterwards governor of New York, but the matter was arranged without a meeting. This long-standing, personal friendship led him to look with more trust upon that aspiring politician than prudence would have dictated, and he paid the penalty when moneys, advanced in matters of joint interest, were used by Burr to further his own questionable projects. When Burr was tried for his misdemeanors, nothing was found which justified proceedings against Mr. Dayton, but, notwithstanding, the complicated condition of things seriously compromised his reputation among those who could be afforded no opportunity to know the facts. This unhappy affair, and the accession of Mr. Jefferson to the Presidential chair, leading to the breaking up of the Federal party, caused his retirement from leadership in the national parties. But in his own State, honored for his faithful service and beloved for his known worth, he was continued in office and chosen to serve several terms in the Senate. His latter days were passed at home in the enjoyment of a comfortable competence, interesting himself in the welfare of the schools, the establishment of a public library, and other benefits to his native town. In connection with John Cleves Symmes and others, he held large tracts of land in Ohio, and the city of Dayton was so named in compliment to his family. When General Lafayette visited America in 1824, Mr. Dayton received him as a guest at Elizabeth, and attended him in his tour through the State. This pleasing event proved to be his last appearance in public, as he died at Elizabeth on the 9th of October in the same year. He was a man of stately presence and appearance, and kept up his formal dignity of manner to the close of his life. He was known as " The last of the cocked hats."

RIGHT, HON. WILLIAM, late of Newark, New Jersey, son of Dr. William Wright, a prominent physician and citizen of Rockland county, New York, and descended from early settlers of Connecticut, was born in Rockland county, New York, in 1791. He was at school in Poughkeepsie, preparing for college, when the death of his father de-

prived him of means of support and compelled him to abandon his intended collegiate course. Learning the trade of harness-making, he not only supported himself during the term of his apprenticeship, but succeeded in saving from his scant wages three hundred dollars, a fund that he applied, upon attaining his majority, to hiring and stocking a small shop in Bridgeport. Here, while working with the energy and industry that characterized his entire career in business and in public life, he continued his interrupted studies; but the ground that he had lost could never be entirely regained, and his education was derived less from books than from men and affairs. Entering into a partnership with his father-in-law, the late William Peet, and Sheldon Smith, he founded a firm for the manufacture of harness and saddles, establishing at the same time a branch house in Charleston, South Carolina. In 1821 the northern manufactory was transferred to Newark, New Jersey—then coming into prominence as a manufacturing town—and during the ensuing thirty-three years his business steadily increased, until it became one of the most important of its kind in the country. In 1854, having, by untiring energy and well-directed commercial talent, amassed a large fortune, he retired from active business life. He took no part in public affairs—unless his services as a volunteer for the defence of Stonington, in the war of 1812, can be held to come under this head—until 1840, when he was elected, without opposition, Mayor of Newark. At that time he was a pronounced member of the Whig party, and was an earnest supporter of Henry Clay. In 1842 he was elected a member of the House of Representatives as an independent candidate, defeating the regular Whig and Democratic nominees; and in 1844 he was re-elected from the same district. In 1851 he abandoned the Whig and entered the Democratic party, and in 1853, as Democratic candidate, was elected a member of the United States Senate for a full term, succeeding the Hon. J. W. Miller. Appointed Chairman of the Senate Committee on Manufactures, his extensive practical knowledge and sound common sense gave weight and point to his utterances; and while he was never prominent in debate, his counsels in committee were always listened to with attention, and were very generally followed. On the Committee to Audit and Control the Expenses of the Senate, his services, while less eminent in degree, were no less eminent in kind. Upon the expiration of his term, in 1859, he was succeeded by the Hon. John C. Ten Eyck; but in 1863 he was again put in nomination by the Democratic party, and was again elected. During that portion of his second term which he was enabled to serve, he displayed the same qualities that had made him so useful when first in office, but at the end of two years failing health disabled him from close attention to his senatorial duties, and for the last twelve months of his life his attendance upon the sessions of Congress was necessarily irregular. He died at his home in Newark, November 1st, 1866.

AAR, DAVID, ex-Judge, Trenton, New Jersey, was born in St. Thomas, Danish West Indies, November 10th, 1800. He is an Israelite, and a direct descendant of one of the families of Spain and Portugal that suffered religious persecution. His progenitor was a resident of Spain in the reign of Ferdinand and Isabella, who to avoid that persecution left the country with the first expedition to South America after the discovery of this country by Christopher Columbus. His destination was Rio de la Hacha, South America, but being wrecked on the island of Curaçoa, he remained there and was succeeded by twelve generations. When fifteen years old David Naar was sent to America to receive his education, returning upon graduation to St. Thomas and entering a large exporting and importing house as an apprentice. Here he was thoroughly drilled in commercial affairs, and after mastering the varied branches of business, founded an establishment of his own, which he conducted successfully for a number of years. During his residence in St. Thomas he held various important offices under the Danish government, the most onerous, and at the same time the most honorable, of these being that of commandant of one of the militia forces of the island, a position that placed upon him responsibilities and entailed upon him duties of a very grave character. In all of his trusts his duties were discharged in the most exemplary and satisfactory manner. In 1834 he removed the seat of his business from St. Thomas to New York, and four years later, 1838, withdrew altogether from mercantile pursuits. In the latter year he purchased a farm near Elizabeth, New Jersey; removed thither and settled down to agriculture. But the quiet life of a farmer was by no means suited to his active temperament, and while retaining a general supervision of the work done on his domain, he gave the greater portion of his time to political affairs. Uniting with the Democratic party, he earnestly and with ardor devoted himself to promulgating and advocating its principles. Naturally a ready and popular speaker, possessing a remarkable talent for foreseeing the ultimate as well as the immediate effects of public measures, and being, moreover, a genial, affable man of the world, he rapidly rose in the favor of his party, and almost from the beginning of his public life he was a leader. In 1843 he assumed his first (in America) official position, being in that year appointed Mayor of the borough of Elizabeth by the New Jersey Legislature. This was previous to the incorporation of Elizabeth as a city, and while it still formed a part of Essex county. In 1843 also he was appointed one of the lay Judges of the Court of Common Pleas of Essex county, an office that he held for a number of years, and the delicate duties of which he very satisfactorily discharged. In 1844 he was elected a Delegate from Essex county to the State Constitutional Convention, and as such exercised an important influence upon the remodelling of the organic law of the commonwealth, his sound common sense and practical legal knowledge enabling him to perceive wherein re-

47

form was needed, and to put his suggestions into working form. During the hotly-contested campaign that terminated in the election of President Polk he was a prominent partisan of the successful candidate, his services being rewarded, and the interest of the country at the same time well served, by his appointment to be Commercial Agent of the United States at St. Thomas. In this position he remained during the term of President Polk's administration, and upon being relieved by his successor, President Taylor's appointee, returned to his home in Elizabeth, where he was shortly elected Recorder of the borough, and a member of the Borough Council. In 1851-52 he again took part in State politics, being Clerk of the General Assembly of New Jersey for two successive sessions. During his public life up to this point, while frequently writing political leaders for one or other of the principal journals attached to the interests of the Democratic party, he had not established himself in any newspaper connection. In 1853 he determined upon entering the profession of journalism, and to this end bought *The True American*, a publication established on a sure financial basis, and being generally regarded as the governing factor in the Democratic party in that portion of the State. His extended personal acquaintance among the leading men not only in his own but in the opposite party, his thorough knowledge and understanding of the political history of New Jersey, and of that of the country at large, and his rare faculty, already alluded to, of perceiving the probable future of the political measures of the present, all united to fit him in an eminent degree for the discharge of the editorial function, and during his incumbency *The True American* was unquestionably the leading Democratic journal of New Jersey. For seventeen years he remained in the editorial harness, and during this long period his paper was steadfastly firm to its political faith; upholding with brilliant vigor the party measures; supporting with earnest warmth the party men, and hitting all the while keen blows among the party's enemies. In 1870 when he resigned his editorship, he had well earned the title of "the Democratic War-horse," for in his long editorial career he had made himself known and felt by every public man in the State, and few there were but had been wisely guided by his counsels, or had come under the stinging lash of his criticism. Five years before his retirement from journalism he was appointed by the joint vote of the Senate and General Assembly of New Jersey State Treasurer, and during the years 1865-66 that he was in office his influence was of an excellently reformatory character. At the close of the year the Republicans came into power and he was displaced. The system of bookkeeping and general accounting that he introduced into the Treasury Department is still retained by his successors, and is greatly superior to any system previously devised. After his retirement from this office, in 1868, he was appointed by ex-Governors Vroom and Olden, the then commissioners of the State Sinking Fund, Secretary to that commission, an office that he still (1877) continues to fill in the most satisfactory manner. For several years he has resided in Trenton, and since his removal to that city has been for two terms a member of the Common Council, and also has served as a member of the School Board, evincing while holding the latter trust, as, indeed, he has done since its inception, a warm regard for and earnest determination to aid the present admirable school system of New Jersey. He has now been in public life in America for nearly forty years; has ably filled many important public offices; has been largely instrumental in the formulation and adoption of many important public measures, and has won the confidence and esteem of a vast number of the leading public men. Throughout his long and useful life he has been unswervingly true to his party and to his friends, and to both he has given far more than he has received. For a long series of years he has been an active member of the society of F. and A. Masons, and is now about the oldest, if not the oldest, member of the 33d degree of the ancient Scottish rite. He was married in February, 1820, to Sarah D'Azevedo, by whom he has had several children, of whom five are now surviving. His wife still lives, and after fifty-seven years of connubial happiness they are surrounded by numbers of grandchildren and great-grandchildren.

———◦◦◦———

HITMAN, WALT, Poet, was born at West Hills, New York, in 1819, and in early life assisted his father in farming and agricultural pursuits, on Long Island. His parents were respectively of English and Dutch descent, and he partakes of the blood and nature of the two races that set in progress the settlement and civilization of New York. In his youth he had listened to the preaching of the famous Quaker iconoclast, Elias Hicks, of whom his parents were followers, and through his valuable teachings he probably secured many of the more important elements in his education and mental characteristics. After leaving his father's farm he taught school for a short time, then became a printer, and subsequently a carpenter. When his first volume appeared he was engaged in the erection of frame dwellings in Brooklyn, and it was set in type entirely by his own hand. He was originally a supporter and partisan of the Democratic party, but when the fugitive slave law was passed, discovered that his ideas and convictions and those of his co-workers in politics were far from harmonizing, and he then openly declared his sentiments and principles in a poem called "Blood Money," one not found in his works, but which was the first he ever wrote. "He confessed to having no talent for industry, and that his forte was loafing and writing poems. He was poor, but had discovered that, on the whole, he could live magnificently on bread and water. He had travelled through the country as far as New Orleans, where he once edited a paper. And in his book will be found all that is himself—his life, works and days;

he has kept nothing back whatever." He continued writing poems, that appeared from time to time in enlarged editions of "Leaves of Grass," which in 1860 reached its sixth edition, until the outbreak of the rebellion, when he repaired to Washington and devoted himself to nursing and conversing with the wounded soldiers who were in the hospitals. His labors among them, for which he never asked nor received any compensation whatever, were unremitting, "and he so won the poor fellows from all thought of their sorrows by his readings and conversation that his entrance was the signal in any room for manifestations of the utmost delight. He certainly has a rare power of attaching people to him." During the years thus occupied it has been computed that in the hospital and on the field he ministered to upward of 100,000 sick and wounded men, giving them personal aid and attention, and retreating from no peril, whether of disease or battle. At the close of the war he was appointed to a clerkship in the Department of the Interior, and in the intervals of official work wrote a new volume of poems, entitled "Drum Taps." A critic, speaking of the work, says: "This volume is entirely free from the peculiar deductions to which the other is liable, and shows that the author has lost no fibre of his force. There is in it a very touching dirge for Abraham Lincoln, who was his warm friend and admirer." In 1865, or 1866, the late Secretary of the Interior, Mr. Harlan, had pointed out to him, "probably by some one who desired Whitman's clerkship," various passages of the "Leaves of Grass," and for this cause removed him from his office. "The indignation which this caused throughout the country proves that Walt Whitman has quietly obtained a very wide influence. After a very curious controversy, chiefly notable for an able and caustic pamphlet written by Mr. O'Connor, showing that the Secretary would equally have dismissed the Scriptural and classical writers, the bard was appointed to an office in the Attorney-General's department." It is understood by his friends that he is writing a series of pieces which shall be the expression of the religious nature of man, which he regards as "essential to the completion of his task." A brilliant writer, in the London *Fortnightly Review*, contributes the following reminiscences: "It was about ten years ago (written in 1866) that literary circles in and around Boston were startled by the tidings that Emerson, whose incredulity concerning American books was known to be as profound as that of Sydney Smith, had discovered an American poet. Emerson had been for many years our literary banker; paper that he had inspected, coin that had been rung on his counter, would pass safely anywhere On his table had been laid one day a queerly-shaped book, entitled, 'Leaves of Grass, by Walt Whitman.' There was also in the front the portrait of a middle-aged man in the garb of a workingman. The Concord philosopher's feeling on perusing this book was expressed in a private letter to its author, which I quote from memory: 'At first I rubbed my eyes to find if this new sunbeam might not be an illusion. . . . . I greet you at the beginning of a great career, which yet must have had a long foreground somewhere for such a start.' Toward no other American, toward no contemporary excepting Carlyle, had Emerson ever used such strong expressions as these." He then at once printed a new edition of his poems, placing on the back of it: "I greet you at the beginning of a great career: R. W. Emerson," which, with the publication of the entire letter at the end of the volume, "annoyed Mr. Emerson very much, for it was a formidable book for any gentleman to carry by his endorsement into general society. Mr. Emerson was afterward convinced, I believe, that Walt Whitman had printed his letter in ignorance of the *bienséances* in such cases, but he was destined to hear of some unpleasant results from it. His book was, in fact, unreadable in many of those circles to which the refined thinker's name at once bore it, and many were the stories of the attempts to read it in mixed companies. One grave clergyman made an effort to read it aloud to some gentlemen and ladies, and only broke down after surprising his company considerably. Nevertheless, the book continued to be studied quietly, and those who read it ceased to wonder that it should have kindled the sage who had complained that the American freeman is 'timid, imitative, tame,' from 'listening too long to the courtly muses of Europe.'" In his poems are the autographs of New York, and of the prairies, savannahs, Ohio and Mississippi, and all powers good and evil. Here is his portrait in 1866: "The sun had put a red mask on his face and neck . . . . his head was oviform in every way; his hair, which was strongly mixed with gray, was cut close to his head, and, with his beard, was in strange contrast to the almost infantine fulness and serenity of his face. This serenity, however, came from the quiet light-blue eyes, and above these there were three or four deep horizontal furrows, which life had ploughed. . . . . When he was talking about that which interested him, his voice, always gentle and clear, became slow, and his eyelids had a tendency to decline over his eyes. It was impossible not to feel at every moment the *reality* of every word and movement of the man, and also the surprising delicacy of one who was even freer with his pen than modest Montaigne." Again : "I found him setting in type in a Brooklyn printing office a paper from the *Democratic Review*, urging the superiority of Walt Whitman's poetry over that of Tennyson, which he meant to print (as he did everything, pro and con), in full in the appendix of his next edition. He still had on the workingman's garb, which (he said) he had been brought up to wear, and now found it an advantage to continue." The following anecdote related of him is characteristic of his nature : He was going the rounds of a prison, and saw a man, pending trial for a slight offence, incarcerated in a very disagreeable and unhealthy cell. "Hearing his account, Walt Whitman turned about, went straight to the governor of the prison and related the matter, ending thus : 'In my opinion, it is a damned shame.' The governor

was at first stunned by this from an outsider, and one in the dress of a laborer; then he eyed him from head to foot, as if questioning whether to commit him; during which the offender stood eying the governor in turn with a severe serenity. Walt triumphed in this duel of eyeshots, and, without another word, the governor called an officer to go and transfer the prisoner to a better room." He was visited by the celebrated Henry Thoreau in 1856, and this scholarly thinker says of him : "Walt Whitman . . . . is the most interesting fact to me at present. I have just read his second edition (which he gave me), and it has done me more good than any reading for a long time. There are two or three pieces in the book which are disagreeable ; simply sensual. . . . . It is as if the beasts spoke. Of course he can communicate to us no experience, and if we are shocked, whose experience is it that we are reminded of? . . . . He occasionally suggests something a little more than human. . . . . Wonderfully like the Orientals, too, considering that when I asked him if he had read them, he said, 'No; tell me about them.' . . . . He is apparently the greatest democrat the world has seen." He has made an equal impression on other men of ability and culture who have visited or have been brought into contact with him ; while in England, by such minds as Rossetti, Meredith, Swinburne, and many more writers of high and unassailable talent and powers, he has been called the great singer of America. He is passionately fond of opera music, and many of his verses have been written while listening to the performance of the Italian, French and German masterpieces. "He notes everything and forgets nothing. His brain is indeed a kind of American formation, in which all things print themselves like ferns in the coal. Every thought, too, signs itself in his mind by a right and immutable word." In one of his private letters is the following : "I assume that poetry in America needs to be entirely recreated. On examining with anything like deep analysis what now prevails in the United States, the whole mass of current works, long and short, consists either of the poetry of an elegantly weak sentimentalism, at bottom nothing but maudlin puerilities, or more or less musical verbiage, arising out of a life of depression and enervation, as their result ; or else that class of poetry, plays, etc., of which the foundation is feudalism, with its ideas of lords and ladies, its imported standard of gentility, and the manners of European high-life-below-stairs in every line and verse. . . . . Instead of mighty and vital breezes, proportionate to our continent with its powerful races of men, its tremendous historic events, its great oceans, its mountains, and its illimitable prairies, I find a few little silly fans languidly moved by shrunken fingers." During the past few years he has resided in the vicinity of Camden, New Jersey, where, as in all places ever honored by his presence, he is regarded with affection and admiration by all classes and all manner of men. He published the first edition of "Leaves of Grass" in 1855; the third edition in 1860; "Drum-Taps" in 1865-66; collected "Poems," 8vo., in 1867; and in 1868 was put forth a volume of his poems selected and edited by W. M. Rossetti, 8vo., London.

ILLETS, COLONEL J. HOWARD, Senator from Cumberland county, was born in Cape May in 1834. He is a son of Dr. Reuben Willets, the family, of English descent, having first settled on Long Island, and afterwards at Willets' Point, Cape May county. He was educated at the Pennington Seminary, and at the West Point Military Academy, where he remained one term, when he resigned and entered the Jefferson Medical College, in Philadelphia, from which he graduated in 1857. Shortly after his graduation he settled at Port Elizabeth, New Jersey, and practised his profession there until the outbreak of the civil war. Sharing in the patriotic uprising so general in New Jersey at that critical period, he volunteered his services and was commissioned a Captain in the 7th Regiment of New Jersey Volunteers, serving with the regiment through the Peninsula campaign, in which he greatly distinguished himself, and elsewhere, till 1862, when he was appointed Lieutenant-Colonel of the 12th Regiment, and a few months later, the colonel, Robert C. Johnson, having resigned on account of ill health, was promoted to the Colonelcy. At the battle of Chancellorsville, in the following May, his regiment behaved with conspicuous gallantry, and suffered heavily, losing 179 in killed, wounded and missing, he himself, at the head of a brigade, being severely wounded in the face and arm. The 12th Regiment, indeed, has passed into history as in every respect one of the finest in the army. "It is the boast of the 12th," says Foster, in his work on "New Jersey and the Rebellion," "as it is that of most of the New Jersey regiments, that it was always in the post of danger; that it suffered in action most severely, and that it could always be relied on for perilous duty. Major-General French regarded the 12th as one of the finest regiments in the army, and the commanding officers of the brigade were always unanimous in its praise. Its losses were very severe in men and officers, and were never supplied by the State, no recruits (except about thirty) having been sent it until after the surrender of Lee. It never lost a color in action, and had very few prisoners taken. It never was broken, and never retreated until the whole line was broken or ordered back. It was composed of the flower and strength of the rural population of South Jersey, and on every field in Virginia they bravely maintained the honor of their flag and State." It was one of his most painful experiences in the war that the wounds he received at Chancellorsville, added to those he had received in the Peninsula, necessitated his parting with this gallant regiment and withdrawing from active service, but being totally disabled, no choice was left him. The War Department subsequently assigned him to duty as President of a Board of Court-Martial, in which capacity he served until the close of the war. He was mustered out of the service, December 20th, 1864, when he returned to Port Elizabeth and resumed the practice of medicine, though the brilliancy of his military records combined with his abilities and popular qualities, soon drew him into the political arena, where, as in every other theatre of action in which he has figured, he won signal distinction. In 1871 he was elected a member of the New Jersey Assembly, and re-elected the following year; and in 1874 he was elected to the State Senate, serving in both bodies on several of the most important committees. His course as a legislator not only secured the respect of his colleagues but proved highly acceptable to his constituents. In 1876 he travelled extensively in South America, visiting most of the important cities on the Pacific side, having previously explored the chief places of interest on the Atlantic coast. Scarcely yet in the prime of his manhood, and thus rich in knowledge and experience, with abilities of a high order well trained, it may fairly be predicted that his countrymen have not heard the last or the best of him.

OODRUFF, HON. AARON DICKINSON, late of Trenton, Lawyer, Attorney-General of the State of New Jersey, was born in Trenton, September 12th, 1762. He delivered the valedictory at the Princeton commencement of 1779; in 1784 was admitted to the bar, and in 1793 was made Attorney-General of the State, and annually re-elected, except in 1811, until his death. He served also in the Legislature, and was influential in having Trenton selected for the State capital. He died at Trenton, New Jersey, June 24th, 1817, while actively engaged in the performance of his numerous and responsible duties as Attorney-General, and Trustee of the Presbyterian Church of his native place. He was buried in the Trenton churchyard, where his epitaph records that: "For twenty-four years he filled the important station of Attorney-General with incorruptible integrity. Adverse to legal subtleties, his professional knowledge was exerted in the cause of truth and justice. The native benevolence of his heart made him a patron of the poor: a defender of the fatherless: it exulted in the joys or participated in the sorrows of his friends."

NGHAM, HON. SAMUEL D., Manufacturer, Secretary of the United States Treasury, 1829–1831, late of Trenton, New Jersey, was born in Bucks county, Pennsylvania, September 16th, 1773, and was of Quaker parentage. His earlier years were spent in the paper manufacturing business, in Easton, Pennsylvania, and until drawn into the arena of political life he was successfully engaged in mer-

Joseph Carr

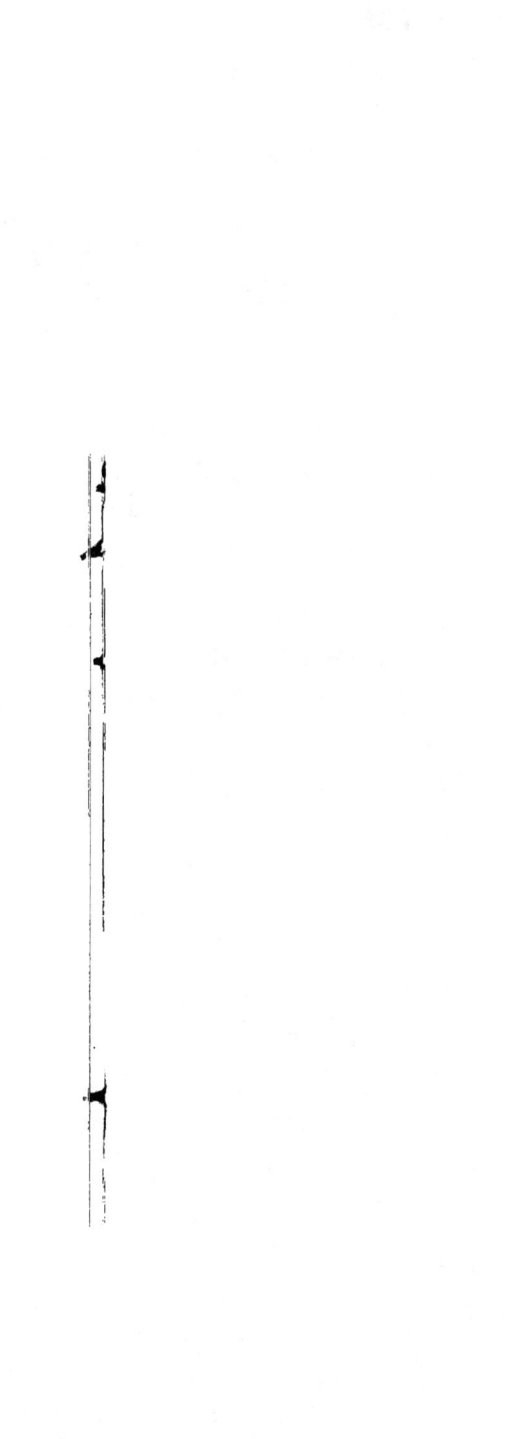

cantile pursuits. He afterward served three years as a member of the Pennsylvania Legislature; and was a member of Congress from his State in the years 1813 to 1818, and 1822 to 1829. From 1829 to 1831 he officiated as Secretary of the United States Treasury; the latter appointment he received from J hn Quincy Adams. He died at Trenton, New Jersey, June 5th, 1860.

ILLER, REV. SAMUEL, D. D., Professor in the Theological Seminary of Princeton, was born in 1769, a few months before the birth of his intimate and illustrious friend, Dr. John Mason. His father, an excellent clergyman of 'Scotch extraction, was born, educated and ordained in Boston, but spent the greater portion of his life in Delaware. His mother, a native of Maryland, was a lady of rare accomplishments and high moral character. At a suitable age he was sent to the University of Pennsylvania, where he enjoyed enviable advantages; while, in his leisure hours, he had access to the best circles of society in Philadelphia and the environs, where he was ever a courted and respected guest and visitor. Upon finishing the prescribed course of studies at the university, he commenced the study of theology under the guidance of his venerable father, and after his decease placed himself under the instructions of the celebrated Dr. Nisbet, then filling the presidential chair of the Dickinson College, Carlisle. He studied the Bible earnestly and constantly, not merely as a source of theological knowledge, but especially as a gracious means of spiritual culture. He was liberal and kindly in sharing his moderate means with those he found deserving pity and support, and in the practical affairs of life was notably careful and systematic. Above all did he act upon the counsel, "Though thine enemies strike and revile thee, thou shalt treat them with pity and compassion;" and once took especial pains to spread a favorable opinion of one who had done him an unmerited injury, and the fact being adverted to, he admitted its truthfulness, but added, mildly, " He was a good man, notwithstanding." In 1791 he was licensed to preach. His early and only settlement as pastor was in the First Presbyterian Church, of New York city, which then embraced more talent, wealth and influence than any other one in the connection. After laboring zealously and efficiently in this field for a period extending over twenty years he was appointed to the Professorship of Ecclesiastical History and Church Government in the Theological Seminary at Princeton. His lectures on the composition and delivery of a sermon, to the students under his charge, have never been surpassed in their line, and take high rank as masterly productions; he was also a judicious critic on all matters relating to public oratory, or speaking, and by those who knew him, and who were competent to

judge, his final opinion and decisions were taken as ultimate and conclusive. His " Treatise on Clerical Manners and Habits," inculcating a courteous and dignified bearing, is widely known, and has been repeatedly quoted, in portions, as an excellent guide for students and the clergy in general. His publications are numerous; his first work of considerable extent being " Retrospect of the Eighteenth Century," written early in his ministry, through which he acquired an enviable reputation both at home and in Great Britain. Several of his works were controversial, and attracted much attention by their perspicuous, logical and well-considered arguments and analyses. He published also several biographical works of extended scope; and his volume on the " Eldership" is a work in high and general repute, Dr. Chalmers asserting that it is the best publication given to the church on that subject. He was the author also of a large number of occasional discourses. Many who were among the most honored in civil life—Dickinson, Jay, Spencer, Boudinot, Rush, Hamilton, and, above all, Washington—were on the list of his personal friends; and with many famous and learned characters in Europe he maintained for many years a close and intimate correspondence. Following is a partial list of his various publications: " Letters on the Constitution and Order of the Christian Ministry, addressed to Members of the Presbyterian Church in the City of New York," 1807; "A Continuation of Letters Concerning the Constitution and Order of the Christian Ministry, being an Examination of the Strictures of the Rev. Drs. Bowden and Kemp, and Rev. Mr. How, on the Former Series," 1809; "Memoirs of Rev. John Rogers, D. D.," 8vo., 1813; "Letters on Unitarianism," 8vo., 1821; "Essay on the Warrant, Nature and Duties of the Office of Ruling Elder in the Presbyterian Church," 12mo., 1831; "Letters to Presbyterians on the Present Crisis in the Presbyterian Church in the United States," 12mo., 1833; "Two Sermons on Baptism, preached at Freehold, New Jersey," 12mo., 1834; "Memoir of Rev. Charles Nesbit, D. D.," 12mo., 1840; "Primitive and Apostolical Order of the Church of Christ Vindicated," 12mo., 1840; besides his "Brief Retrospect" and his "Letters on Clerical Manners and Habits," etc., etc. He died at Princeton, New Jersey, in 1850.

ARR, HON. JOSEPH, Judge of the Court of Common Pleas and Orphans' Court of Burlington county, was born, January 11th, 1821, in the town of Mount Holly, New Jersey, and is the son of Joseph and Ruth N. (Thomas) Carr. His father was a merchant for upwards of fifty years in Mount Holly, and is a native of the State; his mother is a native of Wales, who when ten years of age came to the United States, at the very commencement of the nineteenth century, and is still living. Joseph received but a limited education in the common school, where he remained until ten years of age, and then entered his father's employ, with whom he continued three years. He was next indentured as an apprentice to Nathan Palmer, the proprietor of the *New Jersey Mirror*, a weekly paper then as now published at Mount Holly. In that establishment he learned the whole art of printing; and after acquiring the same he remained in the employ of his patron until the latter's death, in 1842. He then assumed the entire charge of the paper, which he conducted with marked ability and success until 1857, when he was admitted to an equal share or partnership with the remaining heir, as Mrs. Palmer had died at this time. The paper was now vested in the firm of J. Carr, Jr., & Co., which continued without change until 1872, when he disposed of his interests in the same. In the same year, without any solicitation on his part, he was appointed Judge of the Court of Common Pleas and of the Orphans' Court for Burlington county, a position which he still retains. His political creed is that held by the Republican party, who in the campaign of 1876 selected him as the representative of the Second Congressional District on the Electoral ticket for Hayes and Wheeler. He has been for many years a Director of the Farmers' National Bank of Mount Holly, one of the oldest financial institutions in the State. In every movement tending towards the improvement of the town or county he has ever manifested a deep interest, and is respected by all classes as a valuable as well as a public spirited citizen. He was married, June 10th, 1875, to Emily, daughter of John Palmer, of New York.

———◦◦———

AYTON, HON. AARON OGDEN, Fourth Auditor, Treasurer, Department of the United States, late of Washington, District of Columbia, was born at Elizabethtown, New Jersey, October 4th, 1796. Ralph Dayton came from England to Boston, and thence to East Hampton, about 1650; was one of the pioneer settlers in that section of the country, and died in 1657; Jonathan Dayton, one of his descendants, removed to Elizabethtown, New Jersey, about 1720. His father, Elias Dayton, was a son of the preceding; while another son, Robert Dayton, bore the same relation to the eminent jurist and statesman, Hon. William L. Dayton, late Senator in Congress from New Jersey. Elias Dayton was born in 1737; in 1759 was commissioned as lieutenant, and in 1760 as captain, in a regiment of foot of the Province of New Jersey; in 1764 he was sent in command of a military force against the Indians near Detroit. In February, 1776, he was commissioned colonel of a New Jersey regiment, and took part in the defence of Ticonderoga, under General Schuyler. With his brigade he assisted in forming the last line of trenches at Yorktown,

and was present at the opening of the capitulation by Cornwallis. At Kniphausen's invasion of New Jersey, in 1780, he was in command of the force which pursued him. In January, 1783, he was appointed a brigadier-general, on which occasion Washington sent him a letter of congratulation, and said he would keep his commission until he could deliver it to him in person. At the close of the war he was appointed Major-General of the Second Division of New Jersey Militia, which station he filled until his decease. He was for many years a member of the State Legislature; declined the appointment of delegate to the convention formed to frame the Constitution of the United States—an honor which, at his request, was subsequently conferred upon his eldest son, the late Jonathan Dayton—and died in 1807. His father, Elias B. Dayton, who was a minor during the Revolution, distinguished himself in those troublous days as a volunteer in several expeditions, and subsequently was engaged in mercantile pursuits in Elizabethtown, New Jersey. His mother was a daughter of Dr. Thomas Bradbury Chandler, who was one of the most eminent divines of the colonial church of England, was the writer of whom it was said, by one well able to judge, that no man in America could mend his pen. He was sent to school at a very early age, and from a small "character book," still preserved, his general standing there seems to have been unvaryingly creditable to him. His fondness for reading even in his childhood may be inferred from an incident which occurred on the occasion of his first visit to New York. Instead of indulging his curiosity, and hurrying out with eagerness to behold the wonders and novelties of this bustling city, he had no sooner entered his uncle's house than he asked for a book, and sat down to its quiet perusal. When in his fifteenth year he was sufficiently advanced in his studies to enter the junior class in Princeton College; and, though the youngest member in it, passed through his course with such distinction—evincing rare assiduity and power of comprehension—as to graduate at its close, in 1813, with the highest honors. He was a member of the Cliosophic Society, before which he delivered on one occasion a noteworthy address, characterized by scholarly elegance. In the course of the year following his relinquishment of college life, he entered on the study of law under the supervision of the late Governor Ogden, after whom he had been named. While thus engaged his constitution, originally strong, became seriously enfeebled by a nervous disease, from which he never entirely recovered, and which often during a great part of his life unfitted him for strong, sustained mental exertion. With short intervals of rest he continued his studies, however, until the completion of his term, and the usual preparatory training, and, November 13th, 1817, was admitted to the bar of New Jersey as an attorney-at-law. In the opening of 1818, partly through health considerations, partly to judge by actual personal observations, concerning the probable advantages obtainable in his profession in Ohio, he left his home and made a journey to that State on horseback, eventually securing a license there as attorney and counsellor. In autumn of the same year he returned to New Jersey with the intention of settling in Cincinnati in the following spring, but was finally induced to change his mind and remain in his native State. In the summer of 1819, accordingly, he entered upon the active practice of his profession at or near Salem, in the western section of New Jersey. He possessed many natural gifts, which, backed by unwearied diligence, eminently fitted him to attain high rank in his profession; had an acute discriminating and logical mind; a lucid and orderly method in arranging his thoughts, and great case and freedom in expressing them; a quick and intuitive perception of strong points in a case before him; and singular readiness in exposing the weaknesses and fallacies in the arguments and pleadings of opponents. His voice was clear and strong, his enunciation distinct and forcible, his manner earnest and impressive. By his careful reading and just thinking he was well versed in general principles of law, and happy in their application to particular cases; also through his patient industry and tireless research he was enabled to illustrate and fortify his positions by all the precedents that had bearing on the question. He was not only a sound lawyer and an excellent reasoner, but also a persuasive and popular pleader, succeeding at once in securing the attention and respect of bench and bar, and in exercising due influence on the minds of the jury. At the outset of his career he rose rapidly, and, instead of the usual trying slow progress of young lawyers, secured almost immediately an extensive and remunerative clientage. "This stimulated him. He did not confine himself to county courts and employ senior counsel to argue cases before the Supreme Court, but as soon as he became counselor, in the shortest time allowed by rules, i. e., three years from time of license as attorney, argued all his cases himself." This active conduct of his cases naturally brought him into conflict with many of his more learned and experienced brethren, and became a still further incitement to study and ambition. In 1823 he was elected to the State Legislature, and though the youngest member of that body took an active part in many of the most important debates, and was occasionally opposed to William Griffith, a distinguished speaker in the House, and other learned legislators. Richard Stockton, however, advised him not to be a candidate again until he made himself master of his profession, wisely observing how many young and promising men have been disastrously diverted from their studies by the fascination of political life and excitement. Upon this advice he acted, and for a time devoted himself with renewed earnestness to professional theory and practice. But at the time of the exciting presidential contest between Jackson and Adams he once more entered ardently into the political arena, taking up arms for Jackson, who was then somewhat unpopular. The duty was committed to him by the convention of delegates held in Trenton, September 1st,

1824, of which he was the secretary, of preparing an address on the subject under discussion to the people of the State. This address, drafted entirely by himself, elicited warm encomiums from many high quarters, and extensively circulated throughout the country; its effect was pronounced and sudden, and the State, supposed originally by all to be entirely for Adams, gave to Jackson the electoral vote. In the summer of 1825 he removed to Jersey City, and thence to New York in 1826, and in May of this year was admitted to practise as counsellor-at-law in that State. He then again became a warm and open ally of Jackson, and in his cause contributed extensively to the current newspapers and journals, and delivered many addresses and speeches, extorting through his eloquence and abilities the admiration even of his bitterest adversaries. In autumn of 1828 he was nominated by the Democrats of the city and county of New York as a candidate for the Legislature, and was elected by 5,000 majority. His principal efforts centred on the subject of banking, which in the proceedings of that session occupied a very prominent place; and he was an unflinching advocate of the safety fund system, which was adopted in the face of a vehement opposition of the city banks. At the next annual election he was again regularly nominated, but the wealth of those opposing him was an important element in the defeat which followed. He was afterward appointed, by the governor and Senate, Master in Chancery, a lucrative position in such a city as New York. He was subsequently honored by the chancellor with the office of Injunction Master for the First Circuit, which included the city and county of New York, Long Island and Staten Island. This station, inferior only to that of vice-chancellor, he filled with ability and with general satisfaction to the chancellor, the bar and the community at large. His state of health prohibiting a vigorous prosecution of his profession, he accepted, in 1833, the offer of a place in the Diplomatic Bureau of the Department of State, and thus virtually forever abandoned the bar. In March, 1834, he was admitted as Counsellor of the Supreme Court of the United States, and shortly after commenced the preparation of a new edition of "Laws of the United States," which was intended to include a history of legislation on each subject from the establishment of the government down to the current time. The publisher, however, after having put in press a portion of this important projected enterprise, not receiving the expected patronage from Congress, abandoned the further prosecution of the work, and a needed and laudable publication was lost to the country. In 1835, at the invitation of the Society of Cincinnati, of New Jersey, he delivered a eulogy on Lafayette, recently deceased; while in the Department of State he had access to a complete file of the *Moniteur* and other works not often seen in this country, which gave him familiar acquaintance with every important event of the patriot Frenchman's life and career. In 1806 he was made Chief Clerk of the Department of State, an office corresponding with the under-secretaryship of state in Great Britain. During the absence 'of the head of the department, he acted, by authority of the President, as Secretary of State, performing the same duties now pertaining to the Assistant Secretaryship of State. In 1837, just after his marriage, he was offered the situation of Chargé d'Affaires at Bogota, but declined the appointment from domestic considerations. In 1838 he was placed at the head of a bureau in the Treasury Department, as Fourth Auditor, and through several varying administrations until his death filled that position, without changing or concealing his politics—his duty being to oversee all accounts of the Navy Department. He was married in August, 1837, to Mary B. Tuft, of Salem, New Jersey; and died, September 30th, 1858, of a sudden attack of apoplexy, occurring while he was on his way to his home. At his decease resolutions of respect were passed by all heads of bureaus in the Treasury Department; also by those especially connected with the office of Fourth Auditor.

URRILL, ALEXANDER M., Lawyer, Legal Writer, late of Kearney, New Jersey, graduated in 1824 from Columbia College, with the highest honors of the class. Subsequently he entered the office of Chancellor Kent, and for several years pursued a course of legal studies under the supervision and guidance of that able and scholarly jurist. He was remarkable for his elegant precision and discrimination in the use of language; and was the author of "Circumstantial Evidence," "Assignments," "Practice," and a "Law Dictionary." He also aided in compiling "Worcester's Dictionary," and deservedly took high rank as an authority on general pronunciation and definition, and on points of law requiring careful inquiry and lucid explanation. He died at Kearney, New Jersey, February 7th, 1869, aged sixty-two years.

GDEN, REV. BENJAMIN, Sixth Pastor of Hopewell Church, Pennington, New Jersey, late of Valparaiso, Indiana, was the son of John Ogden and Abigail (Bennett) Ogden. He was born in Fairfield, Cumberland county, New Jersey, October 4th, 1797, and was educated at the College of New Jersey, from which institution he graduated in 1817. He early manifested a leaning toward the church, became deeply interested in divinity and theological study, and was eventually one of the subjects of that wonderful work of grace under Dr. Green's presidency, which gave to the church such men as Drs. Charles Hodge, David Magie, John Maclean and Ravaud K. Rodgers, and Bishops McIlvaine and Johns. He prepared for the ministry at the

Theological Seminary of the Presbyterian church, in Princeton, in April, 1821, was licensed as a probationer by the Presbytery of Philadelphia, and by the same presbytery ordained in June, 1822, at Bensalem, Bucks county, Pennsylvania, where he labored as a missionary for one year and six months. In 1823 he was installed as pastor of the church in Lewistown, Delaware, by the Presbytery of New Castle, and in this place remained for a period of three and a half years. In the meantime the Presbytery of Lewes was formed, and November 28th, 1826, he was received from the presbytery of that place by the Presbytery of New Brunswick, when a call from Hopewell Church was placed in his hands, and by him accepted. December 5th, 1826, he was installed pastor of this church by a committee consisting of Dr. Samuel Miller and the Rev. Messrs. Eli F. Cooley and George S. Woodhull. In this field he labored well and wisely. Early in the summer of 1833 he called to his aid Rev. Daniel Dernelle, who began his offices by preaching a series of sermons to Christians from passages in the Fifty-first Psalm. "The word came with power. The hearts of believers were melted, backsliders returned, unceasing prayer was offered mingled with praise, and sinners were brought to repentance." Although it was in the midst of the harvest, there was no hindrance. The farmers rose to their work in the field at about three in the morning and closed at noon. After dining they arrived at the church in time for one service at 3 P. M., and another at 8 P. M., the intervening hours being devoted to meetings for prayer. As a fruit of this work, there was an addition to the communion roll of forty-seven persons. In the winter of 1837-38 came another memorable revival, which is excellently described in an article published in The Presbyterian, signed "N. N.," dated Pennington, April 24th, 1838. On one Saturday and the following Sabbath, the church received an addition of threescore persons, fifty-eight on examination and two by certificate. Of this number, twenty-nine were baptized on Saturday. "It was a pleasing spectacle. Those who witnessed it can never forget it. Amongst the number was an aged man who had been in the world nearly threescore and ten years. He, with two others, of nearly the same age, had gone into the vineyard at the eleventh hour. In this display of Divine grace, it seems as if no age nor class of people were passed by. The youngest of the number received into church fellowship was eleven years of age." On this solemn occasion he preached a touching sermon from the words, "By grace ye are saved," and in speaking of the revival, remarked, "To all other churches could we ardently wish a like stirring up of people's souls, and with might and main shall pray for so divine a result." The whole number received on profession of their faith under his ministry was one hundred and eighty-six. On the completion of his labors in this section, he removed to Three Rivers, Michigan, where by his preaching and example he accomplished beneficent and enduring results, and thence travelled to Indiana, settling eventually at

Valparaiso, his final place of sojourn. He was married to Emily T. Sahsbury, October 15th, 1821, by whom he had ten children—four sons and six daughters—all of whom survived him. One daughter married Rev. James Greer, and another, Rev. J. G. Reiheldaffer, D. D.; one son, Thomas Spencer Ogden, entered the ministry. He was born at Pennington, January 9th, 1832, and baptized in the following May; was licensed as a probationer by the Presbytery of New Brunswick, and was ordained by the same body in the Millstone Presbyterian Church, Monmouth county, New Jersey, August 29th, 1857; after marrying Phœbe Elizabeth Coombs, he set sail for Corisco, Central Africa, on the following October 5th; in that far-off field of labor he was constantly employed in earnest Christian missionary work until the time of his decease, and there was buried after a faithful service of three years, his widow and infant child returning to this country. Of his other children there is no especial mention found in the chronicles of Hopewell Church, of Pennington. He died at Valparaiso, Indiana, January 11th, 1853.

DAYTON, GENERAL ELIAS, late of Elizabeth, was born, May 1st, 1737, at Elizabethtown, and commissioned, March 19th, 1759, as a Lieutenant in the regiment of provincial troops raised in New Jersey, and known as the "Jersey Blues," which were employed in the conquest of Canada from the French. He participated in the battle on the Heights of Abraham, at the gates of Quebec, on September 13th, 1759, and was present at the surrender, five days after. In the succeeding spring he was promoted to Captain, and took part in the campaign which terminated with the surrender of Montreal, and at the same time the ceding of the whole of Canada, with its dependencies, to the British crown. In 1764 he was sent on special service in command of an expedition against the northern Indians near Detroit. A journal kept by him during the five months he passed in that wild region is still in existence, and is full of exciting interest. The objects of the expedition were accomplished, and he received official commendation for his success. After the disbandment of the provincial forces, he engaged in mercantile pursuits in his native town. But the spring of 1774 brought the tidings of British despotism in Boston, and Elizabethtown became from that time the head-quarters of the patriotic movement in New Jersey, giving impulse to the whole country. Mr. Dayton was an Alderman of the town, and became active in determining the people to stand by the Bostonians. In June, 1774, the patriots met to extend sympathy, and adopted resolutions to urge the country to stand firmly united, and inviting provincial conventions to assemble speedily to appoint delegates to a general Congress. In December he was chosen at a meeting of the Town Freeholders, to be a member of the "Committee of Correspondence and Observation, to

favor the more vigorous prosecution of the measures recom. mended by Congress." His father, Jonathan, who was then over seventy-four years of age, also served on the same committee. In the fall of 1775, when recruiting for the Continental army was begun, he was appointed Muster-Master, and assisted in the organization of the first two regiments raised in the province. At the beginning of the year 1776 Congress directed that the 3d Regiment be raised in New Jersey, and elected Mr. Dayton to be its Colonel. On the 23d of January, 1776, he signalized himself by fitting out at Elizabethport an expedition of three armed boats and one hundred and ten men, with which, in conjunction with a boat and forty men under Lord Sterling, he captured the British transport-ship, "Blue Mountain Valley," which lay in the lower bay of New York, loaded with supplies and necessaries for the British army. The prize was brought to Elizabethport, and a resolution of thanks to the captors passed Congress. After being retained for some time in the vicinity of New York to ward off anticipated raids from the British fleet, Colonel Dayton was in April, 1776, ordered to march to the relief of the northern army besieging Quebec, but on his arrival at Albany, General Schuyler changed his destination and gave him command of the Mohawk valley, where he quelled the Toryism which had been fostered by the activity of Sir John Johnson, and kept a check on the Indians of the "Six Nations" in that locality. He built Fort Schuyler, on the site of old Fort Stanwix, at Rome, and Fort Dayton, at Herkimer. In the close of the year he took part in the defence of Ticonderoga and Mount Independence, after which his regiment was returned to New Jersey, and on reaching Morristown was brigaded with the other New Jersey Continentals under General Maxwell. They reached the province in the darkest hour of the patriot cause, almost the whole State being in the possession of the enemy. After much skirmishing the Jersey Brigade reoccupied the country around Newark and Elizabethtown, shortly after the battle of Trenton. Many found their homes in ruins—houses plundered, fences gone and gardens laid waste. Colonel Dayton was among the sufferers. He was stationed at his native town a portion of the winter. In the campaign of the following year he commanded his regiment at the battle of the Brandywine, September 11th, 1777, the Jersey Brigade suffering severely and Colonel Dayton having a horse shot under him. At the battle of Germantown, October 4th, 1777, he had another horse killed under him while engaged near the corner of the famous Chew's house in the village. Although the result of the battle was not favorable to the Americans, they inflicted the greater loss upon the enemy, the New Jersey regiments making famous their title, "The Jersey Brigade." In the winter of 1777-78 he was again posted at Elizabethtown and put in supervision of the secret service for General Washington, getting information of the enemy's condition and movements. In June, 1778, when the British evacuated Philadelphia and retired across New Jersey, Colonel Dayton was with the force detached under General Lafayette to harass and impede them in their march. The British were so severely pressed that they turned and gave battle at Monmouth, June 28th, in which engagement the New Jersey Continentals and militia rendered most valuable service. While the New Jersey Brigade was stationed at Elizabeth and Newark, in February, 1779, a night attack was made on the former place by the 33d and 42d British regiments, who succeeded in burning some buildings, including the academy ; but daybreak revealing their numbers, they were at once attacked by Colonel Dayton's regiment with portions of two others, driven into the mud marshes, and forced to retreat thoroughly demoralized. In June, 1779, the Jersey Brigade marched in General Sullivan's army into northern Pennsylvania and western New York, to punish the Indian confederacy of the Six Nations, who had been the cause of the massacre of Wyoming and other terrible outrages. Colonel Dayton was engaged in the battle on August 29th, near Elmira, New York, when these Indians, under Brant, Butler and Middleton, with a Tory force under Sir John Johnson, were defeated and routed. The troops then overran the country, penetrating as far west as the Genesee valley. The houses and crops were destroyed and lands laid waste. The Indians never recovered from the severe chastising which they received. In October General Sullivan's troops were recalled. During the severe winter of 1779–80, General Washington, with the main army, lay at Morristown, with the Jersey Brigade in the advance posts from Rahway to above Newark. The frozen rivers and arms of the bays enabling troops to cross them necessitated extraordinary vigilance. Colonel Dayton participated in an attack, January 25th, made by 2,500 men, in an effort to capture the 1,200 British stationed on Staten Island. Sleds were used in crossing, and the troops occupied the heights on the island, but were so impeded in their movements by the snow, which was " four to six feet deep," that they failed to accomplish their object. The British retaliated by repeated invasions of Jersey during January and February, and in one of these the court-house at Elizabeth was burned, and also the Presbyterian church, of which Colonel Dayton was a Trustee. In the campaign of 1780 the British made their last important effort in New Jersey. On the night of June 6th an expedition of over 6,000 of the flower of the British army, including the Coldstream Guards, cavalry, flying artillery, and Hessians, under General Knyphausen, landed at Elizabethport, proposing to march upon Washington's main army at Morristown. Colonel Dayton commanded the post of Elizabethtown, from which they encountered the first opposition, his skirmish line mortally wounding the general of their advance division before they entered the town. The alarm signals brought out militia to Colonel Dayton's support, but he fell back skirmishing before the superior force of the enemy to a position behind Connecticut Farms village, where he effected a junction with the other portions of the Jersey Brigade. The

Continentals and militia then made a stand for three hours, twice attacking the enemy and driving his advance upon the main body, but at last, after a very close action, were pushed over the Rahway river into Springfield, but prevented the British from following. The plans of the enemy were thwarted by the delay caused by this obstinate resistance, and in the afternoon they retired to Connecticut Farms, their flanks being harassed by the militia which had been put under the command of Colonel Dayton. The enemy burned the village of Connecticut Farms, where they shot the wife of Rev. Mr. Caldwell, the chaplain of Colonel Dayton's regiment, and retreated the same night, through a drenching storm, to their boats at Elizabethport. Instead of having annihilated General Washington's force and ended the rebellion, they had been thwarted and held at bay by a single brigade of Continentals, aided only by militia. This miserable failure was more than British pride thought it could bear, and the attempt to penetrate to Washington's camp was renewed by the same powerful and well-organized force, with additional artillery, on the 23d of June, under direction and command of Sir Henry Clinton. On Colonel Dayton again fell the first blow. He succeeded in checking them at Connecticut Farms, and then retired to Springfield, where he was given the defence of the town with the bridges leading into it, a duty in which he greatly distinguished himself, holding the place nearly an hour against repeated assaults of the enemy and having his horse shot under him. He then rejoined the remainder of Maxwell's brigade, which, with Stark's brigade, were posted on the heights in the rear of the village, under command of General Greene, with the militia on the flanks. The strength of this position, and information of the approach of troops sent out by General Washington, deterred the British from attempting further advance. After exhausting their valor by burning a score of dwellings, and the Presbyterian church in the village of Springfield, they retreated precipitately, receiving additional punishment by the active pursuit ordered by General Greene. They recrossed to Staten Island immediately, and never again attempted a pleasure trip into Jersey. An officer of the Coldstream Guards estimated the loss of the British in these two June expeditions at about five hundred officers and men. Soon after the battle of Springfield, General Maxwell's resignation was accepted by Congress, and Colonel Dayton assumed command of the Jersey Brigade and held the command during the remainder of the war, although not confirmed as a Brigadier-General until January, 1783. In January, 1781, a portion of the Jersey Brigade, emboldened by the mild treatment used towards the Pennsylvania line, who had mutinied, imitated their example, and demanded the same indulgences, but Colonel Dayton's prompt action forced the surrender of all concerned. In September, 1781, the Jersey Brigade, under Colonel Dayton's command, landed on James river, about five miles from Williamsburgh, and took part in the campaign of the siege of Yorktown, forming the

Garret A. Hobart.

last line of trenches. He was present at the signing of the capitulation by Lord Cornwallis, on the 19th of October. In 1782 he was in charge of the camp of prisoners at Chatham, New Jersey. On the 7th of January, 1783, he was commissioned a Brigadier-General by Congress. General Washington wrote him upon the occasion, congratulating him upon his promotion and informing him that he would keep his commission till he must have the pleasure of delivering it to him in person. The news of the cessation of hostilities was announced in the camp of the brigade April 19th, 1783, and they were discharged November 3d, 1783. General Dayton had taken part in all the battles in which the Continental Line of New Jersey had been engaged. After the war he was commissioned Major-General of the 2d Division New Jersey State Militia, which command he held at the time of his death. Upon the formation of the New Jersey Society of the Cincinnati, General Dayton was chosen its President, and held that office during the remainder of his life. He declined an election to Congress in 1779. In 1787 he was appointed a member of the convention to frame the Constitution of the United States, but favored the appointment of his son. In 1789 he was elected Recorder of Elizabethtown, and from 1796 to 1805 was Mayor of the town, and for several years a member of the Legislature of New Jersey. In private life he sustained a high reputation. He was open and generous, and scrupulously upright, and in manners easy, unassuming and pleasant. In person and bearing he is said to have resembled General Washington so strongly, that with their backs turned it was difficult to distinguish them. He was on terms of intimacy with that illustrious man, by whom he was always treated with distinguished confidence. General Lafayette was also his warm friend. General Dayton died at Elizabeth, October 22d, 1807.

even before his professional one, and a practical career, opening in 1872 with his entrance to the Assembly, and thenceforward advancing without a one toward step, to having been re-elected the following year, when he was chosen Speaker of the Assembly, and subsequently elected to the State Senate, with a clear prospect of still higher honors in the future. During his first term in the Assembly he was placed on the Judiciary Committee, a recognition at the dawn of his public life which foreshadowed his upward course. His party affiliations are Republican, and, as befits an active member of a political society, are close and warm. He is plainly a politician of high promise. As a lawyer his practice is mainly confined to corporations, and is nearly all done quietly in his own office. He belongs to the great class of business lawyers, who in modern times have grown but their area eagle brethren quite off the stage, wisdom of action being much more in requisition than the gift of speech. He is Receiver for the New Jersey Midland Railroad, for the Paterson & Little Falls Horse Railroad, and for the Manhattan Bleaching & Dyeing Company; and was in 1872 appointed Counsel of the Board of Chosen Freeholders, in addition to his being counsel for a number of banks and insurance companies. His first political office in the line of his public service was his appointment as City Counsellor of Paterson, in honor of which he was against his will, and which he shortly resigned. His aptitude for business is extraordinary, in respect to origination as well as despatch, assuring not only the systematic and rapid performance of his immense office work, but the success of his projects and the profit of his investments in a measure that has occasioned his "luck" to pass into a proverb. In his case, however, as in that of most other successful men, it is safe to say that "luck" is only a familiar name for the force of brains. Personally, he is estimable and attractive, of excellent habits, cheerful temper, genial manners and generous feelings.

HOBART, HON. GARRET A., Lawyer, was born in Long Branch, Monmouth county, New Jersey, June 3d, 1844. His father, Addison W. Hobart, was a merchant. His mother's maiden name was Sophhie Vandervere. The mother was a native of New Jersey and of Dutch descent, the father being from New Hampshire and of the same family with the late Bishop Hobart. Garret's education was begun in the district schools, those great foundation-builders of individual culture, and finished at Rutgers College, which he entered in 1860, graduating in the class of 1863. He studied law in the office of Socrates Tuttle, and was licensed as an attorney in 1866, and as a counsellor in 1869, in which last year he was married to E. J. Tuttle, daughter of his late preceptor. He began the practice of his profession at Paterson in 1866, and has pursued it ever since with diligence and success, notwithstanding his pursuit at the same time, with equal success, of a large business career, begun

---

LINDLEY, JACOB, late of New Garden, New Jersey, was born in September, 1744. He was early in life a lover of religious inquiry, "being of an affable and communicative disposition, not willingly giving, nor readily taking offense; and as his natural endowments became seasoned with divine grace, he was fitted to fill with propriety the important station to which he was afterward called." His first appearance in the ministry was about the thirtieth year of his age; his communications were lively and powerful, "reaching the witness in the hearts of those to whom he ministered; and by keeping low and humble, walking in fear, and in obedience to the manifestations of duty, he grew in his gift and became an able minister of the gospel, qualified to divide the word aright to the several states of the people." Being well versed in the Scriptures, he was frequently enabled to open them with instructive clearness.

last line of trenches. He was present at the signing of the capitulation by Lord Cornwallis, on the 19th of October. In 1782 he was in charge of the camp of prisoners at Chatham, New Jersey. On the 7th of January, 1783, he was commissioned a Brigadier-General by Congress. General Washington wrote him upon the occasion, congratulating him upon his promotion and informing him that he would keep his commission until he could have the pleasure of delivering it to him in person. The news of the cessation of hostilities was announced in the camp of the brigade April 19th, 1783, and they were discharged November 3d, 1783. General Dayton had taken part in all the battles in which the Continental Line of New Jersey had been engaged. After the war he was commissioned Major-General of the 2d Division New Jersey State Militia, which command he held at the time of his death. Upon the formation of the New Jersey Society of the Cincinnati, General Dayton was chosen its President, and held that office during the remainder of his life. He declined an election to Congress in 1779. In 1787 he was appointed a member of the convention to frame the Constitution of the United States, but favored the appointment of his son. In 1789 he was elected Recorder of Elizabethtown, and from 1796 to 1805 was Mayor of the town, and for several years a member of the Legislature of New Jersey. In private life he sustained a high reputation. He was open and generous, and scrupulously upright, and in manners easy, unassuming and pleasant. In person and bearing he is said to have resembled General Washington so strongly, that with their backs turned it was difficult to distinguish them. He was on terms of intimacy with that illustrious man, by whom he was always treated with distinguished confidence. General Lafayette was also his warm friend. General Dayton died at Elizabeth, October 22d, 1807.

OBART, HON. GARRET A., Lawyer, was born at Long Branch, Monmouth county, New Jersey, June 3d, 1844. His father, Addison W. Hobart, was a merchant. His mother's maiden name was Sophine Vandervere. The mother was a native of New Jersey and of Dutch descent, the father being from New Hampshire and of the same family with the late Bishop Hobart. Garret's education was begun in the district schools, those great foundation-builders of individual culture, and finished at Rutgers College, which he entered in 1860, graduating in the class of 1863. He studied law in the office of Socrates Tuttle, and was licensed as an attorney in 1866, and as a counsellor in 1869, in which last year he was married to E. J Tuttle, daughter of his late preceptor. He began the practice of his profession at Paterson in 1866, and has pursued it ever since with diligence and success, notwithstanding his pursuit at the same time, with equal success, of a large business career, begun even before his professional one, and a political career, opening in 1872 with his election to the Assembly, and thenceforward advancing without a backward step, he having been re-elected the following year, when he was chosen Speaker of the Assembly, and subsequently elected to the State Senate, with a clear prospect of still greater honors in the future. During his first term in the Assembly he was placed on the Judiciary Committee, a recognition at the dawn of his public life which foreshadowed his upward course. His party affiliations are Republican, and, as befits an active member of a political society, are close and warm. He is plainly a politician of high promise. As a lawyer his practice is mainly confined to corporations, and is nearly all done quietly in his own office. He belongs to the great class of business lawyers, who in modern times have crowded their spread-eagle brethren quite off the stage, wisdom of action being much more in requisition than the gift of speech. He is Receiver for the New Jersey Middle Railroad, for the Paterson & Little Falls Horse Railroad, and for the Manhattan Bleaching & Dyeing Company ; and was in 1872 appointed Counsel of the Board of Chosen Freeholders, in addition to being counsel for a number of banks and insurance companies. His first preferment in the line of his profession was his appointment as City Counsel of Paterson, an honor thrust upon him against his will, and which he shortly resigned. His aptitude for business is extraordinary, in respect to origination as well as despatch, assuring not only the systematic and rapid performance of his immense office work, but the success of his projects and the profit of his investments in a measure that has occasioned his " luck " to pass into a proverb. In his case, however, as in that of most other successful men, it is safe to say that " luck " is only a familiar name for the force of brains. Personally, he is estimable and attractive, of excellent habits, cheerful temper, genial manners and generous feelings.

INDLEY, JACOB, late of New Garden, New Jersey, was born in September, 1744. He was early in life a lover of religious inquiry, " being of an affable and communicative disposition, not willingly giving, nor readily taking offence; and as his natural endowments became seasoned with divine grace, he was fitted to fill with propriety the important station to which he was afterward called." His first appearance in the ministry was about the thirtieth year of his age; his communications were lively and powerful, " reaching the witness in the hearts of those to whom he ministered; and by keeping low and humble, walking in fear, and in obedience to the manifestations of duty, he grew in his gift and became an able minister of the gospel, qualified to divide the word aright to the several states of the people." Being well versed in the Scriptures, he was frequently enabled to open them with instructive clearness.

In times of internal commotion and strife in the country he was deeply concerned; earnestly cautioning Friends, especially the young men, to watch against the delusive spirit of war, in its various appearances, so desolating in its progress and destructive to the human species; and his labors therein were productive of salutary effects. He was one of those who bore a faithful testimony against the improper use of ardent spirits, at a time when the minds of Friends in general were less awakened to the magnitude of the evil than has since been the case. The descendants of the African race found in him a zealous advocate, their wrongs and sufferings obtaining his tender sympathy. On the day of his death he appeared in the meeting at New Garden in a lively and affecting communication, "delivered with heart tendering energy and clearness;" in the course of which he intimated an apprehension that there might be those present who would not see the light of another day; adding, "and perhaps it may be myself." After meeting he appeared in his usual cheerful disposition; when toward evening, by a fall from a chaise, he was suddenly deprived of life. His decease was on the 12th of June, 1814, and on the ensuing 14th he was interred in Friends' burying ground at New Garden, where a solemn meeting was held on the occasion.

━━◆◆━━

HIPMAN, JEHIEL G., Lawyer, of Belvidere, son of David Shipman, of Hope, Warren county, New Jersey, was born near that place about 1820. The family is of Norman descent, its founder having been knighted by Henry III., of England (A. D. 1258), and granted the following coat of arms: Gules on a bend argent, betwixt six etoiles, or three pellets; crest: a leopard se jant ar., spotted sa., resting his dexter paw on a ship's rudder az.; motto: *Non sibi sed orbi*. The family seat was at Sarnington, in Nottinghamshire. In 1635 Edward Shipman, a refugee from religious persecution, came to America in company with Hugh Peters, John Davenport and Theodore Fenwick, and settled at Saybrook, Connecticut. From him the American branches of the family are descended. J. G. Shipman's grandfather was one of the first settlers of Morristown, New Jersey, assisting in the erection of the first house built there; three of his uncles served with credit through the revolutionary war, and another relative, James Shipman, died aboard the old Jersey prison-ship in Wallabout Bay. He graduated at Union College, in the class of 1842, which included also Clarkson N. Potter and William A. Beach, of the New York bar, entering soon after his graduation the law office of William C. Morris, of Belvidere, remaining there until admitted to the bar, in 1844. On his admission he immediately began to practise, his first cause having been the celebrated Carter and Park murder case, in which he was retained by the State, the opening of the prosecution falling to him. In the performance of this part he displayed such ability and thoroughness in argument, and such tact and skill in management, as at once to attract the attention of the bar and the public, introducing him to a practice which, nurtured by the qualities that planted it, has grown to be one of the largest and most lucrative in the State. He has been engaged in a number of important criminal cases, among which may be mentioned the celebrated case of the Rev. J. S. Hardin, convicted and hung for wife murder, and that of the Frenchman, Peter Cucle, of Morristown, New Jersey. He practises extensively in all the courts of the State and of the United States, in one of the former of which he argued successfully, in 1861, a case of exceptional importance, involving the right of a State to tax the traffic in coal passing through it from another State. The high quality of his professional character may be inferred from the fact that he is counsel for the Delaware, Lackawanna & Western Railroad, the Morris Canal, the Belvidere National Bank, the Phillipsburg National Bank, and other corporations. Few lawyers in the State manage so great a number of really important cases as he, particularly in railroad litigation and chancery practice. He is remarkable for what may be called the faculty of logical constructiveness, enabling him with surprising ease to master and unfold all the intricacies of a case from the simple developments of the trial as it proceeds. This faculty, rare in all but the greatest lawyers, and not always possessed by them, is in itself sufficient to stamp him as one of the foremost members of the profession. He is perhaps the ablest lawyer in the State, taken in all departments of the law. Mr. Shipman is a pronounced and prominent Republican, and was for a long time a member of the Republican State Executive Committee. He is held in great esteem by his party. He has never sought office, but office may be Said to have sought him, his political friends having frequently urged him to stand for the highest places in the State. As a political speaker he is extremely effective. He is a member of the Presbyterian Church, of which he has been a Ruling Elder for twenty years, and during most of this period Superintendent or Assistant Superintendent of the Sabbath-school, and at all times a consistent and liberal supporter of school and church alike. He was married in 1845 to a daughter of W. C. Morris, Esq., of Belvidere. His son, Geo. M., is a member of the New Jersey bar, and since 1873 has been his law partner, the firm being J. G. Shipman & Son. For one year (1868) Mercer Beasly, Jr., son of Chief-Justice Beasly, was his partner.

━━◆◆━━

HIPMAN, CAPTAIN WILLIAM M., Merchant, of Clinton, and brother of the subject of the foregoing sketch, was born, April 22d, 1823, near Hope, Warren county, New Jersey. Beginning his studies at the country public schools, he completed his education at St. Luke's Seminary, and for a short time afterward was engaged in teaching. In

1846, when the mineral resources of the Wyoming and Lackawánna regions began first to be utilized, he secured an appointment with the then managers of the Lackawanna Coal and Iron Company, G. W. & S. T. Scranton. Here he remained for five years, and here gained his thorough knowledge of business that has made him successful where so many others have failed. From 1851 to 1853 he was engaged in the wholesale trade in New York, after which he established himself in Somerville, in partnership with W. G. Steele, in a general mercantile business. In 1856 the business was removed to Clinton, Hunterdon county, New Jersey, and in 1861 his partner, Mr. Steele, having been elected to Congress, Captain Shipman purchased his interest and has since continued—excepting three years during the war—the business in his own name. When war was declared he assisted General Taylor in raising recruits, making a recruiting office of his store. He received an appointment from Governor Charles S. Olden to the 15th New Jersey Regiment; but owing to the enlistment of his nephew, D. E. Hicks, a gallant young soldier who was killed while charging the rebel works at Chancellorsville, with whom he had an arrangement to leave the care of his business, he was unable to accept the commission from Governor Olden. On the 2d day of May, 1863, he was appointed Provost Marshal of the Third Congressional District of New Jersey, the appointment carrying with it the rank of Captain of Cavalry. He established his headquarters at Somerville, but at the end of a year removed to Elizabeth, the latter town, though less central than the former, affording better facilities for the subsistence of troops. Until the war ended he held the position, not only to the satisfaction of the War Department, but to the satisfaction of the people of the district, the thankless duties of his office being discharged in so obviously an impartial manner as to leave no room for cavilling. His success was the more remarkable, since the people in many portions of the district had openly avowed their intentions to resist the draft, and had actually organized for this purpose. Only the knowledge that the provost marshal was a man of the utmost firmness of character, and would without hesitation use the forces at his command to maintain the authority of the government, prevented draft-riots in his district as violent as those which occurred in New York city. Early in 1864 Captain Shipman became convinced that fraudulent naval certificates of muster were being extensively circulated in his district, and by calling the immediate attention of Commodore Paulding (who was then in command at the Brooklyn Navy Yard) to the fact, caused an order to be issued by him that at once put an end to their circulation in the Third District, and saved the people of the district from being defrauded, as many others were, by the sale to the township committees of these fraudulent papers. After the last draft had been made, and the quotas of the several wards and townships had been filled, a number of gentlemen, belonging variously to the several township and ward committees, and headed by John T. Jenkins, then postmaster of the city of New Brunswick, united in presenting Captain Shipman with an elegant gold watch and chain, accompanied by a very complimentary letter, expressing their appreciation of the impartial manner in which the arduous duties of the office had been performed, and concluding as follows: " We ask you to accept the enclosed watch and chain as a memento of our respect for you as a gentleman of unimpeachable integrity and for the faithful and kind manner in which you have discharged the duties of your office." Coming, as this testimonial did, when the business of the provost marshal's office was practically at an end, and when the donors had no selfish ends to compass in securing the favor of the donee, its value was infinitely enhanced. Captain Shipman replied, thanking the gentlemen for the elegant and costly gift and for the kind expressions of personal regard for himself, disclaiming, however, that all the credit was due to himself for the successful and impartial manner in which the business of the office had been conducted, but that quite as much was due to his associates in the Board of Enrolment, Dr. Ezra M. Hunt, Commissioner, and Dr. Robert Wescott, Surgeon. Captain Shipman's official duties were discharged, as has been already stated, not less satisfactorily to the War Department than to his fellow-citizens, and on the 16th of November, 1865, he received an honorable discharge from the military service of the United States. When peace was restored he made, in company with Colonel W. Henry, an extended tour through the Southern States, with a view to purchasing property and engaging in the cultivation of cotton. Owing, however, to the still unsettled condition of affairs in the South, he abandoned this plan, and, returning to Clinton, repurchased the business that he had disposed of three years previously upon accepting the position of Provost Marshal of the Third District. In politics he was, until the formation of the Republican party, a Whig; and has been, since the Republican organization came into existence, one of the most earnest of its supporters. Captain Shipman was married in 1851 to Samantha A. Furman, daughter of Moore Furman Esq., late of Scranton, Pennsylvania.

<hr />

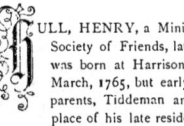ULL, HENRY, a Minister of the Gospel in the Society of Friends, late of Stanford, New York, was born at Harrison's Purchase, New York, in March, 1765, but early in life removed with his parents, Tiddeman and Elizabeth Hull, to the place of his late residence. It appears, from his own account, that he was favored with the tendering impressions of heavenly love very early in life; yet, through unwatchfulness, sometimes gave way to the follies incident to youth, which brought condemnation; but by yielding to the renewed visitation of love and mercy, through the

refining operation of the Divine power upon his heart, he became qualified for usefulness in the church. It was notably about the year 1785 that his exercises and conflict of spirit were great, and that he became impressed with the belief that he should have to stand forth as a public advocate for that cause "which is dignified by immortality, and crowned with eternal life." He travelled much in the ministry, in different parts of the United States and Canada; was specially and importantly identified with the growth and spread, in New Jersey, New York, Maine and New Hampshire, of Friends' societies; and, having for several years felt his mind drawn, in the love of the gospel, to pay a religious visit to Friends of Great Britain and Ireland, embarked at New York for England in the summer of 1810. He was kindly received across the Atlantic, and visited the meetings generally; while, from certificates furnished him, it appears that his labors were truly acceptable and edifying to Friends in that country. While abroad he wrote an address, in gospel love, to the youth, which was extensively circulated in Europe, and afterward reprinted in his native State. Upon his return home, in 1812, his time was considerably occupied in visiting the various meetings in the east and northeast. In 1814, and subsequently until his decease, he performed several extensive journeys within the different yearly meetings in the United States. "Not depending upon past experience, but seeking a renewed qualification for services in the church, and being careful to attend to the voice of the true Shepherd, he became a pillar in the church. . . . . Being quick of discernment in the fear of the Lord, he early bore his testimony against an unsound and spurious ministry, and the many departures from the wholesome order of society, and was zealous for the support of the good order and discipline of the church." His ministry was sound, clear and edifying; manifesting a tenderness and fervor of spirit which showed that he was deeply impressed with the doctrines that he preached. In the summer of 1834 his mind was drawn to attend the yearly meetings of Ohio and Indiana, "and his peace consisted in standing resigned to the service, notwithstanding his age and constitutional debility." Speaking of a memorable experience in New Jersey, he says in the "Memoirs": "I took passage in the steamboat, and reached Rahway, where I met Richard Hartshorne, and was greeted by him with the cordiality of true Christian friendship. I entered on the service which drew me from my home by attending the monthly meeting held at Plainfield, the day following the quarterly meeting for business, and afterward one for worship; in which meetings the cementing influence of gospel love was very precious, an endearing affection engaging the minds of Friends toward each other, in which they encouraged one another to press toward the mark of the prize of their high calling of God in Christ Jesus." Meetings of remarkable power and sweetness were then held (in 1833–34) at Ringwood, Hardwick, Randolph, Plainfield, Stony Brook, Trenton, Crosswicks, Burlington,

Tuckerton, Haddonfield, Salem Quarter, and many other places, and in almost every case were attended by glorious and lasting results. Soon after the close of the Ohio yearly meeting he was confined to his room by a painful illness; and on the 23d of the ensuing October quietly breathed his last. In 1785 he was married to the late Sarah Hallock, daughter of Edward Hallock; and again, in 1814, to Sarah Cooper, of New Jersey.

———◆◆———

DOBBINS, HON. SAMUEL A., of Burlington county, Farmer and Member of Congress from the Second District of New Jersey, was born, April 14th, 1814, in the original township of North Hampton—now known as South Hampton—Burlington county, and is a son of Samuel and Elizabeth (Scroggy) Dobbins. His father was engaged in agricultural pursuits, and both his parents were natives of New Jersey. His maternal grandfather, Thomas Scroggy, was a soldier of the revolutionary war, and an officer under General Washington. He was with the latter at the crossing of the Delaware, prior to the battle of Trenton, and was a participant in that contest. He served throughout the war, and although he was several times wounded, yet recovered and lived many years thereafter; he died in 1828, at a very advanced age. Samuel A. Dobbins received a very good education, attending both the common and private schools until he attained his majority, generally working on his father's farm during the fair months of the year, and devoting the winter to study. When twenty-two years old he married and commenced farming on his own account, and has ever since that time followed the avocation of a husbandman. About the year 1846 he commenced his political career, serving on the township committees for some years, and at a later period filled the position of Chosen Freeholder for the term of three years. In 1854 he was elected by the Whigs of Burlington county to the Sheriffalty, and annually thereafter until the usual three years had elapsed. In 1858 he was elected by the Republicans to the lower branch of the State Legislature, and re-elected three times successively. While a member of that body he served with much ability on several important committees, among which were those on Agriculture, the State Prison, the Insane Asylum, etc. In the fall of 1872 he was elected by the Republicans of the Second Congressional District as their representative in the Federal Legislature, and was re-elected in 1874. In that body he was a member of the Committee on Patents from the time he first took his seat, and also on that of Revolutionary Claims, and Claims during the War of 1812. He has been an active politician for the past thirty years, and has been actively engaged in many campaigns, delivering addresses throughout the State in every important canvass. He is a forcible speaker, and always creates enthusiasm among his listeners. He was a Delegate to the National Convention when Andrew Johnson was nominated for Vice-President. He has always taken a great interest in the temperance movement, and in 1840 was one of the charter-members of the Division of Sons of Temperance which organized at Mount Holly in that year. During the year 1844 he was Grand Worthy Patriarch of the State Division. For nearly twenty years he has been a Trustee of the Pennington Seminary, and for the past ten years President of the Board. He was one of the corporators, and since its organization, a member of the Board of Directors of the Union National Bank, of Mount Holly. He was married, February 4th, 1836, to Damaris Harker, of New Jersey.

ALE, REV. GEORGE, D. D., seventh Pastor of Hopewell Church, Pennington, New Jersey, was a native of the State of New York. After pursuing a preliminary course of studies at Williams College, he graduated from that institution in 1831, subsequently entered Princeton Theological Seminary as a student, and there was graduated in 1838. January 2d, 1839, he was called to the pastorate of Hopewell Church, Pennington, New Jersey, and in the winter of 1841–42 presided over a great revival in the church, which swept over Pennington and its vicinity like a purifying storm. By Sabbath, the 20th of March, 1842, when a sacramental service was held, the beneficent results were made manifest. On that day one hundred and twelve stood up to enter into covenant with God and his church, and sat down for the first time at the communion table; of this number eighty persons were baptized, while the whole number gathered into the visible church through this work of grace was one hundred and thirty-two, forty-nine of whom were heads of families. The hopeful converts were of every age, from twelve up to eighty-two. This revival of 1841–42 prepared the way for the organization of the Titusville Church in 1844. There was another revival in the year 1846. As a result, fifty-six names were added to the communion roll; while the effects of this desirable awakening were continued through the years of 1847–48. From 1850 to 1853 there were several minor revivals which cheered the pastor in his efforts, and incited him to still greater exertions in the gracious field of conversion. The winter of 1857–58 heralded another notable revival, of which the pastor made a record at the time: "It has pleased God recently to visit the church of Pennington, New Jersey, with a gracious outpouring of the Holy Spirit, as the result of which sixty persons have united with the church by a public profession of the faith." Of this number there were ten husbands with their wives; ten female heads of families, three of whom were the wives of church members; and five male heads of families, who were husbands of commu-

nicants—making in all thirty-five heads of families. The remainder were single persons of both sexes ranging from the age of sixteen upward; of the sixty, twenty-two were males and thirty-eight were females. "Among them are found the children of the covenant and the lineal descendants in the fourth and fifth generation of the godly men who, nearly a century and a half ago, laid the foundations of this church, as well as some of the posterity of a former pastor who labored faithfully among this people for almost half a century." On the 18th of November, 1863, being the twenty-fifth anniversary of the day on which he began his regular labors in Hopewell Church, he preached a "Quarter-Century Sermon," from Psalm lxviii. 28. During his ministry of thirty years, 513 persons were added to the church on profession, and 127 by certificate; there were 356 baptized in infancy, and there were 550 funerals, and 275 marriages. In 1867, in consideration of his manifold and harassing labors, with not a day of relaxation through a period so protracted, he was cordially granted leave of absence for six months. On Saturday, May 25th, he sailed from New York for Havre, France, on the steamer "Guiding Star," and on his return in the "Arago," from Falmouth, England, landed in New York, and arrived safely at Pennington, New Jersey, on the evening of Thursday, November 14th, 1867. On Friday two hundred of the congregation met at Evergreen Hall, of that place, and there tendered him a hearty and inspiriting welcome. February 11th, 1869, he was elected, by the Trustees of the General Assembly, the Secretary of the Fund for Disabled Ministers and their families, to fill the vacancy occasioned by the death of Rev. Joseph H. Jones, D. D. Upon the acceptance of the appointment, he offered a letter of resignation to Hopewell Church, March 2d, 1869, and on the 7th of this month the pastoral relation was dissolved.

ANEWAY, REV. JACOB JONES, D. D., Presbyterian Clergyman, Vice-President of Rutgers College, Trustee of the New Jersey College, late of New Brunswick, New Jersey, was born in the city of New York, November 20th, 1774, of George Janeway and Effie (Ten Eyck) Janeway, and grew up amid the religious influences which surrounded him from his birth. His mother was a cultured and pious woman, and in his journal he often speaks of her with reverence and affection. She died soon after his entrance on the ministry, after a period of harassing illness. His parents were members of the Reformed Dutch Church. His father, an ardent Whig, was compelled to leave, with his family, when the British troops took possession of New York. During the seven years of exile the family removed repeatedly, as New Jersey was ravaged by the frequent incursions of the enemy. At the close of the war and on the evacuation of the city, the family returned, and there he remained during the whole course of his education. ' From the excellent " Life" of his father, by Thomas L. Janeway, is taken the following: " Two centuries ago there existed in England, and not far from London, a remarkable family, bearing the name of Janeway—remarkable, not for anything which the world esteems, but for the eminent holiness which adorned them. William, the father, was a minister of Christ, together with four of his sons, and the holy life and triumphant death of his son, John, is cherished amid the sacred literature of the English language. A descendant of this holy seed was an officer in the royal navy, in the reign of William III., and on a visit with his ship to this country, purchased property on Manhattan Island, on the edge of New York, which then hardly passed the present Park and City Hall. Returning at a subsequent period to New York, he intermarried with Mrs. De Meir, and became a resident. He was intrusted with the charter of Trinity Church, granted by Queen Anne, of which church he was named by the crown as one of the vestrymen, and brought the charter to America. His death, judging from the probate of his will, was about the year 1708." His only son and surviving child, Jacob Janeway, settled, on arriving at man's estate, in Somerset county, New Jersey, where he died in early manhood, leaving a widow and three children. One of these, a daughter, died in her minority, and the eldest son, William, was lost at sea. The survivor, George, bereft of his father when but four years of age, and of his mother when twelve, grew up in ignorance of his right to the property purchased by his grandfather, and which had been seized and was held by the city corporation. With his characteristic energy, he indentured himself to a carpenter, and assiduously applied himself to his business. On reaching his twenty-first year, aided by friends, he commenced a suit against the city for the recovery of his property, and after several years of the law's delay, recovered about one-half of the patrimony of his fathers. He lived a long life, honored by his contemporaries; as Alderman, intrusted with important duties, and died in his eighty-fifth year, from mere decay of nature and without any apparent disease. Until the age of eleven years he went to an English school, then commenced the study of Latin and Greek preparatory to college life. At fifteen he entered Columbia College and took its full course of four years. Subsequently, on his recovery from a violent attack of scarlet fever, he turned ardently to religion ; for the fear of death and anxieties about his soul had wrought in him conviction for sin. He was then urged by Dr. Livingston to repose on the imputed righteousness of Christ, and his mind gradually obtained composure. " From this time I began to reform my life, and read the sacred Scriptures. . . . ." May 15th he made a confession of his faith, and was received into full communion with the church. In 1795 he narrowly escaped death in falling from his horse, but escaped the yellow-fever, which was then raging with such terrible results in New York. The year 1797 found him diligent in the use of the means

of grace, and seeking growth in the divine life. He then became a pupil of Rev. Dr. J. H. Livingston, professor of theology in the Reformed Dutch Church, and under him prosecuted the study of Hebrew, etc. Thursday, November 30th, 1797, he was licensed to preach by the Classis of New York; and while still under the paternal roof, embraced every opportunity of preaching in the pulpits of the city, and of making occasional excursions to the city. In company with the late Rev. Dr. J. N. Abeel, he made a journey of some two thousand miles, much of it in the saddle, mainly in pursuit of health, which had been much shattered by the ardor of his studies. Much of the journey was performed through New Englamd, and, while at Charlestown, he preached for Dr. Morse, at the old South Church, in Boston, Massachusetts. At this period his thoughts were directed to a mission among the North American Indians, and he offered himself to those who had charge of the infant missions of that day. He afterward received an urgent request from Rev. Dr. Ashbel Green, then sole pastor of the Second Presbyterian Church, Philadelphia, to remove thither with a view to a settlement. The yellow fever then prevailing, however, it was judged prudent to defer his visit until the pestilence had passed. In the close of the year he preached in Philadelphia with such acceptance that he was unanimously called as a colleague with Dr. Green. This church was then, as it was during the whole of his pastorate, rich in the eldership. Men of high social position and of eminent piety served that people in the gospel of Christ; among them were such names as Latimer, Jandon, Smith, Henry, Ralston, etc. June 13th, 1799, he was ordained by the Presbytery of Philadelphia, in company with John Blair Linn, William Latta, John E. Latta, and Buckley Carl. In the summer of 1803 the eyes of his church were turned toward the desolations in the Northern Liberties, or Campington, whose population was increasing, and as it lay north of the Arch Street Church, it was regarded as its peculiar domain and field of culture. It was to be an outlaying post, and when able to sustain the gospel, to be separate. The connection continued, however, for ten or twelve years, and it was served by the colleague pastors of the Second Church. During the hot season of 1805, Dr. Milledoler being absent, and Mr. Potts prostrated by sickness, the care of all the city churches devolved on him, "the most youthful preacher of them all." As the era of missions dawned on the American church, he manifested a deep interest in its hastening, was familiar with every movement of the church in relation thereto, and rejoiced greatly in the advancement of every project and enterprise. He preached a sermon in order to raise funds to aid British Christians in their efforts to translate the holy word into the dialects of Hindoostan, and was a zealous coworker with Robert Ralston, Captain Wickes, and other pious laborers. In the fall of 1807 he visited Newark, New Jersey, to attend a memorable revival there in progress, and preached sermons while thus engaged. In

1808 "politics ran high, and Philadelphia was the head-quarters of the excitement. The old Federal party was fast losing its power. War with Great Britain was advocated by one party, and deprecated by the other. The rancorous debates were unfavorable to religion, and the hopes of the pious were mocked then, as they have been since. He would have been more than human, not to have felt some of the influences around him. But we see from his journal the jealous guard he maintained over his heart." Late in 1808, he, in union with others, entered upon measures to establish a Bible society to promote the circulation of the word of God. He was one of the four who issued the circular to their brethren of other denominations, to meet in solemn deliberation on this, the first series of measures, "which have resulted in such good to our country and the world." It was on December 11th, 1808, that the prepara-tory meeting was held, and when a constitution previously drafted was adopted, he, with Dr. Benjamin Rush, Robert Ralston, and Dr. Green, "were the men who were honored of God to inaugurate the new movement of mercy." It was the pioneer movement of the kind in the United States, and was followed by similar action throughout the land; and, during his life, the venerable Bishop White was the chief officer of the Philadelphia establishment. In 1812 he published his "Letters on the Abrahamic Covenant," as establishing the right of the children of believing parents to the ordinance of baptism. "He entertained high ideas of the precious nature of the privilege, and the bounden duty of Christian parents to present their infant offspring to God. He did not merely *defend* the received faith of God's church on this matter, but ever insisted upon it as a part of our covenant obligations, from which we could not escape without sin." He was appointed in 1812 to organize the First Presbyterian Church in the Northern Liberties, but continued, in exchange with the minister succeeding him, to preside in a measure over his old pastorate. Early in 1814 he preached in the Presbyterian church at New Brunswick, vacant by the decease of Dr. Clark, on their invitation; and in April received a unanimous call, which he accepted. About this time, also, the College at Middlebury, Vermont, conferred on him the degree of Doctor in Divinity. During the year 1819 he preached a notable sermon, as Moderator of the General Assembly, "full of honest warnings, which proved abundantly prophetic." In May, 1827, he was elected Professor of Theology in the newly-erected Western Theological Seminary, established at Alleghenytown, Penn-sylvania, by the General Assembly, with great unanimity. "After solemn and mature reflection, and after, by prayer and fasting, seeking to know the will of God, to the great joy of his people he declined the call." In the following spring he took a prominent part, until attacked by sickness, in the proceedings of the meeting of the Directors of the Theological Seminary at Princeton, New Jersey. In 1828 he visited Pittsburgh, and finally was inaugurated Professor during the meeting of the Synod, when he delivered his in-augural address, which, with Dr. Swift's address, was pub-lished by the directors. In 1829 he returned with his household to Philadelphia, and eventually severed his con-nection with the seminary. In April, 1830, he removed to New Brunswick, New Jersey, and became pastor of the First Reformed Dutch Church. "The duties were onerous. His preaching was extended to the country parts—his visit-ing laborious." He then labored in New York, in Orchard street, for a short time. In May, 1833, he was elected by the General Synod of the Reformed Dutch Church, Vice-President of Rutgers College and Professor of Belles-Lettres and the Evidences of Christianity, and settled definitely in New Brunswick, which was his home during the remainder of his life. On the retirement of Dr. Mille-doler he was offered, but declined, the presidency of this institution. In 1839 he resigned his offices in the college, and at the same time returned to the Presbyterian Church, wherein he believed was offered a wider field of influence. He was then elected a Trustee in the College of New Jer-sey, which office he had vacated on his removal to the West; and the General Assembly replaced him in the Directors' Board of the Seminary at Princeton, with whose earliest movements he had been connected. He was placed also on the Executive Committee of the Foreign Board of Missions, and to its funds he gave the largest of his contributions. "We have now come to the later stages of his life, still filled with active labor in the work of his Master. Matters connected with the movement of the Bible Society interested him. He had been her life-long friend, and he was true to the end of his days. The dis-tribution of Bibles, chiefly through the county society, ocen-pied his attention. He gave regularly and largely to its funds, and manifested great interest in the resupply of the State of New Jersey." He became greatly interested also in the erection of a new Presbyterian church in New Bruns-wick, attended its worship, and gave largely to its support; and when the present tasteful edifice was erected, con-tributed of his own funds between four and five thousand dollars. In 1850 "the heaviest sorrow of his life fell upon him; the wife of his youth sickened and died." His views of the millennium increased the joy he ordinarily felt in re-vivals, and on the commencement of those works of mercy in 1858, his soul was greatly refreshed and he grew eloquent with pious enthusiasm. In 1857 his health was seriously assailed, and on Sabbath, January 31st, of the same year, he was confined to that bed from which he never arose. Disease obscured his mind and caused confusion and wan-dering, yet, on the subject of religion, or any exposition of the Scriptures, he was clear as ever. At the close of June he became unconscious, and lay for two or three days with-out any communion with the outer world; and June 27th, at sunset, he died. His funeral was attended in the First Presbyterian Church, where Rev. Dr. Hodge preached his funeral sermon. In April, 1804, he was married to Martha G. Leiper, daughter of Thomas Leiper, a respectable and

49

wealthy merchant of Philadelphia. "The Bible was his great study, and other books only as they illustrated the word of God. In early life, while settled in the ministry, he had, in the interval of his parochial duties, paid much attention to the study of the prophecies, and especially in the great aspects of the decline and fall of Antichrist, and written much on this subject. . . . . Himself a true patriot, he was deeply interested in the welfare of his native land; and the sectional agitations which at times threatened it were for him a great grief. He published 'Hope for My Country,' as an exposition of his views, and as such it was warmly received by the clergy and the public in general. The duty of pastoral visitation he recognized and practised, and his systematic habits enabled him to accomplish much in this mattter. Of it he made a conscience, though he often complained of want of disposition and talent to drop a word for God, and render his visits more practical."

———

STAUGH, JOHN, late of Haddonfield, New Jersey, was born in Keldevon, Essex county, England, February 23d, 1776, of estimable parents; but he grew uneasy with the religious professions of both father and mother (they being of different persuasions), and being a seeker, fell in with the Baptists, and "liked them so well, he was on the point of joining them; but a Friend, a neighbor, being dead, it so happened that he was invited to the burial," where that worthy minister of the gospel, Francis Stamper, of London, being led to speak with life and power directly to his state, it made such deep impressions on his tender mind that he at once entered upon a search into the principles of Friends, and finding that he could conscientiously be one with them in belief and sentiment, joined with their society in the seventeenth year of his age. A year later he came forth in the ministry, and grew in his gift, so that in some time he travelled to visit Friends in America, and, having the unity of the brethren, embarked in 1800, and "was enabled by the great hand that drew him forth to perform that service to the great satisfaction of Friends and the reward of peace in himself." Being then, and for some time after, freed from any concern to travel in the service of truth, he married and settled at Haddonfield, New Jersey. "In the forepart of his time he travelled pretty much; but in latter part he was troubled with an infirmity in his head, which rendered him unfit for the service." After several years of indisposition he finally recovered so far as to be strong enough to endure with safety the fatigue of a long journey, and then was filled with a concern to visit Friends at Tortola. This brought on him a deep exercise, but when he was confirmed that it was really required of him so to do, he abandoned himself entirely and gratefully to the teachings of the inward monitor. He first wrote to them, but finding that this would not excuse him, dared delay no longer. August 8th, 1842, ac-

cordingly he departed on his mission; September 8th he arrived at the house of John Pickering with his companion, John Cadwalader, and was there fittingly welcomed. He retained his health until the death of his beloved associate, when, on the occasion of his burial, he was drenched with rain, and soon after attacked by a severe cold. On the following day he went to a small island called Jos Vandicks, accompanied by several friends; but on the next morning complained very much. He persisted, however, in attending meeting, and while there "extended his voice as a trumpet of the Lord's own sounding, but was so inwardly spent he was ready to faint." He went on board the sloop that afternoon, and next morning was prostrated by a shivering fit and high fever, which kept its constant course every day. . . . . And though the last two days he was in much pain, yet he was preserved under it in much patience and resignation, and had his perfect senses to the last, exhorting Friends to faithfulness, etc. And on the Sixth day of the Tenth month, about six o'clock at night, he went away like a lamb, with praises and thanksgivings in his lips but about two minutes before. At the Monthly Meeting at Haddonfield, New Jersey, November 9th, 1843, a touching tribute to his memory was signed by sorrowing Friends. October 1st, 1802, he was married to Elizabeth, his loving and devoted wife.

———

MORSE, DR. ISAAC, Physician, late of Elizabeth, was born in Rahway, New Jersey, August 5th, 1758, of parents who were respected members of the Society of Friends. His ancestor, Robert Morse, arrived in Boston before 1644; his son, Robert the second, was born in the Elizabethtown grants; his son, Robert the third, came into the world at the same place. His father, Joseph Morse, was also born at Elizabeth in 1709, and died in 1779. "He was a short, stout man, with a partially bald head. His society was universally courted, and, while overflowing with mirthfulness, he had courage, firmness, constancy, and perseverance." He was a student of Dr. William Barnet, under whose able preceptorship he acquired an extensive knowledge of the theory and practice of medicine. The following anecdote related of him exhibits him in a characteristic light: "A sloop was loaded with hay half-mast-high, going from Morse's Mill to New York. She got foul of an English vessel. The captain cried out, 'Cut the infernal Yankee shallop's rigging and let her drift.' The doctor, who was on board, called to his colored man to give him a firebrand. Mounting the hay, he cried out in a loud tone, 'I will fire the hay.' Said the frightened Englishman, 'We shall drift down to Hell Gate.' Said the doctor, 'You shan't stop at the gates of hell, if you cut one of my ropes.' The doctor was then invited on board the English vessel, and treated. When asked if there were any more like him, he replied,

'I am not a circumstance to our people generally.'" He owned a useless slave, Pete, who went off in one of William Gibbons' steamers. He sued Gibbons and recovered three hundred dollars. He told Gibbons afterward that if he brought him back he would sue him for three hundred more. Said Mr. Gibbons, "Did you not want him?" "No, I offered him twenty dollars to run away and never come back." . . . . Although a very accomplished scholar, and a charming and intelligent companion, a skilful practitioner, and a brilliant conversationalist when so inclined, he was so fond of practical jokes, that he was not unfrequently rude. Stories of his management of hypochondriacs, his practical pleasantries, and his facetious acts, full of humor, always kind in intent, if apparently harsh, could be multiplied to any extent. He died, after a life of great usefulness and considerable brilliancy, at Elizabeth, New Jersey, July 23d, 1825.

ARRISON, JOHN D., Patent Leather Manufacturer, was born in Morris county, New Jersey, in October, 1829. He is a son of Henry Harrison, a native of Orange, New Jersey, and a grandson of Captain Thomas Harrison, also a native of Orange, and a revolutionary soldier. On the maternal side likewise he is of revolutionary stock, his mother, whose maiden name was Pamela De Hart, having descended from the De Harts famous in the war of independence. He received a very thorough education, attending first the select schools of Orange, and finally the celebrated school of Dr. Wicks, at Newark. On leaving school he proceeded to learn the art of manufacturing patent leather, in which his brother, Charles H. Harrison, was already a proficient, and a few years later entered into partnership with his brother, under the name of C. H. & J. D. Harrison, for the prosecution of that business. A notice of the firm will be found in a sketch of the senior member in another part of this work. The junior member, it may be said here, however, has borne his share in the conduct of the business of the firm, and is entitled proportionately to the credit of its signal success. At the same time he has been somewhat largely interested in outside matters, especially in public affairs, for which he has shown a decided aptitude. He is a zealous and active member of the Republican party, of which he is a prominent leader in the city of Newark. For two consecutive terms of two years each he represented the Thirteenth Ward of Newark in the Board of Aldermen of the city; and in February, 1875, he was elected Sheriff of Essex county, to fill the vacancy made by the death of David Canfield, who died a few months after his election, leaving unexpired nearly his full term of four years. He is, therefore, the present incumbent of the sheriffalty, the responsible duties of which he has performed with the method and precision to be expected from a business man of his high standing, and with the firmness and spirit natural to one

whose veins are filled with revolutionary blood. The sheriffalty, particularly in a mixed and populous community, is one of the severest tests by which the manhood, integrity, and business capacity of a man can be tried, and it is to his abiding honor that he has borne this test with credit. Besides serving his city and county in the stations mentioned, he is a Director of the Manufacturers' Bank, of Newark, and also of the Merchants' Insurance Company. In short, he is in every relation a man of marked prominence and influence in his community. He was married some years since to Marie Dean, of Newark.

IERSON, HON. ISAAC, Physician and Surgeon, President of the Medical Society of New Jersey, late of Orange, New Jersey, was born there, August 15th, 1770, and became an intimate friend and classmate of Dr. David Hosack, of New York. His father, Dr. Matthias Pierson, a contemporary of Dr. John Condit, was also born in Orange, New Jersey, June 20th, 1734, where he spent his life in the practice of medicine, and died May 9th, 1808. He was an alumnus of Nassau Hall, Princeton, a Fellow of the College of Physicians and Surgeons, and in 1827 was President of the Medical Society of New Jersey. He was also a member of the Twentieth and Twenty-first Congress of the United States. He was a distinguished and notably successful practitioner of medicine in Orange, and its vicinity, for a period extending over forty years, and was the father of Dr. William Pierson, Sr., "who is glad to share the mantle with his son, Dr. William Pierson, who will probably secure the succession for at least another generation." Except in the case of Dr. John C. Budd, who was the son of Dr. Berne Budd, and the father of Dr. Berne W. Budd, the grandfather of Professor Charles Budd and Dr. Berne Budd, of New York, none, of whom there is record in New Jersey, can boast of so long a medical ancestry. Cyrus Pierson, his brother-in-law, was born in South Orange, and was also an alumnus of Nassau Hall, Princeton; he practised medicine in Orange, Woodbridge, Caldwell and Newark. While in the latter place he was a partner of Dr. Samuel Hays until his decease, October 7th, 1804.

ONDIT, HON. JOHN S., Physician, late of Newark, was born in Morristown, New Jersey, in 1801, and was the nephew of John Condit, and a son of the late Hon. Silas Condit. In a sermon delivered in the Second Presbyterian Church, in Newark, April 7th, 1848, he is spoken of as a "highly respected fellow-citizen, who was passing the meridian of his days with a vigorous step." He was a graduate of Princeton College in 1817; and, after studying law under the tutorship of the late Hon. Theodore Frelinghuysen, turned his attention to the study of medicine. He was a member successively of the Assembly and Senate of New Jersey. "Purity of private character, strong sense of moral obligations," are terms applied to him by a discriminating friend. He is spoken of also as "a man of strong moral convictions." The distinguished physician and statesman, Lewis Condict, of Morristown, who had three sons who were physicians, descended from a collateral branch of the family, which adhered to the ancient mode of spelling its name. He died, April 7th, 1848, at the age of forty-seven years.

———o———

HALSTED, DR. ROBERT, Physician, Revolutionary Patriot, was born in "Essex District," New Jersey, September 13th, 1746. He was a leading and fearless citizen in the gloomy days of the contest with Great Britain, and a medical practitioner of unquestionable talent and sterling attainments. On one occasion a notorious Tory informed against him as a rebel and an aider and upholder of rebellion, and he was temporarily lodged in the old Sugar House, in Liberty street, New York. On another occasion he saved the life of Colonel Aaron Ogden, who had been seriously wounded by the Hessians while out alone on a military reconnoissance. He was serious, and by some is spoken of as stern; yet he was by all admired and respected, and was a patriot in a time when the title bore a significant and an eloquent meaning. He died 1815-20. His younger brother, Caleb Halsted, was born in Elizabeth, New Jersey, September 15th, 1752, and was also an eminent physician. July 15th, 1825, while confined to his house by illness, he received a visit from General Lafayette, and had the pleasant honor of entertaining that famous son of France. He was travelling at the time from Morristown, under the conduct of the late General Andruss, the father-in-law of Dr. Jabez G. Goble. During the French revolution, many of the refugee nobility settled in and about Elizabeth, and most of these families came under his professional care. He died August 18th, 1827, aged seventy-five years.

———o———

BUDD, DR. JOHN C., Physician, late of Orange, was born in Morristown, New Jersey, May 26th, 1762, and studied under the supervision of Dr. John Condit, of Orange. His father, Dr. Bernard Budd, appears the first on the roll of fourteen who formed the New Jersey Medical Society in 1766, and was a surgeon in the revolutionary army. John Budd, his ancestor, was an English surveyor for the Lord Proprietors; and in him was the title of Powles Hook, at Jersey

City; also that of a great part of "German Valley," in Morris county, New Jersey. At eighty-three years of age he was perfectly erect, and had a pleasing, cheerful face. He was careless in dress and in his business habits; naturally preferred fun to professional toil, but was yet a skilful and trusted practitioner. His humane disposition rendered him a faithful physician, and his fine abilities and power of observation, a counsellor of unusual resources. He had the reputation, in those far-off witch-burning times, of being able to raise the devil. It is said he had something to do with the 'Morristown Ghost,'—but not discreditably—which created so much excitement in 1778 and some years after." He had two famous prescriptions: one he called his Tincture Botanæ, the other, his Diabolical Pill. "The first," he said, "I give when I don't know what else to do, for it is emmenagogue, sedative, cathartic, tonic, and expectorant, and cannot fail to hit somewhere." He died in Orange, New Jersey, January 12th, 1845.

———o———

LOVE. JOHN J. H., Physician and Surgeon, of Montclair, was born in Harmony township, Warren county, New Jersey, April 3d, 1833, and is the eldest son of Rev. Robert Love and Ann Thompson (Fair) Love. He was educated at Lafayette College, Easton, Pennsylvania, and in due time graduated from that institution; his medical degree was obtained in the medical department of the University of New York; and, before enlisting in the United States service, he practised his profession for a period of seven years at Montreal. July 19th, 1862, he was commissioned Surgeon of the 13th Regiment, New Jersey Volunteers, and was mustered into the United States service August 25th, 1862. March 23d, 1863, he was assigned to duty as Surgeon-in-Chief of the 3d Brigade, 1st Division, 12th Army Corps, Army of the Potomac, whose offices he performed, in addition to his regimental duties, until August 1st, 1863, when, under special orders from corps headquarters, he assumed the position and duties of Surgeon-in-Chief, 1st Division, 12th Army Corps. In this important station he was constantly engaged until January 28th, 1864, when he resigned his commission and was honorably discharged from the United States service. He was always engaged in field service, and May 5th, 1862, was sent out as a volunteer surgeon by Governor Olden, and assisted in the transportation and care of the wounded after the battle of Williamsburg, Virginia. He was present and on duty also at the battles of Antietam, September 17th, 1862; Chancellorsville, May 1st, 2d, 3d, 1863; Gettysburg, July 1st, 2d, 3d, 1863; and assisted in caring for the wounded after the battles of Lookout Mountain and Mission Ridge, near Chattanooga, Tennessee, in December, 1863. In his opinion the medical history of the civil war has developed no one fact

G. W. Doane,
Bishop of New Jersey

more prominently than that, to maintain [illegible] effective condition, a constant and enlightened [illegible] must be given by the surgeons and officers to the laws hygiene. He remarks: "From ignorance of these laws the majority of the physicians commissioned to attend to the wants of the soldiers found themselves, when in active service, unable satisfactorily to discharge the duties devolving upon them; particularly was this the [illegible] surgeons from civil practice, who had left [illegible] the idea that their whole duty consisted in [illegible] and operating. These soon learned that to [illegible] ness in their commands was the primary object. [illegible] that the war is over, and they have resumed civil [illegible] the knowledge gained of hygienic laws will be used in the prevention and amelioration of disease among our citizens. Surgeons in active field practice have little or no opportunity to know the results of their practice. No matter how interesting the case in its inception, when the termination is unknown the facts are useless." He is now practising at Montclair, Essex county.

DOANE, RT. REV. GEORGE WASHINGTON, D. D., LL. D., Bishop of New Jersey, late of Burlington, was born in Trenton, New Jersey, May 27th, 1799. His father, Jonathan Doane, was a well-known master builder and contractor; "he was a man of singular perseverance and high principle, commanding and handsome in his appearance, most loving and devoted in all his home relations, and very proud of his son;" his paternal grandmother was "a noble woman, heroic and self-denying. . . . . She was one of the women of the Revolution, no whit less heroes than [illegible] and on her grave-cross is inscribed: 'The Bishop of New Jersey to the Best of Mothers.'" Moving from Trenton when the State House and other public buildings were completed, his second home was in New York, where his early training was obtained under the care of Dr. Barry, whose bishop he afterward became. In 1808 he removed with his family to Geneva, and there continued his studies with Dr. Axtell, a Presbyterian clergyman. Of his experiences at this place he has written: "The Rev. Dr. Orin Clark was the [illegible] of my boyhood. The wax was soft, and the impressions are deep. My father went to Geneva in 1808. The church, what little there was of it, was then 'a stranger in a strange land.' Geneva was an outpost. 'Father Nash' had been there, and the venerable Davenport Phelps. These were the pioneers of the church. They came once a month. . . . . The intervening Sundays were supplied with lay reading by two most excellent men, John Nicholas and Daniel W. Lewis. Judge Nicholas was prominent in political life; Mr. Lewis was a sound and learned lawyer. . . . . There was no church built when we [illegible] 1816, [illegible] of the [illegible] Union College [illegible] dency of Dr. [illegible] the salutatory was [illegible] it on account [illegible] Leaving [illegible] to [illegible] New York, [illegible] a large [illegible] as an [illegible] This, [illegible] but [illegible] consequence of [illegible] consecrate [illegible] study [illegible] New Jersey [illegible] established [illegible] and [illegible] of Dr. [illegible] Trinity College [illegible] the expression [illegible] work with [illegible] except in [illegible] sooner had [illegible] lambs' been [illegible] turned, with [illegible] of effort and [illegible] Mary's Hall and [illegible] the increasing parochial schools [illegible] and the care and attention paid [illegible] all the surrounding parishes of the State to [illegible] are witnesses to the truth of his own [illegible] of his life as the instrument in God's [illegible] promote and perfect the great work of [illegible] in the American church. Previously he [illegible] Hartford, in 1824, and there, in Washington [illegible] filled the position of Professor of Belles Lettres, and also took charge of the whole working system of the institution, his appointment as Bursar laying upon him [illegible] labor. He was warmly interested in the formation of the Historical Society of the State, and was one of its incorporators; also in the organization of a college society, called the Athenæum. His acquaintance with Dr. Croswell began in 1826, and was the result of certain efforts and movements made relating the publication of a church paper. Upon the establishment of *The Episcopal Watchman* he became its editor, with William Croswell as associate and assistant, speaking of whom he said: "Man has never been in closer bonds with man, than he with me, for five and twenty years. Our intercourse was intimate at once, and we never had a feeling,

more prominently than that, to maintain an army in an effective condition, a constant and enlightened attention must be given by the surgeons and officers to the laws of hygiene. He remarks: "From ignorance of these laws the majority of the physicians commissioned to attend to the wants of the soldiers found themselves, when in active service, unable satisfactorily to discharge the duties devolving upon them; particularly was this the case with regimental surgeons from civil practice, who had left their homes with the idea that their whole duty consisted in treating disease and operating. These soon learned that to prevent sickness in their commands was the primary object. And now that the war is over, and they have resumed civil practice, the knowledge gained of hygienic laws will be used in the prevention and amelioration of disease among our citizens. Surgeons in active field practice have little or no opportunity to know the results of their practice. No matter how interesting the case in its inception, when the termination is unknown the facts are useless." He is now practising at Montclair, Essex county.

——◦○◦——

OANE, RT. REV. GEORGE WASHINGTON, D. D., LL. D., Bishop of New Jersey, late of Burlington, was born in Trenton, New Jersey, May 27th, 1799. His father, Jonathan Doane, was a well-known master builder and contractor; "he was a man of singular perseverance and high principle, commanding and handsome in his appearance, most loving and devoted in all his home relations, and very proud of his son;" his paternal grandmother was "a noble woman, heroic and self-denying. . . . . She was one of the women of the Revolution, no whit less heroes than its men," and on her grave-cross is inscribed "The Bishop of New Jersey to the Best of Mothers." Moving from Trenton when the State House and other public buildings were completed, his second home was in New York, where his early training was obtained under the care of Dr. Barry, whose bishop he afterward became. In 1808 he removed with his family to Geneva, and there continued his studies with Dr. Axtell, a Presbyterian clergyman. Of his experiences at this place he has written: "The Rev. Dr. Orin Clark was the pastor of my boyhood. The wax was soft, and the impressions are deep. My father went to Geneva in 1808. The church, what little there was of it, was then 'a stranger in a strange land.' Geneva was an outpost. 'Father Nash' had been there, and the venerable Davenport Phelps. These were the pioneers of the church. They came once a month. . . . . The intervening Sundays were supplied with lay reading by two most excellent men, John Nicholas and Daniel W. Lewis. Judge Nicholas was prominent in political life; Mr. Lewis was a sound and learned lawyer. . . . . There was no church built when we

went to Geneva; indeed my father was the builder of Trinity Church. The Rev. Orin Clark, then a young man, came in aid of the Rev. Mr. Phelps. . . . . I was catechised by him, and prepared by him for confirmation." After preparing for college, under Ransom Hubbell, in 1816, he entered the second term of the sophomore year in Union College, Schenectady, New York, under the presidency of Dr. Nott. In 1818 he graduated, taking an honor; the salutatory was then assigned to him, but he failed to deliver it on account of his inability to return to the commencement. Leaving college at the end of the term he went to New York, to cultivate still further the seed of his collegiate sowing, that it might bear fruit for the good of others. In 1819 he became a candidate for holy orders in the Diocese of New York, and found support for himself in teaching in a large school of the metropolis. Then he thought of going as an assistant in Rev. Dr. Rudd's school at Elizabethtown. This, however, was never accomplished, but his course in consequence of it brought him closely in contact with Bishop Hobart, under whose directions he was studying. His first teaching was in New York, where he established a classical school for boys; and here his success and popularity were so great that he attracted the attention of Dr. Brownell, who secured him for a professorship in Trinity College, and there he was installed in 1825. At the expiration of three years his absorption in parochial work withdrew him for a time from the sphere of teaching, except in the pulpit and at the chancel-rail. "But no sooner had the full commission to St. Peter 'to feed the lambs' been given him, in the apostolic office, than he returned, with renewed earnestness and further reaches, both of effort and success, to the great work of education." St. Mary's Hall and Burlington College; the increasing parochial schools throughout his diocese, and the care and attention paid through all the surrounding parishes of the State to the duty of catechising, are witnesses to the truth of his own estimate and use of his life as the instrument in God's hands to found, and promote and perfect the great work of Christian education in the American church. Previously he left New York for Hartford, in 1824, and there, in Washington College, filled the position of Professor of Belles-Lettres, and also took charge of the whole working system of this institution, his appointment as Bursar laying upon him much detail of financial labor. He was warmly interested in the formation of the Historical Society of the State, and was one of the incorporators; also in the organization of a college society, called the Athenæum. His acquaintance with Dr. Croswell began in 1826, and was the result of certain efforts and movements made relating to the publication of a church paper. Upon the establishment of *The Episcopal Watchman* he became its editor, with William Croswell as associate and assistant, speaking of whom he said: "Man has never been in closer bonds with man, than he with me, for five and twenty years. Our intercourse was intimate at once, and we never had a feeling, or a thought to part us." When he went to Trinity Church, Boston, "the unhelped and lonely labor drew heavily on the mind and heart of Dr. Croswell." An effort was then made to reunite the friends and colaborers, and in the year in which he was ordained, having discontinued his connection with the paper, Croswell also went to Boston, first as assistant, then as rector of Christ Church. His coming was announced, and for some time he was known as "Mr. Doane's friend." They were again associated in Boston in the editorship of the *Banner of the Church*, and upon his removal to New Jersey, almost his first thought was to get Croswell nearer to him, as the editor of the *New York Churchman*. Regarding the decease of this valued friend, he spoke to his convention as follows: "His heart was large enough to take in all the world. His generosity was unbounded. If he excelled in any one relation, after his service to Christ's poor, it was in all the acts and offices of friendship. . . . . On Sunday, in the Church of the Advent, in the city of Boston, at the request of the wardens and vestry, I preached a sermon, commemorative of the late rector, Rev. William Croswell, D. D.; as the sermon has been published, I need not dwell upon his beautiful and blessed memory." The *Watchman* was fearless in tone and utterance, and unvaryingly true to its principles, which were at the time by no means the prevailing views, either in the diocese of its publication or in the country generally. It was undertaken, March 26th, 1827, on the suspension of the *Churchman's Magazine* and the *Gospel Advocate*, to disseminate pure and undefiled religion in "what is believed to be the scriptural and most effectual way," also to elucidate and defend the doctrines, discipline and worship of the American Protestant Episcopal Church, and to uphold the truthfulness of "the perfectness of the gospel only in the church." Among other notable points may be cited his admiration of painted glass in churches; his line of argument against fraternizing with the denominational ministers, whose enforcement brought down such torrents of abuse, on the last year of his episcopate; his love for the Liturgy, as the great preserver of truth and the rebuker and preventer of error in doctrine; his opposition to the progressive idea of religion, set on the sliding platform of human science; his happy adaptation of his thoughts to children's comprehension; his zealous care for the support of the general institutions of the church, its unity, and the duty of her members to support it; and his enthusiasm in missionary and educational work and reform. While editing the *Banner* he made it "an out and out expression of uncompromising churchmanship, with the same stress laid upon all missionary and educational work;" and he counted it his chief delight to be esteemed emphatically a "missionary bishop," and found glory also in being regarded as a missionary editor. In one of his articles occurs a logical yet ardent plea for the daily service, then (1832) nowhere real-ized in the American church; and in the same year he wrote an essay full of force and significance concerning the

insertion of the prayer for Congress during its session, advocating it even in family prayers; while, during the latter years of his episcopate, when special political dangers threatened the country, he urged the families of the diocese, in his conventional address, to make daily use at home of the prayer for Congress. Fully convinced, both in theory and practice, of the importance of a church newspaper—the *Banner* having been discontinued—he established the *Missionary*, the first number appearing April 20th, 1834. It was continued uninterruptedly until January 1st, 1838, and was renewed again for a few years' life in 1847. After 1850 the publication of the *Missionary* was discontinued. Its very low price, and the very large number to whom it was sent free, made it impossible that it should be self-supporting. "Like most of his luxuries, it was for the good of others; and with his luxuries this ceased when his means were gone." But the influence of these papers was very great, and by their instrumentality he urged upon many who could not be reached from the pulpit, or by private intercourse, the great importance of missions and Christian education, and the weekly offertory, and many other things besides, which owed to him their earliest and incessant inculcation through the church in America. "His dealings with the press were manifold, in the publication of his own sermons, etc., and in the issuing of the catalogues of the schools. In the printing office he was much at home, and a most thorough and accurate proof-reader. He learned this in Mr. Bogert's printing office in Geneva during his boyhood."—"I have known three printers brought into the church from 'setting up' his very many publications." The *Episcopal Watchman*, of April 12th, 1828, contained the announcement of his unanimous election as assistant minister of Trinity Church, Boston; and at the death of Dr. Gardiner he was unanimously elected Rector, December 3d, 1830. In that city his position was very influential, and indeed through the whole diocese; and in all that could advance the interests of the church he was a prominent and active mover. He was identified also with the Church Scholarship Society of Connecticut, and with the Massachusetts Missionary Society; also with the formation of Diocesan Sunday-school Unions, auxiliary to the General Union. "But of the great points to which the energies of his soul and mind, his thoughts and words, his efforts and prayers were given, the cause of missions came perhaps first. Reaching first to the full limits of his own cure, and then over the surface of the city, and then through the borders of the diocese, they grew into the glorious Catholicity of the present missionary organization of the American church, which, without invidious distinction, I may claim as the creation of his wisdom and earnestness. His interest in it did not begin in Boston, but was maturing there." In Hartford he was much interested in an auxiliary society to the Domestic and Foreign Missionary Society. Upon the organization, in 1828, of the African Mission School Society, with the purpose of educating colored schoolmasters, catechists and missionaries, to be sent to Africa under the direction of the General Society, he was a prominent Director, and acted as one of the Executive Committee. In 1830 he was called to preach the sermon before the missionary society in Philadelphia; it was entitled "The Missionary Argument," and is on the text, "Go ye into all the world, and preach the gospel to every creature." November 27th, 1831, he preached his memorable sermon, "The Missionary Spirit," in Christ Church, Boston. "But his greatest work and service to this glorious cause was rendered late in life. He was one of a Committee of the Board of Directors of the Missionary Society, in 1835, to consider the organization of the society. It was the very opportunity of his life. He brought to it years of thought and prayer, and all the earnestness and energy of his nature, in its very prime. And the original draft of the report, in his own writing, with scarce an alteration, ... shows how, for all time, the American church owes to him a debt (always acknowledged but once and by one man) of unforgetting gratitude." He preached the sermon at the consecration of Dr. Kemper, the first missionary bishop of the American church; and his famous four sermons, "The Missionary Spirit," "The Missionary Argument," "The Missionary Bishop" and "The Missionary Charter," are "wells of unfailing refreshment for all painfulness of work; shadows from the Great Rock in the weary land of missionary toil." The sermon at the consecration, on the text, "How shall they preach except they be sent," is full of exuberant joy at the completion of a long-cherished desire; and of the exulting and overcoming hope, in the working of a thoroughly thought-out plan. The last of the four sermons is on the whole of the apostolic commission, as recorded by St. Matthew, and was preached when he ordained Dr. Wolff, in September, 1837. Upon the refusal of the lower house, in 1841, to accede to the bishops' desire of sending missionary bishops to Texas and Africa, which seemed to indicate a lessening interest in the cause he looked upon with such sincere affection, he spoke strongly and frankly in his conventional address, "with the eloquent and earnest plainness of deep-seated conviction." To the convention of 1839 he wrote of two subjects, often in his heart as connected closely with each other—Christian missions and Christian education; and to the Diocese of Maryland, of which he had charge in 1840, he spoke, as he could with no personality, as to the proper and just support of the episcopate. While, generally speaking, "the perfectly independent way in which he battered the solid front of his convictions, against the wall of popular opinions, was another element of his character and work. Of all walls, none is more solid and brazen than the prevailing notion which considers the commission to evangelize the world as given mainly to Sunday-school teachers. He had not so learned," and would have been sorry to think of the Sunday-school, as such, as a permanent idea in the church. He did not care to see it stereotyped in brick and mortar; looked upon it as the offspring of a superficial, labor-saving, self-sparing age, as an idea which has freed parents and sponsors from the sense of their responsibility in the religious care of children; and declared that it had cheated pastors with the notion of an easier way of doing what Jesus laid on Simon, as the highest test of love, the feeding of his lambs. "It has puffed up multitudes with the conceit of knowledge, and almost of a new order in the church. And it has substituted in the minds of children the most superficial smattering for that sound, patient, thorough instruction in the faith and practice of the gospel which Christ intrusted to his church, for which he holds her accountable, and for which she makes the fullest and most adequate provision." Of the incorporation of Burlington College, in 1846, he writes: "I have singular pleasure in announcing to the convention the incorporation of Burlington College, with a charter securing its direction, forever, to the church. . . . . For many years I have earnestly expressed my conviction of the importance of such an institution for the diocese. . . . . A body of men of higher intelligence and more entire devotion to their enterprise than the Board of Trustees I have never been permitted to co-operate with. As my best approval of their spirit and exertions, I have accepted their appointment as agent to procure a suitable endowment for it. I design to devote myself to it unreservedly, and shall count on a generous reception from my brethren of the clergy and laity. . . . I need not repeat here . . . . my strong conviction of the eminent fitness of the Diocese of New Jersey for all the purposes of education; and chiefly for what concerns us most, of education in the church." The plan of hiring clergymen was always odious to him. To one who proposed it once he wrote in curt response: "I do not ordain coachmen." His aversion to doing everything by societies has kept from the diocese, as it took from the general church, the missionary organization which prevails generally; his own theory being the rule that the church is the brotherhood, the missionary society, the Bible distributer, by divine right. "The prominence, and the faithful discharge, of public catechizing, his greatest greatness, which in his own parish was monthly, and whenever it could be in all his visitations, shows his appreciation of the charge to Simon. A greater conformity to the requirements of the 'Prayer Book' in daily prayers and weekly and holy-day eucharists, and a far more rubrical performance of the services than existed before, attest the influence of his frequent teaching and the power of his example. . . . . For his monuments, one may stand anywhere and look around and see them, in the churches, the parsonages, the school-houses that dot the land. And in Burlington, St. Mary's Church, St. Mary's Hall and Burlington College are enduring memorials of his incessant, undaunted works of faith and love which God has blessed so richly." In the American Colonization Society he was always warmly interested, and regarded it as one of the wisest works of mercy that the age has produced. To all concerns of state he devoted keen attention, and, though never mixing in mere politics, was a discerning and thoughtful statesman. At the formation of the Historical Society of New Jersey he was one of the earliest members, for many years attending their meetings, and finding time in 1846 to write an address to be delivered before them, by their invitation, in which he stands on the broad ground, "A Jerseyman in New Jersey." In 1845 he delivered the oration before the venerable Society of Cincinnati; and on every fitting occasion his cheering voice was heard in lyceum, lecture-room, pulpit and academy, urging his listeners on to generous deeds and kindly measures. In 1851 he delivered the introductory lecture before the Mechanics' Library and Reading Room Association, on "The Diffusion of Useful ⟨nowledge;" and, at the death of President Harrison, delivered at Burlington an address, at the invitation of the Common Council. At the decease of Taylor, also, he preached a sermon on its lessons, at the request of the students, and also addressed to the people of his charge a solemn and touching pastoral letter. While famine was desolating Ireland he was the first to move the plan by which his native State should assert, and substantially, its sympathy, and the first resolution of the Newark meeting was to adopt his proposition bearing on the subject, "Resolved, That we approve of the proposition of the Rt. Rev. Bishop Doane to charter a Jersey ship, and to freight her with the least possible delay." His English correspondence was very extensive and interesting, comprising such names as Hugh James Rose, Pusey, ⟨eble, Newman and Manning, Dr. Hook, Archdeacon Harrison, Bishop Terrot and Bishop Forbes, Rev. J. H. Horne, the Bishops of Oxford and New Zealand, Archbishop Howley, Sir Robert Inglis, Hope, Gladstone, Acland, Mrs. Southey, Wordsworth, etc. In 1841 he received and accepted from Rev. Dr. Hook, Vicar of Leeds, an invitation to preach the sermon at the consecration of his new parish church, the act permitting the clergy of the American church to officiate in England having recently been passed. In 1858 he urged the observance of the Rogation days, and authorized a form set in a letter to the clergy and laity of the Diocese of New Jersey; and it was "a happy return to the liturgical treasures of better days," that gave back to his diocese, in the Second Evening Service, which he authorized, the Magnificat and Nunc Dimittis, and the unmutilated Benedictus and full Versicles of the English "Prayer Book." Speaking of his numerous trials, triumphs, etc., Dr. Ogilby writes: "Our bishop, as everybody knows, has been the butt of accusations as gross as those which caused St. Athanasius . . . . to be twice condemned by synods of his peers. . . . . Unlike the great champion of antiquity, however, Bishop Doane, though accused, has never been condemned. The charges brought against him were solemnly dismissed by his peers. . . . . With an easy path before him, whose way was smoothed by concessions and compromises, ... he chose

the steep way, the rough way, to clear for himself, to struggle up alone; and in such heart he conquered." And with unflinching courage, and in the face of timidity and prejudice, he asserted and reasserted, before the Court of Bishops, his conviction of the entire innocence of the Bishop of New York; "to proclaim his firm belief, that, and the scandal and partisanship of that persecution, were more harmful to the church than would have been the truth of the false charges against him; and so to invite to himself the revived bitterness of all that cruel storm." Says Rev. Dr. Mahan: "To the more solid and essential traits he added also the lighter graces and accomplishments. . . . . He was skilful in song, as well as mighty in the severer labors of life; . . . . an elegant scholar, an orator, a poet. . . . . He was the poet of works, with whom song is but the blossom that prepares the way for solid fruit. Burlington College and St. Mary's Hall are his two great poems. Such, however, was the exuberance of his genius that blossom and fruit, in his case, sprang side by side, as it were, on the selfsame bough; and his poetical powers, like his practical, continued fresh and vigorous to the last." And in all his poems may be found two sterling characteristics, sweet fervid simpleness, and deep devotional ˙ feeling. Again: " His poetical writings were simple necessities. He could not help them. His heart was full of song. It oozed out, in his conversation, in his sermons, in everything that he did. . . . . Never sarcastic, he had a great capacity for severity. His power of reproof was most searching and severe, often most uncomfortable. He seemed always to try not to say it; but sometimes it would come out, generally with some softening word after it. . . . . Often he had an endurance of impertinence and insult which amazed me. And a playful rebuke came much more freely from him, when it would meet the case." Again, in Dr. Mahan's sermon: " He was a mighty Preacher. Of him it might eminently be said, that his preaching was not in word only, but in power. Mighty in the Scriptures, he had hardly a thought, varied and original as all his thoughts were, which did not spontaneously arm itself, as it were, in the panoply of inspiration. And the theme of his preaching was always Christ. . . . . " And in Dr. Ogilby's sermon: "As a preacher no bishop surpassed him. He has published more sermons than the whole House of Bishops—able sermons, which will be perpetual memorials of his intellectual powers and of his zeal for the church." He died, April 27th, 1859, in the twenty-seventh year of his episcopate. From the *Church Journal* is gathered the following: " The hour for the funeral was fixed at one o'clock, on Saturday, April 30th, at which time, from every part of the diocese, clergy and laity came up to render this last homage of reverence and love to their departed bishop; while Philadelphia and New York, and even more distant parts of the church, were largely represented; and Burlington itself was out *en masse*. . . . . The body lay in an apartment of his late residence at Riverside, where it was viewed by thousands of persons. The Bishop of Vermont, Bishop Potter, of New York, and Bishop Southgate, being in attendance, together with more than a hundred clergymen in surplices, beside many others. . . . . On reaching the gate of St. Mary's churchyard, the opening sentences of the burial service were said by the venerable rector of Trinity church, New York. . . . . The lesson was read by Bishop Southgate. . . . . The concluding prayers and benediction were said by Bishop Potter." "The Life and Writings of George Washington Doane, D. D., LL. D., for twenty-seven years Bishop of New Jersey, containing his Poetical Works, Sermons, and Miscellaneous Writings, with a Memoir by his son, William Croswell Doane," four vols., was published in New York in 1860, and simultaneously in London, where, as at home, it met, and deservedly, with a warm and appreciative reception, both from the clergy and the laity.

SELDEN, J. CAREY, Physician, Acting Assistant Surgeon of the Ward United States Hospital, in Newark, New Jersey, late of that city, was born in Powhatan county, Virginia, in 1824, and was a graduate of the medical department of the New York University. He was for two years the Assistant-Surgeon at Ward's Island Hospital, New York, where he gained considerable reputation as a physician and surgeon; and in 1860 established himself in Broad street, Newark, New Jersey. He served several years also as Acting Assistant Surgeon of the Ward United States Hospital in that city. He was found dead in his office, November 14th, 1865, having died soon after coming in from a professional visit early in the morning, and was supposed to have died in one of the epileptic paroxysms to which he was subject. "He died at the age of thirty-one, and was never married. He was large and tall, pleasant and sociable, honorable in his business relations, and had made many friends."

HENDRY, BOWMAN, M. D., late of Gloucester county, was born in Woodbury, Gloucester county, New Jersey, October 1st, 1773. His grandparents emigrated from England at an early period in the colonial history of America, and settled in Burlington, New Jersey, where his father, Dr. Thomas Hendry, was born. After some years the family removed to Woodbury. His father secured an extensive practice, and maintained through life an enviable professional reputation in Woodbury and its vicinity. His mother was an English lady, remarkable for those traits of character which command respect and call forth the affections in all the social and domestic relations. The family name was Bowman, and hence the origin of his Christian

50

name. His childhood was passed in his native village, where, among his early associates, were the late Commodore Decatur and his brother, the late Captain Lawrence, and the celebrated Andrew Hunter. In company with these, and many other distinguished citizens of the State and times, he received his education as an academy boy. Under the tuition of a Mr. Hunter, a gentleman of high literary attainments and a classical scholar of ample ability, he received an education far more liberal than was generally obtainable, even by youth of respectable parentage, at that early period, when the whole country was struggling to recover from the ruinous results of the Revolution. His literary course was concluded with distinction, and he left the academy with its highest honors; and, at the age of seventeen years, commenced the study of medicine under the preceptorship of his father, whose age and ability amply qualified him for the correct initiation of his son into the theory and practice of this noble science. He was afterward sent to Philadelphia for the purpose of pursuing his medical studies under a distinguished practitioner of that metropolis and attending medical lectures at the University of Pennsylvania. He there became resident, as a pupil, in the family of the late Dr. Duffield, where the various relations which render life desirable and pleasant were displayed in the most attractive form. During the time of his attendance at the university, he enjoyed the opportunity of hearing and profiting by the lectures of some of the most eminent professors of that or any other period. Such were those of Professor Shippen, on midwifery, anatomy, and surgery; the venerated Benjamin Rush, on the institutes of medicine and clinical practice; Woodhouse, on chemistry; Professor A. Cuhn, on the practice of physic; and Professor Ewing, on natural philosophy, etc. He attended also many occasional lectures, together with the actual demonstrations of the clinical and anatomical departments of the Pennsylvania Hospital, and reaped such practical advantages as were then afforded by the Philadelphia Almshouse. About the time that his novitiate was drawing to its close, the "Western Insurrection" broke out, and he, fired by the prevalent patriotic enthusiasm, became engaged in the expedition then preparing for the field, and shouldered his musket, as a private in the ranks. He then marched with the troops until the town of Lancaster was reached, when, being a slim and delicate youth, he was nearly overcome by the unusual exertion. Subsequently, through the kindly exertions of Professor James, he became an assistant in the surgical department. Previously, however, he was compelled to pass a very rigid examination, "but he came forth triumphantly from the 'Green Box,' and eventually received the legitimate diploma from the hands of the provost and professors." On his return from the bloodless field of insurrection he was discharged with honor, and, after a brief sojourn with the Duffield family, where his preceptor's daughter was the magnet attracting him in that direction, he proceeded to his paternal home in Woodbury to commence the active duties of life upon an independent footing. After a survey, having for end the choice of a proper theatre of action, it was resolved that he should enter upon his medical career in Haddonfield, Gloucester county; and accordingly, in 1794, he commenced practice as a physician and surgeon in that town and its vicinity. But there existed, previously to that time, a colonial act, entitled, "An act to regulate the practice of physic and surgery in the colony of New Jersey," passed September 26th, 1772, prohibiting the practice of those professions by any person whatsoever, until " examined, approved, and admitted " by two judges of the Supreme Court, aided by such persons as they might see fit to call to their assistance in the execution of their duties. The operation of this salutary law was, of course, temporarily suspended by the confusion resulting from the Revolution; but on the 26th of November, 1783, an act of similar import and intention was passed by the Assembly of the State, a Board of Examiners being therein appointed, as aids to the judicial authorities in carrying out its provisions. He thus became liable to those provisions, although already armed with the diploma of the first medical school in the country; and that the act had not sunk into desuetude when he commenced his career is sufficiently proved by a document still in existence, which contains the necessary legal certificate of his professional qualifications, signed by the members of the Board of Examiners, Drs. Nicholas Bellville and Ebenezer Elmer; and also the authorization of the judges of the Supreme Court, Hon. James Kinney, and Hon. Isaac Smith, dated March 11th, 1796. In a very brief space of time he became the doctor of Gloucester county, his rides extending from the Delaware to the seaboard, and being not unfrequently pushed, at the request of other practitioners, to the very extremities of the State. During about fifteen years of the early part of his professional career, he rode upon the saddle, and by night or day, in heat or cold, in storm or sunshine, was on horseback. At length, resolving upon an improvement in his mode of travelling, he purchased at a vendue an old-fashioned sulkey, of the kind used in those days by the wealthier portion of the community only. "An old Friend, who had witnessed this extravagance—an outlay of thirty dollars— quietly remarked : ' Doctor, I fear thee is too fast in making this purchase. Thee will not be able to stand it, and make thy income meet thy expenses.' This remark furnishes a strong proof of the primitive simplicity of those times." During a period of about thirty years the general amount of daily travelling performed by him was from thirty to fifty miles ; but his journeys sometimes extended to the almost incredible distance of seventy-five miles in a single day ; and the necessary rapidity of his movements on such occasions was sufficient to tire out four horses in succession. " It has been computed that, during his entire career of professional usefulness, more than five hundred of these noble animals were completely exhausted in his service." He was ever peculiarly fortunate in the department of obstetrics,

which, previously to his time, had been almost monopolized for years by female *accoucheurs ;* and certainly no other individual in West Jersey ever introduced into the world so many children, with so much honor to himself, and ease to the mother and infant. " It is much to be regretted that there exists no detailed record of the very numerous operations which he performed, from time to time, during his long course of practice ; yet evidence enough remains to show that many of them were difficult and dangerous, such as are sufficient, when performed in the great medical institutions of capitals, and made public through the press, to establish an enviable reputation for the operator. In the theory of medicine his conceptions were clear, correct and decided, his tact in diagnosis remarkable, and his clinical practice rich in original prescriptions. " How, in the midst of such engrossing professional labors, he managed to keep pace with the progress of his profession, it is difficult to conjecture, ... but that he did so, with remarkable success, is not to be disputed." He was a subscriber to the principal medical periodicals, both foreign and domestic, and was always found prepared to converse and to act upon the scientific discoveries and professional improvements of the day. Nothing can tend more strongly to substantiate the justice of this statement than the frequency with which he was called in consultation by the most prominent physicians of New Jersey and the men of science of the country. For many years also he had charge of the Gloucester County Almshouse, and consented to serve as Surgeon to a volunteer company of cavalry, formed in 1805 by Captain J. B. Cooper, from the young gentlemen of Woodbury, Haddonfield and the adjacent country. His political opinions, though decided, were never blazoned abroad ; he never entered into political contests, but, steadily performing his private political duties and maintaining his right to individual judgment on such subjects, suffered none to invade that right, and never invaded the similar rights of others. In religion, as in politics, he cautiously avoided those controversies which, without benefiting any one, might have lessened the sphere of his professional usefulness ; but was never backward in the simple statement of his faith. His freely-avowed sentiments were those of a churchman, and through life, he manifested, on all proper occasions, a decided preference for the Episcopalian service over any other mode of divine worship. For the Society of Friends, many of whom were ranked among his deeply valued associates and most intimate acquaintances, he always entertained the highest esteem. The natural consequence of his excessive and continual exertions was the access of a premature old age ; and as an additional evidence of decay, he was attacked by that terrible and, at his age, hopeless affliction, epilepsy. Until this fatal illness, he had never been known to travel for recreation or amusement; but now his excellent friend and attentive physician, Dr. Spencer, persuaded him to visit New York for the benefit of change of scene and air. In that city he became the honored guest of his medical adviser's particular friend, the late Major Gamble, U. S. A., of whose genuine hospitality he retained a pleasing remembrance until death. The visit had the effect of cheering his mind, but permanent relief was beyond all human art. The absolute necessity of relinquishing the practice of his profession became daily more apparent, and an effort was made to settle his temporal affairs. In this undertaking his friends encountered difficulties productive of most painful feelings. "Instead of being a man possessed of vast riches, as many, recollecting his extensive practice, naturally supposed, he was found comparatively poor. His liberality on all occasions, but more especially the neglect of his account books and the collection of just debts, resulted in this state of his affairs at last. No remedy could be applied; the time and opportunity were gone, and thus the condition of his pecuniary circumstances became the proudest monument of his lifelong and self-sacrificing liberality." For two years immediately preceding his death he had declined entirely the practice of his profession, being generally confined to his chamber or the house. He was married in 1796 to a daughter of Dr. Duffield; and died, April 23d, 1838.

ODD, JOSEPH SMITH, Physician, late of Bloomfield township, New Jersey, son of General John Dodd, was born in that place January 10th, 1791, and graduated at Princeton College in 1813. He commenced the practice of medicine in his native village in 1816, and there was professionally engaged without any interruption of moment for more than thirty years. He was a contemporary of Drs. John C. Budd, Isaac Pierson, John Ward, Uzal Johnson and Abraham Clark. In 1842 he was elected to the Council (afterward called the Senate) of New Jersey, to which office, after serving one term, he was re-elected under the new constitution of the State. While in the Senate he took an active and leading part in originating and establishing the State Lunatic Asylum; was the Chairman of the Committee having charge of that subject, and contributed greatly by his exertions to the successful inauguration of that institution. About this time he became associated with Dr. Joseph A. Davis, now a prominent physician of Bloomfield, as a partner, and, with the gradual failure of his health, began to retire from active professional life. He had a large practice, embracing the principal part of Bloomfield township, and extending into the townships of Livingston and Caldwell. "His unremitting devotion to it impaired, at a comparatively early age, the vigor of his constitution, never very robust, and contributed to bring on the disease of which he died. He was decidedly of a reflective cast, and evinced this in the careful and considerate treatment of his patients, as well as in the ordinary intercourse of life. The sound-

ness of his judgment was perhaps the conspicuous feature of his character." It is a remarkable fact that, in a practice of thirty years, he never lost a patient in labor. He was a man of scholarly tastes and retained through life the love which, in his youth, he had for general studies, especially the mathematical and classical. He was a member of the Presbyterian church, and a devout and thorough student of the Scriptures, with which, and the psalms and hymns of Watts, his memory was largely stored. "He met death September 5th, 1847, with an undisturbed Christian hope, and left behind him the influence and fruits of a pure, laborious and useful life." His son, Amzi Dodd, is a resident of Newark, New Jersey.

MITH, LYNDON A., Physician, late of Newark, New Jersey, was born at Haverhill, New Hampshire, November 11th, 1795, and was the son of Rev. Ethan Smith. He graduated at Dartmouth College in August, 1817, and in that institution took also his medical degree in 1822. In July, 1827, he removed to Newark, New Jersey, from Williamstown, Massachusetts, and there resided till the time of his decease. He was a valued and prominent member of the Essex District Medical Society, and his name is, from April 28th, 1829, down to 1865, to be seen on almost every page of its "Transactions." While in the enjoyment of his usual health, there was suddenly developed disease of the prostate gland; and, although he rallied at times, it caused his death in about eight weeks. The sentiment of the profession and the public was admirably expressed in the resolution passed at the special meeting of the Essex Society, whose members attended his funeral in a body: "Resolved: That in the death of Dr. Smith, this society suffers no common bereavement. Eminently social and genial in his feelings, cordial in his friendships, kind to his equals in age, fatherly toward his juniors, and ingenuous and open in all his intercourse, he had won a warm place in our fraternal regard. Educated at one of New England's oldest seats of learning, and trained for his profession in one of our best medical schools, he united, with a generous, general culture, a thorough knowledge of the principles of the liberal science to which he purposed to devote his life; and, under the guidance of a discriminating judgment and a conscientious sense of responsibility, he applied this knowledge with distinguished skill and success to the relief of suffering humanity through a period of more than forty years. Holding in just appreciation the noble mission of his profession and its exalted rank among secular pursuits, he was warmly interested in every effort to add to its stores of knowledge, to extend the limits of its resources and elevate the standard of literary and scientific preparation to be required of those who would seek admission to its mysteries. Hence, the various associations, local and national, instituted with reference to those objects, found in him an ardent friend, a constant, ever present helper. . . . . Humane in all his impulses, every work of philanthropy had a place in his sympathies; a sincere and consistent Christian, the church and all her enterprises of benevolence and charity received his earnest co-operation and advocacy; a patriotic and loyal citizen, he gave his whole heart to his country's cause, and in the day of her calamity laid the son of his old age a sacrifice upon her altar." Dr. Abraham Coles, President of the Medical Society of New Jersey, at the Centenary Anniversary, held January, 1866, also paid an eloquent tribute to him as a physician and a Christian gentleman. He died in Newark, New Jersey, December 15th, 1865.

LMER, JOHN C., Physician, late of Springfield, New Jersey, was born in Goshen, Orange county, New York, April 7th, 1817, and graduated at the College of Physicians and Surgeons, New York, in the class of 1840. In the course of the same year he settled in Mendham, New Jersey, and in 1852 removed to Springfield, where he remained until the time of his decease. He had studied medicine under the preceptorship of Dr. John B. Johnes, of Morristown, New Jersey, in his day one of the most eminent men in the State. He was a student and practitioner of ripe experience, and was regarded as especially skilled in diagnosis. "He was very faithful to his patients, and had a strong hold upon their affections. His mind was powerful and discriminating, and he was patient in research. He was a very tall, stout man; his face bore ample evidence of kindness of heart and quiet thinking, common to many men of sympathetic temperaments. He was a man, however, of strong will and very decided opinions." He died, October 17th, 1863.

USCHENBERGER WILLIAM S. W, Surgeon, Naturalist, Traveller, Author, was born in Cumberland county, New Jersey, September 4th, 1807, in which year his father died, though his mother is still living at the age of ninety-two, enabling him in his seventieth year to enjoy the rare privilege of a mother's care, or the care of a mother, which is perhaps the keener enjoyment of the two. After pursuing his academical course in Philadelphia and New York, he began the study of medicine in August, 1824, under the direction of Dr. J. P. Hopkinson and Dr. Nathaniel Chapman, of Philadelphia, subsequently entering the medical department of the University of Pennsylvania, from which he graduated in March, 1830. He had been appointed, August 10th, 1826, Surgeon's Mate in the United States navy, in the service of which he spent the whole of his active professional life, visiting nearly all the strange lands and seas of this planet, seeing the sights thereof, and, what is more, telling of them in racy and graphic books. In the course of the eight years that immediately followed his entrance into the navy, he made two voyages to the Pacific and about it, giving the result of his observations to the world in a work entitled "Three Years in the Pacific," published in Philadelphia in 1834, and the next year in London. Thus early did he find his true bent, and thus successfully, at the opening, did he work it. From March, 1835, to November, 1837, he was Fleet Surgeon of the East India Squadron, in which he circumnavigated the globe, recording his experiences in another volume, entitled "A Voyage Round the World," published in Philadelphia in 1838, and the same year in London, with the omission of certain strictures on the British government, which were probably too true to be palatable to the British public. This work received flattering notices from the *Edinburgh Review*, the *London Athenæum*, the *Southern Literary Messenger* and the *North American Review*, which last pronounced it "the most readable account of foreign travel" that had lately appeared. He was in charge of the United States Naval Asylum at Brooklyn, New York, from 1843 to 1847, during which period he organized the Naval Laboratory, for supplying the service with unadulterated drugs. In this important matter he displayed conspicuously the practical side of his character and talents, proving that he could devise and execute measures for the good of the mariners as well as provide amusement for the marines. In 1848 he again visited the East Indies, giving an account of his visit in "Notes and Commentaries during a Voyage to Brazil and China, in 1848," published in Richmond in 1854; and in 1849 he was appointed, in further recognition of his practical abilities, a member of the Board to draw up plans and regulations for the United States Naval Academy. His services on this Board, it is unnecessary to say, were judicious and valuable. In October, 1854, he sailed as Surgeon of the Pacific Squadron, making his third voyage to the Pacific, of which, however, he published no account, not caring, possibly, to indulge in "thrice-told tales." He was afterwards appointed Medical Director in the navy, and finally, September 4th, 1869, retired, thus closing his long, eventful and brilliant career in the service. His whole life, indeed, has been one of diversified and honorable activity. He has done many great things, and done them well, insomuch that out of his achievements, it is no exaggeration to say, a good title to fame might be carved for half a dozen men. As an author he has not by any means confined himself to books of travel, but has handled, and handled with masterly force and clearness, some of the largest and most interesting branches of science. He published in Philadelphia, in 1850, a work entitled "Elements of Natural History," in two volumes; also published in separate parts under the following titles: I. Anatomy and

Physiology; II. Botany; III. Conchology; IV. Entomology; V. Geology; VI. Herpetology and Ichthyology; VII. Mammalogy; VIII. Ornithology. In the same year he published a "Lexicon of Terms Used in Natural History;" and in 1852 "A Notice of the Origin, Progress and Present Condition of the Academy of Natural Sciences of Philadelphia." He has published, besides, several pamphlets on the rank of medical officers in the navy; edited with notes the work of Dr. Henry Marshall, of the British army, on "Enlisting, Discharging and Pensioning Soldiers;" and contributed numerous papers and reviews to the *Medical Examiner*, the *American Journal of the Medical Sciences*, the *Journal of Pharmacy*, and other medical and scientific periodicals. His distinguished and varied services to science and literature have been acknowledged by his election to the membership of many of the principal learned societies in this country, including the American Medical Association; the College of Physicians, of Philadelphia, of which he has been Secretary and Vice-President; the Academy of Natural Sciences, of Philadelphia, of which he has been Vice-President and President; the American Philosophical Society, and the Historical Society of Pennsylvania. His rounded life of activity and honor is one of the treasures of his native State, and as such will ever be cherished. He was married in October, 1839.

HOMPSON, COLONEL RICHARD S., Lawyer, was born at Cape May Court House, Cape May county, New Jersey, December 27th, 1837. His father, Richard Thompson, was a prominent citizen of southern New Jersey, an extensive landowner, and largely interested in vessels engaged in the coast trade. When fourteen years old he entered the Norristown Seminary, at Norristown, Pennsylvania, where he remained three years, and then was placed under the private tuition of Rev. A. Scovel, a Presbyterian clergyman of Bordentown, New Jersey, continuing under his charge for four years, and receiving in this time a comprehensive and thorough education. Upon the expiration of this pupilage he commenced to read law, at the time continuing his literary studies under the direction of Asa I. Fish, LL. D., of the Philadelphia bar, widely and popularly known as the editor of the "American Law Register," "Selwyn's Nisi Prius," "Todd's Practice," "Williams on Executors," and of the newest and best publication of "Troubat and Haley's Practice," the only complete digest of English exchequer reports. These are all works of estimable and well-deserved reputation. Under the supervision of this scholarly and profoundly learned barrister he remained for two years preparation for practice, and then passed to the Dane Law School of Harvard College, from which he graduated with distinction in 1861. Returning

to Philadelphia, he spent another year in the office of his preceptor, Mr. Fish, and in 1862 was admitted to the bar, having passed a very creditable examination by the board of Examiners, then presided over by Hon. Eli K. Price. After his admission he made an extensive tour of the country, and, inspired with martial ardor by the opening of the civil war, returned to his native State and raised a company of soldiers, who were attached to the 12th New Jersey Volunteers, becoming Captain of Company K, which he had recruited. While at Ellicott's Mills he was appointed Assistant Provost Marshal, under General Wool, with head-quarters at the mills until his regiment was ordered to the front. It was subsequently first attached to the Second Brigade, Third Division, Second Army Corps, then to the Third Brigade and Second Division of the same corps, and at the close of the war formed part of a provisional corps. During these changes, however, it served with the Army of the Potomac. Colonel Thompson participated in all of the hard-fought battles save for a short time when absent on detached duty. At Chancellorsville, when the Union line was hard pressed, several regiments having given way, and his own commander, Colonel Willetts, having been wounded, he took command of the companies which remained, and succeeded in stemming the onslaught until the broken line had fallen back and reformed. For this gallant service, which saved the line at a moment of greatest peril, he was highly complimented. At Gettysburg his regiment was on the right centre, and successfully opposed Pettigrew's North Carolina brigade, which formed the left of Longstreet's charging column. He participated in the hot engagements at Falling Waters, Auburn Mills, Bristow's Station, Blackburn's Ford, Robeson's Farm, and at Mine Run, where the fighting lasted three days. In that series of terrible engagements, which marked the progress of Grant's army towards Richmond, Colonel Thompson's regiment was conspicuous for its gallantry. At Deep Bottom he acted as corps officer of the day, and it became his duty to hold the lines until the main body of troops under General Hancock, who was making a demonstration on the north side of the James river, had recrossed. This was an important and dangerous position, as this line was more than four miles in length and in some places scarcely fifty feet from the enemy's pickets. He, however, succeeded with slight loss, and received from Hancock himself a personal compliment for this service. In a successful charge by his regiment and others, in the autumn of 1864, to dislodge the enemy from a strong position at Ream's Station he was severely wounded by the explosion of a shell. Soon after he was taken to Philadelphia, where he remained until December, and while still on crutches was assigned to duty as President of a General Court Martial sitting in that city. In this capacity he continued to act until February, 1865, when, ascertaining from his physician that his wounds would incapacitate him for active service for a long time, he resigned his commission. The character of the service he saw may be estimated when it is known that his regiment was mustered in with 992 men, and was mustered out with only ninety-three, and all of these bearing honorable wounds. Colonel, afterward Brigadier-General, Thomas A. Smith, commanding the brigade, wrote Governor Parker, under date of March 2d, 1864, as follows: " The majority of the 12th New Jersey is now vacant. I take pleasure to recommend to your notice Captain Richard S. Thompson. He is a gallant officer and a good disciplinarian. As an executive officer he has few equals. His assiduous attention to his duties has upon several occasions won the highest encomiums of his superior officers." On January 14th, 1865, General Hancock asked to have him commissioned as Colonel in a veteran reserve corps, for his valor at Deep Bottom and Ream's Station, and President Lincoln indorsed the recommendation. Colonel Thompson removed to Chicago, October 24th, 1865, and entered upon the practice of law. In 1867 he became a member of the firm of Leaming & Thompson, which still exists. In 1869 he was chosen a member of the Board of Trustees of Hyde Park, and soon after was elected its attorney. In 1872 he was nominated on the Republican ticket as candidate for State Senator from the Second Illinois District, and was returned by a handsome majority. His ability as a legislator, his keen knowledge of parliamentary law, his constant advocacy of all measures for the public weal, his official integrity, have achieved for him a reputation second only to that which he won upon the battle-field. He is the leading member of the Senate, a position which he has secured by a fearless performance of all the duties rightly devolving upon him as a representative of the people. He distinguished himself in the session of 1875, during the agitation over the repeal of the Liquor Law, by holding at bay temporary majorities until a full house was present to decide the issue, and again in the debate upon the contested election of Senator Marshal. He was married, June 7th, 1865, to Catharine S. Scovel, daughter of Rev. A. Scovel, at that time a resident of Bloomington, Illinois.

———◦◦◦———

IERSON, EDWARD A., Physician, late of Newark, New Jersey, was born in that city, March 22d, 1836, and was a lineal descendant from Rev. Abraham Pierson, the first pastor of the First Presbyterian Church in Newark. He studied medicine with Dr. John F. Ward, and graduated at the College of Physicians and Surgeons, in New York, in the class of 1858. At the commencement of the sectional conflict he at once entered the service as Assistant-Surgeon of the 1st Regiment New Jersey Volunteers, and continued to serve in this capacity till the expiration of the three months term for which he had enlisted. He performed the duties of his office with zeal and fidelity,

and in due time was honorably discharged. He soon after presented himself for examination, and was appointed Assistant-Surgeon in the United States navy. January 24th, 1862, he was assigned to the frigate " St. Lawrence.' While on board this vessel, in the memorable contest with the rebel ram " Merrimac," he narrowly escaped injury from a shell which entered his room and struck within a few feet of his head. He afterward accompanied her to Key West, and there was attacked by yellow fever, from which he escaped with life, but in so precarious a condition that it was deemed advisable for him to return to his home for the purpose of recuperation. After a short stay he was detached to the " Penobscot," which was at that time engaged in the blockading service off Wilmington, North Carolina. On the morning of the 22d of May, 1862, a rebel steamer was discovered trying to run the blockade, upon which the " Penobscot " at once started in pursuit. At this juncture a shell from Fort Fisher crashed through the woodwork of his room, and he was struck by a large splinter of wood that fractured the occipital bone. He became immediately unconscious, and before the expiration of the second hour from the time of the occurrence had breathed his last. He had but a few minutes before laid out his instruments and prepared his medicaments and bandages, and was fully prepared to meet the wants of his expected patients. " He was a young man of rare personal beauty, of vivacious manners, of remarkable memory, of great good nature, and a consistent Christian. He was the life of the social medical circles of Essex District, and will be long remembered." He was buried in Mount Pleasant Cemetery, New Jersey, and his funeral was attended in a body by the members of the Essex District Medical Society, which passed a suitable resolution expressive of its regret at a loss so mournful, and of its high esteem for him as a prac- titioner, and an upright friend and intrepid patriot.

———◦◦◦———

 CKERS, OSCAR J., M. D., Physician, late of Newark, was born in Bloomfield, New Jersey, in 1823, and was a graduate of the College of Physicians and Surgeons, in New York. " He will be long remembered on account of his admirable social qualities and sincerity. He was an honest, reliable man. He was the soul of honor, and his integrity none ever called in question." "Adelphos," in the Daily Advertiser, writes of him: " Sleep well, beloved brother, whose life was laid down on the altar of duty. Earth can have no greener spot than the turf that covers thy true heart;" while, at a meeting of the Essex District Medical Society, the following resolutions are the first two of the five adopted on the occasion of his decease: " Resolved, That the many excellent qualities of the deceased, his geniality and kindness of heart, his sound judgment and ample information, especially upon topics connected with his profession, give us great and unusual reason to mourn his loss. Resolved, That this painful event adds another to the many instances often too little appreciated, in which physicians have sacrificed themselves on the altar of professional duty, and that this consideration may legitimately assuage the grief of his sorrowing friends." He was married in December, 1860, to Mrs. Mary Cole; and died at his residence in New street, Newark, April 9th, 1861, in the thirty-ninth year of his age.

HOMAS, LUTHER G., Physician, late of Newark, New Jersey, was born in this city, January 27th, 1830, and was the son of Frederic S. Thomas, and grandson of the late Luther Goble, one of the earliest and most prosperous merchants of his native town. He graduated at Princeton College in 1849, was secretary at the first class-meeting, and made a valuable statistical report. His later studies in medicine were prosecuted under the supervision of the late Dr. L. A. Smith, who wrote an obituary notice of his former pupil, published in the "Transactions of the State Medical Society for 1865." As a student he was industrious and quick of apprehension; as a physician attentive, skilful, and courteously affable. His name also has honorable place in the army record, as may be seen in the adjutant-general's "Official Report" of 1863-64. After receiving his medical diploma, in 1852, from the College of Physicians and Surgeons of New York, he was constantly engaged in professional labors until 1863, when he set out for the scene of war as Surgeon of the 26th Regiment, New Jersey Volunteers. He died suddenly and unexpectedly, it is said, of congestion of the brain, in May, 1864. He was a valued member of the South Park Presbyterian Church, and also of the Essex District Medical Society, whose members accompanied his remains to their last resting-place.

HITE, REV. WILLIAM C., Pastor of First Presbyterian Church, Orange, late of Orange, New Jersey, was born in Sandisfield, Berkshire county, Massachusetts, January 16th, 1803. He was of Puritan stock and a lineal descendant of Peregrine White, the first child of pilgrim exiles, who was born on the "Mayflower," after her arrival at Plymouth harbor in 1620. His parents, of whom he was the second son, were Rev. Levi White and Mary Sergeant White, the latter being the oldest daughter of the Rev. John Sergeant, for many years an eminent and zealous missionary among the Stockbridge Indians. He entered Williams College soon after Dr. Griffiths became president of that institution, graduating in 1826, when twenty-four years of age, with

one of the highest honors of his class. At the expiration of three years from that time he entered upon a course of theological studies at Princeton; in the autumn of 1832 was licensed to preach by the Berkshire Association, but wisely continued the prosecution of his studies at the seminary through another year, and found his first field of labor at East Machias, Maine, where he was absorbed in pastoral work with special blessing for four months. The ensuing six months found him engaged in Tyringham, Massachusetts, where he remained until the summer of 1832. In October of the same year he accepted an invitation to visit the parish of the First Presbyterian Church, of Orange, New Jersey, shortly after Hatfield's temporary labors had closed, and while the church was still filled with gladness and rejoicing over the fruits of a sweeping and precious revival. The result of the meeting between him and the people of that place was the presentation of a call, which he decided to accept over two or three others that had been tendered him from other fields. On the 13th of the following February, the day after Dr. Hillyer's dismission, he was ordained and installed by the Presbytery of Newark, New Jersey. On this occasion Dr. Weeks preached, Dr. Hillyer gave the charge to the pastor, and Dr. Fisher that to the people; the text of the day was 1 Timothy iv. 16: "Take heed unto thyself and unto the doctrine; continue in them; for in doing this thou shalt both save thyself and them that hear thee." It was worthy to have been the motto of a ministerial life characteristically studious and single-aimed. He was, at his ordination, thirty years of age, and had been married about eighteen months. Since the settlement of his predecessor the circumstances of the parish had greatly changed, the population become less homogeneous, and many divided in feeling and sentiment by new denominational rivalries. Two new Presbyterian churches had sprung up, which had taken from the First Presbyterian Church one hundred and fifty members, and from the congregation a much larger number. The circumstances environing his advent at Orange were far from being of the most favorable kind; he came in the wake of a great religious excitement, which is generally followed in churches by a long calm; the church had just reaped a harvest; a long husbandry was necessary to prepare the field for a similar awakening. The funds of the church were not then in a very prosperous condition, and he was settled with a salary of six hundred dollars; the old parsonage still brought in a small rent to the society as a tenement, but was of no service to the pastor. After boarding three months, he hired a small new cottage on Main street; and afterward lived two years in Scotland street, near the present bend of the railroad—his rent for the second year being paid by the parish. In 1836 a new parsonage was built by subscription and contract for eighteen hundred and seventy-five dollars. It was entered in the following year, and was the pastor's home until his removal to the "house not made with hands." In 1842 the church received another bountiful refreshing, and the April report shows an addition of fifty persons to the communion of the church, of whom thirty-six were admitted by profession. The year 1850 was still another year of blessing, when thirty-four persons were added to the church. His health was in a precarious condition for several years preceding his resignation, yet he struggled on until the opening months of 1855, when he yielded to necessity, and April 18th his pastoral relations were dissolved, after a ministry of twenty-two years. The chosen associate of his life and ministry was Clarissa Dart, daughter of Joseph Dart, of Middle Haddam, Connecticut, to whom he was married in August, 1831, soon after the completion of his preparatory studies. He died on the evening of February 7th, 1856, aged fifty-three years, leaving three sons and one daughter, the latter but two years of age.

———◦———

DELL, HON. and REV. JONATHAN, Physician, Poet, Refugee, etc., was born in Newark, New Jersey, September 25th, 1737, was Master of Arts of Nassau Hall, educated for the practice of medicine, and served as Surgeon in the British army; he left the army while stationed in the West Indies, went to England and prepared for holy orders. He was ordained deacon December 21st, 1766, in the Chapel Royal of St. James' Palace, Westminster, by the Rt. Rev. Dr. Terrick, Bishop of London; and in January, 1767, was advanced to priest's orders. On the Christmas day preceding he had been appointed by the Society for Propagating the Gospel in Foreign Parts as Missionary to Burlington, New Jersey, where he arrived July 25th, 1767, and was the next day inducted into St. Mary's Church, Burlington, by his excellency, William Franklin, Esq., Governor of the Province of New Jersey. In October 12th, 1768, he was the leading spirit at a voluntary convention in New Brunswick, New Jersey, which drew up a scheme with sixteen articles, and afterward was one of a committee of two from each of the three provinces of New York, New Jersey, and Pennsylvania, to solicit a charter for the Corporation for the Relief of the Widows and Orphans of Deceased Clergymen in said provinces. In the charter thus obtained he was constituted Secretary of this corporation. In 1769, through his efforts, the church building in Burlington was extended westward twenty-three feet, a new bell placed in the belfry, and elegant hangings and furniture given by Mrs. Franklin, the governor's wife, for "the pulpit, desk, and table." On the 25th of July, 1771, in addition to the care of his parish, Dr. Odell resumed the practice of medicine, generously declining the contributions of his parishioners until the debt incurred for the enlargement of the church should be cancelled. On the 6th of May, 1772, he was married in Burlington, by the missionary of Trenton, to Annie De Cou. In 1774, without the usual examination,

he was unanimously admitted a member of the New Jersey Medical Society, and appointed Chairman of a committee to confer with the attorney-general with reference to an application to the governor for a charter of incorporation. At the outbreak of the revolutionary war, as a subject of Great Britain and clergyman of the Church of England, who had taken the most solemn "oath of supremacy" at his ordination, he used all the efforts he could discreetly to promote peace. In October, 1775, among papers seized by the local Committee of Inspection and Observation, two letters from Dr. Odell were found, whereupon he was paroled, and the matter referred to the Council of Safety, and afterwards to the New Jersey Provincial Congress, before whom he prayed, by memorial, to appear. After hearing and deliberation, the "Congress declined passing any public censure against him." Meanwhile Dr. Odell was indulging his muse. He and Mr. Stansbury were the two most important loyal versifiers of their time. "As a political satirist," says Winthrop Sargent, in his collections of "The Loyalist Poetry of the Revolution," "Dr. Odell is entitled to high rank. In fertility of conception, and vigor and ease of expression, many passages in his poems will compare favorably with those of Churchill and Canning." In a few days after the Declaration of Independence was signed, Dr. Odell's parole was taken, restricting him to a circle within eight miles of Burlington. The people of Burlington were almost unanimous in their aversion to independence. They were lovers of peace and good order, yet, as the months went by, they were not without molestation by the agitators. In December, 1776, a message was received by Dr. Odell that a party of armed Tory-hunters were in search of him. He was hidden, by a Quakeress, in a secret chamber of her house, and in the evening taken to town by her and placed in other lodgings, whence, on the 18th, he left the town and a wife and three children (the youngest not five weeks old), to ramble as a refugee, because he would not sacrifice his principles. He reached New York at last, and was occasionally employed as a Deputy Chaplain in the army. The vestry at Burlington, on the Easter after he left, voted that his salary should be continued, notwithstanding his absence, a pleasing proof of their friendliness towards him. Early in 1782 standards were presented to the King's American Dragoons with imposing ceremonies, when the Rev. Dr. Odell made an address, in the presence of a large number of distinguished officers of the British army and navy, including Prince William Henry (afterwards William IV.), who was at that time in New York. When the British forces left that city, November 5th, 1783, Dr. Odell accompanied them to England. When the province of Nova Scotia was divided, Dr. Odell was called to a seat in the King's Council in the Province of New Brunswick, and became the Secretary, Registrar and Clerk of the Council, with a salary of a thousand pounds sterling. There, after a long separation from them, he was rejoined by his family. For thirty years he faithfully discharged the duties of these offices. He died at Frederickton, New Brunswick, November 25th, 1818, aged eighty-one years. The above has been gleaned from the valuable " History of the Church in Burlington, New Jersey," by the Rev. George Morgan Hills, D. D., in which may be found, at length, many original letters of Dr. Odell, and some of the best specimens of his poetical powers.

RANT, GABRIEL, Physician and Surgeon, graduated at Williams College, Massachusetts, in the class of 1846, and in the College of Physicians and Surgeons of New York in the class of 1851. After practising medicine for some time in Newark, he entered the United States service, June 13th, 1861, as Surgeon of the 2d Regiment, 2d Brigade, New Jersey Volunteers, under command of General Kearny, and served with the regiment at the first battle of Bull Run. At Washington he was examined by the United States Army Medical Board, and at the same date promoted to the position of Brigade Surgeon of Volunteers, afterwards designated by act of Congress as Surgeon of United States Volunteers. November 4th, 1861, he was assigned to Palmer's brigade of cavalry. This brigade organization being subsequently abandoned, he was assigned, December 12th, 1861, to French's brigade as Brigade Surgeon, and afterward as Division Surgeon-in-Chief, and served in the battles of Fair Oaks, Gaines' Mill, Peach Orchard Station, Savage Station, White Oak Swamp, Malvern Hill, second action at Bull Run, Antietam and Fredericksburg, and attended the wounded at Williamsburg and South Mountain. He then accompanied General Stoneman as one of his Staff Surgeons in the grand reconnoissance of March 14th, 1862; and organized the Brigade Hospital at Camp California, and the Division Hospital at Harper's Ferry. February 18th, 1863, he was assigned as Medical Director of Hospitals, at Evansville, Indiana; and while on duty there, was sent, May 29th, of the same year, by order of General Burnside, commanding the Department of the Ohio, to Vicksburg, in charge of the steamer "Atlantic," to transport to his own hospitals the wounded belonging to the State of Indiana. This large steamer was fitted up with all the appointments of an extensive hospital—surgeons, stewards, nurses, and complete stores of medical and surgical supplies. At Columbus the steamer was stopped by General Asboth, in command at that place, and loaded with a regiment of infantry, a battery of artillery, and stores of ammunition. With these materials 'of war he was sent ninety miles up the Yazoo river, in the rear of Vicksburg, and arrived at Sartatia as Blair and Kimball were fighting the rebel General Johnson. This was the most critical period of the campaign; General Grant was investing Vicksburg; Pemberton had come out from the city to attack

him, and the enemy, with stubborn desperation, was throwing every available force on the rear and flank of the Union army. The hot southern climate, malaria, and inadequate supplies, surrounded with great difficulties the alleviation of the sufferings of those sick and wounded; and the medical officers, as well, suffered extremely from fatigue and the same depressing influences of exposure and climate. " The services rendered by the surgeons engaged with the army in the several fights in the rear of Vicksburg will probably never be recorded, for they are in the shadow of the grand capitulation. But the toilsome march, the exhausting care of sick and wounded under an almost tropical sun, was endured by them cheerfully, in the consciousness of deserving well of their country and profession." He was present also at the bombardment of Vicksburg, and from there returned with the wounded to Indiana, where he resumed his ordinary duties. September 4th, 1863, by order of General Burnside, at the request of Medical Director Carpenter, he was placed in command of the Madison United States Army Government Hospital, at Madison, Indiana. This institution was then in an incipient state of erection, and by him was completely established and organized. About seventy buildings were erected *en echelon*, and 2,095 beds were officially reported. The enlarged accommodations, during the latter part of its existence, increased it to 3,000 beds. The highest number of patients was 2,760, principally from the battle-fields of Georgia and Tennessee. The whole number of different patients was 7,300; the mortality was 120, being 1.66 per cent.; the average length of time each patient was in the hospital was twelve weeks. After serving a year and a half in this institution he resigned, January 13th, 1865, and was relieved from duty February 4th, 1865. Brevet Brigadier-General C. S. Wood, Assistant Surgeon-General United States Army, thus refers to the management of the hospital in a letter addressed to him: "While you were in charge of the Madison General Hospital, a very large establishment, your various administrative and professional duties were performed with efficiency and to the entire satisfaction of this office."

ARD, JOHN, Physician, late of Newark, was born in Orange, New Jersey, April 26th, 1774, and studied medicine with Dr. Condit, also of Orange. He afterward removed to Bloomfield, and thence to Newark, where he resided until his decease.

In 1830 his office was at the corner of New and Broad streets; later he moved to Orange street, and subsequently built the house adjoining the residence of Hon. Marcus L. Ward, there remaining till 1836. He was eminent as an obstetrician, "although he never attended but one hundred and fifty cases per annum," " had great powers of endurance, was very kind and pleasant in his manners, and attentive to his business; and was an eminently religious man." He was a contemporary of Dr. Hayes, and was succeeded in his practice by his brother-in-law, Dr. J. B. Jackson. The following well-known medical gentlemen may claim him with justifiable pride as their common ancestor: Drs. Eleazar Ward, John F. Ward, Edward Ward, George Ward, Augustine Ward, Monroe Ward, and J. R. Ward. Dr. Samuel L. Ward, of Belleville, belongs to a collateral branch. He died June 24th, 1836, aged sixty-two years.

——◆◦◆——

OWLER, HON. SAMUEL, M. D., Physician, Manufacturer, Member of the New Jersey Legislature and of the Twenty-fourth and Twenty-fifth Congresses, late of Franklin, was born, October 30th, 1779, at the family homestead, built by his father, near Newburgh, Orange county, New York, and which is still standing, a pleasant and well-preserved edifice. He came of English ancestry. Joseph Fowler is mentioned as a first settler near Mispat Cills, Long Island, New York, as early as 1665. John Fowler, the father of Samuel, and sixth in descent from Joseph, resided at Newburgh, and married his cousin, Glorianna Fowler, the daughter of his uncle, Samuel Fowler. The subject of this sketch received a thorough academic education at the Montgomery Academy, and his medical education under the instruction of Dr. David Fowler, of Newburgh, and attended the lectures of the Pennsylvania Medical College, at Philadelphia, an institution which included at that time Drs. Rush and Physic in its faculty. After completing his medical studies and lectures, he removed to Hamburgh, Sussex county, New Jersey, and was licensed to the practice of medicine in that State on the 17th day of March, 1800, he being then a little over twenty-one years of age. In 1808 he married Ann Breckenridge Thompson, the daughter of Colonel Mark Thompson, of Changewater, New Jersey, one of the representatives in Congress from this State during the administration of Washington. After pursuing the practice of his profession at Hamburgh for a few years, he removed to Franklin, a small village, about three miles distant, situate in the valley of the Wallkill, and there his first wife died, leaving one child, a daughter, the wife of Moses Bigelow, of Newark. In 1816 he married his second wife, Rebecca Wood Platt Ogden, the daughter of Robert Ogden, Esq., formerly of Elizabethtown, but at this time of Sparta, Sussex county, New Jersey, to which place he had removed in 1786. The children of this marriage were four sons and three daughters, viz.: Samuel, Mary Estelle, Henry Ogden, Robert Ogden, John, Rebecca Ogden and Clarinda. He died at Franklin, of heart disease, on February 20th, 1844, aged sixty-five years. An interesting account of the estimation in which he was held as a physician is given by Dr. Thomas Ryerson, in his Report to the Medical Society of New Jersey at their centennial meeting, held at New Brunswick, 1866. Dr. Ryer-

son, in speaking of the early physicians of Sussex county, says: "The leading mind was Dr. Fowler; he came into the county a few years prior to its division, and soon compelled all its physicians either to take license or retire. Into his hands speedily passed the consultation business, and his opinion may therefore be taken as a fair indication of the scientific status of the profession at that time." A very able practitioner of the present day, who was contemporaneous with the last years of Dr. Fowler, says of him: "He was by far the best naturally endowed practitioner I ever knew." Of acute perception, vivid imagination, and yet of judicial mind and an original thinker, his native talents placed him far in advance of his day, when Cullen and his disciple, Gregory, shaped the theory and practice of the country. He was familiar with Brown and Davison, as with Cullen and other writers of his time. There are indeed very few practitioners of experience, though of defective education, who fail to acquire a set of principles which they act upon if they cannot express. But it is equally true that some "remain mere empirics in the midst of the rubbish with which reading and observation have furnished them." But Dr. Fowler was neither; to use Bacon's simile, "He was neither an ant nor a spider;" neither a collector of others' ideas nor a weaver of his own fancies, but a bee, who, by proper mingling and analyzing, elaborated and utilized the various products of his industrious observation. He was fond of saying that "The whole art of medicine consisted in knowing when to stimulate and when to depiete; an aphorism that requires but slight modification to be level with the present knowledge." The District Medical Society for the County of Sussex was formed in 1829 by him and several others. In person he was large and tall, of dignified and agreeable presence, courteous and affable in his manners. His head and physiognomy indicated native strength of character and mental activity. He was strictly temperate, and exemplary in all his habits; an early riser, and of untiring industry, and endeavored to devote all his leisure moments to the attainment of useful knowledge. He was for many years owner of the iron works at Franklin Furnace, which in their various branches he conducted, while at the same time attending to the arduous duties of his profession; his regular medical practice being more extensive perhaps than that of any country physician in the State, including, besides his own county of Sussex, the neighboring ones of Passaic, Morris and Warren, and extending even into the adjoining county of Pike, in Pennsylvania, and Orange, in New York. He also found time to take an active and leading part in national and State politics, representing his county in the upper branch of the State Legislature, and afterwards his State in the Twenty-fourth and Twenty-fifth Congresses during the administration of General Jackson, of whom he was a warm supporter, and one of the earliest friends in New Jersey. As a mineralogist and geologist he is estimated by men of science as among the first in the country. Dr. Charles T. Jackson, the discoverer of the somnific powers of ether, in speaking of him in connection with four other mineralogists of equal eminence, says: " They were at the head of their profession, and it will be long before we look upon their like again." It is evidence of the estimation in which he was held in these branches that he was made a member of many of the leading scientific societies of his day, among which were the Geological Society of the State of Pennsylvania, and the New York Lyceum of Natural History; an honorary member of the Literary and Philosophical Society of the State of New Jersey; a corresponding member of the Academy of Natural Sciences of Philadelphia, etc. He was also an honorary member of the Scientific Society of London and Dublin, and of other European scientific societies. He was an intimate friend and correspondent of Thomas Nuttall, the well-known English naturalist, at one time, while in this country, Professor of Natural History at Harvard University; a correspondent and friend of Baron Charles Leaderer, minister from Austria to this country during the third decade of the present century; of John Torry, Professor of Chemistry at West Point Military Academy from 1824 to 1827, afterward Professor of Chemistry and Botany in the College of Physicians and Surgeons of New York, and, later, Professor of Chemistry at Princeton College; of Dr. Troost, State Geologist of Tennessee; of Adam Seybert, William Mead, John Holbrook, George Carpenter, a correspondent to the *American Journal of Science and Art*, and Professor Keating, of Philadelphia. Among his occasional correspondents were Professor Benjamin Sylaman, Professor Berzelius, of Stockholm, Sweden; Professor Vannuxen, of the South Carolina College; John Finch, M. C. C.; Professor Griscom, Frederic Cozzens, Professor Benedict, of New York, and Dr. J. N. Phillips. The rare mineral known as "Fowlerite," first discovered by him at Franklin and brought to public notice, was named in his honor by his brother mineralogists. Early in life he became interested in the valuable mines and mineral localities of the region in which he resided, and for many years made efforts to bring them to the notice of the scientific world. By his extensive correspondence with the naturalists and generous distribution of minerals he induced men of science from all parts of the country to visit the place. It was soon discovered that in this sequestered region the rarest and most valuable American minerals were to be found, many of them peculiar to these localities and found nowhere else in this country or in Europe, and applications from many quarters were made to him to make a business of the exchange of minerals. As indicating the modesty of his character, as well as the disinterestedness with which he pursued his researches, to one who thus applied he answered, " My object is the promotion of science, and not to make a trade of the business, and when gentlemen of science have applied to me for minerals I have furnished what they requested from the locality, and received in return such specimens as they thought proper to give me." In 1825

he published in *Silliman's American Journal of Science*, vol. ix., "An Account of some New and Extraordinary Minerals Discovered in Warwick, Orange county, New York." In 1832, in same journal, vol. xxi.: "An Account of the Sapphire and other Minerals in Newton township, Sussex county, New Jersey." He also contributed to " Gordon's Gazetteer and History of New Jersey " an article on the " Franklinite, Red Oxide of Zinc, and other Minerals found in the valley lying at the foot of the Hamburgh and Franklin mountains; " and also a notice of the geology and mineralogy of the same region for " Cleavland's Mineralogy," new edition. He is supposed to have given the name of " Franklinite " to the ore of iron now so extensively known by that name, the great value of which he foresaw, although no means were discovered during his lifetime of working it with success. He made it known to mineralogists by sending specimens to all parts of this country, and to many eminent naturalists in Europe; among others to Berzelius, of Stockholm, and Professor Thompson, of Glasgow, by whom it was analyzed, and awakened an interest in it, which has since resulted in its successful development and manufacture. The extensive zinc mines of Sussex, now worked with great profit and affording the only red oxide of zinc known in the world, were at this time owned by him, but were disposed of before his death. In regard to his connection with these mines, A. C. Farrington, geologist and mining engineer, says, in his " Report of the New Jersey Zinc Company," published in 1852: " The late Dr. Fowler, about thirty-five years since, became the owner of these mines, and, to scientific attainments uniting practical business talents of the highest order, appears to have been really the first one to appreciate their true value. He made several efforts to have them worked, and offered liberal inducements to others to join him in the enterprise. But the untried nature of the ore, and the difficulties in obtaining competent operatives, caused a failure of his plans, without lessening in his mind the value of the ore and the ultimate success that would be likely to attend future attempts to work it. While he was a member of the House of Representatives of the United States Congress, a law was passed directing the Secretary of the Treasury to cause a standard set of weights and measures to be prepared for the use of the government in the different custom houses. F. R. Hasler, LL.D., then Superintendent of the Coast Survey, was intrusted by the secretary with the execution of this important duty, and Dr. Fowler succeeded in having New Jersey red oxide of zinc reduced to alloy with copper to form the brass used for these standards, mining and transporting many tons of the ore from his mines at Franklin to Washington City." His remains are interred in the valley of Hardyston, which near half a century before his death he sought as a youthful stranger, with no fortune but that which he carried in his own brave heart— a will to use with industry and faith the talents which Providence had given him.

OWLER, COLONEL SAMUEL, Franklin, New Jersey, eldest son of the celebrated scientist, Dr. Samuel Fowler, of Franklin, New Jersey, was born, March 25th, 1818, at Ogdensburg, at the homestead of his grandfather, Robert Ogden. His mother, Rebecca Ogden, was a lineal descendant of the Sir John Ogden knighted by Charles II. for services rendered in assisting Charles I. to escape after the battle of Worcester. He received an ample preparatory education, and subsequently, having determined.upon law as his profession, entered as a student the office of the late Governor Haines. In 1844 he was admitted to practise at the New Jersey bar. Two years later he married Henrietta ·L., daughter of D. M.,Brodhead, Esq., formerly of Philadelphia, and shortly after his marriage took up his residence at Port Jervis. Here he built a fine mansion, surrounded by handsomely laid-out grounds, on the bank of the Neversink river, and in honor of his wife he called the domain Glen-nette. Through his means and influence the village of Port Jervis was rapidly developed into a thriving town, and his eminent public services in this respect made him the most prominent man of the locality. In politics he was a recognized leader, and the Democratic party, of which he was an earnest member, was a considerable gainer by his counsels and active exertions in its behalf. He was for a time Chairman of the New York Democratic State Committee. He was also nominated to represent the counties of Sullivan and Orange in Congress, but was defeated by a small majority. In 1855 he left New York and returned to his native State, where he continued to reside until his death. Sussex county, New Jersey, is celebrated for its great mineral wealth, and more particularly for its Franklinite, a very rare mineral, composed of the red oxide of zinc and iron, and found nowhere else in the world. Colonel Fowler owned several valuable mineral claims at Sterling Hill, and at Franklin, a small village on the banks of the Wallkil river, where he resided on his farm with his family. The State is largely indebted to him for the development of its ores, in which he invested both labor and capital. *The Newton Herald and Democrat*, of October 21st, 1869, says: "All remember Colonel Samuel Fowler's magnificent zinc boulder of 5,000 pounds which he contributed to the World's Fair Exposition at London some fifteen years since, which so astonished the savans of Europe. . . . . At that fair Sussex minerals won three prizes—zinc, iron and paints." He was the inventor of the zinc paint from which so many fortunes have been made, and which is so celebrated not only in our own but in foreign countries. The first idea of its manufacture he relates as follows: "At a certain time a chimney connected with the furnace at Franklin was found deficient in draught. This was attempted to be remedied by fixing a bottomless barrel to the top of the chimney; through this barrel many volatilized ingredients from the contents of the furnace passed, forming incrustations on the inside of the barrel. When the barrel, after months, per-

haps after years, was taken down, I investigated the deposit and scraped off with my jack-knife the first zinc-white of the kind ever known." In 1862, when the second levy of New Jersey volunteers was called for, he was most zealous in his efforts to secure a prompt response to the call, and mainly to him was due the enrolment and organization, effected within thirty days, of the 15th New Jersey Regiment; and he was scarcely less active in assisting to raise the 1st New Jersey Cavalry. Of the 15th he was commissioned Colonel, July 10th, and a few weeks later his command was doing good service in the field. While in the army he was twice prostrated by severe attacks of illness, and in March, 1863, his health quite broken down, he reluctantly resigned his commission. He returned to Franklin, where he gradually recovered, but aware that he was physically unfitted for army life he did not again enter the service. John Y. Foster, in his "New Jersey in the Rebellion," says of him, speaking of the receipt of the order for his regiment to march: "But one thing was universally regretted, and that was the inability of Colonel Fowler, the chivalrous commander, who was dangerously ill with typhoid fever, to accompany the regiment. His ability and energy had been manifested in recruiting and rapidly preparing for the field an unusually fine body of men, but his high ambition to lead them into actual combat was never gratified, and he never after assumed command." During the remaining two years of his life his time and means were devoted to strengthening the government in the rear, and so giving moral support to the men who were fighting for the government in the advance. Before and during the war he took a prominent part in every political campaign. Possessing remarkable eloquence as a speaker, his services on the stump were in constant demand. After his return from the army his friends were desirous of nominating him for State Senator, but he declined being a candidate, although his chances of success were excellent. He accepted a seat in the Eighty-ninth Legislature. He had been ill about ten days before leaving his home, and as there was a tie in the Assembly, his duty to his constituents and the Democratic party, and the pressure from his political friends, urged him on. He arrived in time to be present at the opening, took the oath as a member, voted once and returned to his hotel. The intense cold and fatigue of the journey increased the disease under which he was laboring, pleura-pneumonia, and from which he died on the following Saturday, January 14th, 1865, in the forty-seventh year of his age, and a martyr to his party. Of his character and life one of his most bitter political antagonists wrote: "He was a man of superior abilities and the.most determined will and energy. Open and fearless in disposition, he never disguised his sentiments, nor resorted to dissimulation. He went in before us, year after year, a leading man in all enterprises and movements which his judgment approved, and always remarkable for his power over his fellow-men. Had he steadily directed his energies to any particular object, no matter how eminent, his success would have been sure. Able as he was generally considered, the popular estimate of his intellect and acquirements was much below their true value. We knew him well, and though constantly opposed to him in politics, always respected and honored him as a generous antagonist."

OWLER, LIEUTENANT JOHN, was born in Sussex county, New Jersey, on the 26th day of January, 1825. He was the son of the late Dr. Samuel Fowler, whose sketch appears above, and Rebecca Ogden, who was a daughter of Robert Ogden, and granddaughter of Dr. Zopher Platt, of Huntington, Long Island. John Fowler devoted some time to the study of medicine, but becoming convinced that he had no taste for professional life, gave it up, engaging in the lumber business and farming. In 1850 he was in California, carried away, like many others, with the gold fever excitement, and fascinated with mining life; in 1855 in the lumber business in Sullivan county, New York, and from that time until the rebellion broke out he was settled on his farm in Sussex county, New Jersey. The summer of 1861 proved the sincerity of his patriotism. Fully roused to the danger which threatened his beloved country, his sympathies met with a quick response to that thrilling cry: "To arms!" He rode night and day to secure recruits for the 1st New Jersey Cavalry (16th Regiment), and the assistance which he rendered his brother, Colonel Samuel Fowler, in raising four companies of that regiment, two from Sussex and two from Warren, Morris and Passaic counties, was most efficient. In August, 1861, he was appointed Second Lieutenant of Company K, 1st New Jersey Cavalry, and on the 4th day of November, 1861, accepted the position of Regimental Quartermaster in that regiment. His duties were very arduous; to purchase arms, clothing and supplies for 1,200 men was no easy task, and his time was constantly occupied from daylight until midnight. He writes from Camp Stanton, January 27th, 1862: "I have been almost constantly in the saddle, and had but little rest at night since yesterday morning a week." The regiment was engaged in the fall in drilling their men and preparing them for active service. The officers felt keenly the inefficiency of their commander; arrests and courts-martial were the order of the day, and insubordination reigned. When the discontent of the officers and men was at its height, and the colonel was threatened with arrest, Colonel Samuel Fowler was suggested as the commander of the regiment, which appointment was favored by the public press. This report soon reached the camp, and from that time every one by the name of Fowler was in disgrace. Lieutenant Fowler, writing from the camp, says: "Things possible and impossible are expected of me; an order given one moment is contradicted the next, and everything that goes wrong is

laid to Quartermaster Fowler." On February 10th, 1862, he resigned his position. Soon after he and Captain John P. Fowler were ordered before the Board of Examiners in Washington, without warning or time for preparation. The board sent in an unfavorable report of their examination, and they were mustered out of the regiment without ceremony. No opportunity was given Lieutenant Fowler to defend himself from the imputation of inefficiency, and this unjust act was censured by all the officers and men in the regiment. Sir Percy Wyndham took command on the 21st day of February, 1862. Lieutenant Fowler was urged by Colonel Wyndham and all the officers of the regiment to make an effort towards reinstatement, but he preferred to wait for another appointment. The position of Regimental Quartermaster was again offered him by Colonel Wyndham and declined. In July, 1862, he enlisted in the 15th Regiment New Jersey Volunteers, Colonel Samuel Fowler commanding. The 15th was one of the five regiments called for in July. Its organization was first perfeeted without bounties, by Colonel Fowler, in the counties of Sussex, Warren, Somerset and Hunterdon, within thirty days from the date of his commission. While stationed near Washington the men were employed on the defences of the city, Fort Kearny being constructed entirely by their labor. When the regiment moved across the Potomac, October 31st, 1862, Lieutenant Fowler took command of the Brigade Ambulance Corps. In December, 1862, the 15th was under fire for the first time at the battle of Fredericksburg; this took place on the 13th, and among the killed was Sergeant-Major John P. Fowler, who fell in action. He was struck in the leg by a ball, and bled to death in a few minutes. His name had just been proposed for a commission. Lieutenant Fowler retained command of the Brigade Ambulance Corps until April 15th, 1862, when, anticipating the movement of the army, he returned to his regiment as First Lieutenant of Company C. The battle of Salem Heights took place on the 3d day of May, in a pine woods, about three miles from Fredericksburg, and during this battle the carnage in the 15th Regiment was greater than at any other time during the war, the command losing in killed, wounded and missing 150 men. Among the killed was Lieutenant John Fowler. He was in command of his company, and while endeavoring to rally his men was struck in the left side with a ball, and it is supposed was instantly killed. Immediately after his fall the enemy advanced and took possession of the field, and our troops were obliged to retreat. Every effort was made to secure Lieutenant Fowler's remains, but in vain. His grave "knoweth no man, only the All-seeing One." May 15th, 1863, a comrade writes of him: "The untimely death of Lieutenant John Fowler has cast a gloom over the whole regiment. Advised to go to the rear, as he was suffering very much from a lame shoulder: 'No!' he said, 'I will stick to my men.'" The same comrade says: "I saw Lieutenant Fowler; he was cheering on his men; he was seen to pick up a rifle and shoot five or six times. He was struck in the left side, near the heart, and fell to the ground dead." A brother officer writes: " Of all we lost that terrible day no one was more sincerely mourned than Lieutenant Fowler. In battle he was cool, brave and collected. He fell with his face to the foe, while cheering on his company and discharging his duty manfully. His men loved him as they would a brother, and would have risked their lives at any time for his sake. His kindness to the sick was one of the many characteristics which endeared us to him." His generous and sympathetic nature, ever ready to lend a helping hand to a brother in distress, combined with great gentleness of disposition, endeared him not only to his comrades but made him the favorite of the home circle.

TICKNEY, CHARLES W., Physician and Surgeon, was born near Milford, Pike county, Pennsylvania, January 4th, 1833, the son of Benjamin Stickney. He studied medicine under the preceptorship of Dr. William Wetherill, at Lambertville, Hunterdon county, New Jersey, and graduated at the University of Pennsylvania in the spring of 1858. He then entered immediately upon the active practice of his profession at Pompton Plains, New Jersey. August 3d, 1863, he joined the United States service as Assistant Surgeon of the 33d Regiment New Jersey Volunteers, to serve three years. After the organization of this body it was assigned to the Army of the West, under the command of Major-General Sherman, and he participated therefore in the succession of battles commencing at Chattanooga, Tennessee, May 1st, 1864, and ending in the fall of Atlanta, Georgia, in September. On the 27th of this month, by order of Major-General Geary, he was ordered for duty at the 2d Division, 20th Corps Hospital, and there remained through the campaign of General Sherman's march to the sea, which was consummated by the taking of Savannah, December 21st, 1864. January 27th, 1865, he left the city of Savannah with his regiment, then connected with the left wing of the army, under command of Major-General Slocum, and was with the main army until it arrived at the Savannah river, when, by special orders, he was directed to take charge of the sick and wounded men belonging to the left wing of the Army of Georgia, and report the same to Savannah. There were then thirty cases of small-pox, in all stages, which were under his special care, and in order to separate them from the main body of sufferers, he was obliged to seize a schooner lying in the river loaded with sutler stores, and to place those cases on board. The result of his treatment exhibits the undesirableness of the old manner of treatment by the use of warm stimulating drinks and heated rooms. These men lay upon the deck of the schooner for want of room below, and were sheltered only by pieces of canvas. " This was on the 5th of February. On the 6th and 7th a severe rain-storm was experienced, to which the invalids were exposed. They were provided with no medicine except whiskey, which was occasionally given. The patients were permitted to drink plentifully of cold water. They did not reach Savannah until the evening of the 8th, when the patients were placed in the Small-Pox Hospital. Although subject to these severe exposures, they all recovered in a few days." After remaining in Savannah a few weeks, he joined his command at Goldsboro', North Carolina. The war having terminated, however, the regiment was ordered to Washington, by way of Richmond, Virginia, where it arrived May 19th, 1865. After a stay in the capital of several weeks, his regiment was sent to the State rendezvous, at Newark, New Jersey, where he was honorably discharged, July 17th, 1865.

ECK, GEORGE, Surgeon in the United States Navy, was commissioned an Assistant Surgeon in the navy February 25th, 1851; cruised in the West Indies and off the coast of Central America in the corvette " Cyane " from August, 1851, until September, 1854, crossing, meanwhile, the Isthmus at Panama and making the journey to the Pacific by way of Nicaragua and its lakes. He was on recruiting service at the naval rendezvous at New York from September, 1854, to October, 1855; was examined and found qualified for promotion March, 1856; cruised in the flagship " St. Lawrence " on the coast of Brazil, and the waters of the La Plata, from August, 1856, to May, 1859; was attached to the receiving-ship " North Carolina " from July, 1859, to March, 1860; and during the same month reported for duty aboard the " Seminole," at Pensacola, with which he cruised on the coast of Brazil and waters of the La Plata until the outbreak of the rebellion, when he returned to the United States. In May, 1861, he was promoted and commissioned as Surgeon; in the following July was engaged in the blockade off Charleston, and eventually joined the Potomac flotilla, which was frequently engaged in action with the Confederate batteries along the Virginia shore. In October he sailed with Admiral Dupont's fleet, and joined in the attack upon the rebel batteries at Port Royal. After its bombardment, he was in the Savannah blockading squadron; joined in the expedition against Fernandina, and after its capture was ordered to the North Atlantic Squadron, under Admiral Goldsborough, at Hampton Roads. He was an active participant at the attack upon the enemy's batteries at Sewall's Point, and upon Norfolk, Virginia; and was in the blockading service in the waters of the Chesapeake and tributaries until July, 1862, when the " Seminole " went out of commission. In the following August he was ordered upon the recruiting service in New

York; in September, 1864, was detached from the rendezvous and ordered to the iron-clad "Dictator," and joined the North Atlantic Squadron, under Admiral Porter, at Hampton Roads. In September, 1865, he was transferred from the "Dictator" to the "Vanderbilt," and sailed in company with the iron-clad "Monadnock" to the north Pacific; in July, 1866, was detached from the "Vanderbilt," at San Francisco; and finally returned to the Atlantic States by the overland route, arriving at his destination in the following September. On May 28th, 1871, he was commissioned Medical Inspector, with the relative rank of Commander.

———◦◦◦———

OBLE, HON. JABEZ G., Physician, President of the New Jersey State Medical Society, late of Newark, New Jersey, was born in that city, November 13th, 1799, and was the son of Luther Goble, who, with Robert Camfield and William Rankin, contributed mainly to lay the deep foundations of the manufacturing celebrity which Newark now enjoys. He was educated from early life for a professional career, and graduated at Hamilton College, in the class of 1819. He was a student of Dr. Isaac Pierson, of Orange, and an office-pupil of the late Dr. David Hosack, of New York; took his medical degree at the College of Physicians and Surgeons, in New York, when under the conduct of Hosack, Hammersley, Macnevin, Mitchell, Mott and Francis; and during his student course distinguished himself as a member of the Medico-Chirurgical Society. He was for many years the Resident Physician of Newark, New Jersey, an office which combined the duties of Health Physician, District Physician and Jail Physician; and in 1839 was President of the New Jersey State Medical Society. He eventually relinquished general practice, and devoted himself to the interests of the Mutual Life Insurance Company, of New York, whose affairs, within his sphere, he managed with fidelity and consummate skill. He was always warmly interested in the political measures and movements of his day; was a fluent, able speaker; served as President of the Common Council, and was an influential member of the State Legislature. In all works of Christian benevolence, also, he was an active mover and co-worker; was conspicuous in the colonization cause, which owed its success in New Jersey greatly to his exertions, and was a Deacon in the Third Presbyterian Church in Newark. In 1835 he visited Europe, and his correspondence, relating to his foreign travel and experience, evinces considerable literary ability. "He was a man universally known—was one of the institutions of Newark. He was tall, erect, scrupulously neat in his dress, punctual in his engagements, and gentlemanly in his manners. His *suaviter in modo* made him many friends. He was seldom abrupt, still always in haste, and his manner was singularly persuasive. When he died,

almost everybody felt that he had individually lost something. He could stand at the post-office and shake hands with more people than almost any other man in the city. Perhaps the two men most missed from Newark by the most people were Dr. Jabez G. Goble and Rev. James Scott, D. D. It seemed as if they could not be spared." He died suddenly, of inflammation of the bowels, and was visited in his last illness by his early friend, Dr. John W. Francis, of New York. The date of his demise is February 7th, 1859.

———◦◦◦———

LARK, ABRAHAM, Physician, Secretary of the State Medical Society of New Jersey, one of the founders of the District Medical Society of the County of Essex, late of Cinderhook, was born in Rahway, New Jersey, in October, 1767. His father was Abraham Clark, the New Jersey signer of the Declaration of Independence, who was the only son of Thomas Clark; the manner of his death is related as follows by the late Rev. Daniel A. Clark, father of the well-known J. Henry Clark, A. M., M. D., President and Historian of the Essex District Medical Society: "He was superintending the erection of a bridge in his meadow, in the autumn of 1794, when he felt the effects of a *coup de soleil*. He was aware of his danger, said that he should not live, stepped into his chaise and drove home, accompanied by the narrator, who remained with him till he died, about two hours afterward." He remembered vividly the frequent shifts of his family during the war, to avoid the pursuit of the enemy and the destruction of their homestead; and two of his older brothers were in the revolutionary service, and eventually became prisoners of war—one in the New York Sugar House, the other in the Jersey Prison-ship. After studying medicine under the preceptorship of Dr. John Griffiths, afterward his father-in-law, he graduated in the University of Pennsylvania, under Professors Shippen, Wistar and Rush; and subsequently was one of the original eleven who formed the District Medical Society of the County of Essex. He entered upon the active practice of his profession first in Elizabeth; thence removed to New York, where he continued for a time engaged limitedly in professional labors, and settled finally in Newark, New Jersey, there securing an extensive and remunerative practice. He was a delegate to the Continental Congress, in 1794. He was a skilful physician, and was, moreover, familiar with general literature, and fond of scientific inquiry. He acquired a large store of varied information in the course of his wide experience; possessed considerable conversational power, and was an instructive and amusing companion. In his profession he was industrious and ingenious, and was an excellent chemist and pharmacist. "He was a man of medium height, slender, of nervous manner, scrupulously neat in his attire, and always gentlemanly in his manners. He wore invariably a light-colored cloth frock coat (in that day dress coats were the rule), and a ruffled shirt. . . . . In his latter days, in Newark, he was invariably followed by a small black and white spaniel."—Dr. J. H. Clark. He practised medicine in Newark until 1830, when he retired from business and removed to ⟨ inderhook, where, at the home of his daughter and only child, he quietly rested from his labors until his decease. In 1824 he was one of the Secretaries of the State Medical Society. His former residence in Newark, New Jersey, still stands upon the southwest corner of the canal and Broad street, but is converted into offices and stores. The canal originally passed directly through his garden; and, in common with many Newarkers of his day, he believed that the success of the canal enterprise would greatly benefit the city; while it is said even that he gave the right of way. In an indirect line there are several medical descendants from him: J. Henry Clark, A. M., M. D., Dr. Ephraim Clark and his son, and Dr. James Guion Clark, the two latter of Staten Island. He died at ⟨ inderhook, in July, 1854.

ARRIS, PHILANDER A., M. D., Physician, of Dover, was born, January 29th, 1852, at Johnsonburg, Warren county, New Jersey, and is a son of Cummins O. Harris. His youth was passed on his father's farm and in attendance upon the district school, near his birthplace, known as the Quaker settlement. In November, 1867, he became a pupil in the seminary at Schooley's Mountain, New Jersey, then under the superintendence of Rev. L. J. Stoutenburgh, where he completed his education. In August, 1869, he entered the office of Dr. John Miller, of Andover, Sussex county, New Jersey, and commenced the study of medicine. In the autumn of 1870 he matriculated in the medical department of the University of Michigan, and attended the course of lectures delivered in that institution during that winter, a part of the session being devoted to practical analytical work in the chemical laboratory. He also was in attendance upon the lectures during the winter of 1871–72 in the same institution, and in March, 1872, passed his examination successfully for the degree of Doctor of Medicine; but not being at that time of the required age, the degree was subsequently conferred. He passed the summer of 1872 in study and in active practice under his preceptor, Dr. Miller. In the fall of the same year he went to New York city, where he attended the lectures delivered in the College of Physicians and Surgeons, and in February, 1873, took an ad eundem degree in that school. Returning to New Jersey he commenced the practice of medicine at Mine Hill, Morris county, in March, 1873, a thickly populated neighborhood, about three miles southwest of Dover. Shortly after establishing himself in Morris county

he opened a correspondence with various physicians in different parts of the county, having in view the reorganization of the Morris District Medical Society, which had ceased its existence in 1858. The leading physicians became interested in the scheme for its resuscitation, and the society was reorganized, December 29th, 1873; and was subsequently received in full connection with the State society, and has since become a strong and influential organization. In view of a more permanent location, Dr. Harris removed to Dover in September, 1875. A large proportion of the inhabitants of that town and its vicinity are engaged in iron mining, and the casualties incident to this occupation afforded him an opportunity for surgical study seldom met with in civil practice. Possessing a natural inventive genius, with a fondness for the practice of this branch of the profession, he has frequently had the opportunity of participating in some of the higher operations, and has proved eminently successful in their treatment. He was among the first in this country—as nearly as can be ascertained—in civil practice, to perform successfully excision of the upper extremity and head of the thigh-bone for compound comminuted fracture (vide "Transactions of the New Jersey Medical Society" for 1874). He is an earnest advocate for the use of plaster of paris in the treatment of certain fractures, and has devised an apparatus to facilitate the application of this article for dressing in cases of fracture of the thigh (vide Medical Record, September 18th, 1875). He has also originated a method of preventing the filling up of the inter-digital space, and the consequent reunion of the raw surfaces, after the operation for the cure of web-fingers; and practised the same successfully in October, 1875. The operation consisted of simply dissecting up a long, narrow, rectangular slip of skin from the dorsum of the hand, or one of the fingers, carrying it between the fingers which had been separated and uniting it to the skin on the palm of the hand by a suture. The opposing fingers were then kept well separated until the slip was found to be united sufficiently to maintain its place, when the suture was removed. Dr. Harris, although only at the threshold of manhood, and less than five years a practising physician, has taken a front rank in the profession, and bids fair to maintain it. He was married, November 15th, 1876, to Maggie Rowson, of Paterson, New Jersey.

OHNSON, HON. UZAL, Physician, late of Newark, New Jersey, was born in that city, April 17th, 1751. "He was a short, red-faced, well-fed man; had a stiff knee; and drove a low, small-wheeled carriage, made especially to suit his infirmity, upon the panels of which was emblazoned the motto, 'Non nunquam paratus.'" He was appointed to the Provisional Congress in 1775, but refused the appointment and entered the British service. He was then one among the English pensioners either until his decease, or till the war of 1812. At that time certain, if not all such, persons were required to remove into Canada, or to forfeit their pensions. It is said that he contracted to call every day upon the family of the late Colonel Samuel Ogden (whose house was demolished a few years ago, in order to straighten Broad street above the stone bridge), to learn whether any of the family were ill, for which service he received an annual stipend. He was abrupt in his manner and address; was more humorous than witty; and bore the reputation of being an eminently agreeable companion. He belonged to the class in which were found Drs. Budd, Morse, John Darcy, and others of that period. He lived in Broad street, near Commerce street, on the spot where was formerly the residence of Dr. L. A. Smith.

GDEN, UZAL, D. D., Clergyman and Author, was born in Newark, New Jersey, about 1744, and was ordained in the Church of England by the Lord Bishop of London, September 21st, 1773. In 1784 he published a Masonic sermon, and at a later date "The Reward of Iniquity." In 1788 he became rector of Trinity Church, Newark, New Jersey, and in 1795 published "The Antidote to Deism." In 1798, from the College of New Jersey, he received the degree of D. D. At an adjourned Convention of the Protestant Episcopal Church in the State of New Jersey, held at New Brunswick, August 15th and 16th, 1798, he was elected Bishop in the State of New Jersey, and the canonical testimonials were laid before the General Convention in Philadelphia, July 14th, 1799; and, after postponement until the 18th, were met with the following: "Whereas, doubts have arisen in the minds of some members of the convention, whether all the priests who voted in the election of the Rev. Uzal Ogden, D. D., to the office of a Bishop, in the State of New Jersey, were so qualified as to constitute them a majority of the resident and officiating priests in the said State, according to the meaning of the canon in this case made and provided: and, whereas, in a matter of so great importance to the interests of religion and the honor of our church, it is not only necessary that they who concur in recommending to an office so very sacred should have a firm conviction of the fitness of the person they recommend, but that they should also be perfectly satisfied with respect to the regularity of every step which had been taken in the business; Resolved, therefore, That in the opinion of the House of Deputies all proceedings respecting the consecration of the Rev. Uzal Ogden, D. D., ought to be suspended until a future convention in the State of New Jersey shall declare their sense of the subject." At a special Convention of New Jersey, October 16th, 1799, for the express purpose

of reconsidering and declaring their sense of the regularity of the election of Dr. Ogden to the episcopal office, after full and free discussion, three resolutions were adopted, declaring the election "regular in every respect." An "Address" was then signed, recapitulating the matter to be sent to the several standing committees in the different States, requesting their consent to the proposed consecration. This address was adopted by the following vote: Clergy, yeas two, nay one; laity, by congregations, yeas ten, nays three, and one divided. The matter did not rest after this action; for in the "Journals of the Conventions of New Jersey" appears the following: "At a special Convention in the State of New Jersey, held at Perth Amboy, December 19th, 1804—called 'for the purpose of taking into consideration and adopting such measures as may bring to a termination certain controversies existing between the Rev. Dr. Uzal Ogden, Rector of Trinity Church, in Newark, and the vestry and congregation of said church, which appears to be of such a nature as cannot be settled by themselves, and which threatens to destroy the peace and prosperity of the said church'—as soon as the convention was ready to proceed to business, the Rev. Dr. Ogden read 'a declaration that he withdrew himself from the Protestant Episcopal Church; but that he would still continue to discharge his duty as Rector of Trinity Church, in Newark, and as a minister of the Church of England, conformably to the constitution and charter of his church, and his letters of orders, and license to preach, under the hand and seal of the Rt. Rev. Father in God, Richard, late Lord Bishop of London; a copy of which declaration he handed to the president and instantly retired.'" In the afternoon the convention adopted the following: "It appearing to this convention that certain controversies are now existing between the Rev. Dr. Uzal Ogden, Rector of Trinity Church, at Newark, and the vestry and the congregation of said church, which have proceeded to such lengths as to preclude all hope of a favorable termination, it is resolved that this convention do earnestly recommend and advise the said Dr. Ogden to relinquish his title to the Rectorship of said church within thirty days from this date, and give notice thereof to the Chairman of the Standing Committee of this State: and we do also earnestly recommend and advise the congregation and vestry of said church, upon such his resignation, to allow and secure to Dr. Ogden the sum of $250 per annum during his life. And if Dr. Ogden refuse to comply with the terms above mentioned, that then authority is hereby given by this convention to the Standing Committee, with the aid and consent of a bishop, to proceed to suspend said Dr. Ogden from the exercise of any ministerial duties within this State." The deputation from Trinity Church, Newark, informed the convention that, in behalf of their church, they were willing to accede to the conditions. At the convention, held June 5th, 1805, the Standing Committee reported that "Dr. Ogden had refused to comply with the recommendations of this convention, and that with the aid and consent of Bishop Moore, of New York, they did unanimously resolve to suspend the said Rev. Dr. Ogden from the exercise of any ministerial duties within this State, and he was thereby suspended accordingly." On motion the following were agreed to: "Whereas, the Rev. Dr. Ogden has been suspended from the exercise of any ministerial duties within the State of New Jersey, and in consequence of that suspension Trinity Church, at Newark, is destitute of the stated services of the ministry; Resolved, that the wardens and vestry of the said church be authorized to invite, occasionally, any minister of our communion to officiate in their church; and every minister of the church in this State is permitted and requested to accept such invitation, during the pleasure of this convention; Resolved, further, that the Bishop of the Church in the State of New York be requested to assist the said church by occasional supplies. In the meantime, the Rev. Dr. Wharton, of Burlington, and the Rev. Mr. Jones, of Amboy, are particularly requested to officiate there on Sundays, the 16th and 23d of the present month, and as often afterwards as either of them conveniently can attend." Soon after Dr. Ogden became a Presbyterian, and died in Newark, New Jersey, November 4th, 1822.

HAYES, SAMUEL, Physician, late of Newark, New Jersey, was born in that city, in 1776, and graduated at Princeton, in the class of 1796. He was a student under the guidance of Dr. John B. Rodgers, father of the late Dr. I. Kearney Rodgers, from 1795 to 1799, when he was appointed apothecary of the New York Hospital. In November of the latter year Drs. John R. B. Rodgers, Wright Post, Richard A. Kissam and Valentine Seamen "testify to his diligence, assiduity, and competence to practise medicine, as well as his integrity, uprightness and virtue." From June to August, 1803, he was engaged in the drug business as one of the firm of Kurze & Hayes, a step taken after his return from India, whither he had made a voyage as Surgeon of the ship "Swan," in 1800. In 1804 he was associated with Dr. Cyrus Pierson, in the practice of medicine in Newark, till the death of his colleague, October 7th, 1806, dissolved the relations previously existing between them. Within a few years of his decease he removed from his house, where the Mechanics' Bank now stands, to the old homestead, near the residence of Cornelius Walsh, then remote from the town, where he passed the remnant of his days, and died July 30th, 1839. "He was a man of excessive modesty, and of acknowledged skill in the management of fevers. He was tall, somewhat bent, and had a small head; was a scholarly man, and very faithful to the interests of his patients. He was excessively sensitive, also, and unwilling to present a professional bill, although he never received over twenty-five cents a visit. He ever

maintained a high Christian character, and was universally esteemed." His son, Dr. James Hayes, graduated at Princeton, in the class of 1840, and took his medical degree in the College of Physicians and Surgeons, in the class of 1844.

MARTIN, JOSEPH W., Rahway, son of Joseph and Julia A. (Barney) Martin—his father a native of Rahway, his mother a native of New Haven, Connecticut—was born in New York, November 3d, 1838. His parents moving to Rahway while he was still an infant, his early education was received in that town, and he subsequently attended schools at Woodbridge and Port Colden, New Jersey; Bethlehem, Pennsylvania, and Ellington, Connecticut; finally entering Rutgers College, whence he graduated in 1855. In the year of his graduation from college he entered an importing house in New York city, and having a natural aptitude for business he achieved rapid and permanent mercantile success. In 1861, upon the first call for troops, he raised a battery of heavy artillery in Rahway—where, although doing business in New York, he had retained his residence —and with his command offered his services to Governor Olden. The quota of troops from New Jersey having been filled, his offer was declined, and he thereupon offered his battery to the Governor of New York, by whom it was promptly accepted. For similar reasons, it may be stated, the services of very many gallant Jerseymen were at this time lost to the State, the prompt filling of the quota preventing the governor from enrolling hundreds of men who, determined to have a part in putting down the rebellion, were compelled to enlist in Pennsylvania and New York regiments. Attached at first to the 9th New York Infantry, Captain Martin's battery served for a time with that organization; was subsequently made an independent force, and as the Sixth Horse Battery did good work during the whole of the remaining portion of the war, being the only volunteer horse battery in the service. His gallantry was most distinguished, and not only was he a brave soldier, but he was a singularly efficient officer, the discipline and *morale* of his command being unsurpassed in the army. On the close of the war he returned home and to mercantile pursuits, in which he is still engaged.

FREEMAN, JOSEPH ADDISON, Physician and Surgeon, late of Orange, was born in Paterson, New Jersey, June 25th, 1833, and was the son of A. H. Freeman, of Orange, New Jersey. At the completion of a preparatory course of studies he entered Princeton College, and graduated from that institution in 1852. His medical degree was received at the College of Physicians and Surgeons, in New

York, in 1856. He first settled at Liberty Corners, where he remained for about three years. At the expiration of that time he returned to Orange, and subsequently entered the army. In the memorable "Seven Days' Fight" he was an active participant, and in one of the numerous scattered engagements fell into the hands of the enemy. Upon his release he received a commission as Assistant Surgeon in the 13th Regiment, New Jersey Volunteers; and after the battle of Gettysburg took the place of Dr. Love, who resigned, and was commissioned as Assistant Surgeon in the Volunteer Corps. He was then assigned to hospital duty at Nashville, Tennessee, where he died, a martyr in the cause of the Union. "His death was due undoubtedly to the exposures of the service. Although but thirty years of age, his medical judgment was mature. When he died one of our best young men was sacrificed upon the altar of a preserved nationality." He died, on the scene of his heroic exertions and unselfish labors, December 29th, 1864.

ELSEY, HON. HENRY COOPER, Secretary of State of the State of New Jersey, was born in Sparta, Sussex county, New Jersey, in 1837. His father, John Ĉelsey, was an old resident of that place, and came from a family long associated with the county, some of its members being among the earliest settlers thereof. His mother belonged to the Van Ĉirk family. After receiving a sound elementary education at the public schools, he, at an early age, entered upon a mercantile career by becoming a clerk in a general store at Sparta. Here he gained an experience that enabled him subsequently to succeed his father as proprietor of a store at Huntsville, where he prosecuted business until 1858. In that year he removed to Newton and engaged in merchandising there, at the same time taking an active interest in public affairs. His political tendencies drew him into close affiliation with the Democratic party, and to promote its success his most earnest labors were always devoted. Very naturally these services met with recognition. In 1859 President Buchanan appointed him to the postmastership of Newton, then, as now, the most important post-office in Sussex county. Bringing into his official life the business ability, strict integrity, and uniform courtesy which had been marked characteristics of his previous career, he became a very popular officer. Still continuing his mercantile operations, he fulfilled the duties of this public position until the summer of 1861, when custom required that he should give way to the successful political party. During the same year he purchased the *New Jersey Herald*, the Democratic organ of Sussex county; also the *Sussex Democrat*, the organ of the Douglas Democrats, founded in 1858. These two journals he merged into one under the name of the former, and relinquishing all other business, he addressed himself unreservedly to journalism. For eight years he conducted the *Herald* with conspicuous ability and success, increasing its value and widening its influence, which, as the paper was always one of the ablest Democratic sheets in the State, had always been extensive. In 1869 he sold the property to an association of leading Democrats, he himself, and Mr. Thomas G. Bunnell, who has since been its editor, being members of the association. During the spirited canvass of 1868 the Democratic cause was admirably advocated by the *Herald*, and its advocacy contributed materially to the success won by the party in that year. Soon after the inauguration of Governor Randolph, the then Secretary of State, Hon. II. N. Congar, resigned, and in July, 1870, Mr. Ĉelsey appointed by the governor to fill the unexpired term. So well were his duties in this new and responsible position performed that, on the assembling of the Legislature in 1871, he was nominated by the governor and confirmed by the Senate, notwithstanding that body was Republican, to fill the office for the full term of five years. On the expiration of this term, in 1876, he was appointed by Governor Bedle for a second term of like duration, and again confirmed by a Republican Senate. He is therefore still holding the position, his tenure of which will not expire until 1881. The duties, at once arduous and delicate, have been discharged by him in a manner satisfactory to fair-minded men of all shades of political faith, and he enjoys the high esteem of the community at large. Notwithstanding his heavy official responsibilities and cares he finds time for indulging a strongly developed taste for agriculture as the owner and manager of an extensive farm near Newton. In 1872, his health suffering from close and continuous application to public and his individual affairs, his physicians recommended the relaxation of foreign travel, and in accordance with their advice he visited Europe, spending several months in Italy. Mr. Ĉelsey is *ex officio* a Commissioner of Insurance, and in this capacity has rendered the public valuable service in ferreting out and bringing to account a number of worthless concerns that had by false showings been covering their worthless condition and preying on the public. His investigations will, it is believed, effectually purify the insurance business in the State. He was married in 1861 to a daughter of Judge John Townsend, of Newton, New Jersey.

ICHOLS, JAMES, Physician, late of Newark, New Jersey, was born in that city, January 30th, 1815, and was a classmate of Dr. J. Henry Clark, in the College of Physicians and Surgeons of New York, and graduated from that institution in the class of 1839. "He was studious, reticent, nervous, quick of apprehension, and, while he could be, diligent in his business. He lived long enough to gain, to a high degree, the confidence of the people, and at the time of his death was President of the Essex District Medical Society. He was tall and spare, and somewhat stooped; had a very serious, long, pale, thin face ; and, while regarded as in health, had an invalid appearance." He was for some time the business partner of Drs. John S. Darcy and Whitfield Nichols. He married Cornelia Baldwin, daughter of J. Baldwin, of Elizabeth, New Jersey, by whom he had one child, a daughter, who died in early youth, probably of inherited pulmonary disease. He died in Newark, New Jersey, January 17th, 1849, at the age of thirty-four years.

ENDRICKSON, CHARLES ELVIN, Lawyer, of Mount Holly, son of Jacob and Mary M. Hendrickson, was born in the village of New Egypt, Ocean county, New Jersey, January 8th, 1843. He prepared for college at an academy in his native place, under the direction successively of P. S. Smith and George D. Horner, A. M. ; and in September, 1860, entered the sophomore class at Union College, Schenectady, New York, where, however, he remained but one term, preferring, chiefly from motives of State pride, to enrol himself in the old historic College of New Jersey, from which he graduated at the age of twenty. The intellectual proficiency and love of State which thus marked his collegiate course have been exemplified in all his subsequent life. He is still one of the truest sons of New Jersey, and at the same time one of the brightest. On leaving college he took charge of a classical academy at Pemberton, New Jersey, which he conducted with distinguished credit for one year, when he began the study of law in the office of the Hon. A. Browning, of Camden, continuing there until May, 1865, and finishing his legal studies under the Hon. Garrit S. Cannon, of Bordentown. He was admitted to the bar of New Jersey at the November term of the Supreme Court in 1866, displaying in his professional novitiate the same rapid proficiency that had characterized his academical career. Soon after his admission to the bar he settled at Mount Holly, New Jersey, and in March, 1870, was appointed, by Governor Randolph, Prosecutor of Pleas, and in March, 1875, reappointed by Governor Bedle—appointments which attest at once his ability as a lawyer and his fidelity as an officer. In 1868 he was elected to the New Jersey Assembly from the Third District of Burlington county, and proved to be not less proficient and efficient as a legislator than he had proved as a lawyer and a scholar, proving also that he was the same devoted lover and admirer of his native State that he was when he left the halls of Union that he might cleave unto Princeton. The boy was father of the man. State pride is indeed an excellent stock on which to engraft all the other civic virtues, and in his case the fruitage has been rich and abundant. He was admitted in 1869 as counsellor-at-law. His practice, now large, is steadily increasing, as is his popularity with the people. Among the young men of New Jersey he stands in the front rank. He already has achieved much, and his future, both political and professional, is full of high promise. Nor is this promise the less high or full that he is a zealous Christian, alike in practice and profession, being a prominent member of the Methodist Episcopal Church, by the New Jersey Annual Conference of which he was elected a lay delegate to the General Conference that met at Baltimore in May, 1876, the bishops at this conference appointing him one of the Committee of Fifteen to revise the hymn-book of the church. On this work of revision, for which his taste and scholarly attainments eminently qualify him, he is now engaged in the intervals left him by the more pressing engagements of his profession. His interest in educational questions, as in all others affecting the welfare of New Jersey, is deep and active, manifesting itself in constant endeavors to enlarge the facilities and elevate the standard of education in the State, as well as in the generous support of established institutions. He is at this time President of the Board of Trustees of Pennington Seminary, at Pennington, New Jersey.

OWELL, SAMUEL BEDELL, M. D., Physician and Scientist, was born in Camden, New Jersey, September 20th, 1834. His father, Richard W. Howell, was widely esteemed as a sound lawyer, a man of high moral worth and a Christian gentleman ; in various offices of trust, held for many years, he manifested distinguished usefulness as a citizen of the town and the State. The family on the father's side originally came from Wales, settled on the Delaware, and for two or three generations has held the estate between Red Bank and Gloucester. One of his uncles, after whom he is named, belonged to the medical profession, and occupied the chair of Anatomy and Physiology in the Princeton College, New Jersey, until his death. Another uncle, Joshua Howell, was a lawyer in good standing in the western part of Pennsylvania ; on the outbreak of the war he raised a regiment, was afterwards made a Brigadier-General of Volunteers, and was killed before Petersburg, Virginia. His brother went out with the New Jersey volunteers, and was killed at the battle of Fair Oaks, when General McClellan's army retreated to Harrison's Landing. His mother is a direct descendant of Samuel Carpenter, one of the original proprietors in Philadelphia with William Penn, and through her, in direct and collateral lineage, he is connected with a large circle of relatives embracing many names of worth and note. Having passed through the usual course of school training in his native town, and in the city of Philadelphia, he was prepared for college by Rev. Dr. Knighton, formerly tutor in Princeton. He early developed a strong taste for the natural sciences, studying them in all the works he could obtain, and in the fields and in the mountains ; he also showed some natural taste for drawing and painting. While preparing for college, his health began to fail, and he was sent off on a pedestrian tour through the New England States, spending a season camping and gunning through Maine and into Canada. Returning home with improved health, he resumed his studies, availing himself always of every opportunity for practical investigations in the laboratory of a neighboring chemist and mineralogist. In the contemplation of the evidences of the slow and silent working of the forces modifying the face of nature, he was guided by one who was a practical mineralogist and geologist, and enthusiastic lover of nature. Manifesting these tastes, it was natural that he should choose medicine for his life work. He matriculated in the medical department of the University of Pennsylvania, and though interrupted in his studies by uncertain health, he persevered, and graduated with honor in March, 1858. By the advice of his uncle, Dr. James Carpenter, he began practice in the Schuylkill mining region, where constant exercise in the mountain air conferred health and strength, permanently establishing his constitution. Appointed, soon after, physician and surgeon to the mining towns of the Hicksober collieries, an extensive field of usefulness opened before him. During his residence in this region he earnestly pursued his studies in practical geology. In 1865 he removed to Philadelphia, and began practice in that larger sphere, availing himself also of the peculiar local facilities for studying chemistry, mineralogy and geology. He had been a member of the Academy of Natural Sciences since 1855, and in 1868 he was elected its Secretary, an office he still holds. For some years he has manifested a strong interest in the welfare of the freedmen of the South and the colored men of the North, holding a liberal Christian culture to be the best means for elevating them to a comprehensive conception of their own interests and responsibilities. In 1868 he was appointed by the Board of Trustees of Lincoln University, Chester county, Pennsylvania, Professor of the Natural Sciences, the duty of forming and developing the department of science, including medicine, being intrusted to him. In this university, which possesses in real estate and invested funds over two hundred thousand dollars, some two hundred students are resident. His services to this admirable institution have been of a distinguished character. In September, 1868, he was elected to fill the Chair of Chemistry and Materia Medica, formerly held by Professor Henry Morton, and afterward by Professor Leeds, in the Philadelphia Dental College. In the preceding April he had been made a Fellow of the time-honored College of Physicians of Philadelphia, and in 1872 he was a delegate therefrom to the American National Medical Association. On December 4th, 1872, he was chosen to occupy the Chair of Mineralogy and Geology in the auxiliary department of the University of Pennsylvania, vacant by the resignation of Professor F. V. Hayden, United States Geologist. He was married, on April 13th, 1859, to the

daughter of the late Rev. William Neill, D. D., of Philadelphia, formerly President of the Dickinson College, Carlisle, Pennsylvania. He is a member and Ruling Elder in the Presbyterian Church.

ILLIAMS, HON. JOHN D., Physician, first President of the Essex District Medical Society, late of Orange, was born in that section of New Jersey, November 5th, 1765. He affords an important connecting link between the Halsteds and Burnets and Barnets, of the ante-revolutionary period; and studied medicine with Dr. Daniel Babbitt, in the office of Dr. John Condit, of Orange. At an early period he settled at Connecticut Farms, and must have been there during the latter years of Dr. Caleb Halsted, or have immediately succeeded him. He was a Magistrate under appointment of the elder Governor Pennington, whose sister he married; and was the first President of the Essex District Medical Society. He died at Orange, January 5th, 1826; and on the ensuing January 7th a special meeting of the society was called at South Orange, when its resolution paid a deserved tribute of respect to a senior and highly-esteemed member. He was buried in the old Orange burying-ground.

ICHOLS, WHITFIELD, Physician, Vice-President of the State Medical Society of New Jersey, late of Newark, New Jersey, was born there February 6th, 1807, and was the brother of Dr. James Nichols. He graduated at Princeton College in 1825, having entered the junior year in the class with Shippen, Ramsey, Rush, Hosack, and other distinguished men since deceased. He was a student of Dr. Samuel Hayes, and early gave evidence of high promise; and after taking his medical diploma in New York at a medical institution called "The Medical Faculty of Geneva College," whose professors were Hosack, Mott, Francis, Macnevin, Goodman, and subsequently Bushe, opened his office in Newark, and soon after entered into partnership with Dr. John S. Darcy. In 1836, on account of a lung affection, he was obliged to relinquish the practice of his profession and go to the West Indies; while, even from an earlier date to the close of his life, he struggled against the insidious disease which confined him to his chamber for five or six months prior to his decease. He was a man of scholarly attainments and upright principles; and on his accession to the Vice-Presidency of the State Medical Society, delivered an able address on the "Diseases Incident to Old Age," which elicited many glowing eulogiums from his brethren and the association. "He was consistent in his walk and conversation; candid and sincere; was broad in his judgments, and honorable and courteous in his intercourse with the profession and the public." He was also a Director in one of the largest and most important banking establishments in Newark, New Jersey, and his judgment on financial matters ever commanded the attention and respect of his colleagues. At his demise, the State Medical Society, and also the Essex District Medical Society, passed appropriate resolutions, while the latter organization attended his funeral in a body. His first wife was Mary Taylor, daughter of the late John Taylor; his second wife is still living. He, like his brother, died of consumption, December 9th, 1851, aged forty-four years.

ETHERILL, WILLIAM, M. D., of Lambertville, was born in Wrightstown, Bucks county, Pennsylvania, January 1st, 1819. His father, for whom he is named, was a minister of the Methodist Episcopal Church, a very devoted and greatly beloved man. William received his literary education at the Newtown Academy, then under the able direction of Mr. Parsons, and soon after leaving school began reading for his chosen profession, medicine, under the superintendence of Dr. C. W. Smith, of Wrightstown. With this preceptor he remained for four years, during which time he took two courses of lectures at the Jefferson Medical College, Philadelphia, from which he was graduated with the class of 1846. Among his classmates were Dr. R. T. Gill, of Poughkeepsie, New York, and Dr. Linderman, director of the United States Mint. Immediately after graduating, in the spring of 1846, he removed to Lambertville, New Jersey, and commenced practice. In this field of labor he has remained ever since, has built up a large practice, and won the esteem, not only of his professional brethren, but of the community at large. Jealous for the honor of his profession, and concerned for the safety of the public, he has always given earnest attention to the subject of regulating the practice of medicine, and was mainly instrumental in getting through the Legislature the present law regulating practice in the State. He was married in Bristol, Pennsylvania, to Rebecca S., eldest daughter of Captain Hawke, of Bristol, Bucks county, Pennsylvania.

RUMLEY, J. D., Physician and Surgeon, of Newark, was born in New Jersey, and had a peculiarly checkered career and experience as a medical officer in the service of the Union army during the rebellion. May 23d, 1863, at the solicitation of Lieutenant-Colonel A. N. Dougherty, he entered as a "contract surgeon," upon a single day's notice. He was first assigned to duty with the 7th Michigan Volunteers, in the brigade of which Colonel Dougherty

was chief surgeon. The period of his "contract" ending just before the "Seven Days' Fight," he remained at the request of his officers, and after the action at Savage Station, having remained to take care of the wounded, was taken prisoner by the enemy. After a detention of one month in Libby Prison, Richmond, he made another "contract," and at once entered upon duty. He went before the Board of Examiners, at Washington, and was accepted as Assistant Surgeon of Volunteers, but the Senate delaying his confirmation, he again entered by "contract," January 2d, 1863, and was assigned to hospital duty at St. Louis, Missouri. Upon receiving his commission he was ordered to Memphis, Tennessee, and there was placed in charge of the General Hospital. In January, 1864, he was ordered to close his hospital and proceed to Louisville, Kentucky, and to take the general superintendence of all the hospitals in that vicinity. At the expiration of two months he was assigned to duty as Chief Surgeon of the 1st Division of the 4th Army Corps, Department of the Cumberland, and remained with this body, filling the positions also of Medical Inspector and Medical Director, until the autumn of 1865. After the capture of Richmond, he was ordered with his army corps to Texas, where eventually it was disbanded. He remained, however, as Chief Surgeon of the Central District of the Department of Texas till mustered out, March 15th, 1866. While connected with the army "he did service in every rebel State except two, and in nearly all of the Northern States east of the Mississippi river."

AIL, HON. DAVID W., late of New Brunswick, New Jersey, was born near that place, September 8th, 1796. His progenitors, who are believed to have been Huguenots, migrated from Normandy to Wales, and from Wales to America; the will of Samuel Vail, his great-great-grandfather, who died at Westchester, New York, is dated June 19th, 1733. "He came to New Brunswick in early boyhood, and was a fine example of industry, prudence and piety." His father was a member of the Society of Friends, and his mother a Baptist; but he, being converted under the preaching of Mr. Huntington, united with the Presbyterian church under his care in the fall of 1817, being then in the twentieth year of his age. He was one of the most active and useful members of the community in which he lived; and the estimation in which he was held was evidenced in his being sent to the State Legislature in 1831 and 1832, his holding the office of Recorder for several years, and his election to the mayoralty in 1840. The same energy displayed in civic affairs he brought with him into the church; and he was made a Ruling Elder, October 2d, 1826, and a Trustee in 1831. "For sixteen years he discharged the functions of an elder with exemplary fidelity and zeal, and was ever ready

Eng'd by E.B. Hall & Sons 62 Fulton St. N.Y.

Joseph P. Bradley

ASSOC'ATE JUSTICE, SUPREME COURT OF THE UNITED STATES

college he was particularly distinguished for his proficiency in mathematics, and for many years after his graduation he prosecuted this branch of study merely as a relaxation from the labors of his profession. In early life he had intended entering the ministry, but shortly after leaving Rutgers—having, meanwhile, conducted an academical school at Millstone, Somerset county, New Jersey—he determined upon law as his profession, and in accordance with this determination began reading in the office of the late Archer Gifford, acting as Inspector of the Customs under that gentleman as Collector, and thus gaining his living while studying. In 1839 he was admitted to the New Jersey bar: but it may be said of him that he has been a law student all his life. This is of course to a certain extent true of all lawyers, but it is especially true of him, for his studies have been prosecuted far beyond the lines of his practice. He has thoroughly investigated the broad field of primitive and developed law as existing in the middle and lower ages; has traced the evolution and formulation of principles and of forms of practice from the earliest times to the present day; and, contemporaneously with these studies, he has exhaustively examined mediæval and modern history and literature. He is, unquestionably, one of the best read men of the present day, and that he has extended his studies over so broad a range is due to his exceptional habit of mind that enables him to rapidly grasp and memorize salient facts while passing over irrelevant and distracting details. His success as a barrister, as may be inferred from the foregoing, was immediate, and he rapidly rose to be one of the leaders of the New Jersey bar—a bar always distinguished for its erudition and practical ability. As a corporation lawyer he was particularly distinguished. For many years he was a Director in and counsel to the Camden & Amboy Railroad Company, and he was also counsel to that not less impor-

Circuit Court, and his service . . . . claimants under . . . . ment in the State court . . . Supreme Court so . . . . . mystery of the affair, so . . . . also appeared in the New Jersey . . . . Land case; the interior 1860 . . . . minister, hung for murdering his . . . . assassinated his friend . . . . won from him by the murdered . . . by . . . barrister, the Judge was successful . . . . the higher courts; he did not exceed before . . . In . . . . until called upon to discharge the high trust of deciding arbiter in the Hayes-Tilden Electoral Tribunal, he has taken no active part. Originally a Whig, he became upon the formation of the Republican party one of its most earnest members, but not one of its active workers. Twice only has he accepted nomination to office. In 1862 he was nominated to represent the Fifth Congressional district of New Jersey, but was defeated, by a somewhat large majority, by Nehemiah Perry, and in 1868 he headed the Grant and Colfax electoral ticket in his State. His elevation to the bench of the Supreme Court of the United States occurred in February, 1870. President Grant had previously nominated Attorney-General E. R. Hoar to the vacant seat, but this nomination had been adversely acted upon by the Senate on the ground that the nominee was not a resident of the Circuit—the Fifth Judicial Circuit, comprehending the districts of Georgia, northern and southern Florida, northern and southern Alabama, Mississippi, Louisiana, and eastern and western Texas—over which he would be called upon to preside. Mr. Bradley's name was put in nomination by the President on the 7th of February, and was received by the Senate with similar objections upon similar grounds. The

to encourage the heart and hold up the hands of his pastor. His decided attachment to the standards of the church made him keen to detect, and resolute to oppose, the insidious entrance of error ; and in the trying times of the Act and Testimony he stood firm as a rock." On the 16th of January, 1842, he died suddenly, of an affection of the heart, in the forty-sixth year of his age. Mr. Birch preached a sermon on the occasion, which made a deep impression, and the trustees solicited a copy for publication ; from motives of modesty, however, it was never put into their hands.

———◦✦◦———

RADLEY, JOSEPH P., Associate Justice United States Supreme Court, was born at Berne, near Albany, New York, March 14th, 1813. His early education was of a limited character, yet when sixteen years old he obtained a position as a school teacher, and so supported himself while preparing himself for college. In 1833 he entered the sophomore class at Rutgers, and in 1836 graduated with honors. While at college he was particularly distinguished for his proficiency in mathematics, and for many years after his graduation he prosecuted this branch of study merely as a relaxation from the labors of his profession. In early life he had intended entering the ministry, but shortly after leaving Rutgers—having, meanwhile, conducted an academical school at Millstone, Somerset county, New Jersey—he determined upon law as his profession, and in accordance with this determination began reading in the office of the late Archer Gifford, acting as Inspector of the Customs under that gentleman as Collector, and thus gaining his living while studying. In 1839 he was admitted to the New Jersey bar : but it may be said of him that he has been a law student all his life. This is of course to a certain extent true of all lawyers, but it is especially true of him, for his studies have been prosecuted far beyond the lines of his practice. He has thoroughly investigated the broad field of primitive and developed law as existing in the middle and lower ages; has traced the evolution and formulation of principles and of forms of practice from the earliest times to the present day ; and, contemporaneously with these studies, he has exhaustively examined mediæval and modern history and literature. He is, unquestionably, one of the best read men of the present day, and that he has extended his studies over so broad a range is due to his exceptional habit of mind that enables him to rapidly grasp and memorize salient facts while passing over irrelevant and distracting details. His success as a barrister, as may be inferred from the foregoing, was immediate, and he rapidly rose to be one of the leaders of the New Jersey bar—a bar always distinguished for its erudition and practical ability. As a corporation lawyer he was particularly distinguished. For many years he was a Director in and counsel to the Camden & Amboy Railroad Company, and he was also counsel to that not less impor-

tant organization, the Delaware & Raritan Canal Company, In suits brought by or against these great companies, and in countless other leading cases, he was constantly in the higher courts of the State, being very frequently in opposition to one or other of his old classmates at Rutgers, Hon. Cortlandt Parker, or Senator Frelinghuysen. Among his leading cases may be mentioned the Passaic Bridge causes, which were conducted by him on one side and Hon. Cortlandt Parker on the other, reaching the Supreme Court of the United States in 1861 ; and the famous and peculiar Muller will case, which occupied the Jersey courts from 1852 to 1860, when the alleged forged will was established as to part of the realty, though repudiated as to the personalty and never set up as to the land not directly sued for in the one suit brought. In this case, Messrs. Bradley, A. C. M. Pennington, William Pennington, and O. S. Halsted appeared for the disputed will, and Runyon, Frelinghuysen, C. Parker, and Asa Whitehead against it. The question was raised first in the Orphans' Court and then by appeal in the Prerogative Court, where the acknowledged will of the testator was proved ; then ejectment was brought in the United States Circuit Court, and the disputed will established ; then the claimants under the prior acknowledged will brought eject-ment in the State courts, and obtained a verdict which the Supreme Court set aside. This closed the litigation, but the mystery of the will has never been cleared up. Mr. Bradley also appeared in the New Jersey Zinc case; the Belvidere Land case; the murder case of Harding, the Methodist minister, hung for poisoning his wife, and of Donnelly, who assassinated his friend at Long Branch to get back money won from him by the murdered man by gaming. As a barrister, the Judge was strongest in law arguments before the higher courts; he did not excel before juries. In politics, until called upon to discharge the high trust of deciding arbiter in the Hayes-Tilden Electoral Tribunal, he has taken no active part. Originally a Whig, he became upon the formation of the Republican party one of its most earnest members, but not one of its active workers. Twice only has he accepted nomination to office. In 1862 he was nominated to represent the Fifth Congressional district of New Jersey, but was defeated, by a somewhat large majority, by Nehemiah Perry ; and in 1868 he headed the Grant and Colfax electoral ticket in his State. His elevation to the bench of the Supreme Court of the United States occurred in February, 1870. President Grant had previously nom-inated Attorney-General E. R. Hoar to the vacant seat, but this nomination had been adversely acted upon by the Senate on the ground that the nominee was not a resident of the Circuit—the Fifth Judicial Circuit, comprehending the districts of Georgia, northern and southern Florida, northern and southern Alabama, Mississippi, Louisiana, and eastern and western Texas—over which he would be called upon to preside. Mr. Bradley's name was put in nomination by the President on the 7th of February, and was received by the Senate with similar objections upon similar grounds. The

Southern senators were particularly urgent in their opposition to his appointment, and the opposition was more or less general upon the Democratic side of the House. Upon his stating that if appointed it was his intention to reside within the confines of his circuit, his case was considerably improved; and, finally, upon the 21st of March, he was confirmed, the vote standing forty-six to nine—the minority including all of the Southern senators. A year later, in April, 1871, he came prominently before the public by the delivery of a dissenting opinion on the question of the right of the federal government to levy and collect a tax upon the income of State officers. In May of the same year he delivered the preliminary decisions in the cases of Knox *vs.* Lee, and Parker *vs.* Davis; and in January, 1872, was one of the five Justices who—confirming these decisions—declared the validity and constitutionality of the Legal Tender act. Inasmuch as this act had been previously declared invalid by the Supreme Court in banc by a vote of five to three—as it was held that Justices Bradley and Strong had been elevated to the bench for the express purpose of reversing this decision —and as, in fact, such result flowed from their appointment, their action was severely criticised by leading members and journals of the Democratic party, being condemned as a purely partisan measure. Justice Bradley has abundantly vindicated his character from this reproach by several subsequent decisions in which his opinion has traversed the interests of his party: notable among these being his decision, rendered in the Grant Parish cases, declaring the Enforcement act to be unconstitutional. The crowning event of his life—an event which made him for the time being the most important man in the whole nation, and which, it cannot be doubted, has exerted upon the future of the nation an influence so potent as to be quite inestimable—was his selection, January 30th, 1872, by Justices Clifford, Miller, Field and Strong as the fifth arbiter in the judicial division of the tripartite Electoral Tribunal charged with determining the result of the Presidential election in the preceding year. He is married to Mary, daughter of the late Joseph C. Hornblower, Chief Justice of the Supreme Court of New Jersey.

——◦◦◦——

OEBLING, JOHN AUGUSTUS, Engineer, late of Trenton, was born in Muhlhausen, Prussia, June 12th, 1806. He was educated at the Polytechnic School in Berlin, and emigrated to America, and settled near Pittsburgh, Pennsylvania, in 1831. He was engaged as Assistant Engineer on the Slackwater navigation of the Beaver, and on the Sandy and Beaver Canal, the feeder of the Pennsylvania Canal. His labors on these enterprises proving his high abilities, he was appointed to a position on the survey for a route across the Allegheny mountains. Upon this survey, adopted for the Pennsylvania Central Railroad, he was engaged for three years. But these labors were only the prelude to the great works of his life, from which such vast benefits are enjoyed by the community and are yet to be enjoyed. He introduced the manufacture of wire rope into this country, beginning his operations at Pittsburgh, and afterward removing them to Trenton, New Jersey, where he erected extensive works, capable of turning out two thousand tons of wire-rope yearly. But not only did he introduce the manufacture of the wire-rope—he was the first to use them in the construction of suspension bridges. His first work was the suspended aqueduct of the Pennsylvania Canal across the Allegheny river, completed in May, 1845. He afterward constructed the Monongahela suspension bridge at Pittsburgh, and some suspension aqueducts on the Delaware & Hudson Canal. In 1851 work was begun by him upon the famous suspension railroad bridge over the Niagara river, just below the falls. It is one of the finest structures of the kind in the country, and perhaps in the world. Its span is 821 feet, and its deflection 59 feet. In the cables 14,560 wires are employed, and their ultimate strength is estimated at 12,000 tons. The elevation of the railroad track above the water is 245 feet, and so great is the stiffness of the roadway that ordinary trains cause a depression of only three to four inches. Work on the bridge was completed in 1855, and although its endurance is severely tested by the continual passage of heavy trains, it has thus far proved a most complete success. About this time, in the year 1854, he removed the Belview bridge at Niagara, and replaced it by one constructed by himself, and more adequate to the demand upon its powers of resistance. Afterward he built the magnificent suspension bridge over the Ohio river at Cincinnati, and this work greatly added to his now wide reputation as a builder of bridges. It has a total length of 2,220 feet, and a clear span of 1,057 feet; is 103 feet above low water in the river. The two cables supporting the roadway are twelve inches and a half in diameter. This structure was completed in 1867, and to this day remains one of the sights of Cincinnati, which all residents are proud of showing to visitors. In 1858-60 he built a fine wire bridge over the Allegheny river at Pittsburgh. His latest design was for a bridge across the East river from New York to Brooklyn, a work that has been in progress for some years; which is the most remarkable undertaking of the kind ever projected, and which promises immense results. Its conception stamps Mr. Roebling as one of the greatest engineers of the age, and its success will cause his name to be held in grateful remembrance forever by the immense populations of the two great cities of New York and Brooklyn, whose dependence upon the uncertain mode of transportation furnished by ferry boats has been so mutually disadvantageous. It is now (1877) in process of construction under the charge of his son, Washington A. Roebling. The bridge will be 3,475 feet long between the anchorages, with a clear span over the East river of 1,595 feet, the bottom chord of which will be 132 feet above the water. The superstructure will consist of an iron framing, eighty five feet wide, suspended from four main cables, each sixteen inches in diameter, composed of galvanized cast steel wire having a strength of 160,000 pounds per square inch of section, while the aggregate strength of the main span will be 5,000 tons. Mr. Roebling is the author of a valuable treatise on "Long and Short Span Bridges," published in New York in 1869. He died in Brooklyn, New York, July 22d, 1869, and is succeeded in the business by his son.

———⋆◆⋆———

HAPMAN, REV. JEDEDIAH, Pastor of the First Presbyterian Church, Orange, New Jersey, late of Geneva, New York, was born in East Haddam, Connecticut, September 27th, 1741, and was a descendant in the sixth generation of the Hon. Robert Chapman, of Hull, England, who came to America in 1635 and settled at Saybrook. He was a theological student of the celebrated Bellamy. At the conclusion of the usual preparatory course of studies at Yale College he graduated from that institution in 1762; two years afterward received his license; and having in the spring of 1766 preached as a candidate, was ordained and settled over the church on the following 22d of July. "He entered the parish in his twenty-fifth year, unmarried and poor. We make the latter statement on authority of tradition, which represents that the attention of his parishioners was at first divided somewhat between the wants of his wardrobe and the word that he preached. It was enough, however, that he was clothed with salvation. They could furnish the rest." During the exciting times of the revolutionary struggle he warmly espoused the American cause, ever upholding it with example, voice and pen; and on account of his outspoken and fearless loyalty was more than once in danger of being kidnapped by the enemy, and carried a prisoner to the British camp. On several occasions soldiers were sent to capture him, but he eluded them in every case, yet several times was obliged to flee the parish and seek temporary asylum behind the mountains, as did many of the families of his flock. After the conclusion of the war, on the occasion of the Fourth of July ceremonies and rejoicings, he walked in the procession and always exhibited an intense enthusiasm in that cause for which he had risked his reputation and his life. He was elected to preside over the Synod of 1787, which is notable as being the last meeting of that body previous to the formation of the General Assembly of the church; and on the 17th of May, 1796, an academy was opened, of which he was chosen to officiate as President. In May, 1800, the General Assembly elected him missionary to the northwestern boundaries of the country, which then lay in western New York, and accordingly his relations with his former pastorate were dissolved. He then established his family at Geneva, where he supplied a congregation for many years, while perform-

ing laborious missionary duty in the surrounding region. To him was assigned by the General Assembly, to which he reported annually, the surveying and superintendence of the whole missionary field in western New York. The oldest churches in that region—those of Geneva, Romulus, Ovid, Rushville, Trumansburg—were organized by him; and he lived to witness the accomplishment of that to which all his powers were for years devoted—a complete union between the Presbyterian and Congregational churches in western New York. About ten months after his settlement over the Geneva church as its senior pastor, and after a service of more than half a century in the ministry, he rested from his labors in the seventy-third year of his age. His last illness came upon him in the pulpit while preaching from the words, "I have fought a good fight, I have finished my course: henceforth there is laid up for me a crown of righteousness," etc. The second year after his settlement at Orange, New Jersey, he married Blanche Smith, of Huguenot descent on the maternal side, and of a family that intermarried with the Adamses, of Massachusetts. By this marriage he had three children: William Smith, Robert Hett and John Hobart, the last of whom died in infancy. November 21st, 1773, soon after the death of the infant son, his wife also died in the twenty-ninth year of her age. His second wife was Margaret Le Conte, daughter of Dr. Peter Le Conte, of Middletown, Connecticut. This lady, who was slightly his senior in years, adorned to a good old age the station she was called to fill. He died May 22d, 1813.

———⋆◆⋆———

ILSON, PUSEY, M. D., of Moorestown, New Jersey, was born, March 8th, 1827, in Northampton township, Chester county, Pennsylvania. His father, Jonathan Wilson, was a farmer by occupation, but spent many years of his life in Wilmington, Delaware, where he filled acceptably the office of Treasurer of the Farmers' Mutual Fire Insurance Company of Delaware, and where he died in 1850. His mother was a Miss Sarah M. Jackson, of Delaware. He received his early education in the public schools of Wilmington, from which he passed in 1845 to the Kennett Square (Pennsylvania) Academy, graduating at the latter institution in 1849. On leaving school he entered the office of the Hon. John M. Clayton, at Wilmington, with the intention of making the law his profession; but, his father dying a year later, he was called from his studies to look after the business affairs of the family, and eventually led to abandon that intention. The Farmers' Mutual Fire Insurance Company promptly chose him to succeed his father as Treasurer, and he served in that capacity for some three years, discharging the duties of the place to his own credit and the satisfaction of the company. In 1855 he began the study of medicine with Dr. S. S. Brooks, of Philadelphia, Professor of the Practice of Medicine in the Hahnemann Medical College, at which he afterwards attended the regular course of lectures, receiving his diploma in March, 1862, having meanwhile, however, practised three years with Dr. Brooks. In 1862, after formally receiving his degree, he removed to Moorestown, where he has since resided, in the active and successful practice of his profession. The Hahnemann Medical College at Philadelphia, his *Alma Mater*, mindful of his proficiency as a student, and of his abilities as a practitioner, recalled him in 1864 to fill its chair of Anatomy, which he held during that year and the following one, accepting then the chair of surgery in the same institution, and holding it until the close of 1867, when, in consequence of his large and increasing practice at home, he resigned. As a medical teacher he achieved marked distinction. Thoroughly grounded in the principles of his profession, versed in its literature, and skilled in its practice, with a wide and varied experience of life, and rare powers of exposition, he at once divined the intellectual needs of the student and effectively supplied them, so that the facts and doctrines he inculcated were not merely understood, but assimilated, becoming organized knowledge, instead of undigested elements in the memory. Not content with instructing, he sought to discipline and equip, to the end that the student, while acquiring positive knowledge, should acquire also the power of using it, and, still better, the power of self-acquisition. This end, the only one at which a teacher worthy of the name should aim, he attained with a measure of success that proved him to be a man of general abilities of a high order, as well as a master of his profession. Had he felt himself at liberty to remain in the faculty of his *Alma Mater*, there can be no doubt that he would have won yet greater eminence as a Professor, and contributed largely to the strong impulse under which homœopathy is spreading in this country. It may be readily imagined that his college took leave of him with regret, not only on its own account, but on account of the system of practice it represents. Such men are not too numerous in any cause, and it is only natural that the cause so fortunate as to number one of them among its representatives and defenders should send him to the front, and strive to keep him there. He, however, deemed that·his true sphere was practice rather than instruction, and, when the two could no longer be reconciled with each other in his case, resigned the latter for the former, to which he has since exclusively devoted himself. As may be supposed, this devotion has been suitably rewarded. A practitioner whose practice is based on so complete a mastery of theory could hardly fail of distinguished success, especially when to this round of professional qualifications are added personal tact and geniality, which in the sick-room are sometimes not less medicinal than medicine itself. He certainly has been eminently successful as a practitioner. In 1875 he was elected President of the West Jersey Medical Society, and was a delegate to the American Institute of Homœopathy, held at Philadelphia in June of that year. Al-

though he has never either held office or sought it, he has been a zealous and active member of the Republican party from its first organization, having been a delegate, while residing in Delaware, to the National Convention that nominated Fremont for the Presidency. And to the sponsorship which he thus undertook he still remains faithful. He was married in 1851 to Rebecca Pusey, of Chester county, Pennsylvania.

ASHINGTON, HON. BUSHROD, Lawyer, one of the Justices of the Supreme Court of the United States, Presiding Justice of the United States Circuit Court for the District of New Jersey, late of Philadelphia, Pennsylvania, was born in Virginia in 1759, and was a favorite nephew of General George Washington, who devised to him his estate at Mount Vernon. He studied law, under the direction of his uncle, with James Wilson, of Philadelphia, an eminent practitioner, afterward one of the Justices of the United States Supreme Court. On the completion of his studies, he entered on the practice of his profession in Virginia, acquired an extensive business, and rapidly won a high reputation as an able lawyer, and, in the House of Delegates and conventions of that State, as a talented and influential member. At the age of thirty-six he was nominated by John Adams, and confirmed as one of the Justices of the Supreme Court. He was eminently fitted for his high office; and his moral and intellectual qualities, his learning, integrity, his tireless, patient attention, the knowledge that every case would be subject to the most searching and unbiased investigation, made him always the object of profound respect. "He had that temperate but inflexible firmness which resulted from confidence in himself, and is the courage of superior minds. His manners and his language, spoken and written, were simple and free from anything approaching to arrogance. He had that great faculty so important for a judge, and so difficult of attainment, of regarding only the essential merits of a cause, without being influenced by any of its surroundings. He knew the cause only by the evidence, and decided it by the law." Once a case tried before him at Philadelphia, in 1809, exhibited his peculiar qualities in a very striking and instructive manner. It was an indictment against General Bright and others for obstructing the process of the United States court, and grew out of a contest respecting certain prize money between the State of Pennsylvania, as the owner of a privateer, and an individual of the name of Olmstead. A certain portion of the money had been paid to David Rittenhouse, as Treasurer of the State, and at his death remained in the hands of his daughters as executors. The case having been carried into the Continental Court of Appeals, that court reversed the decree of the State Admiralty Court, and awarded all the money to Olmstead. He obtained a decree in the Court of Admiralty of the United States for the payment of this money to him. The Legislature of the State then passed an act requiring the executors of Rittenhouse to pay the money into the State Treasury; and this act was passed upon the ground that the Court of Appeals had no jurisdiction of the case, and that its decree of reversal was null and void. This act also required the Governor of the State to protect the persons and property of the lady executors from any process which might be issued out of the courts of the United States. In this state of things the case was submitted to the Supreme Court, which, after a hearing, commanded the District Court to issue the required process to enforce its judgment. But, by order of the Governor of the State, General Bright called out and took command of a body of the militia, which surrounded the houses of the ladies, and then opposed with force the efforts of the marshal to serve his process. "But, as might be supposed, the ladies were not quite pleased to be thus made prisoners, and, it was said, soon contrived to surrender themselves to the custody of the marshal. At any rate, the process was served, and the State, instead of continuing the war, relieved the ladies by paying the money." For the resistance Bright and others were indicted, and brought to trial. "The learning, the patient hearing, the clear and discriminating sagacity, and the unhesitating fearlessness of the Judge, then won for him universal approbation. His charge was a fine manifestation of his power to impress a jury with their duty to conform to the law; and the defendants were found guilty, and adequately punished." He was accustomed to charge the jury very fully and explicitly, seldom leaving it doubtful how he thought the verdict should be rendered. "I remember that in a case which involved merely a question as to the running of a boundary line, he mistook the facts, so that the jury, upon which there happened to be a very competent surveyor, found directly contrary to his charge. He received the verdict with very evident surprise, but said quietly that he would look into the facts of the case very carefully. After doing so, he promptly acknowledged his error, and thanked the jury for their care to be right, in a matter of fact which belonged to them to decide. Most judges would have done substantially the same, but his manner of correcting his own error was very simple and pleasant."—Hon. Lucius Q. C. Elmer, LL.D. The four volumes of Washington Circuit Court Reports contain most of the opinions delivered in the Circuit Courts of New Jersey and Pennsylvania during the time he presided. In the opinion of an eminent jurist and scholar, his style is a fine model of plain, perspicuous English, resembling that of Addison and Blackstone. These volumes were carefully made up in manuscript, and carried with him, before they were printed, to the circuits, lest, as he would at times very pleasantly remark, "he might some time inadvertently overrule himself, which would be worse than merely overruling some other judge." The case of Corfield vs. Coryell, reported in 4 Wash. C. R. 371, grew

out of transactions in New Jersey, and ever since has been considered as establishing the right of a State to prohibit the inhabitants of other States from catching oysters in oyster beds within its limits. A vessel owned in Philadelphia was seized in the year 1820, while engaged in catching oysters in Maurice river cove, in pursuance of the act originally passed as early as 1798; later the seventh section of the act for the preservation of clams and oysters, revised in 1846. Several of the persons engaged in making this seizure were sued in Philadelphia by the owners of the vessel. One case was tried before Judge Ingersoll, in the District Court of the city, and under his direction the jury rendered a verdict for the defendant. The case against Coryell was removed into the Circuit Court of the United States. The great point then insisted on for the plaintiff was that the act of the Legislature of New Jersey was in violation of that clause of the Constitution of the United States which provides that "the citizens of each State shall be entitled to all privileges and immunities of citizens in the several States." He held that the privileges and immunities protected by this clause were only those which are in their nature fundamental, which belong of right to the citizens of all free governments, and which have been at all times enjoyed by the citizens of the several States which compose the Union, from the period of becoming free, independent and sovereign, and did not extend to the privilege of interfering with the rights of the citizens of a State to have the exclusive privilege of catching fish and oysters within its waters. The expense of this litigation was defrayed by the State of New Jersey. To quote again from the admirable "Reminiscences of New Jersey," by Hon. L. Q. C. Elmer, LL.D.: "I have in my possession, however, one elaborate opinion, the last I believe that he prepared, just before his death in 1829, which was not printed. The case was argued before him and Judge Rossell, at Trenton, about a month before he died, by George Wood for the defendant, and by myself for the plaintiff. The case had been removed from the State court by the defendant, a citizen of Pennsylvania, for the express purpose of obtaining a decision, that when a bond had been assigned and the payment guaranteed by the assignor, if the assignee was directed to proceed against the obligor, his omission to do so would be a sufficient defence to an action upon the guarantee, which in this case was under seal. The judge, however, adhered to the principle established by the Supreme Court of this State (New Jersey) in the case of Stout vs. Stevenson (1 South. R. 178), namely, that a general guarantee or warranty of payment by the assignor of a bond is absolute and co-extensive with the instrument assigned, so that the warrantor becomes a surely for the payment of the money at the day, if it is assigned before the day of payment, and on demand, if it is assigned afterward." In private intercourse he was a very agreeable companion, and often told an excellent story, or recounted an amusing anecdote, with much effect and humor. He never brought with him to Trenton his family coach and servants, but came in a hired vehicle with hired servants, except a female servant of Mrs. Washington, who was in the habit of accompanying her, although a confirmed invalid. When not engaged in court he devoted himself to her with marked and affectionate assiduity. "I am happy to be able to say that I believe he was a sincere Christian. I know that he had the habit of regularly reading prayers in his private room. If I was asked, Who of all the judges you have known, do you consider to have been the best fitted for that high office, taking into the account integrity of character, learning, deportment, balance of mind, natural temper and disposition, and ability to ascertain and regard the true merits of a cause, as determined by the law that he was called to administer? I should say, Bushrod Washington."—Judge Elmer. He continued to fill the position of Presiding Justice of the United States Circuit Court for the District of New Jersey, from his first appointment in 1798 until his death in Philadelphia, November 26th, 1829.

ELCH, ASHBEL, Civil Engineer, was born in Madison county, New York, December 4th, 1809. His father was originally a farmer, living near Windham, Connecticut, on land occupied by his ancestors of the same name since about 1680. His grandmother was a great-great-granddaughter of William Bradford, who came over in the "Mayflower." When he was six or seven years old, the family removed to the neighborhood of Utica, where some years later he attended the school of Ambrose Kasson. One of his classmates there was Horatio Seymour, and one of the younger scholars was Ward Hunt. He afterwards studied mathematics and natural philosophy at the Albany Academy, under Professor Henry, now of the Smithsonian Institution. In his eighteenth year he left school (though he never discontinued his studies), and commenced his professional career under his brother, Sylvester Welch, on the Lehigh Canal. Among his associates in that hard-working corps were W. Milnor Roberts, Solomon W. Roberts, and Edward Miller, all of whom afterward became eminent civil engineers. In 1830 he entered the service of the Delaware & Raritan Canal Company, under Canvass White, one of the ablest and most original of American engineers. Since then he has been a citizen of New Jersey, and since 1832 a resident of Lambertville. In 1836 he took charge of the works of the canal company, and retained that charge for many years, in the meantime constructing several other works, among which was the Belvidere Delaware Railroad, commenced in 1850 and finished in 1854. On the 20th of December, 1852, the stockholders of the canal company suddenly determined to double the capacity of their locks and canal. Mr. Welch organized his staff, drew his plans and specifications, procured his materials, employed and officered a force of 4,000 men, and finished the work in

three months, and all within his estimate. One of the items of work was 20,000 cubic yards of cement masonry, laid in the dead of winter, and kept from freezing by housing and artificial heat. From 1862 to 1867, as Vice-President of the Camden & Amboy Railroad Company, he was the executive officer of the "Joint Companies," whose works extended across New Jersey. At the beginning of 1867 he, with others, effected the consolidation of the New Jersey Railroad Company with the "Joint Companies," thus bringing the whole system of railroads and canals between New York and Philadelphia into one interest and under one management. He was appointed General President of the Associated Companies, Hon. Hamilton Fish being vice-president, and Hon. Joseph P. Bradley, secretary. This position he held until December 1st, 1871, when the Pennsylvania Railroad Company took possession of the works under their lease. His policy was to improve the works connecting the two great cities of the Union in such a manner as to remove all ground of complaint and all fear of competition. Those associated companies are now merged into "The United New Jersey Railroad and Canal Company." He is still President of the Belvidere Delaware and some smaller railroad companies, all operated by lessees. Mr. Welch is not merely an administrator, but especially an originator. In 1863 he originated and put in operation a system of safety signals on the line between New York and Philadelphia (since, we believe, extended to Pittsburgh), which has entirely prevented the most dangerous class of accidents, previously so frequent and so fatal. The value of this system was especially shown during the rush of the Centennial season. It is sometimes confounded with the English "Block System," from which, however, it differs essentially, and from which Mr. Welch received no hint. The system was described in a report by him to the National Railroad Convention held in New York in 1866. In 1866 he invented a pattern of steel rail, more economical and forming better connections than those in previous use, the principles of which are stated at length in his "Report," made to the American Society of Civil Engineers at its annual convention in 1874. These principles have since been extensively recognized and adopted. Mr. Welch's efforts have not been confined exclusively to his profession. From 1840 to 1845 he was associated with Captain Robert F. Stockton in his operations which resulted in building the war steamer "Princeton," the first propeller-ship ever constructed in America, and in the introduction of cannon of extraordinary size, since followed up by Rodman and others. On the invasion of Pennsylvania during the late civil war, Professor Bache, to whom had been intrusted the defences of Philadelphia, called him to his counsel, but the battle of Gettysburg soon made the further consideration of the subject unnecessary. In 1843 the College of New Jersey, at Princeton, conferred on him the honorary degree of A. M. He has been a member of the Presbyterian Church since 1832, and an Elder since 1844,

Ashbel Welch

and has several times been a member of the General Assembly of that church. He is an occasional contributor to the *Princeton Review*, the principal organ of the Presbyterian Church in America, his last article being " The Perpetuity of the Sabbath." In it he takes the position, never before suggested, that many Hebrew local laws were declaratory of the moral law, just as many English statute laws are declaratory of the common law. For more than a quarter of a century he was Superintendent of the Sabbath school, and he now conducts the congregational Bible class in the Rev. Dr. Studdiford's church. For many years he has been a most diligent student of the word of God. Thoroughly orthodox in his belief, he is also independent and original in his Bible investigations, taking nothing at second hand, but seeking to find for himself the meaning of the sacred text. Few laymen have given as much attention as he to the study of the Bible, and not many of the clergy are better versed in the principles of its interpretation. In politics he is not tied to either party organization, but has decided opinions, one of which has long been in favor of civil service reform. He was married in 1834 to Mary H. Seabrook, who died in 1874, leaving five children, the oldest of whom is the widow of Mr. William Cowin, of Lambertville, and the youngest daughter the wife of Rev. R. Randall Hoes, of Mount Holly. His eldest son is interested in iron and machinery works at Lambertville. Mr. Welch is loved and honored by a large circle of friends, among whom, as well as in the world at large, his influence has ever been potent for good. Cautious and conservative, yet kind and conciliatory, he eminently "follows after the things which make for peace." Earnest and independent in his search for truth, wise in counsel, public-spirited as a citizen, liberal as a benefactor, firm and conscientious in the maintenance of right, true and faithful in all the relations of life, he combines in himself qualities which make him one of the most valuable members of society.

LACKWELL, HON. JONATHAN HUNT, of Trenton, Merchant, and Senator from Mercer county, was born at Hopewell, Mercer county, New Jersey, December 20th, 1841. His parents, Stephen and Franconia (Hunt) Blackwell, came from families resident in this section of the State for several generations. Among his maternal ancestors were several who participated in the war of the Revolution, doing gallant service in the patriot cause. His father is a merchant at Hopewell, and highly respected. Jonathan received his early educational training at the public schools in the vicinity of his native place, and it was continued in the New Jersey Conference Seminary, at Pennington, and Claverack Collegiate Institute, on the Hudson. At the age of eighteen, on leaving school, he commenced his mercantile career as clerk in his father's store at Hopewell. Thus

employed he grew to man's estate. On attaining his majority, desirous of obtaining experience in a wider field, he entered the extensive wholesale grocery establishment of William Dolton. Here he remained for twelve months, and shortly afterward engaged in business in New York city, where he continued until 1864. In that year he returned to Trenton and became associated as a partner with his former employer, William Dolton. This partnership has continued till the present time, and their business is probably the largest of its character in the State. A man of large activity and great public spirit, Mr. Blackwell has always manifested great interest in the affairs of the city and the State, devoting much time to the promotion of all movements calculated in his judgment to develop their natural resources and to improve their government. In political affiliation he is a Democrat, and has been honored by his party with various positions of trust and responsibility. In 1873 he was elected a member of the Trenton Common Council for three years, and in that body he served with great credit to himself and satisfaction to his constituents. During the succeeding year he was nominated as candidate for State Senator, and some idea of his popularity is conveyed in the fact that, while the Republicans had previously represented the county in the Senate, he was elected by a good majority of a largely increased vote, the total being 10,531, against 9,107 in 1871. Although the youngest member of the Senate, with his party in the minority, his ability received immediate recognition in his appointment on several important committees; among them those on Education and on Banks and Insurance Companies. During the session of 1877 he was Chairman of the first-named committee, and also of that on Claims and Pensions; a member of those on Militia, on Lunatic Asylums, on State Library, and on Printing; of the latter he was also Chairman. His career as a legislator has deepened the good opinion entertained of him by the community, for while warmly attached to the Democratic party and desirous of promoting its interests, he has never been actuated by partisanship to support any measure which he did not deem for the public good. Both as a business man and as a politician he commands the highest respect and esteem of his fellow-citizens. He was married, October 5th, 1865, to Susan Weart, daughter of Spencer Weart, Esq., of Mercer county, New Jersey.

ROWN, WILLIAM MORTIMER, Physician, late of Newark, New Jersey, was born in this city, September 8th, 1816. He was one of the most faithful, active and influential members of the Essex District Medical Society, and was always at his post and punctual in every appointment. Also, as one of the deacons of the Third Presbyterian Church, he was active in every good work and enterprise. For many years preceding his decease he was in a feeble state of health, and had a marked predisposition to disease of the lungs which rendered it unsafe for him to expose himself at night. " The disease, however, slowly but insidiously advanced till about all available lung was consumed. He sunk to his grave ' calmly, like one who wraps the drapery of his couch about him, and lies down to pleasant dreams.' His manners were quiet and retiring. He was a good physician, and enjoyed to a high degree the confidence of his fellow-practitioners. He regarded with especial interest the *esprit du corps* of the profession, and was ever mindful of its honor and dignity. He was a man of medium size, slim, sallow, and bore for years evidence of consumptive tendencies."—Dr. J. H. Clark. In 1865 Dr. S. H. Pennington published, in the "Transactions of the State Medical Society," an eloquent and elegant poetical tribute to his memory. He died in Newark, April 4th, 1864, in the forty-eighth year of his age.

EWITT, HON. CHARLES, President of the Trenton Iron Company, was born in the city of New York in 1824. His father, John Hewitt, was of English birth; the ancestors of his mother, a Miss Gurneé, left France at the time of the St. Bartholomew massacre. Hon. Abram Hewitt is his brother. Charles attended one of the public schools of New York until eleven years of age, when, having reached the highest class, he was taken from school and placed as a clerk with an insurance company in Wall street, where he remained about six years. During this service, by devoting all spare time at his clerk's desk and the evenings to study, he qualified himself to receive, at seventeen years of age, an appointment as teacher in the Grammar School of Columbia College, then under the control of the eminent linguist and author, Professor Charles Anthon. After a few months' service as assistant teacher, he was appointed Principal of the third department of the school, a position which he continued to hold until 1845, when he accepted a situation in the iron works at Trenton, then being erected by the distinguished philanthropist, Peter Cooper. In October of this year, and before he had attained his twenty-first year, Columbia College conferred on him the honorary degree of A. M., thereby indicating the high estimation which his talents, scholarship and character had won. In his new position he had at first charge of the commercial department of the business transacted at the works, but in a few years' thereafter, when they passed under the control of corporate organizations, the sphere of his duties was enlarged, and he became the General Manager, controlling both the commercial and manufacturing departments of the business at Trenton. The two large establishments now belonging to the New Jersey Steel and Iron Company and the Trenton Iron Company were for many years operated under one corporate organization, and were during that time managed by him. He is now the President of the Trenton Iron Company, Edwin F. Bedell being secretary, and James Hall, treasurer. This corporation was organized in 1847. In 1854 it owned the Andover, Roseville, and other mines, and the Ringwood estate; three blast furnaces (now the property of the Andover Iron Company) at Phillipsburg, New Jersey; a rolling and puddling mill (now the property of the New Jersey Steel and Iron Company) at Trenton, and the Trenton Water Power, besides a rolling mill and a wire mill in the last-named city. Only the last two are now retained by the company, it having been found desirable to divide the various former interests. The capacity of the rolling mill is 14,000 tons per annum; it has 6 heating furnaces; 4 trains of rolls, 19, 12, 10 and 8 inch respectively; 2 steam hammers; 12 sinking fires, and 2 refining fires. Of the wire mill the capacity is 7,000 tons per annum. The products are bar-iron, wire and brazier rods; market, fence, telegraph, screw, bridge, rope, weaving, coppered and tinned, bale, hay-bale, spring (iron and steel), buckle, square, flat, and half round, cast-steel, Martin steel and Bessemer steel wire, and fence staples. So judicious is the management of the works, that even in the troublous labor agitations, through which the country has passed of late years, strikes have been unknown. The men now in the employ are to a great extent those who have grown up with the works, and when a change in values renders a reduction in wages a business necessity, Mr. Hewitt invariably gives notice of the proposed reduction several weeks before it takes effect. During this interval any arguments advanced by the workmen are patiently listened to, any demonstrated injustice remedied, and so in all cases the change is explained satisfactorily to the men. By this course the hands are kept in full sympathy with their employer. The advantage of this to the works is very apparent. Feeling that their personal interests and the prosperity of the company are one and the same, the men at the furnace and at the rolls labor with their best energies to maintain, so far as in them lies, the welfare of the concern. Mr. Hewitt is eminently a man of affairs, manifests a large public spirit, and is characterized by an apparently inexhaustible energy. Besides carefully conserving and promoting the interests of the industrial institution to which his attention is primarily directed, he has been and is now prominently identified with various public and corporate bodies. Within the last thirty years he has been Vice-President of the New Jersey Steel and Iron Company, President and Superintendent of the Trenton Water Power Company, President of the National Pottery Company, a member of the Common Council of the city, and President of its Board of Trade. He is now President of the Trenton Iron Company, a Manager of the Trenton Savings Fund Society, and one of the Managers of the State Lunatic Asylum, at Trenton. In 1871 he was elected to represent Mercer county in the State Senate, and was appointed

Chairman of the Committee on Education, also of that on State Prison, and a member of several others of importance. During his senatorship he took the leading part in the work and discussions which led to the enactment, in the last year of his term, of the general railroad law, and at all times displayed an active interest in the educational affairs of the State. He has, in common with other members of the Trenton Board of Trade, labored effectively to promote the growth and prosperity of that city, and especially for the better utilization of the water-power of the river Delaware. And not only is his genius administrative, it is inventive. He has perfected a number of inventions that have proved of great value in the manufacture of iron, among which may be especially mentioned an arrangement for moving iron at the rolls, by means of which the manufacture of rolled beams and girders, and other heavy iron, has been greatly facilitated. Indeed, his career has been wholly honorable and successful, whether as a business man or a mover in public affairs, and he very naturally holds a high place in the confidence and esteem of the community for whose best interests he has labored so intelligently and conscientiously.

OSSELL, HON. WILLIAM, Judge of the District Court of the United States for New Jersey, late of New Jersey, was born in 1755-65. "He was an honest, industrious judge, of excellent character and good judgment, who was elected by the Republicans, as he once said to me himself, because they had no good lawyer of the party in the western part of the State, willing and fit to take the office, and because, being an active and influential politician in Burlington county, where he resided, he had been for that reason persecuted by some of the Federalists."—Hon. L. Q. C. Elmer. For many years after he became Judge he was one of the most prominent leaders of the Democratic party in the State, but was never accused of allowing his political views and sentiments to influence his conduct on the bench. "His good sense led him generally to concur with the chief-justice, and some of his reported opinions read very well. But his total lack of legal knowledge, especially in matters of practice and pleading, was so much complained of by the lawyers of the circuit which he attended," that, in 1820, an act was passed, requiring the justices of the Supreme Court so to arrange the several circuits in the State, there being no judicial districts established by law, as now, that no justice should hold the Circuit Court in the same county two terms in succession, unless in the opinion of the court there should be a necessity therefor. This stringent law continued in force and was complied with, to the serious inconvenience of the judges, until 1846. When it was passed, there were two Circuit Courts held each year in all the counties, thirteen in number, except Cape May, in which there was but one. The other courts had four terms in each year until

1855, when a reduction to three was effected, and the Circuit Courts in all the counties were required to have three terms yearly. Upon the death of Judge Pennington, in 1826, he was strongly recommended for, and received the appointment of, Judge of the District Court of the United States for New Jersey, a place at that time of great respectability and very little labor, "like the common bench in England at the same period," to which judges were glad to retire from more arduous duties. When he relinquished his seat on the bench of the Supreme Court, a meeting of the bar, under the lead of Hon. Mr. Frelinghuysen, adopted resolutions highly complimentary of his faithful performance of the duties of his office. He died in 1840, at an advanced age.

CLENAHAN, ROBERT MILLS, M. D., late of New Hampton, was born at Pennington, New Jersey, October 19th, 1817, and was the son of Rev. Mr. McLenahan, a preacher of the Methodist Episcopal Church. His early education was obtained in his native place, where he also commenced the study of medicine with Dr. Joseph Welling. He afterward graduated at the New York Medical College in 1836. Soon after receiving his degree he commenced practice at New Hampton, New Jersey. His genial and winning manners, combined with professional abilities of a high order, soon won him a reputation and a practice of proportions seldom reached by a country physician. Indeed, so extended did his responsibilities become that, about 1860, he invited Dr. Howard Service to come to New Hampton, and render him the relief that his failing health rendered it absolutely essential that he should have. After entering into this arrangement he gradually withdrew from practice. His health continued to fail, and on April 28th, 1864, he died, being then in his forty-seventh year. He was greatly missed by a large circle of friends and acquaintances, to whom a lifetime association had endeared him. He was twice married, his first wife being Christiana, daughter of the late Aaron Van Syckel, Esq., who died March 8th, 1856; and his second a Miss Johnston, who survives him.

OUTHARD, HENRY, M. D., late of Somerville, son of the Hon. Isaac Southard, and a grandson of the Hon. Henry Southard, of revolutionary fame, was born in Somerset county, New Jersey, March 27th, 1811. Having studied medicine, he was duly licensed by the State Board of Censors, and after practising successively at Flemington, Asbury Danville, Belvidere, and Phillipsburg, he finally established himself in Somerville, Hunterdon county, where he remained in active practice for a number of years. He was a member of the Hunterdon County Medical Society, of which he was for a time Secretary; was a member of the New Jersey Medical Society, and in 1847 was a member of the State Board of Censors. During his residence in Phillipsburg he married Louisa Maxwell. He died October 13th, 1859.

ELSEY, ENOS, Merchant, Revolutionary Patriot, Treasurer of Princeton College, late of Princeton, was a native of New Jersey, and was born in the middle of the last century. After his graduation from Princeton College he settled as a merchant in the city of his *Alma Mater*, and there resided, engaged in business pursuits, until the time of his decease. During the troublous days of the Revolution he held a responsible office in the Clothier-General's office, under the State government. There is a letter of his preserved in the "Revolutionary Correspondence of New Jersey," addressed to the Speaker of the Assembly, dated October 4th, 1779, in which he makes an estimate of the cost of clothing the Jersey troops. "He proposes to go himself to Boston and make the purchases, and thinks that by the proposed scheme he can save the State ten thousand pounds in the purchase." He was intimately identified with Princeton College, and for many years officiated as Treasurer of that institution. He died in Princeton, New Jersey, in 1809 or 1810.

ALHOUN, JAMES THEODORE, Physician and Surgeon, late of Rahway, New Jersey, was born there, September 17th, 1838, and commenced the study of medicine at the age of sixteen, in the office of Dr. Samuel Abernethy, also of Rahway, who always evinced a warm interest in him. March 17th, 1859, he graduated at the University of Pennsylvania, Philadelphia, and at once entered upon the active practice of his profession at Rahway, where he was engaged during the ensuing two years. In June, 1861, he entered the Union army, as Assistant-Surgeon of the (5th Excelsior) 74th New York Volunteer Regiment; in May, 1863, received an appointment as Assistant-Surgeon in the regular army; and, September 24th, 1864, was assigned to duty as Surgeon in charge of the Ward United States Army General Hospital. In September, 1865, the hospital at Newark was discontinued, and he superintended the sales of the government hospitals in the Department of the East, after which he became Medical Director of Transportation at New York city, where he remained from December, 1865, until the middle of May, 1866, when he was placed on the board of officers appointed by the government to examine and decide upon cholera disinfectants, more particularly the "Phœnix Disinfectant," upon which he did not report

favorably. He visited several places for the purpose of trying it, including David's Island, New York harbor, where he tried it upon spoiled eggs. He was about to be ordered to Augusta, Maine, when an exchange was made between Assistant-Surgeon Harvey Brown and himself, and he was ordered, on the 4th of June, 1866, to Hart's Island, as Post Surgeon, relieving Dr. Brown. He took an active part with his regiment at the siege of Yorktown; also in the battles of Williamsburg, Fair Oaks, and those of the Seven Days' Fight; and was present at the siege of Richmond and the action known as Hooker's Malvern; also at the battles of Bristow's Station, second Bull Run, and Chantilly, of Pope's campaign. "I was present with my regiment at the battle of Fredericksburg, and, under the new regulations of the Medical Department, was detailed as 'operating surgeon' of my brigade. I passed a satisfactory examination before the Regular Army Medical Board, and immediately thereafter, without solicitation on my part, I was appointed Surgeon-in-Chief of the Second Division, Third Corps, commanded by Major-General Berry." While in command at Newark he planned and constructed a new hospital, its enclosure containing twenty-four acres of ground; and he served respectively upon the staffs of Major-Generals Berry, Binney, Sickles, Humphrey, Mott, Prince, Carr, Hancock, French and Graham. While at Gettysburg the medical director of the corps, Dr. Thomas Sims, was called upon to accompany General Sickles to Washington, and this occasioned his placing on duty as Acting Medical Director of the corps. How well he acquitted himself of the heavy responsibilities then thrown upon him is best told by the fact that, although at this time almost the junior Assistant-Surgeon of the regular army, he was continued on duty as Acting Medical Director of the corps through its subsequent marches in pursuit of the Confederate army, including the affair at "Wapping Heights," and until it went into camp at the Rappahannock, when he rejoined his division. Dr. Dougherty also bears ample testimony to his activity, his faithfulness and his executive ability: "While at Brandy Station we had a Division Medical Society, which was probably the most vigorous and useful of any in the army. Its efficacy was mainly due to his earnest endeavors and professional prelections. . . . . During General Grant's campaign to Petersburg he displayed admirable qualities. The wounded had implicit confidence in him, and preferred his attentions to those of any other; while his superior energy and activity caused him to be selected for the charge of the colored hospital at City Point. He raised it from a despicable position to the first rank, eliciting the warm commendation of the chief medical officers. . . . ." At Gettysburg, also, where he assisted in the amputation of the leg of General Sickles, Dr. Dougherty says of him: "In this bloody fight his energies and resources were taxed to the utmost, but he was never found wanting; " while the same able physician declares that "he not only systematized and improvised his hospitals, but he was the best operator in them." While quite young in the profession he wrote an excellent article on the "Influences of Mill-Dams" in Rahway, which contributed greatly to accomplish their removal, and consequently a notable change in the healthfulness of the town; while in a series of articles, published in the Philadelphia *Medical Reporter*, he gave to the profession some of the results of his observations and experience during the war. May 3d, 1865, he was married to Nora C. Orr, by whom he had one child, which died at Newark, New Jersey, of cholera infantum, July 28th, 1866. He died July 19th, 1866, at Hart's Island, New York, of Asiatic cholera. His remains were ultimately removed, in accordance with a request made by him before death, to Rahway, New Jersey; and, February 22d, 1867, the funeral services were held at the Second Presbyterian Church, of which he had been a member. After the service the regulars, escorted by the New Jersey Veteran Volunteers and the New Jersey Rifle Corps, marched to the cemetery of Hazelwood, where they met the remains. The coffin was enveloped in the United States flag, and on it were laid his sword, sash and cap; a crown of immortelles, and an anchor and cross of white flowers. His deceased son, Charles, was placed in the same tomb with him, after which Rev. Mr. Hodges read the conclusion of the burial service, and the permanent party from Governor's Island fired the military salute. Many distinguished characters, public and private, attended the funeral, and the people of Rahway united their efforts to testify their respect to his memory; the houses were draped with mourning, and the flags placed at half-mast throughout the place. He received two brevets for faithful and meritorious services during the war, dating from the 13th of March, 1865; and since his death the President has brevetted him Lieutenant-Colonel in the regular army, "for distinguished and meritorious services at Hart's Island, New York, where cholera prevailed, to date from the 19th of July, 1866."

ARCLAY, REV. DAVID, Clergyman, late of Punxatawny, Pennsylvania, was born in New Jersey, in the last quarter of the past century, and studied at Princeton College, graduating in 1790–92 from that institution. After leaving Princeton he applied his time and attention to the study of theology; and, December 3d, 1794, was ordained by the Presbytery of New Brunswick, and installed as pastor of the church at Bound Brook, where he remained until April, 1805. At this date, on account of some troubles, he abandoned his charge there, and in June became pastor of Knowlton, Oxford and Lower Mount Bethel churches, New Jersey, there continuing his labors until 1811. He was a man of decided ability; quick, earnest and energetic in his motions and his speech; of stout, athletic frame, but

of an impetuous and imprudent temperament. He was constantly involved in troubles and disputes with his congregations, and one of his elders, Jacob Ker, published a volume of more than 400 pages, entitled "The Several Trials of David Barclay before the Presbytery of New Brunswick and Synod of New York and New Jersey." On the 25th of April, 1819, he was dismissed to the Presbytery of Redstone, and took up his residence in Punxatawny, Pennsylvania, where he died in 1846.

ART, JOHN SEELY, LL. D., Scholar and Author, late of Philadelphia, Pennsylvania, was born in Old Stockbridge, Berkshire county, Massachusetts, on January 28th, 1810; but when he was only two years old his father, with some other families, removed into Pennsylvania, and settled in Providence township, on the Lackawanna, which was then a wilderness. Here he continued until 1823, when his father acquired a mill-privilege at Laurel run, then about two miles above Wilkesbarre, in the valley of Wyoming. When a boy he was very sickly, and adjudged unfit for any employment requiring physical strength; so arrangements were made to get him educated for a teacher, and in his fifteenth year he entered the Wilkesbarre Academy. By diligent use of the opportunities afforded him here, in three years he was well fitted for college. In the fall of 1827 he entered the sophomore class of the College of New Jersey, and graduated in 1830, with the first honors of his class. He then went South, and was for one year Principal of the academy at Natchez, Mississippi. Returning to New Jersey, in the fall of 1831 he entered the Theological Seminary at Princeton. During the last two years of his attendance at the seminary he acted as tutor in the college, and in 1834 he was appointed Adjunct Professor of Ancient Languages. During this period he paid much attention to the study of Hebrew and Arabic, studying the latter under Addison Alexander. He was licensed to preach by the Presbytery of New Brunswick in 1835, but in the following year he was induced to become Principal of the Edgehill Fitting School, at Princeton, and, regarding it as a permanent field of usefulness, requested the presbytery to take back his license, which was formally cancelled. He continued in the management of the Edgehill for five years. In September, 1842, he was elected Principal of the Central High School, of Philadelphia. It was here that he became best known to the citizens of Philadelphia, and under his management the High School flourished and became extremely popular. This position he occupied until 1859, receiving during his incumbency, in the year 1848, the degree of LL. D. from the University of Miami. Some time after his retirement from the High School, in the year 1860, he became connected with the American Sunday-

School Union, as the editor of its publications. During this engagement he projected the *Sunday-School Times*, of which he remained the senior editor until the spring of 1871. From 1862 to 1871 he was connected with the New Jersey State Normal School, at Trenton—one year as head of the model department, and the remainder of the time as principal of the institution. After much solicitation on the part of Dr. McCosh and the faculty at Princeton, and much hesitation and many refusals on the part of Professor Hart, he was in 1872 induced to take the Professorship of Rhetoric and of the English Language and Literature in that institution, agreeing to remain only until a successor could be found. He occupied this chair about two years, having been a teacher over forty years and having had over 7,000 pupils confided to his direct care and training. His literary works are exceedingly numerous and valuable, and several of them are used as text-books in the public schools of Philadelphia. He commenced to write for publication as early as his twenty-fifth year, contributing to the *Princeton Review* a series of articles on "Jenkyn on the Atonement;" "The English Bible;" "Tyndale's New Testament;" "The Revised Webster;" "An Argument for Common Schools;" "Normal Schools;" and "The English Language." In 1844 he edited the *Common School Journal*, "Hart's Class Book of Poetry" and "Hart's Class Book of Prose." In 1845 he edited the philological volume of the "United States Exploring Expedition," during the absence of Mr. Hale, its author, in Europe. In the same year he published "An Exposition of the Constitution of the United States for the Use of Schools," and an "English Grammar." In 1847 he published his first original volume, "An Essay on Spenser, and the Fairy Queen." From January, 1849, to July, 1851, he edited *Sartain's Magazine*. In 1851 he published "The Female Prose Writers of America," an enlarged edition of which was issued in 1856. In 1853 he published "A Greek and Roman Mythology." About this time he was also engaged in editing some eight or ten literary annuals. From 1862 to 1870 he published a series of pamphlets and minor writings. "The Bible as an Educational Power Among the Nations;" "Mistakes of Educated Men;" "Pennsylvania Coal and its Carriers;" "Thoughts on Sabbath-Schools;" "Counsels for the School Room;" "The Golden Censer;" and "Thoughts on the Lord's Prayer." These were succeeded by several works on practical piety, the "Sunday-School Idea, its Objects, Organization, etc." In 1870 he published two such works, viz.: "Removing Mountains," and "Life Lessons from the Gospels." His latest publications have been of an educational character, such as "A Manual of Composition and Rhetoric," and "First Lessons in Composition," 1870; "A Manual of English Literature," 1872; "A Manual of American Literature," 1873; "A Short Course in Literature, English and American," 1873; and since then "An Analysis of English Grammar," and "Language Lessons." The two latter were published after he returned from Princeton.

He was also a large contributor to the periodical press. A day or two after the accident which resulted in his death, he said to his publisher that he should probably be confined to his room for several months, and that during that time he proposed to prepare for the press a work which should be the masterpiece of his life—a grammar of grammars—the materials for which he had been collecting for many years. This accident occurred on January 17th, 1877. He had consented to read and criticise a manuscript submitted to him by a young lady of literary aspirations, and, having completed his self-imposed task, started on that evening to return the manuscript to its author. On the way he slipped and fell on the icy sidewalk, breaking his hip, and sustaining severe internal injuries. A few days later he fell into a comatose condition, in which he remained almost constantly until his death, on March 26th, 1877. The accident interrupted a course of noon-day lectures on Shakspeare, being delivered at the Girls' Normal School. He was for many years a leading member of the Tenth Presbyterian Church, Philadelphia, and was Superintendent of the Sunday-school up to the time of his accident. He left a widow and one son, Professor J. Morgan Hart, of the University of Cincinnati, Ohio. His scholarship was extensive and varied, and he was an excellent teacher. He had the art of exciting an interest in the topics of which he wrote or spoke, and he personally commanded the affectionate respect of his pupils, so that the many hundreds of young men who have been under his care will acknowledge their indebtedness to him for much of their literary training. With all his amiability of character, he was a man of great firmness, a good disciplinarian and a good business man, and his long career as a teacher and a writer was both useful and successful. He made many friends and kept them, and left behind a justly honored name. Respecting the man and his influence in the cause of education, the *Evening Telegraph*, of Philadelphia, on the day following his death, said: "It seems proper to say that Mr. Hart was one of the strongest and most devoted workers in that cause that this country has produced. He was an enthusiast—and this notwithstanding the fact that he had an indrawn and undemonstrative nature. Again, he made serious sacrifices in devoting himself to teaching. Though a good teacher, he would have made a better lawyer; he had the real analytic legal brain, and all who knew him well made no secret of their belief that he might have ranked among the luminaries of the Philadelphia bar if he had so chosen; but he looked at life as involving something more than personal ambition and success. The educational cause was a profound matter of conscience with him, and the whole labor of a long life, with the exception of various literary relaxations, was given to what may be called, in opposition to a more brilliant career which he might have chosen, humble and self-sacrificing toil. There are not many such instances in our school history, and when they occur they should be noted with especial honor.

Professor Hart's name is associated with Princeton College, with the New Jersey Normal School, and with other large educational interests, but in this locality he is chiefly known through his long direction of the Boys' High School. In point of fact, he placed that now representative American school on a solid foundation—of discipline and accomplishment, and of popular confidence. He found it in a state of feebleness, and at a time when it was highly unlikely that the scheme of so advanced a shoot of the public school system could flourish—and in his term of office he demonstrated very clearly that this mingling of school and college could be made a reality. He had many pupils in this locality who, from under his wise and careful ruling, passed into the working world to take places of honor and trust, and few men could be followed to the grave with a larger respect than will be offered him, and with greater sympathy and sense of personal obligation."

———— ·◇· ————

ILES, GENERAL JAMES, Lawyer, Officer in the Revolutionary Army, President of the Cumberland Bank, late of Bridgeton, New Jersey, was born in New York, in 1759. His parents were from England, and do not appear to have had any relatives in this country. His father subsequently returned to the mother country, to be ordained as a minister of the Episcopal Church; on his return the vessel in which he came was wrecked, in a violent snow storm, at the entrance of Delaware Bay, and be with others found there a watery grave; his body was said to have been buried in an old graveyard at New England Town, in Cape May county, now nearly or quite washed away by the encroachment of the bay; but the exact situation of the grave has never been satisfactorily defined. At an early period of the revolutionary struggle he was appointed to a Lieutenancy in the 2d, or New York, Regiment of Artillery, and continued in service until 1782, in which year he became a student at law with Joseph Bloomfield, then resident at Trenton. In 1780 he attached to the command of Lafayette, and served under him in Virginia, being one of the officers who received from the gallant hero a sword, brought from France, which is now in the possession of the Historical Society of New Jersey. When his old commander revisited this country, in 1824, this sword was handsomely remounted, and worn when he was received by the Society of Cincinnati of New Jersey, of which he was a member. It was said at the time that the general received him with great cordiality, immediately recognized him, and warmly greeted him by name. He was for several years General of the Cumberland brigade of militia, and was commonly addressed by that title. In 1783 he was licensed as an attorney, and in due time as a counsellor, and in 1804 was made a serjeant-at-law. Shortly after

he was licensed he married the sister of General Bloomfield, and took up his residence in his native city, where he was admitted to the bar. "In the first 'Directory' of that city, published in 1786, in the list of lawyers is found the name, 'James Giles, Esq., 65 Maiden lane.'" In 1788 he removed with his family to Bridgeton, where he resided during the remainder of his life. In the ensuing year he was appointed by the Legislature, in joint meeting, Clerk of the county; and, being twice reappointed, held that office during a period of fifteen years. Being at that time entitled also to practise law, he had quite an extensive and, for that day, lucrative business. In 1793 he built for his own ocen-patiou a mansion, which, with its ornamental grounds and rich furniture, was the finest residence in the place; and also accumulated the largest library, both of law and miscellaneous books, in South Jersey. He was a well-read lawyer and safe counsellor, and excellent, though not brilliant, as an advocate. "He was a small man, precise in his dress, and remarkably erect and graceful, but very slow in his movements and in all he did. At the circuits he was one of the most genial and delightful companions. The legal documents he drew were marked by great neatness and precision." About 1805 his friends confidently expected that he would be elected one of the justices of the Supreme Court, although a majority of the joint meeting was politically opposed to him; but the result was that the law authorizing three associate judges was repealed. During the latter years of his life he held the position of President of the Cumberland Bank; and died at Bridgeton, New Jersey, in 1825. He had a large family of children, most of whom died young. James G. Hampton, educated for the bar, who graduated at Princeton in 1835, and represented the First District in Congress two terms, and who died in 1863, was a grandson. "Now all have passed away; not a single individual of kin to General Giles, and only remote kindred on the side of Mrs. Giles, remain in the State. His name will be found a few times as counsel in the early reports; but his business was nearly all confined to the counties of Cumberland and Cape May. A beautiful daughter, who married Mr. Inskeep, of Philadelphia, of the firm of Bradford & Inskeep, booksellers, removed many years ago to New Orleans, and had several daughters, who inherited some of their mother's beauty, whose descendants are still living there, and occupy respectable positions in society."

———— ·◇· ————

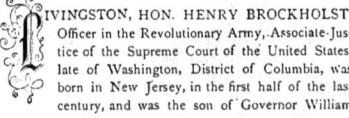

IVINGSTON, HON. HENRY BROCKHOLST, Officer in the Revolutionary Army, Associate Justice of the Supreme Court of the United States, late of Washington, District of Columbia, was born in New Jersey, in the first half of the last century, and was the son of Governor William Livingston, of New Jersey. He graduated at Princeton

College.. In 1776 he entered the military family of General Schuyler, Commander of the Northern army, and was subsequently attached to the suite of Arnold at the time of the capture of Burgoyne. In 1779, when Mr. Jay, who had married his sister, repaired to the Court of Spain, he accompanied him as his Private Secretary. After three years' absence he returned to his native country, and, at the expiration of the usual period of study and probation, was admitted to the bar in 1783. On the 8th of June, 1802, he was appointed Judge of the Supreme Court of New York; and in November, 1806, was appointed Associate-Judge of the Supreme Court of the United States. "His mind was acute and powerful, and he was distinguished as a scholar and a jurist." He died in Washington, during a session of the court, March 18th, 1823.

LAGLER, THOMAS B., M. D., Physician, of Morristown, was born, August 21st, 1823, in the town of Lagrange, Dutchess county, New York. His father was Abraham Flagler, a farmer and himself a native of Lagrange; and his mother was Elizabeth (Burtis) Flagler. The Flagler family is of Dutch origin, and the founders of the American branch, bearing then the name of Van Vluglen, came from Holland to this country in the early part of the seventeenth century. The Van Vluglens established themselves at the village of Nine Partners, so named from the fact that the land on which it stands was owned and the village founded by nine men in partnership; and there the family has ever since been strongly represented. The education of Thomas B. Flagler was received at Poughkeepsie. He was an earnest and industrious student, and his advancement in his studies was rapid and marked. In considering the choice of a profession, he had early decided upon that of medicine, and in the year 1839 he commenced his preliminary medical studies in the office of Dr. John Cooper, of Poughkeepsie. His habit of close and diligent study, added to great natural aptitude for the profession he had chosen, insured his rapid advancement under the instruction he received, and he was soon well grounded in the elements of professional knowledge. In due course of time he commenced attending the College of Physicians and Surgeons, in New York, in which institution he went through two regular courses. In addition to this he attended a course of lectures at the Albany Medical College. He received his diploma in the year 1844, and immediately thereafter commenced the practice of his profession in Poughkeepsie. He remained there a year, gaining in that time rapid and substantial professional success. At the end of the year he removed to Morristown, New Jersey, where he has ever since remained. His large medical knowledge, his zeal in his profession and his high natural qualifications for meeting all its requirements, insured his

success as a practitioner, and he speedily became possessed of a large, increasing and lucrative practice. He is devoted to his profession, and, still retaining his habits of study, he keeps himself fully up with the progress made in medical science, and thereby he has won a high and recognized position in the front rank of medical practitioners. He is one of the Judicial Council of the United States Medical Society, and other official honors bestowed upon him from time to time attest the estimation in which he is held by his professional brethren. His devotion to his profession does not prevent his being active as a public-spirited citizen, and he has always been prominent in works of public improvement and benefit. He was one of the incorporators of the Morris County Savings Bank, of which institution he is one of the Directors. He is also a Director of the Evergreen Cemetery, at Morristown. He was married, in 1849, to Mary E. Wetmore, of Morristown.

UNT, REV. HOLLOWAY WHITEFIELD, late of Hunterdon county, was born in New Jersey, in the last quarter of the eighteenth century, and graduated from Princeton College. He received license from the Presbytery of New Brunswick about 1792, and on the 17th of June, 1795, was ordained and settled as pastor of the churches at Newton and Hardiston, New Jersey. In 1804 he removed to Hunterdon county, and took charge of the united churches of Kingwood, Bethlehem and Alexandria. "He was a tall, portly man, of a very fair complexion; and, in later years, his hair white with age. He was a man of fair abilities, and in his prime was a popular preacher." His manners were bland and attractive, and he had the faculty of attaching to him very strongly the people of his charge. In the latter years of his life he gave up the active duties of the ministry, on account of growing and harassing infirmities. He died in Hunterdon county, New Jersey, in 1858.

OHNSON, COLONEL ROBERT G., Member of the Legislature of New Jersey, Vice-President of the New Jersey Historical Society, late of New-haven, was born in the last quarter of the past century, and was a son of Robert Johnson, of an old family of Salem county, New Jersey. His father was a man of wealth and station, his mother a descendant of early and wealthy settlers from England. He was a graduate of Princeton College. On one occasion his father complained bitterly to Dr. Witherspoon that his son had not been advanced as he expected. After bearing considerable reproach, the doctor exclaimed, with the strong Scotch accent that characterized his warmer utterance, "I tell you, sir, the boy wants capacity!" Soon after graduating

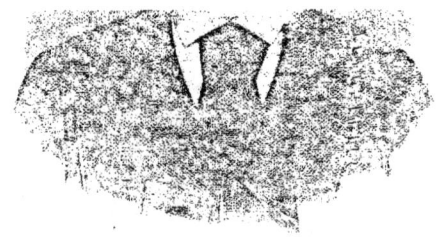

Galaxy Pub. Co. Philad.ª

he became Captain of a troop of cavalry, and eventually rose to the station of Colonel. In 1794 he served in the army raised to quell the whiskey insurrection, acting on that occasion as a paymaster. He was in his own right, and in the right of his wife, probably the largest landholder in Salem county. In 1821, and from 1823 to 1825, he was a member of the Legislature of New Jersey. "He was a man of truth and honor, but so fixed in his convictions as not always to be tolerant of those who differed with him. He was very hospitable, and beyond question a true Christian, but, owing to this peculiarity of temper, was unpopular with many." He was fond of historical research, and was Vice-President of the New Jersey Historical Society from its foundation in 1845 till near the time of his decease. To its valuable collections he added much historical matter of importance; among other things, a "Memoir of John Fenwick," the early proprietor of New Jersey. He died at Newhaven, New Jersey, in October, 1850.

———————

MITH, HEZEKIAH B., Inventor and Manufacturer of Woodworking Machinery, of Smithville, Burlington county, was born in Vermont in 1816. His ancestors can be traced back for two hundred years to American origin. On the paternal side his grandfather and several of his brothers were sea-captains trading to foreign ports, and principally to the West Indies. At the outbreak of the war of independence, their trade being destroyed, they took out letters of marque and engaged in what was then and is still known as privateering, or in other words legalized piracy. In this business they were unfortunate; as far as known all met violent deaths. The father of the subject of this sketch was thus early in life left penniless and fatherless, and the bereaved mother was compelled to apprentice her son to learn tanning, currying, and shoemaking. He was subjected to all the toils, hardships, and privations of that old pernicious system of English apprenticeship. He served his time faithfully for seven years, and at its expiration, being tired and weary of the scenes of his labors and sufferings, it was with a light heart that he set out for the wilds of Vermont. He halted at Bridgewater and there renewed his trades for himself; being a man of more than ordinary natural intellectual ability he soon took to reading and study, and soon made up in a degree for early deficiencies in scholarship. After a time he established a fine library, which occupied one end of his shop, and it was his greatest delight to pore over these books after his day's toil was ended. On the maternal side his origin may be traced back to the old Roger Williams stock. The relation of a tragical incident which occurred in the family of one of his ancestors, and which resulted in giving the name of Hezekiah to the subject of this sketch, may not be out of place here. His great-grandfather

Williams settled in Vermont when it was nothing but a wilderness. He had two sons—Roger, who was named for his ancestor, and Hezekiah. It was their custom every evening to go for the cows: the elder one always carried a gun as a protection against bears, wolves, Indians, etc.; while Hezekiah, the younger, went along to help drive the cows home. One evening the boys started out as was their custom; Roger trudging along in front with gun over shoulder, when suddenly stubbing his toe, he fell, the gun went off, and two balls passed directly through Hezekiah's head, killing him almost instantly. To perpetuate the name and to commemorate the sad event the subject of this sketch was named Hezekiah. With such sturdy New England blood flowing in his veins it is no wonder that he early developed remarkable mechanical genius. As early as thirteen he became a deep thinker, and hearing his father and uncle discuss their beliefs in the feasibility of perpetual motion, he quickly made up his mind to test the matter. Constructing a wooden key to his father's workshop, thither he repaired on Sunday, it being the only day he could work without interruption, to test the truth or falsity of this much mooted theory. After three days of toil the simple fact flashed upon his mind that a weight in falling one foot would produce a certain amount of power, but it must be raised back to the starting point before it could produce power by falling the foot again. Thus his hopes were dashed, and he has never since attempted to work in opposition to nature's laws. He continued until the age of sixteen to attend school for three months in summer and three months in winter. At the age of seventeen, his father giving him his time, he "let" himself to a man named Mills, to learn the cabinet business. In a short time he became master of his trade. He then began business for himself as a cabinet maker, chair maker, sash, door, and blind manufacturer, etc., etc. While thus engaged his genius took distinct and definite form. From earliest boyhood his mind had been filled with visions of mechanical contrivances—saw-mills filled with new and curious machinery, and brooks whose water-power was conserved and applied to useful purposes by water-wheels of peculiar construction. Machinery has always exercised and still continues to exercise a perfect fascination for him. He early perceived, as he progressed in his business, the necessity for the introduction into woodworking of machinery that would quicken and cheapen production of every class. Gradually the visions of younger life assumed tangible form, and his ready invention suggested contrivances of the most valuable kind for the saving of labor and overcoming of obstacles to cheap and superior production. One after another has been added to the list which now includes hundreds of different woodworking machines of various degrees of intricacy, but all rendering easy, simple, and cheap the accomplishment of work previously only performed slowly, laboriously, and expensively by hand-power. Coming before the public as the first introducer of rapid motion in this class of machinery, and constructing his machines entirely of iron and steel, thus avoiding the warp and twist incident to the old wooden frames, and which formed so marked a defect in other makes of machines, he has obtained wide popularity for his inventions, which have forced their way into favor by their superior merits, and by reason of the exceptionally fair and honorable manner in which all purchasers are treated. His machines are to be met with all over the world, and everywhere have given the most complete satisfaction, while inaugurating a new era in woodworking. Some of his best patents were invented when their inventor lived by necessity on a low diet, which only seemed to have the effect of making his intellect burn more brightly and clearly. Always a shrewd business man, availing himself of all openings, he has never been known to resort to sharpness or trickery in his dealings. By his ability, industry, and perseverance he has accumulated a handsome competency in his legitimate business, which was started with no foundation but his active brain and ready hands. The early part of his life was spent in Massachusetts; he removed to Smithville, Burlington county, New Jersey, in 1865. Long before leaving the East, and ever since settling in New Jersey, he has stood at the head of the manufacturers of woodworking machinery. By the excellence of his inventions, and his indomitable will in forcing public recognition of them, he has driven many of his competitors out of the market. Arriving in New Jersey he purchased the land and a portion of the buildings now occupied by his extensive manufactory, which to-day comprises about two acres and a half of floor room, the lower floors being of iron. He has, in fact, worked no less than one thousand tons of iron into real estate. When running at its full capacity the factory is capable of giving employment to from seven to eight hundred men. For the material comfort and mental and moral improvement of this large number of employés he manifests constant and generous solicitude. Adjoining the mills he has erected a large boarding-house for his "boys," as he calls them, to which is attached a well-appointed and well-stored reading-room, and a very beautiful hall for their free use. From among the "boys" a fine hand has been organized and equipped by Mr. Smith, and a room in the hall has been fitted up expressly for them to practise in. In fact, the entire village, which consists of some fifty houses, a post-office, store, and newspaper office, belongs to him, and he is even the publisher of the newspaper, a very neat little weekly sheet, ably edited by his wife, a lady of excellent family and many accomplishments. Indeed, nothing is left undone by him that would tend to elevate the character of his men and afford them pleasure. He is not only their employer but their best friend. Surrounding the village, he owns and cultivates a farm of about five hundred acres. It is maintained in a high state of cultivation, and he takes great delight and pride in its products and in the raising of fine stock. His residence is a fine, substantial edifice, and the extensive grounds are so

beautifully laid out, so choicely stocked and so well-cared for as to present a fairy scene of color and beauty. Here he dispenses a generous hospitality, and receives unmistakable evidence of the wide esteem in which he is held. Most emphatically the architect of his own fortunes, his career offers at once an example and an encouragement to youth. None could have had more adverse circumstances to contend with than beset his early career; none with the results his energy and industry have achieved before them need despair of final triumph, if only they will bring the same qualities to bear in the struggle. He never aspired to any political position, having many times received invitations to accept office but always replying that his taste and ability belonged to mechanics, not politics; but he at one time received the unanimous nomination for Congress in the Second District of New Jersey, unsolicited and undesired by him, but under circumstances in which he could not honorably decline. Although running in a district strongly opposed to him politically he was only defeated by a small majority; and much to the surprise of everybody he carried his own county by a handsome majority, which had never before been done by his party.

———❦———

SBORNE, JOSEPH D., Physician and Surgeon, was born at Suckasunny, New Jersey, September 6th, 1833, the son of Rev. Enos A. Osborne. August 17th, 1861, he received the appointment of Assistant-Surgeon, United States Volunteers, and went out with the 4th Regiment, New Jersey Volunteers. In October of the same year he was appointed Surgeon of the 2d Regiment, New Jersey Volunteers; and was then transferred to the 4th Regiment, with which he remained until mustered out, November 19th, 1864. He was Chief of Brigade by virtue of date of commission; in 1863 was Assistant Operator of Division; and in 1864 was Operating Surgeon of Division. From July to October of 1863 he was Executive Officer of Hospitals, and was placed in charge of the transfer of the wounded at Gettysburg. From January to July of 1864 he was on duty in the Ward United States Hospital, in Newark.

———❦———

OLCOMBE, SAMUEL, Grain Merchant, late of New Brunswick, was born in Amwell, New Jersey, whither his father had removed from England, in 1768. He was made a ruling elder in Amwell church while it was under the pastoral care of Rev. Mr. Grant, but in what year is not certainly known. In 1809 he removed to New Brunswick, where he carried on a heavy business in the grain trade. He was irreproachable as a man of business, and exemplary as an elder of the First Presbyterian Church, to which office he was chosen December 30th, 1810. "He was assiduous in visiting the poor, and liberal in aims-giving. He was of a lovely disposition, being very even-tempered, and never known to be angry even by his family. His death was like his life, happy and Christian. It took place December 17th, 1838, in the seventieth year of his age."

ALLACE, JOSHUA MADDOX, of Burlington, was born in the city of Philadelphia, October 4th, 1752. His father was Mr. John Wallace, a native of Scotland, who, emigrating in his twenty-third year from his paternal home at Drumellier, upon the Tweed, arrived in the year 1742 in Newport, Rhode Island. His name is there found among those of other persons, including several natives of Scotland, members of a literary society through whose organization the Redwood Library in that ancient town was subsequently founded. Having resided for some time in Newport, Mr. Wallace removed to Philadelphia, then becoming the principal city of America, and in this place married Mary, only child of Joshua and Mary Maddox; the former an honored citizen of Philadelphia, and for many years one of the justices of the courts there, a councilman of the city, a founder and trustee of the college, and a warden of Christ Church.. The subject of this notice was placed at an early age under the care of the best teachers of the time; and having been thoroughly instructed in rudimentary learning, was entered at the College of Philadelphia. He was graduated there November 17th, 1767. After exercising for a short time in that same year the office of a tutor in the college, he was placed in the counting-house of Mr. Archibald McCall, a well-known merchant of old Philadelphia. How long the subject of this notice remained in this excellent school for the acquisition of mercantile knowledge is not now known; but the singular integrity, method and accuracy which marked his own transactions of business in after life, and his scrupulous punctuality in all his engagements, would indicate that while there his time was given with effect to a comprehension and to a practice of the duties which the situation imposed. But though qualified, as might be inferred, for affairs of commerce, he does not seem, on leaving the counting-house of Mr. McCall, to have entered upon them. The uncertain state of our British relations may have induced him to postpone doing so, and his tastes, it is probable, combining with his excellent education, found stronger affinities in literature and science. These apparently occupied his early manhood. A few years after his marriage in 1773 with Tace, the daughter of Colonel William Bradford—a lady of uncommon virtue, intelligence and refinement—he went to occupy his estate of Ellerslie, a large and beautiful farm upon the Raritan, Somerset county, New Jersey. He retained his estate of Ellerslie for many years, and during the heats of summer occasionally resided there. But thinking that there was some ground to suppose the region insalubrious, he fixed his abode in 1784 at Burlington, New Jersey, near which place the family of his wife, in the maternal lines, had been settled from the foundation of the province. He continued to reside at Burlington until the close of his life, A. D. 1819, maintaining "that ancient, native, genuine character" described by Edmund Burke, but now apparently departed from the earth, of "a country gentleman," and using his leisure and ample inheritance greatly to the benefit of the place and its inhabitants. In the office of Judge of the Pleas of Burlington County, which he accepted from the Council and General Assembly of the State in the year 1784, "he was very highly useful in administering justice, maintaining the police, relieving the distresses and improving the morals of the common people." He greatly interested himself to advance agriculture, and particularly those attractive branches of it, ornamental gardening, and the culture of fruit trees. He was instrumental in establishing an academy of learning, and in bringing good teachers to the place. The public library of the town was a subject of his interest and contributions. He took much pains to introduce for the benefit of the townspeople supplies of pure and wholesome water, and also to establish engines, with a well-appointed police, to prevent the ravages of fire; and was, in short, an energetic, disinterested and most useful citizen. He was a Trustee for more than twenty years of Princeton College, President of the Trustees of the Burlington Academy, and President of the Society in New Jersey for the Suppression of Vice and Immorality. His name appears in the Journals of the General Convention of the Episcopal Church, as a representative from his State of New Jersey, for the years 1786, 1795, 1808, 1811, 1814 and 1817, the last which he lived to witness; and it is constantly found through the same long series of years, in the Journals of the New Jersey Conventions, as a representative of the ancient parish of St. Mary's, Burlington. In 1796 he was appointed, along with his friend Mr. Croes, afterwards Bishop of New Jersey, to the responsible office of framing a Constitution and Canons for the ecclesiastical polity of that State, Rules for Conducting its Business in Convention, Rules for the Government of Congregations, and such recommendations from the convention to the churches generally as were calculated to advance its prosperity. The Journal of the following year contains the report "as agreed to and adopted by the convention." Devoted, however, as he was to the theology of his own church, his love for it was characterized by a most catholic spirit. With his friend and near kinsman, the venerable Elias Boudinot, he took an early and active part in the formation of the American Bible Society, and was chosen President of the Convention which formed it, in acknowledgment of his zeal and services in promoting the great object for which that body was assembled. Of the Bible Society in his own State he was a manager from its foundation till the time of his death—

a term of about nine years; and it is recorded of him that he brought a larger amount to its treasury than was ever brought to it by any individual at one time. Though his tastes did not lead Mr. Wallace to mingle actively in the conflict of parties, he well understood the duties which belong to a citizen of the republic. He was a member of that convention which, in 1707, ratified, in behalf of the State of New Jersey, the Constitution of these United States. And acting throughout his life upon the principle that it was the duty of the government to give this instrument a fair interpretation, and fairly to exercise its powers in furtherance of its professed design, it need scarcely be added that his political principles were those of the Federal school: the principles of Washington and Hamilton, of Jay and Marshall. To these he steadily adhered, avowing and maintaining them as deep laid in the economy of our popular institutions; the only principles, in short, upon which this government could be administered with permanent justice, dignity or success. He represented the county of Burlington in the Assembly of New Jersey during a most critical term in the history of our country, and in this capacity contributed, by his steadiness of judgment and the influence of his acknowledged probity, much to hold the State to that anchorage of sound political morality from which so many parts of our country were carried by the tempest of the revolution in France. Mr. Wallace died on the 17th of May, 1819, in the sixty-eighth year of his age. His illness had been but short, and the intelligence of its issue produced in the city of Burlington, which for more than thirty-five years had been the witness of his honorable and useful life, a sensation of general sorrow. His remains were followed to the grave by a large concourse of citizens, including many persons from adjoining places. And on a following Sunday an impressive discourse upon his life and character was pronounced by the Rev. Mr. Carter, of Trenton, in St. Mary's Church, Burlington, with which venerable edifice the person of Mr. Wallace, as a warden and worshipper, had long been identified. Obituary notices of this distinguished citizen of Burlington are found in *The Christian Journal and Literary Register* of June, 1819, published in New York, and in the (London) *Christian Observer* of March, 1820. Mr. Wallace was the father of the late well-known lawyer, John Bradford Wallace, Esq., of Philadelphia, for some time a representative from Crawford county in the Legislature of Pennsylvania, and a most efficient advocate of its early internal improvements.

LPAUGH, WILLIAM C., M. D., Physician and Surgeon, of High Bridge, was born in the town of Twexbury, Hunterdon county, New Jersey, September 14th, 1841. His ancestors were of German extraction, and among the earliest settlers of the State. One of them was a captain in the war of the Revolution, and distinguished himself by his gallantry during that patriotic struggle. The family has always been noted for its piety and integrity, and love for liberal institutions. The father of Dr. Alpaugh is a farmer of considerable means, a man of the highest character, and an unflinching adherent to and exponent of his principles. An illustration of this trait was frequently afforded during the late civil war, when he was constantly threatened with personal violence, because of the boldness with which he denounced the rebels and their Northern sympathizers. The subject of this sketch obtained his earlier education at the public schools, and assisted his father on the farm until his sixteenth year. For two years thereafter he taught school, and then entered the Presbyterian Seminary at Hackettstown, New Jersey, at that time under the direction of Professor Budd. After studying there for a period of two years, he placed himself under the tuition of Mr. O. H. Hoffman, for a course of classics and mathematics; meanwhile beginning the study of medicine with the late Dr. Barclay, of Lebanon, New Jersey. His preliminary reading with this physician having convinced him that his career lay in the medical profession, he entered upon close preparation therefor, devoting his leisure hours to literary labor in the shape of contributions to newspapers and periodicals. In 1865 he entered the Bellevue Hospital Medical College, attended the usual course of lectures, and in 1867 was admitted to practise in the Charity Hospital connected with the college. In 1868 he graduated, standing second in a class of over one hundred students. Looking abroad for a field of action, he settled temporarily near Coaxburg, New Jersey, and began practice. There he remained until the spring of 1869, having in that short time acquired considerable practice and reputation, particularly through the treatment of some cases of chronic diseases, which had previously been treated by the resident physicians of the county for years without success. In consequence of the solicitations of Dr. Fields and a number of the most influential citizens of High Bridge, he was induced to settle at that place. At first he was associated in partnership with Dr. Fields, of Clinton, but this connection was dissolved in 1872, and since that time he has practised alone. At the present time he enjoys a practice and reputation second to none in the county, while he is frequently called in consultation into adjoining counties. Although successful in a wide range of cases, he has been especially remarkable for his treatment of fevers. In the famous Brennan murder case he took a conspicuous part, being called on to make the post mortem examination, and becoming, in consequence, one of the principal witnesses on the part of the State on the trial. One of the attorneys for the defence had very evidently been "cramming" for the cross-examination of the doctor, and his discomfiture at the ready and intelligent manner in which Dr. Alpaugh explained his theory to the court and jury was palpable to all present. After the trial, he published an article conclusively demonstrating the fallacy of the theory for the defence. He stands high in the estimation of his medical brethren, by whom he was elected a member of the Hunterdon County Medical Society in 1874. In 1877 he was appointed surgeon for the High Bridge branch of the New Jersey Central Railroad. On April 29th, 1865, he was married to Miss Solliday, a lady much respected in a wide circle, and has one child. His home and surroundings evince the possession of taste and liberal culture.

IVINGSTON, WILLIAM, the First Governor of New Jersey under the constitution of 1776, was born in Albany, New York, in the year 1723. He belonged to a family worthily conspicuous for many years in the history of the United States.

He was the grandson of Robert Livingston, a very distinguished minister of the Established Kirk of Scotland. After the restoration of the monarchy in the person of Charles II., this minister with his son fled to Holland, whence Robert came to America about the year 1675, in 1679 married Alida, the widow of Nicholas Van Rensselaer, and resided at Albany. He made extensive purchases of land from the Indians, and in consideration thereof the manor and lordship of Livingston was granted to him in 1686, and confirmed by royal authority in 1715. It was the second largest of the five great manors granted in the province of New York, which in more recent times have been so fruitful of anti-rent troubles, and comprised nearly one hundred and fifty thousand acres of land, commencing about five miles south of the present city of Hudson, running twelve miles along the east bank of the Hudson river, and extending back to the line of Massachusetts. It was in a measure divided at an early period, but the greater part of it was strictly entailed and transmitted through the next two generations, in the hands of the eldest son and grandson. Philip, the father of William, was the second son of Robert; but the elder brother having died, he succeeded to the manorial estate. His wife was Catharine Van Brugh, a member of a respected Dutch family of Albany. William was their fifth child. He was accorded the best education the country afforded. After due preparation he entered Yale College, from which institution he was graduated in 1741 at the head of his class. As illustrative of the educational customs of the day, it may be mentioned that, according to general report, there were, at that time, besides himself and three elder brothers, only six persons not in orders, in the province of New York, who had received a collegiate education. William was brought up for the legal profession, and began study therefor with James Alexander, a most distinguished lawyer of New York city, and a sturdy advocate of popular rights and opponent of ministerial assumptions. Some idea of young Livingston's life at this period may be obtained from a letter written by him to his father in 1744 : " I have received your letter of

November 21st, whereof the first two lines are, ' I am concerned to hear that you neglect your study, and are abroad most every night.' As to neglecting my study, I am as much concerned to hear it as my father, having read the greatest part of this winter till twelve and two o'clock at night, and since I have had a fire in my room have frequently risen at five in the morning and read by candle-light, of which I suppose your informer (whatever ingenious fellow it be) was ignorant, as it was impossible he should know it without being a wizard. As to my being abroad almost every night, I have for this month stayed at Mr. Alexander's till eight and nine o'clock at night, and shall continue to do so all winter, he instructing us in the mathematics, which is indeed being abroad." Studying thus diligently, he in due course was licensed to practise law in 1748. Such close study being combined with great natural ability and qualifications for a lawyer, it is not surprising to learn that he soon won a high position at the bar, and was retained in most of the important litigations of the day, not only in New York, but in New Jersey. Among other notable engagements in his legal career, he was in 1752 one of the counsel of the defendants in the great suit in chancery, between the proprietors of East Jersey and some of the settlers, which, although never brought to a final decision, has been much referred to in respect of the title to a considerable part of East Jersey. Brought up in the Reformed Dutch Church, he engaged earnestly in the controversies which arose with the Episcopalian party, in reference to an established religion. It was not a little owing to the feelings so strongly excited in Congregationalists and Presbyterians by these discussions, that the resistance eventually advanced to the attempted imposition of taxes on the American colonies by the British ministry arose, and the unanimous support by the colonies of antagonistic measures resulted. Livingston's most earnest sympathies were enlisted in the cause of the colonists, and he wrote very much on the various topics which grew out of the dispute. In 1772 he changed his residence to Elizabethtown, New Jersey, where he had acquired by purchases at different times an estate of about one hundred and twenty acres, which was carefully cultivated and upon which he planted various species of fruit trees, imported by him from abroad. Upon this estate he built a handsome residence, which continued his home during life. As at this time he was possessed of property considered sufficient for the maintenance of his family, he intended settling down to a quiet country life, but the failure of some of his debtors, and the loss by payments of others in depreciated Continental money, reduced his income considerably, and caused him in a measure to abandon his intention. He had been admitted to the bar of New Jersey in 1755, and at it he continued to practise his profession, but not in any very close fashion. To him was submitted the case of Stephen Skinner, treasurer of the eastern division of the province, whose public-money chest was broken open and robbed of six or seven thousand

55

pounds in coin and paper. The treasurer was held respon-sible for this sum, on the ground of negligence, by a majority of the Assembly, and although he was supported by Gov-cruor William Franklin, he eventually resigned, and an action was brought to recover the amount, but it never reached trial, and Skinner throwing his services on the British side, his New Jersey property was finally confiscated and sold. In 1774 Livingston was chosen a Delegate to the Continental Congress by the committee which met at New Brunswick in July of that year, and became a member of the committee of that body, appointed to prepare the ad-dress to the people of Great Britain. He signed and ad-hered to the non-consumption and non-importation pledge. In January, 1775, he was re-elected Delegate to the Con-gress by the Assembly, and served on the most important committees thereof. He was again delegated in February, 1776, by the Provincial Congress, and labored on the same committees with Adams, Jefferson, and Lee. During the ensuing June, however, he left the Congress at Philadelphia, In order to take command of the militia of New Jersey as a Brigadier-General, this position having been accorded him some time previously by the Provincial Congress. While thus patriotic in spirit and doing everything in his power to advance the American cause, he was yet among those, and the number included many pronounced Whigs, who doubted the expediency of the Declaration of Independence at the time it was made. On this subject he says, in a letter dated in February, 1778: "As to the policy of it, I then thought, and I have found no reason to change my sentiments since, that if we could not maintain our separation without the assistance of France, her alliance ought to have been secured, by our stipulation to assert it on that condition. This would have forced her out into upen .day, and we should have been certain either of her explicit avowal, or of the folly of our dependency upon it." Holding these sentiments, however, he would not hesitate to accept all risks in a cause so dear to his heart, or to enter military life on its behalf, and this without any military training or ex-perience. Relative to this he says, in another letter: "We must endeavor to make the best of everything. Whoever draws his sword against his prince, must fling away the scabbard. We have passed the Rubicon, and whoever at-tempts to cross it will be knocked in the head by the one or the other party, on the opposite banks. We cannot re-cede, nor should I wish it if we could. Great Britain must infallibly perish, and that speedily, by her own corruption, and I never loved her so much as to wish to keep her com-pany in her ruin." While this extract does not do much honor to his quality as a prophet, so far as the downfall of the British empire is concerned, it demonstrates very clearly the patriotic impulses of his heart. In June, 1776, by de-sire of Congress he took command of the militia destined for New York, and established his head-quarters at Elizabeth-town Point. There is good reason to believe, however, that he would have much preferred to continue a delegate to the

Continental Congress, in which case he would undoubtedly have signed the Declaration of Independence. Indeed, his correspondence indicates this feeling very plainly. In military duty he nevertheless proved himself remarkably efficient, while conscious of his need of precise knowledge, for he says, in a letter written to Congress in July: "I must acknowledge to you that I feel myself unequal to the present important command, and therefore wish for every assistance in my power;" and again, in a letter to a Con-gressman in Philadelphia, in August: "I received yours of yesterday's date, just after I had got into my new habita-tion, which is a marque tent in our encampment. You would really be astonished to see how grand I look, while at the same time I can assure you I was never more sensible (to use a New England phrase) of my own nothingness in military affairs. I removed my quarters from the town hither to be with the men and to inure them to discipline, which by my distance from the camp before, considering what scurvy subaltern officers we are ever like to have, while they are in the appointment of the mobility, I found it impossible to introduce. My ancient corporal fabric is almost tottering under the fatigue I have lately undergone, constantly rising at two o'clock in the morning to examine our lines, which are —— and very extensive, till daybreak, and from that time till eleven in giving orders, sending despatches, and doing the proper business of quartermasters, colonels, com-missaries, and I know not what." Soon after this his family were obliged to find a safer residence than their home, and for three or four years lived at Parsippany. It was not long that Livingston served as a soldier, his abilities being called into play in a position where they were calcu-lated to prove of far greater value to his country. A new constitution having been adopted, and a Legislature chosen under it, that body assembled at Princeton, and on August 27th, 1776, proceeded in joint convention to elect a gov-cruor. The vote was by a secret ballot, and it resulted for a time in a tie between him and Richard Stockton. By next day, however, an arrangement had been reached, and Livingston was elected Governor, Stockton being chosen chief-justice of the Supreme Court. The former accepted, but the latter declined. For a while after installation, Governor Livingston, by resolution of the Legislature, used his own seal at arms as the great seal of the State, but in a short time it was replaced by a seal of silver, engraved in Philadelphia, which bore the devices still in use, and was lettered, "The great seal of the State of New Jersey," the word colony, used in the constitution, being entirely dis-carded. On September 13th the Governor made an address to the Legislature, in which he says: "Considering how long the hand of oppression had been stretched out against us, how long the system of despotism, concerted for our ruin, had been insidiously pursued, and was at length at-tempted to be enforced by the violence of war; reason and conscience must have approved the measure had we sooner abjured that allegiance from which, not only by a denial of

protection, but the hostile assault on our persons and properties, we were clearly absolved. That, being thus constrained to assert our own independence, the late representatives of the colony of New Jersey, in Congress assembled,
did, in pursuance of the advice of the Continental Congress,
the supreme council of the American colonies, agree upon
the form of a constitution which, by tacit consent and open
approbation, hath since received the consent and concurrence
of the good people of the State; and agreeably to this constitution, a Legislative Council and Assembly have been
chosen, and also a governor. Let us, then, as it is our indispensable duty, make it our invariable aim to exhibit to
our constituents the brightest examples of a disinterested
love for the common weal; let us, both by precept and example, encourage a spirit of economy, industry and patriotism, and that public integrity and righteousness that cannot
fail to exalt a nation; setting our faces at the same time
like a flint against that dissoluteness of manner and political
corruption that will ever be the reproach of any people.
May the foundation of an infant State be laid in virtue and
the fear of God, and the superstructure will rise glorious
and endure for ages. Then may we humbly expect the
blessings of the Most High, who divides to the nations
their inheritance and separates the sons of Adam." From
an expression in this address the Governor is said to have
derived a name he bore for some time, "Doctor Flint."
From year to year he was re-elected Governor, while he
lived, occupying the combined office of Governor and Chancellor nearly fourteen years. Occasionally slight opposition
was manifested, but quickly overcome. From August 31st
to November 1st, 1777, there was an interregnum, his term
of a year having expired and the second Legislature not
meeting until two months thereafter. For some two years
after election his task was onerous and not without great
danger. In every part the State was exposed, and suffered
more from military operations than any other. Shortly after
his inauguration the upper part of it was occupied by the
enemy, and until the happy turn of affairs occasioned by the
victories at Trenton and Princeton, during the winter of
1776–77, everything was in jeopardy. Many, hitherto sanguine, despaired and accepted British protection. The
Legislature became a wandering body, now meeting at
Trenton, and then at Princeton, at Pittstown, in Hunterdon
county, and at Haddonfield. But the Governor was immovable and labored unremittingly for efficient militia laws
and the organization of the new government upon a solid
foundation. Among the first laws passed was one providing for the taking of an oath renouncing allegiance to
the king of Great Britain and of allegiance to the new
State government, and another for the punishment of traitors
and disaffected persons, and those who sought in any way
to uphold British authority. During the session at Haddonfield, lasting some two months, an act was passed establishing a committee of safety, consisting of twenty-three persons,
the governor or vice-president being one. This committee

was to act as a board of justice in criminal matters; fill up
vacant military offices; apprehend disaffected persons and
commit them to jail without bail or mainprise; could call
out the militia to execute their orders; were to send the
wives and children of fugitives with the enemy into the
enemy's lines; cause offenders to be tried, and persons refusing to take the oaths to government to be committed
to jail, or to send them, if willing, into the enemy's lines;
make any house or room a legal jail; negotiate exchanges;
disarm the disaffected, etc. During the two months' gubernatorial interregnum this committee was of especial importance. So determined and able a man as the Governor was
naturally in danger. His family residence was despoiled,
and he was most bitterly denounced in *Riverton's Gazette*,
the organ of the British party in New York. As an offset
to this journal, a patriotic paper was started in December,
printed by Isaac Collins, of whom a sketch appears elsewhere in this volume, sometimes at Trenton and sometimes
at Burlington, under the title of *The New Jersey Gazette*.
To it the Governor contributed largely, and many of his articles exerted a potent influence for good. But while popular among patriots, the Governor did not escape all criticism.
On October 27th, 1779, just before his re-election, a virulent
attack was made upon him in the *New Jersey Gazette*, over
the signature of "Cincinnatus." The following day this
resolution was passed by a large majority in the Council:
"Whereas by a late publication, inserted in the *New Jersey
Gazette*, called 'Hints humbly offered to the consideration
of the Legislature of New Jersey, in the future choice of a
governor,' signed 'Cincinnatus,' being apparently designed
to have an undue influence in the ensuing election of a
governor of this State, and, though in an ironical way, fully
and clearly implies, not only a slur upon the seminary of
learning in this State, and the president and tutors thereof,
but also a tacit charge against the Legislature of this State,
as being greatly deficient in point of integrity, or ability and
judgment, in the choice of a governor, and an express
declaration against our excellent constitution, and also an
unjust, false, and cruel defamation and aspersion of his excellency, the Governor; all which evidently tends to disturb
the peace of the inhabitants and promote discord and confusion in the State, and to encourage those who are disaffected to the present government; and notwithstanding
the freedom of the press ought to be tolerated as far as is
consistent with the good of the people and the security of
the government established under their authority, yet good
policy, as well as justice, requires that those who speak anything that directly tends to encourage the enemy and disaffected, and to discourage or disquiet the minds of the
good people of this State, ought to be detected and brought
to such punishment as may be agreeable to law and justice;
therefore, resolved, that Isaac Collins be required immediately to inform the Legislature of this State who is the
author of the aforesaid publication, and at whose request the
same was published." This resolution was forwarded to

the Assembly, where it was negatived by seventeen nays to eleven yeas. Thereupon the Council, on the next day, passed a resolution requiring Isaac Collins to furnish it with the information, and a copy was served on Collins, but he declined to make any answer, and the matter dropped. Livingston was re-elected by a vote of twenty-nine to nine for Philemon Dickinson, but for some time the Governor ceased to write for the *Gazette.* By other authority it is asserted that this temporary cessation of journalistic work was owing to the remonstrance of some legislators, who judged it undignified. However this may be, all are now agreed that he was peculiarly fitted for the very difficult duties he was called upon to perform. Whenever appealed to, in regard to the enforcement of the laws of the State, making the Continental money a legal tender, he always sustained them, though he always opposed the passage of such laws, and would not take advantage of them himself. On the proclamation of peace he quitted Trenton and returned to his house at Elizabethtown. In June, 1785, he was appointed by Congress Minister to the Court of Holland, but, while he was at first disposed to accept, eventually declined. During the succeeding year he became a member of the society in New York for promoting the emancipation of slaves, and emancipated the two he owned. He was appointed by the Legislature in May, 1787, a Delegate to the convention that formed the national constitution, and subsequently, in a message to the Legislature, expressed his gratitude to God that he had lived to see its approval and adoption by the States. Yale College in the next year conferred on him the degree of LL. D. He was a man of strong literary inclinations, and during both his earlier and later life wrote largely on political subjects, indulging also occasionally in poetical effusions. In the year 1745 he married Susannah French, whose father had been a large proprietor of land in New Jersey; she died in 1789. His own death occurred June 25th, 1790. Of his thirteen children, six died before him. One son, Brockholst Livingston, became a distinguished lawyer in New York, sat for several years on the Supreme bench of that State, and in 1807 was elevated to that of the United States, occupying his seat thereon until his death in 1823.

ARCLAY, ALEXANDER, JR., M. D., late of New Germantown, Hunterdon county, son of Dr. Alexander Barclay, of Newburgh, New York, was born in Aberdeen, Scotland, January 9th, 1832. Having read medicine under his father, he attended medical lectures, was graduated M. D., and in 1860, being duly licensed by the State Board of Censors, established himself in practice at New Germantown. On the 15th of September, 1862, he was commissioned Assistant Surgeon in the United States volunteer army, was attached to the 13th New Jersey Regiment, and

served until the 5th of March, 1863, when he resigned his commission. Returning to New Germantown he resumed his private practice, continuing actively engaged until June 18th, 1865, when he was thrown from his carriage and killed. He was a member of the Hunterdon County Medical Society, and in his profession his standing was excellent. He married a Miss Waldron, of New Germantown.

GDEN, ISAAC, M. D., late of New Brunswick, was born about the middle of the last century; graduated from the College of New Jersey in 1784; studied medicine, was licensed as a physician, and established himself at Six Mile Run, a village adjacent to his native town. Here he was married to a daughter of Elder Peter Stoothoff, the only child by this marriage becoming in early life the wife of the Rev. Isaac N. Wyckoff, D. D., of Albany, New York. He subsequently removed to Whitehouse, a few years later to New Germantown, and in 1809, relinquishing his practice in favor of his nephew, Dr. Oliver Barnet, to New Brunswick. As an obstetrician he attained to considerable celebrity, and was also successful as a general practitioner. He was an earnest student of astronomy, and during the latter portion of his life gave the greater portion of his time to that science. For several years he published an almanac in which, beside the usual tables, etc., he presented prognostications—generally in rhyme—of the weather for the coming year; a work that had at the time a very extensive circulation, and of which, preserved as curiosities, copies are still to be found in out-of-the-way country houses, and in the hands of book collectors. In 1821 he was one of the founders of the Hunterdon County Medical Society, was President of that organization in 1823, and in 1826, on leaving the county, was elected the first honorary member. He died suddenly, of apoplexy, some few years after his removal to New Brunswick.

ARRISON, JOSIAH, Lawyer, late of Salem, was born in Essex county, New Jersey, in 1795; was licensed as an attorney in 1800, and as a counsellor in 1803. After teaching a classical school for a few years at Deerfield, Cumberland county, he settled as a lawyer in Salem, where he married a lady of great respectability and worth. " He was a man of small stature, and had a respectable business as a conveyancer and attorney." The most remarkable circumstance in his professional career was his connection with the will of John Sinnickson, a citizen of Salem, who died without descendants, leaving a large property, consisting principally of real estate, about the year 1815, whose final instrument he drew and witnessed. The contest about this will lasted several years, was of a very exciting character, and divided the society of the town into two very hostile parties, "making breaches in very respectable families, which are hardly healed to this day." The principal opponent of the will was Dr. Rowan, who married a niece of the deceased. Probate of the will was refused by the Orphans' Court, and upon an appeal to Governor Mahlon Dickerson, as judge of the Prerogative Court, he affirmed this decree. He then removed his residence to Philadelphia, and filed a bill in the Circuit Court of the United States for the establishment of the trusts in the will. An issue of will or no will being ordered, the case was brought on before Judge Washington, and a jury which, after a protracted trial, rendered a verdict establishing the will. The case is reported in 3 Wash. C. C. R., p. 580, Harrison vs. Rowan. A motion for a new trial being made, was decided in 1820. Judge Washington declared himself perfectly satisfied with the verdict; but as Judge Pennington, who sat with him, was not so, a new trial was ordered. The parties then compromised and allowed a decree to be entered establishing the will, releases and other papers being executed by the heirs and devisees. A life-estate was thus settled on Dr. Rowan, who lived to extreme old age. After this trial, his wife having died in the meantime, he resided for several years in Camden, New Jersey, and carried on business as a printer. During that time he acted also as Reporter of the Supreme Court. Removing subsequently to Salem, he resided there permanently until his decease, which occurred in the year 1865.

WOODRUFF, HON. GEORGE WHITEFIELD, Lawyer, United States District Attorney, late of Trenton, was born at Elizabethtown, New Jersey, March 16th, 1765, and was a brother of A. D. Woodruff, who graduated at Princeton in the class of 1779. He pursued his studies in the *Alma Mater* of that brother, and after graduation studied law, and was admitted to practise as an attorney at the April term of the Supreme Court in 1788. He then removed to the State of Georgia, and in that State acquired a position of much respectability at the bar. Subsequently he was appointed, by President John Adams, United States District Attorney. Having acquired an ample fortune, he returned to New Jersey, and took up his residence near Trenton. Here he lived "in much companionship with books, withdrawn from active business, but not from constant amiable intercourse with men, until his death," which occurred in 1846, at the advanced age of eighty-two years. At the time of his decease he was the oldest member of the New Jersey bar. It is said that his most intimate friends never knew him to be betrayed into an angry deed or word. Possessed of fortune and a well-cultivated and richly stored mind, he exercised, notwithstanding his retiring manners,

the influence which wealth and intelligence confer. One of his sons graduated from Princeton College in the class of 1836.

NEEDHAM, LEWIS RANDOLPH, M. D., late of Perryville, New Jersey, was born in East Haddam, Connecticut, in 1808. He was for some time a school teacher in Sussex county, New Jersey; read medicine a short time with Dr. Jepthah B. Munn; subsequently with Dr. John Blane; attended medical lectures in New York, and in 1835 received his degree of M. D. Having been duly examined and licensed by the State Board of Censors, he entered into partnership with Dr. Blane, under whom he had studied, and this partnership was continued up to the time of his death. In practice he was highly successful, and for his ability, as well as for his genial manner and true kindliness, was very generally esteemed. He was a member of the Hunterdon County Medical Society, and was elected Secretary of that organization in 1836. He married Susan F. Sayre, of Madison, Morris county, New Jersey, by whom he had two children, one of whom, a son, is still living. He died November 12th, 1841.

SCHENCK, HENRY H., M. D., late of Readington, New Jersey, oldest son of Dr. Henry and Ellen (Hardenberg) Schenck, was born in February, 1782; his father removing a few years later to Neshamie, New Jersey. His strong love of adventure led him to enlist in the United States army when a mere lad, but being a minor, his enlistment was cancelled by his father before he had seen service. His next performance, when he had arrived at the mature age of seventeen years, was to get married; the lady of his choice being Jane Herder, who, being sixteen years old, was no less endowed with gravity and discretion than was her husband. Being married, he deemed it proper to settle down in life, and to this end entered vigorously upon the study of medicine under the supervision of his father. But medicine was monotonous, so one morning he left his books and his bride, and the next that was heard of him he was once more a soldier. This time his father concluded to give him his head, trusting to the many drawbacks to army life to cure him of his military proclivities. But he did not cure easily, and it was a round seven years before he lapsed back to the life of a civilian, having in the meantime fought through the war of 1812, up to the battle of Queenstown Heights, and after that event having passed his time as a prisoner in the British lines. His seven years of service quieted down his love of adventure, and during the remainder of his life he practised medicine vigorously and with very uniform success. As a matter of course he was extremely popular in the communities where he lived, his energetic habit and bright, cheerful manner making him hosts of acquaintances, and these, when they came to know his real kindliness of heart, rarely failed to become his warm friends. He was for some time in practice at Quakertown, removed thence to Readington, (about) 1810, and remained in practice at Readington until the time of his death, December 20th, 1823.

———◦◦◦———

COTT, MOSES, Physician and Surgeon, Revolutionary Soldier and Officer, late of New Brunswick, New Jersey, was born in 1738, and at seventeen years of age accompanied the unfortunate expedition under Braddock, and shared in all the privations and perils of the time and circumstances. At the capture of Fort Duquesne, three years afterward, he had risen to be a commissioned officer. In the course of the following year he resigned his commission, on account of the invidious distinction made between royal and colonial officers; and, by the advice of Dr. Ewing and Mr. Beattie, entered upon a course of studies in medicine. His first residence was at Brandywine, but about 1774 he removed to New Brunswick. When the revolutionary struggle commenced he took an active part on the patriotic side, and was appointed, July 2d, 1776, Physician and Surgeon-General of the State forces, and Director-General of the Military Hospitals. He then procured a supply of medicines and surgical instruments from Europe, partly by his own means and credit; but, unfortunately, a great portion of his needed and valuable store fell into the hands of the enemy on their sudden invasion of New Brunswick, at which time he barely saved himself from capture. "He was just sitting down to the table when the alarm was given, and the enemy, entering soon after, took possession of his house and regaled themselves on his deserted dinner. A tory neighbor told them that the boxes of medicine which they found had been poisoned by the rebel doctor, and left there purposely to destroy the British troops; whereupon they lost no time in emptying them into the street." In 1777 Congress took the entire direction of the medical staff, and he was commissioned as Senior Physician and Surgeon of the Hospitals, and Assistant Director-General; and in the discharge of the numerous and responsible duties attendant on his station he won universal encomiums. He was present at the battles of Trenton, Princeton, Brandywine and Germantown; and at Princeton was near the gallant Mercer when he fell. On the restoration of peace he resumed the practice of his profession in New Brunswick, New Jersey. He was one of the most active workers in raising the First Presbyterian Church of that city from its dilapidated and embarrassed state; and his is a prominent name on the committees called for the purpose of securing

its restoration to a flourishing condition. "It was through his agency, and partly, it is believed, by his gift, the ground was procured for the building." Having made a profession of religion at an early age, he was during his entire life a main pillar of the church; and for many years was an efficient and zealous Elder, and Treasurer of the Board of Trustees. His death occurred, December 28th, 1821, at the advanced age of eighty-three years.

———◦◦◦———

TTO, JOHN C., Physician and Surgeon, late of Philadelphia, was born near Woodbury, New Jersey, March 15th, 1774, and was the son of Bodo Otto, an eminent physician, and a distinguished public character in the stirring days of the revolutionary conflict. His literary education was obtained at Princeton College, and he graduated from that institution after the usual course of study and examination. He then entered the office of Dr. Rush, and in 1796 received his medical diploma from the University of Pennsylvania. He soon attained a highly respectable rank among his contemporaries, and in 1798 was elected one of the physicians of the Philadelphia Dispensary, an institution which he faithfully served for a period of five years. In 1813 he was appointed to succeed Dr. Rush (lately deceased) as one of the physicians of the Pennsylvania Hospital. Here his untiring devotion to the sick, his sound medical knowledge, his matured judgment, and a deep and ever-present sense of the responsibilities of the post, proved him to be the right man for the important position. He held this office during a period of twenty-two years. His clinical lectures while connected with the hospital were models of conciseness, simplicity and truthfulness. One of his pupils, himself afterward eminent as a physician, writes: "Who cannot look back with lively satisfaction and recall the slender and slightly-stooping frame of this venerable physician, as he passed around the wards of the hospital, stopping at each bed as he passed, kindly saluting his patient, making the necessary inquiries into his condition, and then, in the most unaffected and yet impressive manner, addressing himself to the assembled class, and fastening upon their minds some valuable medical precept." In addition to this responsible position, he was connected and identified with several other public charities. During twenty years he served the Orphan Asylum, where he was greatly beloved by the children and by all connected with the institution. He was also Physician for many years to the Magdalen Asylum, in whose prosperity he always evinced a deep and generous interest. In 1840 he was elected Vice-President of the College of Physicians, a position which he occupied at the time of his decease. In social life he was remarkable for the simplicity and ease of his manners, and for the vast amount of instructive and suggestive matter that generally pervaded his conversation. He was warmly attached to the Presbyterian forms and teachings, but was also of a truly liberal and catholic spirit; and his religion was peculiarly vital and practical. He read the Scriptures morning and evening, and rarely passed a day without perusing a portion of Thomas À Kempis' "Imitation of Christ." He died as he lived, an humble and devout Christian, beloved and respected by all, June 26th, 1844. He published "Medical Papers" in the New York *Medical Repository*, 1803; contributions to *Coxe's Medical Museum*, 1805; essays in the *Eclectic Repository;* and articles on medical and scientific subjects in the *North American Medical and Surgical Journal*, 1828, 1830.

———◆———

IRCH, REV. ROBERT, late of New Brunswick, New Jersey, was born in New York city, in January, 1808, and was the son of an eminent physician of that city. While an infant he was attacked by a severe inflammation of the brain, and life was despaired of, insomuch that his mother made his shroud while watching at his couch. He was saved, however, by the opening of a vein in his head; but he always suffered somewhat from the effects of that illness to the end of his days. At a very early age he lost his father, and with him his expectation of a liberal education. He was then taken from school and placed in a counting-house, for the purpose of acquiring a practical and thorough knowledge of mercantile transactions and affairs. "Becoming pious, he was received to the communion of the Cedar Street Church, under Dr. Romeyn, at the age of twelve. The fatherless and sprightly boy then attracted the notice of Dr. John Breckinridge, and was induced by him to resume his studies." After graduating at Dickinson College he taught a classical school, first at Lancaster, and subsequently at Savannah, where he gained many friends of high standing and distinction. His theological studies, commenced at Andover, were completed at Princeton; and after his licensure, by the Presbytery of New York, he preached for a short time to a new church in a hall in Broadway, from which he was called to New Brunswick, on a salary of $1,000. March 14th, 1839, Rev. Thomas Smyth, D. D., of Charleston, South Carolina, having declined an invitation to serve as successor to Dr. Jones, he was chosen pastor of the First Presbyterian Church, Father Comfort presiding. The sermon was preached by the late Professor Dod, from Psalm xcvii. 1; the charge to the minister and that to the people being both given by Rev. Ravand K. Rodgers, Rev. James Alexander, who had been appointed to the latter duty, being taken suddenly ill. His pastoral career was brief, but full of zeal and promise; and his interest in the young was evinced in the pains he took to get up a course of winter evening lectures of a popular

character. After his decease, September 12th, 1842, in the thirty-fifth year of his age, the congregation erected, in the new cemetery, a handsome marble monument to his memory.

———◆———

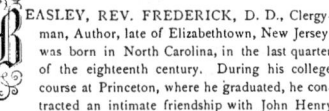

EASLEY, REV. FREDERICK, D. D., Clergyman, Author, late of Elizabethtown, New Jersey, was born in North Carolina, in the last quarter of the eighteenth century. During his college course at Princeton, where he graduated, he contracted an intimate friendship with John Henry Hobart and Henry Kollock, which was terminated only by death. After graduating he studied theology with President Samuel Stanhope Smith, acting at the same time as tutor in the college. In 1801 he was ordained deacon by Bishop Moore, of New York, and priest by the same divine in 1802. In September of this year he became Rector of St. John's Church, Elizabethtown, but in the following spring resigned his charge and accepted a call to the Rectorship of St. Peter's Church, Albany. Here he remained until 1809, the date of his removal to Baltimore, where he became Rector of St. Paul's Church. In 1813, his health being in a precarious condition, and feeling the need of a position where lighter and less trying service would be required, he resigned his charge and accepted the office of Provost of the University of Pennsylvania, a place that suited admirably his intellectual tastes and habits; and during the ensuing fifteen years he discharged the duties of that station with acknowledged fidelity and ability. The office of Provost he resigned in 1828, and in 1829 became Rector of St. Michael's Church, Trenton, New Jersey, where he remained until 1836. His health becoming very much impaired, he relinquished also his charge at Trenton, and removed to Elizabethtown, where he spent the remainder of his days. He received the honorary degree of Doctor of Divinity from Columbia College, and from the University of Pennsylvania in 1815. "He was a man of slight frame, below the ordinary height, and was very easy and rapid in his movements. He was remarkably social and frank in all his intercourse." His acquirements in literature were extensive and varied, and his chief delight was found in reading, studying and meditation. His sermons were terse, well-written, and cogent in reasoning, and while his studies lay mainly in the direction of mental philosophy, he had no relish for the Scotch philosophers, but admired John Locke above all others. He published "A Discourse before the Ladies' Society, instituted for the Relief of Distressed Seamen in the City of Albany," 1808; "Inaugural Sermon," in St. Paul's Church, Baltimore, 1810; "A Sermon on Duelling," 1811; an anonymous pamphlet, entitled "Serious Reflections addressed to Episcopalians in Maryland, on the State of their Church generally, but more particularly on the Pending Election of a

Suffragan Bishop," 1813; "A Sermon before the Diocesan Convention of Pennsylvania," 1815; "American Dialogues of the Dead," 1815; "A (second) Sermon on Duelling," 1822; "A Search of Truth in the Science of the Human Mind :. Part I.," one volume, 8vo., 1822 (he left in MSS. Part II. complete); '"A Vindication of the Argument *a priori* in Proof of the Being and Attributes of God, from Objections of Dr. Waterland," 1825; " Review of Brown's Philosophy of the Human Mind," 1825; "A Vindication of the Fundamental Principles of Truth and Order in the Church of Christ, from the Allegations of Rev. William E. Channing, D. D.," 1830; "An Examination of No. 90 of the Tracts for the Times," 1842. He edited also the two volumes of Dr. Samuel Stanhope Smith's posthumous sermons, and wrote the memoir of his life, prefixed to the first volume; and contributed largely to the periodical literature of the day. He died at Elizabethtown, New Jersey, November 1st, 1845.

AVARD, HON. JOHN, Colonel in the Revolutionary Army, Mayor of New Brunswick, late of that place, was born on Bohemia Manor, in Cecil county, Maryland, August 11th, 1738. His father left no will at his decease, and he, being the eldest son, became entitled, by the laws of his native State, to the whole real estate. Such, however, was his affection for his twin brother that no sooner had he reached the age of manhood than he conveyed to him half the estate. After receiving an academical education, under the preceptorship of Dr. Finley, he was placed as a subordinate in the counting-house of John Rhea, a well-known merchant of Philadelphia. " It was here that the seeds of grace began first to take root, and to give promise of those fruits of righteousness which afterward abounded." He early became a communicant of the Presbyterian church, under the charge of Gilbert Tennent, of Log College fame. Some years after his marriage he was chosen to occupy the station of Ruling Elder, and filled this place with acceptance and energetic zeal. Mr. Whitfield, while on his visits to America, became intimately acquainted with him; formed for him an affectionate and enduring attachment; and in company with him made several extended tours." In 1770 he lost his only brother, Dr. James A. Bayard, a man of promising talents, of prudence and skill, and of a most amiable disposition, and growing reputation. The violence of his sorrow at first produced an illness which confined him to his bed for several days. " But by degrees it subsided into a tender melancholy, which for years after would steal across his mind, and tinge his hours of domestic intercourse and solitary devotion with pensive sadness." At the death of that brother's widow he adopted the children and educated them as his own. One of them became an eminent statesman, and placed his name high on the tablets of

national fame and honor. ' At the opening of the contest with Great Britain he was fearless in the enunciation of his opinions and views, and took an open and decided part in favor of the patriot revolutionists. At the head of the 2d Battalion of the Philadelphia Militia he marched to the assistance of General Washington, and was present at the battle of Trenton. He was also a valued and influential member of the Council of Safety, and for many years presided with marked ability and firmness as Speaker of the Legislature. In 1777, when a report was spread that his house and property had been destroyed by the British army, and that his servant, who had been intrusted with valuable personal effects, had decamped with his trust and found refuge within the enemy's lines, William Bell, with whom he had served his apprenticeship, and who had accumulated several thousand pounds, insisted that his patron should receive one-half of his estate; this generous offer was not accepted, however, as the report was without foundation. " Reiterated afflictions induced a deep depression of mind, and for some time he was no longer relieved by the avocations of business." But in 1785 he was appointed a member of the old Congress, then sitting in New York. In the following year, however, he was not included in the delegation. In 1788 he removed to New Brunswick, New Jersey, where he filled in turn the positions of Mayor of the city and Judge of the Court of Common Pleas. He was also a Ruling Elder of the church in this place; and conspicuous as a tireless coworker in all measures and movements calculated to raise the local standard of education, political and literary, and of morality and religion. His death occurred at New Brunswick, New Jersey, January 7th, 1807, aged sixty-eight years.

AN DOREN, REV. ISAAC, Clergyman, Educator, late of Perth Amboy, was born in New Jersey, in the last quarter of the eighteenth century, and secured his literary education at Princeton College, where he graduated in due time and season.

He subsequently applied himself to the study of theology under the guidance of Professor Theodore Dirck Romeyn, and completed his preparations for the ministry with Dr. Livingston. He was licensed by the Classis of New York, and was ordained about the year 1798. In 1800 he became pastor of the Reformed Dutch Church at Hopewell, Orange county, New York, where, during a pastorate of twenty-three years, he was blessed with eminent success. Leaving his charge, he removed to Newark, New Jersey, and during the ensuing four years presided as principal over an academy in that place. Later, in conjunction with his eldest son, he established the Collegiate Institute on Brooklyn Heights. He removed from there to Lexington, Kentucky. After spending several years in teaching in the West, he returned to New Jersey, where his later years were passed happily and usefully among his children. "He was eminently social, given to hospitality, the gifted counsellor of young clergymen and of all who sought his advice." He died at Perth Amboy, New Jersey, August 12th, 1864. His only publication was a tract entitled "A Summary of Christian Duty," compiled from the Douay Bible.

AYLOR, AUGUSTUS R., Physician, late of New Brunswick, was born in that town in 1793' or 1794, and was the oldest son of Colonel John Taylor. His medical education was conducted under the supervision of Dr. Scott, of New Brunswick. He was for many years a member of the Board of Trustees of the First Presbyterian Church; and was widely and highly esteemed for his good judgment, well-balanced mind, and thorough medical skill and abilities. He was married, in 1804, to Catharine Neilson. He died in 1841, at the age of fifty-eight years. Resolutions of eulogy and condolence were then passed by the New Jersey Medical Society, and transmitted to the family. During his last illness he was admitted to church membership; "but that his mind had long been sensible of the obligations of religion was inferred from a copy of a prayer found after his death, in his own handwriting. The prayer was that beautiful and appropriate one drawn up by Dr. John Mason Good, for his own use before entering on his daily round of practice."

---

cCARTER, THOMAS NESBITT, Lawyer, Newark. John McCarter, founder of the family in America, was an educated Scotch-Irish Presbyterian, who emigrated in 1774 to this country, and settled in Morristown, New Jersey. Upon the breaking out of the revolutionary war he warmly espoused the cause of the colonies, and enlisted as a private in the Continental army; was shortly thereafter promoted to be Assistant Commissary with the rank of Major, and in this capacity served, until peace was declared. After the war he returned to Morristown, and was for a number of years clerk of Morris county. His son, Robert H. McCarter, succeeded him in this office, and subsequently was for fifteen years a Judge of the Court of Common Pleas of Sussex county; for many years a Commissioner of the Supreme Court of New Jersey, and was at the time of his death, 1851, a Judge of the Court of Errors and Appeals. Thomas Nesbitt McCarter, son of Robert H. McCarter, was born at Morristown, January 31, 1824. Prepared for college at the Newton Academy, he entered the junior class at Princeton in 1840; was graduated thence B. A. in 1842; immediately

upon receiving his degree began the study of law in the office of the Hon. Martin Ryerson, at Newton, and was admitted to the New Jersey bar as an attorney in October, 1845, and as a counsellor in January, 1849. Upon being licensed, he formed a partnership with Mr. Ryerson, that proved highly satisfactory to both parties, and that was continued until 1853, when the senior member of the firm removed to Trenton, and in a little time was appointed a Justice of the Supreme Court of New Jersey. After the disruption of this partnership he practised alone in Newton until 1865, when he removed to his present location, Newark. Already well known by reputation to the bar of that city, one of the strongest in the State, he was at once accorded a prominent position; and in a few years was one of the recognized leaders. In 1868, his practice having greatly increased, he entered into a partnership with Oscar Keen, Esq., a partnership that still continues. For a number of years his standing as a corporation lawyer has been of the highest, and beside being specially retained in many of the great suits brought in recent years in the New Jersey courts, he is the regularly appointed counsel of several of the most important corporate organizations of, or doing business in, the State. While resident in Newton he was a Director in and Counsel to the Sussex Railroad Company; has been for a number of years a Director of and Counsel to the Morris Canal and Banking Company; has been Counsel to the Lehigh Valley Railroad Company; to the Delaware, Lackawanna & Western Railroad Company; to the Morris & Essex Railroad Company; to the New Jersey Railroad and Transportation Company, etc., etc. Aside from his professional connections, he has been and continues to be prominently identified with various influential corporate bodies as a Director. Of the People's Mutual Insurance Company; of the Republic Trust Company—both of Newark; and of the Easton & Amboy Railroad Company, he was one of the original incorporators; and in each of these companies, since their foundation, he has been a Director, and has taken an active part in their management. He has twice been tendered a seat upon the bench of the Supreme Court of New Jersey—by Governor Olden in 1860, and again by Governor Ward in 1866—but on both occasions his desire to remain at the bar led him to decline the proffered honor. The only professional position of a public character that he has accepted has been that of Chancery Reporter, tendered him in 1864 by Chancellor Green; and this, after issuing two volumes of reports, he was compelled to resign by reason of his constantly increasing practice to resign. For many years he has taken an active part in State and national politics, and had he chosen to relinquish his profession his opportunities for advancement in public life were exceptionally excellent. While resident in Newton, he was for three years Collector for Sussex county, and in 1861 was elected thence, on the Democratic ticket, a member of the State Assembly—his election being remarkable in that no opposition candidate was placed in the field and

56

that he received in common the vote of both political parties. During his term of office he served as Chairman of the Committee of Ways and Means, taking an active part in all the deliberations of that body—composed of an unusually large delegation of able and influential men—and impressing in a marked manner his own personality upon all important measures reported by it for legislative action. In 1862 he declined to be a candidate for re-election, and in the following year—strongly objecting to its pronounced opposition to the prosecution of the war—he definitely abandoned the Democratic party. In the Presidential campaign of 1864 he earnestly advocated on the stump—and proved the sincerity of his advocacy by his vote at the polls—the re-election of President Lincoln; and since that date he has been thoroughly identified with the Republican party, and in its interest has taken an active part in every important canvass. He has twice been nominated a Presidential Elector: on the Douglas ticket in 1860, and on the Hayes and Wheeler ticket in 1876, being elected on the former. He married, December 4th, 1849, Mary Louisa Haggerty, daughter of Uzal C. Haggerty, Esq., of Sussex county, New Jersey.

HEPARD, JOSEPH FLAVAL, M. D., of Phillipsburg, was born, March 30th, 1819, in Ranton township, Hunterdon county, New Jersey. He is a son of the late Jacob Shepard, a farmer of Ranton. Receiving an ordinary education in the schools of Hunterdon, he began in 1843 the study of medicine with the venerable Dr. Schenck, of Flemington, with whom he remained five years, practising with him for a portion of the time, and also attending, in 1851 and 1852, a course of lectures at the Medical Department of the University of New York, from which he graduated in 1853. He first settled at Hightstown, New Jersey, whence, after a short residence there, he removed to Phillipsburg, where he settled permanently. For about twelve years he was the only physician in Phillipsburg, which, at the time he took up his residence in it, was a village of less than two hundred inhabitants; *Harper's Gazetteer*, published a year or two later, putting its population at one hundred and seventy-five. It now contains between five and six thousand inhabitants, and its growth measures roughly the growth of his practice, which from a small beginning has become as large, perhaps, as that of any other physician in the county of Warren. He is a member of the Phillipsburg Medical Society, of which he is President, and of the Warren County Medical Society; and in 1877 represented Warren county in the State Medical Society. For eleven years he has been a member of the Phillipsburg School Board, of which for the last five years he has been Treasurer; has been for several years a member of the Phillipsburg Town Council, is Treasurer of the Phillipsburg Building Loan Association, Nos.

1 and 4, and also a member of the Masonic order. A man of strong and rounded character, combining general abilities with special training, he touches the community in which he lives at many points besides the strictly professional one, exerting through each a wholesome and decided influence. He was married, in 1856, to Miss Cummings, of Belvidere, who died the following year; and again, in 1871, to Mrs. Hannah Stears, of Plainfield.

OTT, GERSHOM, Trenton, Keeper of the New Jersey State Prison, late Major-General United States Volunteer Army, son of Gershom Mott, and descended from a German family long resident in New Jersey, was born near Trenton, April 7th, 1822. Having received at the Trenton Academy the groundwork of a solid English education, he began his business career, when but fourteen years of age, in a commercial establishment in New York. Mercantile affairs, however, were not to his taste—he was destined to move in a broader field—and shortly before the breaking out of the Mexican war he had relinquished his position in New York, and was temporarily residing with his father in New Jersey. When Congress, in May, 1846, voted ten millions of dollars for the prosecution of the war against Mexico, and at the same time authorized President Polk to accept the services of fifty thousand volunteers, the opportunity that he required was presented, and he eagerly accepted it. Promptly upon the publication of President Polk's proclamation calling for volunteers, he offered his services to the government, was commissioned a Second Lieutenant, and was assigned to the 10th United States Infantry. With this organization he served during the entire war, distinguishing himself for his coolness in danger and for his exactness as a disciplinarian—not only in seeing that his own orders were obeyed, but in rendering prompt obedience to the orders addressed to him by his superiors. On the triumphant termination of the war he willingly relinquished his military rank, having no desire to be a soldier in times of peace; while in recognition of his meritorious services he was offered by President Polk the position—previously held by Gershom Mott, Sr.—of Collector of the Port of Lamberton (now a part of Trenton). This office he accepted, retaining it until the spring of 1849, when he was removed to make room for President Taylor's appointee. About this time he was tendered and accepted a clerical situation in the office at Bordentown of the Delaware and Raritan Canal Company, remaining thus employed until 1855, when he was appointed Teller in the Bordentown Bank. It was while he held this latter position that the final acts were wrought out of the long chain terminating in the war of the rebellion. All his life long he had been a sincere believer in the principles espoused by the Democratic party; but when the Southern division of that political organization declared and acted upon what its leaders styled the right of secession from the Federal Union, he promptly ranged himself on the side of union and law, and loyally offered his services to the government in defence of its menaced integrity. When the famous Second New Jersey Brigade—composed of the 5th, 6th, 7th, and 8th Regiments—was formed, under a requisition made by President Lincoln on the 24th of July, 1861, he was appointed (August 4th) by Governor Olden Lieutenant-Colonel of the 5th Regiment. Practically—Colonel Starr being ranking officer and acting Brigadier-General—he was the Colonel of the 5th; and under his supervision—his previous military training admirably fitting him for the task—its men were thoroughly disciplined and drilled. Early in December, 1861, the regiment was deemed ready for the field, and was accordingly ordered forward from the camp at Meridian Hill, near Washington, where it had lain since mustered into the service, and with the remainder of the brigade was attached to General Hooker's division, at Budd's Ferry, Maryland. In March, 1862, it entered upon its brilliant career of service in the field; on the 10th of that month a detail of five hundred men, under Lieutenant-Colonel Mott, being sent across the Potomac to occupy the rebel works at Cockpit Point, abandoned the previous day by General Beauregard in his retreat from Manassas, and a few weeks later—having been transferred to the Peninsula—went into action for the first time at the battle of Williamsburg. In this battle the New Jersey Brigade took a leading part, holding for a time the entire rebel army in check, and the 5th Regiment was for more than nine hours exposed to a frightfully destructive fire. For the gallant manner in which he held his ground, Lieutenant-Colonel Mott was promoted (May 7, 1862) to be Colonel of the 6th New Jersey Regiment; and while in command of the 6th his soldierly qualities became more and more conspicuous. In the official report of the battle of Seven Pines, General Hooker made especial mention of his "distinguished services in the field;" and Acting Brigadier-General Starr, in his official reports, again and again speaks of his intrepidity and coolness whilst under fire. Throughout the Peninsular campaign his record is distinguished, notwithstanding the heroic qualities of the men by the side of whom he fought. In the second Bull Run battle, July 28th, 1862, he was severely wounded in the arm, and was compelled for a time to relinquish his command; and it was while thus absent on sick-leave that he was unanimously commended by his superior officers for promotion. Acting upon this commendation, President Lincoln promoted him (September 7th, 1862) to be Brigadier-General, and when he returned to duty (December 4th) he was assigned, at the urgent request of General Hooker, to the command of the Second New Jersey Brigade; or, as it was in fact, the Third Brigade of the Second Division, Third Army Corps. In the battle of Chancellorsville (May 3d, 1863) the Jersey troops were again placed in the thick of the fight, and were held up to their work by General Mott with his accustomed cool-

ness ano courage. Early in the day he had a narrow escape, a rifle-ball passing between his bridle-arm and body, and at a later period of the engagement his left hand was struck and shattered. After receiving this wound he remained for a considerable time upon the field, and it was only when greatly weakened by loss of blood that he at last consented to go to the rear. During the action a section of Dimmick's battery, 1st Artillery, was in great danger of being captured, the artillerymen and horses having all been killed, and in order to rescue it General Mott ordered Captain Nicholls, with a detachment of men from the 8th New Jersey, to bring it off by hand. The battery was being raked by a pitiless fire, and for a moment the resetting party wavered. Promptly General Mott seized the colors, sprang forward and said that he himself would lead the detail, and the men—with a ringing cheer for their plucky commander—rallied at once, put themselves down to their work, and the battery was saved. His wound, though not dangerous, was an ugly one, and it was not until the end of August that the surgeons would permit him to rejoin his brigade. On the 15th of the following October the brigade fought the spirited little engagement at McLean's Ford, on Bull Run, the ordering of the fight resting entirely with General Mott, and resulting in successfully holding the ford against a superior force of the enemy. When the grand advance was ordered by General Grant, in the spring of 1864, General Mott was placed in command of the Second Division of the Third Army Corps, a position that he held until the end of the war. As had been his custom from the outset, during the campaign of the ensuing summer he was utterly regardless of his personal safety, looking only to the effectiveness of his command, and it was owing to this regardlessness that (before Petersburg, August 19th, 1864) he was again—though not seriously—wounded. His management of his division was as able as had been his management of his brigade and regiment, and on the 10th of September he was deservedly brevetted a Major-General. Just at the end of the war (April 6th, 1865), in a skirmish at Amelia Springs, he was again wounded, and while the wound was but slight it was sufficient to temporarily disable him, and so prevent him from being in at the death with the brave Jerseymen of his command. On the dissolution of the army General Mott was placed in temporary command of the Provisional Corps, and when, in July, that body was disbanded, his services were still retained, and he was ordered to Washington. In August he was detailed to serve on the Wirz commission, and in the ensuing November was detailed to serve on the commission appointed to investigate the difficulties between the State of Massachusetts and the Austrian government, growing out of the enlistment of Austrian subjects by the former. While engaged in this last service he received his final promotion, being made (December 1st, 1865) a full Major-General of Volunteers. He was thus the first soldier from New Jersey to receive the brevet of Major-General, and was the only Jerseyman who attained to the full rank. On the 20th of February, 1866, his resignation, tendered some time previously, was accepted, and with hearty expressions of esteem from Secretary Stanton and other members of the government, he retired from the service to which he had so constantly done honor, and the interests of which he had so constantly advanced. The following is a partial list of the battles in which he personally took part: Yorktown, Williamsburg, Fair Oaks, Seven Pines, Savage's Station, Glendale, Malvern Hill, Bristow's Station, Second Bull Run, Chantilly, Centreville, Fredericksburg, Chancellorsville, Wapping Heights, McLean's Ford, Mine Run, the Wilderness, Todd's Tavern, Po River, Spottsylvania, Spottsylvania Court House, North Anna River, Toloposomy Creek, Cold Harbor, before Petersburg, Deep Bottom, Mine Explosion, North Bank of the James, Fort Sedgewick, Poplar Spring Church, and Amelia Springs. Upon returning to his home in New Jersey, he was offered and accepted the important position of Paymaster in the Camden & Amboy Railroad Company. In 1867, while holding this office, the regular army was increased, and General Mott was appointed Colonel of the 33d Infantry, but he declined the commission. Although the nomination was in a high degree complimentary to the reputation he had made as a soldier, and would certainly have proved only a stepping-stone to further preferment, he could not bring himself to a soldier's life in time of peace. When his country needed him he had not been found absent, but the war over he preferred civil life. He therefore continued in his railroad appointment, and discharged his duties with marked ability and efficiency until March 1st, 1872, when the Camden & Amboy Company's lines were leased to the Pennsylvania Railroad Company. Shortly after this event, September 1st, 1875, he was appointed to a much higher office, to wit: that of Treasurer of the State of New Jersey—his presentation to the treasurership having been made by Governor Bedle to fill the vacancy caused by the removal of Sooy. The management of the treasury at this particular juncture was of course a matter of some little delicacy, but by the efficient manipulation of the forces at his command he rapidly restored order throughout the department, and during the entire period of his incumbency he evinced a quite exceptional financial ability. On February 15th, 1876, upon the appointment of his Republican successor, he relinquished his trust; and on the 29th of the following March, 1876, was appointed to his present position of Keeper of the New Jersey State Prison. In tendering him this office, Governor Bedle recognized the fact that his habit of enforcing rigid discipline would admirably well fit him for the discharge of its responsible duties, and the record of his administration up to the present time has abundantly justified this belief. In his present, as was the case in all his past professions, General Mott keeps ever before him one single word—duty. It is this honesty to himself that has made his life so exemplary. He married, August 8th, 1849, Elizabeth, daughter of John E. Smith, Esq., of Trenton

ING, REV. BARNABAS, D. D., late of Rockaway, Morris county, New Jersey, was born in New Marlborough, Massachusetts, June 2d, 1780; graduated at Williams College, September 5th, 1804, and in the fall of 1805 was licensed to preach by the Berkshire Association. On the following 24th of December he first stepped upon the soil of New Jersey, and soon after began his labors at Sparta, Sussex county; occasionally, also, at Berkeshire Valley, and Rockaway, Morris county; his first sermon in the latter place having been preached Friday evening, January 24th, 1806, at a private house, on the text: "To everything there is a season, and a time to every purpose under the heavens."—Ecclesiastes iii. 1. At various times during that year he supplied the Rockaway pulpit; but in October, 1807, made an agreement to supply it regularly, and also the one at Sparta, on alternate Sabbaths. His labors were so acceptable that, on the 25th of September, 1808, he was called to be pastor of the church at Rockaway, the call being signed and attested by Rev. James Richards, D. D., of Morristown, as moderator of the parish meetings; and December 27th was ordained and installed pastor by the Presbytery of New York. The services took place in the old church, "which was less comfortable than many a modern barn, and which had no stove to warm it." Among the eminent men who were present were Drs. Griffin, Hillyer, Richards, John McDowell, Perrine, and Rev. Aaron Condit. Dr. McDowell, then in the third year of his ministry, preached the sermon; and Dr. Perrine, then the pastor of the "Bottle Hill Church," as Madison was called, and afterward the associate of Dr. Richards, in the Auburn Theological Seminary, delivered the charge to the pastor. "As a mark of the times, it may be stated that the services were held in that rude and uncomfortable church on a very cold day; they were begun with a congregational prayer-meeting at ten o'clock, and continued until three in the afternoon. There is no tradition of a single complaint, either by the clergymen or people, although it is said that the young pastor was so thoroughly chilled, that when seated at the dinner-table, it was shaken by his trembling."—"Sketch" by Rev. Joseph F. Tuttle, D. D. His parish included a circle of territory whose diameter was ten or twelve miles. In that region he was for several years the sole minister; he visited with strict regularity every family; and, in addition, held such frequent public services in the church, the school-house, or private house, as often to amount, for weeks together, to ten each week. These abundant labors, accomplished by the most rigid adherence to rule in regard to his health, studies, and time, were attended with extraordinary success. The growth of the church was rapid, and healthful in tone and character, and with that there was a marvellous and desirable change in society. Schools sprang up, many young men sought the culture of the college, business prospects grew brighter and more extended, the wealth of the mines was discovered and appreciated, and the refinements of an elegant social life increased. In 1848 he preached his fortieth anniversary sermon, which was published, and preserved among the pamphlets of the New Jersey Historical Society. "The greatness and value of the good man's labors are related in that discourse with far too much modesty, in view of the results flowing from his residence in the State." In December, 1853, he pronounced his forty-fifth anniversary discourse, which he was unwilling to publish. December 24th, 1854, he again preached an anniversary sermon, the forty-sixth of his pastorate, and the forty-ninth of his ministry in the one church, since he preached his first discourse in Rockaway, January 24th, 1806. December 12th, 1858, the session of the Presbyterian Church at Rockaway adopted a minute, and directed a copy of it to be sent to him, its senior pastor, in view of the fact that the fiftieth anniversary of his installation as pastor was at hand. In this minute the session speak in terms expressive of gratitude to God for sending such a faithful man to be their pastor, and for the abundant results of his ministry. "Let it be added that he was spared to his people more than three years after the occasion referred to. He sometimes preached, but oftener exhorted, and always with acceptance. His mental faculties remained unimpaired, and his interest in everything pertaining to his friends, the church, and the country, was as warm as in early manhood. The Monday night the news of the Bull Run disaster gave such horrible unrest to vast multitudes in the loyal States was spent by him in sleep as trustful and sweet as an infant's; and he said: 'Children, it cost us seven years of dreadful war to give us a nation, it will cost us years of more dreadful war to save that nation; but you need not fear as if it were not to be saved. It shall live, and not die.' In the spring of 1862 it was thought best by himself that he tender his resignation formally to the parish; but, to their honor, his faithful people refused to receive it, professing to him an unabated attachment." He had then filled the pastorate fifty-three years and several months. "On the second Sabbath in March, 1862, he had performed his last official act in public, with a singular fitness, it being on the occasion of his last communion with the church, at the close of which he stretched forth his hands and with such pathos and beauty pronounced the apostolical benediction, recorded in the thirteenth chapter of the Epistle to the Hebrews, that many were moved to tears, and some even said they had never heard the words before." More than fifty-six years before he had preached for the first time in that congregation, and more than fifty-four years (from October, 1807,) had been preaching there regularly, lacking only less than a year of being their pastor during that long period. Thus writes Rev. Dr. Joseph F. Tuttle: "The first half of this century was marked by no event more important in its results to the region of country of which Rockaway, Morris county, is the centre, than the entrance of the Rev. Barnabas King upon his duties as pastor of the First Presbyterian Church in that town; the moral force he exerted effecting

an entire change in the character of the people coming within the sphere of his influence." On the day that his resignation was laid before the parish he was stricken down by sickness; and after several days of suffering, he passed from earth "as peacefully as a little child passes into sleep." In his able and interesting history of the Presbyterian Church, Dr. Gillett thus describes him: "Frail and feeble in appearance, and supposed by all to be consumptive, he was spared to the discharge of a long and useful pastorate. But while faithful to his special charge, he did not neglect the missionary field around him. With the best men of the Jersey Presbytery he bore his full share in itinerant evangelization, going from Powles Hook to the Delaware, to tell the destitute of Christ. The monuments of his success were scattered around him far and near. One of the most eminent of his contemporaries, the Rev. Albert Barnes, remarked that he "knew of no minister whose walk and labor and success had been so admirable as those of Mr. King, of Rockaway. His great ambition was to win souls. His one book was the Bible." As a preacher, he was simple and scriptural; and his whole course was characterized by good sense, consummate judgment, earnestness of purpose and devotion to his work; and usefulness he placed high above eloquence or learning. Yet his utterance was always forcible and manly, and at times touchingly fervent. He rested from his labors on the 10th of April, 1862, and on the 13th his remains were consigned to the grave, "in the midst of such a concourse of people as was never before gathered in the old yard at Rockaway." At his own request, the funeral sermon was preached by his colleague in the pastorate of the church.

ONES, REV. JOSEPH H., D. D., late Pastor of the First Presbyterian Church of New Brunswick, New Jersey, was born in Tolland county, Connecticut, and graduated at Cambridge, Massachusetts, wherefrom, by appointment, he became a tutor in Bowdoin College. At the expiration of one year he removed to Wilkesbarre, Pennsylvania, and after spending two or three years in that place prosecuted his theological studies at Princeton Seminary. He was then engaged one year as stated supply of Woodbury, New Jersey, and subsequently was called to New Brunswick, with a salary of nine hundred dollars. "The church prospered greatly under him; and his pastoral attention was unremitting." Every successive year of his ministry here brought with it new evidences of prosperity. A parsonage was built in 1827, at a cost of three thousand three hundred and fifty dollars; and in 1832 a new frame session-house was erected adjoining the church, at a cost of two thousand six hundred and ninety-six dollars. The old session-house was sold with permission of the session, and the proceeds, with rents amounting to one hundred and seventy-nine dollars and forty-four cents, were divided among the owners *pro rata*.

At a later period the congregation had increased so much that the project of a second organization was entertained, and ventilated in a public meeting called for the purpose, but after a warm discussion the subject was indefinitely postponed. But, although the project was discountenanced by the majority, there were a few who continued to uphold it; and eventually a second church was organized. "As in consequence of the determination to erect a new edifice the pretext of want of room was obviated, it was shrewdly suspected that theological differences were at the bottom of this scheme; and these suspicions grew into belief when, on the division of the General Assembly in 1838, the second church elected to adhere to the new school, while the first church adhered to the old. It is gratifying to be able to add that the second church having in the course of time become freed from its original elements, has since returned to the old school connection, and the congregation are now worshipping in a new and tasteful building, erected chiefly by the liberality of three individuals. Although there was no small debate about it, it was at last determined by the old congregation to take down their house and erect a larger one nearly on the same site, viz., on the corner of George and Paterson streets." In the interval that elapsed, the consistory of the Dutch church courteously offered the use of their house on Sabbath afternoons, which was gratefully accepted, the morning service being held in the lecture-room. The new church was dedicated on Thursday, December 15th, 1836; Dr. John Breckinridge preaching in the morning, and Dr. McClelland in the afternoon, to crowded auditories. The amount of money disbursed was twenty-three thousand three hundred and twenty-eight dollars and fifty-six cents, of which six thousand dollars were borrowed. This debt was shortly after generously assumed in different proportions by ten gentlemen, viz.: Charles Smith, James Neilson, John W. Stout, Frederick Richmond, Joseph C. Griggs, Samuel Holcomb, F. R. Smith, Peter Dayton, A. S. Neilson, and Augustus R. Taylor. A lien was given them on the unsold pews, and the income arising from them; but when it was soon after discovered that there was still a further debt on the church property to the amount of two thousand eight hundred and twenty-six dollars, they voluntarily proposed to relinquish their lien, on condition that the rest of the congregation would raise money sufficient to wipe off this remaining incumbrance. The condition was fulfilled; fresh subscriptions were made, and the congregation had ultimately the satisfaction of occupying their new church, without fear of sheriff's writs or foreclosure of mortgages. In 1837 a remarkable revival of religion occurred, "altogether unprecedented in the history of New Brunswick," whose fruits were the addition of one hundred and forty-nine persons to the communion of the Presbyterian church, and of about three hundred and fifty to the other churches of the city. During that period of grace, the pastors were relieved in their arduous duties by the visits of eminent clergymen from other places, among whom were Dr. John Breckin-

ridge, Professor Dod, Mr. Ródgers, Drs. Murray, Archibald, James W. Alexander, David Abeel, Thomas L. Janeway, and Armstrong. From New Brunswick, the revival spread to the neighboring towns; and the churches of Bound Brook, Somerville, Plainfield, and Piscataway, in particular, largely shared the blessing. "In the First Presbyterian Church there have been other seasons of refreshing, but for power and extent the revival of 1837 stands without a parallel, either before or since. In attempting to account for it, he is of opinion that no natural causes were adequate; neither the cholera of 1832, the tornado of 1835, the commercial embarrassments of a later period, the predisposition of the people, or the ordinary means of grace; in short, he prefers to ascribe it to that mysterious and divine agency which, like the wind, bloweth where it listeth. It only remains to add that the great mass of the converts have done credit to their profession." The singular success of his ministry drew on him the attention of the Sixth Church of Philadelphia, which was languishing, and turned to him as one likely to promote their resuscitation. At first he declined the invitation, and his people fearing to lose his services, at once raised his salary to twelve hundred dollars with the parsonage. Eventually, however, yielding to urgent importunities and the advice of the Princeton professors, he conceived it to be his duty to go, and accordingly gave up his charge in New Brunswick, in the spring of 1838, thus closing an honorable and useful career of thirteen years, amid the profound and openly expressed regrets of his people. "His name and services still continue fragrant in the memory of New Brunswick." At the time of his departure, April 24th, 1838, the session reported the large number of four hundred and eleven communicants.

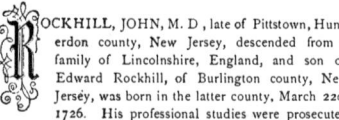

OCKHILL, JOHN, M. D , late of Pittstown, Hunterdon county, New Jersey, descended from a family of Lincolnshire, England, and son of Edward Rockhill, of Burlington county, New Jersey, was born in the latter county, March 22d, 1726. His professional studies were prosecuted under the supervision of Dr. Thomas Cadwallader, of Philadelphia, and upon being admitted to practise he established himself at Pittstown, where he was actively engaged during the ensuing fifty years. The range of country over which his functions were exercised was enormous, being limited only by the Blue mountains on the north, and the Delaware on the west, and extending on the south and east fairly into the territory covered by the physicians of Burlington, Raritan and New Brunswick. Owing to the troublous state of the times, his practice was largely surgical, one of his notable cases being a most dangerous gunshot wound that he treated with remarkable skill and success. During a foray on the part of the Indians living to the north of the mountains, the house of a settler named Wedges was attacked, captured, plundered and burned; and while the family were escaping to the woods, one of the children, a girl of twelve, was shot directly through the lungs. She fell, as was supposed, dead, but when her people returned the next morning, she was found in the brush, very much exhausted, but yet alive. Dr. Rockhill was sent for—the distance to Pittstown was nearly forty miles, and the roads were little more than blazed tracks through the woods—and by his exertions saved her life. She entirely recovered, subsequently married a son of Edward Marshall—the Edward Marshall who took the famous "long walk" along the Delaware—and reared a family of twelve children. Beside attending to his large and far-reaching practice, Dr. Rockhill found time to transact a large amount of other business as well, being considerably engaged in public affairs, and being for a number of years employed as Surveyor to the West Jersey Board of Land Proprietors. He married a Miss Robeson, by whom he had several children. The brother of this lady married Dr. Rockhill's sister, George M. Robeson, late Secretary of the Navy, being a greatgrandson of the latter couple.

AIGHT, CHARLES, Lawyer and ex-Member of Congress, of Freehold, New Jersey, son of Thomas G. and Ann Eliza (Van Meter) Haight, and descended from William Haight, one of three brothers who emigrated to this country from Germany, was born at Colt's Neck, Monmouth county, New Jersey, January 4th, 1838. Entering the College of New Jersey, Princeton, as a sophomore, in 1854, he graduated from that institution in 1857, and in the same year began the study of law in the office of that eminent barrister, Joel Parker, sometime Governor of New Jersey. Completing his legal education in the office of Messrs Cummins, Alexander & Green, counsellors and attorneys-at-law, New York, he was licensed to practise as an attorney at the bar of New Jersey in 1861, and as a counsellor in 1865. Upon being admitted to the bar he established himself at Freehold, where he rapidly built up an extensive practice. From early manhood he has taken an active and important part in politics—a sphere in which his father was also distinguished. In 1860 he was elected, on the Democratic ticket, a member of the State Legislature, and in the session of 1861-62 was Speaker of the House, a position the delicate duties of which he discharged in a manner satisfactory to both parties. In 1867 he was elected to Congress from the Second Congressional District (comprising Burlington, Mercer, Monmouth and Ocean counties), and in 1869 was re-elected from the same district. While in Congress his record was highly creditable, and in 1872 his name was brought prominently before the State Democratic Convention as that of a candidate for the governor-

ship. He has frequently been a Delegate to the conventions of his party—was a member and Chairman of the New Jersey delegation in 1872 to the convention that nominated Horace Greeley for the Presidency—and in conventions and party councils generally his opinions are listened to with respect and have a considerable influence in moulding the line of policy adopted. He is regarded as one of the leaders of the younger bar of New Jersey, and in 1873 was appointed, by Governor Parker, Prosecutor of the Pleas for Monmouth county. He was married, in 1862, to Mary B., daughter of Dr. J. L. Taylor, of Trenton, New Jersey.

OLCOMBE, HENRY, M. D., late of Everittstown, Hunterdon county, was born in Hunterdon county, August 5th, 1797. Having graduated from the College of New Jersey in 1818, he read medicine with his cousin, Dr. George Holcombe, of Allentown, Monmouth county, New Jersey—a physician who at that time stood at the head of his profession in the State—subsequently entered the medical department of the University of Pennsylvania, and from that institution received his degree of M. D. in 1821. Having been duly licensed to practise as a physician in New Jersey, he settled at Rowland's Mills, on the south branch of the Raritan, but in the ensuing year (1822) he removed to Everittstown, where he was engaged in active practice during the ensuing thirty-seven years. His exceptionally thorough education gave him a decided advantage over the medical men of the locality, and his services were soon in general demand; in a few years his practice extended over almost the entire county, and even across the river into Pennsylvania. In 1821 he was one of the founders of the Hunterdon County Medical Society, was Treasurer of that organization in 1825-26-27-28, and a member of the Board of Censors in 1825. He was also an honorary member of the Philadelphia Medical Society. He married Catherine, daughter of Samuel Case, Esq, by whom he had one daughter, Elizabeth, subsequently the wife of Baltus Pickel, Esq, of Trenton. In agricultural pursuits he took much interest, owning a large farm, the affairs of which he managed with remarkable skill and success. He died on the 7th of April, 1859.

HETWOOD, HON. WILLIAM, Lawyer, late of Elizabethtown, New Jersey, was born in that place in 1770, and was the son of John Chetwood, one of the Justices of the Supreme Court. His family were originally Quakers, and settled first in Salem county, but, after the removal of Judge Chetwood to Elizabethtown, became connected with the Episcopal Church. He was educated at Princeton Col-

lege, graduated from that institution in 1792, and subsequently pursued a course of studies in law, under the
guidance and care of his father. During the memorable
" Whiskey Insurrection," he became a volunteer, and served
on the staff of General Lee, having the rank then, or afterward, of Major, by which title he was usually addressed.
He was licensed as an attorney in 1796, as counsellor in
1799, and in 1816 was made a serjeant-at-law. He was
elected a member of Congress by the Jackson party, being
one of those Federalists who preferred him to Adams.
Afterward, however, he acted chiefly with the Whigs. He
accumulated a very handsome estate, a considerable part of
which was invested in New York insurance companies, and
ultimately lost by the great fire of 1835, leaving him, however, a competent support. He was for many years a constant attendant on the sittings of the Supreme Court at
Trenton, and "was one of those indefatigable workers,
who, by persistent industry, are pretty sure to succeed." A
story was formerly told of him that is not without piquancy :
On one occasion he attended court in his own carriage, as
the custom then was, expecting to remain only a day, and
without a change of linen. Unexpectedly detained, it became necessary for him to go to Sussex county without
returning home ; and he turned his shirt, in order to appear
as decently as circumstances would permit. But before it
was possible to procure a change, he found it expedient to
turn it back again, and so arrived at home about as he left,
but with a shirt rather the worse for wear. He married a
daughter of Colonel Francis Barber, who was killed during
the revolutionary war by the falling of a tree. He died at
Elizabethtown, New Jersey, in 1857, at the advanced age
of eighty-six years and six months.

USENBERY, HENRY, of Jersey City, was born
in New Hampton, New Jersey, April 21st, 1828.
He is a son of Joseph Warreu Dusenbery, of
New Hampton, formerly engaged in the mercantile and milling business there, and a grandson
of Major Henry Dusenbery, a merchant of Philadelphia, who afterwards settled at New Hampton. He
attended the village school at New Hampton until he was
fifteen years of age, when he became a clerk in the service
of Benjamin Shackleton, a merchant at Quakertown, New
Jersey, whose head-quarters were at Belvidere, Warren
county, of which the Quakertown business was a branch.
He remained in that position for three years, engaging then
in the same capacity with M. S. Stiger, of Clinton, the
first mayor of that town, and remaining with him for about
the same period. Leaving the employment of Mr. Stiger,
he went to Imlaysdale, Warren county, and set up in business as a general storekeeper on his own account, conducting the business for three years; after which he returned to
Mr. Stiger's employment at Clinton. In 1854 he removed
to New York city, and served as clerk in the house of
Young, Bonnell & Sutphen, on the dissolution of which, in
1856, he became a partner in the reconstructed firm of
Young, Bonnell & Co. Four years later Young retired from
the firm, when the style was altered to A. Bonnell & Co.,
and afterwards to Bonnell, Dusenbery & Co., and finally on
the 1st of May, 1869, this latter partnership was dissolved
to make way for one composed of himself and his brother,
Joseph Warren, under the name of Dusenbery Brothers, in
West street, New York. Thus was his business career
crowned. Never was commercial success more gradual,
regular, or legitimate, the way for each forward step in his
course having been made smooth by the preceding one.
After faithfully toiling at the bottom of the ladder, and
slowly but surely mounting the rounds, he reached at last
the top, where he has since stood, and now stands, not only
a thoroughly successful man of business, a commercial
leader in the commercial metropolis of the land, but a
citizen universally esteemed and implicitly trusted. It is
safe to assume that a success thus attained will be steadily
maintained at its full height. He finds time to discharge
with acceptability all his civic and social duties, but none
for the mere contests of party. In religious belief he is a
Presbyterian, and is a Ruling Elder and President of the
Board of Trustees of the First Presbyterian Church, Bergen,
Jersey City, New Jersey. He is a Director of the Library
Association of Bergen, and President of the Central Savings
Bank of Jersey City; but, though several times nominated,
he has always declined political office. He is married to
Emily A. Stiger, daughter of Adam Stiger, of Clinton, an
old resident and merchant of Hunterdon county.

USENBERY, JOSEPH WARREN, younger
brother of the subject of the preceding sketch,
was born at New Hampton, New Jersey, March
12th, 1830. He was educated principally at the
village school, which he attended until he was
seventeen years of age, when he entered St.
Matthew's Hall, Port Colden, New Jersey, where he pursued
his studies for one year, and then, accoutred as he was,
plunged into the "angry flood" of life. He first entered the
employment of Benjamin Shackleton, at Quakertown,
serving him as clerk for some three years, at the end of
which he went to Clinton, New Jersey, and in the same
capacity served Joseph Stiger for about the same length of
time. His service with Mr. Stiger having been terminated
by that gentleman's death, he formed a partnership in the
general mercantile business with Alexander Bonnell, at
Clinton, under the name of Bonnell & Dusenbery, which
continued for ten years or thereabouts. During his membership in this firm he was chosen a Director of the Clinton
Bank. His integrity, talents and success as a business man

had already given him an enviable standing in the community. Subsequently he established himself in business on his own account in the same town, prosecuting the enterprise for about two years, after which he removed to New York city, where he became a partner in the firm of Bonnell, Dusenbery & Co., on the dissolution of which he united with his brother Henry in establishing the present house of Dusenbery Brothers, in West street, New York. In this house his fortunes, like his brother's, and through remarkably similar vicissitudes, have culminated, capping with substantial and visible success a long, patient, faithful, energetic and honorable course of mercantile toils and ventures. When the prizes of life are so won, they can excite only satisfaction in the beholder, as they should bring nothing but happiness to the possessor. He has been twice married: first to Chrissie Dunham, daughter of Nehemiah Dunham, a farmer of Clinton, New Jersey, of which he was an old resident, who died in 1862; and a second time, to Mary De Witt, daughter of Charles A. De Witt, superintendent of the United States Express Company, Jersey City, whose father, Charles G. De Witt, was at one time associated with President Jackson's administration, and in 1833 was appointed Chargé d'Affaires to Guatemala, in Central America.

WOODRUFF, REV. BENJAMIN, Clergyman, late of Westfield, was born in Elizabethtown, New Jersey, and was the son of Samuel Woodruff, an eminent merchant of his native place, and for nearly twenty years a Trustee of Princeton College. After graduating he pursued the study of theology, probably with his pastor, Elihu Spencer. In due time he was licensed to preach, and on March 14th, 1759, was ordained pastor of the Presbyterian Church of Westfield, New Jersey. During the forty-four years of his useful and zealous ministry there, he greatly endeared himself to his people by his earnest preaching, sincere piety and charitableness, and his pastoral intercourse. He is described as small in person, dignified and precise in his manners, scrupulously exact and fastidious in his dress, with small-clothes, silk hose, buckles, cock-hat and ruffles, everywhere the same, and always commanding respect. He died suddenly, April 3d, 1803, and with him went a well-beloved link that connected the old time and the new, and a revered and exemplary spiritual guide and exhorter.

STEVENS, JOHN, Inventor, Prominent Citizen of New Jersey, late of Hoboken, New Jersey, was born in New York in 1749. In 1787, happening to see the imperfectly constructed steamboat of John Fitch, he at once became interested in steam propulsion, and during the ensuing thirty years was constantly engaged in experimenting on the subject.

In 1789 he petitioned the Legislature of New York for a grant of the exclusive navigation of the waters of that State, his petition being accompanied with draughts of the plan of his steamboat. The right demanded was, however, not granted. In 1804 he constructed a propeller, a small open boat worked by steam, and success meeting this venture, he built the "Phœnix," a steamboat which was completed but a short time after Fulton had finished the "Clermont." Fulton having obtained the exclusive right to the navigation of the Hudson, his coworker placed his boats on the Delaware and Connecticut. In 1812 he published a remarkable pamphlet, urging the government to make experiments in railways traversed by steam carriages, and proposed the construction of his projected railway from Albany to Lake Erie. "The railway engines," he thought, " might traverse the roads at a speed of fifty miles, or even more, per hour, though probably in practice it would be found convenient not to exceed twenty or thirty miles per hour." The details of construction of the roadway, and of the locomotives and carriages, are given with such minuteness and accuracy, that "it is difficult to realize that their only existence at that time was in the mind of the inventor." He died at Hoboken, New Jersey, in 1838.

STEVENS, ROBERT LIVINGSTON, Inventor, President of the Camden & Amboy Railroad, son of the inventor, John Stevens, late of Hoboken, New Jersey, was born in that place in 1788. Inheriting his father's mechanical genius and his deep interest in propulsion by steam on land and water, he, while still a youth, commenced a course of discovery and improvement on these subjects which has given him a very high rank among the inventors of this century. At the age of twenty he constructed a steamboat with concave water lines, the first application of the wave-line to ship-building; subsequently used for the first time vertical buckets on pivots in the paddle-wheels of steamers, suspended the guard-beam by iron rods, and adopted a new and original method of bracing and fastening steamboats. In 1818 he discovered the advantage of using steam expansively, and of employing anthracite coal as fuel for steamers. In 1822 he substituted the skeleton wrought-iron walking-beam for the heavy cast-iron one previously in use; first placed the boilers on the guards, and divided the buckets on the water-wheels in order to lessen the jar of the boat. In 1824 he applied artificial blast to the boiler furnace by means of blowers; and in 1827 adapted the "hog-frame" to boats, to prevent them from bending at the centre. In the course of the ensuing twenty-two years he made numerous other improvements, in the way of balance-valves, tubular-boilers, steam-packing, cut-offs, cross-propellers to turn boats as on a pivot, the forcing of air under the bottom of the steamer "John Wilson," to lighten the

57

draft, etc. During this period he also invented and put into use the T rail, and used successfully anthracite coal as a fuel for fast passenger locomotives. At an early age he had established steam ferry-boats on the Hudson river; and on the organization of the Camden & Amboy Railroad, took a warm interest in its management and development, and was for many years its President. In 1813-14 he invented an elongated bomb-shell of great destructive power, and imparted to the government the secret of its construction, in consideration of which he received a large annuity. In 1842 he commenced experiments with a view to the construction of an iron-plated war-steamer, or battery, which should be shot-and-shell-proof, and whose construction was begun in 1858, at Hoboken, New Jersey, under a contract made by him with the Navy Department in 1849. The actual construction of this vessel was commenced, however, in 1856. The following were her principal dimensions: extreme length, 415 feet; breadth, 48 feet; depth, 32 feet 4 inches; displacement in tons, 5,840; indicated steam-power at 50 pounds pressure equal to 8,624 horses; 10 large boilers; 8 driving-engines; 45½-inch cylinder; 3½ feet stroke; 2 propellers; 9 subordinate engines for various purposes, such as pumping, blowing, starting, etc. He also devoted much time and expense to an elaborate series of ordnance experiments, and entertained no doubt of the practicability of making his battery shot-and-shell-proof. His vessel was intended to operate in the waters of New York bay and harbor, from Sandy Hook upward, and in March, 1858, was about two-thirds completed, all her machinery, boilers and dependencies being in place; in February, 1862, the propriety of finishing this huge war-instrument was earnestly advocated by those who foresaw the duration and probable magnitude of the sectional conflict. A more detailed and fuller account of his various inventions, improvements, etc., will probably be found in the later volumes of the "Annual of Scientific Discovery." He died at Hoboken, New Jersey, April 20th, 1856.

OODHULL, REV. GEORGE SPAFFORD, Pastor of the Presbyterian Church at Cranberry, late of Middletown Point, New Jersey, was born in New Jersey in the last quarter of the past century, and was the son of Rev. John Woodhull, of the Princeton class of 1766. He also studied at Princeton College, and in due time and season graduated from that institution. He subsequently studied law for two years, and medicine for one year; but, determining to enter the ministry, was licensed by the Presbytery of New Brunswick, November 14th, 1797. June 6th, 1798, he was ordained and installed as pastor of the Presbyterian Church at Cranberry, New Jersey. Here he remained until 1820, when he was chosen pastor of the church of Princeton, where, for twelve years, he labored faithfully and success-

fully. In 1832 he resigned his charge, and spent the last two years of his life as pastor of the Presbyterian Church at Middletown Point, New Jersey, where he died, December 25th, 1834. He was eminently blameless and exemplary in his life, eminently peaceful and happy in his death. Three of his sons graduated at Princeton; one in 1822, and two in 1828.

ILLER, WILLIAM W., Lawyer, late of Paris, France, was born in Hunterdon county, New Jersey, in 1797. "Although living in the country, which commonly presents so many more alluring pastimes for a boy, and having the companionship of a large family of brothers and sisters, yet his fondness for and his application to study was so great, that at the age of twelve years he was prepared to enter the freshman class at college." The regulations of the institution not permitting this, he pursued his studies alone, and at the age of fourteen entered the junior class of Princeton College, half advanced. Before attaining his sixteenth year he graduated, taking one of the honors of his class, several members of which were afterward distinguished characters in public life. Owing to his youth, he was advised not to enter immediately upon his professional studies, but to review those to which he had so successfully applied himself while laboring as a student. For this purpose he went to Somerville, and there instructed in the languages a class of young men, all older than himself. Shortly afterward, however, he entered upon the study of the law with Theodore Frelinghuysen, and was licensed as an attorney in 1818, and as a counsellor in 1821. He then commenced practice as a lawyer in Morristown, where he was professionally occupied during the ensuing five or six years, removing subsequently with his family, consisting of a wife and three children, to Newark. His reputation as a public speaker began at this time to attract attention, not only in his own neighborhood, but also in the city of New York, so that frequent calls were made upon him to address public meetings. His speech in behalf of the Greeks, then struggling to relieve themselves from the oppression of the Turks, made in Trinity Church, Newark, July 13th, 1824, won for him applause which rang through the whole country, and is still spoken of as a master-piece of eloquence. In February, 1825, he was retained as counsel for a minister of the Dutch church, who had sued his son-in-law in New York for a gross slander. The case was one that excited universal interest, and the City Hall was every day crowded to excess while it was in progress. The celebrated Thomas Addis Emmet was one of the counsel of the defendant; so that every circumstance was calculated to enlist the sympathy and stimulate the ambition of a young lawyer. He spoke nearly three hours on this occasion, during which time the excitement of the crowd assembled was intense, and when at last he sank exhausted into a chair, Emmet embraced him, and the defendant sobbed so violently as to be heard all over the court-room. The cause was gained, but it was the last effort of the gifted orator; that night he was prostrated by a hemorrhage of the lungs. By the advice of his physicians he then left home and repaired to the south of France, and for a time seemed on the road to a complete recovery; but on the 24th of July, 1825, he was again attacked by a hemorrhage, at a hotel in Paris, and there died, at the early age of twenty-eight years and a few months. He lies buried in the well-known cemetery of Père la Chaise, where an iron railing marks his grave, and which is visited with melancholy interest by his American friends. On the news of his death, a meeting of the bench and bar was held in the court-room at Trenton, of which Richard Stockton was chairman and Peter D. Vroom secretary, and highly complimentary resolutions were duly adopted. Says Hon. L. Q. C. Elmer: " I well remember his reputation for splendid oratorical powers, and his high character as a Christian gentleman. His Greek speech was published, and universally admired."

———◆◇◆———

RUTHERFURD, HON. JOHN, President of the New Jersey Historical Society, President of the Tuckerton Railroad in Ocean county, and of the Council of Proprietors for the Eastern Division of New Jersey, and of the New Jersey Coal Company, Director in the Sussex Railroad, etc., late of Newark, New Jersey, was born at the residence of his maternal grandfather, Lewis Morris, of Morrisania, Westchester county, New York, July 21st, 1810, and was the son of Robert Walter Rutherfurd and Sabina (Morris) Rutherfurd. His paternal grandfather, after whom he was named, John Rutherfurd, was a country gentleman and large landed proprietor, living on his estate at Edgerton, on the Passaic river, known as Rutherfurd park; he married the sister of Lewis Morris, "thus making a double tie of consanguinity in the ancestors of Mr. Rutherfurd": he was also well known throughout the State as a public-spirited and energetic citizen, and is recorded as a United States Senator in the "Senate Journal" of the First Session of the Third Congress, which met in Philadelphia in 1793; his only son was Robert Walter Rutherfurd. The paternal great-grandfather was a British officer of the rank of colonel, who was prominent in several actions attendant on the old French war; and letters are still extant in the family, describing his sufferings in the campaign on Lake Ontario and in Canada; he married a sister of Lord Stirling, and the daughter of James Alexander, who holds an enviable and distinguished position in the colonial history of New Jersey and New York. His maternal grandfather, Colonel Lewis Morris, was a son of the signer of the Declaration of Independence; he was the oldest of six sons, "most of

whom, excepting the youngest, joined the Continental army on reaching the age of sixteen; the youngest, fearing the war would close before he was of that age, joined when only fifteen." When the British forces entered New York the officers took possession of the Morris country place, the family hastily escaping with their servants, horses and furniture, in a flat-boat across the Hudson to Weehawken, and to Round Valley, Hunterdon county, where they remained until the close of the conflict. "Thus, while this sturdy patriot was contending against the enemy with voice and pen in the Continental Congress, he sends his six sons into the field as soon as they can shoulder a musket—his family, meantime, seeking refuge in a secluded valley among the Jersey hills." At the age of two and a half years he went to live with his grandfather, at Edgerton, situated on the east bank of the Passaic, about seven miles above Newark; the old mansion there existed until quite recently, when it was altered and enlarged for a hotel, and ultimately destroyed by fire. "It was in its day the scene for the dispensation of elegant hospitality; and there are yet many old neighbors and former residents on the river who cherish very delightful recollections of the old place, and the pleasant and joyous times they have had within its hospitable walls." As a child he seems to have given token of some precocity of intellect; an extract from an old diary will serve to illustrate the fact: "July 21st, 1817. John Rutherfurd is seven years old to-day, and has commenced reading history with the Bible." .... "July 24th. Read an extract of Egyptian and Persian history, with some extracts in third volume of Rollins' 'Belles-Lettres.'—Reading Goldsmith's 'Abridged History of Greece,' and an abridgment of Alexander's Life and Conquests, from 'Flowers of History.'— We began Goldsmith's 'Rome,' the number of the different states rendering Grecian history rather complicated for a child of seven years of age." At nine years of age he was sent to school, at the Newark Academy, then presided over by Andrew Smith, "a very respectable old Scotchman," and "probably because the distance was too far for the young boy to go to and fro each day, he was placed at board with the family of his teacher, who lived across the Passaic, in what is now known as East Newark, on the turnpike road near to the crossing of the Morris & Essex Railroad, from which place he, in company with four other boys, walked in daily to the academy, which then stood on the site of the present post-office." From this school he was sent to the famous educational institute of Dr. Brownlee, at Basking Ridge, to be fitted for college. It was intended that he should go to Princeton, and be educated by the venerable *Alma Mater* under whose shadow his father had won his scholarly attainments; "but here we have an early instance of his strongly marked character, and decision of purpose as impressed by nature herself. One day he went to Princeton to pay a visit to an old schoolmate then in college, and living, as the custom of the times was, in 'commons;' but the boy, accustomed from his infancy to the observance of all the nice proprieties of refined life, took such a disgust at the scenes he witnessed among the youths at dinner that he at once resolved he would look elsewhere for an education." Accordingly, and without consulting any one, he went to New Brunswick and applied for admission to Rutgers College; and there, after the ordeal of a two hours' examination, conducted by the Dutch professors who had charge of the curriculum of that institution, secured a favorable verdict, becoming a member of the sophomore class at the early age of fifteen years. He graduated while in his eighteenth year, and soon after entered the law office of Elias Van Arsdale, in the city of Newark. After being admitted to the bar, and practising law for about two years, he abandoned his profession in order to assist his grandfather in the care and management of his large landed estate. He continued to live at Edgerton until the death of his grandparents, after which his two aunts, Mary and Louisa Rutherfurd, built an elegant residence on the same bank of the Passaic, about two miles distant from Newark, " which the refinement and taste of those ladies rendered conspicuous for all that is attractive in rural life." He then took up his residence with them at " Eastridge," as the grounds were named, and commenced there his married life. He possessed remarkable executive ability; had a far-sighted vision as to the future of the State; and furthered materially the many enterprises set on foot to develop its interests and resources. " His great self-control, his tact in management of all embarrassing questions, his whole-souled generosity, his entire abnegation of self, and slowness to suspect anything wrong in the motives of others, caused him to be almost worshipped among his tenantry, and there was probably no one in the entire county of Essex who had equal popularity with him." One of his favorite projects was the uniting of the waters of the Delaware and Hudson by a continuous route of railway; this led him to originate the Warwick Railroad, which was commenced on the line of the Erie road, at Chester, and continued to the State line, a distance of ten miles. He was also largely interested in the construction of the Pequest Valley Railroad, and was a Director and able worker in the Midland Railroad; "his counsels and energetic action in this corporation will be sadly missed." He was President of the Tuckerton Railroad, in Ocean county, where, with other members of his family, he was very largely interested in the Pine Barrens, which are now giving place to cultivated lands, fulfilling and realizing the Scripture prophecy, "The desert shall blossom as the rose." He was also the President of the Council of Proprietors for the Eastern Division of New Jersey; was an hereditary proprietor in this board, and had been its presiding officer for many years. " His influence in that body was so great, and the confidence in his inflexible uprightness and sound judgment so general, that he never failed, by expressing his opinion, to control the action of the board, no matter how divided the sentiment might be." He was also the President of the New

Jersey Coal Company, in which enterprise he was warmly interested, his faith in it being so great that he believed—from the value of their lands and the superior quality of their coal—that it could not fail to become a very wealthy corporation. He was a Director also in the Sussex Railroad, in which county was his home, his residence being known as Maple Grange. Beyond these official positions he held several others; was a Director in the New Jersey State Agricultural Society, and in several financial institutions; and was also the honored head of the New Jersey Historical Society, in whose prosperity and promotion he ever manifested a deep and generous interest, contributing to its funds with no sparing hand, and seeking by every means in his power to advance its aims and objects. " Many of the priceless manuscripts, documents and literary curiosities contained in our library are the gifts of Mr. Rutherfurd and his family, and there is enough to-day in that library to keep his name ever fresh in grateful remembrance."—R. S. Swords. He was elected a member of the society November 6th, 1845, and made Vice-President January 19th, 1865. Speaking of him the same writer remarks, further: His versatile talents enabled him to devote himself with fidelity to every duty he assumed. His memory was tenacious to an extraordinary degree, and he was wont to depend upon it to an extent that hardly another man would have felt safe in doing. He never forgot a business engagement, or failed to keep an appointment; in such matters he was the promptest of the prompt. There was probably no man in the State whose time was more entirely engrossed, and yet it is recorded of him that "he never brought his business affairs into his family." In his dealings with his fellow-men he was just and generous; no friend ever appealed to him in vain for sympathy or aid. No man could be more simple and unaffected in manner; and yet, so careful was he of wounding the feelings of others that, in most cases, where he had the right to be severe, he preferred silence to delivery of just resentment. His last sickness was sudden and severe. He came from Newport early in the fall, suffering from an attack of malarious fever, complicated with the beginning of the painful malady which was to end his days. He then remained temporarily at his city residence in Newark, in order to recuperate under the watching of his physician; and subsequently returned to his home in Sussex, where he improved slightly, and became strong enough to ride about the country. Being advised to return to Newark, where he could receive more attention and find higher medical skill, he started on his return, and on the night of his first day's journey was prostrated by a fresh attack while resting at the house of a friend. After reaching Newark his malady speedily assumed the most serious and alarming aspect; his naturally powerful frame and strength of constitution enabled him to endure for a time what any other man of less vigor would at once have succumbed to; but on the 21st day of November, 1872, at 8 o'clock A. M., he breathed his last, "conscious to the extremest moment," and "was gathered unto his fathers, having the testimony of a good conscience; in the communion of the catholic church, in the confidence of a certain faith, in the comfort of a reasonable, religious and holy hope; in favor (as we devoutly believe) with his God; and in perfect charity with the world." His funeral took place from Trinity Church, Newark; and he was buried in the yard of Christ Church, Belleville, where are interred the remains of his father and mother, his aunts, and one of his own children. In this church he had grown up and become a communicant, and afterward for many years was one of its vestrymen; he also frequently represented the parish in the diocesan conventions of the Episcopal Church in New Jersey.

ERRINE, REV. MATTHEW LA RUE, Clergyman, Professor of Ecclesiastical History and Church Polity, late of Auburn, New York, was born in the last quarter of the eighteenth century, and belonged to a distinguished and influential family of Monmouth county, New Jersey. After graduating at Princeton College he studied theology under Dr. John Woodhull, of Freehold, New Jersey, and was licensed to preach by the Presbytery of New Brunswick, September 18th, 1799. On the 24th of June, 1800, he was ordained, and for four months acted as a missionary in western New York. On the 15th of June, 1802, he was installed as pastor of the Spring Street Church, New York. Here he continued till the summer of 1820, when, at his own request, the pastoral relation was dissolved. In 1821 he was elected to the Professorship of Ecclesiastical History and Church Polity in the Auburn Theological Seminary. He continued actively engaged in the discharge of his various duties till near the close of his life. In 1818 he received the honorary degree of Doctor of Divinity from Allegheny College. "His personal appearance was altogether agreeable. His countenance indicated great mildness and benignity, mingled with thoughtfulness and intelligence; his manners were urbane and winning; his temper amiable and benevolent." He was naturally of a speculative and metaphysical turn, and in theology harmonized with Dr. Emmous; as a preacher he was always instructive and interesting, but could not be called popular. His style was correct and perspicuous, but, in a great measure, unadorned; yet in the mellow and gentle tones of his voice there lurked a great and enduring charm. He had the reputation of being an accurate and thorough scholar. He published "Letters Concerning the Plan of Salvation, addressed to the Members of the Spring Street Church," New York, 1816; "A Sermon before a French Missionary Society in New York," in 1817; and "An Abstract of Biblical Geography," 1835. He also contributed several

essays and articles to the current magazines and journals of his day. He died, February 11th, 1836.

ANNERS, HON. JOHN, M. D., Physician, Lawyer and State Senator, late of Clinton, son of John and Rachel Manners, was born in Hunterdon county, New Jersey, April 8th, 1786. Having received his preliminary education—including, probably, a full course in the College of New Jersey—he entered the medical department of the University of Pennsylvania, and from that institution received, in 1812, his degree of M. D. While prosecuting his professional studies at the university he was also an office student with Drs. Benjamin Rush and Thomas Cooper, the latter of whom became in due course of time his father-in-law, and with the former of whom he maintained for many years a more or less close friendship. Shortly after his graduation he applied to the New Jersey Board of Censors for permission to practise in the State; was examined, passed and licensed. He at first established himself at Flemington; subsequently removed to a handsome country-seat (to which he gave the name of Belvoir), near Clinton, and finally settled in the town of Clinton. He became a member of the Hunterdon County Medical Society on the revival of that organization, in 1836, but as the society immediately fell to pieces again, and was not permanently revived until 1846, he lost interest in it, and during the few years previous to his death that it was in active operation he was but an irregular attendant at its meetings. He married, August 2d, 1810, Eliza, daughter of Dr. Thomas Cooper, of South Carolina, a connection that brought him into intimate relations with many eminent Southerners, and led to a development on his part of a very sincere respect and admiration for southern character and customs. The latter to a certain extent he introduced at Belvoir, patterning that establishment, as nearly as circumstances would permit, upon the model of a southern homestead. He was an earnest believer in blooded stock, and his horses were the best bred in all the country side; and the same was true of his cows, pigs and chickens. After practising medicine for some years he determined upon entering the legal profession also; and to this end read law in the office of James M. Porter, of Easton, Pennsylvania. After the usual course he was examined and admitted to the bar. Although qualified to practise at the bar of both the State and United States courts, he does not seem to have been very largely employed in either, and it is probable that he studied law mainly with the view of making it a stepping-stone to political preferment. For three years previous to his death he represented Hunterdon county in the State Senate, being during the last year of his term President of that body. That he would have risen to greater prominence in public life, had he lived, is extremely probable, for he is represented as having displayed while in office more than ordinary legislative ability. He died, June 24th, 1853. By his will, he ordered that his body should be buried in the cemetery at Trenton, and that over his grave should be erected, "of the best Italian marble," a monument bearing this inscription: "Erected to the memory of Hon. John Manners, Esq., A. M., M. D., and Counsellor at Law of the Supreme Court, United States of America. The Friend and Medical Pupil of Benjamin Rush, M. D., LL. D., Philadelphia. The Friend, the Pupil and the Son-in-law of Thomas Cooper, M. D., LL. D., etc., of South Carolina; and the Friend and Correspondent of Thomas Jefferson, LL. D., of Virginia, formerly President of the United States."

IERSON, CLARK, Journalist, of Lambertville, was born in Lambertville, New Jersey, July 13th, 1836. He was educated at the private school of Mr. Parson, which he attended until he was twelve or thirteen years of age, when he entered the printing office of the Lambertville *Telegraph*, in which he remained for several years, passing through all the grades of the craft, and ending with the superintendence of the job work, an excellent course of training for one destined to be a journalist. He did not, however, immediately take his seat on the tripod, but first added another chapter to his preliminary experience, becoming in 1856 a clerk in the office of the Belvidere Delaware Railroad, where he remained until 1858. In the latter year he bought the *Beacon* newspaper (formerly the *Telegraph*), editing and publishing it till 1869, and then disposing of it. But he made this disposition with no thought of retiring from the newspaper business, his eleven years' experience in which had not dulled his partiality for it, or failed, as may well be imagined, to perfect his mastery of it, particularly as those eleven years included the period of the civil war, during which American journalism, in all its branches, underwent an improvement so rapid and vast that it may be said to have been born anew. On the contrary, the sale of the *Beacon* establishment was but a step in his journalistic career—a step that he followed up by a stride in 1872, when he founded the Lambertville *Record*, which at once took a prominent place among the journals of New Jersey, and of which he is still the proprietor and editor. In politics he is a Republican, as he has been since the outbreak of the civil war, previously to which he was a Democrat of the Douglas school; but as a journalist he is accustomed to follow his own convictions, which enlist his pen and the influence of his paper in the service of every praiseworthy reform, whether set down in the party platform or not. He is especially identified with the cause of temperance, of which he has proved himself an effective advocate, his strictures on the Lambertville Common Council, for instance, the majority of whose members he deemed to have sacrificed the welfare of the people to the interests of the rumsellers, telling with such effect that at the next election the faithless members were all defeated and their places filled by temperance councilmen, no license to sell liquor being granted for the three succeeding years. He is also a devoted friend of education, and in 1861 his fellow-citizens gave him an opportunity to make his devotion fruitful by electing him Superintendent of the Public Schools of Lambertville, an opportunity which, it need not be said, he turned to good account. He was the first President of the Young Men's Christian Association of Lambertville, in the organization of which he bore a leading part. To religion, temperance and education, in the cause of each of which he is an efficient worker, he adds philanthropy, being, to cite no further evidence, a Free Mason, belonging to the Lambertville Lodge and Chapter. In 1876 he was the Republican candidate, in the First Legislative District of Hunterdon, for the State Assembly; but, the district being largely Democratic, he was defeated. His standing in his own immediate community was shown in 1877 by his triumphant choice as Postmaster of Lambertville, the appointment having been left to a vote of the people. But the character in which he is best known and most influential is that of conductor of the Lambertville *Record*. As a journalist he is an acknowledged power in his section of the State.

CÒTT, COLONEL WARREN, Lawyer, was born in New Brunswick, New Jersey, toward the close of the last century, and graduated from Princeton College. He subsequently studied medicine for a short time with his father, and also paid some attention to theology, "a science congenial to his intellect and early education." On one occasion he attended court in New York, and became greatly interested in the able argument of one of the lawyers, and this was the incentive that led him to adopt the law as his profession. He was admitted an attorney of the Supreme Court of New Jersey at the February term, 1801, and as a counsellor in February, 1804. In February, 1816, he was called to the position of serjeant-at-law. In criminal cases he showed great power and almost resistless eloquence. He argued his last case at the age of eighty, and spoke for several hours with very little apparent weariness, considering his years. Hon. Hamilton Fish, Secretary of State of the United States, on hearing of his death, writes: "Genial and bright in intellect and wit, fourscore and ten years had not, when last I met him, quenched the ardor of his warm and impulsive nature; and I shall ever remember Colonel Warren Scott as one of the most attractive talkers and agreeable companions whom it has been my fortune to meet." He died, April 27th, 1871.

ICIIOLS, ISAAC A., M. D., of Newark, was born in that city on the 24th of February, 1828. Having received an ample preparatory education, he decided upon adopting medicine as his profession, . and in accordance with this determination matriculated at the College of Physicians and Surgeons of New York. After duly attending lectures, he was graduated thence, with distinction, in 1850; received his degree of M. D., and in the same year entered upon the practice of his profession in his native city. From the outset of his career, both as a physician and surgeon, he was successful, and he has now been for many years one of the leading medical men of Newark. In 1858 his standing was such that he was appointed City Physician, a position that he has since, during a period of nineteen years, continued to hold. As a surgeon, his reputation is quite exceptional, his practice in this branch of his profession being so skilful as to lead to his appointment as surgeon to Saint Michael's Hospital, Newark, and also as surgeon to the Pennsylvania Railroad Company. In his profession, among his brother physicians, his standing is of the highest; a fact evidenced by his election in 1873 to the Presidency of the Essex County Medical Society. Of the Newark Medical Association, and of the New Jersey Academy of Medicine, he is also a distinguished member, taking a prominent part in the discussion of all important matters, and being a member of the leading committees of both organizations. He was married in 1854.

HITEHEAD, HON. ASA, Lawyer, late of Newark, New Jersey, was born in Essex county, New Jersey, and was the son of Hon. Silas Whitehead, who was appointed, in 1817, Clerk of the county of Essex. He was licensed as an attorney in 1818; as a counsellor in 1821; and was one of those called to the degree of serjeant-at-law in 1837, after which time that degree ceased to be conferred. He was subsequently commissioned by the Governor to fill the position of Clerk of the county of Essex, made vacant by the death of his father; and, at the meeting of the Legislature in 1819, was regularly appointed to the office. Being reappointed in 1824, he occupied that station for a period of ten years. Connected with the Pennington family by marriage, his politics were like theirs, Democratic, until the contest between Adams and Jackson, after which he became a Whig, and continued an active and influential supporter of this party as long as it existed. His term of office as Clerk expiring in 1819, when the Jackson party was largely in the majority, and political feeling running very high, he failed to be re-elected at the moment, " very much to his regret." Chief-Justice Ewing remarked at the time, however, that " it would prove a great benefit to him, for the reason that although he did not seem himself to be aware of it, he had the ability to make a 'first-class lawyer,

and now he would be obliged to rely upon his profession." The opinion thus expressed proved to be entirely correct. He rapidly took rank as a reliable counsellor and an able advocate, so that, during the last twenty years of his life, he stood, if not at the head of the profession in the northern part of the State, yet among those relied upon in all important cases. In the years 1833-1834 he was a member of the Assembly; and in 1848, after the adoption of the new Constitution, was chosen a member of the State Senate for three years. " Of unimpeached integrity, and thoroughly imbued with the conservative spirit of the old school politicians, he exercised a salutary influence in legislation, and was active in promoting the success of the Whig party." —Hon. L. Q. C. Elmer. He was a leading member of the delegates from New Jersey to the Whig Convention of 1840, and united with them in voting for General Scott, " without even consulting Mr. Southard, upon whom Henry Clay laid the blame of their not voting for him, as he expected." Although he did not favor the selection of General Harrison as the Whig candidate for the Presidency, he cordially supported him at the election, and aided materially in securing for him the vote of New Jersey. He died in the spring of 1860.

ALBOT, RIGHT REV. JOHN, M. A., Founder and first Rector of Saint Mary's Church, Burlingtou, New Jersey, and the first Bishop in America. The earliest information at hand concerning this noteworthy clergyman is, that he was once Rector of Freethern, in the county of Gloucester, England, and then chaplain on the ship "Centurion," which sailed from the Isle of Wight, April 28th, 1702, bringing to America the first missionaries from the Society of the Propagation of the Gospel in Foreign Parts— George Keith and Patrick Gordon. All that follows is quoted from a sermon preached at the Ninety-third Annual Convention of the Diocese of New Jersey, in Saint Michael's Church, Trenton, May 30th, 1876, by the Rev. George Morgan Hills, D. D., Rector of Saint Mary's Church, Burlingtou, New Jersey: "During their six weeks' voyage, a warm friendship sprung up between Keith and Talbot. So like-minded were they that, before the ship reached her moorings, Keith proposed and Talbot consented—if the Society approved—that they should be associated. 'Friend Keith and I,' writes Talbot from New York, 'have been above five hundred miles together, visiting the churches in these parts of America, viz., New England, New Hampshire, New Bristol, New London, New York, and the Jerseys as far as Philadelphia. We preached in all churches where we came, and in several Dissenters' meetings, such as owned the Church of England to be their mother church, and were willing to communicate with her and to submit to her bishops, if they had opportunity.' The many letters of

Mr. Talbot to private persons, as well as for the public eye, present him to us a well-furnished priest of apostolic simplicity, resolute, fearless, transparently honest, intent only on the kingdom of God and the righteousness thereof. 'God bless Queen Anne,' he exclaims, in one of his letters to a personal friend, 'and defend her that she may defend the faith; and her faithful councellours, if they have any piety or policy, I'm sure will take some course with these heathens and hereticks, for if they be let alone to take the sword (which they certainly will when they think they are strong enough) we shall perish with it, for not opposing them in due time.' When we reflect that this utterance was made seventy years before the armed hostilities of revolution, we must regard it as a prophecy remarkably fulfilled. There was not only timid temporizing in managing the government of the colonies, but culpable neglect in manning the church. And yet what openings there were! 'It grieves me much,' writes Mr. Talbot, 'to see so many people here without the benefit of serving God in the wilderness. I believe I have been solicited to tarry in twenty places where they want much, and are able to maintain a minister, so that he should want nothing.' The earnest determination of Mr. Talbot finds vent when he says, 'I believe I have done the church more service since I came hither than I would in seven years in England. Perhaps when I have been here six or seven years, I may make a trip home to see some friends (for they won't come to me), but then it will be *Animo Revertendi*, for I have given myself up to the service of God and his church *apud Americanos*; and I had rather dye in the service than desert it.' . . . 'I use to take a wallet full of books and carry them a hundred miles about, and disperse them abroad, and give them to all that desired them, which in due time will be of good service to the church.' In November, 1705, the clergy of New York, New Jersey, and Pennsylvania, met at Burlington, and drew up an address to the Society, the whole burden of which was that a Suffragan Bishop might be sent to them. This address was signed by fourteen clergy, some of whom belonged to the Church of Sweden— (a beautiful instance of the catholic inter-communion of those days)—and with it was their united letter to the Bishop of London, commending Mr. Talbot, who was deputed to carry it across the ocean. The following March Mr. Talbot was in London, 'soliciting for a suffragan, books and ministers;' and two years afterwards we hear from him in New Jersey once more. August 24th, 1708, he writes: 'I am forced to turn itinerant again, for the care of all the churches from East to West Jersey is upon me; what is the worst is that I can't confirm any, nor have not a deacon to help me.' Three years more elapsed, and in October, 1712, the famous property of John Tatham, at Burlington, a 'great and stately palace, pleasantly situated on the north side of the town, having a very fine and delightful garden and orchard,' and embracing in its domain 'fifteen acres,' was bought by the Society for six hundred pounds,

sterling money of England, or nine hundred pounds current money of New York, for a Bishop's Seat. A bill was ordered to be drafted to be offered in Parliament for establishing bishoprics in America. Everything presaged success; but, before the bill was introduced, its great patroness, Queen Anne, died. The first George was absorbed by what politicians regarded as more important than religion in the colonies. He alienated many by the course he pursued both in church and state; and Mr. Talbot, it was rumored, omitted from the litany the suffrage that the king might have 'victory over all his enemies.' Whether this was only rumor, we are unable to say. We know that he and three of the most distinguished laymen in New Jersey, ex-Governor Bass, Hon. Colonel Coxe, and Alexander Griffiths, Attorney-General, were charged by Governor Hunter, in a very scurrilous letter, with 'incorporating the Jacobites in the Jerseys.' Mr. Talbot's vestry, who had known his doctrine, manner of life, and purpose, with whom he had been at all seasons for twelve years, united in a formal disavowal of the charge, pronouncing it 'a calumnious and groundless scandal,' and indorsing their rector as 'a truly pious and apostolic person.' During the next twelve months one of Mr. Talbot's bills was ordered to lie by for a half a year, and a missionary was sent over to take his place in case of his removal. Of this he writes in 1716, 'I suffer all things for the elect's sake, the poor church of God here, in the wilderness. There is none to guide her among all the sons that she has brought forth, nor is there any that takes her by the hand of all the sons that she has brought up. When the apostles heard that Samaria had received the word of God, immediately they set out two of the chief, Peter and John, to lay their hands on them, and pray that they might receive the Holy Ghost; they did not stay for a secular design of salary; and when the apostles heard that the word of God was preached at Antioch, presently they sent out Paul and Barnabas, that they should go as far as Antioch, to confirm the disciples, and so the churches were established in the faith, and increasing in number daily; and when Paul did but *dream* that a man of Macedonia called him, he set sail all so fast, and went over himself to help them; but we have been here these twenty years, calling till our hearts ache, and ye own 'tis the call and the cause of God, and yet ye have not heard, or have not answered, and it is all one. I must say this, that if the Society don't do more in a short time than they have in a long, they will, I fear, lose their honor and character too. I don't pretend to prophesy, but you know how they said the kingdom of God shall be taken from them, and given to a nation that will bring forth the fruits of it.' These and such like appeals, petitions, remonstrances, and warnings, were made persistently, not only by Mr. Talbot, but by all whom he could associate with him, for a period of eighteen years. Finally, in 1720, Mr. Talbot went to England, and received the interest on Archbishop Tenison's legacy as a retired missionary. He was absent nearly two

Richard A Terhune M.D.

years and a half, and during this time made the acquaint-ance of the nonjuring bishops who had perpetuated their succession from the days of Sancroft and Ken. In 1722 he received consecration from this source, and returned to America. On his arrival he did more as a missionary than ever before. He instituted the daily service in Burlington, with frequent communions, preaching on Sunday mornings, and catechising or homilizing in the afternoon. He urged the establishment of a college, and suggested that the Society's house in Burlington be devoted to that purpose. He travelled from the capes of Delaware to the mountains in East Jersey. He visited Trenton and Hopewell and Amwell, preaching and baptizing nineteen persons in one day. He visited persons that were sick, in one instance going all the way from East Jersey to Burlington and back, to get the elements, that he might administer the holy communion to some converts eighty years of age who had never received it. He set up a schoolmaster to read prayers, and controlled the churches of Pennsylvania and New Jersey with the magnetism of his warm and honest heart. Two years he was thus engaged, 'no man forbidding him,' when another nonjuring bishop, one of his consecrators, Robert Welton, arrived and took charge of the church in Philadelphia. Contrasted with the establishment in Great Britain, the nonjurors were a 'feeble folk,' yet in the transatlantic world, they could 'make their houses in the rocks.' The government became alarmed. His Majesty's 'Writ of Privy Seal' was served on Welton, commanding him upon his allegiance to return to England. Talbot was 'discharged' the Society, and ordered to 'surcease officiating.' Welton went to Lisbon, where he shortly died. Talbot remained in Burlington, universally respected and beloved. More than one memorial was sent to the authorities in his behalf. The church people of Philadelphia, Bristol, and Burlington united in praying for the removal of his inhibition, declaring with solemn deliberation 'that by his exemplary life and ministry, he had been the greatest advocate for the Church of England, by law established, that ever appeared on this shore.' The next information comes from a news-paper, dated 'Philadelphia, November 30th, 1727.—Yesterday, died at Burlington, the Rev. Mr. John Talbot, formerly minister of that place, who was a pious, good man, and much lamented.' On his widow's will I discovered, within a few months past, his episcopal seal—a mitre, with a plain cross upon it, and beneath, the monogram, 'J. Talbot.' Such, in outline, is the career of one who did what he could to act the good Samaritan to the 'half dead' church in the wilderness, which the priest and the Levite of the court passed by. Because he acknowledged that he had the oil of the apostolate, as well as the wine of the priesthood, he was buried—a confessor for the truth. His character, his acts, his motives, examined through every available medium, fail to furnish him with a harsher epitaph than 'the zeal of thine house hath eaten me up.' In spirit, he resembled Ridley; in fidelity, Juxon; in suffering,

58

Sancroft; in devotion, Ken. He sought no emolument, he claimed no jurisdiction, he assumed no title, but a hundred and fifty years after his entombment, we, members of a free church in a free State, custodians of his sepulchre and trustees of his memory, arise up and give him the title emeritus, 'First Bishop of the Continent of America.'"

———◆◇◆———

IERSON, WILLIAM, Jr., M. D., was born in Orange, New Jersey, November 20th, 1830. He comes of a line of physicians, being a son of Dr. William Pierson, a grandson of Dr. Isaac Pierson, and a great-grandson of Dr. Matthias Pierson. He was educated at Nassau Hall, taking the degree of A. M., as well as that of A. B., and studied medicine in the medical department of the University of the City of New York, from which he graduated, settling in his native town. His specialty is surgery, in which he has attained marked distinction. He is a member of the Essex Medical Union; of the Essex District Medical Society, of which he was President in 1865; of the Medical Society of New Jersey, of which he has been Secretary; and of the New Jersey Academy of Medicine, of which he is now Vice-President. He was Surgeon of the Board of Enrolment for the Fourth Congressional District of New Jersey during the civil war. In 1851 and 1852 he was House Physician and Surgeon to the Brooklyn City Hospital. He is at present Surgeon to the Orange Memorial Hospital, and Consulting Surgeon to Saint Barnabas Hospital in Newark. His reputation alike as a physician and as a man is high and clear. He was married in 1856.

———◆◇◆———

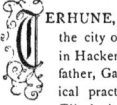

ERHUNE, RICHARD A., M. D., Physician, of the city of Passaic, was born, January 9th, 1829, in Hackensack, Bergen county, New Jersey. His father, Garrit Terhune, is one of the oldest medical practitioners in the State; his mother was Elizabeth (Zabriskie) Terhune—the former a native of New Jersey, and the latter of New York State. Richard A. Terhune received a very careful home education, his father taking the utmost pains to ground him solidly and thoroughly in the studies he was to pursue, and to secure for him the utmost mental discipline and development. This course of home education was supplemented by attendance at the public schools, and the two agencies secured for him a good degree of training and a large stock of practical and carefully selected knowledge. Influenced partly by the fact that his father was an eminent physician, and partly by the natural bent of his own inclinations, he decided upon entering the medical profession, and in the year

1846 he commenced a regular preliminary course of profes-sioual study, under the direction of his father. His pre-paratory course completed, he entered the College of Physicians and Surgeons in New York and attended three courses there. He graduated and received his diploma in 1850. On receiving his diploma he at once commenced practice in Passaic, in association with his father. This association continued until the year 1861, when he commenced independent practice, in which he has ever since continued. He speedily won the confidence of the community by the extent and thoroughness of his professional knowledge, by the skill which characterized his practice, and by the zeal and energy with which he performed the duties of his calling, and in consequence a large and valuable patronage was soon at his command. He is a member of the Passaic County Medical Society, in which body he has from time to time held official positions. Besides being a devoted professional man, he is an active and public-spirited citizen, interesting himself in all movements for the benefit of the community in which he lives. He is President of the Town Water Company, and was President of the Board of Council of the city of Passaic for three years. He was married, in 1861, to Mrs. Emily L. Morrell, widow of Richard Morrell, of Jersey City, and daughter of the late Alanson Randal, of Newburgh, New York.

----◆◆◆----

OLEMAN, JAMES BEARES, M. D., of Trenton, was born in 1806. He is descended from ancestors who long before the Revolution lived in Trenton and the immediate neighborhood. His great-grandfather, Edmund Beakes, as far back as 1716 resided in Trenton, and was for a long period Surveyor-General of West Jersey. The only child of Mr. Beakes married Job Pearson, of one of the William Penn Quaker families of Pennsylvania. He resided on a farm two and half miles above Trenton, in Lawrence township, at the period of the Revolution. His only living child, a daughter, married James Coleman, of an adjoining township. The Colemans were the first settlers of that district. James Coleman was a man highly esteemed by his acquaintances for his intelligence and manly qualities. His death occurred at middle age. He left a family of four children, two boys and two girls. One of the daughters, an accomplished and intelligent woman, died many years since; the other still lives, a blessing to those who depend on her for sympathy and counsel. The oldest son, Dr. Isaac Pearson Coleman, died November 4th, 1869, at Pemberton, New Jersey. He was eminent as a physician and surgeon, and was sought in counsel in most of the difficult cases that occurred in his district. He was President of the New Jersey Medical Society in 1858. So kindly was he regarded by his brothers of the profession that the Burlington County Medical Society have erected to his memory a costly monument in Mt. Holly cemetery. Dr. James Beakes Coleman was educated in Trenton, and spent some years with an apothecary, during which time he devoted himself particularly to chemistry, and became for one of his age, and at that period, an excellent practical chemist. He read such books as could be procured, sought advice from a Philadelphia friend engaged in the same pursuits, and was able, under the difficulty that then attended chemical studies, to succeed in making experiments, even making sulphate of quinine, a remedy that had within that year been introduced from France. He began the study of medicine when nineteen years of age with Dr. Nicholas Belleville, of Trenton, attended three courses of lectures at Yale College, and graduated in 1829. He read a thesis, as was the custom at that school, before the assembled professors and examiners appointed by the State Medical Society. The subject of the thesis was the "Similarity of the Nervous and Galvanic Fluid," a matter little investigated at that time. In the discussion that occurred in defence of the doctrines advanced, the late Professor Silliman strongly advocated the theories of the thesis, and assisted in removing the objections of some of the examiners. After graduating, nearly two years were spent in Philadelphia, when the prospect of a better immediate practice offered in Burlington county, New Jersey, which was accepted. Here an easy country practice, in a delightful neighborhood, occupied six years. During this interval, besides attending patients, some of the time was occupied lecturing to lyceums on subjects connected with medical studies, as natural philosophy, chemistry, vegetable physiology, phrenology, and battling with the Thompsonians, who then were popular and infested the neighborhood. Against them he wrote and had printed a Hudibrastic pamphlet of twenty-one pages, which seemed to have the effect in that region of quieting their clamorous advocates, and driving away their troublesome doctors. The pamphlet was called "Number Six, or the Thompsonian conferring the degree of Steam Doctor on Sam Simons, with Practical Advice." Practice, although pleasant from all its associations in this neighborhood, was necessarily limited, not enough to occupy the whole time of one who was desirous to gain a position in a profession that requires, along with other qualifications, that of much and varied experience. The last move was to return to Trenton, his native place. Here, since 1837, he has remained without interruption engaged in general practice; the time absent during this long period would not amount to more than five weeks, and part of this time away has been occasioned by professional calls. Although a general practitioner he became better known as a surgeon, for cases in this department are more under the public eye. Soon after establishing himself in Trenton, while yet young in his profession, the higher operations in surgery were frequently performed by him. As early as 1842 he extirpated successfully the parotid gland of John Gibbs, in Lamberton, an operation the formidable character of which speaks well of his skill and nerve as a surgeon. Gibbs died some time afterward of consumption. Many plino-plastic operations, relieving great deformities, such as lost noses restored by flaps cut from the forehead, and limbs distorted by burns relieved by transferring skin to the contracted part; lithotomy, cataract, strabismus, club-foot, trèpanning, strangulated hernia, hardly an operation of importance that he has not been successful in performing. Mechanical knowledge, invention, and a ready use of tools, enabling him to construct without assistance almost any implement or apparatus he may require, have qualified him particularly for the surgical branch of his profession. The skill of a physician is hardly as demonstrable as that of the surgeon; our only estimate is formed from the regard in which he is held by his patients, and by the members of his own profession, and by his writings. Judging from these he is entitled to high rank. His patients have been amongst those of the first position and intelligence, and they regard him as authority; his brother physicians accord him knowledge of his profession in a high degree, theoretic and practical; his communications to medical societies show that he is original in thought, and industrious in research. A report to the New Jersey Medical Society, "On the Effects of Mercurial Preparations on the living Animal Tissues," read before the society in 1853, and published in their Transactions of that year, had it met the eye of Surgeon-General Barnes during the early part of the rebellion, when he was about ordering the army surgeons to prescribe no mercury for the soldiers, would have been the document of all others upon which to base his action and authority. A paper on Malaria, for the same society, published in their Transactions of 1866, took the position that malaria is the product of diseased action in vegetables, not of vegetable decomposition, but poisonous emanations caused by perverted functions, as in animals when suffering from infectious diseases. This new and reasonable analogy has been received with much favor, and as a matter of general interest was republished in *Beecher's Magazine* in 1871. Many papers have been read by him before the Mercy County Medical Society on practical surgery, such as knee-joint operations, illustrated by his own cases; apparatus for fractured clavicle; the propriety of immediate operations in cases of severe wounds, confirmed by railroad and machinery wounds, in which limbs have been amputated before reaction came on, showing the effect of the knife was to stimulate life and cause reaction, while the operation caused less pain during the prostration that followed the shock of the accident. These communications stated his experience had been that all cases thus promptly treated had done better in every respect, and without anæsthesia than others in which there had been the ordinary delay. He also contributed a series of articles, published in *Beecher's Magazine*, on natural and artificial mechanism, making in all a good-sized volume. The first attempt, of which there is any record, of forced ventilation of public

buildings to drive the circulation of hot air by a blowing-fan, was in the New Jersey Penitentiary, in 1841. At that time he was Physician to the prison. The former plan of heating this establishment was by hot water circulating through the ranges of cells: it was the Perkins' plan, and adopted in many public buildings; heat without ventilation radiated from hot pipes, and as a consequence the cells became very offensive. The new plan was conceived from a hint given by a visit to Hanover furnace, where they had adopted the hot-air blast to facilitate the reduction of iron ore. The air here was found hot enough to burn a shingle as it rushed through the tuyere in the lower part of the furnace. A description of a new way to warm the prisoners, and at the same time to ventilate perfectly, was drawn up, and submitted to the inspectors. It was approved and brought before the Legislature. An appropriation of $5,000 was made for the purpose. The apparatus was constructed, and Professor Henry was called to witness the experiment and give his opinion as to the value of the method. He said it was a new thing and he doubted its practicability. This is the plan by which all well-ventilated and well-warmed public buildings are now managed, and it was thrown out of the New Jersey Penitentiary because they had not power to spare from their other work to drive the fan. Almost as soon as electroplating was made known to the public he conceived the idea of applying the process to forming raised cuts to be used after the manner of wood-cuts in printing. He traced pictures through a wax coating on copper plates, filled up with more wax the broad spaces between the lines of the drawings, covered the edges and back of the plates with a still further coat of wax, and by proper arrangement submitted the prepared drawing to galvanic action in a solution of sulphate of copper. He succeeded in forming a precipitate of pure copper that filled all the lines and around all the intervening spaces, which, when separated from the copper plate, showed the drawing in relief. These were backed, mounted, and used in the printing press more than a year before Palmer, of London, published his first pictures, and after this identical plan. The writer of this has seen some of these old plates, made in 1845. He is the originator of a plan for firing large ordnance, such as the fifteen or twenty-inch guns, by a central chamber, on which the ball rests, with the main charge of the powder around this chamber, so that it cannot take fire until the inner chamber has been fired and the inertia of the heavy ball has been overcome by its lift from its bed. Thus started, it is accelerated in its motion by the main body of the powder taking fire from the fount after the whole of the charge in the central chamber has been exploded. Commodore Robert F. Stockton, who led the way in heavy guns, as well as steam war vessels, when the results of the adoption of this plan to a fowling-piece were named to him, said it was the only method by which good, quick powder could be used in heavy cannon. To overcome the inertia of the huge ball suddenly was too great a shock for the guns, and this would be the remedy. Mr. Edwin Stevens, who was present, had his attention called to it, and determined in case his battery was accepted by the government to experiment on the plan, confident that it would succeed. The late John A. Roebling was so taken by this plan to set heavy balls in motion that he made efforts to have it brought before the Ordnance Department. Apart from his profession and the useful allied arts, he seems to have indulged in painting and poetry, particularly in the earlier years of his life. Many of his pieces appeared in the Philadelphia *United States Gazette*, when it was edited by Joseph R. Chandler, and were extensively copied. One, "The Cities of the Plain," was published as anonymous in a Boston collection of select poems. A ready sketcher, many excellent likenesses and good paintings of his early friends are still to be found. One, the portrait, three-quarter length, of his old preceptor, Dr. Belleville, would do credit to many a professed artist. During the United States Bank troubles, when General Jackson made war upon it, the celebrated "Gold Humbug" caricature was published in New York, in the style of a large fifty-cent ticket. Thousands were struck off and sent to all parts of the country; more profitably to himself, the publisher said, than anything of the kind he had attempted. Another, executed when John R. Thompson ran for Governor of New Jersey, representing the railroad running over the backs of the people, contributed greatly, it was thought at the time, to the success of Stratton, the opposing candidate. He was President of the Medical Society of New Jersey in 1855; has been President of the Mercer County Medical Society at different times; President of the Board of Health, of Trenton, for the last five or six years; one of the Board of Managers of the New Jersey Asylum for the Insane, and of the United States Board of Examining Surgeons for Pensions.

———◆◇◆———

TUDDIFORD, JAMES HERVEY, M. D., late of Lambertville, son of the Rev. P. O. Studdiford, D. D., for forty-five years pastor of the Presbyterian Church at Lambertville, was born in that town, September 12th, 1832. His preliminary education was received in the College of New Jersey, whence he was graduated with honors in 1852. In the same year he began the study of medicine under his uncle, Surgeon Josiah Simpson, of the Medical Staff, United States Army, and in the winter of 1852–53 attended lectures in the medical department of the University of Pennsylvania. The ensuing winter he attended lectures at the University of New York, and in the spring of 1854 received from that institution his degree of M. D. In 1856, having, after due examination by the State Board of Censors, received his license to practice as a physician in New Jersey, he established himself at Quakertown, Hunterdon county, as the

successor to Dr. A. J. Clark; in 1857 removed to St. Paul, Minnesota, and in 1857 returned thence, and finally settled in Lambertville. He was a prominent member of the Hunterdon County Medical Society, being elected Vice-President of that organization in 1866, and President in 1867, and in all its affairs taking an active interest and leading part. For several years he was a Ruling Elder in the Presbyterian Church of Lambertville. At the time of his death he had attained to an extensive practice, and was esteemed no less for his professional ability than for his moral worth. He died March 23d, 1870.

———◆◇◆———

OODRUFF, ABNER, later of Perth Amboy, was born in Elizabethtown, New Jersey, December 28th, 1767, and was the son of Elias Woodruff, also of Elizabethtown; George W. Woodruff was his brother; in 1772 his father settled in Princeton. In February, 1779, Abner joined the grammar school in Nassau Hall, and, as he says, "Commenced the rudiments of education." In 1780 he entered the Freshman Class of Princeton College. Soon after graduating he took up his residence in Sussex county, New Jersey, where he was engaged in mercantile operations until 1787. In September of that year he returned to Princeton, and was there admitted to the degree of Master of Arts. In September, 1794, having resumed business in Sussex county, he, with his partner, both belonging to a volunteer troop of horse, joined the expedition organized and fitted out to quell the whiskey insurrection in western Pennsylvania. He then acted as a Paymaster of the 2d Regiment of New Jersey Cavalry. In December of the same year he returned to his native State. In 1798 he received an appointment as Midshipman in the navy, and continued in the service until 1803, when he resigned his commission and removed to Georgia, where he resided for a number of years. He afterward took up his residence at Perth Amboy, New Jersey, where he died, January 11th, 1842.

———◆◇◆———

ALL, JOHN, M. D., late of Pittstown, Hunterdon county, New Jersey, was born, in 1787, in Solebury, Bucks county, Pennsylvania, and received his professional education under Dr. John Wilson of the latter place. About 1807 he succeeded Dr. McKissack, at Pittstown; acquired a considerable practice and became in that locality extremely popular. The kindly regard so generally felt for him was based largely upon his success in the treatment of disease, but it was probably mainly owing to the fact that his charges for professional services were very small, and that he rarely took the trouble to collect even these. If the

recovered patient left a jug of apple brandy at the doctor's door, it was considered in the light of full payment of a long bill: and while in the end his too free use of his liquid for tended to throw his practice into other and steadier hands, it is none the less true that his professional ability was quite exceptional. He was very fond of out-door sports—hunting, fishing and riding—and in such passed much of his time. He died September 12th, 1826.

MOREHOUSE, GEORGE READ, M. D., was born, March 25th, 1829, at Mount Holly, Burlington county, New Jersey. He is a son of the Rev. George V. Morehouse and Martha Read, descendants respectively of Colonel Andrew Morehouse and Major Z. Russell, of the Revolution. He is a graduate of the College of New Jersey, from which he received also the degree of A. M., having graduated in 1848, and been made Master of Arts in 1851. He studied medicine in the Jefferson Medical College and the medical department of the University of Pennsylvania, graduating from the latter in 1851, and settling in Philadelphia, where he has since resided. He is a member of the Philadelphia County Medical Society; of the College of Physicians of Philadelphia; of the Philadelphia Academy of Natural Sciences; of the Pathological Society of Philadelphia; of the Biological Society. He has enriched medical literature with numerous writings, some of which at least, it is safe to say, the profession "will not willingly let die;" as, for example, "Respiration in Chelonians," Smithsonian Institute, 1858; "Reflex Paralysis as the Result of Gunshot Wounds;" "Malingery, Especially in Regard to the Simulation of Diseases of the Nervous System;" "Gunshot Wounds and Other Injuries of the Nerves," Philadelphia, J. B. Lippincott & Co., 1864; "Laryngo-Tracheotomy," also the Use of Atropia in Prolapsus Iridis." From 1862 to 1864 he was Acting Assistant Surgeon in charge of the general hospital for Nervous Diseases, at the corner of Christian street and Turner's lane.

LINDSLY, HARVEY, M. D., was born, January 11th, 1804, in Morris county, New Jersey. He is descended through both lines (Lindsly and Condict) from English stock, the representatives of which emigrated to this country more than two hundred years ago, and settled in New Jersey. He prepared for college in Somerset county, New Jersey, at the classical academy of the Rev. Dr. Finley, afterwards president of the University of Georgia, graduated at Princeton College, and studied medicine in the city of New York and Washington, District of Columbia, graduating at the latter place in 1828, and settling there immediately, where he has ever since resided. He retired from general practice in 1872, not less full of honors than of years. For several years he was Professor of Obstetrics, and subsequently of the Principles and Practice of Medicine, in the National Medical College, in the District of Columbia. He is a member of the Medical Society of Washington; of the American Medical Association, of which he has been President; and of the Washington Alumni Association of Princeton College, of which he was elected President, December 23d, 1876; and an honorary member of the Rhode Island Medical Society, the Historical Society of New Jersey, and numerous other societies in different quarters of the country. He has published articles on a variety of medical subjects in the *American Journal of Medical Science* and other medical journals, as also literary and scientific articles in the *North American Review, Southern Literary Messenger*, and other periodicals of the kind. In 1833 he was elected President of the Board of Health of Washington, and held the position for many years. He was for thirty years a member of the American Colonization Society, and Chairman of its Executive Committee. Philanthropist, sanitarist, and author, as well as physician, he has borne well his part alike in his avocations and in his green vocation, wherein especially he has walked worthy of it, so that now, when nature in him stands on the "verge of life sublime," he may enjoy the sweet solace of looking back over a long and busy life spent in usefulness and crowned with honor.

BLANCKE, FERDINAND F., Capitalist and Insurance President, of Linden, was born, January 31st, 1831, in Manden, Prussia. His parents were Frederick A. Blancke, a merchant of the city just named, and Anna (Snider) Blancke, of Duesberg, on the Rhine. He came to this country in the year 1854, and established himself in New York, where for nearly ten years he was prosperously engaged in the confectionery business. In the year 1864 he removed to New Jersey, locating himself in what was then the little town of Wheatsheaf. Here he purchased four hundred acres of land, and inaugurated a series of improvements which have resulted in the thriving town now known as Linden. The success which has attended his ventures here well illustrates the energy and executive ability of the man. His character has inspired esteem and confidence in his neighbors, and they have given practical expression thereto by placing him in various positions of trust and responsibility. He has been twice elected to the State Legislature; is President of the Germania Fire Insurance Company, of Elizabeth, which position he has filled since the organization of the company in 1871; is President of the Union Manufacturing Company of Elizabethport; is a Director of the First National Bank of Elizabeth, and has

recovered patient left a jug of apple brandy at the doctor's door, it was considered in the light of full payment of a long bill; and while in the end his too free use of his liquid fees tended to throw his practice into other and steadier hands, it is none the less true that his professional ability was quite exceptional. He was very fond of out-door sports—hunting, fishing and riding—and in such passed much of his time. He died September 12th, 1826.

OREHOUSE, GEORGE READ, M. D., was born, March 25th, 1829, at Mount Holly, Burlington county, New Jersey. He is a son of the Rev. George Y. Morehouse and Martha Read, descendants respectively of Colonel Andrew Morehouse and Major Z. Russell, of the Revolution. He is a graduate of the College of New Jersey, from which he received also the degree of A. M., having graduated in 1848, and been made Master of Arts in 1851. He studied medicine in the Jefferson Medical College and the medical department of the University of Pennsylvania, graduating from the latter in 1851, and settling in Philadelphia, where he has since resided. He is a member of the Philadelphia County Medical Society; of the College of Physicians of Philadelphia; of the Philadelphia Academy of Natural Sciences; of the Pathological Society of Philadelphia, and of the Biological Society. He has enriched medical literature with numerous writings, some of which at least, it is safe to say, the profession " will not willingly let die; " as, for example, " Respiration in Chelonians," Smithsonian Institute, 1858; " Reflex Paralysis as the Result of Gunshot Wounds; " " Malingery, Especially in Regard to the Simulation of Diseases of the Nervous System; " " Gunshot Wounds and Other Injuries of the Nerves," Philadelphia, J. B. Lippincott & Co., 1864; " Laryngo-Tracheotomy," and the " Use of Atropia in Prolapsus Iridis." From 1862 to 1865 he was Acting Assistant Surgeon in charge of the Special Hospital for Nervous Diseases, at the corner of Christian street and Turner's lane.

INDSLY, HARVEY, M. D., was born, January 11th, 1804, in Morris county, New Jersey. He is descended through both lines (Lindsly and Condict) from English stock, the representatives of which emigrated to this country more than two hundred years ago, and settled in New Jersey. He prepared for college in Somerset county, New Jersey, at the classical academy of the Rev. Dr. Finley, afterwards president of the University of Georgia, graduated at Princeton College, and studied medicine in the city of New York and Washington, District of Columbia, graduating at the latter place in 1828, and settling there immediately, where he has ever since resided. He retired from general practice in 1872, not less full of honors than of years. For several years he was Professor of Obstetrics, and subsequently of the Principles and Practice of Medicine, in the National Medical College, in the District of Columbia. He is a member of the Medical Society of Washington; of the American Medical Association, of which he has been President; and of the Washington Alumni Association of Princeton College, of which he was elected President, December 23d, 1876; and an honorary member of the Rhode Island Medical Society, the Historical Society of New Jersey, and numerous other societies in different quarters of the country. He has published articles on a variety of medical subjects in the *American Journal of Medical Science* and other medical journals, as also literary and scientific articles in the *North American Review*, *Southern Literary Messenger*, and other periodicals of the kind. In 1833 he was elected President of the Board of Health of Washington, and held the position for many years. He was for thirty years a member of the American Colonization Society, and Chairman of its Executive Committee. Philanthropist, sanitarist, and author, as well as physician, he has borne well his part alike in his avocations and in his great vocation, wherein especially he has walked worthy of it, so that now, when nature in him stands on the " verge of her confine," he may enjoy the sweet solace of looking back over a long and busy life spent in usefulness and crowned with honor.

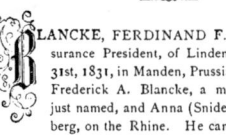LANCKE, FERDINAND F., Capitalist and Insurance President, of Linden, was born, January 31st, 1831, in Manden, Prussia. His parents were Frederick A. Blancke, a merchant of the city just named, and Anna (Snider) Blancke, of Duesberg, on the Rhine. He came to this country in the year 1854, and established himself in New York, where for nearly ten years he was prosperously engaged in the confectionery business. In the year 1864 he removed to New Jersey, locating himself in what was then the little town of Wheatsheaf. Here he purchased four hundred acres of land, and inaugurated a series of improvements which have resulted in the thriving town now known as Linden. The success which has attended his enterprise here well illustrates the energy and executive ability of the man. His character has inspired esteem and confidence in his neighbors, and they have given practical expression thereto by placing him in various positions of trust and responsibility. He has been twice elected to the State Legislature; is President of the Germania Fire Insurance Company, of Elizabeth, which position he has filled since the organization of the company in 1871; is President of the Union Manufacturing Company of Elizabethport; is a Director of the First National Bank of Elizabeth, and has

been for the past six years; has been a Director of the New Jersey State Agricultural Society for the past eight years; is the Manager of the Rahway Savings Bank, and is a Director of the Mechanics' Savings Bank, of Elizabeth. In politics he is thoroughly independent, always voting for the men and the measures best calculated in his judgment to advance the welfare of the city, the State, and the nation. He was married, April 3d, 1855, to Caroline Brake, of Balefeld, Germany.

TRYKER, SAMUEL STANHOPE, M. D., was born at Trenton, New Jersey, May 4th, 1842. He is not only a native but a descendant of natives, his ancestors being American for many generations back. He received his preparatory education at Lawrenceville, New Jersey, and his classical at Princeton, studying medicine at the University of Pennsylvania, from the medical department of which he graduated in March, 1866. He settled in West Philadelphia, where he now resides. He is a member of the Pathological Society of Philadelphia, and of the Philadelphia Obstetrical Society. As yet he contents himself with drawing from the fountain of medical literature, instead of contributing to its treasures, except indeed as every successful practitioner, especially in a great city, cannot help doing, seeing that practice furnishes the material of literature. He is at present Visiting Accoucheur to the Philadelphia Hospital. Still on the sunny side of his prime, of excellent general culture, and of acknowledged professional skill, he has a firm footing on the ladder of fame, and will, it may be safely predicted, steadily ascend the shining rounds.

LARK, WILLIAM PATTERSON, M. D., late of Belvidere, New Jersey, son of the Rev. Joseph Clark, was born in New Brunswick, in which town his father was for many years pastor of the First Presbyterian Church. After graduating in 1819 from the College of New Jersey, Princeton, he studied medicine, was licensed as a physician, and for a short time was engaged in practice in Wilkesbarre, Pennsylvania. He subsequently removed to Clinton, Hunterdon county, and in 1821 was one of the founders of the Hunterdon County Medical Society. He was the second Treasurer of that organization (elected May 7th, 1822), and at the same time served as a member of the Board of Censors. His essay, "A Cursory Analysis of the Theory of Health, Predisposition, and Disease," read at the first semi-annual meeting of the society (October 23d, 1821), was the only paper read at that meeting, and was the first of any sort read before the society. In 1836-37 he was Third Vice-President of the New Jersey State Medical Society. He

removed to Belvidere in 1825, and was there actively engaged in practice until the time of his death, occupying a leading place among the physicians of that locality, and possessing to a remarkable degree the confidence and esteem of the entire community. He died September 4th, 1857.

URVEE, REV. PHILIP, Pastor of the Reformed Dutch Church at English Neighborhood, and late of Morristown, New Jersey, was born in New York in 1775 or 1776. In November, 1828, he was called from Saratoga, New York, to the church at Bergen, to succeed Rev. Mr. Abeel. His installation took place December 21st, 1828, on which occasion Rev. Benjamin C. Taylor preached the sermon, and Rev. Staats Van Santvoord addressed the pastor and the people, immediately after which he delivered his introductory discourse, on Mark xvi. 15: "Go ye into all the world, and preach the gospel to every creature." Having, in his former field of labor, taken great pleasure and labored diligently in rearing new churches, while fostering the interests of his principal charge; and, being possessed of a kind spirit and gentleness of manner, he knew excellently well how to seek and follow the things which secure peace; with mild persuasion he gained many friends at English Neighborhood, and labored diligently and lovingly in his holy calling. About this time occurred the foreclosure of a mortgage covering the schoolhouse at New Durham, which had been executed by the seceding Consistory. The case was decided in favor of the mortgagee, and a heavy amount had to be raised to meet the claim. The Reformed Dutch Church at Bergen then aided their involved brethren to the amount of one hundred dollars, and the Collegiate Church in New York appropriated to them three hundred dollars, received by them in 1836. Thus relieved from these temporal difficulties, "God was pleased, in the winter of 1837-38, to visit them with spiritual blessings," and at the February communion nineteen persons were admitted to church membership on confession of faith. In 1839, in consideration of the growth of population at New Durham, and the increased desire for more frequent service there, the Classis, in September, recommended the attention of the English Neighborhood Consistory to the propriety of organizing a district church at New Durham. On the 1st of October the Consistory expressed their view of its inexpediency, and on the 7th of that month determined that it would not "at present" advance the interests of the church. The measure was not effected until March 27th, 1843. It was effected kindly, however, and the English Neighborhood Consistory agreed to convey to the New Durham Church the lecture-room owned by them at this place. In 1847 he requested his Consistory to take measures for calling another minister, in consideration of his increasing bodily infirmities, but they postponed acting on his request for some time. On the 6th of February, 1848, he requested the Consistory to join him in asking of Classis the dissolution of the ecclesiastical tie which had so pleasantly subsisted between them for nearly twenty years. The kindness of his feeling for this flock was attested on the occasion by the following statement: "There is a considerable sum due me for wood and hay, also in money. These arrearages I give to my Consistory, hoping that it may encourage all my friends to have my place filled." On the 3d of April, 1848, the Classis, as requested, dissolved the connection between him and the church, and adopted a resolution expressive of "their esteem for this honored servant of Christ, and their appreciation of his valuable pastoral labors." Under his ministry there were added to the communion of his church eighty-four persons on confession of faith, and twenty-eight on certificate—in all, one hundred and twelve. Shortly after his resignation of his pastoral charge he removed to Morristown, New Jersey, to reside with his son-in-law, Richard W. Stevenson, M. D. There, on the 24th of February, 1850, he passed away. In 1834 he was honored by the Trustees of Rutgers College with the degree of Doctor of Divinity. His widow, his daughter—Mrs. Stevenson—and his son, Abraham Duryee, survived him. On the west wall of the English Neighborhood Church is a white marble plate, placed there as a memorial of him by Thomas H. Herring.

—◦✦◦—

EPUE, HON. DAVID AYRES, Justice of the Supreme Court of the State of New Jersey, was born at Mount Bethel, Northampton county, Pennsylvania, October 27th, 1826. He is of Huguenot descent, and his ancestors were among the earliest settlers of Pahaquarry, Warren county. When Samuel Preston, in 1787, went out with a party into Northampton county on his first surveying tour, he met with two members of the family, and experienced at their hands great hospitality, and from them gained much valuable information. Writing to *Hazard's Register* in June, 1828, respecting the Meenesink settlement, this surveyor says, that "at the venerable Samuel Dupuis' they found great hospitality and plenty of the necessaries of life;" also, that "Samuel Dupuis told them that when the rivers were frozen he had a good road to Esopus (now Kingston) from the mine holes on the mine road some hundred miles; that he took his wheat and cider there for salt and necessaries. . . . . They were of opinion that first settlements of Hollanders in Meenesink were many years older than William Penn's charter." Samuel Dupuis (or Depue) treated the surveying party so well that they concluded to make a survey of his claim "in order to befriend him, if necessary." But the Indians thought they ought to say something about this time. So, when the men

began to survey, the Indians gathered around and watched for a while. At length an old Indian laid his hand on the shoulder of one Nathaniel Scull, and said, "Put up iron string; go home." This injunction seemed likely to be followed up by further demonstrations of Indian disapproval, so the surveyors "quit and returned." In another letter the same writer says: "I found Nicholas Dupuis, Esquire (son of Samuel), living in a spacious stone house in great plenty and affluence." From him the surveyor obtained much information as to the means of communication with the outside world enjoyed by the settlers, when and by whom the mine road was made, the ores that were dug, and the formation of the original settlement; but he only gave it as tradition, there being no records of any kind. At the time of this interview, June, 1787, Nicholas Dupuis was about sixty years of age. The settlers then were by no means clear whether they were living in the jurisdiction of New Jersey or Pennsylvania. Judge Depue's ancestors continued to reside in this section, and his father, Benjamin Depue, was a citizen thereof. The family moved, however, in 1840, to Belvidere, Warren county, New Jersey. After a sound preliminary training, the subject of this sketch entered Princeton College, matriculating in 1843. At the conclusion of a three years' course he was graduated, and soon thereafter began the study of law under the direction of John M. Sherrerd. In due course he was admitted to the bar, July, 1849, and began practice at Belvidere in the same year. He met with encouraging success, and prosecuted his profession until the year 1866, when Governor Marcus L. Ward offered him a seat on the Supreme Bench, to succeed Judge Daniel Haines. The nomination was accepted, and his commission bears date November 15th, 1866. On the expiration of his term, in 1873, he was reappointed by Governor Joel Parker. Being himself a Republican, and originally appointed by a Republican, this renomination by a Democratic governor is all-sufficient testimony to the ability, impartiality and integrity of his administration of justice. On appointment he was assigned to the Essex and Union Circuit, and in order to be convenient to the sphere of his duty he removed to Newark, where he has since resided. He received the honorary degree of LL. D. from Rutgers College in 1874. The judiciary of New Jersey has always ranked deservedly high, alike for ability and integrity, and this eminence will never be lost so long as the bench is occupied by men like Judge Depue. No purer or more thoroughly conscientious jurist ever wore the ermine. With a singularly even-balanced mind, a keen discrimination, and vast capacity for work, joined to profound knowledge of the law, he fills precisely the popular estimate of the upright, incorruptible judge, and his rulings and decisions carry with them an influence and weight which make them practically irresistible, whether as statements of law or interpretations of evidence. Judge Depue, with all his learning, is a man of exceptionally simple and unaffected manners, and in his intercourse with his fellows is genial and kindly to the last degree. In his leisure hours he finds great delight in the perusal of favorite authors, and there are few men of his years who are more familiar than he with the best thoughts of the kings and priests of litera-ture. He has a fine appreciation of humor in its higher forms, and the happy faculty, moreover, of seeing the sun-shine of things rather than the shadow. Such a man— pure, able, broad in all his views, steady in the discharge of duty, inflexible in his detestation of wrong, squaring his life by the perfect standard established by the Master—is not merely a blessing to the community which his virtues illuminate: he is a model and a helper, by as much as he reinforces the moral forces of the world, to the whole brotherhood of man.

INDSLEV, JOHN BERRIEN, M. D., was born at Princeton, New Jersey, October 24th, 1822. His family, in the paternal line, were among the first colonists at Morristown, New Jersey, while his maternal ancestors, the Lawrence family, set-tled at Hell Gate, Long Island, as early as 1660. He was educated at the University of Nashville, Tennessee, from which he graduated in 1839, taking the degree of A. M. in 1842, and after attending the session of 1841–42 at the medical department of the University of Louisville, entered the medical department of the University of Penn-sylvania, from which he graduated in March, 1843, with William Walker, of Nicaragua fame, subsequently attending the session of 1849–50 at the medical department of the University of Louisville. His home has been at Nashville since 1824, when his father, having declined the présidency of Princeton College, took charge of the Nashville Univer-sity. In October, 1850, he became Professor of Chemistry and Pharmacy in the Medical Department of the University of Nashville, and Dean of the Faculty, devoting six years mainly to the duties of the deanship, the school meanwhile growing from nought to over four hundred students. In 1873 he resigned his professorship. From February, 1855, to May, 1870, he was Chancellor of the University of Nash-ville, preserving it unharmed throughout the war. He is a member of the American Medical Association, and a very faithful one, having attended nine of its annual meetings; and of the Numismatic and Antiquarian Society of Phila-delphia, and a Fellow of the American Association for the Advancement of Science. He is the author of a " Eulogy on R. M. Porter, M. D.," 1856; and of an " Introductory Lecture," 1858; and is now engaged on the " Medical Annals of Tennessee," at the request of the State Medical Society. He is also engaged now on a work to be entitled, " Sources and Sketches of Cumberland Presbyterian His-tory," his literary efficiency in behalf of Presbyterianism having already earned for him the degree of D. D., from the College of New Jersey. In conjunction with Dr. J. G. M. Rumsey, of Knoxville, he will publish in the course of the

present year (1877) the "Abridged Annals of Tennessee." In 1875 he was Secretary of the State Board of Education of Tennessee. He was Acting Post Surgeon at Nashville in February, 1862, by General A. S. Johnston's request. In 1874 he was Professor of Materia Medica in the Tennes-see College of Pharmacy, and in 1876 Health Officer of Nashville. He was married, February 9th, 1851, to Sarah McGavock, daughter of Jacob McGavock, of one of the old families of Nashville.

IELD, CHAUNCEY MITCHELL, M. D., of Bound Brook, New Jersey, was born in Brooklyn, New York, in 1850. The Field family is of English extraction, but has long been settled in New Jersey. Several of its members served in the Continental army during the revolutionary war, while in later years, in civil life, the name has been no less distinguished. The Hon. David Dudley Field, a recognized leader of the New York bar, and the Rev. M. S. Field, D. D., the able editor of the *Evangelist*, may be mentioned, as typical representatives at the present day. Dr. Field's father, R. R. Field, Esq., was the founder of the house of Field Brothers, extensive cloth dealers of St. Louis; subsequently changing his residence to Brooklyn. Here, as already stated, Dr. Field was born. Entering, when a lad, the Lawrenceville Classical and Commercial High School, he was graduated thence with first honors; and from the College of New Jersey, Princeton, he was graduated with similar distinction in 1871. Immediately upon taking his B. A. degree, he began the study of medi-cine under Dr. Markoe, of New York, subsequently entered the College of Physicians and Surgeons of New York, and was graduated thence M. D. in 1874. For some six months after his graduation he continued his professional studies in the New York hospitals, and then established himself in Bound Brook, taking the practice of the well-known Dr. Smith, of that town. Although so recently entered upon his professional career, he has already acquired something more than a local reputation, his skilful treatment of disease, joined to his success in a number of difficult surgical opera-tions, having given him a distinctive and honorable stand-ing among medical men.

AN HORN, REV. WILLIAM, Pastor of the Church of Scotch Plains, New Jersey, Chaplain in the Revolutionary Army, was born in New Jersey in 1746, and was the son of Peter Van Horn. He was educated at Dr. Jones' academy, in Pennepek, New Jersey, and was ordained at Southampton, Pennsylvania, where he continued for a period of thirteen years, laboring zealously in all times and seasons and serving for several years as chaplain in the army during the war. In 1785 he became the pastor of the church of Scotch Plains, remaining in this relation until 1807, when he resigned, and removed with his wife and seven children to the West, designing to settle near Lebanon, Ohio. He died of dropsy, *en route*, at Pittsburgh, Pennsylvania, October 31st, 1807.

CLARK, REV. JOSEPH, Clergyman, late of New Brunswick, was born in Elizabethtown, New Jersey, October 21st, 1751. He early felt the power of religion, and was admitted to the communion by that distinguished Christian and patriot, Rev. James Caldwell. At the age of seventeen he was apprenticed to learn the trade of a carpenter, and had great difficulties to contend with in obtaining the elements of learning. After working all day at his trade, he studied the Latin grammar at night by the light of a pine-knot; and thus, by indefatigable diligence, made himself acquainted with the classics. In two years after commencing this course he presented himself as a candidate for admission to Princeton College, and after a creditable examination was received into the junior class. The war soon afterward broke up the tenor and systematic regularity of the instructions at this institution, and he joined the army, and with his patriot comrades in arms served valiantly and efficiently for several years. While thus engaged in a military capacity, he received flattering testimonials from several distinguished military characters for his fidelity and ability in the discharge of various important trusts. After many interruptions he eventually returned to college and the prosecution of his studies, and in 1781 obtained his bachelor's degree. He then applied himself to the study of theology, and at the expiration of two years was duly licensed to preach the gospel. October 21st, 1783, he took charge of the congregation at Allentown, whence he was translated in 1797 to New Brunswick. "The Rev. John Woodhull, of Freehold, having been called, and having declined the call, an invitation was given in 1796 to the Rev. Joseph Clark, pastor of the united churches of Allentown and Nottingham. His people made a vigorous opposition, but they were finally overruled by the Presbytery; and Mr. Clark was installed January 4th, 1797, with a salary of £250. President S. Stanhope Smith preached the sermon, 2 Timothy i. 13, and also presided, and gave the charge." He continued in this connection for sixteen years, until his decease. He was "a solid, serious, and impressive preacher;" was capable of moving the feelings in a notable degree; and "wept freely himself; while the tears of his auditors attested the power which he exercised over them. He blended great dignity with affability. Few ministers have enjoyed to a greater degree the confidence and affection of their people. As a proof of their esteem, in 1809 they raised his salary from $666.66, on his request, to $800." He was

highly esteemed by his brethren in the ministry, and his counsel and judgment were greatly prized in the ecclesiastical courts. He was for many years a Trustee of the College of New Jersey, and a Director of the Theological Seminary; and was also one of the most successful agents in collecting funds for rebuilding Nassau Hall after its destruction by fire. The only production of his pen that was given to the world is a "Sermon on the Death of Governor Paterson;" who, after an exemplary and useful life, died peacefully, September 9th, 1806. That discourse was so eloquent and acceptable that the trustees ordered the printing of five hundred copies. "It was written in a clear, manly style; first defining the character of a Christian statesman, and then applying the description to the deceased. The closing part of the discourse was a masterly appeal to the conscience and feelings of the different classes of hearers addressed. The number of communicants at his decease was one hundred and twenty-seven, nearly double what it had been at his accession. He died in New Brunswick, New Jersey, October 20th, 1813." The Sunday before his death, he preached from the text: "The time is short," 1 Corinthians vii. 29. On Tuesday night he retired to bed in his usual health, and suddenly expired about three o'clock the next morning. A handsome monument to his memory was erected by private subscriptions, and two quarters' salary were voted to his widow, subject to the deduction of $36 for supplies.

TUDDIFORD, REV. PETER OGILVIE, D. D., Pastor of the Presbyterian Church of Lambertville, son of Rev. Peter Studdiford and Phœbe (Vanderveer) Studdiford, was born at Readington, New Jersey, January 11th, 1799. "His childhood was marked by his dutiful conduct to his parents, his unexceptionable deportment generally, his unusual tenderness of conscience, and deep thoughtfulness on the subject of personal religion. Having been devoted to God in covenant by baptism in his infancy, and having received a faithful religious training under the parental roof, he early consecrated himself to the service of Christ, and became a communicant in the church at Readington, of which his father was then the pastor." He pursued his classical studies in part at the academy in Basking Ridge, in the care of Rev. Robert Finley, D. D., and in part at Somerville, under the tuition of Cullen Morris. Having completed his preparation, he entered Queens (now Rutgers) College, at New Brunswick, and in the summer of 1816, when but seventeen years of age, graduated at that institution with the highest honors of his class. After leaving college, he was occupied for about three years in teaching, first in Bedminster, subsequently in Somerville, "and with great acceptance, although many of his pupils were older than himself." July 8th, 1819, he entered the Theological Seminary of the Presbyterian Church, at Princeton, where he remained proseeuting his studies for the ministry until September 29th, 1821. On the 27th of April in the same year, at a meeting of the Presbytery of New Brunswick in Trenton, he was licensed to preach the gospel, together with nine of his fellow-students, only one of whom was surviving in 1867. During the spring vacation he preached in the employ of the General Assembly's Board of Missions about Bristol and Tullytown, Pennsylvania. On Wednesday, November 28th, 1821, in the Presbyterian Church at Trenton, he was ordained as an evangelist by the Presbytery of New Brunswick, at the same time with Rev. Charles Hodge, D. D., and the late Rev. William I. Armstrong, D. D.; and on the following Sabbath, December 2d, commenced his labors at Lambertville, having agreed to supply that church, and the one at Solebury, Pennsylvania, alternately, for one year. In September, 1822, upon the application of seven persons, the church of Lambertville and Georgetown was organized by Rev. Dr. Hodge, under the direction of the Presbytery of New Brunswick; and Emley Holcombe and Jonathan Pidcock were chosen ruling elders. "On the fly-leaf of the session-book, in the handwriting of Dr. Studdiford, penned at the time of the first meeting of the session, is the motto: 'Who hath despised the day of small things?' How significant in view of subsequent changes and results since reached!" In June, 1825, he was formally installed pastor of the churches of Lambertville and Solebury, public services being held in the morning at Solebury, and in the afternoon at Lambertville. Some time in the course of this year he opened a classical school in his own house; and from that date to the commencement of his last sickness, for forty-one years, continued engaged in the instruction of youth; several of whom, including two of his own sons, have entered the Christian ministry, while others are occupying stations of usefulness and honor. As a testimonial of the estimate in which he was held as a scholar, in 1821 the trustees of the College of New Jersey conferred upon him the honorary degree of Master of Arts; and in 1844 that of Doctor in Divinity. "It is due to him and to this church (Lambertville, New Jersey) to state that on several occasions he had been called to the pastorate of other churches with promising expectations; in the year 1826 to the Reformed Protestant Dutch Church of Readington, as successor to his father, then recently deceased; in 1837 to the church of Scraalenburg, also to the church in Bedminster, where he had been engaged in teaching for a season, and to the church of Lodi in New York, besides having received flattering overtures from several other churches. But all these invitations he declined, because both his deliberate judgment and the feelings of his heart prompted him to abide with this people, and carry forward the work which he had commenced with such a small beginning. I need not say what this church owes to him, grown as it has from seven communicants to about three hundred, or how much this town (in whose prosperity he felt a lively interest) is indebted to him, having increased during his residence from a population of some one hundred and fifty persons, dwelling in scattered houses, to an incorporated borough of three thousand inhabitants. . . . . He was indeed the patriarch of this community, and one of the greatest blessings God could have bestowed upon it. For the first four years this was truly missionary ground, only twenty-five additions having been made to the church in that time, and fifteen of these by certificate; but he, without ambitious aspirations, humbly and patiently persevered through all the discouragements of his position, and has founded a church which will, we trust, by God's favor, live to be a lasting blessing."—"Funeral Sermon," of Rev. George Hale, D. D. During a ministry of great length and eminent usefulness he was an untiring worker, and zealous in good counselling and tender deeds; his labors were abundant in extra preaching services at home and abroad, in systematic pastoral visitations, in calls upon the sick, in ministering comfort to the afflicted, in advising the anxious inquirer, in rejoicing with his people in their joys, and sharing in their sorrows. He solemnized five hundred and ninety marriages, and officiated at more than twice that number of funerals. In the church at Solebury he baptized seventy-one adults and eighty-three infants; in the church at Lambertville two hundred and sixty adults, and two hundred and twenty-four infants, making, in both churches, a total of six hundred and thirty-eight baptisms. While in charge of the Solebury church—for twenty-six years, until 1848, when the pastoral relation was dissolved owing to the increased demand at Lambertville for all his services—one hundred and fifty-four persons were received into the communion of the church on profession of their faith, and fifteen by certificate. At Lambertville five hundred and seventy have been received on profession, and two hundred and ninety-two by certificate from other churches. As the result of his labors, nine hundred and thirty-one communicants have been taken under his pastoral care, of whom seven hundred and twenty-four were admitted on profession of their faith, making an average of a little more than sixteen persons each year received on confession. During his pastorate, also, "there were not less than eight precious seasons of the outpouring of the Holy Spirit,"—in 1833-34, 1837-38, 1841-42, 1845-46, 1854, 1856, and 1863. The largest ingatherings were probably in the winter of 1841-42, and 1845-46. "If to this part of his work were added his frequent services in other congregations and among the destitute, services always willingly rendered, and all the precious fruits brought together, it would be manifest that few ministers have wrought more earnestly, or have been more richly blessed." He was a diligent student through his life from childhood; his reading was varied and extensive, and few could "eviscerate" a book with equal rapidity and thoroughness. He was also a sound and able theologian; an independent thinker, investigating for himself the great questions that claimed his attention; and a judicious, discriminating and most instructive preacher. He seized with eagerness every book coming from the press which promised to throw light on the word of God—his constant study in the original Hebrew and Greek. "He was mighty in the Scriptures, and sought to make his people so; and the fruit of his efforts has been seen in the interesting and profitable Bible-classes which characterized his ministry." In his "Diary," at the date, February 11th, 1822, is found this record: "I must cultivate more intercourse with my people. Besides writing one sermon weekly, Theology, Church History, the German, French, Greek and Hebrew languages claim my attention." One of his last public exercises was the giving of the charge to his son, Rev. Samuel Studdiford, at his instalment as pastor of the Trenton Third Church; and his last sermon was preached at the funeral of his venerable and life-long friend, Rev. Jacob Kirkpatrick, D. D., of Ringoes. Urged by his people (who made liberal provision for his journey) to take some rest he repaired to Baltimore, and there gathered his family and kindred around him for the last time." His final exclamation was: "Into thy hands I commit my spirit." He then engaged in prayer, but his speech was too feeble and broken to be understood; and waving his hand, as if to request the family to leave his bedside—"evidently desiring to be alone with God"—he went to the eternal home. Thus closed a life of sixty-seven years, a ministry of forty-five years, a fruitful pastorate of forty-four and a half years, on Tuesday, June 5th, 1866.

———

YLE, JOHN, Silk Manufacturer, of Paterson, New Jersey, was born in Macclesfield, England, noted for its silk fabrics, in the manufacture of which his brothers, Reuben and William, have for many years borne a leading part, supplying the London and Manchester markets. He emigrated to this country in 1839, and being already an expert in his business, engaged the following year in the manufacture of silk at Paterson. His products at first were limited to the ordinary varieties of sewing and floss silks, but in 1843 he attempted weaving, succeeding perfectly in producing marketable articles, though not, unfortunately, at a profitable cost, for which reason he gave up the attempt. Among his products of that period was the beautiful flag, which waved over the Crystal Palace at the great exhibition in New York in 1852. In 1860 he renewed the attempt, but in consequence of the civil war and the lack of encouragement from the government, he was again constrained to abandon it. His ill fortune in weaving, however, was compensated by his success with his sewing silks, which during this period attained a high reputation, and have since been regarded everywhere as equal in quality to the standard. Some day, no doubt, when the conditions of the manufacture are improved, he will again renew the work of weaving, twice relinquished, and carry it through successfully, since he is a man of commercial nerve, and not likely in the line of his business to yield to any difficulty not absolutely insuperable. Meanwhile, the

department in which he first set out gives fair scope to his energies and skill. The business in his hands has grown to immense proportions, the mechanical provisions for it having of course kept pace with it. On May 10th, 1869, the Murray Mill, as the factory was then called, was destroyed by fire, entailing a loss of $550,000, against which there was no insurance. In order to more readily recover from the effects of this misfortune, Mr. Ryle caused to be chartered and organized the Ryle Silk Manufacturing Company, and the mill was rebuilt and fitted with the newest and best appliances. In this manufactory all the processes are performed, including dyeing and finishing, as to the former of which he has been particularly successful, as he has been particularly solicitous, the dyeing department being under the superintendence of a Macclesfield dyer of long experience. Macclesfield, indeed, as his native place, as still the home of his brothers, and as a great centre of the silk manufacture, in which his brothers are themselves leaders, is a storehouse to which he is probably indebted for much, besides skilled workmen, that has profited him in his bold venture here, serving as a rich subsoil of knowledge and methods, so to speak, into which his enterprise might strike its roots and draw up nourishment. However, the part of this subsoil that has chiefly nourished him is doubtless the part he brought over with him when he transplanted himself into this country, where his flourishing growth must be set down to the vigor and vitality of the plant as much as to all other things put together. Be this as it may, the fact of his distinguished success is patent. And richly does he deserve it, personally as well as commercially. After doing business in connection with the company organization for about three years, Mr. Ryle, who had in that time become the owner of nearly all its stock, retired from business in March, 1872. During the after part of that year, however, he sustained such serious losses that he was compelled to resume business. At the present time he has employed in the extensive works, which are built upon the site of the mill burned in 1869 and on a large tract of adjoining property, about four hundred operatives, whose average annual wages, even at the present low rate, is over $150,000. His efforts in the present manufacturing enterprise are aided and seconded by the well-known firm of Leister & Summerhoff, of New York city, who are the sole consignees of the silks produced at the establishment, and whose facilities for selling, combined with the facilities possessed by Mr. Ryle for producing every variety of goods in the silk market, constitute one of the ablest organizations in the country. Mr. Ryle has been a benefactor to Paterson, not only in establishing a new branch of manufactures of great importance, but in promoting civic improvements tending to increase the attractions of the city as a place of residence. The waterworks, which furnish the city with an abundant supply of pure water, were erected mainly through his exertions and means; and the grounds around the "cottage on the cliff" and the Falls, that afford a delightful breathing place to the citizens, especially the operatives in the factories, were adorned by him and thrown open freely to the public. He is not more shrewd and able than he is generous and public-spirited.

―――――◦◦◦――――

COTT, LIEUTENANT-GENERAL WIN-FIELD, United States Army, late of Elizabeth, New Jersey, was born in Petersburg, Virginia, June 13th, 1786, of parentage of Scotch descent. He was left an orphan in early boyhood; was educated at William and Mary College, whence he graduated in 1804; subsequently studied law, and in 1806 was admitted to the bar. After a few years' practice of his profession he was appointed, May 3d, 1808, a Captain of the Light Artillery, and was stationed at Baton Rouge, Louisiana, in the division commanded by General Wilkinson. At a later date certain remarks uttered by him, expressive of an opinion of General Wilkinson's complicity with Burr's conspiracy, were made the basis of a prosecution, and led to his suspension from the score of disrespect to his commanding officer. He then returned to Virginia, and turned to advantage his year's absence from his post by again devoting his time and attention to legal studies. In July, 1812, he was promoted to a Lieutenant-Colonelcy, and ordered to the Canada frontier. Upon arriving at Lewiston, while the affair of Queenstown Heights was in progress, he crossed the river, and entering instantly into action saw the field won under his direction; it was eventually lost, however, and, owing to the refusal of the troops at Lewiston to cross to his assistance, he and his command fell into the hands of the enemy. "The war of 1812 had arisen, in part out of the claim of the British government to the right of impressing seamen into her service, Great Britain acting on the maxim, 'Once a subject always a subject,' while the American government insisted upon the right of expatriation. The British officers attempted to enforce practically the doctrine of their government in the case of the prisoners taken at Queenstown, and were in the act of selecting the Irish and other foreign-born citizens out of Colonel Scott's command, to send them to England to be tried for treason, when he ordered the men not to answer any question or make known the place of their nativity. He threatened the retaliation of his government, and upon being exchanged procured the passage of a law to that effect; and he caused a number of British prisoners, equal to that of his own men who had been sent to Europe, to be set aside for the same fate that those should receive. The result was the safe return of his men to the United States after the close of the war." Shortly after the capture of York, Upper Canada, he joined the army under General Dearborn, as his Adjutant-General, with the rank of Colonel; and in the combined naval and land attack on Fort George, May 27th, 1813, was in command of the advance,

in surf-boats. Upon landing, under a severe fire of musketry, the line was formed on the beach, below an abrupt elevation of ten or twelve feet held by 1,500 of the enemy. He was repulsed at the first onslaught, but finally carried the position by a vigorous rally, and pushed on to Fort George, which was abandoned by the enemy after they had attached slow matches to the magazines. One of these exploding, he was thrown from his horse by a flying piece of timber, and severely injured. Two officers snatched away in time the matches from the other magazines, while he with his own hands tore the British flag from its staff. In the autumn of 1813 he commanded in the advance of Wilkinson's descent of the St. Lawrence, in the operations directed against Montreal, "but which was abandoned on wholly insufficient grounds, at a time when the place could have been easily captured and the campaign closed with honor." In the opening of 1814 he was made a Brigadier-General, and established a camp of instruction at Buffalo, New York, where he introduced the French system of tactics, and put them in practice from April to July, "with such success that the three brigades and the battalion of artillery under him were as thoroughly instructed as is requisite for all the purposes of war." On the following July 13th his and Ripley's brigades, with Hindman's artillery, crossed the Niagara river, captured Fort Erie and a part of its garrison, and the next day advanced upon Chippewa, skirmishing the entire distance to the point occupied by General Riall, and on the 5th succeeding in repulsing the enemy and driving them beyond the river. Twenty days later was fought the battle of Lundy's Lane, or Bridgewater, near Niagara Falls, in which he had two horses killed under him and was twice severely wounded; his wound of the left shoulder, especially, was critical, and his recovery painful and slow, and when completed his arm was left partially disabled. Before operations were resumed on the Canada frontier the treaty of peace was concluded, and he then was offered, and declined, a seat in the Cabinet as Secretary of War, and was promoted to the rank of Major-General. After assisting in the reduction of the army to a peace establishment, he visited Europe in a military and diplomatic capacity; and, arriving in France shortly after the battle of Waterloo, enjoyed the great advantage of consultation and intercourse with many of the leading captains who had fought under Napoleon. After the peace of 1815 he made several needed contributions to American military literature; and his "General Regulations for the Army" supplied at the time a great desideratum, and contains much useful information for the garrison and field. The "Infantry Tactics," from the French, and published under a resolution of Congress in 1835, "is the basis of that department of military knowledge in this country." He also aided materially in the preparation of other works of a similar kind, and wielded an able pen in various departments of literature. In the hostilities of 1832 against the Sacs and Foxes, which were terminated by the battle of Bad Axe, he

Winfield Scott

Winfield Scott

was an active and prominent participant. On the passage of his troops to Chicago the cholera attacked them with great severity, and for the time utterly prostrated the command; and again, on his arrival at the Mississippi, he encountered the same scourge in the army under General Atkinson. In the same year occurred the Nullification troubles in South Carolina, foreshadowing an unwelcome collision between the authorities of that State and of the United States. "Great prudence, tact, self-restraint and delicacy were called for on the part of the chief military man commanding at that crisis the forces of the general government in the harbor of Charleston. Boldness, decision, energy, so valuable in their effect at other times, might then have precipitated a result fatal to the peace of the country. The qualities actually required by the situation were conspicuously displayed by Winfield Scott." During the war with the Seminoles in Florida, which began in 1835, he was present for a short time at the scene of action in the Indian territory, was then called to the Creek country, and from there was ordered before a court of inquiry to answer for the failure of the campaigns in the Creek country and in Florida. The finding of the court was, without qualification, in his favor. During the time of the Cherokee troubles, in 1838—which arose from the policy adopted by the United States government, and the nature of the attitude necessarily assumed—his personal and official influence was ably and considerately exerted to induce the incensed Indians to submit to the dictates of their masters, abandon their grounds in Georgia and remove to the banks of the Arkansas. At the time of the Canadian rebellion, which developed into the "Patriot War of 1837," he was called upon to prevent the outbreak of a fresh conflict that would have been a violation of treaties, and in defiance of international law, between Great Britain and the United States; and eventually accomplished his difficult mission in a most efficient and honorable manner. In the spring of 1839, while actual hostilities were impending between the State of Maine and the Province of New Brunswick, owing to a bitter dispute about their respective bonndary lines, he arrived at Portland, Maine, in the character of a pacificator, and at once reopened communications with Major-General Sir John Harvey, the Lieutenant-Governor, who, through his earnest efforts, assisted him in smoothing the way to a reconciliation with Governor Fairfield, and in establishing a temporary convention between the State and the province. The whole question and matter of dispute were then referred to Washington, where the difficulty was finally settled by the treaty arranged in 1842 between Webster and Ashburton. He had in the meantime, by the death of General Macomb, become Commander-in-Chief of the Army of the United States. After the capture of Monterey, September, 1846, he was assigned to the chief command of the army in Mexico, and decided to direct an army upon the capital of the republic, with Vera Cruz as the base line. March 9th, 1847, his 12,000 men landed safely at their destination, and at once the city was invested from shore to shore. The mortar battery opened on the 22d, and the siege pieces on the 24th, and after receiving nearly 7,000 missiles, fired day and night, the city and the castle of San Juan d'Ulloa capitulated on the 26th, and on the 29th the garrison of 5,000 men marched out of the city and grounded their arms. April 8th the march toward Jalapa was begun, and on the 17th the army was in front and on the flank of the mountain position of Cerro Gordo, while Santa Anna, with an army of double the numerical strength of the Americans, occupied the fortifications. His order, on that occasion, begins: "The enemy's whole line of intrenchments and batteries will be attacked in front, and at the same time turned, early in the day, to-morrow, probably before ten o'clock A. M."; and "the order that directed what was to be done, became, after it was done, the narrative of the performance." The enemy was driven from every point of his line, and, following in pursuit, the American army captured Jalapa April 19th, Perote on the 22d, and Puebla May 15th, where it remained, drilling and awaiting reinforcements, till August 7th. He had always opposed the policy of occupying an armed frontier line, either the Rio Grande or the Sierra Madre, and had designated the base line of Vera Cruz, and the line of operations from that place to the city of Mexico. For the preparatory measure of the campaign, whatever its plan should be, he, as the commanding General of the army at Washington, had proposed to the administration that the new troops should be assembled at convenient and healthful points within the United States, there to be organized and disciplined, and suggested that the new line could not be placed upon the Rio Grande earlier than September. The proposal, however, met with ridicule and rejection, but time vindicated it with exactness, and brought its convincing testimony of bitter experience to honor his slighted wisdom. "The army was delayed at Puebla to do there what should have been done at home beforehand; the sickness and losses upon both Taylor's and Scott's lines were excessively increased by the unfitted state of the new troops for the field; and Santa Anna had time to create a new army, and to fortify the capital." Up to the time of his arrival in Mexico there was no law to punish offences committed by Americans upon Mexicans, and by Mexicans upon Americans. Congress had adjourned without providing for the difficulty, the most flagrant crimes passed by unpunished, and terrible barbarities were continually occurring. The discipline of the army also was in peril, and daily its morale was being undermined by the state of anarchy in which it existed. To meet and correct this state of affairs he issued, at Tampico, in February, his "General Order, No. 20," which specified the classes of crimes and offences hitherto unprovided for, deduced a code of laws from the articles of war and the general criminal jurisprudence of the United States, and established tribunals under the name of military commissions. August

7th–10th the divisions were set in motion from Puebla along the national road, the whole force numbering 10,740 men, the advance of the army coming in view of Mexico at the latter date. The road from Puebla was defended by the fortified mound El Peñon, which, it was decided, could not be attacked with any desirable degree of success; while for reasons deemed sufficient the route by Mexicalcingo also was declined. He then ordered an examination through General Worth, to ascertain whether a possibly practicable route could be found or made around lakes Chalso and Xachimilco. A way being found, a detour was made around the lakes to the southern avenue of the city, the Acapulco road; and the last division of the army withdrew from before El Peñon on the 16th, up to which time it was supposed that the initial action would take place at the mound. "The detour was a stroke of strategy which had long been premeditated as a likelihood by the general, and as such imparted to his staff." After the capture of Contreras and Cherubusco, August 20th, the capital lay at the mercy of the invaders, but it was deemed advisable to afford an opportunity for negotiations, through the peace commissioner, Mr. Trist, who was present for that purpose. On the 21st a truce was asked by Santa Anna, an armistice entered into, and negotiations carried on, which were continued until September 7th, when another series of operations was begun on the southwest avenue, the Toluca road. On the morning of September 14th, after the most gallant and heroic exertions on the part of the American officers and soldiers, and valiant and stubborn resistance in many cases on the part of the enemy, the army passed into the conquered city, Quitman's division leading into the Grand Plaza and running up the United States flag on the national palace. At nine A. M. he also rode into the square amid the wildest enthusiasm. "Mexico was humiliated and cast down. Her 32,000 soldiers had disappeared, and her lines of fortifications were silent and abandoned." There was afterward some street-fighting, and firing upon the troops from the buildings, on the part of disbanded soldiers, released criminals and the street beggars; but these futile reprisals were suppressed completely before nightfall. Order was then established, and a contribution levied on the city of $150,000 for the army, two-thirds of which sum he remitted to the United States as a fund for the creation and erection of military asylums. Taxes to raise revenue for the support of the troops were laid, the sphere of the military commission was extended and defined, and a civil organization created under the protection of the troops, who were spread over various parts of the country to give it an order and security which it had long ceased to enjoy; "all which made the presence of the American army in Mexico not the scourge that invading and victorious forces generally are, but acceptable and a blessing to the people of the country, whose best citizens saw its withdrawal approaching with regret." The treaty of Guadaloupe-Hidalgo, negotiated by Mr. Trist, was signed March 2d, 1848, and Mexico was soon after evacuated by the American armies. The general, in May of the same year, returned to Elizabethtown, New Jersey, which had been his home for some years. Subsequently a court of inquiry was called, "but the result only redounded to the fame of General Scott." In 1852 he was the unsuccessful nominee of the Whig party for the Presidency, receiving 1,386,580 votes, to 1,601,274 for the Democratic candidate, General Pierce. In 1855 the brevet rank of Lieutenant-General was revived, in order that it might be conferred upon him, and was expressly so framed that it should not survive him. In 1859, serious differences as to the boundary line of the United States and British America through the straits of Fuca having arisen, and a disputed military possession occurring, he was ordered to that locality, where he succeeded in establishing a satisfactory state of affairs, and settling the difficulty. During the war of the rebellion he was a staunch and zealous upholder of the Union, and during the latter portion of Buchanan's term "urged the wisest precautions to prevent the armed withdrawal of the eleven seceded States from the Union." He secured the safe inauguration of President Lincoln, the defence of the national capital, the organization of the Union army, and its establishment upon the strategic points of the country. "At his advanced age he has exerted an astonishing energy in the efforts to hold together the interests, the affections, and the doctrines of the republic." November 1st, 1861, he retired from active service, retaining, by a special provision in the act of Congress, passed at its extra session in the summer of 1861, his full pay and allowances, and, November 9th of the same year, sailed from New York for Europe, expecting to build up anew there his waning health. His later days he devoted to the preparation of his "Autobiography," two volumes, 8vo, published in 1864. He died at West Point, New York, May 29th, 1866.

OISNOT, JAMES M., M. D., was born, July 20th, 1836, in Somerset county, New Jersey. He was educated at Trenton, New Jersey, and at Carlisle Seminary, in Schoharie county, New York, and studied medicine at the University of Pennsylvania, from which he graduated in March, 1858. He settled in Philadelphia, where he became a lecturer on Anatomy and Operative Surgery. Among his notable cases is the successful reduction by manipulation of a double dislocation of the hip-joint, followed by a perfect recovery. This case he made the subject of a paper in the *American Journal of the Medical Sciences*. He is a member of the Northern Medical Society and of the Philadelphia County Medical Society. He has been a frequent and valued contributor to the medical journals of the day. In the civil war he was Surgeon of the 98th Pennsylvania Volunteers.

HARTON, CHARLES HENRY, D. D., Clergyman, Scholar, Poet, Author, etc., was born in St. Mary's county, in Maryland, on the 25th of May, O. S., 1748. His ancestors were Roman Catholics, and the family plantation, called Notley Hall, from a governor of that name, was presented to his grandfather by Lord Baltimore. From him it descended to the father, Jesse Wharton, and at his death in 1754 became the property of Charles Henry, his eldest son. When not quite seven years old he was attacked by a furious dog, which had already torn off part of his scalp, when his father, with signal presence of mind and promptitude of action, seizing a loaded gun from behind the door, shot the dog while the child's head was still in its jaws. In 1760 he was sent to the English Jesuits' College at St. Omer's. At the close of two years the college was broken up by the expulsion of the Jesuits from France. The teachers and scholars retired to Bruges, in Flanders. "Sequestered from all society," he writes, "beyond the walls of the college, and of course a total stranger to everything inconsistent with the strictest discipline, in acquiring classical attainments, and those habits of devotion which were deemed essential to a Roman Catholic youth, I applied myself very diligently to my studies, and became prominent among my associates, in a very accurate knowledge of the Latin language, which became nearly as familiar as English, as we were obliged to converse in it during our ordinary relaxations from our studies." His Letters of Orders bear date in 1772, having been admitted in June of that year to the Order of Deacons, and in September to that of Priests, in the Roman Catholic Church. At the end of the war of the American Revolution, he was residing in Worcester, England, as Chaplain to the Roman Catholics of that city, deeply interested on the side of his country, and anxious to return. He employed his pen at this time in a poetical epistle to General Washington, with a sketch of his life, which was published in England for the benefit of American prisoners there. His mind was at this period much agitated on the subject of his religious creed. He returned to this country in 1783, in the first vessel which sailed after the peace. In May, 1784, he visited Philadelphia for the purpose of publishing his celebrated Letter to the Roman Catholics of Worcester. "This production," says Bishop White, "was perused by me with great pleasure in manuscript. The result was my entire conviction that the soundness of his arguments for the change of his religious profession was fully equalled by the sincerity and disinterestedness which accompanied the transaction." On the death of his father he was the legitimate heir to the paternal estate. Upon taking orders he immediately conveyed it to his brother. After the controversy had taken place with Archbishop Carroll, occasioned by the Letter to the Roman Catholics of the city of Worcester, it appeared that the conveyance was not complete. A meeting took place in the most amicable manner, the paper was executed, and an es-

tate of great value—the whole patrimony of the conveyer—given the second time to a younger brother. For the first year after his return to America, Mr. Wharton resided at the paternal mansion, on leaving which, in July, 1784, the principal residents of the vicinage presented him, unasked and unsolicited, with a most honorable testimonial of his worth as a gentleman, a scholar, a Christian, and a Christian minister. It is a document of singular excellence in sentiment, spirit, and expression, and does high honor to them who freely gave as well as to him who worthily received it. While Rector of Immanuel Church, New Castle, Delaware, he was an influential member of the General Convention held in Philadelphia in 1785. On the 28th of September, in that year, he was on the committee "to prepare and report a draft of an Ecclesiastical Constitution for the Protestant Episcopal Church in the United States." On the 5th of October he was on the committee " to prepare a Form of Prayer and Thanksgiving for the Fourth of July," and also on a committee "to publish the Book of Common Prayer with the alterations, in order to render the Liturgy consistent with the American Revolution and the Constitutions of the respective States." On the 21st of July, 1786, he was elected a member of the American Philosophical Society. Between this date and 1792 he was connected with the Swedish Church at Wilmington, Delaware, from which time until 1798 he resided on his estate at Prospect Hill, in the neighborhood of that town, in feeble health. On the 20th of August, 1796, the vestry of St. Mary's Church, Burlington, New Jersey, made proposals to him with reference to the rectorship soon to be vacant, and on the 5th of September following unanimously elected him Rector. It was not, however, until March 15th, 1798, that he arrived at Burlington with his family. In less than three months his wife, who had been long an invalid, died at Philadelphia, and was buried in St. Peter's burial-ground. This was the occasion which evoked from his pen that most touching and melancholy production, evincing very high poetic talent, called "An Elegy to the Memory of Mrs. Mary Wharton, by her Husband." In October, 1801, he was unanimously elected President of Columbia College, New York, which he accepted so far as to preside at the commencement; but his vestry at Burlington consenting to his conditions of remaining with them, he declined the presidency of the college. In 1803 he was powerfully urged to become Principal of the College at Beaufort, South Carolina, and Rector of the parish there, but declined. He was at this time, and so continued to be until the day of his death, the most scholarly and influential clergyman in the Diocese of New Jersey. He was President of the Standing Committee, and Senior Deputy to the General Convention. Under his ministry in 1811, the church building at Burlington was rearranged internally, and a semi-circular chancel extension made on the east end. At the annual convention of the diocese, August 30th, 1815, he preached the opening sermon, and, by resolution, received the thanks of the convention for the same. It was at this convention, when the Rev. John Croes, D. D., was chosen Bishop of New Jersey, that the Rev. Dr. Wharton was the only other person who received any ballots for that office. Dr. Croes, only two months previous, had been elected to the Episcopate of Connecticut, and it was while the committee from that diocese was in correspondence with their bishop-elect in regard to his support, consecration and removal, that the convention of New Jersey met and elected him—an exhibition of human nature of which it is not the only instance in electoral bodies. At the convention held May 28th, 1828, Dr. Wharton offered two resolutions which showed him to be fully abreast, if not ahead of the times. The first was "recommending all congregations in the diocese to repeat distinctly all the responses and prayers as the rubric directs," and the second was "highly approving the objects and designs of the Domestic and Foreign Missionary Society," and "recommending it to the attention and patronage" of the diocese, both of which were unanimously adopted. "It was not my good fortune," writes Bishop George W. Doane, "to know Dr. Wharton until within a short time previous to his death. I had indeed known him by reputation as a pillar and ornament of the church, adorning with his life the doctrines which with his voice he proclaimed, and with his pen so ably advocated. I knew him as among the first in scholarship of the clergy of America, a sound and thoroughly accomplished divine, a practised and successful controversialist, a faithful parish priest, a patriarch of the diocese in which he lived." "He fell sweetly asleep, even as an infant sinks to rest upon its mother's bosom, on Tuesday morning, July 23d, 1833, having entered nearly two months upon his eighty-sixth year, and having been for more than sixty-one years a minister of Christ—the senior Presbyter, if I mistake not, of the American Protestant Episcopal Church." Dr. Wharton was twice married—the second time to Anne, daughter of Chief Justice Kinsey, who survived him. He had no children.

———◦✧◦———

IEGLER, GEORGE JACOB, M. D., was born, March 6th, 1821, at Long-a-coming (now Berlin), Gloucester county, New Jersey. He is the third child of George E. and Elizabeth Ziegler, who, when he was still a youth, removed to Philadelphia. He acquired his general education in the public schools of Philadelphia, supplemented by private tuition and self-culture. His medical studies were begun under Dr. George W. Patterson, and completed at the University of Pennsylvania, from which he graduated in 1850, his thesis on the occasion being recommended for publication. He settled in Philadelphia, where he has ever since resided. His specialty is nervous, pulmonary and chronic diseases, his

practice dealing more particularly with these diseases in women and children. He is a member of the Philadelphia County Medical Society; of the American Medical Association; of the Academy of the Natural Sciences of Philadelphia, etc., etc. The literary promise he gave in his graduating thesis has been fulfilled by the performances of his riper years, his medical writings being both numerous and valuable, and presenting the fruits of original investigation as well as the flowers of speech. They embrace publications on "Zooadynamia," "Researches on Nitrous Oxide," "Human Rights as Exemplified in the Natural Laws of Marriage," "Legitimacy," and "Life." He is also the author of papers on "Tubercolosis," "Reproduction," "Reparation of Bone," and many other subjects. He was for years an editor of the *Dental Cosmos*, and later editor and publisher of the *Medical Cosmos*. He was Accoucheur and subsequently Physician to the Philadelphia Hospital, but was obliged to resign on account of ill health, his delicate constitution having in fact greatly restricted his professioual activity in general. The wonder is that with his feeble health he has been able to achieve so much that is useful and excellent in the field of practice and of literature. His achievements under the circumstances do hardly less honor to his tenacity of purpose than to his vigor and fertility of intellect.

———◦✧◦———

XTELL, REV. HENRY, D. D., late of Geneva, New York, was born in Mendham, New Jersey, June 9th, 1773, and was a son of Henry Axtell, a farmer and a revolutionary officer. His studies were pursued at Princeton College, where he duly graduated. Subsequently he taught school for several years in Morristown and Mendham, and in 1804 removed to Geneva, New York, where he was also for several years at the head of a flourishing educational institute. On the 1st of November, 1810, he was licensed to preach by the Presbytery of Geneva, and, after laboring zealously and with eminent usefulness in various places, was, in 1812, installed as colleague pastor with Rev. Jedediah Chapman, at Geneva, where he spent the remainder of his life. The degree of Doctor of Divinity was conferred upon him by Middlebury College in 1823, as a mark of his scholarship in theology. He was a bold and faithful preacher, and when unusually warmed by favoring circumstances, or spurred on by exceptional difficulties, became very powerful and singularly endowed with the fire of grace. He was both practical and argumentative, and eminently Scriptural in his preaching. In stature, he was rather above the average, and was of a broad and athletic build. "He died in the utmost peace, February 11th, 1849." He published a "Sermon" preached at the ordination of Julius Steele, in 1816.

THOMPSON, HON. RICHARD P., Lawyer, Attorney-General of the State of New Jersey, late of Salem, New Jersey, was born in that town in 1805. He studied law with William N. Jeffers, and was licensed as an attorney in 1825, and as a counsellor in 1828. "He was, within the sphere of his knowledge, a very adroit and respectable advocate." His expertness in the trial of causes and in the transaction of business was very great, and for several years his practice was extensive and lucrative. For several years he prosecuted the pleas of New Jersey with noteworthy ability and success; and, while holding this office, was appointed, by Governor Haines, Attorney-General of the State, to fill the vacancy occasioned by the death of Attorney-General Molleson. At the expiration of the term of that temporary office, he resumed the duties of Prosecutor, and was met by a writ of *quo warranto* sued out by the late Judge Clawson. The Supreme Court decided that, by the acceptance of the office of attorney-general, that of prosecutor was vacated, the two offices being incompatible. Concerning that case the Hon. L. Q. C. Elmer writes: "Although as his counsel I was dissatisfied with this decision, on the ground. that, admitting the two offices to be incompatible, it was the office of attorney-general that could not be legally held, it was not thought advisable to carry the case into the Court of Errors, Mr. Clawson having relinquished all claim to the fees received as prosecutor." In 1852 he was appointed, by Governor Fort, Attorney-General; and, being confirmed by the Senate, held the office the full term. He succeeded also in inducing the Legislature, by the act passed in 1854, to place that office upon its present respectable footing, relieving the attorney-general from the necessity of taking upon himself the ordinary prosecution of criminals, giving him a respectable salary, and extra compensation for his aid in all extraordinary cases. On the last day of the year 1852 he carried through the prosecution of Treadway, for the murder of his wife, "in a manner that strikingly contrasts with many modern cases of this kind, and therefore deserves special mention." The case was well tried on both sides. The Court of Oyer and Terminer of the county of Salem, for this trial, was opened at 9 A. M.; thirty witnesses were examined; the case was ably summed up on both sides; Mr. MacCulloch being the counsel for the defendant; the jury retired at ten o'clock in the evening, and at eleven returned with a verdict of guilty of murder in the first degree. The criminal afterward confessed his guilt and was executed. "Although the evidence was circumstantial, it was entirely satisfactory. . . . . The defendant, several days before he had committed the crime, had been heard to threaten it; he was shown to have had a gun, and to have purchased powder and buckshot in the morning, and the shot precisely of the kind extracted from the body of his victim; he was shown to have been seen, late in the afternoon, with his gun, in the neighborhood of the house where his wife was.

She stood near a window in the evening, employed at a table on which there was a lamp, when she was shot through the window, several buckshot penetrating her body and heart, so that she ran into an adjoining room, fell down, and immediately died. The place where the person stood who shot her was easily determined, and upon being examined the next morning, a slight rain having fallen during the night, the paper wadding of the gun was found, discolored, but whole, and this, upon being pressed smooth, exactly fitted the torn part of a newspaper found in the criminal's pocket. The Attorney-General had made himself fully acquainted with all the circumstances of the case, and had arranged the evidence so that each witness testified to the material facts known to him, and nothing else. No case ever tried before me, during an experience on the bench of fifteen years, was better conducted, or more satisfactory in the result."—Hon. L. Q. C. Elmer. He died in Salem, New Jersey, in 1859.

KER, REV. NATHAN, Clergyman, and formerly Pastor of the Church of Springfield, was born at Basking Ridge, New Jersey, in 1735. He was the great-grandson of Walter Ker, who was banished from Scotland, September 3d, 1685, and came to America, settling at Freehold, New Jersey, where he was regarded as one of the principal founders of the town and the local church; his son, Samuel, had two sons, Samuel and Joseph; the grandson, Samuel, also had two sons, Jacob and Nathan. The last named graduated at the College of New Jersey in 1761, and with his brother, Jacob, was ordained by the Presbytery of New Brunswick, July 17th, 1763. Shortly after this he was transferred to the Presbytery of New York, and took charge of the church of Springfield, New Jersey. He continued here but two years, and at the expiration of that time removed to Long Island, and in 1766 to Goshen, New York, where he continued in the faithful discharge of his ministry until his decease, December 14th, 1804. His brother, Jacob Ker, graduated also at the College of New Jersey, in 1758, was a tutor in his *Alma Mater* from 1760 to 1762, and afterward became a highly respectable minister of the Presbyterian Church in Delaware.

BURNET, HON. WILLIAM, Judge, Physician, late of Elizabethtown, New Jersey, was born in that place about the middle of last century, and was the son of Ichabod Burnet, a distinguished physician of his native place. After graduating, he studied medicine with Dr. Staats, of New York, but the trouble with Great Britain dwarfing all other events, public and private, he relinquished a lucrative prac-

60

tice, and entered actively into the political and aggressive movements of the day and the patriot citizens. He presided as Chairman of the Committee of Public Safety, which met daily at Newark; in 1775 was Superintendent of a Military Hospital, established on his own responsibility in the same city; and in the winter of 1776 was elected a member of the Continental Congress. Early in the session, however, Congress divided the thirteen States into three military districts, and he was appointed Physician and Surgeon-General of the Eastern District. He accordingly resigned his seat in Congress, and entered at once upon his office, the arduous duties of which he continued to discharge with zealous ability until the close of the war in 1783. He was for a time stationed at West Point, and on a certain occasion was dining with a party of gentlemen at the house of General Arnold, when the officer of the day entered, and reported that a spy had been taken below who called himself John Anderson. It was remarked by the persons who were at the table that this intelligence, interesting to the general as it must have been, produced no visible change in his conduct or behavior; that he continued in his seat for some minutes, conversing as before; after which he rose, saying to his guests that business required him to be absent for a short time, and desiring them to remain and enjoy themselves till his return. The next intelligence they had of him was, that he was in his barge, moving rapidly to a British ship-of-war, the "Vulture," which was lying at anchor a short distance below the Point.—(On authority of his son, Hon. Judge Jacob Burnet, of Ohio.) At the termination of the contest he returned to his home and family, and devoted himself to agricultural pursuits. He was subsequently appointed Presiding Judge of the Court of Common Pleas by the Legislature of New Jersey, and was also elected President of the State Medical Society. Being a fine classical scholar, on taking the chair he read an elaborate essay in Latin, "On the Proper Use of the Lancet in Pleuritic Cases." He died October 7th, 1791.

OOLE, HENRY B., M. D., late of South River, Middlesex county, New Jersey, son of Cyrus Poole, was born in Enfield, England, April 24th, 1791. In 1801 his parents emigrated to America, settled at New Brunswick, and in that town his father was for a long time principal of a very well-conducted and popular school. Under his father's supervision he was prepared for college, entered Rutgers, and in 1809 graduated from that institution with first honors. He was subsequently engaged for several years as a teacher, being for a time Principal of a high school, and then private tutor to the children of the patroon of Albany, receiving, while occupying the latter position, the very high salary (for

the times) of a thousand dollars a year. In 1816 he married Olivia M., daughter of Samuel Jacques, of Middlesex, and in the same year entered the office of Dr. Augustus R. Taylor, and began the study of medicine. Applying for examination in 1818 to the Censors of the District Medical Society of Somerset county, his term of study was regarded as too brief, and he was subjected to an examination of altogether unusual severity. From this he came out with credit, was recommended for license, was licensed on the strength of the Censors' approval, and at once began the practice of his profession in Flemington. While resident at Flemington he was one of the founders of the Hunterdon County Medical Society (in 1821); was the first Secretary of that organization, serving until 1826; was in that year elected Vice-President, and repeatedly served on the Board of Censors. He was also a member of the New Jersey State Medical Society, serving as a Censor of that body and, in 1822, as Vice-President. In 1827-28 he practised in New York; returned to New Jersey in the latter year and established himself at South River, Middlesex county. Here he remained actively engaged until 1855, when he was disabled by a stroke of paralysis. He died six years later, December 2d, 1861.

AN SYCKEL, CHESTER, Lawyer, of Flemington, New Jersey, son of the late Aaron Van Syckel, Esq., was born in Union township, Hunterdon county, New Jersey, June 6th, 1838. Having received his preparatory education at the well-known school of the Rev. John Vanderveer, at Easton, he entered Lafayette College in 1859; was a student in that institution for two years; entered the junior class in the College of New Jersey, at Princeton, and was graduated thence in 1859. Immediately upon graduation he was entered at the New Jersey bar, began his legal studies in the office of his brother, Bennett Van Syckel, Esq.—now one of the judges of the New Jersey Supreme Court—and in 1862 was licensed as an attorney. For some two years he was associated with his brother; was licensed as a counsellor in 1865; shortly after became a member of the law firm of Bird, Vorhees & Van Syckel—subsequently Vorhees & Van Syckel—with which he continued until 1872. Since 1872 he has practised alone. For several years he has been a Special Master in Chancery, and also a Commissioner of the Supreme Court; is attorney for the Clinton National Bank, and independently of these sources commands an extensive practice. He is a member of the Democratic party, but is in no sense a politician; his professional duties amply engrossing his time and affording full scope for his exceptional ability. At the bar, as well as among his fellow-citizens, his standing is of the best.

OWNE, JOHN, M. D., late of Ringoes, New Jersey, was born in Monmouth county, New Jersey, September 2d, 1767. Graduating from the academy at Freehold, where he received an unusually thorough classical education, he began his professional studies in the office of Dr. Moses Scott, of New Brunswick, at that time president of the New Jersey Medical Society, and one of the most prominent medical men in the State. He subsequently attended lectures in the medical department of the University of Pennsylvania—at the same time studying under the supervision of Professor William Shipman, of Philadelphia—was graduated M. D. in the spring of 1791, and on the 3d of August in that year was licensed to practise as a physician in New Jersey. In the fall of 1791 he entered upon the duties of his profession at Prallsville, removing thence in 1796 to the farm near Ringoes, where he resided for more than sixty years. Of the New Jersey State Medical Society he was for a long period a very prominent member, being repeatedly elected to office, and receiving from it the honorary degree of M. D. In 1821 he was one of the founders of the Hunterdon County Medical Society; was the second President of that body (1822); was Vice-President in 1825; was again President in 1846, and was Chairman of the Board of Censors in 1821, 1824-25, 1827-28. He was also a member, elected in 1818, of the Cliosophic Society of Nassau Hall, Princeton, and for more than fifty years was a Ruling Elder in the Second Presbyterian Church of Amwell. His practice was very extensive, stretching over a tract of country some twenty miles long by six wide, and as the roads were few and bad his professioual rounds were uniformly made upon horseback. All told, something more than thirty years of his life was passed in the saddle. In temperament he was sanguine, in manner decided, and the confidence that he had in the remedies which he prescribed tended to produce the effect desired, tended largely to assure his patients, and materially helped him in his treatment of disease. His life was prolonged to the unusual length of ninety years, and up to a comparatively short time before his death he continued actively engaged. He died November 4th, 1857.

AYS, HON. JAMES L., of Newark, was born in Philadelphia' in 1833, and was educated in the public schools of that city. Being designed by his parents for a business career, he was early trained therefor, and in 1853, when only twenty years of age, engaged in mercantile pursuits in Rock Island, Illinois, whither he drifted in the tide of emigration which about that time swept westward. After three years of western experiences, he returned to the East, and in 1856 located in Newark, New Jersey, where he still resides. Here he in a few years built up a large and successful business, and by his activity and ability achieved a prominent position in the community. A man of ardent impulses and great natural enthusiasm of character, he was among the foremost, when rebellion assailed the national flag, to engage in patriotic labors and especially in the work of organizing the loyal sentiment of his adopted State. He was one of the founders of the Union League, an organization which at one time exercised a controlling influence upon the politics of New Jersey; and his influence and means were at all times freely given in aid of the cause of patriotism and national unity. A Republican by conviction, he was from the first an uncompromising supporter of the principles and policy of that party, and consequently the measures framed by the administration and Congress which were employed for the suppression of the rebellion. And no consideration of self-interest, or menace of a loss of patronage or social favor, ever swerved him a hair's breadth from his convictions of duty or his fidelity to principle. In 1863 Mr. Hays was elected a member of the Common Council, then embracing some of the best men of Newark; and, illustrating in this position his high capacity, he was, in 1865, chosen to the lower branch of the Legislature, where he at once took a leading place. The following year, the people of the county having discovered in him precisely the qualities needed in a representative, he was elected to the State Senate. His term of service in that body, three years, covered a most important period in the history of the State. The questions growing out of the war and the abolition of slavery were all, so far as New Jersey was concerned, settled within that period, and as to them all Mr. Hays sustained an honorable and influential relation. The Legislature of 1866 proposing to withdraw the assent of the State, previously given, to the adoption of the Fourteenth Amendment to the Constitution, he presented an eloquent and able protest, which attracted wide attention from its comprehensive statement of the legal objections to such a course. As to matters of purely State concern, Mr. Hays occupied an equally prominent position, some of the most important acts of legislation having been consummated through his influence. He was always on the side of economy in expenditure and the largest possible development, consistently with the public demands, of the resources of the State. The educationalist interest had in him an earnest supporter, and all measures looking to the purification of the public morals uniformly commanded his active sympathy. In the care and protection of the interests of his own constituents he was at once vigilant and conscientious. He thrice defeated a stupendous "job," known as the Newark Park bill, thereby saving millions of dollars to the tax-payers of the city. He was chiefly instrumental in securing for his city, against a powerful opposition, a new line of railroad communication with New York, and also in defeating a project for the division of the county which was strongly urged by an influential and discontented element of its population. Since his retirement from the Senate

Mr. Hays has held no public position, except that of a member of the Board of Education, being absorbed in the management of his personal interests and in the performance of less ostentatious but equally important duties in connection with some of the leading charitable and religious organizations of the city. Mr. Hays is a forcible writer and an able speaker, and both pen and voice have been liberally used in furtherance of Christian and patriotic enterprises. He possesses great firmness and decision of character, is tenacious in his friendships, and generous to a fault. What he does he does effectually; what he believes he believes absolutely and unchangeably. In his personal manners he is suave, genial, frank, but he is never undignified where dignity best befits the man. He is and has been for many years a member of the Methodist Episcopal Church, and that large and prosperous denomination has no man in its ranks who is prouder of its traditions and history, or more faithful, in his daily life, to the principles or standard of duty which it maintains.

————◆————

ALENTINE, MULFORD D., Manufacturer, of Woodbridge, was born in that town, October 26th, 1843. His father, James Valentine, a brick manufacturer, was born in New York, and his mother, Catherine (Ackerman) Valentine, daughter of James Ackerman, Esq., was also a native of New York. Mulford Valentine received his education at the district schools of the vicinity in which he lived. His attendance at school continued, with some interruption, until he had reached the age of eighteen. By that time the war of the rebellion had broken out, and he, like multitudes of the young men of those days, felt that he had a part to play in the great drama of the time. So he entered the army of the Union as a private in the 28th New Jersey Infantry. His term of enlistment was for nine months, and at the expiration of that time he returned with his regiment to the Army of the Potomac, and participated in a number of engagements. He was finally mustered out of service, July 1st, 1863, and on leaving military life he entered Eastman's Business College, at Poughkeepsie, New York, where he remained for about six months. Leaving there, he went to New York city, and took a position as bookkeeper for the firm of L. T. Valentine & Co., proprietors of a large paper warehouse. He remained in this situation from 1864 to 1866, when, having determined to enter business on his own account, he returned to his home at Woodbridge, New Jersey, and associated himself with his brother, J. R. Valentine, under the firm-name of M. D. Valentine & Co., for the manufacture of fire-brick and drain tile. Their commencement in business was on a small scale, and for the first year they only undertook the manufacture of Bath brick, sometimes known as Bristol brick, for the cleaning of cutlery. Their success in this branch

was not encouraging, and at the end of a year they commenced the manufacture of drain-pipe in addition to their former specialty. A year later, in 1868, the enterprising young firm added to their rapidly growing business the manufacture of fire-brick. They have occupied from the first the present site of their manufactory, and their beginnings in all their several departments were small. Year by year they have added to their business and to their establishment, until to-day the firm ranks among the foremost fire-brick manufacturers in the country. Indomitable energy, strict devotion to business, and an integrity and uprightness that none could question have accomplished the result. Their manufacturing establishment consists of half a dozen large two-story brick buildings. The largest is 80 by 125 feet in extent, and the others range from eighty feet square to forty by fifty feet. There are four kilns, the capacity of all being very great, baking from 22,000 to 52,000 bricks at one time. They are of the old English, round style, and are known as the " up-draught." The capacity of the works is upwards of 4,000,000 bricks per annum, and besides the various kinds of brick turned out, they produce very heavily of drain tile, stove linings, etc. When working to their full capacity, the works employ about one hundred hands. The products of the establishment are noted everywhere, and the market for them is national, orders being received from North, South, East, and West. Fortunately, the facilities for shipment are very great, and goods can be loaded on boats or cars. The premises have a frontage of three hundred feet on the creek, and a siding of the Pennsylvania Railroad has been laid beside the factory. Mulford Valentine, the head of the firm, was married, September 10th, 1868, to Rachel V. Camp, of Ocean county, New Jersey.

————◆————

AYLOR, JOHN, Packer, etc., of Trenton, was born in Hamilton Square, Mercer county, New Jersey, October 6th, 1836. When he arrived at the age of ten years his father died, leaving the family without any means of support. John sought and obtained work in a brickyard, and from that time assumed the care of his mother and three younger brothers and sisters, and was their chief dependence. At the age of fifteen he entered as clerk a retail grocery store in the city of Trenton, and remained in that capacity for five years. During the last year of his service he was intrusted with the purchase of stock in Philadelphia and New York, and thus acquired a knowledge of business and formed an acquaintance with business men which largely aided him in his subsequent operations. At the age of twenty years he started a retail grocery store under his own name, with a cash capital of fifteen dollars. In this he continued for three years, and then tore out counters and shelves and boldly launched out into the wholesale trade. It was the first venture ever made in the city of Trenton of a distinctively wholesale business of any kind. Many careful and sagacious business men doubted the expediency of the undertaking and predicted its failure. The first year he sold $250,000 worth of goods, and the annual sales thenceforward steadily increased until 1870, when they reached over a million of dollars. The wholesale trade which grew out of this successful pioneer experiment has now become the most important element of mercantile life in the city. During the year 1870 he sold his interest in the grocery business, and built a packing-house and slaughtering establishment, which he is now successfully operating. He has served two terms in the Trenton Common Council, and in that capacity secured the passage of an ordinance submitting to a vote of the people the question of removing the public markets from Greene street, and the abandonment by the city of the market business. By his zealous labors for two years he procured the success of these projects. This question was one of the most interesting and exciting local contests that had agitated the community for several years. He contributed liberally to the stock in private market associations, and several new and handsome markets have been erected, one of which, in honor to him, bears the name of Taylor. In 1866 he conceived the project of erecting an opera house, and by taking half the stock himself and energetically canvassing for the remainder he secured the success of the enterprise. The building was begun the same year and opened to the public in 1867. It cost $125,000, and is the finest structure of the kind in New Jersey. Many sagacious people also predicted that this enterprise would be a disastrous failure, but there is now nothing in the city in which the citizens take a greater pride than in the Taylor Opera House. He was also chiefly instrumental in organizing Company "A," of the National Guard, one of the finest military organizations in the State. In the directions indicated and in various other ways he has successfully labored to foster a spirit of public improvement in Trenton.

RUNYON, HON. ENOS W., Lawyer and Judge, was born, February 24th, 1825, in Somerset county, New Jersey. He is the son of Squire Runyon. His family is of Huguenot descent, his ancestors having left France on the Revocation of the Edict of Nantes, settling first in England, from which one branch emigrated to this country, taking up their residence in the Carolinas, whence some of their descendants removed to New Jersey. He was educated at the Plainfield Academy, and afterwards taught school until his 25th year, at the same time preparing himself for the bar. He began the study of law with Cornelius Boice, and finished his preparatory course with Joseph Annin, a relative of President Edwards. He was admitted to the bar, June 8th, 1854, and at once entered upon the practice in Plainfield. At that time he and Mr. Boice, his late preceptor, were the only lawyers in Plainfield; but, though the laborers were few, the harvest was not plenteous, and he had to depend on the growth of the town for the growth of his practice. This dependence, however, did not fail him in the end; Plainfield has grown, and his practice with it, until both are large and flourishing, his practice having become lucrative in all branches of the profession. Meanwhile, in 1856, when his practice was not yet absorbing, he founded the *Plainfield Gazette*, and conducted it for about three years, placing it on a sound footing, financially and journalistically. In 1862 his brother, Nelson Runyon, became his law-partner, the name of the firm being E. W. & N. Runyon. Most successful lawyers, in the smaller cities at least, are drawn, soon or late, into politics, and he has not proved an exception, owing in some measure, possibly, to his former connection with the press. In 1867 he was elected to the New Jersey Legislature, in which he took a leading part in favor of conferring the right of suffrage on the colored people of the State, being the most outspoken and fearless of all the advocates of the measure, and doing more, perhaps, than any other member to secure its passage. It was not a popular measure at the time, and his prominent connection with it no doubt contributed to prevent his return to the next Legislature, but he had the consolation of success in the line of duty, to which has since been added the general admission that he was right, the bitterest opponents of the measure then conceding now its justice and wisdom. In April, 1873, he was appointed Law Judge of Union county, a position which he still holds, and the duties of which he has discharged to the satisfaction of the bar and the public. He was married, February 20th, 1850, to Miss Vail, daughter of Stephen Vail, of Plainfield.

MAXON, WILLIAM B., Lawyer, of Plainfield, was born in May, 1829, at Unadilla Forks, Otsego county, New York. He is a son of the Rev. Wm. B. Maxon, of the Seventh-day Baptist Church. The Maxon family came to this country from England in the seventeenth century, and settled in Rhode Island, where the whole family was murdered by the Indians, except one boy, the great-grandfather of the subject of this sketch, who was also a minister of the Seventh-day Baptist Church. The mother of the present subject was Lucinda Le Roy, whose mother was a native of Stonington, Connecticut, and, when a young girl, signalized her revolutionary spirit by secretly entering the British lines, in company with another girl, and bringing off the British flag in triumph. The descendant of this spirited maiden, whose life is now to be sketched, received a classical education at the Du Ruyter Institute, and at the age of eighteen went to New York city, where he was employed in the Novelty Iron Works, then operated and partly owned by Mr. Thomas Stillman. Six months in this establishment convinced him that he had no aptitude for the mechanical arts and he accordingly relinquished the study of them. In 1849 he went to California, in which he cast his first vote for President, voting for General Scott in 1852. Finally discovering what he believed to be his true bent, he began the study of law, reading with Mr. Wheelan, formerly law-partner of Ex-Governor Smith, and in 1854 was admitted to the California bar. He practised in San Francisco until 1859, when he was elected to the California Legislature, wherein he served with credit for one term, declining a re-nomination. Previously, however, he had held the office of Judge of the Court of General Sessions of San Mateo county, during his incumbency of which the Terry-Broderick duel took place, the first hostile meeting of the parties being frustrated by their arrest under a warrant issuing from him. Their second meeting, as is well known, eluded the officers of the law, with a result fatal to Senator Broderick. To return, while in the Legislature he was a member of the committee to investigate the necessity of an expedition against the Indians, making a minority report in opposition to the measure, and in favor of protecting the Indians rather than fighting them. This report, especially notable as coming from one who tracks his lineage through pools of innocent blood shed by Indians, was ultimately adopted, whereby the State was saved certainly a great expense and probably a great shame. After spending sixteen years in California, including the turbulent times in which the Vigilance Committee bore sway, a stern but necessary rule as he believes, he returned, in 1867, to the East, settling at Plainfield, New Jersey, though entering into a legal partnership with Judge Titsworth, of Newark. He continued this partnership for two years, when he was elected Superintendent and Agent of the American and Mexican Railroad and Telegraph Company, organized to construct a railroad and telegraph line from Guaymas, in Sonora, to El Paso, in Texas. He spent two years in the service of this company, whose enterprise, owing to the unsettled state of the country and the death of Judge Whiting, one of the principal projectors, was eventually abandoned. In 1873 he resumed his practice and his residence in the city of Plainfield, where he has since attained great distinction in his profession, particularly as a jury lawyer, in which respect his reputation may fairly be said to have become national. His recent defence of a young girl accused of larceny was remarked upon at the time by the press of the metropolis, and of the country at large, as an effort of surpassing ability and eloquence. In politics he was a Whig so long as the Whig party existed, after which he adhered to the Republican party until the nomination of Mr. Greeley, in 1872, when he took his place among the Liberal Republicans. Since 1874 he has been Corporation Counsel for the city of Plainfield. He was married, in 1867, to Miss Titsworth, daughter of the late Judge Titsworth, of Plainfield.

OOK, LEWIS C., M. D., was born in December, 1818, at Stewartsville, Warren county, New Jersey. He was a son of Dr. Silas C. Cook, of that county. He graduated at Princeton College in 1838, and studied medicine in the medical department of the University of Pennsylvania, from which he graduated in 1842. He succeeded his father in the practice of medicine at Stewartsville, and subsequently formed a partnership with Dr. Rea, which lasted until the latter retired from practice, when he formed a new partnership with his younger brother, Dr. John S. Cook. The latter partnership continued until he removed to Chicago, Illinois. After four years of successful practice in that city his declining health induced him to return to the East, upon which he renewed his partnership with his brother at Hackettstown, in his native county, where he resided for the remainder of his life. He was an active and leading member of the Warren County Medical Society, which he frequently represented in the State Medical Society. His profession in all its relations was the object of his ardent devotion, a devotion which never flagged while his life endured, and which was reflected back in the esteem and admiration accorded to him by his fellow-practitioners throughout the wide circle of his acquaintance and the still wider circle of his reputation. Personally he was a man of fine appearance, graceful address, refined and genial manners, and warm social feelings, unstinted in his charities, tenacious in his friendships, steadfast in his convictions, and above all, unfaltering in his faith, the type, in short, of a Christian gentleman. He died on the 11th of January, 1874, of typhus fever, after an illness of sixteen days, dying as he had lived, in the full possession of the Christian faith as taught by the Presbyterian Church, of which he had long been an exemplary member. He was married, in March, 1852, to Miss Janet Eaton, whom he survived, though but for a few years.

OOK, JOHN S., M. D., was born, June 19th, 1827, near Stewartsville, Warren county, New Jersey. He is a son of Dr. Silas C. Cook, a prominent physician of that county. Having prepared for college at Easton, Pennsylvania, he entered Lafayette College in 1844, remaining at that institution until 1846, when he left it to enter Union College, from which he graduated in 1847, completing the curriculum in three years, which would seem to imply an unusually thorough preparation at the outset, or unusual proficiency in the course, if not both. He began the study of medicine with his father, and finished it in the medical department of the University of Pennsylvania, at which he graduated in 1850. Soon after his graduation he entered upon the practice of his profession at Hackettstown, New Jersey, where he has since pursued it, acquiring an extensive practice, and establishing an enviable reputation both as a physician and a man. For a number of years he was associated in the practice with his elder brother, the late Dr. Lewis C. Cook, a physician of distinction, and in all respects an ornament to the profession, as indeed may be as truthfully said of the younger brother, whose professional abilities and personal character are held in the highest regard by the community which they serve and adorn. He is a member of the Warren County Medical Society; of the New Jersey Academy of Medicine; and of the State Medical Society, of which he is Vice-President. He was married, in 1855, to Georgia Lewis, of Columbus, Ohio.

—◦—

ATEMAN, ROBERT MORRISON, M. D., of Red Bank, New Jersey, son of Dr. B. Rush Bateman, and a grandson of the Hon. Ephraim Bateman, United States Senator from New Jersey, 1826–28, was born at Cedarville, Cumberland county, New Jersey, September 14th, 1836. Having received his preparatory education at Harmony Academy, Cedarville, and at Edgehill Grammar School, he entered the College of New Jersey, and was graduated thence B. A. His professional education was received in the medical department of the University of Pennsylvania, and by that institution, in March, 1859, he was granted his degree of M. D. In the same year he established himself as a general practitioner in his native town, and in a short time acquired a very satisfactory practice. This was interrupted for a time by the war. In 1862 he was appointed Acting Assistant-Surgeon to the 25th New Jersey Regiment; was subsequently promoted to be Surgeon, and rendered efficient service in these capacities until the latter part of 1863. He then resumed practice at Cedarville, where he remained actively engaged until May, 1877, when he removed to Red Bank. He is a member of the American Medical Association; a member of the New Jersey State Medical Society, essayist in 1874 and in 1875, and while resident at Cedarville was one of the most prominent members of the Cumberland County Medical Society, being reporter in 1865, president in 1866, and historian in 1867. In the latter capacity he prepared his valuable "History of the Medical Men, and of the District Medical Society of the County of Cumberland, New Jersey," a work of present interest and of permanent value. His literary productions, professional and non-professional, have been quite extensive, including contributions to the leading medical periodicals and to the literary magazines of the day. He is also well and favorably known in the rostrum, being an exceedingly popular lecturer before the religious and literary societies of Cumberland and the adjacent counties. His high professional and social standing has led to his appointment to numerous positions of local importance: he has

been County Examiner of Public Schools; President of the Cumberland County Sunday-School Association; member of the Board of Trustees of the West Jersey Academy; member of the Board of Directors of the Cumberland County Bible Society, etc. He has also for a number of years been Medical Examiner to the American, of Philadelphia, and the Mutual and Ætna, of New York, Life Insurance Companies. He has married twice: first, April 7th, 1859, to Caroline H. Bateman, who died August 23d, 1874; and, second, June 14th, 1876, to Louise L. Goff.

—◦—

ARRISON, CHARLES, M. D., late of Swedesborough, Gloucester county, New Jersey, was born about 1800. His professional education was received in the medical department of the University of Pennsylvania, whence he graduated, M. D., in 1821. In the same year, having been examined, passed and licensed by the District Board of Censors, he settled at Deerfield, Cumberland county, New Jersey; removed in less than a year to Clarksborough, Gloucester county, and thence in a few months to Swedesborough. Here for half a century he was engaged in active practice, being during the greater portion of this period the leading physician of southwest New Jersey. In obstetrics alone he attended 9,000 cases. He was a prominent member of the Gloucester County Medical Society, and also of the New Jersey State Medical Society, and for many years contributed largely to current medical literature. He married a sister of Dr. Joseph Fithian, of Woodbury, New Jersey. He died April 12th, 1875.

GARRISON, REV JOSEPH FITHIAN M D., of Camden, New Jersey, son of the preceding, was born at Deerfield, Cumberland county, January 25th, 1822. Having received his preparatory education at the Bridgeton Boarding School, he entered the College of New Jersey, Princeton, whence he was graduated with the second honor. He subsequently attended medical lectures at the University of Pennsylvania, receiving from that institution, in the spring of 1845, his degree of M. D. During the ensuing nine years, in partnership with his father, he was actively engaged in the practice of his profession at Swedesborough; being a member of the State and county medical societies, and contributing occasional papers to the leading medical periodicals. In 1855 he entered holy orders, and for the past twenty-two years has been Rector of St. Paul's Protestant Episcopal Church at Camden.

GARRISON, CHARLES GRANT, M. D., of Swedesborough, New Jersey, son of the preceding, was born in Swedesborough, August 3d, 1849. Having received his preparatory education at Edgehill School, Princeton, he entered the classical department of the University of Pennsylvania; was graduated thence B. A.; entered the medical department, and was graduated thence, M. D., in 1872. In the same year he established himself at Swedesborough, where his own ability and the prestige of his name led to his rapid acquisition of an extensive practice. He is a member of the New Jersey State Medical Society, of which he has been Reporter since 1872, and of the Gloucester County Medical Society, of which he has for the past two years been Secretary. He has contributed a number of valuable reports of cases and monographs to the leading medical periodicals of the day.

ICKES, STEPHEN, M. D., of Orange, New Jersey, son of Van Wyck and Eliza (Herriman) Wickes, and a descendant of Thomas Wickes, grantee in 1666 of the site of the present town of Huntington, Long Island, was born at Jamaica, Long Island, March 17th, 1813. His preparatory education was received at Union Hall Academy, in his native town, whence he passed to Union College, Schenectady. From this institution he graduated, B. A., in 1831 (receiving three years later the degree of M. A.), and with a view to fitting himself for the profession of medicine was, during the ensuing year, a student of the natural sciences at the Rensselaer Polytechnic Institute. In the fall of 1832 he entered the medical department of the University of Pennsylvania; graduated thence, M. D., in the spring of 1834, and shortly thereafter began practice in the city of New York. In 1835 he removed to Troy, New York, where he remained for something over fifteen years, being for a considerable portion of this time in partnership with Dr. Thomas W. Blotchford, under whom he had read medicine previously to entering the University of Pennsylvania. In April, 1852, he finally established himself in Orange, where for a number of years he has been one of the leading physicians. During his residence in Troy he was a Trustee of the Rensselaer Polytechnic Institute; was President of the Rensselaer Tract Society, and was a Ruling Elder in the First Presbyterian Church. In 1856 he was made a Ruling Elder of the First Presbyterian Church of Orange; has for a number of years been a member of the Essex County Bible Society, and in 1872 was President of that organization. He is a member of the American Medical Association; a member of the New Jersey State Medical Society, Chairman since 1861 of the Standing Committee; an honorary member of the New York State Medical Society; a member of the National Sanitary Association; a member of the New Jersey Sanitary Association; a member of the New Jersey Historical Society, etc. His most important literary work is a volume entitled "Annals of New Jersey Medicine Prior to 1800"—at present (1877) in manuscript and scarcely completed—a compilation necessitating most careful research, and destined to be of permanent value and interest. In a measure supplementing this are the annual reports which he has furnished since 1861 to the New Jersey State Medical Society upon the current medical history of the State; and during the same period he has edited the society's *Transactions.* The industry required to produce so much literary matter, while attending to the duties of a large practice, may be readily estimated, especially when it is added that, beside his private professional employment, he is Physician to Memorial Hospital, at Orange. He has twice married: first, in 1835, to Mary Whitney, daughter of Isaac Heyer, Esq., of New York; and, second, in 1841, to Lydia Matilda, widow of Dr. William Vandinderer, and daughter of Joseph Howard, Esq., of Brooklyn.

OHNSON, WILLIAM, M. D., late of Whitehouse, Hunterdon county, son of Thomas P. and Mary (Stockton) Johnson, was born at Princeton, New Jersey, February 18th, 1789. Having read medicine under Dr. John Van Cleve, of Princeton, he entered the medical department of the University of Pennsylvania, and from that institution received, in the spring of 1811, his degree of M. D. In April of the same year he was examined by the State Board of Censors, and was licensed to practise as a physician in New Jersey, and in the ensuing July he established himself at Whitehouse. In 1821 he was one of the founders of the Hunterdon County Medical Society; was first Vice-President on the foundation, and held the same office in 1848 and in 1856; was President in 1824, 1836, 1849 and 1857, and was for many years a member of the Board of Censors. He was also a member of the New Jersey State Medical Society, serving as Vice-President in 1823. For more than fifty years he was one of the leading practitioners of Hunterdon, being highly successful in his treatment of disease, and attaining to high professional standing as well as to far-reaching personal popularity. Among his office-students were a number of subsequently eminent physicians. He died January 13th, 1867.

EN EYCK, HON. JOHN CONOVER, of Mount Holly, Lawyer, and United States Senator from 1859 to 1865, was born in Freehold, Monmouth county, New Jersey, on March 12th, 1814. His classical education was very carefully conducted by private tutors, and was of a thorough character. Inclining to the legal profession, he in due time began the study of law in the office of Hon. Joseph F. Randolph, late a Justice of the Supreme Court of New Jersey, and having followed the prescribed course was admitted to the bar as an attorney in 1835, and as counsellor in 1838. He settled for practice in Burlington, going into partnership with Hon. Garret D. Wall, then United States Senator from New Jersey. In the year 1839 he was appointed Prosecutor of the Pleas for Burlington county, and held the appointment for ten years, performing all the duties of the office with ability and conscientious regard to the public interests. He has always manifested an active interest in public affairs, his opinions leading him into affiliation with the Whig and Republican parties. When the convention called to revise the constitution of the State met, in 1844, he took his seat as a delegate, and, although next to the youngest member, made his influence felt in the deliberations of that body. He was elected to the United States Senate for the term commencing in 1859 and terminating in 1865. While a member of the Senate he served, among other committees, upon those on Commerce, Patents and the Judiciary. Recently he was again called upon to assist in the revision of the constitution of the State of New Jersey, being appointed a member of the commission formed in 1873 to prepare a comprehensive series of amendments. Of this commission he was chairman. The commission was a distinguished body, and the labor cast upon it was most worthily performed, the results meeting with the emphatic approbation of the community.

RANDIN, JOHN F., late of Hampden, son of Philip and Eleanor (Forman) Grandin, was born in Hunterdon county, New Jersey, in 1760. He read medicine under Dr. James Newell, of Allentown, New Jersey, and upon being admitted to practise as a physician was appointed a Surgeon in the United States navy. In this capacity he served during the latter part of the revolutionary war; subsequently visited Holland, and upon returning to America established himself in practice at Hampden. He married Mary, daughter of Dr. James Newell. For upwards of twenty years he was a prominent physician in Hunterdon, practising with fair success, and being generally esteemed both in and out of his profession. He died July 21st, 1811.

ERLIN, ISAAC NEWTON, M. D., was born at Burlington, New Jersey, May 27th, 1834. He is a son of Joseph Kerlin, of Burlington county, New Jersey, and Sarah A. Ware, of Philadelphia. After receiving a common school and academical education he entered the medical department of the University of Pennsylvania, from which he graduated in 1856. He settled in Philadelphia, where he was Resident Physician of Wills Hospital for one year. From 1857 to 1862 he was Assistant Superintendent of the Institution

for the Feeble-Minded, at Media, Pennsylvania, of which he has been Superintendent-in-Chief since 1864. His professional life has been chiefly occupied with the delicate and responsible duties of this office. He is a member of the Delaware County Medical Society, of which he was Secretary for many years; of the State Medical Society of Pennsylvania; of the American Medical Association, his membership of which is permanent; of the American Public Health Association; and of the Association of Superintendents of Institutions for the Feeble-Minded, of which he is Secretary. In 1858 he published a small volume entitled "Mind Unveiled," giving his experiences in the early days of his work in the care and treatment of idiots and imbeciles. In 1862 and 1863 he was connected for ten months with the Sanitary Commission, having charge of the field-work of the Army of the Potomac. He was married, September 7th, 1865, to Harriet C. Dix, of Groton, Massachusetts.

UTPHEN, HON. JOHN C., M. D., of Plainfield, was born at the old Sutphen homestead, in Somerset county, New Jersey, in 1836. His ancestors on his father's side emigrated from Sutphen, Holland; and from this ancient city the family name is derived. Both of his grandmothers were of English (Puritan) descent. His preparatory education was received at his home, and in 1852 he entered the College of New Jersey, at Princeton, whence he was graduated, B. A., in 1856; his brother, the Rev. Morris C. Sutphen, D. D., being his classmate and fellow-graduate. In the ensuing year he entered the medical department of the University of Pennsylvania, and from that institution received, in 1859, his degree of M. D. During the ensuing eight years he was actively engaged in the practice of his profession at Liberty Corner, Somerset county, and in 1867 removed to Plainfield, where he has since resided. Immediately upon his arrival at Plainfield he was chosen City Physician, under the new city charter then just adopted, and in the year following was elected a member of the Common Council, and was appointed chairman of several of the leading committees. During this time his practice s eadily increased; reliance in his professional skill and regard for his sterling qualities as a public-spirited citizen being greatly augmented by his fearless and largely successful labors during the memorable small-pox pestilence. His heroic exertions on this occasion were in a measure recognized by his nomination and election, in 1874, and re-election in 1875, to the position of Mayor of Plainfield, an office that he filled to the entire satisfaction of his fellow-citizens and to the permanent benefit of the city. Since the nomination of Mr. Greeley for the Presidency he has been a member of the Liberal wing of the Republican

party—as he was previously of the Republican party proper —and is in entire sympathy with the policy adopted by President Hayes.

——— ◆◆◆ ———

WINDS, GENERAL WILLIAM, Revolutionary Hero, late of Rockaway, Morris county, New Jersey, was born in Southhold, Long Island, in 1727 or 1728. From "a list of the names of Old and Young, Christians and Heathens, Freemen and Servants, white and black, etc., inhabittinge within the Townshipp of Southhold," it would appear that the Winds family, early in the last century, was quite numerous. William removed to New Jersey when a young man, and purchased a part of the Burroughs tract of land on "Pigeon Hill." After improving several acres of that estate he ascertained that the title under which he held it was not reliable, and with a frank statement of the fact, sold his right, giving a quit-claim deed. He then bought a large tract of land only a short distance from the village of Dover, where he resided until the time of his decease. The barn which he built is still standing, and the foundations of his house are yet to be seen. He sold from his original purchase several farms, retaining for his own use what is still known as "the Winds Farm." His wealth as a landholder and his natural force of character gave him great influence in the community, at a time when the savages yet infested New Jersey, and the whole country was agitated with the contest between England and France. At such a period, naturally, a leader who could be relied upon for timely counsel and shrewd action was respected and looked up to by his neighbors and the State. "Besides this, he was so chivalric in his bravery, and so decided in his views, and withal there was in him such a blending of courage with great physical powers, that his fellow-citizens naturally turned to him in times where ordinary gifts were insufficient to meet the emergencies which were constantly arising. In the old French war, a brigade was raised in New Jersey to aid in the conquest of Canada, and in that force he was commissioned as an officer. On their march, a great way north of Albany, the troops were exposed to the enemy, and, whilst being attacked, were forbidden by their own commander to return the fire, or even to offer any resistance. He, although a subordinate, then ran up to the general officer, and remonstrated with him, whereupon his superior menaced him with his sword. "The warm-blooded Winds, seconded by the enraged troops, made such answer to this that the commander put spur to his horse and fled for his life. Winds now assumed the command, and brought off the troops with honor." In 1758 a battalion was raised in New Jersey, the term of enlistment being for one year, and he then received a royal commission as Major—"but Mr. Losey is mistaken in the rank he assigns him at that period, since, in the records of the Presbyterian Parish of Rockaway, on January 29th, 1771, he is called Captain Winds,

and his name as Major Winds is not given until the record of April 20th, 1773." The same authority states further that he was not present at the capture of Quebec, by Wolfe, in 1759, the term for which the New Jersey troops were enlisted having expired. Yet he was actively engaged in many attendant and often severe skirmishes, and assisted in taking many prisoners. His treatment of these was so considerate and generous that several accompanied him back to New Jersey, and there settled as permanent residents. Among these was a man named Cubbey, to whom he became greatly attached, and presented a deed for twelve acres of land in the vicinity of Dover. This man acted as a sort of body-servant to him for many years. His conduct in that campaign was favorably reported by his soldiers, and he became more than ever a popular man at home. In this, as in all his campaigns, also, he gained the love of his troops by intrepidity, and by his careful protection of their interests in standing between them and greedy speculators, who, through his efforts, were prevented from preying mercilessly on the means of the common soldier. With slight variations, the tradition concerning his exploit on the expedition to Canada is confirmed by Colonel Joseph Jackson, of Rockaway, who was personally acquainted with him, and whose father served under him repeatedly during the revolutionary war. That New Jersey sent troops to Canada in 1758 is certain, and also that they formed a part of the army which Abercrombie led to the attack on Ticonderoga in July of that year. This probably affords the clue to the relation. In that disastrous battle Montcalm commanded the French; and Abercrombie, scorning the sound advice of Stark (the husband of "Molly Stark"), and also various English officers, calling them "Rehoboam counsellors," precipitated his gallant troops upon a foolish and bloody defeat. His conduct was severely reprobated by the survivors of his army, and by the authorities at home. "And here, in all probability, is the seed from which grew the Morris county tradition." At home he was not merely a brave man, but the bravest of the brave; and in some respects was the most noted man in the county, holding there a relative position which was not so obvious in an army made up of valiant spirits from England and Scotland and the New England colonies, which, among other noted spirits, had sent Wolfe, Putnam and Stark. It is a matter of uncertainty whether he engaged in military service during the period intervening between the French war and the Revolution. Meanwhile he received a commission from the English authorities as one of the king's justices of the peace for the county of Morris. This was previous to 1765, a year famous in American history for the passage of the odious stamp act. In common with the masses of his countrymen, he regarded that act as an intolerable oppression, and resisted its practical enforcement, a step more difficult than common in his case as a justice of the peace. The bold resistance of the New England colonies has found a place in history, and yet the mountains of Morris county furnished as singular an evasion of the act as any on record. To avoid the use of the stamped paper, he substituted the bark of the white birch. Warrants and writs, bonds and executions, were not then so numerous as in these days of litigation, and the simplicity of the times allowed a brevity in those legal documents which might now be considered indecorous. "But when the constable displayed a warrant to arrest 'Richard Roe,' and bring him before me, William Winds, there was no one bold enough to deny the summary authority." If there be another instance of a sworn justice of King George nullifying the stamp act with white birch bark, it has as yet escaped historical notice. He was connected with the Presbyterian Church of Rockaway, which was organized about 1752; made a public profession of religion during the pastorate of Rev. James Tuttle, the first pastor, and was a liberal contributor toward the church expenses and building the first meeting-house, "although it must be acknowledged that his warm imperious temper betrayed him into some extravagances scarcely consistent with his profession." For instance, one Sabbath morning, when the congregation was surprised by a messenger on horseback bringing the news that the enemy were on the march to Morristown, he exhibited the most wrathful impatience because the "minute men" had come to church without their arms. A woman who witnessed the scene says that he never attended meeting in those days without his arms, and that on this alarm he "spoke, or rather bawled, so loud that he might have been heard to the Short Hills." He sometimes led in prayer when the congregation, lacking a pastor, held deacons' meeting; at such times his voice was usually low and gentle until he began to plead for the cause of American freedom, when his excitement became explosive, and his "voice was raised until it sounded like heavy thunder!" In his "Revolutionary Reminiscences," Dr. Ashbel Green says: "He was of gigantic frame and strength, and no one doubted his courage. But the most remarkable thing about him was his voice. It exceeded in power and efficiency (for it was articulate as well as loud) every other human voice I ever heard. It was indeed a stentorophonic voice." Mrs. Anderson, who lived more than half a mile in an air line from his house, the valley of the Rockaway river intervening, says that she has frequently heard distinctly the various orders he issued at intervals to the laborers in his fields. The anecdote of his frightening off a detachment of British soldiers by crying out at the top of his voice: "Open to the right and left, and let the artillery through!" is familiar to every Jerseyman. The scene of this anecdote was on the Hackensack river, as was testified by Stephen Jackson, father of Colonel Joseph Jackson, who was present when the fictitious order was given. When he sang in church it was said that he not only drowned the combined voices of the entire congregation, but that "he seemed also to make the very building itself shake." In his home everything was planned and executed with military precision; he insisted

on literal obedience to his orders, even when his own interests suffered in consequence thereof. From Mrs. Winds to his slave, no one dared vary a hair's breadth from his commands, "under such a storm as it was fearful to encounter." His favorite laborer, for this reason, was a man called Ogden, and on one occasion his prompt attention to orders was seriously to the cost of his employer: he was starting for Norristown one morning, when he saw that his sheep had broken into a grain-field; greatly excited, he called out: "Ogden, go and kill every one of those sheep!" and springing on his horse rode off at full speed, which was not abated until his steed had covered more than a mile. Then, "remembering that his man was a terrible literalist, he wheeled his horse and rode back at as swift a rate, at every leap of the animal," roaring out like the report of a brass field-piece: "Ogden, hold your hand! Ogden, hold your hand!" But Ogden had executed orders so far as to have slaughtered seven of the sheep before he received counter commands. In the greatest good-humor, he commended the man for his promptness, but assured him that he had done enough for the present. He had reason to regret a great while one of his orders, which was to a niece, to whom he was greatly attached, to execute some errand on the horse he himself usually rode, and which was as fiery and headstrong as its master. The young woman, not daring to disobey, mounted the animal and was thrown from his back. The fall made her a cripple for life. During her tedious illness he watched over her with untiring care and tenderness, and, at his death, left her a legacy amounting to one-twentieth of his whole estate. Yet all accounts depict him as a man of boundless generosity to the poor and distressed; he had a rough manner, but a kind heart; was imperious and petulant, yet constantly swayed by generosity and magnanimous promptings. As a magistrate he regarded equity and not technicalities, and dispensed justice in modes more consonant with martial than with civil law; as a Christian, he shrank from no pecuniary obligation to religion, and was as punctilious as a Pharisee in all religious duties; as an employer, he suffered no interference with his plans, and those who obeyed him most closely enlisted his kindest regards; as a military officer, he was always ready for duty, and his soldiers were devotedly attached to him—his very eccentricities endearing him to them, for even these were employed in their behalf. The date of his commission as Lieutenant-Colonel in the 1st New Jersey Battalion was Tuesday, November 7th, 1775, and by appointment of the Continental Congress. Previously, on October 28th, of the same year, the 1st Battalion of New Jersey had elected the very officers who were subsequently commissioned by Congress. From a letter bearing date "Mendham, December 7th, 1775," it is learned that about this time he was vigorously engaged in scouring the country for the purchase of arms. On December 10th, 1775, Major de Hart wrote to Lord Stirling that some complaints had been made of "the price and quality of some of the arms purchased by Colonel Winds." An order, also, is in existence, under date of November 21st, 1775, from Stirling, requesting him to lead three companies, of which Captain Morris' and Captain Howell's were two, to the Highlands, but the order was probably countermanded. During the contest between Governor Franklin and the Assembly, he was at Perth Amboy, the seat of government, in command of a detachment of troops, subject to the order of his Colonel, Lord Stirling. Under date of January 10th, 1776, Stirling writes to the President of the Continental Congress that he has ordered him to secure the person of the governor and remove him to Elizabethtown, where he had "provided good and genteel lodgings for him." Two days previous to this, Winds wrote the following letter to Franklin: "Barracks at Perth Amboy, January 8th, 1776. Sir—I have hints that you intend to leave the province in case the letters that were intercepted should be sent to the Continental Congress. As I have particular orders concerning the matter, I therefore desire you will give me your word and honor that you will not depart this province until I know the will and pleasure of the Continental Congress concerning the matter." Franklin replies the same day: "I have not the least intention to quit the province; nor shall I, unless compelled by violence." But meanwhile, as the required pledge had not been given, he stationed his sentinels at the governor's gate, "which in keeping his resolution." This calls out an indignant letter the next day, January 9th, which concludes with this significant sentence: "However, let the authority, or pretence, be what it may, I do hereby require of you, if these men are sent by your orders, that you do immediately remove them from hence, as you will answer the contrary at your peril." To this he instantly replied: "As you, in a former letter, say you wrote nothing but what was your duty to do as a faithful officer of the crown; so I say, touching the sentinels placed at your gate, I have done nothing but what was my duty to do as a faithful officer of the Congress." The situation of Franklin was uncomfortable enough, since on the 10th of January, Lord Stirling sent a message to him by the outspoken Winds, "which kindly invited him to dine with me at this place," Elizabethtown; and such was the decision of the messenger, that "he at last ordered up his coach to proceed to this place." The intervention of Chief Justice Smyth, who prevailed on him to make the promise which Winds demanded, saved the governor from a disagreeable ride, under a guard, to Elizabethtown. From Franklin's second letter to him, it comes to light, incidentally, that he was not only a Lieutenant-colonel, but an elected representative also of the people of Morris in the Assembly. From December 21st, 1775, to January 14th, 1776, his troops were on duty around Perth Amboy and Elizabethtown; on the 14th of that month they searched Staten Island for tories, and on the 18th marched from Bergentown to New York city, thence to Hellgate, Newtown, Jamaica, and Rockaway, on Long Island, always in pursuit of tories. On the 22d, at Elizabethtown, he stood sentry over a ship lately taken from the enemy. In February of this year he informed Congress that he was stationed at Perth Amboy with a part of the Eastern Battalion of the Continental forces; that he was destitute of ammunition; and that he stood in pressing need of speedy supplies. Congress, by their President, then requested the committee of Somerset county to furnish him with four quarter-casks of powder, and the committee of Middlesex county to furnish him with one hundred and fifty pounds of lead. On Thursday, March 7th, 1776, he was promoted to the Colonelcy of the 1st New Jersey Battalion; and the news of his promotion was accompanied with a special and flattering letter from John Hancock. From the depositions of several soldiers applying for pensions is gathered the fact that, early in May, 1776, his regiment set out to join the expedition against Canada, in which Montgomery lost his life the previous year; it proceeded as far as the town of Sorel, if not to Three Rivers. In the following July he took post on the Onion river, under instructions from General Sullivan, for the purpose of protecting the inhabitants of the several towns in the New Hampshire grants. The journals of the Provincial Legislature show that on February 3d, 1777, he was, by the joint meeting, elected Colonel of the Western Battalion of Militia in the county of Morris, "lately commanded by Colonel Jacob Drake;" and that on March 4th, 1777, he was elected by ballot a Brigadier-General of the Militia of New Jersey. Previously, on the 6th of November, 1776, he had left Ticonderoga and was afterward with Washington during his retreat. During the summer of 1777 he was stationed on the North river, to aid in preventing a junction between Burgoyne's army from the North, and that of Sir Henry Clinton from New York. In 1778 he was for several months in active service in the region of Elizabethtown and Hackensack, and during this time several severe skirmishes were fought with the enemy. After the battle of Monmouth he led a detachment of troops to Minisink, on the Delaware, to repel a threatened incursion of Indians; and during the remainder of the summer and fall guarded the lines on the Passaic and Hackensack with noteworthy courage and prudence. On several occasions he attacked the enemy, and repulsed them in all their attempts to cross the rivers. The venerable David Gordon, when ninety-one years of age, once repeated to Rev. Joseph F. Tuttle a speech made by him during the campaign, which is sufficiently characteristic. The troops were at Acquackanonk; and one Sabbath morning he paraded, and thus addressed them: "Brother-soldiers, to-day by the blessing of God, I mean to attack the enemy. All you that are sick, lame, or afraid, stay behind, for I don't want sick men, lame men can't run, and cowards won't fight!" He subsequently managed so adroitly an attack on a party of Hessians as to take, according to one witness, thirty, and according to another, seventy prisoners, near Connecticut Farms, perhaps in Elizabethtown. In the following year he was "not much in active service," and, owing to the feeling

M. Hutchinson.

the control of an extensive and lucrative line of patronage. In 1853 he was elected on the Whig ticket a member of the Legislature, from the First district of Burlington county; that being the first year when the district system was adopted in that county. While a member of the House in 1853 and 1854, he served on several important committees, chief among them being those on the Judiciary, the Educational and on the Insane Asylum; he declined a nomination for the year 1855. He was appointed in 1860, by Governor Olden, Prosecutor of the Pleas for Burlington county, which position he retained for five years. He has likewise been commissioned as one of the Commissioners of the Supreme Court of New Jersey. Also United States Commissioner, and in addition, holds the position of a Master and Examiner in Chancery. He has served as a member of the Public School Board for three years, and at the present time is President of the Board of Trustees of the Bordentown Female College. He has been for the past eighteen years a Director of the Bordentown Bank; and is also a Director of the First National Bank of Trenton. He has ever taken an active interest in the affairs of his State, especially in connection with the various lines of railway, which have been constructed within the past twenty-five years. Since the disintegration of the Whig he has united with the Republican organization. He was married ... 1848, to Amy N., daughter of Caleb ...

McKISSACK, WILLIAM D., late of Millstone, Somerset county, New Jersey, was born in Somerset county, and was the only son of Dr. William McKissack, long an eminent practitioner at Bound Brook, and a zealous Whig during and after the revolutionary war. His education was the best that the country afforded, beginning with a careful school course at Basking Ridge ... course at Princeton ... office study in the ... ville, of Trenton ... New York. In the latter part of ... the end of ..., where for some ... years ... was the leading representative of ... a prominent member of the New Jersey State Medical Society, being for twelve years ... Secretary of that organization, and serving also as ... and (in 1826) as President. In the Somerset County Medical Society he was likewise a leader, filling at various times the several offices, and taking an active part in the conduct of the affairs of the society. During the war of 1812 he was commissioned Captain of a company of volunteers raised for the defence of the State, and after the war remained in the militia and eventually

excited against him in connection with the battle of Monmouth, resigned his commission as a Brigadier-General. His resignation bears date of June 10th, 1779. From this time he is not to be considered as a member of the active army, but did not desert his country's cause. When the battle of Springfield was fought in 1780 he was present, and did good service. In 1781 also he was instrumental in furthering the aims of his fellow-countrymen. When Washington was driving Cornwallis before him, and had begun the siege at Yorktown, it was deemed of the highest necessity to keep the British in New York until the arrival of the French fleet in the Chesapeake should cut off Cornwallis' retreat by water. Lafayette, accordingly, was sent to make a great demonstration on the enemy in New York. For this purpose he began to collect all the boats in the surrounding waters, even seizing those above Patterson Falls, on the Passaic. These were carried on wagons to be launched at Elizabethtown, apparently for an attack on Staten Island. On one particular night the rain poured down furiously and in torrents, and several of the wagons broke down at Crane-town (West Bloomfield). These annoyances filled Lafayette with great vexation. " General Winds was then in command of a detachment, and performed excellent and efficient service in aiding to better the general condition of things. His voice vied with the tempest as he cheered and directed his men." In 1788 he, with William Woodhull and John Jacob Faesch, were elected by Morris county to the State Convention which ratified the present Constitution of the United States. On the 12th of October, 1789, he died, of dropsy in the chest. He had in his family, at the time of his death, one of his soldiers, named Phelps. This man insisted that his old commander should be buried with the honors of war, although opposition was encountered in some quarters. Accordingly, Captain Josiah Hall, who had frequently served under him, assembled a company of his former soldiers, and he was finally buried in accordance with military customs.

———◦◆◦———

UTCHINSON, MAHLON, Lawyer, was born, May 10th, 1823, in the city of Philadelphia, Pennsylvania, and is a son of the late Randel Hutchinson, Jr., who married Mary Keeler, both natives of that State; the former being of Welsh descent, while the latter was of German lineage. Mahlon received his preliminary education at the Lawrenceville High School; he subsequently entered Princeton College in 1840, and remained there until 1841. Having determined to embrace the legal profession, he entered as a student the office of the Hon. Henry W. Green, with whom he remained until he completed the prescribed course of reading; and was licensed as an attorney in 1845, and as counsellor in 1854. He immediately entered upon the practice of his profession, locating at Bordentown, where he has remained ever since engaged in legal pursuits, and has

the control of an extensive and lucrative line of patronage. In 1853 he was elected on the Whig ticket a member of the Legislature, from the First district of Burlington county; that being the first year when the district system was adopted in that county. While a member of the House in 1853 and 1854, he served on several important committees, chief among them being those on the Judiciary, the Educational and on the Insane Asylum; he declined a nomination for the year 1855. He was appointed in 1860, by Governor Olden, Prosecutor of the Pleas for Burlington county, which position he retained for five years. He has likewise been commissioned as one of the Commissioners of the Supreme Court of New Jersey. Also United States Commissioner, and in addition, holds the position of a Master and Examiner in Chancery. He has served as a member of the Public School Board for three years, and at the present time is President of the Board of Trustees of the Bordentown Female College. He has been for the past eighteen years a Director of the Bordentown Bank; and is also a Director of the First National Bank of Trenton. He has ever taken an active interest in the affairs of his adopted State, especially in connection with the various lines of railway, which have been constructed within the past twenty-five years. Since the disintegration of the Whig party he has affiliated with the Republican organization. He was married, February 23d, 1848, to Amy N., daughter of Caleb Shreeve, of Burlington county.

———◦◆◦———

cKISSACK, WILLIAM D., late of Millstone, Somerset county, New Jersey, was born in Somerset county, and was the only son of Dr. William McKissack, long an eminent practitioner at Bound Brook, and a zealous Whig during and after the revolutionary war. His education was the best that the country afforded, beginning with a careful school course at Basking Ridge; continuing with a full collegiate course at Princeton, whence he graduated in 1802; then office study in medicine under the famous Dr. Nicholas Belville, of Trenton, and with medical lectures in New York. In the latter part of 1805, or the early part of 1806, he entered upon practice at Pittstown, Hunterdon county, but at the end of some two years removed thence to Millstone, where for something over forty years he was the leading representative of his profession. He was a prominent member of the New Jersey State Medical Society, being for twelve years Recording Secretary of that organization, and serving also as Vice-President and (in 1826) as President. In the Somerset County Medical Society he was likewise a leader, filling at various times the several offices, and taking an active part in the conduct of the affairs of the society. During the war of 1812 he was commissioned Captain of a company of volunteers raised for the defence of the State, and after the war remained in the militia and eventually became a Brigadier-General. In 1835-36 he was a member of the State Legislature. Both professionally and socially he was highly esteemed, his liberal habit of practising without fee among his poorer patients rendering him especially popular. He married Margaret, only daughter of Peter Ditmars, of Millstone, having by this marriage five children. He died March 6th, 1853.

MITH, ABRAHAM CARPENTER, M. D., Banker, of Bloomsbury, Hunterdon county, only son of William B. and Elizabeth Smith, was born in Greenwich township, Warren county, New Jersey, December 11th, 1840. Having received a careful preparatory education, he entered Lafayette College and was graduated thence B. A. Shortly after his graduation he began the study of medicine, and, after office-study and a collegiate course, received his degree of M. D. For some years he was engaged in practice at Mauch Chunk, Pennsylvania, but upon the foundation of the Bloomsbury National Bank, he relinquished his profession in order to accept the position of Teller, tendered him by the Board of Directors of that corporation. This position he continues to retain, holding in financial affairs a leading position.

ALENTINE, HON. CALEB H., Lawyer, of Hackettstown—a grandson of Judge Caleb H. Valentine, who, previous to his elevation to the bench of the Court of Errors and Appeals, was successively a member of the lower and upper houses of the New Jersey Legislature—was born at Hackettstown, July 22d, 1838. Having been prepared for college under the tutorship of the Rev. H. N. Wilson, D. D., pastor of the Presbyterian Church of his native town, he entered Yale, and was graduated thence B. A. in 1863, ex-Governor Chamberlain, of South Carolina, being one of his classmates and fellow-graduates. Shortly after leaving college he began the study of law in the office of J. G. Shipman, Esq., of Belvidere, and at about the same time was commissioned Colonel of the 3d (militia) Regiment of Warren county. In 1865 he temporarily relinquished his legal studies for the purpose of visiting the oil regions of Pennsylvania, and here, by judicious speculation, he in a short time acquired a handsome competency. Returning to Belvidere, he resumed his course of reading and in 1869 was admitted to the New Jersey bar. On being licensed he established himself in Hackettstown, where he rapidly acquired a large practice, and is now regarded as one of the leading barristers of the county, being especially successful with cases in the criminal courts. During the past few years he has devoted a considerable portion of his fortune

to the purchase and improvement of landed property, and is at present one of the most extensive owners of improved real estate in Warren. His social and professional prominence has naturally led to his selection as county Representative in the State Assembly, and in 1869-70-71 he did good service in the Legislature. He was one of the originators and a most earnest promoter of the present admirable free-school system, the adoption of which has done so much honor to New Jersey; showing in his labors for this, and other measures of scarcely less importance, a liberal and far-seeing statesmanship. In 1876 he was named as a candidate for Representative from the Fourth Congressional District of New Jersey, but as Somerset county claimed the right of nomination, he withdrew his name and heartily supported the Somerset nominee. From early manhood he has been a consistent member of the Democratic party, holding that personal claims should not be pressed at the risk of party success—a belief the honesty of which was sufficiently established in the instance just mentioned. He married, in 1863, Miss Russling, daughter of Robert Russling, Esq., of Hackettstown.

ORTER, EDMUND, M. D., late of Frenchtown, Hunterdon county, New Jersey, was born in Haddam, Connecticut, June 18th, 1791. His medical education was received in New England, and shortly after being licensed to practise he settled in Easton, Pennsylvania. He thence migrated to Union county in the same State; then drifted down to the West Indies, and finally, returning to North America, established himself in June, 1820, at Frenchtown, where he remained until his death, on the 12th of July, 1826. In 1821 he was one of the founders of the Hunterdon County Medical Society, and was one of the first delegates from that body to the Medical Society of New Jersey. In practice he was generally successful, was of a cheerful, sanguine temperament, and was extremely popular in the community where the latter part of his life was passed. He was twice a candidate for the Assembly, and on being put in nomination the second time, was elected. In all matters relating to his profession he was exceedingly methodical, keeping a regular set of books, in which he noted all his cases, giving symptoms, disease, prescriptions, medicine actually administered, quantity, doses, effects produced from day to day, and result; also a record of the daily state of the weather, with the effects of changes upon his patients. He was for the times a voluminous writer upon medical, political and miscellaneous subjects, contributing quite largely to the medical and newspaper press of the day. Not content with writing for the present, he cherished a desire to write for posterity, and to this end deposited in the cellar wall of a house built for his use in Frenchtown, in

·1823, a curious document, from which are extracted the following paragraphs: "To futurity I address myself, in the year of our Lord 1823. Perhaps this memento may be of service or curiosity to future generations, if found among the rubbish of this mansion erected by order of Edmund Porter, M. D., physician and surgeon; member of and principal founder of the Medical Society of Hunterdon County, New Jersey; licentiate of the Connecticut Medical Society, also of the Medical Society of St. Bartholomew's (West Indies), and Union Medical Society, of Pennsylvania, and author of a number of medical essays, political pieces, to be found in the *New York Medical Repository* and *American Medical Recorder*, the *New England Journal of Medicine*, and in the newspapers, viz., the Trenton *True American*, *The Spirit of Pennsylvania*, the *Eastern Sentinel*, etc., etc." Under the heading, "existing facts," he briefly writes : " James Monroe, President of the United States. W. II. Williamson, Governor of New Jersey." Then follows a long list of the names of the several persons engaged in the building of the house, " previously to the deposition of this memorandum in the cellar wall;" the " architects of this building," the " persons who assisted at the several parties in digging Seller, tending masons, quarrying stone and carting the same." Then, launching out into the broader sphere of contemporaneous history, he continues: " The 4th of July is to be celebrated in this town on the approaching anniversary, it being the forty-seventh of American independence. William Voorhis and John Clifford, Esquires, and Samuel Powers and David R. Warford, presidents and vice-presidents of the day. Dr. Albert Tyler is to deliver the oration, Dr. Luther Towner the invocation, and the Hon. Joshua B. Colvin is to read the Declaration of Independence. The Rev. Mr. Hunt is requested to make a short address. Captain John Scott is appointed marshal of the day, and Captain Ezra Brewster will appear with the Kingwood Uniform Company, equipped and in uniform. A dinner, toasts, music, and the roar of cannon to conclude the festivities of the day." Then follows this brief autobiography: "Edmund Porter was born in Haddam, Connecticut, June 18th, 1791, emigrated to Pennsylvania in 1815, married Mary More, September the 28th, 1816. Have three children [names and dates of birth]. Commenced the practice of medicine in this town, June 10th, 1820. Intermitting fever makes its appearance after an absence of twenty years; has been common along the banks of the Delaware river, and dysenteria interiorly; charcoal pulverized proved a useful adjunct in the latter complaint." His fondness, already mentioned, for recording meteorological observations, crops out in a paragraph to this effect: ⁱ· The seasons for five years past have been remarkably dry. The present year, 1823, has thus far been cold and inclement; frost and ice seen on the 5th and 6th of May. Crops look well, June 1st." In conclusion he adds; " Finder of this document, know that I wrote it to amuse; if it should afford you any, remember the end of all things,

and prepare yourself to die, as all of us have done whose names you see enrolled on this memorial. We all of us had our virtues and vices; each of us was of service to society in their several capacities in life. We are no more. We look to future generations to preserve unimpaired the liberty and independence which thus far we have assisted to perpetuate at the risk of our lives and fortunes. This voice from the tombs admonishes you to do the same as we have done for you!!! Farewell." His deposit in his "seller wall " did not remain hidden nearly so long as he had intended, a party of investigative antiquarians taking if upon themselves some twenty-five years ago to discover his records. According to their own statement this was done in the interest of historical and archæological research. Of Dr. Porter's children, none, it is believed, now survive; nor has he any living descendants. His portrait, presented by a collateral relative, is in the possession of the Hunterdon County Medical Society. The several record books, in which the history of his professional life was so carefully set forth, and which would now be veritable medical curiosities, have unfortunately been lost.

———◆◇◆———

ERGEANT, LAMBERT H., Lawyer, and Mayor of Lambertville, New Jersey, was born in 1841, near Flemington in that State, and is the son of Gershom C. Sergeant, who was engaged in agricultural pursuits; the family is of German lineage.

Young Sergeant until his eighteenth year assisted his father in the management of the farm, and attended also the public schools of the neighborhood, subsequently entering the Flemington High School, where he completed his education after a two years' course in that institution. With a view of acquiring first-class legal attainments, he became a student in the office of B. Van Syckel, now Judge of the Supreme Court, where he passed four years; and subsequently entered the law department of the University of Albany, from which institution he graduated as Bachelor of Laws in May, 1868. He then returned to the office of Judge Van Syckel, where he remained until the November term of the Supreme Court, and was then admitted to the New Jersey bar. In December, 1868, he removed to Lambertville, where he opened an office and commenced the practice of his profession; and his attainments, together with his high integrity of character, soon won for him the confidence of the public, and as a consequence he was rewarded with a large share of legal business of the county. In 1873 he was appointed, by the Common Council, City Solicitor, and reappointed in April, 1876. In 1874 he was nominated by the Democrats of the city of Lambertville as their candidate for Mayor, and was elected by a large majority. Again, in 1875, he was renominated by the same organization, and re-elected by an increased majority, although the majority of the ticket was defeated. He was elected a third time, in 1876, and still holds the position. He has the control of an extensive practice, not only as a business lawyer, but also in litigated cases. He is shrewd and efficient in the management of a case, preparing it thoroughly, and always brings it before court in the most presentable manner. He was married, May 6th, 1874, to Sadie, daughter of William Scarborough, of New Hope, Pennsylvania.

ROE, REV. AZEL, D. D., Revolutionary Patriot, late of Woodbridge, New Jersey, was a native of Long Island, whence he removed to New Jersey for the purpose of becoming a student in Princeton College. In 1760 he was licensed by the Presbytery of New York, and two years later was ordained. In 1763 he became pastor of the Presbyterian Church at Woodbridge, New Jersey, afterward connected with Metuchen. During the revolutionary contest he proved his patriotism in many ways and on many occasions. The part of New Jersey in which he resided was constantly annoyed by marauding parties sent out from the British forces stationed at Staten Island. On one occasion a brave Continental captain, who had done great execution in driving off or annoying those predatory bands, was very anxious to attack a party which had encamped near the Blazing Star Ferry, but could not induce his men to follow him. As many of them belonged to his congregation, he determined to bring into action the influence their pastor might possess over the weak and wavering, and ask his assistance. "Accordingly he called and stated his difficulty, and found Mr. Roe more than willing to second his efforts. The good minister accompanied the captain to the place where his men were, and addressed a few words to them, exhorting them to their duty, and enforcing his exhortation by telling them that it was his purpose to go into the action himself. And into the action he went, every man following readily. But when the bullets began to fly among them, they promised that, if he would keep out of harm's way, they would do the business for the enemy. And seeing that their spirits were sufficiently excited, he did retire, and, as he afterwards acknowledged, very much to his own comfort." One night the tories united with the British, and, seizing him while with his family, carried him off as a prisoner to New York, where he was lodged in the famous "Sugar-House." As they were on their way to New York, it was found necessary to ford a small stream. The officer in command, "who seemed to have taken a fancy to Mr. Roe and treated him politely, insisted that the captured minister should allow him to carry him over on his back. When they were about the middle of the stream, Mr. Roe, who relished a joke and was not wanting in ready wit, said to the officer: 'Well, sir, if never before, you can say after this, that you were once priest-ridden.' The officer was so convulsed with laughter that he had well-nigh fallen under his burden into the water." When they arrived in New York, an excellent breakfast was sent him by the father of Washington Irving, who had been informed of his capture and imprisonment. He was a Trustee of the Princeton College twenty-nine years, from 1778 to 1807. In 1800 the honorary degree of Doctor of Divinity was conferred on him by Yale College. His preaching was distinguished for substantial excellence, rather than for those qualities which attract and dazzle the multitude; and he was universally and highly esteemed as a pastor, and was in charge of the same flock for fifty-four years. He died in November, 1815.

BELVILLE, NICHOLAS, M. D., late of Trenton. This eminent physician was born in France in 1752, was educated in that country, and in 1781 emigrated to America. Settling at Trenton, he rapidly acquired a large practice, and in time came to be one of the medical pillars of the State, being constantly sought in consultation, and the favor of studying under his supervision being eagerly solicited by young men desirous of adopting medicine as a profession. His manner was quick and peremptory—occasionally to the hither verge of rudeness—but it was manner only, his nature being kindly to a degree. He was one of the founders (in 1821) of the Hunterdon County Medical Society (Trenton at that time being included within the limits of Hunterdon), and was of that society the first President. When Joseph Bonaparte was resident in Bordentown, he was the regularly appointed physician to the ex-king. His personal character was on a par with his professional standing, his strict integrity, no less than his success as a physician, winning for him the respect and esteem of the community in which for half a century he lived. He died December 17th, 1831, and was buried in the graveyard of the Presbyterian Church at Trenton.

LILLY, JOHN, M. D., late of Lambertville, one of the most eminent physicians of East New Jersey during the first half of the present century, son of Samuel Lilly, Esq., barrister, was born in Staffordshire, England, in 1783. His parents emigrated to America while he was still a child, settling first in the city of New York, subsequently in Albany, and finally in Elizabeth, New Jersey. His father was for several years engaged as a teacher in New York and in Albany; while in the latter city he took holy orders, and was for many years Rector of St. John's Episcopal Church at Elizabeth. While in charge of St. John's, Lord Bolingbroke being then a resident of Elizabeth, he performed the

Lewis Jemison M.D.

marriage ... John Lilly, being ... profession, was... to Dr. Samuel Stringer, ... surgeon of Albany, and ... of four years, was duly ... 1807. During the ensuing ... professional duty in Lansingburg, ... in 1808 removed to New Jersey, and ... at Readington, Hunterdon county. ... to the State Medical Society for authority to practise ... he was examined by the then Board of Censors, of which the venerable Dr. Moses Scott, of New Brunswick, was chairman; and being found properly qualified, was made a licentiate of that organization. At this time he married Julia Moodie, a lady with whom he had become acquainted in Lansingburg, and who had come upon a visit to the Lane family, of Readington, shortly after his establishment in that town. In the spring of 1809, as the successor to Dr. Kroesen, then recently deceased, he finally settled at Lambertville (then called Georgetown), where, during the ensuing thirty-nine years, he remained actively engaged in the duties of his profession. In 1821 he was one of the founders of the Hunterdon County Medical Society, and until his death was, through all its ... (including two actual disruptions), one of the most ... and enthusiastic members of that body. He was President in 1825 and in 1847; Vice-President in 1823 and in 1846; Treasurer from 1836 to 1846; a member of the Board of Censors from 1821 to 1825 inclusive, and in 1847-48; and was repeatedly a delegate to the annual conventions of the New Jersey State Medical Society. Of the State Society he was also a leading member, being Corresponding Secretary in 1827, and again in 1832; a member of the Standing Committee in 1831, and a member and Chairman of the same committee in 1847. Dr. John Blane, the able historian of the Hunterdon County Medical Society, who was for many years his intimate friend, writes of him: "His ... and character were those of a refined gentleman; ... pure and chaste in ... acts and words. The writer, during a close intimacy of ... twenty years, during which he has seen him in all kinds of company, never heard a word or an intimation pass ... which could not have been uttered in the most refined circle. This purity and refinement was very prominent in all his writings, he being a frequent contributor to the periodicals of the day, and frequently appearing before his fellow-citizens in the character of a lecturer before the local literary societies. As a physician he was very attentive to his patients; his judgment sound and clear, and his practice in emergent and dangerous cases prompt and energetic. He was not slow to adopt any new or improved mode of treatment, if it had the approbation of his judgment. His success was as that of the most successful. He was always a stickler for the most rigid professional ethics. He never permitted himself to be betrayed into the violence ... condemn such ... inferred from the ... ligious convictions. ... the Protestant Episcopal Church ... death was a consistent ... tion. For many years he ... siderable period was Senior Warden ... Church, at Lambertville. ... politician, he took much interest ... that he filled with credit to himself, and to the satisfaction of his constituents. He died in June, 1848.

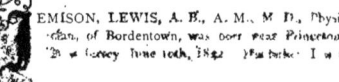

EMISON, LEWIS, A. B., A. M., M. D., Physician, of Bordentown, was born near Princeton, ... Jersey, June 10th, 1842. ... I ...

... of the ... decided upon ... the medical profession, and ... gave up teaching to enter upon the study of medicine. This he did in Princeton, in the office of Professor J. Stillwell Schanck, LL. D., ... professor of chemistry in the College of New Jersey, at Princeton. Having completed his preliminary studies, he attended the regular course at the University of Pennsylvania, at Philadelphia, and received his ... in 1878, being now a qualified practitioner, he ... Hightstown, New Jersey, and commenced ... but a short time, however, and then ... residence in Bordentown, where he ... actively engaged in the practice of his ... profession has always been ... a practitioner remarkable. He is ... careful in ... tive, requisite ... those eminent results ... for success ... popular natural powers, a quick insight, ... judge ... and trained skill. He rapidly gained ... important practice, and is, as it was, is high in the confidence of the community, and in the regards of his professional brethren. He is a member of the Burlington County Medical Society, and was its President during 1870. He has never taken any active part in politics, but has devoted his time and energies to his profession exclusively. He is the United States Examining Surgeon in his section of the State for applicants for pensions

marriage ceremony for that exotic nobleman. John Lilly, being desirous of entering the medical profession, was—after the custom of the time—apprenticed to Dr. Samuel Stringer, a prominent physician and surgeon of Albany, and after serving an apprenticeship of four years, was duly licensed as a practitioner in 1807. During the ensuing year he was engaged in professional duty in Lansingburg, near Albany, but in 1808 removed to New Jersey, and established himself at Readington, Hunterdon county. Applying to the State Medical Society for authority to practise, he was examined by the then Board of Censors, of which the venerable Dr. Moses Scott, of New Brunswick, was chairman; and being found properly qualified, was made a licentiate of that organization. At this time he was married to Julia Moodie, a lady with whom he had become acquainted in Lansingburg, and who had come upon a visit to the Lane family, of Readington, shortly after his establishment in that town. In the spring of 1809, as the successor to Dr. Kroesen, then recently deceased, he finally settled at Lambertville (then called Georgetown), where, during the ensuing thirty-nine years, he remained actively engaged in the duties of his profession. In 1821 he was one of the founders of the Hunterdon County Medical Society, and until his death was, through all its vicissitudes (including two actual disruptions), one of the most prominent and enthusiastic members of that body. He was President in 1825 and in 1847; Vice-President in 1823 and in 1846; Treasurer from 1836 to 1846; a member of the Board of Censors from 1821 to 1825 inclusive, and in 1847–48; and was repeatedly a delegate to the annual conventions of the New Jersey State Medical Society. Of the State Society he was also a leading member, being Corresponding Secretary in 1827, and again in 1832; a member of the Standing Committee in 1831, and a. member and Chairman of the same committee in 1847. Dr. John Blane, the able historian of the Hunterdon County Medical Society, who was for many years his intimate friend, writes of him: "His mind and character were those of a refined gentleman; scrupulously neat in his personal habits, pure and chaste in all his acts and words. The writer, during a close intimacy of nearly twenty years, during which he has seen him in all kinds of company, never heard a word or an intimation pass his lips which could not have been uttered in the most refined circle. This purity and refinement was very prominent in all his writings, he being a frequent contributor to the periodicals of the day, and frequently appearing before his fellow-citizens in the character of a lecturer before the local literary societies. As a physician he was very attentive to his patients; his judgment sound and clear, and his practice in emergent and dangerous cases prompt and energetic. He was not slow to adopt any new or improved mode of treatment, if it had the approbation of his judgment. His success was as marked as that of the most successful. He was always a stickler for the most rigid professional ethics. He never permitted himself to be betrayed

62

into the violation of the strictest code, and was not slow to condemn such violation on the part of others." As may be inferred from the foregoing, he was a man of decided religious convictions; in early life he became connected with the Protestant Episcopal Church, and to the time of his death was a consistent member of that religious organization. For many years he was a Vestryman, and for a considerable period was Senior Warden of St. Andrew's Church, at Lambertville. While by no means an active politician, he took much interest in politics, and in 1840–41 was elected a member of the Legislative Council, a position that he filled with credit to himself, and to the satisfaction of his constituents. He died in June, 1848.

———————

EMISON, LEWIS, A. B., A. M., M. D., Physician, of Bordentown, was born near Princeton, New Jersey, June 10th, 1832. His father, Isaiah Jemison, a farmer, and his mother, Elizabeth (Major) Jemison, were both natives of New Jersey. His early education was received at the select school of George W. Schanck, in Princeton, and when he had finished his preparatory course, in 1849, he entered Princeton College. He was a close and successful student in college, and graduated with honors in the year 1853. After leaving college he went to Haverstraw, New York, and taught for some time in the classical department of the institute there. He had decided upon adopting the medical profession, and at length gave up teaching to enter upon the study of medicine. This he did in Princeton, in the office of Professor J. Stillwell Schanck, LL. D., now professor of chemistry in the College of New Jersey, at Princeton. Having completed his preliminary studies, he attended the regular course at the University of Pennsylvania, at Philadelphia, and received his diploma in 1858. Being now a qualified practitioner, he removed to Hightstown, New Jersey, and commenced practice. He remained there but a short time, however, and then took up his residence in Bordentown, where he has since lived, actively engaged in the practice of his profession. His professional devotion has always been great, and his success as a practitioner remarkable. He is a patient student, a careful and exhaustive reader, and, in addition to these eminent qualifications for success, he possesses peculiar natural talents, a quick insight, accurate judgment and trained skill. He rapidly gained a large and important practice, and to-day stands high in the confidence of the community, and in the regards of his professional brethren. He is a member of the Burlington County Medical Society, and was its President during 1870. He has never taken any active part in politics, but has devoted his time and energies to his profession exclusively. He is the United States Examining Surgeon in his section of the State for applicants for pensions

He was married, in 1859, to Martha D. Allison, of New York. She died April 4th, 1860, and he was again married, January 1st, 1863, to Rebecca S. Wray, of Philadelphia.

CUDDER, HON. EDWARD W., Lawyer, and one of the Justices of the Supreme Court of New Jersey, is a native of Mercer county, New Jersey. He was admitted to the bar of the State in 1844, at the September term, and was made counsellor in October, 1848. He practised extensively in all the courts of the State until 1869, when he was appointed by Governor Randolph one of the Justices of the New Jersey Supreme Court, and after serving a full term of seven years was reappointed by Governor Bedle, in 1876, and is still holding the position, his tenure of which will expire in 1883. His career as a lawyer and judge has been such as to add to the reputation and dignity of the New Jersey bench and bar, and consequently to the high estimation in which they are held throughout the United States.

---

cCOSH, REV. JAMES, D. D., LL. D., President of Princeton College, was born in Ayrshire, Scotland, April 1st, 1811. His father, Andrew Mc-Cosh, was a farmer on the banks of the Doon, respected for his intelligence and integrity. In 1830 Andrew McCosh died, leaving a widow and seven children, six daughters and this son. The widow continued the farm and sent James to the parochial school. From here, at the age of thirteen, he was sent to Glasgow University, where he remained five years, applying himself with success to the study of philosophy. From here he went to Edinburgh University, where he had for his instructor the eminent scholar and theologian, Dr. Chalmers. Another five years was passed at this university, during which time the youthful metaphysician wrote his " Essay on the Stoic Philosophy," which gained for him the honorary degree of Master of Arts. After leaving Edinburgh he continued the study of theology, begun at Glasgow, with Dr. Thomas Guthrie, the famous preacher. A year later, in 1834, he was licensed to preach the gospel in connection with the Church of Scotland, and soon afterwards he was ordained minister to Abby Chapel, Arbroath, in the eastern part of Scotland. His ministry here was very successful, terminating after three years of incessant labor in a call to the charge of the city of Brechin, a parish in Forfarshire, which he accepted. Even at this early date he was taking an active interest in church politics, and attracting attention by the breadth and liberality of his views. He was one of the little band of Scotch Presbyterian ministers, led by Dr. Chalmers, who signed away their livings and founded the Free Church of Scotland. In 1845 he married a daughter of Alexander Guthrie, a physician as eminent in his profession as his brother, Thomas Guthrie, the divine—McCosh's former teacher—was distinguished in the ministry. The next five years were largely devoted to the service of the church which he had aided in establishing, but that he found time to continue his philosophic studies is evidenced by the publication, in 1848, of his first great work, " The Method of Divine Government, Physical and Moral," which at once attracted much attention, especially among metaphysicians, and gained for the author warm praise as well as criticism in Europe and America. He was soon after called (1851) to the Professorship of the newly created chair of Logic and Metaphysics in Queen's College, Belfast, which position he accepted and occupied until his removal to this country, in 1868. The same year, 1851, he published an essay on " Typical Forms " in the *North British Review*, which he afterwards elaborated in connection with Dr. Dickie, also of Queen's College, into " Typical Forms and Special Ends in Creation." In 1860 his " Intuitions of the Mind Inductively Investigated " brought him still more prominently into notice as a profound scholar and theological essayist. " In this, as in his previous publications, he diverges from the English school of Locke, by maintaining the existence and essential importance of ' a priori' conceptions and beliefs. They are the conditions of an empirical and concrete knowledge, and without them ethics, theology and all the science are impossible. But by investigating these intuitions inductively, he claims that he departs from the method and avoids the results of the German transcendental school, shunning the two extremes of sensationalism and idealism. It is his aim to grasp and unite the truth in each. In this spirit he treats the topics which lie at the foundation of knowledge and faith, as time, space, quantity, power, idealty, causation, substance, being, the infinite, personality, freedom and moral worth." While at Belfast he also wrote and published " The Supernatural in Relation to the Natural," 1862; " Examination of J. S. Mills' Philosophy, being a Defence of Fundamental Truth," 1866; and numerous articles for the periodical press of the day, which won him great distinction as a keen controversialist, a ready logician and a master metaphysician. In 1858 he visited Europe with a view to studying the educational systems obtaining in the great universities, especially in those of Germany. On his return the educational question in Ireland was occasioning much feeling, and he at once entered into the discussion with his accustomed vigor. Indeed, during his sixteen years' residence in Ireland he was the devoted friend of the working classes, laboring for the extension of education and the social improvement of the people. His singleness and sincerity of purpose won him the respect even of those to whom he was opposed by his convictions. In 1866 he visited this country, making an extended tour and examining our several colleges and theological seminaries. While at Princeton he read his essay on "The Method of Divine Government," which made a profound impression upon the trustees of the college; and when the venerable Dr. Maclean signified his intention of severing his connection of over fifty years with that institution, Dr. McCosh was unanimously chosen to supply the presidential chair. He was elected April 29th, 1868, and signified his acceptance the next month. When this was made known the college was universally congratulated on its acquisition, and the learned societies of Great Britain expressed their regrets at his loss to that nation and their good wishes for his success in his new field of.labor. Harvard College conferred upon him the degree of LL. D. He was inaugurated President of the College of New Jersey on the 27th of October, 1868, and entered upon the duties of his office immediately. In his inaugural address, "Academic Teaching in Europe," he presented the views of education which have since been followed at Princeton with such eminent success. He thoroughly identified himself with the college, and was unremitting in his exertions to raise it to the highest standard of excellence. The course of study was reorganized, enlarged, and. the standard of scholarship raised. A judicious adjustment of voluntary and elective studies was made. Incentives to study were added by the establishment of prizes and fellowships. The fruits of his labors are visible. Since 1868 the number of students has increased fifty per cent.; nine fellowships and a Professorship of Modern Languages have been founded; the material resources and accommodations have been enlarged and improved; several new and imposing college buildings have been erected, one of these latter, Reunion Hall, commemorating the union of the Presbyterian churches. In college reform one of his first acts was to suppress the scandalous secret paper which used to be circulated just before commencement day; a later and more radical change was the abolition of the secret societies, which, however, was not accomplished without considerable difficulty. Being at the head of the principal educational institution in New Jersey, Dr. McCosh also took a lively interest in the educational progress of the State, seeking to elevate and enlarge the public school system. In this purpose he delivered an address before the House of Assembly during the winter of 1871, in favor of the establishment of a system of high schools. Shortly after this he was appointed by Governor Randolph on an educational commission for the revision of the school laws of the State, and the suggestion of such amendments as this investigation might reveal a necessity for. This commission made a thorough and exhaustive report, suggesting reforms in this particular which will be of great benefit to the community. The movement to bring into closer relations all church organizations holding Presbyterian doctrines and using the Presbyterian form of government originated with Dr. McCosh. It may be said to have started at the tercentenary celebration of the birth of John Knox, held in Philadelphia, in November, 1872. He stated at that time that there were

20,000 congregations of Presbyterians, including the Reformed churches, and 34,000,000 population. It had long been a favorite idea of his to bring these churches together in a Pan-Presbyterian council. He had written of the scheme to the *Weekly Review*, of London, and had spoken of it to the Irish Presbyterian Assembly, and to the Old and New School Assemblies, at St. Louis, in 1866. At the World's Conference of the Evangelical Alliance, held in New York, in October, 1873, a meeting of the Presbyterian delegates present was called by him, and their assent to the idea of confederation was secured. A committee, with Dr. McCosh at the head, was appointed "to correspond with individuals and with organized bodies, in order to ascertain the feeling of Presbyterians in regard to such Federal Council, and to take such measures as may in their judgment promote this object." This committee issued an address to the Presbyterians of the world, asking each Presbyterian organization, "First, to express in a formal manner its approval of the scheme," and, second, to appoint a committee to arrange for a convention to organize the federation; and it also set forth the benefits that would result from the proposed union. The movement also received a great impetus from a visit which Dr. McCosh made to Europe in the summer of 1874, during which he made frequent addresses in London and elsewhere in furtherance of the project. Concerning this visit he wrote: "My late visit to Great Britain was simply for the purpose of seeing my friends; but, being there, I put myself in connection, in an unofficial way, with persons interested in the scheme. I was happy to find that all the Presbyterian churches of the three kingdoms, including the Established Church of Scotland, the Free Church of Scotland, the United Presbyterian Church of Scotland, the Covenanting Church of Scotland, the Presbyterian Church of Ireland and the Covenanters of Ireland, the Welsh Calvinistic Church and the Presbyterian Church of England, have passed strong and decided resolutions on its behalf, and appointed committees with full power to carry out the grand design. I was able to hold quiet meetings in London, in Belfast and in Edinburgh, and I put the question in each place, What step are we to take next? And in answer I got valuable suggestions, all pointing in the same direction. I may add, that I have had communications from the French churches, the Belgian, the Swiss evangelical churches, the Waldensians; from Dr. Dorner, of Berlin, and Professor William Kraft, of Bonn, and from distant Australia—all favorable. We need only the blessing of heaven to secure success, and let us pray for that." One of the results of this visit was the formation of a committee representing the State Church of Scotland, the Free Church of Scotland, the United Presbyterian Church, the Reformed Presbyterian Church, the Presbyterian Church of Ireland and the English Presbyterian Church, which committee had a session in November, 1874, and discussed the programme of the great meeting held in London, in July, 1875. This committee made a suggestion, which was acted upon, that the gathering should be strictly representative, and should be composed of commissioners appointed by the churches. It also recommended that, in regard to the English-speaking churches, the Westminster Confession should constitute a doctrinal basis of union; but that, in regard to other churches having Presbyterian government, a general agreement with the Reformed symbols of doctrine should be required. On the 20th of April, 1875, a committee, under the presidency of Dr. McCosh, met in New York and adopted a draft of a constitution to be presented to the council in London for consideration. In this draft it was proposed that the alliance be called "The Confederation of the Reformed Churches holding to the Presbyterian System;" but when the question was considered at the London council, in July, it was found that a large majority of the council preferred the title and form of an alliance, rather than a confederation, as less restricted in scope, and it was ultimately agreed that the alliance of all the Reformed churches throughout the world should be formed. The name given to the union, in accordance with this resolution, was the "Alliance of Reformed Churches throughout the World." Since his residence in the United States, Dr. McCosh has written several works; notably, "Logic," 1869; "Christianity and Positivism;" "A Series of Lectures to the Times on Natural Theology and Apologetics," 1871; and "The Scottish Philosophy, Biographical, Expository, Critical; from Hatchem to Hamilton," 1874. The lectures mentioned above were originally delivered in New York, and being in refutation of the teachings and deductions of Huxley, Darwin, Spencer and that school of thinkers, evoked a very deep interest in the religious world, where the work is very highly esteemed. Concerning his philosophy as compared with Sir William Hamilton, a writer says "it was what physiology is compared with anatomy; while he did not lack the acuteness of the dialectician, he clothed his skeletons with flesh and blood, and they readily took their places as living organisms in the world of progress." His mental characteristics are given by Dr. Shedd in his introduction to Dr. McCosh's greatest work, "The Intuitions of the Mind Inductively Investigated." He says: "The first feature that strikes the reader is the fidelity of the author to his nationality in rejecting all idealism in philosophy, realism in perception; that objects have an existence independent of the mind, that there is a substance in which properties inhere, that our perceptions of God, the soul, and even of infinity and eternity, are positive, and not merely negative. These and such like are the positions taken by this writer with decision, and maintained with power. In this particular we regard him as doing an excellent service in counteracting the influence of some recent speculations which tend to unsettle all scientific thinking and to convert the hightest department of human thought into a sphere of airy and unreal fictions. Though holding a high estimate of philosophy as a branch of human inquiry, he does not fall into the error of those who suppose that it is capable of solving all problems and becoming a system of infinite knowledge. . . . . In respect to the great theme of morals and religion, Dr. McCosh agrees with that lofty and influential class of thinkers from Pliny to Kant, who believe that genuine philosophy is in harmony with man's religious needs and instincts, and that these views of man are impossible without true views of God." A pen portrait of Dr. McCosh, as he appeared when he came to this country to assume the Presidency of Princeton College, sketches him as a tall, handsome man, with dark, penetrating eyes, a pleasant smile and most engaging manners. His forehead is high and clear, and his mouth indicates him as a man of great firmness and strength of will. He has just enough of the scholarly stoop to betray his sedentary avocations, yet his step is elastic, and in all respects he seems like a vigorous man, to whom the exercise of mental or bodily powers is never fatiguing.

———◆———

MITH, JOHN JAY, Librarian, Editor, Author, great-grandson of James Logan, of New Jersey, was born in Burlington county, New Jersey, June 16th, 1798. From 1829 to 1851 he presided as Librarian of the Philadelphia and Loganian Libraries. He is the author of "Notes for a History of the Philadelphia Library Company," published in 1831; "Guide to Laurel Hill Cemetery," published in 1844; "A Summer's Jaunt," two volumes, published in 1846; "American Historical and Literary Curiosities," published in 1861; and, in the "National Portrait Gallery," of lives of Franklin, Rittenhouse, Keaton, Montgomery and A. Washington. He has also been engaged extensively in editing various works and periodicals: The Saturday Bulletin, 1830–32; The Daily Express, 1832; "Waldie's Select Library," 1833–49; "Waldie's Portfolio," two volumes, quarto; "Smith's Weekly Volume," 1845–46, three volumes; Walsh's National Gazette and Downing's Horticulturist, 1855–60. He is a man of varied and scholarly attainments; is fond of antiquarian research, and though long-continued study of the earlier annals of the States has grown to be a recognized authority on the subject of American and colonial literature and history.

———◆———

AMPBELL, GEORGE, M.D., late of Frenchtown, Hunterdon county, New Jersey, son of James Campbell, was born at Newtown-Stewart, county Tyrone, Ireland, August 15th, 1758. He was educated at the University of Dublin, entering the medical department after graduating from the department of arts, and being during the time that he attended medical lectures an office student with Dr. Mc-

Farling. He ...... his degree .... the American war ...... Revolution ......; and sympathizing ...... with the ...... colonies, ... immigrant ...... this country ...... the Continental army. He was soon ...... and in this capacity ...... until ...... When the army was disbanded, he ...... where his exceptionally thorough ...... extensive surgical experience ...... to throw into his hands a very large ...... married Rachel, youngest daughter ...... by whom he had two children. ...... rely engaged in his profession until ...... was prostrated by a stroke of paralysis. ...... never entirely recovered, and his death, followed ...... stroke, occurred in August, 1818

BENTLEY, PETER, Lawyer, late of Jersey City, son of Christopher and Eleanor (Althouse) Bentley—the former of English, the latter of Dutch descent—was born at Half Moon, Saratoga county New York, September 7th, 1805. ...... he was enabled to ...... ter months in a country school-house, ... evenings by the mingled light of pine-knots and the broad open fire; but these scant advantages he utilized to the utmost, and on the slender foundation that, even when best used, they afforded he reared in after life, by determined effort, the superstructure of a liberal English and a very fair classical education. Alternating with his brief days of schooling was the wholesome exercise of outdoor life and labor upon his father's farm; and by the years thus spent in honest, hard work in the open air he acquired that physical vigor and endurance which gave him strength for his coming battle with the world. In 1825, when twenty years of age, without the aid of capital, or that of the sustaining power of influential friends, he came to Jersey City. Entering the establishment of Yates & McIntyre; who at that time owned many of the lottery grants of the country, he acquired the art of printing, and was thus brought within the sphere of the movements of that period. Here he formed an acquaintance with the members of that firm, who were then prominent men, and, with some of their successors, he was on terms of friendship until they all passed away. The profession of the law then, as now, was regarded as the way to honorable distinction and fortune. Notwithstanding his limited means of early education he determined to enter a higher position. After remaining five years with Yates & McIntyre in the early part of 1830 he began the study of the law with Samuel Cassedy, at that time the leading attorney in the old county of Bergen, which stretched from Rockland county, New York, to Kill Von Kull. Not

being an idle or ...... many of the details ...... him the business of ...... court were mere ...... erty at that time was ...... in banks and insurance companies, and the ...... justices' courts were often participated in by lawyers of the first talent in the State. That was the ...... the young professional aspirant, and ...... holders were often assembled before the ...... to settle controversies which now would be ...... volving amounts too small to merit serious attention. ...... nest, zealous, and pertinacious, he here made his ...... attracted attention, and the Dutch descendants who predominated in Bergen county, soon became acqu...... and appreciated his sterling qualities. The confidence the Dutch thus early reposed in his integrity and worth remained unshaken throughout his entire life. Squire Paradise, as he was called, a peculiar and eccentric man, who had a personal deformity from a curvature of the spine near the neck, held his court as a justice of the peace in York street, at Pawles Hook, and Mr. Bentley, from his efficiency ...... Clay ...... the early title of the municipal corporation. He was admitted to the bar of New Jersey in the May term of the Supreme Court, 1834, and took the degree of Counsellor in September term, 1839. He at once showed his sagacity. The Pawles Hook ferry was then at the foot of Grand street. On that street stood Billy Anderson's tavern, the proprietor of which was famous in those days for his humor and drollery, and along it passed all the travel to New York from the counties of Essex and ...... and a large part of the county of Bergen. On this street, the first square from the ferry, he purchased a lot and erected a neat and commodious office. His success was almost immediate. Many matters of ...... trusted to him in the first few years of his practice, and his able management of these gave him a permanent standing at the bar. ...... the breath of ...... death, the ...... from his hands the simple reason that he ...... trusted, and could display ...... He had an instinct of success which made ...... What he could do himself he could do ...... and he always in his cases showed his judgment in selecting the best assistants. He was ...... master of chancery. He came early in contact with the leading men in the profession, by calling ...... on the important cases in which he was engaged; and his practical judgment and acumen were

Farling. He received his degree of M. D. while the American war of the Revolution was in progress; and sympathizing heartily with the cause of the rebel colonies, he immigrated to this country and entered the Continental army. He was soon promoted to be Surgeon, and in this capacity served until peace was declared. When the army was disbanded, he settled at Frenchtown, where his exceptionally thorough education, and his extensive surgical experience during the war, combined to throw into his hands a very large practice. Here he married Rachel, youngest daughter of Jeremiah Thatcher, by whom he had two children. He remained actively engaged in his profession until 1812, when he was prostrated by a stroke of paralysis. From this he never entirely recovered, and his death, following a second stroke, occurred in August, 1818.

ENTLEY, PETER, Lawyer, late of Jersey City, son of Christopher and Eleanor (Althouse) Bentley— the former of English, the latter of Dutch descent —was born at Half Moon, Saratoga county, New York, September 7th, 1805. In his early youth he was enabled to receive but little knowledge from books, only such as could be gathered during the winter months in a country school-house, and in the winter evenings by the mingled light of pine-knots and the broad open fire; but these scant advantages he utilized to the utmost, and on the slender foundation that, even when best used, they afforded he reared in after life, by determined effort, the superstructure of a liberal English and a very fair classical education. Alternating with his brief days of schooling was the wholesome exercise of outdoor life and labor upon his father's farm; and by the years thus spent in honest, hard work in the open air he acquired that physical vigor and endurance which gave him strength for his coming battle with the world. In 1825, when twenty years of age, without the aid of capital, or that of the sustaining power of influential friends, he came to Jersey City. Entering the establishment of Yates & McIntyre, who at that time owned many of the lottery grants of the country, he acquired the art of printing, and was thus brought within the sphere of the movements of that period. Here he formed an acquaintance with the members of that firm, who were then prominent men, and, with some of their successors, he was on terms of friendship until they all passed away. The profession of the law then, as now, was regarded as the way to honorable distinction and fortune. Notwithstanding his limited means of early education he determined to enter a higher position. After remaining five years with Yates & McIntyre, in the early part of 1830 he began the study of the law with Samuel Cassedy, at that time the leading attorney in the old county of Bergen, which stretched from Rockland county, New York, to Kill Von Kull. Not

being an idle or mere formal student, he took charge of many of the details of office business. His preceptor gave him the business of the justices' courts. Affairs in that court were more important then than now. Personal property at that time was confined chiefly to mortgages, shares in banks and insurance companies, and the struggles in the justices' courts were often participated in by lawyers of the first talent in the State. That was the training-ground for the young professional aspirant; and six or twelve freeholders were often assembled before the magistrate as jurors, to settle controversies which now would be regarded as involving amounts too small to merit serious attention. Earnest, zealous, and pertinacious, he here made his mark and attracted attention, and the Dutch descendants, who predominated in Bergen county, soon became acquainted with and appreciated his sterling qualities. The confidence that the Dutch thus early reposed in his ability and worth remained unshaken throughout his entire life. Squire Paradise, as he was called, a peculiar and eccentric man, who had a personal deformity from a curvature of the spine near the neck, held his court as a justice of the peace in York street, at Pawles Hook; and Mr. Bentley, from his efficiency and zeal, while yet a law student, became the Attorney-General in that tribunal. His native sagacity and practical sense supplied the want of erudition; and confidence, the parent of success, was here acquired. In 1833 he was Clerk of the Board of Select Men of Jersey City, that being the early title of the municipal corporation. He was admitted to the bar of New Jersey in the May term of the Supreme Court, 1834, and took the degree of Counsellor in September term, 1839. He at once showed his sagacity. The Pawles Hook ferry was then at the foot of Grand street. On that street stood Billy Anderson's tavern, the proprietor of which was famous in those days for his humor and drollery, and along it passed all the travel to New York from the counties of Essex and Middlesex, and a large part of the county of Bergen. On this street, in the first square from the ferry, he purchased a lot and there erected a neat and commodious office. His success was almost immediate. Many matters of importance were intrusted to him in the first few years of his practice, and his able management of these gave him a permanent standing at the bar. His Dutch clients constantly increased, and he invested their money on bond and mortgage; managed and settled their estates when the ownership was changed by death, and money flowed into his hands from the simple reason that he showed that he could be trusted, and could display sagacity in its use. He had an element of success which marks all able men. What he could not do himself he could find the right man to do, and he always in his cases showed his judgment by selecting the best assistants. He was essentially a manager of affairs. He came early in contact with the leading men in the profession, by calling in their assistance in the important cases in which he was engaged, and his practical judgment and acumen were always most valuable aids in any controversy. He became the attorney of the Select Men of Jersey City, and was engaged in the celebrated cause of The Select Men against Dummer, in which, in 1842, the doctrine of dedication by maps was decided. In 1843 he was elected Mayor of Jersey City. Such a selection at that period was not so much a matter of party success as an expression of confidence and good-will among neighbors. In his temperament he was earnest and zealous; and this quality imported force and energy to his character. He had one rare quality to a rare degree. He stuck to his friends. He would turn out of his way to render assistance to those who, when he was struggling to rise, aided him; and the children of his benefactors, unaware of the motives which impelled him, were frequently helped in the time of need. Though never claiming to be deeply read, he possessed a good working library, and took pleasure in keeping it up. He was familiar with where to find the needed information, and with a few practical suggestions and directions, urged students to work out their own difficulties. His advice was sound and practical. He had a quick and excellent perception of the right of a case, and of its reasonable probabilities. He was noted for bringing about settlements, and fought his clients' battles as cunningly and with as much tact, ingenuity and success in office conferences as many others do before the court. His shrewd judgment of the probabilities of success was well shown (in 1843) in his adoption, with persistent energy and confidence, of the celebrated case of Mrs. Bell, involving the question of the right of the State to lands below high-water mark. After twelve or fourteen years of contest, in which he secured the aid of some of the ablest counsel in the State, and when it seemed likely that final success in the United States Supreme Court would justify his views, a satisfactory settlement was reached. The sale of the valuable rights in question to the Long Dock Company initiated the series of vast improvements which now line the Jersey City shores for miles, and whatever may be said of the sure result, sooner or later, of the natural advantages of this shore, the persistent energy of Mr. Bentley greatly aided in hastening the advent of these improvements. Banking facilities thirty years ago were rare in Jersey City. The old North River Bank, in Greenwich street, was generally the resort of Jerseymen on the west banks of the Hudson. The banking enterprises in Bergen county had generally been disastrous. The Hudson County Bank was founded in the year 1851, and Mr. Bentley conceiving the need of another institution, and having, as already stated, the confidence of capitalists, organized the Mechanics' and Traders' Bank in the year 1853, and became its President. He evinced in that position his usual ability, and though he retired from that office on account of the conduct of others, who did not fully appreciate the delicacy of their position, the institution prospered under his management and won the confidence of the public. He became a prominent Trustee in the Provident Institution for

Savings in Jersey City, and was its legal adviser to the time of his death. His general advice was to invest in land, and instead of trusting to investments in corporations his maxim was, that he could best manage his own capital. In the purchase of lands, his preference was to acquire those on which there were some improvements, that interest and taxes might not absorb the value of the investment; a rule the soundness of which has been demonstrated by the disasters of recent times. While in the pursuit of business he had a maxim, which with him was successful in practice: that to get in debt for that which was fully equivalent to the responsibility incurred, stimulated to exertion, and led to success. On the 13th of October, 1842, he married Margaret E., daughter of John W. Holmes, of Jersey City, who was of English descent. His married life was harmonious, and he derived from that source an incentive to activity and progress. The strength and confidence which a man of well-constituted mind derives from happy domestic relations lead to great exertions; and the conviction that disaster will wreck more than one introduces the elements of prudence and caution. In the year 1854 he made a purchase of lands on the western slope of Bergen Hill, and there erected a commodious residence. This was his home for the remainder of his life; and some relative, some friend or neighbor could daily be found under his hospitable roof. His wife, a lady of cultivated manners and kindly disposition, contributed her share to the entertainments. He had two children, a son and a daughter, and he lived to see his son engage in the profession that he himself so long had honored, and to see his children's children grow up around him. He thus enjoyed that paternal pride which in imagination looks forward to future generations to perpetuate a name, and to whom he could transmit the fruits of his labors. Opposed to municipal extravagance, Mr. Bentley took an active part in all those plans designed to protect property from unnecessary taxes and wasteful assessments. Finding that extravagant and unjust assessments, provocative of serious litigation, had been imposed on property in Jersey City, he conceived in 1873 the plan of creating a commission, to be composed of men of high character, who should be empowered to review all such cases; and adjust them on sound and equitable principles. With his usual energy he carried his project before the Legislature; had a commission appointed, of which Judge Haines, who had been the Governor of the State, and Justice of the Supreme Court, was made the head; and the result was a more just and proper distribution of the public burthens, and the assessments having been fairly established have been for the most part collected. Instead of shrinking from responsibility he was ever ready to oppose projects designed to oppress the property-holder, and on many occasions he showed how much success could be obtained by earnest and persevering effort. He was Treasurer of the Jersey City and Bergen Plank Road Company; a Director in the Gas Company, and at one time Treasurer; and executed many trusts relative to property where individuals were concerned. He was also Vice-President of the Savings Bank of Jersey City. Towards the close of his life he spent much time in travel; visiting Europe and the Pacific coast, and wherever he went making friends by his genial disposition. In politics he was originally a Democrat, and acted with that party; but no party ties were strong enough to control his action in a direction which his conscience did not approve; and when, in 1848, the Democratic party, at the dictation of the South, proclaimed its purpose to force slavery into all our Territories, his free spirit revolted, and uniting with similar spirits in the State, he took an active part in organizing the " Free Soil " party. Although the ticket then nominated received at the election in November following but about one hundred and forty votes in the State, the principles of that party which he then advocated took deep root in the nation, and he lived long enough to see their complete triumph in the absolute overthrow of the hated institution of slavery. In the great struggle that led to this consummation the nation contained no truer patriot or more staunch supporter than he. His patriotism, it is true, was not of that noisy and boisterous kind which characterized many who acquired a reputation for intense loyalty to the government, and found their reward in profitable contracts, moieties, and commissions; but of that quiet, retiring kind that watched passing events with intense interest, and spared not his wealth, when needed, to fill up and maintain our armies in the field. After the war was over he felt a deep interest and took an active part in politics, continuing to within but a short period of his death to give to his city and State the benefit of his counsel in public affairs. He died September, 1875. Peter Bentley was one of the active men who laid the foundations, who helped to plan the municipal corporations, and draft the laws and charters upon which the institutions of the county of Hudson have been reared; as a lawyer he was possessed of great ability, as a man, of no less great integrity, and in all relations of life he so conducted himself that at his death he left to his children that most honorable of all heritages—an unsullied name.

---◦◦◦---

ILLETTE, FIDELIO BUCKINGHAM, M. D., of Plainfield, was born in Nile, Allegany county, New York, October 30th, 1833. He is a son of the Rev. Walter Bloomfield Gillette, a Baptist clergyman. His grandfather and great-grandfather were physicians, the latter having been a Huguenot, banished from France during the religious persecutions in that country. His family, indeed, has been noted for the number of physicians and preachers it includes. When he was four years of age his father had charge of a Baptist church in Middlesex county, New Jersey, in the public schools of which he received his early education. At the age of fifteen he entered the Du Ruyter

Institute, where he remained two years, attending subsequently the Union Academy, from which he graduated in 1853, entering the same year the medical department of the University of Pennsylvania, at which he graduated in 1856. On receiving his medical diploma he settled in Belleville, New Jersey, and at once began the practice of his profession. Shortly afterwards he accepted an appointment as Surgeon on a New York and Liverpool vessel, which, on the completion of his first round voyage in her, suffered an outbreak of yellow fever while in quarantine, and, the assistant health officer failing to report, he volunteered to supply his place for the emergency, which he did so acceptably that, in recognition of his promptitude and efficiency, he was soon after appointed to fill the place regularly, receiving a commission as Assistant Health Officer of the Port of New York. This position, so honorably conferred, he held for one year. The following year he spent in perfecting his knowledge of surgical dentistry, and in the spring of 1858 settled at Dantown, New Jersey, where he remained until the breaking out of the civil war, when he was commissioned Assistant Surgeon of the 9th New Jersey Volunteers, serving with the regiment in every engagement after the battle of Newbern till the close of the war, having meanwhile been commissioned a full Surgeon. He was mustered out with the regiment at Trenton, in August, 1865. His partiality for military service, however, survived the war, and induced him not to quit the army. In November of the same year, accordingly, he reported to Dr. Goodman, Medical Director at Vicksburg, and, receiving the contract of Acting Assistant Surgeon in the United States army, was ordered to Natchez, and placed in charge of the hospital there, in which capacity he served till the spring of 1868, when he was ordered to Texas as Medical Officer on the staff of General Gillem. Arriving at Galveston, he was made Post Surgeon, filling the position for three months, after which he filled the same position at Indianola, where he remained until the post was broken up. Later he was Post Surgeon at Corpus Christi, at which, however, after a few months, the post was also broken up; whereupon he crossed the plains with his family, who had joined him just before the close of the war, to Ringgold Barracks, near Camargo, and, after remaining there a few months, proceeded to Brownsville, Texas. In July, 1872, he resigned his position in the army, and, returning to New Jersey, settled in Plainfield, principally for the sake of securing educational advantages to his children. During the second year of his residence at Plainfield he was appointed City Physician, and in 1876 was appointed County Physician for the county of Union. The checkered, rough-flowing course of his professional career at last runs smooth in the midst of peace and its triumphs. He was married, in 1856, to Sarah E. McPherson, of Salem county, New Jersey. Whilst serving with the famous Third Division in the South he had the misfortune to lose his youngest daughter, who died at Greensborough, North Carolina.

WELCH, WILLIAM M., M. D., was born, September 12th, 1837, in Bethlehem, Hunterdon county, New Jersey. His father was a farmer at Bethlehem, the family being American as far back as it has been traced. He pursued his medical studies in the University of Pennsylvania, from which he graduated in 1859, settling the following year in Philadelphia. He is a member of the Philadelphia County Medical Society, of which he was elected Treasurer in 1869; of the Northern Medical Association, of which he was President in 1869; of the Pennsylvania State Medical Society; and of the American Medical Association. He published in 1871-2 a Report on Epidemic Small-Pox, and has written a few papers, able though few, on medical topics. In the civil war he served for two years as Acting Assistant Surgeon in the United States army. He has been one of the Attending Physicians to the Northern Home for Friendless Children, in Philadelphia, since 1865; and in 1870 he was appointed Physician-in-charge of the Municipal Hospital. For five years he served as Attending Physician to the Northern Dispensary, to which he is now one of the consulting physicians. He was for five years a member of the Medical Board of the Charity Hospital. He was married in 1863.

KENNEDY, HON. HENRY R., ex-State Senator, was born at Kennedyville, Greenwich township, Warren county, New Jersey, on the 10th of January, A. D. 1815. He is the only remaining son of Judge Robert H. Kennedy, and grandson of Robert Kennedy, who was of Scottish descent, and emigrated to America with his father in 1748, and located first near Tinicum, Bucks county, Pennsylvania; thence he removed in the year 1770 to Greenwich township, Warren county, New Jersey, and finally settled on the Powhatcong creek, where he built a flour mill; and when the Revolution against Great Britain occurred, Robert Kennedy placed himself and his mills at the service of his country, acting in the capacity of Brigade Wagon Master under General Washington; filling orders for flour and feed from his mills 'to the army at Morristown and the Short Hills, discharging his duties faithfully during the war, and thereafter lived a quiet and unostentatious life, loved and revered for his kindness and benevolence. He died in 1812, and was interred in Greenwich cemetery, where in a plot forty feet square lie the remains of General William Maxwell, Captain John Maxwell, Captain Benjamin McCullough, Conrad Davis, Thomas Kennedy and William Kennedy, brave and honored men of the Revolution. Robert H. Kennedy, born in 1787, succeeded to the beautiful homestead on the Powhatcong, being endowed with a kindly heart, which, in connection with his urbanity of manner and noble deportment, secured him the regard and esteem of all. He early became the ensample of benevolence in the Presbyterian Church, and every call of charity met his prompt response. He served his township and county in divers official capacities, and in 1835 was elected to State Council for Warren county, being returned for a term of four years, faithfully fulfilling the trusts confided to him. He died in 1859, and lies buried in the family plot in Greenwich cemetery. The mother of Henry R. Kennedy, the subject of this sketch, was the youngest daughter of John Key, Esq., who, with his brother Francis Key, the author of the "Star-Spangled Banner," took an active part for American freedom. Senator Kennedy was at an early age placed under the care and tuition of the Rev. John Vanderveer, of Easton, Pennsylvania, and completed his academic course at Rutgers College. He married in 1838 a daughter of General John Frelinghuysen. Mr. Kennedy being gifted with a goodly portion of the genial temperament and integrity of character so prominent in his father's career, early attained the respect and confidence of the community in which he has served. Reared in the Presbyterian faith, he united with the church in early life. He has served in the capacity of Ruling Elder nearly twenty years, liberally and conscientiously discharging the important duties of the position. He has served in many official positions, and has won the trust and confidence of those he serves. In the year 1863 he was elected to the Senate of New Jersey, and served three years in that body, to the satisfaction of his constituents. For a number of years he has been one of the Board of Managers of the State Lunatic Asylum at Trenton; is President of the Bloomsbury National Bank, and Chaplain of the H. R. Kennedy Lodge, A. F. and A. M., named in honor of him.

DUER, EDWARD LOUIS, M. D., was born, January 19th, 1836, at Crosswicks, Burlington county, New Jersey. He is a son of Dr. George S. Duer, of New Jersey, being of Scottish ancestry. He was educated at Yale College, from which he graduated in 1857, studying medicine at the University of Pennsylvania, and graduating from the medical department of that institution in 1860. For two years he was Resident Physician of the Philadelphia Hospital, after which he practised medicine with his father for one year, when he settled permanently in Philadelphia. His specialty is obstetrics and diseases of women. He is a member of the College of Physicians; of the Pathological Society; of the Obstetrical Society, and of numerous other societies. He has written only a few short papers, which, however, suffice to show that he should write more, as he doubtless will when increased years have somewhat abated his ardor in the practice for which, notwithstanding his fine attainments and thorough culture, he has a manifest and decided preference. He was for three years Acting Assistant Surgeon in the United States army. He is Accoucheur and Clinical Lecturer on Diseases of Women and Children, and Visiting Physician to the Preston Retreat, as also to the State Hospital for Women. He was married, October 29th, 1863, to Miss Naudain, of Philadelphia.

ONDICT, REV. IRA, Vice-President of Rutgers College, Trustee of Princeton College, late of New Jersey, was a graduate of Princeton, and, after the completion of his studies at that institution, engaged in teaching school in Freehold. He afterward studied theology with Rev. John Woodhull. In April, 1786, he was licensed by the Presbytery of New Brunswick, and in 1787 installed pastor of the Presbyterian Churches of Newton and Shappenac, New Jersey. In 1793 he became pastor of the Reformed Dutch Church in New Brunswick. At the revival of Queen's College, afterwards Rutgers, in 1808, in effecting which he had an important agency, he was chosen Vice-President. Dr. Livingstone was the President, but the office was a nominal one, as he confined himself almost exclusively to his theological professorship, so that his colleague was virtually the President until his decease in 1811. He had a strong, athletic frame, and was considerably above the medium height; had dark eyes and hair, with an expression of countenance which indicated a vigorous masculine intellect. He was a man of great reserve and remarkable gravity.

HANDLER, THOMAS BRADBURY, D. D., Protestant Episcopal Clergyman, late of Elizabethtown, New Jersey, was born at Woodstock, Connecticut, April 26th, 1726. He was a descendant of William Chandler, who, with his wife, Hannah, and four children, Hannah, Thomas, John and William, came to this country from England, and settled at Roxbury, Massachusetts, in 1637. His son John, born in England in 1635, united in 1686 with several of his neighbors in the settlement of Woodstock, Connecticut, of the church of which he was chosen deacon, and where he died April 15th, 1703. Thomas' early years were spent on the paternal farm, and he graduated at Yale College in 1745. In 1747 he was invited to serve as Catechist at North Castle and Bedford, Westchester county, New York, but declined in favor of St. Peter's Church, Westchester. Immediately after the decease of Rev. Mr. Vaughan, however, he went to St. John's, in Elizabeth, New Jersey, about the 1st of December, 1747, and, highly recommended, was appointed by the "Venerable Society," in May, 1748, their

63

Catechist at Elizabethtown, New Jersey, on a stipend of ten pounds per year, the church obliging themselves, in case he should be appointed to the mission, "to raise the sum of fifty pounds current money of the province per annum," in addition, and to provide him a convenient parsonage. On the 11th of December, 1749, the church purchased of Captain John Emott, step-son of Mr. Vaughan, and son-in-law of Elias Boudinot, Sr., for a hundred and sixty-two pounds, a parsonage lot of about four acres, with the old dwelling-house built in 1696-97 by Andrew Hampton. The wardens at this time were John Halsted and Henry Garthwait, and the vestrymen William Ricketts, Jacob De' Hart, Peter Trembly, Matthias De Hart, Jonathan Hampton, and Matthias Williamson. During the same year Rev. Mr. Wood was appointed missionary to New Brunswick, with instructions to "spend a Sunday or two every month at Elizabethtown." At the close of May, 1750, that minister had made but two visits to the town, his duty at New Brunswick permitting him to officiate there only on every fourth Sunday. The most urgent representations were then made to the society for a resident rector, one who could give them his whole time, and Mr. Chandler, in response, was appointed in 1750 to be their missionary at Elizabeth, if, upon his arrival in England, "he shall be found worthy to be ordained a deacon and priest." Among the considerations urged was the fact that "the Dissenters in this town have five ministers settled, constantly to officiate in publick, to visit them in private, ready to serve on any particular occasion, and, in a word, that are always in and among them." In the summer of 1751 he repaired to England, was admitted to the priesthood by Dr. Thomas Sherlock, Bishop of London, and early in September sailed again for America, arriving at home, after a passage of nine weeks, about the 1st of November. His salary was fixed at thirty pounds sterling from the society, and sixty pounds New Jersey currency, with a house and glebe from the people. At the close of 1754 the congregation included eighty-five families, and communicants numbered ninety. In 1757, during the prevalence of the small-pox, he was prostrated by the terrible scourge, and did not recover from its ill effects for nearly three years. In addition to his labors here as parish priest, he performed a large amount of missionary work in visiting and officiating in the remote parts of the town back of the mountains, and in the town of Woodbridge. His ministrations at the latter place, at the commencement of the year 1762, had required of him more than three thousand miles of travel, and nearly two hundred sermons, for all of which he had received in gratuities not more than five guineas. As he had been bred an Independent, and had in early youth become a convert to Episcopacy, "it was natural for him to magnify the importance of the Episcopal peculiarities." With all the zeal, therefore, of a proselyte, he sought to widen rather than to narrow the breach between "the church" and "the meeting." This object he sought to promote principally by the circulation of controversial tracts, copies of which he desired might be sent him from abroad. "But that supply being precarious, his own pen was presently called into action." On the occasion of Rev. George Whitefield's visit to Elizabeth in November, 1763, he refused to grant him the use of his pulpit. Popular as he was among all classes, this refusal created a division in the parish, and many people were offended at what they considered a discourteous action. The number of communicants was reduced to about seventy-five, of whom seldom more than fifty were gathered together at one time. The revival of religion which prevailed in the town during 1764 also tended to embarrass him in his ministrations, opposed as he was to everything of the kind. Matters began to wear a more hopeful appearance at the close of the ensuing half year; the church services were better attended, and an enlargement of the parsonage was provided for by a generous subscription. But, at the opening of the following year, he was constrained, in consequence of the stamp act agitation, then at its height, to feel and say that "the duty of an Episcopal missionary in this country is now become more difficult than ever." While deprecating the continuance of the policy of the government, he still professed his fixed resolution to abide by the cause of Parliament rather than by that of the people—a resolution from which he never swerved. In 1766 the University of Oxford conferred on him, at the solicitation of Rev. Dr. Johnson, of New York, the degree of Doctor of Divinity. Up to this time he had published nothing. The struggle in reference to an American Episcopate was now in progress, and exciting deep and wide-spread interest. Several pamphlets had already appeared on both sides, from the pens of Mr. Apthorp and Drs. Johnson and Caner for, and of Dr. Mayhew against the project. At the request of Dr. Johnson, whose infirmities would not allow of his undertaking the work himself, and by appointment of the clergy of New York and New Jersey, met in convention at Shrewsbury, October 1st, 1767, he, "stimulated thereto, doubtless, by the anti-Episcopal Convention at East-town in November," prepared and published in New York in June, 1767, his "Appeal to the Public in behalf of the Church of England in America: Wherein the Original and Nature of the Episcopal Office are briefly considered, Reasons for sending Bishops to America are Assigned, the Plan on which it is proposed to send them is stated, and the objections against sending them are obviated and confuted." Rev. Dr. Charles Channey, of Boston, Massachusetts, responded, 1768, in a pamphlet entitled "The Appeal to the Public Answered, in behalf of the non-Episcopal Churches in America, containing Remarks on what Dr. Thomas Bradbury Chandler has advanced," etc. Soon after this he published "The Appeal Defended, or The Proposed American Episcopate Vindicated," etc. This drew forth a rejoinder from Dr. Channey, January, 1770, with the title: "Reply to Dr. T. B. Chandler's Appeal Defended," which was answered in 1771 in a pamphlet of two hundred and forty pages, entitled "The Appeal

Farther Defended, in answer to the farther Misrepresentations of Dr. Channey." Notwithstanding this pamphlet controversy, he continued in the regular discharge of his parochial duties, occasionally going forth on missionary tours. In July, 1770, he refers to the fact that "the Dissenters, of late, have become more friendly in appearance than ever," sometimes exceeding in number, in their attendance on special occasions, his own people. In the course of the two or three following years, the congregation had increased so greatly as to determine the people to enlarge the capacity of the church edifice. In 1774, however, it was resolved to erect an entirely new building; materials were collected, and money subscribed to defray the expenses. But the first shock of war put an end to the work, not to be resumed by that generation. He then found his situation painful and unpleasant, as well from the active part which he deemed it his duty to take, as from the violent feeling generally entertained against the church of which he was a minister. These considerations caused him to think of leaving the colonies and crossing over again to England. Just before his departure he received a letter from John Pownall, Under-Secretary of State, bearing date April 5th, 1775, as follows: "I am directed by the Earl of Dartmouth to acquaint you that His Majesty has been graciously pleased, from a consideration of your merit and services, to signify His Commands to the Lords Commissioners of the Treasury that they do make an allowance to you, out of such funds as their Lordships shall think proper, of two hundred pounds per annum, the said allowance to commence from the first of January last." He continued to officiate in Elizabeth until the middle of May, 1775, when, probably alarmed by the sacking of the house of his friend, Dr. Myles Cooper, at New York, on the night of the 10th of May, he found refuge with him on the "Kingfisher," Captain James Montague, a British ship-of-war, lying in the harbor of New York. On the 24th of May, in company with Dr. Cooper and Rev. Samuel Cook, he sailed in the "Exeter" for Bristol, England. The congregation were then left without a supply for the pulpit; public worship was at length suspended, and the church edifice became unoccupied on the Sabbath. As houses were needed for hospitals and barracks, resort was had occasionally to the churches. The fences were used for fuel, and even wooden memorial tablets, etc., consumed in the hour of need. St. John's suffered most severely, as it was not used on the Sabbath; nearly all the wood-work of the interior was destroyed, while "two attempts to burn the building by putting fire under the pulpit were providentially defeated." About 1779 or 1780 the congregation began to reassemble in a private house for public worship on the Sabbath. After the destruction of the Presbyterian Church, in January, 1780, many, who had been accustomed to worship there, resorted to the Episcopal Church, especially when Mr. Ogden, Mrs. Caldwell's cousin, was to preach. Dr. Caldwell remained in exile the full period of ten years—a pensioner upon the royal bounty—his family continuing to occupy the rectory, as before, through all the gloomy period of the conflict. The home government gladly availed themselves of his long experience in American affairs, and often sought of him information and advice. Says Professor McVickar: "From a manuscript journal kept by Dr. Chandler during his absence, and now (1836) in the possession of the author, we find him still laboring for those whom he had left; raising funds for his destitute brethren; urging upon the government plans of conciliation, and upon the bishops with whom he seems to have lived in habits of intimate friendship the completion of his long-cherished plan of an American Episcopate." Dr. Berrian affirms that "he was received with such a marked and universal respect into the society of the most distinguished persons as has very rarely been rendered to any one from our country in private life." In the State Paper Office at London is preserved a "Petition of Thomas Bradbury Chandler, D. D., Rector of St. John's Church, Elizabethtown, New Jersey, and others, to the King," supposed to have been presented early in 1777, to the effect that "in consideration of their eminent services to His Majesty, and that, having at considerable expense discovered a tract of land on the waters of the Ohio, in the Province of Canada, the settlement of which must soon take place," they pray His Majesty to grant them a mandamus for 100,000 acres of land in the said spot. He continued to cherish "almost to the last" the expectation of the restoration of the royal authority in America; and, as late as December 3d, 1781, wrote from London to Rev. Abraham Beach, of New Brunswick, New Jersey: "The late blow in Virginia (Cornwallis's surrender) has given us a shock, but has not overset us. Though the clouds at present are rather thick about us, I am far, very far, from desponding. I think matters will take a right turn, and then the event will be right." About the year 1780 a small scab on his nose, a relic of the small-pox of 1757, developed in the form of a cancer, and gave him much concern. Every expedient for a cure proved unavailing. He spent a summer on the Isle of Wight, living mainly on goat's milk, but did not reap the anticipated benefit. In May, 1783, after the proclamation of peace, several of the Episcopal clergy of New York and Connecticut, Drs. Leaming, Inglis and Moore, with others, wrote, by Rev. Dr. Seabury—on his way to obtain the episcopate—to the Archbishop of York a letter of commendation, in which, strengthened by the warm support of Sir Guy Carleton, they requested his appointment as Bishop for the Province of Nova Scotia. It was estimated that not less than 30,000 refugee royalists had removed from the States to Nova Scotia, many of whom were from New York and its vicinity. Hence the zeal to provide an episcopate for their benefit, as very few of them pertained to any other body than the Church of England. Dr. Chandler desired the appointment, but a decision was so long delayed that he finally, pressed by the necessity of change for his health, desired to forego all claim thereto and return to his family and parish. Archbishop Moore would not consent to the abandonment, but consented that he should visit his family. He accordingly sailed for America, and reached New York, Sunday, June 19th, 1785, but found himself too infirm to resume his parochial charge. In the course of the following year the long-sought episcopate of Nova Scotia was offered him, but his health was too seriously impaired for him to think of performing its duties, and he was compelled to decline it. At his suggestion the office was conferred on his friend, Rev. Charles Inglis, D. D. He was very rarely able to perform any official services after his return, five times only officiating in the marriage service (for Elias B. Dayton, George Joy, Michael Hatfield, Aaron Ogden, and Captain Cyrus de Hart), and occasionally at a funeral. At the request of the vestry, however, he retained the rectorship and rectory as long as he lived. He was married, in 1752, to Jane Emott, daughter of Captain John Emott and Mary (Boudinot). Emott, daughter of Elias Boudinot, Sr., and died, at his home, June 17th, 1790, in the sixty-fifth year of his age. He had six children, one of whom married a son of General Elias Dayton, and another Rev. John Henry Hobart, afterward Bishop of the Diocese of New York.

DARBY, REV. JOHN, M. D., Presbyterian Minister, of Parsippany, Morris county, New Jersey, late of that place, was born in New Jersey, about 1725, and was a son, or grandson, probably, of William Darby, of Elizabethtown. He graduated at Yale College in 1748; was licensed by the Presbytery of Suffolk, Long Island, in April, 1749; and appointed to preach at Lower Aquebogue and Mattituck, remaining in this service for two years. During the ensuing six years, and more, he supplied other congregations on the island, and subsequently, November 10th, 1757, was ordained by the same Presbytery as an Evangelist at Oyster-Ponds (Orient). His ministry at Connecticut Farms commenced in 1758, and continued about two years. In 1772 he withdrew from the Presbytery of New York and connected himself with the Presbytery of Morris county. After leaving the farms he settled at Parsippany, Morris county, where he not only preached the gospel, but practised medicine, having acquired a medical education. "As such he made himself quite useful during the revolutionary war." His degree of M. D. was conferred by Dartmouth College in 1782. He died in December, 1805, aged ninety years. He was twice married. By his first wife he had one son and two daughters; the eldest, Hester, married a British officer named Fox. His second wife was Hester White Hunting, a widow of East Hampton, Long Island; by her he had one son, Henry White Darby, M. D., of Parsippany, and two daughters, Helen, wife of General O'Hara, and Lucinda, wife of Christian de Wint.

ONGSTREET, HENRY H., M. D., Physician, of Bordentown, was born, January 11th, 1819, in Monmouth county, New Jersey, and is a son of Hendrick and Mary (Holmes) Longstreet; his father was engaged during life in agricultural pursuits, and both parents were also natives of New Jersey. Dr. Longstreet received his preliminary education at a select school in the village of Middletown Point, now known as Mattawan, New Jersey, and completed the same in a seminary at Lenox, Massachusetts. Having determined to embrace the medical profession, he became a student under the supervision of Dr. Robert W. Cooke, of Holmdel, and continued his studies with Dr. John B. Beck, Professor of Materia Medica and Jurisprudence in the College of Physicians and Surgeons, in the city of New York; in which institution he subsequently attended several courses of lectures delivered there, and duly graduated with the degree of Doctor of Medicine in 1842. In the month of May of that year he commenced the practice of his profession at Bordentown, New Jersey, where he has since continued to reside, and where he has been constantly engaged in the control of an extensive and lucrative practice; and during all this time, being over one-third of a century, has never been absent three months altogether from the scene of his labors. He is thoroughly devoted to his profession, and takes great interest in the several medical societies with which he is connected; and has held many offices in both the County and State Medical Societies, having been a delegate to the latter organization very many times. He has also been prominently identified with all the improvements that have been projected in and around Bordentown since he first became a resident, and is at present a Director of the Bordentown Banking Company; also in the Water Company, and of the Vincentown Mail Company. In political belief he is a strong and ardent Democrat, but is not an active worker in the party, as his time is wholly engrossed by his professional duties. He was married, in 1848, to Hannah Ann Taylor, of New Jersey, who died in 1857. He was married a second time, in 1869, to Elizabeth, daughter of the late Joseph Newbold, an old merchant of Wrightstown, New Jersey.

OOD, GEORGE, Lawyer, late of New York, was born in Burlington county, New Jersey, about 1780; graduated at Princeton in 1808; studied law under the supervision of Richard Stockton, and was admitted to the bar in 1812, taking up his residence in New Brunswick, New Jersey. "It was not long before he rivalled his master, to whom in some respects he was superior. His intellect was of the highest order, entitling him to rank with Mr. Webster. His power of analogical reasoning was very striking; the most difficult subject seemed to arrange itself in his mind in its true pro-

portions. He had the faculty attributed to Lord Mansfield, of so stating a question as to make the mere statement a sufficient argument."—Hon. L. Q. C. Elmer. He generally spoke from mere short memoranda in pencil, and was so accurate in the use of language that what he said would, when written down, prove entirely correct. After a few years practice at the bar of New Jersey he removed to New York, where he took rank among the leaders, and showed himself the equal of all, if not their superior. Until his death in 1860, he was constantly engaged in the most important causes, not only in New York but in other States; and was among the few eminent lawyers of the country who held no office. Upon the decease of Judge Thompson in 1845, he was strongly recommended to President Tyler to take his place on the bench of the Supreme Court of the United States, and "there can be no doubt he would have adorned the station." His political education inclined him to take sides with Federalist views and measures, but he never manifested any marked desire to interest himself personally in the political questions or conflicts of the day, and never supported the Republican party. Not long before his demise he spoke at a public meeting in New York, strongly in favor of maintaining the compromises of the constitution, and thus obtained from several of the Radical papers the honorable and honoring designation of "Union-Saver." "In my early practice it was my fortune several times to encounter him at the bar, and a most formidable adversary he was: The last time I heard him was in the year 1855, when he appeared before the New Jersey Court of Appeals, in the case of Gifford vs. Thorn, reported in 1 Stock. 708. I have always thought his speech in that case, upon the whole, the ablest to which I ever listened. It combined almost every kind of eloquence; in solid reasoning quite equal to that of his leading opponent, Charles O'Connor; in playful wit, in occasional appeals to the sympathy of the judges, and in impassioned declamation quite superior." On one noteworthy occasion, Mr. Van Arsdale, an old lawyer of Newark, was his opponent in a case which was conducted with singular dexterity. He had filed a bill to foreclose a mortgage more than twenty years due; and set out with great particularity several payments alleged to have been made on it by the mortgageor. The answer sworn to by Van Arsdale positively denied the alleged payments, and denied also that any payments had been made. When he took the ground on the argument that, after twenty years, payment of a debt was to be presumed, the chancellor remarked with an amused smile, "How can I presume a payment which the party himself positively denies?" The dilemma seemed then for the first time to be perceived by the counsel, and the ludicrous manner in which he exclaimed, "Is my client to lose his money by such a trick as that?" caused a general laugh, in which the court could not help participating. One of the more remarkable cases in which he was engaged was that of Smith vs. Wood, a bill in chancery for the sale of mortgaged premises to raise a large sum of money. It lasted

Engraved by J.D. Mitchell

Henry H. Longstreet M.D.

Henry H. Longstreet M. D.

ten years, and was argued nine times—three times before a master; once before Chancellor Williamson, who went out of office before he had time to make a decree; once before Chancellor Vroom, whose opinion is reported in Saxton Ch. R. 74; three times before the Court of Errors and Appeals; and once before Chancellor Philemon Dickerson. He died in New York in 1860.

IRKPATRICK, HENRY AUGUSTUS, M. D., late of Stanton, Hunterdon county, New Jersey, son of the Rev. Jacob Kirkpatrick, D. D., for more than half a century pastor of the United Presbyterian Churches of Amwell, Hunterdon county, was born in 1816. Having read medicine in the office of Dr. Cicero Hunt, of Ringoes, he entered the Jefferson Medical College, was graduated thence M. D. in the spring of 1841, and in the same year established himself at Stanton. During the remaining ten years of his life he acquired a large practice, being skilful as a physician and popular as a man. He was twice married: first to Mary Servis, of Ringoes, and second to the daughter of Mr. Jacques Quick, of Readington. He died September 29th, 1851.

RIFFIN, REV. EDWARD DORR, late of Newark, formerly pastor of the First and later of the Second Presbyterian Church of that city, and for some years President of Williams College, was born in East Haddam, Connecticut, January 6th, 1770. His father, George Griffin, was a wealthy farmer of a strong mind and a good education; his mother, Eve (Dorr) Griffin, was a sister of Rev. Edward Dorr, of Hartford, Connecticut. From a very early age his parents destined him to the ministry; and while yet a child of only four or five years he was the subject of deep religious impressions. "But though once and again strongly exercised on the subject of religion, and once to such an extent as to venture for a time to hope he was a true Christian, his conversion does not appear to have taken place till after the close of his course in college, when he had abandoned the purpose with which his early training and his parents' wishes had inspired him, and, according to his own account, devoted himself to the law, and made up his mind to be a man of the world." The means of awakening him to a just sense of his spiritual need was a severe illness with which he was overtaken in the gayest period of his life. Having given his heart to God, he now resolved to resume his original purpose, and devote himself to the service of Christ in the work of the ministry. He graduated with the first honors of his class at Yale College in 1790, became a member of the church in Derby in the spring of 1792, and having pursued his theological studies under the direction of Dr. Jonathan Edwards, son of the first President Edwards, at New Haven, was licensed to preach the gospel by the Association of New Haven West, on the 31st of October, 1792. On the 10th of November following, he preached his first sermon, and having supplied several pulpits for varying periods of time in New Salem, Farmington, Middlebury, and other places, in one of which he received a call, but did not actually settle, he was ordained as pastor of the church in New Hartford, June 4th, 1795. There he remained, carrying on the work of the ministry with marked success, till 1800, when he departed on a journey on account of his wife's health, and spent the ensuing winter in the vicinity of Newark, New Jersey. The people of Orange, where he preached during a part of this period, and where fifty persons were added to the church under his ministrations, were desirous of inviting him to become their pastor; but on the reception of a call from the First Church in Newark his pastoral relations with the church in Hartford were dissolved, and he was installed as colleague pastor with Dr. Macwhorter by the Presbytery of New York on the 20th of October, 1801, in the thirty-second year of his age. Dr. Macwhorter presided, Dr. McKnight preached a sermon from 2 Corinthians ii. 16, the last clause, and Dr. Rodgers gave the charge to the people. He took the charge of this congregation in the full spirit of a new era in the church's history, which he thoroughly believed began to dawn about the time of his entrance upon the ministry, and was destined to culminate only in the meridian of millennial glory. This belief he lost no opportunity of expressing in the strongest terms. " In the year 1792," said he, " three series of events commenced, which needed not a fourth to fill the earth with the knowledge of glory of the Lord. First, the series of missionary and charitable efforts. . . . Secondly, the series of revivals of religion. . . . Thirdly, the series of judgments intended to destroy the nations which had given their power and strength to the beast." This belief, says Dr. J. F. Stearns, acting upon a lively imagination, an enthusiastic temperament, a powerful intellect, and an affectionate and devoutly pious heart, is the true key to many of the peculiar excellencies, and to what some may be disposed to mention as the peculiar defects of his character and actions. It nerved his strength, it fired his eloquence, it animated his hopes anew, when his heart would otherwise have sunk under discouragement; it made him bold in discarding obsolete customs, and regardless of trifling difficulties, in carrying into effect what he considered as the best measures for the conversion of men, and the advancement of the kingdom of Christ. With these impulses was his whole ministry identified in an eminent degree. No sooner did he begin to preach than converts began to be numbered by hundreds. This was also the case in New Haven, when he was preaching there, even before his ordination; and likewise in East Hartford, during his mission of five years in that place; and in Orange, where he spent the winter just before his invitation to Newark. His ministry in the last mentioned city, too, was exceedingly rich in spiritual fruits; and the next year after he entered upon his pastoral duties a sweeping revival occurred. It continued two years, and about one hundred and thirty persons were added to the church on profession, of whom one hundred were received in the course of twelve months. In the spring of 1803 he engaged zealously in making preaching tours in the neighborhood of Newark, and even to a considerable distance in the surrounding regions, leaving the pulpit in the care of his venerable colleague. The present (1853) parsonage house, on Mulberry street, was built about this time for his and his family's accommodation. The old one was a stone building two stories high, and stood upon the west side of Broad street, below the corner of William street. The site of the new structure was purchased of Rev. Aaron Burr. In the spring of 1807 commenced a very powerful effusion of divine influences. A deep impression had been made upon the congregation by the death of Dr. Macwhorter, and it was confirmed and made more intense through the labors of Rev. Gideon Blackburn, who preached in Newark several times with stirring earnestness. The influence was felt in Orange and Newark at the same time, and during the month of March, 1808, ninety-seven persons joined the church in Newark, and seventy-two that in Orange. But his ministry in this church, recent as it was, was now drawing to a close. As early as the year 1805 he had been invited to leave his post for the purpose of taking charge of the First Reformed Dutch Church in Albany; but that call, though it cost him no little doubt and perplexity, he at length judged it his duty to decline. But later, two invitations, each having attached peculiar claims, pressed themselves simultaneously on his attention—one to the chair of Pulpit Eloquence in the Theological Seminary in Andover, the other to become the stated preacher in the New Church in Park street, Boston. The path of duty seemed plain; and, having first obtained the consent of his people, he was released from his pastoral charge in April, 1809, and, on the 28th of May following, took a solemn leave of his flock in an eloquent farewell sermon. "During the eight years of his ministry in this congregation, less than two of which he was the sole pastor, sixty-two persons were received into the church from other churches, and three hundred and seventy-two on a profession of their faith. When he came here the church consisted of two hundred and two members. During his ministry the number had more than doubled, including, when he took his dismission, five hundred and twenty-two persons." He left Newark, May 29th, 1809, taking with him five young men who had consecrated themselves to the work of the ministry under his influence; and who were desirous of availing themselves of his instruction in his new sphere of service. He was inaugurated to the office of Professor in Andover, June 21st, and held that station two years, preaching at the same time on the Sabbath to the church in Boston. But, finding it impossible to fulfil the duties of both offices, he eventually resigned his professorship, and was installed as pastor of the Park Street Church, Boston, July 31st, 1811. In the summer of 1815 he left his charge

in Boston, and became the pastor of the Second Presbyterian Church in Newark, New Jersey, where he remained about six years. In October, 1821, he assumed the Presidency of Williams College, whose duties he discharged with eminent success during a period of fifteen years. "And now, the evening of life drawing on, he returned to Newark, to which he still looked, amidst all his changes, as the home of his affections; and, becoming an inmate of his eldest daughter's family, he passed the little remnant of his days in domestic love and cheerfulness, and died in hope, November 8th, 1837, in the sixty-eighth year of his age." He was married, May 17th, 1796, to Frances Huntington, daughter of Rev. Joshua Huntington, D. D., of Coventry, and adopted daughter of her uncle, Governor Samuel Huntington, of Norwich, Connecticut.

BUCHANAN, JAMES, Lawyer, was born at Ringoes, New Jersey, June 17th, 1839. He is the son of Samuel Buchanan, a farmer, of Hunterdon county. His family is of Scotch origin, having emigrated to this country several years previous to the Revolution. He was educated in the public schools of Hunterdon, and at the Clinton Academy in Clinton. In 1860 he began the study of law with the Hon. J. T. Bird, of Flemington; and in 1863, having fairly mastered the principles of the science under his able preceptor, entered the law school of the Albany University, in which he remained until 1864, when he was admitted to the bar of his native State. He at once began the practice of his profession at Trenton, where he has since resided. In 1866, before his practice had become absorbing, he was elected Reading Clerk of the New Jersey Assembly, serving during the session of that year, but, in consequence of the rapid increase of his practice, declining a re-election offered to him. In 1868 he was admitted to practise in the United States Circuit Court, as in the previous year he had been admitted to the United States District Court, and in these courts he rapidly established an extensive practice. His vivid conception of the great principles of the law, and his skill in applying them, combined with his resources as an advocate, and his force and persuasiveness as a speaker, made him a prominent figure at the bar. He was elected in 1868 a member of the Trenton School Board, in which he served two years, declining a re-election. In 1872 he was a member of the Republican National Convention that renominated General Grant; and in 1874 was appointed by the New Jersey Legislature to succeed Judge Reed as Law Judge of the County of Mercer, a position which he still holds. The University of Lewisburg, Pennsylvania, in recognition of his learning and ability, conferred on him in 1875 the honorary degree of A. M. In his activities, as in his sympathies, he is many-sided, taking not only a lively interest, but an active part in all the more important movements of society. He is a member of the Trenton Board of Trade; one of the Trustees of the Peddie Institution; and has been since 1873 President of the State Convention of the New Jersey Baptists. He was married in 1873 to Mary Isabel Bullock, of Flemington, New Jersey.

OLLESON, HON. GEORGE P., Lawyer, Attorney-General of the State of New Jersey, late of New Brunswick, was born in New Jersey, May 25th, 1805, and was the son of Elias Molleson, a descendant from one of the twenty-four proprietors of East Jersey. Upon embracing the profession of the law, he met with much and merited success, and, the possessor of promising talents and popular manners, rapidly attained distinction as a practitioner of thorough skill and ability. He was chosen three times successively to the lower house of Assembly, and there took a prominent and leading part in the current measures and movements. Declining a re-election, he was appointed Prosecuting Attorney for the County of Middlesex, from which post he was, in the course of the following year, promoted to the more important office of Attorney-General of the State. During the three years in which he held this station, he acquitted himself with great credit in the midst of unusually arduous and harassing circumstances. It was about the year 1837 that he became deeply sensible of the value of religion. In the church he grew to be a decided favorite, on account of his many amiable qualities. He was chosen Superintendent of the Sabbath-school, which flourished greatly under his care; and, March 5th, 1843, was ordained Ruling Elder. "His personal popularity, his honored ancestry, his affable manners, and his evident sincerity, gave him unbounded influence; his presence was everywhere welcome, and his persuasions were sufficient to reconcile contending parties. Thus he gave fair promise of usefulness, when his career was suddenly arrested by that mandate which none can resist. His disease was the same as that which carried off his father—dropsy on the chest." He died May 17th, 1844, in the thirty-ninth year of his age.

INNICKSON, HON. CLEMENT H., Lawyer, of Salem, was born in Salem county, New Jersey, September 16th, 1834, where the family have long been residents, one of his great-uncles having served as member of Congress from the same county as early as 1789. His uncle, Thomas Sinnickson, also from the same county, was elected to Congress from the same district in 1828. Clement H. graduated at Union College, New York, with the class of 1855, and the same year commenced his preparation for the bar

with the late Hon. William L. Dayton, at Trenton, New Jersey. He was admitted in 1858, and commenced practice in his native county. The civil war soon afterward interrupted his progress in the profession. On the breaking out of the war he was commissioned Captain of the 4th New Jersey Volunteers, and served until the term of enlistment of that organization expired, when he returned to Salem and resumed the practice of his profession, and has since resided there. In 1874 he was nominated by the Republicans of the First District as their candidate for Congress, the district including the counties of Cape May, Camden, Cumberland, Gloucester and Salem, and notwithstanding the reverses to the Republican party that year, he received a handsome majority. He is a decided Republican, and proved an efficient Representative.

ARNAHAN, REV. JAMES, D. D., President of the College of New Jersey, at Princeton, late of Newark, New Jersey, was born in Cumberland county, Pennsylvania, November 17th, 1775. In November, 1798, he entered the junior class in the College of New Jersey, and received the first degree in the arts in September, 1800. He subsequently devoted himself to the study of theology under the guidance of Rev. John McMillan, D. D., in the western part of his native State. In 1801 he returned to Princeton as tutor, but ceased to act further in that capacity in the fall of 1803. In April, 1804, he was licensed by the Presbytery of New Brunswick, which was then assembled at Basking Ridge, to preach the gospel; and selected the vicinity of Hackettstown, Oxford and Knowlton, as his field of labors. January 5th, 1805, he was ordained and installed pastor of the united churches of Whitesborough and Utica, in the State of New York. In February, 1814, he removed on account of health considerations to Georgetown, District of Columbia, and there opened a classical and mathematical school, where he was engaged in teaching for about nine years. In May, 1823, he was chosen President of the College of New Jersey, was inaugurated August 5th, 1823, and, after a service of thirty years, resigned in 1853. His connection with that institution was dissolved in June, 1854. He was, in different capacities, identified more or less prominently with the college for a period of thirty-five years, viz., two years as a student, two as a tutor, and thirty-one as President. He was one of the Trustees also of Princeton at the time of his death, and President of the Board of Trustees of the Theological Seminary. During life he was associated with many illustrious persons of his time, and was one of the last of the venerable men who, for so many years, rendered Princeton renowned for its intellectual and moral greatness. During the long period he presided over the college, he was zealous and untiring in his devotion to its interests. In 1823, the date of his entry into office, the faculty consisted of a president, vice-president, a professor of mathematics, and two tutors—total, five. In 1854 there were six professors, two assistant professors, three tutors, a teacher of modern languages, and a lecturer on zoology —total, with the president and vice-president, fifteen. In the annual catalogue for the year 1823 there were the names of 125 students; in that of 185), the names of 254 students. The whole number of graduates to 1859, 107 years, was 3,390; number of graduates before 1823, seventy-six years, 1,680; from 1823 to 1854, inclusive, thirty-one years, 1,710. So that he, as President, conferred the first degree upon a greater number of alumni, by thirty, than had all his predecessors taken together. He died at the residence of his son-in-law, William C. McDonald, in Newark, New Jersey, March 2d, 1859, in the eighty-fourth year of his age. His remains were removed to Princeton, the scene of his longest and most important services, and the funeral took place on the 8th instant. The services were held in the First Presbyterian Church, which was crowded with sympathizing friends, and the deserted appearance of the business streets of the city showed that for a time the ordinary transactions of its inhabitants were relinquished as a mark of respect to one revered and loved. His faithful friends, the alumni of the college at Newark, New Jersey, sent a deputation with the remains, which arrived at Princeton in the morning train on the day of the funeral. The sermon was preached by Rev. Dr. Macdonald, from 1 Corinthians xv. 12-20. Dr. Stearns, of Newark, and Dr. Cooley, of Trenton, assisted in the services at the church. A funeral procession was formed to the grave headed by the students of the college, and followed by those of the seminary, with the professors of both institutions. Said Hon. William Pennington, at a meeting of the alumni of the college: " He was a wise man; his judgment was remarkable. . . . . It was his habit to let others express their sentiments freely upon any subject; but before the matter was decided he gave his opinion modestly and with diffidence, and time and again those opinions settled the controversy. Wisdom, I think, was the chief characteristic of the man. He was noble, too, with great generosity, and looked at things upon a broad scale. He was a learned man; his scholarship was fine, ... and he acted in the College of New Jersey as a helm does to a ship; and the young men found in him a safe head to guide them."

REARLY, HON. DAVID, Chief Justice of the State of New Jersey from 1779 to 1789, was born in the State in the year 1745, received a good education, and was practising his profession at Allentown, Monmouth county, at the time of the breaking out of the war of independence. His sympathies led him into warm support of the patriotic cause and into the patriot army, wherein he held a commission as Lieutenant-Colonel in Maxwell's brigade, of the Jersey line. At the time of his nomination as Chief Justice, June 10th, 1779, the army was on its march, under the command of General Sullivan, to subdue the Indians in the western part of New York. Some persuasion was necessary to secure his acceptance of the position and resignation of his commission. He presided over the Supreme Court for a period of nearly eleven years, when he resigned, November, 1789, to accept the appointment of Judge of the United States District Court for New Jersey. The duties of this office he continued to discharge until his death, in 1790. His reputation as President of the Supreme Court rests upon tradition only, no reports of its decisions during that period being published. He is regarded as having proved a faithful, reliable judge, and that he enjoyed the high esteem of his contemporaries is very clear. The College of New Jersey, at its commencement in 1781, conferred upon him the honorary degree of Master of Arts. Two years later he was elected one of the Vice-Presidents of the State Society of Cincinnati, and held the position until his death. In 1787, while still Chief Justice, he was appointed by the Legislature of New Jersey a delegate to the convention which framed the constitution of the United States, and he took his seat in that body, participated in its deliberations, and signed the instrument when it was agreed upon. He was afterwards a member of the State convention which ratified it. A deep interest was ever manifested by him in public affairs, and he exercised an influence in politics that was entirely wholesome. In 1788 he was a Presidential Elector, and he aided to secure the election of General Washington.

EED, ALFRED, Lawyer, was born, December 23d, 1839, in Ewing township, Mercer county, New Jersey. He attended the Lawrenceville High School in 1856, and the Model School at Trenton in 1857-58, entering Rutgers College, at New Brunswick, in 1859. In the fall of 1860 he was matriculated at the State and National Law School, Poughkeepsie, New York, and in the summer of 1862 admitted to the practice of law in the State of New York. Not content with the legal proficiency thus attested, however, he returned to Trenton, and renewed his study of the law, being admitted to the bar of New Jersey at the June term in 1864. The seed sown in his unusually thorough preparation for the bar has already borne him a harvest of abundant honors in and out of the profession, though he is not yet forty. In the spring of 1865 he was elected to the Common Council of Trenton, of which he was made President. He was elected Mayor of Trenton in 1867, serving for one term. In the spring of 1869 he was appointed President Judge of the Common Pleas and Special Sessions of Mercer county, a position he held for a full term of five years; and April 8th, 1875, he was appointed by Governor Bedle a Justice of the Supreme Court of the State. He is the youngest member of the Supreme Court, as in fact all his previous honors were attained at an age remarkably early, having been President of the Trenton Common Council when twenty-six, Mayor of the city when twenty-eight, and Law Judge of Mercer county when thirty. So much, in part at any rate, for getting thoroughly ready before he started. The lesson is worth heeding by the rising generation. The rapidity and degree of his advancement is the more noticeable that he has about him nothing of the intriguing politician, but, on the contrary, is distinguished as greatly for manly candor and straightforwardness in public matters as for legal ability and personal worth. His record, political, judicial and private, is without a stain. In politics he is a Democrat.

———◦✦◦———

EASLEY, HON. MERCER, LL. D., Lawyer, and Chief Justice of the Supreme Court of New Jersey, was born in Mercer county, New Jersey, about 1815. He graduated at Princeton College with the class of 1834, which institution has since conferred on him the honorary degree of LL. D. After leaving college he began his preparation for the New Jersey bar, to which he was admitted in the June term, 1838, and was made counsellor in 1842. He practised his profession in the city of Trenton and acquired an extensive and lucrative practice. In politics an earnest Democrat, he yet avoided taking active part in any of the violent political agitations, devoting his talents and energies exclusively to his profession, and soon becoming recognized as one of the leaders of the New Jersey bar. In 1864 his ability and legal attainments were recognized by Governor Parker, by whom he was appointed Chief Justice of the Supreme Court of New Jersey. At the expiration of his term of service in 1871, he was reappointed by Governor Randolph, and is now serving his second term of seven years, which will expire in 1878. His career as Chief Justice has been eminently satisfactory to the bar and people of the State. His son, Mercer Beasley, Jr., is the present Prosecutor of the Pleas for Mercer county, and a young man of ability, rapidly rising in the profession.

———◦✦◦———

ABERNETHY, HUGH HOMER, M. D., of Philipsburg, New Jersey, of Scotch-Irish descent, son of Samuel Abernethy, a farmer, was born at Tinicum, Bucks county, Pennsylvania, December 12th, 1808. His family was founded in Bucks about the middle of the last century; has since then taken a prominent part in county affairs, his father and grandfather having severally held various offices

64

of trust and importance. Having received a sound English education, supplemented by a careful classical course under the late Rev. Dr. Studdiford, of Lambertville, he began the study of medicine in 1827 under Dr. Stewart Kennedy, of Greenwich, and afterwards of Easton, Pennsylvania. A year later he entered the medical department of the University of Pennsylvania, under the office instructions of Professor Dewees, and in 1830 was graduated thence M. D. Among his classmates and fellow-graduates were a number of since eminent medical men, including his brother, the late Dr. Samuel Abernethy, of Rahway, New Jersey; Dr. J. C. Kennedy; Dr. Ferguson. From the date of his graduation until 1841 he practised at Greenwich, New Jersey, and in partnership with Dr. Green, of Belvidere. In that year (1841) he began a partnership with his former preceptor, Dr. Stewart Kennedy, in Easton. The association lasted only a few months, failing health compelling Dr. Kennedy to retire, leaving the practice in his hands. In 1853 Dr. Abernethy was himself compelled by the same cause to relinquish for a time the practice of his profession. Dr. Kennedy retired to Chambersburg, Pennsylvania, and lived but a short time. During the ensuing fourteen years his time was spent partly upon his farm at Greenwich, partly in travel. In 1867, establishing himself in Phillipsburg—where, and in Jersey City, he has since continued to reside—he resumed practice, and has during the past ten years been more or less actively engaged. Among the many physicians whose professional study was begun under his supervision may be mentioned Drs. Fields, C. V. Robbins, H. Race, G. Sandt, R. Ritchey, L. D. Grey and Asher Riley. Throughout his long career his standing has been of the highest, his reputation extending beyond the limits of the State, and his services being very generally sought in consultation in extreme or unusual cases. For the past few years his practice has been restricted almost entirely to consultation. In politics, while taking no active part, he steadily voted with the Whig party until that organization was merged in the Republican, and since the formation of the Republican party he has been one of its most earnest members. He married, in 1831, Mary J., daughter of the late John Maxwell, of Phillipsburg; since 1864 he has been a widower.

———◦✦◦———

LITTELL, SQUIRE, M. D., was born in Burlington, New Jersey, December 9th, 1803. His ancestors in both lines (Littell and Gardiner) were among the earliest settlers of the State, although no generation of the family has been more honorably distinguished than the one of which he is a prominent member, his eldest brother being that eminent literary benefactor of the American public, Eliakim Littell, of *Littell's Living Age*, and another brother, John Stockton Littell, having signalized himself by his researches into the unwritten history of the revolutionary period; while his cousin, the late William Littell, LL. D., was a legal author of repute and a noted member of the Kentucky bar, at which he was the early associate of Clay, Grundy, and the rest of the constellation of statesmen and orators that shone in the legal firmament of Kentucky during the first quarter of this century. He studied medicine at the University of Pennsylvania, from which he graduated in 1824, settling in Philadelphia, where he still resides. In 1825 he made a voyage to South America, practising for a time in Buenos Ayres, with such skill and success as to win from the Academy of Medicine of that city the degree of Licentiate. His specialty is ophthalmology, in which he has acquired an extensive reputation, not only from his practice, but from his original investigations. He is a member of the various medical societies of the city and county of Philadelphia, and of the College of Physicians of Philadelphia. In 1828-29 he was editor of the *Journal of Foreign Medical Sciences*, published by his brother, the present proprietor of the *Living Age*, and for several years he was connected with the editorial department of the *Museum of Foreign Literature and Science*, also published by his brother. He is the author of a work entitled "Manual of Diseases of the Eye; or, A Treatise on Ophthalmology," of which two editions were published, the first being reprinted in London and receiving the highest commendation from the *British and Foreign Medical Review*. "It is replete with information," said that authority, "yet so terse in style and compressed in bulk as at once to entice and repay perusal." In 1853 he edited Haynes Walton's treatise on "Operative Ophthalmic Surgery," being the first American from the first London edition. He has also written a memoir on "Granular Ophthalmia," published in the "Transactions of the *Congress D' Ophthalmologie de Bruxelles*;" a discourse on "Electrical Fluctuations, or Variations of Electrical Tension, as the Cause of Disease," in "Transactions of the American Medical Association for 1866;" papers on "The External Remedial Use of Cold Water," "Non-Malarial Origin of Disease," and other medical subjects; a report on a "Case of Morbid Growth in the Sphenoidal and Ethnoidal Cells," *Dunglison's Medical Intelligencer*, with many other reports on various cases; and "Medical Obituaries," chiefly of members of the Philadelphia College of Physicians, before which they were read. His literary activity, however, has not been strictly confined to the sphere of his profession. For a number of years he edited the Philadelphia *Banner of the Cross*, and has from time to time contributed articles, in prose and verse, to the literary periodicals of the day, it being his custom, as it was that of his cousin, the Kentucky Doctor of Laws, to relieve his more abstruse studies by original excursions into the domain of polite literature. From 1834 to 1864 he was Surgeon to Wills' Ophthalmic Hospital, in Philadelphia, to which he is now Emeritus Surgeon, an honor which he won by a career of service not more distinguished by duration than by ability

and success. He is at present Consulting Physician to the Philadelphia Dispensary, and Councillor of the College of Physicians of Philadelphia. He was married in 1834.

 LOAN, JOHN, M. D., late of Easton, Pennsylvania, son of the Rev. William B. Sloan, for many years pastor of the First Presbyterian Church in Greenwich, Warren county, New Jersey, was born in that town, May 26th, 1799. After being licensed as a physician he established himself in Bloomsbury, Hunterdon county, New Jersey, and in 1821 was one of the founders of the Hunterdon County Medical Society. He subsequently removed to Washington, Warren county; thence in a short time to Easton, Pennsylvania; thence to New York city, where he opened an apothecary shop, and also engaged in practice; thence to Utica, New York; thence to Asbury, Warren county, New Jersey, and finally, about 1835, returned to Easton, where he died on the 10th of February, 1849. His roving disposition prevented him from achieving any great measure of success in his profession, yet his ability was above the average, and as a practitioner he was popular. He was disposed to analytical investigation of disease—a taste by no means common among country practitioners of his time—and in the archives of the Hunterdon County Medical Society is still preserved a well-written essay by him, on "Intermittent Fever," read before that body at the semi-annual meeting in October, 1822.

LOAN, REV. WILLIAM B., Pastor of Greenwich, and late of that place, was born in Lamington, New Jersey, in the last quarter of the past century, and removed thence to Princeton, where he pursued his studies and became eventually a graduate of the college. At the completion of his general and literary studies he devoted himself to theology under the guidance and preceptorship of Dr. John Woodhull, of Freehold, New Jersey, and May 31st, 1797, was licensed by the Presbytery of New Brunswick. In 1798 he was ordained by the same presbytery and installed as pastor of the United Congregations of Greenwich and Mansfield. For seventeen years he served, with noteworthy zeal, fidelity and usefulness, the two congregations, and at the expiration of that time became pastor of Greenwich only. Ultimately, through increasing infirmities, he was compelled to resign also the latter charge, and his pastoral relations with it were dissolved in October, 1834. "He was a man of noble presence, above the medium height, erect, slender, but well-formed; his features were finely chiselled, yet manly and dignified in expression; his eye was a clear, expressive blue; and his gait and bearing were stately, yet unconstrained. His talents were respectable, though not great;

his style simple and unaffected. He was not a very vigorous thinker, but was an earnest and affectionate preacher." He died July 3d, 1839.

cDOWELL, REV. JOHN, D. D., Trustee of Princeton College, late of Philadelphia, Pennsylvania, was born in Lamington, New Jersey, September 10th, 1780, and reared on the paternal farm. He was the son of Matthew McDowell, whose father, Ephraim McDowell, migrated in 1746 from the north of Ireland, where his ancestors, fleeing from persecution in Scotland during the previous century, had found an asylum. Ephraim purchased a tract of 400 acres of wild land on the western borders of Somerset county, New Jersey, in what has since been known as the village of Lamington, about ten miles northwest of Somerville. Here Matthew McDowell was born, in 1748, and through his life was engaged in farming and agricultural pursuits; he married Elizabeth Anderson, whose parents also were from the north of Ireland. Both were exemplary members of the Presbyterian Church of Lamington. At the age of eleven years " he experienced religion," and entered upon a course of study for the ministry, under the instructions of Rev. William Boyd, then teaching in the neighborhood of his home. In 1799 he entered the junior class of the College of New Jersey, at Princeton, graduating with honor in 1801, in the same class with Nicholas Biddle, afterward eminent as an able and remarkable financier. He studied theology under the direction, first, of Rev. Holloway W. Hunt, of Newton, New Jersey, and then of Rev. John Woodhull, D. D., of Freehold, New Jersey. At the latter place he made public profession of his religion in September, 1802. April 25th, 1804, he was licensed by the Presbytery of New Brunswick, at their meeting in Basking Ridge. He was then providentially directed to Elizabethtown, and there preached his first sermon on the first Sabbath of July. The call was presented August 21st, 1804, and he was duly installed on the following Wednesday, December 26th, at eleven o'clock A. M. On this occasion Rev. Dr. Macwhorter, of Newark, presided, offered the ordaining prayer and gave the charge to the minister; Rev. Amzi Armstrong, of Mendham, New Jersey, preached from Titus i. 5; and Rev. Edward D. Griffin, of Newark, New Jersey, gave the exhortation to the people. In the faithful and laborious discharge of the duties of his office, as pastor of the First Presbyterian Church, of Elizabeth, he continued for a period of twenty-eight and a half years, greatly favored of God and honored of man. The attendance on his ministrations steadily increased until it reached the full capacity of the church edifice; so that, in February, 1820, measures were adopted for the gathering of a second Presbyterian church. The number added to his church during his ministry, on profession of faith, was 921; and on certificate

223; in all, 1,144. The baptisms numbered 1,498, of whom 282 were adults. This notable success in his work was brought about by repeated outpourings of the Holy Spirit upon the congregation. The more remarkable of these seasons were the years 1807-8, 1813, 1817 and 1826. In 1808 the additions to the church by profession were 111; in 1813, " the year of hostility," 100; in 1817, 167; and in 1826, 138. Other seasons of refreshing, but of a less general and extended character, were enjoyed, also adding to the church on profession, in 1820, fifty-nine; and in 1831, forty-four. The number of communicants in 1804 was 207; in 1820, 660. In the year 1818 the honorary degree of Doctor of Divinity was conferred upon him by the University of North Carolina and by Union College. He was then already high in repute as a preacher, a scholar and an author. As a Trustee of the College of New Jersey, and as a Director of the Theological Seminary at Princeton, he rendered the most important services to the cause of education and of religion. Calls were extended to him, at different times during his ministry in Elizabeth, from the Collegiate Reformed Dutch Church and the Wall Street Presbyterian Church, both of the city of New York, and from the Presbyterian Church of Princeton, New Jersey. Overtures were made to him also from other quarters, but were not entertained. He was chosen a Professor in the Theological Seminary at Allegheny, Pennsylvania, and in the Union Theological Seminary of Virginia. He was also appointed Secretary of the Board of Missions. In pastoral labors he ranked among the most useful ministers of the church. Every portion of his extensive charge was regularly visited at set seasons every year; Bible-classes, embracing a very large proportion of the youth in his congregation, were regularly instructed. Sunday-schools were introduced in 1814-16, and vigorously conducted; while all the benevolent operations of the church found in him an earnest and powerful advocate. In consequence mainly of his strenuous opposition, repeated attempts at Sabbath-profaning and horse-racing were effectually frustrated; and his influence was felt all over the town, in all its interests, only for good. A call was extended to him in April, 1833, by the Central Presbyterian Church, of Philadelphia, which he accepted; and, being released by the presbytery from his pastoral charge, he bade his people farewell, May 12th, and on the following June 6th was duly installed in his new field of labors. He married, at Newark, a few weeks after his installation there, February 5th, 1805, Henrietta Kollock, daughter of Shepard Rollock, and sister of his predecessor in the pastoral office. His death occurred February 13th, 1863, nearly thirty years after his removal from Newark, New Jersey, the whole interval having been filled with faithful, laborious and effective service, in his Master's vineyard. In the churches to which he so happily ministered, in the benevolent and educational boards of which he was a member, in the presbytery, the synod and the General Assembly (of the last of which he was for eleven years Permanent Clerk, and four years Stated Clerk), his memory is precious, and his good works reverently remembered. "Few men in this or any other community have left behind them a more grateful savor; and to none with more propriety could the Master say at the last, 'Well done, thou good and faithful servant; enter thou into the joy of thy Lord.' "—Rev. Dr. E. F. Hatfield.

AYRE, LEWIS ALBERT, M. D., was born, February 29th, 1820, at Madison, Morris county, New Jersey. He is a son of Ephraim Sayre, Quartermaster on General Washington's staff in the Revolution. In his youth he attended the Madison Academy and the Wantage Seminary, at Deckertown, subsequently entering the Transylvania University, at Lexington, Centucky, from which he graduated in 1839, going the same year to New York city, where he began the study of medicine with Dr. David Gunn, and graduated from the College of Physicians and Surgeons, March 1st, 1842. He at once settled in New York. Shortly after his graduation he was appointed Prosector of Surgery in the College of Physicians and Surgeons. In 1844 he organized the Pathological Society of New York. From 1844 to 1866 he was Hospital Surgeon of the 1st Division of the New York State Militia. In 1853 he was appointed Surgeon to Bellevue Hospital, a position which he still fills. From 1857 to 1871 he was Surgeon to the Charity Hospital, to which he is now Consulting Surgeon. From 1857 to 1866 he was Resident Physician of Charity Hospital. His specialty is surgery, in which his name stands among the very first in America. He is a member of the New York County Medical Society; of the New York State Medical Society; of the American Medical Association; of the New York Academy of Medicine; of the Pathological Society of New York; of the New York Neurological Society; and of the Medico-Legal Society of New York; and an honorary member of the New Brunswick Medical Society and of the Medical Society of Norway; and in 1872 was created by the Cing of Sweden a Cnight of the Order of Wassa. His medical writings, valuable, though not voluminous, comprise a paper on the "Exsection of the Head of the Femur," 1854; a report on "Morbus Coxam," 1860; a paper on "Compulsory Vaccination," 1862; a treatise on the "Mechanical Treatment of Diseased Joints," 1865; a report on the "Contagion of Cholera," 1866; a paper on "Club-Foot," 1869; an essay on "Reflex Paralysis and Incordination from Genital Irritation," 1870; an exposition of a "New Treatment of Fractured Clavicle," 1871; a report on "Fractures," 1874; a paper on "Anchylosis," 1874; a treatise on "Orthopedic Surgery and Diseases of the Joints," 1876; a report on "Pott's Disease," Transactions of the American Medical Association, 1876; a paper on

"Lateral Curative," Transactions of the New York State Medical Society, 1876; and one on "Hip Disease," read before the Medical Congress, in 1876. He is not a politician, but nevertheless he has very distinct and rooted political convictions, being a Democrat of the strictest sect, taking for his guide the Constitution as interpreted by the great chiefs of the Democracy, and rejecting all measures and all men that fall short of that standard. Personally he is one of the most genial and attractive of men. Although he early became an adopted son of New York, and is cherished as a son by Centucky, in whose blue-grass region he pursued his academical studies, New Jersey still claims him as her own by right of nativity, and asserts her title to share in his brilliant professional renown. Happily for him and for them his renown is great enough to go all round. He was married, January 25th, 1849, to Eliza A. Hall, daughter of Charles H. Hall, of Harlem.

CHUREMAN, REV. JOHN, Pastor of the Reformed Dutch Church at Millstone, New Jersey, Vice-President of the New Brunswick College, late of New Brunswick, was born near that place, October 19th, 1778. In 1795 he graduated from the college there, and, after pursuing his theological studies under the guidance of Dr. Livingston, was licensed to preach in 1800. In the course of the following year he settled at Bedminster, where he remained for six years. The Consistory of Millstone, possessing no parsonage, had disposed of all interest in their last property to Six Mile Run church; he lived, after accepting the call of April 20th, 1807, on the place afterward occupied by Jacob Van Cleeve, near Blackwell's mills. During his ministry an important reformation in the management of the finances of the church was attempted, and met with partial success. Many of the pew-holders surrendered their old deeds to the consistory, and received new ones in return, in which the pews were made directly assessable for all the expenses of the church. But his short pastorate there prevented the plan from being carried out fully, and in 1828, at the removal of Dr. Condict, he received, meanwhile, successive calls from the church of New Brunswick, and in the spring of 1813 was installed as its pastor. "But his poor health, in three months, compelled him to give up this charge." In 1815 the church, appreciating his abilities,

[continued on the following page] plan from being carried out fully, and in 1828, at the removal of Dr. Condict, he received, meanwhile, successive calls from the church of New Brunswick,

appointed him Professor of History and Church Government. Dr. Livingston writes concerning him: "He was mild and pleasant; discerning and firm; steadfast, but not obstinate; zealous, but not assuming. The frequent hemorrhage of his lungs, and the habitual weakness of his constitution, prevented him from close and intense studies; yet he was a good belles-lettres scholar. His style was correct and pure; and he made such progress in the official branches of his professorship that his lectures upon ecclesiastical history and pastoral theology were highly acceptable and very useful. The suavity of his manners and the propriety of his conduct endeared him to the students, and recommended him to the respect and affection of all who knew him. He was growing into extensive usefulness, and, had he lived and progressed as he began, would have become a treasure to the Theological College." He died at New Brunswick, in May, 1818.

ABRISKIE, REV. JOHN L. ("Father Zabriskie"), Pastor of the Reformed Dutch Church at Millstone, New Jersey, was born March 4th, 1779. He was of Polish extraction, having descended from Albert Saboroweski, who arrived in this country in the ship "Fox," in 1662, and settled at once in Hackensack, New Jersey; he had studied for the Lutheran ministry, it is said, but was in some manner impressed into the army, and at a favorable moment availed himself of an opportunity which offered to effect a safe flight to the new world. He purchased from the Indians a large tract of land, called Paramus, where many of his children resided permanently, and whence the family has sent forth numerous members and branches. He graduated at Union College in 1798, being a member of the first class in that institution, and in 1801 was licensed to preach by the Classis of Rensselaer. He first settled over the united churches of Greenbush and Wynantskill, succeeding Rev. J. V. C. Romeyn, and where he continued for about eight years. "He preached here for the first in the month of February, 1810, and moved to Millstone in May, 1811, and was installed by Rev. Mr. Cannon." The church, at the time of his settlement, had not more than about seventy members and eighty-four families; and his ministry began about the time when the incipient steps were in progress of all those great union associations of piety and philanthropy "which have since so greatly blessed, and are still blessing, our world." He was among the earliest friends of the New Jersey Bible Society, the first of those State societies which, when their numbers had increased, merged themselves into the one grand American Bible Society. "It seems to have been his work to build up this church to strength and numbers through the Spirit's influence, that she might then take an active and important, yea, a prominent, part in these great plans of God." Shortly after his settlement, early in 1812, the consistory again provided a parsonage property for themselves. They bought the lot, afterward occupied by Dr. Fred. Blackwell, of Daniel Disborough for $1,250, and immediate repairs bestowed swelled this amount to $2,232. During the first eighteen years of his ministry he preached in the old church. The building had received a slight repairing during the Revolution, and a more considerable one in 1783; again in 1800 it was very thoroughly renovated, and the pews rearranged; in 1805 was agitated the matter of putting in a gallery, but the project did not meet with success. The old building continued to be occupied till April 22d, 1828, the subject of rebuilding "having been agitated for twenty-five years, without a majority being able to agree on the best course." On May 26th, 1827, however, a memorial was presented to the consistory, signed by eighty persons, respectfully requesting a call to the congregation for a meeting to devise means for enlarging or rebuilding the church edifice. Frequent meetings were held, and finally the consistory determined that, in conformity with the wishes of a large portion of the congregation, a new church should be erected, the edifice to be built after the model of the new structure at Six Mile Run. The Building Committee consisted of Stephen Garretson, Daniel H. Disborough and Abraham Beekman, subject to the direction of the consistory. The corner-stone was laid June 8th, 1828, and an address delivered by the pastor from Gen. xxviii. 22. The church was dedicated on Christmas, Sabbath, 1828. His ministry, respecting additions to the church during the occupancy of the old building, had been quite successful; and during his whole ministry in the new church, of twenty-two years, he received 280 on profession of faith, and 118 by certificates from other churches; while, during his whole pastorate of forty years, the total number received was 446 by profession, and 162 by certificate. His last report to classis, in the spring of 1850, makes the church membership to be then 291, and 176 families. "Father Zabriskie died August 15th, 1850, at the age of seventy-one years. His dust lies in the adjoining churchyard, where his memorial monument reminds the passer-by of the venerable 'minister of God' of more than half a century's service."

YOUNG, NELSON, Merchant and Banker, of Somerville, New Jersey, was born near Flemington, Hunterdon county, in that State, in 1814. His father was William P. Young, an old and highly-esteemed citizen of Hunterdon. He received a fair business education, and during several years was engaged with his brother in the milling business near Flemington. In the year 1842 he removed to the city in which he at present resides, and entered into the grain trade there. Here he continued by himself till 1848. In that year the firm of Young & Bound was organized, for wholesale and retail business in the same line of trade, and the seat of business removed from Flemington to New York. It soon became one of the largest establishments in the grain trade in New York, and continued to hold that position till 1863, when Mr. Young relinquished business, retired from the firm, and, returning to Somerville, took up his permanent residence there. On the organization of the First National Bank, of Somerville, which took place about that time, Mr. Young was elected its Vice-President, a position which he held till the retirement of Colonel Hope from the presidency of that institution, in 1874. He was then elected its President, an office he still holds. He is also President of the Dime Savings Bank, of Somerville, and has been since that institution was organized. He is a strong Republican, and has belonged to the party from the earliest date of its formation. He is, however, neither an active politician nor an office-seeker, having never either sought or held office. In 1842 he married the daughter of Mr. Jones, of Flemington, New Jersey.

———————

AN FLEET, HON. ABRAHAM V., Vice-Chancellor of the State of New Jersey, was born in Hunterdon county, New Jersey, about 1825; was admitted to the bar in the November term, 1852, and made counsellor in 1858. He opened his first law office in Flemington, New Jersey, where he soon acquired an extensive and lucrative practice. Although an ardent Republican and sincere believer in the doctrines of that party, he has taken no active interest in politics, devoting himself to the interest of his profession. In 1875 he was appointed by Chancellor Runyan, and commissioned by Governor Bedle, Vice-Chancellor of the State of New Jersey for five years; his term of office will expire in 1880. In the office of Vice-Chancellor he has confirmed his previous reputation of being one of the finest chancery lawyers of the State.

———————

GILVIE, ALEXANDER, Merchant, late of Elizabeth, was born in Stirling, Scotland, August 2d, 1767. Of his father he had but little remembrance, but of his mother he often spoke with the tenderest affection. The minister of his childhood was Rev. Mr. Stuart, of whose person and preaching he had a most vivid recollection, and to whose fidelity he bore the strongest testimony. He became, early in life, a communicant of the church, and was a scrupulous and pious Christian. He arrived in New York in 1794, and at once connected himself with the church in Cedar street, of which the late Dr. John M. Mason was the youthful and eloquent pastor. Subsequently he removed his membership to the church in Pearl street, then under the pastoral care of Rev. Dr. Phillips, of which he was ordained an elder in February, 1823. In the vigorous and faithful discharge of the duties of that office he continued during the pastorate of Dr. Phillips, Mr. Monteith and Drs. Rice and Rowland, until his removal to Elizabeth, New Jersey, in the spring of 1836. For the church there, its pastors and its members, he maintained an affection peculiarly strong. Soon after his connection with it he was elected to the office of Ruling Elder, and was installed March 4th, 1837. "His life-business in New York was that of a merchant. And whilst he was successful in his calling, and twice met with reverses that swept from him much of his gains, his high integrity was never questioned." He died in Elizabeth, New Jersey, in the spring of 1857.

———————

COVEL, HON. ALDEN CORTLANDT, Lawyer, of Camden, son of the Rev. Alden Scovel, some time Principal of the Hudson River Seminary, New York, was born at Princeton, New Jersey, June 13th, 1830. His preliminary education was received mainly under the able tuition of his father; and having determined upon law as his profession he went through the prescribed course of study, and in 1856 was admitted to practise as an attorney at the New Jersey bar. In the same year he established himself in Camden, and in 1859—having been, meanwhile, admitted as a counsellor—he formed a partnership with the Hon. George M. Robeson that continued until the latter was appointed Secretary of the Navy. Early identifying himself with the Republican party, he has now for a number of years been prominent in local and State politics, and has been elected to various positions of importance in both the municipal and State governments. For a considerable period he was Clerk to the Board of Chosen Freeholders of Camden, and at the same time was counsel to that body; in 1867 was elected, by popular vote, City Solicitor of Camden for a term of two years, and in 1869 was re-elected for a term of three years. He has also served for three years in the Camden City Councils. The esteem in which he is held in the business community of the city may be inferred from the fact that he is a Director of and counsel to the National State Bank of Camden—one of the oldest and most substantial financial institutions in New Jersey. His career in State politics began in 1874, when he was elected to the Assembly, a position to which he has since been annually re-elected. At the beginning of the first session of 1877 he was made, by acclamation, the Republican nominee for Speaker, and was only defeated in the election for that office through the change of vote of four members of his party. In all the public positions which he has held, and especially since his election to the Assembly, he has served his constituents faithfully and well; and the manner in which he has been constantly advanced to places of increased trust and responsibility is the best evidence that, reciprocally, his constituents have appreciated and held in proper esteem his efficient services.

----◆----

USTIN, REV. DAVID, generally known as the "Prophet," and formerly Pastor of the Presbyterian Church at Elizabethtown, was born in New Haven, Connecticut, in 1760, and was a descendant of John Austin, who married, November 5th, 1667, Mercy, daughter of Joshua Atwater, and died in 1690. His father, David Austin, was a highly respectable and prosperous merchant, who held for some time the position of collector of the customs. His daughter, Mary, who resided with her brother in Elizabethtown, became the wife of Rev. Professor Andrew Yates, D. D., of Schenectady, New York. From early childhood David was trained in pious ways; graduated at Yale College in 1779, having been associated in study with such men as Joel Barlow, Josiah Meigs, Zephaniah Smith, Noah Webster, Oliver Wolcott, Elizur Goodrich, and Roger Griswold; and pursued his theological studies under the direction of Dr. Joseph Bellamy, at Bethlehem, Connecticut. In May, 1780, he was licensed at North Guilford, by the New Haven East Association. Young as he was he preached with singular acceptance, and was earnestly solicited to settle in the ministry. But, declining all such proposals, he went abroad at the close of the war. After spending some time in foreign countries he returned to America, and temporarily supplied the pulpit of the Chelsea (Second) Congregational Church, Norwich, Connecticut, where he became acquainted with the family of Dr. Joseph Lathrop, whose daughter, Lydia, he eventually married. The *New Jersey Journal*, of Wednesday, September 10th, 1788, says: "Yesterday, in a crowded and solemn assembly, the Rev. David Austin was ordained pastor of the Presbyterian Church in this town (Elizabeth). The Rev. Mr. Roe preached the sermon, Dr. Rogers, who presided, gave the charge to the minister, and Dr. Macwhorter to the people." The erection of the church there was then prosecuted with increased energy; he secured the building of its "graceful spire," and obtained subscriptions for the purchase of a bell. He also evinced a deep interest in the cause of education, and in the promotion of everything connected with the public welfare. One of the first literary enterprises in which he embarked was the publication, bi-monthly, of *The Christian's, Scholar's and Farmer's Magazine*, whose initial number was for "April and May, 1789." It was printed at East Town, by Shepard Kollock, one of the proprietors. At the close of the first year it was spoken of as a success, and was continued through the second year. About the year 1790 he began the publication, by subscription, of "The American

Preacher," a serial, containing some of the choicest discourses of living American divines, without respect to denomination; the first two volumes were issued January 1st, 1791. Other gentlemen were associated with him in the enterprise, "but it was his work almost wholly." As early as January 1st, 1791, he had begun to take an interest in prophetic studies. "Nor was he, at the time, singular in this respect. The pulpit resounded with earnest utterances on the downfall of Babylon, and the speedy coming of the Millennial reign of Christ and his saints." In pursuing the study of these mysterious oracles he was but yielding to the prevailing current of popular opinion. In the spring of 1793 he preached a remarkable discourse, first to his own church, and then, on the evening of April 7th, at New York, that produced a profound sensation. This discourse, delivered from short notes, he subsequently wrote out, amplified, and illustrated with numerous citations. It was printed by Mr. Kollock, and made its appearance, May 1st, 1794, as "The Downfall of Mystical Babylon; or, a Key to the Providence of God, in the Political Operations of 1793-4." In connection with the sermon he republished Rev. Dr. Bellamy's "Discourse on the Millennium," and Edwards' "Humble Attempt," etc., the whole forming an octavo volume of four hundred and twenty-six pages, with the title, "The Millennium, or the Thousand Years of Prosperity," etc. At the time his teachings were deemed sound and scriptural; the method of interpretation and the style of argument differed not at all from what was then almost universally accepted. In the year 1795, after a violent visitation of scarlet fever, he became perfectly convinced that he had ascertained the precise day of the advent of Christ; and delivered a series of discourses, with wonderful animation, and in language of surpassing eloquence. The congregation were deeply moved, "some not knowing what to believe, a few utterly unbelieving, but the greater part carried away with the holy fervor of their beloved pastor. The excitement spread through all the region round about." At length, May 8th, 1796, he announced that the Lord would surely come on the ensuing Lord's day, the 15th. Of course a prodigious excitement followed such a startling piece of intelligence. In the midst of the ferment, he "made his arrangements to receive his adorable Lord in a becoming manner. Several young females were selected, for whom white raiment was prepared, that they might attend upon the Lord at his coming." Much of the time during the week was, not unreasonably, occupied with religious exercises; and on the evening of the 14th a crowded and deeply agitated meeting was held in the Methodist church. The long-expected day arrived, the bell tolled, the church was full to overflowing, but the sky was troubled by no unusual visitation. After "long and wearisome waiting," he preached, taking for his text, "My Lord delayeth his coming." A slight error in the computation of dates had been made—so it was suggested—and some satisfied themselves with the explanation. But the congre-

gation was distracted, the more substantial portion disaffected and deeply grieved. He then took the vow of a
Nazarite, and gave himself up almost wholly to the work
of announcing Christ's coming. His labors were incessant;
often he preached thrice a day, and went everywhere,
through all the neighborhood, calling upon men to repent.
In April, 1797, a meeting of the congregation was held in
the church, and a committee appointed to wait on him. In
his answer to it, he declared that it was his fixed and un-
alterable determination to institute a new church, and to set
up a new order of things in ecclesiastical concerns, independent of presbytery, of the synod, or of the General Assembly. He professed to have received an extraordinary
and direct call from God to engage in the work. The congregation then again met, April 19th, and determined to
apply to the presbytery for a dissolution of the pastoral
relation. At its meeting, in New York, the application was
received, and on the following day the presbytery called
upon him to know if he concurred in it. He thereupon
renounced that body's jurisdiction, and withdrew; and the
presbytery, after due deliberation, granted the application,
and put on record their sense of the whole matter. He
supplied for a time, in 1797–98, the pulpit at Greenfield, in
Fairfield, Connecticut, and afterward removed to East Haven,
and found a home at the house of his uncle, Rev. Nicholas
Street, his wife having returned to her father's house in
Norwich. At New Haven, he embarked in a building
enterprise, involving a large outlay of money, by which he
exhausted his resources, and incurred obligations that he
was unable to meet. In November, 1799, after returning
to Elizabethtown, and "embracing every opportunity of
resuming his ministerial work," he announced, in the
Journal, the publication of "The First Vibration of the
Jubilee Trump." At the announcement of the death of
Washington, the corporation, December 24th, requested
him to deliver a funeral oration in the Presbyterian church,
and he complied with the request. On the following day
he performed the same service at the cantonment on Greek
Brook, Scotch Plains; and again at Springfield, on the 1st
of January. He sought to make converts to his views, and
to defend himself against opposers, by a communication in
the *Journal*, of January 28th, 1800, signed "The Pharez
of God." He died, it is supposed, in New Jersey, in the
earlier years of the present century.

UDD, REV. JOHN CHURCHILL, D. D., Pastor
of St. John's (Episcopal) Church, of Elizabethtown, New Jersey, was born at Norwich, Connecticut, May 24th, 1779. He was the eldest
child of Jonathan Rudd, and Mary Huntington,
daughter of Deacon Barnabas Huntington; his
grandfather, Samuel, was, probably, a great-grandson of
Jonathan, who was at New Haven in 1644. His ancestors
were of Puritan faith, and he, inclining to their church,

was reared as a Congregationalist. He was fitted for college under the tuition of Rev. Samuel Nott, of Norwich,
West Farms, now Franklin, Connecticut, but was not
favored with a collegiate course. Upon attaining his
majority he went to New York, and made that city his
home, connecting himself there with the Episcopal Church.
Having prepared for the ministry, under the direction of
Bishop Moore, and Rev. J. H. Hobart, he was ordained by
the former as a deacon, April 28th, 1805, and thereafter was
employed for several months as a missionary on Long
Island. J. H. Hobart, having married some years previously a daughter of Rev. Dr. Chandler, "doubtless introduced him to the pulpit of St. John's Church," where he
preached, for the first time, July 21st, 1805. The congregation then seldom exceeded a hundred souls, and the communicants were sixty in number. A new steeple was
erected in 1807, and other improvements were made in the
church edifice. In 1808 the length of the house was increased seventeen feet, and the interior entirely renovated.
In 1810 his salary was raised from $500 to $600. In 1813
he became the editor of a new series of *The Churchman's
Magazine* and the place of publication was changed from
New York to Elizabethtown. Other improvements were
made in the church edifice in 1818; and the parsonage
house was rebuilt, at an expense of about $3,000. For
several years he conducted also a classical school in his
house with great and merited success. July 31st, 1823, the
University of Pennsylvania conferred on him the degree of
Doctor of Divinity. Owing to the loss of health, and particularly of his voice, he was released from his parochial
charge June 1st, 1826, and in the course of the ensuing
month removed to Auburn, New York, where, and at
Utica, New York, as teacher, rector, and editor of *The
Gospel Messenger*, his remaining days were spent. After
suffering greatly, and for many years, from a rheumatic
affection, he died at his home in Utica, November 15th,
1848, greatly lamented by his own church and others. His
remains, at his own request, were brought to Elizabethtown,
and buried, on the 19th, in St. John's church-yard. He
was married, January 22d, 1803, at New York, Dr. Hobart
officiating, to Phebe Eliza Bennett, daughter of Edward
Bennett, of Shrewsbury, New Jersey; she died in October,
1867, aged eighty-eight years, having survived him nearly
nineteen years. In addition to his editorial work, he published, at various periods, more than a dozen discourses,
sermons, etc.

ORRELL, REV. THOMAS, known as "Father
Morrell," Officer in the Revolutionary Army, late
of Elizabethtown, was the eldest child of Jonathan
Morrell, and was born at New York, November
22d, 1747. His father was a native of Newtown,
Long Island, and a grandson of Thomas Morrell,
who was at Gravesend, Long Island, in 1650, and at New-

town as early as 1655, where he died about 1704. When tidings of the battle of Lexington reached Elizabethtown, a company of volunteers was immediately gathered, of which he, being a leading spirit among his fellows, was chosen Captain. He was in command of one of the boats that captured the "Blue Mountain Valley," off Sandy Hook, January 23d, 1776; and took an active part in the measures adopted to protect the town and neighborhood, during the following summer and autumn, against the British and Hessians. In June, 1776, he received a captain's commission, with orders to muster a company of seventy-eight men, and report to General Washington, then at New York. Two companies of militia were parading in front of the Presbyterian church, and from these, by means of a fiery harangue, he filled his quota. They were equipped and ready, at New York, for service, six days after the Declaration of Independence. They were attached to the New Jersey Brigade, under General Heard, of Woodbridge, and in the fatal engagement at Flatbush, August 27th, 1776, were nearly cut to pieces. Their captain fell, severely wounded, and barely escaped destruction. He was removed, first to New York, and then to his father's house in Elizabethtown, where he remained, unable to report for duty, until the advent of Cornwallis and his army of invasion, when he found a place of refuge at the house of Rev. Jonathan Elmer, at New Providence. He was subsequently appointed a Major in the 4th Jersey Regiment, and served through the campaign of 1777, or until the attack on Germantown, Pennsylvania, October 3d, in which he was an active participant. He also distinguished himself in the action at Brandywine, September 11th. His health had now become so much impaired that, with the reluctant assent of Washington, who esteemed him highly, he withdrew from military service, and resumed his mercantile pursuits, in which he continued thenceforward for a period of nearly ten years. The change which then ensued is best told in his own words: "In the month of October, 1785, I was awakened by the preaching of Rev. John Hagerty, and in March, 1786, received the witness of God's Spirit of my acceptance. In June, 1786, I began to preach as a local preacher, in Elizabethtown, and in several parts of the circuit. In March, 1787, I began to ride as a travelling preacher, and rode on Elizabethtown Circuit twenty months with Robert Cloud. At the Conference in New York, in October, 1788, I was ordained deacon (nearly forty-one years old) and appointed to the Trenton Circuit, with John Merrick and Jethro Johnson. At the June Conference, in New York, in 1789, was ordained an elder, and appointed for that city, with Brother Cloud, who was with me twelve months, and Brother Merrick, four months." He continued at New York, most of the time, for nearly five years, residing at No. 32 John street. During the first six months he built the Forsyth Street Church, the funds for which he raised himself. The church was dedicated November 8th, 1789. A great revival followed, resulting in four hundred conversions,

and two hundred accessions to the society, within nine weeks from January 1st, 1790. At the Conference of that year he was appointed Presiding Elder for the district including New York, East Town, Long Island, New Rochelle, and Newburgh Circuits. In the winter of 1791-92 he travelled with Bishop Asbury through the Southern States. He was stationed several months at Charleston, and returned to New York in June, 1792. In March, 1794, he left the city, and retired to Elizabethtown, having found in the society at the former place, in 1789, about three hundred members, and left it with more than eight hundred and fifty. During the ensuing winter he was stationed at Philadelphia, but, in consequence of a severe illness, was laid aside for about four years. In 1799 he was stationed at Baltimore, Maryland, and there remained for two years. In May, 1801, though appointed to New York, he returned to his home and there remained for about a year. In 1802, with his newly-married wife, he consented to be stationed at New York; but in February, 1804, he retired from the itinerant connection, and became a permanent resident of Elizabethtown. The meeting-house of the Methodist Society had been built soon after the organization of the church; it was a small frame building, adapted to the wants of a feeble congregation. In this humble structure once, at least, every Sabbath, he took delight in preaching to all who came. At the time of his return to the town he was preaching in the Presbyterian church. When the congregation voted against continuing him in their service, his friends procured for him the use of the Methodist church. The division in the Presbyterian church then induced quite a number of families to attach themselves to his lively and energetic ministry. During a period of more than thirty-four years he continued in the faithful discharge of his duties as a Christian minister, rarely failing to preach once every Sabbath, until he had attained his eighty-seventh year. As "Father Morrell," he was known, revered, and greatly honored by all classes of people in the town, many from the other churches, the young as well as the old, "resorting frequently to hear the old soldier discourse of the great salvation." He took an active part in all measures for the improvement of the town, and especially in those designed for the advancement of morality and religion. On all patriotic occasions—Fourth of July celebrations, etc.—he was invariably present as actor or spectator. During the war of 1812-15 his counsels and other services were freely tendered, and were invaluable; and, so late as July 4th, 1828, at fourscore years of age, he delivered an oration in the Presbyterian church, "full of patriotic fire, and worthy of the occasion." On the 9th of August, 1838, after a severe illness of six months' duration, he died, in his ninety-first year, having been a faithful and honored minister of the gospel for more than fifty-two years. "He was rather short in stature, but strongly built. His neck was short, his head not large, his eye bright and blue, his lips thin, and his whole appearance indicative of much more than ordinary firmness." He was

65

thrice married. The name of his first wife, whom he married about October 1st, 1759, has not been preserved; she was the mother of two children, Elizabeth B., and Catharine, who married Benjamin Wade. His second wife—Bishop Asbury officiating—was Lydia, a daughter of George Frazee, of Westfield, she had three children: Francis Asbury, Catharine, who married Rev. William A. Wilmer, and Francis Asbury (2d), who married Mary, a daughter of Jonathan Griffith. His third wife was Eunice, widow of Theodorus James Hamilton, a well-known merchant of Elizabethtown; she was the daughter of Uzal Woodruff and Elizabeth, daughter of Samuel Ogden and Hannah Hatfield; she had but one child, Eunice Theodosia, who became the second wife of Hon. Apollos Morrell Elmer, a grandson of Rev. Jonathan Elmer.

RANE, GENERAL WILLIAM, Patriot of the Revolution, late of Elizabethtown, New Jersey, was born in that place, in 1748; and was the son of Hon. Stephen Crane, a prominent and useful citizen of the troublous period of the contest between America and Great Britain; he was the son of Daniel, and grandson of Stephen Crane, "the Planter," of Elizabethtown. Being in the full vigor of his early manhood at the beginning of the revolutionary war he at once espoused his country's cause, and, in common with several of his townsmen, attached himself, as Lieutenant of an artillery company, to the Canada expedition, under Montgomery. At the time of his commander's fall, before Quebec, December 31st, 1775, he received a bomb-shell wound in one of his ankles, from which he suffered until his death, nearly forty years afterward. Says Rev. Edwin F. Hatfield, in his excellent "History of Elizabeth": "One act more of aggressive hostility, on the part of citizens of this town, March, 1783, remains to be narrated. It will be told in the words of Major William Crane, the leader of the enterprise, as written the next day : ' I have the pleasure to inform you of the capture of the sloop " Caty," of twelve double-fortified twelve-pounders, containing one hundred and seventeen puncheons of Jamaica spirits, lying, at the time of capture, within pistol-shot of the grand battery at New York, and alongside the ship "Eagle," of twenty-four guns, which we also took, but were obliged to leave there, as she lay aground. The captains and crews of both the vessels were brought up by us in the sloop to this place, where we have them secure. This was performed on the night of the 3d of March (Monday), by six townsmen, under the command of Captain Quigley and myself, without the firing of a musket by any of our party.' " The vessel and cargo were sold at auction, at Elizabethtown, Monday, March 17th, following. For various acts of bravery, and eminent services on the field, he was promoted, after the war, to a Brigadiership of militia. In 1807 he was appointed Deputy-Mayor of the borough, and from that date also was a Trustee of the Presbyterian Church until his decease. The *New Jersey Journal*, of July 12th, 1814, has this notice : " Died on Saturday last (9th), General William Crane, in the sixty-seventh year of his age. In the year 1775 he entered the Continental service, and at the reduction of St. John's, or Montreal, received a wound in his leg, which was never cured. About seventeen months since, his leg was amputated, with flattering prospects, but that last resort had been too long deferred, and he fell a victim to the incurable wound. His character as a citizen and soldier stood pre-eminent, and he lived beloved, and died lamented. His funeral was attended, on Sunday, by a vast concourse of people from this and the neighboring parishes, who testified his worth as a man."

RANE, COMMODORE WILLIAM M., United States Navy, son of General William Crane, who served as an officer in the revolutionary army, was born in Elizabethtown, New Jersey, February 1st, 1776. In May, 1799, he entered the navy as Midshipman; in July, 1803, was made a Lieutenant, and served before Tripoli, under Commodore Edward Preble, and was present at all the attacks made on the city. He was serving on board the "Chesapeake" at the time of her action with the "Leopard." At the commencement of the war with England he was appointed to the command of the brig "Nautilus," of fourteen guns, in which he was captured, in July, 1812, by a British squadron, soon after sailing from New York. On his exchange he was ordered to the Lakes, where, in command of the "Madison and Pike," in the squadron of Commodore Chauncey, he served with distinction for the remainder of the war. From 1815 until the time of his decease he was very constantly employed in important services. During one cruise of over four years in the Mediterranean he commanded successively the "Independence" ship-of-the-line, the "Erie" sloop, and the frigates "Constellation" and "United States." In 1827 he was appointed to command the American squadron in that sea, the "Delaware" ship-of-the-line bearing his flag. While on this service he acted as joint Commissioner with Mr. Offley, United States consul at Smyrna, to open negotiations with the Ottoman government preliminary to a commercial treaty, which was soon afterward concluded. In 1841 he was appointed Navy Commissioner; and in 1842, when the Navy Department was reorganized, was made Chief of the Bureau of Ordnance and Hydrography, which he administered until near the close of his days. In this last-named position he demonstrated yet more conspicuously his high administrative ability, his department being managed with admirable efficiency and economy. He died in Washington, District of Columbia, March 18th, 1846.

Frederick A. Kinch, M.D.

INCH, FREDERICK A., M. D., Physician and Surgeon, in Westfield, was born in New York city, March 12th, 1822. His parents died while he was quite young, consequently he was thrown upon his own resources and energy for his future in life. This circumstance, which would have discouraged many, seems in his case to have served an an incentive. He attended the public schools during his boyhood and youth, and on arriving at years of maturity engaged in teaching in Mount Hope, Orange county, New York, and at the same time he spent his leisure and evenings in the study of medicine and surgery under the instruction of Drs. Wm. C. Terry and D. F. Wyckoff. After the study of medicine and surgery for four years, including his attendance upon lectures in the University of the City of New York, be was admitted to practise by the New York State Medical Society; and in 1849, removing to Westfield, New Jersey, commenced the practice of medicine and surgery in that place. In accordance with the laws of the State then in force, he submitted to an examination before the State Medical Society of New Jersey, and received his license May 1st, 1851. He has continued to practise in Westfield and vicinity up to the present; having acquired a comfortable competence and a happy home, and having devoted all his time and ability to relieve suffering humanity and assuage the maladies of mankind, he feels rewarded by a grateful people, and the smiles of a kind and beneficent Providence. He was married to Harriet Little, daughter of Colonel William S. Little, of Mount Hope, Orange county, New York, February 6th, 1850. He is a member of the District Medical Society of the County of Union, and in 1873-74 occupied the Presidential

---

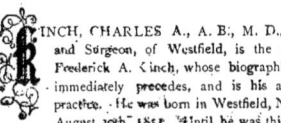

INCH, CHARLES A., A. B., M. D., Physician and Surgeon, of Westfield, is the son of Dr. Frederick A. Cinch, whose biographical sketch immediately precedes, and is his associate in practice. He was born in Westfield, New Jersey, August 30th, 1851. Until he was thirteen years of age he attended the public school of his native town, and was then transferred to Grammar School No. 35, Thirteenth street, New York city. In regular course he entered the College of the City of New York, and graduated with honor in the year 1870. He was awarded a special prize in chemistry by Prof. R. O. Doremus. He received the degree of Doctor of Medicine from the College of Physicians and Surgeons, New York, in the year 1873, and at once entered upon the practice of his profession. On 24th, 1876, he married Carrie E., the eldest daughter of the late Charles Cheney, Esq., of Elizabeth, New Jersey. He is a member of the District Medical Society of the County of Union.

OBART, REV. JOHN HENRY, D. D., Pastor of Christ's Church, New Brunswick, New Jersey, Bishop of the Protestant Episcopal Church in the Diocese of New York, late of Auburn, New York, was born in Philadelphia, Pennsylvania, September 14th, 1775. His ancestors, in 1663, had emigrated from Norfolk, England, and settled in Hingham, Massachusetts; his father, Enoch Hobart, was commander of a merchant ship. In 1788 he entered the College of Philadelphia, whence, in 1791, he was transferred to Princeton College, where he graduated in 1793. At first, owing to certain family considerations, he reluctantly undertook to fit himself for mercantile life in the counting-house of his brother-in-law; but finding, after a brief experience, that his tastes and inclination led him in another direction, he resolved to enter upon a course of preparation for the ministry. Receiving at this time an invitation to a tutorship at Princeton, New Jersey, he accepted the post, and began the discharge of his duties in January, 1796. At the same time he studied theology under the guidance of Dr. Samuel Stanhope Smith, the president of the college. In the spring of 1798 he resigned his tutorship and removed to Philadelphia, where he pursued his studies under the supervision of Bishop White, by whom he was admitted to deacon's orders, June 3d, 1798, and was invited to take charge of two suburban parishes near Philadelphia. In 1799 he was called to Christ's Church, New Brunswick, New Jersey, where he remained until he became Rector of St. George's Church, Hempstead, Long Island. Subsequent he declined the Rectorship of St. Mark's Church, New York; in the following September, however, he accepted an invitation to become an assistant minister of Trinity Church, New York. In 1801 he was ordained Priest by Bishop Provoost. He had already been Secretary of the House of Bishops, and was elected Secretary of the Convention of New York, Deputy to the General Conventions of 1801, 1804, and 1808, and on the last two occasions was Secretary to the House of Clerical and Lay Deputies. In 1806 Union College conferred upon him the degree of D. D. In February, 1811, Bishop Moore, of New York, having been disabled from public service by a paralytic stroke, he was elected Assistant Bishop, and was consecrated on the 29th. In consequence of Bishop Moore's infirmities he was then charged with the entire duty of overseeing the church throughout the State of New York. In 1812 he was made Assistant Rector of Trinity Church, and, on Moore's death, in 1816, became Bishop of the diocese, and was also called to the Rectorship of Trinity Church. He was specially active in forming a theological seminary in New York, and the result of his efforts was the establishment of the General Theological Seminary of the Protestant Episcopal Church. In 1821 he consented to undertake the duties of Professor of Pastoral Theology and Pulpit Eloquence in that institution. His health failing under his severe labors, in the latter part of 1823 he embarked for England, and,

INCH, FREDERIC A., M. D., Physician and Surgeon, in Westfield, was born in New York city, March 12th, 1822. His parents died while he was quite young, consequently he was thrown upon his own resources and energy for his future success in life. This circumstance, which would have discouraged many, seems in his case to have served as an incentive. He attended the public schools during his boyhood and youth, and on arriving at years of maturity engaged in teaching in Mount Hope, Orange county, New York, and at the same time he spent his leisure hours and evenings in the study of medicine and surgery under the instruction of Drs. Wm. C. Terry and D. F. Graham. After the study of medicine and surgery for four years, including his attendance upon lectures in the University of the City of New York, he was admitted to practise by the New York State Medical Society; and in 1849, removing to Westfield, New Jersey, commenced the practice of medicine and surgery in that place. In accordance with the laws of the State then in force, he submitted to an examination before the State Medical Society of New Jersey, and received his license May 1st, 1851. He has continued to practise in Westfield and vicinity up to the present; having acquired a comfortable competence and a happy home, and having devoted all his time and ability to relieve suffering humanity and assuage the maladies of mankind, he feels rewarded by a grateful people, and the smiles of a kind and beneficent Providence. He was married to Harriet Little, daughter of Colonel William S. Little, of Mount Hope, Orange county, New York, February 6th, 1850. He is a member of the District Medical Society of the County of Union, and in 1873-74 occupied the Presidential chair.

INCH, CHARLES A., A. B., M. D., Physician and Surgeon, of Westfield, is the son of Dr. Frederick A. Finch, whose biographical sketch immediately precedes, and is his associate in practice. He was born in Westfield, New Jersey, August 30th, 1851. Until he was thirteen years of age he attended the public school of his native town, and was then transferred to Grammar School No. 35, Thirteenth street, New York city. In regular course he entered the College of the City of New York, and graduated with honor in the year 1870. He was awarded a special prize in chemistry by Prof. R. O. Doremus. He received the degree of Doctor of Medicine from the College of Physicians and Surgeons, New York, in the year 1873, and at once entered upon the practice of his profession. October 24th, 1876, he married Carrie E., the eldest daughter of the late Charles Cheney, Esq., of Elizabeth, New Jersey. He is a member of the District Medical Society of the County of Union.

OBART, REV. JOHN HENRY, D. D., Pastor of Christ's Church, New Brunswick, New Jersey, Bishop of the Protestant Episcopal Church in the Diocese of New York, late of Auburn, New York, was born in Philadelphia, Pennsylvania, September 14th, 1775. His ancestors, in 1663, had emigrated from Norfolk, England, and settled in Hingham, Massachusetts; his father, Enoch Hobart, was commander of a merchant ship. In 1788 he entered the College of Philadelphia, whence, in 1791, he was transferred to Princeton College, where he graduated in 1793. At first, owing to certain family considerations, he reluctantly undertook to fit himself for mercantile life in the counting-house of his brother-in-law; but finding, after a brief experience, that his tastes and inclination led him in another direction, he resolved to enter upon a course of preparation for the ministry. Receiving at this time an invitation to a tutorship at Princeton, New Jersey, he accepted the post, and began the discharge of his duties in January, 1796. At the same time he studied theology under the guidance of Dr. Samuel Stanhope Smith, the president of the college. In the spring of 1798 he resigned his tutorship and removed to Philadelphia, where he pursued his studies under the supervision of Bishop White, by whom he was admitted to deacon's orders, June 3d, 1798, and was invited to take charge of two suburban parishes near Philadelphia. In 1799 he was called to Christ's Church, New Brunswick, New Jersey, where he remained until he became Rector of St. George's Church, Hempstead, Long Island. Subsequently he declined the Rectorship of St. Mark's Church, New York. In the following September, however, he accepted an invitation to become an assistant minister of Trinity Church, New York. In 1801 he was ordained Priest by Bishop Provoost. He had already been Secretary of the House of Bishops, and was elected Secretary of the Convention of New York, Deputy to the General Conventions of 1801, 1804, and 1808, and on the last two occasions was Secretary to the House of Clerical and Lay Deputies. In 1806 Union College conferred upon him the degree of D. D. In February, 1811, Bishop Moore, of New York, having been disabled from public service by a paralytic stroke, he was elected Assistant Bishop, and was consecrated on the 29th. In consequence of Bishop Moore's infirmities he was then charged with the entire duty of overseeing the church throughout the State of New York. In 1812 he was made Assistant Rector of Trinity Church, and, on Moore's death, in 1816, became Bishop of the diocese, and was also called to the Rectorship of Trinity Church. He was specially active in forming a theological seminary for the church, and the result of his efforts was the foundation of the General Theological Seminary of the Protestant Episcopal Church. In 1821 he consented to undertake the duties of Professor of Pastoral Theology and Pulpit Eloquence in that institution. His health failing under his severe labors, in the latter part of 1823 he embarked for England, and,

November 1st, arrived safely at Liverpool. While abroad he visited Great Britain, France, Switzerland, and Italy, and spent much of his time in investigations and inquiries relative to the progress of religion, and the social and moral condition of Europe. His first sermon, after his return home in 1825, was glowing and patriotic " to an unusual degree." Theological education, Sunday-schools, domestic and foreign missions, the Bible and Prayer-Book Society, the Protestant Episcopal Tract Society, and other associations of a similar character, commanded his warm and steady support. In 1818 he visited the Oneida Indians, and again in 1826, and it was through him that Eleazar Williams (who was afterward thought by some to be the lost Dauphin, Louis XVII.) was admitted to orders, and officiated among the aborigines. He represented the " old-fashioned high-churchman " of his day, and never scrupled to set forth with all boldness the views and sentiments which necessarily brought him into collision with Christians of other denominations, and which were not wholly approved of by many in his own church. In addition to a large number of pamphlets, occasional sermons, and charges, he was the author, or editor, of several publications, which have had a very wide circulation. Among his more important works are : " Companion for the Altar," " Companion for the Festivals and Fasts," "Apology for Apostolic Order," " State of Departed Spirits," " Communicant's Manual," " Clergyman's Companion," " Christian's Manual of Faith and Devotion," and an edition of D'Oyley and Mant's " Commentary on the Bible." He was married in May, 1800, to a daughter of Rev. Dr. Chandler, of Elizabethtown, New Jersey, and died in Auburn, New York, September 10th, 1830.

LARK, HON. ABRAHAM, one of the Signers of the Declaration of Independence from New Jersey, late of Rahway, was born at Elizabethtown, New Jersey, February 15th, 1726. His grandfather, Thomas, was the son of Richard (who emigrated to Elizabeth in 1678), and resided on the Upper or Western Road, about midway between Elizabethtown and Rahway; he had at least three sons and one daughter : Thomas, Abraham, and James, and Mrs. Day. Captain Abraham Clark, commander of the troop, outlived his brother Robert but fifteen days ; Thomas, the eldest, was named in the first charter of the borough as one of the aldermen—"he was judge, and, I believe, keeper of the king's arms, as many muskets and cartouche boxes with the letters ' G. R.' on their covers remained in the house until used by our patriots."—Dr. Abraham Clark. He secured a good English education under competent teachers, and was markedly addicted to the study of mathematics and of civil law. A constitution naturally weak and a slender form prevented him from engaging in laborious pursuits, to which, although reared as a farmer, he was almost wholly unaccustomed. His principal occupations in early life were surveying, conveyancing, and giving legal advice. He was not by profession a lawyer, but tendered advice gratuitously, a task for which he had rendered himself competent by the ardent pursuit of his favorite study. This generosity, which in those more primitive times was held in high estimation, procured him the honorable title of " the poor man's counsellor." His frequent services as an arbitrator of litigated titles to land in different counties of the State indicate the high estimation in which his integrity and the correctness of his judgment were held beyond the immediate circle in which he lived ; and this opinion is confirmed by the appointment of the General Assembly, which empowered him to settle undivided commons. Previous to the commencement of his congressional duties, the confidence reposed in his zeal and ability by his fellow-citizens had been variously manifested. As High Sheriff of the County of Essex, and Clerk of the Colonial Assembly at Amboy, under the royal dominion, he had won distinction through official assiduity and capacity. When the tempest of the Revolution began to agitate the land, he had already passed the meridian of life, and arrived at an age when the actions of men are more frequently guided by principle than by passion ; and it was, therefore, under a well-settled and solemn conviction of the justice of the cause, that he appeared in the first ranks of the revolutionary phalanx, and devoted his remaining years to the service of his country. In the commencement of the conflict he distinguished himself as an active member of the Committee of Public Safety, as a constant attendant and assistant at popular meetings, and as a persevering promoter of patriotic feelings by private communication. After an unremitting series of services in his native province he was summoned to exercise his talents upon a more extensive stage. On the 21st of June, 1776, he was appointed by the Provincial Congress, in conjunction with Richard Stockton, John Hart, Francis Hopkinson and Dr. John Witherspoon, a delegate to the Continental Congress. They were instructed to unite with the delegates of the other colonies in the most vigorous measures for supporting the rights and liberties of America, and, should it be deemed necessary or expedient for this purpose, to join with them in declaring the united colonies independent of Great Britain. He then applied himself zealously to the loyal discharge of his new duties, and for a long time was one of the leading members of the Jersey delegation. His abilities and perseverance in the business of committees, and his plain, clear view of general measures, rendered him a valuable member of the House ; while his fervid patriotism and unswerving integrity attracted the respect and admiration of his colleagues. " His faith and firmness were amply tested a few days after he took his seat by his cordial co-operation with those who advocated the immediate proclamation of independence, and it is believed that his strong conviction of the propriety of that measure united with his many political virtues in promoting his appointment." One of the first duties which devolved on him as a member of the great national council, involving personal safety and fortune, and above all, the liberties of his country, was discharged with alacrity; and he affixed his name to the Declaration of Independence " with those feelings of pride and resolution that are excited by a noble but dangerous action." November 30th, 1776, he was again elected by the Provincial Congress of New Jersey, and continued, with the exception of the session of 1779, to be annually re-elected a delegate from that State until November, 1783. During this long period of service his necessary intimacy with the proceedings of Congress, and the course and nature of the arduous and protracted affairs which frequently demanded a great extent of attention, memory and judgment, rendered him an active and eminently useful member. In 1788 he again took his seat in the national legislature. The intervals of his non-election to Congress were not devoted to leisure, nor applied to that relief from public cares which the feebleness of his constitution required. His exertions and services in the State Legislature, of which he was a member during those periods, were properly appreciated, and his influence became so extended that he personally incurred popular praise or reproach, in proportion to the applause or odium excited by the general acts of the Legislature. An act to regulate the practice in the courts of law in New Jersey, in some degree curtailing the emoluments of practitioners, was called "Clark's law" by the members of the bar; and they, in general, manifested a strong spirit of enmity toward him as the supposed framer of the act. He was styled the "father of the paper currency," although he opposed the emission with the whole weight of his influence, until popular meetings were convened to devise a plan for arresting the course of justice and closing the courts. Contrary to the advice of his friends, who urged a consideration of the personal danger he incurred, he attended one of these meetings, and there explained and enforced the reasons which induced him to desire the postponement of the emission until the fate of similar experiments, then in train in the neighboring States, might afford a practical view of their results. He was instrumental for a time in calming the popular ferment, but was ultimately compelled to coalesce in a measure which appeared unavoidable. He possessed the reputation of being a rigid economist in all things relating to the public treasure; and was one among the earliest promoters of those measures which led to a convention for the purpose of framing a more stable and efficacious constitution for the government of the States. In 1787 he was appointed a member of the general convention which framed the Federal Constitution, but was prevented by ill health from joining in the deliberations of that illustrious assembly. He was opposed to the constitution in its primitive form, but his objections being removed by subsequent amendments, it met with his cordial approbation and support. In the winter of 1789–90 he was appointed a commissioner to settle the accounts of his State with the United States, which office he held until the ensuing election, when he was elected a Representative in the Second Congress, and continued to hold that honorable appointment until a short time previous to his decease. In the Congress of 1794 he exerted his influence and talents in support of the resolutions submitted by Madison, relative to the commerce of the United States. He was also prominent during the troublous period of the Genet complications; and on one occasion moved a resolution to prohibit all intercourse with Great Britain, " until full compensation was made to our citizens for the injuries sustained by them from British armed vessels, and until the Western posts should be delivered up." Exhausted by his political toils and increasing infirmities, he finally retired from public life on the adjournment of Congress, June 9th, 1794. In the following autumn, September 15th, he was stricken down by sunstroke, which terminated his existence in two hours. He died in the sixty-ninth year of his age, and was buried in the church-yard at Rahway, New Jersey.

ICHARDS, REV. AARON, Revolutionary Patriot and Presbyterian minister, late of Rahway, was born in Newark, New Jersey, in 1718. His great-grandfather, Thomas Richards, born in England about 1602, came to America, settled in Hartford, Connecticut, about 1637, and there died in the course of the following year; his son, John, born in 1631, married as early as 1656 Lydia Stocking, and died in 1712, at Newark, New Jersey; one of his sons, John Richards, was born in 1687, and married in 1717 Jane, daughter of Deacon Azariah Crane, of Newark, New Jersey, and died in that town, March 16th, 1748; Mrs. Jane Richards, his wife, died September 12th, 1741, in her fifty-sixth year; they had three sons: Moses and Aaron, twins, and David, born in 1720. In 1743 Aaron graduated at Yale College, having associated there with such men as Governor William Livingston, Samuel Hopkins, D. D., Samuel Buel, D. D., James Sproat, D. D., Noah Welles, D. D., William Peartree Smith, D. D., Eliphalet Williams, D. D., William S. Johnson, President and LL. D., Thomas B. Chandler, D. D., and others; Caleb Smith, of Orange, New Jersey, was his classmate. He was ordained by the Presbytery of New York, November 15th, 1748, and installed the first pastor of the Presbyterian Church of Rahway, New Jersey, where he retained the pastoral charge during an uninterrupted period of forty-two years. His usefulness and happiness were much impaired by a morbid hypochondria, to which he was more or less subject during the greater part of his ministry. He is spoken of, in 1753, as "a pious minister under the deepest melancholy and temptation, harassed with perpetual suggestions to cut his own throat. Naturally, however, he was gay and lively." Having espoused the cause of his country during the war of the Revolution, he was compelled to flee from the British invaders in 1776, and to reside a few months at South Hanover, New Jersey, where he ministered to the Presbyterian Church until the time came when he was enabled to return to his home in safety. With advancing years he became more than ever a victim of the most distressing hypochondria, "so that at length, at the age of seventy-two, he desisted entirely from preaching." The pastoral relation was dissolved November 2d, 1791, and he died at Rahway, May 16th, 1793, in the seventy-sixth year of his age and the forty-fifth of his ministry. His wife, Susannah Smith, a native of England, survived him but a few months. They had seven children : Smith, Alexander, William, Samuel, Vroom, Mary, who married Joseph Barnett, of Rahway, and Betsy, who became the wife of James Brown, of Woodbridge.

AN ARTSDALEN, REV. JACOB, at one time Pastor of the Springfield Presbyterian Church, was born at Somerset, New Jersey, February 8th, 1745, and was, as his name indicates, of Dutch extraction. Symon Jansen Van Arsdalen emigrated from Holland to New Amsterdam in 1653, locating at Flatlands, Long Island, where he was classed among the first and most respected citizens; he died about the year 1710, leaving two sons, Cornelius and John, the prolific source of all the Van Arsdale family in America: Cornelius had six sons—Derick, John, Simon, Philip, Abraham and Jacobus—who settled in Somerset county, New Jersey, as early as 1726; he had also three daughters—Alletta, Petronella and Mary. John was the great-grandfather of the late Cornelius C. Van Arsdale, D. D., of New York ; Philip, born February 12th, 1701, at Flatlands, Long Island, married, April 30th, 1726, Jane Van Dyck, of Red Mills, Long Island (born February 23d, 1703), and had eight children—Cornelius, Hendrick, Mary, Isaac, Philip, John, Jacob and Abraham: he died in his ninety-seventh year, June 17th, 1797, at Somerset, New Jersey. The subject of this sketch was educated at Princeton College and graduated from that institution in 1765, a classmate of Judges Bacon and Rush, of Drs. Halsted and Rumsay, of Robert and Jonathan Ogden, of Rev. Samuel Kirkland, of Rev. Drs. Joel Benedict and Jonathan Edwards, college presidents, and other worthies. June 19th, 1771, he was ordained by the Presbytery of New Brunswick, in whose connection he continued until the latter part of 1774, when he was received by the Presbytery of New York, and put in charge of the church of Springfield, New Jersey. He continued in the orderly and faithful performance of the duties of this office, as far as his health permitted, more than a quarter of a century. In the spring of 1797, and again three years later, he was, by reason of long-continued illness, disqualified for preaching, and, at his request, supplies

for his pulpit were provided by the presbytery. He was eventually compelled to relinquish the pastoral office, and was dismissed from his charge, May 6th, 1801. He married Mary Sutphen, of Monmouth county, New Jersey, who survived him and died at Somerset, and had four children. Mary, wife of Grover Coe; Jane, wife of Mr. Stewart, of Elizabethtown; Elizabeth Ryerson, wife of Isaac Van Arsdale, of Somerset; and Elias Van Arsdale, LL. D., of Newark. He died at Springfield, New Jersey, October 24th, 1803.

AMILTON, HON. ROBERT, Lawyer, of Newton, was born at Hamburg, Sussex county, New Jersey, 1811. His father was General Benjamin Hamilton. He received a substantial education, directed his attention to the study of law, was admitted to the New Jersey bar in 1836, and was made counsellor three years afterward. He served two terms as Prosecutor of the Pleas of Sussex county, and for several years was Director of the Board of Chosen Freeholders. In 1862 he was nominated by the Democrats as their candidate for Assembly, was elected both that and the succeeding year, and served during the sessions of 1863-64. During the latter session the Speaker, Mr. Taylor, died, and Mr. Hamilton was elected to succeed him. In 1872 he was nominated by the Democrats of the Fourth Congressional District as their congressional candidate. The district is composed of the counties of Hunterdon, Warren, Somerset, and Sussex. He was elected by over 2,000 majority. In 1874 he was renominated and again elected by an increased majority. Mr. Hamilton is an able lawyer, and previous to his election to Congress had an extensive practice in all the State courts. He is an unflinching Democrat, and an earnest advocate of the doctrines of that party.

OSS, HON. MILES, Merchant, of New Brunswick, was born at Raritan, New Jersey, in 1828. When quite young he removed with his father to New Brunswick, New Jersey, where he was educated, and engaged with his father in the vessel trade. He was for some time one of the Chosen Freeholders of New Brunswick, Mayor of the city, and was for two years successively elected to the New Jersey Assembly. He is largely engaged in the wholesale coal trade, was for a long while a leading Bank Director, a member of the Board of Street Commissioners, and variously interested in the public institutions of New Brunswick. In 1874 he was nominated by the Democrats of the Third District as their candidate for Congress, and although the district had elected a Republican representative two years previously, he was elected by over 2,000 majority. The Third District is composed of the counties of Middlesex, Monmouth and Union. His congressional career has been a satisfactory one, and he has the entire confidence of his party.

EFFERS, HON. WILLIAM N., Lawyer, late of Camden, New Jersey, was born in New York, and after being admitted to the bar of that State, went to New Orleans in the employ of John Jacob Astor. After a shórt stay in the South he removed to Cincinnati, and undertook to practise as a lawyer; but soon became involved in some transaction which occasioned an indictment to be found against him in the criminal court of that city, for the forgery or falsification of a bond. He was, however, permitted to put in bail of a nominal character, and to leave without a trial. He came to New Jersey about the year 1813, and after a short residence in Mount Holly, where he secured the friendship and patronage of Judge Rossell, who remained his warm friend as long as he lived, was in 1814 examined and licensed as an attorney. He then took up his residence in Salem, and in 1817 was admitted as a counsellor. In 1834 he was called to the degree of serjeant-at-law. "He was never a well-read lawyer, but had some remarkable characteristics. He was a very handsome man, and distinguished for polite manners and a winning address." He rapidly acquired an extensive and lucrative practice in his profession, and as an advocate before a Court of Common Pleas, or a jury, won merited distinction as a most astute and formidable adversary; and he had also the faculty of always retaining his clients, who seemed never, when worsted even, to attribute blame to him in the slightest degree. At an early period he engaged in the political movements of the hour, taking sides with the Democratic party. In 1827, and in several years afterward, he was elected a member of the Assembly, and in 1829 was a candidate in the caucus of the Jackson members for the position of Governor, but did not succeed in obtaining the nomination. He was also named for the Senate of the United States, and at one time confidently expected to succeed. "Salem has always been a warmly contested county, sometimes on the one side, sometimes on the other." He was one of the first who engaged personally in canvassing for votes, now so common a habit as to occasion no surprise, and for this step was strongly condemned by many who deemed it undignified and unbecoming. Although he had warm personal friends, he contrived to create equally violent opponents, and much injustice may have been done him by those toward whom he showed a hostile attitude, or who were politically opposed to him. He was intimately identified with the early management of the Salem Bank, originally chartered in connection with a steam flour-mill, and in some way was interested in the setting up of a manufacturing company in the name and under the direction of a brother; and in connection there-

with was accused, justly or unjustly, of blamable transactions, which occasioned a legislative investigation. In the early part of Jackson's administration he was appointed Minister to one of the South American republics, and had proceeded as far as Mobile on his way to the mission. In the meantime, however, some of those persons whose enmity he had provoked procured a copy of the old indictment against him, and he was recalled before he left the country. This occasioned his renunciation of politics, and he eventually removed to Camden, New Jersey, where he resided and was actively engaged in his profession, holding only the office of Prosecutor of Pleas, until his death in 1853, at the age of about sixty-five years.

ITSWORTH, HON. CALEB S., President Judge of the Court of Common Pleas, of Newark, was born at Metuchen, Middlesex county, New Jersey, September 16th, 1826. His father, Abraham D. Titsworth, was engaged in farming and the manufacture of clothing. The lad attended the schools of his native place and remained at home till the age of sixteen, being brought up on the farm. He then became a pupil at the De Ruyter Institute, Madison county, New York, with the view of preparing for college. Here he remained for about eighteen months, and subsequently engaged in teaching in the public schools of Middlesex county for about six months. When eighteen years of age he went to Shiloh, Cumberland county, and took charge of the Shiloh Academy. During this latter period he entered his name as a student-at-law in the office, at Bridgeton, of Judge Nixon, now of the United States District Court, and read law during his hours of leisure from teaching. The summer of 1847 he spent at Rutgers Grammar School, New Brunswick, and in the fall of that year entered the sophomore class of the Union College, then under the charge of the late venerable Dr. Eliphalet Nott. He was graduated therefrom in 1850 as A. B., with high honors. In consequence of too close application to study his health had by this time become materially impaired, and he determined upon a trip to the South, partly for the purpose of recruiting himself physically, partly for observation, and partly to seek an opening for a career. Gradually he drifted down to Mississippi, where he engaged as classical teacher in Brighton Grammar School, situated about nine miles from Natchez. This institution was then under the charge of a noble old Virginian, John S. Moseley, now deceased. Mr. Titsworth filled this position until March, 1853, when he returned to his father's home, which had been removed to Plainfield, New Jersey, and entered the office of Joseph Annin, in that place, as law student. With him he studied for a year or two, and then moved to Newark, where he completed his law course in the office of the present Chancellor Runyon. Admitted to the bar in November, 1855, he worked hard at his profession, and at the same time took an active part in public affairs. He was especially active in the campaign of 1856, and was among the first to aid in the formation in Jersey of the Republican party, of which he has ever since been a staunch and consistent supporter. His convictions on the subject of slavery were crystallized and deepened by his residence in the South and his personal experience of the working of the "institution," and he thus naturally became a most pronounced Republican and strongly opposed to the extension of the system to other States. In January, 1866, he was elected City Councillor for the city of Newark, was re-elected in 1867, and continued to hold the office until appointed Prosecutor of the Pleas for Essex county in March, 1867, when he resigned. He prosecuted the county pleas for one term, that is, until 1872, when the politics of the State undergoing a change, he was not reappointed. During his term of office some important trials occurred, which he conducted most successfully; indeed, he fulfilled the responsible position with an ability and fidelity highly satisfactory to the community. In 1874 he was elected by the Legislature, in joint convention, under the old constitution, as President Judge of the Court of Common Pleas, and now holds the appointment. He is a Director and counsel for the Merchants' Insurance Company, of Newark, which he was instrumental in organizing and has taken great interest in from the beginning. He was married in November, 1858, to Fanny C. Grant, daughter of Charles Grant, an old and highly respected resident of Newark. Judge Titsworth is a man of high ability, and adds to his intellectual strength both conscientiousness of purpose and dignity of character. In the performance of his judicial duties he has displayed a decision and independence of external influences, and a fidelity to personal convictions of right, which have crowned his career with the approval of all right-thinking people. In his private life he enjoys the cordial esteem of all who know him, his daily walk and conversation showing him to be one of the manliest and most genial, as well as one of the most upright of men.

AYLOR, WILLIAM JOHNSTON, President of the North Jersey Iron Company, was born, January 5th, 1836, at High Bridge (then called Solitude), Hunterdon county, New Jersey. He is a son of Lewis H. Taylor and his wife, Jane C., whose maiden name was Johnston. His family has long resided at High Bridge, his great-grandfather having pursued the manufacture of iron there before the war of the Revolution, acquiring in the vicinity valuable landed estates, with extensive water-power and large deposits of iron ore. A sketch of his father, and also of his uncle, George W. Taylor, will be found in this work. He received his early education in the schools of his native county, attending subsequently St. Mary's College, at Wilmington, Delaware. The interval between the time of his leaving school and the attainment of his majority was spent at home in the discharge of clerical duties in the iron works, thus while still a youth familiarizing himself with the humbler operations of the business in which he was destined to pass the greater part of his life and achieve the highest distinction. Nevertheless he did not immediately enter upon this business. In 1857 he went to Philadelphia, where he engaged in mercantile pursuits, which he followed until the outbreak of the civil war, when he received the appointment of Sutler to the 3d Regiment of New Jersey Volunteers, and served in that capacity for about two years. Returning to Philadelphia he became the prime mover in the organization of the Coastwise Steamship Company of Philadelphia. This enterprise, in which he was associated with Mr. E. C. Knight and other well-known merchants and capitalists of Philadelphia, did not in the end prove successful, however, and he turned his attention to the building of ocean steamers. Among the products of his skill in this line was the model propeller known as the "Electric Spark," which was placed on the mail line between New York and New Orleans, and on her second voyage was captured by the notorious "Alabama," a disaster which, in the interest of the stockholders of the ill-fated steamer, he made it his personal business to endeavor to repair, and which, after fighting for the resulting claim step by step before the Alabama Claims Commission, and jealously guarding the interests of the rightful owners against false or imaginary claimants, he has lately had the satisfaction of repairing, by paying over to the stockholders $227,000, the sum awarded by the commission. Though the claim was undoubtedly just, the stockholders clearly realize, in view of the endless slips between the cup of the best claim and the lip of the claimant, that they have only him to thank for their ultimate indemnification. In 1866 he returned to High Bridge and regularly entered upon his destined vocation, taking charge at once of the iron works, which in 1868 were incorporated as "The Taylor Iron Works," having been enlarged and a cam-wheel foundry and machine-shop added in the course of the two previous years. The capital of the company was then $350,000, but in 1871 the capital was increased and the works were enlarged to their present capacity, which is probably greater than that of any other establishment of the kind in the country. Its specialty is the manufacture of cam-wheels, car-axles, and car and locomotive forgings. He continued in charge of the works until 1875, when he resigned his position as Treasurer and General Manager, to accept that of President and Treasurer of the Union Iron Company, now known as the North Jersey Iron Company, which he was chiefly instrumental in organizing. This company, having a capital stock of $300,000, is largely engaged in the mining and

smelting ores... conn y,... mines being
ne r Chester and its ft... at Po... the pre ent
northern terminus of the I gh Bria... t l ad Besides
his effi ent s rv ces as the l ead of the c mp... e las in
vented a furnace for roasting the... tes of Ne
Jersey whe by the sulphu... sep... at d from... ore, an
invention that bi s fair to... vo... considerable
measure, the iron manuf turing bu ss of the State, and
which certa ly shows n co... on w h his successful
administration, that as h chief of an iron com pa v he s
the right n in right place. In... wi h his
fathe... ated the High Bridge Rail... b th having
been offi a'l connected with it ntil it was completed an 1
was... over to the New Jersey Central. The High Bridge
road wa chartered in 1872, and compete l in 1876. I
for s th... ut ct f r the iron mines of Mo t s c nty;
and, no w l tanding the depression of the times since its
completi on, its re ght business has quite exceed l xe on
tion, and with a... n of prosperity o the iron in... rs... l
no doubt prove one of the l... t j.yi g roads in... Se t...
The prominent part he took in... on... i r

twice m n... in 1858 u... k... c f... t.

he is held by his fello v-Sen t... appear... he numbe... f
res onsible ar l ion... p... t ons... h... v have assigned hi... the l t ne of l g... i... lu l...
Ch rm nshi of the c mm... on... p rations, the...
mittee Is e l c... br s, the Committee n T de trial
... C r... e Comm tee... l diers
dress Home...... a mun ber of the t mor t...
on Municipal Cot pora... d l v... u... her... po tan
committees. When it is con... l... e is not a law
that he has had no spec al... c t ti g, a l that h
ent red the Sena e without... ve experi c... av
that acqu red in three short terms of civ... he Assembl
these positions, conferr d on him y l e lle gues, speak
signifi antly, it must be owned, of the strength a l quick
ness o h s u first nding as well as of his s erling moral
qu e... l e... n trut a ance s rong and pene... ng
mon s n e u facult hich, when reinforced by a
sound moral e se, is ja e of dealing uccessiu y at
tty short notice with mo t of tl e problems of busines

... l t... one ab... all I,... De nou ie t

P he ... ult r of Pe I he o I can yl an

ILVERTH N, H N W 1
was born in 1823, in Warren cou... t... H is son of Daniel S lverthorn a... mc of
W r... His fam a of Germ n desce... and
a... g the Id r sidents of that section of... te.
He was educa ed in the public chools
of his native co nty, afte leaving which he engaged in
agricultu al... rsuits u... l he was twen... fiv... years o... g,
when he embarke l... e b siness of a drover and stock-
dealer, which he ha... con ucted with ste dily nc...
success unt'l it has grown to be very extens ve.
ene gy, abili y and in grity which he displayed as
n ss mat o n gave hi... nence in the c mm... y,
and led... n to the public service, for which he a... ou...
prove l h... h... and in... h accordingly, th...
an interruption he has sinc e cnt nued. In 1858 he wa...
elected Coll... r W rren cou... ling the po i o...
1861. He ft... of Treasu r of the Borough of P...
vid re for on... y... as... so been a member of the Tow n
Council of Be... 9 he w. s e ected a m ber o
the S a e Assm... ec e l n 1871 and 1872, each
time w hout oppos... I llican p rty n k ng
nominations. In 1875... lected to the State Senate, oi
wb eh h... l a me... k ng among the... est and
mos tr sted of the body... erti v among the m
d ligent, vigilant and fa thf... h g... tio n w ie

ONDY, JOSEPH IARI... N... D. I hv ici n
of J rsey C tv, w... b rn, O... e oth 18 9,
the I rovince of New Brunswi k. Down on of
Canada a... l... s... t Thom and Margaret
P... o y... I... a lur a t t f th I'

h... e ered th off... or li N

ii... ntl of J...... m t at Jerse Ci
where he... where he has since re-
sid J...... an as ured o e from he hr
and h... ing practitioners of th city.
He is a c...... l... s rict Medical Socie y of Hu l o...

smelting of ores in Morris county, its principal mines being near Chester, and its furnace at Port Oram, the present northern terminus of the High Bridge Railroad. Besides his efficient services as the head of the company, he has invented a furnace for roasting the sulphurous ores of New Jersey, whereby the sulphur is separated from the ore, an invention that bids fair to revolutionize, in a considerable measure, the iron manufacturing business of the State, and which certainly shows, in connection with his successful administration, that as the chief of an iron company he is the right man in the right place. In conjunction with his father he originated the High Bridge Railroad, both having been officially connected with it until it was completed and passed over to the New Jersey Central. The High Bridge road was chartered in 1872, and completed in 1876. It forms the main outlet for the iron mines of Morris county; and, notwithstanding the depression of the times since its completion, its freight business has quite exceeded expectation, and with a return of prosperity to the iron interest will no doubt prove one of the best paying roads in the State. The prominent part he took in constructing it entitles him to the lasting gratitude of the great interest of which he is so worthy and distinguished a representative. He has been twice married: in 1858, to Ellen Knight, of Philadelphia, who died in 1865; and, in 1868, to Mary Alward, of Auburn, New Jersey.

ILVERTHORN, HON. WILLIAM, of Belvidere, was born in 1823, in Warren county, New Jersey. He is a son of Daniel Silverthorn, a farmer of Warren. His family are of German descent, and among the old residents of that section of the State. He was educated in the public schools of his native county, after leaving which he engaged in agricultural pursuits until he was twenty-five years of age, when he embarked in the business of a drover and stock-dealer, which he has conducted with steadily increasing success until it has grown to be very extensive. The energy, ability and integrity which he displayed as a business man soon gave him prominence in the community, and led him into the public service, for which he at once proved his fitness, and in which, accordingly, with scarcely an interruption, he has since continued. In 1858 he was elected Collector for Warren county, filling the position until 1861. He held the office of Treasurer of the Borough of Belvidere for one year. He has also been a member of the Town Council of Belvidere. In 1869 he was elected a member of the State Assembly, and re-elected in 1871 and 1872, each time without opposition, the Republican party making no nominations. In 1875 he was elected to the State Senate, of which he is still a member, ranking among the ablest and most trusted of the body, as he is certainly among the most diligent, vigilant and faithful. The high estimation in which

66

he is held by his fellow-Senators appears in the number of responsible and laborious positions to which they have assigned him in the business of legislation, including the Chairmanship of the Committee on Corporations, the Committee on Miscellaneous Bills, the Committee on Industrial Schools for Girls, and the Committee on Soldiers' Children's Home. He is, besides, a member of the Committee on Municipal Corporations, and of various other important committees. When it is considered that he is not a lawyer, that he has had no special intellectual training, and that he entered the Senate without any legislative experience, save that acquired in three short terms of service in the Assembly, these positions, conferred on him by his colleagues, speak significantly, it must be owned, of the strength and quickness of his understanding, as well as of his sterling moral qualities. He is in truth a man of strong and penetrating common sense, a faculty which, when reinforced by a sound moral sense, is capable of dealing successfully, at pretty short notice, with most of the problems of business and of life. In politics he is a Democrat, and a staunch and true one, abiding tranquilly by the Democratic principles and the Democratic organization alike through evil and through good report, and exhibiting neither bitterness in the long night of defeat nor vindictiveness in the breaking day of triumph. He not only believes in his party, but is proud of it; and his party, as all must allow, has reason to be proud of him. He was married, in 1847, to Miss Pipher, daughter of Peter Pipher, of Pennsylvania.

ONDY, JOSEPH HARRISON, M. D., Physician, of Jersey City, was born, October 9th, 1829, in the Province of New Brunswick, Dominion of Canada, and is a son of Thomas and Margaret (Biggs) Vondy. His father, a native of the Isle of Man, was engaged in mercantile pursuits, but retired from business some years ago; and his mother, at the time of her marriage to his father, was a widow—Mrs. Margaret (Biggs) McCullum. His early education he received at a private school, after which he attended a grammar school in the town of Chatham, New Brunswick. Having determined upon entering the medical profession, he entered the office of Dr. K. B. Forbes, in that town, where he pursued his studies for a year, and in the autumn of 1848 went to New York city, where he matriculated at the university of that city. After attending the usual prescribed courses of lectures, delivered in that institution, he graduated therefrom in the spring of 1851. In the following month of June he established himself at Jersey City, where he commenced practice, and where he has since resided. His success has been an assured one from the first, and he ranks among the leading practitioners of the city. He is a member of the District Medical Society of Hudson county, and has been a delegate to the American Medical Association. Since the organization, by Drs. Hunt and Morris and himself, of the Jersey City Charity Hospital, in 1868, he has been a member of its medical staff; and has also filled a similar position in the Hudson County Church Hospital. He was married, in 1853, to Mrs. J. T. Gilbert, *née* Merritt Wilson, of New York city.

———————

EASBEY, ANTHONY Q., of Newark, Lawyer and United States District Attorney for the District of New Jersey, was born, March 1st, 1824, in Salem, New Jersey. His ancestors were among the earliest settlers of Salem county, the capital of which, Salem, was the first place settled in West Jersey, having been founded in 1675 by John Fenwick, the English Quaker, who then claimed authority as chief proprietor over that section of the province. Edward Keasbey, the great-grandfather of the subject of this sketch, bore a prominent part in the public affairs of New Jersey during the period that ushered in the war of independence. In November, 1763, he "was returned a representative to serve in the General Assembly for the colonies of Salem and Cumberland," in which capacity he served until 1769. He was elected one of the Deputies for Salem to the Provincial Congress, which assembled at Trenton in October, 1775, and attended the session of that Congress held at New Brunswick in 1776, at which a State constitution was adopted, the Statehood of New Jersey and the nationality of the United Colonies dating from the same year. In 1778 he was appointed a member of the Council of Safety. His son, Anthony Keasbey, was for a long time Clerk of the county of Salem, and from 1798 to 1801 represented that county in the General Assembly. The father of the present subject, Edward Q. Keasbey, born in 1793, was a physician, having studied with Dr. Philip Physick, of Philadelphia, and been engaged in active practice until his death, in 1847. His learning, however, extended beyond the bounds of his profession, as did his training and activity; insomuch that, February 27th, 1840, he was appointed a Judge of the Court of Common Pleas, and in 1844 was chosen a Presidential Elector by the Whigs, of whose peerless leader, Henry Clay, he was a strong supporter. He resided all his life in Salem. Anthony Q. Keasbey, the son, was graduated at Yale College in 1843, and shortly afterwards began the study of law, studying with Francis L. McCulloch, in Salem, and subsequently with Cortlandt Parker, in Newark. He was admitted to the bar in October, 1846, and began the practice of the law in Salem, where he pursued it until 1852, at which time he removed to Newark, and in 1855 entered into partnership with Cortlandt Parker, his former preceptor, the firm, which was the first formed in the State after the passage of the law authorizing legal partnerships, continuing for twenty years.

In April, 1861, he was appointed, by President Lincoln, United States Attorney for the District of New Jersey, and in April, 1865, reappointed; but, his new commission not having been signed at Mr. Lincoln's death, he was provisionally appointed by President Johnson till the next session of the Senate, when, in 1866, he was regularly appointed, being reappointed by President Grant in 1870, and again in 1874. He has thus held the office continuously since the spring of 1861, a period of unbroken incumbency longer than that of any other United States district attorney in the Union. Of his fidelity as an officer and his ability as a lawyer no clearer or stronger proof than this record could be asked. It is a testimonial, so to speak, of his official, professional and personal merit, signed by the President and Senate of the United States, and countersigned by the bar of the State. After the dissolution of his long partnership with Mr. Parker he associated with him in the practice of the law his two sons, Edward Q. and George M., under the style of A. Q. Keasbey & Sons, and this connection now subsists. He is a man of polite attainments, it should be said, as well as of professional learning, adding to distinguished legal abilities and acquirements the culture and tastes of the scholar. His wife is the daughter of the Hon. Jacob W. Miller, for two consecutive terms a representative of New Jersey in the Senate of the United States.

———————

OD, REV. THADDEUS, Presbyterian Minister, of Cross Creek, was born near Newark, New Jersey, March 7th, 1740 (o. s.), and was the son of Stephen Dod. He spent his youthful days in Mendham, whence his father, who was a native of Guilford, Connecticut, had removed from Newark. From early childhood he had strong religious impressions, and the private record of his exercises through a series of years shows that he was the subject of almost constant internal conflicts, until 1764, when he believed that he experienced a decisive change of character. In the course of the following year he was admitted to the communion of the church in Mendham. At a very early period "he began to develop an extraordinary taste and talent for mathematics," and was earnestly desirous of obtaining a collegiate education; but the straitened circumstances of his father forbade the expectation of it, except as it should be accomplished through his own efforts. By teaching school at different times, and studying in leisure hours, he at length succeeded in fitting himself to enter college and in acquiring the means of meeting his expenses there. In the spring of 1771 he joined the sophomore class of the College of New Jersey, and was graduated in the fall of 1773, under the presidency of Dr. Witherspoon. He subsequently settled in Newark, and entered on the study of theology under the direction of Rev. Dr. Macwhorter. After remaining there about one year he removed to Morristown, where he continned his studies under Rev. Timothy Johnes, who had been his first teacher in Latin. In 1775 he was licensed to preach by the New York Presbytery. In the winter of 1776–77 he was prostrated by a severe attack of inflammatory rheumatism; but in March, though still unable to dress himself without assistance, he resolved on making a tour to the West. After preaching in parts of Virginia and Maryland, he crossed the mountains and visited the settlements of George's Creek, Muddy Creek and Dunlap's Creek, thence proceeding to Ten Mile. As there were at the latter place a number of families who had removed from Morris county, "it is not improbable that they had invited him to visit them, and that his journey was undertaken with special reference to that purpose." This emigration had taken place about the year 1773, when there had been for several years peace with the Indian tribes; but by a fresh outbreak, in the spring of 1774, these people were driven back, and took refuge in a fort near Monongahela river. The next year they returned and built a fort, to which they could resort in time of danger. In the summer season, for several years, they were compelled frequently to remain together in the defences, the men going out in armed parties to work on their farms; and in the winter, when the Indians had retired to their wigwams and hunting-grounds, they returned to their habitations. Such was the state of things when he went among them; and as they were his old friends, and some of them associates with him in the scenes of an interesting revival in New Jersey, in 1764, the meeting must have been, on both sides, one of uncommon interest. The frequent incursions of the savages, however, had put a stop to immigration, and prevented the increase of their numbers, and consequently delayed what was ardently desired, the establishment of a church and the administration of its ordinances among them. After preaching for some time in that comparatively desolate region, he returned to New Jersey in August, 1777. The people at Ten Mile during his sojourn there expressed a strong desire that he should take up his residence among them as their minister; and though there were not more than ten men within their bounds who were professors of religion, and not one man of wealth among them all, they unanimously agreed to support him and his family, if he would cast in his lot with them. He ultimately yielded to their wishes, and was ordained accordingly by the Presbytery of New York, sine titulo, in October, 1777, with a view to finding his home in that then wild part of the country. He then left New Jersey, with his family and also two of his brothers, to carry out his purpose in regard to an ultimate settlement. By the 10th of November they had arrived at Patterson's creek, in Hampshire county, Virginia; but hearing while there of an attack by the Indians on the fort at Wheeling, and of the consequent confusion and terror prevailing throughout the West, they deemed it imprudent to proceed farther at that time. But after remaining a few days with his family, he

left his brothers, and, crossing the mountains alone, proceeded to Ten Mile, where he preached in the forts and baptized the children. After his return he remained at Patterson's creek for nearly two years, during which time he was employed in preaching there, and in the adjacent counties in Virginia and Maryland, where, it would seem, no churches had yet been organized. His labors in this field were attended with a manifest blessing, and when he was about to leave, a vigorous effort was made to retain him, and a much better support offered than he could expect at Ten Mile; "but he could not be diverted from his purpose." In September, 1779, accordingly, he, with his family, proceeded on his way, and crossed the mountains on pack-horses. On reaching the place of his destination "he found a dark and forbidding state of things," yet entered upon his labors with great zeal and self-denial. August 15th, 1781, he organized a church consisting of twenty-five members. The first administration of the Lord's Supper was in a barn, in May, 1783, and the first house of worship was erected in the summer of 1785. As he "had an exquisite taste for music, and withal was well acquainted with it as a science, he caused special attention to be given to the performance of that part of public worship." He was specially attentive to the interests of education, frequently visiting schools and counselling and encouraging the teachers; and in the spring of 1782 opened a classical and mathematical school. September 24th, 1787, in conjunction with Messrs. Smith and McMillan, he instituted an academy at Washington, Pennsylvania, and secured a charter for it. At the fall meeting of presbytery he was appointed to preach at Cross Creek, and accepted that charge. He died May 20th, 1793. Says Rev. Dr. Eliot: "As an academy, it soon acquired distinction by having for its first president the Rev. Thaddeus Dod, one of the early literary pioneers of western Pennsylvania."

ARDENBERGH, HON. AUGUSTUS A., Member of Congress, of Jersey City, was born in that city, May 18th, 1830. He is a son of the late Cornelius L. Hardenbergh, LL. D., of New Brunswick, who was during his lifetime a leading member of the New Jersey bar, and for many years prominently connected with Rutgers College, of which institution Rev. J. R. Hardenbergh, D. D., another of his distinguished ancestors, was the first president and founder. Augustus entered Rutgers in 1844, but continued in college only one year, the failing health and sight of his father rendering the son's assistance as amanuensis necessary. Two years later he entered a counting-house in New York, and took up his residence in Jersey City. In 1852 he became connected with the Hudson County Bank, and in 1858 was appointed its Cashier. For some years previously he had manifested an interest in politics. In 1853 he was elected by the Democrats to the New Jersey Legislature from Jersey City, and although quite a young man, took an active part in legislative affairs. He was five times elected Alderman of Jersey City—in 1857, 1858, 1859, 1860 and 1862. During the last-named year he was chosen President of the Common Council. In 1868 he removed to Bergen, and during the first year's residence there was almost unanimously elected to the town council. During the same year he was elected State Director of Railroads by the New Jersey Legislature, and in 1872 represented the Fourth Congressional District as their delegate to the Baltimore National Convention. He again removed to Hudson county in 1873, and has since continued to reside there. In 1874, at the solicitation of his friends, he became the Democratic candidate for Congress, and although the district had gone Republican two years previously by over one thousand majority, he was elected by nearly five thousand majority. He is a ready and graceful speaker, a cultivated gentleman, and is a representative who reflects honor on himself and his State. He was again elected in 1876.

————

OBESON, WILLIAM PENN, Lawyer and Jurist, was the son of Morris Robeson and Tacey Paul, his wife. He was the third son of a large family of children, and was born in Philadelphia, November 10th, 1798. His ancestor, Andrew Robeson, came to Warren county, New Jersey, from England with William Penn, and was a member of Governor Markham's Privy Council. He had a son, Andrew, who was sent to England and educated at Oxford University. The second Andrew had two sons, Jonathan and Edward. Jonathan Robeson was one of the pioneers in the iron manufacture in America. He built a blast furnace called "The Forest of Dean," in what was then called the "Highlands of York," in the province of New York; the "Weymouth" Furnace, in what is now Ocean county, New Jersey; and "Oxford" Furnace, in what is now Warren county, New Jersey. This last-named furnace was commenced in 1741, and the first iron was run from it March 17th, 1743. The same furnace, now belonging to the Oxford Iron Company, is still in successful operation, and the iron mines on the same estate are among the most valuable in the State. Jonathan Robeson had two sons, John and Morris. John was the father of Judge James M. Robeson, of Belvidere, and several other sons, most of whom are now dead. Morris, the father of William P., lived a portion of his life in Philadelphia and another portion at Oxford, where he died in 1823. William P. was a large landowner in Warren county, engaged a large portion of his life in agricultural and mercantile pursuits, and for a long time occupied a position on the bench of the Common Pleas, over which he presided for more than twenty-five years.

He was married early in life to Anna Maria Maxwell, the daughter of Hon. George C. Maxwell, and sister of Hon. John P. B. Maxwell, both of whom at different times represented the State of New Jersey in the United States Congress. She is the granddaughter of Captain John Maxwell and grandniece of General William Maxwell, both of the Continental army. His wife still survives him, and resides at Camden, New Jersey. Judge Robeson was an ardent Whig in politics, and occupied a prominent position in the party in the upper portion of the State, but as that region was during his entire career largely Democratic, he was never elected to any important office. During the latter years of his life he was a decided Republican, but took less interest in politics. He was by birth a Quaker in religious belief, but afterwards connected himself with the Episcopal Church, of which he was a prominent supporter. He resided for several years after his marriage at Oxford Furnace, which then belonged to his brother-in-law and himself, but had for a long time been out of blast. About the year 1832, having rented the furnace to Messrs. Henry Jordan & Co., who at that time put it in operation, he removed to Belvidere, where he resided until his death. He died at Belvidere, December 2d, 1864, leaving his widow and four children surviving him, viz.: George Maxwell, the present Secretary of the Navy; William Penn, who served with honor as Colonel of the 3d New Jersey Cavalry under Sheridan in the war of the rebellion, and was brevetted as a Brigadier-General; Emily Maxwell, married to Joseph M. P. Price, of Philadelphia; and Anna M.

————

cCAULY, REV. THOMAS, D. D., Presbyterian Clergyman, was born February 28th, 1818, in Franklin county, Pennsylvania, and is a son of Thomas McCauly, a merchant of that county. The family are of Scotch-Irish origin; the grandfather of the subject of this sketch emigrated to this country, and with his associates settled at Ringgold Manor, in Maryland. His son not liking the institution of slavery, removed to Pennsylvania, where Thomas, as already stated, was born. He was prepared for college at Greencastle Academy, and in 1848 entered the College of New Jersey, at Princeton, where he was graduated with the class of 1852, together with Senator Magie, of Elizabeth, New Jersey, Donald Cameron, late Secretary of War, and President Kendal, of Lincoln University. The same year he entered the Theological Seminary, and was graduated therefrom in 1855. Immediately upon graduation he entered the ministry as pastor of a Presbyterian church on Long Island, where he remained for nine years. Then he moved to Philadelphia, and became Secretary of the Presbyterian Board of Education. In 1867 he accepted a call to the Presbyterian Church of Hackettstown, New Jersey, where he has since continued to officiate. At the present time he is

Moderator of the Presbyterian Synod of New Jersey. He was married, October 1st, 1857, to Maria Louisa Dunton, of Philadelphia.

ACDONALD, REV. JAMES M., D. D., lately Pastor of the First Presbyterian Church of Princeton, was born at Limerick, Maine, in 1812, the son of Major-General John Macdonald. He received the advantages of an excellent education; graduated from Union College, New York, in 1832, and from the Divinity School in New Haven soon afterwards. Drawn towards the ministry of the Presbyterian Church, he was ordained in 1835. For a time he was pastor of the Fifteenth Street Presbyterian Church in New York, and for twenty-three years he was pastor of the First Church in Princeton, filling the position once occupied by the late President John Witherspoon, of the College of New Jersey. His first book, "Credulity, as Illustrated by Successful Impostures in Science, Superstition, and Fanaticism," appeared in 1843. Five years later he published his "Key to the Book of Revelation," of which there was a second edition in 1848. In 1847 he issued a short "History of the Presbyterian Church of Jamaica, Long Island," where he was once settled as pastor. In 1856 appeared "The Book of Ecclesiastes Explained," a scholarly commentary widely and favorably reviewed. A few years later he printed a volume of sermons with the title of "My Father's House; or, the Heaven of the Bible," and at the time of his death he was engaged in preparing another work for the press. He died at Princeton, April, 1877, leaving a wife and six children.

IFFORD, HON. C. L. C., Lawyer and Jurist, late of Newark, was born in that city in November, 1825. He was a son of the late Arthur Gifford, one of the most esteemed of the old residents of Newark, whose estate he inherited and occupied at the time of his death. He graduated from the Vale Law School in 1844, and afterwards studied with his father. In 1847 he was licensed as an attorney-at-law, and was admitted as counsellor-at-law in January, 1850. For four years he was Deputy Collector for the port of Newark. Mr. Gifford was elected to the House of Assembly in 1857, and in 1858 appointed State Senator, which position be held for two years, during the second year of his term being chosen President of the Senate. Although a Democrat, he received the Republican nomination for Mayor in 1862, but was defeated by the late Moses Bigelow. On the 29th of June, 1872, he was sworn in as Presiding Judge of the Essex County Court of Common Pleas, to fill the unexpired term of Judge Frederick H. Teese, and remained upon the bench until the appointment of Judge Titsworth,

in 1874. Mr. Gifford was endowed with a strong constitution, and although he is supposed to have overworked himself in early life, when prominent in politics and the cause of temperance, retained an unusual amount of health and vigor until the closing years of his life. He was first taken ill during the early part of 1875, and in the spring of that year made a trip to Europe in the hope of recovering his health, but failed to derive any permanent benefit from it. Throughout his final illness he was attended by a devoted wife, whose care and patience were unremitting. He was a genial, kindly gentleman, beloved by many friends and respected by all who knew him. His death occurred March 31st, 1877.

OUDINOT, ELIAS, was born in Philadelphia, May 2d, 1740. His ancestors were French Huguenots, who came to America soon after the revocation of the Edict of Nantes. He received a classical education, and having resolved upon the law as his profession, entered the office of Richard Stockton, the elder, of New Jersey. Being admitted to the bar, his agreeable manners, good principles, practical qualities and ready abilities as a speaker, early opened the way to a lucrative practice at the provincial bar, a way made more easy, perhaps, by his marriage with a sister of his preceptor in the law, Mr. Stockton, himself already at the head of the New Jersey bar of that day, as also by the marriage of Mr. Stockton with the sister of Mr. Boudinot. But in every part of the colonies the troubles with the mother country soon began to direct to the political and military fields all the abilities of the bar. Mr. Boudinot, with his brother Elisha and his wife's family connections, the Stocktons, early espoused the cause of the colonies, and in 1777 he was appointed Commissary-General of Prisoners, an office for which his humanity and sympathetic disposition, combined as these were with an inflexible sense of justice, a deep feeling at the treatment received by our own prisoners at the hands of British officers, and great dignity of person and manner, peculiarly fitted him. In the same year he was elected a member of the Continental Congress. In 1782 he was made President of that body, and signed in 1783 our treaty of peace with Great Britain. In common, however, with most intelligent men in public life, he had perceived long ere this time the entire inadequacy of the existing form of government to conduct with efficiency the affairs of the nation. And early relations of friendship existing between himself and Alexander Hamilton, who as a youth had indeed been almost domesticated in the family of Mr. and Mrs. Boudinot, led the subject of our notice into active endeavors to bring about a far stronger system of national government. From the beginning of the effort to change the system established by the articles of confederation, he advocated all the ideas and supported all the efforts of Hamilton, and in 1789 had the happiness to see them crowned by the adoption of the " Constitution of the United States of America;" a constitution not indeed quite so national or so strong as he would have desired (for like Hamilton he would have had one where some control emanating from the central source should have operated on all State legislation which affected the general welfare— a feature which, had it been adopted, would have rendered impossible the late rebellion)—but one, nevertheless, which, if interpreted in furtherance of its professed ends, and not in defeat of them, he looked upon from the time of its adoption as likely to secure even those immeasurable blessings which, under it, the nation has since enjoyed. As an appropriate recognition of his services in the line just spoken of, Mr. ·Boudinot was elected to the first Congress of the United States under the present Constitution, and re-elected during six years. Having, while attending upon the Congress, fixed his residence in Philadelphia, where he built and resided in the handsome mansion still standing at the southeast corner of Arch and Ninth streets, and where his only child had married the Hon. William Bradford, Attorney-General of the United States, one of the most eminent men of his time, and so being no longer eligible as a member of Congress from New Jersey, Mr. Boudinot in 1796 was appointed by President Washington, who long had had opportunies of witnessing his abilities and integrity, Director of the Mint, an office which he held till 1805. He was among the very few officers appointed by Washington that Mr. Jefferson, who had come into power on ·the 4th of March, 1804, exhibited no disposition to remove. However, Mr. Boudinot had been in public life now for nearly thirty years; advancing years were coming upon him; the death of his accomplished son-in-law, Mr. Bradford, in the very bloom of life, had deeply affected him; and the triumph of Democracy in all departments of the federal government, as also in those of the State of Pennsylvania, made it more agreeable to him, blessed as he was with ample fortune, to retire from official life. The names of himself and his brother, Elisha Boudinot, were honored ones everywhere throughout New Jersey, and in the politics of that State still exerted, as they continued during their lives to do, a controlling influence. The attractions of the city of Burlington, then distinguished above almost any place in the State for an assemblage of distinguished and excellent men, among whom may be gratefully recalled by this day the Rev. Dr. Wharton, William Griffith, William Coxe, Joseph McIlvaine, Joseph Bloomfield, Joshua Maddox Wallace, and different members of the families of Smith, the historian of New Jersey, Lawrence, so well known in our naval annals, and Fenimore Cooper, not less known in that of literature, led him, by the advice of his friend and near kinsman, Mr. Wallace, to fix his residence in that then beautiful and salubrious place. He built there the noble mansion still standing, though in a form greatly changed, at the extreme west end of Broad street, laying out its surrounding grounds,

about ten acres in size, and planting them in the best style of ornamental garden. In this elegant abode, with his wife and daughter, he devoted himself to a liberal hospitality and to benevolent and literary pursuits. He became an active Trustee of Princeton College, into the board of whose trustees he had been elected so far back as 1772, and endowed it with a cabinet of natural history. In 1812 he was a member of the American Board of Commissioners for Foreign Missions, and in 1816 was made the first President of the American Bible Society; an institution in which he ever took great interest, and to which in a single donation he gave $10,000, a great sum of money at the time he gave it. During his whole residence in Burlington, there being at that time no Presbyterian church there, Mr. Boudinot was a devout worshipper and communicant in St. Mary's Protestant Episcopal Church, as also in his life and death a liberal benefactor to it. As both his own education and his wife's were in the Presbyterian denomination, and as his preferences were probably for it, his constant interest in St. Mary's must be regarded as a proof of a truly catholic disposition. Mr. Boudinot died at his residence in Burlington, October 24th, 1821, and is buried in the grounds of St. Mary's Church, where his daughter, wife, and many of his connections are also interred. It is much to be regretted that no life of this eminent citizen of New Jersey has been written. His familiar letters were singularly agreeable, while those on public subjects have superior value. One of these, a letter addressed to Mr. James Searle, who.in behalf of the Congress of the United States had apparently offered to him a valuable commercial post at the disposal of the government, gives us an idea of Mr. Boudinot's wisdom and integrity, and affords so valuable an example to men in public office that we give it entire :—" Philadelphia, April 5th, 1779. Dear Sir : I have been seriously considering the proposal you ·were kindly pleased to make me last evening, and am induced to answer it in the negative for the following reasons : I have ever made it a principle of my conduct in life not to eat the bread of the publick for nought, which, did I accept your proposal, would in some measure be the case in the present instance, as far as I am unequal to the task. I esteem it a most useful piece of wisdom to know what department in business one can fill with propriety, and to be careful not to aspire to any beyond my reach. I consider myself so totally inferior to this department in mercantile knowledge, especially when compared with many who might fill it with reputation, that it appears to me a little like publick robbery to accept a lucrative employment which from the generous provision of the contract is apparently designed for a man of abilities in this particular branch of business. And lastly : in the present stage of public affairs an honest man must expect to be herded together with the general complexion of office, which must wound the delicacy of public spirit or love to one's country. My plan of life is to avoid as much as possible being too much entangled in public business. My family

is small; my wants are few. In retirement and obscurity I can enjoy domestic happiness, which is the summit of my wish. I am nevertheless equally obliged to you for your kind attention as if I had accepted it, and am, dear sir, Yours, affectionately, ELIAS BOUDINOT. To Hon. James Searle, Esq."

UTLER, REV. MANASSEH, LL.D., Clergyman, Chaplain in the Revolutionary Army, was born at Killingly, Connecticut, May 28th, 1742, and graduated at Yale College in 1765. He then entered upon a course of legal studies, and in due time was admitted to the bar. Edgarton, Martha's Vineyard, was eventually selected as a field of labors, and there he was engaged for some time in the practice of his profession. He subsequently devoted himself to the study of theology; September 11th, 1771, was ordained, and at once installed pastor of the Congregational church in Hamilton, then Ipswich Hamlet, Massachusetts. He served also during two campaigns in the war of the Revolution as chaplain in the American army. In 1786 he had become associated with a company, afterward known as the Ohio Company, whose leading spirits were revolutionary officers, organized with a view to the purchase of land north of the Ohio. In June, 1787, he went to New York, as the company's agent, to negotiate with the American Congress for the purchase of a large tract, somewhere in the new country, west of Pennsylvania and Virginia. "With consummate tact he accomplished his mission, and made a contract for the purchase of over a million and a half of acres, at two-thirds of a dollar per acre. He kept a journal of his journey and his proceedings at New York, from which it appears that his plan could only be carried out by allowing some private parties to make an immense purchase of Western lands under the cover of the contract of the Ohio Company." The bargain included five millions of acres, one and a half millions of which were for the Ohio Company, and the remainder for the parties operating through him. In his journal, under date of Friday, July 27th, 1787, he gives this account of the closing of his mission to New York: "At half past three I was informed that an ordinance passed Congress on the terms stated in our letter, without the least variation, and that the Board of Treasury was directed to take order and close the contract. This was agreeable but unexpected intelligence. Sargent and I went directly to the board, who had received the ordinance, but were then rising. They urged me to tarry the next day, and they would put by all other business to complete the contract, but I found it inconvenient, and, after making a general verbal adjustment, left it with Sargent to finish what was to be done at present. Dr. Lee, a brother of the famous Virginia orator, congratulated me, and declared he would do all in his power to adjust the terms of the contract, so far as was left to them, as much in our favor as possible. I proposed three months for collecting the first half million of dollars and for executing the instruments of the contract, which was acceded to." By this ordinance was obtained the grant of over five millions of acres of land, amounting to three million five hundred thousand dollars; one million and a half for the Ohio Company, and the remainder for private speculation, in which many of the principal characters in the Eastern States were then concerned. "Without connecting this speculation, similar terms and advantages could not have been obtained for the Ohio Company. On my return through Broadway I received the congratulations of my friends in Congress, and others with whom I happened to meet." "It is an interesting fact," says Rev. Joseph F. Tuttle, D. D., "that he was in all these negotiations in constant communication with Colonel William Duer, of the Treasury Board, and closely related to several of our New Jersey and New York families." Dr. Tuttle continues: "I cannot bring myself to drop this part of Dr. Cutler's history without referring to two facts, as I fully believe them to be such. The ordinance to be submitted to Congress was placed in his hands for examination, and his two grand suggestions were adopted. The first was the exclusion of slavery forever from the Northwest Territory, and the second was the devotion of two entire townships of land for the endowment of an university, and section sixteen in every township of land and fractional township in that vast purchase for the purpose of schools. Those two ideas adopted by all the new States made the great West what it is." At a certain stage of his negotiation with Congress, in 1789, he made a trip to Philadelphia, and thence made an extended tour through New Jersey, whose lands, manners, towns, etc., are described at length in various parts of his journal. In the course of the following winter the first colony, under General Rufus Putnam, made its way across the mountains, and on the 7th of April landed on the east side of the Muskingum river, where it enters the Ohio. In July he also made a journey thither in his sulky and on horseback, meanwhile keeping a journal for the amusement of his daughter. In this journey he crossed New Jersey twice, and both the records concerning that State and his journey thither are of great interest. In 1789 he received from Yale College the honorary degree of LL.D. He was regarded as one of the most learned botanists in the United States, and in many other respects was a talented and remarkable man. In 1787, in a published pamphlet, he predicted that "many then living would see the Western rivers navigated with steam, and that within fifty years the Northwestern Territory would contain more inhabitants than all New England." His first night in New Jersey was at "Walling's tavern, kept by one Sears, a surly old fellow, very extravagant (in his charges), and an empty house. . . . . Went on to Sussex Court House; road good fourteen miles. Breakfasted at a tavern just above the court house, kept by Jonathan Willis. This is a pretty village on the eastern side, and near the summit of a high hill; land good; houses indifferent. . . . . At Log Jail, or Log Town, is a miserable tavern, kept by Jones, a Jew. Six miles from Log Town is Hope, commonly called Moravian Town. This is a small, new, but very pretty village. Houses mostly stone, built in Dutch style." In describing Bedford, the shire-town of the county, he says that which "should interest Jerseymen and Buckeyes also:" "Judge Symmes, John Cleves had taken lodging at the best tavern; we, however, made shift to get lodgings in the same house, Mr. Wert's, a Dutchman. Judge Symmes was complaisant. I had a letter to him from his brother at Sussex Court House, New Jersey. He had his daughter with him, a very pretty young lady." Dr. Tuttle speaking of this extract, at a reading of the New Jersey Historical Society, says: "Well might these two remarkable men treat each other 'with complaisance,' as they met in Bedford on their way to a country whose destiny was to be so greatly affected by their plans and energy." The following is from a letter dated July 11th, 1787: " . . . . Two miles from the Hook is Bergen-town, a very compact village of considerable extent. It is inhabited entirely by the Dutch. There is a large Dutch church built with stone, and a handsome steeple. The houses are mostly built with stone, in the Dutch style. After leaving Bergentown I entered a very extensive marsh which goes far into the country. . . . . Newark is a small village situated on a plain; it has no considerable build-ings; there is a small church, a Presbyterian meeting-house, and a Dutch church. . . . . Elizabethtown is a very pretty village, several handsome houses, one meeting-house, and another new building. . . . . I passed through Spanktown (now Rahway), but the meeting-house and the thickest of the buildings were at some distance. It is a small village of no consideration. New Brunswick is a large town, and well built. Many of the buildings are brick and stone. There seems to be considerable trade carried on in this town, though the shipping consists of very small craft. . . . . Princeton is a small town, or rather has but a small num-ber of houses in the most compact part. . . . . Trenton is spread over a considerable space of ground. There is only one small meeting-house and one church in this town. I therefore conclude that the people are not much disposed to attend public worship, for the two houses, I presume, are not sufficient to hold one-third of the inhabitants." He died July 23d, 1823, aged eighty-one years, in the fifty-second year of his ministry. His oldest son, Judge Eph-raim Cutler, of Warren, Washington county, Ohio, who died July 8th, 1853, was a remarkable man, and was hon-ored in the Ohio Constitutional Convention as the successful leader of the opposition to an attempt to introduce slavery into that State, an attempt which at one time seemed sure of triumph. "Thus the name of Cutler is an honored one in the history of the great West and Northwest, and is still most worthily borne by William P. Cutler, the son of Eph-raim, who still resides on the goodly acres which consti-

tuted his patrimony." The foregoing sketch is valuable as a part of the present volume on account of the insight which it affords into the early condition of many parts of the State, and into the history of a scheme for the development of the West in which New Jersey manifested a deep and active interest.

ANKIN, WILLIAM, of Newark, was born, in December, 1787, in Nova Scotia. His family was of Scotch extraction, his father having emigrated from Scotland. When he was still a child, his parents removed to Albany, New York, where he was educated, and whence, be-fore he was out of his teens, he went to Elizabeth, New Jersey, to learn the trade of a hatter. In 1812, having learned his trade, and learned it well, he removed to Newark and set up hatting there on his own account, conducting his business with an energy and industry and prudence that soon made it both large and profitable. In 1831 he took his son-in-law, Peter S. Duryee, into partnership with him, and the firm had a successful career for many years. He retired from the firm in 1845, the business being con-tinued by Mr. Duryee and his partners until about the year 1871. In 1836, when Newark was proclaimed a city, he was elected an Alderman in the first City Council. He was also Vice-President of the Mechanics' Insurance Com-pany in Newark. His reputation as a business man and a citizen was high. Although a Republican in politics, and a man of political convictions, so that he could pro-mote the public good, he cared nothing for party. He was married early in life to Abigail Ogden, of Elizabeth, whose family were old residents of that place. He died at his home in Newark, December 15th, 1869.

KINNER, D. M., Assistant-Surgeon in the United States Navy, of Newark, New Jersey, upon passing the necessary examination, was appointed in September, 1861. He then served one month on the receiving-ship "North Carolina," and six months upon the frigate "Sabine." During that time the lost "Vermont" was found, which vessel had left Boston for Port Royal, but encountering a heavy gale when but a few days out, lost anchor, sails and rudder, and drifted about at the mercy of the winds and waves until found by the "Sabine," when she was assisted in shipping a temporary rudder, finally reaching her destina-tion in safety. He was about one year on the sloop-of-war "Vincennes," attached to the West Gulf Squadron, and was then ordered to duty with the army besieging Port Hudson, and there, after the surrender, placed in charge of the General Hospital. Early in August, 1863, he was ordered to the United States steamer "Calhoun." This vessel was Admiral Farragut's flag-ship in the attack upon Fort Powell, situated at the entrance from Mississippi Sound into Mobile Bay. In April, 1864, the "Calhoun" being ordered to New Orleans for repairs, he was permitted to return to the North. In June, 1864, he was ordered to the Naval Academy, then located at Newport, Rhode Island, and there remained until he resigned, in May, 1865.

————◆————

ABE, HON. RUDOLPH F., Lawyer and Speaker of the State House of Representatives in the session of 1877, was born in Germany in 1841. He received a classical education in his native country, from which, at the age of fifteen, he emigrated to the United States, settling in New York city, where he engaged at first in mercantile pursuits, pursuing them until 1862, when he began the study of law in the office of Connable & Elliott. Subsequently he entered the Columbia Law School, from which he graduated in 1869, and was admitted to the bar of New York, at which he has since practised, although his residence for the last thirteen or fourteen years has been in Hoboken, New Jersey. For a time he was one of the proprietors of the *Hudson County Journal*, published in Hoboken. His practice in the New York courts is large and general, extending to all branches of the profession. He is a lawyer of decided ability, and of equal versatility, the latter quality, so far from diminishing or diluting the former, serving rather to strengthen and enrich it. For some years he has been the junior member of the law firm of Browne & Rabe. In politics he is a Democrat, staunch and true, yet fair and dispassionate. Though a strong partisan, he is an honorable one. In 1873, on his return from a visit to Europe, he was elected to the New Jersey Assembly, in which he is now serving his fourth consecutive term. His quality as a legislator is sufficiently disclosed in the fact that, besides having been a member of all the more important committees, he has been Chairman of the Committee on the Judiciary, and of the Committee on Commerce and Navigation, and, still more amply, in the organization of the Assembly in 1877, when, there being a party tie, thirty Democrats to thirty Republicans, he was elected Speaker, after a struggle of two days, terminated by his receiving the votes of a number of Republicans, in addition to those of all the Democrats. It is pleasant to be able to record that this mark of confidence on the part of his political opponents has been justified by the uniform and manifest impartiality of his rulings, which have been accepted with satisfaction by both parties alike. The opportunity was a rare one, and he has proved himself equal to it, thereby at once confirming and enlarging his reputation. Henceforward the way to high honors will be apt to be open to him, but should it not be, he will probably know how to open it. Young, able, well educated, well informed, a man of character as well as of intellect, he is not likely,

in the pursuit of a just ambition, to succumb to obstacles or surrender to adversaries. He is married to Miss Lusby, of New Jersey.

————◆————

ATHERS, THOMAS B., of Woodbury, was born, December 15th, 1831, at Germantown, Pennsylvania, his father, Thomas Mathers, being then a resident of Philadelphia, where the family had been old residents. He received his education in the public schools of Philadelphia, after leaving which he engaged with his uncle in stock-dealing and butchery in that city. When he was nineteen years of age he went to Woodbury, Gloucester county, New Jersey, where his parents had gone some years before, and there established himself in the business of a drover and butcher, which he carried on with such industry, judgment and thrift, that he soon became a prominent man in the community. His business qualifications, personal energy, and public spirit won for him the confidence of his fellow-citizens to such a degree that in 1869, having previously filled several local offices, he was elected by a large majority Sheriff of Gloucester county, and, so acceptable was his discharge of the office, re-elected three times in succession. The sheriffalty is an office that tries the mettle of a man as thoroughly as any other civil office whatever, insomuch that one who comes out of it with general applause may pretty safely be taken for a man of courage and sense as well as of integrity; and in this point of view his successive re-elections to the office speak much more significantly than any ordinary series of re-elections could have done. They attest the public sense not merely of his business capacity and executive vigor, but of his manhood and his probity. In 1875 the Republican party, of which he is a staunch member, nominated him for the office of State Senator, and elected him by the full vote of the party in the district. His term in the Senate is still unexpired, but he has served long enough to show that he is an able, faithful and intelligent legislator. He is at present a member of the Committee on Commerce; of the Committee on Printing, and of the Committee on Engrossed Bills. His constituents and his colleagues alike hold him in high esteem as a Senator. As a man and a citizen he has the warm regards of all who know him. He was married in 1853 to Rebecca Graves, of Glassborough, who died November 22d, 1873.

————◆————

ODGE, REV. ARCHIBALD ALEXANDER, Minister and Author, was born in Pennsylvania, July 18th, 1823, and is the son of Professor Charles Hodge, of Princeton, the eminent theologian and author. He graduated at the College of New Jersey in 1841. Three years later he became a tutor in the institution, and held that position

67

until 1846. He graduated at the Princeton Theological Seminary in 1847, and subsequently went to Allahabad, India, as a missionary, under the auspices of the Presbyterian Board of Missions, remaining there and laboring with much fidelity and success until 1850. Returning to this country, he became the pastor of a church at Nottingham, Maryland, in 1851. Four years later he accepted a call to Fredericksburg, Virginia; in 1861, one to Wilkesbarre, Pennsylvania; and in 1866, one to Allegheny City. Two years previously, in 1864, he was appointed Professor of Didactic, Historical and Polemic Theology in the Theological Seminary in Allegheny City. He published "Outlines of Theology," New York, 1860; translated into Welsh, 1863; "The Atonement," 1867; "Commentary on the Confession of Faith," 1869; and "Presbyterian Doctrine Briefly Stated," 1869.

———◦◦◦———

RICK, GENERAL JOHN STOCKTON, of Vincentown, was born at the old Irick homestead, in North Hampton (now known as South Hampton) township, Burlington county, New Jersey, August 4th, 1811. His father, William Irick, was a native of New Jersey, a farmer, and also a surveyor and scrivener. His mother was Margaret Stockton, a member of the eminent Stockton family of New Jersey. His early education was received at the common schools of his native county, and was completed at the well-known academical institute at Burlington, of which John Gummerie was principal. When twenty years of age he began farming upon his own account, and throughout his life he has always taken an active interest in agricultural affairs. In early manhood he identified himself with and became an earnest worker in the Whig party; and since the foundation of the Republican party he has been no less active in the service of that organization. For a number of years he held the position of chosen freeholder, relinquishing this in 1847, when he was elected a member of the State Assembly. In 1848, and again in 1849, he was re-elected to the Assembly, and during the three years that he remained in office—serving on the finance and other important committees—he manifested a quite remarkable legislative ability. Although never again permitting his name to be put in nomination for a public elective office, he has continued to take a zealous interest in the government of the State, and has exercised a potent influence in moulding and directing its policy. With an enlightened comprehension of the necessity for developing the great natural resources of the commonwealth, and with a clear, well-balanced mind, capable of adapting means to ends, and of adjusting practice to theory, he has for years been prominent in advancing all measures tending to the public good, his intimate acquaintance with the leading men of the State enabling him to place his suggestions in such position and in such shape as to assure their speedily taking form in action. Nor has he confined himself to advice alone, being always ready to back his public-spirited schemes with his own capital. The Vincentown National Bank, of which, in 1864, he was elected President, was created through his exertions, and by the liberal aid of his means; the Camden & Burlington County Railroad, now a section of the United Railways of New Jersey Division of the Pennsylvania Railroad, was strongly urged by him, and was in part built with his money; the Vincentown Branch of this line was almost wholly his work; and the St. Mary's River Timber Company and the Vincentown Marl Company were likewise mainly created by his effort. Of all of these corporations he has from the outset taken a leading part in the direction, his business ability being exercised in their guidance, as his formulative ability was exercised in their foundation. Of the Morris Canal Company, and of other equally important corporate organizations of the State, he is also a Director, his administrative and executive talent naturally bringing him to the front in all business enterprises with which he becomes connected. During the late war he served for eighteen months as an Aide-de-Camp on Governor Olden's staff, being during this period Adjutant-General, and Master of Military Transportation. He married, May 18th, 1832, Emeline S. Bishop, of Burlington county, New Jersey.

———◦◦◦———

RICK, HON. HENRY J., of Vincentown, son of the preceding, was born in South Hampton township, March 13th, 1833. His early education was received at a select school in the immediate vicinity of his home; he was subsequently, 1844-49, a student at Treemount Seminary, Morristown, where among his classmates was the present Governor of Pennsylvania, John F. Hartranft, and in 1849-51 concluded his education at the Freehold, New Jersey, Institute. For three years after leaving the institute he was employed upon his father's farm; then moved to and took charge of the homestead farm, where he remained until 1863; was for several years resident in Vincentown while engaged in milling, and has latterly resided upon one of the several farms owned by the family near that town. Like his father, he has since early manhood been prominent in politics. Joining the Whig party upon attaining his majority, he worked and voted with that organization until the Republican party was formed, and he has since continued an earnest supporter of the newer political faith. In the fall of 1862 he was elected to the lower house of the State Legislature from the old Fourth District of Burlington county by a majority of thirty-five; was re-elected in 1863 by a majority of one hundred and ninety, and again in 1864 by a majority of one hundred and sixty. During his three years in the House, he served upon a number of important committees, and in 1864 was one of the Special Committee appointed to adjust the dead-lock in the Legislature. In 1870 he was

Lewis Drake M. D.

nominated as State Senator from Burlington county, and was elected by a majority of one hundred and fifty-five, running very considerably ahead of his ticket. In 1871, and again in 1872, he was re-elected. In the Senate, as in the House, he was appointed a member of important committees, serving on the Judiciary, Engrossed Bills as Chairman, Education, and Soldiers' Orphans' Homes. He also served as Chairman of the Committee on Railroads at the time of the very serious difficulty between the Pennsylvania Railroad Company and the Hamilton Land and Improvement Company. In local enterprises he has taken a prominent part, and at present he is a Director and Secretary and Treasurer of the Vincentown Railroad Company, a Director of the Vincentown Loan Association, and Secretary and Treasurer of the Vincentown Marl Company. In 1862 he married Harriet R. Clement, a niece of ex-Senator John H. Roberts, of Camden county, New Jersey.

RACE, LEWIS, M. D., Physician, of Rahway, was born, August 26th, 1803, in Middlesex county, New Jersey, and is a son of the late Reuben and Marion (Piatt) Drake, both of whom were natives of New Jersey. His father was a descendant of one of the Drake brothers, who, according to a family tradition, was a connection of the famous navigator, Sir Francis Drake, and who came to America about the year 1660. On first leaving home for school, Dr. Drake went to Basking Ridge, where he entered Dr. Brownley's grammar school. A few months subsequently Dr. Brownley received a call to take a professorship in Rutgers College, which he accepted. Thereupon Lewis Drake left the academy and soon after went to Amherst, Massachusetts, and entered the grammar school of that place. At the expiration of two terms he returned home and took lessons in Latin and Greek of a minister residing not far away from his father's residence. In a few months this preceptor sickened and died, whereupon his pupil decided to proceed no further in this course of study, but to begin at once a thorough preparation for the medical profession. For this purpose he placed himself under the direction of Dr. Taylor, of New Brunswick, in whose office he pursued his studies for about eighteen months. He then went to Philadelphia and placed himself under the tuition of Dr. Samuel Jackson, who was at that time Professor of the Practice of Medicine in the University of Pennsylvania. He likewise attended three separate courses of lectures at that institution, from which he graduated in the spring of 1829 with the degree of Doctor of Medicine. Returning to New Jersey, he located at first at Woodbridge, where he commenced the practice of his profession, but only remained there a short time; and finally settled at Rahway, where he has since discharged his professional duties, covering a period of forty-seven years, and is the oldest resident practitioner of medicine in

Union county. He took an active part, in the years 1855 and 1856, in causing the passage of an act by the Legislature whereby the mill dams on the Rahway river, within the city limits, were removed, as it was shown conclusively that they were the cause of much sickness to the population. He was married, in 1832, to Charity S. Freeman, who died April 28th, 1842. After a widowerhood of three years he was again united in marriage, in 1845, to Mrs. Julia Anna Martin; she died September 2d, 1874.

LOCE, WILLIAM, the Editor of the Trenton, New Jersey, Daily and Weekly *State Gazette*, was born in the county of Kent, England, February 18th, 1842. His ancestry was among the most ancient and honorable yeomanry of that county, dating back, by authentic family records, to the time of the conquest. The subject of this sketch was brought to this country in 1848, the family first settling in New York city, and removing thence in 1850 to Monmouth county, New Jersey, where Mr. Cloke, Sr., followed the farming business for a short time. This proving neither lucrative nor congenial, he entered into the business of a country merchant, where William assisted him in the capacity of clerk. When he was about seventeen years of age William began teaching a country school, and followed this occupation until 1860, when he was summarily dismissed for the aggressive and outspoken character of his abolition sentiments. In 1861 he was given entire editorial and business management of the Monmouth *Herald and Inquirer*, a weekly Republican journal published at Freehold, the county-seat. He conducted this paper with such vigor and ability as to attract considerable attention, and the paper immediately rose to a position of influence and authority. It was while defending the principles of the Republican party and the cause of the Union in this sphere that he attracted the notice and won the lasting friendship of the late Horace Greeley. In a letter to the Secretary of War in 1864, Mr. Greeley said: "Mr. Cloke is one of the best and most promising young men in New Jersey." The sale of this paper, a few years later, left Mr. Cloke without employment, and he went South and engaged in the culture of sea island cotton at Hilton Head. Returning North, he took charge, as principal, for one year, of the Freehold Academy, and the next year, the spring of 1867, was offered the position of city editor or reporter of the Trenton *State Gazette*, which he promptly accepted. He performed the duties of this position with such fidelity and acceptability that when the editor-in-chief, Mr. Enoch R. Borden, died, in 1871, Mr. Cloke was at once promoted to the vacant chair. In this position the force and character of his mind have had full opportunity to display themselves. From early boyhood he had had a taste and genius for newspaper work. When a lad at school, he drew with his pen and pencil an amateur newspaper, which excited the astonishment and delight of his teacher. Later he corresponded every week with the local press, and the whole bent of his mind seemed to be strongly and irresistibly in the direction of a journalistic career. As editor of the *State Gazette*, he has made a decided mark in New Jersey journalism. The paper has, under his editorship, steadily and rapidly risen in public favor and in influence and character. No newspaper in New Jersey ever before exerted so widespread an influence upon the thought of the State. It goes to every post-office in the State, to readers in the remotest sections, and its utterances are eagerly consulted by a very large circle of devoted admirers. Mr. Cloke's editorial writings are characterized by profound sincerity, an intelligent and wide grasp of subjects of current interest, a masculine vigor of style, and by a moral earnestness which wins the confidence of honest minds. During the time that he has been editor he has been twice elected Assistant Secretary of the New Jersey Senate. He is emphatically the architect of his own fortune, having won his way in life entirely by his own exertions, and through the force of a vigorous mind and a strong and resolute character. He is regarded as one of the foremost editors in New Jersey, and as a rising man.

———◦—◦———

UCAS, JOHN, Manufacturing Chemist, eldest son of Thomas Lucas, and a descendant of the John Lucas of Ashburn, Derbyshire, who was the warm friend and long-time companion of Izaak Walton, was born at Stone, Staffordshire, England, November 25th, 1825. After receiving a liberal education at Fieldplace Commercial Academy, near his native town, and after passing a sufficient length of time in his father's tea and general grocery establishment to determine that mercantile pursuits as then obtaining in England were not to his liking, he entered upon the study of agricultural chemistry. This he prosecuted with much earnestness, and to his proficiency as a chemist he owes his subsequently successful business career. Previously to establishing himself in business he made—leaving England in 1844—an extended tour of the United States and Canadas; and so well pleased was he with the former that he returned to Great Britain only to the end that he might make preparations to become an American citizen. Various hindrances delayed his intended emigration, and it was not until 1849 that he was enabled to sail. Upon his arrival in this country he selected Philadelphia as his home, and with characteristic energy immediately embarked in active business, establishing a foreign commission house, obtaining the agency of several large firms in Europe, and laying a broad foundation generally, upon which he has since built his very extensive trade. His first store was at No. 33 North Front street, his operations being confined almost exclu-

sively to paints, oils and colors; but finding it a difficult matter to ascertain, through the medium of the wholesale trade, the most salable articles for the American market, he made arrangements for bringing himself into direct contact with consumers. To this end he removed to a large store on Fourth street north of Arch, the centre then as now of the oil and color trade, and himself served behind the counter, being thus brought into close relations with practical painters. The immediate result of his enterprising method of investigation was the discovery that a pressing need existed for a good green paint to take the place of the Paris or arsenical green, the latter not only having an injurious effect upon those using it, but being also deficient in body. Applying his chemical knowledge, he began a series of experiments that resulted in the discovery of an economical formula productive of the article desired; and pursuing his investigations in a different direction, he made valuable improvements in the machinery necessary to its manufacture. Upon the latter he has taken out letters patent. In 1852, for the purpose of enlarging his business, he took into partnership an old and experienced color manufacturer, his relation, Mr. Joseph Foster. In the same year he removed his store to No. 130 Arch street, and purchased a considerable tract of land, on which was a large sheet of remarkably pure water, entirely free from lime or iron, in Camden county, New Jersey. Upon this tract he erected the Gibsboro' White Lead, Zinc and Color Works. The purity of the water enabled him to produce the beautiful and permanent "Swiss" and "Imperial French" greens, now so favorably known and so extensively used throughout the United States and Canadas. The perfection to which he has brought the white oxide of zinc, effected by continued and careful chemical experiment, may be understood when it is stated that the best judges of the article have pronounced it to be not only superior to any manufactured in this country, but fully equal to the world-renowned Vieille Montaigne Company's production. The pulp steel and Chinese blues, and primrose chrome yellow, have superseded the French and English makes, and are now used by all the leading manufacturers of paper-hangings in the United States. In 1857 Mr. Foster withdrew from the firm, and the senior partner was joined by his brother, Mr. William H. Lucas. The latter, under the new arrangement, took charge of the salesroom and financial department generally, leaving the former at liberty to devote his undivided attention to the manufacturing and chemical departments, an arrangement that has enabled the firm to reach and maintain its present pre-eminence in the trade. Having become, by naturalization, a citizen of the United States, Mr. Lucas has thoroughly identified himself with his adopted country. At the outbreak of the rebellion he threw all his heart and energy into the Union cause, being instant to assist in organizing, drilling and equipping volunteers for the army. The location of his large interests in New Jersey has naturally caused him to feel a lively concern in the prosperity of the Camden & Atlantic Railroad Company, upon whose line his works are situate, and, consequent to this, in the welfare of the town at the seaward terminus of the road. For a number of years he has been prominent in the Board of Direction of the Company, and for years has been its President. His manufactory, near White-Horse Station, materially contributes to the revenues of the road, a large amount of freight being received at and shipped from this point under his orders. Personally, he is genial and affable, combining the shrewd business man with the polished gentleman. Among the members of the mercantile community his name for honesty and integrity stands second to none.

————◆◆————

HILLDIN, ALEXANDER, Merchant, of Philadelphia, was born in that city, January 28th, 1808. His father, Captain Daniel Whilldin, a native of New Jersey, and a resident, in early life, of Cape May, was a well-known shipmaster at the beginning of the present century. In 1812 Captain Whilldin sailed from a French port for America and was never heard of again. His widow, with her son and two daughters, removed to the old homestead at Cape May, and on the farm there the son remained until he was sixteen years old, receiving in the winters such education as was obtainable in the country schools. In 1824 he returned to Philadelphia, and entered a store as an apprentice, his honesty, industry, and ability rapidly gaining for him the confidence and esteem of his employers and of all with whom he was brought in contact. After eight years of. faithful service, during which time he was advanced to positions of trust and considerable emolument in the firm, he determined upon beginning business on his own account, and to this end, in 1832, established himself as a commission merchant in cotton and wool, the first year with a partner who brought in needed capital; after the first year alone. The business then founded, almost half a century ago, has since grown to immense proportions, and the house of Alexander Whilldin & Sons is now one of the foremost in America, dealing in wool, cotton, and yarns. In the development of this great commercial establishment he showed, from the outset, rare business talent. Prudent, sound in judgment, courteous, industrious, self-reliant, and possessed of indomitable energy and remarkable administrative and executive ability, he could not fail to achieve success; and although at one time, during a period of unusual depression in mercantile affairs, he was very considerably embarrassed in his resources, he was enabled to triumph over the temporary obstruction, honorably meeting every obligation that he had assumed, and to turn what had seemed to be the wreck of his hopes and efforts into the sure foundation of a fortune well won and rarely well-applied. In 1836 he married Jane G. Stites, descended from a family resident for over a century and a half in Cape May county, New Jersey. The three sons born to him in this marriage have for several years past been his business partners, and their assistance in the conduct of the house has given him leisure for a long-contemplated tour in Europe and the Holy Land, and for closer attention to the interests of the many philanthropic and religious schemes in which he is prominently engaged. For forty years a devoted Christian, and for a great portion of that time a Ruling Elder in the Presbyterian Church, a very large part of his time has been given to furthering the various charitable and benevolent institutions founded by the Presbyterian and other evangelical denominations, and besides subscribing freely to their support he has given, as a Director, the benefit of his counsel in the guidance of the Presbyterian Board of Publication, Hospital, and Home for Widows, and also in that of the American Tract Society, American Sunday-School Union, Union Temporary Home for Children, Seamen's Friend Society, and other scarcely less well-known organizations. But the work which will cause his name to live longest in grateful remembrance was the founding of Sea Grove, in New Jersey, adjoining the city of Cape May. The site of Sea Grove was purchased of "The West New Jersey Society," in England, by Jonathan Pyne, the elder, through Jeremiah Basse; was inherited by Jonathan and Abigail Pyne; was deeded by them and Robert Courtney, Abigail Pyne's husband, to Henry Stites in 1712, and was eventually inherited by Jane G. Stites, wife to Alexander Whilldin. The property possessed more than ordinary natural advantages as a seaside resort, having, beside a fine beach and surf, a fresh-water lake and numerous shade-trees; while rapid communication with Philadelphia was assured by established railway and steamboat lines. In 1875 Mr. Whilldin, having the hearty co-operation of his wife, determined upon founding upon this site "a moral and religious seaside home for the glory of God and the welfare of man, where he may be refreshed and invigorated, body and soul, and better fitted for the highest and noblest duties of life." On the 18th of February, 1875, under the corporate title of "The Sea Grove Association," an organization was effected, and shortly thereafter a liberal charter was obtained from the New Jersey Legislature. Under this charter the company was empowered to insert in every lease or conveyance a clause absolutely forbidding the sale of intoxicating liquor upon the premises so leased or purchased, and also to forbid any act, either in the character of business or amusement, opposed to morality or religion. Saving these especial clauses, the charter was of the same general character as those ordinarily held by the proprietors of park towns, compelling conformity on the part of tenants or freeholders with the general scheme of improvement adopted at the outset, with liability to such additional, reasonable regulations as might from time to time be adopted by the Board of Direction. Under this charter work was at once begun, and the waste beach was rapidly transformed into a charming park, well graded, well watered, well shaded, and laid out in conven ient lots intersected by well-made roads. The first building erected was a pavilion, capable of holding twelve hundred persons, intended for religious or other meetings; after this a commodious hotel; and when the seaside season opened Sea Grove was dedicated to its excellent purpose by a series of religious meetings participated in by many of the most eminent divines and laymen of the Christian church. Fol lowing the erection of the hotel handsome cottages were erected by the several proprietors and by the various pur chasers of lots, and when the season of 1876 opened a village of delightful rural homes had been created, and a population had been secured calculated in every way to carry out the Christian and rational views of its founder. In order to insure conformity with the original plan the lots were sold at an almost nominal price, and arrangements were entered into with the West Jersey Railroad Company, by which residents should have, in proportion to the extent of their improvement of the property purchased, free passes over the line for one, two, or three years. In short, it was an enterprise undertaken for the general good of his fellows by an earnest Christian who was at the same time a good man of business, and who, in carrying out his scheme for the common welfare, gave to those whom he benefited not only comfortable homes for pleasure and recreation, but also the help of his judgment, large experience, and administrative talent. Above all other of his many good deeds this, the creation of Sea Grove, stands eminent, for by it he has most largely, most directly, and most diffusely benefited his fellow-men. It is a signal act, fitly marking the final period of his useful, honorable life—a life so well spent in every way that its record may rightly stand as a lasting exemplar.

———•◦•———

ODD, JOHN R., M. D., late of Lebanonville, received his professional education in the New York College of Physicians and Surgeons, whence he was graduated M. D., in March, 1864. On the 15th of the following April he was commis sioned an Acting Assistant Surgeon in the United States Volunteer Army, and was attached to the 2d New Jersey Cavalry. Although entering the army at the begin ning of the last year of the war he saw quite as much ser vice in the field as many surgeons appointed in 1861, for the 2d Cavalry, under the gallant Yorke, was one of the hardest fighting regiments in the whole army. He joined the regiment in time to take part in the disastrous foray (under Sturgis) against the rebel General Forrest, and, later, in Grierson's brilliant raid through Mississippi; both affairs giving him ample professional employment. On the 1st of November, 1865, he was honorably discharged from the service; and in January, 1866, having been examined and licensed, he established himself at Lebanonville, Hunter don county. Here, in a short time, he acquired a very fair

practice; was made a member of the Hunterdon County Medical Society, and was in excellent standing both in the profession and as a citizen. Here, too, he married a daugh ter of W. Johnson, Esq. In April, 1871, he removed to Omaha City, but in a few years failing health compelled him to abandon practice, and he returned to Lebanonville, where he died in 1876.

———•◦•———

ORRIGAN, M. A., RIGHT REV., Bishop of Newark, and President of Seton Hall College, South Orange, New Jersey, was born in Newark, New Jersey, August 13th, 1839. His parents were well-to-do Irish-Americans, who sent their son, when quite young, to St. Mary's College, near Emmetsburg, Maryland, to be educated. His ability and beauty of character speedily won the esteem and affec tion of his teachers and associates, and in 1859 he was graduated from the college with the highest honors. Im mediately afterwards, having determined to enter the priest hood, he went to Rome to study theology, and entered the American College there, where he remained four years. In 1863 he was ordained a Priest by Cardinal Patrizi. The next year he was invested with the degree of Doctor of Divinity. In 1865 he returned to this country, and on the retirement of Rev. Dr. Braun was appointed Vice-President of Seton Hall College under Father McQuaide, the first President of that institution. When the latter was appointed Bishop of Rochester, Dr. Corrigan was made President of the college, and his brother, James A., likewise in the priesthood, was made Vice-President. Under his able management the college grew rapidly in prosperity and in fluence. In 1873 Dr. Corrigan was appointed to succeed Bishop Bayley, who founded Seton Hall College, as Bishop of Newark; and on May 3d, of that year, he was consecrated in St. Patrick's Cathedral, in that city, with grand and im posing ceremony. Previous to this, and from the time of Bishop Bayley's elevation to the Archbishopric of Baltimore, Father Corrigan was made Administrator of the Diocese and Vicar-General. At the time of his elevation to the prelacy Bishop Corrigan was but thirty-four years old, and the youngest bishop in the country. In person he is small of stature and slender. He is a good, earnest preacher; a fine student, and a man of much learning.

———•◦•———

ARLL, REV. BUCKLEY, Pastor of the Presby terian Church, of Rahway, late of Deerfield, was born in New Jersey, in 1770. In 1799 he became the pastor of the Presbyterian Church of Pitts grove, New Jersey. In the summer of 1802 a call was extended to him by the church at Rah way, and met with acceptance. He was received by the

Presbytery of New York, October 6th, 1802; and at its meeting, at Connecticut Farms, November 16th, 1802, " Mr. David Hetfield, a commissioner from the congregation of Rahway, appeared in Presbytery, requesting the instalment of Mr. Buckley Carll as their pastor as soon as convenient. Whereupon the Presbytery agreed to install him pastor of the congregation of Rahway, on the fourth Tuesday of December, at 11 o'clock A. M. Mr. Griffin to preach the sermon; Dr. Roe to preside; and Mr. Hillyer to give an exhortation to the people." He was dismissed in 1825, "broken down by disease," and returned to the neighborhood of his former charge, where, four miles from Deerfield, he purchased a farm, on which he resided until within a short period of his decease. He died at Deerfield, May 22d, 1849, in his eightieth year, and was buried at Pittsgrove. His first wife, Naomi, died in Rahway, August 28th, 1804, in the thirty-fifth year of her age. His second wife, Abigail, survived him, and after his decease resided in Bridgeton, New Jersey.

———◦◦———

INNEY, HON. WILLIAM BURNET, was born at Speedwell, Morris county, New Jersey, in September, 1799, his ancestors being among the early settlers of the country. His father was a son of Sir Thomas Kinney, Baronet, who came from England to explore the mineral resources of the State, and settled in Morris county, which then included Sussex. He was appointed by the crown High Sheriff, and held that office till the Revolution changed the government. His mother was a daughter of Dr. William Burnet, a distinguished physician, who was descended from Bishop Burnet, the historian of his own time. He was a member of the Continental Congress and organized the medical department of the army, taking the Eastern Division under his own supervision. One of his sons was an aide to General Greene, of revolutionary fame, and attended Major Andre at his execution. Another, Jacob, was a pioneer in the West, wrote its history, and represented the State of Ohio in the national Senate for several terms. A third, David G., was an early settler in Texas, and the first president of that republic before its admission into the United States. Abraham Kinney, the father of William B., was an officer in the war of 1812, and destined his son, who was then a boy, for the army. He was used to carry despatches during the hostilities, and was afterwards admitted to West Point as a cadet, but his father died about this time, and his mother, who had other views, withdrew him, under the impression that the gifts of oratory, of which he gave early promise, would open for him a larger field of future usefulness. To this end he was placed under the care of Mr. Whelpley, author of " The Triangle," and father of the late Chief Justice Whelpley; afterwards he became a pupil of

the late Rev. John Ford, D. D., an eminent classical teacher of the time, at Bloomfield. His elder brother, Thomas T. Kinney, being a prominent member of the bar, and Surrogate of Essex county, William B. entered his office as a lawstudent, and afterwards continued his course with Mr. Hornblower, who was his cousin by marriage, and afterwards Chief Justice of the State. His tastes, however, ran more in the direction of literature and metaphysics, and he demonstrated unusual brilliance as a writer and speaker. This brought him into direct intercourse with the press, and he became editor of the *New Jersey Eagle*, a weekly paper at Newark, about the year 1820; from which he retired after the election of President Adams in 1825, and went to New York to pursue his favorite studies. There he took an active part in the establishment of the Mercantile Library, and became intimate with the Harper Brothers, who had just begun their publishing business and sought his advice. His judgment in the selection of books became extremely valuable to them, and their intercourse ripened into a mutual and life-long friendship. His excessive application impaired his health, and about the year 1830 he returned to Newark, where political excitements soon drew him into public action again as an earnest advocate of the principles of the Whig party, and in promotion of his friend, Henry Clay. About this period he became the editor of the *Newark Daily Advertiser*, the first daily paper issued in the State, and united it with the *Sentinel of Freedom*, one of the oldest weekly papers in the country, both of which he conducted with distinguished ability and increasing success. He became especially famous for his eloquence as a lecturer, and was called by literary societies in all parts of the Union to deliver addresses, which he did so far as possible, but he always declined compensation for such services. He also became an earnest advocate of popular education, and was foremost in promoting the establishment of the present free school system of the State. In 1836 the College of New Jersey, at Princeton, conferred upon him the honorary degree of Master of Arts, and in 1840 he was elected a Trustee of that institution, which he resigned in 1850, previous to his departure from the country. In 1843 he was nominated for Congress by the Whig Convention of the Fifth District, against his will, but was constrained to accept the position; and after one of the most excited contests ever known in the State he was defeated by a coalition of Independents and Democrats, with the late Hon. William Wright as their candidate. This coalition caused a political revolution in the State. In 1844 he, with the late Chancellor Green, was a Delegate-at-large to the National Whig Convention at Baltimore, and was chiefly instrumental in securing the renomination of a Jerseyman—the late Theodore Frelinghuysen—for Vice-President, on the ticket with Mr. Clay. Both, however, were defeated at the election by the Democratic nominees, Polk and Dallas. In 1851 he was appointed United States Minister to Sardinia by President Taylor, and on the eve of his departure was complimented by a banquet at the Park House by the leading members of both parties. At the court of Turin he became a great favorite of the ministry of that government, and was in constant consultation with them on the practical operation of the republican system in this country, which probably influenced the establishment of the present liberal institutions of Italy. He was also in active sympathy and intimate relations with the British minister, Sir Ralph Abercrombie, in the promotion of religious and political freedom in that country, and received a flattering acknowledgment from their prime minister, Lord Palmerston, on behalf of her Majesty's government. It was about the same period that Kossuth was brought to America from Constantinople in a national ship detached from the Mediterranean squadron, which was under Mr. Kinney's jurisdiction, and his position enabled him to give early information and advice to our government as to the character and objects of the distinguished exile, and thwarted his efforts to enlist it in a complication with foreign powers. Upon the expiration of his term of office at Turin he went to Florence, where he remained for several years among congenial friends, devoted to the cultivation of literature and art, including the Brownings, Hiram Powers, and others. He returned home in 1864, and delivered the oration at the celebration of the 200th anniversary of the settlement of Newark, on May 17th, 1866, in the old First Church. This was his last appearance in public, and he is now enjoying the evening of his days near the place of his birth.

NANNATTA, HON. JACOB, Lawyer, and late Attorney-General of New Jersey, was born in Morris county, New Jersey, about 1825. He was admitted to the bar in the October term, 1849, and made counsellor in the February term, 1853. On commencing the practice of law at Morristown, New Jersey, his energy and great natural ability soon placed him in the front rank of his profession. He has been and is attorney for some of the leading New Jersey railroads, and has an extensive practice in all the courts of the State and United States courts. In 1875 he was appointed, by Governor Bedle, Attorney-General of the State of New Jersey, a position he resigned in 1877 in consequence of its duties interfering with his extensive law practice. The announcement that he had concluded to take this step was received with very general regret, as the office had been admirably administered by him. He is politically a Democrat, taking an active part in the advancement of his party's interest and the general welfare of the county. Although he has been repeatedly urged for the highest offices of the State, he has, with the single exception of his two years' service as Attorney-General, steadily declined office or nomination for political position of any character whatever.

WOODHULL, REV. JOHN, D. D., late Pastor of the Presbyterian Church of Freehold, Trustee of the College of New Jersey, was born in Suffolk county, Long Island, January 26th, 1744, and was the son of John Woodhull, a man of wealth, probity and distinction, connected in marriage with Elizabeth Smith, daughter of William Smith, Esq., of St. George's Manor, Long Island. The Woodhull family emigrated from Great Britain to Long Island at an early period in the settlement of this country, and are descended from illustrious ancestors through a long line, which has been preserved entire from the Norman conquest, A. D. 1066. He received his classical instruction, preparatory to entering college, in a grammar-school under the care of Rev. Caleb Smith, his maternal uncle, who resided at Newark Mountains, now Orange, New Jersey. In the commencement of his education, when about sixteen years of age, he was seriously inclined "and importunate with God for his blessing." While in the College of New Jersey, soon after, under the presidency of the learned and pious Dr. Finley, "it pleased the great Head of the church to pour out his spirit in a remarkable manner upon the youth assembled there," and he, with others, obtained sudden and delightful relief, and saw his future open out more clearly before him. He soon gave evidence of warm and established piety, so that when he called on Dr. Finley to converse on the subject of the approaching communion, a business committed to the president of the college at that time, he scarcely waited for the young convert to express his desire, before he lifted both hands, and exclaimed, " Oh, go, go, and the Lord go with you ! " In 1766 he received the first degree in the arts and at once proceeded to Fags' Manor for the purpose of pursuing theological studies with Rev. John Blair. While thus engaged he was strongly solicited by some pious young men, who had been his classmates in college, from New England, to come over and study with them, alleging that they enjoyed there superior light. They pressed the invitation so urgently that he resolved on this change of situation, and went hope to obtain his father's approbation. This was given, the arrangements made, and time set for his departure from Long Island. " The morning came, and he awoke, he thought, as well as usual, and sprang with alacrity out of bed; but in attempting to dress he found himself unable to stand, and eventually was compelled to lie down again, when he was seized with an alarming fever that confined him there many weeks. His sickness was severe; his recovery very slow. This dispensation of Providence he considered of great importance, as influencing materially the whole course of his after life." He then returned to Mr. Blair, finished his preliminary studies, and, August 10th, 1768, was licensed by the Presbytery of New Castle to preach the gospel. Of the several calls which he subsequently had under consideration at the same time, a sense of duty inclined him to prefer that of Laycock Congregation, Lancaster, Pennsylvania, where,

August 1st, 1770, he was ordained to the holy ministry. In 1779 he was translated from this charge to the large and respectable congregation at Freehold, New Jersey, which was regularly organized June 3d, 1730; before this date it had nominally existed a short time and enjoyed the pastoral labors of Rev. Joseph Morgan. In 1780 he was elected a Trustee of the College of New Jersey, at Princeton, and to this institution he unceasingly devoted his most faithful attention. In 1798 he received from Yale College the degree of Doctor of Divinity, a tribute of respect, of which it was universally admitted he was eminently worthy. His fame as a preacher of the gospel was already extensive, and his influence in ecclesiastical judicatories well known. "His eminence and usefulness were both increased by his uncommon diligence and fidelity in conducting for many years near his residence, a grammar-school, which sent forth a succession of accomplished scholars, a good proportion of whom have shone with distinction in the learned professions, and some have occupied offices of dignity and trust in the nation." His character also as a theological teacher was widely diffused, and during a period of thirty years a great number of candidates for the sacred office from different and distant parts of the church availed themselves of the advantages of his pleasant situation, his hospitable mansion, his kind pure and attention, his well-selected library, and his richly furnished mind. The labors of this sort he declined after the establishment of the Theological Seminary at Princeton, in whose prosperity he always manifested a deep interest, and in whose affairs and their direction he bore an important part for many years. "His intellectual endowments were by nature uniquely of the first order. By native soundness of judgment, deepness of penetration and extent of view, comprehensiveness of mind and tenaciousness of memory, mildness of disposition, dignity of aspect and suavity of manners, fertility of mental resource and masculine powers of eloquence, prudence in difficulty, patience, perseverance in enterprise and benevolence to the wretched, he was placed by the Hand that formed him in the first grade of his species. And his acquired furniture for the sacred office was rich and appropriate."—Sermon, by Rev. Isaac V. Brown, eminent clergyman of Princeton, New Jersey. Mathematical science absorbed his mind, classical reading was his amusement, and history his delight through the college course; while his engagements in New Jersey, as teacher of languages and of candidates for the sacred desk, made him familiar with the whole circle of classics and led him to explore thoroughly the treasures of sacred literature. When the church in this State was young and destitute, in many parts almost shepherdless, he performed an incredible amount of labor, besides the care of his own flock, in organizing churches, establishing the principles of orthodox religion and Presbyterian church government, reconciling differences and repairing desolations in the congregations, and raising up and sending forth laborers into the vast field then unoccupied.

"The churches looked to him as their counsellor and guide in Christ, and they have long since, from ample experience, by universal suffrage, conferred upon this apostolic man the imperishable distinction of being one of the most orthodox and evangelic divines of the last and present century. . . The church is by his death bereaved of a burning and shining light, the Presbytery of New Brunswick mourn the loss of a father, and Bible societies the departure of a steady adherent and able advocate; the State of New Jersey gives up to-day a patriot, enlightened, ardent, inflexible—one who has long shone splendidly in the bright constellation of her illustrious citizens." In 1772 he was united in marriage to Sarah Spafford, of Philadelphia; and with this pious and excellent woman lived more than half a century. His granddaughter, Cornelia Neilson Woodhull, daughter of S. Woodhull, of Princeton, New Jersey, was ranbury, New Jersey, May 16th, 1803, and died in 1824.

RAVEN, JOHN JOSEPH, M. D., of Jersey City, was born in New Jersey, September 8th, 1822, apprenticed when a lad to David G. Ayres, house carpenter, of New Jersey, and upon attaining his majority entered the employment of John Grigg, of Newark, carpenter and millwright. He was immediately employed in the construction of the Passaic Chemical Works, and when the works went into operation he was retained in the employ ment of William Clough, practical chemist, as Superintendent of the staple product of the works and it is from the quality of the value and it was from the manufacture employed the first steps research. While holding this position he was married to Catherine S., daughter of Mr. Samuel Tichenor, of Newark. In 1845 Morse's telegraph across New Jersey was in course of construction, the Newark office being located in the court-house of that city. During the erection and testing of the first instruments, he became greatly interested in the new science; became acquainted with Professor Morse and others connected with the Magnetic Telegraph Company, and, resigning his position in the Passaic Chemical Works, entered the service of the company as Superintendent of Construction. Under his supervision the line connecting Newark, Paterson, Hackensack and Fort Lee was erected, and having finished this work he remained for some time at Fort Lee, under the instruction of Professor Morse, experimenting in the construction of submarine telegraph cables. The attempts in this direction, made in the latter part of 1845 and during 1846, were unsuccessful, a proper insulation of the wire presenting a difficulty that seemed to be wholly insurmountable. In 1847, however, he was shown, as a curiosity, some gutta-percha—a substance not then

August 1st, 1770, he was ordained to the holy ministry. In 1779 he was translated from this charge to the large and respectable congregation at Freehold, New Jersey, which was regularly organized June 3d, 1730; before this date it had nominally existed a short time and enjoyed the pastoral labors of Rev. Joseph Morgan. In 1780 he was elected a Trustee of the College of New Jersey, at Princeton, and to this institution he unceasingly devoted his most faithful attention. In 1798 he received from Yale College the degree of Doctor of Divinity, a tribute of respect, of which it was universally admitted he was eminently worthy. His fame as a freacher of the gospel was already extensive, and his influence in ecclesiastical judicatories well known. "His eminence and usefulness were both increased by his uncommon diligence and fidelity in conducting for many years, near his residence, a grammar-school, which sent forth a succession of accomplished scholars, a good proportion of whom have shone with distinction in the learned professions, and some have occupied offices of dignity and trust in the nation." His character also as a theological teacher was widely diffused, and during a period of thirty years a great number of candidates for the sacred office from different and distant parts of the church availed themselves of the advantages of his pleasant situation, his hospitable mansion, his kind parental attentions, his well-selected library, and his richly furnished mind. But labors of this sort he declined after the establishment of the Theological Seminary at Princeton, in whose prosperity he always manifested a deep interest, and in whose affairs and their direction he bore an important part for many years. "His intellectual endowments were by nature unquestionably of the first order. By native soundness of judgment, deepness of penetration and extent of view, comprehensiveness of mind and tenaciousness of memory, mildness of disposition, dignity of aspect and suavity of manners, fertility of mental resource and masculine powers of eloquence, prudence in difficulty, patience, perseverance in enterprise and benevolence to the wretched, he was placed by the Hand that formed him in the first grade of his species. And his acquired furniture for the sacred office was rich and appropriate."—Sermon, by Rev. Isaac V. Brown, eminent clergyman of Princeton, New Jersey. Mathematical science absorbed his mind, classical reading was his amusement, and history his delight through the college course; while his engagements in New Jersey, as teacher of languages and of candidates for the sacred desk, made him familiar with the whole circle of classics and led him to explore thoroughly the treasures of sacred literature. When the church in this State was young and destitute, in many parts almost shepherdless, he performed an incredible amount of labor, besides the care of his own flock, in organizing churches, establishing the principles of orthodox religion and Presbyterian church government, reconciling differences and repairing desolations in the congregations, and raising up and sending forth laborers into the vast field then unoccupied.

"The churches looked to him as their counsellor and father in Christ, and they have long since, from ample experience, by universal suffrage, conferred upon this apostolic man the imperishable distinction of being one of the most orthodox and evangelic divines of the last and present century. . . . The church is by his death bereaved of a burning and shining light, the Presbytery of New Brunswick mourn the loss of a father, and Bible societies the departure of a steady adherent and able advocate; the State of New Jersey gives up to-day a patriot, enlightened, ardent, inflexible—one who has long shone splendidly in the bright constellation of her illustrious citizens." In 1772 he was united in marriage to Sarah Spafford, of Philadelphia, and with this pious and excellent woman lived more than half a century. His granddaughter, Cornelia Neilson Woodhull, daughter of Rev. George S. Woodhull, of Princeton, New Jersey, was born at Cranbury, New Jersey, May 16th, 1803, and died in 1824.

———————

RAVEN, JOHN JOSEPH, M. D., of Jersey City, was born in New Jersey, September 8th, 1822. He was apprenticed when a lad to David G. Ayres, house carpenter, of Newark, New Jersey, and upon attaining his majority entered the employment of John Grigg, of Newark, carpenter and millwright. He was immediately employed in the construction of the Passaic Chemical Works, and when the works went into operation he was retained in the employment of William Clough, proprietor, and a practical chemist, as Superintendent of Construction and Repairs. The staple products of the works were acids and dry salts, and it was from the study of the various processes of manufacture employed that he first acquired a taste for scientific research. While holding this position he was married to Catherine S., daughter of Mr. Samuel Tichenor, of Newark. In 1845 Morse's telegraph across New Jersey was in course of construction, the Newark office being located in the court-house of that city. During the erection and testing of the first instruments, he became greatly interested in the new science; became acquainted with Professor Morse and others connected with the Magnetic Telegraph Company and, resigning his position in the Passaic Chemical Works, entered the service of the company as Superintendent of Construction. Under his supervision the line connecting Newark, Paterson, Hackensack and Fort Lee was erected, and having finished this work he remained for some time at Fort Lee, under the instruction of Professor Morse, experimenting in the construction of submarine telegraph cables. The attempts in this direction, made in the latter part of 1845 and during 1846, were unsuccessful, a proper insulation of the wire presenting a difficulty that seemed to be wholly insurmountable. In 1847, however, he was shown, as a curiosity, some gutta-percha,—a substance not then

68

known commercially—and he was at once struck by its adaptability to the very purpose that he had in hand. In the month of August, 1847, in his own house, with the assistance of his wife, he covered with gutta-percha a copper wire, submerged it in water, and by repeated electrical tests satisfied himself that his discovery was in every way a success. The wire that he had prepared being of sufficient length, he submerged it in the Passaic river at the railroad draw-bridge at Newark, and, by the consent of the Magnetic Telegraph Company, connected it with the land wires on each side. Careful tests showed the new method to be entirely effective, and the inventor had the satisfaction of knowing that he had won a great scientific victory—how great that victory was in the end to be, even he little imagined. This at Newark was undoubtedly the first application of gutta-percha as an insulating substance for submarine telegraph purposes. In the latter part of 1847, gutta-percha having at that time been placed in our markets, he prepared wires for use at various points where it was desirable to carry telegraph lines across navigable streams, and all of these, when put into use, proved entirely satisfactory in their working. As he had unquestionably discovered the practical value, and had applied gutta-percha for the first time to telegraphic purposes, and as his discovery was evidently one of great commercial value, he took measures in 1848 to protect his rights by patenting the process which he had devised. By a quite unpardonable error of judgment on the part of the Commissioners of Patents, his application was refused; the very insufficient reason given for such refusal being that Professor Faraday had already mentioned gutta-percha as being a non-conducting substance. This was unquestionably true; but Professor Faraday had not remotely hinted at the invaluable purpose to which it had been applied by the American inventor, and the essential excellence of a patent rests quite as much upon application as upon discovery. It is a disgrace to the Patent Office that so excellent an invention was refused recognition, and that an inventor of such merit was defrauded of his reward. The Hon. William D. Kelley, in his address delivered in Philadelphia at the cable celebration (1858), thus alluded to the man who made submarine cables possible : " But we celebrate the laying of a submarine cable, and let me with my poor efforts draw from the obscurity into which it is fallen the name of that toiling worker of days-work who first laid a magnetic telegraph wire, coated in gutta-percha, under a body of water near his native town of Newark, New Jersey. He laid four thus coated, and for the use of one of them he received, from a powerful corporation, one dollar and twenty-five cents per day. He applied for a patent, but on grounds which, if I understand the case rightly, were very inadequate for such a decision, his claim was rejected, and he lost even his poor revenue from the work which the corporation used. John J. Craven, of Newark, New Jersey, made and laid the first practical, substantial, available submarine telegraph; and

let his name stand out in its proper place." In the same strain is the following extract from the Newark *Courier*, of January 15th, 1870: "A former citizen of Newark was the first person to suggest the utility of submarine telegraph cables, and to carry his suggestion into effect by practical experiment. There is much truth in the old adage that prophets are never honored in their own country, but we are glad to observe one exception at least in a rule which has such general application. A recent scientific report of pre-eminent authority very properly conceded the claim of the submarine cable inventor, and hands down to the rightful honor which awaits it the name of our former townsman, Dr. John J. Craven. Since Dr. Craven first undertook in a small, but nevertheless convincing way, to test the practicability of submarine telegraphic cables, the matter has received the attention of the scientific men of both sides of the Atlantic, and everybody knows the results obtained. Within a few years an electric current has bound the old world to the new, thus affording for intelligence a magnificent triumph both over space and time. In point of communication, London and Paris are almost as near to us to-day as New York and Brooklyn. It is both proper and right to applaud the efforts of Field and others, whose energy and means contributed so much to this final demonstration of practical science. Yet, while we cheerfully accord these indomitable spirits their just deserts, it is fitting that we should also remember the comparatively humble pioneer in this great undertaking, who has been rewarded in nothing but the late recognition of his just claim." Notwithstanding the difficulties with which the inventor had to contend, he had a profound faith in his invention, and in a letter written in the early part of 1848 he prophetically says: " I have surely struck it. I have now in my possession a wire that is, in a short circuit beneath a stream, in connection with a main line, doing its work faithfully. Mark my words: it will yet cross rivers, bays, seas and oceans, and connect continents." Having had his material prepared, he then, under the direction of the officers of the Magnetic Telegraph Company, laid down, on the 15th of June, 1848, a cable uniting New York and Jersey City, and making complete the line between New York and Washington. As at first laid this cable extended from the Cunard dock in Jersey City to the (then) Albany dock, at the foot of Cortlandt street, New York. This location he selected on account of its being almost in the track of the New York and Jersey City Ferry, hoping thereby to escape the dangers of disturbance from anchorage. In a few days, however, a less exposed situation was in a little time selected. Meanwhile his only pecuniary return for his labor and skill was the small salary paid him by the Magnetic Telegraph Company, and in the hope of bettering his fortunes he sailed early in 1849 for the then just discovered gold-fields of California. His success upon the Pacific coast was not brilliant, and in 1851 he returned to the States, and in the same year began the study of medicine, and subsequently placed himself under the preceptorship of Dr. Gabriel Grant, of Newark. Having attended lectures at the College of Physicians and Surgeons of New York, he entered upon the practice of medicine in Newark, and remained in successful practice in that city until 1861. On the breaking out of the late war he was offered and accepted the appointment of Surgeon of the 1st New Jersey Regiment, and served with that organization during the three months' term of its enlistment. Having returned he was invited by the Secretary of War to appear before a Board of Army Surgeons, then sitting in the city of Washington, as a candidate for Brigade Surgeon. Passing through this examination successfully, he was appointed Brigade Surgeon and attached to the staff of General H. G. Wright, in Sherman's expeditionary corps. In February, 1862, he was promoted to be Chief Medical Officer of General Wright's brigade, and accompanied that force to Florida; was subsequently assigned to duty on Tybee island, Georgia, and while active in this capacity, was selected by the medical director of the department for Chief Medical Officer to General Gilmore's command during the investment of Fort Pulaski. In September, 1862, he was made Medical Purveyor of the Department of the South, with head-quarters at Hilton Head. In May, 1864, he was made Chief Medical Officer of Field Operations against Forts Wagner, Gregg and Sumpter. On the reduction of the works General Gilmore organized the 10th Army Corps, with which Surgeon Craven proceeded to Virginia as Medical Director, and was in the following August detailed for thirty days as a member of a Board for the Examination of Hospitals in the Department of the East, saving which time he remained with the 10th Corps until 1865. On the 17th of January, by special order, he was assigned to duty as Medical Purveyor and Chief Medical Officer of the Department of Virginia and North Carolina, with head-quarters at Fortress Monroe. In March, 1865, he was brevetted Lieutenant-Colonel for faithful and meritorious services during the war, and on the 16th of December he was honorably discharged from the service. While on duty at Fortress Monroe he attended lectures at the Baltimore Academy of Medicine, and from that institution received his degree of M. D., a formality scarcely necessary, since in the school of the army he had successively taken the degrees of Surgeon of the Regiment, Surgeon of the Brigade, Surgeon of Division, Surgeon of Corps, Surgeon of the Army, and finally Chief Medical Officer of a Department, winning each of these positions by his acknowledged professional and executive ability. In 1867 he again began the practice of his profession in New Jersey, establishing himself in Jersey City. About this time, as will be remembered, the great abattoir at Communipaw was figuring prominently in the New Jersey courts; had been formally declared to be by the chancellor—as it certainly was—a nuisance, and by the same authority its conduct had been enjoined. In this strait, the president of the abattoir company applied to Dr. Craven, on the ground of his extensive chemical and sanitary knowledge, to devise some plan by which the business might be unobjectionably conducted. Entering into the work with great interest and enthusiasm, he entirely succeeded in bringing it to a successful issue, although in the course of so doing he was compelled to invent processes, and to, moreover, invent machinery for putting such processes into action. He is now the recognized authority upon establishments of this sort, and during the last ten years his advice has been sought by the projectors of the large abattoirs in this country. In this present instance his inventions have deservedly redounded to his own profit, and he can now contemplate with coolness the millions lost to him through the bungling of the Patent Office over his gutta-percha-coated wire. Oddly enough, he has himself come of late years to be a recognized expert in patent cases of a scientific character, too late, however, to be of any service to his own claims. One of his most important inventions, as yet unmentioned, is a process for the transportation of fresh meat for long distances, a process that is now in successful use and seems to entirely fulfil all reasonable conditions. But the list of his successes is too long to be enumerated; from what has been written the rest must be inferred. He is a typical, self-made man, of humble origin and without any early advantages of education; with, indeed, almost insuperable natural disadvantages to weigh him down, he has by sheer force of nerve and strength of intelligence raised himself to a commanding position in the community. Summing him up, intellectually and personally, one of his fellow staff-officers wrote, a dozen years ago: " He is a very excellent, kind, skilful and conscientious medical attendant. A vigorous follower of field sports; rather spare of habit; pure Roman features, set off to advantage by military whiskers and moustache; a voice of excellent modulation, and manners of great courtesy and politeness. He is a devotee of science in all its branches, and more fully fills my idea of a savant than any other medical man it has been my fortune to meet in the army."

————◆◇◆————

EWELL, HON. WILLIAM A., was born in Ohio and graduated at Rutgers College. Moving to New Jersey when still a young man, he took an active interest in politics, and was shortly afterwards elected upon the Republican ticket a Representative to Congress from 1847 to 1851. Abraham Lincoln was a member of the same Congress, and the two men sat beside each other in the House, roomed and boarded together, and became intimate friends. In 1856 Mr. Newell was elected Governor of New Jersey by a Republican majority of about 1,000. In 1864 he was a Delegate to the Baltimore Convention, and was re-elected to the Thirty-ninth Congress, Mr. Lincoln at that time

being President, and the friendship between them was renewed. He served on the Committees on Foreign Affairs
and Revolutionary Claims, and was an indefatigable worker.
In 1868 and 1870 he was a candidate for re-election to Congress, but was both times defeated. In 1871 he was a candidate for the United States Senate, and for a number of
years he held the office of Vice-President of the National
Union League.

ALLANTINE, PETER, of Newark, New Jersey,
Brewer, was born in 1791 in Ayrshire, Scotland,
memorable, among other things, as containing
the birthplace of the poet Burns, and the Allo-
way-Kirk, in which Tam O'Shanter had his
midnight vision. In 1820 he came to this country, and went to Albany, New York, where he entered the
service of Robert Dunlop, a brewer, and one of the most extensive at that time in the country, with whom he learned
the process of brewing, though more from close observation
of the work as done by others than from direct instruction.
Such was his docility and mother wit, however, that he soon
mastered the business, and was employed as brewer and
malster by several leading firms in succession at Albany
and the vicinity, and subsequently became a partner in the
firm of Fidler, Ryckman & Co., in which he remained
about six years. He was now not only an expert but an
experienced manager in the business. In 1840 he removed
to Newark, New Jersey, and rented there a brewery, which,
though it had never been operated successfully before,
he carried on with steadily increasing success from the beginning, in the face not merely of the competition of
the most celebrated brands in the country, but of the bad
reputation of the ales previously brewed in the establishment. At the end of the eighth year he had increased his
annual production to eleven thousand barrels, which, being
the limit of the facilities then at his command, necessitated
the erection of new buildings; whereupon he bought in
1848 a tract of land adjacent to the Passaic river, on which
he built a malthouse of thirty thousand bushels capacity, and
in the following year a new brewery, communicating with
his new malthouse, and having a capacity of one hundred
barrels a day. His business was at last in the full tide of
prosperity, and flowed on with ever increasing volume, insomuch that the difficulty was not to accelerate it but to
keep pace with it, new facilities being constantly required to
meet the new demands. The sales continued to grow until
from brewing four times a week he was compelled to brew
every day, and sometimes twice a day. He, however, kept
his swelling business well in hand by dint of wisely yielding to its successive exactions, building first another malthouse of twenty thousand bushels capacity; next enlarging
his brewery; then building a third malthouse of sixty

thousand bushels capacity, which he afterwards enlarged to
eighty thousand bushels; and, finally, building still another
malthouse, two hundred feet long, forty-eight feet wide, and
six stories in height. In these ample accommodations he
rests for the present, but as his business is as active and progressive as ever, there is no telling how soon it may outgrow
even such immense facilities. It should be stated that his
establishment supplies malt to other brewers, producing consequently much more than is consumed in his own breweries.
His house is thus a kind of mother-brewery, standing to
others in something of the same relation that the metropolis
bears to other cities. It is assuredly a grand monument of
his energy and skill. During the first five years of his business career in Newark he was in partnership with Mr. E.
Patterson, and since 1859 his three sons have been associated with him, under the firm-name of P. Ballantine &
Sons, one of them having charge of the principal depot in
New York city, whence all the shipping is done and all the
city trade supplied. But the father has been the head of
the concern in fact as in name. He is now a patriarch not
only among brewers but among men, being eighty-six years
of age. All the most important improvements in his business have come in under his eye. He has seen hand labor,
exclusively used in breweries when he began, superseded
almost wholly by the appliances of modern invention; the
old cumbrous and costly motive powers replaced by steam,
with the consequent revolution in his own as in all other departments of industry; and brewing, once thought practicable during only about eight months of the twelve, continued
throughout the year, sound ale being brewed alike in July
and in January. And all these improvements, as they have
appeared one after another, he has been quick to seize and
utilize for the benefit of his customers as well as himself,
until he has succeeded not simply in amassing a fortune, but
in raising the reputation of Newark ale in this country to a
height scarcely less than that of Munich beer in Germany,
keeping at the same time his own reputation, amid all vicissitudes, free from spot or tarnish. Well does he merit, what
he receives in full measure, the respect and veneration of his
fellow-citizens.

HOMPSON, REV. STEPHEN OGDEN, Presbyterian Minister, of Connecticut Farms, New Jersey,
was born in Mendham, New Jersey, and was a descendant of "Goodman Thompson," one of the
founders of Elizabethtown, and a pioneer settler
of extended reputation. His parents were Jacob
and Hannah (Beach) Thompson, daughter of Elisha Beach;
his grandfather, Stephen Thompson, was nineteen years old
when his father, Joseph, migrated from the old home at
Elizabethtown to the head spring of the Passaic, in what is
now known as the village of Mendham; Joseph, the great-
grandfather, was the son of Aaron, and the grandson of

Goodman Thompson; the grandfather of Stephen O. having died at thirty years of age, the widow married Dr. Joseph Ogden. The subject of this sketch studied at the College of New Jersey, and graduated from that institution in 1797. He was then, October 18th, 1798, taken under the care of the Presbytery of New York; and licensed to preach, October 9th, 1800. A call for his services as pastor was presented to the Presbytery, June 15th, 1802, from the church of Connecticut Farms; and he was ordained pastor thereof on Tuesday, November 16th, 1802, at eleven o'clock A. M.; Rev. Asa Hillyer, of Orange, New Jersey, presided; Rev. Aaron Condict, of Hanover, preached the sermon; and Rev. James Richards, of Morristown, gave the exhortation to the people. Thrice during his ministry, in 1808, 1813-14, and in 1817, his people were favored with notable revivals of religion. In 1834 he was dismissed. He subsequently removed to Indiana, N. E., and became a member of the Presbytery of St. Joseph (N. S.), in which he continued till his decease, May 31st, 1856, in his eighty-first year. February 24th, 1803, he was married to Henrietta Beach, a daughter of Major Nathaniel Beach, of Newark. The ceremony was performed by Dr. Macwhorter, with whom, probably, he had studied for the ministry.

ORST, DANIEL P., Merchant, of Trenton, was born in New Hope, Bucks county, Pennsylvania, April 11th, 1822, and is the son of William H. Forst, of that place, a merchant and member of the firm of Daniel Parry & Co. After attending for some years the schools and academy of New Hope, Daniel completed his education at Plainfield, New Jersey. On leaving school he commenced his business life as a clerk in the employment of the firm of which his father was a member during his lifetime. In this engagement he continued until 1841, when, being then in his twentieth year, he removed to Bristol, Pennsylvania, and commenced operations on his own account in the coal, lumber and general mercantile business. Success attended his enterprise. In 1855, desirous of a wider sphere, he removed to Trenton, New Jersey, and opened a general store business on Broad street, which he prosecuted energetically for a period of three years. In 1858 the firm of Forst & Taylor was organized, the copartners being Daniel P. Forst and John Taylor, of whom a biographical sketch appears in another part of this volume, and it became one of the pioneers in the wholesale trade of Trenton. Its sales, which have now reached nearly a million of dollars per annum, at the time of the formation of the copartnership amounted to less than two hundred thousand. After an association of twelve years Mr. Taylor retired from the firm in 1870, and Mr. W. H. Skirm became a member, the style being D. P. Forst & Co. Since that date C. W. Leeds and Joseph M. Forst, son of the senior member of the firm, have been admitted to an interest in the business. The first store occupied by Forst & Taylor was a comparatively small one at the corner of Green and Hanover streets, and in it they continued for one year. More commodious premises were then found at the northeast corner of Green and Academy streets. In 1866 their constantly increasing business demanding considerable enlargement of their facilities, their present handsome and capacious building was erected. The store and the business transacted therein are upon a scale fairly rivalling the concerns of the same class in New York and Philadelphia. The development and prosperity of the establishment are the natural results of the energy, integrity and fine business qualifications brought to bear by Mr. Forst. He is a very public-spirited man, and labors in and out of season to advance the commercial and social status of his adopted city. He is an active member of the Board of Trade; Director in the Mechanics' National Bank, and in the People's Fire Insurance Company. In politics he is a Republican, but he only takes a citizen's interest in political affairs.

CARBOROUGH, RT. REV. JOHN, D. D., Protestant Episcopal Bishop of New Jersey, was born in New York in 1827. He received his early education in that State, and afterwards entered Trinity College, Hartford, Connecticut; after graduating at this institution he entered the General Theological Seminary of the Protestant Episcopal Church in New York city, and was graduated in the class of 1857. At the seminary he was esteemed for his many brilliant and scholarly qualities, and for his zeal in missionary and Sunday-school work among the poor of the parish of Trinity Church. His first office was with the venerable Rev. Dr. Thomas W. Coit, of Christ Church, Troy, New York, to whom he was assistant for several years. His next care was to Poughkeepsie, New York, where he had charge of a large and flourishing parish. From here he removed to Pittsburgh, Pennsylvania, to become the successor of Rev. Dr. Swope at Trinity Church, the most prominent Protestant Episcopal Church in that city. Dr. Scarborough's ministrations in his new parish were very successful and acceptable to his congregation, who during his incumbency erected the present elegant and costly church edifice. In November, 1874, he was elected, after a protracted struggle, to the Bishopric of the Diocese of New Jersey, which State had been divided into a Northern and Southern diocese, and Bishop Odenheimer, formerly the Bishop of both, having selected the Northern diocese as his own. The Southern diocese includes the counties of Cape May, Cumberland, Salem, Gloucester, Camden, Burlington, Mercer, Hunterdon, Atlantic, Ocean, Monmouth, Union, Middlesex and Somerset. The Burlington College for Boys, and the Female College, St. Mary's Hall, both at Burlington, and the Episcopal residence of Riverside are included in this diocese. On February 2d, 1875, Bishop Scarborough was consecrated in St. Mary's Church, Burlington. Like his predecessors before the division of the seat, he has since made Burlington his residence. Bishop Scarborough is a man of great zeal and unusual ability, and his rare executive ability has been shown in his administration of the Episcopal office in New Jersey.

ORKE, HON. THOMAS JONES, Merchant, of Salem—a descendant of Thomas Yorke, some time a High Sheriff in England during the reign of Henry VIII.; more recently of Simon Yorke, a native of and landed proprietor in Wiltshire, and afterwards a resident of Dover, in Kent; and fifth in descent from Thomas Yorke (brother of Joseph Yorke, some time Mayor of Dover, and Minister to the Hague under George II.), who immigrated to America from Yorkshire in 1728—was born in Salem, New Jersey, March 25th, 1801. Having received a substantial English education at the Salem Academy, he entered the store of his grandfather, Thomas Jones, a merchant of Salem, and thence in 1817 entered the counting-house of James Patton, at that time a leading shipping merchant of Philadelphia. Four years later he returned to Salem, and established in partnership with his uncle, Thomas Jones, Jr., a general business under the firm-name of Jones & Yorke. This business he continued until 1847, when the pressure of other affairs, public and private, compelled him to relinquish its conduct. Early in life he associated himself with the Whig party, and with that political organization and with its successor, the Republican party, he has since been prominently identified. Having held various local offices in his native county, his broader public career was begun in 1835 by his election to the State Assembly. The ensuing year he was elected a member of the National House of Representatives, and until 1843 continued to be a member of that body. During his term of office occurred the famous " Broad seal war," and it was also while he was a member of the House that Morse made his application to Congress for aid in building the first line of telegraph. He was one of the members who voted in favor of the appropriation of $40,000 for the construction of the Baltimore and Washington line. His fine business ability naturally brought him into connection with numerous corporate organizations, and his money and judgment were given with equal freedom in stimulating and developing the resources of his native State. In 1853 he was elected a Director and was made Secretary and Treasurer of the West Jersey Railroad Company; held these offices until 1866, when he was elected President of the road, and since 1875—when he resigned the position of President—has continued to be a member of the Board of Directors. Within the past twenty-

five years it is safe to say that this line of railway has more than doubled the productiveness, and has more than quadrupled the value of the section of country that it drains. For very much of this appreciation in usefulness and value Mr. Yorke is directly responsible; his management of the road having been based on a policy of enlightened liberality calculated to induce the mutual prosperity of the owners and patrons of the line. In his management of the Cape May & Millville Railroad Company, and of the West Jersey Express Company—of both of which he is President—a similar policy has been uniformly maintained; and a like policy has been urged by him in the conduct of the West Jersey Mail and Transportation Company; in that of the Salem Railroad Company, in that of the Swedesboro Railroad Company, and in that of the Camden & Philadelphia Ferry Company, in all of which corporations he is a Director. Besides holding the various positions already named, he has been for the past twelve years President Judge of the Court of Common Pleas of Salem County. For this latter office he was especially fitted by a course of legal study, undertaken not with a view of practising law as a profession, but for the purpose of gaining additional knowledge to be used in the management of his own affairs, and of the affairs of the various trusts the discharge of which have been laid upon him, and so beneficial has this knowledge proved to him that he caused both of his sons to pursue a similar course of study, although neither intended to enter upon a legal career. During the late war he was earnest and outspoken in his maintenance of the Federal Union, but his only active military service was during the war of 1812, when—a mere lad—he was for a considerable period employed as a scout to note the movements of the British forces at the time of the blockade of the Delaware. The duty to which he was then detailed was intelligently and effectively discharged, and was of material service to the American forces. He was twice married—first to Mary Ann, daughter of Jonathan Smith, Esq., of Bucks county, Pennsylvania; and, second, to Margaret Johnson, daughter of Thomas Sinnickson, Esq., of Chester county, Pennsylvania. His eldest son, Louis Eugene, was educated as a civil engineer at Rensselaer Institute, New York; was subsequently employed on the Pennsylvania Railroad, Memphis & Charleston Railroad, and in 1860 was engineer in charge of the Bergen tunnel. Resigning this position he entered the United States volunteer army as a member of the 7th New York Regiment; served with that organization during its term of enlistment; entered the regular army and was commissioned a Captain in the 14th United States Regiment; was with Sherman in his march to the sea; was wounded in the Arkansas campaign, and at the end of the war—at which time he held the brevet rank of Colonel—resigned his commission and resumed the practice of his profession. He died in Cincinnati in 1873. Mr. Yorke's second son, Thomas, is a member of the firm of Sinnickson & Co., of Philadelphia.

ILL, HON. JOHN, Merchant, of Boonton, was born at Catskill, New York, June 10th, 1821, and received a substantial business education in the schools of his native place. On leaving school he devoted himself to mercantile pursuits. In 1844 he removed to New Jersey, locating at Boonton, an iron manufacturing town of Morris county, and engaging in merchandising. His unquestionable integrity and large public spirit rapidly won for him the esteem and confidence of his fellow-citizens. He identified himself thoroughly with the town, and manifested at all times a deep interest in the welfare and progress of its institutions. It followed very naturally that he should be asked to serve the community in official relations. Repeatedly he was elected to local offices, and in 1860 he was elected as a Representative to the New Jersey Assembly, and was re-elected in the following year. During the succeeding period of war he earnestly and ably sustained the general government in all measures necessary to suppress the rebellion, freely devoting his time and means in the raising of troops, and in extending aid and comfort to the soldiers in the field, often visiting the camps and rendering the men every assistance in his power. This patriotic course he pursued so long as an army remained in the field, so long as sick and wounded had to be cared for. In 1865 he was again elected to the New Jersey Assembly, and was chosen Speaker of the House, in which position he proved exceptionally efficient and reliable. During that session of the Legislature he introduced and carried through the House and passed the Senate the joint resolutions of thanks to the soldiers and sailors of New Jersey who enlisted to put down the late rebellion, and which have been issued in the form of a certificate and sent to all soldiers and sailors whose place of residence could be found. At the general election in the fall of 1866 he was returned to the Fortieth Congress, and was re-elected two years later to the Forty-first, and again in 1870 to the Forty-second. During his career in Congress he served on the Committee on Post-Offices and Post-Roads, and his well-directed efforts to secure reforms in the postal service secured him a national reputation. It is not too much to say that the country is probably more indebted to him than to any other member of Congress for those two almost inestimable reforms—the present postal card system, and the abolition of the franking privilege. In the Fortieth and Forty-first Congresses he was also member of the Committee on Coinage, Weights and Measures, and in the Forty-second, Chairman of the Committee on Expenditures of the Department of the Interior. While working for national interests he was by no means unmindful of those more immediately appertaining to his constituency, the mining, manufacturing and agricultural affairs in which his district is so largely concerned receiving careful and constant attention at his hands during his congressional career. Believing in the principle of "protection to American industry," he was fully awake to the importance of protecting labor, and

was ever on the alert to defend the interests of the working-man. Among other congressional labors mention must be made of his active efforts in procuring an appropriation, on April 13th, 1861, for the "life-saving service on the New Jersey coast," or, "for the purpose of more effectually securing life and property on the coast of New Jersey," whereby additional stations, with crews at each, and improved surf-boats, have been secured, which have proved the means of saving great loss of life and of property since they went into operation. On his return home from Congress his constituents marked their high sense of "his important services in behalf of protection to American industry, postal reform and the general interests of his country, State and district, during three terms in Congress," by the public presentation of a very handsome testimonial consisting of a service of silver; while the members of the Manufacturers' Silk Association of Paterson presented him with an elegantly engrossed expression of thanks for his labors on behalf of the silk interest of the United States. Leading men from all parts of the State participated on the occasion, which was in the nature of a very enthusiastic ovation. In 1874 he was elected to the State Senate from Morris county, and has proved one of the ablest members of that body. While the Republicans were in a majority he served on several of the most important committees, and was Chairman of those on Education and Soldiers' Children's Home. During the recent session (1877) the Democrats controlled the Senate, and ability and fitness on the Republican side had no opportunity. But he put forth then, as previously, earnest efforts on behalf of retrenchment and reform in the expenditures of the State, such as have attracted universal attention throughout the State, and have marked him out as a man eminently fitted to lead his party in the State. His friends are therefore warmly advocating his nomination as Republican candidate for Governor at the ensuing election. It may very certainly be said that he would prove a popular candidate, for probably no man could be nominated who possesses in so great a degree the confidence and esteem of the people of the State.

———◆◇◆———

REEN, HON. ASHBEL, Lawyer, born November 17th, 1825, in Princeton, New Jersey, is a descendant of a family intimately connected with the culture and advancement of that State. His grandfather, the Rev. Ashbel Green, for many years President of Princeton College, was distinguished for his learning and eloquence, and was at one time chaplain to Congress. His father, James S. Green, Esq., was a prominent lawyer of New Jersey, and educated his son for that profession. The lad was educated at Princeton, and graduated from Princeton College with distinction in 1846. After studying law for three years he was admitted to the bar in 1849. His father's position as a director and counsel of the Camden & Amboy Railroad, and Delaware & Raritan Canal Company, of which corporations he was one of the original promoters, directed Ashbel Green's attention to the study of corporation law, in which specialty he has a great reputation. He early took an interest in politics, allying himself with the Democratic party, speaking throughout the State and contributing to that party's advancement by every means in his power. In 1867 he was elected Judge of the County Court of Bergen, New Jersey. In 1876 he was chosen one of the Tilden Electors, and took an active part in the events connected with the contest. In 1877 he was defeated by John R. McPherson in the caucus nomination for United States Senator. In the argument before the Electoral Commission he was associated, by the Democratic National Committee, with Lyman Trumbull, of Illinois, Matthew H. Carpenter, of Wisconsin, and Jeremiah Black, of Pennsylvania, to manage the great case. Judge Green is known as a man of fine literary culture and taste, and of refined feeling; in his profession he is not only a learned lawyer, but an eloquent and effective orator.

———◆———

OXE, HON. DANIEL, Associate-Justice of the Supreme Court of New Jersey, late of Trenton, was a son of Dr. Daniel Coxe, of London—well known in colonial days as the greatest proprietor of West Jersey—and was born in 1664, probably at Burlington. Having studied law, he was admitted to the New Jersey bar, and rapidly acquired a leading position. In 1710 he was appointed by Governor Robert Hunter, who succeeded Lord Lovelace, a member of the Provincial Council, and in 1734 he was made an Associate-Justice of the Supreme Court of New Jersey. He died April 25th, 1739. As a public-spirited citizen, as a barrister and judge of no ordinary ability, and as a zealous member of the Church of England, Mr. Justice Coxe did much in his day and generation towards laying the firm foundation of law and morality upon which the great State of New Jersey has since been builded. Had his labors ceased here, he would have deserved only the grateful remembrance of those who, living in New Jersey, are now reaping the benefit of his good works. But it may be said that he has laid the whole American nation under obligations of gratitude to him; for he it was who first formulated the scheme of confederation which, a full half century later, was, in but a slightly modified form, used to bind together the Thirteen United States. In 1722 he published in London a volume bearing the ponderous title : "A Description of the English Province of Carolana, by the Spaniards cali'd Florida, and by the French *La Louisiane,* with a large and curious Preface, demonstrating the Right of the English to that Country, and the unjust Manner of the French usurping it ;

their prodigious Increase there, &c., and the inevitable Danger our other Colonies on the Continent will be exposed to, if not timely prevented; interspersed with many useful Hints in Regard to our Plantations in General." It is in the "curious Preface" that the scheme alluded to is presented. After dilating at some length upon the danger to be feared from the encroachments of the French, he presents the following : "The only expedient I can at present think of, or shall presume to mention (with the utmost deference to His Majesty and His Ministers), to help and obviate these absurdities and inconveniences, and apply a remedy to them, is, that all the colonies appertaining to the crown of Great Britain on the northern continent of America be united, under a legal, regular and firm establishment; over which it is proposed a Lieutenant, or Supreme Governor, may be constituted, and appointed to preside on the spot, to whom the governors of each colony shall be subordinate. It is further humbly proposed, that two deputies shall be annually elected by the council and assembly of each province, who are to be in the nature of a great council, or general convention of the estates of the colonies; and by the order, consent or approbation of the Lieutenant, or Governor-General, shall meet together, consult and advise for the good of the whole; settle and appoint particular quotas or proportions of money, men, provisions, etc., that each respective government is to raise for their mutual defence and safety, as well as, if necessary, for offence and invasion of their enemies; in all which cases the Governor-General or Lieutenant is to have a negative; but not to enact anything without their concurrence, or that of the majority of them. The quota or proportion, as above allotted and charged on each colony, may, nevertheless, be levied and raised by its own assembly, in such manner as they shall judge most easy and convenient, and the circumstances of their affairs will permit. Other jurisdictions, powers and authorities, respecting the honor of His Majesty, the interest of the plantations and the liberty and property of the proprietors, traders, planters and inhabitants in them, may be vested in and cognizable by the aforesaid Governor-General or Lieutenant, and grand convention of estates, according to the laws of England, but are not thought fit to be touched on or inserted here, this proposal being general, and with all humility submitted to the consideration of our supervisors, who may improve, model, or reject it, as they in their wisdom may judge proper. A coalition, or union, of this nature, tempered with and grounded on prudence, moderation and justice, and a generous encouragement given to the labor, industry and good management of all sorts and conditions of persons inhabiting or, any ways, concerned or interested in the several colonies above mentioned, will in all probability lay a sure and lasting foundation of dominion, strength and trade, sufficient not only to secure and promote the prosperity of the plantations, but to revive and greatly increase the late flourishing state and condition of Great Britain, and thereby render it once more the envy and admiration of its neighbors. Let us consider the fall of our ancestors, and grow wise by their misfortunes. If the ancient Britons had been united amongst themselves, the Romans, in all probability, had never become their masters; for, as Cæsar observed of them, *Dum Singuli pugnabant, Universi vincebantur*—whilst they fought in separate bodies the whole island was subdued. So, if the English colonies in America were consolidated as one body, and joined in one common interest, as they are under one Gracious Sovereign, and with united forces were ready and willing to act in concert and assist each other, they would be better enabled to provide for and defend themselves against any troublesome ambitious neighbor, or bold invader. For union and concord increase and establish strength and power, whilst division and discord have the contrary effects." In his "Colonial History" (vol. ii. p. 199), Grahame writes: "In this plan we behold the germ of that more celebrated, though less original, project, which was again ineffectually recommended by an American statesman in 1754; and which, not many years after, was actually embraced by his countrymen." Chief-Justice Field, in his "Provincial Courts of New Jersey," is even more plainly outspoken, and his words fitly sum up the case and direct the verdict. He writes: "It was in fact the very plan which was recommended by Dr. Franklin to the convention at Albany, in 1754, for the purpose of forming a league with the Six Nations, and concerting measures for united operations against the encroachments of the French. This plan of Dr. Franklin's has been much talked of as 'the Albany Plan of Union'; figures largely in all our histories, and is thought to have been one of those grand and original conceptions for which he was so famous. And yet it was little more than a transcript of the design sketched by Daniel Coxe, many years before, and which would seem to have originated with him. To him, therefore, a citizen of New Jersey, belongs the credit of it, and the truth of history requires that from him it should no longer be withheld."

AN VORST, HON. CORNELIUS, Officer in the Revolutionary Army, late of Hudson county, New Jersey, was born there, November 25th, 1728. "He was popularly known as 'Faddy;' was one of the wealthiest men in the county, and full of fun and practical jokes; was fond of fast horses, and drove the best team in the vicinity." He established the race-course on Paulus Hoeck, in 1753, and was the lion of that "Derby." But, while loving the genial side of life, he did not neglect its weightier duties. In 1764 he established the Jersey City ferry; and at the outbreak of the Revolution took decided ground on the side of his country. At a meeting of the inhabitants of Bergen county, held at Hackensack, June 25th, 1774, he was appointed one of a

"committee for corresponding with the committees of the other counties in this province, and particularly to meet with the other county committees at New Brunswick, ... in order to elect delegates to attend a General Congress of Delegates of the American Colonies." June 29th, 1776, the Provincial Congress appointed him Lieutenant-Colonel of a battalion of foot militia in the county of Bergen. It is doubtful, however, if he ever was in actual service. Shortly after the capture of New York by the British, and the fall of Paulus Hoeck, his house at Harsimus was occupied by the officers of a detachment of cavalry, while he and his family were crowded into the kitchen. The fact that he continued to reside on his place while it lay in the hands of the enemy aroused suspicion that he had begun to harbor tory inclinations; and, November 10th, 1776, he was charged before the court with having joined the British; after a thorough investigation he was, however, honorably acquitted. "During this occupancy of his house by the enemy, the officers, for their own amusement, were in the practice of discharging muskets up the chimney. One day, his mother being sick, he requested them to desist. This they haughtily refused to do. Being a powerful man, he proceeded to vindicate his rights by administering a drubbing to the insolent soldiers." Incarceration in the old sugar-house was the consequence of attempting to administer justice *inter arma*. Sir Henry Clinton, then in command at New York, was one of his old school companions, and at once released him, with the admonition "not to let such a thing occur again." But, being impetuous as well as muscular, he was soon entangled in a fresh difficulty by espousing the cause of an injured cobbler: an officer refused to pay for the repair of his boots, whereupon he satisfied the shoemaker by thrashing the trooper. For this he was again locked up in New York, and again discharged with a severe admonition. The presence of the enemy, always offensive to the sturdy patriot, finally became unendurable. They not only lived in his house, but seized his horses and confiscated his cattle. Determined to separate from their company, "which he loathed," he took his family to Pompton, and there resided with Philip Schuyler. On his return he went to Paulus Hoeck, and there lived in the ferry-house until the close of the war. Like his opulent neighbors, "he was a practical believer in the patriarchal institution, and always kept his spacious kitchen well stocked with slaves. Among the number was a character known as Half-Indian Jack, who died at Harsimus Ferry, February 2d, 1831, at the age of 102 years, and was buried on what is now the rear of lot No. 153 Wayne street. Jack ran away from Van Vorst during the revolutionary war, and became a spy for the British. He was generally in the company of a white spy named Meyers. Both did their work for pay—Jack for whiskey, Meyers for gold. Meyers deposited his money in a box, which he kept buried. Whenever he was in a condition to add to the deposit, he and Jack would unearth the treasure. When uncovered,

Jack would be dismissed, and Meyers buried the money in a different place. The story, as told by Jack, was, that as often as he had helped Meyers dig up the box, he had never seen it buried, nor was it ever buried twice in the same place. At last the patriots entrapped and shot Meyers, but Jack was too wary, and escaped. After Meyers' death great efforts were made to discover his treasure. His widow, ever looking for the 'end of the rainbow where rests the pot of gold,' every spring, when the ground was soft, would go over what was recently the Fourth and Fifth Wards of Jersey City, prospecting with an iron rod, which she pushed into the ground, hoping to strike the box. She never succeeded, though she worked and hoped while she lived. It is possible that the old spy's box of British gold yet lies buried in that part of the city, awaiting its resurrection by the spade of some lucky finder." April 21st, 1753, he married Annetje Van Horn; and died September 30th, 1818.

———◆◆◇———

ROELIGH, REV. SOLOMON, Pastor of the Reformed Dutch Church at Millstone, and Patriot of the Revolution, was born at Red Hook, near Albany, New York, May 29th, 1750 (0. s.) In his fourteenth year his mind was deeply impressed with religious convictions, he being then under the pastoral care of Rev. John Schenema, the minister of Catskill and Coxsackie. While in his eighteenth year he was placed under the care of Rev. Dirck Romeyn, the pastor of Marbletown, Warwarsing and Rochester, to begin the study of Latin and Greek. "He never received any assistance from his father, but assisted himself by teaching school." Subsequently he removed to Hackensack, New Jersey, and entered the celebrated academy of Dr. Peter Wilson. Here he made such progress that Princeton College conferred on him the degree of A. B. He then proceeded to the study of theology, under Rev. John H. Goetschius, minister at Hackensack. October 1st, 1774, he was licensed to preach the gospel; and, June 11th, 1775, ordained pastor of the four united churches of Long Island. "With his ardent nature he could not help taking sides in the great struggle between the colonies and the mother country." The district in which he lived was noted for its disaffection to the cause of independence; yet in the midst of enemies he labored and prayed boldly for his country's freedom. Shortly after the battle of Long Island, in August, 1776, which occurred in the territory of his congregations, he found it necessary to flee to save his life. He then fled to Jamaica and Newtown; and, having been concealed one night in the house of Mr. Rapalje, at Hurl-gate, was guided across the river to Harlem. He went first, however, to Hackensack, and while there preached a most patriotic sermon from 2 Chron. xi. 4, exhorting the inhabitants not to fight against the cause of freedom, to which

many of the residents of that place were only too strongly inclined. Dr. Laidlie, the colleague of Dr. Livingston, heard him on that occasion, and warmly commended his action and utterances. In his flight he lost his cattle, furniture, books and clothing. In company with Dr. Livingston, both being on horseback, he started for Poughkeepsie, keeping on the west side of the Hudson; and during the ensuing three years supplied the pulpits of Fishkill and Poughkeepsie (1776-79). In the spring of 1780 he appeared in Millstone, one year after Mr. Foering's death, and the consistory at once appointed Ernestus Van Harlingen to wait upon him, and try and secure his services till he could return to his churches on Long Island. They offered to give him, as salary, 268 bushels of wheat per year, each bushel to weigh sixty pounds; but he declined entering into a temporary arrangement, and said he would accept a call. This the consistory gladly extended, and he moved into the parsonage, June 5th, 1780. The consistory paid his expenses of moving, which, in the money of the day, amounted to $1,455, one dollar in gold being worth at the time forty dollars of the continental currency. But it was impossible for him to obtain a formal dismission from his churches on Long Island, as the enemy held both the island and the city. But the synod, meeting in October, 1780, at New Paltz, appointed a committee to settle a question of dispute between the Millstone congregation and the three neighboring congregations, in respect to the bounds of each; and, if they succeeded in effectually reconciling all differences, they were then empowered, in the name of the synod, to approve the call, and in this very unusual case to dismiss him from his congregations on Long Island. But during the summer of 1780, and before the call was acted on from the Millstone congregation, Nechanic sought to unite with it, and thus secure a part of his services, Nechanic and Sourland being then under the care of Rev. John M. Van Harlingen. Articles of agreement were entered into, and his call, as finally approved, stands in the name of the two churches, and is dated September 4th, 1780. He was to preach two Sundays out of three at Millstone, and one at Nechanic, and was to alternate between the Dutch and English. October 1st, 1782, the synod met in the church of New Millstone; New York was their general place of meeting, both before and after the war, but during its progress all meetings were held at places remote from the scene of hostilities; and in 1782 "our defaced and desolated church, almost unfit to be occupied, welcomed the synod of the denomination within its blackened walls." Rev. Harmanus Meyer, the pastor at Paterson and Pompton Plains, presided over the body, which consisted, however, of only nine members. It was at this meeting that Simeon Van Arsdale was examined and licensed. Afterward, while on Long Island, soliciting funds to be devoted to the repairing of the church at Millstone, "his old charges tried hard to keep him, as he had never been regularly dismissed; but he said he was now united to another, and refused to remain." In 1786 he received a call to the two congregations of Hackensack and Schraalenberg, which he accepted; and in these two places he continued to labor until his death, October 8th, 1827. In 1791 he was elected Professor of Theology, in place of Dr. Meyer, of Pompton, who had died. In his new field he found his churches divided into two parties, with two consistories, on account of a difficulty which had begun fifty years before; and having tried to unite them, and failed, "he took sides with the party which was very strenuous in doctrine, and opposed to the commingling of Christians of different names, virtually exalting doctrine above practical religion, and refusing to unite in the great efforts of Christian union and fraternization, under the power of which the Bible, and Tract and Missionary, and other union societies, were organized." Finally, he, with four others, seceded from the Dutch Church in 1822, when he was seventy-two years of age, thirty-six years after his departure from Millstone. He was accordingly deposed from the professorship and the ministry by General Synod; and although the True Reformed Dutch Church which he organized continued to increase for six years quite rapidly, it has since that time been steadily declining, " and but few congregations of any strength remain."

———❦———

URPHY, JOHN L., of Trenton, Proprietor of the State Gazette, was born on the 19th of June, 1828, in the city of Trenton, State of New Jersey. At the age of eleven years he entered the weekly State Gazette newspaper and printing office, as errand-boy and news-carrier. In that capacity he carried the first tri-weekly and the first daily newspaper published in Trenton. At the age of sixteen years he was regularly apprenticed to James T. Sherman, to learn the printing business. He served his time out, and worked with the firm (then Sherman & Harron) as journeyman until 1856. In that year Enoch T. Borden started the Free Press, in opposition to the Camden & Amboy Railroad monopoly, and Mr. Murphy went with him as foreman. At the expiration of six months the paper suspended, and Mr. Murphy bought the material and started a job office. He went into business with a cash capital of about $500, saved up out of his wages as journeyman printer. At that time there was no regular job printing office in the city, and he was therefore the pioneer of the business in the capital of New Jersey. Three months after setting up in business for himself he took in Mr. Charles Bechtel, a young man of about his own age, as equal partner, and they removed to the building on the corner of State and Greene streets, the present site of the large newspaper and printing establishment of John L. Murphy. Being practical men, the young firm were enabled to do work cheaper and better than the newspaper offices, and they gradually built

up a large and thriving business. In 1869 the firm purchased the State Gazette, daily and weekly newspaper, regarded from time immemorial as the " State organ" of the Republican party of New Jersey. At the time they purchased it, the paper was greatly run down in circulation and influence, and under their vigorous and enterprising management it at once started upon a new and unexampled career of usefulness and prosperity. Its daily circulation was about 700, and is now 2,200; its weekly circulation was 2,000, and is now 7,127. In July, 1875, Mr. Murphy bought out the interest of his partner, and has since conducted the entire business of newspaper publisher, job printer, book-binder and stationer himself. During his career Mr. Murphy has held several important positions of public trust. He was twice elected Collector in the city of Trenton, was United States Internal Revenue Assessor for the Second District of New Jersey, from 1868 until the office was abolished by act of Congress and its duties merged in that of Collector; was then Collector until January, 1876, when he resigned in order to devote himself more exclusively to his extensive and increasing business. He is now the sole proprietor of (with one exception) the largest and most valuable newspaper and printing establishment in New Jersey. He is entirely a self-made man, and his success in life is due to great natural shrewdness and far-seeing business sagacity, boundless energy, an enterprising spirit that is dismayed or turned aside by no obstacles, and an unwavering adherence to honorable and upright principles.

———❦———

RANE, REV. DANIEL, Clergyman, Educator, late of Chester, was born in Essex county, New Jersey, in the last quarter of the past century, and graduated from Princeton College. In 1803, having spent some time in preparing himself for the ministry, he was licensed by the Morris County Presbytery, and in the course of the following year was ordained by the same presbytery, and settled as pastor of the Presbyterian church at Chester, New Jersey. He remained in this charge until 1808, when he became pastor of the church at Fishkill, New York, June 7th, and there for thirteen years labored with notable zeal and success. In July, 1821, he took charge of the First Congregational Church in Waterbury, Connecticut, still retaining his connection with the presbytery. In 1825 he returned to Fishkill, and taught there in a select school for about two years, and then accepted a call to his old charge in Chester. He was installed July 18th, 1827, and continued his labors in that field until September 14th, 1831, at which time he tendered his resignation, and his pastoral relations were amicably dissolved. The remainder of his life was spent in preaching and good works, as health and opportunity permitted. He died April 1st, 1861.

SMAN, LEWIS M., M. D., of Philipsburg, son of Joseph Osman, farmer, was born in Independence township, Warren county, New Jersey, November 2d, 1837. Some years later his father removed to Virginia, engaging in real estate operations in Prince William and adjacent counties, and in Virginia his preliminary education was received. Having read medicine under his uncle, Dr. L. C. Osman, he entered the National Medical College, and in 1860 received from that institution his degree of M. D. In the same year he entered upon the practice of his profession in Pike county, Pennsylvania, where he remained until 1862. He was then appointed a member of the medical staff of the Methodist Church Hospital at Alexandria, Virginia, and some six months later, upon receiving a similar appointment in the Emory Hospital, removed to Washington. In August, 1865, he established himself permanently in Philipsburg, his excellent professional qualities enabling him to rapidly build up an extensive practice in that town. For several years past he has been Surgeon to the Middle & Eastern Division of the Delaware, Lackawanna & Western Railroad Company, and is also Assistant Surgeon to the Central Railroad Company of New Jersey. Among the medical men of the section in which he practises he occupies a leading position, being one of the most active and influential members of the Warren County Medical Society, and holding at present the position of Vice-President in that organization.

UGH, HON. JOHN HOWARD, M. D., of Burlington, son of Elijah, and Lettice (Barnard) Pugh—the former fifth in descent from Daniel and Catherine Pugh, immigrants to this country from Wales in the early part of the last century; the latter descended from Godfrey Barnard, of French origin, who died and was buried at Wareford, England, in 1240, and one of whose descendants immigrated to Pennsylvania in 1685—was born in Chester county, Pennsylvania, June 23d, 1827. Having received a thorough academic education, he was for some three years associated with Professor Wickersham, now the able Superintendent of Public Instruction in Pennsylvania, as his assistant in the conduct of an academy at Marietta, his leisure time during this period being utilized for a continuation of his studies in classical and general literature. Relinquishing his position in the Marietta Academy, he began the study of medicine, and after regular attendance upon lectures in the medical department of the University of Pennsylvania, he was in 1852 graduated with honors, and received from that institution his degree of M. D. Immediately upon graduation, he established himself as a physician at Bristol, Bucks county, Pennsylvania, but within a few months failing health compelled him to temporarily

relinquish practice, and as a sanitary measure he betook himself to the mining regions of Lake Superior. A year in this bracing climate thoroughly restored his health, and returning to the seaboard States, he permanently established himself, in the spring of 1854, in Burlington, where he has since continued to reside. His skill as a physician, and his strong traits of personal character, enabled him to quickly win and constantly hold the confidence of the community of which, as an entire stranger, he had become a part, and he rapidly rose to take rank with the most prominent and influential of his fellow-citizens. Aside from his professional ability, he has displayed in his management of the Mechanics' National Bank of Burlington, of which he has been President for the past eight years, remarkable judgment and administrative talent as a financier. During the late war he was a zealous supporter of the Federal government, laboring with voice and pen to secure its triumph, and giving a practical proof of his loyalty by attending without compensation the sick and wounded soldiers in the United States General Hospital at Beverly. In September, 1876, he was nominated by the Republican State Convention to represent the Second Congressional District of New Jersey. The nomination was on his part unsought and unexpected, but received the unqualified approval of the Republican party and Republican press of the district. In the election that took place in the ensuing November he was elected by a handsome majority, and is at present (1877) efficiently discharging the duties of his high office.

ALDWIN, MILTON, M. D., of Newark, was born in Newark, October 22d, 1821. Having received an ample preparatory education, he began the study of medicine at the University of New York, and in 1843 received from that institution his degree of M. D. In the same year he established himself as a physician in his native town, and in a very short time—his pleasant social qualities uniting with his professional skill to render him popular—built up an extensive and lucrative practice. In 1848, although then one of the youngest physicians in the city, he was elected Coroner by a handsome majority, and in 1851-52 was elected by a similar full vote a member of the Board of Education. In 1854 he was again elected Coroner, and was re-elected during four successive years. During the last two years (1857-58) of his service as Coroner, he also held other important municipal offices, being an Alderman of the city of Newark in 1857, and President of the Common Council in 1858. Finding the duties of public life incompatible with the duties of his greatly increased practice, he has since 1858 declined all save professional offices, and has given his time wholly to his profession. In October, 1862, he entered the medical department of the United States volunteer army as an Acting Assistant Surgeon; was assigned to the Ward General Hospital at Newark, and until June, 1865, rendered faithful and efficient service in that institution. The discharge of this duty of course involved a considerable (temporary) loss of practice and very greatly increased labor; but on neither account did he permit his earnest loyalty to be discouraged, and until the end he remained true to his self-imposed trust. From the outset of his career his personal popularity has been a potent factor in his success. Naturally buoyant and cheerful in disposition, courteous in manner, warm-hearted and outspoken in his friendships, and true to his friends, his genial, kindly qualities have paved the way for a recognition of his professional skill, and have assured to him the merited esteem of all who have known him either casually or well.

----◆----

HODGE, REV. CHARLES, D. D., LL. D., Clergyman, Author, and Professor of Didactic, Exegetical and Polemic Theology in the Theological Seminary at Princeton, was born in Philadelphia, December 28th, 1797, and graduated from the New Jersey College in 1815. In 1819 he became a graduate of the Princeton Theological Seminary; in 1820 was appointed Assistant; and in 1822 Professor of Oriental and Biblical Literature in that institution. In 1840 he was made Professor of Didactic and Exegetical Theology, a position for which he was admirably qualified by his innate bent and sterling attainments. Twelve years later polemic theology was added, and the chair thus constituted he still holds. In 1825 he founded the *Biblical Repertory and Princeton Review*, enlarging its plan in 1829, and conducting it until it was changed into the *Presbyterian Quarterly and Princeton Review* in 1872. The most important of his contributions to this journal were reprinted in the "Princeton Theological Essays," two volumes, 1846-47, and in his "Essays and Reviews," issued in 1857. In 1846 he was elected Moderator of the General Assembly of the Presbyterian Church, Old School, and in 1858 he was appointed a member of the committee intrusted with the revision of the Book of Discipline. On the 24th of April, 1872, the semi-centennial anniversary of his appointment to the professorial dignity, a notable celebration occurred at Princeton. Between four and five hundred classmen and former pupils assembled, and by appropriate exercises and ceremonies conveyed to the eminent scholar and teacher their congratulations on the happy occasion, and marked their great love and esteem for the man and the professor. The proceedings were subsequently published in book form, and in that shape have had large circulation among the graduates of the institution. Among the principal works which have proceeded from Dr. Hodge's pen may be mentioned his "Commentary on the Epistle to the Romans," published in Philadelphia in 1835, issued in abridged form in 1836, rewritten and enlarged and republished in 1866; "Constitutional History of the Presbyterian Church in the United States," two volumes, published in 1840-41; "The Way of Life," 1842; "Commentaries on the Ephesians," 1856; "Commentaries on the First Epistle to the Corinthians," 1857; "Commentaries on the Second Epistle to the Corinthians," 1860; "Systematic Theology," three volumes, 1871-72; "What is Darwinism?" 1874. A ripe scholar, a profound theologian, and a most estimable gentleman, he enjoys, in a high degree, the respect and esteem of a very wide circle.

----◆----

PERRY, NEHEMIAH, Retired Manufacturer and Statesman, of Newark, New Jersey, was born at Bridgefield, Connecticut, March 30th, 1816. His father was a farmer. He was educated at the Wesleyan Seminary of Bridgefield, and intended to study medicine, but, his health failing, he was compelled to give up that intention. At the age of sixteen he became a clerk in the dry-goods store of George St. John, at Norwalk, Connecticut, with whom he remained in that capacity for two or three years, performing his duties with fidelity and marked cleverness. His employer was more than satisfied with his services; but, stirred by a just ambition to do greater things, he resolved to seek a sphere where greater things were to be done. Pursuant to this resolution, he went to the city of New York, where, shortly after his arrival, he engaged as a clerk in a clothing store on the corner of Greenwich and Cortlandt streets. This, however, was not by any means the entertainment to which he had invited himself, and, while diligently performing the duties of his clerkship, he kept his eyes and ears open to catch the clew or cue to some larger opportunity. It presently came in the shape of a tempting report about Newark, which finally induced him to visit that city, where, though only twenty years of age, and a total stranger, he soon made the acquaintance of influential citizens, and, what was more to the purpose, made an excellent impression on them, the result at last being the establishment of the cloth and clothing manufacturing firm of N. Perry & Co., through which he built his fortune, and laid the foundations of his fame. He continued at the head of this firm for sixteen years, during which it grew to be one of the most extensive establishments of the kind in the United States, having branch houses in St. Louis, Omaha, Chicago, Cincinnati, Louisville, Lexington, Nashville, and Petersburg, Virginia, and being distinguished alike for its enterprise, its financial resources, and the perfect system upon which its vast business was conducted. He showed himself a prince among business men, and, as the reward of his rare energy and sagacity, was able in 1866 to retire with an ample fortune. He did not, however, retire from all business, but rather transferred his capital to new forms of investment, entailing less toil and vigilance in the management, and leaving him some portion at least of that leisure to which his means and his achievements entitled him. Confiding, as he does, and as he well may, in the future of Newark, he has, for one thing, invested largely in real estate there; but he is, besides, connected more or less prominently with most of the leading business corporations, and a Director of the Mutual Benefit Life Insurance Company, one of the most important institutions of the kind in the whole country, of the American Insurance Company, of which he is now Vice-President, and of the New Jersey Railroad and Transportation Company. While the weight of his immense establishment still rested on his shoulders, though, he found time, without compromitting in the least his business interests, to enter upon a political career, and pursue it with a success and to a length which few unoccupied men are able to reach. He was elected in 1852 a member of the Common Council, of which he was the presiding officer for several terms. In 1850 he was elected to the State Assembly from the Newark District, and in 1856 re-elected, being at his second term the caucus nominee of his party for the position of Speaker of the House. In 1860 he was nominated by the Bell-Everett or Constitutional Union party for Congress against William Pennington, and elected by a majority of four hundred and ninety-nine. He was re-elected in 1862, by a majority of three hundred and eighty-four, over Joseph P. Bradley, then a leading lawyer of Newark, now a member of the Supreme Court of the United States. As a representative in Congress, he displayed ability and efficiency, serving with credit as a member of the Committee on Commerce, and of other important committees, and, though speaking but seldom, speaking always with discretion and effect. One of the most sensible and cogent speeches made in the House during the critical period of the war was his speech in 1862 on the state of the Union, closing with this inspiring and eloquent forecast of the issue: " Though everything may be dark and foreboding, still behind the cloud of rebellion the sky is clear and beautiful. Soon the breath of heaven will sweep across the threatening mass, and one by one the stars on that dear banner will reappear; then we can count the thirty-four, and thank God that they are all there." His remarks, in the following session, on the death of Senator Thomson, of New Jersey, were charged with subdued pathos and beauty. " Let us all strive," he said exquisitely in conclusion, " so to live that, when gradually sinking into the ocean of eternity, we may leave on the fluctuating waves of time a golden tint." At this time his political affiliations were Democratic, he having joined the Democracy on the dissolution of the Whig party, of which he had been a consistent and devoted adherent for the preceding twenty years. In 1868 he was a candidate before the Democratic State Convention for the gubernatorial nomination, and, but for differences in the Newark delegation, would have received it, in place of Mr. Randolph. The Democrats in 1873

nominated him for the Mayoralty of Newark, and, the personal views he announced on the occasion being acceptable to both parties, he was triumphantly elected, his vote exceeding the party strength. In the Presidential canvass of 1876, however, he deemed it his duty to support Mr. Hayes as against Mr. Tilden. What effect this step will have on his political connections hereafter remains to be seen. He is evidently a man with whom party ties are less strong than personal convictions, and whose personal convictions, moreover, are formed with perfect independence. His services to the city of his adoption have been long-continued, constant and effective. Since the organization of the first city government in Newark in 1836, he has been prominently identified with nearly all the improvements that have tended to make it so prosperous and beautiful a city, raising it from a population of fifteen thousand at the date of its municipal organization, to one of over a hundred and forty thousand. He may without vanity claim to share with Themistocles in the boast, that although he " never learned how to tune a harp or play upon a lute," he knows " how to raise a small and inconsiderable city to glory and greatness." He has made two visits to Europe, during which he travelled over the whole continent, observing as well as enjoying keenly, and turning his travels to rich account as a source of knowledge not less than of healthful pleasure. In person he is well-proportioned, erect, and active, with a large head and face, high, broad, and full brow, small, clear eyes, a mouth expressive of resolution and decision, and manners courteous and genial. He looks the refined and ready man he is.

————◦◦◦————

LAMBERT, HON. JOHN, one of the most distinguished citizens of New Jersey during the latter part of the past and the early part of the present century, was born in 1746, in the township of Amwell, New Jersey. His father's name was Gershom, and his mother's Sarah Merriam. His grandfather was John Lambert, who married Abigail Bumstead in 1713. The subject of this sketch cultivated a large tract of land in his native town, where he lived a long and useful life. For many years he was a member of the New Jersey Council, the higher branch of the State Legislature, in which body he ably served the interests of his section and constituents. From 1795 to 1800 he was Vice-President of that body, and during the years 1802 and 1803 he performed with vigorous efficiency the duties of Acting Governor of the State. He was a representative in Congress from New Jersey from 1805 to 1809, and from 1809 to 1815 was an influential member of the United States Senate. He was married in 1765 to Susannah Barber, by whom he had seven children. His second wife was Hannah Dennis (née Little), by whom he had six children, the oldest of whom was Jerusha (married Abraham Holmes), and the next in age, Merriam, who married James Seabrook.

Merriam and James were the parents of Mary Hannah Seabrook, the wife of Ashbel Welch, Esq., of Lambertville. John Lambert was a devoted lover of literature, and was especially familiar with the English classics. He owned the best library in Hunterdon county, which at that time included within its limits the city of Trenton. He was a man of great decision of character, and thoroughly honest and outspoken, even in those days of extreme party bitterness. He died on the 4th of February, 1823, aged seventy-seven.

NAPP, HON. MANNING M., Lawyer, and Justice of the Supreme Court of New Jersey, was born about 1823 in Bergen county, New Jersey. After receiving a liberal education he prepared for the New Jersey bar, to which he was admitted during the July term, 1846, and was made counsellor in 1850. He acquired an extensive practice in the courts of New Jersey, and in 1875 he was appointed by Governor Bedle one of the Justices of the Supreme Court for a term of seven years. In this conspicuous and trying position he has fully sustained his previous reputation as a man of fine legal attainments.

ICHARDS, REV. JAMES, D. D., formerly Pastor of the First Presbyterian Church of Newark, New Jersey, was born at New Canaan, Connecticut, October 29th, 1767. He was the son of James Richards, a farmer of excellent character, and a descendant of Samuel Richards, who came to this country from Wales during the reign of Queen Anne; his mother's maiden name was Ruth Hanford. When but thirteen years of age, he undertook the charge of a common district school, and managed its affairs with such success as to secure the offer of the same post for a second term. It was his early wish "to obtain a public education;" but as his father was not in a condition to encourage and sustain the project, he apprenticed himself, at the age of fifteen, to the business of cabinet and chair-making, together with house-painting, and labored for a short time in a cabinet-maker's shop in the city of New York. He united with the church in Stamford, Connecticut, September 17th, 1786, and immediately began to look forward with strong desires to the work of the Christian ministry. With many discouragements and interruptions, he completed his preparatory studies through the assistance of two excellent female relatives, and entered Yale College in 1789. But at the close of his freshman year his studies were interrupted, first by want of pecuniary means, which compelled him to leave college, and afterward by severe illness; so that, although his diligence and perseverance overcame the obstacles in the way of a private education, he did not go through col-

lege with his class, but received his degree of Bachelor of Arts out of course, in 1794. In 1793 he was licensed to preach the gospel by an association in Fairfield county, Connecticut, and having labored for a time in Wilton, Ballaston, Shelter Island, and Sag Harbor, he commenced the work of the ministry in Morristown, in June, 1794, and was ordained as pastor of the church in that place, by the Presbytery of New York, May 1st, 1795. Dr. Macwhorter preached the ordination sermon, Dr. Rodgers presided, and Rev. Mr. Austin gave the charge to the people. His ministry there was signally successful; and in three memorable instances his labors were attended with peculiar manifestations of divine influence, in 1791, in 1803-4, and in 1808. Urgent applications were then made to him, after the removal of Dr. Griffin, to take charge of the church in Newark, New Jersey; and when a call was unanimously offered him, the path of wisdom and duty seemed plain, and, with the consent and approbation of the presbytery, he accepted it, and his connection with the church in Morristown was dissolved. He was installed at Newark, June 7th, 1809. Dr. Romeyn, of New York, preached the sermon, Dr. Rowe presided and gave the charge, and Dr. Miller, of Princeton, delivered the exhortation to the people. November 14th, 1809, the Presbytery of New York, with which this church had been connected ever since its formation in 1738, was divided into two by erecting a portion of its churches into a new presbytery bearing the old name, and changing the name of the remaining portion, of which this church was one, into the "Presbytery of Jersey." Its first meeting under the new arrangement was held in Morristown, April 24th, 1810. The First Church had been, hitherto, during nearly a century and a half, the only Presbyterian church in Newark, except those of Orange and Bloomfield, which had now become separate towns. But the time had come when the need of greater facilities for the accommodation of a large and growing population was manifest to all. In the spring of 1809, accordingly, the business of church extension was entered upon with commendable zeal and enterprise. The whole transaction, which resulted in the establishment of the Second Presbyterian Church of Newark, took place with his entire approbation, and was forwarded also by his active assistance. At the service of organization he delivered an address on the words, "Let brotherly love continue." For a time the two pastors exercised a sort of joint ministry in the two congregations, officiating in each other's pulpit in the afternoon of every Sabbath. During his ministry, the first Sabbath-school in the congregation was established, under the superintendency of Moses Lyon, and held its meetings, for a brief period, in the gallery of the church. The first lecture-room, a low brick building, was erected in 1813. His ministry, especially its early part, was notably fruitful in conversions. Between the years 1812 and 1813 there was a very desirable revival of God's work; and in 1816–17 occurred a remarkable season, whose fruits were, in nine-months, one hundred and thirty-five, of whom sixty-nine were added to the church at one time. When he first took charge of the congregation, the number of communicants was about five hundred and thirty; and, in the course of fourteen years, five hundred and fifty-six were added thereto, three hundred and thirty-two by profession, and two hundred and twenty-seven by certificate; making in all one thousand and eighty-six to whom, in the course of that period, he statedly administered the sacred ordinances. Under him, the church contained the largest number of communicants that ever belonged to it at one time, viz., about seven hundred, and that notwithstanding the dismission of the large colony that united in the formation of the Second Church. But Providence had now other work for him to perform, in another and still more responsible station. By his constant devotion to study, he had made large attainments in theological knowledge; and by his careful and discreet management of affairs intrusted to him, public and private, had acquired a reputation which marked him as one of the first men in the church, in respect to qualifications for the head of a theological institution. In the autumn of 1823, accordingly, having been a second time solicited to take the Professorship of Theology in Auburn Theological Seminary, he accepted the appointment, and, having resigned his charge in Newark, was inaugurated to that office, October 29th, 1823. He took charge of that institution when it was suffering under great embarrassments, and left it in a strong and prosperous condition. He died August 2d, 1843, in the seventy-sixth year of his age. He published several lectures and sermons. His successor at Newark was Rev. William T. Hamilton.

ISH, BENJAMIN, of Trenton, was born November 15th, 1785, in what was then Trenton township, in Hunterdon county, but in the course of the mutations of almost a century has become Ewing township, in the county of Mercer. His father, whose Christian name he bears, was a farmer, on whose farm he spent the early years of his life, acquiring the ordinary education furnished by the common schools of that remote day. In the spring of 1808 he took up his residence in Trenton, where, with the stability characteristic of a strong mind in a strong body, he has resided ever since, a period in itself equalling the span of human life as defined by the Psalmist. During the war of 1812 he took in hand the business of forwarding merchandise and munitions of war across the State from Trenton to New Brunswick, continuing it, with the necessary changes, after the close of the war, at the same time instituting a new forwarding line, by vessels and steamboats, from Trenton to Philadelphia. He merits the distinction of being regarded as one of the pioneers of transportation in this country. Nor was he a pioneer merely, for he not only prepared the way for the railroad and the canal, but took the lead in preparing those modern courses of intercommunication themselves. He was one of the projectors and incorporators of the Camden & Amboy Railroad, and of the Delaware and Raritan Canal, as also a member of the first Board of Directors, and, for that matter, of every subsequent board, he having served as a Director until the property was leased to the Pennsylvania Railroad, and formed, as he still forms, one of the new board under the new organization. The work on the Camden & Amboy Railroad, it may be stated, was begun in 1830, and completed in about two years and a half, while the Delaware and Raritan Canal was not completed till some time later. He has been a Director of the Trenton Banking Company for over forty years. He is President of the Freehold & Jamesburg Railroad, and a Director of the other roads belonging to the United Company of New Jersey. Previous to the building of railroads in this country, he, like Commodore Vanderbilt, was largely interested in steamboats and stages, though afterwards, like the commodore again, he transferred his energies and his capital to the new means of locomotion. In 1833 and 1834, he was a member of the New Jersey Legislature, showing in that position the sagacity and public spirit which have marked his entire career, to the vast and manifold advantage of the commonwealth. His life, indeed, has been one of unswerving devotion to the best interests of New Jersey, as well as of unintermitting activity. Although now in his ninety-third year, he is still a hale man, in the full possession of his faculties, and retaining a vivid recollection, at once comprehensive and minute, of the history of those great public improvements with which he has been so closely and thoroughly identified. It is an occasion of just regret that this sketch cannot be enriched with some account of his personal habits, in respect to diet, exercise, rest, etc., whereby, in a measure at least, it may be presumed, his life has been thus remarkably prolonged. Autopsy is properly regarded as a source of much information important to the preservation of human life, but on this topic such a man living could afford more information of value than scores of dead men; his autobiography would be worth a hundred autopsies. He was married in 1812, and has two children living, one a son, A. I. Fish, Esq., of Philadelphia, the other a daughter, married to John C. Chambers, Esq., of Trenton.

AYLEY, JAMES ROOSEVELT, Archbishop of the Province of Baltimore, was born in New York, in 1814, and brought up in the faith of the Protestant Episcopal Church. He received his college education at Trinity (then Washington) College. He was graduated in 1836, and having determined to become a clergyman, he became a student

Avery Pub. Co. Phila Pa

of theology with Dr. S. F. Jarvis, at Middletown, Connecticut. After his ordination he was assigned to a parish at Harlem, where he remained until called to a pastoral charge in western New York. From there he moved to Hagerstown, Maryland, where he was some time rector of a church. In the meantime his religious views having undergone a gradual change, he finally decided to adopt the Roman Catholic faith. With this view he resigned his position in the Protestant Episcopal Church, and entered St. Sulpice College, Paris, where he pursued the necessary preliminary course of study. From Paris he returned to this country and completed his studies at the Ecclesiastical Seminary at St. John's, Fordham, New York. On the 2d of March, 1842, he was ordained priest by Bishop Hughes, in St. Patrick's Cathedral, New York. For a time he officiated as parish priest on Staten Island, from whence he was called to act as Secretary to Archbishop Hughes. His rise in church was rapid. He was appointed Professor of Belles-Lettres at St. John's College, Fordham, New York, and subsequently became Vice-President and acting President of that institution. When the college was transferred to the Jesuit Fathers, the Rev. Mr. Bayley was made Chancellor of the Archdiocese. He held this position until 1853, when, at the recommendation of Archbishop Hughes and his suffragans, the Pope appointed him Bishop of the new see of Newark. He was the first bishop of the diocese which was created from the old diocese of New York, and included all the State of New Jersey. He was consecrated in St. Patrick's Cathedral, New York, on the 30th October, 1853, by the Most Reverend Cajetan Bedini, afterward Cardinal, who was on an apostolic visit to this country. The ceremonies of consecration were of the most imposing character, all the bishops of the archdiocese, including the Rt. Rev. Bishop Rappe, of Cleveland, Ohio, and the Rt. Rev. Bishop McCloskey, assisting. His presenters were the Rt. Rev. Bishops Fitzpatrick, O'Reilly and Timon. The sermon was preached by Archbishop Hughes. The new bishop at once entered upon his duties and labors in New Jersey, and during the nineteen years of his administration he devoted his personal attention to the elevation and advancement of its affairs. He may be truly said to have created one of the most prosperous and flourishing dioceses of the Roman Catholic Church in the United States. During his administration he founded Seton Hall College, at Orange; the Academies of the Sisters of Charity at Madison, and the Houses of the Brothers of the Christian Schools at Newark and at Jersey City. He built many large and beautiful churches throughout the State, and introduced into his diocese a priory of Benedictine monks in Newark, and a convent of Benedictine nuns at Elizabeth, the Convent of the Passionists of St. Michael's, at West Hoboken, and the Jesuits' establishment at St. Peter's, Jersey City. On the 30th of July, 1872, Bishop Bayley was elevated to the Archdiocese of Baltimore (to succeed Archbishop Spaulding, deceased) by a papal bull signed on that

day. The decree reached Archbishop Bayley on the 25th of August, and two months later he had severed his official relations with the see of Newark, where he had labored so long and well, and began the work in the new field to which he was called, and where he still remains. The Archbishop "has written much, but published little." Among his printed works are a "Sketch of the Early History of the Catholic Church on the Island of New York," written while he was Secretary of the Diocese of New York, a "Biography of Bishop Bruté," of Vincennes, Indiana; and "Pastorals for the People," dealing mainly with the subject of temperance, for which he has always been an earnest advocate and worker. He is also known to the general public as a popular lecturer, in which capacity he has addressed audiences in several of our eastern cities and towns.

LUTKINS, ALFRED A., M. D., of Jersey City, was born in New York city, in October, 1826. His father, Stephen H. Lutkins, was a native of New Jersey, and for many years held the position of magistrate in New York; his mother was Eliza La Rue. The family moved to Jersey City when Alfred was two years old, and it was here that the lad obtained his early education. Destined for the profession of medicine, he matriculated at the University of New York in 1846, and after taking two courses of lectures he was licensed by the New Jersey State Medical Association, having, as a preliminary, passed the required examination before its Board of Censors in May, 1848. On receiving his diploma, he commenced practice in Jersey City, where he has since been constantly engaged in the active duties of his profession, and has built up a most extensive and successful practice. An earnest student, and thoroughly in love with his profession, he has kept himself well abreast with medical progress, and is highly esteemed by his brethren as a well-read and eminently efficient physician, so much so that his services are frequently called in consultations. He has been a member of the District Medical Society of Hudson county for many years, and was President of that body in 1873. Since the organization of the Jersey City Charity Hospital, he has been a member of its medical staff, and he is also connected with the Hudson County Hospital. For five years he was City Physician of Jersey City, and during his term of office the duties and responsibilities were exceptionally heavy, owing to the prevalence of the well-remembered cholera epidemic. While a public-spirited citizen, discharging faithfully his duties to the community, he has not suffered his attention to be drawn beyond his profession, devoting himself to its service, and being content to find his rewards therein. He married Julia Demotte, of Hudson county, New Jersey.

of theology with Dr. S. F. Jarvis, at Middletown, Connecticut. After his ordination he was assigned to a parish at Harlem, where he remained until called to a pastoral charge in western New York. From there he moved to Hagerstown, Maryland, where he was some time rector of a church. In the meantime his religious views having undergone a gradual change, he finally decided to adopt the Roman Catholic faith. With this view he resigned his position in the Protestant Episcopal Church, and entered St. Sulpice College, Paris, where he pursued the necessary preliminary course of study. From Paris he returned to this country and completed his studies at the Ecclesiastical Seminary at St. John's, Fordham, New York. On the 2d of March, 1842, he was ordained priest by Bishop Hughes, in St. Patrick's Cathedral, New York. For a time he officiated as parish priest on Staten Island, from whence he was called to act as Secretary to Archbishop Hughes. His rise in church was rapid. He was appointed Professor of Belles-Lettres at St. John's College, Fordham, New York, and subsequently became Vice-President and acting President of that institution. When the college was transferred to the Jesuit Fathers, the Rev. Mr. Bayley was made Chancellor of the Archdiocese. He held this position until 1853, when, at the recommendation of Archbishop Hughes and his suffragans, the Pope appointed him Bishop of the new see of Newark. He was the first bishop of the diocese which was erected from the old diocese of New York, and included all the State of New Jersey. He was consecrated in St. Patrick's Cathedral, New York, on the 30th October, 1853, by the Most Reverend Cajetan Bèdini, afterward Cardinal, who made on an apostolic visit to this country. The ceremonies of consecration were of the most imposing character, all the bishops of the archdiocese, including the Rt. Rev. Bishop Rappe, of Cleveland, Ohio, and the Rt. Rev. Bishop McCloskey, assisting. His presenters were the Rt. Rev. Bishops Fitzpatrick, O'Reilly and Timon. The sermon was preached by Archbishop Hughes. The new bishop at once entered upon his duties and labors in New Jersey, and during the nineteen years of his administration he devoted his personal attention to the elevation and advancement of its affairs. He may be truly said to have created one of the most prosperous and flourishing dioceses of the Roman Catholic Church in the United States. During his administration he founded Seton Hall College, at Orange; the Academies of the Sisters of Charity at Madison, and the Houses of the Brothers of the Christian Schools at Newark and at Jersey City. He built many large and beautiful churches throughout the State, and introduced into his diocese a priory of Benedictine monks in Newark, and a convent of Benedictine nuns at Elizabeth, the Convent of the Passionists at St. Michael's, at West Hoboken, and the Jesuits' establishment at St. Peter's, Jersey City. On the 30th of July, 1872, Bishop Bayley was elevated to the Archdiocese of Baltimore (to succeed Archbishop Spaulding, deceased) by a papal bull signed on that

day. The decree reached Archbishop Bayley on the 25th of August, and two months later he had severed his official relations with the see of Newark, where he had labored so long and well, and began the work in the new field to which he was called, and where he still remains. The Archbishop "has written much, but published little." Among his printed works are a "Sketch of the Early History of the Catholic Church on the Island of New York," written while he was Secretary of the Diocese of New York, a "Biography of Bishop Bruté," of Vincennes, Indiana, and "Pastorals for the People," dealing mainly with the subject of temperance, for which he has always been an earnest advocate and worker. He is also known to the general public as a popular lecturer, in which capacity he has addressed audiences in several of our eastern cities and towns.

LUTKINS, ALFRED A., M. D., of Jersey City, was born in New York city, in October, 1826. His father, Stephen H. Lutkins, was a native of New Jersey, and for many years held the position of magistrate in New York; his mother was Eliza La Rue. The family moved to Jersey City when Alfred was two years old, and it was here that the lad obtained his early education. Destined for the profession of medicine, he matriculated at the University of New York in 1846, and after taking two courses of lectures he was licensed by the New Jersey State Medical Association, having, as a preliminary, passed the required examination before its Board of Censors in May, 1848. On receiving his diploma, he commenced practice in Jersey City, where he has since been constantly engaged in the active duties of his profession, and has built up a most extensive and successful practice. An earnest student, and thoroughly in love with his profession, he has kept himself well abreast with medical progress, and is highly esteemed by his brethren as a well-read and eminently efficient physician, so much so that his services are frequently called in consultations. He has been a member of the District Medical Society of Hudson county for many years, and was President of that body in 1873. Since the organization of the Jersey City Charity Hospital, he has been a member of its medical staff, and he is also connected with the Hudson County Hospital. For five years he was City Physician of Jersey City, and during his term of office the duties and responsibilities were exceptionally heavy, owing to the prevalence of the well-remembered cholera epidemic. While a public-spirited citizen, discharging faithfully his duties to the community, he has not suffered his attention to be drawn beyond his profession, devoting himself to its service, and being content to find his rewards therein. He married Julia Demotte, of Hudson county, New Jersey.

CHULTZE, GENERAL JOHN, State Senator, Manchester, Ocean county, a grandson of Henry Frederick William Schultze, some time a member of the Prussian diplomatic service, one of the commissioners appointed to determine the boundary between Prussia and Russia, and, during the latter part of his life, President of the University of Halle, and son of H. F. W. Schultze, who immigrated to America in 1815, settled in Centre county, Pennsylvania, and there married Sarah Watson, a descendant of the Williamson family, members of which were among the early settlers of the Cumberland valley, and were also distinguished in the war of the Revolution, was born in Centre county, September 1st, 1836. Having received a liberal education, begun in the public schools of his native county, continued at the Lock Haven Academy, and ended at Dickinson Seminary, Williamsport, he engaged in the manufacture of iron, and was in a short time made Superintendent of the Millhall Iron Works and Washington Iron Works in Clinton county. From 1855 to 1858 he was Superintendent of the Roaring Creek Iron Works, the output of the works being anthracite pig-iron, and in the latter year was appointed General Superintendent of the works of the Farrondale Iron and Coal Company, a corporation engaged in the manufacture of boiler iron and of fire-brick, and also extensively engaged in mining and shipping bituminous coal. While conducting this general business for the company, he also conducted a considerable trade in lumber on his own account. Thus employed, he remained until 1861. In August of that year, when the second call for troops was issued, and it had become evident that not a mere mutiny had occurred in a single Southern State, but that the whole South had risen in rebellion, he relinquished his profitable and well-established business and entered the United States volunteer army. Of the company recruited among his own and the Farrondale employés, he was commissioned First Lieutenant, and the command was assigned to the Fourteenth (subsequently the Ninety-third) Pennsylvania Regiment. In all the hard fighting during the Peninsula campaign he took an active part, and while serving for a considerable period on the staff of General Couch (in charge of the transportation of material) he always managed to be with his regiment when it was ordered into action. During the campaign he was three times wounded—at Williamsburg, at Fair Oaks, and at Malvern Hill. After the army was withdrawn from the Peninsula, he took part in the battles of Chantilly and second Bull Run, and served through the Maryland campaign that terminated in the battle of Antietam. Immediately after Williamsburg he was raised two grades at a step, being promoted from Lieutenant to be Major, and shortly after Antietam he was promoted to be Lieutenant-Colonel. On receiving this latter promotion he was again attached to the staff of General Couch, as Chief Quartermaster of the Second Army Corps; but, as before, his connection with his regiment was not severed, and he took part

in all its engagements. At Chancellorsville and Fredericks-burg his gallantry was especially conspicuous, and in the latter battle he was severely wounded. Soon after the Chancellorsville fight, General Couch was assigned to the Department of the Susquehanna, and at the same time Colonel Schultze was made Adjutant-General of the Department of Pennsylvania, a position that he retained until after the battle of Gettysburg. During the remainder of the war he served in this department, being promoted to be Brigadier-General in 1864, and in 1865 receiving the brevet of Major-General. The war being ended, he resigned his commission, and the resignation was accepted in May, 1866. Upon returning to civil life he became, and has since continued to be, the business agent of Mr. James Brown, of New York, in the charge of varied properties of that gentleman in New Jersey, including tracts of land in Ocean county aggregating twenty-five thousand acres; several slate quarries; a large iron mill; extensive mining operations; and important interests in a number of feeder and main lines of railway. The management of this great and heterogeneous trust necessarily implies the possession on the part of the trustee of business tact and ability of the highest order. Since assuming its duties he has resided in Manchester. On his own account he conducts a manufactory of gunny cloth, and is also prominently connected with various leading corporations. As his war record implies, he is an earnest member of the Republican party, and since he has been a resident of New Jersey he has taken an active part in State politics. In 1872 he was elected a member of the Assembly, and in 1873 refused a renomination, as he was desirous of visiting Europe. Having returned to America, he was elected, in 1874, a member of the State Senate, and still (1877) retains his seat in that body. A request to be congressional candidate for his district, with the certainty of election, he was compelled to refuse, the requirements of his very extensive business preventing him from accepting the offer. In the State Legislature he has served on several of the leading committees, and both in committee and in debate has displayed a broad knowledge of the principles of good government, and a remarkable faculty of reducing his principles to practice—qualities which, in a modified form, have been no less conspicuous in his brilliant military and business career.

———————

AYLOR, HON. JOHN W., Lawyer, of Newark, was born at Buckland, Massachusetts, about 1830, and was educated in that State. Like so many young men, in New England especially, he spent the years of his earlier manhood in teaching, first in his native State, and then at Morristown, New Jersey. He studied law with ex-Vice-Chancellor Dodd, was admitted to the bar in 1857, and began practice in Newark. Always taking an active part in public affairs, he was elected a member of the Board of Education of the City of Newark from the Second ward in October, 1869, and was re-elected in 1871, serving as Chairman of the Committee on High Schools. In 1869 the Republican party put him forward, without any seeking on his part, as their candidate for Senator for the county, and he was elected. So well pleased was the party with its choice, so amply did his career in the Senate justify their confidence, that a re-election in 1872, by a greatly increased majority, followed naturally. In the session of 1873 he was unanimously elected President of the Senate, and a similar honor was conferred upon him in the succeeding session. He proved himself a most efficient presiding officer, displaying intimate knowledge of parliamentary practice, holding the scales evenly between both parties, and at all times upholding the dignity of the position and of the Senate. He has always pursued his profession in Newark, and is justly regarded as one of the first lawyers in the State. For several years he has been Counsel to the Chosen Board of Freeholders of Newark.

OLFAX, GENERAL WILLIAM, Captain of Washington's Life-Guard, late of Pompton, New Jersey, was born in Connecticut, July 3d, 1756, and "was of the staunchest New England stock. An ancestor of the same name was one of the early settlers of Weathersfield, Connecticut, and the births of four of his children are recorded as occurring in that ancient village about 1653–59. He was probably the grandfather of John Colfax, of New London, Connecticut, who married Ann Latimer, September 3d, 1727, the young couple being admitted to the church in New London on profession of their faith, and their son, George (born December 25th, 1727) baptized March 17th, 1728. The records also note the births of these other children of John Colfax: Ann, 1728; Jonathan, 1736; John, 1739; William, 1748.—George married Lucy, daughter of Ebenezer Avery, and their children were: Sarah, 1750; George, 1752; Ebenezer, 1753; Lucy, 1755; William, 1756; Jonathan, 1758; Ann, 1760; Robert, 1761; John, 1763; Mary, 1766. Captain George Colfax, the father of this numerous progeny, died in 1766, leaving an estate of £807. Lucy, his widow, survived him nearly forty years, dying in September, 1804, aged seventy-five." Of his early life little is certainly known, and nothing of noteworthy importance can be gleaned concerning his career as a youth. "Doubtless it was the same as that of every other young farmer in New England—full of the rugged toil and self-dependence that taught the Yankees their power, and made them the readier to exercise it when the time came for them to assert their right to their independence, their ability to maintain which had long been evident. He often used to tell his family that he participated in the battle of Bunker

Hill, June 17th, 1775. It is probable that he never left the army from that day till the liberties of his country were secured." He appears to have enlisted in a Connecticut regiment, and in the records of the comptroller's office of that State is credited with service in the Continental army to January 1st, 1780, £184 3s. 11d. On January 1st, 1781, he received for balance of service £106 1s. 4d. While the American army was encamped at Valley Forge, Washington issued an order, dated March 17th, 1778, directing that "one hundred chosen men are to be annexed to the guard of the commander-in-chief, for the purpose of forming a corps, to be instructed in the manœuvres necessary to be introduced into the army, and to serve as a model for the execution of them." These men, taken from the various States, were required to be from five feet eight inches to five feet ten inches in height, from twenty to thirty years of age, and of robust constitutions and good character. They were to be American-born, and the motto of the guard was, "Conquer or Die.' Into this honorable corps he was drafted, and his fine appearance and gallantry in the field soon made him a favorite with the general, and it was not long ere he became a Lieutenant, subsequently succeeding Caleb Gibbs, of Rhode Island, as Captain Commandant, though it appears that he was never commissioned a Captain. He was thrice wounded in battles, once dangerously; one of these wounds was received at the battle of White Plains, New York, in October, 1776. Upon one occasion, while in the act of giving the word of command to his men, a bullet struck his uplifted sword, shattering the blade, and, glancing, skinned one of his fingers. In another engagement, a bullet struck his forearm, severing the integuments, and passing between the bones without touching them. Again, while riding on horseback in an exposed position, a bullet was sent through his body, just above the hip, and below the bowels, entering in front and coming out behind. In the excitement of the battle he did not notice the wound, but galloped from point to point over the field delivering orders, until one of his men saw the dripping stream, and cried out, "Captain, the blood is running out of your boot." Glancing down, he perceived his condition for the first time, saw that the wound was serious, and rode over toward the field-hospital. Dr. Ledyard looked at the wound, and bade him go at once into the hospital and stay there. Later, Washington, "seeing the state of his trusted captain, said to him : 'You are in a deplorable condition; I will give you a furlough that you may go home till you recover.' He persisted in staying with the army, however, till they went into winter quarters at Morristown in the winter of 1779–80." During that season he went home to Connecticut, on the saddle the entire distance; while in March the snow had fallen so heavily that in many instances he rode over the covered fence-tops. Eventually, he returned greatly improved in health, and remained with his comrades-in-arms until the close of the war. At the surrender of Lord Cornwallis, at Yorktown, in October, 1781, he was, at his own particular request, permitted to occupy a prominent position on horseback, near his beloved chief, and in after years was never weary of describing that memorable scene, with all its attendant incidents. He was a personal friend of Lady Washington, as well as of the general, and the family still preserves a sort of net for his cue, knitted of linen thread by her, and given to him as a present. His descendants have also one of a brace of pistols given to him by Washington. " He was a man of fine presence; about five feet ten inches in height, large frame, well-proportioned, and weighing about one hundred and ninety or two hundred pounds. He had dark hair, a clean-shaven face, with massive square-set under-jaw, a clear, florid complexion, and beautiful blue eyes. His hair was powdered and worn in a cue, tied with a black ribbon, till his later years. A pretty miniature of himself, painted about the end of the revolutionary war for his sweetheart, shows that his coat was dark blue, with collar and facing of scarlet; his waistcoat was doubtless buff, although the color is now faded; a ruffled shirt-bosom overflows the upper part of the waistcoat, and there appears to be a black cravat about his neck, with a white collar turned partly over it. This neatness of dress characterized his appearance all his life." While the army was at Pompton Plains, northern New Jersey, the citizens showed the officers various courtesies. About a quarter of a mile above the Pompton Steel Works, the road to Wanaque and Ringwood leaves the old Hamburgh turnpike, and at the southeast corner of these roads stands an ancient yellow frame-house, two stories high in front, with roof sloping almost to the ground in the rear; a covered verandah in front, and quaint half-doors, show that it is a mansion of the olden time. This was the residence, during the Revolution, of Casparus (Jasper) Schuyler, grandson of Arent Schuyler. The young officers found here a great attraction in the charming daughter, Hester Schuyler—who, in accordance with a custom of Dutch families, was named after her grandmother, Hester, daughter of Isaac Kingsland. "And the valiant young Colfax, brave as he was in battle, surrendered at discretion before the flash of her bright eyes." Soon after the close of the war, he took up his residence at Pompton, and August 27th, 1783, was married to the belle of the village. There, for more than half a century, he lived quietly and peacefully as a farmer, " seeing his children grow up around him, and witnessing the wonderful development of the nation for whose existence he had fought so long and well in his youth. He was honored, trusted, and revered by his neighbors, and was repeatedly elected or appointed to various responsible positions in the town, county or State. By appointment of the Legislature, he was for many years a Justice of the Peace, and a Judge of Common Pleas ; in 1806–7, 1809–10 and 1811, was a member of the General Assembly from Bergen county, New Jersey ; and in 1808, 1812 and 1813, served prominently in the Legislative Council. He was always warmly interested in military affairs and measures; in 1811 filled the position of

Brigadier-General of the 2d Division of Infantry, Bergen Brigade; and in the war of 1812 was in command at Sandy Hook; " while at the elaborate and enthusiastic celebrations of Independence Day, which were customary a half century ago, his presence was deemed indispensable at the demonstrations in his neighborhood." In 1824 or 1825, on the occasion of the great parade in Newark, in honor of the French hero, the Marquis de Lafayette, he participated as one of the most conspicuous revolutionary heroes of the day. " He preserved his faculties to the very last, and died after but a few days illness, 9th September, 1838, aged eighty-two years and two months." He was buried on his own estate with military honors, the militia of Paterson and vicinity turning out en masse on the occasion, with martial music, under the command of General Abraham Godwin, the younger, and Colonel Cornelius G. Garrison, both of Paterson. The services were held in the Dutch Reformed Church at Pompton, Rev. Isaac S. Demarest officiating, while the people came in crowds from all the country around, to testify by their presence to their respect for one whom they had so long reverenced and admired. On the sites of the houses built by Brockholls (or Brockholst) and Schuyler are now two spacious and inviting country mansions, occupied, the one by the venerable Dr. William Washington Colfax, the other by his nephew, Major William Washington Colfax. A short distance above the doctor's residence, in an enclosed field, and but a few feet from the roadside, is an unostentatious white marble pyramidal shaft, about five feet high, resting on a simple brown stone base, and bearing this inscription : " General William Colfax, Captain of Washington's Life-Guards." He left six children : George Washington, born November 3d, 1784, married Eliza Colfax; Lucy, born November 18th, 1789, married Henry P. Berry; Schuyler, born August 3d, 1792, married Hannah Delameter Stryker (father of Schuyler Colfax, Vice-President of the United States, 1869–73); Elizabeth, born August 8th, 1794, married James L. Baldwin; William W., born April 26th, 1797, married Hester Mandeville ; Maria, born July 3d, 1800, married Abraham Williams.

POTTS, HON. FREDERICK A., of Pittstown, was born in Pottstown, Pennsylvania, in 1836. After receiving a liberal education he engaged in the mining and shipping of coal, and for a number of years has conducted an extensive wholesale coal business in New York. About 1862 he purchased a farm—originally the property of one of his ancestors— near Pittstown, Hunterdon county, New Jersey, and while still maintaining his business in New York, has since this date made his home in New Jersey. In early life he identified himself with the Republican party; was an earnest supporter of the administration of President Lincoln,

Theo. F. Randolph

and has since his removal to New Jersey been prominent in local and State politics. In 1870 he was nominated State Senator from Hunterdon county, and was defeated; the county being notoriously strongly Democratic. In 1872 he again led the forlorn hope, accepting in that year the congressional nomination from the Fourth District. He was again defeated, but he succeeded in greatly reducing the ordinary Democratic majority in the district from about six thousand to about two thousand; while in his county, that on previous important elections had given a Democratic majority of from fifteen hundred to two thousand, he was defeated by but five hundred and seventy-six votes. In 1873 he was once more the Republican nominee for State Senator from Hunterdon, and on this occasion was elected by a majority of three hundred and eighty-seven—being the only Senator ever elected over a Democrat in the county. While a member of the Senate he was Chairman of the Committee on Commerce and Navigation; was a member of various other important committees; and throughout his term of office displayed legislative ability of a high order. In 1872 he was chosen a member of the Republican State Executive Committee, and in the deliberations and actions of that body his counsel and energetic labor have done much toward strengthening the New Jersey division of the party. Always manly and outspoken in his political views; never seeking office, and accepting nomination in the face of almost certain defeat and at a considerable personal sacrifice; thoroughly honest in his convictions, and at all times determined to use his best efforts for the good of the whole people, he has uniformly succeeded in winning the personal esteem of his political enemies, and, as his record shows, has actually turned several thousand of his political enemies into his political friends. Already his name has been prominently mentioned by the leading men of his party in connection with the gubernatorial office, and should he receive the nomination for Governor his chances of election seem of the best.

ANDOLPH, HON. THEODORE F., Lawyer, was born in New Brunswick, Middlesex county, New Jersey, June 24th, 1826. His family are of old revolutionary stock, dating back to the progenitor of the Randolphs of Roanoke, Virginia. His father, James F. Randolph, was for thirty-six years the publisher and editor of the *Fredonian*, an able and influential journal of the Whig party, published at New Brunswick. He was an able statesman, and for eight years represented his party in Congress. Theodore was liberally educated, and adopted the profession of the law, being admitted to the bar in 1848. He was brought up by his father in the Whig school of politics, and when quite young he became a writer on his father's paper. When quite a young man he went to Mississippi for a season, where he cast his first vote. In 1850 he returned to New Jersey and took up his residence in Hudson county, where he remained twelve years. In 1852 he married a daughter of Hon. W. D. Coleman, member of Congress from Kentucky, and a granddaughter of Chief Justice Marshall. When, in the same year, the Whig party suffered its famous defeat, Mr. Randolph allied himself with the Native American or Know Nothing party, and took a prominent part in its proceedings, and generally in State politics. During the struggle over the slavery question in 1860 Mr. Randolph and other Know Nothings formed a coalition with the Democratic party, by which he was elected to the House of Assembly from the First District of Hudson county, and was offered but declined the Speakership of that body. He was the first Democrat who ever carried that district. In 1861 he presided as Chairman over the Special Committee on the Peace Congress, and was one of those who inaugurated the measure for the relief of soldiers' families. In the same year, 1861, he was elected to the State Senate to fill an unexpired term, and the following year he was re-elected and served until 1865. The year of his re-election he was appointed Commissioner of Draft for Hudson county. In 1867 he was unanimously elected President of the Morris & Essex Railroad Company. In the fall campaign of 1868 he became the Democratic candidate for Governor, and was elected by a majority of 4,618 votes over John I. Blair, the Republican nominee. He was inaugurated in 1869, and held the office three years, during which time he used the veto power freely for the purpose of defeating whatever he considered corrupt legislation, proving himself an efficient as well as a popular officer. During his governorship he caused the repeal of the transit tax on persons travelling through the State, and established a general railway law; he made the State Prison system self-supporting; passed a bill for the punishment of bribers in elections; suggested the plan for the State Lunatic Asylum; settled the feud between the Erie and Delaware Railroads, and various other important acts. He also signed the resolution of the Legislature which ratified the Fifteenth Amendment to the Federal Constitution. During his last year of office Governor Randolph showed his independence of character by his action in regard to the Orangemen's procession, July 12th, 1871. The day before Superintendent Kelso, of New York, had issued a proclamation, forbidding the Orangemen's procession in that city. This caused great excitement, loud and angry demands being made on the authorities to accord to them, the Orangemen, the same privileges which had always been accorded to other organizations, and, always before, to them. The news of the order by Superintendent Kelso having been telegraphed to Governor Randolph, who was at Newark, he immediately issued the following proclamation, which has become famous: "A portion of our citizens desiring to celebrate what is deemed by them an anniversary day, and it having come to my knowledge that interference with the contemplated celebration may possibly take place, by reason of which a serious disturbance of the peace of this State would probably ensue; therefore, I, Theodore F. Randolph, Governor of the State of New Jersey, do hereby proclaim that both the letter and spirit of the Constitution of our State of New Jersey, as well as the long-established custom of our people to permit and protect all peaceful gatherings of the inhabitants of this State, irrespective of political or religious creed, makes it the lawful right of any body of peaceful citizens to assemble together, and that right cannot be abridged or interfered with by any unauthorized body of men of any nationality, creed, or religion, whatever the real or supposed provocation may seem to be; and I do therefore enjoin upon all good, law-abiding and peaceful citizens of this, our State of New Jersey, to assist in every way in preserving the peace, good order, and dignity of the same, not only by abstinence from provocation, but by acts of toleration, forbearance, and true manliness. And I do hereby warn all persons from other States who may seek by acts of provocation to interfere with the peaceful assembling of the inhabitants of this State, that such offence against the peace and good order of the commonwealth will be promptly and rigorously punished by our authorities, whom I do further enjoin and command to enforce this proclamation, assuring all such properly-constituted authorities that, in the event of the insufficiency of the ordinary local power, then the entire power of the State will, if necessary, be called into exercise to compel, at any cost, respect for and obedience to our laws. And I do further enjoin upon the members of the society, especially, professing to assemble together to-morrow, the exercise of the utmost patience, care, and discretion in the pursuance of their rights, bearing in mind that, to a large portion of our fellow-citizens, the peculiar occasion of their gathering is deemed an unnecessary revival of an ancient political and religious feud, of no general interest to the great body of our American citizens, and, though they were sustained, as in their right to peacefully assemble together, they are by no means sustained, as I firmly believe, by any large number, of sincere, patriotic, and Christian people in the expediency of the exercise of that right at this time. Given at the executive chambers, in the city of Trenton, this 11th day of July, in the year of our Lord 1871, and the independence of the United States of America the ninety-sixth. Theodore F. Randolph. Attest, Samuel C. Brown, Private Secretary." Speaking of the matter afterwards, Mr. Randolph said that when he read Superintendent Kelso's order he immediately determined, without having time or opportunity to consult with any one, to issue his proclamation, as he felt that the result of this order would be to throw into New Jersey the riotous elements of New York. By one o'clock the proclamation was written, sent to the telegraph, and ordered to be printed in hand-bills and posted. By half-past three o'clock all the necessary military orders had been given. When the ammunition was forwarded, Governor Randolph said he ordered that no blank cartridges be sent, as he felt that to fire blank cartridges in such a situation would be to instigate riot rather than to quell it. During the day he was constantly alert to see that no New York organization crossed the river, and for the same purpose he remained on a tugboat, on the watch, all night. Fortunately, no attempt was made, and in the trouble of the next day the civil authority showed its ability to cope with the situation without the direct interference of the military. All through his conduct of this emergency Governor Randolph proved himself a ruler of singular firmness and ability in an emergency. On the expiration of his office Mr. Randolph devoted himself to farming and mining. On his home, at Morristown, New Jersey, where he has resided since 1862, comprising ninety acres, he pursued his agricultural tastes and fondness for stock-raising. On January 20th the New Jersey Democratic caucus nominated him as successor, in the United States Senate, to Hon. John P. Stockton, whose term expired in March of that year. His opponent was Hon. George M. Robeson. At the election, a week later, he received the entire vote of all the Democratic members of both houses. In March, 1875, Mr. Randolph was placed on the Committees on Military Affairs, Mines and Mining, and Civil Service and Retrenchment. March 9th, 1877, he was placed on the Committees on Commerce and Military Affairs.

BUCKLEY, BENJAMIN, Manufacturer, of Paterson, New Jersey, son of Joseph Buckley, was born in Oldham, Lancashire, England, January 29th, 1808. From his sixteenth to his twentieth year he served as an apprentice to Samuel Lees & Son, machinists, of Oldham; remained with the firm for six months after the termination of his term of apprenticeship, and in 1831 immigrated to America. Settling at Paterson, he worked at his trade in the establishments of Rogers, Danforth, and others; and in 1844 began the manufacture, upon his own account, of spindles and flyers. This business he still continues under the firm-name of Benjamin Buckley & Co., his two sons having for some time been associated in partnership with him. In April, 1871, he was elected President of the Second National Bank of Paterson, a position that at present (1877) he still holds. He is also a Director of the Paterson Fire Insurance Company. For a number of years he has taken a prominent part in politics. In 1856 he was elected to the State Assembly, was re-elected in 1857-58, and subsequently served for nine years as a member of the State Senate, being in 1867 President of that body. Able in committee and sound in debate, his legislative career has been highly honorable; its appreciation by his constituents being evidenced by his repeated re-elections, and also by his election, in 1875-76-77, as Mayor of Paterson. He married Mary, daughter of Mr. Wilson, of Paterson.

ANSOM,· STEPHEN BILLINGS, Lawyer, of Jersey City, was born at Salem, Connecticut, October 12th, 1814, being the son of Amsa Ransom, a farmer long resident in that place. He was educated at Bacon Academy, Colchester, Connecticut, until 1835. During the latter part of this term he was engaged in teaching, which occupation he pursued for the following six years at Mendham, Belvidere, Hope, New Germantown and Chester. In 1841 he began the study of law under the direction of Phineas B. Kennedy, then county clerk at Belvidere, and finished his course under William Thompson, of Somerville. He was admitted to the bar of New Jersey on September 5th, 1844. For three years he practised his profession at New Germantown, Hunterdon county. In April, 1848, he removed to Somerville, where he resided and prosecuted the law until 1856. Two years previously to the last-mentioned he had opened an office in Jersey City, to which after a while he removed his residence, and where he still continues to practise. In politics he was originally a Democrat, and supported Van Buren for President in 1848. Four years later he advocated the Free Soil platform, and voted for Pierce, the political elements with which he then found himself crystallizing into the Republican party. He supported Horace Greeley for the Presidency against the re-election of Ulysses S. Grant. Always a prohibitionist, he cast at the last Presidential election the only vote recorded in Jersey City for Green Clay Smith, the prohibitionist candidate. In 1845 and 1846 he commanded a company of militia at New Germantown. He married, May 14th, 1845, Maria C. Apgar, daughter of Jacob Apgar, a merchant of Hunterdon county,.who went to California on the discovery of gold, and died there in 1849. In the following year Mrs. Ransom died. He was married a second time, in July, 1856, to Eliza W. Hunt, daughter of Stephen R. Hunt, lawyer, of Somerville.

member of the Middlesex County Medical Society, having served as President of that organization in 1870, and having been for nine years past its representative in the annual conventions of the State Medical Society. In this latter body he holds a no less leading place, having repeatedly been chosen its delegate to the annual conventions of the medical societies of other States, and having also represented it at the meetings of the American Medical Association—the supreme head of the medical profession in America. He is also a member of the New Jersey Microscopical Society; of the New Brunswick Historical Society, of which he has been Secretary since 1868; of the Phi Beta Kappa, Rutgers College Chapter, of which he was Secretary in 1875-76, and was re-elected to the present year (1877); and of the order of Ancient Free and Accepted Masons. In February, 1862, he was appointed an Acting Assistant Surgeon in the United States volunteer army, was subsequently promoted to be Surgeon, served until the end of the war, and was honorably discharged in 1865. He was present and rendered efficient service at the battles of Hanover, Fair Oaks, Gaines' Mill, and Savage's Station; was taken prisoner in the latter engagement, and was for some time confined at .Libby and at Belleisle. On being released he rejoined his command, and was with the army of the Potomac during the retreat down the Peninsula to Fortress Monroe; was in Suffolk during the siege by Longstreet's corps, took part in the engagements before Petersburg and Richmond, and was in Fort Yorktown at the time of the explosion of the magazine. Beside his very active field service, he rendered service no less valuable in the hospital department,—being detailed as Assistant Surgeon to the hospital at Craney's Island, and to the United States General Hospital at Plampton, Virginia, and as Post Surgeon at Fort Yorktown during the winter of 1863-64. He married Charlotte B., eldest daughter of Dr. Anthony Bournonville, a leading physician of Philadelphia.

OORHEES, CHARLES HOLBERT, M. D., of New Brunswick, New Jersey, descended from emigrants to America from Holland in 1670, a grandson of David Voorhees, a soldier in the Continental army during the revolutionary war, and a son of the late Ira C. Voorhees, Esq., was born in New Brunswick, August 3d, 1824. After a creditable course at the well-known Rutgers College Grammar School, he entered the Jefferson Medical College, at Philadelphia, and from that institution received in the spring of 1850 his degree of M. D. Immediately upon graduation he entered upon the practice of his profession in his native town, and, save during a temporary sojourn in Plainfield,.and during the late war, has since remained established there, in the enjoyment of a constantly increasing practice and the esteem of his townsmen. In his profession his standing is of the best. For a number of years he has been a prominent

HAPMAN, REV. ROBERT HETT, D. D., Pastor of the Presbyterian Church at Rahway, President of the University of North Carolina, late of Winchester, Virginia, was born in Orange, New Jersey, March 2d (or 5th), 1771, both dates being given in "The Chapman Family." He was a descendant, in the seventh generation, of Robert Chapman, who was born at Hull, England, in 1616, and came to Boston in 1635, settling eventually at Saybrook, Connecticut, in April, 1642; his son, Robert, had a son, Robert, who was one of the first settlers of East Haddam, Connecticut; he was the father of Robert the fourth, and the grandfather of Jedidiah, of Orange, New Jersey, father of Robert Hett Chapman, who was born in East Haddam, Connecticut, September 27th, 1741, and died at Geneva, New York, May 22d, 1813. Robert Hett was the second son of Rev. Jedidiah Chapman and Blanche Smith, and graduated at the College of New Jersey in 1789, in the same class with David Hosack, Mahlon Dickerson, Isaac Pierson and Silas Wood. After a full course of theological study he was licensed to preach by the Presbytery of New York, October 3d, 1793. In the winter of 1794-95 he visited the Southern States on a missionary tour, and on his return supplied for a time the newly organized church of Wardsesson (Bloomfield), New Jersey. The call from Rahway was laid before the presbytery October 12th, 1796, and was accepted. The ordination and installation took place January 5th, 1797; and among those present were Rev. Messrs. Woodruff, Roe, Chapman, Austin, Fish, Hillyer, Condict, Cook, Richards, Armstrong and Force. Mr. Hillyer preached, Mr. Chapman presided, and Mr. Condict gave the exhortation to the people. His first pastorate was short, since, October 2d, 1799, he was dismissed for want of adequate support, the people being unable to fulfil their engagements. He was subsequently the honored President of the University of North Carolina; received the degree of D. D. from Williams College in 1815; and died, while on a journey, at Winchester, Virginia, June 18th, 1833. He was married, February 14th, 1797, to Hannah, daughter and sixth child of Isaac Arnett and Hannah White; she was the sister of Mrs. Shepard Kollock, of Elizabethtown, and the granddaughter of James Arnett, who was one of those who were admitted Associates of the Town in 1699. They had twelve children, four of whom were born at Rahway.

---◆---

WARE, REV. THOMAS, Celebrated Itinerant Methodist Preacher, Soldier in the Revolutionary Army, late of Salem, New Jersey, was born in Greenwich, New Jersey, December 19th, 1758. His paternal grandfather was an Englishman by birth and a captain in the British service under Queen Anne. In his sixteenth year he left his native town and went to live with an uncle in Salem, New Jersey, an ingenious mechanic and a ready wit, but lax in his moral and religious principles; and there his religious creed and convictions were made the subject of biting and incessant ridicule. " Habitually listening to the skeptical conversations of those who frequented his house, I soon imbibed the spirit and sentiments, and joined with them in their merriment." Also while residing in Salem, the quarrel with Great Britain grew more threatening, and he became deeply imbued with the spirit of patriotic resistance, and openly declared for the colonial as against the royal cause. His uncle was, on the opening of the struggle, on the side of America, but on the declaration of independence again became a loyalist. Influenced by the views and feelings nurtured by his love of liberty, he then abandoned his roof and volunteered as a soldier in the service; and in 1776

was one of the nine thousand quartered at Perth Amboy. "After we had lain there a short time, to make a show of our strength, as was supposed, our general reviewed us in full view of the enemy. As was expected by some, they opened their artillery upon us. Had their fire been directed with skill, many must have been slain. But they shot over us. . . . . This was indeed a useless exposure of life." After being quartered one month at Perth Amboy he volunteered to reinforce Washington on Long Island, and was marched thence to Powles' Hook. Before arriving there, however, the British had secured the Hudson river, and a passage was thus rendered impossible. Upon his volunteering at Perth Amboy to aid in strengthening Washington's position, in consequence of the refusal of the ensign to go, he was given the colors as a reward for being the first to follow his captain, who was the first in the regiment that turned out and called for volunteers. He subsequently was greatly exercised about his spiritual condition, and, retiring from the army, meditated solemnly over his past, present, and future life. " From this time I considered my country safe, nor ever after sickened at the thought of wearing the chains of civil bondage. But, alas ! I wore chains infinitely more galling than any ever forged by an earthly tyrant. My soul was in bondage to sin. . . . . I had been led to infer, from the effect my reading of the catechism and Confession of Faith produced on my mind, that no human being was ever properly in a state of trial, not even Adam himself. . . . . I was silenced, however, by my mother's fears and tears at my doubts and questionings. But I could no longer hold to this system. In leaving it, however, I did not find the right way. I resorted to nature's laws as my guide, preferring to believe that the Deity had revealed no will, rather than admit that he had revealed one so much at variance with himself and the dictates of reason." Eventually, however, after a season of trials and harassing experiences, he became, through the chance instrumentality of a wandering preacher, Mr. Pedicord, acquainted with the Methodist doctrine and several of its adherents, and was greatly affected by what he saw and heard concerning them and their mode of belief and practice. After attending a meeting he hastened to his lodgings, and falling upon his knees in prayer, spent much of the night in penitential weeping. He then relinquished his former studies in navigation, and abandoned all company but that of the pious. The New Testament he read over and over, and was charmed with the character of God our Saviour as revealed in it. Mount Holly, Burlington county, New Jersey, was the place of his spiritual birth. Soon after he joined the Methodist Society, Messrs. Pedicord and Cromwell were removed from his circuit, and Dudley and Ivy appointed in their place. From the time he made a public profession of religion, many of his brethren thought he was called to preach. " But I believed them not. The affectionate solicitude I felt for the salvation of sinners, which had prompted me to some bold acts that I had performed from a sense of duty, I did not construe as a call to the ministry, but as a collateral evidence of my adoption into the family of God. . . . . I was a leader and an exhorter, and more than these I never expected to be." Such were his views and feelings when Bishop Asbury came to New Mills, and sent for him to come and see him. The result of his interview with that eminent Methodist was his appointment to take the Dover Circuit, which had but one preacher on it; and in September, 1783, accordingly, he turned toward the peninsula, where he was received with warmth and kindliness. In the spring of 1784 he attended the conference which sat at Baltimore. "There was quite a number of preachers present. : . . . The whole number of itinerant preachers at that time in America was eighty-three; stations and circuits, sixty four; and members in society, 14,988. . . . . Among these pioneers, Asbury, by common consent, stood first and chief; next to him, in the estimation of utany, stood the placid Tunnell, the philosophical Gill, and the pathetic Pedicord." He was afterwards appointed, with James O. Cromwell and William Lynch, on the Kent Circuit, Eastern Shore of Maryland; and here, as on Dover Circuit, found a great number of young people, some of them connected with the first families; and when, in 1800, he had charge of the whole peninsula, he found many journeying toward the holy land, who, in sixteen years, had advanced from babes in Christ to fathers and mothers in Israel. The Methodist Episcopal Church in the United States was organized in 1784, soon after the close of the Revolution; and it was impracticable, during the war, for Wesley to furnish an organization suited to the necessities of this country. After its termination, however, Mr. Asbury made application to the father and founder of the Methodist societies in behalf of those of the new nation. Wesley, accordingly, resolved without delay to send over Dr. Coke, whom he first set apart by the imposition of hands to the office of superintendent, with instructions to carry his plan into effect. The doctor was then furnished with forms of ordination for deacons, elders, and superintendents, and appointed, jointly with Asbury, to preside over the Methodist societies in America. It was already agreed to have a conference, to meet in Baltimore on the ensuing 25th of December. "Nearly fifty years have now elapsed since the Christmas Conference; and I have a thousand times looked back to the memorable era with pleasurable emotions. I never often said it was the most solemn convocation I ever saw. I might have said, for many reasons, it was sublime. . . . . After Mr. Wesley's letter had been read, analyzed, and cordially approved by the conference, the question arose, 'What name or title shall we take?' I thought to myself, I shall be satisfied that we be denominated The Methodist Church, and so whispered to a brother sitting near me. But one proposed, I think it was John Dickens, that we should adopt the title of Methodist Episcopal Church, ... and the motion was carried, I think, without a dissenting voice. There was

71

not, to my recollection, the least agitation on the question. Had the conference indulged a suspicion that the name they adopted would be, in the least degree, offensive to the views or feelings of Mr. Wesley, they would have abandoned it at once; for the name of Mr. Wesley was inexpressibly dear to the Christmas Conference, and especially to Mr. Asbury and Dr. Coke." After the organization they proceeded to elect a sufficient number of elders to visit the quarterly meetings and administer the ordinances; and this it was which gave rise to the office of presiding elder among the Methodists. From this conference he returned to the peninsula, in every part of which Methodism was flourishing, and where the administration of the ordinances at the quarterly meetings "was singularly owned of God." His after course and career for a time is thus summarized in his "Life," as a preliminary heading: "Dr. Coke visits the peninsula. Multitudes flock to hear the word, receive the sacrament, and get their children baptized. Mr. Ware's labors interrupted by sickness. He partially recovers and resolves to return home. Is induced to change his course by an extraordinary manifestation of divine influence at a meeting he attended, just about the time he had made arrangements to leave. Has a second attack. Did not attend conference, and wrote to be discontinued for at least one year. Was, however, continued, and appointed to Salem Circuit. Had to contend with error. Saw many of his relatives brought into the church. Prosperity of the work. His reflections on the benefits of having the ordinances. Extension of the work. He is sent to Long Island, New York. Crosses over on the main shore, and visits New Rochelle, Bedford and Peekskill. Detained at a public house. His detention proves a blessing to the landlord and his wife." In the spring of 1787 Dr. Coke again visited this country, and called the preachers to meet in conference at Baltimore on the 1st of the ensuing May; during its progress he took part in the proceedings—which were especially notable and of high importance as affecting the relations existing between Wesley and his American brethren—and volunteered to accompany Mr. Tunnell to the Holston country, afterward called East Tennessee, where a fair field of labor lay ready for the sower. There, notwithstanding violent opposition from many and various quarters, societies were formed and a number of log chapels erected; and on the circuit three hundred members were received the first year. In the fall of this year he was sent to form a circuit low down on the Holston and French Broad; and the first conference in Holston was held in 1788. His next appointment was to East New River, where he was instructed, in conjunction with his colleague, to enlarge his borders from a two to a four weeks' circuit. In the spring of 1789 his circuit was visited by Bishop Asbury, and with him he journeyed to North Carolina; and the following conference was held at McKnight's Church, commencing on the 11th of April. Caswell Circuit was his next field of labor, and his second year in the Southern section was passed on a district consisting of eight circuits, embracing a part of Virginia. After spending two years in that country he returned to the North, and arrived in time to attend the Philadelphia Conference for 1791, and was appointed to Wilmington, Delaware, and in the spring of 1792 to Staten Island, New York, where he labored a short time with "much satisfaction and some success." He then took charge of the Susquehanna District, and thenceforward, until 1808, continued to fill this very laborious office, "which was, I believe, a longer time in regular succession than had fallen to the lot of any other man since we became a church." In the spring of 1793 he took charge of the Albany District, which was constituted of ten circuits, embracing a portion of New York, Connecticut, Massachusetts and Vermont. September 30th, 1796, the Annual Conference commenced its session in New York city, and from there he went with Bishop Asbury to the Philadelphia Conference, which commenced on the 20th of October. Here he was appointed to the charge of the Philadelphia District, extending from Wilmington, Delaware, to Lake Seneca, New York. He did not enter upon its duties, however, until after the General Conference, whose session opened in Baltimore on the same day. In 1800 he was appointed to a district on the peninsula, and his first year there "was one of the happiest in his whole life." Previously to entering upon the charge of this district he attended the third Baltimore General Conference, where, as at other past meetings, he deplored the neglect of providing for superannuated preachers, and eloquently advocated the speedy adoption of needed measures relating to the subject. He was present also at the Annual Conference at Smyrna, and participated in a great revival which, continuing during the session, added one hundred members to the church at its close. A meeting was then appointed by request at Dover, to be called the Yearly Meeting; a season followed of extraordinary power and gracious influence. Leaving the district at the end of the third year, he returned to the charge at Philadelphia, and in 1803 took charge of the Jersey District, continuing on it four years. He afterward labored two years in the St. George's charge, Philadelphia; in 1808 was attacked by serious illness; in the spring of 1809, on account of his debility, was obliged to take a supernumerary relation, and in the following year was superannuated. In 1811 Lancaster Town became the field of his labor, and at the General Conference held at New York in 1812 he was elected one of the Book Agents. In that office he continued four years, and was then appointed to Long Island. "From this time, 1816, I continued to be effective till 1825, so that I was an effective travelling preacher, in all, forty years." He attended also the General Conference in 1832. While Strasburg Circuit was the place of his residence, he formed an acquaintance with Barbary Miller, "a person whom I selected, above all others, as a suitable companion for me; and on the 15th of October, 1797, we were joined in holy matrimony, she being thirty-five years of age, and I

thirty-eight." In the "Preface to Memoir of Rev. Thomas Ware" are the following characteristic lines: "The writer has neither capacity nor disposition to employ his pen merely for the purpose of amusing his fellow-men. But having been called in the order of Providence to act a part upon the stage of life at a period when everything connected with the history of this great nation was stamped with interest, he may without ostentation perform the humble task of recording some things which passed under his observation, and thus preserving from oblivion incidents connected with those days which might otherwise be lost. . . . . He has lived to witness great changes. . . . . His 'old companions dear' are all gone. He lives as in a new world; yet not new, because, though other men inhabit it, they are engaged in the same cause. Methodism, in its radical principles and prominent features, is the same as when the writer first entered the field. That it may continue so to the end of time, and equal the highest expectations of its early friends and advocates as an instrument of spreading evangelical holiness through these lands, is his sincere prayer." He died some years since.

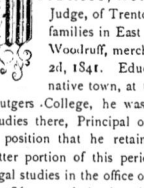

OODRUFF, HON. ROBERT S., Jr., Lawyer and Judge, of Trenton, a member of one of the oldest families in East New Jersey, and son of James H. Woodruff, merchant, was born at Newark, April 2d, 1841. Educated in the public schools of his native town, at the State Normal School, and at Rutgers College, he was appointed, while pursuing his studies there, Principal of the Rutgers Grammar School, a position that he retained for six years. During the latter portion of this period he read law, completing his legal studies in the office of Lewis Parker, Jr., Trenton, and in 1869 was admitted to the New Jersey bar. Establishing himself in Trenton, he was in the same year elected a member of the Common Council for a three years' term, but in 1870 resigned his seat. In 1874 he was elected a member of the State Assembly, and during the ensuing session served on the Judiciary and other important committees. A renomination, tendered him in 1875, he declined, his practice having so greatly increased as to command his undivided attention. Early in 1877 an act was passed by the New Jersey Legislature creating District Courts in all cities of New Jersey containing more than fifteen thousand inhabitants, and soon after this act became a law he was tendered by and accepted from Governor Bedle the position of Judge of the District Court of Trenton. His appointment was confirmed by the Senate during the extra session in March, 1877, and under his direction the new court was at once organized. His management of its business has thus far been highly successful, greatly expediting the administration of justice in civil suits, and going a long way toward breaking down the strong feeling against the operation of the act that has been aroused in several cities of the State. Beside his other public offices, Judge Woodruff has been since 1868 a prominent member of the Trenton School Board.

———◆◆———

ALE, THOMAS N., Silk Manufacturer, the founder and principal owner of the Dale Manufacturing Company, of Paterson, New Jersey, was born at Springfield, Massachusetts, April 25th, 1813, of respectable and unpretending parentage. He was the youngest of three children—two sons and one daughter—and was left fatherless at an early age. The common district school teachings of New England, with two winter terms at the High School, at Springfield, were all the education his mother, who had married again, was able to give him. At the age of sixteen he was sent to Pittsfield, Massachusetts, to learn the trade of gun-making, at the establishment of Mr. Lemuel Pomeroy. Some difficulty, which occurred between himself and one of Mr. Pomeroy's sons, caused him to leave in the autumn of the year and return to his home. A few weeks afterward he was engaged as clerk with Mr. Marvin B. Avery, a retailer of dry-goods, groceries, hardware and crockery. He remained in this employment until the spring of 1833, when, Mr. Avery having failed, he left Springfield and went to New London, where he shipped himself as a sailor on board the ship "Georgia," Captain Brewster, bound on a two years' whaling cruise to the Indian ocean. This voyage was not a financial success to the young sailor, though rich in experience. In October, 1835, he was installed as clerk in the house of Levi Cook & Co., of New York, a Pearl street jobbing house, in what was then known as the notion and fancy trade. He remained with this house, except during a temporary suspension in the summer and winter of 1837, until January, 1840, when, with the sum of forty-five dollars, the balance due him for his salary, he joined in business another clerk from the same house, who had ninety dollars. The name of the firm was Dale & Maxwell, and their place of business was at No. 2 Cedar street. They were the first to introduce into this country a specialty known as "tailors' trimmings." The business was profitable and the house successful until 1844, when it was dissolved, and Mr. Dale continued the business under his own name. In January, 1845, he married a daughter of Alfred S. Monson, M. D., of New Haven, Connecticut. His business increased rapidly, and it was in the latter part of that year that he realized his want of knowledge of the nature and value of silk, of which his stock was largely composed. He advertised for a silk weaver, and found an Englishman from Macclesfield, whom he engaged, and with whom he made the experiment of weaving a piece of silk vesting. Mr. Dale attended in person to the buying

and dyeing of the silk, and watched very attentively all the operations in manufacturing this piece of silk. When it was finished, the reed was reserved, the remaining machinery sold, and the vesting disposed of, the whole operation resulting in a loss of $100. This experiment qualified him to become a successful purchaser of silk goods. In 1848 he went to Europe to purchase goods, for the first time, and made semi-annual trips until 1851. At this time, having a young family, and his business being greatly increased, he was induced to take two of his clerks into partnership, under the firm-name of Thomas N. Dale & Co., and move his family to Paris, France, where they resided until the autumn of 1864, Mr. Dale making frequent visits to this country, occasionally accompanied by his family. During his residence in Paris he was active in, and sympathized with, all that was American in character. The success of the American chapel in Paris, founded by Mr. Anson G. Phelps and Rev. Dr. Kirk, was largely due to his active co-operation with other American residents in Paris, and many Americans in distress found relief at his hands. He returned to this country with his family in 1864. He was identified with many patriotic movements originating with the Union League Club at the commencement and close of the slaveholders' rebellion. On the passage of the tariff bill of 1864 he became convinced that silk manufacture would be one of the great industries of this country, and under this conviction he organized the Dale Manufacturing Company, and constructed the Dale mill, at Paterson, for the purpose of supplying the house of Thomas N. Dale & Co., and its branches in Philadelphia and Cincinnati, with the class of goods in which they dealt. The mill was finished in the summer of 1866, and commenced operations; but the over-purchase of foreign goods by his house compelled the mill to diminish its product and partially suspend its operations. Mr. Dale finally became the purchaser of the largest portion of the stock of the company; and his house in New York having gone into liquidation, he turned his attention to the reorganization of the mill company; but not succeeding in securing such an organization as he desired, and the business outlook not being inviting, in the spring of 1873 he commenced reducing his operations, sold part of the machinery, and rented the largest portion of the mill. Since then he has confined himself principally to the manufacture of silk braids and trimmings. But his active mind has been interested in questions of economy and the industrial education of the laboring classes. He has been prominent as the first Vice-President of the Silk Association of America, has taken an active part in matters connected with the Paterson Board of Trade, and was appointed Centennial Commissioner for the Fifth District of New Jersey. On this commission his usual activity was displayed, and he shared with his fellow-commissioners the gratifying commendations of the public. He was instrumental in urging upon the Legislature the passage of the bill presented by the Centennial Commission, creating a commission to examine and report to the next Legislature upon the subject of technical education, and establishing industrial schools in the State of New Jersey.

GREEN, HON. CALEB S., Lawyer, was born, February 18th, 1819, in Lawrence township, near Princeton, New Jersey. He is a son of Caleb Smith Green, a farmer of that township. He was educated at the Lawrenceville High School, from which he graduated in 1834, and at Princeton College, graduating from that institution in the class of 1837, which included, among others who have since acquired greater or less distinction, Joseph Branch, of North Carolina, Charles J. Biddle, of Philadelphia, and Rev. J. H. McIlvaine, D. D. Immediately after graduating he entered the law office of his brother, the late ex-Chancellor H. W. Green, with whom he completed his legal studies, being admitted to the bar in 1843. He at once settled in the city of Trenton, and began the practice of his profession, which he pursued with such diligence and effect that he soon took rank among the ablest of its members, his practice becoming both lucrative and extensive, not always synonymous terms in the practice of either law or medicine, as many overworked practitioners of one and the other can testify. He is a man of strong political convictions, which unite him with the Republican party; but he is not a partisan, his devotion to his profession, as well as the judicial temper of his mind and character, keeping him aloof from the ordinary and perennial strife of parties. He belongs, indeed, to the class of men who, believing with the fathers of the republic that office should be neither sought nor declined, generally have offices of trust thrust upon them, while inferior men help themselves to the offices of profit; a pretty fair result, perhaps, in a rough way, after all, so far at least as the public is concerned, it being more important, from the public point of view, that offices of trust should be filled by trustworthy men, than that trustworthy men should fill the offices of profit, where of course the two qualities are not combined in the same office. Be this as it may, he has not escaped the honorable fate of his class. In 1862 he was appointed one of the Managers of the New Jersey State Lunatic Asylum, and has held the position ever since. In 1873 he was appointed to fill a vacancy in the Court of Errors and Appeals, and in 1874 appointed for the regular term of six years. For the past twenty years he has been a Director of the Trenton Banking Company, and since 1854 President of the Trenton Savings Fund Association. He is also a Trustee of Princeton College and of the Princeton Theological Seminary. It will be noticed that every position to which he has ever been appointed he still fills, the periods of his incumbency ranging from four years to the full period of a generation of men, a fact, considering the rule of unresting rotation which obtains in official

life in this country, very significant of his solid qualities both of character and of intellect. He was married, in 1847, to the youngest daughter of the late Chief-Justice Ewing, of Trenton, New Jersey.

SPRAGGS, REV. SAMUEL, Rector of St. John's Church, Elizabethtown, late of Mount Holly, was born in England, about the middle of the last century. His first appointment, after being admitted on trial, as a Methodist itinerant preacher, was to Brunswick Circuit, in southeastern Virginia, May 25th, 1774. In May, 1775, having been admitted to full connection, he was appointed to Philadelphia, and reappointed in May, 1776. In May, 1777, he was appointed to the Frederick Circuit, in Maryland. After the capture of Philadelphia by the British army, September 26th, 1777, he again returned to Philadelphia, and in the course of the following winter, or spring, removed to New York. As the only travelling preacher there in the connection, he took charge of the old John street chapel from that time to the close of the war, in 1783. In common with his fellow-itinerants, he was regarded by the British authorities as a loyalist, and so neither he nor the chapel was disturbed at any time. His ministry there terminated in July, from which time his name is missing from the connection. It is probable that about this time he married and settled at Mount Holly, New Jersey. It is not known certainly how he was occupied during the next few years. He had, in all probability, become connected with the Episcopalians, and been ordained a deacon. January 1st, 1791, he was appointed to succeed Rev. Dr. Chandler, as Rector of St. John's Church, in Elizabethtown. His ministry, however, which had given promise of great usefulness, was cut short by his unexpected decease, September 7th, 1794.

RUNYON, HON. THEODORE, LL. D., Lawyer and Chancellor of New Jersey, was born at Somerville, Somerset county, New Jersey, October 25th, 1822, the son of Abraham Runyon, of that town. The family is of Huguenot origin, and was among the original settlers at Piscataway township, Middlesex county, their ancestor being Vincent Rognion, a Huguenot who came to this country with the Stelles and other French families. Theodore was educated partly in New Jersey and partly in New York, whither his father removed when the lad was quite young. Having been fitted for college at Plainfield, he became a student at Yale, where he was graduated as A. B. in 1842, and subsequently received his degree as A. M. Having elected the law for a career, he began his legal studies in the office of Asa Whitehead. In due course he was admitted to the bar of New Jersey, in July term, 1846, and three years later he was called as counsellor. He began practice in the city of Newark, immediately after his admission, and without intermission continued its prosecution in the same place until his appointment as Chancellor. His marked ability soon gave him great prominence in his profession, and secured a practice at once extensive and lucrative. For many years he was City Solicitor of Newark. He always manifested great interest in military matters, and did more to organize the militia of the State than any other man.—indeed what of military organization existed in the State at the outbreak of the war owed its being mainly to him. He was appointed Brigadier-General of Militia for the county of Essex on May 8th, 1857. On the commencement of hostilities, in 1861, he was appointed Brigadier-General of the 1st New Jersey Brigade, and this force, moving under his command, was the first fully equipped and organized brigade of troops that went to the defence of Washington. Other States had previously sent regiments and detachments, but to New Jersey belongs the honor of furnishing the first full brigade. President Lincoln issued his call for troops April 15th, 1861 ; the first company of the New Jersey quota under that call was mustered in, April 23d; General Runyon received his commission from Governor Olden, and took command April 27th, and on the 30th of April the quota was declared full. And, notwithstanding the difficulties in the way of obtaining transportation, ammunition and supplies, in reducing this large body of un-disciplined men, drawn from all positions in life, and wholly without previous military training, into effective condition, General Runyon set about his anything but light task with such well-directed energy, and was so generously supported by his assistants and the patriotic people of the State generally, that on May 3d the brigade embarked on the propellers of the Delaware & Raritan Canal. The command arrived at Annapolis on the 4th, and reported at Washington May 6th, thirteen days after the first man had been mustered. The appearance of this large organization did much to quiet the apprehensions entertained for the city of Washington. General Runyon served with the brigade until they were mustered out, at the end of their term of enlistment, during which they were engaged on the fortifications in Virginia, opposite Washington, where Fort Runyon, named after him, was erected. He returned home in August, 1861, but before quitting the field he received the thanks of President Lincoln, personally tendered in the presence of the Cabinet, for his services in connection with the New Jersey Brigade. Subsequently resolutions complimentary to his patriotism and efficiency as a soldier were passed by the Legislature of New Jersey, and he was, on February 25th, 1862, appointed, by Governor Olden, Major-General by brevet, in compliance with the recommendation of the House of Assembly, in testimony of his patriotic and meritorious services in the field. He was appointed Major-General commanding the National Guard of the State of New Jersey on April 7th, 1869, and held the position until 1873, when he resigned on accepting the Chancellorship. For many years he bore a prominent part in the management of the political affairs of the State, as a member of the Democratic party. He was a Presidential Elector in 1860, was elected Mayor of the city of Newark in 1864, and held that office during that and the following year, his high integrity, superior ability, kindly feeling and invariable courtesy winning for him great popularity. In August, 1865, he received the nomination of his party for Governor of the State, and after a very exciting campaign was defeated by the Republican nominee, Marcus L. Ward, by only a bare majority. On April 29th, 1873, he was appointed a member of a commission to prepare amendments to the constitution of the State, and about the same time was nominated by Governor Joel Parker as Chancellor of the State for a term of seven years. The nomination, accepted by General Runyon, was confirmed by the Senate, and his commission issued bearing date May 1st, 1873. Upon assuming this high and responsible office he resigned the presidency of the Manufacturers' National Bank, which he had held from the organization of the corporation, in 1871. As Chancellor he has proved a worthy successor of a long line of profound lawyers and worthy men, who have shed lustre upon the records of the Court of Chancery in the State. He has received the honorary degree of LL. D. from two institutions—the Western University, Middletown, Connecticut, on August 15th, 1867; Rutgers College in 1875. He was married on January 20th, 1864, to Clementine, daughter of William D. Bruen, Esq., a retired merchant of Newark.

OOLMAN, FRANKLIN, Surveyor and Conveyancer, of Burlington, New Jersey, was born in that city, March 25th, 1814, and in it has always resided. He is descended from a family which were among the oldest settlers in that vicinity, and whose name has ever borne with it an honorable reputation. The American head of the family, John Woolman, arrived from England in 1681. He was a member of the Society of Friends, and he sought in America the shelter and peace which, owing to his religious views, he was prevented from enjoying in the old country. He located a tract of land about four miles from Burlington in 1686; it extended from the city of Burlington to Rancocas creek, a distance of about five miles, and comprised about 8,000 acres; part of the land still remains in the possession of the family. A man of education and ability, a surveyor, and the owner of an extensive property, he naturally occupied a prominent position in the community, and became a member of the Council of Proprietors. His son, Samuel, was also a prominent surveyor, and devoted much attention to the farming of his land. Samuel had two sons, John and Jonah. The former was the celebrated Quaker preacher and philanthropist, and the first person who opposed slavery. His life has been published several times, and his "Journal" edited by the poet Whittier. The latter is perhaps one of the most beautiful idyls in prose in the English language. The other son, Jonah, followed his father's occupation of surveying and farming, and he, in turn, was succeeded by his son, Burr, who added conveyancing; he was appointed Surveyor-General of the Western Division of New Jersey in 1814, and held the office for thirty years. Franklin Woolman, the subject of this sketch, is the son of Burr. He received a sound education, and studied with a view to inheriting his father's business, into which in due course he was admitted. On the death of his father he was appointed to the Surveyor-Generalship, and has held the office ever since, in connection with the old-established conveyancing and surveying business. He has made an especial study of titles and matters connected with real estate in Burlington county, and has gained the reputation of being the most thoroughly informed person on this subject in that section of the State. His capacity in the management of estates and his high character have caused him to be very frequently selected as executor and administrator, and it is probable that in these capacities he has settled more estates than any other person in West Jersey. His business ability has also been called into requisition in connection with several corporate and other associations, among which may be named the Burlington Savings Institution, of which he is Vice-President, the Burlington National Bank and the Burlington Library, in each of which he is a Director. A man of public spirit, and especially interested in the advancement of the social and moral condition of the community with which his interests are so intimately bound up, he takes an active part in all movements calculated to accomplish that end. He is a prominent Episcopalian, attending St. Mary's Church, of which he is a vestryman and the Treasurer. He was married, in 1848, to Jane, daughter of John Conrad, a well-known citizen of Philadelphia and Mayor of the Northern Liberties, and sister of Judge Conrad, the first Mayor of the consolidated city of Philadelphia. Mr. Woolman is one of the best known citizens of West Jersey, and he is as widely respected and esteemed as known.

———◦◦◦———

LAIR, JOHN I., Railroad- Promoter, of Blairstown, was born in Warren county, New Jersey, near that place, about the year 1810. He received an ordinary business education, and at a very early age was thrown upon his own resources, with very indifferent prospects. When a mere boy he commenced work for his own support as a clerk in his uncle's small country store in his native county. As he neared manhood he opened a similar business for himself at a place then known as Gravel Hill, but now

called Blairstown, in his honor. Here he continued for many years, applying himself industriously to his business and managing it with marked economy and judgment. What may be termed his first start was obtained by a speculative transaction on a small scale in cotton. It yielded a fair profit, and on this was laid the foundation of his ample fortune. The section of the State in which his early lot was cast was then comparatively wild and uninhabited; but it was ascertained to possess valuable resources, and he was one of the first and most active spirits in the development of its agricultural and mineral wealth. By small investments in the coal and iron interests of New Jersey and Pennsylvania, he gradually became a master-spirit among capitalists of that particular branch of industry, and employed all his earnings for a time exclusively in the expansion of the coal and iron trade. Extending his interests to the Lackawanna and Wyoming valleys, of Pennsylvania, he became one of the original founders of the city of Scranton, and largely interested in the coal and iron enterprises of that place. With a view to providing an outlet for the products of this region, he took part as one of the promoters in the construction of the main line of the Delaware, Lackawanna & Western Railroad. This road has been the principal means of developing the extensive natural resources of the Lackawanna and Wyoming valleys, and for many years was the only eastern outlet for the coal and iron of the region. In the welfare and prosperity of this corporation he has ever continued to manifest the warmest interest, and is still one of its managing directors. He also holds a managing interest in the Lackawanna-Coal and Iron Company, a separate organization, as well as important shares in other mining and banking stock concerns of Scranton. Railroad enterprises have always claimed large attention at his hands. He has been extensively engaged in various undertakings of the kind both in the West and South, in most cases taking the entire contract, and personally superintending the work, and all those in which he has held a controlling interest have proved successful. He displayed wonderful mechanical skill in the rapid construction of the Sioux City Railroad, in Missouri, which he completed under contract in one year, the road-bed and other track accessories extending a distance of 100 miles. This was considered by practical men a splendid achievement. In one instance he is said to have built 300 miles of road in eight months. Although his varied interests have occasioned an extraordinary amount of travelling, so much so that he may be said to have lived and slept in railroad cars, with occasional intervals in prairie huts, he has still regarded Blairstown as his home, and has managed to return thither to spend some time with his family, to look after his home concerns and to take needed rest. In the advancement of the town he has always manifested the liveliest activity. Originally a mere village, it is now a thriving town of some thousands of inhabitants. Through his exertions and aid, banks, churches and institutions of learning have been established.

He built the Blairstown Academy, with its boarding-house attached; burned during the winter of 1867–68, he at once set about its rebuilding, at a cost of some $40,000. Of the Belvidere Bank, one of the most substantial financial institutions in the State, he was elected President in 1860, having been for some years previously a Director and its largest shareholder; he has always been able to discharge the duties of President down to the present time, notwithstanding his multifarious engagements. In educational matters he has proved a munificent benefactor. Beyond his large expenditure in this direction, directly in Blairstown, he some years since endowed a professorship at Princeton with $30,000, and he has also given $10,000 to the Lafayette College, at Easton, Pennsylvania. Other educational establishments have experienced his generosity, and any deserving charity finds in him a liberal friend. Politically, he was a Whig until the organization of the Republican party, when his warm sympathies were enlisted on behalf of that organization, although as a rule he has refrained from personal share in the actual work of politics, only on one occasion permitting his name to be offered for any public office. . This was in 1868, when he accepted the Republican nomination for Governor of New Jersey. As, however, the State was Democratic, he was defeated by Hon. Theodore F. Randolph, the candidate of that party, by a small majority. · Although he has now passed the meridian of life, Mr. Blair enjoys robust health, being as hale and vigorous, physically and mentally, as when in early manhood. This is in a great measure due to the out-door life and exercise he has pursued. With an intellect naturally clear and vigorous, he has supplied the deficiencies of early education and overcome the obstacles presented to his youthful ambition, and now stands forward a noteworthy example. of a self-made man—a pure, strong, well-balanced character, a developed mind, and a successful financier. Of a family of several children he has but one surviving son.

———◦◦◦———

TETSON, DAVID S., Merchant, was born in Bath, Maine, May 22d, 1819. Bred among seamen, at a very early age he determined to adopt a seafaring life, and when only fourteen years old he went as cabin boy in the ship "New England," bound from Bath to New Orleans, and thence to Havre. His rise in his profession was unusually rapid: when only eighteen years old he was made first officer of the ship "Manco," and when scarcely twenty-one he was given the command of the "Maria," brig. In the "Manco" he came for the first time to Philadelphia, and was subsequently engaged in the Gulf and South Atlantic trade. The "Maria" he commanded for four years, trading between Philadelphia and the West Indies. In 1844 he built the brig "James A. Marple," an unlucky vessel that was soon after wrecked upon the Bahamas. With characteristic energy he repaired his loss immediately by building the brig "Ida," continuing in her in the West India trade during the ensuing three years. In 1846 he married a daughter of Mr. T. H. and Susan Sickels, of Philadelphia, and the ensuing year he determined upon abandoning the sea. Associated with Mr. J. Baker under the firm-name of Baker & Stetson, he established himself in Philadelphia as a ship-chandler, his store being situated upon Delaware avenue, north of Arch street. In 1856 Mr. Baker withdrew from the firm, whereon Mr. Stetson formed a partnership with Mr. W. F. Cushing, at the same time changing the character of his business to that of shipping and commission. Founded just before the financial panic of 1857, the firm of D. S. Stetson & Co. was seriously affected by the failure of many prominent houses with which it had dealings; but while sorely pressed, the firm maintained its credit intact. Every obligation was met as it became due, and at the end of the season of disaster and reverse, although weakened in capital, the credit of the firm was unimpeachable. The losses of '57 were more than made good during the flush years of the war, an immense business being done under contract with the government in coaling and supplying the naval vessels and stations of the Gulf, and in forwarding supplies for the use of the armies operating in the Southern seaboard States. From the punctual manner in which these contracts were fulfilled, the government was an even greater gainer than were the contractors: it is not too much to say that the success of the naval force operating in the Gulf, and of the military force in the interior, was very largely due to the faithfully rendered services of the firm of D. S. Stetson & Co. In 1872 Mr. Cushing retired from the firm, and D. S. Stetson, Jr., who had for a number of years been actively engaged in the executive departments of the establishment, became his father's partner: a young man of exceptional business ability, fine address, and a thorough comprehension of the trade, West India and Mediterranean, in which the house is mainly engaged, he has of late succeeded to a considerable share in the control of the large and still increasing business, thus enabling his father to take the rest which, by his laborious, useful life, he has so abundantly earned. Mr. Stetson has been prominent in the development of two thriving towns in New Jersey—Merchantville, on the eastern border of Camden county, and Ocean Grove, near Long Branch. In the former, a village of handsome villas, he has for many years resided, being prominent alike in the Methodist Church and in furthering all works looking to the moral or material advancement of the welfare of the town; and in the latter he is the owner and summer ocenpant of a charming cottage. He is a man of commanding presence: his manner, somewhat bluff and smacking of the sea, is tempered by geniality and an innate courtesy; while his absolute honesty in all relations of life assures him the respect and esteem of all with whom he is brought in contact.

ILCHRIST, HON. ROBERT, Lawyer, of Jersey City, was born in the first quarter of the present century. He studied law, and in due course was called to the bar, where he holds a high position, being regarded, by general consent, as one of the leading lawyers of the State. Always taking an earnest interest in public affairs, he has been called upon to discharge some high and responsible trusts. Politically, he was a member of the Whig party until it was merged into the Republican organization. During Mr. Lincoln's administration he acted with the moderate Republicans, protesting against the radical measures of the government, and finally breaking away from the party upon the question of reconstruction. In the summer of 1866 he joined the Johnson movement, and became the Democratic candidate for Congress in the Fifth District. The Republicans, however, were successful, electing their nominee, George A. Halsey. In May, 1869, he was nominated by Governor Randolph as Attorney-General of the State, to succeed George M. Robeson, appointed Secretary of the Navy, accepted the nomination, and was confirmed by the Senate. During his term of office an important question arose, and his public-spirited, unpartisan decision upon its submission to his judgment doubtless prevented what might have proved a serious trouble. It concerned the right of negroes to vote in New Jersey. The question was submitted by the Mayor of Princeton in the following form on April 2d, 1870:—" Borough election, Monday. Have the negroes a right to vote?" His reply came promptly on the same day in the following terms:—" E. R. Stoneaker, Esq., Mayor Princeton, New Jersey—The Fifteenth Amendment makes void so much of our State Constitution as on account of color denies the right of any citizen of the United States to vote. The Thirteenth Amendment made all the colored people who were before in slavery free: If a free colored native was not a citizen before, the text of the Fourteenth Amendment makes him so. Three questions are made on the Fifteenth Amendment. First. Is it in force or legally adopted? Second. Does it operate upon State elections? Third. Does it destroy old provisions of the Constitution as well as prevent future provisions denying the right to vote on account of color? In my opinion, the judges of election should treat the matter as a practical one, and answer all these questions in the affirmative, though they may believe as I do, that unconstitutional force was the means of procuring the ratification of the amendment, and though on this ground it may finally be held by all branches of the government never to have been in force. Nothing but disorder will result if the judges of election in any State, by concert, now, answer these questions in the negative. Yet if any judge thinks these questions should be answered in the negative and desires to make a case, and thinks he can practically do so, by refusing a colored person's vote, he may without moral guilt refuse it, but will undoubtedly subject himself to the penalty of the law (if any there be imposed upon a judge) for the refusal, and if the courts decide he is wrong, to a civil suit; and the person elected may, if the votes refused would have defeated him, lose his election. One or two cases in the whole State will be all that can be productive of any good whatever, if it shall be deemed wise to contest the right. As a practical, present question of the hour, the right of the colored man to vote, if he is otherwise qualified, should be treated as settled in his favor—Robert Gilchrist." In April, 1873, he was appointed by Governor Parker on a special commission to revise the Constitution of the State. In January, 1875, he retired from the Attorney-Generalship, and was succeeded by ex-Governor Joel Parker. During the same month his name was brought before the Democratic caucus of the Legislature for the nomination for United States Senator, and he received large support; but ex-Governor Theodore F. Randolph eventually obtained the nomination and was elected.

AY, HON. ANDREW K., of Winslow, was born in Massachusetts about 1817. Removing to New Jersey, he became engaged in the manufacture of glass at Winslow, and has in the course of a number of years built up an extensive business in that town. He is also largely interested in real estate, and has under cultivation in the vicinity of Winslow several fine farms. During the existence of the Whig party, he was a member of that organization, and from 1849 to 1851 represented his district in Congress. Since the foundation of the Republican party he has been one of its staunchest members, and while declining office, has been an earnest worker for the success of Republican principles. In 1872 he was a Grant and Colfax elector.

LUMMER, HON. SAMUEL, of Salem, was born in Salem county, New Jersey, September 13th, 1813. He is of English extraction. In youth he was put to the coach-making business, but was soon drawn into political life, being elected Assessor of Pyle's Grove Township. Subsequently he became the first Justice of the Peace in that township elected under the new Constitution. In 1848 he removed to Penn's Grove; in 1852 was elected Sheriff of Salem county; in 1855 and 1856 a member of the New Jersey Assembly. In 1864 and 1865 he was appointed under the United States Internal Revenue law Assessor-at-large in the First Congressional District, and was also President of the Board of State Prison Inspectors. In 1866 he was elected to the State Senate from Salem county by the Republicans, and in 1869 became United States Marshal for the District of New Jersey; reappointed in 1873, he declined being an applicant in 1877. He married a daughter of E. Woodruff, Esq., of Bridgeton, New Jersey.

for the refusal, and if the courts deci ... the person elected may ... votes refused would have defeated him, lose his elec... ... one or two cases in the whole State will be all that ... can be productive of any good whatever, if it shall be ... contest the right. As a practical, present ... of the hour, the right of the colored man to vote, ... should be treated as settled in ... mayor ... In April, 1873, he was ap... on a special commission to re... State. In January, 1875, he ... halship, and was succeeded ... During the same month his ... of the ...

... of the State ...

... in this term

... K. C. Winslow was born in Massachusetts ... 1817. Removing to New Jersey, he became engaged ... glass at Winslow, and has ... a number of years built up an extensive business in that town. He is also largely interested in real ... or cultivation in the vicinity of Winslow ... During the existence of the Whig ... member of that organization, ... Republican party ... of its ...

... several ...

... means of ... New Jersey Assembly ... under the United ... ing but dis- ... age in the First Con... by gross ma... was also President of the Board ... of State ... 1876 he was elected to he ... State Se... by the Republicans, and in ... counted being an applicant ... 1877 ... of L. Woodruff, Esq.,

INDEX.

THE END.